Great American Women *of the* 19th Century

Great American Women of the 19th Century

a biographical encyclopedia

Edited by
Frances E. Willard &
Mary A. Livermore

Humanity Books

an imprint of Prometheus Books
59 John Glenn Drive, Amherst, New York 14228-2197

Published 2005 by Humanity Books, an imprint of Prometheus Books

Great American Women of the 19th Century: A Biographical Encyclopedia.
Introduction copyright © 2005 by Patricia Lengermann and Jill Niebrugge-Brantley.

Inquiries should be addressed to
Humanity Books
59 John Glenn Drive
Amherst, New York 14228–2197
VOICE: 716–691–0133, ext. 207
FAX: 716–564–2711

09 08 07 06 05   5 4 3 2 1

Library of Congress Cataloging-in-Publication Data

Great American women of the nineteenth century : a biographical encyclopedia /
    edited by Frances E. Willard and Mary A. Livermore ; with an introduction by
    Patricia Lengermann and Jill Niebrugge-Brantley
        p. cm.
    Originally published: American women. Rev. ed. New York : Mast, Crowell &
Kirkpatrick, c1897.
    Includes bibliographical references (p.).
    ISBN 1–59102–211–8 (alk. paper)
    1. Women—United States—Biography—Encylopedias. 2. United States—
Biography—Encyclopedias. 3. Biography—19th century. I. Willard, Frances
Elizabeth, 1839-1898. II. Livermore, Mary Ashton Rice, 1820-1905. III. Title.

CT3260.A4725 2004
920.72'0973'09034—dc22
                                                                        2004052375

Printed in the United States of America on acid-free paper

INTRODUCTION

PATRICIA LENGERMANN, GEORGE WASHINGTON UNIVERSITY,
AND JILL NIEBRUGGE-BRANTLEY, AMERICAN UNIVERSITY

I n 1897 *American Women: Fifteen Hundred Portraits* was published as the second, expanded edition of *A Woman of the Century*, published in 1893. *A Woman of the Century*, as its subtitle says, contained "fourteen hundred-seventy biographical sketches accompanied by portraits of LEADING AMERICAN WOMEN in All Walks of Life." *American Women* added thirty biographical sketches and an index listing the women subjects by the "walks of life" in which they had achieved most public prominence. Both editions are inscribed as "edited by Frances E. Willard and Mary A. Livermore, assisted by a corps of able contributors." Willard and Livermore were among the most influential women of their day—a time their introduction proclaims "woman's century." Willard was president of the Woman's Christian Temperance Union (WCTU), the largest women's organization in the United States and the world, and at the height of her influence she was the most famous woman in America and probably second only to Queen Victoria in world renown. Livermore was a Civil War hero and a major spokesperson for progressive causes, most particularly temperance and woman suffrage. That both are relatively unknown today underscores the ongoing struggle to maintain women's history and the importance of this volume, which of all the writings credited to these two women, is probably still the most used and referenced.[1] (There is still no biography of Livermore and no definitive study of Willard, though Ruth Bordin's 1987 *Frances Willard* is an intelligent introduction to this extraordinary life.)[2]

The book's durability is probably because it offers scholars an extraordinary example of the kind of artifact that their contemporary Harriet Martineau, the first sociologist to study America[3] (and the subject of one of Livermore's lectures), urged the social scientist to seek: "The grand secret of wise inquiry into Morals and Manners is to begin with the study of THINGS. . . . The voice of a whole people goes up in the silent workings of an institution; the condition of the masses is reflected from the surface of a record . . . whether architectural remains, epitaphs, civic registers, national music, or any of the thousand manifestations of the common mind."[4] But, as Martineau well knew, artifacts do not speak for themselves. In this introduction we try to determine exactly what this volume is a record of, describing its authorship, purpose, content, and historical context, and assessing how well it achieves its original purpose and the purposes to which it can be put today.

AUTHORSHIP

The question of authorship remains both important and puzzling—important because it affects our assessment of what this is a record of; puzzling on two counts, the exact relationship of Willard and Livermore to the volume and the identities of the "corps of able contributors."

We have several reasons for uncertainty about Willard's and Livermore's roles in the volume's construction. First, neither woman seems to have claimed public credit for the volume, although other works by them—for example, Livermore's *My Story of the War* (1888) and Willard's *Glimpses of Fifty Years* (1889)—are heavily advertised in the 1890s. Livermore makes no mention of this volume in her autobiography, *The Story of My Life, or The Sunshine and Shadow of Seventy Years*, which, in what she feared might be her final illness, she undertook to write in 1896–1897. Neither the preparation nor publication of the volume is noted in the *Union Signal*, the WCTU newspaper, or the *Woman's Journal*, the suffrage newspaper of which Livermore was the first editor in chief; yet both periodicals steadily reported on Willard's and Livermore's activities in the 1890s. Further, the preface to the 1893 edition is dated "Christmas 1892," but Willard had been in Britain since November and was in a period of crisis—her mother, to whom she was devoted, had died in August; she was in ill health;

and she was engrossed in a significant new relationship with Lady Henry Somerset. There are also records of Willard signing her very bankable name to works in the production of which she may have had only a minor part.[5]

Nevertheless, it seems reasonable that Willard and Livermore were the organizing intelligences for the volume,[6] because of the breadth of their reach into circles with access to the information contained in *American Women* and their records of speaking and writing on women's contributions to US history and producing biographical sketches of other women.[7] Further, the volume's content, purpose, and execution reflect the principles that marked Willard's political genius:[8] an ability to grant freedom of action to individuals and units within organizations she headed, a willingness to let other women shine, an inclination to respond to disagreement with tolerance and equanimity, and a deep interest in coalition building. These qualities are reflected in the volume's eclecticism as to the range of activities and views of individual subjects (e.g., suffrage and antisuffrage, abolitionist and Confederate) and the positive entries on persons with whom Willard had reconciled after disagreement. This general philosophical guidance would have been complemented by Livermore's own feminism, her availability in 1892, and her practical editorial experience with the *Woman's Journal* and as associate editor for her husband's Universalist newspaper—all of which would have led her to a modest standardization of the entries while preserving the voices of the contributors. And internal evidence suggests her authorship of several sketches (e.g., Mrs. Edna Chaffee Noble).

Whatever their particular roles, Willard and Livermore were massively assisted by the "corps of able contributors" who surely did most of the actual research and writing. The host of intimate details and the personal photographs accompanying most entries point to direct contact between contributor and subject. We had originally assumed that the corps was drawn from Willard's and Livermore's numerous acquaintances through the temperance, women's club, and woman suffrage movements and that there would be an easily accessible public record of the solicitation of contributions. While our research leads us to believe that the first part of this thesis remains true, we have yet to find a record of how the women subjects or the contributors were selected. But we have located definite sources for a few of the sketches, which may give a clue as to how the volume was compiled. The sketch of Mrs. Sarah Doan La Fetra is abbreviated from a *Union Signal* article of September 12, 1889, written by Miss Ida Hinman, a journalist also profiled in *American Women*. The sketch of Lucy Stone was written by her daughter Alice Stone Blackwell, appearing originally in the *Housekeeper's Weekly* of 1892 and reprinted in the *Woman's Journal* on April 15, 1893, and again at Stone's death in October 1893. Harriet B. Kells, an editor of the *Union Signal,* did a profile of Miss Jessie Ackermann in the issue of July 27, 1893 (19, no. 30), that mirrors the sketch in *American Women.* An anonymous memoriam of Miss Rachel L. Bodley, a scientist and doctor of medicine, in the *Woman's Journal* on June 24, 1888 (14, no. 25), is reprinted in abbreviated form in *American Women.* And many of the biographical subjects either contributed to or have their activities mentioned in the *Union Signal* or the *Woman's Journal* of the 1880s and 1890s. The corps of contributors is a sign of the enormous strength of the women's movement, of Willard's and Livermore's organizational skills, and of the cultural feminist approach that underlies the volume. The decision, by design or chance, to allow the individual voices of the contributors to emerge lets the volume approach the record Martineau dreamed of—if *American Women* is not quite "the voice of a whole people," it is a commentary on and by a significant sample.

PURPOSE AND CONTENT

Our analysis is on both a reading of all 1,500 sketches and a content analysis of 163 entries selected by random sample. Because of the book's multiple authors, it is necessary to distinguish among its purpose, manifest content, and latent content; the manifest content explicitly supports the volume's stated purposes; the latent content either implicitly serves those purposes or provides unintended information (which may contradict those purposes).

PURPOSE

In their preface to the 1893 edition, cited at length here because it was not reprinted in 1897, Willard and Livermore envision the volume as a record and stock taking of the accomplishments of American women in the nineteenth century done at the end of that century and looking to the next:

> Among all cyclopedias and books about famous women, this is intended to be unique and to supply a vacant niche in the reference library. This book is not alone a book [or] record of famous names, but one which aims to show what women have done in the humbler as in the higher walks of life. It is a record of American women offered, at the close of four centuries of life in the New World, to the consideration of those who would know what the nineteenth century of Chris-

tian civilization has here brought forth, and what are the vast outlook and the marvelous promise of the twentieth century.

This purpose needs to be set against the background of the status of women in the United States in the 1890s, a world alive with women's growing sense of the power they could wield through social activism in a vast array of causes, manifest in the biographies in this volume. One way to pattern this activism is to consider women as a class in a materialist feminist sense—a group of persons assigned to the same role in production, in women's case the work of the home, family, and aide to the men in their lives. Some of women's activism in the 1890s is as what Marx calls "a class-in-itself," as women make common cause with others around a particular issue arising from their lived experience but not perceived as systematically related to other issues affecting women. Thus, this volume shows women working for temperance because of their experience of what alcohol addiction did to home life but not identifying with woman suffrage or other women's issues.

Recognition and conscious pursuit of the interests arising from their shared position in social production marks the existence of "class for itself" as in the suffrage movement promulgated by Elizabeth Cady Stanton, Susan B. Anthony, and others.[9] *American Women* features innumerable women whose activism focused on woman suffrage specifically and women's rights in general.

But this traditional Marxist division of class must be expanded in the case of women's activism to include a third form: that of "a class-beyond-itself," a class that responds to duties beyond the immediate interests of its own people, duties to a larger society. In this volume, the abolitionist movement is the clearest example of this.[10]

Willard's great political achievement was to bring these three strands of activism together. By first creating a rallying cry for temperance and suffrage in the slogan "the Home Protection Ballot" and then expanding women's concerns from temperance and suffrage to what she called "the larger home of Society and Government,"[11] she drew to suffrage and women's rights women who began their activism in the class-in-itself mode, acting for temperance, or in the class-beyond-itself mode, acting for the African American slave or for other disempowered groups. Under Willard, Progressives supported temperance,[12] and the WCTU championed a host of Progressive causes from the eight-hour day to kindergartens, Native rights, and prison reform. This amalgamation means that when *American Women* reports a woman working for temperance, she should be understood as progressively engaged with social issues.

MANIFEST CONTENT

The manifest content of *American Women* is the compilation of life stories that show women as agents in United States life, most particularly in the public sphere.[13] The fifteen hundred biographical sketches uniformly begin by giving the subject's full name (not, in the case of married women, the husband's name),[14] her major area of public achievement—for example, temperance worker, suffragist, poet, educator—and her date and place of birth. Proceeding chronologically, the biography describes parents, upbringing, early life, education, and marriage and then focuses on public achievement, handling of private responsibilities, and qualities of character. The sketches vary in length from under one hundred words to over three thousand, with the vast majority between five hundred and seven hundred words. The length correlates not only with the subject's public prominence but also with the degree of knowledge the writer seems to have about her— from intimacy to acquaintanceship to reputation only. The women represented range from the most famous names in social reform—Willard, Livermore, Anthony, Stanton, Stone—to biographies of those of modest achievement—for example, Mrs. Mary A. Saunders, businesswoman; Miss Ella Maynard Kelley, telegrapher; Miss Lizzie Thayer, train dispatcher; Mrs. Anna Augusta Truit, local philanthropist and temperance worker. The reasons for the selection are part of the historical puzzle discussed above.

The sketches support four main themes about women in American life by showing that their subject (1) is an agent in the public sphere, (2) wants and is able successfully to balance public agency with responsibility for the private sphere, (3) possesses qualities of character fitting her for both private and public sphere, and (4) could do even greater things if men/society would let women have more opportunities.

The effectiveness of this argument is due in part to the subjects' accomplishments; in part to the sheer massing of data, especially data about women of limited prominence, which produces a sense of literally thousands more women like them; and in part to the contributors' use of *texture,* that quality in a text which survives after a paraphrase of the argument. In almost any portrait over five hundred words, the writer moves with extraordinary economy to bring the reader into the subject's life, giving details of the actual work and skills, direct quotation from the subject or those who know her, and vivid anecdotes. This stylistic consistency is particularly remarkable given the potential number of "the able corps of contributors."

Public Life

The volume's index of women by area of endeavor presents eighty-six separate kinds of public sphere activity and a "miscellaneous" category. The major career fields indexed are: literary contributors, 248 women, including some who wrote only irregularly and not necessarily for income; authors, 178; temperance workers, 122; educators, 99; physicians, 78; philanthropists, 73; and suffrage workers, 53. We can interpret these categories as part of a total social system by using Martineau's key social indicators: domestic state (economy, health, and marriage), general moral notions, and ideas of liberty and progress. In the domestic state, the volume shows women participating in the paid economy as business persons, professionals (e.g., doctors, educators, lawyers, and scientists), skilled technicians (e.g., telegraphers and stenographers), and, as a subset, as an aide to a husband's career (e.g., wives of US presidents and ministers). Women's role in society's "general moral notions" is illustrated by achievement in the arts (e.g., novelists, poets, journalists, actors, elocutionists, and musicians). Women participate in the shaping of "the idea of liberty" and "progress" as suffragists, temperance workers, missionaries, club women, and advocates for the disempowered (e.g., orphans, the aged, the disabled, racial minorities, and labor). Women's public sphere activity is shown as important whether paid, unremunerated, or combining advocacy and earning a living (e.g., lecturing or social organizing).

The texture of the individual sketches reveals the relevances that shaped both the contributors and, presumably, their subjects. For instance, the biographer of Mrs. Annie White Baxter interprets her subject's career as a county clerk through a detailed job description: "by far the most complicated and laborious of any office in the county, embracing the entire tax levy . . . of more than 50,000 people, . . . and collection of interest on a public school fund of over $225,000, loaned out to citizens of the county, and . . . settlements with the state treasurer"; a history of Mrs. Baxter's career path, culminating in her nomination and election in 1890, defeating "a popular and competent" male opponent to become "the first woman in the United States elected by the people and qualified under the law to fill the office of clerk of a court of record"; an analysis of her qualities of character: "keen perception, intuitive acumen, mathematical precision, untiring application, energy, and directness, and . . . pleasing address and manner," and an affirmation of her femininity: a "womanly refinement and modesty" which lets her bear "her honors and responsibility with unconscious ease and natural grace."

For the women whose prominence comes from social activism, the sketches emphasize both the details of the career and the qualities of moral fiber—especially a responsiveness to injustice. The biographer of Mrs. Amelia Quinton, "President of the Women's National Indian Association," shows how "presented with the facts about the national wrongs to Indians, Mrs. Quinton's heart and conscience at once responded, 'Something must be done'"; she is then shown as she "studied in libraries, prepared literature" and a petition "three-hundred feet long . . . presented to Congress in February 1880." For women in the arts, there is an emphasis on both talent and popularity. Novelist Mary Jane Holmes's popularity is vividly recounted: "statistics of a wholesale bookstore . . . show that next to [male author] E. P. Roe's works, Mrs. Holmes' novels are the most popular of any American author . . . more than one-million copies of her books have been sold. . . . [L]ibraries . . . keep twenty and thirty sets of her books on their shelves."

Private Sphere Responsibility

A general fear about women's public achievement, both then and now, is that it will weaken their commitment to home and family. *American Women* sets out to show that marriage, home, and family remain secure and central, and the sketches treat marriage in terms of its relation to women's public agency. We find five main patterns. About 15 percent of the portraits of married women show a happy conventional relationship with the husband's earnings supporting the wife's activities (e.g., Mrs. Kate Smeed Cross, "social leader": "the wife of a banker and business man" who "in their charming home, 'Elmwood,' . . . with their little daughter live and dispense hospitality").

For about 55 percent of the marriages, women are partners in their husbands' undertakings, either with him fully active—as with the wives of ministers (e.g., Mrs. Esther Baldwin), journalists (e.g., Mrs. Mary G. Charlton Edholm), educators (e.g., Mrs. Emma Atwood Edwards), and labor agitators (e.g., Mrs. Eva McDonald Valesh)—or with the husband in some way impaired, so that the wife assumes full responsibility for the business. Mrs. Frank Leslie offers a spectacular instance of this. Her husband, the publisher of *Leslie's Lady's Magazine*, ran into debt in the panic of 1877, "developed a tumor," and knowing "that his fate was sealed . . . said to his wife: 'Go to my office, sit in my place, and do my work until my debts are paid.' She undertook this task without hesitation, and she accomplished it with ease . . . and brought success out of what seemed chaos." In about 10 percent of the portraits, the quality of the marriage relationship is not reported (e.g., Fannie J. Crosby and Maude Howe Elliot). Two other patterns dealing with problem marriages are discussed below under "Latent Content."

General Moral Notions

In explaining why these women are worthy of attention, the contributors draw on what Martineau would call "general moral notions" (prevailing ideals of conduct) and measure these notions in five of the ways she suggests: the events from which epochs are dated, the "love of kindred and birth-place," the qualities in which a person may take pride, the celebrities respected, and literature and philosophy. Three key events emerge—the abolitionist movement and Civil War, the Ohio Crusade and the beginning of the modern temperance movement, and the early conventions of the women's suffrage movement. To have been in any way active in those events is always treated as laudatory (for Southern women, struggle in the Confederate cause is so treated, though the volume is overwhelmingly pro-Union). The "love of kindred and birth-place" is present in nearly every biography as women's qualities of character are typically attributed to inheritance from worthy ancestors or upbringing by virtuous parents—that is, to that private sphere that is a woman's special responsibility. Persons whom it is clearly an honor to claim an association with—no matter how fleeting—include major figures of the Revolutionary and Civil Wars and the suffrage and temperance movements, literary luminaries (e.g., John Greenleaf Whittier), European royalty, US presidents and governors, and stars of opera and stage.

The qualities of character praised in the women are those that would be seen by a reform-minded class as most necessary to ascendancy: intelligence and talent, courage, a sense of sympathy and justice, and a love of home. The descriptions of physical and moral courage illustrate the dramatic levels contributors could reach. For instance, Mrs. Annie Wittenmeyer, the first president of the WCTU, is pictured as "under fire at Pittsburgh Landing, and . . . under the guns in Vicksburg every day during the siege, when shot and shell were flying and balls filled the air with the music of death. When warned of her danger, her reply was: 'I am safe; He covers me with His feathers and hides me under His wings.'"

Protesting Sexism

Women in nearly every line of work in the paid economy are presented as struggling to overcome male prejudice: physicians cannot find schools to admit them, and when they do, male students harass them; businesswomen have to prove they are not incompetent; teachers fight constantly for equal pay. Women's success is typically recounted in detail, with any "first" noted and perseverance for fairness applauded. For instance, Mrs. Edna Chaffee

Noble, "elocutionist," is cited as the first woman to teach school in Rochester, Vermont, and commended for firmness when the hiring committee asked her terms: "'The same you have paid the gentleman whose place you wish me to fill, unless there is more work to do, under which circumstances I shall require more pay.' . . . [A]t length they engaged her for one term, but kept her two years."

LATENT CONTENT

There are three types of latent content in *American Women*—covert, contradictory, and serendipitous. The main covert—that is, unspoken—content lies in the overall portrait of "representative American women." While Willard and Livermore suggest they are creating a universal portrait of "woman," the volume in fact is a portrait of the agency of particular women: the agency in public life of white, middle-class women. The reader at the beginning of the twenty-first century is immediately struck by two absences: that of working-class women and that of women of color—indeed, there are only a few Catholics and less than a half dozen Jews. Working-class women are partially represented by those women who work their way from manual jobs to positions for which they are included, most notably labor organizers. While the volume indexes 86 separate kinds of activity, the 1900 census listed women in 295 out of 303 occupational categories; of the 18 of these, largely manual jobs, which accounted for nearly 87 percent of women's employment,[15] *American Women* indexes only four—bookkeepers, musicians and teachers of music, professors and teachers, and stenographers and typewriters. Conversely, other careers are overrepresented in the volume, most especially writers of all sorts—whose high visibility supports Ann Douglas's thesis of "the feminization of American culture"[16] and may provide a clue to the process of inclusion in the volume.

People of color find their way into the biographical sketches only as the subjects of those sketches name their abolitionist roots, links to the Union's military efforts, or service on behalf of newly freed slaves. Frederick Douglass is mentioned as what Martineau would term "a popular idol" in the biography of Miss Anna Gardner, as is Sojourner Truth in the biography of Caroline Maria Seymour Severance. The broader literature of the period reporting white women's activism shows awareness of the activism of women of color: for instance, the *Union Signal* regularly devoted space to the actions of "Colored" WCTU chapters, reviewed the work of Ellen Watkins Harper, and included notice of publication of Monroe Majors's

Notable Negro Women (1893) in its column "The Library Table"(19, no. 32 [September14, 1893]). Yet no woman of color is given her own biography.[17] The volume thus reflects the stance of the white women's rights movement in the 1890s, a period of growing frustration for suffrage women that led them to criticize the enfranchisement of immigrant and Negro men but the denial of white women and to reach out for support to white women and white legislators in the South.

The contradictory latent content argues against the main messages and is most visible in the treatment of marriage, where a fifth of the sketches show marriage inhibiting the wife's capacity for public work temporarily or permanently. Women with artistic talent find that they must limit their activities or change direction of expression after marriage. For example, poet Mrs. Mary Van Densen is described as "sacrificing the pleasures of 'dream life' that she might minister more constantly to her husband and children." Even women who moved into seeming partnerships sometimes seem to regret the changes brought by marriage; as a minister's wife Mrs. Margaret Bloodgood Peeke found that "for fifteen years, she attended only to family and parish duties, and the cherished thought of a literary life was abandoned." Occasionally, the women are portrayed as having made an unhappy marriage, the ending of which propels them into their own agency (e.g., Mrs. Antoinette Van Hoesen Wakeman).

The serendipitous latent content is apparent in two ways. First, the fact of "a corps of contributors" produces an "unevenness" in the volume in accuracy, clarity, and tone. But this unevenness rather than being a weakness gives authenticity to the volume and is a spur to further reading—one literally does not know what will turn up next. For instance, two marriages that have in common the husband's collapse in some way are told in totally different tones: Mrs. Harriet M. [Fales] Rathbun's first marriage is described in the hushed tones of stately struggle: "At last husband and child were laid at rest, in 1886, and Mrs. Fales returned alone to New York City." Mrs. Harriet Hubbard Ayer's marriage is brusquely dismissed: "Reverses came in 1882 and Mr. Ayer failed for several millions. Disheartened by the blow, he became a wreck." These are not canned biographies sanitized by some powerful editorial hand but voices directly from the field. (Indeed, sometimes one wonders if these are autobiographical statements written in the third person, so intimate is the level of detail.)

A second serendipitous latent content is the texture of the entries; slipping through the intended purpose of praising famous and obscure women are the details of daily living—irrelevant, poignant, melodramatic, humorous, revealing, human. Unlike a standard *Who's Who* entry, which may give, as an Enid Bagnold character says, "the shadow and substance of a life with the accidents of truth taken out,"[18] the portraits here are rich in those accidents, revealing what one may accurately call a woman's eye for the details of a life. One example may suggest this richness. Mrs. Corelli Simpson, "a poet" of apparently modest achievement, is nevertheless sketched vividly as the author of the *Tête-à-tête Cook Book*, produced originally for benefit of the Young Men's Christian Association in Bangor, Maine, and now in a second edition. She is introduced in terms of her unusual first name: "Her mother was Corelli Caswell, whose father, Cyrus Caswell, a lover of music, gave to his daughter the Italian name of Corelli, from an air he was fond of playing on his violin. She handed it down by giving to her twin daughters the names Corelli and Salome. So much alike were these little girls, that they were distinguished by their pink and blue ribbons, and in maturer life the resemblance is still remarkable."

If the reader accepts this volume for what it is, a portrait of the agency of white, middle-class women in a society shaped by patriarchy as fundamentally as by capitalism and racism, then it is a work from which a new generation may draw pleasure and strength.

NOTES

1. Historian Carolyn De Swarte Gifford, editor of *Writing Out My Heart: Frances E. Willard, 1855–1896* (Urbana: University of Illinois Press, 1995), personal communication, October 1, 2003.

2. Mary E. Livermore, *The Story of My Life, or The Sunshine and Shadow of Seventy Years* (Hartford, CT: A. D. Worthington & Co., 1897); Ruth Bordin, *Frances Willard* (Chapel Hill: University of North Carolina Press, 1986). Other treatments of Willard include: Mary Frances Earhart, *Frances Willard: From Prayers to Politics* (Chicago: University of Chicago Press, 1944); Anna A. Gordon, *The Beautiful Life of Frances Willard* (Chicago: Woman's Temperance Publishing Association, 1914); and Lydia Jones Trowbridge, *Frances Willard of Evanston* (Chicago: Willett, Clark & Company, 1938).

3. The fullest account of Martineau as a sociologist is Susan Hoecker-Drysdale, *Harriet Martineau: First Woman Sociologist* (Oxford: Berg, 1992).

4. Harriet Martineau, *How to Observe Morals and Manners* (London: Charles Knight and Company, 1838), pp. 61–62.

5. See Bordin, *Frances Willard*, p. 116.

6. The volume's publisher, Charles Moulton, who seems to have spent very little on publicity, is credited in *Who Was Who in America* (vol.1, pt. 2, 1897–1942) "as publisher and editor has issued about 150 vols., notably *A Woman of the Century* (in assn. with Frances E. Willard and Mary A. Livermore)."

7. For example, Frances Willard, *Woman and Temperance* (Hartford, CT: Park Publishing, 1883); and Livermore, *The Story of My Life*, pp. 493–94.

8. See Bordin, *Frances Willard*, p. 106, for an analysis of Willard's political acumen in the fight for the WCTU presidency.

9. A good discussions in line with this point is Ellen DuBois, "The Radicalism of the Woman Suffrage Movement: Notes toward the Reconstruction of Nineteenth-Century Feminism," in *U.S. Women in Struggle*, ed. Claire Goldberg Moses and Heidi Hartmann (Urbana: University of Illinois Free Press, 1995), pp. 42–51.

10. See Jean Fagan Yellin and John C. Van Horne, eds., *The Abolitionist Sisterhood* (Ithaca, NY: Cornell University Press, 1994).

11. Cited in Bordin, *Frances Willard*, p. 13, from Willard, Presidential Address 1894, WCTU Convention *Minutes,* 177 WCTU Series, reel 4.

12. See Bordin, *Frances Willard*, chap. 1, for an energetic summary of this point.

13. The volume also contains several biographies of Canadian women and a few English women. The Canadians are often linked to temperance; the selection of English women seems arbitrary.

14. Thus, a typical entry for a married woman begins: "MEECH, Mrs. Jeannette Du Bois" not in the conventional manner as "Mrs.W. W. Meech." There are 1,093 married—or once married—women and 407 never-married women profiled in the volume, about the same percentages as in the population in the census of 1900.

15. Data are from Edith Abbott and Sophonisba Breckinridge, "Employment of Women in Industries—Twelfth Census Statistics," *Journal of Political Economy* 14 (January–December 1906): 14–39.

16. Ann Douglas, *The Feminization of American Culture* (New York: Knopf, 1977).

17. The one exception may be Pauline Johnson, a Canadian poet, born of an English mother and a Mohawk father.

18. Enid Bagnold, *The Chalk Garden* (New York: Random House, 1956).

Great American
Women *of the* 19th Century

FRANCES E.
WILLARD.

MARY A.
LIVERMORE.

ABBATT, Miss Agnes Dean, artist, born in New York City, 23rd June, 1847. She still resides in her native city. Her paternal ancestors were English, and she is of French Huguenot descent on her mother's side. Her great-grandfather and his family came from England to this country in the latter part of the last century. They settled in what is now Pleasant Valley, Dutchess county, NY, where William D. Abbatt, the father of Agnes, was born. He passed his life in business in Poughkeepsie, Philadelphia and New York. Miss Abbatt's grandmother, Mrs. Dean, an English woman, was an art amateur of unusual talent and accomplishments. Of her children, nearly all possessed the talent for painting, but of all the descendants Agnes alone has adopted art as a profession. She showed in early childhood a marked talent for drawing, but it was not till 1873 that she took up the study of art as a profession. In that year she entered the Cooper Union art-school. She won a medal for a head of Ajax in the first year of her studies, and on the merit of that achievement she was admitted to the art-school of the National Academy of Design in New York. So decided was her progress that, at the end of the first year in that institution her first full-length drawing was one of those selected for exhibition. As it was not her intention to become a figure-painter, she left the Academy and devoted herself to the study of landscape painting. That branch of art she studied for several years under R. Swain Gifford, N.A., and James D. Smillie, N.A., constantly showing new powers and making rapid progress. At the same time she was gratifying her tastes in another direction, and she won distinction as a water-colorist and also as a flower-painter. Her first pictures, two panels of flowers, were shown in the exhibition of the Brooklyn Art Club in 1875, where they attracted much attention and found purchasers. Her next picture, "My Next Neighbor," was shown in New York, and was the subject of much favorable comment. In the Water Color Society's exhibition, in 1880, she showed a composition named, "When Autumn Turns the Leaves," which was one of the most conspicuous features of the exhibition. In the same year Miss Abbatt was elected a member of the American Water Color Society, at once taking high rank in that somewhat exclusive organization of artists. She is the second woman on its list of members. She has given especial attention to the painting of chrysanthemums. Besides the picture entitled "When Autumn Turns the Leaves," she has painted others that are noteworthy, among which are "The Last of the Flowers," "Flowers of the Frost," "Our Japanese Cousins," "From the Land of the Mikado," "Autumn Colors," and "A Japanese Embassy," all devoted to the royal chrysanthemum. In the landscape field she has confined her work mostly to the rural scenes in Westchester, county, NY, the picturesque nooks of the eastern end of Long Island, and the coast of Maine and Massachusetts Bay. Among her notable productions in landscape are "Near Barnstable, Cape Cod," "The Noisy Geese that Gabbled o'er the Pool." "A Summer Afternoon on the New England Coast," and "In Lobster Lane, Magnolia, Mass." The last named picture won for her a silver medal in the exhibition of the Charitable Mechanics' and Tradesmen's Association of Boston, MA. She works with equal facility and success in oil and water colors, and she has also made a study of pastel work. In addition to her own extended creative work, she has been a successful art-teacher, in studio and in field. Aside from her home studio, she has taught classes in Washington, DC, Troy, NY, and in New Haven, CT, while her field instruction has been given in New York, Massachusetts and Maine. She is a genuine enthusiast in art, both as creator and instructor, and in these two fields, calling for so widely differing powers, she has been equally at home. Her work is distinct in character, in outline and tone in shades and lights, and her proud position among the painters of the United States is a one legitimately won and successfully held.

ABBOTT, Mrs. Elizabeth Robinson, educator, born in Lowell, MA, 11th September, 1852. Her maiden name was Elizabeth Osborne Robinson. She is the youngest daughter of William S. and Harriet H. Robinson. Through the writings and conversations of Miss Elizabeth P. Peabody she became interested, in her girlhood, in the kindergarten method of teaching, and would gladly have taken up

that branch of educational work at the time when the death of her father made it necessary for her to become self-supporting. But circumstances prevented, and she therefore sought other ways of earning her living. Successively, she taught a district school in Maine and "boarded round," kept a little private school of her own, tried bookkeeping and learned to set type. After giving three months to learning type-setting, she hardly earned enough to pay her board out of the low wages given to women compositors. About that time two positions were open to her, one to "tend store" and the other as "second assistant" in Mrs. Shaw's charity kindergarten and nursery at the North End in Boston. The latter position meant simply to be the kitchen-maid or cook, and nothing more; but, preferring this position to that of shop-girl, and thinking it might eventually lead or open the way into higher kindergarten work, she accepted the offer. While there, Miss Phoebe Adam, the manager, became interested in the "second assistant" and, knowing her desire to become a kindergartner, with money helped her to carry on her studies, and kindly allowed her the privilege of taking time for her lessons out of the afternoon hours of her work. She was one of the early pupils of Miss Lucy H. Symonds, of Boston, and was a graduate of the class of 1883. So, after waiting seven years for the fulfillment of her cherished desires, Mrs. Abbott began her work as a kindergartner. Her first teaching was done in a summer charity-school in Boston. She then went to Waterbury, CT, and introduced this method into the Hillside Avenue school. There she taught until her marriage, in 1885, to George S. Abbott, of that city. After her marriage Mrs. Abbott did not lose her interest in kindergarten work, but continued her class until most of her little pupils were graduated into primary schools. Since that time she has encouraged and helped others to keep up the work she so successfully began, having for two years given part of her home for use as a kindergarten. Thus Mrs. Abbott has created and maintained in the city where she now lives a lasting interest, and she may be considered a pioneer of kindergarten work in Connecticut. She is now secretary of the Connecticut Valley Kindergarten Association, an association of kindergartners embracing western Massachusetts, Connecticut and Rhode Island. Mrs. Abbott is not well known as a writer or speaker, but she is interested in and works for all that relates to the advancement of women. She is chairman of the correspondence committee for Connecticut of the General Federation of Women's Clubs, one of the founders of Old and New, the woman's club of Maiden, MA, and the chief founder of the Woman's Club of Waterbury, CT.

ABBOTT, Emma, prima donna, born in Chicago, IL, in 1850. Her father was a music teacher, and he encouraged her and her brother George to develop the musical talents that each showed at a very early age. Emma was a singing child, and under her father's training she sang well and became a proficient performer on the guitar. Professor Abbott moved from Chicago to Peoria, IL, in 1854. There his patronage was so small that his family was in straitened circumstances. He gave a concert in 1859, in which the young Emma was prima donna and guitar player, and her brother was her support. The entertainment was a success, and Professor Abbott and his two talented children gave a large number of concerts in other towns and cities, with varying fortunes. In 1866 the finances of the family were at a low ebb, and Emma took a district school to teach in order to assist in supporting the household. Emma's early lessons on the guitar and her brother's on the violin were not entirely paid for until she had become a successful concert singer in New York. At the age of thirteen she taught the guitar with success. Her education was acquired in the Peoria public schools. When she was sixteen years old she sang in the synagogue in Peoria. At that age she joined the Lombard Concert Company, of Chicago, and traveled with them in Iowa, Illinois, and Wisconsin. When the company disbanded Emma found herself in Grand Haven, MI, friendless and moneyless. With her guitar she started out alone and gave concerts in Michigan and the neighboring States, and thus worked her way to New York City, where she gave parlor concerts in the hotels in which she staid, and in that way earned the money for her expenses. Failing to gain notice in New York, she borrowed money and returned to the west. She tried a concert season in Chicago and Milwaukee, but was unsuccessful. She then tried a number of smaller towns and ended her tour in a failure in a hotel in Toledo, OH. Among her hearers in that slimly attended concert was Clara Louise Kellogg, who recognized her merit and gave her money enough to go to New York, with a letter to Professor Errani. In 1870 she began to study with him, and was engaged to sing in Dr. Chapin's church at a salary of $1,500 a year. In 1872 Mr. Lake, with the aid of Dr. Chapin's congregation, raised $10,000 to send her to Europe for musical training. She went to Milan and studied with San Giovanni, and afterward to Paris, where she studied under Wartel for several years. She studied with Delle Sadie also. While in Paris, she suffered an illness that threatened the destruction of her voice. She made a successful début, however, and she had there a warm friend in the Baroness Rothschild. Numerous enticing offers were made to her by European managers. She made an engagement with Manager Gye in London, but refused, on moral grounds, to appear in the opera, "La Traviata." In this she was supported by Eugene Wetherell, her husband. He was a member of Dr. Chapin's church and had followed her to Europe, where they were secretly married. Her refusal to sing that rôle ended in the cancellation of her engagement with Mr. Gye. In 1876 she returned to the United States, and with C. D. Hess organized an opera company. She appeared in the Park Theater, Brooklyn, NY, in her famous rôle of Marguerite. Soon after she became her own manager, and her husband and Charles Pratt attended to her business until Mr. Wetherell's sudden death in Denver, CO, in 1888. Miss Abbott, for she always retained her maiden name, was successful from the start. In spite of abuse, ridicule and misrepresentation, she drew large audiences wherever she appeared. The critics at first derided her in every possible way, but the public did not heed the critics and crowded to hear the courageous little woman who could maintain her good temper under a shower of ridicule, the like of which never before fell upon the head of a public personage. She grew artistically every year, and her stainless character, her generosity to her company, her gifts to charity, and her industry and perseverance at length won over the critics, who had simply made manifest their inability to write down a really meritorious artist. Miss Abbott sang throughout the United States, and in an incredibly short time she had amassed a fortune of several millions of dollars. Her voice was a pure, clear, long-range soprano of

great flexibility. Her rôles included Norma, Semiramide, Elvira, Martha, Lucia, and Marguerite, and in her last years she appeared in costumes more magnificent than any other singer had ever worn. She died in Ogden, Utah, 4th January, 1891, after an illness of less than a week. Her funeral was held in Chicago on 9th January, her body was cremated, in accordance with a provision of her will, and its ashes were deposited in the magnificent mausoleum she had built in Gloucester, MA. Her large fortune was divided by her will among her relatives and friends, and various churches and charitable societies.

ACHESON, Mrs. Sarah C., temperance worker, born in Washington, PA, 20th February, 1844. She is descended on the paternal side from English and Dutch families that settled in Virginia in 1600, and on the maternal side from Col. George Morgan, who had charge of Indian affairs under Washington, with headquarters at Fort Pitt, and of whom Jefferson, in a letter which Mrs. Acheson has in her possession, says, "He first gave me notice of the mad project of that day," meaning the Aaron Burr treason. Among her ancestors were Col. William Duane, of Philadelphia, editor of the Philadelphia "Aurora" during the Revolution. Her girlhood was spent in the town of her birth, where she was married, in 1863, to Capt. Acheson, of the same place, then on Gen. Miles's staff, the marriage taking place while the Captain was on furlough with a gunshot wound in the face. He left for the front ten days after, encouraged by his young wife. Dr. and Mrs. Acheson moved to Texas in 1872. During their residence in Texas Mrs. Acheson has been a moral force. Her influence has been strongly felt, not only in the city where she resides, but throughout the State. Her generous nature has been shown in heroic deeds of a kind which the world seldom sees. When a cyclone struck the village of Savoy, many of its inhabitants were badly wounded, some were killed, others made homeless. Mrs. Acheson reached them as speedily as a train could take her, doing duty as nurse and special provider for the suffering. She gave three years of active service to the Woman's Christian Temperance Union. She was State president at a time when a strong leader was greatly needed, guiding their bark into a haven of financial safety. Her life is active along all lines of duty. She is abreast of the advanced thought of the age. The world's progress in social, scientific and religious reform is not only an open, but a well-read book, to her. Her home is in Denison, TX.

ACKERMANN, Miss Jessie A., president of the Woman's Christian Temperance Union of Australasia, born in Boston, MA, 4th July, 1860. As befits a Fourth-of-July child, she has the ring of American independence. She is a descendant of the Pilgrim Fathers on her mother's side, and is of German extraction on her father's. Her inherited virtues and talents have been developed by liberal educational advantages. She was instructed in law, and spent much time in the study of elocution. She took a private course of study in theology, while drawing and painting and instruction in household matters were not neglected. She had the advantage of extensive travel through her native land and spent much time in the Southern States, immediately after the close of her school-days. At twelve years of age she was taken to a Good Templars' Lodge, where she received her first temperance teaching, and gave her first temperance talk. She began public work as grand lecturer and organizer for that society in 1881, and continued until, in 1888, the wider scope and higher spiritual tone of the Woman's Christian Temperance Union, with its special opportunities for work among women, won her heart, and she began to serve in its ranks. She succeeded amid extraordinary difficulties in organizing unions at Sitka and Juneau, in Alaska. She also traveled and organized in British Columbia with success. She gladly responded to the call to go round the world, and receiving her appointment at the National Convention held in New York, in October, 1888, she sailed from San Francisco for the Sandwich Islands on 29th January, 1889. She reached Honolulu on 6th February, and was cordially welcomed at the residence of the W.C.T.U. president. The Japanese Consul-General, a cultivated Christian gentleman, president of a temperance society of 1,400 mem-

bers, was much interested in her work and acted as interpreter at the meetings she held among the Japanese residents, the other foreigners and the native Hawaiians. She spent some time in the Islands. The history of her mission in New Zealand and the Australian colonies was recorded in the "Union Signal" by her letters during 1889. Successful and enthusiastic missions were held in the North and South Islands of New Zealand and in the Island of Tasmania. She visited Melbourne on the way for Adelaide. She remained two months in South Australia, traveled over the greater part of the colony, organized twenty-four local unions, called a convention in Adelaide, formed a Colonial Union, and left a membership of 1,126. Workers responded to her call in every place, and money was forthcoming for all needs. Finding the work in Victoria well organized under the care of Mrs. Love, of America, she stayed only a few days, in which she spoke in the crowded meetings of the Victorian Alliance, which is very influential in Melbourne. Her stay in New South Wales was very brief, for she found that outside help was not at that time welcomed in that oldest and most conservative colony, although a good work was doing by the several local unions. She was most cordially welcomed to Queensland, but stayed only long enough to attend their annual convention, as the way to China and Japan seemed open before her. A sense of duty rather than inclination took Miss Ackermann to China, but from the time she landed in Hong Kong she was well received everywhere. As there seemed no opportunity to organize in Hong Kong, she decided to proceed to Siam, by way of Swatow. Her visit to Bankok was prolonged through an attack of malarial fever, which greatly reduced her strength. While in that city, she obtained an audience with His Royal Highness, Prince Diss, who is at the head of the department of education in Siam. She was also presented to His Majesty, the King of Siam, who received her graciously. She returned again to Hong Kong, on the way to Canton, which she reached by river. The northern ports of China being closed, Miss Ackermann proceeded to Japan, going to Yokohama. There she did much work and formed a union. She next visited Tokio. A very successful mission was held at Numadza, where a union of forty members was formed. Meetings were held in Nagoya, and also under the auspices of the temperance society in Kioto, where Miss Ackerrnann addressed the

Congregational Conference, then in session. There she also spoke in the theater to six hundred Buddhist students, on "What Christianity has done for the World." She addressed nine hundred students in the Doshisha school. Osaka was visited at the invitation of the Young Men's Christian Association. Returning to Shanghai, she enjoyed the privilege of attending and making an address before the General Missionary Conference of China. The last was held thirteen years earlier. At that time a woman was called upon to bring her work before the conference, at which the chairman vacated the chair, and many left the meeting in sore grief and indignation. On this occasion, however, all women delegates present, including missionaries' wives, were made voting members of the conference with all the privileges of the floor, amid storms of applause. Miss Ackermann was able to form a National Woman's Christian Temperance Union for China. Successful missions were conducted in Cooktown, Townsville, Mount Morgan, Rockhampton and Brisbane, and she again went into New South Wales. The work was very hard. In the first month she traveled seven-hundred miles, held forty-two meetings, and made more than one hundred calls in search of leaders for the work. The results were gratifying, being twenty new unions, a reorganized Colonial Union, and fifteen Colonial superintendents. The Good Templars were her faithful friends in that colony, and she spoke in the annual meetings of the Grand Lodge, where about three-hundred delegates were present. She called a convention in Melbourne for May, 1891, which was attended by forty-nine delegates. Miss Ackermann was elected president. A constitution was adopted providing for a triennial convention, the next to be held in Sydney in 1894, and Miss Ackermann was elected president of the Woman's Christian Temperance Union of Australasia for the ensuing term of three years. Since October, 1888, she has traveled more than forty-thousand miles, spoken through interpreters in seventeen different languages, formed more than one-hundred unions, taken five thousand pledges, and received over four thousand women into the union. The suppression of the opium traffic and of gambling, and the religious education of the young are questions to which she is devoting much thought. Since the Australasian convention she has traveled and organized in Victoria and South Australia. Miss Ackermann writes modestly of her platform ability, but she is really a speaker of no mean order. Her audiences are held by her addresses and fascinated by her lectures.

ADAMS, Mrs. Abigail, wife of John Adams, second President of the United States, born 22nd November, 1744, in Weymouth, MA. She was a daughter of the Rev. William Smith, for forty years minister of the Congregational church in Weymouth. Her mother was Elizabeth Quincy, a great-great-granddaughter of Rev. Thomas Shepard, an eminent Puritan clergyman of Cambridge, and a great-grandniece of the Rev. John Norton, of Boston. Abigail Adams was one of the most distinguished women of the Revolutionary period. She was in delicate health in youth and unable to attend school, but she became a far better scholar than most of the women of her day. She read widely and wrote in terse, vigorous and elegant language. Her youth was passed in converse with persons of learning, experience and political sagacity. She was married on 25th October, 1764, to John Adams, then a young lawyer practicing in Boston. During the next ten years her quiet and happy life was devoted to her husband and her four children, three sons and one daughter. Then came the troubled times that were marked by the disputes between the Colonies and England. Mrs. Adams seconded her husband in his opposition to the English oppression, and encouraged him in his zeal and determination in urging the Colonies to declare their independence. She remained in Braintree, MA, while Mr. Adams was absent as a delegate to the Continental Congress and afterward on diplomatic missions in Europe. In 1784 she joined her husband in France, and in 1785 they went to London, whither Mr. Adams was sent as Minister Plenipotentiary to the Court of Great Britain. Remembering the patriotic zeal and independence of Mrs. Adams during the Revolution, George III and his queen, still smarting over the loss of the American Colonies, treated her with marked rudeness. Mrs. Adams remembered their rudeness, and afterward wrote: "Humiliation for Charlotte is no sorrow for me." After spending one year in France and three in England, Mrs. Adams returned to the United States in 1788. In 1789, after her husband was appointed Vice-President of the United States, she went to reside in Philadelphia, PA, then the seat of government. In 1797 Mr. Adams was chosen President. In 1800, after his defeat, they retired to Quincy, MA, where Mrs. Adams died 28th October, 1818. She was a woman of elevated mind and strong powers of judgment and observation. Her letters have been collected and published with a biographical sketch by her grandson, Charles F. Adams, in a volume entitled "Familiar Letters of John Adams and his Wife, Abigail Adams, During the Revolution."

ADAMS, Mrs. Florence Adelaide Fowle, dramatic reader and teacher, born in Chelsea, MA, 15th October, 1863. Her maiden name was Fowle. Her father's family, originally from England, have been for many generations residents of the old Bay State. On her mother's side she is descended from the Earl of Seafield, who was her mother's great-grandfather, and from the Ogilvies, Grants, Gordons and Ichmartins of Scotland, tracing their ancestry back to 1300. She was graduated from the Chelsea public school and afterward attended the girl's Latin school in Boston. She learned readily, making particularly rapid progress in the study of the languages.

During childhood she gave promise of great dramatic power. This, combined with her pretty childish face and happy disposition, won her much attention, while it held out flattering prospects for the future. She was graduated from the Boston School of Oratory in 1884, under the late Prof. Robert R. Raymond. In June, 1888, she was married to George Adams, a direct descendant of the statesmen and presidents. Her marriage has not interfered with her chosen line of work. Naturally of a sympathetic disposition, she has devoted much time and talent to charities. Having had from time to time many pupils to instruct, she felt the need of a text-book that should set forth the principles of the Delsarte system in a form easily grasped by the student. This led to the publication of her book "Gestures and Pantomimic Action" (Boston, 1891). Mrs. Adams was her own model for the numerous illustrations used in the volume, and in this, as throughout the work, she

had an invaluable critic in the person of her mother, who is also a graduate of the Boston School of Oratory. One distinguishing trait of Mrs. Adams' character is her great love for animals, not confined to a few pampered pets, but extended to the whole brute creation. Her personal appearance is pleasing. She is youthful looking and is fond of society in which she has ever been a general favorite.

ADAMS, Miss Hannah, the first woman in the United States to make a profession of literature was born in Medfield, MA, in 1755, and died in Brookline, MA, 15th November, 1832. Her father was a well-to-do farmer of considerable education and culture. Hannah was a delicate child fond of reading and study. In childhood she memorized most of the poetical works of Milton, Pope. Thomson, Young and others. Her studies were varied, including Greek and Latin, in which she was instructed by the divinity students who made their home with her family. In 1772 her father lost his property, and the children were forced to provide for themselves. Hannah supported herself during the Revolutionary War by making lace and by teaching school. After the war she opened a school to prepare young men for college, in which she was very successful. Her principal work, a volume entitled "A View of Religious Opinions," appeared in 1784. The labor necessary for so great a work resulted in a serious illness that threatened her with mental derangement. That book passed through several editions in the United States and was republished in England. It is a work of great research and erudition. When the fourth edition was published, she changed the title to "A Dictionary of Religions." It was long a standard volume. Her second work, "A History of New England," appeared in 1799, and her third, "Evidences of Christianity," in 1801. Her income from these successful works was meager, as she did not understand the art of making money so well as she knew the art of making books. Her reputation extended to Europe and won her many friends, among whom was Abbé Grégoire, who was then laboring to secure the emancipation of the Jews in France. With him she corresponded, and from him she received valuable aid in preparing her "History of the Jews," which appeared in 1812. Her next book, "A Controversy with Dr. Morse," appeared in 1814, and her "Letters on the Gospels" in 1826. All her books passed through many editions. Miss Adams was a woman of great modesty and simplicity. Her life was very quiet; her only journey by water was the ten-mile trip from Boston to Nahant and her longest land journey was from Boston to Chelmsford. The closing years of her life she spent in Boston, supported by an annuity settled upon her by three wealthy men of that city. She was buried in Mount Auburn, being the first one to be buried in that cemetery. Her autobiography, edited with additions by Mrs. Hannah F. Lee, was published in Boston in 1832.

ADAMS, Mrs. Jane Kelley, educator, born in Woburn, MA, 30th October, 1852. Her father was a member of a prominent firm of leather manufacturers. Her family had gone from New Hampshire, her mother being a descendant of the Marston family that came over from England in 1634. Mrs. Adams as a child showed great fondness for the schoolroom and for books. When three-and-one-half years old she "ran away" to attend the infant school, of which she became a regular member six months later. From that time her connection with school work, either as student, teacher, or committee-woman, has been almost continuous. As a student, she worked steadily, in spite of delicate health and the protests of physician and friends. She was graduated from the Woburn high school in 1871, and from Vassar College in 1875. In 1876 she became a teacher in the high school from which she was graduated, leaving in 1881 to become the wife of Charles Day Adams, a member of the class of 1873 in Harvard, and a lawyer practicing in Boston. Since her marriage, as before, her home has been in Woburn, and, although a conscientious housekeeper and the mother of two children, she has found time within the last ten years, not only to have occasional private pupils, but also to identify herself fully with the public work of her native city. In 1886–7 she was president of the Woburn

Woman's Club. Within that time she organized three parliamentary law clubs among her women friends. Later, she was one of the founders of the Woburn Home for Aged Women and was one of its vice-presidents. She has served as a director and an auditor of the Woman's Club, as president of a church society, and as chairman of the executive committee of the Equal Suffrage League. In 1888 she was elected to a position on the Woburn school board, and in 1890 served as its presiding officer. In the spring of 1891, feeling from her work on the board of education the great need the students had of instruction in manual training, she was instrumental in establishing classes in sewing, sloyd and cooking, which were largely attended. Besides her work in her native town, Mrs. Adams has found time to be active in the various societies for college-bred women in the neighboring city of Boston. She is of a social nature, has a great interest in her husband's work, and it is not impossible that she will become a student of law.

ADAMS, Mrs. Louise Catherine, wife of John Quincy Adams, born in London, England, in 1775. She was a daughter of Joshua Johnson, of Maryland, but passed her early years in England and France. Her father's house in London was the resort of Americans in England. She was married to Mr. Adams in 1797. Mr. Adams had been resident minister at The Hague, and when his father was elected President of the United States, he went as minister to Berlin, Germany. There the young wife sustained herself with dignity in social and political life. In 1801 she returned with her husband to the United States. Mr. Adams was elected to the United States Senate, and they passed their winters in Washington, DC, and their summers in Boston. In 1808 Mr. Adams was appointed by President Madison the first accredited minister to Russia. Mrs. Adams accompanied him to Russia, and she was the first American woman presented at the Russian court. She made an eminently favorable impression on Russian society. She passed one winter alone in St. Petersburg, while Mr. Adams was in Ghent negotiating a treaty between the United States and England. In the spring, accompanied by her eight-year-old son and servants, she set out to travel to Paris by land. The journey was a memorable one to her, as the times were troublous, the traveling very bad and the country full of soldiers. She reached Paris in March, 1815. There she witnessed all the momentous affairs that preluded the famous "Hundred Days." Mr. Adams was next appointed Minister to England, and they made their home near London. In 1817 they returned to the United States. Mr. Adams served as Secretary of State for eight years, and Mrs. Adams did the honors of their home in Washington. When her husband was elected President, she became the mistress of the White House. There she displayed the same quiet elegance and simplicity that had distinguished her in so many prominent situations. Failing health forced her into semi-retirement. She ceased to appear in fashionable circles, but still presided at public receptions. After the expiration of President Adams' term of office, her retirement was complete. The closing years of her life were spent in the care of her family and the practice of domestic virtues. She died on 14th May, 1852, and was buried by the side of her husband in the family burying ground at Quincy, MA.

ADAMS, Mrs. Mary Mathews, poet, born 23rd October, 1840. She is of Irish birth and parentage, but having come to this country when she was a mere child, she may easily claim America as her mental birthplace. Her home was in Brooklyn, NY, and she was educated mainly at Packer Institute, and taught for nine years. Miss Mathews was married to C. M. Smith, and five years after was left a widow. Her enthusiasm as a student, which she always has been, finds its best result in her Shakespearian study and her parlor lectures. The refined literary appreciation manifested in this work reveals itself in her poems. The "Epithalamium" is perhaps the best known. In 1883 she became the wife of A. S. Barnes, the well-known publisher. He lived but a short time, and in London, in 1890, Mrs. Barnes was married to Charles Kendall Adams, the President of Cornell University, and brought to her position marked mental and social gifts.

ADKINSON, Mrs. Mary Osburn, temperance reformer, born in Rush county, IN, 28th July, 1843; the daughter of Harmon Osburn. Miss Osburn was educated in Whitewater College, Centerville, IN. She began her married life as a pastor's wife in Laurel, IN. Removing to Madison, she was four times elected president of the Madison district association of the Methodist Episcopal Church. Since 1873 she has actively engaged in temperance work, and is now superintendent of the Woman's Christian Temperance Union among the colored people in the State of Louisiana. Mrs. Adkinson is also matron and teacher of sewing and dressmaking in New Orleans University, over which her husband presides.

ADSIT, Mrs. Nancy H., art-lecturer, born in Palermo, Oswego county, NY, 21st May, 1825. At the age of thirteen years she assumed entire charge of herself and her fortunes. The expenses of a collegiate course, in Ingham University, were met by teaching and journalism. Her earlier work was mostly in the line of poetic effusions and several series of "Lay Sermons" under the signature of "Probus." These sermons aroused intense antagonism in clerical circles. "Probus," the unknown, was adjudged by a general council "guilty of heresy," and the sermons were denounced and condemned. The series was completed, however, and her identity was held sacredly between herself and the editor, and not until many years later, by her own voluntary confession, was the writer identified. Mrs. Adsit was married to Charles Davenport Adsit, of Buffalo, NY, 13th December, 1862. They removed to Milwaukee, WI, in 1865, where Mr. Adsit died in 1873, and his wife immediately assumed the entire charge and management of a general insurance agency. She was the first woman in general insurance in this country, and, so far as is known, in the world. Mrs. Adsit, after a successful career, sold the business and resumed the pen. Her contributions to the London "Art Journals,"

Grace Addison.
From Photo by B. J. Falk, New York.

Fanny Davenport.
From Photo by Baker, Columbus.

many years since, brought a request for a series of articles on the "White and Black in Art," or "Etching and Engraving." An entire year was consumed in preparing this work. Months before the articles were completed the demand for parlor conversation on the topics which so absorbed her induced Mrs. Adsit to open her home to classes for study. During the last thirteen years she has given her lecture courses in nearly all the principal cities east and west. Her name is now prominently identified with art education, both in this country and abroad.

AGASSIZ, Mrs. Elizabeth Cabot, naturalist. She is the daughter of Thomas Graves Cary, of Boston, MA. She was married to Professor Louis Agassiz in 1850. She accompanied her husband on his journey to Brazil in 1865–6 and on the Hassler expedition in 1871–2; of the second she wrote an account for the "Atlantic Monthly," and was associated with him in many of his studies and writings. She has published "A First Lesson in Natural History" (Boston, 1859), and edited "Geological Sketches" (1866). Her husband died in 1873, and Mrs. Agassiz edited his "Life and Correspondence" in two volumes (Boston, 1885), a very important work. Mrs. Agassiz resides in Cambridge, MA, and has done much to further the interest of Radcliffe College from its beginning when known as the Harvard "Annex."

AHRENS, Mrs. Mary A., lawyer and philanthropist, born in Staffordshire, England, 29th December, 1836. When she was fifteen years of age her family moved to America and settled in Illinois. Mary was a pupil in the seminary in Galesburg for several years, and a close student until her first marriage in 1857. In her home she took up the study of medicine and earned her diploma. She felt impelled to labor for the elevation of the recently emancipated colored race, and was the first woman teacher in southern Illinois for that ignorant and long-neglected people. For years after her removal to Chicago Mrs. Ahrens devoted herself largely to the lecture field, for which she is well qualified. Soon after her marriage to Louis Ahrens, an artist of ability, this woman of many talents entered the Chicago Union College of Law, and was graduated with honors in 1889. Her success as a practitioner has been marked. As vice-president of the Protective Agency for Women and Children, Mrs. Ahrens

has been of great service to that benevolent organization. Mrs. Ahrens was made chairman of the Woman's School Suffrage Association, of Cook county, and her efforts to secure to the women citizens their legal right to vote at school elections entitle her to the gratitude of every woman in the State. She is a member of the Illinois Woman's Press Association. Her home is in Chicago.

AIKENS, Mrs. Amanda L., editor and philanthropist, born in North Adams, MA, 12th May, 1833. Her father's name was Asahel Richardson Barnes. Her education was received in Maplewood Institute, Pittsfield, MA. After her marriage to Andrew Jackson Aikens she removed to Milwaukee, WI. In November, 1887, Mrs. Aikens began to edit "Woman's World," a special department of "The Evening Wisconsin," of which her husband was one of the proprietors, published in Milwaukee. She was at one time president of the Board of Local Charities and Corrections, two years president of the Woman's Club of Milwaukee, two years chairman of the Art Committee, and has been vice-president of the Wisconsin Industrial School for Girls, and for ten years the chairman of its executive committee. During the Civil War she was an indefatigable worker. It was she who made the public appeals and announcements through the press when the question of a National Soldiers' Home was agitated. In the history of Milwaukee, published in 1881, there is a long account of her various labors for suffering humanity in that time of strife and bloodshed, the War for the Union. She traveled extensively in Europe, and her newspaper letters were really art criticisms of a high order. She was one of the most enthusiastic and successful of those who raised money in Wisconsin for the Johns Hopkins Medical School in Baltimore, for the purpose of admitting women on equal terms with men. She helped largely in organizing the first Woman's Republican Club of Wisconsin, and was a State delegate to the

National Conference of Charities when it met in Baltimore. In 1891 she read a paper before the State Conference of Charities in Madison, WI. Mrs. Aikens had much to do with the introduction of cooking into the public schools of Milwaukee. She was long identified as an officer or director with the Art Science Class, a literary organization for the purpose of developing a taste in architecture, painting, sculpture, and science. One-hundred-fifty ladies belong to this class, and it has done more for the direct education of women in the arts and sciences than any other society in the State. Mrs. Aikens will long be remembered as a talented woman in the literary sense of the word, a loyal wife, a devoted mother, and a philanthropist of the truest and tenderest type. She died at her home in Milwaukee, 20th May, 1892. Few, if any, local interests concerned in the advancement of women but lost a thoughtful, efficient promoter at her death.

ALBANI, Mme. Emma, operatic singer, born in Chambly, near Montreal, Province of Quebec, Canada, in 1851. Her maiden name was Marie Emma La Jeunesse. Her parents were French-Canadians, descendants of Frenchmen that settled in Canada long before the conquest. Her father was a musician, a professor of the harp, and he conducted her early musical studies. In 1856 the family removed to Montreal, where Emma entered the convent school of Notre Dame de Sacré Cœur. There she studied singing. In 1863, when she was twelve years old, she went on a starring tour with her sister. She made her first appearance in Albany, NY, and displayed the vocal and dramatic endowments that have since made her famous. In 1864 her family removed to Albany, where she was engaged to sing in the Roman Catholic cathedral. The bishop was so impressed by her talent that he urged her father to send her abroad for training. A public concert was given in Albany to raise money to enable her to go to Europe. Accompanied by her father, she went to Paris, remaining two years with the Baroness Lafitte, to study under Duprez, and next went to Milan, Italy, where she was trained by Lamperti. In 1870 she sang in Messina with success, and

was at once engaged for Malta. She adopted the stage-name "Albani," in remembrance of Albany, whose citizens had been her generous friends and patrons. In 1871 she sang at the theater La Pergola, in Florence, Italy, where she created successfully the rôle of Mignon in Ambroise Thomas's opera, which had been condemned in four Italian theaters. In 1872 she made her first appearance in England, at the Royal Italian Opera in London, where she made an extraordinary success as Amina in "La Sonnambula." She strengthened her reputation by her presentation of Lucia, Marta, Gilda, and Linda. In November, 1872, she sang as Amina in Paris with marked success. She returned to London and was enthusiastically received. There she added Ophelia to her list of triumphs. In 1874 she revived Mignon. In the winter of 1874–5, she made a successful tour of the United States. In May, 1875, she was again in London, England, where she sang the rôle of Elsa in "Lohengrin," brought out by manager Gye in Covent Garden theater. In Nice, in 1876, she made a deep impression. In Paris she revived the fortunes of the Théâtre Ventadour by her rendition of Lucia and of Gilda in "Rigoletto." In 1877, in the Royal Italian Opera in London, she sang the rôle of Elizabeth in "Tannhäuser," scoring a great success in that majestic character. In August, 1878, she was married to Ernest Gye, the oldest son of Frederick Gye, director of the Royal Italian Opera in London, England. During the winter of 1878 she sang in the Imperial Opera in St. Petersburg, Russia, and afterward in Moscow, Milan and Brussels, always with increasing popularity. In 1879 and 1880 she appeared in Covent Garden, London, as Gilda, Amina, Marguerite, Elvira, Elsa, Mignon, and Ophelia. In the last-named rôle she has no rival. In 1883 she sang in "Faust" and "Rigoletto" in Washington, DC, and closed her operatic tour in Philadelphia in April of that year in "The Flying Dutchman." On 3d April, 1884, she sang in Gounod's "Redemption" in the Trocadéro, Paris, where that composer conducted his own work. In March, 1884, she sang in the Royal Opera house in Berlin. Her operatic career has been one long line of successes. Her voice is a pure soprano of great flexibility and wide range, and her dramatic powers are of the highest order. She is equally successful in concert and oratorio. Her repertoire includes most of the famous rôles. In May, 1886, at the opening of the Colonial Exhibition in London, she sang the ode written for the occasion by Tennyson. Among her acquaintances in Europe is Queen Victoria, who visits her at Mar Lodge, Albani's home in the Scotch Highlands, and meets her as a friend. Madame Albani-Gye is unspoiled by her successes.

ALBRIGHT, Mrs. Eliza Downing, church and temperance worker, born in Philadelphia, PA, 13th March, 1847. She is descended from Puritan ancestry, dating back to that goodly company of 20,000 emigrants, Englishmen of the adventurous and thrifty class, whose sails whitened the Atlantic between 1630 and 1640. At the age of eleven years Eliza Downing was graduated from the public schools of Philadelphia, and later she studied under private teachers and in some of the institutes in which the city at that time abounded. In 1867 she was married to the Rev. Louis M. Albright, D. D., a graduate of the Ohio Wesleyan University and a minister of the Methodist Episcopal Church. After marriage she was engaged with her husband in teaching mathematics and natural sciences in the Ohio Wesleyan Female College, in Delaware, OH. Later she was a teacher of mathematics in Lewis College, Glasgow, MO, and De Pauw Female College, of which Dr. Albright was president. More recently, in the itinerancy in Ohio, Mrs. Albright has been occupied in good work as a pastor's wife in connection with the churches and districts in which her husband has successively served. For the last six years they have resided in Delaware, OH. When the temperance crusade began, Mrs. Albright threw herself into that new movement. She became corresponding secretary of the Ohio Woman's Christian Temperance Union at its organization, in 1877, and for three years, until family cares made necessary her resignation, she did a large amount of work in the way of correspondence and public speaking. She has been identified with the Woman's Foreign Missionary Society of the Methodist Episcopal Church, as district secretary and speaker. At present she is one of the national officers of the Woman's Home Missionary Society and is also chairman of the State executive committee of the Young Woman's Christian Association. A clear and effective speaker, she is in constant demand for public addresses in the interest of these and other causes. While in sympathy with every movement for reform, Mrs. Albright counts her duties to her family first and highest. Naturally a student, with strong physique and great energy, she turns to account every opportunity for personal improvement.

ALCOTT, Miss Louisa May, author, born in Germantown, PA, 29th November, 1832. Her birthday was the anniversary of the birth of her father, the late A. Bronson Alcott, the "Sage of Concord." Louisa was the second of four daughters, only one of whom, Mrs. J. B. Pratt, is now living. Surrounded in childhood by an atmosphere of literature, she began to write at an early age, her reading including Shakespeare, Goethe, Emerson, Margaret Fuller, Miss Edgeworth and George Sand. Her first poem, "To a Robin," was written when she was eight years old. In 1838 the Alcott family removed to Boston, and she lived in or near that city until her death. Concord was longest her home. Their life in this latter town was interrupted by a year spent in an ideal community, "Fruitlands," in the town of Harvard, where they abstained from meat as food. The experience Miss Alcott described in an amusing sketch, "Transcendental Wild Oats." Returning to Concord, the Alcotts lived for a while in a house that was afterward Hawthorne's home. Her father, a distinguished lecturer and teacher of his time, was one of the first to insist that gentleness was more influential than the rod, and to show that education should bring out the best that was in a child's nature, not simply cram a young mind with facts. Miss Alcott received her instructions chiefly from Henry Thoreau. Emerson was Mr. Alcott's most intimate friend, and very early in her life Miss Alcott became his favorite. When she was fifteen, Mr. Emerson loaned her a copy of "Wilhelm Meister," from the reading of which dated her lifelong devotion to Goethe. At the age of sixteen Miss Alcott began to teach a little school of twenty members, and continued to do work of this kind in various ways for fifteen years, although it was extremely distasteful to her, and at the same time she began to write stories for publication. Her first published book was "Flower Fables" (Boston, 1855). It was not successful. She continued to write for her own amusement in her spare hours, but devoted herself to helping her father and mother by teaching school, serving as nursery governess, and even at times sewing for a living. Many of the troubles of those early years have been referred to in the sorrows of Christie in her volume called "Work," published after her name was widely known. After awhile she found there was money in sensational stories, and she wrote them in quick succession and sent them to many papers; but this style of writing soon wearied her and she had conscientious scruples about continuing it. In 1862 she became a nurse in the Washington hospitals and devoted herself to her duties there with conscientious zeal. In consequence, she became ill herself and narrowly escaped death by typhoid fever. While in Washington she wrote to her mother and sisters letters describing hospital life and experience, which were revised and published in book-form as "Hospital Sketches" (Boston, 1863). In that year she went to Europe as companion to an invalid woman, spending a year in Germany, Switzerland, Paris and London. Then followed "Moods" (1864); "Morning Glories, and Other Tales" (1867); "Proverb Stories" (1868). She then published "Little Women," 2 volumes, (1868), a story founded largely on incidents in the lives of her three sisters and herself at Concord. This book made its author famous. From its appearance until her death she was constantly held in public esteem, and the sale of her books has passed into many hundred thousands. Most of her stories were written while she resided in Concord, though she penned the manuscript in Boston, declaring that she could do her writing better in that city, so favorable to her genius and success. Following "Little Women" came "An Old-Fashioned Girl" (1870); "Little Men" (1871), the mere announcement of which brought an advance order from the dealers for 50,000 copies; the "Aunt Jo's Scrap-Bag" (1871), 6 volumes; "Work" (1873); "Eight Cousins" (1875); "A Rose in Bloom" (1876); "Silver Pitchers and Independence" (1876); "Modern Mephistopheles," anonymously in the "No Name Series" (1877); "Under the Lilacs" (1878); "Jack and Jill" (1880); "Proverb Stories" a new edition revised (1882); "Moods" a revised edition (1884); "Spinning-Wheel Stories" (1884); "Jo's Boys" (1886). This latest story was a sequel to "Little Men." "A Garland for Girls" (1887).

With three exceptions her works were all published in Boston. Miss Alcott did not attempt a great diversity of subjects; almost everything she wrote told of scenes and incidents that had come within her personal knowledge. The sales of her books in the United States alone amount to over a half-million. Her "Little Women" reached a sale of 87,000 copies in less than three years. She wrote a few dainty poems, but never considered that her talents lay in versifying. Her death occurred 6th March, 1888, just two days after the death of her father. She was buried on 8th March in the old Sleepy Hollow graveyard in Concord, the funeral being a double one and attended only by the immediate relatives. Miss Alcott's will directed that all her unfinished manuscripts, including all letters written by her, should be burned unread.

ALCOTT, Miss May, see NIERIKER, MME. MAY ALCOTT.

ALDEN, Miss Emily Gillmore, author and educator, born in Boston, MA, 21st January, 1834. In infancy her parents removed to Cambridge, and her education was pursued in the public schools of that city, and in Mt. Holyoke Seminary, South Hadley, MA. Her career has been chiefly that of a teacher in Castleton, VT, and in Monticello Seminary, Godfrey, IL. In this latter institution she now has charge of the departments of history, rhetoric, and English literature, and of senior classes for graduation. Her literary work, stimulated probably by the scope of her teaching and her experience as an enthusiastic and truly artistic educator, has been the recreation of her years, and her poems have the delicacy and spontaneity that belong to genius. Miss Alden comes of Pilgrim ancestry, being of the eighth generation in lineal descent from the Mayflower. She is singularly retiring in manner, courts no admiration for her work, and holds ever her daintiest verses in most modest estimation. She shrinks from publicity, and her first efforts were offered under a pen-name. An early critic, detecting an artistic touch in her poetic fancy, insisted that the mask should be dropped, and since then her poems have reached a very appreciative circle of readers under her own signature.

ALDEN, Mrs. Isabella Macdonald, author, born in Rochester, NY, 3d November, 1841. Her maiden name was Macdonald. While she was still a child, her father moved to Johnstown, NY, and afterward to Gloversville, in the same State. Her pen-name "Pansy," by which she is known so widely, was given to her by her father on the occasion when Isabella, a mere child, had plucked every blossom from a treasured bed of pansies grown by her mother. As the child showered the blossoms in her mother's lap, she said they were "every one for her," and Mr. Macdonald gave her the name which has become so famous. Her father and mother, both persons of intellect and education, encouraged her in every way in her literary work, and her progress was very rapid. When she was only ten years old, she wrote a story about an old family clock which suddenly stopped after running many years, and her father had it published. As a girl, Isabella was an aspiring and industrious author. She wrote stories, sketches, compositions, and a diary in which she recorded all the important events of her life. Her articles were accepted and published in the village papers, and "Pansy" began to be known. Her first book was published when she was yet a mere girl. A publishing house offered a prize for the best Sunday- school book upon a given subject. She wrote "Helen Lester," a small book for young people, partly to amuse herself, and sent the manuscript to the publishers, not expecting to hear from it again. To her surprise the committee selected her book as the best of those received. From that time her pen has never been idle. More than sixty volumes bear the name "Pansy," and all are good, pure books for young and old alike. Miss Macdonald was married in May, 1866, to the Rev. G. R. Alden, and she is a success as a pastor's wife. She composes easily. Her mornings are given to literary work. Some of her books are: "Esther Reid," "Four Girls at Chautauqua," "Chautauqua Girls at Home," "Tip Lewis and His Lamp," "Three People," "Links in Rebecca's Life," "Julia Reid," "Ruth Erskine's Crosses," "The King's Daughter," "The Browning Boys," "From Different Standpoints," "Mrs. Harry Harper's Awakening," and "The Pocket Measure." Story-writing by no means is all her work. She writes the primary lesson department of the "Westminister Teacher," edits the "Presbyterian Primary Quarterly" and the children's popular magazine "Pansy," and writes a serial story for the "Herald and Presbyter" of Cincinnati every winter. Mrs. Alden is deeply interested in Sunday-school primary teaching, and has had charge of more than a hundred children every Sunday for many years. She is interested in temperance also, but delicate health and a busy life hinder her from taking an active part in the work. She gives liberally to the cause, and four of her books, "Three People," "The King's Daughter," "One Commonplace Day," and "Little Fishers and their Nets," are distinctively temperance books, while the principle of total abstinence is maintained in all her writings. Mrs. Alden is a constant sufferer from headache, which never leaves her and is often very severe, but she refuses to call herself an invalid. She is a model housekeeper in every way. Her physician limits her to three hours of literary work each day. The famous Chautauqua system of instruction is warmly advocated by her. She has been prominently identified with that movement from its beginning. Her books are peculiarly adapted to the youth of this country. Most of them have been adopted in Sunday-school libraries throughout the United States. Rev. and Mrs. Alden are now pleasantly located in Washington, DC.

ALDEN, Mrs. Lucy Morris Chaffee, author, born in South Wilbraham, New Hampden, MA, 20th November, 1836. She is a daughter of Daniel D. and Sarah F. Chaffee. Among her maternal ancestors was Judge John Bliss, of South Wilbraham, who on the eighth of April, 1775, was appointed sole committee "to repair to Connecticut to request that Colony to co-operate with Massachusetts for the general defense," and who, under the constitution was chosen to the first and several succeeding senates. Miss Chaffee spent a year at Monson Academy, twenty years in teaching school, and three years as a member of the school board of her native town. She was left alone by the death of her mother in 1884, and was married in July, 1890, to Lucius D. Alden, an early schoolmate but long a resident on the Pacific coast, and she still occupies her father's homestead. Her poetic, and far more numerous prose, writings have appeared in various newspapers of Springfield,

Boston, Chicago, and Minneapolis, in several Sunday-school song-books, and in quarterly and monthly journals. One doctrinal pamphlet of hers has lately been translated by a British officer and missionary in Madras into the Hindusani tongue, and many copies printed. Copies of another were voluntarily distributed by a county judge in Florida among members of his State legislature. Two years ago, under an appropriation, made by an association whose conferences reach from Maine to California, of a sum to be distributed among writers of meritorious articles, Mrs. Alden was selected to write for Massachusetts.

ALDRICH, Miss Anne Reeve, poet and novelist, born in New York City, 25th April, 1866. From her earliest childhood she showed a fondness for composition, spending hours from the time she learned to print in writing stories and verses, although she had the usual healthy childish tastes for romping and all out-of-door sports. At the death of her father, which occurred in her eighth year, her mother removed to the country, where she at first took charge of her daughter's education, which was afterward carried on by competent tutors. Miss Aldrich displayed remarkable proficiency in compostion and rhetoric, which was counterbalanced by what she herself calls an amusing inaptitude for mathematics, so that, while she was translating French and Latin authors for amusement, she was also struggling over a simple arithmetic, whose tear-blotted leaves she still preserves. In her fifteenth year a friend suggested to her to send a poem to "Scribner's Magazine." Although the verses were returned, with them she received a friendly note of encouragement and praise from the editor, who from that time often criticized the young girl's work. She wrote constantly and voluminously, usually destroying her work from month to month, so that but few of her earlier verses are extant. She also read widely, her taste inclining to the early English poets and dramatists and to mediæval literature. When she was seventeen, her first published poem appeared in "Lippincott's Magazine," followed by others in the "Century" and various periodicals. In 1885 Miss Aldrich's mother moved back to New York.

Her first book was "The Rose of Flame and Other Poems of Love" (New York, 1889), and she published one novel, "The Feet of Love" (New York, 1890). Miss Aldrich disliked country life and was fond of society. Her ancestors were Tories in Revolutionary days, and their large estates were confiscated by the American government because of their allegiance to the crown. She died in New York City, 28th June, 1892.

ALDRICH, Mrs. Flora L., doctor of medicine, born in Westford, NY, 6th October, 1859. Her maiden name was Southard. Her father was a farmer, and her childhood was spent on a farm known as "Sutherland Place." Her paternal ancestors were among the original Dutch settlers of the Hudson river valley at Kinderhook and Hudson. Among them are the names of Hoffman and Hubbard. Of the Southard family little is known, as the great-grandfather was an adopted child of a Hudson merchant and could remember only that his name was Southard, and that he was stolen from a port in England. From all that can be gathered he is believed to be of good English family, and probably Southworth was the original name. Her maternal ancestors were of the Sutherland family, who have a clear connection with the nobility of England and Scotland. Her early education was conducted almost entirely by her mother, who ranked among the educated women of her day. Before Flora was eleven years old she could trace nearly every constellation of stars, and knew the names and characteristics of flowers, insects, and birds in that section of her native State. When she was in her twelfth year her mother died, and her education subsequently was academic and by instruction under private teachers. When eighteen years old she was an advanced scholar in many branches. Interest in the sick and suffering was uppermost in her mind, and her chosen life-work would have been that of a missionary. Her marriage with Dr. A. G. Aldrich, of Adams, MA, in 1883, resulted in her beginning immediately the study of medicine and surgery. A year later they removed to Anoka, Minn., where they now reside. She was graduated in 1887 from the old Minnesota Medical College, now the Medical Department of the State University, and has since taken postgraduate courses in the best schools in this country. She is now preparing for a course of study in Europe. In addition to her professional attainments, Dr. Aldrich has talent as a writer, and has nearly ready for publication a volume of almost two hundred poems. In religious belief she is Episcopalian. Though, exceedingly busy in her profession, both as physician and surgeon, in social life and the literary and scientific world, she is at the head of several literary and social organizations, and is greatly interested in charitable and philanthropic work.

ALDRICH, Mrs. Josephine Cables, author and philanthropist, born in Connecticut. She was but a few years old when her mother died, leaving her in the care of two Puritan grandmothers of the most severe school, strict in the observance of what they considered their religious duties. They believed that a free use of the rod was necessary to save the child's soul from destruction. This severe treatment taught her that the Golden Rule was by far the best maxim for morality and happiness, and no sooner was she in control of a home of her own in Rochester, NY, than she gave such instruction for the betterment of humanity by word and deed that her home became a sort of Mecca for advance thinkers, not only of America, but pilgrims came from Europe, Asia and Africa to confer with her. In 1882 she began in Rochester, NY, the publication of "The Occult World," a little paper devoted to advanced thought and reform work. Her editorials taught liberality, justice and mercy. Her greatest work has been in private life, and her influence for good over the individual was remarkable. She was at one time secretary of the Theosophical Society of the United States, and president of the Rochester Brotherhood. She is now in affluent circumstances in a home in Aldrich, AL, a mining town named for her husband Mr. Aldrich fully sustains his wife in all her work, and she is in turn assisting him to carry out a plan of his, whereby persons accused of crime shall be defended before the court, at the public expense, as diligently and ably as such persons are now prosecuted. The town of Aldrich is a

quiet, peaceful, moral and refined community, where the rights of all are respected, and where drink and tobacco are almost unknown. Mrs. Aldrich is vice-president of the Woman's National Industrial League, vice-president of the Woman's National Liberal Union, and one of the founders of the Woman's National University and School of Useful and Ornamental Arts.

ALDRICH, Mrs. Julia Carter, author, born in Liverpool, OH, 28th January, 1834. She was the fifth in a family of seven children. Her maiden name was Carter. Her paternal ancestors were New Englanders of English stock. Her mother's parents, born and reared in Richmond, VA, were of Scotch and German descent. Miss Carter began to write when quite young, making a successful attempt at the age of fourteen years. At seventeen she began to teach in a large village school, following that vocation for four years. During all the busy period of study and teaching, frequent contributions from her pen, both of verse and prose, found place in various periodicals. In October, 1854, she was married to Joseph Aldrich, of New York. During the earlier years of her married life literary work was somewhat neglected, but believing that many fountains of evil had their origin in bad home management, for several years she did much earnest work for the home circle under various pen-names, "Petresia Peters" being the best known. Her articles written in the interests of humanity would make volumes. Mrs. Aldrich is the mother of three sons. Her husband died in 1889, at their country place, "Maple Grove Home," near Wauseon, OH.

ALDRICH, Mrs. Mary Jane, temperance reformer, born in Sidney Plains, NY, 19th March, 1833. Her paternal great-grandfather, the Rev. William Johnson, a Scotch-Irish Presbyterian minister, as also her grandfather, Col. Witter Johnson, was in the Revolutionary army. Her father, Milton Johnson, was a farmer possessing uncommon intellectual ability, and her mother, Delia Hull, a well educated woman of deeply religious nature. Beyond the public school, three terms in Franklin Academy supplied the school privileges

Adele Block.
From Photo by Baker, Columbus.

Viola Allen.
From Photo by Morrison, Chicago.

of Miss Johnson. She was married in 1855 to John Aldrich, and removed soon after to Nebraska, where for ten years her married life was full of pioneer experiences. In 1866 she removed with her husband, son and daughter, to Cedar Rapids, IA, her present home, where her youngest child, a son, was born. Her uneventful life was spent in caring for her husband and children and in Sabbath school and missionary work. From childhood a "total abstainer" and in full sympathy with prohibitory law, she was not even a member of any temperance society until the crusade. That movement touched the deepest springs of her being. At the organization of the Woman's Christian Temperance Union of Iowa, 3d and 4th November, 1874, the Raising of Lazarus was her text for more earnest temperance work by Christian people. Later, at a county Woman's Christian Temperance Union convention, she delivered her first address, and ere long became widely known as a forceful, entertaining and logical speaker. She was a vice-president of the National Woman's Christian Temperance Union at its organization, in 1874, when she visited different localities, and in 1875 was corresponding secretary of the Woman's Christian Temperance Union of Iowa, leaving the latter office in 1876 to spend more time in the field. There are few counties in Iowa in which she has not spoken. Elected president of her State union in 1883, she declined reelection in 1885 because unable to give to the work all the time it required, but was elected corresponding secretary by the Union, which office she still holds. When the National Union, at the St. Louis Convention in 1884, declared in favor of political temperance work by the union, Mrs. Aldrich, with the majority of the Iowa delegation, voted against the resolution. Subsequently she was the efficient co-worker of Mrs. J. Ellen Foster, the president, who represented the Woman's Christian Temperance Union of Iowa in its open opposition to political Woman's Christian Temperance Union work, and its final withdrawal from the auxiliaryship to the National, on that account, in October, 1890. She attended the convention held in Cleveland, OH, in 1890, at which the Nonpartisan National Woman's Christian Temperance Union was organized. As secretary of the department of evangelistic work she has been a member of the executive committee from its organization. By church connection she is a Presbyterian.

ALDRICH, Miss Susanna Valentine, author, born in Hopkinton, MA, 14th November, 1828. She is the only child of Willard and Lucy (Morse) Aldrich. From her earliest years she showed a decided literary bent. Her studies were interrupted by a severe illness lasting for years. A victim to insomnia, she always kept paper and pencil within reach in order to jot down the fancies that thronged upon her. Encouraged by the Rev. J. C. Webster, her pastor, also one of the directors of the academy which Miss Aldrich attended, some of her compositions were offered to a magazine, and were accepted. For many years Miss Aldrich contributed both prose and poetry to a number of papers and magazines. Since 1879 she has made her home in the Roxbury District of Boston, MA.

ALEXANDER, Miss Jane Grace, pioneer woman-banker, born in Winchester, NH, 26th October, 1848. She is a daughter of Edward and Lucy Capron Alexander, who were of Puritan ancestry. Miss Alexander finished her educational course in Glenwood Seminary, Brattleboro, VT. After graduating she taught school for a time, and then accepted a position in the Winchester National Bank. For more than twenty years she has pursued the path of her choice, and has long been assistant cashier of the National bank just mentioned. In 1881, at the time of the incorporation of the Security Savings Bank, Miss Alexander was elected treasurer, being the first woman to fill such a position. As superintendent of a Sabbath school and president of a Chautauqua class, she has long been a leading spirit in the village, and she has abundantly shown what a true-hearted, earnest woman may attain in the line of business.

ALLEN, Mrs. Elizabeth Akers, poet, born in Strong, Franklin county, ME, 9th October, 1832. Her mother died when Elizabeth was yet an infant, and the poet's girlhood was passed in Farmington, ME. Her verses were received with marked favor, and were widely copied. Her earliest verses were written when she was only twelve years old. In 1855 she became assistant editor of the Portland, ME, "Transcript," and the next year published her first volume of poetry, "Forest Buds from the Woods of Maine." It proved a success financially, and she was able to spend some time in Italy, France and Germany. In 1860 she was married to her first husband, Paul Akers, the sculptor, who died in Philadelphia, PA, in the spring of 1861, at the age of thirty-five, just as a brilliant career was opening to him. Their only child died shortly afterward, and Mrs. Akers, rallying from a long mental and physical prostration, returned to Portland and took her old situation in the "Transcript" office. In 1863 she received an appointment in the War Office in Washington, DC. Her second volume of verse, "Poems by Elizabeth Akers," was brought out in 1866, and was successful. In the fall of 1866 she was married to E. M. Allen, and went with him to Richmond, VA. The now celebrated poem, "Rock Me to Sleep, Mother," was written by Mrs. Allen, in 1859, and sent from Rome to the Philadelphia "Post," and that journal published it in 1860. In 1872 her husband engaged in business in New York City, which is now her home, and where she is a member of Sorosis.

ALLEN, Mrs. Esther Lavilla, author, born in Ithaca, NY, 28th May, 1834. While she was a child, her parents removed to Ypsilanti, MI, and she was educated in the seminary of that town. In 1851 she was married, and for some years her home has been in Hillsdale, MI. Beginning her literary career in earnest in 1870, she wrote stories, sketches and poems for prominent periodicals, her productions being widely copied. Much of her work has been devoted to temperance and missionary lines. Being a fine reader she has often read her poetical productions in public, mainly before college societies.

ALLEN, Mrs. Esther Saville, author, born in Honeoye, Ontario county, NY, 11th December, 1837. Her parents were Joseph and Esther Redfern Saville, natives of England. Her father was a man of refined literary taste. Before she was ten years old she made her first public effort in a poem, which was published. At the age of twelve years she wrote for Morris and Willis a poem which they published in the "Home Journal." Her father judiciously, so far as possible, repressed all precocious display, but the passion was her master, and while a pupil in the common schools of western New York, and in the academy in Rushford, NY, she wrote and published many poems under the pen-name of "Winnie Woodbine." She became a teacher in the public schools of western New York and continued to write for eastern papers, assuming her proper name, Etta Saville. Moving to Illinois in 1857, she taught in the public schools until 1859, when she was married to Samuel R. Allen, a lawyer in Erie, IL. Since her marriage all her literary productions have appeared under the name of Mrs. S. R. Allen. Since 1872 she has resided in Little Rock, Ark. She is probably the author of more productions, both in prose and verse, than any other woman of her State. Much of her work has been widely copied and recopied. Devoted to charity, organized and practical, her writings in that cause have promoted the institution and development of much useful work, or revived and reinvigorated it. Though retiring by nature and disposition, she is fearless and vigorous in action when occasion calls and the right demands it. Her life-work, by her own choice, has been the faithful and efficient discharge of every duty in her home and social relations. She is a true outgrowth and exemplification of the greatness of American women, to whose devotion to duty and rich display of intellect and truth in domestic relations is owing a great proportion of the might of the Nation in the past and present, and its hope for the time to come.

ALLEN, Mrs. Mary Wood, physician, author and lecturer, born in Delta, OH, 19th October, 1841. She is the daughter of George Wood, who emigrated from his English home when just of age, and in the wilds of southern Michigan met and married Miss Sarah Seely. The young couple settled where the village of Delta now stands, but at that time there were but two dwellings in the place. In one of these Mary was born, and there her childhood was passed. Even in those early days her future was shadowed forth, for she never played with dolls except to doctor them in severe illnesses. They often died under her treatment and then she enjoyed having a funeral, in which she figured as chief mourner, preacher and sexton, as she had neither brother nor sister, and her playmates were few. At fourteen she had exhausted the resources of the village school. She manifested a love for study, especially of music, and before fifteen years of age had established herself in central Ohio as a music teacher with a class of twenty pupils. Her talent in music was a direct inheritance from her mother who had a remarkable voice. As a music teacher Mary earned money to begin her college course in Delaware, OH, where she proved an ardent student, putting four years work into three and, as a result breaking down in health. After graduation she taught music, French and German in a collegiate institute in Battle Ground, IN, continuing there until her marriage to Chillon B. Allen, a graduate of the classical department of the Ohio Wesleyan University in Delaware, OH, and of the Ann Arbor Law School. Her own delicate health led her into the investigation of many therapeutical measures, and after the death of her first child in infancy she, with her husband, began the study of medicine, first in her own country and then in Europe, where she spent three years, returning to graduate in medicine from Ann Arbor in 1875. In Newark, NJ, where she settled and practiced her profession, her first important literary work was done. This was the beginning of the "Man Wonderful and the House Beautiful" (New York, 1884), an allegorical physiology. The first ten chapters appeared in the "Christian Union," and received such a recognition that their expansion into a book was began, and she and her husband united in completing the volume. Dr. Allen has also been a contributor of both prose and poetry to many leading periodicals, her poem entitled "Motherhood" having won for itself immediate fame. It is, however, as a lecturer that Dr. Allen has won her brightest laurels. A paper upon heredity which she presented at the State convention of the Woman's Christian Temperance Union in Cortland, NY, was both eloquent and logical and aroused the interest of the whole convention, and as a result Dr. Allen was appointed national lecturer of the Woman's Christian Temperance Union in the departments of heredity and hygiene. Since then she has received calls from various parts of the United States to lecture upon these and kindred topics. A demand soon arose for her instruction in teachers' institutes and normal colleges upon the subject of temperance physiology. Her presentation of the topic gave general satisfaction. At present Dr. Allen has her home in Toledo, OH, whence she goes forth into the lecture field. Glorious as has been her work for temperance, that which she has done, and is doing, for social purity is more beautiful. Upon this subject, so difficult to handle, she has spoken Sabbath evenings in many pulpits, and has received the unqualified praise of such noted clergymen as Dr. Heber Newton, Dr. Theodore Cuyler and Dr. Pentecost in the East, and Dr. McLean upon the Pacific coast. She manifests a peculiar fitness for giving wise counsel to girls, and has done acceptable work in this line in schools and colleges. During several winters, by invitation of Miss Grace Dodge, she has spoken to the Working Girl's Clubs of New York City. It is a scene of absorbing interest when, with rare tact and delicacy, she addresses large audiences of young men on the work of the White Cross. Her mission in the work of reform and philanthropy demands a peculiar talent which she possesses in an unusual degree; a scientific education which enables her to speak with authority; a winning presence; a musical voice which makes itself heard in the largest building with no apparent effort, and which by its sympathetic quality arrests attention and touches the heart, while her words appeal to the reason, and a gentle womanly manner which converts the most pronounced opposer of woman's public work. To those who hear her on the platform or in the pulpit, she is a living voice, alluring her hearers to lives of truth and purity, and to those who know her personally she is a sweet womanly presence, the embodiment of those graces which are the power in the home.

ALLERTON, Mrs. Ellen Palmer, poet, born in Centerville, NY, 17th October, 1835. Her ancestors were of Knickerbocker blood. She received a district-school education and afterward spent a few terms in academies, but never graduated. Her marriage to Alpheus B. Aller-ton took place in 1862, soon after her removal to Wisconsin. Mr. and Mrs. Allerton were both in-valids in Wisconsin, but in 1879, traveled to Kansas in a wagon, cook-ing their own meals and get-ting health and happiness out of the journey. They selected for a home an unim-proved farm, a-quarter section, on very high land in Brown county, in sight of Padonia, Hamlin, Falls City and Hiawatha. They now have a hand-some home and every comfort that prosperity brings in its train. Mrs. Allerton composed and recited verses before she could write, but offered little to the press until she was past thirty years of age. Her first poems were published in "The Jef-ferson County Union," Ex-Governor Hoard's paper. Later she contributed to Milwaukee and Chicago papers, and was at one time book-reviewer for the Milwaukee "Sentinel." She has published one volume, "Poems of the Prairies," (New York, 1886). She is considered one of the leading authors of Kansas. As a woman and as a writer she is quiet and sensible. At her home in Padonia she has a wide circle of loving friends, and throughout the West the hearts that hold her dear are legion.

ALLYN, Mrs. Eunice Eloisae Gibbs, author, born in Brecksville, a suburb of Cleveland, OH. Her father, Dr. Sidney Smith Gibbs, was a native of Schoharie county, NY, and her mother, Eunice Lucinda Newberry, was a native of St. Lawrence county, in the same State. Dr. Gibbs was prac-ticing in Brecksville when he married Miss New-berry, who was a cultured and successful teacher. He was a relative of Sidney Smith, and was natu-rally of a literary turn. Mrs. Gibbs possessed sim-ilar talents, and many articles from their pens were published in the press of the day. Their family consisted of four chil-dren, of whom Eunice was the third. After various changes of climate in search of health, Dr. Gibbs died in compara-tively early manhood, leaving his wife with three young children to provide for. The devoted mother most nobly filled her trust. After his death the family moved from Jackson, MI, to Cleveland, OH, where Eunice was graduated with honors from the high school. She intended to become a teacher, but her mother dis-suaded her and she remained at home, going into society and writing in a quiet way for the local papers. Her articles were signed by various pen-names in order to avoid displeasing one of her brothers, who did not wish to have a "blue-stocking" in the family. Her first published poems appeared in the Cleveland "Plain Dealer," when she was only thirteen years old. Besides com-posing poems for recitation in school, she often wrote songs, both words and music, when she could not find songs suited to various occasions. In 1873 she was married to Clarence G. Allyn, of Nyack, NY. After spending several years at Nyack, New London, CT, and Auburn, NY, they moved to Dubuque, IA, where they now live. Mrs. Allyn is a prominent member of the Dubuque Ladies' Literary Union, and for eight years she has served as president of the Dubuque Woman's Christian Temperance Union. She has been con-nected with the local press at times, and she has also won distinction as an artist. She is a member of the Episcopal Church, is broad in her views, while strictly orthodox, and is an ardent admirer of Oriental philosophy. Before her marriage she gained valuable experience as Washington corre-spondent of the Chicago "Inter-Ocean," a position which she filled for a year, during which time she also wrote numerous articles for the St. Louis "Globe," the New York "World," and before and since then for various New York, Boston, Indi-anapolis, Philadelphia and Chicago journals. She is a pointed, incisive writer, and all her work, prose or poetry, has an aim, a central thought. In her own city she has quietly inaugurated many reforms and educational movements, doing the work, not for notoriety, but prompted by her inborn desire to do something toward lifting up humanity.

ALRICH, Mrs. Emma B., journalist, author and educator, born in Cape May county, NJ, 4th April, 1845. She was the first child of fond parents, and no attempt was made to guard against precocity. At the age of three years a New Testament was given her as a prize for reading its chapters, and at five years she picked blackberries to buy an arith-metic. At twelve years of age she joined the Baptist Church. At that time she began to write for the county paper. At sixteen she taught the summer school at her home. In 1862 she entered the State Normal School in Trenton, NJ, going out for six months in the middle of the course to earn the money for finishing it. She was graduated in June, 1864, as valedictorian of her class. She began to teach in a summer school on the next Monday morning after her graduation. In 1866 she was married to Levi L. Alrich, who had won laurels as one of Baker's Cavalry, or 71st Pennsylvania Regiment. Her first two years of married life they spent in Philadelphia, PA. In 1876 the Centennial opened up new possibilities and Mr. and Mrs. Alrich moved to the West and settled in Cawker City, KS. There she again entered the school-room, was the first woman in Mitchell county to take the highest grade certificate, and the only woman who has been superintendent of the city schools. She was a warm supporter of teachers' meetings, church social gatherings, a public library and a woman's club. In 1883 her husband's failing health compelled a change in business. He bought the "Free Press," and changed its name to the "Public Record." All the work of the office has been done by their own family, and each can do every part of it. Besides her journalistic work, she served two years on the board of teachers' examiners. She was one of the forty who organized the National Woman's Relief Corps, one of the three who founded the Woman's Hesperian Library Club, and was the founder of the Kansas Woman's Press Association. Her busy life leaves her but little time for purely literary work.

AMES, Mrs. Eleanor M., author, born in 1830. She now lives in Brooklyn, NY. She has written a number of books, under the pen-name "Eleanor Kirk" designed to assist young writers, and she publishes a magazine entitled "Eleanor Kirk's Idea," for the same purpose. Her works. include "Up Broadway, and its Sequel" (New York, 1870), "Periodicals that Pay Contributors" (Brooklyn), "Information for Authors" (Brooklyn, 1888); and as editor, "Henry Ward Beecher as a Humorist" (New York, 1887), and "The Beecher Book of Days" (New York, 1886).

AMES, Mrs. Fanny B., industrial reformer, born in Canandaigua, NY, 14th June, 1840. In her childhood she was taken with her father's family to Ohio, where she was for some time a student in Antioch College, under the presidency of Horace Mann. Her first experience in practical work was gained in military hospitals during the war. For five years she was a teacher in the public schools in Cincinnati. She was married in 1863 to the Rev. Charles G. Ames, and during his ministry in Philadelphia she engaged in the work of organized charity, was president of the Children's Aid Society, traveled widely in Pennsylvania, assisting in the organization of county branches of that society, visiting almshouses, and getting up the provisions by which dependent children were removed from almshouses and placed in private families under the supervision of local committees of women. Under State authority she was for five years one of the visitors of public institutions, with power to inspect and report to the Board of State Charities. She thus became familiar with the methods, merits and abuses of those institutions, her knowledge of which not only qualified her to prepare the reports of the Philadelphia Board of Visitors, but led her into wide and careful study of the causes of poverty and dependence, quickening her natural sympathy with the struggling classes, at the same time elevating her estimate of the social service rendered by wisely-used capital and fairly-managed industries. She was for two years president of the New Century Club of Philadelphia, one of the most active and influential women's clubs of this country. Mrs. Ames now resides in Boston, her husband presiding over the Church of the Disciples. She read a paper before the National Council of Women in 1891 on the "Care of Defective Children." She was appointed Factory Inspector in Massachusetts, 8th May, 1891, by Governor Russell, in accordance with an act passed by the State legislature.

AMES, Miss Julia A., editor and temperance reformer, born near Odell, Livingston county, IL, 14th October, 1861. She was the daughter of a well-known wealthy citizen of Streator, IL. She was a graduate of Streator high school, the Illinois Wesleyan University, and of the Chicago School of Oratory. Her work in the Woman's Christian Temperance Union began in Streator, where she proved herself a most valuable and efficient helper to Mrs. Plumb, the district president of the

Woman's Christian Temperance Union. Her peculiar talents for temperance work soon brought her into prominence, and she was drawn into the central union in Chicago. There, in addition to her elocutionary talents and executive capacity, she showed herself the possessor of the journalistic faculty, and she was soon placed where she could make good use of that faculty for the noble organization of temperance workers. The first of the Chicago daily newspapers to publish a Woman's Christian Temperance Union department was the "Inter-Ocean." In her first interviews with the editors, Miss Ames received many charges and cautions, all of which she tried faithfully to heed. Yet, in spite of her care, everything she sent was sharply scanned and often mercilessly cut. At first only a few inches of space were given to her. This was gradually increased as the editors learned they could trust her, till, before she gave the department into other hands, she usually occupied nearly a column, and editors ceased to cut her manuscript. Other and more important work soon came to her hand. The national superintendent of press-work, Mrs. Esther Housh, found her labor too great for her strength, and Miss Ames was appointed her assistant. She performed all the necessary work in this field until her duties on the "Union Signal" forced her to give the work into other hands. Her connection with the central union brought her into intimate contact with many noble women, among whom were Helen Louise Hood, Mrs. Matilda B. Carse, Mrs. Andrew and Miss Willard. Her intercourse with them molded her views and life visibly, and her progress was rapid. Position after position called her, and in each she did earnest, noble work without stint. When Mrs. Andrew felt that, on account of her health, she must give up her work on the "Union Signal," the question of her successor was earnestly discussed. The thoughts of the leaders at once turned to Miss Ames, and despite her youth, she justified the choice of those who urged her to follow Mrs. Andrew. Up to 1889 her special province was the difficult one of news from the field and children's department. She originated the department of illustrated biography and the queen's garden. In all her work she showed a thoroughness, patience and courtesy absolutely indispensable to success, yet seldom found united in one person. Her forte was not so much writing, though she was ready with her pen, as it was that higher faculty which instinctively told her what to choose and what to reject of others' writing, and the winning power to draw from them their best thoughts. In 1889 she had sole charge of the "Union Signal" in the absence of the editor. She took a vacation trip to Europe in 1890, spending a month in London, England, and visiting Lady Henry Somerset at Eastnor Castle. Miss Ames was received with honor by the British Woman's Temperance Association. While in London, she organized the press department of that society on lines similar to those of the American organization. She traveled through Europe with a chosen party conducted by Miss Sarah E. Morgan, under the auspices of Mrs. M. B. Willard's school for girls. She witnessed the Passion Play at Oberammergau, visited Rome and other famous cities and returned to the United States refreshed in mind and body to resume her editorial duties on the "Union Signal." She attended the Boston convention in November, 1891, in her editorial capacity. She assisted in editing the daily "Union Signal," prepared the Associated Press dispatches each night, and was the chairman of one or two committees. She was not well when she left Chicago, and she contracted a severe cold, which through the pressure of her work developed into typhoid pneumonia, of which she died 12th December, 1891. Miss Ames was a member of the Woman's Temperance Publishing Association Circle of King's Daughters and was president of that organization when she left Chicago for her European tour. The silver cross and the white ribbon were the symbols of her life. She was an efficient worker, a thorough organizer and the possessor of more than ordinary executive capacity. She was direct, positive earnest, amiable and indefatigable.

AMES, Miss Lucia True, author, born in Boscawen, NH, 5th May, 1856. She has written two books, "Great Thoughts for Little Thinkers" (New York, 1888), and "Memoirs of a Millionaire" (Boston, 1889), a work of fiction. The first is an attempt to present modern and liberal thought on scientific and religious questions in a simple form which shall supplement home and Sunday-school instruction. The second volume treats of experiments in modern social reforms. Miss Ames has been to Europe several times and traveled extensively. She has for some years conducted numerous large adult classes in Boston and vicinity in studies in nineteenth century thought, taking Emerson, Lowell, Carlyle, Webster and Bryce as the bases for study. She has been a contributor to various periodicals. She is a woman suffragist and an earnest worker in furthering measures that shall promote good citizenship. She is a niece of Charles Carleton Coffin, the author of books for boys. Her home is in Boston, MA, in which vicinity she has spent the greater part of her life.

AMES, Mrs. Mary Clemmer, see HUDSON, MRS. MARY CLEMMER.

AMIES, Mrs. Olive Pond, educator and lecturer, born in Jordan, NY. She was two weeks old when her father died, and the mother and child went to the home of the grandparents in New Britain, CT. There the mother worked untiringly with her needle for the support of herself and her two children. The older child, a boy, was placed in the care of an uncle, and to Olive the mother took the place of father, mother, brother and sister. When Olive was four years old, the mother and child left the home of the grandmother and went to the village to board, that Olive might be sent to school. Soon after this the mother married Cyrus Judd, a man of influence in the town of New Britain. Olive passed through the course of the New Britain high school, was graduated from the State Normal School, and later, after several years of teaching, was graduated from the Normal and Training School in Oswego, NY. She was always a leader in school and became eminent as a teacher. For five years in the State of New York and two in the State of Maine she was in constant demand in the county teachers' institutes. She founded the training school for teachers in Lewiston, ME, and graduated its first classes. In 1871 she was married to the Rev. J. H. Amies, pastor of the Universalist Church, Lewiston, ME, though she had been brought up a Methodist and had become, in later years, an Episcopalian. In 1877 she began to edit

the primary department of the "Sunday School Helper," published in Boston, the exponent for the Universalist Church of the International Lessons. Since January, 1880, she has never failed with a lesson, excepting two months in 1884, during a severe illness. Mrs. Amies feels that her husband's encouragement and assistance have been the moving power in her work. She holds State positions in the Woman's Christian Temperance Union and the Woman Suffrage Association, and delivers lectures on the different themes connected with those two organizations. She also speaks on kindergarten and object teaching, and her "Conversations on Juvenile Reforms" have been exceedingly popular wherever given. Her home is now in Philadelphia, PA. She has had a family of six children, of whom one son and one daughter died while young.

AMORY, Mrs. Estelle Mendell, educator, and author, born in Ellisburgh, Jefferson county, NY, 3d June, 1845, passed her childhood on a farm. In 1852 her family moved to Adams, where her father, S. J. Mendell, engaged in business. The Mendell home was a home of refinement and culture, where were entertained many prominent persons, intercourse with whom did much to inspire the young girl with a desire to make a mark in literature. Her father served in the army throughout the war, rising to the rank of colonel by brevet. Estelle had developed meanwhile into a studious young woman, and had taught her first school. She studied in the Hungerford Collegiate Institute in her home town, and in Falley Seminary, Fulton, NY. In 1866 the family moved to Franklin county, IA. In 1867 she returned to the East and re-entered Falley Seminary, from which institution she was graduated with honors in 1868. Then followed seven years of earnest work as a teacher. In 1875 she became the wife of J. H. Amory, of Binghamton, NY, and went to Elgin, IL, to live. During all those years Mrs. Amory had written much but published little. Ready acceptance of offered work now encouraged her, and soon she became a regular contributor to standard periodicals. Her well-known "Aunt Martha Letters," in the Elmira "Telegram," and the more famous "Aunt Chatty" series in the Minneapolis "Housekeeper," made her name a household word. Among the score of journals that have given her articles to the public are the "Ladies' Home Journal," "Mail and Express," Cincinnati "Enquirer," "Union Signal,"

"Babyhood," and "Golden Days." Mrs. Amory's family consists of a son and a daughter, and her home is now in Belmond, IA.

ANDERSON, Mary, Mme. Navarro, actor, born in Sacramento, CA, 28th July, 1859. Her maiden name was Mary Antoinette Anderson. Her mother was of German descent, and her father was the grandson of an Englishman. In January, 1860, her parents removed from Sacramento to Louisville, KY, where she lived until 1877. Her father joined the Confederate army at the beginning of the Civil War, and was killed at Mobile, AL, in 1862. Her mother was married again in 1864, to Dr. Hamilton Griffin, a practicing physician in Louisville. Mary and her brother Joseph had a pleasant home. Mary was a bright, mischievous child, whose early pranks earned her the name of "Little Mustang." Afterward, when her exuberance was toned down and she had settled seriously to study, she was called "Little Newspaper." In school she was so careless of books and fond of mischief, that at the age of thirteen years she was permitted to study at home. There, instead of the usual studies, she spent her time on Shakespeare. Fascinated by the world that the poet opened to her, she began to train her voice to recite striking passages that she committed to memory. The desire to become an actor was born with her. At the age of ten she recited passages from Shakespeare, with her room arranged to represent the stage scene. Her first visit to the theater occurred when she was twelve years old. She and her brother witnessed the performance of a fairy piece, and from that moment she had no thought for any profession but the stage. Her parents attempted to dissuade her from this choice, but she was known to possess dramatic talent, and friends urged her parents to put her in training for the stage. In her fourteenth year she saw Edwin Booth perform as Richard III in Louisville, and the performance intensified her desire to become an actor. She repeated his performance at home, and terrified a colored servant girl into hysterics with her fierce declamation. The performance was repeated before an audience of friends in her home, and in it she achieved her first success. Her interrupted course in the Ursuline Convent school in Louisville was supplemented by a course of training in music, dancing and literature, with the idea of a dramatic career. By the advice of Charlotte Cushman she made a thorough preparation, studying for a time with the younger Vanderhoff in New York. That was her only real training—ten lessons from a dramatic teacher; all the rest she accomplished for herself. Her first appearance was in the rôle of Juliet, on 27th November, 1875, in Macauley's Theater, Louisville, in a benefit given for Milnes Levick, an English stock actor, who was in financial straits. Miss Anderson was announced on the bills simply as "Juliet, by a Louisville Young Lady."

The theater was packed, and Mary Anderson, in spite of natural crudities and faults, won a most pronounced success. In February, 1876, she played a week in the same theater, appearing as Bianca in "Fazio," as Julia in the "Hunchback," as Evadne, and again as Juliet. Her reputation spread rapidly, and on 6th March, 1876, she began a week's engagement at the opera house in St. Louis, MO. She next played in Ben de Bar's Drury Lane Theater in New Orleans, and scored a brilliant triumph. She next presented Meg Merrilies in the New Orleans Lyceum, and won a memorable success. Prominent persons overwhelmed her with attentions, and a special engine and car bore her to Louisville. She now passed some time in study and next played a second engagement in New Orleans.

Her first and only rebuff was in her native State, where she played for two weeks in San Francisco. The press and critics were cold and hostile, and it was only when she appeared as Meg Merrilies the Californians could see any genius in her. In San Francisco she met Edwin Booth, who advised her to study such parts as "Parthenia," as better suited to her powers than the more sombre tragic characters. Her Californian tour discouraged her, but she was keen to perceive the lesson that underlay ill success, and decided to begin at the bottom and build upward. She made a summer engagement with a company of strolling players and familiarized herself with the stage "business" in all its details. The company played mostly to empty benches, but the training was valuable to Miss Anderson. In 1876 she accepted an offer from John T. Ford, of Washington and Baltimore, to join his company as a star at three-hundred dollars a week. Accompanied by her parents, as was her invariable custom, she went on a tour with Mr. Ford's company and everywhere won new triumphs. The management reaped a rich harvest. On this tour Miss Anderson was subjected to annoyance through a boycott by the other members of the company, who were jealous of the young star. She had added Lady Macbeth to her list of characters. The press criticisms that were showered upon her make interesting reading. In St. Louis, Baltimore, Washington and other cities the critics were agreed upon the fact of her genius, but not all agreed upon her manner of expressing it. Having won in the West and Southwest, she began to invade eastern territory. She appeared in Pittsburgh in 1880, and was successful. In Philadelphia she won the public and critics to her side easily. In Boston she opened as Evadne, with great apprehension of failure, but she triumphed and appeared as Juliet and Meg Merrilies, drawing large houses. While in Boston, she formed the acquaintance of Longfellow, and their friendship lasted through the later-life of the venerable poet. After Boston came New York and in the metropolis she opened with a good company in "The Lady of Lyons" Her engagement was so successful there that it was extended to six weeks. During that engagement she played as Juliet and in "The Daughter of Roland." After the New York engagement she had no more difficulties to overcome. Everywhere in the United States and Canada she was welcomed as the leading actor among American women. In 1879 she made her first trip to Europe, and while in England visited the grave of Shakespeare at Stratford-on-Avon, and in Paris met Sarah Bernhardt, Madame Ristori and other famous actors. In 1880 she received an offer from the manager of Drury Lane, London, England, to play an engagement. She was pleased by the offer, but she modestly refused it, as she thought herself hardly finished enough for such a test of her powers. In 1883 she also refused an offer to appear in the London Lyceum. In 1884–5 she was again in London, and then she accepted an offer to appear at the Lyceum in "Parthenia." Her success was pronounced and instantaneous. She drew crowded houses, and among her friends and patrons were the Prince and Princess of Wales, Lord Lytton and Tennyson. She played successfully in Manchester, Edinburgh and other British towns. During that visit she opened the Memorial Theater in Stratford-on-Avon, playing Rosamond in "As You Like It." Her portrait in that character forms one of the panels of the Shakespeare Theater. In 1885–6 she played many engagements in the United States and Great Britain. In 1889 a serious illness compelled her to retire from the stage temporarily. In 1890 she announced her permanent withdrawal from it, and soon after she was married to M. Antonio Navarro de Viano, a citizen of New York. They now live in England.

ANDREWS, Miss Alice A., composer and director, born in St. Peter, MN. She is a member of the musical Andrews family, now grown into the well-known Andrews Opera Company. It has been said of her that she could sing before she could lisp a word, as she began to sing at the early age of two years. When she was nine years of age, she started out with her brothers and sisters as one of the family concert troupe, giving sacred concerts in the churches throughout the State. After a few musical seasons she left the concert stage for the school-room, where she spent her time for several years, taking a trip with the family now and then in the summer vacations. As a child she had a remarkably strong voice, but at twelve years of age it failed completely, and for six years she did not sing a note. After that time she regained it in a measure, but not in its completeness, and she has since turned her attention more to instrumental music, being for eight or nine years the pianist and musical director of the company. She has composed several vocal pieces, which she is now having published. She has a remarkable talent for transposition, and could transpose music as soon as she could read it. The Andrews family is of

Spanish descent by the line of the father who was a man of much intellectual ability. The paternal grandfather came to this country when quite a young boy, leaving his parents upon large landed estates to which he, the only child, would one day be heir. Here he married, and his wife would never consent to his returning to look after his interests in far-away Spain. Much of the musical and dramatic talent of his grandchildren is doubtless an inheritance, brought to them by him from the land of the vine and the olive, of sunshine and song.

ANDREWS, Miss Eliza Frances, author and educator, born in Washington, GA, 10th August,

1847. Her father was Judge Garnett Andrews, an eminent jurist and the author of a book of amusing sketches entitled "Reminiscences of an Old Georgia Lawyer." Among others of her immediate family who have distinguished themselves are her brother, Col. Garnett Andrews, a brave Confederate officer and the present mayor of Chattanooga, and her niece, Maude Andrews, of the Atlanta "Constitution." Soon after the death of her father, in 1873, his estate was wrecked by one of those "highly moral" defaulters, whose operations Miss Andrews has vividly portrayed in her novel, "A Mere Adventurer" (Philadelphia, 1879). The old homestead was sold, and Miss Andrews was reduced to the necessity of toiling for her daily bread. Though wholly unprepared, either by nature or training, for a life of self-dependence, she wasted no time in sentimental regrets, but courageously prepared to meet the situation. Journalism was hardly at that time a recognized profession for women in Georgia, and Miss Andrews, whose natural timidity and reserve had been fostered by the traditions in which she was reared, shrank from striking out into a new path. She did a little literary work secretly, but turned rather to teaching as a profession. For six months she edited a country newspaper, unknown to the proprietor himself, who had engaged a man to do the work at a salary of forty dollars a month. The pseudo-editor, feeling himself totally incompetent, offered Miss Andrews one-half of the salary if she would do the writing for him, and, being in great straits at the time, she accepted the unequal terms, doing all the actual work, while the duties of the ostensible editor were limited to taking the exchanges out of the post-office and drawing his half of the pay. After a few months the senior member of this unequal partnership, finding employment elsewhere, recommended Miss Andrews as his successor, a proposition to which the proprietor of the paper would not hear, declaring in his wisdom that it was impossible for a woman to fill such a position. Even when assured that one had actually been filling it for six months, he persisted in his refusal on the ground that editing a paper was not proper work for a woman. This, with exception of a few news letters to the New York "World," written about the same time, was Miss Andrews' first essay in journalism, and her experience on that occasion, together with

similar experiences in other walks, has perhaps had something to do with making her such an ardent advocate of a more enlarged sphere of action for women. In spite of this unpromising beginning, she has been successful both as writer and teacher, and had gone far toward retrieving her shattered fortunes when her health failed. She spent eighteen months under treatment in a private hospital, and for two years more was compelled to withdraw from active life. Even under these adverse circumstances her energetic nature asserted itself, and "Prince Hal," an idyl of old-time plantation life, was written when she was so ill that she often had to lie in bed with her hands propped on a pillow to write. After a winter in Florida, in which she wrote a series of letters for the Augusta "Chronicle," she recovered her strength so far as to be able to accept an important position in the Wesleyan College in Macon, GA, where she has remained for six or seven years, and in that time has added to her literary reputation that of a successful platform speaker. Her lectures on "The Novel as a Work of Art," "Jack and Jill," and "The Ugly Girl," delivered at the Piedmont Chautauqua, Monteagle, TN, and other places, have attracted wide attention. Besides being a fine linguist, speaking French and German fluently, and reading Latin with ease, she is probably the most accomplished field botanist in the South. Her literary work has been varied. From the solemn grandeur that marks the closing paragraphs of "Prince Hal" down to such popular sketches as "Uncle Edom and the Book Agent," or "The Dog Fight at Big Lick Meetin' House," her pen has ranged through nearly every field of literary activity. It is, perhaps, in what may be called the humorous treatment of serious subjects that her talent finds its best expression, as in her witty reply to Grant Allen on the woman question ("Popular Science Monthly"), or her "Plea for the Ugly Girls" ("Lippincott's Magazine"). "A Family Secret" (Philadelphia, 1876) is the most popular of her novels. This was followed by "How He was Tempted," published as a serial in the Detroit "Free Press." "Prince Hal" (Philadelphia, 1882) is the last of her works issued in book form. Her later writings have been published as contributions to different newspapers and periodicals. Her poems have been too few to warrant a judgment upon her as a writer of verse, but one of them, entitled "Haunted," shows how intimately the humorous and the pathetic faculties may be connected in the same mind.

ANDREWS, Mrs. Judith Walker, philanthropist, born in Fryeburgh, ME, 26th April, 1826. She was educated in Fryeburgh Academy with the intention, so common with New England girls, of becoming a teacher. Her brother, Dr. Clement A. Walker, one of the first of the new school of physicians for the insane, having been appointed to the charge of the newly established hospital of the city of Boston, his sister joined him there. Although never officially connected with the institution, which had already gained a reputation as a pioneer in improved administration of the work for the insane, Miss Walker interested herself in the details of that administration, and by her personal attention to the patients endeared herself to them. No better school of training could be found for the activities to which she has given her life. She was married while in the institution, on 15th January, 1857, to Joseph Andrews, of Salem, a man of generous public spirit, who gave much time and labor to the improvement of the militia system of the commonwealth, both before and during the Civil War. He died in 1869. They had three children, all boys, to whose early education Mrs. Andrews gave the years, only too few, of a happy married life. Removing to Boston in 1863, she became a member of the South Congregational Church (Unitarian), and in 1876 was elected president of its ladies' organization, the South Friendly Society. Her service of sixteen years in that office is only one of five such terms in the history of the society. Under the influence of its pastor, Dr. Edward Everett Hale, the South Congregational Church has had wide relations both inside and outside denominational lines, and these relations have brought to Mrs. Andrews opportunities for religious and philanthropic work to which she always has been ready to respond. While most of these, though requiring much work and thought, are of a local character, two lines of her work have made her name familiar to a large circle. Elected, in 1886, president of the Women's Auxiliary Conference, she was active in the movement to enlarge its scope and usefulness, and in 1889, when the National Alliance of Unitarian and Other Liberal Christian Women was organized, she became its first president, declining re-election in 1891. Since 1889 she has been a member of the Council of the National Unitarian Conference. Having become interested in the child-widows of India, through the eloquence, and later the personal friendship, of Pundita Ramabai, she was largely instrumental in the formation of the Ramabai Association, to carry out the plans of Ramabai and to systematize the work of her friends throughout the country. To the executive committee of that association, of which Mrs. Andrews has been chairman from the begining, is entrusted the oversight of the management of the school for child-widows, the Shâradâ Sadana at Poona and the settlement of the many delicate questions arising from a work so opposed to the customs, though fortunately not to the best traditions, of India.

ANDREWS, Mrs. Marie Louise, story writer and journalist, born in Bedford, IN, 31st October, 1849. She was the second daughter of the late Dr. Benjamin and Louise A. Newland, who were educated and intellectual persons. Her early life was spent in Bedford. She was educated mainly in private schools. She was a student in St. Mary's-of-the-Woods, in St. Agnes' Hall, Terre Haute, IN, and in Hungerford Institute, Adams, NY. The last-named institute was destroyed by fire shortly before commencement, so that Miss Newland was not formally graduated. She was married on 15th May, 1875, to Albert M. Andrews, of Seymour, IN. In 1877 they removed to Connersville, IN, where Mr. Andrews engaged in the drug business. They had one child, a son. Mrs. Adams died on 7th February, 1891, in Connersville, IN. She was thoroughly educated. She spoke French and German and was familiar with Latin and the literature of the modern languages. Her literary tastes were displayed in her earliest years. She wrote much, in both verse and prose, but she never published her productions in book form. She was the originator of the Western Association of Writers, and served as its secretary from its organization until

June, 1888, when she insisted on retiring from the office. Among her acquaintances were many of the prominent writers of the West, and at the annual conventions of the Western Association of Writers she was always a conspicuous member. She foresaw the growth of literature in the West, and her ideas of that growth and of the best means of fostering it are embodied in the organization which she founded. That association has already been the means of introducing scores of talented young writers to the public, and it alone is a worthy monument to Mrs. Andrews. She was a brilliant conversationalist and an effective impromptu speaker.

ANDREWS, Mrs. Mary Garard, Universalist minister, born in Clarksburgh, VA, 3rd March, 1852. She is of good old Pennsylvania ancestors in whom the best Quaker and Baptist blood mingled. Her maiden name was Garard. Always fondly proud of the home of her adoption, Iowa, she calls herself a thoroughly western woman. She was left motherless at the age of five years and her father was killed in the service of his country a few years later. Thus early left to struggle with the adverse elements of human life, she developed a strong character and marked individuality, and overcame many difficulties in acquiring an education. In spite of ill health, the discouragement of friends and financial pressure, she maintained her independence and kept herself in school for eight years. She spent two years in the academy in Washington, IA, three years in the Iowa State Industrial College, and three years in Hillsdale College, MI. While in the last-named place she completed the English Theological course with several elective studies, having charge of one or two churches all the time and preaching twice every Sunday during the three years. She says: "I never spent much time over the oft controverted question, 'Shall woman preach?' I thought the most satisfactory solution of the problem would be for woman quietly, without ostentation or controversy, to assume her place and let her work speak for itself." After five years of faithful, fruitful service in the Free Baptist Church, convictions of truth and duty caused her to sever ties grown dear and cast her lot with a strange people. For eight years she was engaged in the regular pastoral work of the Universalist Church, during which time she was a close and thorough student, keeping well informed on the questions of the day. Never satisfied with present attainments, she pursued a more advanced theological and philosophical course, in which she passed an examination and received the degree of B.D. from Lombard University, Illinois. She has been an interesting, successful and beloved pastor. Besides doing well and faithfully her parish work, she was an enthusiastic temperance and Grand Army worker, and for two years was National Chaplain of the Woman's Relief Corps. In April, 1888, she was married to I. R. Andrews, a prosperous attorney of Omaha, NE, where she now resides.

ANGELINI, Mme. Arabella, evangelical worker, born in Elton, MD, 8th July, 1863. Her maiden name was Chapman. On her mother's side she is descended from a Huguenot family, the De Vinneys, who settled in Maryland over a century ago. Her father died when she was only four years old and Arabella was taken to Europe at the age of eight years, by Miss Mary Gilpin, of Philadelphia, for the ostensible purpose of learning music and languages. On reaching Germany, Miss Gilpin developed a strange mania for abusing her little charge. They spent several months in Germany and Switzerland and passed on to Italy, stopping first at Verona. In that city the police were instructed to watch Miss Gilpin closely, as her erratic behavior attracted attention. In Florence her cruelty to her charge caused the police to interfere. They took charge of Arabella, who was less than nine years old, and Miss Gilpin left her to her fate among strangers, whose language she did not understand. She found shelter in the Protestant College in Florence and was there cared for until her health was restored. She remained in the institution nine years and at the end of that time was married to the Rev. Luigi Angelini, a minister of the Evangelical Church of Italy. After their marriage they settled in a small village in northern Italy, Bassignana. In 1884 the board of the Evangelical Church of Italy nominated Dr. Angelini as its representative in the United States, and thus, after a long absence, Mme. Angelini returned to her native land only to find herself quite as much a foreigner as though born in Italy. When brought face to face with her mother, she could not speak her native language. Long disuse had not effaced the English language from her memory, however, and the words soon came back to her. Mme. Angelini is aiding her husband to arouse an interest in the churches of America, and in organizing undenominational societies for the support of the native Evangelical Church of Italy. She looks forward to a career of usefulness in Italy, aiding the women of her adopted country in their struggle for elevation.

ANTHONY, Miss Susan B., woman suffragist, born in South Adams, MA, 15th February, 1820. If locality and religious heritage have any influence in determining fate, what might be predicted for Susan B. Anthony? Born in Massachusetts, brought up in New York, of Quaker father and Baptist mother, she has by heritage a strongly marked individuality and native strength. In girlish years Susan belonged to Quaker meeting, with aspirations toward "high-seat" dignity, but this was modified by the severe treatment accorded to her father, who, having been publicly reprimanded twice, the first time for marrying a Baptist, the second for wearing a comfortable cloak with a large cape, was finally expelled from "meeting" because he allowed the use of one of his rooms for the instruction of a class in dancing, in order that the youth might not be subject to the temptations of a liquor-selling public house. Though Mr. Anthony was a cotton manufacturer and one of the wealthiest men in Washington county, NY, he desired that his daughters, as his sons, should be trained for some profession. Accordingly they were fitted, in the best of private schools, for teachers, the only vocation then thought of for girls, and at fifteen Susan found herself teaching a Quaker family school at one dollar a week and board. When the financial crash of 1837 caused his failure, they were not only teaching and supporting them-

selves, but were able to help their father in his efforts to retrieve his fortunes. With a natural aptitude for the work, conscientious and prompt in all her duties, Susan was soon pronounced a successful teacher, and to that profession she devoted fifteen years of her life. She was an active member of the New York State Teachers' Association and in their conventions made many effective pleas for higher wages and for the recognition of the principle of equal rights for women in all the honors and responsibilities of the association. The women teachers from Maine to Oregon owe Miss Anthony a debt of gratitude for the improved position they hold to-day. Miss Anthony has been from a child deeply interested in the subject of temperance. In 1847 she joined the Daughters of Temperance, and in 1852 organized the New York State Woman's Temperance Association, the first open temperance organization of women. Of this Mrs. Elizabeth Cady Stanton was president. As secretary Miss Anthony for several years gave her earnest efforts to the temperance cause, but she soon saw that woman was utterly powerless to change conditions without the ballot. Since she identified herself with the suffrage movement in 1852 she has left others to remedy individual wrongs, while she has been working for the weapon by which, as she believes, women will be able to do away with the producing causes. She says she has "no time to dip out vice with a teaspoon while the wrongly-adjusted forces of society are pouring it in by the bucketful." With all her family, Miss Anthony was a pronounced and active Abolitionist. During the war, with her life-long friend and co-worker, Elizabeth Cady Stanton, and other coadjutors, she rolled up nearly 400,000 petitions to Congress for the abolition of slavery. Those petitions circulated in every northern and western State, served the double purpose of rousing the people to thought and furnishing the friends of the slave in Congress opportunities for speech. In Charles Sumner's letters to Miss Anthony we find the frequent appeals, "Send on the petitions; they furnish the only background for my demands." The most harrassing, though most satisfactory, enterprise Miss Anthony ever undertook was the publication for three years of a weekly paper, "The Revolution." This formed an epoch in the woman's rights movement and roused widespread thought on the question. Ably edited by Elizabeth Cady Stanton and Parker Pillsbury, with the finest intellects in the Nation among its contributors, dealing pungently with passing events, and rising immediately to a recognized position among the papers of the Nation, there was no reason why there should not have been a financial success, save that Miss Anthony's duties kept her almost entirely from the lecture field, and those who were on the platform, in the pulpit and in all the lucrative positions which this work was opening to women, could not and did not feel that the cause was their own. After three years of toil and worry a debt of $10,000 had accumulated. "The Revolution" was transferred to other hands but did not long survive. Miss Anthony set bravely about the task of earning money to pay the debt, every cent of which was duly paid from the earnings of her lectures. Miss Anthony has always been in great demand on the platform and has lectured in almost every city and hamlet in the North. She has made constitutional arguments before congressional committees and spoken impromptu to assemblies in all sorts of places. Whether it be a good word in introducing a speaker, the short speech to awaken a convention, the closing appeal to set people to work, the full hour address of argument or the helpful talk at suffrage meetings, she always says the right thing and never wearies her audience. There is no hurry, no superfluity in her discourse, no sentiment, no poetry, save that of self-forgetfulness in devotion to the noblest principles that can actuate human motive. A fine sense of humor pervades her arguments, and by the *reductio ad absurdum* she disarms and wins her opponent. The most dramatic event of Miss Anthony's life was her arrest and trial for voting at the presidential election of 1872. Owing to the mistaken kindness of her counsel, who was unwilling that she should be imprisoned, she gave bonds, which prevented her taking her case to the Supreme Court, a fact she always regretted. When asked by the judge, "You voted as a woman, did you not?" she replied, "No, sir, I voted as a citizen of the United States." The date and place of trial being set, Miss Anthony thoroughly canvassed her county so as to make sure that all of the jurors were instructed in a citizen's rights. Change of venue was ordered to another

county, setting the date three weeks ahead. In twenty-four hours Miss Anthony had her plans made, dates set, and posters sent out for a series of meetings in that county. After the argument had been presented to the jury, the judge took the case out of their hands, saying it was a question of law and not of fact, and pronounced Miss Anthony guilty, fining her $100 and costs. She said to the judge, "Resistance to tyranny is obedience to God, and I shall never pay a penny of this unjust claim," and she glories in never having done so. The inspectors, who received the ballots from herself and friends, were fined and imprisoned, but were pardoned by President Grant. Miss Anthony has had from the beginning the kindly sympathy and co-operation of her entire family, and especially of her youngest sister, Miss Mary S. Anthony, who has freed her from domestic responsibilities. A wonderful memory which carries the legislative history of each State, the formation and progress of political parties, the parts played by prominent men in our National life, and whatever has been done the world over to ameliorate conditions for women, makes Miss Anthony a genial and instructive companion, while her unfailing sympathy makes her as good a listener as talker. The change in public sentiment toward woman suffrage is well indicated by the change in the popular estimate of Miss Anthony. Where once it was the fashion of the press to ridicule and jeer, it is now the best reporters who are sent to interview her. Society, too, throws open its doors, and into many distinguished gatherings she carries a refreshing breath of sincerity and earnestness. Her seventieth birthday, celebrated by the National Woman Suffrage Association, of which she was vice-president-at-large from its formation in 1869 until its convention in 1892, when she was elected president, was the occasion of a spontaneous outburst of gratitude which is, without any doubt, unparalleled in the history of any living individual. Miss Anthony is truly one of the most heroic figures in American history.

ARCHIBALD, Mrs. Edith Jessie, temperance reformer, born in St. Johns, Newfoundland, 5th April, 1854. She is the youngest daughter of Sir Edward Mortimer Archibald, K.C.M.G., C.B., whose family were descendants of Loyalists who emigrated from Massachusetts during the Revolution. Her grandfather on her father's side was called to the bar, where he displayed great talent, and entering public life became Attorney-General of Nova Scotia, Judge of the Supreme Court of Prince Edward's Island, and Speaker of the House of Assembly of Nova Scotia. In 1857 he removed with his family to New York, where he held the British consulship during twenty-seven years, making a record of public life of over fifty-two years. Edith Jessie was educated in New York and London. She was married at the age of twenty years to Charles Archibald, of Cape Breton, where her husband is an extensive property owner and the manager of one of the largest collieries in the island. Their residence is at Gowrie Mines, Cow Bay. Living in a country so isolated and surrounded by the cares of family and home. Mrs. Archibald, who is passionately fond of art, music and literature, has still endeavored to keep in touch with culture, and has recently published a number of poems and magazine articles. She is devoted to reforms and is an enthusiastic member of the Woman's Christian Temperance Union of the Dominion.

AREY, Mrs. Harriett Ellen Grannis, author and editor, born in Cavendish, VT, 14th April, 1819. Her father's ancestors settled in New Haven, CT, previous to 1655. A hundred years later her grandfather removed from New Haven to Claremont, NH, where he married a daughter of Dr. William Sumner, who had removed thither from Boston. The seventh child of this family was the father of Harriett E. Grannis. The war of 1812 came with its ruinous effects upon the country, followed from 1815 by the two or three cold seasons so well remembered in New England, in which the crops were cut off, and her father was called from his studies to assist in saving the crippled business in which his brothers were engaged. Their best efforts were in vain. When Harriett was three years of age, her father removed to Woodstock, VT, and a year or two later to Charleston, in the township of Hatley, Province of Quebec, where in a few years he became a member of the Provincial Parliament. Losing her mother when in her fifteenth year, the young girl was under the care of relatives in Claremont for the next three or four years. At the end of that time she joined her father at Oberlin, OH, whither he had meantime removed. There she spent some years in uninterrupted study, and then found a position as teacher in a ladies' school in Cleveland, OH, from which place she removed, on her marriage, to Buffalo, NY. From early girlhood a contributor to various papers and magazines, not long after her marriage she became editor of the "Youth's Casket" and the "Home Monthly." Under the double burden of a growing family and her editorial responsibilities, her health failed, and work had to be given up. Soon afterward her husband was called to the principalship of the State Normal School in Albany, NY, and in that city she spent a few pleasant years. A serious illness and a railroad accident following close upon it had prostrated her husband. When his health began to improve, he accepted the principalship of the State Normal School, then opening in Whitewater, WI. Mrs. Arey went into the school with him, holding for years the position of lady principal. Later, in her old home in Cleveland, for some years she edited a monthly devoted to charitable work, being at the same time on the board of the Woman's Christian Association. She was one of the founders and the first president of the Ohio Woman's State Press Association. She has been for many years president of a literary and social club. Her principal writings are "Household Songs and Other Poems" (New York, 1854).

ARMBRUSTER, Mrs. Sara Dary, business woman and publisher, born in Philadelphia, PA, 29th September, 1862. Her early years were passed in luxury, and she had all the advantages of thorough schooling. When she was seventeen years old, reverses left her family poor, and she was made partly helpless by paralysis. Obliged to support herself and other members of her family, she took the Irving House, a hotel of ninety-five rooms, in Philadelphia, and by good management made it a successful establishment and lifted herself and those dependent upon her above poverty. She was married at an early age. She originated in Philadelphia the Woman's Exchange. Her present enterprise is to furnish a house for the infants of widows and deserted wives in her native city. She is the publisher of the "Woman's Journal," a weekly paper devoted to the cause of women, and her interest in philanthropic movements is earnest and active.

ARMSTRONG, Mrs. Ruth Alice, national superintendent of heredity for the Woman's Christian Temperance Union, born near Cassopolis, Cass county, MI, 30th April, 1850. Her father, Amos Jones, was from Georgia, and her mother, Rebecca Hebron, from Yorkshire, England. She was educated in the public schools, and at the age of eighteen commenced to teach, while she was herself a student in the higher branches. Impressed with the injustice done to women in the matter of salaries, she left her native State for California, but not until she had aided in the organization of the first woman suffrage society of her native county. As a teacher she was successful. In 1874 she was married to Thomas Armstrong, a stockraiser of Trinity county, CA. For four years they lived in idyllic isolation, with no society except that furnished by a well-selected library. Just before the birth of their only child, Ruth, they moved to Woodland, CA. There Mrs. Armstrong organized a Shakespeare Club, and then a lecture bureau, of which she was the first president. She assisted in the organization of a literary society for the study of literature of all nations. She was the first woman ever elected to the office of trustee in the Congregational Church of Woodland. In 1891 she united with the Christian Church. To the Woman's Christian Temperance Union she has given abundantly of time and resources, organizing the county and several local unions, her enthusiasm and common-sense making her a leader and inspirer. She began to plan for the education of women in maternity and other allied subjects. She was made the superintendent of heredity for the town of Woodland, next for the county, and afterward for the National Union. From her pen go out over all the Nation leaflets and letters of instruction to aid in the development of the highest physical, mental, moral and spiritual interest of mankind. Her lectures on "Heredity" and "Motherhood" carry the conviction that, for the highest development of manhood and womanhood, parentage must be assumed as the highest, the holiest and most sacred responsibility entrusted to us by the Creator. At present she is helping to plan and put into execution a womans' building, to contain a printing office,

lecture hail and a home for homeless women and girls. Mrs. Armstrong's helpfulness in the town, in the church, in the Woman's Christian Temperance Union and in the world comes from her belief in the powers of the unit and from the fact that her education has been assimilated into her character, producing a culture which has ministry for its highest aim. Possessed of keen and critical acumen, she ever makes choice of both word and action, endeavoring to say and do what is true, honest and pure, holding herself responsible to God and God alone.

ARMSTRONG, Miss Sarah B., physician and surgeon, born in Newton, near Cincinnati, OH, 31st July, 1857. Her early education was acquired in the schools of Cincinnati. Her family removed to Lebanon, OH, in 1865. She took a course of study in the university located in that town. She became a teacher at the age of sixteen years. In 1880 she took the degree of B.S. in the Lebanon University having graduated with the highest honors in a class of sixty-six members. In 1883 she returned to the university as a teacher and took charge of the art department. While thus engaged, she completed the classical course taking the degree of B.A. in 1887. In 1890 the degree of M.A. was conferred upon her as honorary. In 1886 she took her first degree in regular medicine. She was appointed matron and physician to the college, serving in that capacity while continuing to teach. In 1888 she was appointed assistant to the chair of theory and practice in the Homœpathic College of Michigan, in Ann Arbor. She remained there two years and took a postgraduate degree in 1889. She then returned to Lebanon to serve as a member of the medical faculty of the university. She soon resigned her position and went to New York, where she spent a year in the hospitals, making a special study of surgery. She removed to Bay City, MI, 1st January, 1891, and has successfully established herself in practice in that city. Dr. Armstrong is a musician and is engaged as a soprano singer in the Baptist Church in Bay City. Her professional duties have not kept her from public work. She was elected a member of the city school board in 1891. She is an active worker in the cause of woman's advancement. Her literary talents are displayed in poetical productions of a high order of merit. Dr. Armstrong inherits her liking for the profession of medicine from her maternal great-grandmother, who was the first woman to practice medicine west of the Alleghany mountains. She was not, of course, permitted to take a degree in those early days, but took her preceptor's certificate and bought her license to practice. Dr. Armstrong has been well received as a physician, and her success is positive.

ARNOLD, Mrs. Harriet Pritchard, author, born in Killingly, CT, in 1858. She was an only child, her father being the Rev. B. F. Pritchard, a New England clergyman of Scotch and English descent. In her childhood she evinced no particular fondness for books, but outdoor recreations she enjoyed with keenest zest. Since 1882, when a lingering illness afforded her many hours of leisure, poems and sketches from her pen have appeared in various magazines and periodicals under the signature H. E. P., and her maiden name, Harriet E. Pritchard. In 1886, she became the wife of Ernest Warner Arnold, of Providence, RI, which city has since been her home.

ATWOOD, Miss Ethel, musician, born in Fairfield, ME, 12th September, 1870. Her parents were Yankees, and possessed sterling thrift and independence. The first fifteen years of Miss Atwood's life were passed in a quiet, uneventful way in her native town, but the desire to branch out and do and be something led her to migrate to Boston, where she has since resided. She began the study of the violin when eight years old, but lack of means and competent teachers in her native place prevented her from acquiring any great proficiency as a soloist. After going to Boston she turned her attention to orchestral work. Two years study and experience determined her to have an orchestra of her own. Securing a young woman whose reputation as a violinist and thorough musician was well established in the city, she organized the Fadette Ladies' Orchestra, with four pieces. Then it was that her Yankee shrewdness began to serve her well. She immediately had the name of her orchestra copyrighted and, hiring an office, put out her "shingle." Finding that prompting was essential to success in dance work she went to one of Boston's best prompters and learned the business thoroughly. An elocutionist taught her to use her voice to the best advantage, and now she stands as one of the best prompters in the city and the only lady prompter in the country. Business has increased rapidly in the past few years, and now there are thirteen regular members of the orchestra who are refined young women of musical ability.

AUSTIN, Mrs. Harriet Bunker, author, born in Erie, PA, 29th December, 1844. She is a daughter of Mr. and Mrs. John F. Bunker, descending from New England stock. Her great-grandfather, Benjamin Bunker, was a soldier of the Revolution, and was killed in the battle of Bunker Hill. The hill from which the battle was named comprised part of the Bunker estate. On her mother's side she is related to the Bronson Alcott and Lyman Beecher families. When quite young, she removed with her parents to Woodstock, McHenry county, IL, where she has since resided. Her education was received in the Woodstock high school and Dr. Todd's Female Seminary. At the close of her seminary life she was married to W. B. Austin, a prosperous merchant of that city. She has been a prolific writer, many of her poems having been set to music and gained deserved popularity. She has always taken an active interest in every scheme for the advancement of women, and is ever ready to lend her influence to the promotion of social reforms.

AUSTIN, Mrs. Helen Vickroy, journalist and horticulturist, born in Miamisburg, Montgomery county, OH, in 1829. She is a daughter of Edwin Augustus and Cornelia Harlan Vickroy. Her family on both sides are people of distinction. Her mother was a daughter of the Hon. George

Harlan, of Warren county, OH. Her father was a son of Thomas Vickroy, of Pennsylvania, who was a soldier in the Revolution under Washington and an eminent surveyor and extensive land-owner. When Mrs. Austin was a child, the family removed to Pennsylvania and established a homestead in Ferndale, Cambria county. There her early life was passed. With an inherent love of nature, she grew up amid the picturesque scenes of the foothills of the Alleghany mountains, a poet in thought and an ardent lover of the beautiful. She was married in 1850 to William W. Austin, a native of Philadelphia, at that time residing at Richmond, IN, in which delightful city they lived until, in 1885, the family went East, taking up their residence at Vineland, NJ. Although Mrs. Austin is a domestic woman, she has taken time to indulge her taste and promptings and has done considerable writing. Some of her best work has been for the agricultural and horticultural press, and her essays at the horticultural meetings and interest in such matters have given her a fame in horticultural circles. As a writer of sketches and essays and a reporter and correspondent Mrs. Austin has marked capacity. She is accurate and concise. Much of her work has been of a fugitive nature for the local press, but was worthy of a more enduring place. One of the marked characteristics of her nature is benevolence. She has given much time and used her pen freely in aid of philanthropic work. She has for many years been identified with the cause of woman suffrage, and the various institutions for the elevation and protection of woman have had her earnest help. Long before the temperance crusade she was a pronounced advocate of temperance and while in her teens was a "Daughter of Temperance." Her philanthropic spirit makes her a friend to the negro and Indian. She is a life member of the National Woman's Indian Rights Association. Mrs. Austin is the mother of three children. One of these, a daughter, is living. Her two sons died in childhood.

AUSTIN, Mrs. Jane Goodwin, author, born in Worcester, MA, in 1831. Her parents were from Plymouth in the Old Colony, and counted their lineage from the Mayflower Pilgrims in no less than eight distinct lines, besides a common descent from Francis Le Baron, the nameless nobleman. Believers in heredity will see in this descent the root of Mrs. Austin's remarkable devotion to Pilgrim story and tradition. Her father, Isaac Goodwin, was a lawyer of considerable eminence, and also a distinguished antiquary and genealogist. Her brother, the Hon. John A. Goodwin, was the author, among other works, of "The Pilgrim Republic," the latest and best of all histories of the settlement of Plymouth. Her mother, well-known as a poet and song-writer, was furthermore a lover of the traditions and anecdotes of her native region, and many of the stories embodied in Mrs. Austin's later works she first heard as a child at her mother's knee, especially those relative to the Le Barons. Although Mrs. Austin's pen strayed in various fields of poetry and prose, it finally settled down into a course very marked and very definite. This daughter of the Pilgrims became a specialist in their behalf and pledged her remaining years to developing their story. Her four well-known books, namely: "Standish of Standish," "Betty Alden," "The Nameless Nobleman" and "Dr. Le Baron and his Daughters," cover the ground from the landing of the Pilgrims upon Plymouth Rock, in 1620, to the days of the Revolution, in 1775, and a fifth volume which succeeded completed the series. She wrote a great number of magazine stories and some poems. Her principal books with the dates of their publication were as follows : "Fairy Dreams" (Boston, 1859); "Dora Darling" (Boston, 1865); "Outpost" (Boston, 1866); "Tailor Boy" (Boston, 1867); "Cypher" (New York, 1869); "The Shadow of Moloch Mountain" (New York, 1870); "Moon-Folk" (New York, 1874); "Mrs. Beauchamp Brown" (Boston, 1880); "The Nameless Nobleman" (Boston, 1881); "Nantucket Scraps" (Boston, 1882); "Standish of Standish" (Boston, 1889); "Dr. Le Baron and his Daughters" (Boston, 1890); "Betty Alden" (Boston, 1891). Although a prolific writer, she always wrote carefully and in finished style, and her contributions to the literature of New England possess a rare value from her intimate knowledge of the pioneers of the eastern colonies gained from thorough reading and tradition. Her work is distinctly American in every essential. Mrs. Austin was married in 1850 to Loring H. Austin, a descendant of the fine old Boston family which figured so largely in the Revolution. She had three children. She was instinctively gracious, and those who knew her not only admired her work, but gave her a warm place in their affections. Her home during her later years was with a married daughter in Roxbury, although she passed a part of the winter in Boston, in order to be near her church, and every summer found her ready to return to her studies of gravestones and traditions, as well as written records, in Plymouth. Mrs. Austin died in Boston, 30th March, 1894.

AVANN Mrs. Ella H. Brockway, educator, born in Newaygo, MI, 20th May, 1853. Her father, the Rev. G. W. Hoag, born in Charlotte VT, was of Quaker parentage and a pioneer in the Methodist Episcopal Church in Michigan, having gone to that State in boyhood. Her mother, Elizabeth Bruce Hoag, from Rochester, NY, was gifted with pen and voice, and was a high official in the Woman's Foreign Missionary Society of her church. At the age of twelve Ella went to Albion College, Albion, MI, and was graduated in 1871. In 1873 she was married to L. Hamline Brockway, of Albion, where they lived for fifteen years, when his election as county clerk caused their removal to Marshall. Mr. Brockway died in August, 1887, and Mrs. Brockway with her son, Bruce, aged twelve, and daughter, Ruth, aged six, returned to Albion. In January, 1889, she became preceptress of the college. In that position she displayed great executive ability. Wise in planning, fertile in resources and energetic in execution, her undertakings were successful. She had great power over the young women of the college and exercised that power without apparent effort. She won the friendship of every student, and they all instinctively turned to her for counsel. She had the department of English literature, and also lectured on the history of music. Her earnestness and enthusiasm were contagious, and her classes

always became interested in their studies. Her addresses to the young ladies were especially prized. For ten years she was president of the Woman's Foreign Missionary Society of Albion district. In June, 1891, she resigned her position in Albion College and on 11th August was married to the Rev. Joseph M. Avann, of Findlay, OH. As a speaker she is pleasing and fascinating. Occasionally she gives a literary address or speaks in behalf of some benevolent cause away from home. She makes frequent contributions to the religious press, and is connected with various literary, social and benevolent societies, holding official positions.

AVERY, Mrs. Catharine Hitchcock Tilden, author and educator, born in Monroe, MI, 13th December, 1844. She is the daughter of Hon. Junius Tilden, formerly a prominent lawyer of that State. She was educated in the Framingham Normal School, in Massachusetts, graduating in 1867. In 1870, she was married to Dr. Elroy M. Avery. He was for several years principal of the East high school and City Normal School, of Cleveland, OH, in which positions his wife was his most able assistant. Dr. Avery is the author of many text-books, notably a series on natural philosophy and chemistry. He is now engaged in historical research and writing, in which Mrs. Avery is his efficient helper. She is president of the East End Conversational, a club organized in 1878 and comprising many of the bright

women of the city. She is a member of the executive committee of the Art and History Club and also of the Cleveland Woman's Press Club. She was a delegate from the latter club to the International League of Press Clubs, 1892, and took part in the journey from New York to the Golden Gate. Her letters descriptive of the trip were published in the Cleveland "Leader and Herald." She is the regent of the Cleveland Chapter of the Daughters of the American Revolution. Four of her ancestors served in the Continental Congress and the cause of freedom. Col. John Bailey, of the Second Massachusetts Regiment, was at Bunker Hill and Monmouth, crossed the Delaware with Washington, and was at Gates's side in the northern campaign which ended in Burgoyne's surrender. The Gad Hitchcocks, father and son, served as chaplain and as surgeon. The elder Gad, in 1774, preached an election sermon in which he advocated the cause of the Colonies and brought forth the wrath of Gage and the thanks of the Massachusetts General Court. Samuel Tilden, private from Marshfield, and member of the Committee of Safety, completes the list of her Revolutionary ancestors. Descended from six of the "Mayflower" band, she is proud of the Pilgrim blood that flows in her veins. She has been for twenty years a member of the Euclid Avenue Congregational Church of Cleveland. Mrs. Avery's father died in the spring of 1861. Her husband, when a boy of sixteen years, went to the war, in 1861, with the first company that left his native town. He was mustered out of service in August, 1865.

AVERY, Mrs. Rachel Foster, woman suffragist, born in Pittsburgh, PA, 30th December, 1858. Her father was J. Heron Foster, of the Pittsburgh "Dispatch." Her mother was a native of Johnstown, NY, the birthplace of her Sunday-school teacher and life-long friend, Elizabeth Cady Stanton. When Rachel was a child, Mrs. Stanton lectured in Pittsburgh. Shortly after, a suffrage meeting was held in Mrs. Foster's house, and a society was formed of which she was made vice-president. Thus the young girl grew up in an atmosphere of radicalism and advanced thought. That she is a woman suffragist comes not only from conviction, but by birthright as well. In 1871 the family, consisting of her mother, her sister, Julia T., and herself, the father having died shortly before, moved to Philadelphia, where they at once identified themselves with the Citizens' Suffrage Association of that city, in which Lucretia Mott, Edward M. Davis, M. Adeline Thompson and others were leading spirits. Her sister, Julia, was for many years a most efficient secretary of that society as well as recording secretary of the National Woman Suffrage Association, and seconded warmly the more active work of her sister, Rachel G., as did also their mother, Mrs. Julia Foster. Both mother and sister have passed away, but their works live after them. When about seventeen years old, Miss Foster began to write for the newspapers, furnishing letters weekly from California and afterward from Europe to the Pittsburgh "Leader." Later she took part in the Harvard examinations, traveled extensively in Europe with her mother and sister, and studied political economy in the University of Zurich. In the winter of 1879 she attended the eleventh Convention of the National Woman Suffrage Association, which determined her career. With characteristic promptitude she began to plan the series of conventions to be held in the West during the summer of 1880, including those at the same times and places as the Republican and Democratic national nominating conventions. In the spring of 1881 she planned the series of ten conventions in the different New England States, beginning at Boston, during the May anniversary week. In 1882 she conducted the Nebraska amendment campaign, with headquarters in Omaha. She engaged Gov. John W. Hoyt, of Wyoming, to give a lecture in Philadelphia on "The good results of thirteen years' experience of woman's voting in Wyoming Territory," had the lecture stenographically reported, collected the money to publish 20,000 copies, and scattered them broadcast over the State of Pennsylvania. The 22nd February, 1883, Miss Foster sailed for Europe with Miss Susan B. Anthony, and with her superior linguistic attainments she served as ears and tongue for her companion in their journeyings through France, Italy, Switzerland and Germany. Miss Foster's management of the International Council of Women, held in Washington, DC, in February, 1888, under the auspices of the National Woman Suffrage Association, was the crowning effort of her executive genius. There were forty-nine official delegates to that council, representing fifty-three different societies from seven distinct nationalities. The expense of this meeting made a grand total of fourteen-thousand dollars, the financial risk of which was beforehand assumed by Miss Anthony, supported by Miss Foster. Mrs. Foster Avery is a philanthropist in the broadest sense. Of her independent fortune she also gives largely to numerous reforms and charities. Her marriage with Cyrus Miller Avery took place 8th November, 1888, Rev. Anna H. Shaw assisting in the ceremony. Mrs. Foster Avery holds the office of Corresponding Secretary of the National Suffrage Association, and of the National and the International Councils of Women.

AVERY, Mrs. Rosa Miller, reformer, born in Madison, OH, 21st May, 1830. Her father, Nahum Miller, was an insatiable reader of Biblical and political history and a man of broad humanitarian views. She married 1st September, 1853, Cyrus Avery, of Oberlin, OH. During their residence in Ashtahula, OH, she organized the first anti-slavery society ever known in that village, and not a clergyman in the place would give notice of its meetings so late as two years before the war; and this in the county home of Giddings and Wade. During the years of the war Mrs. Avery's pen was actively engaged in writing for various journals on the subjects of union and emancipation, under male signatures, so as to command attention. During ten years' residence in Erie, PA, besides writing occasional articles for the newspaper world, she disseminated her views on social questions, love, matrimony and religion in romance in the "High School News," over the pen-name "Sue Smith," work which produced much and rich fruition in the years following. About that time her husband was appointed by the Young Men's Christian Association of Erie as visitor to the criminals confined in the city prison. Mrs. Avery usually assisted her husband in his work. As the result of her investigations, she has ever since maintained "there is not a criminal on this broad earth but that there lies back of him a crime greater than he represents, and for which he, we, and everyone suffers in a greater or less degree." For the last fourteen years Mr. and Mrs. Avery have resided in Chicago. Mrs. Avery's special labors have been largely for social purity and equal suffrage, in which interests she has written many able articles, especially in the "Inter-Ocean."

AYER, Mrs. Harriet Hubbard, business woman and journalist, born in Chicago, IL, in 1852. Her maiden name was Hubbard. The Hubbard family tree extended back without a break to 1590. About 1844 its then youngest offshoot left New England for Chicago, and there his youngest daughter was born. Graduated at fifteen years of age from the Convent of the Sacred Heart, she was soon after married to Mr. Ayer, whose wealth enabled her to train and gratify her taste and love for beauty, and her home became a house famous for its refinement and hospitality. She was then, as now, a many-sided woman. She was an indefatigable reader and student, an art connoisseur of trained critical taste, a leader in philanthropic effort, and a business counselor of rare judgment. Her frequent trips abroad made London, Paris, Vienna and Rome second homes to her. She speaks a half-dozen languages. In 1882 Mr. Ayer failed for several millions. Disheartened by the blow, he became a wreck. Mrs. Ayer gave up to her husband's creditors much that she might have legally claimed as her own. Without a dollar and with two little daughters dependent upon her, she left a home of luxury and became a saleswoman in a leading shop in New York. For eight hours a day, and sometimes for fourteen, she worked behind the counter, returning to the tiny apartment where she, her mother and her children were attended by a solitary maid of-all-work, there to write letters, sketches, essays and editorials by the weary hour. Within a year she had an income from her salary in the shop, from the agreed-upon commissions on her sales, from her pen, and from a successful real estate operation, devised and carried out by herself, of more than ten-thousand dollars a year. The strain upon her health was too great. A change became inevitable. She decided to leave the shop and begin to buy goods and furnish houses for her friends upon commission. She succeeded in this departure also, and was soon able to take a house of her own. In an unfortunate moment for herself she offered the Recamier toilet preparations to the public. Within a month the house was filled from top to bottom with women trying to manufacture them fast enough to meet the public demand, so that the home ceased to be a home. The avarice of some of the assistants whom she had gathered about her led to a conspiracy to capture the Recamier Company. The careless generosity with which she had given away some shares of her stock in the company was abused. A desperate, determined fight was made to wrest the control of the company from her, and to deprive her of all share in the profits of her industry and her brain. Mrs. Ayer discovered this conspiracy while in

Carrie Behr.
From Photo by Morrison, Chicago.

Rolande Bainbridge.
From Photo by Baker, Columbus.

Charlotte Crane.
From Photo Copyrighted, 1896, by Morrison, Chicago.

Amelia Bingham.
From Photo by Falk, New York.

Europe. She returned to find her business in the possession of her foes, her offices barricaded against her, and her money used to hire lawyers to rob her of her rights. Alone, ill, reduced to absolute poverty a second time, this undaunted woman at once began the fight, one against many, a pauper against millionaires, and she won. At the close of the litigation she was again in possession of the business, the offices and the money as sole owner. Since that victory Mrs. Ayer has devoted herself to extending and increasing the business of the Recamier Company, of which she is the president and chief owner.

BABCOCK, Mrs. Elnora Monroe, woman suffragist, born in Columbus, PA, 11th January, 1852. Her maiden name was Monroe. She was married at the age of eighteen to Prof. John W. Babcock, of Jamestown, NY, who for the last twelve years has been city superintendent of public schools in Dunkirk, NY, where they now live. From early girlhood she felt the injustice of denying to woman a voice in government, but took no very active part in the reforms of the day until 1889, when a political equality club was organized in Dunkirk, of which she was made president. This club flourished, and before the close of her first year as president of the Dunkirk club, she was elected president of the Chautauqua County Political Equality Club, the most thoroughly organized county in the United States, having twenty-five flourishing local clubs within its borders and a membership of 1,400. At the close of her first year as president of that club she was unanimously re-elected. That office she still holds. On 25th July, 1891, she had the honor of presiding over the first woman suffrage meeting ever held at the great Chautauqua Assembly, where, through the request of the county club, the subject was allowed to be advocated. Aside from the presidency of these clubs, she has served upon a number of important committees connected with suffrage work. Although deeply interested in all the reforms of the day tending to the uplifting of humanity, she has devoted most of her time to the enfranchisement of woman believing this to be the most important reform before the American

people to-day, and one upon which all other reforms rest.

BABCOCK, Mrs. Emma Whitcomb, author, born in Adams, NY, 24th April, 1849. She is now a resident of Oil City, PA, in which town her husband, C. A. Babcock, is superintendent of schools. As a writer, Mrs. Babcock has been before the public for years, and has contributed to journals and magazines, besides doing good work as a book-reviewer, but is probably best known through her series of unsigned articles which during five years appeared in the New York "Evening Post." She was a contributor to the first number of "Babyhood" and also of the "Cosmopolitan." She has published one volume, "Household Hints" (1891), and is about to issue another, "A Mother's Note Book." At present she is conducting a department in the "Homemaker." Mrs. Babcock has written a novel, which embodies many distinctive features of the oil country. Her husband's profession turned her attention to educational subjects, and she has published many articles in the technical journals on those subjects. She is interested in home mission work and is president of a literary club which is known throughout western Pennsylvania, and which has founded a public library.

BABCOCK, Mrs. Helen Louise B., dramatic reader, born in Galva, IL, 13th August, 1867. Her maiden name was Bailey. She early displayed a marked talent for elocution and on reaching woman's estate she decided to make dramatic reading her profession. With that aim she became a pupil in the Cumnock School of Oratory of the Northwestern University, and, being an earnest student, she was graduated with the highest honors. Afterward she became an assistant instructor in the same oratorical school and was very successful in the delicate and difficult work of developing elocutionary and dramatic talents in others. Perfectly familiar with the work, she was able to guide students rapidly over the rough places and start them on the high road to success. After severing her connection with the Cumnock school, she taught for a time in Mount Vernon Seminary, Washington, DC. After the death of her mother, in 1890, she accompanied her father abroad and spent some time in visiting the principal countries of Europe. In 1891 she was married to Dr. F. C. Babcock, of Hastings, NE, where she now lives.

BAER, Mrs. Libbie C. Riley, poet, born near Bethel, Clermont county, OH, 18th November, 1849. Her ancestors on the paternal side were the two families Riley and Swing. From the original family of the former descended the distinguished poet and humorist, James Whitcomb Riley, and from the latter the eminent philosopher and preacher, Prof. David Swing, of Chicago. On the maternal side Mrs. Baer is a descendant of the Blairs, an old and favorably known family of southern Ohio. It is not surprising, therefore, that through early associations, combined with a natural taste and aptitude for literary work, her genius for poetry was shown during childhood. Her first poem, written when she was scarcely ten years of age, was a spontaneous and really remarkable production for one so young. In November, 1867, she was married to Capt. John M. Baer, an officer with gallant military record. She went with her husband to Appleton, WI, where they still reside. Upon the organization of the Woman's Relief Corps, as allied with the G. A. R., Mrs. Baer took an important part in the benevolent work of that order, and has held various responsible positions connected therewith, devoting much time and energy to the cause, solely as a labor of love. Though always proficient in poetical composition, she really began her literary career during the last decade, and the favor with which her poems have been received proves the merit of her productions.

BAGG, Miss Clara B., pianist and music teacher, born in New York City, 26th September, 1861. Her life has been passed in her native city with the exception of a brief residence in Orange, NJ, and a residence in Brooklyn, NY, where her family spent several years. She showed remarkable musical talents at an early age, and as a child she was a skillful pianist, playing difficult classical music with correct expression and great taste. When she was eleven years old, she was placed under training with competent teachers of the piano, and her progress in that art has been rapid and remarkable, her technical and expressional talents seeming to burst at once into full flower. Enthusiastic in her love of music, she has studied earnestly and thoroughly. From the last of her instructors, Rafael Joseffy, she absorbed much of that artist's power, technical skill, fire, force and delicacy. To this she adds her own talent, equipping her for success as a concert performer and as a teacher. She has become well known in the metropolis in both capacities. Although she does not intend to make concert playing her profession, she has appeared with success in Orange, NJ, in Brooklyn, NY, and during the winter of 1891–92 in New York City. As a teacher she is quite as enthusiastic as she is in the rôle of a performer.

BAGGETT, Mrs. Alice, educator, born in Soccapatoy, Coosa county, Ala., 184–. Her maiden name was Alice Phillips. On her mother's side she is descended from the Scotch families of Campbell, McNeill, Wade, and Hampton, of Virginia. On her father's side her ancestors were the Dowds and Phillipses, of North Carolina. Her father, James D. Phillips, was a Whig who clung to the Union and the Constitution, doing all that lay in his power to avert the Civil War. Alice, just out of school, was full of the secessionist spirit, but a strong advocate of peace. Her early desire to enter the profession of teacher was opposed by her parents, but she resolved to follow her inclination, when, at the close of the Civil War, her family shared in the general desolation that lay upon the South. She became a teacher and for several years made successful use of her varied attainments. In 1868 she was married to A. J. Baggett, continuing her school work after marriage. In a few years her husband became an invalid and Mrs. Baggett then showed her mettle. She cared for her family of three children and assisted her brothers and sisters to get their education. Her husband died in 1875.

Since that time she has served mainly as principal of high schools in Alabama. She has done much work for the orphans of Freemasons, to which order her husband had belonged. Wherever she has worked, she has organized, systematized and revolutionized educational matters. She now resides in St. Augustine, Fla., where her work is highly successful. Her family consists of one surviving daughter.

BAGLEY, Mrs. Blanche Pentecost, Unitarian minister, born in Torquay, England, 19th January, 1858. Her father is the Rev. R. T. Pentecost, a Unitarian minister, now of Salem, MA. Miss Pentecost received her early education partly in private schools in London, England, where her family then resided, and partly in a French college in Avenches, Canton Vaud, Switzerland, from which she was graduated. In 1882 the family came to this country and made their home in Chicago, where three of her brothers, architects, still reside. Blanche Pentecost, like the rest of her family, was brought up in the Established Church of England, but she became a Unitarian while visiting a sister, whose husband, the Rev. F. B. Mott, was then studying for the Unitarian ministry. By them she was induced to enter the Meadville Theological School, from which institution she was graduated in 1889. She had first met her future husband, the Rev. James E. Bagley, in Meadville, where they had entered and left school together. Her first experience of preaching outside of the college chapel, was in Vermont, in the little town of Middlesex, where she spent the summer of 1887. After her graduation she took up work as a minister in Reedsburg, WI. There she continued until her marriage, on 4th September, 1889, when she accompanied her husband to All Souls Church, Sioux Falls, SD, to which he had received a call. Mr. and Mrs. Bagley were ordained and installed together there as joint pastors on 17th November, the same year, the ceremony being the first of that kind in the history of the world. It was, however, only returning to the New Testament custom of sending the disciples out two by two. During their residence in South Dakota Mrs. Bagley took an active interest in all public questions and moral

reforms in that State. She usually conducted the evening services in the church and occasionally assisted in the morning service. She was also assistant superintendent of the Sunday-school, chairman of the executive board of the Unity Club a literary organization, a charter member of the board of directors of the Woman's Benevolent Association, a member of the Minister's Association, and with her husband, joint chairman of the executive committee of the Equal Suffrage Association. She was a member of the Relief Corps, of which, a short time before she left the city, she became chaplain. While in Sioux Falls she made the acquaintance of Susan B. Anthony, and the Rev. Anna Shaw, and had the honor of introducing both of these speakers to Sioux Falls audiences. During the first year of her married life she took part in the ordination of two other woman ministers, the Rev. Helene Putnam and the Rev. Lila Frost-Sprague, both of whom had been college friends. Her home is now in Haverhill, MA, where her husband in 1890 was installed pastor of the First Parish Church. They have two children, and Mrs. Bagley is naturally much occupied, as she feels that home duties have the first claim upon her, but she finds time for some outside work, occasionally taking her husband's pulpit and conducting the afternoon service at a little church in the outskirts of the city. She is also local superintendent of the department of scientific temperance instruction in connection with the Woman's Christian Temperance Union. Mrs. Bagley is an accomplished pianist and has an inherited gift for painting which she has found time to cultivate. She has a vigorous constitution and an unusually strong, clear contralto voice, with a distinct articulation, which makes it easy for her to be heard by the largest audiences.

BAILEY, Mrs. Ann, scout, said to have been born in Liverpool, England, about 1725, died in Hamson township, Gullia county, OH, 23rd November, 1825.

BAILEY, Mrs. Anna Warner, patriot, born in Groton, CT, 11th October, 1758, and died there in 1850.

BAILEY, Miss Ellene Alice, inventor, born in Pond Fort, St. Charles county, MO. She is the third daughter of the late Judge Robert Bailey and Lucinda Zumwalt. Pond Fort was founded by her grandfather, Robert Bailey. Her father was a man of liberal thought with an appreciative interest in all new ideas. An owner of slaves, through the force of circumstances rather than from inclination, he and his son Robert were among the first to advocate their freedom. Her father's ancestors were English, her mother's German. Miss Bailey's first invention was the "Pond Fort" boot, a high boot reaching to the knee and close-fitting about the ankle, on which she obtained an American and a Canadian patent in 1880. The next thing was to put it upon the market and that led her to remove to New York. Her second invention was the "Pond Lily powder puff" patented in 1882. Later she invented another puff, the "Thistledown." An interest in this she sold for a fair price. In the spring of 1889 she improved and simplified these two puffs, bringing out the "Floral" puff. In the summer of 1891 she invented and patented the very best of all the "Dainty" powder puff. These all proved of commercial value. One of her principal inventions is the "Dart" needle for sewing on shoe and other buttons, patented in 1884, 1886 and 1888. The man who undertook the setting up of her machinery and the manufacture of the needle, departed abruptly about the time things were ready for business, leaving no one who understood the mechanism. The inventor rose to the occasion and made the first sixty-thousand needles herself. There was more than one crisis to meet, and she met them all in the same businesslike way. For the past three years the needles have been made by a well-known New England firm, and are staple goods. Another patented article, which is successful, is a device for holding on rubber overshoes. One of the ways in which she increased her resources was by designing useful articles for a novelty-loving public. The list includes a silver whisk-broom, patented in 1887, and several other novelties filled with perfume; a music roll which was used first as a Christmas card and then as an Easter card; a shaving case; a manicure case; a wall album for photographs; a desk holder for stationery; a work box; a perforated felt chest protector; a sleeve holder; a corset shield, patented in 1885; copyright photographs of Martha Washington and Mrs. Cleveland; odd nov-

elty clocks; chains for holding drapery; ornamental tables, inkstands, screens, easels and unique boxes for holding candies, a hand pinking device (1892); a leg protector made of waterproof cloth, a combination of legging and overgaiter (1892). She has also taken several crude designs of other inventors and improved them so as to make them salable and profitable. Miss Bailey enjoys the friendship of many of the most womanly women of the country, and she has the respect and confidence of the largest business houses. Her inventions have proved not only useful and practical, but of commercial importance. She is a member of Grace Episcopal Church, New York, and also a member of the Young Woman's Christian Association, in which she is greatly interested. She finds time to keep in touch with whatever is newest and best, and writes an occasional article for the press.

BAILEY, Mrs. Hannah J., philanthropist and reformer, born in Cornwall-on-the-Hudson, NY, 5th July, 1839. Her maiden name was Hannah Clark Johnston, and she was the oldest of a family of eleven children. Her parents were David and Letitia Johnston. Mr. Johnston was by occupation a tanner, but in 1853 he became a farmer, locating in Plattekill, Ulster county, NY. He was a minister in the Society of Friends, and on Sundays the family worshiped in the quiet little church near their home. Hannah passed her busy and studious girlhood on the homestead, and in 1858 she began to teach school. She continued to teach successfully until 1867. In that year she accompanied a woman preacher on a mission to the churches and institutions for criminals and for charity, within the limits of the New England Yearly Meeting of Friends. While on that mission, she met Moses Bailey, a noble and active Christian, to whom she was married in October, 1868. A peaceful, useful train of years followed until his death, in 1882, and she was left with one son, Moses Melvin Bailey, then twelve years of age. At the time of her husband's death Mrs. Bailey was very ill, but afterward rallied to gather up the threads of his life-work and her own, and since then she has carried them steadily forward. Her husband's oilcloth manufactury, and also a retail carpet store in Portland, ME, was carried on under her management until, in 1889, she sold the manufacturing establishment, and in 1891 her son assumed the care and possession of the business in Portland. For thirty years she has been a Sabbath-school teacher, and she continually adds new branches to her church work, holding positions on the Providence and Oak Grove Boarding School committees, and on other important committees of the church and other philanthropic organizations. She is treasurer of the Woman's Foreign Missionary Society of the New England Yearly Meeting of Friends and is always active in its interests. In 1883 Mrs. Bailey joined the Woman's Christian Temperance Union and entered heartily into its work of reform. She was always a strong advocate of peace principles, and in 1887, when the department of peace and arbitration was created, she was appointed superintendent of it. In 1888 she was made the superintendent of that department for the World's Woman's Christian Temperance Union. With active brain, willing heart and generous hand, she prosecutes this work, employing a private secretary, editing and publishing two monthly papers, "The Pacific Banner" and "The Acorn," besides millions of pages of literature. She is State superintendent of the Sabbath observance department of the Maine Woman's Christian Temperance Union, and is also working diligently in the interests of securing a reformatory prison for women in her State. She is the author of "Reminiscences of a Christian Life" (1884). In every branch of philanthropic work she is found to be interested. For the church, for the school, for the young man or woman who is striving for an education, her heart and purse are always open. Her home is in Winthrop Center, ME.

BAILEY, Mrs. Lepha Eliza, author and lecturer, born in Battle Creek, MI, 21st January, 1845. Her maiden name was Dunton. Her father was of Scotch descent. Both parents were born and reared in Georgia, VT, and their family consisted of nine children, all born in Georgia, VT, except Mrs. Bailey, the youngest. From Vermont her parents removed, with their entire family, to Battle Creek in the fall of 1840. Michigan was at that time an unbroken wilderness. In early life Miss Dunton became a contributor to local papers. On 21st October, 1873, she was married to Lewis Bailey, of Battle Creek. Four children were born

to them, two of whom died in infancy. Mrs. Bailey was a useful member of many local organizations, including the Woman's Christian Temperance Union, Sovereigns of Industry, Independent Order of Good Templars, and Grangers, and was an officer of each. When the red-ribbon movement became prominent Mrs. Bailey took an active interest in its development, and she dates her present work as a speaker from her local labor for the Woman's Christian Temperance Union and red-ribbon clubs. At that time Mrs. Bailey edited a department in "Our Age," published at Battle Creek, this she continued for three years. In 1876–77 she wrote much for the "Grange Visitor," and gave talks upon the labor question before assemblies of Grangers, at that time flourishing in Michigan. In 1878 she was invited by the State amendment committee, to canvass her own county on the question of a prohibitory amendment submitted to the people. She gave two-hundred lectures, speaking in every city, village and school district. For two years previous Mrs. Bailey had been speaking occasionally upon the temperance question and woman suffrage, but her active public work began with the amendment campaign in her own State, since which time she has been constantly in field service, having been actively engaged in every State where an amendment campaign has been inaugurated. In 1880 Mrs. Bailey was invited to speak under the auspices of the National Prohibition Alliance. She responded, and worked in the East until that society disbanded, and finally merged with the Prohibition Party, under whose auspices she is at present employed.

BAILEY, Mrs. Sara Lord, elocutionist and teacher of dramatic elocution, born in Tottington, near Bury, England, 9th September, 1856. She is the only child of Mr. and Mrs. Daniel Lord, her parents bringing her to the United States the year following her birth and making their home in Lawrence, MA, where they now reside. She early showed a fondness and talent for dramatic elocution, and it was developed by her participation in amateur plays given in Lawrence under the auspices of the Grand Army posts. She was educated in the Oliver grammar school, passing thence to Lasell Seminary, Auburndale, MA, where she studied two years. She afterward studied under the best teachers of elocution in Boston, and was graduated in 1888 from the Boston School of Oratory. A few years ago she was married to Elbridge E. Bailey, and in 1882 to benefit Mr. Bailey's health they went to the Sandwich Islands where they lived for nearly two years. They were present at the coronation ceremonies of the king and queen in Iolani palace, 12th February, 1883. In 1884 they returned to the United States, and Mr. Bailey went into business in St. Louis, MO, where Mrs. Bailey taught elocution most successfully in the Mission School for the Blind. They afterward removed to Kansas City, where Mr. Bailey has built up a flourishing business. Mrs. Bailey for some time taught elocution and voice-culture in the school of oratory there, but was obliged to return to Massachusetts on account of her failing health. She is devoted to her profession, having several large classes in elocution in Lawrence, besides fulfilling engagements to read in various cities.

BAKER, Mrs. Charlotte Johnson, physician, born in Newburyport, MA, 30th March, 1855. Her maiden name was Charlotte Le Breton Johnson. She was graduated from the Newburyport high school in 1872, spent a year in teaching, and entered Vassar College in 1873. She was graduated from that institution in 1877 with the degree of B.A. During the college year of 1877–78 she served as instructor in gymnastics in Vassar. In 1878 and 1879 she was assistant to Dr. Eliza M. Mosher, surgeon in the Woman's Reformatory Prison in Sherbourne, MA. In the fall of 1879 she entered with advanced standing the medical department of the University of Michigan, from which institution she was graduated in 1881 with the degree of MD. She returned to Newburyport and in 1882 was married to Dr. Fred Baker and they went to Akron, OH. Threatened failure of health caused her to go to New Mexico, where she lived in the mountains for five years. Early in 1888 she and her husband moved to San Diego, CA, where both are engaged in successful practice as physicians. Their family consists of two children. In 1889 Dr. Charlotte received the degree of A.M. from Vassar College for special work in optics and ophthalmology done after graduation. Besides her professional work, Dr. Baker has always identified herself with the Woman's Christian Temperance Union and with all other movements for the advancement of women individually, socially and politically.

BAKER, Mrs. Harriette Newell Woods, author, born in Andover, MA, in 1815. She has published, under the pen-name "Mrs. Madeline Leslie," nearly two-hundred moral and religious tales. She has also written under her own name or initials, and under that of "Aunt Hattie."

BAKER, Miss Ida Wikoff, business woman, born in Decatur, IL, 31st July, 1859. Her father, Peter Montfort Wikoff, was a native of Warren county, OH, who removed with his father to Illinois while quite young. He was a descendant of Peter Cloesen Wikoff, who came from Holland in 1636 and settled on Long Island, where he held a position under the Dutch Government. He married Margaret Van Ness. Mrs. Baker's mother, whose maiden name was Elizabeth Fletcher, was born near Crotches' Ferry, MD. On 25th April, 1878, Ida was married to Joseph N. Baker, then a merchant of Decatur, and now connected with the Citizens' National Bank. Of two children born to them, one, a daughter aged nine, is living. In 1889 Mrs. Baker's sister, Miss Laura B. Wikoff, set on foot a plan to organize a stock company composed of women only, for the purpose of promoting the industrial, educational and social advancement of women, and for literary, scientific and musical culture in the city of Decatur. Articles of incorporation were issued to the Woman's Club Stock Company 15th August, 1889, and a building was finished and occupied by the first tenant 1st November, 1890. Mrs. Baker was named one of the nine directors at the first annual meeting, was elected secretary of the stock company 12th January, 1891, and has served in that capacity ever since. In December, 1889, the Woman's Exchange was established as a branch of the Industrial and Charitable Union. Mrs. Baker was elected president and served until forced by illness to resign. After partly regaining her health, she served as treasurer and business manager. She is a member of the Woman's Club, of the Order of the Eastern Star, and of the Woman's Christian Temperance Union. Her life is one of constant activity.

BAKER, Miss Joanna, linguist and educator, born in New Rochelle, Ogle county, IL, 14th February, 1862. She is professor of Greek, language, literature and philosophy in Simpson College, Indianola, IA. Her name has come conspicuously before the public on account of her early and unusual proficiency in ancient and modern languages. Her parents, Orlando H. and Mary C. Ridley Baker, were both teachers and linguists, and began to instruct her in Greek and Latin as soon as she could speak English clearly. Her father for her amusement taught her, instead of Mother Goose melodies, the conjugation of the verb in Greek and Latin, which she learned merely from the rhythm. It was in her fourth year she was put to the systematic study of three languages, one lesson each day except Sunday. Mondays and Thursdays it was Greek, Tuesdays and Fridays, Latin, and Wednesdays and Saturdays, French. This system of instruction was continued with only the variation of oral exercises, and with scarcely ever an intermission, for several years. The lessons assigned were short, but the standard was perfection. She learned her lessons so easily that it took but a small part of the morning, and she seemed to have as much time for voluntary reading and childish amusements, of which she was very fond, as those children who had no studies. Before she was eight years old, she had thoroughly finished the primary books in Greek, Latin and French. She had read, besides, in Greek the first book of Xenophon's Anabasis and three books of Homer's Iliad. In Latin she had read Harkness' Reader entire, the first book of Cæsar, and two books of Virgil's Æneid. She took daily grammar lessons in Hadley's Greek grammar and Harkness' Latin, and all the grammatical references and notes annexed to the texts both of Latin and Greek. She had read in French a book of fables and stories, and learned Fasquelle's French course. Homer, Virgil and Fasquelle were recited with college classes. These were her studies in language before her eighth birthday. Her parents

removed to Algona, IA, where she became a student in Algona College. At the age of twelve years, besides the above studies, she had read other books of Homer and Virgil, Herodotus, Memorabilia, Demosthenes de Corona, Sallust, Cicero de Senectute et Amicitia, Orations against Catiline, with frequent exercise in Latin and Greek composition. It is not to be supposed that she was wholly occupied with classical studies. She was initiated early into the mysteries of practical housekeeping, from the kitchen up. She read history, biography and such current literature as fell into her hands, and was always ready to take her place with girls of her age in excursions and sports. At twelve years of age she began to study arithmetic and finished it so far as the subject of interest in three months. She took up algebra, geometry and trigonometry in rapid succession, and showed as much ability in mathematics as in languages. Before her fourteenth year she had read several times over Œdipus Tyrannus in Greek, and made a complete lexicon of it, with critical notes on the text. At sixteen she had read most of the Greek and Latin of a college course and, having returned to Simpson College, was appointed by President Berry tutor of Greek. This was the occasion of the first public notice taken of her early linguistic attainments. The notice made of her in the Indianola "Herald" was copied with comments and variations all over America and in many countries of Europe. At eighteen years of age she published an original literal translation of Plato's Apology, which received commendation from eminent Greek scholars. Some years before she had begun the study of music and German. This language became a favorite and she soon acquired a speaking knowledge of it. In 1881 she entered Cornell College, IA, and in 1882 graduated, receiving the degree of A.B. She entered DePauw University in 1886, for special instruction in Greek, German, French and music. After two years of study, during which she acted as tutor of Greek, she received the degree of A.M. *pro merito*, was admitted an alumna of that university, *ad eundem gradum*, and was elected instructor of Latin by the board of trustees, in which position she served for one year. She was re-elected the second year, but, having received an offer of the chair of Greek in Simpson College, a position her father had filled twenty years before, she accepted the latter. A year after she lost her mother to whom she was affectionately attached. She has three younger sisters. The older, Myra, is now professor of German and French in Napa College, California, and the other two are still at home, students in college. Miss Baker is a clear, forcible writer and a ready speaker. Her public lectures are well attended. She is an interesting conversationist, has a pleasing address and is unassuming. She is popular with her students and imbues them with her own enthusiasm and love for the Greek language and its literature. She organized all students of Greek in the college into a club called "Hoi Hellenikoi," especially for the study of Greek home life and customs, mythology and civil polity; and to gain familiarity with choice passages from the best authors in the original Greek. Miss Baker is fond of company, and a member of the Methodist Church.

BAKER, Mrs. Julie Wetherill, author, born in Woodville, MS, in 1858. Her birthplace was the home of her distinguished grandfather, Cotesworth Pinckney Smith, chief-justice of the State of Missis- 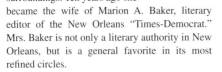 sippi. Born in Mississippi and reared partly in that State, and partly in Philadelphia, PA, the home of her Quaker ancestor, Samuel Wetherill, she shows in her writings the dual influence of her early surroundings. Ten years ago she became the wife of Marion A. Baker, literary editor of the New Orleans "Times-Democrat." Mrs. Baker is not only a literary authority in New Orleans, but is a general favorite in its most refined circles.

BAKER, Miss Louise S., Congregational minister, born in Nantucket, MA, 17th October, 1846. She was the only daughter among five sons. She was educated in Nantucket, her specialty being the languages and elocution. She began to teach at eighteen, and at twenty-two was assistant in the high school in Pawtucket, RI. From 1877 to 1880 she spent much time in Boston, speaking in the interest of the Massachusetts Woman's Christian Temperance Union. On one of her visits home she was invited to preach in the Baptist Church, and

subsequently supplied that pulpit many times. She was the acting pastor of the Old North Church (Congregational) for more than seven years, being ordained by that body in 1884. She was a member of the church, having united with it in 1866. Repeated family bereavements caused her to quit active work for a time, and in 1888 she withdrew from pas-  toral labors. She has preached by invitation in other cities, and is very active in her own community. She has done considerable literary work in essays and lectures, and has published a volume of poems under the title of "By the Sea." Her home is in Nantucket.

BALDWIN, Mrs. Esther E., missionary, born in Marlton, NJ, 8th November, 1840. Her father, the Rev. M. Jerman, was for many years an honored member of the New Jersey Annual Conference of the Methodist Episcopal Church. Esther was constitutionally frail, sensitive and studious. Her first schooling was given her at home. She was graduated from Pennington Seminary, Salem, NJ, in 1859, taking the highest honors. A teacher of higher mathematics, Latin and French in a seminary in Virginia, her sympathies were with the North, and she resigned her position and returned home. In 1862 she was married to the Rev. Dr. S. L. Baldwin, a missionary to China. After her marriage she accompanied her husband to Foochow, China. Besides domestic responsibilities, she soon had supervision of several day schools and of a class of Bible women who were sent out to read the Bible to their country-women. Her voice was the first to ask for a medical woman to be sent to China. For several years she translated the Berean Lessons into the Chinese language, and for two years edited in the same language the "Youth's Illustrated Paper." She saw the missions grow from small beginnings into strong churches of intelligent and self-sacrificing Christians. In the midst of her usefulness sickness came, and, after eighteen years of earnest, patient, hopeful service in the foreign field, she turned her

Marie Burroughs.
From Photo Copyrighted, 1894, by Morrison, Chicago.

Bessie Cleveland.
From Photo by Morrison, Chicago.

face homeward, as the only means of saving her life. For some years Dr. Baldwin has been the recording secretary of the Board of Missions of the M. E. Church. Mrs. Baldwin's health having been largely restored, she spends the full measure of her strength in active benevolence. She has been extensively employed in the interests of the Woman's Foreign Missionary Society, and of the Woman's Christian Temperance Union, as also in lectures on various subjects, and in many charities. She is an ardent advocate of the equality of women with men in State and Church. The misrepresentation and abuse of the Chinese have kindled her indignation. She has been called to speak before large audiences in many places on the Chinese question and has written numerous articles on the subject. She has collected and forcibly stated both the laws and the facts, and has published them in a small volume entitled "Must the Chinese Go?" She has won the distinction of being the "Chinese Champion." Mrs. Baldwin is the mother of seven children, two of whom died in Foochow. She now resides in Brooklyn, NY.

BALL, Mrs. Isabel Worrell, pioneer woman journalist of the West, born in a log cabin near Hennepin, Putnam county, IL, 13th March, 1855. She was educated in public schools and academies, her favorite study being history. Her father was a lawyer, and at the age of thirteen years she began to study with him, gaining a fair knowledge of law. In 1873 her family removed to western Kansas. She rode over the prairies, assisting in herding her father's stock, learning to throw a lasso with the dexterity of a cowboy, and to handle a gun. The outdoor life restored her health. She taught the first public school in Pawnee county, KS, her school district including the whole immense county. She was the second woman to be appointed a notary public in Kansas. She held positions in committee clerkships of the Kansas legislature from 1876 to 1886, and served as press reporter from 1877 to 1890. Her journalistic work began in 1881. In New Mexico and Arizona she had many experiences with the Indians, and gathered much interesting material for future work. She practically "lived in a little gripsack." The Atlantic and Pacific Railroad was being built and she was special correspondent for the Albuquerque "Daily Journal." Her life was often in danger from Navajoe and Apache Indians. Once the boarding train was surrounded by the Indians, and escape entirely cut off by washouts. The little dwelling, a box car, was riddled with bullets, and two men were killed, but Mrs. Ball escaped unhurt. For two years she lived in that wild country, seeing no woman's face, save that of a squaw, for three months at a time. In 1882 she returned to Kansas and acted for three years as editor of the Larned "Chronoscope." Removing to Topeka in 1886, she was made assistant secretary of the State Historical Society. After filling an editorial position on the "Commonwealth," in 1888 she became literary critic of the Kansas City "Daily Times." In 1889 she changed to the Kansas City "Star," and in the fall of 1891 she removed to Washington and entered upon special journalistic work. Meanwhile she had contributed many sketches to eastern periodicals. In ¡889 she was prominent in the formation of the Western Authors' and Artists' Club, which meets annually in Kansas City, and of which Mrs. Ball is the secretary and master spirit. Her marriage to H. M. Ball occurred in 1887.

BALL, Miss Martha Violet, educator and philanthropist, born in Boston, MA, 17th May, 1811. She was a school teacher for thirty years and a Sunday-school teacher for forty years. In 1838, under the auspices of the New England Moral Reform Society, she commenced her labors for fallen, intemperate women and unfortunate young girls. That association has rescued thousands from lives of intemperance, and thousands of young girls have been sought out and furnished shelter. Miss Ball for ten years was assistant editor and seventeen years the editor of the society's publication, "The Home Guardian." She was one among others who in 1833 formed the Boston Female Anti-Slavery Society, and was its recording secretary when the mob, designated as "gentlemen of property and standing," entered the hall and broke up a quarterly meeting. In 1842 Miss Ball was sent as delegate to an anti-slavery convention of women held in Philadelphia. Pennsylvania Hall was attacked by a mob of thousands, the women driven out and pelted with stones, mud and missiles of various kinds, and Miss Ball struck in the chest by a piece of brick. The hall was burned to the ground by the mob. Miss Ball aided in forming the Ladies' Baptist Bethel Society and was its first secretary; she was then elected president, and retained that office for thirty years. In 1860 Miss Ball, with a few others, organized the Woman's Union Missionary Society for Heathen Lands.

BALLARD, Miss Mary Canfield, poet, born in Troy, PA, 22nd June, 1852, on her mother's side is related to Col. Ethan Allen, of Revolutionary fame. At fourteen she was sent to the State Normal School, but, growing homesick, returned to her home in Troy, where she finished her education. She is devoted to painting, music and literature, and has been a prolific contributor to periodicals under the pen-name of Minnie C. Ballard ever since she sent her first poem to William Cullen Bryant, who gave it a place in the "Evening Post." Her early literary efforts were very ambitious ones. When she was only thirteen years old, she wrote a continued story about a hairpin, managing to introduce an elopement, an angry father, tears, repentance and forgiveness. She also wrote an essay on Sappho. She began to write poems at the age of sixteen, but her first published productions made their appearance when she was twenty-one years old. Since her bow to the public in the poets' corner of the "Evening Post," she has contributed occasionally to some thirty periodicals. She has published "Idle Fancies" (Troy, PA, 1883), for private circulation, and a new edition for the general public (Philadelphia, 1884).

BALLOU, Miss Ella Maria, stenographer, born in Wallingford, VT, 15th November, 1852, and has spent her life in her native State. She was educated in the Wallingford high school and immediately after leaving school began life as a teacher, in which vocation she was successful, but was rebellious over what she considered the injustice of requiring her to accept for equal service a much smaller compensation than was paid to a man of equal or less ability. After a few years of labor as a teacher, she learned shorthand and adopted it as a life-work. The persistence and thoroughness that had been a characteristic of her girlhood manifested itself in her work, and she went into the courts and wrote out evidence and argument until she became noted for accuracy and skill, and in 1885, upon the unanimous application of the Rutland County Bar, Hon. W. G. Veazey, Judge of the Supreme Court, appointed her the official reporter of Rutland County Court. Hers was the first appointment of a woman as official stenographer in Vermont, if not in the United States. Her success in her work has been marked and she has also been appointed official reporter of the adjoining county of Addison. When not in court, Miss Ballou does general work in her profession. She has also done some literary work in the line of essays and addresses. Miss Ballou is a practical example of what may be done by women, and while she earnestly claims all her rights as a woman and her full right to have as much pay for her labor as is paid to a man for the same service, she makes no claim to be allowed to vote or hold office. She honors her sex and exalts it to an equality with the other, and yet believes it to be a distinct order of human life.

BANCKER, Miss Mary E. C., author, known by her pen-name, "Betsey Bancker," born in New York City, 1st September, 1860. She is a lineal descendant of that old and historical Knickerbocker family whose name she bears, which came from Holland in 1658. The Bancker family intermarried with the De Puysters, Rutgers, Ogdens and Livingstons. The maternal grandfather of Miss Bancker was Michael Henry, one of the leading merchants of New York, as well as patron of art, and founder and owner of the once famous picture gallery at Number 100 Broadway. Mr. Henry was of Huguenot extraction. His ancestors, driven out of France after the revocation of the Edict of Nantes, during the reign of Louis XIV, established themselves at Henry's Grove, Armaugh, Ireland. Mr. Henry's father, John Sinclair Henry, came to America with the idea of founding a colony in South Carolina. Homeward bound, he stopped in New York, where he met

Leah, of the old Brevoort family, of that city, and, wooing and wedding her, he remained and established a shipping business between this country and Newry, Ireland. Miss Mary, daughter of F. J. Bancker, began to write early. Her maiden efforts were a series of sketches descriptive of outdoor life, appearing in the "Turf, Field and Farm." These articles were well received and extensively copied. Miss Bancker corresponded for the Cincinnati "Enquirer" during several years, and now represents the Montreal "Herald" in New York, her present home, as stall correspondent for that Canadian journal. She is known from Quebec to British Columbia. Miss Bancker produced the Indian Opera "Dovetta" in April, 1889, in the Standard Theater in New York, in conjunction with Mrs. E. Marcy Raymond. Miss Bancker was librettist with Charles Raynaud. She is constantly writing upon a variety of topics, that find their way to American as well as Canadian periodicals. Miss Bancker began her education in New York, and at a very impressionable age traveled extensively in Europe and in the tropics of America. She has a knowledge of the French and Spanish languages.

BANKS, Mrs. Mary Ross, author, born in Macon, GA, 4th March, 1846. On her father's side she is from Scotch ancestry. Her grandfather, Luke Ross, was a man of large wealth for his day, and had a sumptuously appointed home, the furniture of which was hauled in wagons from New York City to North Carolina. A man of unblemished integrity, having stood security for a friend and lost, he sacrificed all his possessions and moved to Jones county, GA, when the present beautiful city of Macon was a small trading port. Mrs. Banks' father, John Bennett Ross, was one of seven brothers and three sisters. The Ross brothers clung together and established themselves in trade about the year 1832. A talent for business and the clannish Scotch blood that kept them together resulted in a splendid commercial success. There were changes in the course of time, some of the brothers embarking in other kinds of business, but John B. Ross continued in the wholesale and retail dry goods and planters' supply business till the end of his days and made so large a fortune that he

was known as "the merchant prince of the South." His home was the center of elegant entertainment, and his children were reared in luxury. He was married three times. His first wife was a Miss Holt; his second, Martha Redding, descended from the Lanes and Flewellens, was the mother of Mrs. Banks; his third wife, a charming woman who still survives him, is a sister of Judge L. Q. C. Lamar, of the Supreme Court of the United States. Mrs. Banks was educated in Wesleyan Female College, in Macon, GA, and in the private school of Mrs. Theodosia Bartow Ford. She was married at seventeen years of age to Edward P. Bowdre, of Macon, at that time a captain in the Confederate army. She went to the army with her husband and did noble service in the hospitals. At twenty-five years of age she was a widow with three sons, and much of the fortune that should have been hers dissipated by the hazard of war and the scarcely less trying period of reconstruction. In June, 1875, she was married to Dr. J. T. Banks, of Griffin, GA, a gentleman of high standing socially and professionally and lived with him in unclouded happiness for four years, when she was again a widow. Crushed by her grief, she realized that her only hope for peace of mind lay in employment and as soon as she had partly recovered from the shock, she went courageously to work to help herself and her boys. With no training for business, and no knowledge of labor, frail in body, but dauntless in spirit, she accomplished wonders in many lines. She was a successful farmer and turned many of her talents and accomplishments into money-making. After raising her sons to the age of independence, she accepted a position in the Department of the Interior at Washington, where she has been assigned to important work in the office of the Secretary, a position she finds both lucrative and agreeable. Her literary fame came to her suddenly and is the result of one book, "Bright Days on the Old Plantation" (Boston, 1882), and a number of sketches and short stories published in various newspapers and periodicals.

BANTA, Mrs. Melissa Elizabeth Riddle, poet, born in Cheviot, a suburb of Cincinnati, OH, 27th March, 1834. Her father, James Riddle, was of Scotch descent, and her mother, Elizabeth Jackson, a Quaker, was of English origin. Melissa Elizabeth is the sole daughter of the house. She attended the Wesleyan Female Institute in Cincinnati until her fourteenth year, when, on the removal of the family to Covington, KY, she was placed in the Female Collegiate Institute of that city, where she was graduated at the age of seventeen years. The same year she made a romantic marriage with Joseph I. Perrin, of Vicksburg, MS. The young couple lived in Vicksburg, where the bride was a teacher in the public schools. A few days after the first anniversary of the wedding day, 11th September, 1853, Mr. Perrin died of yellow fever. That was the year when the fever was epidemic in the South. Mrs. Banta's recollections of that time are vivid. Her poem, "The Gruesome Rain," embodies a grief, a regret and a hint of the horrors of that season. Mrs. Sophia Fox, hearing of her situation, sent her carriage and servants a distance of twenty-five miles to carry the young widow to her plantation at Bovina, MS. There she remained for two months, until her parents dared to send for her. Mrs. Fox, with characteristic southern warmheartedness, had supplied all her needs and refused all proffered remuneration on the arrival of Dr. Mount, the old family physician. After the death of Mr. Perrin, a little daughter was born, but in a few weeks she faded from her mother's arms, and the child-widow took again her place in her father's house. For the sake of an entire change of scene her father disposed of his home and business interests in Covington, temporarily, and removed to Bloomington, IN. It was there Mrs. Perrin met David D. Banta, to whom she was married 11th June, 1856. Soon after the wedding they went to Covington, KY, and in October, 1847, to Franklin, IN, where they have since lived. They have a beautiful home, and this second marriage is an ideal one. Mrs. Banta is the mother of two sons and one daughter. She has been twice to Europe and has visited all the notable places in the United States. Her letters of travel are only less charming than her poetry. She inherits her literary talent from her maternal grandmother, who, though not a writer, was a highly intellectual woman.

BARBER, Mrs. Mary Augustine, educator, born in Newton, CT, in 1789; died in Mobile, AL, in 1860. She entered the Visitation Convent in Georgetown, DC, in 1818, with her four daughters. She founded a convent of visitation in Kaskaskia,

IL, in 1836, remaining there till 1844. She taught in a convent in St. Louis, MO, from 1844 till 1848, and in Mobile until the time of her death.

BARBOT, Mme. Blanche Hermine, musical director and pianist, born in Brussels, Belgium, 28th December, 1842. She is the daughter of Victor and Marie Therese Petit, and inherits her great musical talents from her father, who was a musician and composer of ability and a fine performer on several instruments, but especially noted for the perfection of his playing on the clarinet. From infancy Hermine gave evidence of a decided talent for music. She received from her father the most careful training. At the age of seven she was already so accomplished a pianist that the celebrated French musician, Mme. Pleyel, complimented her most warmly on her playing and predicted for her a brilliant future upon the concert stage, for which her father destined her. Her first appearance in concert was in the Theatre Italien-Francais, in Brussels, in February, 1851. This first success of the little Hermine was followed by many others during a tour she made with her father through the various large cities of Belgium and Holland. While in Holland, she was invited to play before the Queen, who was so delighted by the child's performance that she gave her a beautiful watch as a token of her admiration. The family removed to New York in the spring of 1852, where several concerts were given by the father and daughter. Mons. Petit was induced to visit the South and finally to settle in Charleston, SC, where he was successful as a music teacher. While still a young man, he fell a victim to yellow fever in the epidemic of 1856, leaving his family in such straitened circumstances that all thought of a musical career for his daughter had to be renounced, and she became a teacher at the age of thirteen. When Thalberg visited Charleston, in 1857, he called upon Mlle. Petit, and was so delighted with her playing that he invited her to render with him a duo on two pianos at his concert. In 1863 Mlle. Petit was married to P. J. Barbot, a merchant of Charleston, who died in 1887, leaving six children. Her marriage in no way interfered with her musical work. Although Mme. Barbot is a brilliant pianist with fine technique and great force and delicacy of expression, she has always shrunk from appearing in public as a solo performer, except in response to the calls of charity, to which she has always given her services freely, irrespective of denomination, although she is herself an earnest Roman Catholic. Her peculiar gift is in training and directing large musical forces. She has for years given cantatas, oratorios and operas with the amateurs of the city. To her Charleston is indebted for most of the fine music it has had of late years, as her taste inclines to the serious and classical. In 1875 Mme. Barbot was chosen director of the Charleston Musical Association, a society of about a hundred voices, with which she has since given many important works. She has been organist in St. Mary's and St. Michael's churches, and is now organist of the Cathedral.

BARNES, Miss Annie Maria, author and editor, born in Columbia, SC, 28th May, 1857. Her mother was a Neville and traced her descent in a direct line from the Earl of Warwick. Miss Barnes's position in literature depends upon no family prestige or any adventitious circumstances in life, but upon her own genius and industry. She knows what it is to struggle for recognition in the literary world and to suffer the inconveniences and embarrassments of poverty. Her family was left at the close of the Civil War, like most Southerners, without means. Under the impulse of genius she persevered and by her energy overcame the disadvantages of her situation and the discouragements that usually beset the path of the young writer. Before reaching the meridian of life she has won foremost rank in the one particular line wherein she has sought recognition, that of southern juvenile literature. Miss Barnes developed early in life a taste for literary work, and when only eleven years of age wrote an article for the Atlanta "Constitution," which was published and favorably noticed by the editor, and at fifteen she became a regular correspondent of that journal. She has been a frequent contributor to leading journals north as well as south. In 1887 she undertook the publication of a juvenile paper called "The Acanthus," which, with one excep-

tion, was the only strictly juvenile paper ever published in the South. In literary character it was a success, but financially, like so many other southern publications, it was a failure. Many of Miss Barnes's earlier productions appeared in the "Sunday-school Visitor," a child's paper published by the Methodist Episcopal Church, South, in Nashville, TN. Her first book was "Some Lowly Lives" (Nashville, 1885); then followed "The Life of David Livingston" (1887), and "Scenes in Pioneer Methodism" (1889). Later she wrote "The Children of the Kalahari," a child's story of Africa, which was very successful in this country and in England. Two books from her pen were to be issued in 1892, "The House of Grass" and "Atlanta Ferryman: A Story of the Chattahoochee." Miss Barnes is at present junior editor for the Woman's Board of Missions, Methodist Episcopal Church, South, having charge of its juvenile paper and of all its quarterly supplies of literature. In that capacity she has done her most telling and forceful work.

BARNES, Miss Catharine Weed, photographer and editor, born in Albany, NY, 10th January, 1851. She is the eldest child of the Hon. William Barnes and Emily P. Weed, daughter of the late Thurlow Weed. After receiving an academical education in Albany she entered Vassar College, but was obliged to give up the idea of graduating because of illness resulting from overwork. In 1872 she accompanied her parents to Russia, where Mr. Barnes was an official delegate from this country to the International Statistical Congress in St. Petersburg. She has traveled much in this country and abroad, and is a close student and hard worker. She took up photography in 1886, having previously given much time to music and painting. On her mother's death, in 1889, she assumed charge of her father's household in Albany but gave all her spare time to camera work. After contributing many articles to various periodicals devoted to photography she went on the editorial staff of the "American Amateur Photographer" in May, 1890. She is an active member of the Society of Amateur Photographers of New York, of the New York Camera Club, and the Postal Photographic Club, an honorary member of the Chicago Camera Club and of the Brooklyn Academy of Photography, and has won prizes at various photographic exhibitions as an amateur. She is a member of the National Photographers' Association of America, a professional organization. Miss Barnes is also connected with several literary and musical associations and belongs to the Sorosis Club of New York. She has a special portrait studio carefully planned, in a building separate from her residence, but is continually altering it for her favorite work of making illustrations and character studies. She does all the work in studio, laboratory and printing-room herself and is a thorough reader of everything bearing on camera work. Her great desire is to encourage women to take up this work as a regular profession. Her own preference is for figures and interiors rather than for landscapes. She makes lantern-slides from her own negatives and shows them in her oxyhydrogen lantern, and has read several papers before societies in different cities, besides recording her camera experiences in her own magazine. In 1888 she received a diploma for the excellence of her work exhibited at Boston and a silver medal in 1891 for lantern-slides. She entered the Enoch Arden prize competition in the Washington convention of the Photographers' Association of America for 1890 with three pictures, which were judged entitled to second place by an eminent art critic who examined all the photographs exhibited, and entered the Elaine competition in Buffalo in 1891. She is the first woman amateur photographer who has ventured to compete with professionals and was invited to read a paper in their Buffalo convention. Her new studio and laboratory are well fitted for photographic work, and owe most of their excellence to contrivances of her own designing. Her editorial work on the "American Amateur Photographer" at first covered the ladies' department only, but she has recently became associate editor. She is editing the woman's photographic department in "Outing," and has contributed a series of articles to "Frank Leslie's Weekly." Some of her pictures have been reproduced in art journals, and her reputation as a photographer is national. She was invited to address the Photographic Convention of the United Kingdom at Edinburgh in July, 1892, during her camera trip through England and Scotland.

BARNES, Mrs. Frances Julia, temperance reformer, born in Skaneateles, Onondaga county, NY, 14th April, 1846. Her maiden name was Allis. Her parents and ancestry were members of the orthodox society of Friends, of which she is a member. She received her early education in the schools of her native village and was finally graduated at the Packer Institute in Brooklyn, NY. After her graduation her family resided in Brooklyn, during which time she became interested in church and Sunday-school and mission work. On 21st September, 1871, she was married to Willis A. Barnes, a lawyer of New York, and made her home for a time in that city. In the fall of 1875 professional business called Mr. Barnes to Chicago, IL. Mrs. Barnes accompanied him, and they remained there five years. During that time she became associated with Miss Frances E. Willard in conducting gospel temperance meetings in lower Farwell Hall and meetings in church parlors in the Newsboy's Home, and in visiting jails, hospitals, printing offices and other places. It was while the temperance movement was confined to the object of "rescuing the perishing" the attention of Mrs. Barnes and her co-workers was drawn to the necessity of not merely seeking to reform the fallen, but also of directing efforts to implant principles of total abstinence among young men and women, and enlisting their coöperation while they were yet on life's threshold. In 1878, in the national convention held in Baltimore, Mrs. Barnes was made a member of the committee on young women's work, and in the next convention, held in Indianapolis, in 1879, she made a verbal report, and was at that time made chairman of the committee for the following year, and at its expiration made the first report on young women's work, which appeared in the National Minutes. In 1879 and 1880 twenty Young Women's Christian Temperance Unions were organized in the State of New York, and of the twenty-five unions in Illinois, with a membership of seven-hundred, two-thirds had been formed during the year. In 1880 young women's work was made a department of the National Woman's Christian Temperance Union, and Mrs. Barnes was appointed superintendent. In 1890 she was appointed fraternal delegate to the annual meeting of the British Women's Temperance Association, held in London, 21st and 22nd May, at which time she so acceptably presented the subject that the department of young women's work was immediately organized, and Lady Henry Somerset accepted the superintendency. As an outgrowth of that interest sixteen branches were organized in Great Britain the first year. In 1891 Mrs. Barnes was made the superintendent for the World's Young Women's Christian Temperance Union work. Under her care it has so grown that there is a membership of 30,000 in the United States alone. The members distribute literature, form hygenic and physical culture clubs, have courses of reading, flower missions, loan-libraries, jail visiting, Sunday-school work, in all covering forty different departments of philanthropic and religious labor. During the year she travels extensively through the country, delivers addresses at public and parlor meetings and organizes new local unions. Not only is her voice heard in the cause of temperance, but practical sentiments flow from her ready pen. Mrs. Barnes has edited a manual on young women's temperance work and is a regular contributor both of prose and poetry to the "Oak and Ivy Leaf," the organ of the National Young Women's Christian Temperance Union. She has been president of the Loyal Legion Temperance Society of New York City for ten years, under whose care a free reading-room for working boys has been maintained during that length of time, the attendance aggregating over two-hundred-thousand boys.

BARNES, Mrs. Mary Sheldon, educator and historian, born in Oswego, NY, 15th September, 1850. Her father was E. A. Sheldon, the principal of the Oswego Normal School. As a child she had a passion for study. After going through the high and normal schools and preparing for college with boys and girls who were bound for Harvard and Yale, she decided to go to college, and Michigan University was her choice. She entered that institution in 1871, as a classical sophomore in a class of eighty boys and eight girls. She was graduated in the classical course in 1874. She then went to teach history, Latin and Geeek in the Oswego State Normal School, but was soon called to Wellesley College, where she organized the department of history. She was at the head of that department from 1st January, 1877, to June, 1879. She next went to Europe for two years' study and travel, each of which had for her a strictly historical aim. She visited France, Italy, Egypt and Germany. The second year she spent as a student in Newnham College, Cambridge University, England, where she devoted the time to the study of modern history, under the direction of Prof. J. R. Seeley, regius professor of modern history. On her return to the United States she taught history and literature in the Normal School in Oswego, NY. Meanwhile she had been gathering materials for a text-book on general history which should present the subject on a more scientific method than the mere giving of a narrative.

While in that school she met Earl Barnes. In 1885 they were married, and in that year her first book was published, under the title "Studies in General History" (Boston). It met an immediate and sympathetic welcome from those who understood her plan. It has come rather slowly into popular use, on account of its originality. Her publishers, however, felt warranted in urging her to make an American history on the same plan, which she accordingly undertook. In 1888 that work was interrupted by a literary engagement which took her husband and herself to Europe, where they spent a year in the libraries of London, Paris and Zürich, collecting historical materials. The second book has recently been published under the title "Studies in American History" (Boston, 1892), and is the joint work of herself and her husband. In 1892 Mr. Barnes was called to the Leland Stanford Junior University, at the head of the department of education. Mrs. Barnes has received an appointment as assistant professor of modern history, an appointment obtained without any sort of solicitation, and it is one of the first appointments of the kind made in an institution of that rank. Her "Studies in American History" is having an immediate success. The home of Mrs. Barnes is now in Palo Alto, Santa Clara county, CA.

BARNEY, Mrs. Susan Hammond, evangelist, was born in Massachusetts. Her father, Dr. John A. Hammond, was a prominent physician. She was a contributor to the local press when thirteen years old. It was her desire to become a foreign missionary, but, owing to ill-health and the strong opposition of friends, she reluctantly gave over her purpose. She was married to Joseph K.

Barney, of Providence, RI, in 1854, and has ever since resided in that city, with the exception of several years spent on the Pacific Coast. Her first public speaking was done in the interest of the Woman's Foreign Missionary Society of the Methodist Episcopal Church. She was one of the founders of the Prisoners' Aid Society of Rhode Island, and has always been interested in prison and jail work. She was the first president of the Rhode Island Woman's Christian Temperance Union, a position she held for several years. She is now a national evangelist. The enactment of constitutional prohibition in Rhode Island in 1886 was largely due to her executive ability. She has had much to do with securing police matrons for the station-houses of large cities, her work in that direction being second to none. She is an able platform speaker. Mrs. Barney contributed a chapter on the "Care of the Criminal" to "Woman's Work in America" (New York, 1891).

BARR, Mrs. Amelia E., novelist, born in Ulverstone, on Morecombe Bay, in the district of Furness, Lancashire, England, in 1832. Her maiden name was Amelia E. Huddleston. She was the daughter of Rev. William Huddleston, a representative of the Huddlestons of Millom, a family of ancient and pure Saxon lineage, who furnished a large number of well-known ecclesiastics and of daring navigators. Amelia was a child of precocious intellect. Brought up in an atmosphere of refined culture, she early turned to books for recreation, and later became a thorough student. Her father was a learned and eloquent preacher, and he directed her studies for years. When she was only six years old, she had memorized many of the "Arabian Nights" stories, and was familiar with "Robinson Crusoe" and "Pilgrim's Progress." When she was nine years old, she became her father's companion and reader. Necessarily that work obliged her to read books of a deep nature and beyond her comprehension; however, the sentiments they contained did much toward her mental development. When twelve years old, she read to her father the well-known "Tracts for the Times" and became an adherent of the religious movement they originated. Her education was conducted in an unmethodical manner, and the principal part was derived from reading instructive books. When Miss Huddleston was sev-

enteen, she attended a celebrated school in Glasgow, Scotland, but she derived very little knowledge from that source. When about eighteen she was married to Robert Barr, the son of Rev. John Barr, of Dovehill Kirk, whose writings are still published. Mr. and Mrs. Barr came to America a few years after their marriage and traveled in the West and South. When the yellow fever broke out in 1856, they were in New Orleans, but, fearing to remain there, they left for Texas, settling in Austin, where Mr. Barr received an appointment in the comptroller's office. After the Civil War they removed to Galveston. In 1876 the yellow fever broke out there, and Mr. Barr and their four sons were stricken and died. Mrs. Barr and her three daughters were spared, and, as soon as it was safe, they went to New York. Mrs. Barr took a letter of introduction to a merchant, who directly engaged her to assist in the education of his three sons. She instructed them in ancient and modern literature, music and drawing. When her pupils went to Princeton, Mrs. Barr sought advice from Rev. Henry Ward Beecher, who was then editor of the "Christian Union." He was very encouraging, and she began to write for that paper and has continued to write for its columns. Mr. Beecher introduced her to Dr. Lyman Abbott, through whom she met the Harper Brothers, for whose periodicals she wrote for a number of years. In 1884 she was confined to her chair by an accident, which seemed to be a fortunate one, however, for during that time she wrote her first novel, "Jan Vedder's Wife." In 1885, it was bought and published by a New York house, who have since published her novels. Her first book attracted general notice and gave her an instantaneous success. It ran through many editions and has been widely read on both sides of the sea, and in more than one language. Since 1885 Mrs. Barr has published numerous stories. Scotland has furnished the scene of four of them; two have dealt with life in the English manufacturing districts. "The Border Shepherdess" (1887) lived in a long-debated territory between Scotland and England. "Feet of Clay" (1889) carried its readers to the Isle of Man. "Friend Olivia," a study of Quaker character, which appeared in 1890 in the "Century," recalled the closing years of the Commonwealth in England. "The Bow of Orange Ribbon" (1886) is a charming picture of life in New York in the days when Dutch manners and habits were still in their prime. "Remember the Alamo" (1888) recalls the stirring episode of the revolt of Texas against the Mexican rule. "She Loved a Sailor" combines pictures of sea life with darker scenes from the days of slavery. It will be seen from this brief catalogue that Mrs. Barr's sympathies are with life rather than with classes of people. Her other works are "A Daughter of Fife" (1886), "The Squire of Sandle-Side," "Paul and Christina" (1887), "Master of his Fate" (1888), "The Last of the Macallisters" (1886), "Between two Loves" (1886), "A Sister to Esau" (1890), and "A Rose of a Hundred Leaves" (1891). There is no other writer in the United States whose writings command so wide a circle of readers at home and abroad as Mrs. Barr's, and yet she is so much of a hermit that her personality is almost a mystery to the hundreds of thousands who are familiar with the creations of her intellect. Most of her time is spent at Cherry Croft, her home on the top of Storm King Mountain, at Cornwall-on-the-Hudson, NY. There she lives with her daughters, happy in her literary work and her social surroundings, and almost worshiped by the dwellers on the mountain, who are frequent visitors at the hermitage. Her career has been an admirable illustration of the capacity of woman, under stress of sorrow, to conquer the world and win success.

BARROW, Mrs. Frances Elizabeth, author, born in Charleston, SC, 22nd February, 1822. She was widely known by her pen-name, "Aunt Fanny." Died in New York City, 7th May, 1894.

BARRY, Mrs. Flora Elizabeth, concert and opera singer and musical educator, born in Paris, ME, 19th September, 1836. Mrs. Barry is descended on the paternal side from William Harlow, who came to this country from England prior to 1637, and Richard Thayer, who immigrated into Massachusetts among the earliest Puritans. On her mother's side, the Watermans claim a direct line of descent from Alfred the Great, while the Maxims were of Spanish origin, dating back to the time of Philip and Mary. Mrs. Barry's father, Isaac Harlow, was a cultured gentleman of musical tastes. Her mother possessed talent as a writer and a musician. Mrs. Barry received a superior education and is still an earnest student in every department of learning, French, Italian, Spanish and German receiving careful attention.

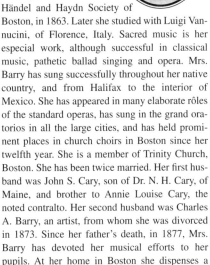

Her musical talent was the dominant one, and she early began the study of that art that she might make herself proficient as a vocalist and teacher. Her first appearances in public were with the Mendelssohn Quintette Club and the Händel and Haydn Society of Boston, in 1863. Later she studied with Luigi Vannucini, of Florence, Italy. Sacred music is her especial work, although successful in classical music, pathetic ballad singing and opera. Mrs. Barry has sung successfully throughout her native country, and from Halifax to the interior of Mexico. She has appeared in many elaborate rôles of the standard operas, has sung in the grand oratorios in all the large cities, and has held prominent places in church choirs in Boston since her twelfth year. She is a member of Trinity Church, Boston. She has been twice married. Her first husband was John S. Cary, son of Dr. N. H. Cary, of Maine, and brother to Annie Louise Cary, the noted contralto. Her second husband was Charles A. Barry, an artist, from whom she was divorced in 1873. Since her father's death, in 1877, Mrs. Barry has devoted her musical efforts to her pupils. At her home in Boston she dispenses a large hospitality.

BARRY, Mrs. Susan E., army nurse, born in Minisink, Orange county, NY, 19th March, 1826. Her maiden name was Hall. Her parents were natives of Orange county, and after forty years' residence on the old farm the family removed to Tompkins county, NY, near Ithaca. The care of the home fell upon Susan from the age of eighteen to thirty. When the farm was given up, after her mother's death, because her father was too infirm to care for it she went to New York City and became a medical student. She attended the lectures and studies in the college of a four-year course, graduating in the spring of 1861, just at the breaking out of the war. A mass meeting was called at Cooper Union to devise ways and means to help the Union soldiers. The Sanitary Commission was formed. The Ladies' Central Relief Association of

New York had been organized. Women were called to volunteer as nurses. Miss Hall gave in her name. The volunteers were required to pass strict examination, then they were admitted to Bellevue and the city hospitals to receive practical instructions. Miss Hall's two months spent in preparatory instruction proved invaluable in her army work. The volunteer nurses received orders 22nd July, 1861, to proceed to Washington and report to Miss Dorothy Dix for duty. When they arrived, all was confusion in the city, with many conflicting reports of the battle and defeat at Bull Run. Miss Hall and her companions received a kind welcome from the surgeon in charge of the Seminary Hospital in Alexandria. These women took turns in doing all the watching at night, with no help except a few contrabands to wait on the men. The nurses who had most experience in wound dressing and in the treatment of surgical cases were always hurried off to the front after battles. Miss Hall and her associate, Miss Dada, after eight months in Alexandria, were sent to Winchester, VA. Later they were sent to Strasburg, and thence they were transferred to Harper's Ferry, next to Annapolis Naval Hospital, then to Georgetown, DC, Warehouse Hospital, which was filled with wounded from the battle of Cedar Mountain. After that came the battle of Antietam, and Miss Hall and six other women nurses, with Miss Dix, were on hand before the dead were buried. Later Miss Hall was again called to Harper's Ferry. The hospitals were crowded, and she remained during the winter. She was next ordered to Gettysburg, immediately after the terrible battle. After several months in that busy field, she was transferred to the Western Department and was assigned to duty in Nashville, and later sent to Murfreesborough. She stayed there seven months, and then went to Chattanooga where she remained till the close of the war, having served the entire period without a furlough. Miss Hall's health was permanently impaired by her long continued labors, and returning home she spent the winter in Dr. Jackson's Sanitarium in Dansville, NY, for rest and treatment. In May, 1866, she was married to Robert Barry, of Chicago. After their marriage they went to California, making their permanent home in San Francisco. Mrs. Barry has not regained strength sufficient to engage in professional or public work.

BARTLETT, Mrs. Alice Eloise, author, born in Delavan, WI, 4th September, 1848. Her maiden name was Bowen, and she is widely known by her pen-name, "Birch Arnold." "The Meeting of the Waters," her first poem, was published in the Madison "Democrat." With all its crudities, it was unique and poetic, and the encouragement received determined her to enter the field of literature as a profession. In 1877 she published her first novel, "Until the Daybreak," which at once gave her a rank among story writers. In 1872 she began to write for the Toledo "Blade" and "Locke's National Monthly." Her articles attracted a great deal of attention, and D. R. Locke (Petroleum V. Nasby) told a friend that he intended to "adopt that promising young man." His (Nasby's) chagrin on learning that the young man was a girl can be imagined. It has often afforded her amusement to find her utterances commented on as the "vigorous ideas of a thinking man." To the world at large she still remains, and is often addressed as, "Birch Arnold, esq." Ill health for several years prevented the continuous effort necessary to pronounced success, but lyrics, essays and miscellaneous writings have from time to time appeared under her signature. In 1876 she was married to J. M. D. Bartlett, of Quincy, IL, and they have two children. As a conversationalist she is interesting, and she is an elocutionist of no ordinary ability. She is extremely sincere and earnest in her life as well as her writings, and her heart is in the work of elevating her sex and humanity in general. Her latest work is a novel entitled "A New Aristocracy" (Detroit, 1891), dealing with women and the labor question. Her home is in Detroit, MI, where she is engaged in literary labor.

BARTLETT, Miss Caroline Julia, Unitarian minister, born in Hudson, St. Croix county, WI, 17th August, 1858. She is a daughter of Lorenzo Dow and Julia A. Brown Bartlett. When she was sixteen years old, she heard a sermon which led her to make the liberal ministry her life-work. After she was graduated at Carthage College, in Illinois, the disapproval of her relatives and friends kept her from entering the ministry at once, and she turned her attention to newspaper work. For about three years she was on the staff of the Minneapolis "Tribune," and later was city editor of the Oshkosh "Daily Morning Times." As a newspaper writer and editor Miss Bartlett was a success. After spending a short time in special study, Miss Bartlett entered on her new calling as pastor of a little Unitarian flock in Sioux Falls, SD. During the three years she remained there, her efforts were greatly prospered. A handsome stone church was built, and the membership increased to many times the number that made up her charge when she undertook the work. The fame of her labors at Sioux Falls brought her an urgent call from the First Unitarian Church of Kalamazoo, MI, which she was induced to accept, as it would give her better opportunity for special study than she could have in South Dakota. Miss Bartlett has been in Kalamazoo three years, and the church of which she is pastor has flourished greatly during that time. Study clubs have been formed under her direction, and the church is an active and important factor in all good work in the community. Miss Bartlett spent the summer of 1891 abroad and preached in many of the Unitarian churches in England. She was received with great kindness, but a woman preacher was such a novelty that it was only by showing the portraits of a dozen other women ministers that she could get the people there to realize that she was not solitary in her vocation. By special invitation she visited the great philosopher and theologian, Dr. James Martineau, in his Scottish Highlands home. In philanthropic investigations while abroad, Miss Bartlett went about with the slum officers of the Salvation Army. Her conversion to the cause of woman's political enfranchisement did not come until after some years of public work, but then it was thorough. She preached the sermon before the National Woman Suffrage Convention in Washington, in 1891.

BARTLETT, Mrs. Maud Whitehead, educator, born in Gillespie, IL, 10th September, 1865. With her parents she removed to Ohio in 1879, and to Kansas five years later. Fascinated with music, she left school before she was graduated that she might, by teaching, be able to finish her musical education. After teaching both day school and music, she finally adopted the former as a profession, and for nine years, the last three of which were spent in the El Dorado, KS, schools, she devoted herself to the duties of the schoolroom, meanwhile steadily pursuing her musical studies. A member of the Methodist Episcopal Church, her life for years has been one constant sacrifice to the happiness of those about her. On 10th September, 1891, she was married to Harry Bartlett, of Denver, CO, which place has since been her home.

BARTON, Miss Clara, philanthropist, was born in North Oxford, Worcester county, MA, about 1830. Her father was a soldier with General Anthony Wayne. She received a good education in the public schools of her native town. After teaching for some years she took a course of study in Clinton, NY. She went to New Jersey, and taught first in Trenton, and then in Bordentown. Overwork in 1853 caused her health to fail, and she went to Washington, DC, to visit relatives and rest. There was at that time much confusion in the Patent Office, where clerks had betrayed secrets of inventors, and Miss Barton was employed to take charge of affairs. The male clerks tried to make her position uncomfortable, employing direct personal insult at first, and slander at last. Her abusers were discharged. She remained in the Patent Office three years, doing much to bring order out of chaos. Removed once on account of her "Black Republicanism," she was recalled by the same administration. When the Civil War broke out, she offered to serve in her department without pay, and resigned her position to find some other way in which to serve her country. She was among the spectators at the railroad station in Washington when the Massachusetts regiment arrived there from Baltimore, where the first blood had been shed. She nursed the forty wounded men who were the victims of the Baltimore mob. On that day she identified herself with army work, and she shared the risk and sufferings of the soldiers of the Union army to the close of the great struggle. Visits to the battle-fields revealed to her the great need of provision for the nursing and feeding of the wounded soldiers. She made an attempt to organize the work of relief, but

and her connection with the great conflict has given her a permanent and conspicuous place in the history of the country.

In 1869 she went to Europe to rest and recover her wasted energies. In Geneva she was visited by the leading members of the International Committee of Relief of Geneva for the care of the wounded in war, who presented to her the treaty, signed by all the civilized nations excepting the United States, under which all who wore the badge of their society were allowed to go on the battle-fields to care for the wounded. Miss Barton had not heard of the society, although its principles were familiar to her from her service in connection with the Sanitary Commission. The society was the Society of the Red Cross. Miss Barton was at once interested in it and began to advocate its extension to cover the United States. In 1870, while she was in

women held back, and Miss Barton herself was not allowed at first to go to the battle-fields. She gathered stores of food and supplies, and finally she prevailed upon Assistant Quartermaster General Rucker to furnish transportation facilities, and she secured permission to go wherever there was a call for her services. She at once went to the front, and her amazing work under the most distressful conditions, her unwearying devotion, and her countless services to the soldiers earned for her the name of "Angel of the Battle-field." During the last year of the war she was called to Massachusetts by family bereavements, and while there she was appointed by President Lincoln to attend to the correspondence of the relatives of missing prisoners after the exchanges. She went to Annapolis, MD, at once, to begin the work. Inquiries by the thousand poured ill, and she established a Bureau of Records of missing men of the Union army, employing several assistants. Her records are now of great value, as they were compiled from prison and hospital rolls and burial lists. At Andersonville she was able to identify all but four-hundred of the thirteen-thousand graves of buried soldiers. In her work she used her own money freely, and Congress voted to reimburse her, but she refused to take money as pay for her services. She managed the bureau for four years,

Berne, the war between France and Prussia broke out. Within three days Miss Barton was asked by Dr. Apia, one of the founders of the Red Cross Society, to go to the front and assist in caring for the wounded. Although herself an invalid, she went with her French companion, the "fair-haired Antoinette," and the two women were admitted within the lines of the German army. They there served after the battle of Hagenau, and Miss Barton realized the enormous value and importance of the Red Cross work, in having supplies of all sorts ready and trained help to do everything required to save life and relieve suffering. Returning to Berne, Miss Barton was called to the court in Carlsruhe by the Grand Duchess of Baden, who wished her to remain with her and give suggestions concerning relief measures. She remained in Carlsruhe until the siege of Strasburg, and, when the gates of that city at last opened to the German army, Miss Barton entered with the soldiers. For her services she received a Red Cross brooch from the Grand Duchess of Baden, the Gold Cross of Remembrance with the colors of the Grand Duchy of Baden from the Grand Duke and his wife, and the Iron Cross of Merit with the colors of Germany and the Red Cross from the Emperor and Empress of Germany. Everywhere in the ruined cities Miss Barton did most valuable work. In Paris, in the closing days of the Commune, she did much work. Monsieur Thiers honored her in signal ways, and she was debarred from receiving the cross of the Legion of Honor only by her refusal to solicit it, as, according to the laws governing its bestowal, it must be solicited by the would-be recipient.

In 1873, utterly broken in health, she returned to the United States, and for several years she was unable to do any work. As soon as she was able to do so, she began to urge the Washington government to accept the Geneva treaty for the Red Cross Society. President Garfield was to have signed the treaty, but his untimely death prevented, and it was signed by President Arthur in 1882. In 1877 an "American National Committee of the Red Cross" was formed in Washington, and it was afterward incorporated as "The American Association of the Red Cross." Miss Barton was appointed to the presidency by President Garfield, and she has since devoted herself to carrying out its benevolences. In the United States Miss Barton's society has done noble work among the fire sufferers in Michigan, and flood sufferers in Louisiana, Mississippi, and Johnstown, PA. During 1891 and 1892 the society worked for the famine sufferers in Russia, the American branch having made large collections of food and money for that purpose. In 1883 Miss Barton was appointed superintendent of the Reformatory Prison for Women in Sherburne, MA, and she divided her time between that work and the work of the Red Cross. She has made that beneficent organization known throughout the United States by its services in times of suffering from fire, flood, drouth, tempest and pestilence. Her later services in supervising the distribution of food and other supplies to the suffering Armenians of Asia Minor, survivors of the dreadful Turkish massacres there, are fresh in the minds of all.

BASCOM, Mrs. Emma Curtiss, woman suffragist and reformer, born in Sheffield, MA, 20th April, 1828. She was the second daughter of Orren Curtiss, and through her mother, Caroline Standish Owen, a direct descendant of Miles Standish. Her early education was received in the Great Barrington Academy, in Pittsfield Institute, Massachusetts, and in Patapsco Institute, Maryland. She became a teacher first in Kinderhook Academy, and later in Stratford Academy, Con-

necticut. In 1856 she was married to John Bascom, at that time professor in Williams College. For years her husband was wholly deprived of the use of his eyes, and she had occasion, during a long period, to share his studies and render him daily assistance in reading and writing. The mother of five children, she cherished a lively interest in all that pertained to the discipline, amplitude and pleasure of the home. She has been an interested observer and eager advocate of those marvelous changes which have, in recent years, opened the doors of opportunity to woman in the social, economic and political world. She was a charter member of the Association for the Advancement of Woman and for many years was one of its board of officers. She was secretary of the Woman's Centennial Commission for the State of Wisconsin. She has been active in the Woman's Christian Temperance Union almost from its first organization.

BATEHAM, Mrs. Josephine Penfield Cushman, temperance reformer, born in Alden, NY, 1st November, 1829. She is descended from a godly New England ancestry. Her parents removed from New York State to Oberlin, OH, when Josephine was five years old. A few years later her widowed mother was married to Prof. Henry Cowles, author of "Cowles' Bible Commentaries," and became a member of the Ladies' Board of Managers of the college. Josephine, soon after graduation, was married to the Rev. Richard S. Cushman, of Attleboro, MA, and went on a foreign mission to St. Marc, Hayti. After eleven months of laborious service Mr. Cushman died, and unable to carry on the new mission single-handed, Mrs. Cushman reluctantly resigned the work and returned home, a widow at nineteen years of age. After teaching a short time in Oberlin College, she was married to M. B. Bateham, editor of the "Ohio Cultivator," and removed to Columbus, OH. There they resided fourteen years, spending part of their summers in travel in

the old world and the new, and jointly editing the "Cultivator," afterward the "Ohio Farmer." Foremost in church and reform work, and widely known by her writings, her home was ever a center of attraction. At Painesville, OH, for sixteen years from 1864, Mrs. Bateham devoted herself to her growing family, to writing, to missionary and temperance work, and was then bereft of her husband. At the opening of the temperance crusade in Ohio, in 1874, Mrs. Bateham became the leader of the Painesville crusade band, and later one of the leaders in the State Woman's Christian Temperance Union. In 1884 she was made national superintendent of the Sabbath observance department of that organization, and her eldest daughter, Minerva, was her secretary till her death, in 1885, after eighteen years of invalidism. Mrs. Bateham removed to Asheville, NC, in 1890, where she devotes her time to the work of the Woman's Christian Temperance Union. During 1890 she traveled sixteen-thousand miles, in nearly every State and Territory and through the Hawaiian Islands, and gave nearly three-hundred lectures. She has written a long line of valuable leaflets on Sabbath questions, of which she sends out more than a million pages every year.

BATEMAN, Isabel, actor, born near Cincinnati, OH, 28th December, 1854. Her family removed to England in 1863, and she first played a juvenile part in 1865 in her sister Kate's farewell benefit at Her Majesty's Theater. She began active theatrical work in 1869. She took leading parts with Henry Irving for six years. She has been very successful in many leading rôles.

BATEMAN, Kate, actor, born in Baltimore, MD, 7th October, 1842. She made her debut in Louisville, KY, at the age of five years. In 1850, as one of the Bateman Children, she appeared in the principal cities of Great Britain. She retired from the stage in 1856, but reappeared in 1860. In 1862 she made her first pronounced success as Julia in "The Hunchback," in the Winter Garden, New York. For several years she played leading parts in Great Britain as well as in the United States. In 1866 Miss Bateman became the wife of Dr. George Crowe, and took up her permanent residence in England. She has appeared in every city of importance in this country as well as in Great Britain.

BATES, Miss Charlotte Fiske, see ROGÉ, MRS. CHARLOTTE.

BATES, Mrs. Clara Doty, author, born in Ann Arbor, MI, in 1838. She was the second daughter of Samuel Rosecrans Doty and Hannah Lawrence, who were among the pioneers of Michigan. Mrs. Bates came of stalwart stock, mingled Dutch and English blood. Her great-grandfather, a Rosecrans, was ninety years old when he died, and the legend goes that at the time of his death "his hair was as black as a raven's wing." Another ancestor was with Washington at Valley Forge. On the mother's side are the Lawrences, and Hannah Lawrence, the great-grandmother, was famous for her gift of story-telling. Clara had a rhyming talent from her earliest days. She wrote verses when she could only print in big letters. Her first poem was published when she was nine years old. The most of her published work has been fugitive, although she has written several books, chiefly for children. Among these are "Æsop's Fables Versified," "Child Lore," "Classics of Babyland," "Heart's Content," and several minor books, all published in Boston. Her life up to her marriage was passed in Ann Arbor. The homestead, "Heart's Content," was well known for its treasures of books and pictures. The location of the State University in Ann Arbor gave better facilities for education than were offered in the usual western village. It was before the admission of women to equal opportunities with men, but it was possible to secure private instruction in advanced studies. This the little flock of Doty girls had in addition to private schools, while the son had the university. Clara Doty was married in 1869 to Morgan Bates, a newspaper man and the author of several plays. Her home was in Chicago, IL, where she was a member of the Fortnightly literary club, and was on the literary committee of the Woman's Branch of the World's Congress Auxiliary. All her manuscript and notes were destroyed by the burning of her father's house several years ago. Among them were a finished story, a half completed novel and some other work. Mrs. Bates was a woman of marked individuality. Died in Chicago, 14th October, 1895.

BATES, Miss Katharine Lee, author and educator, born in Falmouth, MA, 12th August, 1859. Her father was Rev. William Bates of the Congregational denomination; his father was the Rev. Joshua Bates of the same denomination, and also president of Middlebury College, Vermont. Her mother was Cornelia Lee, daughter of Samuel Lee, tinsmith, Northampton, MA. Her father died in 1859, within three weeks of her birth, leaving four children. The family remained in Falmouth until 1871, removing then to the neighborhood of Boston. Miss Bates was educated in the Falmouth primary and grammar schools; the Needham high school, graduating in 1874; the more advanced Newton high school, graduating in 1876; and Wellesley College, graduating in 1880, having been throughout the course president of her class. After graduation she taught mathematics, classics and English in the Natick high school, and then for four years mathematics and classics, gradually concentrating her work on Latin, in the leading preparatory school for Wellesley, Dana Hall. In 1885 she was called to the college as instructor in English literature, in 1888 was made associate professor, and in 1891 professor in charge. In 1890 she went abroad for rest, travel and study. In connection with educational work, she has edited Coleridge's "Ancient Mariner" (Boston, 1889), and a collection of "Ballads" (Boston, 1890), published by an educational firm in their series of English classics. Her general literary work has been always subordinate to the demands of a life closely busied with educational concerns. She has published prose and verse from her undergraduate days to the present time, but irregularly and often too hastily. In prose she wrote stories and sketches as an undergraduate for the Springfield "Republican" and a few other papers, and has since contributed to the "Chautauquan," "Independent," "Christian Union," "Congregationalist," "Youth's Companion," and other publications. She took the first prize, $700, offered by the Congregational Publishing Society for a young people's story, to be published in book form, with "Rose and Thorn" (Boston, 1889). This volume was followed by another juvenile story, "Hermit Island" (Boston, 1890). In verse she took a college prize for a Latin boat-song, another for an English poem, was class poet, and has since served as commencement poet. Outside of college she took a prize offered by the Congregational Publishing Society for the children's poem, "Sunshine," since

issued as an illustrated booklet (Boston, 1887). The same publishers have since issued her two similar booklets, "Santa Claus' Riddle" and "Goody Santa Claus." Her first book venture was a compilation known as the "Wedding Day Book" (Boston, 1882). In 1889 she won a prize of $30 for a quatrain contributed to the "Magazine of Poetry." She has published verses in the "Century," "Atlantic," "Independent," "New England Magazine," "Wide Awake" and many other publications, and has issued two small volumes for private sale in aid of one of the college funds which is under the control of the Wellesley alumnæ.

BATES, Mrs. Margaret Holmes, author, born in Fremont, OH, 6th October, 1844. Her maiden name was Ernsperger, and after five generations on American soil the name preserves its original spelling and pronunciation. Mrs. Bates' father was born and bred in Baltimore, MD. He went with his father's family some time after he had attained his majority and settled in northern Ohio. From Ohio he removed to Rochester, IN, in the fall of 1858. The mother's family, as purely German as the father's, were Pennsylvanians. As a family, they were scholarly and polished, running to professions, notably those of law and theology. In Mrs. Bates' childhood she showed great fondness for books, and, as a schoolgirl, the weekly or fortnightly "composition" was to her a pleasant pastime, a respite from the duller, more prosaic studies of mathematics and the rules of grammar. It was her delight to be allowed, when out of school, to put her fancies into form in writing, or to sit surrounded by her young sisters and baby brother and tell them stories as they came into her mind. In June, 1865, she was married to Charles Austin Bates, of Medina, NY, and since that time her home has been in Indianapolis, IN. Fascinated for several years after her marriage with the idea of becoming a model housekeeper, and conscientious to a painful degree in the discharge of her duties as a mother, she wrote nothing for publication, and but little, even at the solicitations of friends, for special occasions. This way of life, unnatural for her, proved unhealthful. Her poem, "Nineveh," is an epitome of her life, and when health seemed to have deserted her, she turned to pencil and tablet for pastime and wrote much for newspapers and periodicals. Her first novel, "Manitou" (1881), was written at the urgent request of her son. It embodies a legend connected with the beautiful little lake of that name in northern Indiana, in the vicinity of which Mrs. Bates lived for several years before her marriage. "The Chamber Over the Gate "(Indianapolis, 1886), has had a wide sale. Besides her gifts as a writer of fiction, she is a poet, some of her poems having attracted wide attention.

BATTEY, Mrs. Emily Verdery, journalist, born in Belair, near Augusta, GA, about the year 1828. She began her career as a journalist soon after the close of the Civil War, writing first for several Georgia newspapers, and traveling and corresponding for the "Ladies Home Gazette" of Atlanta, under the editorial guidance of her brother-in-law, Col. John S. Prather, an ex-confederate cavalry officer. Mrs. Battey went to New York in 1870, securing editorial positions at once on the "Tablet," the "Home Journal" and the "Telegram" and occasionally writing for the "Star," the "Democrat," the "Herald" and "Harper's Magazine." The "Sun," under the management of Hon. Amos J. Cummings and Dr. John B. Wood, frequently printed reports, special articles and editorials from Mrs. Battey's facile pen. In 1875 she became a salaried member of the staff of the "Sun," which position she held until 1890. While filling that position Mrs. Battey wrote for several syndicates, as well as special articles for newspapers in various parts of the country, signing various pen-names. She is not and never has been one of those workers who desire to acquire notoriety. Her aim has always been to do earnest work, and that work has always been excellent. The story of her career she tells in a lecture "Twenty Years on the Press." Her long experience on the New York press has made her well acquainted with leading women of the world, social, literary, political and religious. No woman knows better than she the history of the founding and progress of the various important women's clubs, guilds, temperance and religious societies and associations of the United States. The fruit of this wide knowledge has ripened for the delectation of those audiences that have heard her lecture, "The Woman's Century." She is a highly cultured and charming woman. Her home is now in

Georgia and Alabama, with her relatives of the Verdery family. Childless herself, she has devoted her earnest life to her family ties and the study and assistance of her own sex.

BAXTER, Mrs. Annie White, business woman, born in Pittsburgh, PA, 2nd March, 1864. She is of American parentage and of English and German extraction. She spent her early school-days in Newark, OH. Her parents removed to Carthage, MO, in 1877, where her education was fin-

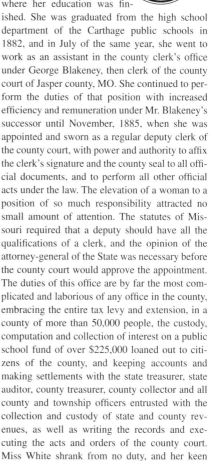

ished. She was graduated from the high school department of the Carthage public schools in 1882, and in July of the same year, she went to work as an assistant in the county clerk's office under George Blakeney, then clerk of the county court of Jasper county, MO. She continued to perform the duties of that position with increased efficiency and remuneration under Mr. Blakeney's successor until November, 1885, when she was appointed and sworn as a regular deputy clerk of the county court, with power and authority to affix the clerk's signature and the county seal to all official documents, and to perform all other official acts under the law. The elevation of a woman to a position of so much responsibility attracted no small amount of attention. The statutes of Missouri required that a deputy should have all the qualifications of a clerk, and the opinion of the attorney-general of the State was necessary before the county court would approve the appointment. The duties of this office are by far the most complicated and laborious of any office in the county, embracing the entire tax levy and extension, in a county of more than 50,000 people, the custody, computation and collection of interest on a public school fund of over $225,000 loaned out to citizens of the county, and keeping accounts and making settlements with the state treasurer, state auditor, county treasurer, county collector and all county and township officers entrusted with the collection and custody of state and county revenues, as well as writing the records and executing the acts and orders of the county court. Miss White shrank from no duty, and her keen perception, intuitive acumen, mathematical precision, untiring application, energy and directness, and her pleasing address and manners won for her the esteem and confidence of the entire population. She was found equal to every occasion and served so well that under the next incumbent of the clerkship she was again appointed and qualified as principal deputy. She was married to C.W. Baxter, of Carthage, MO, 14th January, 1888, and withdrew from official duty to attend to the more pleasant tastes of domestic life, but, the county clerk becoming partly disabled by paralysis, she was again induced to take charge of the office. In 1890, she was placed in nomination for county clerk by the regular Democratic county convention for county clerk. Jasper county had for years polled a large Republican majority, but, although her rival was regarded as a popular and competent man, Mrs. Baxter received a majority of 463 votes at the polls. She took charge of the office as clerk under a commission signed by Gov. D. R. Francis. She is the first woman in the United States elected by the people and qualified under the law to fill the office of clerk of a court of record. Mrs. Baxter retains all her womanly refinement and modesty, maintains a popular position in social life, and bears her honors and responsibilities with unconscious ease and natural grace.

BAXTER, Mrs. Marion Babcock, lecturer and author, born on a farm in Litchfield, Hillsdale county, MI, 12th April, 1850. Her father, Abel E. Babcock, was an Adventist minister in the times when it required courage to preach an unpopular doctrine. Her mother, Mary Babcock, was a gracious woman, to whose love and tender teaching Mrs. Baxter owes all that she is. Mrs. Baxter traces her lineage back to the Reformation in England. Her early childhood was spent in poverty and self-denial, and she was familiar with work, for which she has ever been thankful. In childhood she had few companions, for the Adventist doctrine was so unpopular and the persecution so pointed that even the children caught the spirit and were accustomed to tease her. Many a time she has climbed a tree to avoid their persecution. In her girlhood she developed a very fine voice and was much in demand for concert singing, but she lost her voice suddenly, and turned to the lecture platform. Her first lecture was given in Jonesville, MI, where she had lived since she was five years old. Her subject was "The Follies of Fashion," quite appropriate for one whose life had been spent in comparative poverty. On that occasion the opera house was packed, a band furnished music, and all the world of Jonesville was there. Her first effort was a success in every way, and she eventually became widely known as a lecturer. She was married at the age of twenty-two years to C. E. K. Baxter, a son of Levi Baxter, the head of one of the oldest and most respected families in the state. She is at present the state president of the White Rose League. She has been a member of the Woman's Christian Temperance Union since its organization and has for years been a member of the Congregational church.

BAYLOR, Miss Frances Courtenay, author, born in Fayetteville, AR, 20th January, 1848. She is descended from an old Virginian family of English strain. Her childhood was spent in San Antonio and New Orleans, where her father, an army officer, was stationed. She was educated principally by her mother and her aunt, in her own home. After the Civil War was ended, she went to Europe and spent the years 1865 to 1867 in travel and residence in England and on the Continent. She spent 1873–74 in Europe, and during her sojourn there she gathered the materials for her literary work. Since 1876 she has lived in an old home near Winchester, VA. Her literary career began with articles in various newspapers, and she contributed to "Lippincott's Magazine," the "Atlantic Monthly" and the "Princeton Review." Among her earlier productions was a play, "Petruchio Tamed." She won a prominent position by her novel, "On Both Sides" (Philadelphia, 1885), in which she contrasts the American and English characters, manners and social creeds. Her second book was "Juan and Juanita" (Boston, 1886). Her third was "Behind the Blue Ridge" (Philadelphia, 1887). All these volumes were highly successful, passing through many editions in a short time. The first, "On Both Sides," was republished in Edinburgh. Miss Baylor deservedly ranks high as an author of remarkable powers of observation, of judgment, of humorous comment, and of philosophic generalization.

BEACH, Mrs. H. H. A., composer, born in Henniker, NH, 5th September, 1867. Her parents were Charles Abbott and Clara Imogene Cheney. Mrs. Cheney, born Marcy, was well known as an excellent musician, and it is due to her careful supervision and fostering care that Mrs. Beach's early musical development was so systematic and judicious. The earliest evidences of her musical powers were manifested before she was a year old, and as she was so situated as to hear much good music, she soon acquired the habit of catching the songs that were sung to her. When three years old, to play the piano was her chief delight, and soon she could play at sight any music that her hands could grasp. At the age of four years she played many tunes by ear. She improvised much and composed several little pieces. Among her earliest musical recollections is that of associating color with sound, the key of C suggesting white, A flat, blue, and so on. The exact pitch of sounds, single or in combination, produced by voice, violin, piano, bells, whistles or birds' songs, has always been perfectly clear to her, making it possible for her to name the notes at once. When she was six years old, her mother began a course of systematic instruction, which continued for two years. At the age of seven she played in three concerts. She continued to compose little pieces. Among these were an air with variations and a setting of the "Rainy Day" of Longfellow, since published. Regular instruction in harmony was begun at the age of fourteen. For ten years, with various interruptions, Mrs. Beach received instruction in piano playing from prominent teachers in Boston. She made her first appearance before a Boston audience as Miss Amy Marcy Cheney on 24th October, 1883, at sixteen years of age, playing the G minor concerto of Moscheles with grand orchestra. That performance was succeeded by various concerts and recitals in Boston and other places, in association with distinguished artists. In December, 1885, she was married to Dr. H. H. A. Beach, and since then has frequently contributed her services for the benefit of the charitable and educational institutions of Boston, in recitals and performances with orchestra. Her talent in composition has shown itself in the following list of published works: A grand mass in E flat, a graduale for tenor voice, an anthem for chorus and organ, three short anthems for quartet with organ accompaniment, a four-part song for female voices, three vocal duets with pianoforte accompaniment, nineteen songs for single voice with a pianoforte accompaniment, a cadenza to Beethoven's C minor concerto, and a valse caprice for piano. She has in manuscript other compositions, a ballad, several short pieces for the piano or piano and violin, and songs. The mass was performed on 7th February, 1892, by the Handel and Haydn Society of Boston, with the Symphony Orchestra and a quartet of soloists assisting.

BEASLEY, Mrs. Marie Wilson, elocutionist and dramatic reader, born in Silver Creek, a suburb of Philadelphia, PA, about 1862. When she was seven years old, her father removed to the West and settled on a farm near Grand Rapids, MI. Marie lived on the farm until she was fourteen years old, when her father died, leaving the family to make their own way. Bearing good credentials from the citizens of Paris, Kent county, Marie removed to Grand Rapids. She became a member of the Baptist Church at the age of fourteen years, but is liberal in sentiment toward all creeds that teach Christ and his works. In her youth, while striving to secure an education, she made her needle her support, earning by hard work enough money to enable her to attend Hillsdale College, Hillsdale, MI, for a year. She afterward studied under Professor Walter C. Lyman, of Chicago, and since 1883, when she made her début as an elocutionist and reader, and also as an instructor in the art of elocution, she has taught many who are already prominent in that field, and her readings have brought her a reputation in many States. She was married in January, 1889, to J. H. Beasley, of Grand Rapids, where they now reside. They spent one year in San Francisco and other points in California. Besides her work as an elocutionist and instructor, she has been a successful lecturer, taking an active interest in the relation of women to law and society. The theme of one of her most successful efforts on the lecture platform is "Woman's Rights, or the XVIth Amendment to the Constitution of the United States of America." She is a woman of amiable disposition, much force and decided powers of intellect.

BEAUCHAMP, Miss Mary Elizabeth, educator and author, born in Burleigh, England, 14th June, 1825. The family removed to this country in 1829, establishing themselves in Coldenham, Orange county, NY. In 1832 they removed to Skaneateles, NY, where Mr. Beauchamp went into the book business, to which seven years later he united a printing office and the publication of a weekly newspaper, which still maintains a healthy existence. In 1834 he established a thoroughly good circulating library, of nearly a thousand volumes, which was very successful for many years. His daughter had free range of its carefully selected treasures and early acquired an unusual familiarity with the best writers of the language. The little girl wrote rhymes when she was ten years old, acrostics for her schoolmates and wildly romantic ballads. Before she entered her "teens" she had become a regular contributor to a juvenile magazine, for which, in her fourteenth year, she furnished a serial running through half a volume. From that time she wrote under various pen-names for several papers and had achieved the honor of an illustrated tale in "Peterson's Magazine" before she was twenty. Then her literary career was checked by ill-health, and for ten years her pen was laid aside almost entirely. What she published during that time appeared in religious papers under the pen-name "Filia Ecclesiæ," and some of these pieces found their way into cotemporary collections of sacred poetry. In 1853, accompanied by a younger brother, she visited England, where she remained nearly two years. At the desire of her uncle, a vicar in Wells, she prepared a "Handbook of Wells Cathedral," which was published in different styles with illustrations. After returning home she wrote a series of papers entitled "The Emigrant's Quest" which attracted for a year attention and were republished in a modest little volume some years later. Her mother died in 1859, and the death of her father in 1867 broke up her home in Skaneateles, and in the ensuing year she took the position of teacher in the orphan ward of the Church Charity Foundation, in Buffalo, NY, remaining there twelve years. In 1879 she went to Europe for a year accompanied by a lady who had been happily associated with her in church work. Soon after returning to this country Miss Beauchamp learned that the Mission of the Protestant Episcopal Church to the Onondaga Indians was in temporary need of a teacher. She offered her services and was delighted with the work. She next purchased a residence in Skaneateles, where she conducted a school for the children of summer residents, organized a literary society for young ladies, and had adult pupils in French and drawing. She took her full share in parochial and missionary work and wrote for religious papers. In March, 1890, she was prostrated for some months by cerebral hemorrhage, and has since resided with a married sister in Skaneateles.

BEAUMONT, Mrs. Betty Bentley, author and merchant, born in Lancastershire, England, 9th August, 1828. She was the only child of Joseph Bentley, the great educational reformer of England. Mr. Bentley organized and conducted a society for "the promotion of the education of the people," and wrote and published thirty-three books to improve the methods of education, but he presents another example of the neglect, by public benefactors, of those bound to them by the closest ties of nature. He allowed his child to acquire only the elements of an education, and took her from school in her tenth year and employed her in his business to copy his manuscripts, correct proof and attend lectures. The independent spirit of the little girl was roused by a strange act on the part of her father. He showed her a summing up of the expenses she had been to him in the ten years of her life. To a child it seemed a large amount, and having set her young brain to devise some plan by which she might support herself so as to be of no further expense to her father, she surreptitiously learned the milliners' trade. She loved her books, and her propensity for learning was exceptional, but her opportunity for study was extremely limited. At a very early age she was married to Edward Beaumont, and came to America seven years after her marriage. They lived in Philadelphia for five years and, on account of Mr. Beaumont's feeble health, removed to the South, going to Woodville, Miss. The coming on of the Civil War and the state of feeling in a southern town toward suspected abolitionists are most interestingly described in Mrs. Beaumont's "Twelve Years of My Life." (Philadelphia, 1887). The failing health of her husband and the needs of a family of seven children called forth her inherent energy, and she promptly began what she felt herself qualified to carry on to success, and became one of the leading merchants of the town. Her varied experiences during a period of historical interest are given in "A Business Woman's Journal" (Philadelphia, 1888). That book graphically explains the financial state of the cotton-growing region of the South during the years immediately succeeding the Civil War, the confusion consequent upon the transition from the credit system to a cash basis, and the condition of the suddenly freed blacks. Mrs. Beaumont's books are valuable because they have photographed a period that quickly passed. Her style is simple and unpretending. She is one of the hard-working business women of to-day. She has shown independence of spirit, self-sacrificing courage and remarkable tenacity of purpose. She has a kind and sympathizing heart, and a nature susceptible to every gentle and elevating influence.

BECK, Miss Leonora, educator, born near Augusta, GA, in 1862. At an early age she showed an unusual aptitude for linguistic study, speaking several modern languages when nine years old. She was well grounded in Latin and Greek when fifteen years old. Oxford College, AL, having thrown open its doors to young women, and being the only college for men in the South which received them, Miss Beck entered and received a careful and thorough training for her chosen profession. At the age of sixteen years she was graduated with A.M. distinction and at once accepted the position of young lady principal in the Bowden, Georgia, College, which she held for two-and-one-half years. During her connection with that institution Miss Beck instructed in meta-

physics, Latin and Greek about one-hundred students, ranging from the ages of fifteen to thirty years. Her success as an educator becoming more generally known, she was urged to accept many positions of trust and honor, but declined them. The Jackson Institute was her next field of labor, and that now famous school owes its popularity and success in a great measure to the energy of thought and action which characterized her work while connected with it. In 1889 Miss Beck removed to Atlanta to engage in founding a first-class school for girls. That college, first known as the Capital Female College, is now known as the Leonora Beck College. The success of the school has been remarkable. In everything Miss Beck does there is an earnest purpose. She is an occasional contributor to the periodical press. A series of essays on Robert Browning is, perhaps, her most enduring contribution to literature.

BECKWITH, Mrs. Emma, woman suffragist, born in Cincinnati, OH, 4th December, 1849. Her maiden name was Knight. She graduated at the age of seventeen years from the high school in Toledo, OH, whither her parents went when she was four years old. At the age of nineteen years she was married to Edwin Beckwith, of Mentor, OH. After residing in Pleasantville, IA, a number of years, they removed to Brooklyn, NY. Her sympathies with women have always been on the alert. Upon locating in the East she began to put to practical use her knowledge of bookkeeping, after obtaining the permission of the owner of a building in Nassau street, New York, by promising to be good and not demoralize the men. She began work in April, 1879. She was the pioneer woman bookkeeper in that part of the city, and established a reputation for modesty and uprightness that has helped many another to a like position. Her business education of five years' duration gave her an insight into many matters not general among women. Since leaving business life she has urged young women to become self-supporting. Disgusted with the vast amount of talk and so little practical work among the advocates of woman suffrage, she felt that Mrs. Belva A. Lockwood had struck the key-note when she became a candidate for the presidency of the United States. Her ambition was aroused to the point of emulation; hence her candidacy for the mayoralty of Brooklyn. The campaign of ten days' duration, with but two public meetings, resulted in her receiving fifty votes regularly counted, and many more thrown out among the scattering, before the New York "Tribune" made a demand for her vote. Mrs. Beckwith has compiled many incidents relating to that novel campaign in a lecture. She has entered the lecture field and is an able and entertaining speaker, enlivening her earnestness with bright, witty sayings.

BEDFORD, Mrs. Lou Singletary, author, born in Feliciana, Graves county, KY, 7th April, 1837. Her father was a teacher, and his little daughter was placed in his school at six years of age. She had no special love for books, except for reading, spelling and grammar, but her ambition kept her at the head of most of her classes. She completed her course of study in Clinton Seminary. After leaving school she taught for a year or two. In 1857 she became the wife of John Joseph Bedford, a friend and associate of her childhood. There were six children born to them, four of whom are living. Mrs. Bedford's literary career has in a great measure become identified with Texas, her adopted home. From her sixteenth year she continued to write until her marriage, after which her pen was silent for nearly fifteen years. She has published two volumes of poetry, "A Vision, and Other Poems" (Cincinnati and London, 1881), and "Gathered Leaves" (Dallas, 1889). Mrs. Bedford has for years contributed to various periodicals. Her present home is in El Paso, Texas, where she is social and literary editor of the El Paso "Sunday Morning Tribune."

BEECHER, Miss Catherine Esther, author and educator, born in East Hampton, Long Island, NY, 6th September, 1800, died in Elmira, NY, 12th May, 1878. Catherine was the oldest child of Lyman Beecher and Roxana Foote Beecher, and the first nine years of her life were spent in the place of her nativity, where she enjoyed the teaching of a loving mother and a devoted aunt, the latter of whom was a woman of great beauty, elegance and refinement, and to whose early instructions Miss Beecher often recurred as having a strong and lasting influence upon her life. In her ninth year Catherine removed with her parents to Litchfield, CT. There, in the female seminary, under the care of Miss Sarah Pearse, Miss Beecher began her career as a school-girl. Her poetical effusions, mostly in a humorous vein, were handed about among her school-mates and friends, to be admired by all. As the oldest of the family, her mother's death, when she was sixteen, brought upon her the cares and responsibilities of a large family. Her father married again, and the parsonage became the center of a cultivated circle of society, where music, painting and poetry combined to lend a charm to existence. Parties were formed for reading, and it was that fact which led Miss Beecher again to take up her pen, in order to lend variety to the meetings. Miss Beecher was a frequent contributor to the "Christian Spectator," a monthly magazine of literature and theology, under the initials "C. D. D." Those poems attracted the attention of a young professor of mathematics in Yale College, Alexander M. Fisher, who in due time became her betrothed husband. He went to Europe and never returned, having perished in a storm which struck the vessel off the coast of Ireland. For a time Miss Beecher could see no light through the clouds which overshadowed her. She was sent to Yale, in the hope that the companionship of Prof. Fisher's relatives might have a beneficial effect upon the stricken mind. There she was induced to begin the study of mathematics under the guidance of Willard Fisher, a brother of her late lover. Going back to Litchfield, she united with her father's church, and resolved to let insoluble problems alone and to follow Christ. Shortly after that, Miss Beecher, in conjunction with her sister, opened a select school in Hartford, CT. In four years' time there was not room for the scholars who applied for admittance. She had always enjoyed the friendship of the leading women of Hartford, and when she began to agitate the subject of a female seminary in that town, it was through their influence that the prominent men of Hartford subscribed the money to purchase the land and erect the buildings of the Hartford Female Seminary. With Miss Beecher as principal and a band of eight teachers of her selection, the school grew rapidly in influence and popularity. Her "Suggestions on Education" was widely read and drew attention to the Hartford Seminary from all parts of the United States. In her school of between one and two hundred pupils, she planned the course of study, guided the teachers, overlooked the boarding-houses and corresponded with parents and guardians. She yet found time to prepare an arithmetic, which was printed and used as a text-book in her school and those emanating from it. About that time the teacher in mental philosophy left the institution, and Miss Beecher not only took charge of that department, but wrote a textbook for it of some four or five hundred pages. After seven years of incessant activity her health gave out, and she was obliged to relinquish the school into other hands. Shortly after that the family removed to Cincinnati, OH, and, in connection with a younger sister, Miss Beecher commenced a school in that city, in which the teaching was all done by instructors of her own training. Her later years she devoted to authorship. "Domestic Economy" (1845) was a text-book for schools. Among the works that followed were "Duty of American Women to Their Country" (1845), "Domestic Receipt Book" (1846), "Letters to the People" (1855), "Physiology and Calisthenics" (1856), "Common Sense Applied to Religion" (1857), "The Religious Training of Children" (1864), "The Housekeeper and Healthkeeper" (1873). Her activity of mind and her zeal in education continued to the last.

BEHAN, Miss Bessie, social leader, born in New Orleans, LA, 5th March, 1872. She is a daughter of Gen. W. J. Behan. She was educated at home by skilled governesses, and had all the advantages of much travel. She made her debut in society in New Orleans in 1891, at once taking rank as a belle and winning general popularity. The most coveted of all social honors in New Orleans is to be chosen queen in the Mardi Gras Carnival. She was not yet out of her teens when she was chosen Carnival Queen, the youngest woman yet selected for coronation in that characteristic festival.

BELCHER, Mrs. Cynthia Holmes, journalist, born in Lunenburgh, VT, 1st December, 1827. She is a daughter of the Hon. George E. and Mary Moore Holmes. Her father served as a member of the State Senate and as judge in Essex county. Miss Holmes was educated in the academy in St. Johnsbury, VT. Her father removed his family of seven daughters from St. Johnsbury to Port Byron, IL, when she was eighteen years old. In her twentieth year she was married to Nathaniel Belcher, a descendant of prominent New England people and one of the pioneers in the settlement of Illinois. He held various offices of trust and was a member of the Whig party that nominated General Winfield Scott for the presidency, and was a prolific political writer. Mr. and Mrs. Belcher traveled extensively. In 1881 they visited Colorado, and in 1882 went to California, where they passed a pleasant year. Their tour included all parts of the Union. On one of their visits to Washington, DC, they were received by President Franklin Pierce, and on a later occasion visited President Grant in the White House. After the death of her husband and two children Mrs. Belcher returned to New England and settled in Boston, that she might indulge and develope her literary, artistic and musical talents. She studied singing in the New England Conservatory of Music and gradually became known also as a contributor to leading newspapers. In 1889 she visited Europe and contributed letters on her travels through the different countries, also describing the Paris Exposition. She is a member of the New England Woman's Press Association. Besides her literary work, she has always been identified with all works of reform, and with church and temperance work, the woman suffrage movement in particular receiving much thought and labor from her. All her thought has been in the line of elevating the individual and the community.

BELL, Mrs. Caroline Horton, philanthropist, born in Windham, Green county, NY, 28th December, 1840. Her father, Rev. Goodrich Horton, was a minister of the Methodist Episcopal Church, a descendant of the Goodriches, one of those earnest, pious, old colonial families. Her mother, whose maiden name was Lydia Fairchild, was a granddaughter of John Fairchild, an officer in the war of the Revolution, and also of Joseph Woodworth, a soldier in the same war. She

Nannie Craddock.
From Photo by Morrison, Chicago.

Lida Dexter.
From Photo by Morrison, Chicago.

received a liberal education in a seminary in Springfield, MA. Miss Horton was married 11th October, 1866, to Samuel R. Bell, and they settled in Milwaukee, WI, where they have since resided. Mr. Bell was a soldier of the Rebellion, enlisting in the 28th Wisconsin Regiment and winning an honorable record. Soon after the formation of the department of the Wisconsin Woman's Relief Corps Auxiliary of the Grand Army of the Republic, Mrs. Bell became prominently connected with the order and has filled a number of positions in that organization. The work she has been enabled to accomplish in that line is important. She was a charter member of E. B. Wolcott Corps, served two years as its chaplain, and nearly two as its president, at which time she was also elected department president. Aside from the work of the Woman's Relief Corps, she has been prominently connected with various other charities of Milwaukee. She was a member of the Benevolent Society upon its organization, and afterward of the Associated Charities. She was one of the founders of the first kindergarten established in that city, and for a long time was one of the directors of the Home of the Friendless, and has been a director of the Home of the Aged since its organization. She was president of the aid society of Calvary Presbyterian Church for several years, during which time she assisted in raising money for the Young Men's Christian Association building, and assisted in establishing a mission kindergarten on the west side of Milwaukee.

BELL, Miss Orelia Key, poet, born in Atlanta, GA, 8th April, 1864. Her birthplace was the Bell mansion, a stately Southern home in the heart of the city. The house has become historic, as it was, soon after Orelia's birth, the headquarters of General Sherman's engineering corps, and the room in which she was born and spent the first three months of her life was that used by General Sherman as a stable for his favorite colt. Miss Bell is of gentle birth on both sides of her house, and is very thoroughly educated. A poem by her father, "God is Love," has been the key-note to some of her highest and sweetest songs. She suffered loss of home and property but met her reverses with a brave front and a song in her heart, and her spirit, strong in courage and purity, has voiced itself in countless melodies that have won for her both fame and money. She writes always with strength and grace. Power and melody are wedded in her poems. Her warmest recognition from the press has come from Richard Watson Gilder of the "Century," Page M. Baker, of the New Orleans "Times-Democrat," Charles A. Dana, of the New York Sun." Mrs. Frank Leslie, Henry W. Grady, and Thaddeus E. Horton, and her own home papers the "Constitution" and the "Journal." Her poem "Maid and Matron" has been used by Rhea as a select recitation. To the instructions of her friend, Mrs. Livingston Mimms, leader of the Christian Science movement South, and founder of the first Church of Christ (Scientist) in Georgia, Miss Bell owes the inspiration of her most enduring work, the International Series of Christian Science Hymns, to the writing of which she gave much time.

BELLAMY, Mrs. Emily Whitfield Croom, novelist, born in Quincy, FL, 17th April, 1839. She was educated in Springer Institute, New York City. She taught in a female seminary in Eutaw, Ala., for several years. Mrs. Bellamy has written under the pen-name "Kampa Thorpe" "Four Oaks" (New York, 1867), and "Little Joanna" (New York, 1876). Besides her novels she has written many short prose articles and poems for the periodical press. Mrs. Bellamy now resides in Mobile, AL.

BENEDICT, Miss Emma Lee, author and educator, born in Clifton Park, Saratoga county, NY, 16th November, 1857. The daughter of a quiet farmer, she early gained from the fields and woods a love for nature as well as the foundations of robust health and a good physique. Always fond of books, at the age of twelve years she had read nearly everything in her father's small but well-selected library. At school she was able to keep pace with pupils much older than herself, besides finding time for extra studies. Her first introduction to science was through an old school-book of her mother's, entitled "Familiar

Science," and another on natural philosophy, which she carried to school and begged her teacher to hear her recite from. At seventeen she began to teach, and the following year entered the State Normal College at Albany, from which she was graduated in 1879. After a few more years of successful teaching, she began to write for educational papers and was soon called to a position on the editorial staff of the New York "School Journal," where she remained for more than three years. A desire for more extended opportunities for study and a broader scope for literary work led her to resign that position and launch on the sea of miscellaneous literature. A very successful book by her, "Stories of Persons and Places in Europe" (New York, 1887), was published in the following year, besides stories, poems and miscellaneous articles which appeared in various standard publications. Miss Benedict was a member of the first class in pedagogy that entered the now thoroughly established pedagogical course in the University of the City of New York. Through contributions to the daily papers and interviews with leading educational people she was an active factor in bringing about the general educational awakening in New York City, in 1888, which resulted in the formation of a new society for the advancement of education. Just at that time she was sent for by Mrs. Mary H. Hunt, national and international superintendent of the department of scientific temperance instruction of the Woman's Christian Temperance Union, to go to Washington and assist in the revision of temperance physiologies, which had then been submitted to Mrs. Hunt for that purpose by several of the leading publishers of temperance text-books. In Washington Miss Benedict spent a number of months in the United States Medical Library, occupied in investigating and compiling the testimony of leading medical writers concerning the nature and effects of alcohol upon the human body. The researches there begun have since been carried on in Boston and New York libraries and by correspondence with leading medical and chemical authorities. There is probably no other person more familiar than she with the whole subject of the nature and effects of alcohol upon the human system. At present Miss Benedict is with Mrs. Mary H. Hunt, in the home of the latter in Hyde Park, MA, assisting in laying out courses of study for institute instructors and preparing manuals for the use of teachers on the subject of physiology and hygiene and the effects of narcotics. Miss Benedict is a pleasant, logical and forcible speaker and writer in her special line of educational and scientific topics, and is in frequent demand as an instructor at teachers' institutes.

BENHAM, Mrs. Ida Whipple, peace advocate, born in a farmhouse in Ledyard, CT, 8th January, 1849. She is a daughter of Timothy and Lucy Ann Geer Whipple, and comes from a Quaker family. At an early age she began to write verses. At the age of thirteen years she taught a country school. She was married 14th April, 1869, to Elijah B. Benham, of Groton, CT. She was early made familiar with the reforms advocated by the Quakers, such as temperance, anti-slavery, and the abolition of war. She has lectured on peace and temperance. She is a director of the American Peace Society, and à member of the executive committee of the Universal Peace Union. She takes a conspicuous part in the large peace conventions held annually in Mystic, CT, and she holds a monthly peace meeting in her own home in Mystic. She has contributed poems to the New York "Independent," the Chicago "Advance," the "Youth's Companion," "St. Nicholas" and other prominent periodicals.

BENJAMIN, Mrs. Anna Smeed, temperance worker, born near Lockport, Niagara county, NY, 28th November, 1834. Her father and mother were the oldest children of their respective families, both bereft of their fathers at an early age, and both from circumstances, as well as by inheritance, industrious, energetic and self-reliant in a remarkable degree. A clear sense of right with an almost morbid conscientiousness characterized both. All those traits are markedly developed in their daughter, who, too, was the oldest child. She was educated in the Lockport union school, in Genesee Wesleyan Seminary, and in Genesee College, now Syracuse University. In each of those institutions she ranked among the first in her classes. In 1855 she was married to G. W. Benjamin, a thorough-going business man, who has constantly aided her work for God and home and native land. One child, a son, was born to them. In due time Mrs. Benjamin was drawn into the work of the Woman's Foreign Missionary Society. From that she naturally passed into the Woman's Christian Temperance Union, founded in 1874 as the systematized form of the great Ohio crusade. In that society her abilities at once marked her as a leader. Suffering from a morbid shyness which, as a school-girl, made the simple reading of an essay a most trying ordeal, she sought nothing more eagerly than the privilege of working in obscurity, but circumstances pushed her to the platform, where her own natural abilities have won for her a foremost place. At the convention held in Grand Rapids, MI, in 1874, she was made chairman of a committee to draft a constitution and by-laws for the newly organized Woman's Christian Temperance Union of the Fifth Congressional District. She is now the superintendent of the national department of parliamentary usage, and the drills which she conducts in the white-ribboners' "School of Methods" and elsewhere are attended by persons of both sexes. At the Chautauquas, where she has had charge, these drills, attended by hundreds, have met an ever increasing need and have been among the most popular meetings held. Mrs. Benjamin has for years been a victim to neuralgia, but her remarkable will power has carried her on until she has become one of the leaders in State and national work. She is a logical, convincing, enthusiastic speaker with a deep, powerful voice and urgent manner. She has been elected president of the Woman's Christian Temperance Union for the fifth district of Michigan for thirteen consecutive years, and has built up white-ribbon interests in the Bay View Assembly, until that foremost summer camp has become a model for all others in that particular. Mrs. Benjamin is a notably excellent presiding officer and a skilled parliamentarian.

BENNETT, Mrs. Adelaide George, poet, born in Warner, NH, 8th November, 1848. Her childhood was passed under the shadow of the famed Kearsarge Mountain. She is the daughter of Gilman C. and Nancy B. George and a sister of H. Maria George, who is also well-known in literary circles. She was educated in Contoocook Academy and under private tutors. She taught several years in the public schools of Manchester, NH. In October, 1887, Miss George was married to Charles H. Bennett, of Pipestone City, Minn. Their marriage was quite a romantic one and was noticed by many papers of the country. The fascinating glamour of legend, woven into poetry by the master hand of Longfellow in his "Song of Hiawatha," led her to covet a piece of the 'blood-red mystic stone" for her cabinet of geological curiosities, and she wrote to the postmaster of Pipestone City, then a paper town surveyed within the precincts of the sacred quarry, for a specimen of the stone. The specimen was forwarded by Mr. Bennett, accompanied by a set of views of the quarry and surrounding region, and a correspondence and acquaintance followed, which resulted in their marriage. On their bridal tour, while calling upon Mr. Longfellow, they informed him that he had unwittingly been a match-maker. As they went down the steps of the old colonial mansion, the venerable figure of the immortal poet was framed in the wide doorway as he beamed a benediction upon them and wished them much joy at their "hanging of the crane." Mrs. Bennett wrote no poems for the press until after her marriage. When she did write for publication, it was at the solicitation of her husband. She is a botanist of distinction. During the season of 1883 she made a collection of the flora of the Pipestone region for Prof. Winchell's report on the botanical resources of Minnesota. That collection was, at the request of Prof. Winchell, exhibited in the New Orleans World's Exposition in 1884. She is an active member of the Woman's Relief Corps, and during 1888–89 she held the office of National Inspector of Minnesota. She has quite a reputation throughout the West for the writing and rendition of poems on public occasions. Possessing rare qualifications for literary work, she has principally confined herself to poetry. She has an elegant prose style, as is shown in her correspondence and a number of fugitive newspaper and magazine articles.

BENNETT, Mrs. Alice, doctor of medicine, born in Wrentham, MA, 31st January, 1851. She was the youngest of six children born to Francis I. and Lydia Hayden Bennett. She was educated in Day's Academy, in her native town, and taught in the district schools there from her seventeenth to her twenty-first year. During that period she prepared herself for the step which, at that place and time, was a sort of social outlawry, and at the age of twenty-one she entered the Woman's Medical College of Pennsylvania, from which she was graduated in March, 1876. One of the intervening years was spent as interne in the New England Hospital, Boston, under Dr. Susan Dimock. After her graduation Dr. Bennett went into dispensary work, living in the slums of Philadelphia for seven months. In October, 1876, she became demonstrator of anatomy in the Woman's Medical College of Pennsylvania and during four years devoted herself to the study and teaching of anatomy, in connection with private practice. At the same time she was pursuing a course of scientific study in the University of Pennsylvania, and received the degree of PhD from that institution in June, 1880. Her graduating thesis upon the anatomy of the fore-limb of the marmoset received honorable mention. In the same month she was elected to the important position she still occupies as superintendent of the department for women of the State Hospital for the Insane, in Norristown, PA. The trustees of that hospital, then just completed and about to be opened, did a thing without precedent in placing a woman physician in absolute and independent charge of their women insane, and dire predictions were made of the results of that revolutionary experiment. At the end of twelve years that hospital is the acknowledged head of the institutions of its kind in the State, if not in the country, and from its successful work the movement, now everywhere felt, to place all insane women under the care of physicians of their own sex, is constantly gaining impetus. Since Dr. Bennett entered upon her work, with one patient and one nurse, 12th July,

1880, more than 2,825 insane women have been received and cared for, new buildings have been added, and the scope of her work has been enlarged in all directions. In 1892 there were 950 patients and a force of 95 nurses under her direction, subject only to the trustees of the hospital. Dr. Bennett is a member of the American Medical Association, of the Pennsylvania State Medical Society, of the Montgomery County Medical Society, of which she was made president in 1890, of the Philadelphia Neurological Society, of the Philadelphia Medical Jurisprudence Society, and of the American Academy of Political and Social Science. She has twice received the appointment to deliver the annual address on mental diseases before the State Medical Society, and she was one of the original corporators of the Spring Garden Unitarian Church of Philadelphia, established by Charles G. Ames. She has recently been appointed by Governor Pattison, of Pennsylvania, one of the board of five commissioners to erect a new hospital for the chronic insane of the State.

BENNETT, Mrs. Ella May, Universalist minister, born in Stony Brook, NY, 21st April, 1855. She was the twelfth child of a family of fourteen, of whom all save two grew to manhood and womanhood. Her father's name was Daniel Shaloe Hawkins, and her mother's maiden name was Harriet Atwood Terry. Two of her brothers have been very prominent in political life. When a very small child, Mrs. Bennett thought deeply upon religious matters. She would often ask her mother to go and pray, especially when her mother seemed troubled in any way. From the very first God seemed to her a friend and comforter. When the doctrines of the church which she had always attended were explained to her, she rejected them. When about thirteen years of age, she visited a cousin in northern Pennsylvania, and for the first time listened to a sermon by a Universalist minister. She recognized early ideas of God and heaven. On her return home she was told the Bible gave no authority for such a doctrine. She accepted that statement, gave up all interest in religious matters, and would not open a Bible, and tried to become an atheist. For years she groped in a mental darkness that at times threatened her reason. When about thirty years of age, Mrs. Bennett's mother, a devout woman, who had long been deeply concerned about her daughter's state of mind, presented her a Bible, begging her for her sake to read it. She gave the book with an earnest prayer that the true light from its pages might shine upon her mind. Mrs. Bennett reluctantly promised. She had only read a few pages when, to her surprise, she found authority for the Universalist faith. The Bible became her constant companion, and for months she read nothing else. Mrs. Bennett became anxious for others to know the faith which had so brightened her own life and readily consented, at the request of Edward Oaks, to read sermons afternoons in Union Hall in Stony Brook. The sermon reading gradually changed to original essays, and finally Mrs. Bennett found herself conducting regular and popular sermons. Rev. L. B. Fisher, of Bridgeport, CT, became interested in her work. She united with his church in May, 1889. Her pastor presented her a library of books and assisted in procuring her a license to preach. On 25th September, 1890, she was ordained in Stony Brook. Mrs. Bennett entered the ministry with the determination never to accept a good position and stated salary, but to labor where the faith was new and for the free-will offering of the people, and, although tempted by large salaries, she has never wavered in that determination. Mrs. Bennett published verses at the age of eleven years, and she has through life given a portion of her time to literary work. In 1875 she was married to William Bennett, and they have three children. She divides her time between her home duties and her ministerial labor, doing full justice to both.

BENTON, Mrs. Louisa Dow, linguist, born in Portland, ME, 23rd March, 1832. She is the daughter of Neal Dow and Cornelia Durant Maynard. She was educated in the best schools of her native city, the last and chief of which was the Free Street Seminary for young ladies, Master Hezekiah Packard, teacher. She had, besides these, teachers in French. On 12th December, 1860, she was married to Jacob Benton, of Lancaster, NH. She passed four seasons in Washington, DC, while Mr. Benton was member of Congress. She was physically as well as intellectually strong and active. In the fall of 1887 she contracted rheumatism, of which she thought little at first, but it soon assumed a serious form, when most energetic measures were adopted to throw it off, but all in vain. She went several times to mineral springs in Canada, and to Hot Springs in Arkansas, but derived no benefit from any of them. At last she could not walk nor even stand, and was confined to her chair, where she passed the time away with hooks, pen, drawing and painting. But her hands and arms were so greatly and increasingly affected by the disease that drawing and painting were soon given up, and she devoted herself to the acquisition of languages, a study which was always especially attractive to her. She learned to read freely Italian, Spanish, German, Greek and Russian, all with no teacher except for Greek. After that she took up the Volapük and mastered it easily. She is so well known as a Volapük scholar that correspondence has come to her, from several prominent linguists in Europe, and several European Volapük associations have elected her corresponding member. During her pains and aches from the disease, she has always been cheerful, never discouraged.

BERG, Miss Lillie, musician and musical educator, was born in New York City. Her father was a German of noble birth, and her mother was a New England woman with a proud English ancestry. Miss Berg passed her childhood in Stuttgart, Germany, where she was thoroughly trained in piano, organ and harmony by professors Lebert, Faisst and Stark. She was graduated from the Royal School in Stuttgart, attending at the same time the Conservatory of Music. Professors Lebert and Stark complimented her by sending to her pupils to prepare in piano and harmony for their classes, while under the direction of the organ teacher, Dr. Faisst, she was organist and choir director of one of the most prominent churches in that city. Her precociousness caused such musical authorities as Julius Benedict and Emma Albani to advise her to devote her attention to her voice, predicting for her a brilliant future. Mme. Albani directed her to her own master, Lamperti. Lamperti, soon perceiving the ability of his new pupil, gave her the position of accompanist, which she held for three years, enabling her to note the artistic and vocal training of many of the most famous artists on the operatic and concert stages. In America she holds the position of the foremost exponent of the Lamperti school and she studies every season indefatigably with the famous artists and great teachers of the Old World. Among these have been Theresa Brambilla, Mme. Filippi, Stockhausen, the late Mme. Rudersdorf, Mme. Marchesi, and Della Sedie, of Paris, William Shakespeare and Randegger. She has developed a "method" which is distinctively her own, and she has an extraordinary knowledge of the art of song. She has the friendship of the majority of modern composers of note, and she aims to combine modern progressiveness and dramatic interpretation with strict adherence to purity and beauty of tone production. She passes the spring season of each year in London, England. Miss Berg possesses a clear soprano voice. She is constantly engaged in arranging concerts and classical recitals in and out of New York. She has also organized quartets and choruses. To Miss Berg belongs, it is believed, the honor of being the first woman musician in America to wield the baton at a public performance. In April, 1891, she conducted Smart's cantata, "King René's Daughter," before an audience which crowded the new Carnegie Hall, New York. The amount of artistic work which she accomplishes is the more astonishing, as she personally instructs an extraordinarily large number of private pupils, professionals and distinguished amateurs, conducts and leads classes and choruses in her private music school, and is in constant demand at social gatherings. Miss Lillie Berg is more widely versatile in her intellectuality than is usual with musicians. She is well versed in philosophy, art, history, poetry, political science and social lore, has traveled extensively, and can speak five languages with fluency.

BERGEN Mrs. Cornelia M., philanthropist, born in Brooklyn, NY, 12th July, 1837. Her education was begun in the school of the Misses Laura and Maria Betts, to be continued in the school of Miss Sarah Demorest, and to be finished, when she was eighteen years old, in the well-known institution kept by Alfred Greenleaf.

From the time of her graduation, in 1855, until the present she has been actively engaged in philanthropic work, mostly of a private character. She believes that to succeed, to gain the best results in that field of work, it is necessary to give close and earnest personal effort. She has never associated herself with any particular institution of a charitable nature, but she has every year given generously to a number of philanthropic and charitable enterprises. Her life has been devoted to aiding and encouraging worthy ones, to whom she was attached by bonds of regard and friendship. Her main idea of life is to make lighter, brighter and happier the lives of those less fortunate than herself. Her substantial gifts have been accompanied by personal attention, comforting ministrations and cheering words. Her home life has been varied. She was married 22nd September, 1858, to Jacob I. Bergen, who died in 1885. He was well known in Brooklyn having served as surrogate of Kings county. Their family numbered five children, only three of whom are living. Mrs. Bergen is to-day a youthful woman in appearance, and she has reaped a harvest of love and respect for her benevolence. In 1886 she became a member of Sorosis and of the Society for the Advancement of Women. Later she joined the Seidl Club, and in 1890 she became a member of the Brooklyn Institute. In those societies her influence has been felt in many ways, and her membership in them has greatly widened her field of philanthropic labor.

BERGEN, Miss Helen Corinne, author and journalist, born in Delanco, NJ, 14th October, 1868. She belongs to the Bergen family that came from Norway and settled in New Jersey in 1618, in the place they called Bergen. Her mother was the daughter of the Rev. Isaac Winner, D.D., one of the most eloquent preachers in the New Jersey Conference of the Methodist Episcopal Church. Her father was Colonel George B. Bergen. Helen is the oldest child and only daughter. She has written for the press ever since she

was a child. She passed her youth in Michigan, and later moved to Washington, DC. She has lived in Louisiana and Texas, and has traveled much. She wrote first for home papers in Michigan and then for papers in the South. She has served on the Washington "Post," and is that journal's freelance, and children's department editor. She acts as reporter when necessary, and is an all-round newspaper woman. She writes poetry, sketches, criticisms and stories. She has a wide circle of acquaintances among the prominent people of the day. She believes in equal pay for equal work by men and women. She holds high rank as a musical and dramatic critic. She is building a permanent home in Washington.

BERRY, Mrs. Adaline Hohf, author, born in Hanover, PA, 20th December, 1859. She removed with her parents, at the age of four years, to Maryland, where she spent her childhood days amid the rural sights and sounds along the quiet Linganore. In 1870 her family removed to Iowa, where, as a school-girl in her teens, she first attempted verse. A talent for composition began its development about that time, and sketches from her pen, in the form of both poetry and prose, found their way into the local papers. She gave no particular evidence of a tendency to rhyme until 1884, at which time she resided in Illinois, when the death of a friend called forth a memorial tribute, which received such commendation from personal friends as to encourage her to continue to work in verse, and poems were frequently written by her afterward. She completed the academic course of Mt. Morris College (Illinois) in 1882, and about six months after graduation entered a printing office as compositor. She worked at the case more than four years and in May, 1885, undertook the editing of "The Golden Dawn," an excellent but short-lived magazine published in Huntingdon, PA. On 20th June, 1888, she was married to William Berry, an instructor in vocal music, and soon after rendered him valuable assistance in compiling an excellent song-book, "Gospel Chimes," writing hymns and some music for it. She and her husband are at present happily located in Huntingdon, and Mrs. Berry is editing a child's paper known as "The

Young Disciple." Her family consists of one child, a son, born in February, 1891. She is of mixed ancestry. Her father, Michael Hohf, was of Dutch extraction, and her mother, whose maiden name was Elizabeth Bucher, was of Swiss blood. Born in a community of "Pennsylvania Dutch," that language was the first she learned to speak.

BERRY, Mrs. Martia L. Davis, political reformer, born in Portland, MI, 22nd January, 1844. Her parents were born in New York State. Her father was of Irish and Italian descent. He was a firm believer in human rights, an earnest anti-slavery man and a strong prohibitionist. Her mother was of German descent, a woman far in advance of her times. Martia wished to teach school, and to that end she labored for a thorough education. She began to teach when she was seventeen years of age and taught five years in the public schools of her native town. At the close of the Rebellion she was married to John S. Berry, a soldier who had given to his country four years of service. In September, 1871, she removed with her husband and only child to Cawker City, KS, and has since resided there. For twelve years she did a business in millinery and general merchandise. During eight years she was a superintendent of the Methodist Episcopal Sunday-school and a steward of the church. She organized the first Woman's Foreign Missionary Society west of the Missouri river, in April, 1872. The idea of the Woman's Club in her town originated with her and the club was organized 15th November, 1883. It is a monument to the literary taste and business ability of its founders. On 29th October, 1885, she was elected to the office of State treasurer of the Kansas Equal Suffrage Association, to which office she has every year since been re-elected. On 14th April, 1887, she was placed at the head of the sixth district of the Kansas Woman's Christian Temprance Union. On 28th February, 1889, she was elected to the office of State treasurer of the Union, and her yearly re-election proves her faithfulness.

BERT, Mabel, actor, born in Australia in 1862. Her father was A. C. Scott. The family came to this country in 1865, settling in San Francisco,

CA. Miss Bert was educated in Mills Seminary, Oakland, CA. She left school when seventeen years old, was married and made her début on the stage the following year. For two years she played with various companies throughout California, and in 1885 joined a stock company in San Francisco, for leading parts. For fourteen months she took a new part every week, including Shakespeare's plays, old comedies, melodramas, society plays and burlesques. In 1887 she went east and joined one of Frohman's companies in "Held by the Enemy." Since that time Miss Bert has taken leading parts in various plays, and has appeared in all of the important cities of America.

BEST, Mrs. Eva, author, born in Cincinnati, OH, 19th December, 1851. She is a daughter of the late John Insco Williams and Mrs. Mary Williams, now of Chicago, IL. Her father was an artist and painted the first bible panorama ever exhibited in the United States. Her mother is also an artist of merit and a writer of excellent verse and prose. The daughter inherits the talents of both parents. In 1869 she was married to William H. Best, of Dayton, OH, and her home is now in that city. Mrs. Best began her literary career as a poet. Her first short story appeared in one of the Frank Leslie periodicals. That was followed by stories in other publications. In 1882 her services were sought by the editor of the Detroit "Free Press," and now Mrs. Best is editor of the household department of that paper. She is also a regular contributor to A. N. Kellogg's Newspaper Company and has written several dramas. The first, "An American Princess," is now in its sixth season. A comedy drama, "Sands of Egypt," is in the hands of Miss Elizabeth Marbury, of New York. "A Rhine Crystal" is being used by Miss Floy Crowell, a young New England artist, and her other plays, "The Little Banshee" and "Gemini," the former in Irish dialect, the latter a two-part character piece, were written for Miss Jennie Calef. In all these plays the music, dances, ballads and all incidental scores are distinctively original. A number of ballads have also added to the author's fame. She has devoted some attention to art. She has two children, a son and a daughter, and the latter is already an artist of some reputation.

BETHUNE, Mrs. Louise, architect, born in Waterloo, NY, in 1856. She is of American parentage. Her maiden name was Blanchard. Her father's ancestors were Huguenot refugees. Her mother's family went to Massachusetts from Wales in 1640. Being a delicate child, she was not sent to school until the age of eleven. Meantime she had acquired habits of study and self-reliance which led her through school life to disregard the usual class criterions. In 1874 she was graduated from the Buffalo, NY, high school. A caustic remark had previously turned her attention in the direction of architecture, and an investigation, which was begun in a spirit of playful self-defense, soon became an absorbing interest. For two years she taught, traveled and studied, preparatory to taking the architectural course in Cornell University. In 1876 she received an offer of an office position as draughtsman and relinquished her former intention of college study. The hours were from eight to six, and the pay was small, but her employer's library was at her service. In 1881 she opened an independent office, thus becoming the first woman architect. She was afterward joined by Robert A. Bethune, to whom she was married in December of the same year. During the ten years of its existence the firm has erected fifteen public buildings and several hundred miscellaneous buildings, mostly in Buffalo and its immediate neighborhood. Mrs. Bethune has made a special study of schools and has been particularly successful in that direction, but refuses to confine herself exclusively to that branch, believing that women who are pioneers in any profession should be proficient in every department, and that now at least women architects must be practical superintendents as well as designers and scientific constructors, and that woman's complete emancipation lies in "equal pay for equal service." Because the competition for the Woman's Building of the

Columbia Exposition was not conducted on that principle, Mrs. Bethune refused to submit a design. The remuneration offered to the successful woman was less than half that given for similar service to the men who designed the other buildings. In 1885 Mrs. Bethune was elected a member of the Western Association of Architects. She is still the only woman member of the American Institute. In 1886 she inaugurated the Buffalo Society of Architects, from which has grown the Western New York Association. Both were active in securing the passage of the Architects' Licensing Bill, intended to enforce rigid preliminary examinations and designed to place the profession in a position similar to that occupied by medicine and law. In the last five or six years a dozen young women have been graduated from the different architectural courses now open to them, and Mrs. Bethune has ceased to be the "only woman architect."

BICKERDYKE, Mrs. Mary A., philanthropist and army nurse, born near Mount Vernon, Knox county, OH, 19th July, 1817. She is the daughter of Hiram and Anna Ball. The mother died when Mary was only seventeen months old. The little one was reared by her grandparents. Her grandsire was a Revolutionary soldier named Rogers and a descendant of the Rogers who landed on Plymouth Rock. While young, she was married to Mr. Bickerdyke, and in a few years was left a widow, with helpless little ones to rear. When the Civil War came, she left home and loved ones to offer her services as nurse to the soldiers, who were dying by scores for lack of food and care. When the supplies to the army were sent from Galesburg to Cairo, Mrs. Bickerdyke accompanied them as delegate. After the battle of Belmont she was assigned as nurse to the field hospital. Fort Donelson brought her in sight of battle for the first time. She obtained supplies sometimes by visiting the North and superintending fairs, by a simple note to a pastor at sermon time, and by her famous "cow and hen" mission, by which she furnished the wounded soldiers with a hundred cows and a thousand hens, to provide fresh dainties for the sufferers. During the winter of 1863–64 she made a short visit home, and returned and took part in the establishment of Adams Block Hospital, Memphis, TN. This accommodated about 6,000 men, and from this she became the matron of Gayoso Hospital, in which were more than 700 wounded men brought in from Sherman's battle of Arkansas Post. She took charge in Memphis, TN, of a small-pox hospital and cleansed and renovated it with her own hands, when nine men lay dead with the disease. Through the battles at Vicksburg, Lookout Mountain, Missionary Ridge and Chattanooga Mrs. Bickerdyke nursed friend and foe alike, and when, in 1864, Sherman started on his memorable March to the Sea, always devoted to the Army of the Tennessee, "Mother" Bickerdyke, as the soldiers used to call her, accompanied the 100,000 men who marched away. Resaca, Kingston, New Hope, Cassville, Allatoona, Dallas and Kenesaw Mountain furnished her with 13,000 of those brave men as subjects for her care. When Sherman cut his base of supplies, Mrs. Bickerdyke went to the North and collected immense sanitary stores for the soldiers. When Sherman entered Savannah, she sailed for the South, to take care of the liberated Union prisoners at Wilmington. At Beaufort, Averysboro and Bentonville she pursued her mission, and at the request of General Logan and the 15th Army Corps she marched into Alexandria with the army. At the final review in Washington Mrs. Bickerdyke, mounted upon a saddle-horse, dressed in a simple calico dress and sun-bonnet, accompanied the troops. This dress and bonnet were sold as relics of the war for $100. Since the rebellion Mrs. Bickerdyke has spent her life in procuring homes and pensions for the "boys." She resides with her son, Prof. Bickerdyke, in Russell, KS.

BIERCE, Mrs. Sarah Elizabeth, journalist, born in Sweden, ME, in 1838. Her maiden name was Holden, one well-known in New England. While a schoolgirl, her essays and poems attracted attention, many of them finding place in the columns of eastern journals. Her early education was received in New England. Removing to Michigan, she was graduated in 1860 from Kalamazoo College. During the next six years she taught in both public and private schools. While engaged in school work, she wrote numerous plays, which were first used at entertainments given by her pupils and afterward published. From the time of her marriage, in 1866, to her husband's death, in 1881, Mrs. Bierce wrote little for the press. In 1885 she accepted a permanent position in connection with the Cleveland "Plain Dealer," contributing stories, sketches and special articles to the Sunday issue. Her stories and sketches of home life and pioneer incidents were especially popular. While most inclined to fiction, she has written numerous letters of travel. Her descriptions of life and scenery in California, Arizona, Nevada and Utah were unusually entertaining. She has given much time to the investigation of certain phases of the working-woman problem, and has also written special articles on art subjects. She is a member of the Ohio Woman's Press Association and is at present (1892) corresponding secretary of that body. In 1891 she was chosen delegate to the International League of Press Clubs, formed in Pittsburgh. Mrs. Bierce is, perhaps, most widely known outside of Ohio through her efficient management of the woman's literary and journalistic department of the Ohio Centennial, held in Columbus in 1888. Through her efforts was secured a full representation of the literary women of Ohio, past and present, editors, journalists, authors and poets, scattered far and wide, sending the fruits of their work to the exposition of their native State. She has a family consisting of a daughter and two sons.

BIGELOW, Mrs. Belle G., woman suffragist and prohibitionist, born on a farm in Gilead, MI, 16th February, 1851. Her education was confined to the district school. She has been from early childhood an omnivorous reader. Her mother died when Belle was ten years old. At the age of eighteen she began to teach. In 1869 she was married to George R. Bigelow, of Ravenna, OH. They removed and settled in Geneva, NE, being the first residents of that place. After eight years of quiet home life, the question of the woman suffrage amendment being brought before the people, she entered into its advocacy. Soon becoming known

as a talker and writer on that subject, she was elected president of the county Equal Suffrage Association and sent as a delegate to the State convention in Omaha. There she made her first appearance as a public speaker and her reception encouraged a continuance of work in that line. The next winter, in Lincoln, she was elected to the office of State secretary and traveled over the State in the interest of the amendment, making effective speeches where opportunity offered and awakening much interest in the subject. She was twice a candidate for county superintendent of instruction on the prohibition ticket, and represented the State in the national convention of that party held in Indianapolis in 1888. She has served for five years as secretary of the Lincoln Woman's Christian Temperance Union, being a member of the union in its infancy. She is superintendent of foreign work for the State union, and was elected delegate to the national convention in Boston in 1891. She is known as an interesting writer for the press on both religious and secular topics. She has been the mother of seven children, four of whom are living.

BIGELOW, Mrs. Ella Augusta, musician, born in Malden, MA, in 1849. Her father, Lewis Fisher, and mother, Ruth Benchley, are both of good old English descent. For many years her home was in the town of Milford. Her parents being in good circumstances, the best of instruction was given her. Developing a taste for music, she was placed under the care of the most advanced teachers in Boston. As a church singer she has been well known in Fitchburg and various other cities, singing at intervals with such artists as Carlyle Petersilea and Eichberg with his "Germania Orchestra." In 1873 she went to Germany, residing while there chiefly in Berlin. There she studied with Ferdinand Sieber, court professor of music, and Fräulein Ress, both of whom gave her strong encouragement to choose a musical career. Becoming acquainted with Mr. and Mrs. George Bancroft, he being minister to Berlin at that time, the opportunity was given her, through their kindness, of meeting many celebrities and making many friends. Before returning to America she traveled through Europe. At a later period she was married to Edward L. Bigelow, of Marlboro, MA, where she now resides in an old Colonial house, full of antiques and souvenirs of travel. There she devotes her time to the education of her three children, making home-life attractive and giving to the public frequent helps to intellectual improvement. She has published "Prize Quotations" (Marlboro, 1887), "Venice" (Marlboro, 1890), "Old Masters of Art" (Buffalo, 1888), and "Letters upon Greece" (Marlboro, 1891). She has for years contributed articles for papers both in the East and the West, and has been president of numerous literary clubs as well as musical ones. Full of sympathy for those who are striving for education and true culture, the doors of her home are ever open to pupils of all classes in life.

BIGELOW, Miss Lettie S., author, born in Pelham, MA, in 1849. She is the daughter of the Rev. I. B. Bigelow, an itinerant minister, for more than half a century an honored member of the Methodist Episcopal Church. Her early education was in the public schools of the cities and towns where her parents lived, as they were removed from place to place every two or three years by the decrees of the presiding bishops, according to the economy of their church. In 1866 she entered Wesleyan Academy in Wilbraham, MA, and remained a student there two years. Failing health compelled her to relinquish her course of study in that institution before the completion of the regular course, and she has since made her home with her parents at their various appointments. Four years ago her father left the active work of the ministry and made for himself and family a permanent home in Holyoke, MA, where Miss Bigelow now lives, tenderly caring for an invalid mother. She has done considerable literary work, being always a close student of books and events. She has published no book of poems, but her verses have appeared quite frequently in the New York "Christian Advocate," "Zion's Herald" of Boston, the New York "Independent," the Boston "Journal" and other papers. Her prose writings , consisting of sketches, newspaper articles, and a serial story, have been for the most part under a pseudonym. A few years ago she wrote a book of

Sunday-school and anniversary exercises, published in New York, which had a large sale. Miss Bigelow is also an interesting platform speaker. Her lecture on "Woman's Place and Power" has found special favor and most hearty commendation wherever it has been delivered. Her manner on the platform is easy and her delivery pleasing.

BIGGART, Miss Mabelle, educator and dramatic reader, born in New York City, 22nd February, 1861. She comes of Scotch and English ancestry and is descended from a long line of teachers, authors and collegians. Her great-grandmother on her father's side was named Porter, and was a sister of Commodore Porter, of Revolutionary fame, and a cousin of Jane Porter, the author of "Scottish Chiefs." Her great-grandfather married into the clan of McKies. Thomas Carlyle and Jane Welsh Carlyle were closely related. Her grandfather on her mother's side was Sir Richard Bond, of London, England. Her father was born in Glasgow, Scotland, and her mother was a native of New York. Miss Biggart took a preparatory college course in the State Normal School in Fredonia, NY, and an oratorical and literary course in Philadelphia. Her professional education has been mainly in Philadelphia and New York, and she is still a constant student of dramatic elocution and of languages. Her parents died when she was only a child, and her life has been varied and eventful. She is of an intense, highly strung nature, and not robust, and her close application to her profession and her studies has more than once forced her to rest. She has held several important positions in colleges and seminaries, and for five years she had charge of rhetoric and elocution in the West high school, Cleveland, OH. A bronchial trouble sent her to Denver, CO, where she was instrumental in building up an institution called the Woman's Polytechnic Institute. She gave part of each week to that work, and the remainder was employed in the State College in Fort Collins, seventy-two miles from Denver. During the summer of 1891 she filled a number of Chautauqua engagements in the East. For about two years the Colorado climate proved beneficial to her, but at length the high altitude caused extreme nervous troubles and necessitated another change. She entered upon a new line of dramatized readings from her own interpretations of French, German and English masterpieces. A tour of the United States was undertaken, accompanied by her friend, Miss Marie Louise Gumaer, contralto. Miss Biggart's literary productions are numerous, including a yet unpublished volume of miscellaneous poems and "Songs from the Rockies," short stories and sketches of western life, a book on "Educational Men and Women and Educational Institutions of the West," "Sketches of Popular Living American Authors," a series of "Supplementary Reading Leaflets," recently published, and a work of fiction, nearly completed. Some of her poems have been set to music.

BINGHAM, Miss Jennie M., author, born in Fulton, NY, 16th March, 1859. She is the daughter of Jane Mills and the Rev. Dr. I. S. Bingham. Her father has been for forty-eight years in the ministry of the Methodist Episcopal Church. When poor health shut off the possibility of teaching, Miss Bingham turned to her pen for a livelihood. Her first article offered for publication was a little story entitled "A Hospital Sketch," which appeared in the "Christian Union." Among her early productions was a missionary story, "A Grain of Mustard Seed" (1881). Eight-thousand copies were sold during the first six months after publication, the proceeds of which founded a home in Japan. She works in every department of literature, book-reviewing, essay writing, fiction, poetry, Sunday-school helps and art criticism. Some of her short stories have appeared in "Harper's Young People." She is the author of two books, "Annals of the Round Table" (1885), and "All Glorious Within" (1889), the latter a story embodying the origin and work of the King's Daughters. She has been specially interested in the charities of New York City, and part of her labor has been in visiting them and writing concerning them. The Newsboys' Lodging-house, Five Points Mission, Flower Mission, Florence Night Mission, and Children's Aid Society are among her subjects. Her life has been a busy one, in which literature has only been incidental. Her home is in Herkimer, NY.

BIRKHOLZ, Mrs. Eugenie S., author, born in Garnavillo, Clayton county, IA, in 1853. She is the daughter of Dr. F. Andros, who was the first physician and surgeon, regularly licensed to practice, who settled west of the Mississippi river and north of Missouri. He settled in Dubuque, IA, in 1830. Mrs. Birkholz was educated in the school of the Catholic sisters in Benton, WI, and was in her early life a woman of original thought and sent many literary contributions to the periodicals and papers of the day. In 1881 she was married to John Birkholz, of Chicago, IL, in which city they both resided, and whence they emigrated to Grand Forks, N. Dak., where she has since made her home. Mrs. Birkholz devotes considerable time to literary work.

BISHOP, Anna, singer, born in London, England, in 1814; died in New York City, 18th March, 1884. Her father was a drawing-master named Rivière. She studied the piano-forte under Moscheles, became distinguished for her singing, and in 1831 became the wife of Sir Henry Rowley Bishop. She eloped with Bochsa, the harpist, in 1839, and soon after went on a tour through the princpal countries of Europe, which extended down to 1843. From that time until 1846 she remained in Italy, and was at one time prima donna at the San Carlo, Naples. After her stay in Italy she returned to England. In 1847 she came to this country, remaining here until 1855, when she sailed for Australia. She then again made a brief visit to England, and in 1859 came to this country for the second time. Her stay was prolonged to 1866, with a brief visit to Mexico and Cuba, when she sailed for the Sandwich Islands, visited China, India, Australia, Egypt and England, arriving in the United States again about 1869. Probably no other singer traveled so much or sang before so many people. She visited nearly every country on the globe, and the most of them repeatedly. In 1858 she was married to Martin Schultz, an American, and made it her permanent home in New York City. Her last public appearance was in a concert in New York in the spring of 1883.

BISHOP, Mrs. Emily Mulkin, Delsartean lecturer and instructor in dress, expression and physical culture, born in Forestville, Chautauqua county, NY, 3rd November, 1858. After leaving school she taught four years, serving as assistant principal of the union school in Silver Creek, NY. She afterward gave several years to the study of Delsarte work in various cities. In 1884 she became the wife of Coleman E Bishop, editor of the "Judge," New York. They soon went to Black Hills, Dakota, to live. Mrs. Bishop was elected superintendent of public schools in Rapid City, SD, being the first woman thus honored in the Territory. In the following year she was invited to establish a Delsarte department in the Chautauqua School of Physical Education, in the Chautauqua Assembly, New York. She has had charge of that department for four seasons, and it has steadily grown in popularity. In 1891 it was the largest single department in the Assembly. From the Chautauqua work has grown a large public work in lecturing and teaching. She has written a number of articles for various magazines and has published one book, "Americanized Delsarte Culture." At present Mrs. Bishop's home is in Washington, DC.

BISHOP, Mrs. Mary Agnes Dalryrnple, journalist, born in Springfield, MA, 12th August, 1857. She is the only child of John Dalrymple and his wife, Frances Ann Hewitt. She has always been proud of her old Scotch ancestry and her ability to trace the family back from Scotland to France, where, early in the twelfth century, William de Darumpill obtained a papal dispensation to marry his kinswoman, Agnes Kennedy. It is scarcely a century since her grandfather came to this country. On her maternal side she traces her ancestry to the Mayflower, which brought over her several-times-removed grandmother May. In local papers her childhood poems were printed readily, but the reading of Horace Greeley's "Recollections of a Busy Life," in which he has some good advice for youthful writers, caused her to determine not to be tempted to allow her doggerel to be published, and for years she adhered to her determination. When she was less than two years old, her parents removed with her to Grafton, Worcester county, MA, and at the age of sixteen years she became the local editor of the Grafton "Herald." Beginning the week following her graduation, she taught in the public schools of Grafton and Sutton for many years. During that time she gave lectures quite frequently in the vicinity and often appeared in the home drama, making her greatest success as "Lady Macbeth." Miss Dalrymple was a frequent contributor to the "Youth's Companion" and other publications, never adopting a pen-name and rarely using her own name or initials. In 1887 she accepted an editorial position on the "Massachusetts Ploughman." The position offered her had never been taken by a woman, and, indeed, the work that she did was never attempted previously, for she had the charge of almost the entire journal from the first. A few months after she accepted the position, the proprietor died, and the entire paper was in her hands for six months. In the autumn the paper was purchased by its present owner, but the chief editorial work remained in her hands. The paper was enlarged from four to eight pages in the meantime and, as before, was published each week. In the autumn of 1889 she became the wife of Frederick Herbert Bishop, a Boston business man. Together they engage in literary pursuits and the work and pleasure of life along its varied lines. Their home is located on Wollaston Heights. Mrs. Bishop does not content herself with editorial work, but is interested in literature in general. She is one of the few newspaper women who is a practical reportorial stenographer. She is a member of the executive committee of the New England Woman's Press Association, of which she was one of the first members.

BISLAND, Miss Elizabeth, journalist, born in Camp Bisland, Fairfax plantation, Teche county, LA, in 1863. Her family, one of the oldest in the South, lost its entire property while she was a child and Miss Bisland became impressed, at an early age, with the necessity of doing something toward the support of herself and relatives. Having shown a talent for writing, this, naturally, was the line of work along which she began her career. Her first sketches, published at the age of fifteen, were written under the pen-name B. L. R. Dane, and were favorably received by the New Orleans newspapers to which they were sent. Miss

Bisland did considerable work for the New Orleans "Times-Democrat" and, later, became literary editor of that paper. After a few years' work in New Orleans she decided to enter the literary field in New York and for a time did miscellaneous work for newspapers and periodicals in that city. In a short time she was offered the position of literary editor of the "Cosmopolitan Magazine" which she accepted. It was while engaged upon that magazine that Miss Bisland undertook her noted journey around the earth in the attempt to make better time than that of Nellie Bly, who was engaged to perform the same journey in the interest of the New York "World"; Miss Bly going east while Miss Bisland took the western direction. Although she did not succeed in defeating her rival, Miss Bisland made such time as to command the admiration of the civilized world. In May, 1890, she went to London, England, in the interest of the "Cosmopolitan," and her letters to that magazine, from London and Paris, have been widely read and appreciated. In addition to her journalistic work, she has also written, in collaboration with Miss Rhoda Broughton, a one-volume novel; also a romance and play in conjunction with the same author. She became the wife of Charles W. Wretmore of New York, 6th October, 1891, and they reside in that city.

BITTENBENDER, Mrs. Ada M., lawyer and reformer, born in Asylum, Bradford county, PA, 3rd August, 1848. Her mother's ancestors were New Englanders, and her father's family were partly of New England and partly of German stock. Her father served as a Union soldier throughout the Civil War and died soon after from exposures then endured. Her maiden name was Ada M. Cole. Her early education was acquired mainly in private schools near her home. In 1869 she was graduated from a Binghamton, NY, commercial college. In January, 1874, she entered as a student the Pennsylvania State Normal School at Bloomsburg, where she was graduated in the normal class of 1875. After graduation she was elected a member of the faculty, and taught in the school one year. She then entered the Froebel Normal Institute in Washington, DC, and was graduated there in the summer of 1877. On the same day of her graduation she received a telegram announcing her unanimous call back to her Alma Mater

normal school, to the position of principal of the model school. She accepted that position and taught there until nearly the end of the year's term, when, being prostrated from overwork, she resigned and retired to her mother's home in Rome, PA, for recovery. On 9th August, 1878, she was married to Henry Clay Bittenbender, a young lawyer of Bloomsburg, PA, and a graduate of Princeton College. In November, 1878, they removed to Osceola, NE. Mrs. Bittenbender taught school during their first winter in Nebraska, and Mr. Bittenbender opened a law office. In 1879 Mr. Bittenbender and Clarence Buell bought the "Record," published in Osceola, and the only paper in Polk county. Mrs. Bittenbender was engaged as editor, and for three years she made it an able, fearless, moral, family and temperance newspaper, Republican in politics. She and her husband were equally pronounced in their temperance views. She strenuously opposed the granting of saloon licenses in the town or county. Mr. and Mrs. Bittenbender reorganized the Polk County Agricultural Association, and Mrs. Bittenbender served as secretary, treasurer, orator and in 1881 as representative at the annual meeting of the State Board of Agriculture. She was the first woman delegate ever received by that body. When the Nebraska Woman Suffrage Association was organized in 1881, she was elected recording secretary. She with others worked with the legislature and secured the submission of the woman suffrage amendment to the constitution in 1881. At the first suffrage convention following the submission she was made one of the three woman campaign speakers. At the following annual meeting she was elected president of the association, and the last three months of the campaign was also chairman of the State campaign committee. She retired from the editorship of the "Record" in 1881, and became the editor of the first Farmers' Alliance paper started in Nebraska. That was a journal started in Osceola by the Polk County Farmers' Alliance. While she was editing the "Record," she read law with her husband, and in 1882 passed the usual examination in open court and was licensed to practice law. She was the first woman admitted to the bar in Nebraska. On the day of her admission she and her husband became law partners under the style of H. C. and Ada M. Bittenbender. The firm still exists. They removed to Lincoln, NE, in December, 1882. Mrs. Bittenbender prefers court practice to office work. She ranks as a very successful lawyer, and only once has she lost a case brought by herself. She has had several cases before the Supreme Court, the highest court of the State, which in every instance she has won. She has been admitted to the United States District and Circuit courts for Nebraska. She secured the passage of the scientific temperance instruction bill, the tobacco bill, secured a law giving the mother the guardianship of her children equally with the father, and several other laws. She is the author of the excellent industrial home bill which was enacted by the Nebraska legislature in 1887, which establishes an industrial school as well as home for penitent women and girls, with a view to lessen prostitution. At the International Council of Women held in Washington, DC, in March, 1888, she spoke on "Woman in Law." During several sessions of Congress she remained in Washington, representing the National Woman's Christian Temperance Union as its superintendent of legislation and petitions. She was an indefatigable worker, constantly sending out to the local unions and the press as her base of operations, for petitions, paragraphs, help in the way of influence with Congress to grant prohibition to the District of Columbia and the Territories, protection to women, constitutional prohibition and other measures called for by the national convention. She drafted the bill to accompany the great petition for the protection of women, offered by Senator Blair. That involved much hard work, as she was obliged to go over all the laws of Congress from the first, to learn precisely what had been done already and to make her bill harmonious with existing legislation. It was mainly through her efforts Congress passed the protection bill. She spoke briefly, but with clear, convincing argument, at hearings before the committees of Senate and House in the interest of prohibition in the District of Columbia. On 15th October, 1888, she was admitted to practice in the Supreme Court of the United States. The motion for her admission was made by Senator Blair, of New Hampshire. In 1888 she was elected attorney for the National Woman's Christian Temperance Union, which position she still holds. She is the author of the chapter on "Woman in Law" in "Woman's Work in America" (New York, 1891). In September, 1891, she was placed in nomination on the prohibition ticket in Nebraska for Judge of

the Supreme Court of that State. She received 7,322 votes out of a total of 155,000 cast in the State in 1891, the largest vote in proportion ever given for the head of the prohibition ticket. Her practice has been large, and her activity has been incessant. She has spent much time in Washington, DC. Mrs. Bittenbender is the author of the "National Prohibitory Amendment Guide," a manual to aid in obtaining an amendment to the Federal Constitution which shall outlaw forever the traffic in alcoholic beverages. The "plan of canvassing" contained in her manual has been quite generally indorsed. She is preparing a treatise on the law of alcoholic liquors as a beverage, showing the unconstitutionality of license laws, as deduced from judicial decisions, including procedures in testing the matter and in enforcing prohibition. She and her husband will bring such test cases in the courts to secure decisions. Mrs. Bittenbender has for years borne a wonderful burden of work, showing the capacity of woman to endure the strain of deep thinking and of arduous professional labor. She is a member of the Presbyterian Church and has been an earnest Sabbath-school teacher.

BLACK, Mrs. Fannie De Grasse, singer and pianist, born in Nisouri, Canada, 21st November, 1856. Her maiden name was De Grasse. She moved with her parents to the United States and made her home in Milwaukee, WI, where she was educated in the high and normal schools, graduating in 1874. At ten years of age she began the study of piano and sight singing, continuing until her sixteenth year, when she became a pupil of Prof. William Mickler, formerly director in court to the Duke of Hesse, Germany, studying with him for four years. She sang in public when she was only six years old, and made her début in classic music at the age of eighteen, under the direction of Professor Mickler, in the concerts of the Milwaukee German Musical Society, and has since sung successfully in opera and oratorio. Later on she took up the study of the pipe organ and is now (1892) organist of the Presbyterian church, El Dorado. In 1881 she was married to judge S. E. Black, of El Dorado, KS. Mrs. Black is a thorough scholar, and she believes that only a thorough scholar and student can become a fine musician. She sings equally well in English, German and Italian, and her pleasant El Dorado home is a center of music and refinement.

BLACK, Mrs. Mary Fleming, author and religious worker, born in Georgetown, SC, 4th August, 1848. Her father, Rev. W. H. Fleming, D. D., was a distinguished member of the South Carolina Conference of the Methodist Episcopal Church South, and died while pastor of Bethel Church, Charleston, SC, in 1877. Her parents were both Charlestonians. Her mother, born Agnes A. Magill, was the daughter of Dr. William Magill, a prominent physician of that city. The education of Mrs. Black was begun in one of the city schools of Charleston. She was afterward graduated with honor in Spartanburg Female College, and later took a special course under the instructions of the faculty of Wofford Male College, of which Rev. A. M. Shipp, D.D., LL.D., was president. Soon after the completion of her studies she was married to Rev. W. S. Black, D. D., then a member of the South Carolina Conference. Mrs. Black soon displayed ability as a writer, her prose and verse productions appearing in various newspapers and periodicals. In 1882 she became the editor of the children's department of the Raleigh "Christian Advocate," of which her husband was one of the editors and proprietors. In that relation she continued until the Woman's Missionary Society of the North Carolina and Western North Carolina Conferences established a juvenile missionary paper, the "Bright Jewels," of which she was elected editor. That position she now holds, and she is known by the children as "Aunt Mary." She is superintendent of the juvenile department and corresponding secretary of the Woman's Missionary Society of the North Carolina Conference, and is a member of the Woman's Board of Missions of the Methodist Episcopal Church South. She is a prominent and influential member of the Woman's Christian Temperance Union and of the King's Daughters of her State. She has three sons, two of whom have reached majority while the third is still in college, and one daughter, just

entering womanhood. As the wife of one of the most able and popular ministers of the conference, she faithfully discharged the many and delicate duties of that position, with great acceptability to her husband's congregation. In addition to many duties and labors, she is rendering her husband valuable aid in the management of the Oxford Orphan Asylum, of which he is superintendent.

BLACK, Mrs. Sarah Hearst, temperance reformer, born on a farm near Savannah, Ashland county, OH, 4th May, 1846. Her father's family removed from Pennsylvania to that farm when he was a boy of fourteen years, and Mrs. Black there grew to womanhood. Her ancestors were Scotch-Irish people, all of them members of the Presbyterian Church. Her mother's maiden name was Townsley. Miss Hearst first attended school in a typical red school-house situated on a corner of her father's farm. At thirteen years of age she began to attend school in Savannah Academy, where she completed a regular course of study. She made a public profession of religion in her fifteenth year and soon after became a teacher in the Sabbath-school, and has continued in that work ever since. After completing her course of study, she entered the ranks as a teacher, and that was her employment for more than ten years. In 1878 she was married to Rev. J. P. Black, a minister of the Presbyterian Church, and went with him to his field of labor in Pennsylvania. They removed to Kansas in 1880 and since that time she has borne the labor and self-denial incident to the life of a home missionary's wife in Kansas, Nebraska and now in Idaho. She became actively engaged in Woman's Christian Temperance Union work in 1885, in Nebraska, and was elected president of the fifth district of that State for two years in succession. After her removal to Idaho she was chosen president of the Woman's Christian Temperance Union in that State. Her home is in Nampa.

BLACKALL, Mrs. Emily Lucas, author and philanthropist, born in Salem, IN, 30th June, 1832, and died in New York City, 28th March, 1892. The first ten years of her life were spent in her birthplace amid picturesque surroundings. Her early school days were marked by a quickness of apprehension and an appreciative literary taste that gave indication of the life that was to be in later years. Her parents were Virginians of English descent. During a considerable period, including the years of the late Civil War, her residence was in Louisville, KY, where she was identified with the Baptist Orphans' Home from its beginning until she left the State, and also was treasurer of the Kentucky branch of the Woman's Missionary Society, founded by the late Mrs. Doremus of New York. Removing to Chicago, she became identified with the woman's temperance crusade and aided in forming the Woman's Christian Temperance Union. She was one of a committee of women who appealed in person to the city council to restrain the liquor-saloon influence, and one of a special committee of three appointed to visit the mayor and urge him to carry out a plan for the protection of homes against the saloon. She was one of the founders of the Woman's Baptist Foreign Missionary Society of the West, and was treasurer of that organization until she left Chicago. She was largely instrumental in the formation of the Women's Baptist Home Mission Society, located in Chicago, with which she was actively engaged at the time of her death. In 1882 she became a resident of Philadelphia, PA, where she was identified with various benevolent enterprises. A member of the Philadelphia Women's Council, a member of the Women's International Congress in 1887, and a delegate to the Woman's National Council in 1891, she showed a depth of sympathy and touch with progressive ideas that proved the breadth of her character and her influence. As a presiding officer and public speaker Mrs. Blackall always gave satisfaction and pleasure. As an author she was successful. Her first story, "Superior to Circumstances" (Boston, 1889), was followed by "Melodies from Nature" (Boston, 1889) and "Won and Not One" (Philadelphia, 1891). Short stories and biographical sketches have frequently appeared in various periodicals, and missionary literature has had numerous contributions from her pen. In collaboration with her husband, the Rev. C. R. Blackall, she was joint author of "Stories about Jesus" (Philadelphia, 1890). Her literary style is marked by purity, vigor and correctness. She dealt with social and economic problems in a practical, common-sense manner, writing from experience and broad observation rather than as an idealist, yet always with tenderness and in a spirit of helpfulness. In the various relations of wife, mother, and home-maker, she was eminent for the sweetness of her disposition, the unfailing accuracy of her judgment, and the purity of her life.

BLACKWELL, Miss Alice Stone, journalist, born in Orange, NJ, 14th September, 1857. She is the daughter of Lucy Stone and Henry B. Blackwell. She was graduated from Boston University with honors in 1881, and has been on the staff of the "Woman's Journal" ever since. During the last few years she has also edited a small weekly paper devoted to woman suffrage, called the "Woman's Column."

BLACKWELL, Mrs. Antoinette Brown, author and minister, born in Henrietta, Monroe county, NY, 20th May, 1825. She is a daughter of Joseph Brown, of Thompson, CT, and Abby Morse, of Dudley, MA. Her parents were descendants of early English colonists and Revolutionary soldiers, many of whom were prominent in the early days of New England. Miss Brown joined the Congregational Church when she was only nine years old, and sometimes spoke and prayed in meetings. She taught school when sixteen years old, and later taught several branches in a seminary in order to pay the expenses of a collegiate course. Even her vacations were devoted to extra study, so ambitious was she and so untiring in the pursuit of knowledge. She was graduated from Oberlin College, where she completed the literary course in 1847 and the theological course in 1850. She bears the degree of M.A. Her attention was engaged early in theological questions. In 1848 she published her first important essay, an exegesis of St. Paul on women, in the "Oberlin Quarterly Review." At the completion of the theological course she could not obtain a license, as was customary with students but was told she must preach or be silent on her own responsibility. That she was not afraid to assume, since ability and responsibility belong together. Without regard to sect, she preached whenever and wherever a place offered, but not always did she do this under favorable circumstances. Obstacles melted away under the powerful personality of such a speaker as Antoinette Brown, and, in spite of the objections to women preachers as a class, she finally became the ordained pastor, in 1852, of a Congregational church in South Butler, Wayne county, NY. In 1853 she was ordained by the council called by the church. After preaching for the society awhile she began to have distressing doubts concerning certain theological doctrines, and on that account she resigned her charge in 1854. She was married to Samuel C. Blackwell, a brother of Dr. Elizabeth Blackwell, 24th January, 1856. She began the study of some of the great questions concerning vice and crime and published the result under the title of "Shadows of Our Social System." Her life as a preacher, lecturer and writer has been a very useful one. In the latter direction she has done work that reflects great credit upon her sex, having received much praise for her logical methods of thought. "Studies in General Science" (New York, 1869), "A Market Woman" (New York, 1870), "The Island Neighbors" (New York, 1871), "The Sexes Throughout Nature" (New York, 1875), and "The Physical Basis of Immortality" (New York, 1876), are some of her various works. The most prominent fact to be recorded in the history of Mrs. Blackwell's life, and the one which speaks loudly for her present honorable place among the eminent women of our country, is her love of effort; only by persistent work has she been able to accomplish so much for herself and others. Although a wife and the mother of several daughters, she has kept abreast of the times on the questions of science, art and literature. She has by no means allowed the luster of intellectual gifts to grow dim from disuse. Amid scenes of domesticity she has found even fresh inspiration for public work. Not wholly preoccupied with home cares and duties, she has yet given faithful attention to them, and this fact, in connection with her success as a speaker and writer, should he chronicled. Mrs. Blackwell has always been actively interested in reformatory subjects and has spoken in behalf of the temperance cause. In 1854 she was a delegate to the World's Temperance Convention in New York, but a hearing was refused to her in that body, not because she was not an able representative, but simply because she was a woman. The change in the condition of women is plainly shown in the reminiscences of such women as Mrs. Blackwell. Mr. and Mrs. Blackwell have five children, and now live in Elizabeth, NJ. Mrs. Blackwell still preaches occasionally and has become a Unitarian.

BLACKWELL, Miss Elizabeth, physician and author, born in Bristol, England, 3rd February, 1821. Her father, Samuel Blackwell, was a wealthy sugar refiner, a man of broad views and strong benevolence. At the political crisis of 1830–31 commercial affairs in England were thrown into confusion, and Mr. Blackwell was among those whose fortunes were swept away at that time. He removed with his family to the United States in August, 1832, and settled in New York, where he started a sugar refinery. He was rapidly amassing wealth when the financial crash of 1837 in the United States swept away his fortune through the wreckage of the weaker houses with which he had business relations. He turned his eyes to the West, and in 1838 removed his family to Cincinnati, OH. There he was stricken by fever and died at the age of forty-five years, leaving a family of nine children to their own resources among strangers. Every cent of indebtedness left by the father was paid by his children. The three older daughters, of whom Elizabeth was the third, placed themselves at once at the head of the family. Two sons in school left their studies and took clerkships. The four younger ones were still in the nursery. The older sisters opened a boarding school for young women, and their liberal culture and enterprise won them a large patronage. The sisters felt the restrictions placed upon women in the matter of earning a livelihood, and they became convinced that the enlargement of opportunities for women was the one essential condition of their well-being in every way. After six years of hard work, when all the younger members of the family had been placed in positions to support themselves, the sisters gave up the school. Elizabeth resolved to study medicine, although she had to overcome a natural aversion to sickness of all kinds. She wrote to six different physicians for advice, and all agreed that it was impossible for a woman to get a medical education. She thought differently, however, and in 1844 she took charge of a Kentucky school to earn money for her expenses. In 1843 she went to Charleston, SC, to teach music in a boarding-school, and there added a good knowledge of Latin to her French and German. There she entered the office student class of Dr. Samuel Henry Dickson. In May, 1847, she applied for admission to the Phila-delphia Medical School, but both col-lege and hospital were closed to her. She applied to all the medical schools in the United States, and twelve of them rejected her application and rebuked her for temerity and indelicacy. The college faculty in Geneva, NY, and that in Castleton, VT, considered her application, and the students in Geneva decided to favor her admission. In 1847 she entered the college as "No. 417" on the reg-ister. In January, 1849, she was graduated with the Geneva class. A large audience witnessed the granting of the first medical diploma to a woman. Immediately after graduation. Dr. Elizabeth Blackwell went to Paris, France, where, after months of delay, she was admitted to the great lying-in hospital of the Maternité as a resident pupil, and several other schools permitted her to visit. She also studied under able private tutors. In 1850 and 1851 she "walked" St. Bartholomew's hospital in London, England, studying in the Women's Hospital and under private teachers. She returned to the United States, and in the autumn of 1851 she opened an office in New York City. She succeeded in building up a large practice, in spite of social and professional antagonism and ostracism. The Society of Friends were the first to receive her warmly and support the new move-ment, and she soon became known as a reliable physician. In 1853, with her sister, Dr. Emily Blackwell, she established in New York the New York Infirmary for Women and Children, which was incorporated and was for some years the only woman's hospital. In 1858 and 1859 she visited England and lectured in London, Birmingham and Liverpool on the connection of women with med-icine. In 1859 she was placed on the register of English physicians. Returning to America, she entered with the warmest interest into the ques-tions of the Civil War, and the sisters organized in the parlors of the Infirmary the Ladies' Central Relief Association, sending off the first supplies to the wounded. That association was soon merged in the Sanitary Commission, in which the sisters continued to take an active part. In 1869 Dr. Eliz-abeth lectured in the Medical College of the New York Infirmary, which had been chartered as a col-lege in 1865. At the close of 1869 she went to England and settled in London, where she practiced for some years. There she founded the National Health Society and worked in a number of social reforms. She aided in organizing the London School of Medicine for Women, in which she served as the first lecturer on the diseases of women. In 1878, after a serious illness, she set-tled in Hastings, England, continuing her consultation practice only and working ener-getically for the repeal of the unjust Contagious Diseases Acts. Up to the present time she has con-tinued to work actively for the promotion of equal standards of morality for men and women. Of late she has become an active opponent of vivisection, regarding it as an intellectual fallacy, misleading research and producing moral injury. She gives close attention to municipal affairs, as she feels the responsibility involved in the possession of a vote, which she possesses as a householder of Hastings. She knows in advanced age no diminu-tion of her zeal for right over wrong. In addition to her long and arduous labors as a teacher, as a student and as the pioneer woman physician, Dr. Elizabeth Blackwell has been a prolific author. Naturally, her works lie in the field of her profes-sion. Between 1852 and 1891 she wrote the fol-lowing important medical and scientific works: "The Laws of Life in Relation to the Physical Education of Girls," "How to Keep a Household in Health," "The Moral Education of the Young in Relation to Sex," "Wrong and Right Methods of Dealing with the Social Evil," "Christian Socialism," "The Human Element in Sex," "The Corruption of New Malthusianism," "The Pur-chase of Women a Great Economic Blunder," "The Decay of Municipal Representative Govern-ment," "The Influence of Women in the Medical Profession," "Erroneous Methods in Medical Education," and "Lessons Taught by the Interna-tional Hygienic Conference." Besides these are to be counted her numerous lectures, addresses and pamphlets on many branches of her profession. She is a woman of unbending will and a courage that never recognized defeat as possible. She opened the gate to the medical profession for women in the United States, in France and in Great Britain, and she has lived to see that profession made as easily accessible to women as to men. Dr. Blackwell is a profound thinker, a clear and logical reasoner, and a scientific controversialist of eminent ability. Her career, her achievements, her literary and scientific productions, and her work as a practicing physician make her a standing refutation of the easy-going assumption that women have neither the endurance, nor the intellect, nor the judgment, nor the requisites to serve in the medical profession. She owns a house in Hastings, England, where she resides, with an office in London for occasional work.

BLACKWELL, Miss Emily, physician, born in Bristol, England, in 1826. She is a younger sister of the well-known Dr. Elizabeth Blackwell. The story of her early life is similar to that of her famous sister. In 1848 Emily began the study of medicine, taking a course of medical reading and dissection with Dr. Davis, the demonstrator of anatomy in the medical college in Cincinnati, OH. Like her sister, she was endowed with great determination, good health, high ideals, quick perceptions and an exceptionally strong memory. Her early studies made her thoroughly familiar with French, Latin and German, and in Greek and mathematics she was well versed. She worked as a teacher to earn the funds to pay for her medical education. Dr. Elizabeth Blackwell had graduated at the Geneva Medical College in 1849, and at her graduation the professors had testified that her presence in the school "had exercised a beneficial influence upon her fellow students in all respects," and that "the average attainments and general conduct of students, during the period she passed among them, were of a higher character than those of any other class which has been assembled in the college since the connection of the president with the institution." The college professors having been severely criticised for making such an innovation, when her sister Emily, in 1851, applied for admission, she was met with the discouraging declaration that they were not ready to look upon the case of Dr. Elizabeth Blackwell as a precedent, and that the admission, training and graduation of one woman did not mean the permanent opening of the doors of the Geneva Medical College to women. Emily made application to ten other colleges, and each of the ten refused to permit her to enter. She then went to

New York City, where she was admitted to study in the free hospital of Bellevue Medical College. In 1852 she was admitted to Rush Medical College in Chicago, IL. The following summer she spent in New York in hospital work in Bellevue and study and experiment in the chemical laboratory of Dr. Doremus. Returning to Chicago to begin her second term, she was dismayed to learn that Rush College had closed its doors against her. The authorities of the college had been censured by the State Medical Association of Illinois for having permitted a woman to enter the institution as a student. She next went to Cleveland, OH, where the medical school admitted her. She studied earnestly and was graduated after passing triumphantly a most searching examination. She then went to Edinburgh, Scotland, where she studied under the eminent Dr. Simpson in the lying-in hospital. Then she went to Paris, where she attended clinics under the great physicians of that city in the Hotel Dieu, the Beaujou, the St. Louis and the Hospital des Enfants Malades, living and working in the Hospital of the Maternité. After Paris, she went to London, England, where she "walked" the wards of St. Bartholomew and other hospitals. In 1856 she returned to the United States, bringing the highest testimonials of training, study and acquirement. On her return she discovered that the popular sentiment seemed to have turned against women physicians more strongly than ever before. After the graduation of the Doctors Blackwell, several other schools had graduated women, but the faculties were determined that no more women should be admitted. Then separate schools sprung up. One of the immediate results of this revulsion of sentiment was the establishment of the hospital in New York by the Doctors Blackwell, in connection with a cultured Polish woman, Dr. M. E. Zakrzewska. In 1865 the legislature conferred college powers upon that institution. The new college extended the course of study to three years and was the first college to establish a chair of hygiene. Dr. Emily Blackwell has been from the first, and still is, one of the professors of that college, and the medical head of the infirmary for women and children established by the joint efforts of herself and her sister. The success of the college is a matter of history. The graduates number hundreds, and many of them have won distinction. It has been a "woman's college" throughout, owned, maintained, officered and managed by women. Dr. Emily Blackwell has also a large and lucrative practice and an honorable standing in her profession. She is interested in all the reform questions of the day and has written and published much in connection with her profession. She is one of the vice-presidents of the Society for the Promotion of Social Purity and the better protection of the young, and has written some of the leaflets published by that society, among them "The State and Girlhood," the "Need of Combination among Women for Self Protection," and "Regulation Fallacies—Vice not a Necessity." She is deeply loved and revered by her numerous friends and pupils. Her character is one of rare wisdom, disinterestedness and undeviating principle.

BLACKWELL, Miss Sarah Ellen, artist and author, the youngest daughter of Samuel and Hannah Lane Blackwell, born in Bristol, England, in 1828. She came to America with her parents at four years of age. Her father dying shortly afterward, she was educated by her older sisters in Cincinnati, OH. She began to teach music at a very early age, while pursuing her studies. When nineteen years old, she went to Philadelphia to pursue the study of art in the newly opened School of Design, and while there received her first literary encouragement. "Sartain's Magazine" having advertised for ten prize stories, to be sent in under fictitious names, Miss Blackwell sent in a story of her own under the name "Brandon," and another by one of her sisters that happened to be in her possession. She received an award of two out of the ten prizes. That led to further literary work. Concluding to continue the study of art in Europe, she secured an engagement for weekly letters for two leading Philadelphia papers. She spent four years in Europe. She entered the government school of design for girls in Paris, then under the care of Rosa Bonheur and her sister, Mme. Julie Peyrol, and afterward entered the studio of Mr. Leigh in London, and painted in the National Gallery, spending the summer on sketching from nature in Wales, Switzerland and the Isle of Wight. Returning to New York, she opened a studio and established classes in drawing and painting, but

finally gave up her studio to assist her sisters, the Doctors Blackwell, then greatly burdened with work connected with the New York Infirmary for Women and Children, and the medical college established by them. For several years she was occupied with domestic duties and the care of children in whom she was interested. As these duties lightened, she resumed artistic and literary work, writing occasional articles for magazines and newspapers and republishing the writings of Dr. Elizabeth Blackwell, then in England. A series of letters written by her for the "Woman's Journal," of Boston, concerning Miss Anna Ella Carroll, author of the plan of the Tennessee campaign, having excited much interest, it was followed by an open letter on the same subject published in the "Century" for August, 1890. That increased the interest, and in the Woman's Council and suffrage meetings in the early spring of 1891, in Washington, DC, a large number of subscribers were obtained, and Miss Blackwell was deputed to write a biography of Miss Carroll and an account of her remarkable work. After careful research, she printed, 21st April, 1891, the biography and sketch entitled "A Military Genius: Life of Anna Ella Carroll, the Great Unrecognized Member of Lincoln's Cabinet." Miss Blackwell spends her summers in an old farm-house at Martha's Vineyard, and her winters in New York or Washington, engaged in literary work. Her especial subjects of interest are land and labor reform, woman's suffrage and anti-vivisection, sympathizing as she does with Dr. Elizabeth Blackwell in her opposition to all cruel and demoralizing practices.

BLAIR, Mrs. Ellen A. Dayton, temperance organizer, born near Vernon Center, Oneida county, NY, 27th December, 1827. She was graduated in the classical course from Fort Edward Institute, NY, in 1837, and in the same year accepted the position of preceptress in Upper Iowa University, Fayette, IA. She remained in that institution one year, having charge of the art department. Soon after she was married to Emery H. Blair, of Iowa, at one time professor of mathematics in Clinton Liberal Institute, NY. Both were strong in anti-slavery and prohibition sentiments. During the Woman's Crusade Mrs. Blair discovered her ability as a temperance speaker. Loving the cause and zealous in its behalf, she has ever since been one of its faithful workers. She is the mother of five sons, three of whom are living. Young men were her special care during the Crusade and in Sunday-school work. Moving to Wisconsin in 1881, she began her illustrative talks to children, on the invitation of Mrs. Mary B. Willard, and later was made superintendent of the juvenile department for Wisconsin. In 1885 she was elected to her present position as national organizer and "chalk talker" of the juvenile department of the Woman's Christian Temperance Union. In fulfillment of her duties she has visited nearly every State and Territory, as well as Canada and has been a member of nearly every national convention. Since she removed to Creighton, NE, she has continued her work in the same field. During the prohibitory amendment campaign in that State she was one of the leaders. As superintendent of the Demorest medal contests, which has occupied much of her time and that of several assistants, under her care Nebraska leads the world in that line of temperance work. Mrs. Blair's greatest influence as a temperance worker lies in her illustrative talks, by which she interests young and old. In her hand the piece of chalk becomes a power. She is a natural artist and, when not engaged in public duties, devotes herself to teaching oil painting, drawing and crayon work.

BLAKE, Mrs. Alice R. Jordan, lawyer, born in Norwalk, OH, 10th October, 1864. She bears the distinction of being the first and so far the only woman to be graduated with a degree from Yale College. She received her high-school education in Coldwater, MI, where from childhood she was considered a prodigy in learning. After graduating from the high school, the youngest of her class, she entered the University of Michigan at the age of sixteen years, being at that time the youngest pupil who had ever entered the course. After graduating from the literary department at the end of four years, Miss Jordan decided to study law, and she entered the law department of the University, then under judge Thomas M. Cooley. So diligently did she prosecute her studies that, at the end of the first year, before she had even entered the senior class, she passed a most rigid examination in open court and was admitted to practice in all the courts of Michigan. Being ambitious that the foundation of her future work should be thoroughly assured, Miss Jordan wished to continue her studies, and with that view she applied for admission to the Law Department of Columbia College, but admission was refused because she was a woman. Not daunted by refusal, she applied to Harvard, but with like result. The authorities there were, if anything, more hostile even than those of Columbia had been. Then she opened correspondence with the authorities of Yale, but with the same discouraging reply that the constitution forbade the granting of a degree to a woman. So it did, but by perseverance against every obstacle, the door was finally opened to her, and she entered the senior class. So strange was it to see a young lady passing to and fro in those halls, dedicated only to young men, and to be reciting in the classes, that a few of the more conservative professors anticipated dire results, but in less than a fortnight the refining influence was felt in hall and class-room, much to the satisfaction of the faculty. At first a few of the young men felt that their prerogatives had been invaded and their standard lowered by admitting a young woman to equal standing with themselves, but it was not for long. That feeling soon changed to one of respect and admiration, and cordial relations existed with every member of the class. As the college year drew to a close, Miss Jordan with great credit passed the final examination. A special session of the corporation was called and, notwithstanding the opposition of the president, it was voted to grant the regular degree with full honors. The result of this decision was almost electrifying. A banquet followed, and it was thought at that time that the battle for women to enjoy equal advantages in the college had been fought and won. After leaving college, Miss Jordan continued her studies in California for two years, when she was married to George D. Blake, an attorney and former class-mate. Since her marriage she has resided in Seattle, WA.

BLAKE, Mrs. Euphenia Vale, author and critic, born in Hastings, England, 7th May, 1825. Her father, Gilbert Vale, removed to New York when she was seven years old. Mr. Vale was well known as an author, publisher, inventor, public lecturer, and a professor of astronomy and other branches of mathematics, making a specialty of navigation. Upon her marriage in 1842, Mrs. Blake went to Massachusetts to reside, her husband, Dr. D. S. Blake, being a native of that State. Almost immediately Mrs. Blake began to write for the Newburyport "Herald." She also edited a weekly literary paper, the "Saturday Evening Union," and supplied leading articles for the "Watch Tower." In 1854 she published the history of the town of Newburyport, and a scientific work on the use of ether and chloroform applied to practical dentistry. At that time she was also writing for the "North American Review" and "Christian Examiner," all the editorials for the "Bay State," a weekly published in Lynn, with occasional articles in the Boston "Transcript," Traveller" and "Atlas" One of her articles in the "Atlas" in 1853 started the movement for revising the laws of Massachusetts, and limiting the franchise to those capable of reading the Constitution of the United States. In 1857 Mrs. Blake returned to Brooklyn, NY, where she has ever since resided. She furnished a series of letters to the Boston "Traveller" and wrote essays for the "Religious Magazine." She did much book reviewing, and also wrote for the "Constellation," edited by Park Benjamin. From 1859 to 1861 she regularly supplied the "Crayon," an art magazine published in New York, with elaborate articles on literature and art. To settle a wager between two friends, one of whom bet that no one "could impose on the New York "Herald," Mrs. Blake wrote a "Great Manifesto Declaration of Independence by the States of South Carolina, Georgia, Alabama, Florida and Mississippi. Copy of the instructions sent to France!" etc. This was printed 14th November, 1860, and paid for, and it was a nine-day wonder why the other papers never had it. In 1871 Mrs. Blake furnished historical articles to the "Catholic World" on the "Milesian Race." Next followed articles for the "Christian Union," and a few short stories, and then some essays to the "Popular Science Monthly." One of her productions in the

Brooklyn "Eagle" discussed the riparian rights of Brooklyn to her own shore line. The late Chief Justice Nielson, of the city court, remarked that "the argument was unanswerable." In 1874 she published a book, "Arctic Experiences" (New York). From 1879 she wrote for the "Oriental Church Magazine." Several lectures on historical and social topics that she wrote for a literary bureau in New York have since been repeatedly delivered by a man as his own. She has also written a book on marine zoology and a series of articles on "The Marys of History, Art and Song." She occasionally writes in verse.

BLAKE, Mrs. Lillie Devereux, woman suffragist and reformer, born in Raleigh, NC, 12th August, 1835. Both her parents were descended from the Rev. Jonathan Edwards, D. D., and by other lines of descent were of highly distinguished ancestry. Lillie received every advantage of education at New Haven, CT, to which place her widowed mother had removed, taking the Yale College course from tutors at home. She grew up a beautiful and brilliant girl and was an acknowledged belle until she was married in 1855 to Frank G. Q. Umsted, a young lawyer of Philadelphia. They made their home in St. Louis, MO, and New York City until 1859, when she was left a widow with two children. She had already begun to write for the press, one of her first stories, "A Lonely House," having appeared in the "Atlantic Monthly." A novel, "Southwold," had achieved a decided success. The handsome fortune she had inherited was largely impaired, and the young widow began to work in earnest, writing stories, sketches and letters for several leading periodicals. She made her home mostly with her mother, in Stratford, CT. In 1862 she published a second novel, "Rockford," and subsequently several romances. In 1866 she was married to Grinfill Blake, a young merchant of New York. In 1869 she became actively interested in the woman suffrage movement. A woman of strong affections and marked domestic tastes, her speaking outside of New York City has been almost wholly done in the summer, when her family was naturally scattered. In 1872 she published a novel called "Fettered for Life," designed to show the many disadvantages under which women labor. In 1873 she made an application for the opening of Columbia College to young women, presenting a class of qualified girl students. The agitation then begun

Bessie Carl.
From Photo Copyrighted, 1896, by Morrison, Chicago.

Mlle. Deyo.
From Photo by Sarony, New York.

has since led to the establishment of Barnard College. In 1879 she was unanimously elected president of the New York State Woman Suffrage Association, and held that office eleven years. Her lectures, printed under the title of "Woman's Place To-day" (New York), have had a large sale. Among the reforms in which she has been actively interested has been that of securing matrons to take charge of women detained in police stations. As early as 1871 she spoke and wrote on the subject. Public sentiment was finally aroused, and in 1891 a law was passed enforcing this much-needed reform. The employment of women as census takers was first urged in 1880 by Mrs. Blake. The bills giving seats to saleswomen, ordering the presence of a woman physician in every insane asylum where women are detained, and many other beneficent measures were presented or aided by her. In 1886 Mrs. Blake was elected president of the New York City Woman Suffrage League, an office which she still holds. She has attended conventions and made speeches in most of the States and Territories, and has addressed committees of both houses of Congress and of the New York and Connecticut Legislatures. She is a graceful and logical writer, a witty and eloquent speaker and a charming hostess, her weekly receptions through the season in New York having been for many years among the attractions of literary and reform circles.

BLAKE, Mrs. Mary Elizabeth, poet, born in Dungarven, county Waterford, Ireland, 1st September, 1840. Her father's name was McGrath. In 1846 he brought his family to America, settling in Quincy, MA. Her education was acquired in the public and private schools of Boston and the Convent of the Sacred Heart, Mannhattanville, NY. In June, 1865, she was married to Dr. John G. Blake, long prominent among Massachusetts medical men. Up to the present time she has published the following works: "Poems" (Boston, 1881), "On the Wing" (Boston, 1883), a volume of letters of western travel, "Mexico," (Boston, 1888), a volume of travel, written in collaboration with Mrs. Margaret Sullivan; "A Summer Holiday" (Boston, 1890), an account of her European impressions; and "Verses Along the Way" (Boston and Dublin, 1890). Mrs. Blake has frequently contributed to the Boston "Journal." Essays and poems from her pen have appeared in the "Catholic World," "Lippincott's Magazine," the "Indepen-

dent," "St. Nicholas," and "Wide Awake." On the invitation of the Boston city government she wrote the poem read on the occasion of the Wendell Phillips Memorial Service in that city, and also the poem read on the occasion of similar honors paid to the memory of Admiral Porter.

BLANCHARD, Miss Helen Augusta, inventor, born in Portland, ME. The death of her father and the embarrassment of his estate determined her course as an inventor. She applied her powers to the intricacies of machinery, and in 1876 established the Blanchard Over-seam Company, of Philadelphia, which was the originality of what is now called zigzag sewing, both inside and outside of material sewed, and which achieved a signal success. A number of great industries have sprung from that company. Among her numerous inventions are the Blanchard over-seaming-machine, the machine for simultaneous sewing and trimming on knitted fabrics, and the crocheting and sewing machines, all of which are in use by immense manufactories and are ranked among the most remarkable mechanical contrivances of the age. For the last few years she has made her home in New York City. In all the rush and publicity that have surrounded her she has preserved those qualities of gentleness, dignity and modest which adorn character, and she has a grateful welcome in society. Aiding with open-hearted generosity the meritorious efforts of struggling women wherever she has found them, she has distinguished herself as a benefactor of her sex.

BLAVATSKY, Mme. Helene Petrovna, theosophist and author, born in Russia in 1820, and died in London, England, 8th May, 1891. Mlle. Hahn, as she then was, became the wife of General Nicole V. Blavatsky at the age of seventeen, but, the marriage proving an unhappy one, they separated after three months of married life. Mme. Blavatsky began the studies of mysticism and the languages at an early age. She spoke nearly forty European and Asiatic tongues and dialects, visited almost every part of Europe, and lived for more than forty years in India. Mme. Blavatsky endeavored several times to penetrate the mysteries of

Buddhism in India, but did not succeed till 1855, when, with the aid of an oriental disguise, she succeeded in entering a monastic house of the Buddhists, in Thibet. She afterward embraced that religion, and her book, "Isis Unveiled," which was published in 1877, is the most remarkable work of the kind in existence. In 1878 she organized the Theosophical Society in America, and the following year she returned to India to disseminate its tenets among the natives. She established a society in Egypt for the study of modern spiritualism. She became a naturalized citizen of the United States, and her third and last husband was an American, Henry S. Olcott. Many regarded her as a Russian spy in disguise. Among her esoteric works are "The Secret Doctrine," "Synthesis of Science, Religion and Philosophy," "Key to Theosophy" and "Voices of Silence."

BLOEDE, Miss Gertrude, poet, born in Dresden, Germany, 10th August, 1845. Her father and mother were among the refugees who fled from Germany in consequence of the revolution of 1848. In this country they were intimate friends of Bayard Taylor, at whose house they met Stedman, Stoddard, Aldrich and other well known American poets and authors. Miss Bloede was naturally impelled, by her surroundings and her talents, to literary effort, and in 1878 she published "Angelo." Miss Bloede used the pen-name "Stuart Sterne" in her first works, and even after that name had become widely known, very few readers were aware that its owner was a woman. Before the appearance of "Angelo," she had published a small volume of short poems, which bore no publisher's imprint. The little volume was favorably reviewed at great length in the New York "Times," and she learned, after much inquiry, that the notice was written by Richard Grant White, who was greatly impressed by the quality of the work. That was her first critical recognition, and she dedicated "Angelo," which she had already finished, to Mr. White. That eminent critic read the manuscript, and on his representations a prominent Boston house published it. Its success was instantaneous. Since its appearance, in 1878, it has passed through sixteen editions. Since that year she has published three notable volumes, "Giorgio" (Boston, 1881), a long poem, "Beyond the Shadows and Other Poems" (Boston, 1888), and "Pierod da Castiglione" (Boston, 1890), a story in verse of the time of Savonarola. In all her books she has used her pen-name," Stuart Sterne," which, she says, she adopted, as many other female writers have done, because men's work is considered stronger than women's, and she wished her work to be judged by the highest standards and to stand or fall on its own merits. She has lived in Brooklyn since 1861, making her home with her sister, the wife of Dr. S. T. King. She recently summed up her work and personality thus briefly and modestly: "There is very little to tell. I have published five volumes of poems, and that is all. I live very quietly. I go into society but little, and I do not belong to anything." Miss Bloede professes to find in the city the seclusion which pastoral poets find in rural life. She is an artist in human passions, not in mere word and scene painting. She is dramatic in instinct, and that quality illumines all her work, though none of her productions have been cast in dramatic form. Although she goes into society but little, she numbers among her friends the most prominent literary people of New York. She is not a member of any of the women's organizations in Brooklyn, as she feels that the artwork of societies from which men are excluded amounts to little. She is interested in art and music and is a lover and student of languages, speaking English, French and German with fluency, and reads Dutch, Italian and Latin with ease. Among her latest productions is a novel, "The Story of Two Lives" (New York, 1892).

BLONDNER, Mrs. Aline Reese, musician and educator, born in Georgia. She received a classical education from her father, Rev. Augustus Reese, a graduate of Oxford College. Her first musical instruction was given to her by her mother, Celeste Dewel Reese, who was educated in Troy Female Seminary, Troy, NY. Aline played at first sight, when eight years of age, with facility and skill, memorizing with rapidity and exciting the admiration of all who heard her play, when, as a tiny child, she appeared in many public exhibitions, executing on the piano compositions which required technical skill and ability. She received further musical education from Prof. George Briggs on piano, violin and guitar, and on the organ from Prof. Charles Blondner, of Philadelphia. In 1878 she took lessons from Prof. Asger Hamerik, of Baltimore. In 1879 she went to Leipsic, Germany, where she took private lessons from Herr Carl Reinecke for two years. In the summer of 1881 she went to Weimar, where Liszt received her as a pupil. Mrs. Blondner is now teaching in her own studio in Nashville, TN. She has a class in the Nashville College for Young Ladies. She is organist in the First Baptist Church and is widely known as pianist, organist and teacher.

BLOOMER, Mrs. Amelia, woman suffragist, born in Homer, Cortland county, NY, 27th May, 1818, of New England parentage. When six years of age, she removed with her parents to Seneca county in the same State, where in 1840 she was united in marriage to D. C. Bloomer, of Seneca Falls, and for fifteen years following resided in that place. In 1842 she became member of the Episcopal Church and remained a sincere and devoted communicant of that body until her death. She was first attracted to public life through the temperance reform, which began to be seriously agitated in 1840 and was continued for some years under the name of "Washingtonian." The agitation of that question soon led her to understand the political, legal and financial necessities and disabilities of woman, and, when she saw the depth of the reform needed, she was not slow to espouse the cause of freedom in its highest, broadest, justest sense. At that early day no woman's voice had yet been heard from the platform pleading the rights or wrongs of her sex. She employed her pen to say the thoughts she could not utter. She wrote for the press over various signatures, her contributions appearing in the "Water Bucket," "Temperance Star," "Free Soil Union," and other papers. On the first of January, 1849, a few months after the inauguration of the first woman's rights convention, she began the publication of the "Lily," a folio sheet devoted to temperance and the interests of woman. That journal was a novelty in the newspaper world, being the first enterprise of the kind ever owned, edited and controlled by a woman and published in the interest of women. It was received with marked favor by the press and continued a successful career of six years in Mrs. Bloomer's hands. At the end of that time, on her removal to the West, she disposed of her paper to Mary B. Birdsall, of Richmond, IN, who continued the publication for two years and then suffered it to go down. Mrs. Bloomer was indebted to Mrs. Stanton, Miss Anthony and others for contributions. In the third year of the publication of her journal her attention was called to the neat, convenient and comfortable costume afterward called by her name. She was not the originator of the style, but adopted it after seeing it worn by others, and introduced it to the public through her paper. The press handed the matter about and commented on this new departure from fashion's sway, until the whole country was excited over it, and Mrs. Bloomer was overwhelmed with letters of inquiry from women concerning the dress. All felt the need of some reform that should lift the burden of clothes from their wearied bodies. Though many adopted the style for a time, yet under the rod of tyrant fashion and the ridicule of the press they soon laid it aside. Mrs. Bloomer herself finally abandoned it, after wearing it six or eight years, and long after those who preceded her in its use had doffed the costume they loved and returned to long skirts. In 1852 Mrs. Bloomer made her début on the platform as a lecturer, and in the winter of that year, in company with Susan B. Anthony and Rev. Antoinette L. Brown, she visited and lectured in all the principal cities and towns of her native State, from New York to Buffalo. At the outset her subject, like that of her co-workers, was temperance, but temperance strongly spiced with the wrongs and rights of woman. In 1849 Mr. Bloomer was appointed postmaster of Seneca Falls. On the reception of the office he at once appointed Mrs. Bloomer his deputy. She soon made herself thoroughly acquainted with the details of the office and discharged its duties for the four years of the Taylor and Filmore administration. In the winter of 1853 she was chairman of a committee appointed to go before the legislature of New York with petitions for a prohibitory liquor law. She continued her work in her native State, writing and lecturing on both temperance and woman's rights, and attending to the duties of her house and office until the winter of 1853–54, when she removed with her husband to Mt. Vernon, OH. There she continued the publication of the "Lily," and was also associate editor of the "Western Home Visitor," a large literary weekly paper published in that place. In the columns of the "Visitor," as in all her writings, some phase of the woman question was the subject of her pen. About that time, and in the fall of 1853, she visited and lectured in all the principal cities and towns of the North and West, going often where no lecturer on woman's enfranchisement had preceded her. She everywhere received a kindly welcome and very flattering notices from the press. In January, 1854, she was one of a committee to memorialize the legislature of Ohio on a prohibitory liquor law. The rules were suspended and the committee received with marked respect and favor, and the same evening the legislature, almost in a body, attended a lecture given by her on woman's right of suffrage. In the spring of 1855 Mr. and Mrs. Bloomer removed to Council Bluffs, IA, making it their permanent home. Owing to weariness of her charge, and also the want of any facilities for printing and carrying so large a mail as her four-thousand papers from that new land, at so early a day, Mrs. Bloomer disposed of the "Lily" before leaving Ohio, and intended henceforth to rest from her public labors. But that was not permitted to her. Calls for lectures were frequent, and to these she responded as far as possible, but was obliged, to refuse to go long distances on account of there being at that day no public conveyance except the old stage coach. In the winter of 1856 Mrs. Bloomer, by invitation, addressed the legislature of Nebraska on the subject of woman's right to the ballot. The Territorial house of representatives shortly afterward passed a bill giving women the right to vote, and in the council it passed to a second reading, but was finally lost for want of time. The limited session was drawing to a close, and the last hour expired before the bill could come up for final action. Mrs. Bloomer took part in organizing the Iowa State Suffrage Association and was at one time its president. Poor health eventually compelled her to retire from active work in the cause. She died 30th December, 1894.

BLYE, Miss Birdie, pianist, born in New York City, in 187–. Her parents are Americans of English descent. Miss Blye early manifested a love of music. Her talent was developed under able masters in London, Paris and Germany. When eleven years of age she made her début in orchestral concerts in London and on the Continent, with success. She played from memory concertos, sonatas and other compositions by Mendelssohn, Beethoven, Schumann, Rubinstein, Liszt, Schubert and Chopin, and could play the whole clavichord without notes and transpose in every key. She received many certificates and medals, and was fêted and admired as the little "wonder child." Within the past three years she has played in more than two-hundred concerts and musicales in chief American, English and European cities with gratifying success. She is an excellent violinist, a pupil of the Joachim School of Berlin. Miss Blye is highly educated, is a linguist of note, and paints like an artist in oil and water colors. She studied in the Grosvenor Art Gallery in London. Her first exibited picture, painted when she was fourteen years of age, was sold for seventy-five dollars.

BODLEY, Miss Rachel L., scientist and doctor of medicine, was born in Cincinnati, OH, 7th December, 1831. Her parents were Anthony R. and Rebecca W. Talbot Bodley, who settled in Cincinnati in 1817. Her paternal ancestry was Scotch-Irish. The American head of the family, Thomas Bodley, came from the north of Ireland early in the eighteenth century. His wife was Eliza Knox, of Edinburgh, Scotland. Her maternal ancestry runs back to John Talbot, an English Friend, who settled in Virginia. Rachel was the oldest daughter and the third child in a family of five. Her mother taught a private school, in which Rachel studied until she was twelve years old. She entered the Wesleyan Female College in Cincinnati in 1844, only two years after the opening of that institution, which was the first chartered college for women in the world. She was graduated in 1849, and in 1860 she was made preceptress in the higher collegiate studies. Dissatisfied with her own attainments, she went to Philadelphia, PA, and entered the Polytechnic College as a special student in physics and chemistry. After two years of study she returned to Cincinnati and was made professor of natural sciences in the Cincinnati Female Seminary, which chair she filled for three years. While there she distinguished herself by classifying the extensive collection of specimens in natural history bequeathed to the seminary by Joseph Clark. Her work on that collection is crystallized in a catalogue that was recognized by Asa Gray, the eminent botanist, as a valuable contribution to science. In 1867 and 1868 she gave a series of important lectures on cryptogamous plants of land and sea. In 1865 she was elected to the chair of chemistry and toxicology in the Woman's Medical College of Pennsylvania, being the first woman professor of chemistry on record. In 1874 she was elected dean of the faculty, and she held both of those positions until her death. She was called to the deanship while the college building was being erected. Among her many achievements was the collection of facts in reference to the success of the graduates of the Woman's Medical College of Pennsylvania in their professional work. That work was entitled "The College Story." The graduates were at that time practicing in Utah, Manitoba, India, China and European lands, and in every state in the Union. Their replies to the questions she sent them showed an unbroken line of success. Dr. Bodley received many honors in recognition of her contributions to science and literature. In 1864 she was made corresponding member of the State Historical Society of Wisconsin. In 1871 she was elected a member of the Academy of Natural Sciences of Philadelphia, and in that year the degree of A. M. was conferred upon her by her alma mater in Cincinnati. That college, up to that time, had never given a degree to any of its alumnae subsequent to the degree of A. B. at graduation. Dr. Bodley was one of the first three to receive that honor. In 1873 she was elected a corresponding member of the Cincinnati Society of Natural History. In 1876 she was elected a corresponding member of the New York Academy of Sciences and a member of the American Chemical Society of New York. She was elected first vice-president of the meeting called in 1874 to celebrate the centennial of chemistry, the month of August in that year being the date chosen in honor of the discovery of oxygen by Dr. Joseph Priestly in 1774. At Dr. Bodley's suggestion the meeting was held in Northumberland, where Dr. Priestly is buried. In 1879 the Woman's Medical College of Pennsylvania con-

ferred upon her the honorary degree of MD. In 1880 she was made a member of the Franklin Institute of Philadelphia, and she delivered a course of lectures on "Household Chemistry" in the regular course of the Institute. In 1882 she was chosen a member of the Educational Society of Philadelphia, and in the same year was elected school director of the twenty-ninth school section, in which office she served until 1885. She was again elected to that position, and served until she died, 15th June, 1888.

BOHAN, Mrs. Elizabeth Baker, author and artist, born in Birmingham, England, 18th August, 1849. She is the daughter of Joseph and Martha Baker. They came to America in 1854 and have lived most of the time in Wisconsin. She received her education in the Milwaukee public schools and was for a time a teacher. She was married to M. Bohan, then editor of the Fond du Lac "journal," in 1872. They now reside in Milwaukee, WI, have a pleasant home and are surrounded by four bright children. Mrs. Bohan is the fortunate possessor of a combination of talents. She is a devoted and successful homekeeper, wife and mother. She is a painter of acknowledged ability and of far more than local celebrity. She is something of a musician, and there are many in Milwaukee and other portions of the State who take high rank as painters and musicians who received their first and only instruction from her. From her earliest youth she has practiced composition. As she grew to womanhood the taste for writing increased. She wrote great numbers of poems and a still greater number of prose sketches, but offered none for publication until within the last five or six years. Since then large numbers of her poems and sketches have been published in the best papers and magazines throughout the country. She is a close student, seven days in a week, and stores away everything she learns where it can be drawn upon on the instant. While she has done much literary work the past five or six years, it has always been a secondary consideration. Her daily duties have been as numerous and exacting as those of almost any mother, wife and home keeper, and everything that she has done in a literary way has been accomplished in odd moments, and sometimes when duty to herself required that she be sleeping instead of thinking and writing.

BOLTON, Mrs. Sarah Knowles, author, born in Farmington, CT, 15th September, 1841. She is a daughter of John Segar Knowles, descended from Henry Knowles, who moved to Portsmouth, RI, from London, England, in 1635. Her grandmother, Mary Carpenter, was descended from Elizabeth Jenckes, sister of Joseph Jenckes, Governor of Rhode Island. Mrs. Bolton comes on her mother's side from Nathaniel Stanley, of Hartford, CT, Lieutenant Colonel of First Regiment in 1739; Assistant Treasurer, 1725–49; Treasurer, 1749–55, and from Colonel William Pynchon, one of the twenty-six incorporators of Massachusetts Bay Colony, and the founder of Springfield, MA. At the age of seventeen she became a member of the family of her uncle, Colonel H. L. Miller, a lawyer of Hartford, whose extensive library was a delight, and whose house was a center for those who loved scholarship and refinement. The aunt was a person of wide reading, exquisite taste and social prominence. There the young girl met Harriet Beecher Stowe, Lydia H. Sigourney, and others like them, whose lives to her were a constant inspiration. She became an excellent scholar and graduated from the seminary founded by Catherine Beecher. Her first published poem appeared in the "Waverly Magazine," when she was fifteen years old. Soon after her graduation she published a small volume, "Orlean Lamar and Other Poems" (New York, 1863), and a serial was accepted by a New England paper. Later she was married to Charles E. Bolton, a graduate of Amherst College, an able and cultivated man, and they removed to Cleveland, OH. She became the first secretary of the Woman's Christian Association of that city, using much of her time in visiting the poor. When, in 1874, the temperance crusade began in Hillsborough, OH, she was one of the first to take up the work and aid it with voice and pen. She was soon appointed assistant corresponding secretary of the National Woman's Christian Temperance Union, and as such, says Miss Willard, "She kept articles,

paragraphs and enlightening excerpts before the public, which did more toward setting our new methods before the people than any single agency had ever compassed up to that time." At the request of the temperance women of the country, Mrs. Bolton prepared a history of the crusade for the Centennial temperance volume, and of the Cleveland work for Mrs. Wittenmyer's general history. At that time she published her temperance story entitled "The Present Problem" (New York, 1874). Invited to Boston to become one of the editors of the "Congregationalist," a most useful and responsible position, she proved herself an able journalist. She passed two years abroad, partly in travel and partly in study, that being her second visit to Europe. She made a special study of woman's higher education in the universities of Cambridge, Oxford, and elsewhere, preparing for magazines several articles on that subject, as well as on woman's philanthropic and intellectual work, and on what was being done for the mental and moral help of laboring people by their employers, reading a paper on that subject at a meeting of the American Social Science Association held in Saratoga in 1883. Mrs. Bolton's additional published works are "How Success is Won" (Boston, 1884); "Lives of Poor Boys who Became Famous" (New York, 1885); "Girls who Became Famous" (New York, 1886); "Stories from Life" (New York, 1886); "Social Studies in England" (Boston, 1886); "From Heart and Nature, Poems" (New York, 1887); "Famous American Authors" (New York, 1887); "Famous American Statesmen" (New York, 1888); "Some Successful Women" (Boston, 1888); "Famous Men of Science" (New York, 1889); "Famous European Artists" (New York, 1890); "English Authors of the Nineteenth Century" (New York, 1890); English Statesmen of Queen Victoria's Reign" (New York, 1891); "Famous Types of Womanhood" (New York, 1892). Several of these books have been reprinted in England. Mrs. Bolton's home is an ideal one for the lover of art and literature. Her husband is a man of wide travel and reading, and has given thirteen-hundred lectures during the past nine seasons. They have but one child, a son, Charles Knowles Bolton, graduated from Harvard College in 1890, and an assistant now in the Harvard University Library.

BOLTON, Mrs. Sarah T, poet, born in Newport, KY, 18th December, 1812. Her maiden name was

Barritt. When she was only three years old, her parents removed to Jennings county, IN. Thence they removed to Madison, where Sarah grew to womanhood. She was educated in North Madison. She became a thorough English scholar, and at subsequent periods of her life acquired a knowledge of German and French. When fourteen years of age, she wrote verses. When not more than sixteen years old, several of her poems were published in a Madison paper. The editor was Nathaniel P. Bolton, and her literary ventures led to an acquaintance with him which resulted in marriage. The early years of her married life were passed on a farm west of Indianapolis. Her time and energies were chiefly devoted to home cares, having been blessed with a son and daughter. In the year 1850 William D. Gallagher, William C. Larrabee and Robert Dale Owen each wrote a biographical notice of her, highly commendatory of her personal and intellectual charms. Mr. Bolton was appointed consul to Switzerland in 1855 by President Pierce. He was accompanied to Europe by his wife and children, the latter of whom spent considerable time in Germany, Italy and France. From all these countries Mrs. Bolton wrote poems, besides sending many valuable prose contributions to the "Home Journal" and Cincinnati "Commercial." Hitherto she had known no trouble but that caused by vicissitude of fortune and the hard cares of life, and in November, 1858, her first great sorrow came in the death of her husband. Mrs. Bolton's life was one full of effort. During the Civil War she wrote many stirring songs, among them "The Union Forever" and "Ralph Farnham's Dream." It is interesting to trace Mrs. Bolton's patriotic blood to its Revolutionary source. Her father was the youngest son of Col. Lemuel Barritt, who distinguished himself as an officer in the war of Independence. Her mother was a Pendleton of Virginia and closely related to James Madison. Mrs. Bolton spent several years of her life abroad, her closing years near Indianapolis. She published "The Life and Poems of Sarah T. Bolton" (Indianapolis, 1880). Her last volume, "The Songs of a Lifetime," was edited by Professor Ridpath, of De Pauw University, with a preface by General Lew Wallace. Mrs. Bolton died in Indianapolis, 4th August, 1893.

BONAPARTE, Mme. Elizabeth Patterson, wife of Jerome Bonaparte, king of Westphalia, born in Baltimore, MD, 6th February, 1785, and died there 4th April, 1879. She was the daughter of William Patterson, the son of a farmer in county Donegal, Ireland. Her father came to the United States while he was a boy and settled in Baltimore. He went to Philadelphia, PA, and was there employed in the counting-house of Samuel Johnson. He developed remarkable financial ability and soon became the owner of a line of clipper ships. During the Revolution he traded to France and brought back cargoes of arms and gunpowder. He acquired a large fortune and was the wealthiest man in Maryland, with the exception of Charles Carroll, of Carrollton. Elizabeth Patterson was a young woman of remarkable beauty of person, of strong powers of intellect, and of great fascination of manners, when, in the autumn of 1803, at a ball in the house of Samuel Chase, in Baltimore, she met Jerome Bonaparte, then in command of a French frigate. As the brother of Napoleon I, he was hospitably received. On their first meeting Captain Bonaparte and Miss Patterson fell in love. Marriage was proposed, but her father, foreseeing the grave difficulties implied in such an alliance with the brother of the First Consul, forbade the lovers to meet. Miss Patterson was sent to Virginia. The lovers corresponded, and Jerome procured a marriage license. The wedding was postponed until 24th December, 1803, when Jerome should have passed his nineteenth birthday. On that date the marriage ceremony was performed by Archbishop Carroll. All the legal formalities had been carefully provided for. The contract was drawn by Alexander Dallas, and the wedding was attended by the mayor of Baltimore, the vice-consul of France and many distinguished persons. Napoleon I obstinately opposed the match from first to last. He notified Jerome that, if he would leave "the young person" in the United States and return to France, his "indiscretion" would be forgiven, and that, if he took her with him to France, she should not be permitted to set foot on French territory. He actually gave orders that neither Jerome nor his wife should be permitted to land at any port controlled by France. In spite of that order, Jerome and his wife sailed in 1805, on one of Mr. Patterson's ships, for Europe.

The ship was wrecked between Philadelphia and the Capes. Embarking on another vessel, they sailed for Lisbon. There the wife remained, while Captain Bonaparte went on to Paris, hoping to make peace with his brother. Napoleon I was obstinate and absolutely refused to recognize the marriage. Madame Bonaparte sailed from Lisbon for Amsterdam, but at the mouth of the Texel two French men-of-war met her, and refused to allow her to land. She then sailed for England. So great a throng of persons gathered to see her land at Dover, that Pitt sent a regiment to that port to preserve order. She went at once to Camberwell, where her only child, Jerome Napoleon Bonaparte, was born 7th July, 1805. Her husband continued to send her messages of love and fidelity. Napoleon asked Pope Pius VII to dissolve the marriage, but the pontiff refused to do so. The Imperial Council of State, at Napoleon's order, passed a decree of divorce. In September, 1805, Madame Bonaparte returned to the United States. Her family gave her an ungracious reception. Her father refused to pay the stipulated income, because Napoleon had annulled the union. Jerome soon afterward was married to Princess Frederica, of Würtemburg. He offered his discarded wife the principality of Smalcand, with an annual income of $40,000. Her reply was: "Westphalia, no doubt, is a considerable kingdom, but not large enough to hold two queens." The reply pleased Napoleon, who directed the French Minister in Washington to intimate his desire to serve her. She replied: "Tell the Emperor I am ambitious; I wish to be made a duchess of France." The Emperor promised to confer that rank upon her, and offered immediately a gross sum of $20,000, with a life annuity of $12,000. That she accepted, "proud to be indebted to the greatest man of modern times." She stipulated that the receipts for payment should be signed by her as "Elizabeth Bonaparte." To that the Emperor acceded, and until his dethronement the annuity was regularly paid. Her husband was angry because she refused aid from him and accepted it from his brother, but she retorted that she "preferred shelter beneath the wing of an eagle to suspension from the pinion of a goose." The submission of Jerome to the commands of his brother was rewarded. He received a high command in the Navy of France and showed himself a competent officer. In 1806 he was made a brigadier-general in the army, and in 1807 was created King of Westphalia. Mme. Bonaparte applied to the Maryland Legislature for a divorce, which was granted without difficulty. Her motive for taking this step is not easily comprehended. The Pope had refused to annul a marriage which had received the open sanction of the Church. The social position of Mme. Bonaparte had never been in the least compromised by her domestic misfortunes. After the fall of Napoleon Madame Bonaparte visited France, where she was honorably received. Only once after the separation did she ever see Jerome. In the gallery of the Pitti Palace, in Florence, they met. She simply said: "It is Jerome." He whispered to his wife: "That lady is my former wife." Madame Bonaparte was well received in Florence and in Rome. Returning to the United States, she made her home in Baltimore. She lived economically and amassed a fortune. Her son, Jerome Bonaparte, was graduated from Harvard College in 1826. He studied law, but never practiced. He was married in early life to Susan Mary Williams, a wealthy lady of Roxbury, MA. He visited France and was on intimate terms with his father. He was never naturalized, and always called himself a citizen of France, although the French courts never recognized his legitimacy. He died in Baltimore 17th June, 1870. His two sons, Jerome Napoleon and Charles Joseph, survived him. Madame Bonaparte's later years were passed in quiet. Her proud spirit, her ambitious temper and her misfortunes alienated her from her father and her son, and her wit took a biting turn with old age. She put forward the claims of her grandson to the throne of France, but without hope of success. She left an estate valued at $1,500,000.

BOND, Mrs. Elizabeth Powell, Dean of Swarthmore College, Swarthmore, PA, born in Clinton, NY, 25th January. 1841. Her parents, Townsend and Catherine Macy Powell, belonged to the Society of Friends. The mother was a descendant of the "Goodman Macey" of whom Whittier writes in his poem "The Exiles," and who was, on account of his religious tolerance, driven in 1660 from his home on the mainland to the Island of Nantucket, where, ever since, Macy has been one of the leading and most honorable names. In 1845 Mr. and Mrs. Powell removed to

Ghent, NY, and there on her parents' farm Elizabeth's childhood and youth were spent. A gentle, thoughtful child, endowed with perfect health and "a spirit equable, poised and free," labeled, as she expresses it, a "teacher" almost from her birth, she began early to exercise her powers. At fifteen she was for one winter assistant teacher in a Friends' school in Dutchess county. Graduating at seventeen from the State Normal School, Albany, NY, she taught for two years in public schools in Mamaroneck and Ghent, NY, and afterward for three years carried on a home school in the house of her parents. Among her boarding pupils were colored and Catholic children. As a young girl she developed the spirit of a reformer and began active work in behalf of temperance, personally pleading with intemperate men, whose families she saw suffering, and instituting in the bar-room of the village tavern a series of readings and talks, hoping so to turn its frequenters away from their cups. At that time she was, with her older brother, Aaron K. Powell, identified with the Abolitionists. The anti-slavery leaders, Garrison, Phillips and Pillsbury, were her personal friends. With them she attended and occasionally spoke in anti-slavery and woman suffrage conventions. Public speaking has, however, generally been auxiliary to her other work, that of teaching. In the summer of 1863 she attended Dr. Lewis' normal class in gymnastics, in Boston, and was the valedictorian of the class at its graduating exhibition in Tremont Temple. The two following winters she conducted classes in gymnastics in Cambridge, Boston and Concord, MA. In 1865, soon after its opening, she was appointed teacher of gymnastics in Vassar College, and continued in that position for five years. After a few months of rest at home Miss Powell was invited to Florence, MA, as superintendent of the Free Congregational Sunday-school and as occasional speaker to the society, whose work was conducted by Charles C. Burleigh. After a year's work in that field Miss Powell was married to Henry H. Bond, a lawyer of Northampton, and resigned most of her public duties, though for a time editing, with her husband, the Northampton "Journal," and acting as one of the working trustees of the Florence kindergarten from its founding. Two sons were born to Mr. and Mrs. Bond, one of whom died in infancy. The years 1879–80 were spent in traveling and residence in the South, in search of health for her husband. After his death, in 1881,

Mrs. Bond returned to Florence and devoted herself to the education of her son, gathering about her a class of children, whom she taught with him. In 1885 she resumed her relations with the Free Congregational Society, becoming its resident minister, preparing written discourses for its Sunday meetings, and performing the social duties of a pastor. At the expiration of a year's service Mrs. Bond tendered her resignation to the society and took the position of matron in Swarthmore College. The title matron was, in 1891, changed to the more appropriate one of dean. That co-educational college, founded by and under the management of Friends, offered a field which Mrs. Bond's principles, experience and gifts eminently fitted her to occupy. Her office is that of director of the social life of the college and special adviser to the young women. The religious meetings of the college are conducted according to the order of Friends. Mrs. Bond's published writings are few. Several tracts on the subject of social purity, occasional addresses at educational meetings, and her messages to the Swarthmore students, which have appeared in the "Friends' Intelligencer," comprise the list.

BONES, Mrs. Marietta M., woman suffragist and social reformer, born upon a farm in Clarion county, PA, 4th May, 1842. Her father, James A. Wilkins, was born in Clarion county, where he resided for forty-eight years, when he removed to Iowa, and died six months later. Mr. Wilkins was a noted Abolitionist, known to have maintained an "underground railroad station." The mother's (Jane Trumbull) family, the Trumbulls, were orginally from Connecticut, and were descendants of Jonathan Trumbull, better known by Washington's pet name, "Brother Jonathan." Her education was received in the Huidekooper Seminary, Meadville, PA, and in the Washington, PA, female seminary. Mrs. Bones was elected vice-president of the National Woman Suffrage Association for Dakota Territory, in 1881, and was annually re-elected for nine years. She made her début as a public speaker in an oration at a Fourth of July celebration in Webster, Dakota, in 1882. In September, 1883, she addressed Dakota's

State Constitutional Convention on behalf of woman's enfranchisement. Failing to have her claim for woman's equality before the law recognized in the State Constitution there framed, she earnestly petitioned both houses of Congress to deny Dakota's admission to the Union as a State. Then she carried on several lively newspaper controversies against efforts to make the social question of temperance a political question. She is an active temperance worker and was secretary of the first Non-partisan National Woman's Christian Temperance Union convention in Chicago, in 1889, for which the local Woman's Temperance Union in Webster, over which she had presided the previous year, discharged her, returning her dues, paid nearly three months before, with an official notice "That the ladies of Webster union moved and carried that Mrs. Bones' dues be returned on account of her having joined the secession movement, and also on account of her antagonism to our State president." As a pioneer settler in her town, she secured for it a donation of a block of lots for a courthouse and county buildings, and through her influence Day county was divided and a part added thereto, in order that the county-seat should be centrally located. So interested was she that their State capital should be situated at the geographical center, that the board of trade in the city of Pierre invited her to be the guest of their city. Through her intercession three infirm veterans of the war have been sent, at the expense of her county, to the Soldiers' Home in Hot Springs, SD. Mrs. Bones was an able assistant of Mrs. Matilda Joslyn Gage in organizing the Woman's National Liberal Union. She addressed the convention in Washington, DC, and is one of the executive council of that organization. The energy of Mrs. Bones knows no bounds when work is needed, and her perfect health helps her willing hand.

BONHAM, Mrs. Mildred A., traveler and journalist, born in Magnolia, IL, in August, 1840. She is of southern blood from Virginia, South Carolina and Tennessee ancestry. Her parents removed to Oregon in 1847, settling in the Willamette valley. In 1858 she became the wife of judge B. F. Bonham, of Salem, OR. In 1885 Judge Bonham was appointed Consul-General to British India, and removed his family to Calcutta the same year. Mrs. Bonham had always a liking for literary work, but the cares of a large family and social duties gave her scant leisure, and it was not until her residence abroad the opportunity came. During five years her letters over the name "Mizpah" attracted much attention and were widely copied by the Oregon and California press. Mrs. Bonham has a gift of observing closely, and her descriptions of foreign scenes make a valuable addition to our knowledge of Anglo Indian life and customs. Her letters from the Himalayas, the island of Ceylon and other notable places are the best. Her deepest sympathy was aroused by the miserable condition and soul-starvation of the women of India, and she set about relieving, so far as lay in her power, their cheerless lot. By her personal appeal a Hindoo girl was educated by a number of young ladies of Salem. The child became a home missionary. Through Mrs. Bonham's further efforts a fund of one-thousand dollars was raised to found a perpetual scholarship. Since her return to the United States she has given several lectures on her experiences in the far East, life among the Zenanas, and kindred subjects.

BOOTH, Mrs. Agnes, actor, born of English parents, in Sydney, Australia, 4th October, 1843. Her dramatic tastes and talents were not inherited. She made her début in 1857 in Sydney as a dancer, with her sister Belle, and next she joined a minstrel company. In 1858 she went to San Francisco, CA, where, in 1861, she was married to Harry A. Perry, who died in 1862. After playing leading parts in the company of Mrs. John Wood, she joined Tom McGuire's company, in which she played various parts on a rough tour through the mountains. In 1867 she was married to J. B. Booth, Jr., who died in 1883. She is now the wife of Manager John B. Schoeffel, and she retains her stage name, Agnes Booth. In California she worked hard and studied thoroughly, and her progress on the stage was rapid. She went to New York in 1865, making her debut in the old Winter

Garden with John S. Clarke, the comedian. She next supported Edwin Forrest in Niblo's Garden. She became absolute mistress of all the "business" of the stage, and her dash, spirit, vivacity and fine appearance combined to place her in the front rank of actors. After the Forrest engagement she played with Miss Bateman in "Leah." She made a success in Washington, Chicago and Boston. In Boston she joined the stock company of the Boston Theater, where she remained for five years. After her marriage to Junius Brutus Booth, she played in Edwin Booth's theater in New York, and later in Niblo's Garden, the Union Square Theater and elsewhere. Notwithstanding her signal success as an actor, Mrs. Booth asserts that she does not like the stage. Her ambition is to own a theater and to be the guide of a stock company. Her home is now in New York City, and she possesses on the New England coast, in Manchester-by-the-sea, a beautiful summer home, where she entertains with most lavish and charming hospitality.

BOOTH, Mrs. Emma Scarr, author, born in Hull, England, 25th April, 1835. When she was nine years old her parents emigrated with their little family of three children to America. The father purchased a farm near Cleveland, OH. At the age of twenty-two years Miss Scarr was married to a young Englishman residing in Twinsburgh, OH, and soon began to contribute to some of the periodicals of the day. Her only brother, a soldier in the Union army, died soon after the battle of Shiloh, and her only sister a few months later. Early in April, 1865, while the family were on a visit to her parents, some twenty miles distant, a friend came post-haste on horseback from Twinsburgh to inform them that their house, together with all its contents, had been reduced to ashes during the night. It had been burned by secret enemies, and not an article was saved. Then came the news of the President's murder. Nine weeks later her husband's mills with their entire contents were fired and totally destroyed. This misfortune reduced the formerly well-to-do pair to comparative poverty, and soon afterward they removed to Painesville, OH. There the wife obtained some needlework, while the husband went to the oil regions near Titusville, PA, where, under the influence of lawless associates, he forgot his duties as a husband, and the result was a final separation a few years later. Meanwhile

Emma had removed to Cleveland, OH, and there supported herself by teaching music. After the father's death, in 1872, Emma took up her abode with her mother, in Cleveland, still continuing to give music lessons. In 1873 she was married again. Her second husband was an American. Her home since that time has been in Cleveland. Mrs. Booth has published three volumes in book form, "Karan Kringle's Journal" (Philadelphia, 1885), "A Willful Heiress" (Buffalo, 1892), and "Poems" (Buffalo, 1892). She has composed songs and instrumental pieces, which have been published.

BOOTH, Miss Mary Louise, author, translator and editor, born in Millville, now Yaphank, NY, 19th April, 1831. She was only a girl when her first contributions were published. Her father was a teacher, and in 1845 and 1846 she taught in his school in Williamsburgh, NY. She then turned to literature. She wrote many stories and sketches for newspapers and magazines, and translated several books from the French. For "Emerson's Magazine" she wrote a number of stories. The first edition of her "History of the City of New York" appeared in 1859. It is a work evidencing much study and research. She next assisted in making a translation of the French classics, and she translated About's "Germaine" (Boston, 1860). During the Civil War she translated the writings of eminent Frenchmen who favored the cause of the Union, including Gasparin's "Uprising of a Great People" and "America before Europe," Edouard Laboulaye's "Paris in America," and Augustin Cochin's "Results of Emancipation" and "Results of Slavery." Her work in that field won the commendation of President Lincoln, Senator Sumner and other statesmen. Among others of her translations at that time were the Countess de Gasparin's "Vesper," "Camille" and "Human Sorrows," Count de Gasparin's "Happiness" and Henri Martin's "History of France." In 1864 she published two volumes treating of "The Age of Louis XIV." In 1866 she published two others, the last two of the seventeen volumes, under the title of "The Decline of the French Monarchy." In 1880 she published the translation of Martin's abridged "History of France." Her later translations from the French include Laboulaye's "Fairy Book" and Mace's "Fairy Tales." In 1880 a second revision of her previously enlarged "History of the City of New York" brought that valuable work down to date. Miss Booth was the editor of "Harper's Bazar" from its establishment, in 1867, until the time of her death, 4th March, 1889.

BOTTA, Mrs. Anne Charlotte Lynch, author, born in Bennington, VT, in 1820, died in New York City, 23rd March, 1891. While still a girl she published a number of literary productions. She removed first to Providence, RI, and then to New York City, where she made her hone until her death. In 1855 she was married to Vincenzo Botta, professor of Italian language and literature in the University of the City of New York. For years their home was a literary and artistic center and they entertained many of the famous authors, painters and musicians of Europe and America. In 1870 and 1871, when funds for the suffering women and children of Paris were collected in New York, Mrs. Botta raised $5,000 by the sale of an album of photographs, autographs and sketches by famous artists. The Franco-Prussian war closing before the collection was complete, the money was used to found a prize in the French Academy for the best essay on "The Condition of Women," to be awarded every fifth year, when the interest on the fund should reach $1,000. She excelled as a writer of sonnets. Her literary productions include a great number of stories, essays, poems and criticisms. In 1848 she published her first volume of poems, and in 1884 she brought out a new edition, illustrated by eminent artists. In 1845 she published "Leaves from the Diary of a Recluse" in "The Gift." Her "Handhook of Universal Literature" (New York, 1860) has run through several editions and has been adopted as a text-book in many educational institutions.

BOUGHTON, Mrs. Caroline Greenbank, educator and philanthropist, born in Philadelphia, PA, 9th August, 1854. Graduating from the Philadelphia Normal School in 1874, the same year she began her career as a teacher in Miss Steven's Seminary, Germantown. In 1878 she took charge of the department of history in the Philadelphia Normal School, which position she filled for four years, when she was married to J. W. Boughton, a prominent manufacturer and inventor of Philadelphia. Mrs. Boughton was early chosen a manager of the Woman's National Indian Association, a position she filled during five years, and for three years has been auditor of the association. She was an active member of the Woman's Christian Temperance Union until failing health obliged her to curb her energies in that direction. Mrs. Boughton is a member of the New Century Club of Philadelphia, and also of the Woman's Suffrage Association.

BOURNE, Mrs. Emma, religious and temperance worker, born in Newark, NJ, 5th September, 1846. Her mother was known among temperance workers as "Mother Hill," and was a woman of great strength of character After receiving her diploma from the Newark Wesleyan Institute, Emma spent eight years as a successful teacher in the Newark schools. After her marriage she went abroad with her husband three times, spending several years beyond the Atlantic. During the last seventeen years she has resided in her native city, actively engaged in church and temperance work. For ten years she served as State recording secretary of the Woman's Christian Temperance Union and was then elected its president. For many years she was superintendent of the infant department of her church Sunday-school. Left to bear the burden and responsibility of training and caring for her four children when they were very young, she is realizing a rich reward for her faithfulness as a mother. In her public duties she is gentle, firm and full of tact. With her "The Golden Age is not behind, but before us." In her public addresses she makes no attempt at oratory, but says what is in her heart to say in an unassuming, convincing manner.

BOUTON, Miss Emily St. John, journalist, born in New Canaan, Fairfield county, CT. On her father's side she traces her ancestry to one of the partisans of William the Conqueror, who was knighted for saving the king when in danger. The family bore a prominent part in the Revolution among the Connecticut patriots. Her father moved to the West when she was yet a child. She was graduated in the public schools of Sandusky, OH, but had previously taught a primary school in that city when only fourteen years of age. After graduating, she became assistant high-school teacher in Milan, OH, then in Tiffin, and then, for several years she filled the same position in the Toledo high school. She occupied the chair of English literature in the Chicago central high school for two years, but relinquished her work on account of failing health, going to California for rest and recuperation. In 1877 she returned to Toledo and became a member of the editorial staff of the Toledo "Blade," a position she has so well filled ever since. To many American households she is endeared as the "household editor" of the paper, but the work, original and editorial, of that one department of that journal by no means measures the extent of her labors. She is a literary critic of no mean order, and is a good "all round" newspaper worker. She has done much regular editorial writing in political campaigns in the columns of the paper with which she is connected. Her leaders on political topics are marked by direct and close reasoning, her diction is clear, and her logic is convincing. Of late years she has not been called on so frequently to do that kind of writing, leaving her time free for the, to her, more congenial fields of purely literary work and the management of her own department of the paper. Her special field is in work for women. She is a believer in equal rights for her sex, and her labors are directed to the advancement of woman's sphere through the personal advancement of every individual of the sex. Her literary style is so clear and pleasing that it seems to convey an idea of her personality to her readers. She has written several successful books on topics pertaining to the home circle. Besides her work upon the Toledo "Blade," she has written stories, letters and essays for other papers and magazines. Miss Bouton has a pleasant home in the beautiful residence portion of the city of Toledo, the family circle consisting of her mother, her widowed sister and two nephews. There is dispensed a refined hospitality, and there Miss Bouton, surrounded by her books, in the prime of her days, and with an almost unlimited capacity for work, leads a busy life, devoted to what she believes to be the interests of humanity.

BOWERS, Mrs. D. P., actor, born in Stamford, CT, 12th March, 1830. Her maiden name was Elizabeth Crocker McCollom. Her father was an Episcopal clergyman, who died while she was an infant. She was from early childhood fond of dramatic presentations. In 1846 she made her début in the Park Theater, in New York City, in the rôle of Amanthis. On 4th March, 1847, when only seventeen years old, she was married to David P. Bowers, an actor in the same company. They went to Philadelphia in the same month, and in the Walnut Street Theater she appeared as Donna Victoria in "A Bold Stroke for a Husband." She was successful from the beginning. She next filled a successful engagement in the Arch Street Theater, in Philadelphia, where she remained until the death of her husband, in June, 1857. In December, 1857, she leased the Walnut Street Theater, which she managed successfully until 1859. She then leased the Philadelphia Academy of Music for a season. In 1860 she was married to Dr. Brown, of Baltimore, MD, who died in 1867. Mrs. Bowers retained the name under which she had won her reputation. In 1861 she went to London, England, where she played Julia in "The Hunchback," in Sadler's Wells Theater. She was successful with the London public and played an engagement in the Lyceum Theater, appearing as Geraldine d'Arcy in "Woman." In 1863 she returned to the United States and played an engagement in the Winter Garden, in New York. She soon afterward retired from the stage and lived quietly in a suburb of Philadelphia, until October, 1886, when she organized a strong company and made a successful tour of the United States. Her death occurred in Washington City, 6th November, 1895.

BOWLES, Mrs. Ada Chastina, Universalist minister, born in Gloucester, MA, 2nd August, 1836. On her father's side her ancestry runs through the Choates and on her mother's side through the Haskells, back into staunch old English families. Her youth was spent by the sea, and her outdoor sports laid the foundation for the vigor and health that have always characterized her. She was born with a sound mind in a sound body. Her early opportunities for acquiring education were limited. After easily and rapidly learning all that was taught in the public schools of Gloucester, she was wholly unsatisfied with her attainments and pushed forward with different studies by herself. At the age of fifteen she began to teach in the public schools. She continued in that vocation until she was twenty-two, employing, meanwhile, such leisure as she could command in writing for the press. She was then married to a popular clergyman, Rev. B. F. Bowles, pastor of the Universalist Church in Melrose, MA. Although by that marriage she became the stepmother of three children, and later the mother of three more, she still found time for a variety of church work, including teaching an adult Bible class. Her success with that class led her to deeper theological study, under the direction of her husband. Mr. Bowles desired that his wife should be in all things his companion, and, after giving her a thorough course in theology, he encouraged her to preach the gospel, which she had long felt called to declare. She began in 1869 by supplying vacant pulpits in New England. In 1872 she was licensed in Boston to preach and became the non-resident pastor of a church in Marlborough, MA. Mr. Bowles, at that time settled in Cambridge, soon after accepted a call to the pastorate of the Church of the Restoration in Philadelphia, and Mrs. Bowles was called as non-resident pastor of the Universalist Church in Easton, PA, a position she held for three very successful years, although the church had been for many years dormant. She closed her connection with that parish that she might lay the foundation of a new church in Trenton, NJ, which she accomplished in six weeks of energetic work. She was regularly ordained in 1874 and has preached and lectured since that time in most of the large cities of the United States. When without a church of her own, she has shared the parish work of her husband and has been constantly engaged in charitable and philanthropic work. In addition to all her ministerial work, she lectured in various parts of the country under the auspices of the Woman's Christian Temperance Union, in which organization she has been state superintendent of various departments. She has been national lecturer of the American Suffrage Association and president of State, county and city suffrage organizations, as well as an active member of many other reforms. Notwithstanding all these duties and labors, she is famed among her acquaintances as a wise and affectionate mother and a model housekeeper. One of her most popular lectures is on "Strong-minded Housekeeping," which embodies her own experience in household cares and management. She is an expert swimmer, perfectly at home in or on the water, and can handle a saw, hammer or rolling-pin with equal dexterity. Her public life has never in any way been allowed to interfere with the exercise of a gracious private charity. She is a very popular and convincing speaker. In all that she undertakes Mrs. Bowles is prompt and incisive, and in private life is as constant in good works as she is able in public in inspiring others to all worthy endeavors. Her present home is in Abington, MA.

BOYD, Mrs. Kate Parker, artist, born in New York, 23rd October, 1836. Her maiden name was Kate Parker Scott. She is a daughter of Andrew Scott, of Flushing, NY, who was a son of Andrew Scott, born in Paisley, Scotland. She inherited her talent for drawing from her father, who was a fine amateur artist from his boyhood to his nineteenth year, and whose portfolios of water-colors are a source of delight to artists of the present time. Miss Scott attended the Flushing Female College, then in the charge of Rev. William Gilder. After leaving that school and traveling awhile, she was married in 1862 to Rev. N. E. Boyd. They have lived in Portland, ME, and in Canastota, NY. Their family consisted of two sons, who died at an early age. When circumstances made it necessary, Mrs. Boyd was able to earn a good income with her pencil. Her pictures were exhibited and sold in New York and Brooklyn. She was an exhibitor in the Academies of Design in both of those cities. She won a number of medals and prizes in the Centennial Exposition in Philadelphia, in 1876, and in various State and county exhibitions. They moved to San Francisco, CA, in

1877, and in that city her work was highly successful. She now writes and draws for the "American Garden," New York, and for other periodicals, using the signature K. P. S. B. She is interested in reforms and humanitarian work in general, and is a member of the Society for the Prevention of Cruelty to Animals, of the Association for the Advancement of Women and of the Pacific Coast Women's Press Association. She works zealously for the sailors' branch of the Woman's Christian Temperance Union and for the Sailors' Lend-a-Hand Club.

BOYD, Mrs. Louise Esther Vickroy, author, born in Urbana, OH, 2nd January, 1827.

When she was about four years of age, her parents removed to Ferndale, a picturesque valley among the mountains near Johnstown, PA. Although good schools were scarce in those days, her education was not neglected, and for two years she was a pupil in the select school of Miss Esther R. Barton, in Lancaster, PA. While a young woman she made frequent visits to Philadelphia, and she there became acquainted with many of the authors and literary people of that city. Her first poem was written in 1851. The next year she became a regular contributor to Grace Greenwood's "Little Pilgrim," and frequently, since that time, her poems as well as prose sketches have appeared in magazines and newspapers, among others the "Knickerbocker," "Graham's Magazine," "Appleton's Journal," the New York "Tribune," the Philadelphia "Saturday Evening Post," the Cincinnati "Gazette," "Woman's Journal," the Indianapolis "Journal," "Wide Awake," the "Century," and others. For several years she was engaged in teaching, until in September, 1865, she became the wife of Dr. S. S. Boyd, since which time her home has been in Dublin, IN. Mrs. Boyd's married life was a most happy one. Her husband was a man of fine literary taste and an ardent worker in the cause of humanity, and she was strengthened and encouraged by him in the causes of temperance and woman suffrage. She is well known as an advocate of woman suffrage. Well acquainted with history, she has watched with unfailing interest all the movements of our eventful times, her sympathies ever on the side of the oppressed. She has frequently appeared on the platform, where she has a good presence, is natural, womanly, logical and sprightly. She is greatly interested in creating a State literature, and she has not only furnished much material for it, but has done a great deal toward creating a correct and pure literary taste in her own town and county. She was reared in the faith of the followers of Emanuel Swedenborg, but is now an earnest member of the Christian Church. She has been a widow since 1888.

BRACE, Miss Maria Porter, educator and elocutionist, born in Penn Yan, NY, in July, 1852. Her early life was spent in Leavenworth, Kans. Her father was one of the first settlers in Kansas, and there the family home has always remained. Miss Brace was educated in Vassar College and was graduated in 1872. A special course in elocution followed under Prof. Robert R. Raymond, in the Boston School of Oratory. These studies, preceded by practice in teaching and reading in the West, were followed by an engagement as teacher of elocution in Vassar College. During several years of residence there, a certain time was reserved every winter for work outside of the college community. In teaching as well as in reading Miss Brace has always associated the art of elocution with the interpretation of the best literature. Her annotated readings from the English classics and from recent masterpieces of prose and poetry often formed a supplement to the course in English literature in schools. In 1883 Miss Brace made her first visit to Europe. Through the influence of Monsieur Regnier, the French actor and teacher, she was admitted to the daily sessions of the dramatic classes in the Conservatoire National de Musique et de Declamation, in Paris. A close study of the French classics in the hands of the pupils and of their masters, the four leading actors of the Théatre Francais, proved a valuable lesson in dramatic reading and criticism. In addition to the daily rehearsals in the Conservatoire, there were talks with M. Regnier, who generously gave his criticism of her own work. The course in the Conservatoire was supplemented by frequent visits to the Théatre Francais, where the professors were often seen in their well-known rôles as actors. Miss Brace's interest in the art of acting received a great impulse from that winter in Paris. Upon her return to New York she read, in the Madison Square Theater, an account of the methods of the Théatre Francais as taught in the National Conservatoire. The lecture attracted the attention of actors and critics who were present and has been repeated many times in New York and elsewhere. During the spring of 1884 an effort was being made to establish in New York a school for actors. Miss Brace became actively interested in the undertaking and was at once engaged as a teacher of dramatic elocution and lecturer upon dramatic literature. She has also taught elocution in the Brearley School for Girls since its opening in New York, in 1884. Her lectures and readings have become favorably known in Philadelphia and New York. The topics are "Francois Del Sarto in Paris," "Colloquial Elocution" and "Professional Elocution." Miss Brace has made occasional contributions to periodical literature upon various phases of her chosen subject, and she is constantly collecting material, both at home and abroad, for further essays and lectures, including a text-book of elocution. In addition to her active work in her profession, Miss Brace has been interested in the social life of her cotemporaries. She has been a frequent contributor to the monthly conversations of the Meridian Club. She has represented the alumnae of her own college on the governing board of the College Settlement. That home in the slums of the East Side represents the first organized effort of college-bred women to improve the condition of life among the poor. She was one of the founders and the first president of the Women's University Club of New York.

BRADEN, Mrs. Anna Madge, author, born in Pennsylvania near historic Valley Forge. She is of English and German descent, and her ancestors have lived in or near Philadelphia, PA, for over a century and a half. Her father is John Conver Rile. Her mother's maiden name was Frantz. She is fifth in direct line of descent from Gen. Joseph Reed, of Revolutionary fame, his daughter being her great-grandmother. In 1880 she was married to Findley Braden, of Ohio, and they now reside in Philadelphia. For six years before her marriage she wrote under her maiden name, Madge Rile, and several pen-names, but since her marriage she adopted her husband's name, signing her articles Mrs. Findley Brayden. She began writing for the newspapers and magazines when but a school-girl of fifteen. It is her life-work, and she thoroughly enjoys it. She has written over seven-hundred humorous and pathetic sketches, poems and serials, many of which have appeared in the secular journals of New York, Boston and Philadelphia. She has also written a number of songs that have found their way into public favor. She is equally at home in the five dialects, Scotch, Irish, Negro, Dutch and Quaker. She is a fine elocutionist and is a graduate of the National School of Elocution and Oratory, Philadelphia. Mrs. Braden is a member of the Presbyterian Church and an earnest worker. Her kindly Christian character can best be seen in her own home, which is a model of neatness and cheerfulness. Her life is spent, not for her own gratification, but for the comfort of those around her. She is an ardent student, painstaking and ambitious.

BRADFORD, Mrs. Mary Carroll Craig, correspondent, born in Brooklyn, NY, 10th August, 1856. She comes from a long line of mental aristocrats, being a direct descendant from Charles Carroll, one of the signers of the Declaration of Independence. She never attended school, but was educated privately by masters and governesses. She has traveled extensively both at home and abroad. She was in Geneva, Switzerland, during the year of the Arbitration, and while there met and enjoyed the society of some of the arbitrators. Her first appearance in print was at the age of twelve in a story, but she only began to write regularly and professionally at twenty-two. At the age of nineteen she was married to Lieut. Edward Taylor Bradford, of the United States Navy, a son of the Paymaster-General of the Navy, and grandson of the famous Boston preacher, familiarly called "Father Taylor." Her literary work has been diversified. She has been a regular contributor to the Brooklyn "Eagle," the New Orleans "Picayune," the "Esoteric," the "Commonwealth," "Christian Union," the "Rocky Mountain News," and other magazines and papers. Her lectures have been on glimpses of her travels and on theosophy. Her home is now in Colorado Springs, CO.

BRADLEY, Miss Amy Morris, educator, born in East Vassalboro, ME, 12th September, 1823. She is a granddaughter of Asa Bradley, a soldier of the Revolution who gave his life for his country. She was educated in her native town. In 1840 she began to teach in country schools, and four years later was appointed principal of one of the grammar schools in Gardiner, ME. In 1846 she became assistant teacher in the Winthrop grammar school of Charlestown, MA, and taught until the autumn of 1849, when, prostrated by pneumonia, she was compelled to seek a milder climate. The winter of 1850–51 was passed in Charleston, SC, but with little benefit, and, advised by her physician to seek a country entirely free from frost, in 1853 she went to San José, Costa Rica, whose climate proved a healing balm to her lungs. In three months after her arrival she opened a school. It was a success. She quickly mastered the Spanish language, and her pupils rapidly acquired the English. For nearly four years she continued her educational work in San José, and in the summer of 1857 she returned to New England to her early home in East Vassalboro, where her venerable father died in January, 1858. The thorough knowledge of Spanish acquired by Miss Bradley in Costa Rica led the New England Glass Company, of East Cambridge, MA, to seek her services in translating letters. She was in Cambridge in 1861, when the first gun was fired at Fort Sumter, and immediately after the battle of Bull Run she offered her services as nurse to the sick and wounded soldiers. On the first of September, 1861, Miss Bradley entered the hospital of the Third Maine Regiment, encamped near Alexandria, VA, but was transferred to the Fifth Maine Regiment, and a few days later was appointed matron of the Seventeenth Brigade Hospital, General Slocum's Brigade, of which she had charge during the winter. In the spring of 1862, after the Army of the Potomac went to the Peninsula, Rev. F. N. Knapp, head of the relief department of the United States Sanitary Commission, telegraphed to Miss Bradley to report immediately to him at Fortress Monroe, and she went in the same boat with Miss Dorothea L. Dix. All through the Peninsular Campaign she was on transport boats, which brought the sick and wounded from the battlefields. After the Seven Days Battles she returned to Washington and helped to organize a home for discharged soldiers. In December, 1862, she was sent to Convalescent Camp, Alexandria, and remained in charge of the Relief Department until the close of the war, when, her special work for country and humanity being ended, her heart and mind turned anew to her original calling. In 1866, at the request of the Soldiers' Memorial Society, of Boston, MA, and under the auspices of the American Unitarian Association, she went to Wilmington, NC, as a teacher of poor white children. Her position at first was a trying one, for she was a stranger and a northerner. Modestly and firmly she took her place and began her work. She opened her school 9th January, 1867, with three children, in a very humble building. Within a week sixty-seven pupils were enrolled, and soon two additional teachers were engaged by her, and, as the number of pupils rapidly increased, new schools were opened, the "Hemenway," the "Pioneer" and the "Normal," and the corps of teachers increased accordingly. Such was the character of the instruction given, such the tone, spirit and influence of the schools, that within a few months, instead of being regarded with suspicion and aversion, Miss Bradley and her coworkers had the confidence and the grateful affection of the community, and large-minded citizens co-operated with the trustees of the Peabody Fund and other benefactors in erecting the needed buildings and forwarding the work. On the thirtieth of November, 1871, the corner-stone of the Tileston Normal School was laid, and it was opened in October, 1872. This building was the gift of Mrs. Mary Hemenway, of Boston, MA, who had been deeply interested in Miss Bradley's work from its beginning, and whose appreciation of its importance and beneficence found expression in the annual contribution of $5,000 toward the support of the Tileston Normal School, from its opening in 1872 to its close in 1891. Failing health led Miss Bradley to resign her position in 1891.

BRADLEY, Mrs. Ann Weaver, educator and temperance worker, born in Hartland, Niagara county, NY, 19th May, 1834. Her parents, William and Mary Earl Weaver, removed from New York to Michigan during her infancy, and she was reared in that State. Her early philanthropic tendencies, fostered by home training, prepared her to espouse the anti-slavery cause and to engage heartily in all reformatory efforts. Loving study for its own sake and feeling that in brain culture one could exert an influence for good on humanity, her earliest ambition was to become a teacher. Attaining that position before her fourteenth birthday, she continued thus to labor with never-failing zest for over thirty years. With a power to impress her own personality upon others and to evoke their latent capabilities, her work in the class-room was especially happy, particularly in the department of literature. While attending Hillsdale College, she publicly gave herself to Christ. In 1858 she was married to George S. Bradley, a theologue from Oberlin, then tutor in Hillsdale. Thereafter her influence for good was felt in all his labors, whether as pastor's wife or lady principal in the seminaries under his charge in Maine, Wisconsin and Iowa. While in Wisconsin, her husband, as chaplain of the Twenty-second Wisconsin Regiment, went with Sherman to the sea. While he was in that service, the last one of their three children died. Mrs. Bradley returned to Hillsdale and engaged in teaching. At the close of the war her husband resumed his old pastorate near Racine, WI, and there for two years they worked. Then followed two years of seminary work in Rochester, and six in Evansville, WI. There was born to them their last and only living child, Charles Clement. Wilton, IA, was for the next five years the scene of their labors. Then Mrs. Bradley began her public work for temperance. The Iowa agitation for prohibition roused her to action. Stepping into the ranks of the Woman's Christian Temperance Union, she organized and carried on a union, a temperance school, and lectured in her own town and vicinity. Later, in central and eastern Kansas, where her husband's labors led, her temperance efforts cost her a three-years' invalidism, from which she has never fully rallied. Her husband is at present pastor of the Congregational Church in Hudson, MI, and she is State superintendent of narcotics for the Woman's Christian Temperance Union. Her inherited hatred of those destroying agents, her gift of persistence, her thoroughness of research and her love of humanity especially fit her for this work.

BRADWELL, Mrs. Myra, lawyer and editor, born in Manchester, VT, 12th February. 1831. She is a daughter of Eben and Abigail Willey Colby, Her parents removed to New York State in her infancy. When she was twelve years old, Chicago became her home. Her family were well represented in the War of the Revolution, two of her ancestors having been in the battle of Bunker Hill. Myra was educated in Kenosha, WI, and at the seminary in Elgin, IL, and afterward taught school in Memphis, TN. In 1852 she was married to James B. Bradwell, whose father was one of the leading pioneers of Illinois. She studied law under the instruction of her husband, and passed a creditable examination. She was the first woman in America to ask for admission to the bar, and it was refused because she was a married woman. She immediately set to work, with the aid of her husband, to have this legal disability removed, and the success of their undertaking is a matter of congratulation for all women. Mrs. Bradwell declared that she should never again apply for admission to the bar, but, to her surprise, she one day received a certificate upon the original application from the court that had refused her years before. Mrs. Brad-

well was the first woman who was made a member of the Illinois Bar Association, and also of the Illinois Press Association. The first weekly legal paper published in the Western States was the Chicago "Legal News," established twenty-three years ago by Myra Bradwell, who has always been its manager and editor. The legislature gave her a special charter for the paper, and passed several acts making it evidence in the courts and a valid medium for the publication of legal notices. The law giving to married women their own earnings was drawn by Myra Bradwell, and its passage was secured through her efforts in 1869. Judge Bradwell retired from the bench in order to assist his wife in the large business to which the Legal News Company had grown. The Bradwells made place in their busy lives for much charitable and philanthropic work. During the Civil War they were active helpers among the sick and wounded soldiers, and did good service in the Sanitary Commission. Mrs. Bradwell has been for nearly thirty years a member of the Soldiers' Home Board. She was untiring in her efforts to secure the World's Fair for Chicago, and is one of the Board of Lady Managers and chairman of the committee on law reform of the World's Congress Auxiliary. She is a member of the Chicago Women's Club and of the Illinois Women's Press Association, and is treasurer of the South Evanston Industrial School, of which she was one of the organizers. Four children form her family. Of these, two died in infancy. Thomas and Bessie remain. They are both lawyers. Bessie's husband, Frank A. Helmer, is also an attorney. Notwithstanding her profession and her numerous activities, Mrs. Bradley is a favorite in the society of Chicago.

BRAEUNLICH, Mrs. Sophia, business manager, born in Bethpage, Long Island, NY, 2nd July, 1860. Her maiden name was Toepken. Her parents were Germans, both from old and aristocratic families. When she was twelve years old, she was sent to Europe, where she received a first-class education. She remained there until her sixteenth year, when she returned to her native country and made Brooklyn her home. Shortly afterward she was married, and after a brief time she was left dependent upon her own resources. She then entered Packard's business college in New York, taking a full course there, and after graduating from the college, in 1879, she obtained a situation as private secretary to Richard P. Rothwell, the editor of the "Engineering and Mining Journal" and president of the Scientific Publishing Company. She has risen step by step from the bottom to the top rung of the business ladder in that office. Mrs. Braeunlich displayed such intelligence and energy that ere long Mr. Rothwell availed himself of her services as both secretary and assistant exchange editor. She mastered the technical details pertaining to the paper, attended the meetings of the American Institute of Mining Engineers, and frequently went down into mines on such occasions, thus gaining practical knowledge of various details that increased her usefulness in the office. When the secretary and treasurer of the publishing company resigned his position, Mrs. Braeunlich was elected to fill the vacancy. She displayed such remarkable executive ability, combined with energy and ambition, that at the first opportunity she was promoted to the office of business manager of the entire establishment. She has full charge of the general business and financial departments, and, in addition to the multiplicity of mental labor entailed by her position, she assisted in the government work connected with the collection of gold and silver statistics for the Eleventh Census. The room in which Mrs. Braeunlich spends most of her time, and which she has occupied for over twelve years, is the same one which Henry Ward Beecher used at the time of his editorial work on the "Christian Union." It is brightened with flowers, birds and pictures, and its neatness presents an agreeable contrast to the majority of journalistic business offices. She is described by one of the "Journal's" staff as "a modest, warm-hearted, accomplished and irreproachable woman, of strong character, with an instinctive clearness of vision that seems to be confined to women, and with the sound judgment of a man," and it is added that "she possesses the absolute esteem and goodwill of all the gentlemen in the office, and is always a courteous lady, though a strict disciplinarian. The office, as well as the work, is the better for her influence." Mrs. Braeunlich has for years worked very hard, giving up almost all social and other pleasures, and devoting all her thoughts and time to business.

BRAINARD, Mrs. Kate J., musical educator, born in New York City, 18th February, 1835. Her father, Rev. D. E. Jones, compiler of the first hymn and tune book ever used and made popular in this country, was of Welsh descent. Her mother was a woman of great natural gifts, both of voice and mind, and a regular contributor to the literature of the day. The daughter inherited in a marked degree their musical talent. When but a very little girl, she studied the elements of music under her father and began piano lessons when seven years old. At an early age she surprised her friends by carrying the alto in part-singing,"making it up" with wonderful correctness. At fifteen she was obliged to begin to earn her living by teaching piano. At the same time her musical studies were faithfully carried on under the best masters. Vocal lessons were begun at that time and she made rapid progress in florid singing. Her last year in the East was spent with the best vocal teachers in Boston. In 1855 she moved to Chicago and there became quite noted as a vocalist. In 1858 she was married, and in 1865 moved to St. Louis, where she was looked upon as one of the leading sopranos, receiving a large salary in one of the choirs. In 1866 Mrs. Brainard assumed charge of the music in Mary Institute, the female department of Washington University, numbering in recent years nearly four-hundred girls. Mrs. Brainard's class-work, as systematized and developed in that institute, is remarkable. During her career in Mary Institute she has frequently spent her vacations in the East with some prominent teacher, to obtain new ideas for her work. Among these was a trip to Europe, where she studied in Paris and London with Viardot, Garcia and Sainton Dolby. Many girls with promising voices have been started on their musical career by Mrs. Brainard. During the past twenty-five years her name has been associated with the progress of musical art in St. Louis, and many singers now prominent as professionals or amateurs refer to her as their conscientious guide during their struggles and studies. She has been deeply and actively interested in church work since she was thirteen years old, at which time she united with Dr. Hatfield's church in New York City. During forty-

three years of teaching she has done an enormous amount of labor, having gained a reputation abroad as well as at home. Mrs. Brainard gives a portion of her time to private pupils.

BRAMAN, Mrs. Ella Frances, lawyer and business woman, born in Brighton, now a part of Boston, MA, 23rd March, 1850. She comes of good Puritan stock. In 1867 she was married to Joseph Balch Braman, of the same place, then a member of the Boston Bar. In 1872 they went to the city of Los Angeles, CA, where her husband practiced law until the spring of 1874, when he resumed law practice in Boston. Soon after their return to Boston, Mr. Braman required some one to assist him in his Boston office as commissioner for the different States to which he had just been appointed, and Mrs. Braman volunteered to become his assistant. She proved so competent that it was decided to ask for her appointment also, so that she could act, especially when clients called for a commissioner during Mr. Braman's temporary absence from the office. Each State governor was written to. Governor Long adding his endorsement, but only ten governors could then be found who either believed in a woman's being appointed or thought they had the power to grant the commission to a woman. Soon Mr. and Mrs. Braman removed to New York City to practice, and then it was determined to continue asking for the appointments from the governors until she had them all. She lacks only about eight States, which will shortly fall into line and give her their commission, as President Harrison has recently done. Soon after settling in the metropolis she became a regular partner with her husband. They have a down-town day office in the Equitable Building, 120 Broadway, and an uptown office and residence at 1270 Broadway. Mrs. Braman is a thoroughbred lawyer and is enthusiastic in her liking for the law. The extent and variety of what she accomplishes in a field generally supposed to be the exclusive property of men may be seen in a mere mention of her titles. She is a lawyer, a notary public, a commissioner of deeds for the States, Territories and District of Columbia, the United States Court of Claims, a United States passport agent at New York, and a consular agent. She holds about fifty commissions and appointments from the President of the United States and from governors of States. Mrs. Braman's uptown office is in her residence, and it is never closed. Her theory seems to be that a person who carries on business should always be ready to attend to business, and to that end her office is kept open, night and day, every day in the year, making no exception even for Sundays and holidays. Here she keeps the laws, blanks and forms for all the States. She is an energetic, intelligent, agreeable woman, and her advice and services are sought by women as well as by men having legal business to transact. She has made a good record for accuracy in the intricate work of her profession.

BRAUMULLER, Mrs. Luetta Elmina, artist, born in Monson, MA, 4th December, 1856. Her family name, Bumstead, is still a familiar one in Boston, where it was among the foremost before and after the Revolutionary War. Bumstead Hall, which was built next after Faneuil Hall, and Bumstead Place are still old landmarks in that city. Her line of ancestry on the mother's side is Puritan, the family, Wood, having come to America in 1638 and with others founded the town of Rowley, near Boston. Mrs. Braumuller's earliest recollections are closely allied to the pencil and brush, and at the age of eight years she received her first instruction in art. Since that time until the present, with the exception of a few short intervals, she has applied herself to the study of drawing and painting in all its branches. In 1880 she made her first trip to Europe, and remained nearly one year in the best studios of Berlin. In 1882 she made a second visit to Paris and Sèvres, in which cities she studied porcelain painting exclusively under celebrated ceramic artists, and later in the same year she continued with a noted practical china and glass painter in Berlin. In 1889 she went to Dresden, where she acquired a knowledge of the methods of the Dresden artists. In 1890 she was again in Paris, where she pursued the study of flesh-painting after the method of Hortense Richard. Mrs. Braumuller is distinctly a figure painter, although she has a complete knowledge of every branch of work connected with porcelain painting and firing. As a student and teacher it has been her greatest ambition to advance the art in America. She published a small work entitled "Lessons in China Painting," in 1882, but, believing that a periodical would have a wider circulation and give better results, she established in New York City, in 1887, a monthly magazine devoted exclusively to the interests of amateur decorators, and known as the "China Decorator." It was a success from the first issue and now enjoys a wide circulation both in this country and in Europe. Mrs. Braumuller has the reputation of being one of the best informed women in this country on the subject of modern porcelain and pottery. She is the wife of a well-known piano manufacturer of New York City and is the mother of two children, a son and daughter.

BREED, Mrs. Alice Ives, social-leader, born in Pavilion, IL, 15th January, 1853. At the age of eighteen years she removed to Boston, MA. In 1873 she was married to Francis W. Breed, who is connected with important business interests in Boston and Lynn, MA. Mrs. Breed has traveled much, read much and thought much. She has shown an intelligent sympathy with every movement in the world of music, art and literature, and her home has been a center of attraction for men and women distinguished in all those fields of effort. She is an accomplished musician. Her family consists of five children. Their home is in Lynn, MA. Mrs. Breed has for years served as chairman of the Lynn branch of the Emergency Association, as president of the Woman's Auxiliary of the Young Men's Christian Association, and as vice-president of the Lynn Woman's Club. She is now president of the North Shore Club, a social and literary organization of the highest character, which has a membership of one-hundred-fifty-five and a waiting list of one-hundred. She is a member of the Massachusetts State committee for correspondence of the General Federation of Women's Literary Clubs. She was appointed a member of the Women's Committee of the World's Congress Auxiliary on moral and social reform. She is a woman of marked executive ability, and her energies find expression in religious, philanthropic, literary and social channels. She is especially a social leader who aims to lift the community to a higher level.

BREWSTER, Miss Cora Belle, physician and surgeon, born in Almond, Allegany county, NY, 6th September, 1859. She was educated partly in Alfred University where she studied five years. She left school to take a position as teacher, and her work in the schoolroom covered several years. Her last work as a teacher was done in the high school in Smethport, PA. In 1877 she went west and took a special course in the Northwestern University. While studying in that institution, she decided to abandon pedagogy, and on leaving the school she took a position as purchasing agent for a large millinery establishment in Chicago. The climate of Chicago proved too severe for her, and after three years of active service in that city she moved to Baltimore, MD. There her health was perfectly restored, and she began the study of medicine. She was graduated from the College of Physicians and Surgeons (Boston, MA) in May, 1886. During her course of study she spent eighteen months in Bellevue Hospital in New York, where she gained a great deal of valuable experience in treating the thousands of cases of every sort that are always to be found in that great institution. After graduating, she returned to Baltimore, where, in partnership with her sister, Flora A. Brewster, MD, she began in 1889 the publication of the Baltimore "Family Health Journal," the name of which was in 1891 changed to the "Homeopathic Advocate and Health Journal," and made a hospital journal with a corps of ten editors. She was in 1890 elected gynæcological surgeon to the Homeopathic Hospital and Free Dispensary of Maryland, under the auspices of the Maryland Homeopathic Medical Society. She has achieved marked success as medical writer, surgeon, editor and practicing physician.

BREWSTER, Miss Flora A., physician and surgeon, born Alfred, Allegany county, NY, 26th February, 1852. Her family moved to northern Pennsylvania in 1863. In 1866 she was sent to Alfred University, where, after passing the examinations, she began the scientific course of study, showing great talent for mathematics. In 1868 her father died suddenly, and she was obliged to leave the university in order to attend to the finances of her family. She took a position as copyist in a tax-collector's office, which she soon left to begin work as a teacher. She hoarded her money with the purpose of returning to the university to complete her course of study, but two years of hard work, teaching school and at the same time carrying on her university studies, so seriously impaired her health that she was compelled to devote her time exclusively to teaching. In 1872 she was appointed teacher in the Mansfield Orphan School, in Mansfield, PA, which was then the training-school for the Mansfield State Normal School. In 1875 she took the degree of B.E. in Mansfield, and in 1877 the degree of Master in Elementary Didactics, while still teaching. In 1877 she was forced by failing health to give up teaching. She spent a year in travel in the West and Northwest, and her health was so greatly improved that in 1878 she went to Chicago and took the editorial and business management of the "Newsboys' Appeal," an illustrated journal published in the interest of the Newsboys' Home in that city. The following year she began to read medicine with Dr. Julia Holmes Smith, of Chicago, and conducted a night school on the kindergarten plan in the Newsboys' Home. In 1882 she completed the course in the Chicago Homeopathic Medical College, after which she went to Baltimore, MD, where she spent six months in the office and private hospital of the late Prof. August F. Erich, the noted gynæcological surgeon. She opened an office and began to practice in Baltimore in 1882. At that time only one woman had succeeded in establishing a paying practice in Baltimore. and that one was Dr. Emma Stein Wanstall, who died in September, 1882: No female physician in the city had been entrusted with surgical cases, but Dr. Brewster believed that the field for women physicians in the South was open to sensible, energetic and educated women, and she persevered. For the next four years she worked arduously, acquiring a large practice and doing a good deal of charitable work. In 1886 she formed a partnership with her sister, Dr. Cora Belle Brewster. In 1890 the agitation caused by the application for the admission of women to the medical department of Johns Hopkins University enlightened the people of the entire South in regard to the status of women in the medical profession. Both the sisters were elected surgeons, and they gave clinics in the new homeopathic hospital in Baltimore. Besides their general practice, the doctors Brewster have a large practice in gynæcological surgery, extending over the entire South. They have opened the medical field to the women of the South, and many southern women have become physicians and trained nurses, and are successfully practicing their profession.

BRIDGMAN, Miss Laura Dewey, blind deaf-mute, born in Hanover, NH, 21st December, 1829, died in South Boston, MA, 24th May, 1889. Her parents were Daniel and Harmony Bridgman. Laura was a delicate infant and subject to severe convulsions. Her health improved until she was two years old, at which age she was a very active and intelligent child, able to talk and familiar with some letters of the alphabet. As she was entering her third year, the family were smitten by the scarlet fever. Two older daughters died of the fever, and Laura was attacked by it. For seven weeks she could not swallow solid food, and then both eyes and ears suppurated and her sight, hearing and sense of smell were totally destroyed. For a year she could not walk without support, and it was two years before she could sit up all day. When she was five years old, her health was once more perfect, and her mind, unaffected by her distressful affliction, began to crave food. She had forgotten the few words she knew when she was smitten. Her remaining sense, that of touch, grew very acute. Her mother taught her to sew, knit and braid. Communication with her was possible only by signs that could be given by touch. She was an affectionate, but self-willed, child. Dr. S. G. Howe, director of the Institution for the Blind in Boston, heard of her, and she was placed in his charge 12th October, 1837. Dr. Howe,

assisted by Mrs. L. H. Morton, of Halifax, MA, developed a special system of training that accomplished wonders. A manual alphabet was used, and Laura learned to read and write in sixteen months, having acquired a considerable vocabulary. Her intellect developed rapidly, and she learned mathematical operations to a limited extent. Her case attracted a great deal of attention, and the system of instruction developed by Dr. Howe in her case was applied successfully to other children similarly deprived of their senses. Laura had no conception of religion up to her twelfth year, as her instructors purposely refrained from giving her any ideas of God until she was old enough to take a correct idea. She could not, as has been asserted, distinguish color by feeling. Laura was visited by many prominent persons, among whom were Ms. Lydia H. Sigourney and Charles Dickens. The "Notes on America" mention Mr. Dickens' visit. George Combe, of Scotland, visited Laura in 1842, and at his suggestion arrangements were made to keep a full record of everything connected with the remarkable girl. By dint of training she learned to speak many words. Her imagination developed more slowly than any other faculty, and her moral ideas were perceptibly different, in some phases, from those of ordinary persons. Her education is fully recorded in Mary Swift Lawson's "Life and Education of Laura Dewey Bridgman," published in 1881.

BRIGGS, Mrs. Mary Blatchley, born in Valparaiso, IN, 1st January, 1846. She is of Scotch, English and Dutch descent. The father was a practicing physician and surgeon of prominence in the allopathic school. Mrs. Briggs' early school-days were spent in the public schools of Iowa. Later her education was continued in the young ladies' seminary in Council Bluffs, IA, receiving prizes for excellent scholarship. In the month of August, 1861, her family removed to Quincy, IL, where she resumed her studies and there enjoyed the advantages of the best schools until she was nineteen years old. In religious belief Mrs. Briggs is strictly a Presbyterian, was born "in the faith," and has always lived the practical life of a consistent Christian. Rev. F. S. Blayney, LL.D., the first pastor of the Second Presbyterian

Louise Thorndyke-Boucicault.
From Photo by Thors, San Francisco.

Church of Omaha, writes of Mrs. Briggs's practical and valuable aid during the long and severe trials from 1880 to 1886 in the struggle to found and build his church, she being one of the foremost workers for the society's welfare. She has always taken a vivid interest in public characters and the local and foreign politics discussed in the newspapers. She was married to John S. Briggs, 24th December, 1857, since which time they have resided in Omaha, NE. Mr. Briggs was born in Ohio, but was reared in Iowa, removing to Nebraska in 1856. He is the son of the late Ansel Briggs, first governor of the State of Iowa. To Mr. and Mrs. Briggs three promising children have been born. Mrs. Briggs has filled many important public positions. During eleven years she served as assistant secretary, superintendent, reporter for the press, and manager of county, State and interstate fairs. While on a visit to Idaho, she and her husband prepared a collection of minerals, stalactitic and calcareous deposits, which, at the suggestion of the officials of the Union Pacific Railroad, was sent to the Mechanics' Institute in Boston,

MA. Mrs. Briggs is interested in art and is secretary of the Western Art Association, which has three-hundred members. In literature she has won an assured position by her poems, one volume of which has been compiled and published. Mrs. Briggs was selected by Mrs. Potter Palmer as one of the six representative women of the West to serve on the executive committee of the Board of Lady Managers of the World's Columbian Commission for the Exposition in 1893. She was appointed a member of the bylaws judiciary committee and was elected an honorary and corresponding member of the woman's branch of the World's Congress Auxiliary, and served on several committees. She possesses an intimate knowledge of Nebraska, its history, its resources, its development and its people.

BRINKERHOFF, Mme. Clara M., singer and musical educator, barn in London, England, 8th September, 1828. She is the daughter of Mr. and Mrs. John A. Rolph, cultured people, who came to the United States when Clara was an infant. Her father was an artist, whose specialty was steel engraving. Her mother was an artistic, literary and musical woman, with a fine voice that had been trained in the old Italian school by Maestro Corri. In her first musical season she had the principal parts in "The Seven Sleepers," "Waldenses," "Judas Maccabæus," "Lobgesang" and Spohr's "Last Judgment"; afterward in "Elijah," "Athalie" and "Stabat Mater," and in classical concerts from Gluck, Beethoven, Mozart, Haydn and Wagner, with a full repertoire of the best Italian composers. She was married to C. E. L. Brinkerhoff on 25th December, 1848, and sang the full Christmas service on the morning of her wedding day. In 1861 she visited Europe, where she received much flattering attention. She has lectured before the polytechnic section of the American Institute.

BRINKMAN, Mrs. Mary A., homœopathic physician, born in Hingham, MA, 22nd February, 1845. On arriving at womanhood she visited Europe, where she devoted herself to study and travel. Soon after returning to this country, in 1871, she entered as a student the New York Medical College and Hospital for Women. In 1876, while retaining her professional chair in the Woman's Medical College, she was appointed physician to the New York Dispensary for Women and Children, and later, to the college dispensary, and in those positions she did active service for several years. In 1881 she was chosen professor of diseases of women (gynæcology) in the New York Medical College and Hospital for Women, and continued there until forced by ill health to resign, in 1889. She was appointed, in 1886, visiting physician on the medical staff of the New York College for Women, and in 1889 consulting physician to the hospital. Dr. Brinkman is an active member of the New York State and County Medical Societies, the Christian League for Promoting Social Purity, the New York Woman Suffrage Society, and the Society for Promoting the Welfare of the Insane. On the subject in which she is most interested, the physical education of our young women, she has written articles for the "North American Review" and other leading journals, which have attracted wide attention.

BRINTON, Mrs. Emma Southwick, army nurse and traveler, born in Peabody, MA, 7th April, 1834. She was educated in Bradford Academy, and after the firing of rebel guns on Fort Sumter, she was on the alert to aid the cause and joined the corps of nurses in Mansion House Hospital, Alexandria. A year was spent there; then after a rest at home nearly another year was spent in Armory Square Hospital, Washington. Then came service in the field at Fredericksburg, White House Landing and City Point. In 1873 she spent several months in the Vienna Exhibition, where so much interest was shown by all other countries and so little by the United States, that she resolved to take some active part in our Centennial in 1876 in Philadelphia. She applied for permission to illustrate the ancient life of New England by

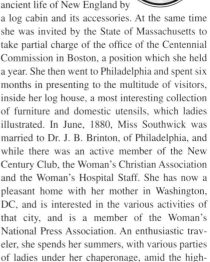

a log cabin and its accessories. At the same time she was invited by the State of Massachusetts to take partial charge of the office of the Centennial Commission in Boston, a position which she held a year. She then went to Philadelphia and spent six months in presenting to the multitude of visitors, inside her log house, a most interesting collection of furniture and domestic utensils, which ladies illustrated. In June, 1880, Miss Southwick was married to Dr. J. B. Brinton, of Philadelphia, and while there was an active member of the New Century Club, the Woman's Christian Association and the Woman's Hospital Staff. She has now a pleasant home with her mother in Washington, DC, and is interested in the various activities of that city, and is a member of the Woman's National Press Association. An enthusiastic traveler, she spends her summers, with various parties of ladies under her chaperonage, amid the highways and byways of the Old World.

BRISBANE, Mrs. Margaret Hunt, poet, born in Vicksburg, MS, 11th February, 1858. She is the youngest daughter of the late Col. Harper P. Hunt, a southerner of the old régime, whose wife was Margaret Tompkins, a member of the well-known Kentucky family of that name. Her childhood was passed in the happy freedom of out-door sport, amid the trees that surrounded the "old house on the hill," as the Hunt mansion was called, and in companionship with bees and birds, flowers and pet horses and dogs, growing up with a naturally poetic temperament, fully developed by her surroundings. Early in life she began to express her musings inverse, and some of her earliest poems gave evidence of the poetical qualities she has revealed in her later and more important work. She has always possessed a sunshiny disposition and a fondness for society, and is a model mother, wife and housekeeper. She was married in 1883 to Dr. Howard Brisbane, of New York, a grandson of Albert Brisbane, of Brook Farm fame. Their family consists of three children. Mrs. Brisbane is a woman of great versatility, of strong womanly sympathies, and of marked refinement. She is a leader in the society of Vicksburg, and Mississippians are proud of her achievements in literature. She is artistic in temperament and aspiration, and in her life she is charitable.

BRISTOL, Mrs. Augusta Cooper, poet and lecturer, born in Croydon, NH, 17th April, 1835. Her maiden name was Cooper, and she was the youngest of a family of ten children. She was a precocious child, and her poetical taste showed itself in her early infancy. Her first verses were written at the age of eight, and she had poems published when only fifteen. She was forward in mathematics and showed in her early life an aptitude for logical and philosophical reasoning. The greater part of her education was acquired in a public school, but she was also a student in Canaan Union Academy and Kimball Union Academy. She began teaching at fifteen and was thus employed summer and winter for seven years. At twenty-two years of age she was married to G. H. Kimball, from whom she was divorced five years later. In 1866 she was married to Louis Bristol, a lawyer of New Haven. CT, and they removed to southern Illinois. In 1869 she published a volume of poems, and in that year she gave her first public lecture, which circumstance seems to

have changed the course of her intellectual career. In 1872 she moved to Vineland, NJ, her present residence, from which date she has been called more before the public as a platform speaker. For four years she was president of the Ladies' Social Science Class in Vineland, NJ, giving lessons from Spencer and Carey every month. In the winter of 1880 she save a course of lectures before the New York Positivist Society on "The Evolution of Character," followed by another course under the auspices of the Woman's Social Science Club of that city. In the following June she was sent by friends in New York to study the equitable association of labor and capital at the Familistère, in Guise, in France, founded by M. Godin. She was also commissioned to represent the New York Positivist Society in an international convention of liberal thinkers in Brussels in September. Remaining in the Familistère for three months and giving a lecture on the "Scientific Basis of Morality" before the Brussels convention, she returned home and published the "Rules and Statutes" of the association in Guise. In 1881 she was chosen State lecturer of the Patrons of Husbandry in New Jersey, and in the autumn of the following year was employed on a national lecture bureau of that order. Since her husband's death, which occurred in December, 1882, Mrs. Bristol has appeared but seldom on the public platform. She is occupied with the care of an estate and in directing the educational interests of her youngest daughter. Some of her philosophic and scientific lectures have been translated and published in foreign countries.

BROOKS, Miss Ida Joe, educator, physician and surgeon, born in Muscatine, IA, 28th April, 1853. She is the daughter of Rev. Joseph Brooks. When she was very young, her parents moved to St. Louis, MO, and she there entered the public schools, beginning in the primary department of the Clay school, when Dr. William T. Harris began his career as a teacher. Her father removed to the South after the war, and Miss Brooks went to Little Rock, AR, in 1870. Two years afterward, in conversation with a friend, she warmly argued that women should earn their own money, and he made a wager that she would not do it herself. As a joke, he found her a school in Fouche Bottom, where the gnats were so thick that a smudge had to be kept continually burning. She accepted the position and taught there faithfully and well. In 1873 Miss Brooks, with a liking for the work, began to teach in the public schools of Little Rock. The following year she was made principal of the grammar school, and in 1876 she was made principal of the Little Rock high school. In 1877 she was elected president of the State Teachers' Association. In the same year her father died, and the family came to shortened means, but were sustained by the independence and noble work of the daughter. In 1881 the Little Rock University was opened. Having become a Master of Arts, she was placed in charge of the mathematical department, where she taught until, in 1888, she entered the Boston University School of Medicine, a course which had for years been her desire. She was graduated there with high honors, and afterward took a post-graduate course on nervous diseases in the Westborough Insane Hospital. She spent one year as house officer in the Massachusetts Homeopathic Hospital, being assigned half the time on the surgical and half the time on the medical work. That was an unusual appointment. Returning to Little Rock in September, 1891, she began the practice of her profession and from the start won recognition and patronage. Dr. Brooks is an earnest woman suffragist and a thorough temperance advocate.

BROOKS, Mrs. M. Sears, poet and author, born in Springfield, MA. She is of English ancestry, descended from the Tuttles, of Hertfordshire, England, who settled in New Haven, CT, in 1635, upon the tract of land now occupied by Yale College, part of which tract remained the family homestead for more than a century. She is of Revolutionary stock, her grandfather being one of Mad Anthony Wayne's picked men at the storming of Stony Point. Her family has been remarkable for strong religious inclination, high regard for education and culture. Some of the most noted names in American letters are descended from this stock. Among them are Presidents Dwight and Woolsey, of Yale, Prescott, the historian, Goodrich (Peter Parley), and many others. Mrs. Brooks received her education in the public and private schools of her native city. After her

marriage she removed to Missouri, in 1859, and subsequently to Madison, IN, in 1863, where she now lives. Her earliest contributions to the press appeared in eastern publications under a pen-name. Latterly her poems, essays and short stories have appeared over her own name in newspapers and magazines in various cities. She has been engaged in regular newspaper work in southern Indiana, as editor and contributor. The advancement of women has been a subject claiming her attention, and for the past two years she has held the office of press superintendent for the State under the Indiana Woman Suffrage Association. Mrs. Brooks partakes in a large degree of the family characteristics, and in associations of prominence, in both State and Nation, her aid and influence have been felt. In her literary work she displays great force and beauty of diction, originality of thought and clearness of perception. She has published in holiday form "A Vision of the Mistletoe" (Buffalo, 1888).

BROTHERTON, Mrs. Alice Williams, author, born in Cambridge, IN. Her family is of Welsh and English descent, with six generations on American soil. Her father resided in Cincinnati, OH, and afterward in St. Louis, MO, then in Cambridge, IN, and again settled in Cincinnati. She was educated mainly in the St. Louis and Cincinnati public schools, graduating in 1870 from Woodward high school, Cincinnati. In October, 1876, she was married to William Ernest Brotherton. Since then she has resided in Cincinnati. Two children, a boy and a girl, compose her family. Her oldest son, a bright boy of eleven, died in 1890. Living from her birth in an atmosphere of books, she was early trained by her mother in careful habits of composition. Her first appearance in print was in 1872. Her specialty is poetry, but she has written considerable prose in the form of essays, reviews and children's stories. From the first her success, in a pecuniary way, has been marked. Writing only when the spirit moves, in the spare moments of a busy home life, she has contributed at intervals to a variety of periodicals, the "Century," the "Atlantic," "Scribner's Monthly," the "Aldine," the "Independent," and various religious journals. Her booklet, "Beyond the Veil" (Chicago, 1886), was followed by "The Sailing of King Olaf and Other Poems" (Chicago, 1887), and by a volume of prose and verse for children, entitled "What the Wind Told the Tree-Tops" (New York. 1887). Her work shows a wide range of feeling and a deep insight into varying phases of life. Many of her poems have been set to music in this country and in England.

BROWN, Mrs. Charlotte Emerson, president of the General Federation of Women's Literary Clubs, born in Andover, MA, 21st April, 1838. She was the daughter of Professor Ralph Emerson, who was for twenty-five years professor of ecclesiastical history and pastoral theology in Andover Theological Seminary, in Massachusetts, and a relative of the philosopher, Ralph Waldo Emerson. Miss Emerson early showed a marked aptitude for linguistic learning. At the age of ten years she could read, write and speak French with facility. She was graduated while young from Abbott Seminary, and then began in earnest the acquirement of several other languages. For many years of her life she devoted from ten to twelve hours daily to intense study. After mastering the Latin grammar and reading carefully the first book of Virgil's Æneid, she translated the remaining eleven books in eleven consecutive week-days. Horace, Cicero and other classical authors were read with similar rapidity. She spent one year in the study of modern languages and music, and as teacher of Latin, French and mathematics in Montreal, with Miss Hannah Lyman, afterward the first woman to serve as principal of Vassar College. Subsequently she spent several years in studying music and languages in Germany, Austria, France, Italy, Greece, Turkey, Egypt and Syria. On her return from foreign study and travel Miss Emerson was able to speak, read and write at least a half dozen foreign tongues almost as readily as she did her native English. On reaching her home in Rockford, IL, whither her parents had removed, she felt the need of a more thorough business education, and at once entered a commercial college in Chicago, and was graduated after a term of six weeks. In order to complete her business knowledge and make it practical, she became for a time private secretary of her brother, Ralph Emerson, the well-known Rockford manufacturer. Subsequently she organized there two clubs that met regularly in her own house; one was a musical club, the Euterpe, and the other a French club, and both were extremely successful. She was at the same time teaching modern languages in Rockford Seminary. In 1879 she was married to Rev. William B. Brown, D.D., then of New York City. Soon after their marriage Dr. and Mrs. Brown went abroad for two or three years, and visited for study the chief art centers of Europe, passing in every country as natives. On their return to America they settled permanently in East Orange, NJ. Mrs. Brown was soon elected president of the Woman's Club of Orange, which greatly prospered under her leadership. She was also engaged in arranging plans of work for the Woman's Board of Missions and was active as a member of the advisory board for the organization and success of the General Federation of Women's Literary Clubs. At the organization convention, in the spring of 1890, Mrs. Brown was elected its first president. There were then fifty literary clubs in the federation. In less than two years that number had increased to over one-hundred-twenty, representing twenty-nine States and enrolling twenty thousand of the intelligent, earnest women of the land. Mrs. Brown was greatly interested in the woman's club movement and gladly devoted her whole time to work for its advancement. She possessed unusual power of memory, mental concentration, energy and business ability, combined with such sweetness of disposition and deference for others as to make it easy for her to accomplish whatever she undertook. She was enthusiastic and inspired others with her own magnetism. She combines the power of general plan with minute detail, and her motto was that what should be done at all should be done promptly and thoroughly. She was the author of many articles that have appeared in magazines and in other forms, mainly in the interests of whatever work she might at the time have had in hand. She carried on a very extensive correspondence and relied largely upon this agency for the full accomplishment of her well-considered plans. Mrs. Brown died in East Orange, NJ, 5th February, 1895.

BROWN, Mrs. Corinne Stubbs, socialist, born in what is now the very heart of Chicago, IL, in 1849. Her mother, Jane Mc-Williams, was born in London, England, and when a child was keenly alive to the part taken by her elder brothers in the repeal of the Corn Laws of England. Coming to the United States when she was seventeen years old, she met and was married to Timothy R. Stubbs, the father of Corinne. He was from Maine, with its hard, stony soil, a stair-builder by trade, and a man of strong and somewhat domineering character. His idea of parental duty led him to keep strict watch on his daughters. He forbade the reading of fiction and insisted on regular attendance at the Sweden-borgian church. The latter command was obeyed, but the former was by Corinne considered unreasonable, and therefore disregarded. She read everything that came in her way, but her vigorous intellect refused to assimilate anything that could weaken it, and to-day fiction has little attraction for her, unless it be of marked excellence or originality. She acquired her education in the public schools of Chicago, continuing after her graduation to identify herself with them as a teacher. Good order and discipline were the rule in her department, and her governing ability led in time to her appointment as principal, a post which she relinquished to become the wife of Frank E. Brown, a gentleman well known in business circles, whose name may be found on the list of officers of many benevolent enterprises. During the quiet of domestic life succeeding her marriage, Mrs. Brown's active mind prepared itself for new fields of thought arid research, and she eagerly seized upon the social problems which began to thrust themselves upon the notice of all thinking people. She read, studied and talked with those who had investigated the causes of the glaring inequalities in social position, and of the increasing number of immense fortunes on the one hand and pauperism on the other. For a time she affiliated with the single-tax party, but its methods did not satisfy her as being adequate to effect the social revolution necessary to banish involuntary poverty. After much research she accepted socialism as the true remedy and Karl Marx as its apostle. Out of this naturally grew her desire to work for the helpless and oppressed, especially among women. She joined the Ladies' Federal Labor Union, identifying herself with working women and gaining an insight into their needs. In 1888 a meeting of that society was called to take action on an exposure of the wrongs of factory employees made in a daily paper. The result of the meeting was the organization of the Illinois Woman's Alliance, to obtain the enforcement and enactment of factory ordinances and of the compulsory education laws. As president of that society, which now includes delegates from twenty eight organizations of women, Mrs. Brown has become widely known. In addition to her work in the Alliance, Mrs. Brown is connected with the Nationalists, the Queen Isabella Association and other societies, chiefly those having for their object the advancement of women.

BROWN, Miss Emma Elizabeth, author, born in Concord, NH. 18th October, 1847. Her girlhood memories are of that comely and prosperous inland city, historic in age and act. There she lived among her own people till the requirements of her work drew her to Boston, MA. She now resides in Newton Highlands. During her school days she sent to the Concord "Monitor" a poem. That was the first of many contributions to various literary and religious newspapers, the "Atlantic Monthly," "Aldine," the "Living Age," and other magazines. Her only volume of poems is a brochure entitled "A Hundred Years Ago" (Boston, 1876). Six volumes of the "Spare Minute Series" are of her compiling, and five of the "Biographical Series" are of her writing. Her Sunday-school books are "From Night to Light" (Boston, 1872), a story of the Babylonish Captivity, and "The Child Toilers of the Boston Streets" (Boston, 1874).

BROWN, Mrs. Harriet A., inventor, born in Augusta, ME, 20th February, 1844. She is of Scotch parentage and early in life was thrown upon her own resources. Mrs. Brown conceived the idea of establishing a regular school of training for women who desired to make themselves self-supporting, and, on the solicitation of many prominent and philanthropic women of Boston, she opened the Dress-Cutting College in that city on 17th October, 1886. In opening her college she had the cooperation of those who induced her to establish such a school in Boston but the underlying ideas, the scientific rules for dress-cutting, the patented system used, and all the methods of instruction, are her own. Mrs. Brown's system of cutting is the result of years of study. All its points she has thoroughly mastered, and has succeeded in patenting rules for cutting, and also obtained the only patent for putting work together. Delegates from the Pratt Institute, Brooklyn, NY, after investigating all the principal European methods, adopted Mrs. Brown's system, and it has been in use for two years in that institution. It is one of the regular features of the Moody Schools, Northfield, MA, where young women are educated for missionary work.

BROWN, Mrs. Martha McClellan, born near Baltimore, MD, 16th April, 1838. On her father's side she is descended from the McClellans, Covenanters of Scotland, and on the mother's side from the old Maryland families of Manypenny and Hight. She was married in her twentieth year to Rev. W. K. Brown, of the Pittsburgh Methodist Episcopal Conference. In the fall of 1860 Mrs. M. McClellan Brown entered the Pittsburgh Female College, and in 1862 was graduated. In 1866 Mrs. Brown, owing to the unexpected death of the principal of the public schools in the county-seat of Columbiana county, OH, where her husband had been appointed pastor, was engaged as associate principal with him. In 1867 she was elected to a place in the executive committee of Ohio Good Templary, and immediately founded the temperance lecture system. In 1868 she took editorial charge of the Republican newspaper of Alliance, OH. Julius A. Spencer, of Cleveland, secretary of Ohio Good Templary in 1868, proposed to Mrs. Brown the formation of an independent political party, and she extended her hand to assist him. The question being further discussed, Mrs. Brown's husband required that, before his wife should unite in the movement for a new party, there must be an agreement to place woman on an equal status with man. Mr. Spencer finally agreed that woman should have equal status in the new party, and that a plank asserting this fact should be inserted in the platform, provided they were not expected to discuss that issue before the people. The Prohibition party was organized in Ohio early in the following year, 1869. In 1870 Mr. Brown purchased the political newspaper of which his wife was editor, and for years that paper was made the vehicle of vigorous warfare against the liquor traffic. In 1872 Mrs. Brown was elected a delegate of Good Templary to Great Britain. Very shortly thereafter she was called to the headship of the order in the State of Ohio. When Mrs. Brown appeared upon the platform in Scotland and England in 1873, audiences of from 5,000 to 10,000 greeted the American temperance woman, and her title of Grand Chief Templar of Ohio was a passport to recognitions of royalty, even so far remote as Milan, Italy. She was elected at the State Grand Lodge of Ohio, held in Columbus in 1873, to succeed herself in the office she held. In her capacity of Chief Templar she issued an order in January, 1874, for a day of fasting and prayer in the three-hundred lodges of Ohio under her jurisdiction, and encouraged that all ministers of religion favorable to the order and the cause of temperance he invited to unite with the Good Templars. Finding that the women who had become active in the out-door work of the crusade were not satisfied to enter the Good Templar lodges, Mrs. Brown, at the suggestion of her husband, prepared a plan for the organization of crusaders in a national society without passwords or symbols, under which plan open religious temperance meetings and work should be prosecuted, women being the chief instruments of such work. She afterward was chiefly instrumental in gathering the women in the first national convention in Cleveland, OH, where she largely assisted in developing her plan, which was made the basis of the permanent organization of the National Woman's Christian Temperance Union. Just after the founding of the Woman's Christian Temperance Union, in August, 1874, Mrs. Brown was elected Right Grand Vice-Templar of the International Order of Good Templars, in Boston, MA. In 1876 Mrs. Brown objected to the attitude of the majority of the Right Grand Lodge of Good Templars in rejecting lodges of colored people, and so withdrew and united with the English delegates. After ten years of separation the two bodies adjusted their issue by providing for regular lodges of colored people, and were reunited in 1886, at Saratoga, NY. In 1877, after repeated personal efforts with leading Republican officials, State and National, had failed to secure any actual, or even fairly promised political, antagonisms of the liquor interests, Mrs. Brown went to New York City and assumed the management of the newly organized National Prohibition Alliance. In October, 1881, Mrs. Brown gathered through personal letters, special circulars and press notices a large national conference of leading Prohibitionists and reformers in the Central Methodist Episcopal Church, New York City. Before that conference she made one of her most impassioned appeals for unity among temperance workers, whereby the National Prohibition Alliance was led to unite formally with the Prohibition Reform party. The success of the New York conference led to a similar conference in Chicago the following year, August, 1882, which was arranged for by Mrs. Brown, and which was more successful than the one held in New York. Many of the old leaders of the Prohibition Reform party were induced to attend the Chicago conference. At that conference Miss Frances E. Willard and her immediate following of Home Protectionists and the Woman's Christian Temperance Union were brought into the Prohibition party, besides many local organizations of temperance workers. Mrs. Brown thereupon dropped the non-partisan National Prohibition Alliance, believing that it had served its purpose. In the summer of 1882 Dr. and Mrs. Brown were elected to the presidency and vice-presidency of the Cincinnati Wesleyan College. The entire management of the institution has since devolved upon them, Mrs. Brown holding a professorship as well as the vice-presidency of the college. Among others she has received the degrees of Ph.D. and LL.D.

BROWN, Miss M. Belle, physician and surgeon, born in Troy, OH, 1st March, 1850. She was educated in the high school of her native town, and in the Oxford Female College, Oxford, OH. Her ancestor, Chad Brown, emigrated from England to Providence, RI, in the year of his arrival. He was one of a committee of four to prepare the first written form of government adopted and continued in force until 1644, when Roger Williams returned from England with the charter and Chad Brown was the first one of the thirty-nine who signed that charter. In 1642 he was ordained the first settled pastor of the Baptist Church. His great grandsons, John and James, repurchased a part of the land that had originally belonged to him and presented it to the college of Rhode Island. In 1770 the cornerstone of University Hall was laid by John Brown. In 1804 the name of that institution was changed to Brown University. Doctor Brown commenced the study of medicine in 1874. In 1876 she went to New York and entered the New York Medical College and Hospital for Women. She was graduated in 1879 and entered immediately upon a general practice in West 34th street, New York, where she still resides. She is one of the few women in medicine who practice surgery. She makes a specialty of diseases of women, and is professor of diseases of women in the New York Medical College and Hospital for Women, and is also secretary of the faculty of that institution. She is a member of the American Institute of Homoeopathy of the New York County Medical Society, a member of the consulting staff of the Memorial Hospital in Brooklyn, and of the New York Homoeopathic Sanitarium Association.

BROWN, Olympia, Universalist minister, born in Prairie Ronde, Kalamazoo county, MI, 5th January, 1835. Though a Wolverine, and always claiming to be a representative Western woman, Olympia's ancestry belonged to what Oliver Wendell Holmes would call "The Brahmin Caste of New England," though both her parents were Vermont mountaineers. On her father's side she traces her lineage directly back to that sturdy old patriot, Gen. Putnam, of Revolutionary fame, and through her mother she belongs to a branch of the Parkers, of Massachusetts. Olympia's parents moved to Michigan, as pioneers, in what was then the remote West. Her birthplace was a log-house, and her memories of childhood are the narrow experiences common to a farmer's

Edith Crane.
From Photo Copyrighted, 1895, by Morrison, Chicago.

Ethel Barrymore.
From Photo by Morrison, Chicago.

household in a new country, with only the exceptional stimulus to mental culture afforded by the self-denial of a mother determined that her daughters should enjoy every advantage of study she could possibly obtain for them. At the age of fifteen Olympia was promoted to the office of mistress of the district school and was familiarized with all the delights of "boarding around." She alternated teaching in a country school in summer with study in the village academy in winter, till, in the fall of 1854, she entered Mount Holyoke Female Seminary, in South Hadley, MA. Though she remained only one year, reviewing branches already quite thoroughly mastered, she there first began to be interested in those theological investigations that have shaped her life. Questioning the doctrinal teaching made prominent in the seminary, she secured the strongest Universalist documents she could find and laid the foundations of a faith never since shaken. Attracted by the reputation of Horace Mann as an educator, she became a student in Antioch College, OH, and was graduated from that institution in 1860. The question confronted her then, "what use shall I make of my life?" To a careful paper, asking advice of the college faculty on that point, she received, as their best deliberate thought, direction to an indefinite course of reading and study, with the one aim of selfish intellectual enjoyment, varied by purely private acts of charity. Against the narrow limitations of such an existence all the activities of her soul rebelled, and, after much thought and in spite of determined opposition from every quarter, she chose the profession of the ministry, and was graduated from the Theological seminary, in Canton, NY, a branch of St. Lawrence University. She was ordained in Malone, NY, in June, 1863, by vote of the ordaining council of the Universalist Church, the first instance of the ordination of a woman by any regularly constituted ecclesiastical body. There had been woman preachers and exhorters in America ever since the days of Anne Hutchinson, but in no case had such preachers been ordained by ecclesiastical council or by the authority of the church of which she was a representative. This public recognition of a woman minister by a body of the church militant opened the pulpit to women so effectively that her ordination was followed by others of other denominations. Her first pastoral labors were as pulpit supply in Marshfield, VT, in the absence of Rev. Eli Ballou, pastor, and preaching every alternate Sunday in East Montpelier. Desirous of better perfecting herself for efficient service, early in 1864 she moved to Boston and entered the Dio Lewis Gymnastic School, taking lessons in elocution of Prof. Leonard. There she received and accepted a call to the church in Weymouth, MA, and was formally installed as pastor on 8th July, 1864, the Rev. Sylvanus Cobb preaching the installation sermon. Early in her pastorate the question was raised concerning the legality of the marriage rite solemnized by a woman. The subject was brought before the Massachusetts Legislature and referred to the judiciary committee, who decided that, according to the definition of legislative statutes, the masculine and feminine pronouns are there used interchangeably, and the statutes, as then worded, legalized marriages by ministers of the gospel, whether men or women. In the spring of 1866 Olympia attended the Equal Rights convention, held in Dr. Cheever's Church in New York, and there met Susan B. Anthony, Parker Pillsbury and other prominent advocates of woman's enfranchisement. From her early girlhood she had taken a keen interest in every movement tending toward a wider scope for girls and women, but on that occasion she was first brought into personal relations with the active reformers of the day. In 1867 the Kansas Legislature submitted to popular vote a proposition to amend their constitution by striking out the word "male." That was the first time the men of any State were asked to vote upon a measure for woman suffrage. Lucy Stone immediately made arrangements with the Republican central committee to send one woman speaker to aid in the ensuing canvass. In response to urgent importunity that she should become the promised speaker, Olympia obtained the consent of her parish, and personally furnished a supply for her pulpit. She set forth on her arduous mission in July and labored unremittingly till after election. A tour through the wilds of Kansas at that time involved hardships, difficulties and even dangers. Arrangements for travel and fitting escort had been promised her, but nothing was provided. Nevertheless, overcoming obstacles that would have taxed the endurance of the strongest man, she completed the entire canvass of the settled portions of the State. Between 5th July and 5th November she made 205 speeches, traveling, not infrequently, fifty miles to reach an appointment. The Republican party, that submitted the proposition and induced her engagement in the field, so far stultified its own action as to send out circulars and speakers to defeat the measure, and yet, by her eloquent appeals, she had so educated public sentiment that the result showed more than one-third of the voting citizens in favor of the change. Olympia's pastoral connection with the church in Weymouth continued nearly six years. But, she said characteristically, the church was then on so admirable a footing she could safely trust it to a man's management and she desired for herself a larger field, involving harder toil. She accepted a call to the church in Bridgeport, CT, then in a comatose condition. Immediately affairs assumed a new aspect, the church membership rapidly increased, the Sunday-school, which had had only a nominal existence, became one of the finest in the city, and the work of the church in all good causes was marked for its excellence and efficiency. She severed her connection with the church in April, 1876. She remained in New England, preaching in many States, as opportunity offered, till February, 1878, when she accepted a call to the pastorate of the Universalist Church in Racine, WI. There she made for herself a home, which is the center of genial I hospitality and the resort of the cultivated and intelligent. She faithfully continued her pastorate with the Racine church, toiling with brain and hand, with zeal unflagging, taxing her resources to the utmost to help the society meet its financial emergencies, till the time of her resignation, in February, 1887. Of her work there, a member of her parish writes: "When she came to Racine some of the parish were groping about in search of 'advanced thought;' some, for social and other causes, had become interested in other churches, and some were indifferent. Her sermons interested the indifferent, called many of the wanderers back and furnished food for thought to the most advanced thinkers. Her addresses were always in point." It is noticeable that all the churches with which Olympia has been connected have continued to be active, working parishes, dating a new life from the time of her union with them, thus showing that her quickening is not the transient development of abnormal excitment, but healthy growth from central, vital truth planting. Since her resignation of her pulpit in Racine, while still keeping the interest of Universalism near her heart, and losing no opportunity to extend its borders and expound its doctrines, and continuing actively in the ministry, Olympia has given

the larger part of her time to the Wisconsin Woman Suffrage Association, of which she has been for several years the president and central inspiration. As vice-president of the National Woman Suffrage Association she has been able to raise an eloquent voice in behalf of progress and has done much to recommend that organization to the people. In the course of her public career she has many times been called to address the legislatures of the several States, and her incisive arguments have contributed much to those changes in the laws which have so greatly ameliorated the condition of women. Olympia has not confined her sympathies to womans' rights or to Universalism. She has been and still is a persevering, faithful temperance agitator, working assiduously for almost a score of years in the orders of the Good Templars and the Sons of Temperance. In April, 1873, Olympia was married to John Henry Willis, a business man, entirely in sympathy with her ideas in regard to woman's position. It is by mutual agreement and with his full consent she retains the maiden name her toil has made historic, and continues her public work. Two children beautify the home, H. Parker Brown Willis and Gwendolen Brown Willis. Perhaps one could hardly answer the sophistries of those who claim that the enlargement of woman's sphere of action will destroy the home-life better than by pointing to its practical illustration in her well-ordered home. Perhaps her most prominent characteristic, and one that has been sometimes mistaken for aggressiveness, is her absolute fearlessness in espousing and defending the right.

BROWNE, Mrs. Mary Frank, philanthropist, born in Warsaw, Wyoming county, NY, 9th September. 1835. She is the youngest daughter of Dr. Augustus Frank, who was born in Canaan, CT, and Jane Patterson, of Londonderry, NH. Andrew Frank, father of Dr. Augustus and grandfather of Mrs. Browne, was a German, coming to America before the formation of the United States government. Professors and men of position in the schools and German universities were connected with the Frank families of the Old World. After the completion of Mrs. Browne's education she was engaged in teaching in

Warsaw for a time, in the school established under the auspices of the Presbyterian Church. Her home remained in Warsaw until 1858, when she was married to Philo D. Browne, a banker of Montreal, Canada. Then began her life of regular, organized Christian activity. She was prominent in the organization of the Young Women's Christian Association of Montreal, and served as its president during its first years. She assisted in forming the Ladies' Canadian Foreign Missionary Society, and was one of its officers. Mrs. Browne aided in establishing and was one of the managers of the Infants' Home in Montreal, and was one of the founders and officers of the Canadian Board of Missions. She removed to California in 1876, where, with her husband and family, she made her home in San Francisco. There she found new fields of usefulness. She at once organized the San Francisco Young Women's Christian Association, and for years was its president. When, later, she had her home in Oakland, CA, she remained its vice-president and one of its most active workers. In 1877 she was elected president of the Woman's Occidental Board of Foreign Missions, an office which she now holds. Many perplexing social and political issues have come into the deliberation of the Occidental Board. The entrance into this country of Chinese women at first, and later the coming of Japanese women of the same class, the management of the home which is intended to be their asylum from slavery, the cases in courts where young Chinese girls are called to appear scores of times before they are finally awarded to the guardianship of the home, as in the famous case of the Chinese child, Woon Tsun, are some of the most perplexing questions for the society. In her broad, catholic spirit, Mrs. Browne was ready to help forward the Hyacinthe movement, under the patronage of Père and Madame Hyacinthe. She has been a constant writer for periodicals and is the author of the interesting temperance book, "Overcome "portraying the evils of fashionable wine-drinking and intemperance. She assisted in organizing the noble army of Christian temperance women of California into the State Woman's Christian Temperance Union, and served the union as president for several years. She was also editor for a considerable period of the organ of the society in California. In 1877 she organized the Young Women's Christian Association in Oakland, in the suburbs of which city is located her "Highland Park" home. Of that organization she is

now president. A home for young women, a day nursery for poor laboring mothers, a kindergarten and station for gospel services are some of the plans provided for in the new building about to be erected by that association. For several years she was president of "The Ebell," an art and literary society in Oakland. The first free kindergarten in Oakland had its inception in Mrs. Browne's Bible class of young ladies. She is the mother of three children, two sons and one daughter.

BROWNELL, Mrs. Helen M. Davis, educator, born in Ossian, NY, 31st January, 1836. Her childhood was spent in a Christian home. At an early age she manifested an eager desire for knowledge, using with avidity the means within reach to fit herself for the position of teacher. She became a prominent educator in the public schools of Bloomfield, Lima and Geneseo, NY. Having attained success as an instructor in English branches, she entered the seminary in Lima, that she might fit herself for more advanced work in her profession. For some years she continued her studies in that school. There she met her future husband, W. A. Brownell, then a student in Genesee college. On the completion of his college course they were married, in July, 1865. In September, 1865, her husband became principal of Red Creek Seminary, NY, and she became preceptress. Later, her husband was called to the chair of Latin in Falley Seminary, NY, where she again took the position of preceptress and teacher of French. At that time Falley Seminary stood in the front rank of collegiate preparatory schools. Upon the call of her husband to the principalship of Fairfield Seminary, NY, she discontinued teaching, and during their three years' residence there her first son was born. In 1871, her husband having accepted a position in the high school in Syracuse, NY, they removed to that city, and there they still reside. Mrs. Brownell gave herself heartily to the making of a home, meanwhile carrying on with enthusiasm her studies in general literature and natural history, particularly in the department of botany. Her home has been not only a safe retreat for her husband and children, but its doors have always been open to receive to its sheltering care young men and women who were struggling to prepare for life's duties. To these young people she has given advice, inspiring and inciting them to the highest aspirations, and aiding and directing them in their studies. She had enjoyed the advantages of travel, both in America and Europe. Within the last few years, since her household duties have been less imperative, she has given herself zealously to the work of the Woman's Home Missionary Society, speaking often in various conventions and conferences.

BROWNSCOMBE, Miss Jennie, artist, born near Honesdale, PA, 10th December, 1850. Her father, a farmer, was a native of Devonshire, England. Her mother belonged to a family conspicuous among the Connecticut pioneers, who came to the Colonies in 1640 with Governor Winthrop. Miss Brownscombe was the only child. She was studious and precocious, and about equally inclined to art and literature. She early showed a talent for drawing, and when only seven years old she began drawing, using the juices of flowers and leaves with which to color her pictures. In school she illustrated every book that had a blank leaf or margin available. Her father died before she left school, and her mother in 1891. When Jennie was eighteen years old, she began to teach school, and at the age of twenty she became a student in the Cooper Institute School of Design for Women in New York, from which she won a medal at the end of a year, and for several succeeding years she studied in the National Academy, winning first medals in the life and antique schools. In the second year of her study she began to make drawings on wood for "Harper's Weekly" and other periodicals, and to teach drawing and painting. She devoted her study mainly to genre figure painting and has made a large number of portraits. Her first important picture was exhibited in 1876 in the Academy of Design in New York. She was one of the first members of the Art Students' League. In 1882 she went to Paris and studied under Harry Moster. On her return in 1883 she was incapacitated from work by an injury to her eyes, and for a year she did but little. Her pictures have been reproduced in photogravures, etchings and engravings for the past six years. Some of her most widely known pictures are "Grandmother's Treasures," "Love's Young Dream," "Blossom Time," "Halcyon Days," "The Gleaners," "Sunday Morning in Sleepy Hollow," "The Recessional" and "The Sirens." Miss Brownscombe now lives in Honesdale, PA.

BRYAN, Mrs. Mary Edwards, author, born in Jefferson county, FL, in 1846. Her father was Major John D. Edwards, one of the early settlers in Florida and a member of the State legislature. Mary was educated by her cultured mother until she was twelve years old. The family moved to Thomasville, GA, where she enjoyed the advantages of good schooling and made rapid progress. When she was sixteen, she was married to Mr. Bryan, the son of a wealthy Louisiana planter, with whom she went to his plantation on the Red river. One year later, under the pressure of painful circumstances, she returned to her father's home. There she began to write for the press. She wrote regularly for the "Literary and Temperance Crusader," published in Penfield, GA. She contributed many columns to that journal, in both prose and verse, and her productions attracted attention. In 1859 the "Crusader" was enlarged, improved and removed to Atlanta, and Mrs. Bryan was engaged as literary editor. She filled the position with brilliant success and brought the journal into prominence. At the end of 1859 she resigned her position on the "Crusader" and became a correspondent of the "Southern Field and Fireside." After the Civil War she became the editor of the Natchitoches, LA, "Semi-Weekly Times," writing political articles, sketches, stories and poems. Her next position was on the "Sunny South," published in Atlanta, GA, which paper she edited for ten years. In 1885 she removed to New York City, where she served as assistant editor of "The Fashion Bazaar" and of "The Fireside Companion." Among her novels are: "Manch" (New York, 1879); "Wild Work," a story of the days of reconstruction in Louisiana (1881), and "The Bayou Bride" and "Kildee" (1886). Mrs. Bryan has a family of four children and several grandchildren. Her home is now in Atlanta, GA, where she has editorial charge of "The Old Homestead," a monthly magazine.

BUCK, Mme. Henriette, educator, born in London, England, 8th January, 1864, during a casual sojourn of her parents, who are Parisians, in that city. Her maiden name was Berdot. Her father, Henri Berdot, is a descendant of a noble Spanish family. One of her aunts, the Baronne de Carbonnel and Marquise de Baudricourt, was a clever author of some reputation. Madame Buck was educated in the best schools in Paris, and after receiving various scholastic honors she obtained the highly prized diploma of the University of France, which entitles the receiver to hold the position of professor in any scholastic position in France. After teaching successfully for several years, she was married to W. Edgar Buck, an eminent bass vocalist and professor of singing, who was a former pupil of Signor Manuel Garcia. Madame Buck and her husband came to America and settled in Montreal, Canada, where they were successful in their respective professions. In June, 1890, Mr. Buck was called to Toronto, Canada, as conductor of the Toronto Vocal Society. Madame Buck formed French classes in that city, and has been very successful in private tuition. She is the leading teacher of French in Toronto. Her literary talent is shown in the comedies and plays which she writes for her classes to perform. She writes fluently in both English and French and is an accomplished musician.

BUCK, Mrs. Mary K., author, born in Ondreor, Bohemia, 1st April, 1849. Her parents carne to America, when she was five years old, and for several years lived in New York City, where she went to school and acquired her knowledge of the English language. From New York they removed to Traverse City, MI, which has since been her home. From a child she was fond of books, reading eagerly whatever came to hand. English books were rare in her Bohemian home, but the little town library, of which she was an unfailing patron, was well stocked with some of the best. Early in life she developed a talent for composition, especially of an imaginative kind, which was encouraged by her teachers and friends. She is happily married, and has three chil-

dren. Always interested in the advancement of women, she has in her own career demonstrated the fact that a woman can at once be a good mother, an excellent housekeeper and a successful business woman. In an exceptionally busy life she has found time to write much for publication. During the summer of 1891 she published, together with Mrs. M. E. C. Bates, a book of short sketches entitled "Along Traverse Shores." She has contributed to the "Congregationalist," the "Advance," the Chicago "Inter-Ocean," the Portland "Transcript," "Good Housekeeping," "St. Nicholas" and many other periodicals.

BUCKNOR, Mrs. Helen Lewis, author, born in New York City, 10th October, 1838. She is of Revolutionary ancestry and New England parentage. Her maiden name was Lewis. Upon the father's side she is descended from the Lewises and Tomlinsons of Stratford, CT. On the mother's side she is descended from the Spragues and Ketchums, of Connecticut originally, but afterward of Long Island. Her grandfather Sprague settled in early times in New York City as a merchant. Her father died when she was a child, and, as she was very delicate, it was decided that she should be brought up in the South by an uncle, the brother of her mother, who had married and settled near Natchez, MS. Her school life was passed there. In her early girlhood she went to the Northwest as a teacher, maintaining herself until the war broke out, when she returned to her southern home and to new and sad experiences. Soon after the close of the war she was married to W. F. Bucknor, of New York City. It was her husband's misfortune to have inherited a large tract of pine lands in Florida. In 1870 he with his wife removed to that State. They were unfitted to endure the privations and discouragements of a pioneer life in that devastated country at that period, and, holding, as they did, strong Republican principles, their experiences were sometimes thrilling in the extreme. Many able articles were published in the press from their ready pens. Mrs. Bucknor's articles of advice to Florida women, who, like herself, were making strenuous efforts to help their husbands to secure homes in that State, were marked by strength and good sense. The Toledo "Blade," the "Home Journal" and other periodicals published her articles. She is possessed of poetic talent, but excels in sharp, pithy, truthful sketches of human nature as she finds it. She is an earnest worker among the King's Daughters and is a member of the Woman's Christian Temperance Union. She now lives in St. Augustine, FL, and is a member of the Flagler Memorial Church in that city.

BUELL, Mrs. Caroline Brown, temperance worker and philanthropist, was born in Massachusetts. Her ancestry was New England and Puritan. She is a daughter of Rev. Thomas G. Brown, of the New England Conference of the Methodist Episcopal Church. Her early life was passed in the way common to the children of itinerant ministers. Hard work, earnest study and self-reliance developed her character on rugged and noble lines. She had a thirst for learning that caused her to improve in study all the time that the only daughter of an itinerant minister could find for books. Arrived at womanhood, she became the wife of Frederick V. H. Buell, a noble and patriotic young Connecticut man, who had enlisted in the Union army at the beginning of the Civil War. During the war her father, husband and three brothers served the Union, three in the army and two brothers in the navy. Her father was the chaplain of her husband's regiment, and in war he earned the name of "The Fighting Chaplain." During those dreary years Mrs. Buell worked, watched and waited, and in the last year of the conflict her husband died, leaving her alone with her only son. She soon became identified with the temperance reform and in 1875 was chosen corresponding secretary of the Woman's Christian Temperance Union of Connecticut, which had been partially organized the previous winter. She entered heartily into the work, and her sound judgment, her powers of discrimination, her energy, her acquaintance with facts and persons, and her facile pen made her at once a power in the association. She came into office when much was new and experimental, and she gave positive direction to the work and originated many plans of procedure. She was the originator of the plan of quarterly returns in Connecticut, a system that has been quite generally adopted in other States. In 1880, in the Boston convention, Mrs. Buell was chosen corresponding secretary of the National Woman's Christian Temperance Union, and in that exalted and responsible position she has done good and effective work with pen, hand and tongue for the association. She has been re-elected to that office regularly for twelve years. She is a dignified presiding officer and an accomplished parliamentarian, and in State conventions she has often filled the chair in emergencies. The war record of her family makes her a favorite with the veterans of the Civil War, and she has, on many occasions, addressed conventions of the G.A.R. Of singularly gentle nature and quiet manners, they are combined with exceptional force of character.

BULL, Mrs. Sarah C. Thorpe, wife of Ole Bull, the famous violinist, is the superintendent of the department of sanitary and economic cookery in the National Women's Christian Temperance Union. She has translated "The Pilot and His Wife" by Jonas Lie (Chicago, 1876), and "The Barque 'Future'" (Chicago, 1879), by the same author. She has also published a "Memoir of Ole Bull" (Boston, 1883.) She was largely instrumental in securing the monument to Ericsson on Commonwealth avenue, Boston. Her home is in Cambridge, MA.

BULLOCK, Mrs. Helen Louise, musical educator and temperance reformer, born in Norwich, NY, 29th April, 1836. She is the youngest daughter of Joseph and Phebe Wood Chapel, from of New England origin. While lacking no interest in other branches, she early possessed a great desire to study music, and at eighteen years of age began to teach piano and vocal music. Some years later she studied the piano with S. B. Mills, and the guitar with Count Lepcowshi, both of New York City. With the exception of two years, she taught music from 1854 to 1886, and was for many years a member of the National Music Teachers' Association. In 1881 she published two books of musical studies, "Scales and Chords" and "Improved Musical Catechism," both of which have had a large sale. When

William A. Pond, who purchased the copyrights, was arranging for their publication, he requested the author's name to be given as H. L. Bullock, in order that the foreign teachers might not know they were written by a woman, and therefore be prejudiced against or undervalue them. At twenty years of age Miss Chapel was married to Daniel S. Bullock, son of Rev. Seymour Bullock, of Prospect, NY. Two children were born to them, a daughter who died at two years of age, and a son who died at the age of twenty-seven. Soon after the death of her son, in 1884, she adopted a little motherless girl five years of age, who has proved a very great comfort. Mrs. Bullock's religious training was in the Presbyterian Church and Sunday-school, but, when converted, her ideas on baptism led her to unite with the Baptist Church, of which she is still a member. She has always been actively interested in the Sunday school and missionary work. From 1871 to 1885 her home was in Fulton, NY, but after a serious illness of pneumonia her physician recommended a milder climate, and the family moved to Elmira, NY. The following April, 1886, a Woman's Christian Temperance Union was re-organized in that city, and she was unanimously elected president. In September of that year Mrs. Mary T. Burt, president of the New York State Woman's Christian Temperance Union, organized Chemung county and urged Mrs. Bullock to go into the adjoining counties of Broome, Schuyler, Tioga and Yates and organize them, which she did. Taking up her public work with great timidity, she was pressed further and further into it, until she was forced to decide as to her future. It was very hard for her to give up her profession, but after much prayerful consideration she devoted the remainder of her life to the uplifting of humanity and the overthrow of the liquor traffic. In 1886 she was appointed State organizer of the New York Woman's Christian Temperance Union, in 1887 State superintendent of the department of narcotics, and in 1888 National lecturer on that subject. She was instrumental in securing the New York State law against selling cigarettes and tobacco to minors. In the interest of that department she wrote the leaflet "The Tobacco Toboggan." In 1889 she was appointed National organizer of the Woman's Christian Temperance Union, and in that work has gone from Maine to California, traveling thirteen thousand miles in one year. In that department she has achieved marked success. During the first five years she held over twelve-hundred meetings, organizing one-hundred-eighty new unions, and securing over ten-thousand members, active and honorary. She is deeply interested in prison and police matron work, and has been president, since its organization, of the Anchorage of Elmira, a rescue home for young girls. In 1892 she was appointed superintendent of the school of methods of the New York State Woman's Christian Temperance Union.

BUMSTEAD, Mrs. Eudora Stone, poet, born in Bedford, MI, 26th August, 1860. In 1862 her parents removed to Nebraska. Her earliest recollections are of the great West, with its prairie billows crested with pleasant homes, its balmy breezes and its sweeping gales. Her parents were highly cultured, and gave her every possible assistance and encouragement. She began to write rhymes in her childhood, and when ten years old a poem from her pen was published in "Our Young Folks," then edited by J. T. Trowbridge. Receiving a good common-school education, she was for a time a successful school-teacher. In 1878–79 she was a student in the Nebraska State University. There she met William T. Bumstead, to whom she was married in 1880. One of their two children, a son, died in infancy, and the other, a daughter, brightens their pleasant home in Ontario, CA. Mrs. Bumstead is of Quaker descent, and is like the Friends in her quiet tastes and sincere manners. Except to a congenial few, she is almost as much a stranger in her own town as abroad. Remarkably well informed and having an analytic mind, she is a keen, though kindly, disputant, accepting nothing as proved which does not stand the test of reason. She has had little time for writing and has used her pen mostly to please the child-readers of "St. Nicholas" and the "Youth's Companion," having been a special contributor to the latter for several years. She thoroughly enjoys her work and asks nothing of fame but to win for her a circle of loving little friends.

BURLINGAME, Mrs. Emeline S., editor and evangelist, born in Smithfield, RI, 22nd September, 1836. Her maiden name was Emeline

Stanley Aldrich. Her father was a public speaker of ability, and her mother was a woman of much energy. After graduating in the Providence high school at the age of fifteen, she pursued a course of study in the Rhode Island Normal School, and then taught five years. In November, 1859, she was married to Luther R. Burlingame and subsequently lived in Wellsboro, PA, and Whitesboro, NY, afterward removing to Dover, NH, and then back to her home in Providence. She early became active in Christian work and, while living in Dover, became a regular contributor to the "Morning Star" and "Little Star," published by the Free Baptists. About the same time she became editor of the "Myrtle," a paper for children. On her removal to Providence she assisted her husband in editing "Town and Country," a temperance paper. In 1873 she was elected president of the Free Baptist Woman's Missionary Society, which position she held for thirteen years, resigning when elected editor of the "Missionary Helper," the organ of the society. She introduced into the magazine features which made it a helper to missionary workers. In 1879 she was elected corresponding secretary and organizer for the Rhode Island Woman's Christian Temperance Union, and began at once to address audiences and to organize unions in different parts of the State. In 1884 she was elected president of the Union and devoted the next seven years to speaking and planning in its interest. In the securing of a prohibitory amendment to the constitution of Rhode Island, the Woman's Christian Temperance Union was the acknowledged leader, and to that work Mrs. Burlingame bent the energy of her life. In 1889 she was a delegate to the General Conference from the Rhode Island Free Baptist Association, that being the first year when women were sent as delegates to that body. In 1890 she was licensed to preach by the Rhode Island Free Baptist Ministers' Association. In 1891, being seriously worn by her prolonged labors for temperance, she resigned the presidency of the Rhode Island Woman's Christian Temperance Union, and was elected National Woman's Christian Temperance Union evangelist. She soon after accepted the position of general agent of the Free Baptist Woman's Missionary Society, and since that time has been traveling, visiting quarterly and yearly conferences and churches, and addressing them on the broadest phases of missionary work, including the important reforms of the day.

BURNETT, Miss Cynthia S., educator and temperance reformer, born in Hartford, OH, 1st May, 1840. She is the oldest daughter of a descendant of the early settlers of New Jersey. Her mother is a Virginian by birth and education. Her early life was divided between home duties and study till the age of seventeen, when she began her career as a teacher in the public schools near her home, a part of each year being spent as a student in the neighboring academy. The Civil War changed the current of her life, and she resolved to obtain the best education possible and to devote her life to the profession of her choice. She studied four years in the Western Reserve Seminary, in her own county, from which she was graduated in the classical course in 1868. She at once accepted the position of preceptress and teacher of Latin in Orwell Normal Institute. Three years later she took the position of teacher of languages in Beaver College. Failing health made a change of climate necessary, and she went to the old home of her mother in Virginia, where for a time she had charge of a training-school for teachers. Two years were spent in the Methodist Episcopal College in Tullahoma, TN. There she became interested in the "New South," and many letters were written for the press in defense of the struggling people. At the first opportunity after the crusade she donned the white ribbon. Her first public work was done in 1879, in Illinois. Later she answered calls for help in Florida, Tennessee, OH and Pennsylvania. In 1885 she was made State organizer of Ohio. The first year she lectured one-hundred-sixty-five times, besides holding meetings in the day-time and organizing over forty unions. Her voice failing, she accepted a call to Utah, as teacher in the Methodist Episcopal College in Salt Lake City. She was made Territorial president of the Woman's Christian Temperance Union. Eight unions and fifteen loyal legions were organized by her. Each month one or more meetings were held by her in the penitentiary. She edited a temperance column in a Mormon paper. Tabernacles and school-houses were open to her, and through the assistance of missionaries and Mormons alike the gospel of temperance was presented in many towns. Unable longer to work so hard, and believing that her real place was in the lecture field, she accepted a call to southern California as State organizer. She spent one year there and in Nevada, during which time one-hundred-fifty lectures were given by her. For efficient service in the West she was made National organizer in 1889, but was soon after called home by the serious illness of her mother, and she has remained near or with her parents ever since. She continued her work as State organizer until recently, when she accepted the position of preceptress in her Alma Mater now Farmington College.

BURNETT, Mrs. Frances Hodgson, novelist, born in Manchester, England, 24th November, 1849. She lived in Manchester until 1864, acquiring that familiarity with the Lancashire character and dialect which is so noticeable in her works of later years. Her parents suffered financial reverses in 1865, her father died, and the family came to the United States. They settled in Knoxville, TN, and afterward moved to Newmarket, TN. Mrs. Hodgson took a farm, where her two sons and three daughters could work and earn their bread. Frances began to write short stories, the first of which was published in a Philadelphia magazine in 1867. She persevered and soon had a market for her work, "Peterson's Magazine," and "Godey's Lady's Book," publishing many of her stories before she became famous. In 1872 she contributed to "Scribner's Magazine" a story in dialect, "Surly Tim's Trouble," which scored an immediate success. Miss Hodgson became the wife of Dr. Luan M. Burnett, of Knoxville, in 1873. They made a long tour in Europe and, returning in 1875, made their home in Washington, DC, where they now reside. Her famous story, "That Lass o' Lowrie's," created a sensation as it was published serially in "Scribner's Magazine." It was issued in book form (New York, 1877), and it found a wide sale, both in the United States and in Europe, running

through many editions. On the stage the dramatized story was received with equal favor. In 1878 and 1879 she republished some of her earlier stories, which had appeared in various magazines. Among those are "Kathleen Mavourneen," "Lindsay's Luck," "Miss Crespigny," "Pretty Polly Pemberton" and "Theo." These stories had appeared in a Philadelphia magazine, and had been published in book form, without her permission, by a house in that city, a proceeding which caused a controversy in public. Her plots were pilfered by dramatists, and all the evidences of popularity were showered upon her. Her later novels, "Haworth's" (New York, 1879), "Louisiana" (New York, 1881), "A Fair Barbarian" (New York, 1882), and "Through One Administration" (New York, 1883), have confirmed her reputation. But her greatest success, on the whole, has been won by her "Little Lord Fauntleroy," which first appeared as a serial in "St. Nicholas," in 1886. It was subsequently published in book form and was dramatized, appearing on the English and American stages with great success. Mrs. Burnett is very fond of society, but her health is too delicate to enable her to give time to both society and literary work. She has been a sufferer from nervous prostration, and since 1885, has not been a voluminous writer. She has published "Sara Crewe" (New York, 1888), "Editha's Burglar" (Boston, 1888), and "Little Saint Elizabeth" and other stories (New York, 1890). Mrs. Burnett is the mother of two sons, one of whom died at an early age. Despite her long residence abroad, she calls herself thoroughly American.

BURNHAM, Miss Bertha H., author and educator, born in Essex, MA, 22nd April, 1866. She is a resident of Lynn, MA. In her early childhood her love for reading and writing was manifested. It was not until her sixteenth year that any of her writings were published, and those possessed the many crudities common to immaturity. Since that time she has written short articles and poems, whenever school duties and health permitted, her themes generally being of a religious nature. Recently her mind has turned toward pedagogical writing, as she has been a successful teacher for the past four years. Her writings have appeared in the New York "Independent," "Wide Awake," Chicago "Advance," "Sunday-School Times," "Education" and other periodicals.

BURNHAM, Mrs. Clara Louise, novelist, born in Newton, MA, 25th May, 1854. She is the oldest daughter of Dr. George F. Root, the eminent musical composer. Her father, becoming the senior partner of the Chicago firm of Root & Cady, 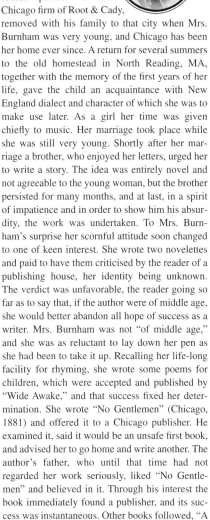 removed with his family to that city when Mrs. Burnham was very young, and Chicago has been her home ever since. A return for several summers to the old homestead in North Reading, MA, together with the memory of the first years of her life, gave the child an acquaintance with New England dialect and character of which she was to make use later. As a girl her time was given chiefly to music. Her marriage took place while she was still very young. Shortly after her marriage a brother, who enjoyed her letters, urged her to write a story. The idea was entirely novel and not agreeable to the young woman, but the brother persisted for many months, and at last, in a spirit of impatience and in order to show him his absurdity, the work was undertaken. To Mrs. Burnham's surprise her scornful attitude soon changed to one of keen interest. She wrote two novelettes and paid to have them criticised by the reader of a publishing house, her identity being unknown. The verdict was unfavorable, the reader going so far as to say that, if the author were of middle age, she would better abandon all hope of success as a writer. Mrs. Burnham was not "of middle age," and she was as reluctant to lay down her pen as she had been to take it up. Recalling her life-long facility for rhyming, she wrote some poems for children, which were accepted and published by "Wide Awake," and that success fixed her determination. She wrote "No Gentlemen" (Chicago, 1881) and offered it to a Chicago publisher. He examined it, said it would be an unsafe first book, and advised her to go home and write another. The author's father, who until that time had not regarded her work seriously, liked "No Gentlemen" and believed in it. Through his interest the book immediately found a publisher, and its success was instantaneous. Other books followed, "A Sane Lunatic" (Chicago, 1882), "Dearly Bought" (Chicago, 1884), "Next Door" (Boston, 1886), "Young Maids and Old" (Boston, 1888), "The Mistress of Beech Knoll" (Boston, 1890), and "Miss Bagg's Secretary" (Boston, 1892). Besides her novels, Mrs. Burnham has written the text for several of Dr. Root's most successful cantatas, and contributed many poems and stories to "Youth's Companion," "St. Nicholas" and "Wide Awake." She resides with her father, and the windows of the room where she works command a wide view of Lake Michigan, whose breezy blue waters serve her for refreshment, not inspiration. She does not believe in the latter for herself. She has a strong love for the profession thrust upon her, and sits down at her desk as regularly as the carpenter goes to his bench. Mrs. Burnham is a cultured pianist. She has no family.

BURNS, Mrs. Nellie Marie, poet, born in Waltham, MA, about 1850. She is a daughter of Dr. Newell Sherman, of Waltham, a descendant of Rev. John Sherman and Mary Launce, a granddaughter of Thomas Darcy, the Earl of Rivers. The family came to America from Dedham, England, in 1642. Her mother's maiden name was Kimball, and she came from the English Brights and Bonds, of Bury St. Edmunds. She was twice married. By her first marriage she was the mother of George C. Cooper, formerly editor of the Rochester, NY, "Union." By her second marriage she became the mother of Mrs. Burns. Nellie became the wife of Thomas H. Burns, the actor, in 1878. She had been a member of the dramatic profession, and she left the stage after marriage, in compliance with the suggestion of her husband. They make their summer home in Kittery Point, ME. Mrs. Burns has written much since 1886 and has prepared her manuscript for publication in book form. She has been a contributor to the Boston "Globe," the Portsmouth "Times," the Waltham "Tribune" and other journals.

BURNZ, Mrs. Eliza B., educator and spelling reformer, born in Rayne, County of Essex, England, 31st October, 1823. From London she came to this country at the age of thirteen, and three years later took up, with her own hands, the battle for bread, a battle she has since maintained unceasingly, and, for the most part, alone and unaided. As an instructor in shorthand she has been successful, and her career as a laborer in her chosen field is a history to which none may point save with pride and commendation. Through the instrumentality of her classes in phonic shorthand in the Burnz School of Shorthand, and in Cooper Institute and the Young Women's Christian Association, in New York City, at least one-thousand young men and women have gone forth to the world well equipped for the positions which they are creditably filling. In addition to these, through the large sales of her text-book, which for many years has been extensively advertised and sold for self-instruction, probably as many more have entered the ranks of the shorthand army as "Burnz" writers. Mrs. Burnz is a member of the New York State Stenographers' Association, and has been its librarian since that body began its collection of stenographic publications. Her popularity among shorthand writers of all schools was shown by her receiving, with the exception of Ed. F. Underhill, the largest number of votes as one of the committee to prepare the Isaac Pitman medal. Aside from her success as a shorthand author and teacher, Mrs. Burnz has for many years been prominently identified with the "spelling reform" movement, having been one of the organizers of the Spelling Reform Association in Philadelphia during the Centennial, in 1876, and for several years a vice-president of that body. Aside from the fact that she has probably published more books and pamphlets in the interest of spelling reform than any other publisher in this country, she has, by her steadfast advocacy of the movement, both in private and public, and by her deep interest at all times in its welfare and advancement, proved herself to be one of the strongest pillars the movement has known. Mrs. Burnz is not only a theoretical, but a practical, spelling reformer, as can be certified by her numerous correspondents. She advocates what is known as the Anglo American alphabet, which was arranged during the formation of the Spelling Reform Association in Philadelphia, in 1876, by Mrs. Burnz and E. Jones of Liverpool, England.

Believing in the old adage, "Never too old to learn," she is now devoting her leisure to the study of Volapük. Although not a strict vegetarian, she is a thorough hygienist. It is to her method of living she attributes the fact that, though puny when a child, she is in good health now. In character she is high-minded, generous to the faults and shortcomings of those with whom she is brought in contact, very strict in her ideas of right and strong in her convictions, not the least important in her eyes being a belief in woman suffrage and equality before the law. She is a stockholder in the Mount Olivet Crematory, located in Freshpond, Long Island, NY, and thoroughly believes in that method of disposing of the body after death. Still a very hard worker, even at her advanced age, she attends to a large amount of teaching, as in years gone by. In her own school she superintends the instruction. She gives class lessons daily for two hours in the Young Women's Christian Association, and, until recently, when her text-book on shorthand was selected for use in the evening schools of the City of New York, she conducted the free evening class in shorthand in Cooper Union. Mrs. Burnz has been twice married, has had four children, and is the grandmother of eight.

BURT, Mrs. Mary Towne, temperance reformer, was born in Cincinnati, OH, of English American parentage. Her father, Thomas Towne, was educated in England for the ministry. After the death of her father, which occurred in her early childhood, her mother removed with her three children to Auburn, NY, where Mrs. Burt received a liberal education, passing through the public schools and the Auburn Young Ladies' Institute. Four years after leaving school she became the wife of Edward Burt, of Auburn. When the crusade opened, in 1873, Mrs. Burt began her work for temperance, which has continued without intermission, with the exception of seven months spent in the sick room of her sister, Mrs. Pomeroy. So deeply was she stirred by the crusade that on 24th March, 1874, she addressed a great audience in the Auburn Opera House on temperance. Immediately after that, Mrs. Burt was elected president of the Auburn Woman's Christian Temperance Union, and served for two years.

She was a delegate to the first national convention held in Cleveland, OH, in 1874, was one of the secretaries of that body, and in the next national convention, in Cincinnati, OH, was elected assistant recording secretary. In the year 1876 in the Newark, NJ, national convention, she was elected a member of the publish committee of the Woman's Temperance Union," the first official organ of the National union. She was afterward made chairman of that committee and publisher of the paper. During the year 1877 she served as managing editor. At her suggestion the name "Our Union" was given to the paper, a name which it held until its consolidation with the "Signal," of Chicago, when it took the name of the "Union Signal." In Chicago, in 1877, she was elected corresponding secretary of the National Union, which office she held for three years, and during that term of office she opened the first headquarters of the National union in the Bible House, New York City. In 1882 she was elected president of the New York State Union, a position which she still holds. During the years of her presidency the State union has increased from five thousand to twenty-one-thousand members and from 179 to 842 local unions, and in work, membership and organization stands at the head of the forty-four States of the National union. Mrs. Burt, with her husband and son, resides in New York. She is a member of the Protestant Episcopal Church.

BUSH, Mrs. Jennie Burchfield, author, born in Meadville, PA, 28th of April, 1858. She is of Scotch, English and Irish descent. Her father was James Burchfield, a prominent journalist of Meadville and a brilliant writer. Her mother, Sarah M. Coburn, also a journalist, was a woman of poetic temperament. The daughter was placed in the State Normal School in Edinburgh, PA, at the age of six years, and remained there until she was sixteen years old. In 1875 she went to Augusta, Kans., where her mother was living, and she has been since then a resident of that State. She became the wife, on the 21st October, 1877, of A. T. Bush, a well-known stockman, of Louisville, KY. Her family consists of two sons. Mrs. Bush was unconscious of her poetical powers

until a few years ago. Since writing her first poem she has made a thorough study of the art of poetic expression. She has published extensively in newspapers and periodicals. Her literary work, while mainly poetical, includes a number of short stories and several serials. Her home in Wichita is an ideal one.

BUSHNELL, Miss Kate, physician and evangelist, born in Peru, IL, 5th February, 1856. She is a descendant of a prominent family that traces its ancestors to John Rogers, the Smithfield martyr. She received a public-school education in her native State and attended the Northwestern University, in Evanston, IL. Selecting the medical profession, she became a private pupil of Dr. James S. Jewell, the noted specialist in nerve diseases. Later she finished her medical education in the Chicago Woman's Medical College, was graduated MD, and became a resident physician in the Hospital for Women and Children. She then went to China, and for nearly three years remained in that country as a medical missionary. Returning to America, she established herself as a physician in Denver, CO. In 1885, complying with earnest requests from the leaders, Dr. Bushnell gave up her practice and entered the field as an evangelist in the social-purity department of the Woman's Christian Temperance Union. It was she who laid the foundation of the Anchorage Mission in Chicago, IL, an institution which has done great good for abandoned women, giving over five-thousand lodgings to women in one year. In 1888 Dr. Bushnell visited the dens and stockades in northern Wisconsin, where women were held in debasing slavery. That undertaking was heroic in its nature, for she took her life in her hand when she dared the opposition of those she encountered. Fearless and undaunted, she finished her investigations, and her report made to the Woman's Christian Temperance Union startled the reading public by its revelations of the utter depravity she had witnessed. As a public speaker Dr. Bushnell is graceful, eloquent and earnest, and as a writer she is well known in her special field. This combination of the woman and the physician, the orator and the author has made her the choice of the

World's Woman's Christian Temperance Union for carrying the gospel of the white ribbon to foreign lands. In 1891 she left Chicago to circumnavigate the earth in the interests of humanity, representing over 500,000 women. Dr. Bushnell went as an evangelist to organize, instruct and encourage. She carried with her the "polyglot petition," a paper that was intended to be signed by at least two-million persons, representing a general protest against legalizing sale of alcoholics and of opium, and it is to be presented to every government on both hemispheres.

BUTIN, Mrs. Mary Ryerson, physician, born near Wilton, IA, 17th August, 1857. She lived on a farm until her eighteenth year, and then took up her residence in the village of Wilton Junction. There, with alternate schooling and teaching, she succeeded in nearly completing the course in the academy in that place, when its financial embarrassments necessitated the closing of its doors. Entering the high school, in one year she was graduated therefrom with the highest honors. At the age of twenty-one she felt the responsibility of choosing her life work. From her earliest remembrance she had heard her mother say that she was to be a doctor. The mother was farseeing and discerned that opening for woman and her fitness for her work. Though timid and sensitive as to the opinions of others, after deliberation she decided that her duty lay in that direction. She turned with keen perception of its responsibilities from the pleasures of a young girl's life and began the study of medicine, with the help and encouragement of the family physician and his partners. She entered the medical college in Iowa City, a co-educational institution, which at that time had enrolled a membership of ninety men and ten women. From that college she came forth a firm opponent of co-education in medical colleges. The following year she attended the Woman's Medical College in Chicago, IL, from which she was graduated in the spring of 1881, afterward entering the South Side Hospital as resident physician. Her duties were so arduous, the lack of nurses making it necessary for her to supply that position sometimes, that, after four months'

service, she resigned and returned home for rest. While on a visit to her brother in Dorchester, NE, her practice became so extensive as to cause her to settle there, where she gradually overcame all opposition among physicians and people to women practitioners. There she met and became the wife, in May, 1883, of Dr. J. L. Butin, a rising young physician. Before she had been in the State a year, she became a member of the Nebraska State Medical Society. She was the first woman to enter that society and was received in Hastings, in 1882. Placed upon the programme for a paper the next year, she has ever since been a contributor to some section of that society. She was elected first vice-president in 1889. She has been a contributor to the Omaha "Clinic" and other medical journals, and was State superintendent of hygiene and heredity for the Woman's Christian Temperance Union, county and local. Untiring in devotion to her profession, she has been ready to lend her aid to all progressive movements, and she has battled and conquered much of the prejudice against woman in the field of medical science.

BUTLER, Miss Clementina, evangelist, born in Bareilly, India, 7th January, 1862. Her father, Rev. William Butler, was commissioned in 1856 to open mission work for the Methodist Episcopal Church. After passing through great perils during the Sepoy rebellion, in 1857, Bareilly was settled as headquarters. The family moved their home seventeen times during the next eight years, according to the needs of the work. Returning to the United States, after a few years' rest, Dr. Butler was requested to organize mission work in Mexico. There the linguistic ability of the daughter was of great service. In 1884 Miss Butler went with her parents to revisit her native land, and her observations during an extended tour in that country have served as the theme of many of her addresses and articles. On account of the infirmities of age and the heavy responsibilities borne so long, Dr. and Mrs. Butler reside quietly in Newton Center, MA, and from their home the daughter goes out to inspire others with her own belief in the glorious possibilities for women in every land, when aided by Christian civilization.

Miss Butler is interested in missionary work of all kinds, medical missions for the women of the East being her favorite subject. As a King's Daughter she works in the slums of Boston, besides pleading in the churches and on public platforms for the needy in the uttermost parts of the earth. A short residence in Alaska gave her an insight into the condition of the people there, and she is an ardent champion of their rights in regard to suitable educational grants and the enforcement of the laws prohibiting the sale of liquor in that Territory. Miss Butler is her father's assistant in his literary labors, by which he still aids the cause he served so long. She uses her pen also for missionary publications.

BUTLER, Mrs. Frances Kemble, see KEMBLE, FRANCES ANNE.

BUTTERFIELD, Miss Mellona Moulton, china-painter, born in Racine, WI, 15th May, 1853. She was educated in St. Louis, MO, and Omaha, NE, and is a graduate of Brownell Hall in Omaha. She was for twelve years engaged in teaching, which vocation she followed with success in Plattsmouth, Grand Island and Hastings, cities of Nebraska. During those years she followed, as devotedly as circumstances would allow, the one art toward which her talents and inclinations tended. At last she gave up other work and applied herself exclusively to ceramic painting, establishing a studio in Omaha. She is one of the best artists in that line in the State. She received the first honorable mention for china-painting in the woman's department of the New Orleans World's Fair, and in 1889 the first gold medal for china-painting given by the Western Art Association in Omaha. She has received many favorable notices from art critics and the press.

BYINGTON, Mrs. Elia Goode, journalist, born in Thomaston, GA, 24th March, 1858. Mrs. Byington is president of the Woman's Press Club of Georgia, and, with her husband, Edward Telfair Byington, joint proprietor, editor and manager of the Columbus "Evening Ledger," a successful southern daily. The flourishing condition of the

Woman's Press Club bears testimony to the deep interest and zeal of its presiding officer. She declares that the work is made easier by the sympathy and approval of her husband. Mrs. Byington is deeply interested in the intellectual and industrial progress of woman, and that her interest is practical, rather than theoretical, is evinced in the fact that, with the exception of the carrier boys and four men for outdoor work, all of the employees of the "Ledger" office are women. A woman is employed as foreman, a woman artist makes the illustrations for the paper, a woman reads the proofs, a woman manipulates the type-writer, a woman is mailing clerk, and all the type is set by women, all of whom receive equal pay with men who are employed in similar capacities. Not content with the help extended to her sisters in her own profession, Mrs. Byington organized a Worker's Club as an aid to the many young girls who, while still burdened with the shrinking southern conservatism, have to go forth to battle with the world. Mrs. Byington comes of a distinguished Georgia family, being the daughter of the late Col. Charles T. Goode, of Americus, and granddaughter of Gen. Eli Warren, of Perry. She is essentially a southern woman, having always lived in her native State, and having received her education in the Furlow Female College, in Americus, and in the Georgia Female College in Madison. She was married in 1877 and, becoming deeply interested in her husband's journalistic labors, began to assist him with her pen, and in that way cultivated a love for the work that has since brought her distinction. Her father was a man of brilliant attainments, while her mother is a perfect type of cultured Southern womanhood. From them Mrs. Byington inherits her intellectual gifts, which, together with her youth, personal beauty and charm of manner, make her a favorite with her friends. She is a constant worker, spending many hours daily at her desk and often working late into the night, but, notwithstanding her numerous duties, she finds time to give to society. She is secretary and treasurer of the Art Club, the leading social and literary organization of Columbus.

CABELL, Mrs. Mary Virginia Ellet, educator, born at the "Point of Honor," Lynchburg, VA, the home of her maternal grandfather, Judge Daniel, 24th January, 1839. Her father, the eminent civil engineer, Charles Ellet, Jr., built the first suspension bridge in the United States, over the Schuylkill river at Philadelphia, presented the first plans for a bridge across the Mississippi river at St. Louis, and built the first bridge across the Niagara below the Falls. He first suggested and advocated a Pacific railroad, and his "temporary track" over the Blue Ridge, at Rock Fish Gap, was the most noted mountain railroad in the world. He was the author of the reservoir plan for the improvement of the Mississippi and Ohio rivers. He invented the steam-ram and constructed and commanded the steam-ram fleet in the victorious battle of Memphis, where he was mortally wounded. Mrs. Cabell's education was directed by her father. At twelve years of age she had thoroughly read Gibbon, and at fifteen she had accomplished a remarkable course of reading, and was in fluent command of the French and German languages. She accompanied her parents to Cuba, remaining there some time. She spent nearly a year at Niagara, crossing the river repeatedly in the famous "iron basket" which first conveyed men and materials, and was the first female to view the Falls from the bridge before its completion. The years of 1854 and 1855 she spent in Europe, studying history and literature. She spent part of the winters of 1860 and 1861 in Richmond, VA, where, under the guardianship of her kinsman, Hon. A. H. H. Stuart and Hon. John B. Baldwin, the two Union leaders in the convention, she followed the proceedings and heard the views of the men who weighed the measure of secession. When the unhappy decision was reached which precipitated civil war, she returned to her family in Washington. After the battle of Memphis Mrs. Ellet and her daughter were permitted to join and nurse Col. Ellet, who sank rapidly from his wound. When the fleet moved to participate in the siege of Vicksburg, Charles Rivers Ellet, who had first hoisted the flag in Memphis, begged to accompany it. The decision was left to his sister, who sent the boy to his brief and glorious career. Col. Ellet died in Cairo, 21st June, 1862, his body was carried to Philadelphia, lay in state in Independence Hall, and was interred in Laurel Hill with military honors. His wife survived him but one week. Charles Rivers Ellet died 29th October, 1862, from exposure and fatigue. The care of the two younger children and of their aged grandmother devolved upon the solitary young girl. After the war Mary Ellet became the wife of William D. Cabell, of Virginia. In 1888 they removed with their family of six children to Washington, DC, and opened a school for girls, Norwood Institute. In 1890 Mrs. Cabell aided in organizing a society of the descendants of Revolutionary patriots, the Daughters of the American Revolution.

CADWALLADER. Mrs. Alice A. W., philanthropist, born in St. Clairsville, OH, in 1832. At an early age she became the wife of Mr. Cochran, a Virginian, who died, leaving her with a family of three small children. Six years after his death she was united in marriage to N. J. White, who was killed in the battle of Antietam. Mrs. White took charge of the sanitary supplies of Jefferson Barracks, Missouri, and served subsequently under the Sanitary Commission on the steamer "R. C. Woods;" at Jeffersonville, IN; and over the White Women's Refugee Hospital, at Nashville, TN. She settled in Nebraska, pre-empting a homestead, on which she lived two years. During that period and for two years afterward she filled the office of Grand Vice-Templar in the order of Good Templars. Then the crusade spirit fired the Great West, and, laying down her Good Templar work, with other sisters, she joined in the crusade against the saloons in Lincoln, NE. In 1880, in Lincoln, NE, she became the wife of Rev. Joseph Cadwallader, of the Congregational Church. On account of his failing health they removed to Jacksonville, FL, where in 1886 she was made president of the State Woman's Christian Temperance Union. In that office she brought the work in that State from a condition of apathy and indifference to a healthy and steadily increasing growth. She resigned her position as State president and is now engaged in the crowning work of her life, the establishment of the Woman's Industrial Home, in Augusta, GA.

Georgia Cayvan.
From Photo by
Morrison, Chicago.

Lillian Blauvelt.
From Photo Copyrighted 1897,
by Aime Dupont, New York.

Madge Edwardes.
From Photo by
Morrison, Chicago.

CADY, Mrs. Helena Maxwell, doctor of medicine, born in New Orleans, LA, 26th April, 1849. She spent most of her youth in Cuba, and was married to Mr. Cady in 1870, and has a family of seven living children. While living in Arkansas after the Civil War, she undertook a course in Homoeopathic School of Physicians and Surgeons in St. Louis. After graduating MD, she practiced for several years in Little Rock, AR. Leaving that city she settled in Louisville, KY. She was for several years one of the staff of physicians of the Little Rock Free Dispensary. She is a member of the Southern Homoeopathic Medical Association and of the Kentucky Homœpathic Medical Society.

CAMERON, Mrs. Elizabeth, editor, born in Niagara, Ontario, Canada, 8th March, 1851. Her maiden name was Millar. Her early years were passed in Montreal and Kingston, and afterward in London, Canada, where she became the wife, 30th September, 1869, of John Cameron, founder and conductor of the London "Ontario Advertiser." She is strongly interested in temperance work, is superintendent of the franchise department of the London Woman's Christian Temperance Union. She conducts, with the co-operation of Miss Agnes Ethelwyn Wetherald, a monthly paper, "Wives and Daughters," which has a large circulation in the United States as well as in Canada.

CAMPBELL, Mrs. Eugenia Steele, temperance reformer, born in Springfield, MI, 31st May, 1843. She is the daughter of Rev. Salmon and Adelaide Ruth Steele. At the age of thirteen years she entered Albion College, and was married to Robert A. Campbell, of New York State, 25th April, 1863. She was among the first to associate herself with the Woman's Christian Temperance Union, and she has spared neither time nor money to help the cause and promote its interests. She has been called continuously to preside in its assemblies, as president of local,

county and district unions. She has for the past eleven years been president of a district, and thus for that time a member of the State executive board of the Woman's Christian Temperance Union of Michigan. For nearly three years she acted as secretary for Henry A. Reynolds, of red-ribbon fame, making his dates and keeping him constantly in the field, winning at that time the name of "Never-say-die Campbell," which was given in a paper read at a State meeting by Mrs. C. H. Johnson. Modest and unassuming, she has by her faculty of perception and indomitable perseverance endeared herself to a large circle of the best workers in both church and temperance causes. She excels in parliamentary drills in her conventions, and in planning and sending through her district the best speakers. For twelve years previous to the Crusade, she conducted a large store in millinery and fancy goods. She is the mother of three sons, one of whom died in infancy. Her two remaining sons now grown to manhood, together with her husband, have given her much aid in carrying on her temperance work. Mr. and Mrs. Campbell have conducted a large hotel for four years past in Manistique, MI.

CAMPBELL, Miss Evelyn, actor, born in Waterloo, England, in 1868. She is the daughter of Conrad and Helen Petrie. Coming to America when she was quite young, the family settled in New York City, where Evelyn entered the Lyceum School for Dramatic Expression, under the charge of L. D. Sargent. She remained there three months, after which she was with a traveling company for two years. She then became a member of Palmer's company in "Jim the Penman." She won a success in the character of the daughter and remained with that company two years. She then joined the Boston Museum Company and is always warmly received by its patrons. Although young, she has earned a fine reputation for a conscientious and natural portrayal of the characters she represents. She is interested in all that pertains to her profession and studies painting as a recreation. She has won the commendation of the fastidious Boston critics, and her career is one that promises future progress.

CAMPBELL, Miss Georgine, artist, born in New Orleans, LA. She is a daughter of Dr. George W. Campbell, a descendant of the distinguished Scotch family of that name. Her father was one of the wealthiest and most influential men in the South, and the family have been prominent social leaders of New Orleans for many generations. Miss Campbell passed her early childhood in New Orleans, going thence to Paris. In that city the Louvre headed the list of attractions for her, and frequenters of the galleries were often surprised to see a little girl pulling her staid "bonne" by the hand to where some masterpiece was hanging, and standing in admiration before it. She spent several years of study in Paris. Loving her art as she does, she could but make it a success, and when, after the death of her father, the family suffered reverses, she used as a profession the art to which she had devoted herself as a pleasure. She made portraiture a specialty and her genius was soon recognized. Among her sitters have been many of the most prominent men and women of the country. She is now one of the successful artists of New York City, where her home and studio are. It is an indescribable touch of life in her pictures that has won for Miss Campbell her laurels. She has received favorable mention on several occasions when her pictures have been exhibited, and in the World's Fair in New Orleans in 1883 and 1884 she received the blue ribbon.

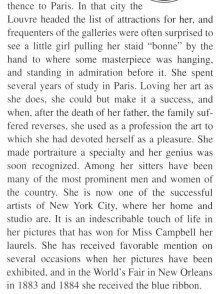

CAMPBELL, Mrs. Helen S., author and editor, born in Lockport, NY, 4th July, 1839. She is of Scotch ancestors on both sides of the house. Twelve months after her birth her father, Homer H. Stuart, removed to New York City, where he lived until his death, in 1890, and where as a lawyer and a citizen he filled with honor various responsible positions. Married at the age of twenty to an army surgeon, she thereafter lived in various portions of the United States, during which time she gained that broad experience which has reappeared in her literary work.

Endowed with abundant vitality, great imagination, power of dramatic expression and a profoundly sympathetic nature, it was impossible for the young woman to live an idle life. At the age of twenty-three, under her married name, Helen C. Weeks, she began work for children, writing steadily for "Our Young Folks," the "Riverside Magazine" and other juvenile periodicals. Like all her subsequent work, these articles were vital, magnetic and infused with both humor and pathos. Soon her stories grew in length, and the "Ainslee Series" was issued in book form. This comprised "Ainslee," "Grandpa's House," "Four and What They Did" and "White and Red." They were exceedingly popular and still find a sale. All of them were reprinted in England. Her next works were "Six Sinners," "His Grandmothers" and "The American Girl's Hand-book of Work and Play." About 1882 she became literary and household editor of "Our Continent," and wrote for its pages the popular novel entitled "Under Green Apple Boughs," followed by the "What-to-do Club." These latter books were preceded by several others, entitled "Unto the Third and Fourth Generation," "The Easiest Way in Housekeeping and Cooking" and the" Problem of the Poor." With the last mentioned book, which gave an impetus to much work along the same lines by other writers, began Mrs. Campbell's special interest in the poor. This appeared in 1880, and drew great attention toward plans for alleviating the miseries of the ignorant and impoverished in New York City. Some of the conclusions reached by Mrs. Campbell appeared in her novel, "Mrs. Herndon's Income," which was printed first as a serial in the "Christian Union," and was afterward issued in book-form. This powerful book at once lifted Mrs. Campbell to an exalted place as a novelist, while her thrilling story won the attention of philanthropists and reformers the world over. Attracted by this volume, in 1886, the New York "Tribune" appointed her its commissioner to investigate the condition of women wage-earners in New York, and that work resulted in a series of papers under the title of "Prisoners of Poverty," which caused a profound and widespread sensation respecting the life of wage-women in the metropolis. It may be regarded as the seed from which has issued a vast amount of literature upon the topic, resulting in great amelioration in the condition of a large, and at that time nearly helpless, body of workers. Soon afterward Mrs.

Campbell went abroad to investigate the lives of wage-earners in London, Paris, Italy and Germany. There she remained eighteen months or more, the fruits of her work appearing, upon her return to this country, in "Prisoners of Poverty Abroad." Following that came "Miss Melinda's Opportunity" and "Roger Berkley's Probation," two short novels, and, later, "Anne Bradstreet and Her Time," a historical study of early colonial life, "A Sylvan City," having already done the same thing for Philadelphia. The latest published work of Mrs. Campbell, "Darkness and Daylight in New York," is a series of graphic portraitures of the salient features of the city. In 1890 Mrs. Campbell received a prize from the American Economical Association for a monograph upon "Women Wage-Earners." She has contributed many articles on economic subjects to reviews and magazines. Her home is in New York City.

CANFIELD, Mrs. Corresta T., physician, born in Chardon, OH, 6th March, 1833. The Canfields, for meritorious service, received from the king of England, in 1350, a grant of land on the river Cam, in Yorkshire, and settled thereon. After occupying that grant for three-hundred years, they came to America, shortly after the arrival of the Plymouth Pilgrims, and were among the first settlers of New Haven, CT. Dr. Canfield is descended from French Huguenots and New England Presbyterians. Her mother, reared at a time when it was thought a sin for a man to kiss his wife or babe on Sunday, did not neglect the moral training of her children. Intellectual, well-read, in advance of her time, the daughter has inherited energy, will power and executive ability. Corresta entered the seminary of Chardon at an early age, but she was soon married. Though a wife and mother, reading and study were kept up. From her childhood she was ambitious to be a physician. Left alone without resources, at the close of the Civil War, the ambitions of early youth revived. In 1869 she entered the Woman's Homeopathic College of Cleveland, OH. With the help of a half year's scholarship Mrs. Canfield finished the first college year. In the second year she became an assistant of the president, Dr. Myra K. Merrick, and gained means to continue in college.

She was graduated with first honors in 1871, having served for some time as demonstrator of anatomy. During the following summer she practiced in Fort Wayne, IN, earning enough to enable her to enter the Men's Homeopathic College of Cleveland. While there, she was demonstrator of anatomy in the woman's department, and practiced enough, visiting patients mornings and evenings, to defray expenses. She attended all the lectures, passed through the whole curriculum and was graduated third in the men's course, the faculty acknowledging that she was entitled to a prize, but would not establish a precedent by awarding it to a practicing physician. A full-fledged MD, she settled in Titusville, PA. Having but fifteen dollars capital, she borrowed enough to buy out a resident physician, and under great opposition so won public patronage as to pay all her debts the first year. There she remained nearly ten years and amassed a snug sum. She next spent a year in traveling. In 1882 she settled in Chicago, where she has built up a large practice and served in many public offices. She is at present a member of the board of censors of the American Institute of Homeopathy, having been elected for the second time. She was the first woman who served in that capacity. One was elected the previous year but was not allowed to serve on the board of censors. Three years before her admission women were not permitted to join that society, and much opprobrium was still attached to those "hybrids" who did. Even women shared in that feeling. After a time, seeing none of her sex actively represented in the society, she felt that, to enjoy its privileges, one should assume its duties. She therefore prepared a paper and read it before the institute. She has served as president, vice-president and secretary of the Woman's Medical Association of Chicago, vice-president of the Hahnemann Clinical for two years, and has been appointed on the woman's committee for a homeopathic congress to be held during the World's Columbian Exposition in 1893.

CAPPIANI, Mme. Luisa, operatic singer and musical educator, was born in Trieste, Austria. Her maiden name was Young. Her paternal grandfather was a noted Scotchman who was a professor in the University of Munich. Her father was a dramatic tenor, and her mother was a German woman of high social rank. At the age of six years Luisa was a musical prodigy, and she received a thorough musical education. At the age of seventeen she was married to Mr. Kapp, an Austrian counselor. Her husband died three years after their marriage, leaving her with two children, a son and a daughter, and with only the usual small pension to support and educate her family. After a period of prostration Mme. Kapp aroused herself and began to make use of her talents and her training. She succeeded and earned ample means to educate her children. When Mme. Kapp began her musical career, she combined her names Kapp and Young, in the usual manner, Kapp-Young. Her teachers had been in Vienna Miss Fröhlich and the tenor Passadonna, and in Italy San Giovanni, Vanucini, Gamberini, the elder Romani and old Lamperti. Her aristocratic friends persuaded her to give two public concerts, which were so successful that Rubinstein and Piatti engaged her for their concerts in Vienna, where she lived with her mother. She was then called to court concerts in Vienna, Prague and Coburg-Gotha. In Munich her concerts brought an invitation to sing in opera. That decided her operatic career. She sang with her brother, Fred Young, in "La Juive," and under his guidance, while he sang Eleasar, her Rachelle was, on 13th May, 1860, a complete success. After that she appeared in London under the auspices and at the residence of Viscountess Palmerston, her crowning triumph being in a concert given by the Queen in the Golden Room of Buckingham Palace to the King of Belgium. Her teachers in dramatic action were her brother, the tenor Young, and his wife, and Lucille Grahn. After appearing in the Royal Theater, Hanover, she was called to Frankfort-onthe-Main, and thence to the Grand Duchy of Hesse-Cassel. At the request of the Intendant she made her début there as Lucrezia. Her Valentine in "The Huguenots," Fides in "The Prophet" and Leonore in "Fidelio" made an impression. Herman Levi, then leader of the Grand Opera in Rotterdam, engaged her after her rendering of Elizabeth in "Tannhäuser." Her appearance in Rotterdam as Ortrud in "Lohengrin" created a furore. After that she appeared in Pesth, Prague and Vienna. The sudden death of her mother caused a severe illness. A sojourn at Como restored her health so that she could sing in

a festival in Bergamo. After that she sang in Italian her great rôle of Valentine in La Scala, in Milan, and then filled engagements for Italian opera in Bucharest and in the Imperial Theater, Nice. The great carnival of Parma followed, and there she created the rôle of Selika, singing it thirty-two times in one carnival. Vianesi, the leader of the Liceo in Barcelona, engaged her after that event. The Imperial Theater of Tiflis, Russia, was her next, though dearly bought, triumph. At the end of the season she contracted bronchitis. Permitted by a foolish physician and over-persuaded by the Intendant and the Prince, she sang, despite her illness. An enthusiastic torchlight procession in her honor closed the evening, but the voice which had entranced the populace was mute to acknowledge the ovation, and that night she was at the point of death by suffocation, in consequence of the ill-advised vocal exertion. September, 1868, the city of Arezzo bestowed upon her, for her singing in a festival, the gold medal of merit by King Victor Emanuel's decree. Six months after, imagining herself cured, she accepted an engagement from Max Maretzek for the Academy of Music, New York. The stormy passage brought on a relapse; still she appeared with remarkable success in "L'Africaine" at the Academy in 1868–69. At that time she discovered in her art fortunate secrets which enabled her to overcome the difficulties brought on her by bronchitis, and the knowledge of which has since made her famous as a teacher. After one season in America she retired from the stage and went to Milan, and there soon and often was called upon to advise young singers. After teaching in Milan two years she accepted an invitation from Boston, and, when singing in a Harvard concert, fused her name into Cappiani, to satisfy an existing popular prejudice. In 1881 she was induced to settle in New York, and there she has been very successful as a trainer. Her essays on the voice are reproduced in many musical papers in this and foreign countries, notably in Germany. When the board of examiners of the American College of Musicians was organized in Cleveland, OH, she was the only woman elected among eighteen professors. At a subsequent meeting in New York she was reëlected.

CARDWILL, Miss Mary E., was born in Louisville, KY. While she was yet a child, her parents moved to New Albany, IN, where she has passed her life. In her early years her health was impaired by too close application to books, and she was forced to give up school work at fifteen years of age, just when it would have been most valuable to her. She began her literary career by working in the interests of reform. Almost every advance movement of the last ten years has received substantial aid from her pen. Some years ago she became very much interested in Shakespeare's dramas. After a course of careful training in that direction, she wrote a number of philosophical and discriminating essays upon the plays. Those articles attracted attention in high literary circles. In June, 1886, in the first convention of the Western Association of Writers, Miss Cardwill contributed a paper on "The Successful Study of Shakespeare." In June, 1888, she was chosen corresponding secretary of that association, and in the following year she was chosen as secretary. In her official capacity, as corresponding secretary, she was associated with Mrs. L. May Wheeler as editor of the "Western Association of Writers Souvenir for 1888," and in the following year she became the sole editor of the souvenir for that year.

CARHART, Mrs. Clara H. Sully, educator and reformer, born in Ottawa, Canada, 30th April, 1845. She is of English parentage. Her maternal grandfather, J. G. Playter, who was a government official from the first settlement of that city, was descended from an old family of English nobility of that name. In early life Mrs. Carhart showed an unusual aptitude for books. Her school duties were ever a source of enjoyment, and she decided to become a teacher. At ten years of age she was sent to a boarding-school in Ottawa, Canada, where she excelled in music. After two years she returned home, and studied in the Buffalo high school, until the removal of her parents to Darien Center, NY, where she attended the seminary. After graduating, she began to teach. In 1861, after the death of her father, the family removed to Davenport, IA. She immediately entered the city school there and for six years held high rank as a teacher. At the solicitation of the schoolboard she inaugurated a system of musical instruction, including every grade of all the city schools. On 5th October, 1871, she became the wife of Rev. Lewis H. Carhart, a young Methodist Episcopal minister, and with him went to live in Charles City, IA. Their family consists of two children. There she entered heartily into his work and seconded all his efforts to build up the church. Soon after the Civil War she went to Texas with her husband, who had been a captain in the Union army, and had volunteered in the work of reorganizing the Methodist Episcopal Church in the South. They had to work in the face of bitter opposition, but, largely owing to Mrs. Carhart's activity and popularity, large congregations were formed and churches were built in Dallas, Sherman and neighboring cities. In 1883 her husband retired from the active ministry, and they went to make their home in Brooklyn, NY, to be near Mrs. Carhart's family. She became much interested in the work of the Woman's Christian Temperance Union, being secretary of one of the largest local unions, and afterward president of the young women's work in Suffolk county. While on a visit in Donley county, TX, she organized a local union, which union so aroused public sentiment that within eight months afterward the saloons in that county were closed by popular vote. She became interested in the social condition of the working-girls of Brooklyn. Prominent women were called together from the churches of the city, and in 1885 they planted the Bedford Club in the heart of a district where shop-girls and factory operatives live. The aim was the bettering of the social condition of those girls, offering them innocent amusements and instruction in practical branches. The work has since grown incredibly. Of that society she was the first president. She was thus the pioneer in establishing girls' clubs, which become such an important factor in the lives of the working-girls of New York and Brooklyn. For six years Mrs. Carhart held the position of corresponding secretary of the Woman's Home Missionary Society of the Methodist Episcopal Church, in the New York East Conference, and she has been a great factor in its success. For six years she was sent as a representative to the national conventions, and in 1889 represented that society on the platform of the National Woman's Christian Temperance

Union in Chicago. She is a member of the advisory council of the woman's branch of the World's Columbian Exposition in Chicago.

CARLISLE, Mrs. Mary Jane, social leader, born in Covington, Kenton county, KY, 28th August, 1835. Her father, Major John Allen Goodson, fought through the war of 1812, and served several terms in the House of Representatives and the Senate, and was for four years mayor of Covington. He bore a strong resemblance to Gen. Jackson, both physically and mentally. He was a man of great will power and personal courage and exerted a strong influence in politics. He married, when forty years of age, Hetty Wasson, of Covington. His daughter possesses much of her father's strength of character. She was educated in the Covington schools and became the wife of John Griffin Carlisle, 25th January, 1837. She is the mother of five children, two of whom are living, William Kinkaed and Lilbon Logan, both lawyers. Mrs. Carlisle's strong personality has much to do with her husband's success in life. She is popular in Washington society, makes many friends and keeps them by being true in her friendships, gladly making sacrifices and suffering inconveniences for others. Her husband, Senator Carlisle, ex-speaker of the House, is known throughout the United States. The support of such women as Mrs. Carlisle is a powerful factor in the lives of all men, and to her more than any other does Mr. Carlisle owe all that is true to himself, that places him in the front rank of the great thinkers and of the great statesmen of the age.

CARPENTER, Mrs. Alice Dimmick, traveler, was born in Milford, PA. She is descended from the English family of Dymokes. The founders of

the American branch came to this country in 1635, and many members of the family have been conspicuous in the social, financial and political history of Pennsylvania and New York. Her father, Milton Dimmick, was a prominent lawyer of Milford, PA. Her mother was Elizabeth Allen, a daughter of Rev. Edward Allen. The early death of Mr. Dimmick left the widow with three young children. Alice was delicate and passed the years of her childhood as an invalid, but she possessed a bright and cheerful disposition that made her life a pleasure despite her weakness. The family lived in various cities. For seven years Mrs. Carpenter lived in Chicago, where she was prominent in art, music and literature, and in club life. She has published one volume of verse, "Poems Original and Translated" (Chicago, 1882). One of her most important productions is a pamphlet entitled "The Man Material," which attempts to prove the doctrine of materialism. She has traveled extensively in this country, Canada and Europe. She passes her winters on the Pacific Coast.

CARPENTER, Miss Ellen M., artist, born in Killingly, CT, 28th November, 1836. While noted in school for correct drawing, it was not until 1858 her attention was called to the study of art. She first studied with Thomas Edward, of Worcester, MA, and afterward drew in the Lowell Institute, Boston, for several years. In 1867 she went to Paris, where she gained a new impetus in study. From that time she has been a popular teacher, having, both in school and studio, numerous classes in drawing, water-color and oil painting. She accompanied some of her students on a European tour in 1873, traveling and sketching extensively. In her own country she has painted from nature numerous scenes in the South, in California and in many noted localities. In 1878 she began seriously to study face and figure, going to Europe for special work. She studied with the portrait painter, Gusson, in Berlin, for a while, and then went to Paris, where she attended Julien's and Carlo Rossi's schools. She copied portraits of several noted Masons for the Masonic Temple in Boston. Her commissions have been numerous. In 1890 she had commissions which took her to Paris, to copy "The Immaculate Conception" and "The Holy Family" by Murillo, and several of the noted modern paintings in the museum of the Luxembourg. In the same year she was in Algiers and Spain, sketching eastern life and manners, and painted several interiors from the Alhambra and Palace in Seville. Her home is in Boston.

CARRINGTON, Miss Abbie, operatic singer, born in Fond du Lac, WI, 13th June, 1856. Her musical talents showed themselves at an early age. In September, 1875, she went to Boston, MA, and studied under J. H. Wheeler. In 1887 she was graduated from the New England Conservatory. She then went to Italy, where she began the study of opera under Giuseppe Perini, and after one year of study she made her début in Milan, in "Traviata." In Cervia and Ravenna she won a triumph as Gilda, in "Rigoletto." She was next engaged for a season of two months in Turin and for one month in Brescia; then she went to Venice to sing during the Carnival season. She made her debut in the United States on 7th October, 1879, in Boston, MA, with the Strakosch Opera Company. She next appeared in New York City with Theodore Thomas and the Philharmonic Society. In January, 1879, she made a tour of the chief American cities, supported by the Mendelssohn Quintette Club of Boston. In 1880–81 she made her first operatic tour with the Strakosch-Hess Grand English Opera Company. In 1881–82 she was re-engaged by Mr. Strakosch to sing on alternate nights with Mme. Etelka Gerster. In 1883–84 Miss Carrington visited Mexico and achieved a pronounced success. In 1887, after six consecutive seasons in grand opera, having sung the leading soprano rôles in twenty different operas, Miss Carrington took a much-needed rest, which resulted in opening a new sphere of work, and since that time she has traveled only with her own company in concert and oratorio. The season of 1890–91 was a tour of the Pacific Coast and British Columbia. Miss Carrington's voice is a soprano. Her home is in Fond du Lac.

CARROLL, Miss Anna Ella, political writer and military genius, born in Kingston Hall, the ancestral residence of her father, Governor Thomas King Carroll, Somerset county, MD, 29th August, 1815. Her mother was Juliana Stevenson, the daughter of Colonel Henry James Stevenson, who had come over in the British army as surgeon during the Revolutionary War. Dr. Stevenson, though a stanch Tory, was beloved for the care bestowed by him upon the wounded of both armies. He settled in Baltimore, became greatly distinguished in his profession and built a beautiful residence on Parnassus Hill. Thomas King Carroll married Miss Stevenson in his twentieth year, and Anna Ella was the oldest child of this youthful couple. She early showed a remarkable character, reading law with her father at a youthful age, and following with interest his political career. She soon began to write for the press. Her first published work was entitled "The Great American Battle, or Political Romanism." This was followed by "The Star of the West," describing the origin of our claims to the western territories, their conditions and their needs, and urging the building of the Pacific railroad. Miss Carroll took an active part in the election of Governor Hicks of Maryland, in 1860, and when the Civil War broke out she used her influence to hold Governor Hicks to the Union, thus saving Maryland from secession and securing the safety of the National Capital. Seeing that slavery was at the root of the rebellion, she freed her own slaves at a great sacrifice and gave herself up enthusiastically to the support of the national cause, using her great social influence and her connection with the press to secure the loyalty of her State. Miss Carroll had become a communicant of the Presbyterian Church in Baltimore, of which Dr. Robert J. Breckenridge, a loyal unionist, was pastor. He was a man of great influence and distinction. His nephew, John C. Breckenridge, at one time a warm friend of Miss Carroll, became a leading secessionist. Immediately after President Lincoln's accession he made a very clever and violent speech, charging Mr. Lincoln and the North with having made the war. This speech was especially designed to carry Maryland out of the Union. Miss Carroll, perceiving at once its baleful effect upon her own State, determined to answer it, and did so in a pamphlet of consummate ability. By the use of documents in her possession she showed that the Southern leaders from the time of Calhoun had been preparing for the war, and that for ten years previous the whole secession movement had been planned, even in its details. Mr. Lincoln and his cabinet were pleased with that vindication, and the Republican party decided that the pamphlet should be used as a campaign document and sent broadcast over Maryland. Thus encouraged, Miss Carroll herself, mainly at her own expense, printed and circulated 50,000 copies. James Tilghman, of the Union Committee of Baltimore, wrote her that he "set his son at the door of his house in Camden street, and that five-hundred men called for the pamphlet in a single day, and that these were the bone and sinew of the city, wanting to know in which army they ought to enlist." Mr. Lincoln and the war department, perceiving Miss Carroll's ability, engaged her to continue to write in support of the government. At their suggestion she prepared a pamphlet on the war powers of the government. Copies of two editions of this pamphlet may be seen side by side in the bound volumes of manuscript in the State department. That paper was followed by one on the "Power of the President to suspend the writ of habeas corpus," and later a paper on "Reconstruction," showing that emancipation could come only as a war measure, the State constitutions giving no opening for emancipation. The examination was made at President Lincoln's express desire. When Miss Carroll was preparing her war papers, it was suggested to her by Mr. Lincoln that she should go to St. Louis and endeavor to form an opinion of the probable success or failure of a most important expedition preparing to descend the Mississippi by means of gunboats. It was a critical time. The Union armies were costing the government two millions a day, and up to that time had met with little else than defeat. The country was deeply despondent, the failure of the Union cause was predicted and the European powers were in haste to grant recognition to the Confederacy. Mr. Lincoln and the administration were in the deepest anxiety, for they felt that defeat upon the Mississippi would be fatal. Miss Carroll repaired to St. Louis, visiting the encampments and examining carefully the topography of the country, conversing with pilots and others. She reported the Mississippi as frowning with fortifications and the tides as unfavorable. She became convinced that the proposed descent by the gunboats would be fatal, and, inquiring carefully concerning the Tennessee river, it occurred to her that that was the true strategic line. The rebel leaders not having perceived this, it had not been fortified. Miss Carroll called in her friend, Judge Evans, of Texas, who had a rare knowledge of the topog-

raphy of that part of the country He was struck by the sagacity and wisdom of her plan and advised her to lose no time in laying it before the war department. He assisted her in drawing up a map to accompany her written plan of campaign, and she hastened to Washington, and on 30th November, 1861, taking both papers to the war department, she laid them before Thomas A. Scott, then assistant secretary of war, explaining her views. Mr. Scott, the great railroad magnate, recognized at once the immense importance of her plans and hastened with them to Lincoln, who evinced the greatest delight at the solution of the problem. He called in Benjamin F. Wade, president of the committee on the conduct of the war, telling him that he felt no doubt that this was the true move, but he feared to inaugurate a movement that was the work of a civilian and a woman. It was decided that the authorship of the plan must be kept secret so long as the war lasted, and urged by Mr. Wade, President Lincoln determined to take the initiative and change the plan of the campaign to the Tennessee. Mr. Stanton was put in office pledged to this measure, and the President was in favor of a plan that promised such fruitful results in the near future. Thomas A. Scott was sent to organize the Western troops, as he testified, to carry out her plans. In furtherance of this secret plan the western armies, to the amazement of the Confederacy, were suddenly transferred from the Mississippi up the Tennessee river. The most brilliant result followed. Fort Henry fell, Fort Donelson was taken, the Confederacy was divided and the rebel armies cut off from their source of supplies. The ultimate triumph of the Federal armies was assured. Great rejoicings took place. President Lincoln issued a proclamation of public thanksgiving, and discussions were held in the Senate and in the House to try to discover how this brilliant plan originated. Miss Carroll sat in the gallery, quietly listening, but made no sign, having been advised that it was absolutely necessary that the authorship of the plan should not be made known. She continued her work, suggesting new moves, by a series of letters to the war department, there placed on file. When repeated reverses were suffered in attempting to take Vicksburg by the river, Miss Carroll prepared another remarkable paper, accompanied by a map showing the fortifications, proving that they could not be taken from the water and advising an attack in the rear. She took those plans to the war office, and Mr. Wade has testified that they were at once sent out to the proper military authorities, and that the fall of Vicksburg and also of Island No. 10 was in consequence of her sagacious suggestions. On subjects connected with the war, and subsequently on reconstruction, Miss Carroll continued her contributions to the press, but, owing to Mr. Lincoln's untimely death, she was left unrecognized, and she presented in vain her very moderate bill to the government for her work in writing the pamphlets. Thomas A. Scott testified that the writings were authorized by the government, and that the bill was very moderate and ought to be paid, but the application met only neglect. After the war Miss Carroll was advised that she ought to make known her authorship of the plan of the Tennessee campaign, proved by a succession of letters in the keeping of the war department and by the direct testimony of Thomas A. Scott, assistant secretary of war, Hon. Benjamin F. Wade, president of the committee for the conduct of the war, Judge Evans, of Texas, and others. Accordingly, in 1871, a military commission under General Howard was appointed by Congress to inquire into the claim. Mr. Scott wrote to the committee, and Mr. Wade and Judge Evans gave their testimony in person. The evidence being incontrovertible, the committee through General Howard, reporting 2nd February, 1871, fully endorsed the claim, but when it came to public acknowledgment and award, political influence caused it to be ignored. Again it was brought up in 1872, and Mr. Wilson left it on record, that the claim was "uncontrovertible." Still it was neglected. In 1879 this claim was again examined by a congressional military committee, who reported through Mr. Cockrell, 18th February, 1879. Although this report was adverse to congressional recognition and award, it admitted the services, both literary and military, even conceding the proposition that "the transfer of the national armies from the banks of the Ohio up the Tennessee river to the decisive position in Mississippi was the greatest military event in the interest of the human race known to modern ages, and will ever rank among the very few strategic movements in the world's history that have decided the fate of empires and people;" and that "no true history can be written that does not assign to the memorialist (Miss Carroll) the credit of the conception." In 1881 a congressional military committee under General Bragg again reported after examining a great array of original letters and testimony. The report confirmed the admission of the claim in the strongest terms, and bills were brought in for the relief of Miss Carroll, now aged and infirm. But the report was reserved for the last day of Congress, and, like the preceding ones, was utterly neglected. Miss Carroll immediately after was stricken with paralysis. For three years her life was despaired of. Although she subsequently rallied, she remained a confirmed invalid, supported and cared for by her devoted sister, Miss Mary H. Carroll, who had been appointed a clerk in the Treasury office, after a season of great privation and trial. In 1885 Miss Carroll's case was brought before the Court of Claims, but, owing to her illness, she could take no part in presenting the evidence. However, the papers were such that the Court of Claims gave its moral assent and retransmitted the case to Congress for action thereon, but nothing was ever done. Each year a number of petitions were sent in from all over the land, praying Congress for Miss Carroll's recognition and award, and quietly the aged and noble authoress awaited the inevitable recognition of the future. During the Woman's Council in Washington, in the spring of 1891, the case was brought up and a great desire expressed for an investigation and a biographical account of Miss Carroll. Subscriptions were secured, and a biography with the congressional documents was prepared by Miss Sarah Ellen Blackwell, and printed under the title, "A Military Genius; Life of Anna Ella Carroll, the Great Unrecognized Member of Lincoln's Cabinet." Miss Carroll died in Washington, 19th February, 1894.

CARSE, Mrs. Matilda B., philanthropist, temperance worker and financier, is of Scotch-Irish origin. Her husband, Thomas Carse, was a railroad manager in Louisville, KY, during the Civil War. In 1869 they went abroad for the benefit of Mr. Carse's health. He died in Paris, France, in June, 1870, leaving Mrs. Carse with three boys under seven years of age. The youngest of those while in Paris had a fall which developed hip disease. He had almost recovered his health, when in 1874, in Chicago, he was run over by a wagon driven by a drunken man and instantly killed. His tragic death caused his mother to register a vow that, until the last hour of her life, she would devote every power of which she was possessed to annihilate the liquor traffic. She early became prominent in temperance work, and has been president of the Chicago Central Woman's Temperance Union since 1878. To Mrs. Carse is due the credit of establishing, under the auspices of her union, the first creche, or day nursery, in Chicago, known as the Bethesda Day Nursery. That was followed in a year or two by the establishment, through her efforts, of a second, known as the Talcott Day Nursery. Beside those nurseries the Union supports two kindergartens among the very poorest class; two gospel temperance meetings; two Sunday-schools; the Anchorage Mission, a home for erring girls; a reading room for men; two dispensaries for the poor; two industrial schools, and three mothers' meetings. Those charities are supported at a cost of over ten-thousand dollars yearly. Mrs. Carse personally raises almost the entire amount. She founded the Woman's Temperance Publishing Association, and in January, 1880, the first number of the "Signal" was published, a large sixteen-page weekly paper. Two years later "Our Union" was merged with it, and as the "Union Signal" it became the national organ of the society. Mrs. Carse also started the first stock company entirely composed of women, as no man can own stock in the Woman's Temperance Publishing Association. It was started with a capital stock of five-thousand dollars, which has been increased to one-hundred-twenty-five-thousand dollars; from having but one paid employee, it now has one-hundred-thirty-five persons on its pay-roll. Mrs. Carse has been the president and financial backer of the association since its first inception. In 1885 she began planning for the great building, the Woman's Temperance Temple in Chicago, the national headquarters of the Woman's Christian Temperance Union. The ground is valued at one-million dollars; the building cost one-million-two-hundred-thousand dollars; the rentals from the building will bring in an annual income of over two-hundred-thousand dollars; the capital stock is six-hundred-thousand dollars, one-half of which is now owned by the Woman's Christian Temperance Union, and it is expected all will be secured to that association. Mrs. Carse is founder and president of the Woman's Dormitory Association of the

Columbian Exposition. That work was done in connection with the Board of Lady Managers of the World's Columbian Exposition, of which she is a member. She was the first woman in Cook county to be appointed on the school board where she served a term of years with great acceptability. Her name appears upon several charitable boards as a director. For years she was a member of the board of the Home for Discharged Prisoners. She is also on the free kindergarten boards, and is a member of the Woman's Club of Chicago, which conducts many philanthropies. In all the wide range of charities to which she has given active help the one that probably lies nearest her heart, and to which she has given a stronger hand of aid than to any other, helping to raise for its buildings and maintenance tens of thousands of dollars, is the Chicago Foundling's Home, the Reverend Dr. George E. Shipman being its founder. She established its aid society, and has been its president since its inception. Mrs. Carse receives no compensation whatever for her services to the public.

CARSON, Mrs. Delia E., educator, born in Athens, NY, 25th January, 1833. Her father, Thomas Wilder, was one of eight brothers who migrated from Massachusetts when the eldest was yet a young man. Several were teachers of prominence, and all were closely identified with the development and progress of Genesee and Wyoming counties, New York, where they ultimately settled. Her mother's maiden name was Hannah Dow. Delia Wilder, afterward Mrs. Carson, was educated in the Alexander Classical Academy. She spent one term in the Albany Normal School and received a diploma therefrom. During 1863 and 1864 she was a teacher in the Ladies' Seminary in Bloomington, IL, from 1865 to 1871 in Beloit, WI, and from 1871 to 1887 she was preceptress of Ladies' Hall, State University of Wisconsin, and teacher of mathematics. In the latter capacity she won high distinction, being possessed of liberal culture and having a remarkably healthful social influence upon the hundreds of young women surrounding her. In addition to other accomplishments, Mrs. Carson has devoted much time to the study of art. During recent years she has become identified with general art interests in Wisconsin, giving courses of lectures and leading classes of women in the study of the history of art. She has traveled extensively in Europe, spending much time in Italy, Sicily, Morocco, Algiers, Egypt and Greece, in pursuit of practical knowledge in her favorite field. She resides in Madison, WI.

CARTER, Mrs. Hannah Johnson, art educator, born in Portland, ME. She is the only child of Jonathan True and Hannah True, his wife. Mrs. Carter's father was a wealthy importer and commission merchant. Her mother died young, leaving her infant daughter to the care of a devoted father who, early recognizing the artistic tastes of his child, gave her considerable training in that direction. In 1868 Miss True became the wife of Henry Theophilus Carter, a mechanical engineer and manufacturer. The marriage was happy and congenial, and with wealth and high social standing life seemed to hold out to the young couple only sunshine, but soon the shadows began to fall. Financial losses, the failing health of her husband, the death of a loved child and the terrible loneliness of widowhood all came in quick succession. Though nearly crushed by the weight of woe so suddenly forced upon her, Mrs. Carter, with noble independence and courage, began to look about for ways and means to support herself and child. Her mind naturally turned to art, and with the life insurance left her by her husband she entered the Massachusetts Normal Art School and was graduated with high standing. After a year's further study with private teachers in first-class studios, she went to Kingston, Canada, to direct an art school, which, if successful, would receive a government grant. Although laboring under great disadvantages, she succeeded in establishing the school on a permanent basis. At the close of the first year she was obliged to return to Boston, as the climate of Canada was too severe for her health. For two years she was associated with the Prang Educational Company, of that city, doing various work pertaining to its educational department, such as illustrating drawing-books and often acting as drawing supervisor where the Prang system of drawing was in use. In the fall of 1887 she was called to New York City to take the chair of professor of form and drawing in the College for the Training of Teachers, and in 1890 she was elected president of the art department of the National Educational Association. In 1891 she was made director of the art department in the Drexel Institute of Art, Science and Industry, in Philadelphia, PA. Mrs. Carter has been appointed on many industrial, educational and art committees. She does not confine her energies to local work, but has an interest in general art education, believing enthusiastically in the necessity of educating and elevating public taste by beginning early with the training of children for a love of the aesthetic, through habits of close observation of the beautiful. Mrs. Carter stands among the leading educators, and is an ardent worker for art education.

CARTER, Miss Mary Adaline Edwarda, industrial art instructor and designer, born in Hinesburgh, Chittenden county, near Burlington, VT. She is the oldest child of Edward H. and Mary Adaline Kellogg Carter. Her parents were natives of Vermont, descended from the early New England settlers, of English and Scotch origin. Her early education was chiefly from nature and object study. After her eighth summer she attended private and public schools in Burlington, VT, and in Vineland, NJ, where her family removed in 1866. The years of country life spent in southern New Jersey during youth were filled with formative influences that laid a broad and sound basis for her life-work. Circumstances and environments led to finding occupations for herself, or to having them given her, that promoted inventive and executive powers and stimulated love for science and art. Thirst for larger opportunities and higher education developed, but adversities came, over-work, intense mental strain, then long and severe illness. After health was restored, she was by degrees led to industrial art as her vocation. Though beset by obstacles that would have turned aside one of less resoluteness, her course has been constantly progressive and largely successful. With simply the intention of becoming proficient as a teacher of drawing, she entered the Woman's Art School, Cooper Union, New York. After graduating with highest honors, in 1876, her services were immediately required as a designer for embroidery. While thus engaged, part of her time was still devoted to art study, and throughout her years of working she has been a constant student in art and other educational subjects. In the Centennial Exhibition, in 1876, she made a special study of the needlework, art embroideries and textiles of all countries. Not long after, her water-color studies from nature attracted the notice of John Bennett, the English painter of art-pottery, and she became his pupil and assistant. In 1879 a number of pieces of faïence decorated by her were sent by invitation to the exhibition of Howell, James & Co., London, England. One of her vases was presented to Sir Frederick Leighton, president of the Royal Academy, and others were sold to art museums in England, to be kept as examples of American art pottery. The same year some of her work in faience was shown in New York, and won much praise. When the Associated Artists began their united enterprise which has done so much in revolutionizing and elevating household taste and interior decoration of American home and public buildings, Miss Carter's services were secured by Louis Tiffany, and she was connected with them several years. At first having to do with all the kinds of work undertaken, glass, mosaics, metals, wood, embroideries, hangings, wall and ceiling coverings, painting or anything else decoratively used in buildings, she was the first woman thus employed. Later, having developed marked ability in plastic art, she had special charge of their pottery and modeling department. Her ornamental relief-work, panels and friezes were often used with heads and figures by St. Gaudens, and combined with work by Colman, Armstrong and other well known artists in the decoration of public and private buildings in New York and different parts of the country. Her designs for memorial and other windows, for decoration of interiors and for different purposes have been used in churches and homes, both east and west. Frequently artists, draughtsmen, teachers and others have sought instruction from her in special subjects. At different times she taught classes of children in drawing, and in the Woman's Art School one in porcelain painting. Since 1886 she has been instructor of the free classes in clay-modeling, applied design and normal training in form-study and drawing for the Young Woman's Christian Association of New York. The courses of study in those classes and all accessories have been planned by her and most effectively carried out. During the past seventeen years Miss Carter has resided with her family in the upper suburban part of New York City. She is a stanch member of the Woman's Christian Temperance Union and strongly interested in the leading questions and reforms of the day.

CARTWRIGHT, Mrs. Florence Byrne, poet, born in Galena, IL, 27th December, 1863. She resided for many years in Grass Valley, CA, where she had charge of the post office until May, 1890. In June 1890, she became the wife of Dr. Richard Cartwright, of Salem, OR, who is a descendant of Edmund Cartwright, D.D., F.R.S., inventor of the power loom, and of Major Cartwright, of colonial fame. Mrs. Cartwright's sympathies are purely Californian, as her parents moved to that State when she was only four months old. Not being strong, she was unable to take a university course, but she had the best of teaching at home. She has traveled extensively. Her future will be devoted to literary work in the Northwest. She is one of the most earnest and enthusiastic devotees of metrical composition on the Pacific Coast, and she has a qualification which few other authors possess, that of taking infinite pains and observing the strictest rules of form, and at the same time producing a careless effect. Her talent runs particularly to old French forms, which appeal to her from their difficulty and novelty, but her favorite style is the sonnet, and her delight in that form never wearies. She has written everything from the simple triolet to the sestina and chant-royal. Her first rondeau was published in the "Californian" in 1882, and her first sestina in the "Overland" in November, 1883. A sestina appearing in "Harper's Magazine" in May, 1884, has been much copied.

CARY, Miss Alice, poet, born near Cincinnati, OH, in April, 1820, died in New York City, 12th February, 1871. The family to which she belonged claimed kindred with Sir Robert Cary, who was a doughty knight in the reign of Henry V of England, and with Walter Cary, who fled with the Huguenots from France to England after the revocation by Louis XIV of the Edict of Nantes. His son Walter, educated in Cambridge, came to the Colonies soon after the landing of the Mayflower and settled in Bridgewater, MA, only sixteen miles from Plymouth Rock. He there opened a grammar school, probably the first one in America. He was the father of seven sons. One of the seven, John, settled in Windham, CT, and of his five sons, the youngest, Samuel, was the great-grandfather of Alice and Phœbe Cary. Samuel was graduated from Yale College, studied medicine and practiced in Lyme. His son, Christopher, at the age of eighteen entered the Revolutionary army. After peace was declared, Christopher received a land grant, or warrant, and settled in Hamilton county, Ohio. His son, Robert, was the father of the famous Cary Sisters, and of several other children, all of whom were persons of poetic temperament and fine intellectual powers. Alice Cary began to show her poetical talent at an early age. She wrote poetry when she was eighteen, much of which was published. Her mother, a woman of English descent, died in 1835, and her father married a second time and maintained a separate home near the cottage in which Alice, Phœbe and Elmira lived. In 1850 Alice and Phœbe decided to remove to New York City. They had won a literary reputation, and they had means to carry out their ambitious projects. Alice made her first literary venture in a volume of poems, the work of herself and her sister Phœbe, which was published in Philadelphia in 1850. Its favorable reception had much to do in causing the sisters to leave "Clovernook" and settle in New York. In 1851 Alice brought out the first series of her "Clovernook Papers," prose sketches of character, which won immediate success. Several large editions were sold in the United States and Great Britain. A second series, issued in 1853, was equally successful. In 1854 she published "The Clovernook Children," a juvenile work, which was very successful. Alice published her first volume of verse in 1853, entitled "Lyra and Other Poems." It met with ready sale, and a second and enlarged edition was published in 1855, which contained "The

Maiden of Tlascala," a long narrative poem. Her first novel, "Hagar," published as a serial in the Cincinnati "Commercial," was issued in a volume in 1852. Another novel, "Married, not Mated," appeared in 1856, and her last novel, "The Bishop's Son," was published in 1867. Her "Pictures of Country Life" appeared in 1859. Alice Cary contributed many articles to "Harper's Magazine," to the "Atlantic Monthly," to the New York "Ledger" and the "Independent." In those periodicals she published her earlier stories as serials. Her latest volumes were "Lyrics and Hymns" (1866), "The Lover's Diary" and "Snow Berries, a Book for Young Folks" (1867). Miss Cary and her sister entertained many prominent persons of their day in their New York home, among whom were Horace Greeley, John Greenleaf Whittier, Bayard Taylor and his wife, Mrs. Croly, Miss Anna E. Dickinson, Madame Le Vert, Elizabeth Cady Stanton, Mrs. Mary E. Dodge and others. Her home was a social and literary center. When Sorosis was formed, she became its first president. She was an invalid for several years before her death, and was tenderly cared for by her stronger sister. She is to-day more generally remembered by her poems than for her numerous and valuable prose works. The one romance of Alice Cary's life is told in the story of an engagement, in her early days of poverty and obscurity, to a young man who was forced by his family to break his plighted troth. Her poems reflect the sadness of her temperament that was supposed to have been influenced by that occurrence. She was a Universalist, and her religion was summed up in the simple creed of serving humanity, doing good and blessing the race.

CARY, Annie Louise, see RAYMOND, ANNIE LOUISE CARY.

CARY, Mrs. Mary Stockly, business woman and philanthropist, born in Allenburg, Canada, 18th August, 1834. Her father, John Galt Stockly, of Philadelphia, PA, whose business interests in Canada led him to reside there for a few years, removed to Cleveland, OH, in 1837. He was a pioneer in the shipping and coal interests of northern Ohio. He built and owned the first

docks in Cleveland harbor. He was of an old Virginia family of Accomac county, and his wife, Catharine Duchatel, was of French descent. Mrs. Cary's paternal grandfather, Captain Ayres Stockly, was the owner of an East India man sailing from Philadelphia, and he was among the first to unfurl the American flag in the harbor of Canton. His vessel was at one time seized by the French government, and he was imprisoned in France, his heirs being among the claimants of the French spoliation funds recently ordered to be distributed by the United States Congress. Mrs. Cary's grandmother, Mary Stockly, was one of the remarkable women in Philadelphia before the Revolutionary War. As a school-girl, Mrs. Cary was quick to learn. Her marriage to John E. Cary, a prominent lawyer of Cleveland, occurred 1st September, 1852. Mr. Cary died in 1874, leaving her with three daughters and two sons. From the time of her husband's death Mrs. Cary, with the management of her property devolving upon herself, exhibited marked and practical business sagacity. Disposing of some of her property, she increased largely her interests in those investments of her husband which she regarded as most promising. She supplied largely the capital required for the development of the Brush electric light system, and, associated with her brother, George W. Stockly, was for many years a director in its board of control. Her wealth is wisely used. Public spirited and generous, she has always taken pride in her city. She is one of the founders of its School of Art and a liberal patron of its charitable and educational institutions. She inherited from her grandfather a love of the sea and of foreign travel, and she has made the circuit of the globe, and during recent years has spent much of her time with her children in European capitals. She is an especial admirer of Japan and its people, and her talk upon the "Houses and Homes of the Japanese," before the Cleveland Sorosis, was original and unique. She is one of the most conspicuous citizens of Cleveland.

CARY, Miss Phœbe, poet, born in Hamilton county, near Cincinnati, OH, 24th September, 1824, and died in Newport, RI, 31st July, 1871. Her early educational advantages were superior to those of her sister Alice, whose constant companion she was through life, and from whom she differed radically in person, in mind and in temperament. Phœbe, like her sister, began to write verses at the age of seventeen. One of her earliest poems, "Nearer Home," written in 1842, has achieved a world-wide reputation. The story of her early life, the loss of her mother, the re-marriage of her father, the want of harmony with the stepmother, and the maintenance of a separate home, is told in the story of her sister's life. Her poems are her chief productions. Her genius did not take kindly to prose. Her verses were very different from those of her sister. Phœbe was a woman of cheerful and independent temper, and her verses were sparkling and hopeful, sunny and cheering, while those of Alice were more somber and redolent of the mournfulness of life. Some of her earlier productions were published in the "Ladies' Repository," in "Graham's Magazine," and in the Washington "National Era." Phœbe was in society a woman of wit and brilliancy, but always kind and genial. She and her sister, in their New York City home, after they had become famous and popular, did many kindly deeds to encourage and bring out obscure young authors of promise. Phœbe was the more robust of the sisters, and, after they had settled in New York City, she from choice assumed the greater share of the household duties, and thereby shortened her time for literary labor, while giving Alice, who was in delicate health for many years, greater opportunities for her literary musings. One of the most touching tributes to the dead ever written is the tribute to Alice, written by Phœbe only a few days before her own death. It was published in the "Ladies' Repository." Phœbe's robust health was not sufficient to carry her through the trial of her sister's death. Weakened by intense sorrow, she began to fail after Alice's death. Her prostration was intensified by a malarial attack, and she was taken to Newport, RI, for a change of air and scenes. The change delayed, but could not avert, the blow. She grew gradually weaker and died there. Like her sister, Phœbe is mainly regarded as a poet. Her contributions to the "Poems of Alice and Phœbe Cary" (Philadelphia, 1850), number one-third of those contained in that volume. Her independent volumes are "Poems and Parodies" (Boston, 1854), "Poems of Faith, Hope and Love" (New York, 1867), and a large number of the poems in

"Hymns for all Christians" (1869). Both of the sisters were women of great native refinement.

CASE, Mrs. Marietta Stanley, author and temperance advocate, born in Thompson, CT, 22nd August, 1845. The Stanleys are of Norman descent. Matthew Stanley, the paternal ancestor of Mrs. Case, came to this country in 1646 and settled in Massachusetts. Her father, Rev. E. S. Stanley, is a retired Methodist clergyman of the New England Southern Conference. While yet a schoolgirl, Miss Stanley wrote short poems for various papers. She wrote the commencement poem upon her graduation in 1866 from the East Greenwich Academy, Rhode Island. She also read a poem at a reunion of the alumnæ of her alma mater in 1890. In June, 1868, she became the wife of A. Willard Case, a paper manufacturer of South Manchester, CT, where they have since resided. She wrote little during the years intervening between her leaving school and the year 1884, for she believed that her domestic duties and the care and education of her children ought to occupy her whole time. She was graduated in Chautauqua in the class of 1888. She has written poems for leading religious and temperance papers, and some of them have been issued in booklet form. Mrs. Case is interested in all work that has the uplifting of humanity for its object, and is especially interested in woman's temperance, home and foreign missionary work. She has three children, two daughters and a son, now in advanced schools. Her husband warmly approves her literary persuits.

CASSEDAY, Miss Jennie, philanthropist, born in Louisville, KY, 9th June, 1840. An invalid for many years, and having burdens herself, she forgets them all in taking upon herself the burdens of others. Her father, Samuel Casseday, was a man of honor and a true Christian. His wife, Eliza McFarland, was the finest type of Christian womanhood, who with one other woman founded a Presbyterian Orphans' Home, which has been a shelter to many homeless little ones. When Miss Casseday was nine years of age, her mother died, and she was left to the care of her aunt, Miss McNutt. Miss Casseday's first work was the flower mission. When the National Woman's Christian Temperance Union met in Louisville, KY, Miss Willard called upon Miss Casseday and inquired into the flower mission work. She was so impressed that she decided to have the flower mission in the Woman's Christian Temperance Union and to appoint Miss Casseday as the superintendent. Thus was formed the National Flower Mission, which carries to the poor, the neglected, the sick and the prisoners in the jails little bouquets with selected texts attached. Subsequently a World's Flower Mission was established, with Miss Casseday as its superintendent. That work is to embrace every country. Miss Casseday appointed 9th June, her birthday, to be observed as the National and Annual Flower Mission Prison Day. On that day the flower missionaries in every State visit all State and local prisons, reformatories and almshouses within their borders. In speaking of the training school for nurses, established in Louisville, Miss Casseday says: "It was born in my heart through the ministry of suffering and a longing to help others, as was my connection with the Shut-In Band." The district nurse work owes its birth to the same touch of pain that makes all the world kin and is an outgrowth of contact with the sick poor through the flower mission. The training school for nurses has been in successful operation for several years. The members of the Shut-In Band consist of men, women and children who are shut in by disease from the outside world, of invalids who seldom or never leave their rooms or beds. The name was selected from the sixteenth verse of the seventeenth chapter of Genesis "And the Lord shut them in." These invalids write to one another and have an official organ, the "Open Window," which contains letters and news for invalid friends. This band has grown from three members to many thousands, living in all parts of the world. Miss Casseday has taken much interest in that work and has written many letters to her invalid friends. Another philanthrophy was the opening of Rest Cottage, as a country home for tired girls and women who have to support themselves. There they can obtain good comfortable board at a dollar a week and rest from their cares for a week or two, entertained by Miss Casseday herself. The King's Daughters have recently established a Jennie Casseday Free Infirmary in Louisville, which is to benefit poor and sick women.

CASTLEMAN, Mrs. Alice Barbee, philanthropist, born in Louisville, KY, 5th December, 1843. She is the daughter of ex-mayor Barbee, of that city. Her father and mother were native Kentuckians and were numbered among the early pioneers. She was their oldest daughter. She became the wife of Gen. John B. Castleman on 24th November, 1868. She is the mother of five children, three

sons and two daughters. Mrs. Castleman was educated in the East. Although she is a social leader, she finds much time for charitable work and is a philanthropist in the broadest sense. Always on the alert to advance the cause of woman, she is progressive, cultured and liberal in her views. She is president of the board of the Louisville Training School for Nurses. She is a prominent member of the Woman's Club, a member of the Woman's Auxiliary of the Board of Missions, Foreign and Domestic, and a member of the National Board of Lady Managers of the Columbian Exposition. She is active in the affairs of the Filson Club of Louisville. In religion she is an Episcopalian and a member of Christ Church, of Louisville.

CATHERWOOD, Mrs. Mary Hartwell, author, born in Luray, Licking county, OH, 16th December, 1847. Mrs. Catherwood's father came from a line of Scotch-Irish baronets, the Scott family. He was a physician and took his young family to Illinois long before the prairies were drained and cultivated. He fell a victim to the arduous duties of his profession in that new and unsettled country. Mary Hart-

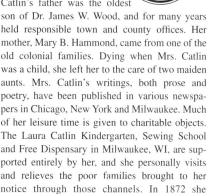

well was graduated in the Female College, Granville, OH, in 1868, and on 27th December, 1887, became the wife of James S. Catherwood, with whom she resides in Hoopeston, IL, a suburb of Chicago.

They have one child. Among her works are "Craque-o'-Doom" (Philadelphia, 1881); "Rocky Fork" (Boston, 1882); "Old Caravan Days" (1884); "The Secrets at Roseladies" (1888); "The Romance of Dollard" (1889), and "The Bells of Ste. Anne" (1889). Mary Hartwell Catherwood was always given to story-making, and she early formed the habit of putting her stories on paper. Her attention was attracted to Canadian subjects while on a visit to the American consul in Sherbrooke. She has made the history of the old French régime a special study. She is best known through her "Romance of Dollard," published as a serial in the "Century." It attracted much attention all over the United States. Her later work, "The Story of Tonty," is the condensed result of much study. In January, 1891, Mrs. Catherwood became associated in an editorial capacity with the "Graphic," a weekly illustrated paper of Chicago. She is a member of the Universalist Church and identifies herself with its work especially among children.

CATLIN, Mrs. Laura Wood, philanthropist born in Rouse's Point, Clinton county, NY, 25th June, 1841. She comes from a family closely connected with the early history of New York State. Her grandfather, Dr. James W. Wood, was taken prisoner while carrying dispatches, during the war of 1812, to Commodore McDonalds' fleet, then stationed at Plattsburgh, NY. He was kept in Quebec a prisoner of war for six months and then exchanged. Mrs. Catlin's father was the oldest son of Dr. James W. Wood, and for many years held responsible town and county offices. Her mother, Mary B. Hammond, came from one of the old colonial families. Dying when Mrs. Catlin was a child, she left her to the care of two maiden aunts. Mrs. Catlin's writings, both prose and poetry, have been published in various newspapers in Chicago, New York and Milwaukee. Much of her leisure time is given to charitable objects. The Laura Catlin Kindergarten, Sewing School and Free Dispensary in Milwaukee, WI, are supported entirely by her, and she personally visits and relieves the poor families brought to her notice through those channels. In 1872 she became the wife of Charles Catlin, a son of Julius Catlin, of Hartford, CT, and since that time has made her home in Milwaukee. Besides her talent for writing, Mrs. Catlin is a thorough musician. She has all her life been active in church work, as Sundayschool teacher and organist.

CATT, Mrs. Carrie Lane Chapman, journalist and lecturer, born in Ripon, WI, 9th January, 1859. Her maiden name was Lane. While yet a child, her parents moved to northern Iowa, where her youth was passed. In 1878 she entered as a student the scientific department of the Iowa Agricultural College and was graduated therefrom in 1880, with the degree of B. S. She was an earnest student and attained first rank in her class. For three years she devoted herself to teaching, first as principal of the high school in Mason City, IA, from which positions she was soon promoted to that of city superintendent of schools in the same place. In 1885 she became the wife of Leo Chapman and entered into partnership with him as joint proprietor and editor of the Mason City "Republican." Within a year Mr. Chapman died. Disposing of her paper, Mrs. Chapman went to California where for a year she was engaged in journalistic work in San Francisco. In 1888 she entered the lecture field and for some time spoke only in lecture courses. The cause of woman's enfranchisement soon enlisted her warmest sympathies, and she accepted a position as State lecturer for the Iowa Woman Suffrage Association. Since that time all her energies have been devoted to that cause and there her earnest, logical eloquence has won her many friends. Three times she has been called as a speaker to the annual convention of the National Association. In 1890 she became the wife of George W. Catt, civil engineer, of New York City. Her home is in Bensonhurst-by-the-Sea, on Long Island.

CAYVAN, Miss Georgia, actor, born in Maine, in 1858. Her childhood was passed in Boston, MA, where she was educated mainly in the public schools. She early showed fine musical and elocutionary talents, and her friends encouraged and assisted her in developing both. At an early age she began to make use of her elocutionary gifts. She gave readings and recitations in New England lyceums, and her ambition was to become an elocutionist. After some experience she went to the Boston School of Oratory, from which institution she was graduated with honors. In 1879, on 14th April, she made her operatic début as Hebe in "Pinafore," with the Boston Ideal Opera Company, in the Boston Theater, and scored a success. She made her début in drama on 10th May, 1879, in the same theater, as Sally Scraggs in "Sketches in India." She was brought to the notice of Steele Mackaye in 1880, and he chose her a member of his Madison Square Theater model stock company. On 7th May, 1880, she made her debut in New York as Dolly Dutton in "Hazel Kirke," and in 1881 she became the "Hazel" of that play, scoring an instant triumph, and then traveled with one of the Madison Square companies until 1882. Early in 1882 she appeared in the memorable production of the Greek tragedy "Antigone" and in the Greek play "Œdipus Tyrannus," in the Boston Globe Theater and in Booth's Theater in New York. On 3rd April, 1882, she appeared as the original Liza in "The White Slave," in Haverly's Fourteenth Street Theater in New York, and on 18th September, 1882, as the original Lura, in America, in "The Romany Rye," in Booth's Theater in New York, both special engagements. She played a successful season with the California Theater stock company, after several years with the Madison Square company. She then played with A. M. Palmer's company, and then returned to the Madison Square company. When Daniel Frohman organized, in New York, the Lyceum Theater stock company, in 1887, he selected Miss Cayvan as leading lady. She appeared in the Lyceum in "The Wife," in "Sweet Lavender," in "The Charity Ball," in "The Idler," in "Nerves," in "Old Heads and Young Hearts," and in "Squire Kate." She is still leading lady in the Lyceum company. Miss Cayvan is a hard worker and a thorough student. Her career has been one of steady growth in her art, and she now ranks among the foremost in her profession. Her home is in New York City with her mother and sister. In social life she is as charming as on the stage. She is now (1892) taking a long vacation and is traveling in Japan and other oriental lands.

CHACE, Mrs. Elizabeth Buffum, anti-slavery agitator and reformer, born in Providence, RI, 9th December, 1806. She was the second child of Arnold and Rebecca Buffum, who were Quakers and were descended from some of the oldest Quaker families in the State. One of the mother's ancestors, Daniel Gould, the first of his name to settle in this country, was arrested on going into Boston in company with the two men who were afterward hung with Mary Dyer, on Boston Common, for the crime of returning to Massachusetts after they had been banished thence because they were Quakers. Gould was sentenced to be whipped because of his religious opinions and the heretical company in which he was taken, and he received his punishment on the Common. Elizabeth Buffum was well educated for her times. During her childhood her family lived in Smithfield, RI, the original home of her father. One of her teachers there was George D. Prentice. Later she attended the Friends' school in Providence. In her youth she was a very devoted Quaker. She became the wife of Samuel Buffington Chace and passed the first part of her married life in Fall River. In 1840 she removed with her husband to Valley Falls, RI, and that place has been her home ever since. Her anti-slavery experiences have been given in her anti-slavery "Reminiscences" (1891, privately printed). That pamphlet has omitted to mention the important work she did in connection with Samuel May, Jr., who was then agent for the Anti-Slavery Society, in getting up anti-slavery meetings and conventions all over the State of Rhode Island. She separated from the Society of Friends because she was dissatisfied with their course about slavery, and after that her religious opinions underwent much modification. In the latter part of her life she has engaged heartily in what was known as the "Free Religious Movement," and found herself in religious sympathy with such men as Theodore Parker, John Weiss, O. B. Frothingham, David Wasson, Samuel Longfellow, T. W. Higginson and Frederic A. Hinckley. Most of these men were personal friends and occasional guests in her house. After the Civil War Mrs. Chace's principal interests centered in prison reform and woman's rights. She was largely instrumental in establishing in Rhode Island a State school and home for dependent children, which should take them out of the pauper and criminal class. It was in great measure due to her efforts that twenty years ago a board of women visitors was appointed to penal institutions, and the recent appointment of women on the boards of actual management of some State institutions is in no small degree the result of her efforts. She was a delegate to the World's Prison Congress held in London, England, in 1872, and read there a paper on the importance of the appointment of women on the boards of control of penal and pauper institutions. Her husband died in 1870, and she had lost by death seven out of her ten children. She felt the need of change, and spent more than a year in travel in Europe with her daughters. Her work for woman suffrage has been unremitting, and she has been president of the Rhode Island Woman Suffrage Association for twenty years. She writes occasionally for the newspapers on such topics as interest her, and, while never a public speaker, she often reads papers at the meetings which she attends. She has always been a consistent believer in total abstinence from the use of alcoholic beverages, and is a strong prohibitionist. She disapproves war under all circumstances. With all her public interests, Mrs. Chace has always been an unusually domestic woman, devoted to her family, solicitous for their education and moral nature, and zealous in her careful housekeeping.

CHAMPNEY, Mrs. Elizabeth W., author, born in Springfield, OH, 6th February, 1850. Her father was Judge S. B. Williams. She was educated in Vassar College and was graduated in 1869. During her girlhood she dreamed of literature as a profession, and she wrote many romances that were never printed. In 1876 she began to publish short stories, poems and romances in large numbers. She contributed to "Harper's Magazine" and the "Century" a series of observations on her travels in England, France, Spain, Portugal and Morocco, as well as other oriental lands. Among these papers was a striking one on Portugal, another on "A Neglected Corner of Europe," and a third, "In the Footsteps of Fortuny and Régnault." Since her return to the United States she has written about a score of volumes. Her novels are "Bourbon Lilies" and "Rosemary and Rue." Her stories for youth include "All Around a Palette" and "Howling Wolf and His Trick Pony." Among her historical stories for youth is "Great Grandmother Girls in New France," suggested by the Indian massacre in Deerfield, MA. One of her most successful works is "Three Vassar Girls Abroad," which consists of ten volumes. Mrs. Champney writes much on solicitation by publishers, and her time is thus too much taken up to permit her to indulge her bent and talent for poems and short stories. Her popularity has dated from the appearance of the Vassar series. She became the wife of J. Wells Champney, the artist, 15th May, 1875. Their union is a singularly happy one in every way. Mr. Champney has done some of his best work in illustrating his gifted wife's books. They have one son, Edward Frère. They make their winter home in New York City, and their summers are spent in "Elmstead," the old-fashioned house built in Deerfield, MA, by Mrs. Champney's grandfather.

CHANDLER, Mrs. Lucinda Banister, social reformer and author, born in Potsdam, NY, 1st April, 1828. Her parents were Silas Banister and Eliza Smith, both of New England birth and ancestry. Mrs. Chandler suffered a spinal injury in early infancy from a fall, and that intensified the susceptibility of a highly nervous organization, and was the cause of a life of invalidism and extreme suffering. As a child she was fond of books and study, and when she entered St. Lawrence Academy, at nine years of age, her teacher registered her as two years older, because of her advancement in studies and seeming maturity of years. At the age of thirteen years her first great disappointment came, when her school course was suspended, never to be resumed, by the severe development of her spinal malady. For several years even reading was denied to her. In her twentieth year she became

the wife of John H. Chandler, who was born and raised in Potsdam. The one child born to them was drowned in his third year. Mrs. Chandler's marriage was a happy one, and the tender devoted care and provision for her relief and benefit by her husband were no doubt the providence that made it possible for her to enjoy a period of usefulness in later life. In the winter of 1870–71 she wrote "Motherhood, Its Power Over Human Destiny," while recuperating from a long illness, and it was so warmly received by a society of ladies in Vineland, NJ, that it was afterward published in booklet form. That introduced her to many thinking women of Boston, where in 1871–72 she held parlor meetings and achieved the purpose of her heart, the organization of a body of women who were pledged to work for the promotion of enlightened parenthood and an equal and high standard of purity for both sexes. The Moral Education Society of Boston has continued a vigorous existence to the present time. Societies were formed in New York, Philadelphia and Washington, DC, by the efforts of Mrs. Chandler and with the cooperation of prominent women. That was the first work in this country in the line of educational standards for the elevation and purity of the relations of men and women, inside as well as outside of marriage. The publication of essays, "A Mother's Aid," "Children's Rights" and the "Divineness of Marriage," written by her, followed and furnished a literature for the agitation of questions that since that time have come to be widely discussed. During one of the long periods of prostration and confinement to her room, to which Mrs. Chandler was subject, she commenced study on the lines of political economy as a mental tonic and helpful agency to restoration. After her recovery she wrote extensively for reform publications upon finance reform, the land question and industrial problems. In Chicago, in 1880, the Margaret Fuller Society was founded, especially to interest women in those subjects and the principles of Americanism. A life-long advocate of the total abstinence principle, Mrs. Chandler served as vice-president of the Woman's Christian Temperance Alliance of Illinois. She was the first president of the Chicago Moral Educational Society, formed in 1882. She is an advocate of Christian socialism, and a firm believer in the final triumph of the Christian idea of the brotherhood of man as a practical and controlling principle in commercial and industrial systems.

CHANDLER, Mrs. Mary Alderson, educator, born near Le Raysville, PA, 16th April, 1849. Her birth place was twenty miles from any town of importance, the only connection with which was the rumbling stage-coach. When other children of her age were profiting by the railroad, the telegraph, music, art, literature and other facilities for unconscious growth and education, she, benightedly, was looking through the little windows of the stone house, dreaming of another world beyond the hills. Her parents were plain English people, whose wealth, they used to say, lay chiefly in their children, of whom there were eight boys and three girls. Her education was begun in the district school, and afterward she spent two years in the State Normal School, Mansfield, PA, graduating with the honors of her class in the spring of 1868. She then began her work as a teacher. The first three years of public-school service were spent in western Pennsylvania, the following nine in California. She was everywhere successful. Being largely endowed with enthusiasm, she invariably left in her wake the spirit of progress. Deciding to become a specialist, she went to Philadelphia as a student. While there she met Willard M. Chandler, whose wife and co-worker she became, and whom she accompanied to Boston, her present home. Mr. Chandler was a gentleman of refinement, intelligence, breadth of thought and unusual power as an orator. Their lives were full of promise, but in a short time he died of consumption. Necessity, a strong commander, decided that stenography, which she had learned more as an aid to her husband than otherwise, should then become her vocation. Summoning courage, she threw herself into that educational work and turned out stenographers of so rare a quality as to attract general attention. That led to the publication of her "Graded Lessons" (Boston, 1889), for which her penetrating mind had discovered the greatest need. Foreseeing the time when shorthand would become a part of a common-school education, she devoted herself to the problem of preparing a work specially adapted to that end, and which she published, "Practical Shorthand for Schools and Colleges" (Boston, 1891). By her strictly logical development she has brought that complicated subject within the ready comprehension of all.

CHANLER, Mrs. Amélie Rives, author, born in Richmond, VA, 23rd August, 1863. Her mother, Miss Macmurdo, was the granddaughter of Bishop Moore, of Virginia, and from her and the grandmother Mrs. Chanler inherits the beauty as marked as her mental gifts. Her father, Colonel Alfred L. Rives, is a distinguished engineer and the son of Hon. William C. Rives, three times minister to France, member of the United States Senate, and the author of a "Life of Madison." Miss Rives passed her childhood between Mobile, AL, and William Rives' country place, Castle Hill, in Albemarle county, VA. When she was about sixteen years old, her father, on the death of his mother, fell heir to the estate, and from that time they made it their permanent home. From the time she was nine years old Miss Rives found her greatest delight in her pen, writing freely and without restraint whatever occupied her fancy for the time. Her writings were never criticised, and rarely read, and to that habit of freedom is perhaps due the strong individuality of style which has carried her so successfully through what has been, so far, a most daring as well as a most brilliant literary career. Her love of art only seconded that of literature, and her life has been spent in pursuit of both. In 1886 Miss Rives published anonymously, in the "Atlantic Monthly," "A Brother to Dragons," a story of the sixteenth century, so powerful that it attracted widespread attention both in this country and in England. The same year a sonnet of great strength appeared in the "Century," signed by Amélie Rives, and she was soon identified as the author of "A Brother to Dragons." Many orders were received by her for stories and poems, but she preferred not to hurry into print, and published the following year, 1887, only two short stories, "The Farrier Lass o' Piping Pebworth" in "Lippincott's Magazine," and "Nurse Crumpet Tells the Story," in "Harper's Magazine." In 1889 appeared in "Lippincott's Magazine" "The Quick or the Dead." That story, or rather study, as Miss Rives called it, at once launched her on the sea of literature as a novelist

of undoubted power. Criticism came from all
sides. The story was translated into French, and
appeared in the "Revue des Deux Mondes." It was
impossible that so daring a venture should escape
censure, but Miss Rives kept her balance through
blame and praise alike, writing steadily and
studying, filled with a purpose to perfect herself in
the art she considers the greatest, determined to
retain her individuality while constantly striving
to throw aside the faults of youth and literary
inexperience. In June, 1888, she became the wife
of John Armstrong Chanler, a grandson of John
Jacob Astor. Mr. Chanler, who has spent much of
his life abroad, was imbued with the same love of
art and literature that had formed the main-spring
of Miss Rives' life, and was anxious that his wife
should perfect her art studies. That summer she
published her first drama, "Herod and Mariamne,"
written three years before, and in April, 1889, she
sailed for Havre. After traveling for some months
she settled in Paris for hard work, but was greatly
interrupted by ill-health. Unable to paint, she continued to write and study, perfecting herself in
French and reading widely in all branches of English literature. None of her European work has
been published, except a study of life in the Latin
Quarter, entitled "According to St. John," which
appeared in the "Cosmopolitan" as a serial, in
1891. In the month of August, 1891, she returned
to America. She was followed shortly by Charles
Lasar, an artist and teacher of prominence in
Paris, under whom she will study at her home in
Castle Hill during the fall and winter months for
several years to come. A second drama, entitled
"Athelwold," was published in "Harper's Magazine" of February, 1892, and has received high
praise from the leading literary papers of the
North. Mrs. Chanler has but just begun a career
which promises to be enduring as well as brilliant.
She is impressed by the feeling that what she has
done is but a preparation, "studies," as she is fond
of expressing it, for the message she feels she has
to deliver, and every power of an intense and
earnest nature is bent on putting to the best uses
the talents which she looks upon with a deep sense
of responsibility.

CHAPIN, Miss Augusta J., Universalist minister, born in Lakeville, near Rochester, NY, 16th
July, 1836. She is a descendant, in the ninth generation, of Samuel Chapin, who came from Wales
to Dorchester, MA, in 1636, and settled in Spring-

field, MA, in 1642. Her father, Almon M. Chapin,
was a native of the latter place. Her family
removed to Michigan while she was very young,
and she was educated in that State. In her childhood she attended the common schools and made
the most of her opportunities. Her father, who was
a man of liberal culture, gave her much instruction
at home. Books for children were few, but she
possessed illustrated copies of the New Testament, Bunyan's Pilgrim's Progress and Robinson
Crusoe. These she read with never-failing delight,
until they were almost memorized, and that early
familiarity with three great books became the
foundation of her life-long love of all that is best
in thought and literature. Of her studies, mathematics and language were her favorites, and so
earnestly and successfully did she apply herself
that, in the spring before her fourteenth birthday,
she received a certificate from the school inspectors of the county authorizing her to teach. She
undertook the charge of a country school the following summer. Soon after, she became a student
in Olivet College, where she remained several
years. Some years later, Lombard University,
Galesburg, IL, acknowledged her high scholarship by conferring upon her an honorary degree.
Miss Chapin is, at the present time, non-resident
lecturer on English literature in that school. After
the opening of the University of Michigan to
women, she entered that institution and was graduated with the degree of M.A. While a student in
Olivet, she became deeply interested in religion
and resolved to enter the Christian ministry. She
preached her first sermon in Portland, MI, 1st
May, 1859. From that time to the present she has
been continuously in active ministerial work. She
was regularly ordained by the Universalist
denomination in Lansing, MI, 3rd December,
1863. Her chief pastorates have been in Portland,
MI; Iowa City, IA; Lansing, MI.; Pittsburgh, PA;
Aurora, IL, and Oak Park, Chicago. The last place
has been Miss Chapin's field of labor for the last
six years, and her church there has enjoyed the
most prosperous period of its
history during her pastorate.
During a continuous min-
istry covering the period
of the coming and going
of an entire generation of
mankind, Miss Chapin
has never once been ab-
sent from her pulpit on

account of sickness. She has been in the active work of the Christian ministry longer than any other living woman. She has delivered more than four-thousand sermons and public addresses, has baptized and received many hundreds of persons into the church, has attended some two-hundred funerals, and has officiated at many marriages. Her vacations have usually been given to missionary work outside her parish, and on those occasions, in addition to many special trips, she has visited and preached in more than half the States and Territories of the Union, and from the Atlantic to the Pacific. She has written considerably for magazines and the denominational press, and has been much sought for in the lecture field. Her lectures are on humanitarian, literary and artistic themes, including lectures on "Temperance," "Woman's Work and Wages," "Shakespeare's Sonnets," "Wordsworth's Ethics" and courses on the "American Poets," "English Cathedrals," "Italian Cities" and other themes. Miss Chapin is an active member of the Art Institute, the Woman's Club and other important local organizations of Chicago, and also, among many others, of the National Society for the Extension of University Teaching. She is the chairman of the Woman's Committee on Religious Congresses in the World's Congress Auxiliary to the Columbian Exposition of 1893. She has traveled extensively in the United States and has been twice to Europe. Miss Chapin has a fine voice, and excellent delivery, and her reading is beyond criticism.

CHAPIN, Mrs. Clara Christiana, woman suffragist and temperance worker, born in Gloucestershire, England, 26th December, 1852. Her maiden name was Morgan. Her father was of Welsh extraction, and her mother came of an old country family the Blagdons, proprietors of the manor of Boddington since the days of William the Conqueror. She was educated in Clifton Ladies' College and passed the Cambridge local examination the only form of university privilege open at that time to girls. She came to the United States with her parents and their five younger children in 1870. The family settled in Fillmore county, NE, and Clara engaged in teaching. In

September, 1872, she became the wife of Clarence C. Chapin, of Sheffield, MA, and shortly after they removed to Franklin county, NE, where both took a prominent part in the development of that new State. Mr. Chapin served as a member of the State legislature, while his talented wife by the use of her pen and personal influence aided in securing the enactment of the famous Slocum license law, at that time supposed to he the panacea intemperance matters. They also aided materially in securing the temperance educational and scientific law for that State. She was particularly interested in all movements for the advancement of women and took an active part in the woman suffrage campaign of 1882. She was a prominent member of the Woman's Christian Temperance Union and wrote much for the press on the woman and temperance questions. Being a little body, Mrs. Chapin commonly went by the name "La Petite" among her co-workers in Nebraska, but, though small of stature, she is of that fine mental acumen which gives great individuality and force of character. Though of English birth, Mrs. Chapin's life-work has been and still is American. She now resides, with her husband, son and two daughters, in one of the pleasant suburban towns of Chicago, IL.

CHAPIN, Mrs. Sallie F., author and temperance worker, born in Charleston, SC. Her maternal ancestors were Huguenots, who came to the Colonies in 1685. Her two great-grandfathers, Vigneron and Tousager, were killed in the Revolutionary War. Her maiden name was Moore, and on her father's side the strain is English. Her father was a Methodist minister. His home in Charleston was burned, and he moved to the northern part of the State. Miss Moore was reared and educated in Cokesburg, Abbeville county. From early childhood she showed a fondness and talent for authorship. Miss Moore became Mrs Chapin while she was still a girl, and her married life has been singularly happy. Her husband was one of the founders of the Young Men's Christian Association of Charleston, and one of its chief officers for years. Mrs. Chapin's father died in the pulpit at a union camp-meeting, during the Civil War, after receiving a dispatch announcing the death of his son in a battle. Mrs. Chapin has written much, but she has published only one book, "Fitzhugh St. Clair, the Rebel Boy of South Carolina." During the war she was president of the Soldiers' Relief Society and worked day and night in the hospitals. The war broke their fortune, and her husband died after the conflict was ended. In the Woman's Christian Temperance Union she has been conspicuous for years, serving as State president, and she has done much to extend that order in the South, where conservatism hindered the work for a long time. In 1881 she attended the convention in Washington, DC, where she made a brilliant reply to the address of welcome on behalf of the South, ending with a telling poem setting forth the intentions of the Woman's Christian Temperance Union. She believes in prohibition as the remedy for intemperance. She is a forcible and brilliant writer and conversationalist. In the Chicago Woman's Christian Temperance Union convention, in 1882, when the Prohibition Home Protection Party was formed, she was made a member of the executive committee, and by pen and voice she popularized that movement in the South. She was at one time president of the Woman's Press Association of the South.

CHAPMAN, Mrs. Carrie Lane, see CATT, MRS. CARRIE LANE.

CHAPMAN, Miss Millie Jane, doctor of medicine, born in Beaver, Crawford county, PA, 23rd July, 1845. She is the daughter of Lewis K. and Robey Ormsbee Chapman. She had a happy early childhood, but reverses came to the family, and at the age of ten 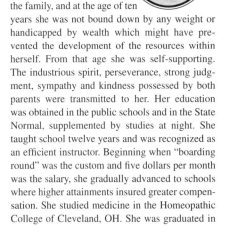 years she was not bound down by any weight or handicapped by wealth which might have prevented the development of the resources within herself. From that age she was self-supporting. The industrious spirit, perseverance, strong judgment, sympathy and kindness possessed by both parents were transmitted to her. Her education was obtained in the public schools and in the State Normal, supplemented by studies at night. She taught school twelve years and was recognized as an efficient instructor. Beginning when "boarding round" was the custom and five dollars per month was the salary, she gradually advanced to schools where higher attainments insured greater compensation. She studied medicine in the Homeopathic College of Cleveland, OH. She was graduated in

February, 1874, and located at once in Pittsburgh, PA, where she still resides. She found it a conservative city, unaccustomed to woman doctors and not realizing a demand for them. It required a great struggle to become established. The pioneer efforts and all influence connected therewith were borne as a necessary ordeal to one entering upon an unusual work. She labored with a firm determination to maintain true professional dignity and general courtesy to all deserving associates, cognizant of the fact that hard study and patient perseverance would be necessary to reach the goal. Her true womanly character in the profession has been endorsed by many exalted positions in local, district, State and national medical organizations. Her faith in God and in the brotherhood of mankind has induced her to make extensive efforts for humanity, for the relief of their physical distress and for their education and reformation.

CHARLES, Mrs. Emily Thornton, poet and journalist, born in Lafayette, IN, 21st March, 1845. She comes of English ancestors, the Thorntons and Parkers. On the paternal side the Thorntons were noted as original thinkers. Her great grandfather, Elisha Thornton, carried a sword in the War of the Revolution. Her grandfather, also Elisha Thornton, resident of Sodus, Wayne county, NY, served in the War of 1812. Her father, James M. Thornton, gave his life to the cause of the Union in 1864, and of her two brothers, Charles lost his life in the Civil War, and Gardner served in Harrison's regiment. The Parkers, her maternal ancestors, were among the primitive Puritans. Deacon Edmund Parker settled in Reading, MA, about 1719, the family removing thence to Pepperell, MA, which town they helped to found. For more than a century, from father to son, the Parkers were deacons and leaders of the choir in the Congregational Church. When Emily's grandfather married, the young couple took a wedding journey in a sleigh to find a new home in Lyons, Wayne county, NY, taking with them their household goods. Twenty years later their daughter, Harriet Parker, was married to James M. Thornton, a civil engineer, son of Elisha. The young couple moved to Lafayette, IN, where Mr. Thornton established a large manufactory. Emily Thornton was educated in the free schools of Indianapolis, and at the age of sixteen she became a teacher. As a child in school she attracted attention by the excellence of her written exercises and her original manner of handling given subjects. She became the wife, while very young, of Daniel B. Charles, son of a business man long established in Indianapolis. At the age of twenty-four she was left a widow, in delicate health, with two little ones dependent upon her. Soon after the death of her husband, 1874, she began to write for a livelihood, doing reportorial and editorial work for Indianapolis papers and correspondence for outside publications. She succeeded well. Having chosen journalism as a profession, she perfected herself in all its branches. She published her first volume of verse under the title "Hawthorn Blossoms" (Philadelphia, 1876). This little book was received with great favor and proved a literary and financial success. From the Centennial year to 1880 she continued to do newspaper work and biographical writing. She was associate editor of "Eminent Men of Indiana." In 1881 she accepted a position as managing editor of the Washington "World." Afterward she established "The National Veteran" in Washington, DC, of which she was sole proprietor and editor. In 1883 Mrs. Charles was prostrated through overwork and was confined to her bed for an entire year. While recovering slowly, she spent a year in revising and preparing for publication her later poems. The work appeared in "Lyrical Poems" (Philadelphia, 1886), a volume of three-hundred pages. That volume fully established her reputation as a national poet. She has appeared upon the lecture platform with success. On the occasion of her departure from Indiana, when a complimentary farewell testimonial was tendered her by the leading citizens of Indianapolis, in 1880, she made a brilliant address. In 1882 she addressed an audience of 1,500 ex-prisoners of war in Cincinnati, OH. Her poetical address on "Woman's Sphere" was delivered before a National Woman's Suffrage Convention. She is a member of the executive committee of the National Woman's Press Association and chairman of the executive council of the Society of American Authors. She has been selected as one of the speakers at the World's Columbian Exposition in 1893. Mrs. Charles writes almost exclusively under the name of "Emily Thornton."

CHASE, Mrs. Louise L., born in Warren, MA, 2nd September, 1840. She is a daughter of Samuel and Mary Bond. Soon after her birth her parents moved to Brimfield, MA, where she received her education, entering the Hitchcock free high school at the age of thirteen. Her attendance in that school was interrupted by a temporary residence in Columbia, CT, where she attended a private school. She returned to Brimfield and finished her course at the age of sixteen. In 1857 she took up her residence in Lebanon, CT, and there became the wife, in 1861, of Alfred W. Chase, a native of Bristol, RI. Mr. and Mrs. Chase soon removed to Brooklyn, CT, and in 1887 to Middletown, RI, the home of Mr. Chase's family, where they still reside. In 1885 she was elected president of the Woman's Christian Temperance Union of Middletown, and in that way became prominent in the work. She was elected State vice-president of the Woman's Christian Temperance Union, and at about the same time State superintendent of the department of Sabbath observance. In 1886 she represented the State in the National Convention in Minneapolis, Minn. She was elected in 1891 State superintendent of scientific temperance instruction in schools.

CHEATHAM, Miss Kitty Smiley, actor, born in Nashville, TN, in 1869. She was educated in the public schools of that city and was graduated at fifteen years of age. While she was still a child, her father died, leaving his family in straitened circumstances. Realizing the necessity of personal exertion and prompted by her love for her mother, whose immunity from want she was anxious to secure, she cast about to see what her hands might find to do. The stage was her dream. She was even in childhood a lover of the theater. Home-made theatrical amusement was her favorite pastime. Mimicry came natural to her. As she grew older her desire to become an actor was made known. By that time she had already won approbation as an amateur of more than average taste and still. Encouraged by critics and friends, she was enabled to overcome the opposition of her family and relatives to her adopting the stage as a profession, and in the spring of 1885 she removed to New York City to study singing under Errani, making such progress as justified her engagement when she was only sixteen years old, as leading lady in the J. O. Barrow "Professor" company. She met a flattering reception throughout the South. The following season she joined Col. Mc-Call's traveling opera company and sang the primadonna parts in the "Black Hussar," "Falka" and "Erminie." The next season she played second parts in the Casino, in New York. Her prospects on that famous stage were flattering, but she foresook them for Daly's company, with which she has since been identified. In the Daly company she has played in "The Midsummer-Night's Dream," "Love's Labor Lost," "The Inconstant," "The Foresters," and as "Kate," a part she created.

CHENEY, Mrs. Abbey Perkins, musical educator, born in Milwaukee, WI, in 1853. She inherits her rare gifts through her mother, from a long line of singing ancestors, the Cheneys of Vermont, who for a hundred years have been famous for their fine and powerful voices and exceptional musical culture. Her mother, Mrs. Elizabeth Cheney Perkins, has a remarkably pure and strong mezzo-soprano voice, and was very successful before her marriage, as a church and concert singer in Buffalo, NY, and subsequently in Milwaukee, WI, and in Leavenworth, Kans. She still enjoys, in her serene silver-haired old age, the musical and literary pleasures of her daughter's San Francisco home. Mrs. Cheney's father, one of the enterprising young business men of Milwaukee in the 50's, was also a music lover. He died in 1861, and his last words to his little daughter were: "Lose no opportunity to cultivate your musical talent." The father's wish decided the child's future. Mrs. Perkins encouraged and aided her daughter in every way, and as her two other children early followed their young father, she was left sadly free from all hindrances to these efforts. The little girl soon achieved such successes that, when only fourteen years old, she was called with her mother to take charge of the music in Ingham University, LeRoy, NY. Two years later they resigned that position in order to go abroad for the prosecution of the daughter's musical studies. They went to Germany, where Miss Perkins entered the Conservatory of Leipsic, and also received private tuition from Louis Plaidy. During that year in Leipsic she was a pupil of Paul, of Coccius, of Reinecke and others on the piano, and of Richter in harmony. But the best teachers in Leipsic were unsatisfactory in point of technique, and through the counsel of honest Coccius, as well as by advice of the master, Liszt, she went to Stuttgart to study with Sigismund Lebert, whom Liszt pronounced the greatest living teacher of technique. The school year at Stuttgart had just closed, and the young American girl presented herself tremblingly to the master for examination, winning such favor that he offered to teach her, contrary to his custom, through vacation, going three times a week to his pupil's house and to the last refusing all compensation. When the school re-opened, the brilliant young musician was admitted to the artists' class, and there for four years she studied with Lebert and with Prückner, the friend of Von Bülow. Then, having received her diploma, she began in Germany her successful career as a musical educator. A term of study with Edward Neupert, the pupil of Kullak, closed her pupil life, but by no means ended her musical studies. She returned to America, thoroughly equipped for the profession, and yet not so wedded to it as to prevent her beng wooed and won by the young musician, poet and littérateur, John Vance Cheney, with whom she went to California in 1876. First in Sacramento, and later in San Francisco, Mrs. Cheney has been the pioneer of a new school of musical technique, and the signal success achieved by her pupils is proof conclusive that in her treatment of piano-playing, primarily from the physiological standpoint, she has enlarged and improved the methods of her masters, Reinecke, Lebert and others. It is proper to state here that the physiological investigations, which have made Mrs. Cheney an originator in her field of work, were instigated by her own great suffering from partial paralysis of the right hand and arm, brought on by over-taxation when completing her studies abroad. It is without doubt, due to this fact that we have the sympathetic broad-minded, self-sacrificing educator in place of the brilliant concert pianist.

CHENEY, Mrs. Armilla Amanda, treasurer National Relief Corps, born in Windham, OH, 27th August, 1845, of Massachusetts and Vermont parentage. Her maiden name was Perkins. She is a lineal descendant of John Perkins, who, over two-hundred-fifty years ago, by strategy, saved the little Puritan colony of Ipswich, MA, from the Indians. Left fatherless at an early age, without brothers or sisters, and with a mother in feeble health, more than ordinary cares and responsibilities came to her in her younger days. Her whole life has been characterized by the ability to do whatsoever her hands found to do. She received a liberal education and was thereby qualified for the useful and responsible positions she has held. She was in school when the war-cry rang out at the firing on Fort Sumter, and became an earnest worker in the home labors that formed so large a part of the daily task of Northern women for alleviating the sufferings of the Boys in Blue. She became the wife of Capt. James W. Cheney, a native of Massachusetts, in May, 1868. Moving to Detroit, MI, in the fall of 1870, where she still resides, she identified herself with one of the prominent churches, and engaged in its work and that of its Sabbath-school, having in charge the infant department for several years. She became a member of Fairbanks Woman's Relief Corps, of Detroit, early in its organization, was appointed department secretary of that order soon after, and in 1887 accepted the office of secretary of the national organization. So faithfully and conscientiously were her duties performed that she won the love and esteem of the order throughout the country, and in Milwaukee, WI, in 1889, was elected national treasurer and was unanimously reelected at the succeeding national conventions, held in Boston, MA, in 1890, and in Detroit, MI, in 1891.

CHENEY, Mrs. Edna Dow, author, born in Boston, MA, 27th June, 1824. There in 1853 she became the wife of Seth W. Cheney, an artist of local prominence, who died in 1856, leaving her with one daughter. The daughter died in 1882. Miss Cheney studied in the Institute of Technology, of which General Francis J. Walker is president, and her memory is preserved by the "Margaret Cheney Reading Room," devoted to the convenience of the women students. Mrs. Cheney's life has been devoted to philosophic and literary research and work. Her early womanhood was passed under the most stimulating influences. She was a member of one of those famous conversation classes which Margaret Fuller instituted in the decade of 1830–40. Emerson, Mr. and Mrs. Alcott, James Freeman Clarke and Theodore Parker were among those who strongly influenced her thought. Her parents, Sargent Smith Littlehale and Edna Parker Littlehale, gave her every educational advantage. In 1851 she aided in forming the School of Design for Women, in Boston, and served as secretary. In 1859 she aided in establishing a hospital in connection with the Woman's Medical School. She took part in a woman's rights convention in 1860. In 1862 she was secretary of the New England Hospital. In 1868 she helped to found the New England Woman's Club and served as vice-president. In 1863 she was secretary of the teachers' committee of the Freedman's Aid Society and secretary of the committee to aid colored regiments. In 1865 she went to Readville and taught soldiers, and attended the convention of Freedmen's societies in New York City, and in the following year the one held in Baltimore, and for several years visited colored schools in various Southern States. In 1869 she assisted in founding a horticultural school for women. She lectured oil horticulture for women before the Massachusetts State Agricultural Society in 1871. In 1879 she delivered a course of ten lectures on the history of art before the Concord School of Philosophy, and the same year was elected vice-president of the Massachusetts School Suffrage Association, of which she is now president. In 1887 she was elected president of the hospital she had helped to found. She was a delegate to the Woman's Council in Washington, DC, in 1888. In 1890 she attended the Lake Mohawk Negro Conference. She has lectured and preached in many cities and has spoken at funerals occasionally. She is vice-president of the Free Religious Association. She has visited Europe three times and has traveled extensively in this country. Her works, all published in Boston, include: "Hand-Book for American Citizens," "Patience" (1870), "Social Games" (1871), "Faithful to the Light" (1872), "Child of the Tide" (1874), "Life of Susan Dimoch" (1875), "Memoir of S. W. Cheney" (1881), "Gleanings in Fields of Art" (1881), "Selected Poems of Michael Angelo" (1885), "Children's Friend," a sketch of Louisa M. Alcott (1888), "Biography of L. M. Alcott" (1889), "Memoir of John Cheney, Engraver" (1888), "Memoir of Margaret S. Cheney" (1888), "Nora's Return" (1890). "Stories of Olden Time "(1890), and a number of articles in books. She has contributed to the "North American Review," the "Christian Examiner," the "Radical," "Index," the "Woman's Journal" and other periodicals. She edited the poems of David A. Wasson (Boston, 1887), and of Harriet Winslow Sewall (Boston, 1889). Much of her work is devoted to religious and artistic subjects. Mrs. Cheney is now living in Jamaica Plain, MA.

CHENOWETH, Mrs. Caroline Van Deusen, vice-consul and educator, born at the summer home of her parents, on the Ohio river, opposite Louisville, KY, 29th December, 1846. She is the youngest daughter of Charles Van Deusen and Mary Huntington, his wife. The winters of her early life were passed in New Orleans, LA, where was also the residence of her mother's family. Her academic training was had in the St. Charles Institute, New Orleans, and Moore's Hill College, near Cincinnati. She became the wife, while still in her girlhood, of Col. Bernard Peel Chenoweth, the son of Rev. Alfred Griffith Chenoweth, of Virginia. Mrs. Chenoweth has always held liberal views relative to woman's work, and the simple naturalness with which she has lived according to her faith is hardly less remarkable than the unusual and brilliant character of her achievements. For fourteen months following her marriage in 1863, she performed faithfully and with patriotic fervor the onerous duties of a military clerk to Col. Chenoweth, thereby returning to duty in the ranks, and as her substitute on the field, the soldier detailed for this clerical work. When Col. Chenoweth was made superintendent of schools in Worcester, MA, Mrs. Chenoweth took the examination required for teachers, that she might be of service in the event of need. It was during her husband's term of office as United States Consul in Canton, China, that she was able to render her most efficient aid. Upon one occasion she sat as vice-consul in an important land case between one of the largest American houses and a wealthy Chinese. She reserved her decision for several days, until it could be submitted to Col. Chenoweth, then some eighty miles distant, under medical care, who promptly returned it unchanged, with direction that she should officially promulgate it as his duly accredited representative. Thenceforth, until Col. Chenoweth's death, several months later, the affairs of the consulate were conducted by Mrs. Chenoweth. She is believed to be the only woman who has ever held diplomatic correspondence with a viceroy of China upon her own responsibility. She was officially recognized in her vice-consular capacity upon her return to Washington to settle her husband's affairs with the Department of State, and was cordially complimented by Hamilton Fish, Secretary of State, for the thoroughness and skill with which her mission was accomplished. The effort was made by influential friends in Massachusetts to return Mrs. Chenoweth to Canton as United States consul, a measure to which President Grant extended his warm approval and the promise of his support, provided his Secretary of State could be won over. The later life of Mrs. Chenoweth has been a most studious and laborious one, the more so that the support and education of her two sons fell to her unaided care. For some years she taught private classes in Boston, and was for a time professor of English literature in Smith College. Her interests are varied, and her literary work is graceful as well as full of energy. Her essays relating to experimental psychology are scholarly and abreast of the freshest thought. She is a member of the London Society for Psychical Research, as well as of many other working societies, among which are the Brooklyn Institute, the New York Dante Society, and the Medico-Legal Society of New York. Her sketches of child-life in China are quaint and sweet. Her "Stories of the Saints" (Boston, 1882) is rich in an old-world charm. The book was written for some children of Dr. Phillips Brooks' parish in Boston, of which she was for twenty years a member. She now resides in New York City.

CHILD, Mrs. Lydia Maria, author, born in Medford, MA, 11th February, 1802. Her father was David Francis. Lydia was assisted in her early studies by her brother, Convers Francis, who was afterward professor of theology in Harvard College. Her first village teacher was an odd old woman, nicknamed "Marm Betty." She studied in the public schools and one year in a seminary. In 1814 she went to Norridgewock, ME, to live with her married sister. She remained there several years and then returned to Watertown, MA, to live with her brother. He encouraged her literary aspirations, and in his study she wrote her first story, "Hobomok," which was published in 1823. It proved successful, and she next published "Rebels," which ran quickly through several editions. She then brought out in rapid succession "The Mother's Book," which ran through eight American, twelve English and one German editions, "The Girl's Book," the "History of Women," and the "Frugal Housewife," which passed through thirty-five editions. In 1826 she commenced to publish her "Juvenile Miscellany." In 1828 she became the wife of David Lee Child, a lawyer, and they settled in Boston, MA. In 1831 they became interested in the anti-slavery movement, and both took an active part in the agitation that followed. Mr. Child was one of the leaders of the anti-slavery party. In 1833 Mrs. Child published her "Appeal in Behalf of that Class of Americans Called Africans." Its appearance served to cut her off from the friends and admirers of her youth. Social and literary circles shut their doors to her. The sales of her books and subscriptions to her magazine fell off, and her life became one of battle. Through it all she bore herself with patience and courage, and she threw herself into the movement with all her powers. While engaged in that memorable battle, she found time to produce her lives of Madame Roland and Baroness de Staël, and her Greek romance, "Philothea." She, with her husband, supervised editorially the "Anti-Slavery Standard," in which she published her admirable "Letters from New York." During those troubled times she prepared her three-volume work on "The Progress of Religious Ideas." She lived in New York City with her husband from 1840 to 1844, when she removed to Wayland, MA, where she died 20th October, 1880. Her anti-slavery writings aided powerfully in bringing about the overthrow of slavery, and she lived to see a reversal of the hostile opinions that greeted her first plea for the negroes. Her books are numerous. Besides those already mentioned the most important are "Flowers for Children" (3 volumes, 1844–46); "Fact and Fiction" (1846); "The Power of Kindness" (1851); "Isaac T. Hopper, a True Life" (1853); "Autumnal Leaves" (1856); "Looking Towards Sunset" (1864); "The Freedman's Book" (1865); "Miria" (1867), and "Aspirations of the World" (1878). Her reply to Governor Wise, of Virginia, and to the wife of Senator Mason, the author of the fugitive slave law, who wrote to her, threatening her with future damnation, was published with their letters in pamphlet form, and 300,000 copies were issued. A volume of her letters, with an introduction by John Greenleaf Whittier and an appendix by Wendell Phillips, was published in Boston, in 1882.

CHURCHILL, Mrs. Caroline M., editor and publisher, born in the township of Pickering, in the Upper Province of Canada, 23rd December, 1833. She lived with her parents in the township of Whitley until thirteen years of age, and was then sent to Lockport, NY, to attend school. How her father, Barber Nichols, came to settle in Canada is a matter not clearly understood by the family, as he was born in Providence, RI, and served in the war of 1812, for which he drew a pension. He lived to be 100 years old. Her mother is now over ninety years old and drawing a widow's pension for the father's service in 1812. Her father was a prosperous tradesman and a leading man fifty years ago in what is now called Ontario. His mother was French, his father English. The mother was Holland Dutch and German, transplanted to the State of Pennsylvania. Mrs. Churchill became the wife of a Canadian, who died in 1862. One daughter, born in 1852, is her only child. In 1869 Mrs. Churchill was attacked with what appeared to be the dread disease, consumption. California was chosen as the best place at that time to overcome a difficulty of that nature. Thither she repaired and took to canvassing for the sake of life in the open air. The result was such that her cough ceased and her health was restored. Her constitution is a light one, however, and without very favorable conditions much development is hardly possible. Mrs. Churchill's most notable public work during six years of traveling life in California was the defeat of Holland's social evil bill by a burlesque. She drew up a bill for the regulation and control of immoral men similar to that introduced for the regulation of the same class of women. A member of the committee to whom the bill was submitted caused the burlesque to be printed and extensively circulated, creating a great deal of amusement at the expense of the advocate of Holland's bill. The latter was never heard from again. An assembly and senate attempted to get the same bill passed in Denver, CO, within a year or two. That burlesque was reprinted and placed upon the tables in both houses, and the bill was defeated. Mrs. Churchill has written two books which have had a sale of over fifty-thousand copies, a little descriptive work called "Little Sheaves," and a book of travel entitled "Over the Purple Hills." While traveling in Texas, she introduced a bill in the legislature, the import of which was to keep the "Police Gazette" from being sold upon the news stands in the State. The bill passed, was signed by Governor Roberts, and has been in force for fifteen years. Feeling the need of preparation for age, Mrs. Churchill settled in Denver, and there established the "Colorado Antelope," a monthly. After publishing it for three years, the paper was changed to a weekly, the "Queen Bee," in 1879. She is a good speaker, but, from press of work in making a home for herself, she has had little opportunity to become known in the lecture field. Mrs. Churchill is by nature aggressively progressive.

CHURCHILL, Miss Lide A., born in Harrison, ME, 9th April, 1859. She is the youngest child of Josiah and Catherine Churchill. From her father she inherited her literary tastes and refined nature, from her mother her strong will and decided traits of character. Three years after her birth Mr. Churchill removed to New Gloucester, ME, where he resided with his family until his death. When quite young, Miss Churchill decided to learn telegraphy, and went to Saundersville, MA, where she partially mastered the art. She took charge of a small office in Northbridge, MA, and without assistance perfected herself in the science. From

that office she was promoted to larger and larger ones, until she had charge of the most important station belonging to the road that employed her. She next mastered stenography without a teacher and practiced it for a time. In 1889 Rev. Charles A. Dickinson, who is at the head of Berkeley Temple, Boston, desired a private secretary, for stenographic and literary work, and offered the position to Miss Churchill, who accepted it. Its duties demand knowledge, skill, tact and literary ability. Miss Churchill has written and published continuously during all the years she has been engaged as telegrapher and literary secretary. Her first book, "My Girls" (Boston, 1882) has passed through several editions. She has also written "Interweaving" and "Raid on New England." She has done much good magazine work.

CHURCHILL, Lady Randolph, social leader and politician, wife of Lord Randolph Churchill, of England, is a native of the United States. She was born in Brooklyn, NY. Her maiden name was Jennie Jerome, daughter of Leonard Jerome, a prominent citizen of New York City. Miss Jerome and her two sisters were educated mainly in Paris, France, where they were thoroughly taught in all the accomplishments common to wealthy women of the time. While visiting the Isle of Wight, England, Miss Jerome met Lord Randolph Churchill, who was then known simply as the second son of the Duke of Marlborough. Their acquaintance ripened to love, engagement followed, and in January, 1874, they were married at the British Embassy in Paris. Lord Randolph's political career began immediately after his marriage, when he entered the House of Commons as a member from Woodstock. Lady Churchill entered into her husband's plans and aspirations with all her native energy and determination, and to her assistance and counsel is credited much of his success in Parliament. Lady Randolph was one of the first members of the Primrose League, the organization of the Conservatives, and it is largely due to her efforts that in Great Britain the order can boast of nearly 2,000 habitations. Lady Churchill is an effective worker in political campaigns, and she has thoroughly mastered all the intricacies of British politics. Besides her activity in politics, Lady Churchill devotes much well directed effort to art and charity, and in British society she is looked upon as a great force. Born in the Republic, she illustrates the self-adapting power of the genuine American in the ease with which she has taken up and mastered the difficult and delicate problems implied in her situation as a wife of a peer of the English realm.

CLAFLIN, Mrs. Adelaide Avery, woman suffragist, born in Boston, MA, 28th July, 1846. She is a daughter of Alden Avery and Lucinda Miller Brown, both natives of Maine, and both of English extraction, although there is a little Scotch Irish blood on the Miller side. Narcissa Adelaide was the second of four children. Her father, although an active business man, had much poetical and religious feeling. He is a prominent member of the Methodist Church, and, on account of his eloquence, was often in earlier life advised to become a minister. Her mother, of a practical, common-sense temperament, had much appreciation of nature and of scientific fact, and a gift for witty and concise expression of thought. So from both parents Mrs. Claflin has derived the ability to speak with clearness and epigrammatic force. Adelaide was sixteen when she was graduated from the Boston girls' high school, and a year or two later she became a teacher in the Winthrop school. Although in childhood attending the Methodist Church with their parents, both her sister and herself early adopted the so-called liberal faith, and joined the church of Rev. James Freeman Clarke. She became the wife of Frederic A. Claflin, of Boston, in 1870, a man of keen and thoughtful mind and generous and kindly spirit. They have for many years resided in Quincy, MA, and have a son and three daughters. In 1883 Mrs. Claflin began to speak in public as an advocate of woman suffrage. In 1884 she was elected a member of the Quincy school committee, and

served three years in that position, being the only woman who ever held office in that conservative town. Although too much occupied with family cares to take a very active part in public life, her pen is busied in writing for the Boston papers, and she finds opportunity to give lectures, and has occasionally been on short lecturing tours outside of the limits of New England. Best known as a woman suffragist, she writes and speaks on various other topics, and her wide range of reading and thinking makes it probable that her future career as a lecturer will not be limited chiefly to the woman suffrage field.

CLARK, Mrs. Frances P., philanthropist, born in Syracuse, NY, 17th September, 1836. She was one of a family of seven children born to Dr. J. H. and Mary P. Parker, who were persons of fine character. Miss Parker was educated in Syracuse, and in November, 1858, became the wife of George W. Clark. In 1860 they moved to Cleveland, OH, remaining there until 1883, when they removed to Omaha, NE, where they have since lived. Their family consists of a daughter and son. After recovering from an apparently incurable disease of long standing, Mrs. Clark, in a spirit of gratitude to God, devoted herself to charitable work, taking up the work most needed to be done and most neglected, as she felt, by Christians, that of care for the so-called outcasts of society. In 1884, in recognition of her ability and services, she was appointed State superintendent of the social purity department of the Woman's Christian Temperance Union of Nebraska. As a result of the agitation begun by Mrs. Clark and her colleagues, the disgraceful statute making the age of consent twelve years was changed by the Legislature, in 1887, raising it to fifteen years. The women had prepared a bill making the limit eighteen years, and the result was a compromise. At the same time they petitioned the Legislature for a grant of $25,000, to be used in establishing an industrial home in Milford, NE. That institution accordingly was founded at once, and through the happy results since flowing therefrom has fully met the expectations of its founders. Mrs. Clark is a member of the board of management of the Milford home, and also of the Woman's Associate Charities of the State of Nebraska, under appointment by the Governor. Besides this, she is the superintendent of a local institution for the same purpose in Omaha, known as "The Open Door," under the auspices of the local Woman's Christian Temperance Union. That institution is supported by subscriptions from the citizens of Omaha. With all these calls upon her time, Mrs. Clark is busy constantly, and she stands in the foremost rank among the women philanthropists of Nebraska.

CLARK, Mrs. Helen Taggart, journalist, born in Northumberland, PA, 24th April, 1849. She is the oldest of three children of the late Col. David Taggart and Annie Pleasants Taggart. She was educated in the Friends' central high school, in Philadelphia, PA. In October, 1869, she made a six months' stay in Charleston, SC, whither she went to make a visit to her father, then stationed in that city as paymaster in the United States army. Miss Taggart became the wife in 1870 of Rev. David H. Clark, a Unitarian minister settled over the church in Northumberland. Four years later they removed to New Milford, PA, to take charge of a Free Religious Society there. In 1875 Mr. Clark was called to the Free Congregational Society in Florence, MA. Attention was first drawn to "H. T. C.," by which some of her earlier work was signed, in 1880, by her occasional poems in the Boston "Index," of which her husband was for a time assistant editor, and in the Springfield "Republican." Her life, as she puts it, has been one of intellectual aspirations and clamorous dish-washing and bread-winning. Mrs. Clark left Florence in 1884, returning to her father's house in Northumberland with her youngest child, an only daughter, her two older children being boys. There for two years she was a teacher in the high school, varying her duties by teaching music and German outside of school hours, story and verse writing and leading a Shakespeare class. In August, 1887, she accepted a position in the "Good Cheer" office, Greenfield, MA, whence she was recalled to Northumberland the following February by the illness of her father. His illness terminated fatally a little later, since

which time Mrs. Clark has made her home in her native town. Mrs. Clark has a large circle of friends, and her social duties take up much of her time, but she contrives to furnish a weekly column for the Sunbury "News," to perform the duties pertaining to her office as secretary of the Woman's Relief Corps in her town, to lead a young people's literary society, and to contribute stories and poems to Frank Leslie's papers, the "Christian Union," the "Woman's Journal" and the Springfield "Republican."

CLARKE, Mrs. Lena Thompson, social leader, born in Americus, GA, 10th January, 1857. Her ancestors were of that sterling Revolutionary stock whose strength of character can be traced through each generation following them. She is the daughter of James Egbert Thompson, and the granddaughter of Judge Amos Thompson, of Poultney, VT. James Egbert Thompson went to St. Paul, MN, and helped to found that city. He founded the First National Bank of St. Paul, which soon became the leading bank of the Northwest. He became influential in the development of the State and was entrusted with numerous offices of importance, which his rare executive ability enabled him to fill with success. He died in the prime of life, with honors still awaiting him and beloved by all who knew him. His widow, a beautiful woman of southern blood, has lived for the most part in Europe since her husband's death. Mrs. Clarke was educated in Germany and thoroughly acquired a cosmopolitan polish of manner. She is an accomplished linguist, and in the midst of a busy life finds time to maintain her reputation as an excellent and sympathetic musician. For years she has been the president of a boarding-home for working women and has been its inspiration. She possesses great energy of character and the courage of her convictions, united with an amiable manner, rare tact and a thoughtful consideration for others. She was chosen commissioner from Minnesota to the World's Columbian Exposition and was appointed a member of the executive committee of the woman's department, chairman of the committee on music in the woman's building, and was elected president for Minnesota of the woman's committee of the World's Congress Auxiliary. Her tastes fitted her to become a valued member of the musical and literary clubs of her city, a feature which has become so helpful in the life of to-day. Above all, it is in her home that she finds her most attractive setting. She has a devoted husband, Francis B. Clarke, a prominent and influential resident of St. Paul, and three children.

CLARKE, Mrs. Mary Bas-sett, born in Independence, NY, 18th November, 1831.  She is the daughter of John C. Bassett, a well-to-do farmer of western New York, and Martha St. John Bassett, both persons of education and refinement. She was the seventh in a family of twelve children who lived to maturity. She was educated in Alfred University. Although ill-health limited her opportunities, she was graduated from the university in 1857. At the age of fifteen she commenced to write for publication, under the pen-name "Ida Fairfield," in the "Flag of Our Union." With some interruption by ill-health, she continued many years to be a contributor to that paper, to the "Rural New Yorker" and to local papers and periodicals. She became the wife of William L. Clarke on 8th September, 1859, and removed to Ashaway, RI, which place has since been her home. For several years her writings, both prose and verse, have been principally given to periodicals issued by the Seventh-Day Baptists, of which sect she is a member.

CLARKE, Mrs. Mary H. Gray, correspondent, born in Bristol, RI, 28th March, 1835. She is the daughter of the late Gideon Gray and Hannah Orne Metcalf Gray. Her father was of the sixth generation from Edward Gray, who came from Westminster, London, England, and settled in Plymouth, MA, prior to 1643. Edward Gray was married to Dorothy Lettice and was known as the richest merchant of Plymouth. The oldest stone in the Plymouth burial ground is that of Edward Gray. Mrs. Clarke's great-grandfather, Thomas Gray, of the fourth generation, was during the war of the Revolution commissioned as colonel. Mrs. Clarke spent her early years on her father's homestead, a portion of the Mount Hope lands obtained from King Philip, the Indian chief. A farm on those famous lands is still in her possession. She attended the schools of her native town and later studied in the academy in East Greenwich. In 1861 she became the wife of Dr. Augustus P. Clarke, a graduate of Brown University, in the arts, and of Harvard, in medicine. During her husband's four years of service as surgeon and surgeon-in-chief of brigade and of division of cavalry in the war of the Rebellion, she took an active interest in work for the success of the Union cause. In the fall of 1865 her husband, continuing in the practice of his profession, removed to Cambridge, MA, where they have since resided. They have two daughters. Mrs. Clarke has written quite extensively for magazines and for the press, principally stories for the young, poems and essays. In 1890, on the occasion of the meeting of the Tenth International Medical Congress in Berlin, Germany, she accompanied her husband and daughters to that place. She has traveled extensively through the British Isles and Europe. In the midst of her duties and responsibilities she has found time to paint many pictures, some in water-colors and some in oils. Much of the writing of Mrs. Clarke has been under the pen-names "Nina Gray" and "Nina Gray Clarke."

CLARKE, Miss Rebecca Sophia, author, born in Norridgewock, ME, 22nd February, 1833. She has spent much of her life in her native town. Miss Clarke is widely known by her pen-name, "Sophia May," which she adopted in 1861 and attached to her first story, published in the Memphis "Appeal." When the story was finished, she signed her middle name, Sophia, and then said: "Well, I'll call it May, for I may write again and may not." Thus the surname was invented that has become so familiar to American boys and girls. Among her early productions were some stories for Grace Greenwood's "Little Pilgrim." She was asked by the editor of the "Congregationalist" to send to that journal all the stories she might write about "Little Prudy." She then had no thought of making a book of the stories. William T. Adams, known as "Oliver Optic," brought them to the attention of Mr. Lee, who published them and paid Miss Clarke fifty dollars for each of the six volumes. These charming stories of "Prudy" and her aunts, sisters and cousins have been said to be portraits, but Miss Clarke disclaims any such delineation. The "Prudy" stories are sold in large numbers every year. In 1891 Miss Clarke published her last book, "In Old Quinnebasset." She resides with her sister, Miss Sarah Clarke, who, as "Penn Shirley," is also a successful author. Miss Clarke's publications, in book form, all issued in Boston, are: "Little Prudy Stories" (1864–6), six volumes; "Dotty Dimple Stories" (1868–70), six volumes; "Little Prudy's Flyaway Series" (1871–74), six volumes; "The Doctor's Daughter" (1873), "Our Helen" (1875); "The Asbury Twins" (1876); "Flaxie Frizzle Stories" (1876–84), six volumes; "Quinnebasset Girls" (1877); "Janet, or a Poor Heiress," (1882); "Drones' Honey" (1887); "In Old Quinnebasset" (1891).

CLAXTON, Kate, actor, born in New York City, in 1848. Her father, Col. Spencer H. Cone, commanded the 61st New York regiment during the Civil War. Her grandfather, Rev. Spencer H. Cone, was a Baptist clergyman, who for a short period was an actor. Kate Claxton first appeared with Lotta in Chicago, soon afterward joined Daly's Fifth Avenue Company, and then became a member of the Union Square Company. She attracted no special notice until she appeared as Mathilde in "Led Astray," in 1873, in which character she won considerable popularity. Her greatest success was Louise in "The Two Orphans" first brought out in the Union Square Theater, and afterward produced throughout the United States. While acting the part in the Brooklyn Theater, the building was destroyed by fire, 5th December, 1876, with much loss of life. Miss Claxton's coolness on that occasion, and at the Southern Hotel fire in St. Louis, MO, shortly afterward, won for her much praise. She has more recently played in Charles Reade's "Double Mar-

riage," in the "Sea of Ice" and in "Bootles' Baby." Miss Claxton was divorced from her first husband, Isidor Lyon, a merchant of New York. In 1876 she became the wife of Charles Stevenson, a member of her company.

CLAY, Mrs. Mary Barr, woman suffragist and farmer, born in Lexington, KY, 13th October, 1839. She is a daughter of Cassius M. Clay and Mary J. Warfield. Her childhood and youth were passed in the country, and she was educated mainly by private tutors from Yale College. She became the wife of John Frank Herrick, of Cleveland, OH, 3rd October, 1860. She was divorced from him in 1872. The position of her father as an advocate of free speech and of the emancipation of the negro slave in a slave State, gave her, who sympathized with him, the independence of thought and action that was necessary to espouse the cause of woman's political and civil freedom in the same conservative community, and she met much opposition, ridicule and slights with equal fortitude. Her realization of the servile position of women under the laws was brought about by attending a convention held in Cleveland, OH, by Lucy Stone, in 1868 or 1869. She then and there subscribed for books and pamphlets and gave them to any one who would read them and wrote articles for the local papers, which the editors published with a protest, declaring that Mrs. Clay alone was responsible for them. She was the first native Kentuckian to take the public platform for woman suffrage. She went to St. Louis in 1879, and, presenting herself to Miss Susan B. Anthony, who was holding a convention there, asked to be admitted as a delegate from Kentucky. Miss Anthony warmly welcomed her and appointed her vice-president for Kentucky, which office she held in that association as long as it existed. In 1879 she organized in Lexington a suffrage club, the first in the State. In 1880 she and Mrs. James Bennett organized one in Richmond which has continued to this time. Mrs. Clay was a member and vice-president for Kentucky for many years of the American Suffrage Association, and was, in 1884, elected president of that association, when it held its convention in Chicago. She was the leading

Kentucky organizer of the first State association, formed in Louisville after the convention held thereby Lucy Stone in 1881. Living in Ann Arbor, MI, for some years, educating her two sons, she organized a suffrage club there and was invited by Mrs. Stebbins to help reorganize the State association. She was made president pro tem, of the convention in Flint, where the present Michigan State Association was reorganized. She edited a column in the Ann Arbor "Register" for some time on woman suffrage. By invitation of the Suffrage Association of Michigan, she spoke before the Legislative Committee, and was invited by the senior law class of the University of Michigan to address them on the "Constitutional Right of Women to Vote." She has petitioned Congress and addressed House and Senate committees for the rights of women. For years she has visited the State Legislature and laid the wrongs of women before that body, demanding as a right, not as a favor, the equality of women under the laws. Mrs. Clay was for years the only worker in the cause except her sisters, and she was the first to demand of the late constitutional convention that they emancipate the women of Kentucky, one-half the adult people of the State. Her letter was read before the convention, and she was the spokesman of the committee of women who were invited to the floor of the convention to hear the plea from the Equal Rights Association of Kentucky. To accomplish the civil and political freedom of women has for years been her chief aim and labor. She is now vice-president of the Kentucky Equal Rights Association.

CLAYTON, Mrs. Florence Andrews, opera singer, born near Le Sueur, MN, in 1862. She is the ninth child of Rev. Mr. Andrews, one of the pioneer Methodist ministers of Minnesota. At that time Le Sueur was well out on the western frontier, and most of the settlers of that region abandoned their homes and crowded into St. Peter during the Indian outbreak. The Andrews family stuck to their farm near the little village. Two of the older sons entered the army of defense against the Indians and were in the battle of New Ulm. Both Mr. Andrews and his wife were natural, though untrained musicians, and all of their ten children, known as the Andrews Family, inherited musical ability. In 1876 Miss Andrews, then fourteen years of age, went upon the stage with her brothers and sisters for their first year with the "Swiss Bells." They played in Minnesota and adjoining States, making trips southward as far as the southern border of the Indian Territory. She has since then been continually before the public, except for longer or shorter vacations. She became the wife of Fred Clayton, of Cleveland, OH, in 1883, who is also with the present Andrews Opera Company. They have two sons. The musical culture of Mrs. Clayton has been received mostly by instruction from and association with some of the most competent vocal artists of the country, while she has been traveling and working with them. She has thus obtained that thorough and practical knowledge of her art which can be secured in no other way. Her repertoire consists of forty operas, tragic and comic. She is not only an excellent vocalist, but also a fine actor, with a natural adaptation to dramatic parts. Her voice is a contralto.

CLEARY, Mrs. Kate McPhelim, correspondent, born in Richibucto, Kent county, New Brunswick, 20th August, 1863. Her parents, James and Margaret McPhelim, were of Irish birth, the former, with his brothers, being distinguished for intellectual ability and business talents. They were extensively engaged in the timber business, and in 1856 her uncle, Hon. Francis McPhelim, was Postmaster-General of New Brunswick, and her father held the office of high sheriff of the county. Her father's death, in 1865, left his widow with three small children and limited means, which she devoted to their education. Kate was educated in the Sacred Heart Convent, St. John, New Brunswick, and later attended other convent schools in this country and in the old. Her pen, which had been a source of diversion and delight to her since she was a little girl, became, when necessity required, an easy means of support. Her first published poem appeared when she was fourteen years old, and from that time to the present she has written almost continuously poetry and fiction. On 26th February, 1884, she became the wife of Michael T. Cleary, a young lumber merchant of Hubbell, NE. Mr. and Mrs. Cleary have kept a hospitable home, welcoming as guests many distinguished men and women. Mrs. Cleary's stories are largely those of adventure and incident, and are published in newspapers quite as much as magazines. She has contributed prose and verse chiefly to the New York "Ledger," "Belford's Magazine," the "Fireside Companion," "Saturday Night," "Puck," the "New York Weekly," the "Current," "Our Continent," the Chicago "Tribune," "St. Nicholas," "Wide-Awake," and the Detroit "Free Press."

CLEAVES, Miss Margaret Abagail, doctor of medicine, born in Columbus City, IA, 25th November, 1848. Her father was of Dutch and English and her mother of Scotch and Irish ancestry, but by birth they were both Americans. Her father, Dr. John Trow Cleaves, was born in Yarmouth, ME, in 1813, and her mother, Elizabeth Stronach, in Baltimore, in 1820. In 1843 they were married in Columbus City, where Dr. Cleaves practiced medicine until his death, which occurred in October, 1863. He was a man who took a deep interest in public affairs, and twice he was elected a member of the Iowa Legislature, first in 1852, and again in 1861. Margaret was the third of seven children. She inherited her father's taste for medical pursuits and as a child frequently accompanied him in his professional visits. Her education was obtained in the public schools and in the Iowa State University, but because of limited means she was unable to finish the collegiate course in the latter institution. After she was sixteen, she alternately attended and taught school for some years. In 1868 the family moved to Davenport, IA. There Margaret resolved to become a doctor instead of continuing a schoolteacher. Her choice of a profession was not regarded with favor by the various members of her family, who entertained the prevailing ideas concerning the limitations of woman's sphere, but her mind was made up, and in 1870 she began to read medicine and against their wishes entered the Medical Department of the Iowa State University. Their opposition did not continue long, for it was soon made manifest

that her choice of a profession had been a wise one. In 1871 she entered the office of her preceptor, Dr. W. F. Peck, who was dean of the faculty and professor of surgery in the university. She was graduated 5th March, 1873, standing at the head of the class. Shortly after graduating, she was appointed second assistant physician in the State Hospital for the Insane, Mount Pleasant, IA. There she was a veritable pioneer, for up to that time only one other woman in the world had occupied the position of physician in a public insane asylum. She remained in the asylum for three years and then resigned her position to commence private practice in Davenport. She was subsequently appointed one of the trustees of the asylum. While practicing medicine in Davenport, she became a member of the Scott County Medical Society, being the second woman to gain admission to that body. For several years she was the secretary of the society. She also joined the State Medical Society, where she was again the second woman to gain admission. She was the first woman to become a member of the Iowa and Illinois Central District Medical Association. During her residence in Davenport she was an active member of the Davenport Academy of Sciences. In 1879 the board of trustees of the State Asylum for the Insane chose her their delegate to the National Conference of Charities, which that year met in Chicago, IL. In that conference she read a paper on "The Medical and Moral Care of Female Patients in Hospitals for the Insane." It attracted widespread attention, and was printed in a volume, "Lunacy in Many Lands," which was published by the Government of New South Wales. In June, 1880, she was appointed by the Governor of Iowa a State delegate to the National Conference of Charities in Cleveland, OH, and thus the distinction was conferred upon her of being the first female delegate from Iowa to that body. She reported for the State to the conference, and her report was subsequently incorporated in the Governor's annual message. That same year she was appointed physician-in-chief in the Female Department of the Pennsylvania State Lunatic Hospital in Harrisburg. After three years of hard work, rendered all the more arduous by her conscientious devotion to the in minutest details of her duties, Dr. Cleaves was compelled by failing health to resign her position. She went abroad in 1883, remaining nearly two years, visiting insane hospitals in Scotland, England,

France, Italy, Germany, Austria, Switzerland and Belgium, everywhere receiving flattering courtesies from men of recognized eminence in the treatment of insanity. She witnessed operations in general hospitals in England, France and Germany, and in Paris she was for several months a regular attendant at lectures and clinics. After returning to the United States, she opened a private home for the reception of patients in Des Moines, IA, conducting also an office practice in connection with her other work. In March, 1885, she was appointed one of the examing committee of the Medical Department of the Iowa State University. It was the first honor of that kind bestowed on a woman by any standard medical school in the United States. In July 1886, she was sent as a delegate to the yearly meeting of the National Conference of Charities, which was held in St. Paul, MN. During her residence in Des Moines she was an active member of the Polk County Medical Society, of the Missouri Valley Medical Association and of the Iowa State Medical Association. Before all those bodies she read papers and she served the last-named body as chairman of obstetrics and gynæcology in the session of 1889. At that time she was the only woman who had received such an appointment. Her work was not confined to medicine alone. She took a deep interest in all that pertains to the welfare and advancement of women. She organized the Des Moines Woman's Club and was its first president. Some time prior to that she had become a member of the Association for the Advancement of Women. Becoming interested in the subject of electro-therapeutics, she went to New York in the winter of 1887 and to Paris in the following summer, to prosecute her inquiries and investigation. After her return she continued to practice for a while in Des Moines, but in 1890 she retired from that field and went to New York, where she opened an office. She there joined the Medical Society of the County of New York, the American Electro-Therapeutic Association and the New York Women's Press Club. In the Post-Graduate Medical School, New York, she is now clinical assistant to the chair of electro-therapeutics. Since she took up her residence in New York, she has read papers before the Medical Society of Kings County, Brooklyn, the New York Medico-Legal Society, the American Electro-Therapeutic Association and the National Conference of Charities. Many of them have been published, and all of

them are distinguished by painstaking research, clearness of statement and logical reasoning. Though a very busy woman, though her chosen fields of labor and study have taken her far away from the paths followed by most women, she has sacrificed none of those sweet, helpful and peculiarly womanly characteristics which endear her to her friends. She is a woman who combines in a most felicitous way gentleness of speech and manner with firmness of character. She has keen insight and quick sympathies, yet cool judgment.

CLEMENT, Mrs. Clara Erskine, see WATERS, CLARA ERSICINE CLEMENT.

CLERC, Mme. Henrietta Fannie Virginie, educator, born in Paris, France, 7th February, 1841. She is the daughter of Alexandre Louis Sulpice Clerc and Marie Josephine Virginie Grand-Fils. Her grandfather, Gen. Le Clerc, fought for the first Napoleon, and was knighted De Saint Clerc by him at the battle of Austerlitz. Sulpice Clerc was too strong a republican to bear any title. He was opposed to the Empire of Napoleon III and was one of the conspirators to take away his life. The plot was discovered, and those who escaped imprisonment were obliged to leave Paris, and all their property was confiscated. Sulpice Clerc and his wife lived in various parts of Europe until their children's education was finished. They had two sons and two daughters. Henrietta, the eldest daughter, was graduated from the Convent of the Dames Benedictines, where she had been since the age of five. The family then came to this country and settled in New York City. In April, 1861, Henrietta was married to her first cousin, Felix Clerc, who was killed the following July in the battle of Bull Run, having entered the Union army as a French Zouave at the outbreak of the Civil War. Since that time Mme. Clerc has supported herself by teaching, at first in a Quaker school in Bristol, then in the Packer Collegiate Institute, in Brooklyn, NY, and in St. Agnes' School, Albany, NY, in each of which schools she remained five years. In 1881 she established a school of her own in Philadelphia, PA, where she is at present training a limited number of girls each year. For the use of her pupils she published several years ago a pamphlet entitled "First Steps in the Art of Speaking French." She is now editing a monthly paper, "L' Etude," for those wishing to perfect themselves in her native tongue.

CLEVELAND, Mrs. Frances Folsom, wife of Stephen Grover Cleveland, the twenty-second President of the United States, born in Buffalo, NY, 21st July, 1864. She is the only child of the late Oscar Folsom, who was killed in a carriage accident in 1875. Her mother is still living in Buffalo, the wife of Henry E. Perrine. Miss Folsom spent her early school days in Madame Brecker's French kindergarten. After Mr. Folsom's death the widow and daughter made their home in Medina, NY, with Mrs. Folsom's mother, Mrs. Harmon. Mr. Cleveland was appointed her guardian-at-law. In Medina Miss Folsorn attended the high school. Returning to Buffalo, she became a student in the central high school, where she was noted for her brightness in study. She next went to Aurora, NY, where she entered Wells College, on her central high school certificate, which admitted her to the sophomore class without examination. She was a favorite in Wells College. She was graduated in June, 1885, her graduating essay being cast in the form of a story. Her future husband was Governor of the State of New York while she was in college, and was elected President before her graduation, on which occasion a gift of flowers was sent to her from the White House. After graduating from college she went abroad for a time for travel and study. She returned from Europe on 28th May, 1886, and was married to Mr. Cleveland, in the White House, 2nd June, 1886. The wedding was the occasion of many pleasant attentions to the President and his bride. Her reign as the first lady of the land, was a brilliant one, marked by tact and unfailing courtesy. She was the youngest of the many mistresses of the White House. When Mr. Cleveland's presidential term ended, in 1889, they made their home in New York City, where their daughter, Ruth, was born. In that city her life has been filled with social duties and charitable work in many directions. She is a member of the Presbyterian Church.

CLEVELAND, Miss Rose Elizabeth, author, born in Fayetteville, NY, in 1846, and moved to Holland Patent, NY, in 1853. She is a sister of ex-President Cleveland and a daughter of Rev. Richard Falley Cleveland, a Presbyterian preacher, who was graduated from Yale College in 1824. Her mother's maiden name was Neal, and she was the daughter of a Baltimore merchant of Irish birth. The Clevelands are of English descent, in a direct line from Moses Cleveland, of the county of Suffolk, England, who came to the Colonies in 1635 and settled in Woburn, MA, where he died in 1701. Miss Cleveland is in the seventh generation. Her father was settled as pastor of the Presbyterian Church in Holland Patent in 1853. Rose was one of a large family. Two of her brothers, Louis and Frederick, were lost at sea in 1872 on the return trip from Nassau. The father died in 1853 and the mother in 1882. One married sister, Mrs. Louise Bacon, lives in Toledo, OH. The parents were persons of marked force of character, morally and intellectually. Rose was educated in the seminary in Houghton. She taught in that school after graduation, and then was called to Lafayette, IN, where she took charge of the Collegiate Institute. She taught later in Pennsylvania in a private school. She then began to lecture on history before classes in Houghton Seminary. Her courses of lectures were well received, and after her mother's death, in 1882, she kept her home in Holland Patent and continued her school work. Her reputation as a lecturer grew, and her services were called for in other schools. When her brother was elected President, she accompanied him to Washington, DC, and presided as mistress of the White House until his marriage, in June, 1886. Her best womanly qualities were displayed in that delicate and difficult position, and she took into the White House an atmosphere of culture, independence and originality that was exceedingly attractive. The brightest men of the time found in her a self-possessed, intellectual, thoroughly educated woman, acquainted with several modern languages and fully informed on all the questions of the day. After her brother's marriage she returned to Holland Patent. She afterward taught history in a private school in New York City. She has not written much. Her published works are "George Eliot's Poetry and Other Studies" (New York, 1885), and "The Long Run," a novel, (Detroit, 1886). She accepted a position as editor of "Literary Life," a magazine published in Chicago, but, not satisfied with the management, she resigned. She has written some verse, but has published very little. She is now engaged in literary work.

CLYMER, Mrs. Ella Maria Dietz, poet, born in New York City. Even as a child she showed many signs of that varied genius which has made her remarkable among the women of her time. Her father died while she was very young, and her mother at first objected to her selection of a theatrical career, but finally gave consent to her daughter's dramatic studies. Early in her teens she married the late Edward M. Clymer, of Pennsylvania, brother of Heister Clymer, who was a member of Congress for several years. Mrs. Clymer made her professional début in New York, in 1872, as Pauline in the "Lady of Lyons." In the spring of 1874 she went to Paris, and in company of her brother and her sister, Miss Linda Dietz, so favorably known in America and in London, she spent some months in studying in the French school of dramatic art. She acted afterward both in London and the provinces, and her performances of the principal Shakespearean parts were very highly commended. Her Juliet was spoken of as "a revelation, poetical and imaginative in the highest degree." In 1881 she brought out a version of "Faust," adapted by herself for the English stage, in which she played Margaret, and was called "the very living reality of Goethe's heroine." The fatigue of stage life proved too much for Mrs. Clyrner's delicate constitution, and she was obliged to abandon the profession. She continued her public readings, however, a department of the dramatic art in which she probably has no peer, and Moncure D. Conway gave expression to the general opinion when he wrote: "As a dramatic reciter and interpreter of modern ballad poetry she is unequaled." Nor was her dramatic gift her only one. She has talent as an artist and has composed many songs full of dainty grace and melody. Her first poems were published in 1873, and since then she has written frequently

for the English and American press. In 1877 she published "The Triumph of Love" (London), and seven years later "The Triumph of Time" (London, 1884), soon followed by "The Triumph of Life" (London, 1885). These are mystical poems, composed of songs, lyrics and sonnets, ranging over the whole gamut of human and divine love, and marked by the same high qualities that distinguished all her work. Notwithstanding all this self-culture, she has not neglected humanity. While in London she was an enthusiastic member of the Church and Stage Guild, and of the religious guild of St. Matthews; she lectured before workingmen's clubs and took part in many other philanthropic undertakings. She has been connected with Sorosis since its beginning, in 1868, and on her return to New York, in 1881, was immediately put upon many of its committees, and served for two years as its president. She has been a leading factor in the Federation of Women's Clubs, which is doing so much to forward the harmonious work of the best women for their own highest good and in the interest of the world.

COATES, Mrs. Florence Earle, poet, was born in Philadelphia, PA. She is descended from Ralph Earle, of Rhode Island, who came from England to the Colonies in 1634, and was one of the petitioners to Charles II for permission to form Rhode Island into a corporate colony. Her grandfather, Thomas Earle, was a noted philanthropist, and the first nominee of the Liberty Party for vice president of the United States. Her father, George H. Earle, is a lawyer of distinction. She was thoroughly educated, having studied in Europe for some time, is an accomplished musician, and possesses strong dramatic talent. The writings of Matthew Arnold have been a great inspiration to her, and have influenced her poetry. During his visits to Philadelphia, Mr. Arnold made his home with her and her husband, Edward H. Coates, who is president of the Pennsylvania Academy of the Fine Arts. He is a generous patron of art and of artists. Mrs. Coates' poems are finished productions. She is a regular contributor to the "Century," "Atlantic Monthly," "Harper's Magazine" and "Lippincott's Magazine," and to other periodicals, and her verses have been widely copied. Her home is in Philadelphia, where she is busied with the relations of a full social and domestic life. She has a summer home situated on the Upper St. Regis Lake in the Adirondacks.

COBB, Mrs. Mary Emilie, educator and philanthropist, born in Elmira, NY, 31st October, 1838. Her father, Dr. George Wells, a descendant of Thomas Wells, one of the earliest settlers of Hartford, CT, and the first colonial governor, was early in life a physician and afterward a preacher of the Disciples' Church. Leaving Connecticut when he was nineteen years old, his life was spent in central New York and northern Pennsylvania. Mrs. Cobb's maternal grandfather was Dr. Ebenezer Pratt, also of an old New England family. A graduate of Middlebury College, Vermont, after a few years spent in the practice of medicine, he became a teacher, in which profession he was for many years prominent in Chautauqua county and in Ovid, NY, and in Troy, PA. Thus the passion for study and literature and the love for teaching, early shown by Mary E. Wells, were an inherited tendency fostered by early influence. At eight years of age she began to write verses, and about the same time to collect, wash, dress and teach the stray and forlorn children of the neighborhood. During her school years she was a contributor to Elmira and Troy papers and to the "Ladies' Christian Annual" and "Arthur's Home Magazine," of Philadelphia. At fifteen she began to teach as an assistant to Dr. Pratt, her grandfather, and under his influence became ambitious to excel in that profession, writing often on topics connected with it, besides her stories and poems for children. She became the wife in 1856 of S. N. Rockwell, of Troy, PA, and resided in Iowa for several years, continuing to teach and write. Previous to 1870 she had published two juvenile books, "Tom Miller" (Philadelphia, 1872), and "Rose Thorpe's Ambition" (Philadelphia, 1875), and had written much for religious and educational publications. "Facts and Thoughts About Reform Schools," in the "Educational Monthly," of New York, and many articles in the "Children's Hour," of Philadelphia, were illustrated by her brother, C. H. Wells, an artist, of Philadelphia. She has contributed some articles to "Scribner's Magazine," and one of her poems, "Acquainted with Grief," was widely copied. Mrs. Rockwell had become deeply interested in reformatory institutions for boys and girls, and she gave herself with enthusiasm to a work which seemed to open just the field for which her preferences and pursuits had prepared her. After some years spent as a teacher in schools of that kind in Philadelphia, New York and Providence, her work as assistant superintendent of the Connecticut Industrial School for Girls, in Middletown attracted the attention of leading philanthropists and reformers, as seeming to give a practical solution of many questions in relation to reformatory and industrial training, which were then widely discussed. In 1876 the National Prison Congress met in New York. Mrs. Rockwell went upon a public platform for the first time and read a paper upon the topic assigned, "The Training and Disposal of Delinquent Children." Early in 1879, having been left alone with a little daughter of eight years, she accepted the position of superintendent of the Wisconsin Industrial School, in Milwaukee. There she remained seven years, during which time the school grew from thirty-eight pupils and three teachers, in one building, to two-hundred twenty-five pupils and twenty assistants, and occupying three large and well appointed buildings, designed, erected and fitted up under her direction. In 1882 Mrs. Rockwell became the wife of Dewey A. Cobb, assistant superintendent of that school, and for four years they remained at its head, removing in 1886 to Philadelphia, where Mr. Cobb entered into business, desiring that Mrs. Cobb should retire from school work, to which she had given twenty-five years of continuous service. In Philadelphia she is an active member of the board of managers of the Woman's Christian Association having been an editor of its organ, "Faith and Works," for three years, and she is one of the editors of the "National Baptist," Philadelphia. As secretary of Foulke and Long Institute and Industrial Training School, she is actively supervising the erection of its new building in Philadelphia. Mrs. Cobb has long been a member of the National Conference of Charities and Corrections and of the Association for the Advancement of Women, and she has several times read papers before those bodies. She is an advocate of institutional training, rather than of the "placing-out" system, for neglected and destitute children. She is earnest and practical in the promotion of manual training and technical education, and to her patient study and efforts much of the success of that movement in several States may be traced. Her more important recent papers have been "The Duty of the State to its Dependent Children," and "Training and Employments in Reformatories."

COBB, Mrs. Sara M. Maxson, art teacher and artist, born in Geneva, NY, 30th September, 1858. She traces her lineage on her father's side to the Maxtons, of Maxton-on-the-Tweed, in Scotland. Her father's family came to America in 1701, after having  been settled in England for generations. Her father, E. R. Maxson, A.M., M.D., LL.D., a graduate of Jefferson Medical College, Philadelphia, PA, had been a lecturer on medical subjects in the colleges of Philadelphia, PA, and Geneva, NY. His "Practice of Medicine" and "Hospitals: British, French and American," are well-known books. Her mother, Lucy Potter Lanphere, was of French-English extraction. Mrs. Maxson-Cobb has lived in Geneva, Adams and Syracuse, NY, in Philadelphia, PA, and Kent's Hill, ME, and now resides in Boulder, CO. When very young she commenced to write for amateur papers. When about eight years of age, happening to read an article on drawing, she tried her pencil at reproducing the simple cuts given in it for copying, with a success so surprising to herself that she then and there resolved in her own mind to become an artist. Her parents had her taught in drawing from youth. In 1883 she was graduated from the Liberal Art College of Syracuse University, Syracuse, NY, and she has since received from it, on examination in a post-graduate course, the degree of PhD. She is a member of the Alpha chapter of the college society, Alpha Phi. In 1886 she was graduated from the Fine Art College of the same University with the degree Bachelor of Painting. Immediately after graduating she was induced to found and conduct an art school in connection with the college and seminary in Kent's Hill, ME. Under her management the school soon became successful. In 1892 she was engaged by the regents of the State University of Colorado to introduce drawing there, and she still has it in charge. Her own artistic productions, though yet comparatively few in number, have been well received. She executes in all usual mediums. A strong literary taste and sympathy for active philanthropic and Christian enterprise have led her into many kinds of work. Her numerous poems, stories told in verse, translations from the German, travel-correspondence and articles on art subjects have found their way into prominent publications. She is a believer in united action, and in the many societies to which she belongs, missionary, temperance, art, literary and scientific, she is recognized as a superior organizer and leader. Geology, microscopy and photography claim a share of her attention, and she has an interesting collection of specimens of her own finding, slides of her own mounting and photographs of her own taking. She delights in music and has a cultivated contralto voice. In March, 1890 she became the wife of Herbert Edgar Cobb, of Maine, a graduate of Wesleyan University, Middletown, CT, and now one of the teachers of mathematics in the State University of Colorado.

COCHRANE, Miss Elizabeth, author, journalist and traveler, known the world over by her pen-name, "Nellie Bly," born in Cochrane Mills, PA, 5th May, 1867, a place named after her father, who was a lawyer and for several terms filled the office of associate judge of Armstrong county, PA. She is a descendant on her father's side of Lord Cochrane, the famous English admiral, who was noted for his deeds of daring, and who was never happy unless engaged in some exciting affair. Miss Cochrane's great-grandfather Cochrane was one of a number of men who wrote a declaration of independence in Maryland near the South Mountains a long time before the historic Declaration of Independence was delivered to the world. Her great-grandfather, on her mother's side, was a man of wealth, owning at one time almost all of Somerset county, PA. His name was Kennedy, and his wife was a nobleman's daughter. They eloped and fled to America. He was an officer, as were his two sons, in the Revolutionary War. Afterward he was sheriff of Somerset county repeatedly until old age compelled him to decline the office. One of his sons, Thomas Kennedy, Miss Cochrane's grand-uncle, made a flying trip around the word, starting from and returning to New York City, where his wife awaited his arrival. It took him three years to make the trip, and he returned in shattered health. He at once set about to write the history of his trip, but his health became so bad that he had to give up his task. Her father died while Elizabeth was yet a child. She was educated at home until 880, when she was sent to Indiana, PA, where she remained in a boarding school until 1881. Impaired health forced her to leave school, and she returned home. The family moved to Pittsburgh, and there she began her literary career. She saw an article in the "Pittsburgh Dispatch" entitled "What Girls are Good For." She wrote a reply to the article, and though the reply was not published, a paragraph appeared in the "Dispatch" the day after she sent the communication, asking for the writer's name. Miss Cochrane sent her name and received a letter from the editor, requesting her to write an article on the subject of girls and their spheres in life for the "Sunday Dispatch." This she did. The article was printed, and the same week she received a check for it and a request for something else. Her next subject was "Divorce," and at the end of the article appeared the now famous signature, "Nellie Bly." Miss Cochrane assumed it on the suggestion of George A. Madden, managing editor of the "Dispatch," who got it from Stephen Foster's popular song. The divorce article attracted attention. She was invited to the office and made arrangements to accept a salary and devote her time to the "Dispatch." Taking an artist with her, she went through the factories and workshops of Pittsburgh, and described and pictured the condition of the working girls. The articles made a hit. Miss Cochrane became society editor of the "Dispatch" and also looked after the dramatic and art department, all for a salary of ten dollars per week. She decided to go to Mexico to write about its people. At that time she was receiving fifteen dollars per week. She went, and her letters printed in the "Dispatch" were full of interest and were widely copied. She had never been out of her State before but she traveled everywhere in Mexico that a railroad could take her. Her mother was her companion on that trip. Returning to Pittsburgh, she became dissatisfied with that field, quit the "Dis-

patch," and went to New York City. She did syndicate work for awhile. One day she lost her pocketbook and all the money she possessed. She was too proud to let her friends know, and she sat down and thought. Before that she had written to the "World," asking the privilege of going in the balloon the "World" was about sending up at St. Louis, but, as final arrangements had been corn-pitted, her suggestion was not favorably received. Now finding herself penniless, she made a list of a half-dozen original ideas and went to the "World" office, determined to see Mr. Pulitzer and offer them to him. Having no letter of introduction and being unknown, she found it almost an impossibility to gain an audience. For three hours she talked and expostulated with different employees, before she finally exhausted their denials and was ushered into the unwilling presence of Mr. Pulitzer and his editor, John A. Cockerill. Once there, they listened to her ideas and immediately offered her twenty-five dollars to give them three days in which to consider her suggestions. At the end of that time she was told that her idea to feign insanity and, as a patient, investigate the treatment of the insane in the Blackwell Island Asylum was accepted. Miss Bly did that with such marked success and originality of treatment, and attracted so much attention, that she secured a permanent place on the "World" staff. She originated a new field in journalism, which has since been copied all over the world by her many imitators. Her achievements since her asylum exposé have been many and brilliant. Scarcely a week passed that she had not some novel feature in the "World." Her fame grew and her tasks enlarged, until they culminated in the wonderful tour of the world in 72 days, 6 hours, 11 minutes and 14 seconds. That idea she proposed to Mr. Pulitzer one year before he approved and accepted it. Owing to delayed steamers, Miss Bly lost fifteen days on land, but she was the first to conceive and establish a record for a fast trip around the world. Since Miss Cochrane "girdled the globe," others have repeated the feat in less time. Her news paperwork resulted in many reforms. Her exposé of asylum abuses procured an appropriation of $3,000,000 for the benefit of the poor insane, in addition to beneficial changes in care and management. Her exposé of the "King of the Lobby" rid Albany of its greatest disgrace; her stationhouse exposé procured matrons for New York police-stations; her exposé of a noted "electric" doctor's secret rid

Brooklyn of a notorious swindler. Miss Cochrane left journalism to do literary work for a weekly publication. She is now a resident of New York.

COE, Miss Emily M., educator, born near Norwalk, OH. She was graduated from Mt. Holyoke Seminary, in 1853, with the honors of her class. For a time she turned her attention to oil painting and other art-work, for which she has a talent. She then taught with success in seminaries and colleges in New England and Pennsylvania, and afterward in the Spingler Institute, in New York City. Realizing more and more the futility of building upon the imperfect foundations of character usually laid in early childhood, she saw clearly that the hope of the world is in the right training of the little children. That led to the establishment of the American kindergarten, the first school of the kind in New York City. The American kindergarten system is the result of more than twenty years of practical work in the school-room. She erected a kindergarten building at her own expense; in the Centennial Exposition of 1876, where material, much of her own invention was exhibited and examined by educators from all parts of the world, in 1872 Miss Coe went to Europe for the purpose of studying educational methods. Her life is an exceedingly busy one. She has given courses of lectures and conducted training classes in Normal institutes in all parts of the country, besides single lectures in many places. At home she conducts the American Kindergarten and Normal Training School in New York City and East Orange, NJ. Miss Coe is editor and proprietor of the "American Kindergarten Magazine," established ten years. She is president of the American Kindergarten Society. She is a member of the Association for the Advancement of Science and a life member of the National Teachers' Association. She is a very earnest Christian.

COGHLAN, Rose, actor, born in London, England, in 1852. Her family was a religious one, and her mother desired Rose to become a cloistered nun. Her brother, Charles Coghlan, threw aside wig and gown to marry a pretty actress. He went on the stage, and he advised Rose, who had shown talent in private the-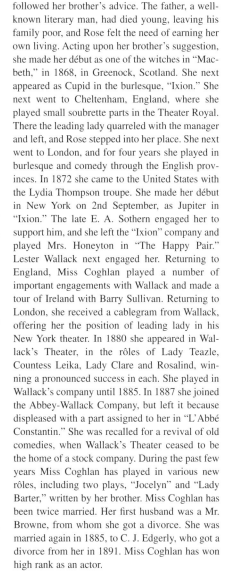atricals, to adopt the profession of actor. Rose, whose only public appearance had been in the rôle of organist and singer in the village church choir, followed her brother's advice. The father, a well-known literary man, had died young, leaving his family poor, and Rose felt the need of earning her own living. Acting upon her brother's suggestion, she made her début as one of the witches in "Macbeth," in 1868, in Greenock, Scotland. She next appeared as Cupid in the burlesque, "Ixion." She next went to Cheltenham, England, where she played small soubrette parts in the Theater Royal. There the leading lady quarreled with the manager and left, and Rose stepped into her place. She next went to London, and for four years she played in burlesque and comedy through the English provinces. In 1872 she came to the United States with the Lydia Thompson troupe. She made her début in New York on 2nd September, as Jupiter in "Ixion." The late E. A. Sothern engaged her to support him, and she left the "Ixion" company and played Mrs. Honeyton in "The Happy Pair." Lester Wallack next engaged her. Returning to England, Miss Coghlan played a number of important engagements with Wallack and made a tour of Ireland with Barry Sullivan. Returning to London, she received a cablegram from Wallack, offering her the position of leading lady in his New York theater. In 1880 she appeared in Wallack's Theater, in the rôles of Lady Teazle, Countess Leika, Lady Clare and Rosalind, winning a pronounced success in each. She played in Wallack's company until 1885. In 1887 she joined the Abbey-Wallack Company, but left it because displeased with a part assigned to her in "L'Abbé Constantin." She was recalled for a revival of old comedies, when Wallack's Theater ceased to be the home of a stock company. During the past few years Miss Coghlan has played in various new rôles, including two plays, "Jocelyn" and "Lady Barter," written by her brother. Miss Coghlan has been twice married. Her first husband was a Mr. Browne, from whom she got a divorce. She was married again in 1885, to C. J. Edgerly, who got a divorce from her in 1891. Miss Coghlan has won high rank as an actor.

COHEN, Miss Mary M., social economist, born in Philadelphia, PA, 26th February, 1854. She is the daughter of Henry and Matilda Cohen, a prominent Jewish family. Henry Cohen was born in London, England, in 1810, came to the United

States in 1844 and went into business in Philadelphia, where he died in 1879. He was identified with many Jewish and unsectarian philanthropic societies. Mrs. Cohen was born in Liverpool, England. She was a woman of fine musical and elocutionary talents and was prominent in charitable work. The daughter, Mary, studied in Miss Ann Dickson's private school in Philadelphia until she was fourteen years old, learning French, English, Latin and drawing. She then went to Miss Catherine Lyman's school, where she continued her studies. After leaving school she took a course in literature under Professor Chase, and studied German for three years. From the age of seven she was taught in music by her mother until prepared for instruction from masters. She began to write short stories when she was thirteen years old. Her first printed essay," Religion Tends to Cheerfulness," appeared in the "Jewish Index," and she has since been a prominent contributor to religious periodicals, both Jewish and Christian, writing under the pen-name "Coralie." Her literary productions cover editing of letters of travel, biography, serial stories and religious articles and essays. She has prepared a number of important papers on Hebrew charities, on subjects of current interest and on social, literary and intellectual problems. She has visited Europe three times and has filled a number of responsible positions in various philanthropic societies. She is a woman of great versatility, a talented author, an artist, a wood-carver, a stenographer and typewriter, and a successful teacher. She has served as the president of the Browning Club of Philadelphia, of which she was the founder, as the corresponding secretary of the Jewish Publication Society of America, as a superintendent of the Southern Hebrew Sunday-school, as president of the society under whose direction the schools are conducted, as a member of some of the leading literary arid art clubs of Philadelphia, such as the Contemporary Club, the Fairmount Park Association, and as a member of the board of directors of the Pennsylvania Museum and School of Industrial Art. When the New Century Club was formed by the executive committee of the Women's Centennial Commission, after the Exposition of 1876 was closed, Miss Cohen became a member, and

was subsequently elected to the executive board. For a year she had charge of the writing class organized by the New Century Guild, and for three years directed a Browning class. In November of 1888 that class developed into an independent society, which now has a membership of nearly six-hundred men and women, including some of the leading people of Philadelphia. In 1884 Miss Cohen was invited by Rev. Dr. H. L. Wayland, one of the directors of the American Social Science Association, to present to that organization a paper on Hebrew charities. The paper was read by its author before the convention held in Saratoga, NY, 12th September, 1884, was favorably received, discussed and published. Miss Cohen was elected a member of the association and placed in the social economy department. In the affairs of the Jewish community Miss Cohen has taken a strong interest and an active part. Receiving her religious inspiration from Rev. Dr. S. Morais, her love for the religion, the history, the achievements and progress of the Jewish people has been deep and abiding. She taught the Bible class in the Northern Hebrew Sunday-school for a number of years. Miss Cohen was chosen to serve on the Philadelphia committee of the Columbian Exposition, in the department of social economy.

COIT, Mrs. Elizabeth, humanitarian and temperance worker, born in Worthington, OH, 10th January, 1820. Her parents, Joseph and Nancy Agnes Greer, were natives of Belfast, Ireland. Elizabeth was the fourth daughter of the family. She was educated in the female seminary in Worthington. After her graduation she was engaged as a teacher in that institution, and held her position until her marriage, 15th April, 1844, to Harvey Coit, of Columbus, OH. Her home has been in that city ever since her marriage. Mrs. Coit is an excellent housekeeper, but she has always found time for a good deal of philanthropic and charitable work outside of her home. She is the mother of eight children, three of whom are now living, the comfort of her declining years. During the Civil War she was one of the members of the committee of three appointed to draft the constitution of the Soldiers' Aid Society. To that organization she devoted much of her time for three years, and her work was invaluable to the society. She is interested actively in all the progressive and reform movements of the time. She was chosen president of the first Woman's Suffrage Association organized in Columbus. For many years she has served as treasurer of the Ohio Woman Suffrage Association.

COIT, Miss Irene Williams, born in Norwich, CT, in 1873. She is the only daughter of General and Mrs. James B. Coit. She won a reputation by success in passing the Yale College entrance examination in 1891, and is by no means insensible to the impetus her venture in knocking at the doors of Yale has been instrumental in giving to the cause of co-education in American colleges. Already that venture has been effective in modifying stringent college laws in various quarters. From her earliest school days she was proficient in her studies. She took the full classical course in the Norwich free academy and was graduated in June, 1891, with highest honors. Her determination to try the Yale examinations with the male classical students of her class, was born solely of her generous ambition. Her instructor, Dr. Robert P. Keep, arranged to have Prof. Seymour, of Yale, give Miss Coit an examination with his class. Besides her aptitude as a student, Miss Coit has long manifested a marked literary capacity. Her first essay in the field of letters some time ago was especially successful. Since the summer of 1891 she has contributed to various newspapers and publications a variety of articles. Miss Coit comes of old New England stock. Her father, General James B. Coit, was a distinguished soldier in the Civil War. In the administration of President Cleveland he was chief of a pension bureau in Washington. Her mother, a refined and charming lady, is a daughter of A. P. Willoughby, representing one of the oldest families in Norwich. Miss Coit lives with her parents in Norwich.

COLBY, Mrs. H. Maria George, author, born in Warner, NH, 1st October, 1844. She is the daughter of Gilman C. and Nancy B. George and the wife of Frederick Myron Colby. She is of English descent on both sides of the family and inherits literary talents from ancestors connected with Daniel Webster of the present century, and on the George side from families whose coat-of-arms dates back to the days of ancient chivalry. Her literary work was the writing of novelettes. Later she wrote considerably for juvenile publications, and she is an acknowledged authority upon domestic topics. Circumstances have rendered it impossible for Mrs. Colby to give her whole time to literary work, but her articles have appeared in the "Housewife," the "Housekeeper," the "Housekeeper's Weekly," the "Christian at Work," "Demorest's Monthly Magazine," "Arthur's Home Magazine," "Youth's Companion," the "Congregationalist," the Portland "Transcript," "Ladies' World," "Good Cheer," the Philadelphia "Press," the Chicago "Ledger," the "Golden Rule," the "Household," "Good Housekeeping" and "St. Nicholas." She was for five years fashion-editor of the "Household." Though naturally fond of society, delicate health and a desire to give her best energies and talents to her literary work have rendered her somewhat retiring. She has made use of various pen-names, but is best known to editors and the public by her maiden name, H. Maria George. A stanch advocate of temperance and equal rights for both sexes, she furthers these as well as every other good work by her pen. Her home is in Warner, NH.

COLBY, Miss Sarah A., physician, born in Sanbornton, NH, 31st May, 1824. She is one of eight children, of whom two survive, herself and a sister, Dr. Esther W. Taylor, of Boston, MA. Dr. Colby was educated in the public schools of her native town and the academy in Sanbornton Square. After leaving school she taught for some time, but failing health compelled her to give up that work. She returned to her home and remained there until her health was improved. During her illness she realized the great need of women physicians, and she became much interested in studying to meet the exigencies of her own condi-

tion. After becoming much improved in health she went to Lowell, MA, where she opened a variety and fancy goods store, continuing the study of medicine and prescribing for many who called upon her. Concluding to make the practice of medicine her life work, she sold out her store and, after preparing herself more fully, located for practice in Manchester, NH, where she was received by the public and by some of the physicians with great cordiality. Dr. Colby gained a large and lucrative practice, which kept her there nine years, when, desiring a larger field, she removed to Boston, MA. One object of her removal was to give her whole attention to gynæology; that she accomplished to a great extent. Dr. Colby was one of the first women physicians in Boston, and she did a remarkable work there. She has been called to meet in consultation, in the large cities of New England, some of the most scientific men physicians of the age, from whom she received every courtesy. In the first fifteen years of her professional experience she was eclectic in practice, but after her sister entered the Hahnemann Medical College of Chicago, she took up the study of medicine of that school, and for fifteen years that has been her mode of treatment, in which she has been very successful. She is still in practice, though her health does not permit her to give her entire time to professional duties.

COLE, Mrs. Cordelia Throop, temperance reformer, born in the town of Hamilton, NY, 17th November, 1833. Her mother, a young and beautiful woman, dowered with the fine instinct of the artist, died when her child Cordelia was but two years of age. In her early womanhood her father died, her nearest then of birth and kin being an only brother, two years younger than herself. She was received into the home of her grandparents and became a favorite among her numerous relatives. Her literary and religious impulses soon asserted themselves. One of the dreams of her early girlhood was a foreign mission. As education was the initial step toward future activities, she entered Hamilton Academy, and just before graduation an alluring offer of a home with an aunt and an uncle in Galesburg, IL, and a position as a teacher in the West was accepted. Her life shaped itself to the vocation of a teacher. In Keokuk, IA, a private institute for young people

was established under the management of R. M. Reynolds, with Miss Throop as associate. From that field of labor Mr. Reynolds and Miss Throop transferred their energies to the North Illinois Institute, in Henry, IL. In December, 1856, Miss Throop became the wife of William Ramey Cole, an earnest student and active philanthropist, a graduate of the Theological Department of Harvard and an ordained minister in the Unitarian Church. Seven children have been born to them, one dying in childhood and one in early manhood. Mrs. Cole served as secretary of the Iowa Unitarian Association, for seven years devoting the mature energies of her mind to that labor of love, preaching in various pulpits of the denomination, creating and carrying on a large correspondence in post-office mission work, attending conferences, forming religious clubs and lending a hand to any agency for the promotion of human welfare. She also, by special request, gave the charge at the ordination of Mary A. Safford in Humbolt, IA, in 1880, and a year later performed the same service at the ordination of Volney B. Cushing, in Iowa City. She took a conspicuous part in the temperance crusade, riding many miles to meet an appointment, with the mercury twenty degrees below zero, sometimes holding three or four meetings at different points in twenty-four hours. In 1885 she was made the Iowa superintendent of White Shield and White Cross work of the Woman's Christian Temperance Union. The new crusade against the subtle foe of impurity aroused the conscience, heart and brain of the wife and mother, and she gave herself unreservedly to that work, making hundreds of public addresses, handling the subject with rare delicacy and skill, and winning the sympathy and warm appreciation of all right-thinking people. Her earnest talks to women have been a marked feature of her work, and more recently her published leaflets, "Helps in Mother Work" and "A Manual for Social Purity Workers," are admirable. In 1889 she received the offer of the place of associate national superintendent, but, loyal to her feeling of duty to the non-partisan side of the dividing lines, she declined. The home of Mrs. Cole, in Mt. Pleasant, IA, is a center of generous hospitality to all humankind. There the outcast have been sheltered, the stricken comforted, the tempted strengthened, the sinful forgiven, the cultured and aspiring made glad.

COLE, Miss Elizabeth, author, born in Darien, WI, 16th January, 1856. Her father's name was Parker M. Cole, and her mother's maiden name was Amelia Y. Frey. The latter was a descendant of the Freys and Herkimers whom Harold Frederic describes so accurately in "In the Valley." She was also a descendant of one of the early settlers of Detroit, named St. Martin, who was a man of note in those days, and whose house. 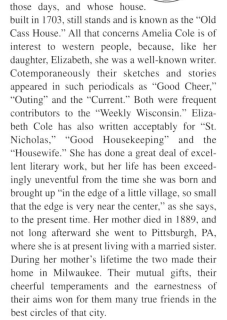 built in 1703, still stands and is known as the "Old Cass House." All that concerns Amelia Cole is of interest to western people, because, like her daughter, Elizabeth, she was a well-known writer. Cotemporaneously their sketches and stories appeared in such periodicals as "Good Cheer," "Outing" and the "Current." Both were frequent contributors to the "Weekly Wisconsin." Elizabeth Cole has also written acceptably for "St. Nicholas," "Good Housekeeping" and the "Housewife." She has done a great deal of excellent literary work, but her life has been exceedingly uneventful from the time she was born and brought up "in the edge of a little village, so small that the edge is very near the center," as she says, to the present time. Her mother died in 1889, and not long afterward she went to Pittsburgh, PA, where she is at present living with a married sister. During her mother's lifetime the two made their home in Milwaukee. Their mutual gifts, their cheerful temperaments and the earnestness of their aims won for them many true friends in the best circles of that city.

COLLIER, Mrs. Ada Langworthy, poet, born in Dubuque, IA, 23rd December, 1843, in the first frame house ever built within the present bounds of the State of Iowa. Her father, a descendant of New England pioneers, was among the very first to explore the lead regions of Iowa, and he was one of the founders of the city of Dubuque. Her mother was a member of an old Baltimore family. None of the hardships and privation that go with pioneer life were known to the little Ada. The lead mines were a source of wealth to her father and his brothers, and soon a group of spacious brick mansions arose on a beautiful bluff above the city, wherein dwelt the Langworthy households. In one of these Ada grew up, a strong, vigorous, attractive child. In early girlhood she was for a time a pupil in a girls' school taught by Miss Catherine Beecher in Dubuque. Afterward she went to Lasell Seminary, Auburndale, MA. Having always found she could accomplish anything she chose to undertake, she there thought she could do the last two years' work in one year, and had nearly succeeded, when she was taken ill of brain fever. In spite of that she was graduated in 1861, at the early age of seventeen. In 1868 she became the wife of Robert Collier, and has since lived in Dubuque. She has one son. She began to write for periodicals in her girlhood. She is the author of many sketches, tales and short poems, of several novels, and of one long, narrative poem, "Lilith" (Boston, 1885). The last is her greatest work, nor can there be any doubt that she should be accounted a poet rather than a novelist.

COLLINS, Mrs. Delia, educator, philanthropist and reformer, born in Franklinton, Schoharie county, NY, 25th November, 1830. Her mother died when she was a young woman, and her father soon afterward moved to Michigan. Miss Delia Krum at the age of fourteen years entered the State Normal School in Albany, NY, and was graduated after the usual course. In 1846 she accepted the assistant principalship of a school in Geneseo, NY, associated with Henry W. Collins as principal. He was a graduate of the State Normal School. They were married in Franklinton in 1849. They moved to Elmira, NY, and Mr. Collins was largely instrumental in the surveying and laying out of that city. In 1855 they moved to Janesville, WI. Mr Collins was elected superintendent of the city schools for several terms, and was connected with the founding and building up of the Institute for the Blind in Janesville. He was the first president and one of the founders of the Northwestern Mutual Life Insurance Company, of Milwaukee, WI. In 1865 he became an invalid, and was confined to the house for eleven years. It was at that time the public life of Mrs. Collins began. Mr. Collins had founded a large business. His excessive labors brought on nervous paralysis, from which he never recovered. There were two sons and a daughter born to them in Janesville. Their daughter died, and business matters involved their property with great losses. Mrs. Collins, in the pressure of home matters, the continued and hopeless illness of her husband, opened a select school for young women, and taught French and German and English literature. Her influence among the literary societies of the city was extensive. In 1876 Mr. Collins died. In 1884 Mrs. Collins became interested in Bible study, Woman's Christian Temperance Union work, church and city charity, and did much in those lines. Her health became impaired, and, becoming acquainted with Miss Carrie Judd, of Buffalo, NY, known as the publisher of "Triumphs of Faith," she accepted the doctrine of "Divine Healing" and was healed of a long-standing spinal trouble, and has since been sustained in both health and the faith work. She is now established in Fort Worth, Texas, where she moved with her sons in 1888. In connection with Woman's Christian Temperance Union work, she, with Mrs. Belle Burchill, of Fort Worth, opened a bootblack's home, which finally resulted in the founding of an orphanage. A building was given for their work, and the home now contains nearly seventy children. She also assisted in opening the Union Bethel Mission of Fort Worth. Its purpose is to reach the people on the street and the children. Mission Sunday-schools are founded and carried on, also nightly gospel meetings and tent gospel meetings. Her next work was the opening and founding, with other women, of a woman's home, a home for unfortunate women on the streets. A foundling home in connection with it has been started. She was engaged in the winter of 1891–1892 in delivering lectures throughout Texas in behalf of the home. She has had the State social purity department work of the Woman's Christian Temperance Union in charge, and is also the president of the Woman's Board of Foreign Missionary Work of the Cumberland Presbyterian Church of North Texas.

COLLINS, Mrs. Emily Parmely, woman suffragist, born in Bristol, Ontario county, NY, 11th August, 1814. She is of New England parents, who were early settlers of the "Genesee Country."

Before the end of her first decade she became an industrious reader, especially of history and poetry. A large part of her second decade was spent in teaching country schools. As an evidence of her success, she received a salary equal to that given to male teachers, something as unusual in those days as in these. She always advocated equal freedom and justice to all. Quite possibly an early bias was given to her mind in that direction, while sitting on her father's knee, listening to his stories of the Revolutionary War in which he participated. The efforts of Greece to throw off the Turkish yoke enlisted her sympathy, which expressed itself in a poem, giving evidence of remarkable depth of mind in one but twelve years of age. Naturally she became an Abolitionist, even before the general anti-slavery agitation. With public affairs and political questions she was always familiar. The full development of woman's capacities she believed to be of supreme importance to the well-being of humanity and, chiefly through the press, has ever advocated woman's educational, industrial and political rights. According to the "History of Woman Suffrage," she organized the first woman suffrage society and sent the first petition for suffrage to the legislature. That was in 1848 in her native town. During the Civil War she went with her two sons, one a surgeon, to the battlefields of Virginia and did efficient service as a volunteer nurse. In 1869 she with her family removed to Louisiana, where she buried her second husband. In 1879, as a new State constitution was being framed, a paper from Mrs. Collins, giving her ideas of what a just constitution should be, was read to the delegates and elicited praise from the New Orleans press. For the last twelve years she has resided in Hartford, CT. In 1885 she, with Miss F. E. Burr, organized the Hartford Equal Rights Club, and she is its president. She wrote occasional stories, to illustrate some principle, for the "Pacific Rural" and other journals. Not ambitious to acquire a literary reputation, and shrinking from publicity, she seldom appended her name. For several years she wrote each week for the Hartford "Journal," under the pen-name "Justitia," a column or two in support of human rights, especially the rights of woman. She also urged the same before each legislature of Connecticut. As a solution of the liquor problem, some years since she advocated in the Hartford "Examiner" the exclusive manufacture and sale of liquor at cost by the government. She also urged a change from the present electoral system to that of proportional representation, and industrial cooperation in place of competition. Always abreast or in advance of the world's progressive thought, her pen is ever busy. Dignified and quiet, modest to a fault, she is justly noted among the intellectual inhabitants of Hartford.

COLLINS, Miss Laura Sedgwick, musician, dramatic reader and amateur actor, was born in Poughkeepsie, NY. At an early age she gave unmistakable evidence of marked ability, and even genius, both as a musician and an elocutionist. She studied under able masters and was graduated several years ago from the Lyceum School of Acting, New York City. She is a skilled pianist, a reader of established reputation, and, though not upon the professional dramatic stage, has appeared in many difficult rôles for the benefit of charities, in the theaters of New York, Brooklyn and other cities. She has studied vocal music and has a sympathetic voice of wide range. She has composed music, much of which is published, and has a large collection of songs, part-music and pianoforte selections and a volume of poems yet to be brought out. "The Two Republics," a march which she wrote, was played at the unveiling of the Statue of Liberty, and Monsieur Bartholdi expressed to her his compliments upon its merits. She composed a minuet for the first performances in English in this country of "Les Précieuses Ridicules," given at the Lyceum Theater, New York. She was also prominently identified with the performance of Sophocles' tragedy of "Electra," which was given in March, 1889, in the Lyceum Theater, New York, and subsequently in the Hollis Street Theater, Boston, MA, and by the request of the Faculty in Harvard College, Cambridge, MA. She composed all of the music for that play and taught it to the chorus, which contained only a few persons who could read music. On 10th December, 1889, at Proctor's Twenty-third Street Theater, New York, was the occasion of the first presentation of a character sketch in four acts, entitled "Sarah Tarbox, M.A.," which was written especially for Miss Collins by Charles Barnard. In that work she won a brilliant success. She spoke with imaginary characters, rode in an imaginary railroad train, went to the theater, attended a reception; yet no one was before the audience but herself. She interpreted vividly all the different parts throughout the entire play; she held the audience during the phases of a scene on Broadway, New York, a scene in a boarding-house room, closing with a scene in St. Luke's Hospital, without the aid of any properties and with but two plain chairs on the stage. In the play she used her various gifts and figured as composer, pianist, singer, dancer and reciter. The achievement was unique in the history of the stage. She has since brought out other successful monologues. Her versatility is coupled with high merit in each line of effort.

COLLINS, Mrs. Miriam O'Leary, actor, born in Boston, MA, in 1864. Her father, William Curran O'Leary, of London, England, was an artist and designer by profession. Her mother's maiden name was Miriam Keating, and at the time of her marriage she was on a visit to Boston from Halifax, Nova Scotia, her native place. Their daughter Miriam was their first child. She received her education in the public schools of Boston, and attended the Franklin grammar school and the girls' high school, and was graduated from both with honors. Her aim throughout her years of preparation was to fit herself as a teacher. After her father's death, encouraged by her cousin, Joseph Haworth, and by other friends, she chose the stage as her profession and began at once her efforts in that direction. Her first success was as Rosalie in "Rosedale" during the engagement of Lester Wallack in the Boston Museum. She spent one season in the company of Edwin Booth and Lawrence Barrett, after which she returned to the Boston Museum, and is now (1892) a member of the stock company of that theater. She has appeared in many widely different rôles, ranging from Smike in "Nicholas Nickleby," Topsy in "Uncle Tom's Cabin," and Sophia in "The

Road to Ruin," to Jess in "Lady Jess." On 25th January, 1892, she became the wife of David A. Collins, a prominent physician of Boston.

COLMAN, Miss Julia, temperance educator and worker, born in the valley of the Sacandaga, Fulton county, NY. She is of Puritan and Huguenot ancestry. In 1840 the family removed to Wisconsin, her father, Rev. Henry R. Colman being sent as missionary to the Oneida Indians near Green Bay. In 1849 she entered the preparatory department of the Lawrence University, in Appleton, WI. She was graduated in the collegiate course in Cazenovia, NY, in 1853, her specialties being natural history and languages. After teaching for a time, she entered the Sunday-school union and tract department of the Methodist Publishing House, in New York City, where she became known as "Aunt Julia" of "The Sunday-school Advocate," and by other literary work. While there, she started anti-tobacco leagues for boys, numbering over one-hundred in various parts of the country. In pursuing medical and hygienic studies she first learned the leading facts about the character of alcohol, and especially that it could be dispensed with in medicine. Always an abstainer, she then saw how she could work for total abstinence successfully, and she began in 1868 to write and lecture on the subject. She took partial courses in different medical colleges, that she might learn their teachings about alcohol and obtain a sound physiological basis for further studies. She spoke before local temperance societies, teachers' institutes and Methodist conferences, delivering upward of one-hundred lectures previous to the crusade. Other engagements prevented her from taking an active part in the uprising, but in 1875 she entered the local work and originated the first "temperance school." That marked a new departure in the temperance work among the children, in that it was largely intellectual, the scholars being arranged in classes, reciting to teachers and reviewed by a superintendent, aided throughout by the systematized use of text-books, tracts, charts and experiments. Those educational methods commended themselves to the National Woman's Christian Temperance Union, and Miss Colman was elected editor of one page of the national organ for one year, to push that elementary work, which soon became

the prevailing model throughout the woman's work and in other temperance organizations. In 1875 Miss Colman was appointed superintendent of literature in the Woman's National Christian Temperance Union, which position she held for fifteen years. During that time she wrote or edited and published upward of five-hundred books, tracts, pamphlets and lesson leaves. Among the books and pamphlets from her pen are: "The Catechisms on Alcohol and Tobacco" (1872), which has reached a circulation of 300,000; "The Juvenile Temperance Manual for Teachers"; "The Primary Temperance Catechism"; "The Catechism on Beer"; "The Sunday School Temperance Catechism"; "The Temperance School"; "Alcohol and Hygiene"; "The Temperance Hand-Book for Speakers and Workers"; "An Evening with Robinson Crusoe," and smaller pamphlets, tracts and leaflets for juveniles and adults. She edited during that time "The Young People's Comrade" and "The Temperance Teacher." She has issued many chromo cards with temperance mottoes for birthday, holiday, Easter, Valentine and everyday use. An effective testing apparatus, capable of showing a variety of helpful chemical experiments, has been put together by her, and with its aid she has delivered courses of illustrated lectures in Silver Springs, Ocean Grove, Toronto and other places, her main object being to simplify scientific teachings and make them attractive to persons of all ages. Her specialty in literary work for adults is the system of tract distribution by topics suited to the educational needs of communities, especially in the total abstinence line, laying a solid foundation for other wise and effective temperance work. She prepared a series of sketches of the State Woman's Christian Temperance Union presidents, published in "Demorest's Magazine." She has written much on health topics and the wholesome preparation of food for "Moore's Rural New Yorker," for the "Ladies' Repository." the "Phrenological Journal," "Good Health" and other periodicals. She is now superintendent of the health department of the National Woman's Christian Temperance Union, with her office in the Bible House, New York City, where it has been for years. From girlhood she has been a devout evangelical Christian, a member of the Methodist Episcopal Church, and her main object in all her philanthropic work is to aid others in attaining a physical development which shall enable them better to serve God, themselves and their fellow men.

COLMAN, Mrs. Lucy Newhall,

anti-slavery agitator and woman suffragist, born in Sturbridge, Worcester county, MA, 26th July, 1817. Her maiden name was Danforth. Her mother was a Newhall and a direct descendant of John Alden and Priscilla. She was early a student of the puzzling problem of slavery in a land of freedom. In 1824 and up to 1830 a revival of religion swept over New England, and Lucy was again puzzled to understand the benefit of such a revival if human beings were elected to be saved from the beginning. She turned to the Bible and read, but her confusion became deeper. The result was that she became a Liberal in religion, a free thinker and a free speaker. She joined the Universalist Church while young, but afterward became a Spiritualist. At the age of eighteen years she was married and went to Boston, MA. Her husband died of consumption in 1841. In 1843 she was married a second time. In 1846 she began to agitate for equal rights for woman and for the emancipation of the slaves. In 1852 her husband, who was an engineer on the Central Railroad, was killed in a railroad accident, leaving her alone with a seven year old daughter. Mrs. Colman, left with a child and no resources, asked the railroad company for work, but they refused the favor. She applied for the position of clerk at the ladies' window in a post-office, for work in a printing office, and for other positions, but was in each case rejected because she was a woman. She then began to teach in Rochester, NY, doing for $350 a year the work that a man received $800 for doing. The "colored school" in Rochester was offered to her, and she took it, resolving that it should die. She advised the colored people to send their children to the schools in their own districts, until the school was dead. This was done in one year. Mrs. Colman was invited by Miss Susan B. Anthony to prepare a paper to read at a State convention of teachers. The paper caused a sensation. Mrs. Colman urged the abolition of corporal punishment in the schools of Rochester. Wearying of

school work, she decided to begin her labor as an abolitionist. She delivered her first lecture in a Presbyterian church near Rochester, which had been secured by her friend, Mrs. Amy Post. She attented the annual convention of the Western Anti-Slavery Society in Michigan, and that meeting was turned into a spiritualistic gathering. She lectured in various towns in Michigan, OH, Indiana and Illinois. Her meetings were disturbed, and she and her co-workers were subjected to all kinds of annoyances and to malicious misrepresentation in the press on many occasions. She attempted some work in Iowa and Wisconsin, but the reformers were few in those sparsely settled States. In Pennsylvania and New York she did much in arousing public sentiment on slavery and woman's rights. In 1862 her daughter, Gertrude, entered the New England Woman's Medical College, and died within two weeks. The funeral was conducted by Frederick Douglass. Then Mrs. Colman went to Washington to serve as matron in the National Colored Orphan Asylum. She afterward was appointed teacher of a colored school in Georgetown, DC. She has held many other positions of the philanthropic kind. In late years she has been conspicuous among the Free-thinkers. Her home is now in Syracuse, NY.

COLYAR, Mrs. Pauline Shackleford,

author, born on a cotton plantation in Southern Mississippi. She belongs to one of the oldest and most aristocratic families of the South, and although her own experience began since the war, she is familiar with every phase of life south of Mason and Dixon's line. This knowledge, coupled with a keen sense of humor and a talent for character drawing, has been used to the best advantage in her literary work. It fell to her lot, when a girl, to attend school in the Tennessee mountains, for

a period of four years, and she thus became familiar with the queer "types" found only in that region, besides acquiring an exhaustible fund of incident and a complete mastery of the "cracker" dialect. Since her marriage she has resided in Chattanooga, TN, where she is recognized as one of the brightest women in society. The public is familiar with her literary work through her contributions to "Lippincott's," "The Youth's Companion," "Woman's Home Companion" and other magazines. Her negro character sketches and stories of the South display a talent scarcely inferior to that of Joel Chandler Harris.

COMFORT, Mrs. Anna Manning, doctor of medicine, born in Trenton, NJ, 19th January, 1845. In her childhood Miss Manning's parents removed to Boston, MA, where she received her academic education. An early liking for the studies of anatomy and physiology was discovered by her aunt, Mrs. Clemence Lozier, MD, the founder and for twenty years the dean of the New York Medical College for Women. Miss Manning entered Dr. Lozier's office as a student. Dr. Lozier's large and generous hospitality brought to her house many of the leading reformers of the time, and from intercourse with them Miss Manning drew much of that sympathetic inspiration and breadth of view which marked her personality in later years. She was a member of the first class in the New York Medical College for Women. At the graduating exercises of that class speeches were made by Henry Ward Beecher, Horace Greeley, Henry J. Raymond and Hon. S. S. Cox in behalf of enlarging the sphere of woman's activities, and especially on her entering the domain of medicine. At that time the opposition to women students, which almost amounted to persecution, was manifested to the first class of lady students, among other things, by the rude treatment they received from the men students and even from some of the professors while attending the clinics in Bellevue Hospital. After graduation Miss Manning began the practice of her profession in Norwich, CT, being the first woman graduate in medicine to practice in that State. By her strong personality and her professional success she soon won a large and important patronage in Norwich and eastern Connecticut. She there strongly espoused, in the press and otherwise, the cause of woman suffrage and of woman's equality with men in all moral, social and civil relations. In 1870 she removed to New York City, where she successfully practiced her profession, was appointed lecturer in the college from which she

graduated, and was elected a member of the newly founded society of Sorosis. In New York Dr. Manning met the gentleman whom she married in 1871, Prof. G. F. Comfort, L.H.D., the distinguished scholar in linguistics and art criticism, who became the founder and dean of the College of Fine Arts of the Syracuse University. In 1872 they removed to Syracuse, where Dean Comfort entered upon his work in the newly established university in that city. Dr. Comfort relinquished her medical practice for some years, till her children had grown beyond the need of a mother's constant cares. On resuming practice she confined her work to gynæcology, which had before been her chief department, and in that field she has achieved success and distinction. In 1874 Dr. Comfort wrote "Woman's Education and Woman's Health," in reply to Dr. Clarke's "Sex in Education," in which he attacked the higher education of woman. In 1887 and 1891 she traveled extensively in Europe, where she visited many important hospitals and medical institutions. Her tastes and accomplishments are varied and versatile; she has marked histrionic powers, and could have achieved distinguished success as an artist, musician or actor, or on the lecture platform.

CONANT, Mrs. Frances Augusta, journalist and business woman, born in West Burlington, NY, 23rd December, 1842. Her parents were Curtis and Martha R. Hemingway. She was educated in the western part of the State and in Brooklyn, where she became the wife, in 1864, of Claudius W. Conant, of New York. In early girlhood she became a contributor to New York publications. Since 1882 Mrs. Conant has been a resident of Chicago, IL. She usually passes the winters in traveling through the South. She was for several years a special correspondent of the "Living Church" and a contributor to the "Advance" and other religious publications of Chicago, as well as to some class journals, and, occasionally, short stories of hers appeared in leading New York and Philadelphia publications. During the New Orleans Exposition of 1884–85 she was the only special woman correspondent in that city for a mechanical and scientific journal, ably representing the "Industrial World," of

Chicago. She often writes as a collaborator with her husband, who is connected with the "American Field," and they frequently do editorial work interchangeably. Mrs. Conant is an earnest advocate of the cause of industrial education, and she was editor and business manager of the "Journal of Industrial Education" in the early days of its publication. Her reputation as a writer of short sketches of travel led to an engagement as editor of the "American Traveler and Tourist," published in Chicago, which position she held for two years, until she became interested in a commercial enterprise. Though rarely working in any associations, she has developed decided ability as a promoter and organizer. She was one of the founders of the Woman's National Press Association, formed in New Orleans, in 1885, for the purpose of fostering State auxiliaries like the Woman's Christian Temperance Union. She was the principal promoter of the Illinois Woman's Press Association, the first independent State organization for the purpose of affording practical assistance to women in literary pursuits. She was secretary of that association for the first two years, and received an honorary life membership in recognition of her services. Mrs. Conant is noted for being most generous in giving time and thought to all appeals for help. It has been said by a long-time friend that if she had been half as zealous in forwarding her own interest as in advancing those of other people she would have made a great financial success in her career. Like all women in public work she has been the constant recipient of the most touching appeals from other women, usually those without technical training, for assistance to occupations by which they could earn their bread. She became oppressed by the problem: "What shall we do with this unskilled army?" When a plan for employing large numbers of these untrained applicants was presented to Mrs. Conant she withdrew from editorial work, in 1891, to engage in the promotion and organization of a corporation projected to give, eventually, remunerative employment to thousands of women in all parts of the country. She was secretary of the company during its first year arid took an active part in the business management, then she resigned her trust to others, having made a record of phenomenal success. The year closed with the company well established.

CONANT, Miss Harriet Beecher, physician, born in Greensboro, VT, 10th June, 1852. Her

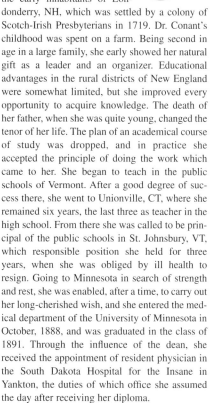

father, E. Tolman Conant. was a life-long resident of that town. His immediate ancestors were natives of Hollis, NH, and those more remote lived in Salem, MA, and were of Puritan descent. Her maternal ancestors were among the early inhabitants of Londonderry, NH, which was settled by a colony of Scotch-Irish Presbyterians in 1719. Dr. Conant's childhood was spent on a farm. Being second in age in a large family, she early showed her natural gift as a leader and an organizer. Educational advantages in the rural districts of New England were somewhat limited, but she improved every opportunity to acquire knowledge. The death of her father, when she was quite young, changed the tenor of her life. The plan of an academical course of study was dropped, and in practice she accepted the principle of doing the work which came to her. She began to teach in the public schools of Vermont. After a good degree of success there, she went to Unionville, CT, where she remained six years, the last three as teacher in the high school. From there she was called to be principal of the public schools in St. Johnsbury, VT, which responsible position she held for three years, when she was obliged by ill health to resign. Going to Minnesota in search of strength and rest, she was enabled, after a time, to carry out her long-cherished wish, and she entered the medical department of the University of Minnesota in October, 1888, and was graduated in the class of 1891. Through the influence of the dean, she received the appointment of resident physician in the South Dakota Hospital for the Insane in Yankton, the duties of which office she assumed the day after receiving her diploma.

CONE, Miss Helen Gray, educator, born in New York City, 8th March, 1859. She was graduated from the New York City Normal College in 1876, in which institution she became instructor in English literature. At her graduation she gave evidence of her poetical gift by the composition of the class song. Since that time she has contributed to the "Atlantic Monthly," the "Century," "Harper's Magazine," "St. Nicholas" and other periodicals. She was a helper in the preparation of thc "Century Dictionary," and assisted Miss Jeannette L. Gilder in editing "Pen Portraits of Literary Women." She has published two volumes of poems, "Oberon and Puck, Verses Grave and Gay" (New York, 1885) and the "Ride of the Lady and other Poems" (Boston, 1891).

CONKLIN, Mrs. Jane Elizabeth Dexter, born in Utica, NY, 7th July, 1831. Her great grandfather, George Grant, of Abernethy, Scotland, came to America in 1774. He joined the Continental Army and served during the Revolutionary War. Her mother was the daughter of William W. Williams, an architect of Albany, NY. An uncle of Mrs. Conklin, Asahel Dexter, was a captain in the War of 1812. Mrs. Conklin's father was born in Paris, NY, his parents having removed to that place from Mansfield, CT, in the latter part of the last century. He was a cousin of John G. Saxe, the poet. Miss Dexter received her education in the Utica Female Academy and in Mrs. Brinkerhoff's school for young ladies, Albany, NY. Her first composition was written in verse. When she was fourteen years old, her poems were first published, and since that time she has been almost continuously writing. While none of her poems are strictly hymns, many of them are sung in religious meetings. She was, for many years, a contributor to the Utica "Gospel Messenger." She also wrote for a New York weekly, and for several local papers, prose articles as well as poetry. In December, 1865, she became the wife of Cramer H. Conklin, a veteran of the Civil War, and since that time she has lived in Binghamton, NY. Mrs. Conklin always took great interest in the War of the Rebellion and in the defenders of the Republic. When the Grand Army of the Republic post, to which her husband belongs, formed a Relief Corps of the wives and daughters of the members, her name was one of the first signed to a call for a charter. Shortly after the corps was organized, she was elected its president, and for three years held that office. In 1884 she published a book of poems, which was favorably received. She has in preparation a second volume of poems.

CONNELLY, Mrs. Celia Logan, see Logan, Celia.

CONNELLY, Miss Emma M., author, born near Louisville, KY, where she lived until 1880. Her father was a Virginian who went to Kentucky with his parents in his early youth. The family was connected with that of the English Governor of Virginia. One branch remained loyal to the king, but the immediate ancestors of the young Kentuckian had borne an active part in the struggle for freedom. Her mother's family were from Pennsylvania. Both her grandmothers were of a Quaker family, Douthett, of Welsh descent. Her mother died in the daughter's infancy, the father in her girlhood. Her first effort was a school-girl story, never thought of for publication till after her father's death, when it was sent to the Louisville "Courier Journal." It was merely a story written because she liked to write, and so alarmed was she to see her thoughts in cold print, with her name attached, that she ran away to the country while it was being published. When Mr. Watterson afforded her the opportunity of the editorial incognito in a daily column on his paper, she gladly took the place, but, the unusual confinement of journalistic life proving too much for her, she gave it up at the close of the year. Of her father's estate sufficient remains to allow her careful study and deliberation in writing. Her taste has led her more and more from the story to the didactic, yet, with the highest aims, she has never given herself over wholly to moralizing. Her "Tilting at Windmills" (Boston, 1888) surprised every one by its strength, its breadth of view, and the knowledge it evinced of human nature. Then followed her "Story of Kentucky" (Boston, 1891) for a historical series, "Stories of the States." Miss Connelly has but one near relative, a brother, John Allison Connelly, of Savannah, GA. She makes her home mainly in New York City.

CONNER, Mrs. Eliza Archard, journalist and lecturer, was born on a farm near Cincinnati, OH. Her ancestors were among the pioneers of southern Ohio, and one of them founded the town of New Richmond. Her maiden name was Eliza Archard. She was educated in Antioch College, Yellow Springs, OH, taking the full course in classics and higher mathematics. In 1869 she became the wife of Dr. George Conner, of Cincinnati. In her early years she was a teacher, part of the time instructor in Latin and German in the Indianapolis high school. There her persistent refusal to accept less wages than had been previously paid to a man teacher for doing the same work resulted in the passing of a rule by the school board that teachers of both sexes in the high school should receive the same salary, a rule that remains in force to this day. Her first newspaper contribution was printed when she was thirteen years old. In 1865 she became a regular contributor to the "Saturday Evening Post," of Philadelphia, under the name of "Zig." Later she wrote for the Cincinnati "Commercial," signing the initials E. A. Her contributions attracted attention. In 1878 she became a member of the editorial staff of the "Commercial." She went to New York City in 1884 as literary editor of the "World." In 1885 she accepted a place on the editorial staff of the American Press Association syndicate in New York.

She is a member of Sorosis and of the New York Women's Press Club. Mrs. Conner has probably written as much newspaper matter as any other woman living. In editorial writing she furnishes regularly two columns daily of a thousand words each. She has done all kinds of newspaper work, from police-court reporting up. Her letters to the Cincinnati "Commercial" from Europe were published in a volume called "E. A. Abroad" (Cincinnati, 1883). She has also written several serial stories. An important part of her work for the American Press Association has been the preparation of a series of newspaper pages of war history, descriptive of the battles of the Civil War. In her girlhood Mrs. Conner entered enthusiastically into the struggle for the emancipation and advancement of women. She originated classes in parliamentary usage and extempore speaking among women. Wherever occasion permitted, she has written and spoken in favor of equal pay for equal work, and of widening the industrial field for women. As a speaker she possesses the magnetic quality. She is deeply interested in psychological studies and in oriental philosophy, accepting the ancient doctrine of repeated incarnation for the same individual. She is an enthu-siast on the subject of physical culture for women, believing that mankind were meant to live outdoors and sleep in houses.

CONNER, Mrs. Elizabeth Marney, dramatic reader and educator, born in Rouse's Point, NY, 26th February, 1856. At the age of eighteen she became the wife of Marcus A. Conner, of Burlington, VT, who died in 1881, leaving her with two young sons to care for and educate. It was then Mrs. Conner turned her attention to developing tastes and satisfying ambitions which heretofore had lain dormant. With decided abilities for music, literature and the drama, circumstances led her to choose some form of dramatic work, and she began the careful study of elocution. In January, 1884, the Buffalo School of Elocution was opened by Mrs. Conner, and since then she has rapidly won her way as teacher and artist in her profession, having gained for herself and school an enviable local reputation, and being well-known in a far wider territory. She is a devotee to the art of which she is a true exponent, and every instinct of her being is absorbed in the success of her pupils and the advancement of that branch of education. Her lecture on "Expression" with illustrative readings has been in demand from school, pulpit and platform. She has published recitations in both prose and verse under the pen-name "Paul Veronique," and is the author of the popular operetta "Eulalie." Although her success as a teacher and reader is exceptional, it is considered by many that her true place is on the stage. For that profession she is gifted in a high degree with the essentials of success. She has a strong personality and magnetic presence, intense dramatic fervor, a fine voice and versatile powers of expression. She possesses in addition indomitable pluck, a cheerful, vivacious temperament, and is altogether one of the sunshiny people of the world.

CONVERSE, Mrs. Harriet Maxwell, author and philanthropist, born in Elmira, NY. She is Scotch by ancestry, American by birth and Indian by adoption. She is a daughter of Thomas Maxwell and Maria Purdy Maxwell. The history of the

Maxwells, lineal descendants of the Earls of Nithsdale, is full of romance. The grandfather of Mrs. Converse was born on the shores of County Down, Ireland, his father and mother being cast there shipwrecked, having embarked for America in 1770. After the babe was some months old, they finally reached America and settled in Berkley, VA, in 1772. In 1792 the baby, Guy Maxwell, was a young man and removed to the spot now Elmira, NY. Of the children of Guy who became prominent, the father of Mrs. Converse, Thomas Maxwell, was remarkable. A man of ability, he was an influential factor in a region of country where it is yet said, "The word of a Maxwell was law." He served as a member of Congress and occupied various important positions. He was a graceful writer and a contributor to the "Knickerbocker Magazine." From him his daughter Harriet inherited her characteristics. Left motherless at a tender age, she was sent to Milan, OH, and there put to school under the care of an aunt. Early married, she became a widow while her former companions were yet girls, and in 1861 she was married to her second husband, Mr. Converse. For five years after her last marriage, she traveled in the United States and Europe, writing prose and verse under a pen-name. Not until 1881 did she begin to make use of her own name in print. She then set herself seriously to her work and published her first volume of poems, "Sheaves" (New York, 1883), which has passed through several editions. In 1884 Mrs. Converse was formally adopted by the Seneca Indians, as had been her father and grandfather before her. It was soon after the occasion of the re-interment by the Buffalo Historical Society of the remains of the famous Red Jacket, and her adoption made her the great granddaughter of Red Jacket, with all the rights and honors pertaining to the relation. Mrs. Converse is an industrious writer of prose and a contributor to several magazines and newspapers. Among the works written by her are the historical volumes, "The Religious Festivals of the Iroquois Indians" and "Mythology and Folk Lore of the North American Indians." She has always defended the rights of the Indians of New York, and effectively aided the Indian delegation at Albany in 1891 to oppose a bill before

the Assembly which would have deprived them of their lands. The bill was killed in committee. Before the hearing of the Indians by the committee, Mrs. Converse had been invited to sit in their Six-Nation Council held in Albany, an honor never before bestowed upon a white woman, save Mary Jemison. After the bill was killed, when the Seneca National Council, in session at Carrollton, Cattaraugus county, NY, in the Allegany Reservation, was called, an application was laid before the body to the effect that, "by love and affection," it was the desire of the Indians that Mrs. Converse should be received into their nation as a legal member of it. Upon this appeal a vote was taken, and it was unanimously resolved that she be at once invited to appear before the Council and receive her Indian name. To this summons Mrs. Converse responded, and on her arrival at Carrollton was met by a delegation of Indians and escorted to the Council House, where she was received by the marshal of the nation and presented by him to the President and Board of Councillors. A runner was immediately sent out to notify the Indian people, and three-hundred of them gathered in the Council House, when Mrs. Converse was nominated by the Indian matrons to sit with them. Taking her place between two of the "mothers" at the head of the Council House, the ceremony proceeded, conducted by a head chief of the Snipe clan, of which Mrs. Converse had been made a family member in 1881. The resolution of the Council was then read in the Seneca language and interpreted to her. Then an eloquent address was made by the head chief of the Snipes, to which Mrs. Converse responded, recalling her inherited claim upon their friendship by reason of the adoption by their ancestors of her grandfather in 1794 and her father in 1804. After her address, she was presented by her "namer," the chief of the Snipe clan, to the president and members of the Council and the other Indian men and women who were present, with whom she shook hands individually. The name given Mrs. Converse is Yä-ih-wah-non, which signifies "ambassador," or the "watcher." This is a clan name, and the last bearer of it was the wife of the celebrated Gy-ant-wa-ka, or Corn-planter. In the fall of 1891, in a Six-Nation Condolence Council, held on the Tonawanda Reservation, NY, Mrs. Converse was nominated, elected and installed as a Six-Nation chief, thereby receiving a title never before bestowed upon a woman in all the history of the

North American Indians. As a defender of the red man, Mrs. Converse is generally known among them as "our good friend," a distinction of which she is justly proud.

CONWAY, Miss Clara, educator, is a native and resident of Memphis, TN. She began her educational career as a public-school teacher. Her study of educational methods inspired her with the desire to establish a system of education for girls which should be based on absolute thoroughness. Her idea was and is that women should be so taught that, if conditions make self-support necessary, they can fill professional careers. She was the first woman in Tennessee to assist in the organization of teachers' institutes, and she was the first southern woman to attend the teachers' summer-school in the North. At the first session of the Martha's Vineyard Summer Institute she was the only representative of the South. At the meeting of the National Educational Association in Madison, WI, 18th July, 1884, she read a paper on the needs of southern women. In 1886 she read a paper in the Saratoga convention, and in 1887 she was elected a member of the National Council during the San Francisco convention, although she was not present. She took a prominent part in the meeting of the Southern Association at Lookout Mountain in 1891, and in the meeting of the National Council in Toronto, Canada, in the same year. Her connection with the famous school that bears her name dates from 1878, when she originated the work with fifty pupils, one assistant and $300 of borrowed money. The growth of the school was remarkable. In 1884 Miss Conway's pupils numbered 250, and it became apparent that permanent accommodations must be provided. A few public-spirited citizens, impressed with the determination of the woman, who had fought such heavy odds, formed a stock company, incorporated the school and had a building erected. It was Miss Conway's proposition that it be called the Margaret Fuller school, but the trustees decided promptly that it should be named in honor of its founder, the Clara Conway Institute. The institute in 1891 had three-hundred pupils, a senior class of thirty, school property valued at $75,000, a strong

faculty, nine of whom, former pupils, have been trained for special departments in the best schools of this country and of Europe, while its graduates are filling many useful positions in life.

CONWAY, Miss Katherine Eleanor, journalist, born in Rochester, NY, 6th September, 1853. She is the daughter of cultivated Celtic parents, who came to this country from the west of Ireland. Upon her mother's side are traditions of scholarship for many generations, several of her kindred having been prominent ecclesiastics in the Church of Rome. The name is of remote Welsh origin, and there is a slight trace of English blood in their veins, but the family pride is all in their Irish blood, and the Conways are "good rebels, every one." The name Conway has been notable in teaching and journalism. Katherine's sister, Miss Mary Conway, is the head of the Collegio Americano, in Buenos Ayres, Argentine Republic. Several of the same name and blood have been prominently associated with journalism in New York, and her kinsman, Rev. John Conway, edits a journal in St. Paul, MN. The father of Katherine Conway, a successful railroad contractor and bridge builder, was also active in politics. From the age of four to fifteen years Katherine was in school. The years from eleven to fifteen were spent in St. Mary's Academy, Buffalo, NY, where her inclination to literature was strengthened by a gifted English teacher. At the age of fifteen, when her first poem appeared, Katherine was under the impression that ten dollars was the price usually paid to an editor for the honor of appearing in his columns in verse, and she supposed that, wishing to please her, some one of her family had been guilty of this blamable extravagance. Her busy mind was ever instinctively outreaching for wider fields of usefulness, and in her aspirations she was assisted by her sympathetic friend and adviser, Bishop McQuaid, of Rochester, NY. Her first work in journalism was done on the Rochester "Daily Union and Advertiser." She edited for five years the "West End Journal," a little religious monthly. She was assistant editor of the Buffalo "Catholic Union and Times" from 1880 to 1883. In that year Miss Conway was invited to visit Boston to recuperate her failing health. There she met for the first time the editor who had given her the earliest recognition for her poems by a check for their value, John Boyle O'Reilly. An opportune vacancy occurring upon the staff of the "Pilot," Mr. O'Reilly tendered it at the close of her visit to Miss Conway, who accepted and entered upon her new duties in the autumn of 1883. Besides a liberal salary, opportunities for outside literary work were often put in the young editor's way by her generous chief. Two years previous to that change, in 1881, Katherine Conway had gathered her vagrant poems into a volume, which was published with the appropriate title, "On the Sunrise Slope." Miss Conway's next venture through the hands of the publisher was in editing Mrs. Clara Erskine Clement Waters' collection, called "Christian Symbols and Stories of the Saints as Illustrated in Art." She has lately brought out a very successful little volume, "Watchwords from John Boyle O' Reilly," with an introductory chapter on O'Reilly as poet and literary writer. Miss Conway is a woman without a grievance. Her toil has been hard and long, but she has won recognition and made steady progress. Her influence is wide. She organized the first Catholic reading circle in Boston, of which she is still president. For years the chosen chairman of the literary entertainments of the New England Woman's Press Association, which office she has resigned, she has made an admirable presiding officer on occasions when any notable literary visitors to Boston were gathered about the board, and has done much to advance the dignity and preserve the harmony of that organization. In the spring of 1891 Miss Conway was invited to give before the Woman's Council in Washington, DC, her paper upon "The Literature of Moral Loveliness." She was the first and is thus far the only Catholic who has appeared before the Educational and Industrial Union of Boston to speak upon a religious theme. In addition to that, during that year she read before the Women's Press Club papers on "Some Obstacles to Women's Success in Journalism," "Personal Journalism," and "On Magnifying Mine Office," a neat satire. Besides all this, her poems have appeared in the Providence "Journal" and "Life," with thoughtful articles of literary trend in the Catholic and secular periodicals. Miss Conway has lately been honored by being chosen president of the press department of the Isabella Association, in connection with the Columbian Exposition in Chicago. She is still on

the "Pilot," associate editor, with James Jeffrey Roche, chief editor. Miss Conway's life has been a full and generous one, overflowing with thought and help for others.

COOK, Miss Amelia Josephine, littérateur, born in Ballston Spa, NY. She is the daughter of Morton C. Cook, of French extraction, and the son of a Unitarian minister. Her mother, Phebe A. Griffin Cook, was a Connecticut Quaker. Amelia was one of a family of six children. She was educated in the public schools in childhood, and subsequently studied in a select school, in a private seminary for young ladies, in an academy for both sexes, and finally in the State Normal School, where she studied with the object of becoming a teacher. From her father she inherited a talent for poetry, which early revealed itself in connection with a remarkable facility for prose composition. Her specialty in literature is the short story. Much of her work is designed for the boys and girls of the land. Her recent work in various periodicals has appeared under several pen-names. She has used her full name very seldom, preferring to remain unknown to the public. She is a member of the Women's National Press Association and of the Incorporated Society of Authors.

COOK, Miss May A., pianist, born in Paw Paw, MI, 4th December, 1869. Her father, Prof. E. Cook, was born in Genesee county, NY. During the Civil War he served in the Eighth New York Heavy Artillery as a member of the band, and saw the surrender of Lee's army at Appomattox Court House. When the regiment was discharged, he returned to his native State and resumed his studies in the normal school in Brockport, NY. Afterward his attention was devoted wholly to music. While teaching in Michigan, he became acquainted with Miss C. A. Tyler, and they were married in 1868. Miss Cook showed an early predilection for music, and has always been an industrious student. At the age of sixteen years she was known as the finest pianist of the Pacific Northwest. She was the first pianist to present to the musical public of that section the works of the great masters, and concertos by Weber, Beethoven and Schumann, with full orchestra, were successively given, and in such an artistic manner as to make them popular. A remarkably clear technic and great expression characterize her playing. In the summer of 1891 Miss Cook, accompanied by her mother, went to Germany, where she purposes to spend some years in musical study. Her home is in Portland, OR.

COOKE, Mrs. Rose Terry, author, born on a farm near Hartford, CT, 17th February, 1827. Her father was Henry Wadsworth Terry, and her mother's maiden name was Anne Wright Hurlbut, and she was a daughter of John Hurlbut, of Wethersfield, CT, who was the first New England shipmaster who sailed around the earth. When Rose Terry was six years old, her parents moved into Hartford. Her father educated her in outdoor lore, and she was familiar with birds, bees, flowers and sunshine. She was carefully trained at home, and in school she was brilliant and noted for the ease with which she learned and for her skill in versification when only a child. She was graduated in 1843, and, although only sixteen years old, became a teacher in Hartford. She afterward taught in New Jersey. Family needs called her home, and she then began to study with the intention of becoming an author. She published poems in the New York "Tribune," and at once won a reputation. She published her first story in "Graham's Magazine," in 1845. Her reception was encouraging. Other productions followed, and in a short time she published a volume of verse. She contributed to "Putnam's Magazine," "Harper's Magazine" and the "Atlantic Monthly" poems and stories, and her productions were in general demand. In 1872 she became the wife of Rollin H. Cooke, a Connecticut manufacturer, and they lived in Winsted for some years. Her most important works are "Poems by Rose Terry" (Boston, 1860), "Happy Dodd" (Boston, 1879), "Somebody's Neighbors" (Boston, 1881), "Root-Bound" (Boston, 1885), and "The Sphinx's Chil-

dren" (Boston, 1886). Her short stories, humorous and descriptive, of New England life would fill several volumes. She died in Pittsfield, MA, 18th July, 1892.

COOKE, Mrs. Susan G., of Knoxville, TN, though for many years a resident of the South, was born in the State of New York. She is the daughter of George Spaulding Gale, one of the most prominent surgeons of Vermont, and a granddaughter of Gen. Summers Gale, of the same State, a hero of the War of 1812. Her mother, a woman of brilliant intellectual and social qualities, was a member of one of the oldest families in her section of the State of New York. From both her parents Mrs. Cooke inherits the energy and resolution which characterize all her

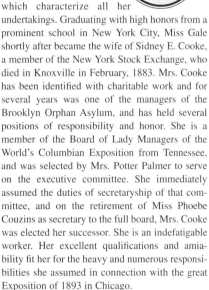

undertakings. Graduating with high honors from a prominent school in New York City, Miss Gale shortly after became the wife of Sidney E. Cooke, a member of the New York Stock Exchange, who died in Knoxville in February, 1883. Mrs. Cooke has been identified with charitable work and for several years was one of the managers of the Brooklyn Orphan Asylum, and has held several positions of responsibility and honor. She is a member of the Board of Lady Managers of the World's Columbian Exposition from Tennessee, and was selected by Mrs. Potter Palmer to serve on the executive committee. She immediately assumed the duties of secretaryship of that committee, and on the retirement of Miss Phoebe Couzins as secretary to the full board, Mrs. Cooke was elected her successor. She is an indefatigable worker. Her excellent qualifications and amiability fit her for the heavy and numerous responsibilities she assumed in connection with the great Exposition of 1893 in Chicago.

COOLBRITH, Mrs. Ina Donna, poet, was born in Illinois. Her parents were New Englanders. The family removed to Los Angeles, CA, when she was a child, and there her youth was passed. She became a voluminous contributor to the "Overland Monthly," and she contributed also to the "Californian," the "Galaxy," "Harper's Magazine" and other important periodicals. Her recognition by the press, by the poets and by the critics was instantaneous. In 1874 circumstances forced her to accept the office of librarian in the free library of Oakland, CA, where she has remained until the present time. In 1881 she published a small volume of poems, "A Perfect Day," most of which had been written before 1876. In 1876 her mother died, and since then her life has been one of self-sacrifice for those who depended upon her. Since the publication of her volume she has written very few poems.

COOLEY, Mrs. Emily M. J., religious and and temperance worker, born in Lima, NY, 1st November, 1831. Her maternal ancestry was of the French nobility who, for religion's sake, left title, fortune and home, and, casting their lot with the persecuted Huguenots, found in New Jersey, among the Quakers, a refuge and a home where they might worship according to their faith. Many of the descendants became distinguished soldiers during the national struggle. On her father's side she is descended from the Puritans of 1636. They settled in North Adams, MA, and some of the eminent men of that State are of kindred blood. Till the age of sixteen she attended the public schools, and then was a student for a year each in Buffalo, in Rochester and in Aurora Academy, now Wells College. She was for five years a teacher in Buffalo, and then became the wife of Rev. R. Cooley, of the Methodist Episcopal Church, a graduate in Meadville, PA. After that for one year she was preceptress of Cooperstown Seminary. They moved to Wisconsin in 1862, and she began her public work in the Woman's Foreign Missionary Society. She was for several years vice-president of the society in Wisconsin Conference and organized many auxiliaries. Her temperance work was begun in 1869. When once awakened to the extent of the liquor evil, she became one of its most determined foes. Though grown white-haired in the service, she is still an

indefatigable worker in the cause of prohibition. In 1880 her husband was transferred to the Nebraska Conference. She had resolved to enjoy home rest for a season after that change, but her fame preceded her in letters to the State officers from Miss Willard and others. She was made State organizer for the Woman's Christian Temperance Union of Nebraska, in her first year with that body. She served four years as State and three years as National organizer, speaking in every State of the Union. She has been for several years president of the second district Woman's Christian Temperance Union of Nebraska. Not alone in the temperance cause has Mrs. Cooley been known as a power for good. Though not an ordained minister of the M. E. Church, being a woman, she was known as an "exhorter," and she was twice appointed by the presiding elder to supply the pulpit of a church without a pastor. Each time her labors were successful and the membership greatly increased.

COOLIDGE, Mrs. Harriet Abbot Lincoln, philanthropist, author and reformer, born in Boston, MA. Her great-grandfather, Amos Lincoln, was a captain of artillery and one of the intrepid band who, in 1773, consigned the tea to the water in Boston harbor. He was in the battle of Bunker Hill, attached to Stark's brigade, in action at Bennington, Brandywine and Monmouth, and aided in the suppression of Shays's Rebellion, and was also one of Governor Hancock's aids. On 14th June, 1781, he was married to Deborah, a daughter of Paul Revere of revolutionary fame, which makes Mrs. Coolidge a great-great-granddaughter of that famous rider. Amos Lincoln's first ancestor in this country was Samuel Lincoln, of Hingham, MA, one of whose sons was Mordecai, the ancestor of President Lincoln. The father of Mrs. Coolidge, Frederic W. Lincoln, was called the War Mayor of Boston, as he held that office all through the Civil War and was reëlected and served seven years. Mrs. Coolidge was delicate in childhood, and her philanthropic spirit was early shown in flower-mission and hospital work in Boston. For several years she was instructed at home, and she was sent to the private boarding-school of Dr. Dio Lewis, of Lexington, MA. In November, 1872, Harriet Abbott Lincoln became the wife of George A. Coolidge, a publishing agent of Boston. With maternal duties came the untiring devotion of conscientious motherhood. Mrs. Coolidge gave her children her best thoughts and studied closely the best methods of infant hygiene. She soon began a series of illustrated articles for the instruction of mothers in a New York magazine, and while residing in that city studied for three years and visited the hospitals for children. Ill health obliged her to return to Washington, DC, where, before going to New York, she was interested in charities and hospitals for children. Meeting the mothers of both the rich and the poor, and seeing the great need of intelligent care in bringing up little children, she soon found a large correspondence on her hands. Her devotion to the waifs of the Foundling Hospital in Washington, and the great hygienic reformation she brought about, gave that institution a record of no deaths among its inmates during the six months she acted as a member of its executive board of officers. Frequent inquiries from mothers desiring information on hygienic subjects relating to children suggested the idea of a series of nursery talks to mothers and the fitting up of a model nursery in her residence, where every accessory of babyhood could be practically presented. "Nursery Talks" were inaugurated by a "Nursery Tea," and five hundred women from official and leading circles were present. Classes were formed, and a paid course and a free one made those lectures available for all desiring information. Even into midsummer, at the urgent request of mothers, Mrs. Coolidge continued to give her mornings to answering questions. She remained in Washington during the summer, guiding those who did not know how to feed their infants proper food, and, as a consequence, her health was impaired, and she was obliged to give up her nursery lectures until her health was restored. She then commenced a scientific course of hygienic study, and was made president of the Woman's Clinic, where women and children are treated by women physicians, free of charge or for a mere trifle. Mrs. Coolidge is always busy. She is an active member of four of the leading charity organizations in Washington, a valued member of the Woman's National Press Association and devoted to every movement in which women's higher education is considered.

COOLIDGE, Susan, see WOOLSEY, MISS SARAH CHANNING.

COOPER, Mrs. Sarah Brown Ingersoll, educator, author and evangelist, born in Cazenovia, NY, 12th December, 1836. She was graduated from the Cazenovia Seminary in 1853. She subsequently attended the Troy Female Seminary. When but fourteen years of age she opened a Sunday school class in a village adjoining Cazenovia, and that class was the germ which finally grew into a church congregation. When she started her school some of the committeemen came to her and told her that, while they believed her to be qualified in every way to teach, at the same time they would all like it better if she would go home and lengthen her skirts. When twelve years old, she appeared in print in the village paper, the "Madison County Whig," and from that time to the present she has been more or less engaged in literary work on papers and magazines. After her graduation from college she went to Augusta, GA, as a governess in the family of Governor Schley. On the Governor's plantation there were five-hundred or more slaves, and Mrs. Cooper, then Miss Ingersoll, used to gather them about her to teach them the Scriptures. While in Augusta she became the wife of Halsey Fenimore Cooper, also a Cazenovia Seminary graduate, who had been appointed by President Pierce to the office of surveyor and inspector of the port of Chattanooga. Mr. and Mrs. Cooper were living in Chattanooga at the breaking out of the Civil War, but soon after removed to Memphis, where Mr. Cooper was appointed assessor of internal revenue. There Mrs. Cooper was elected president of the Society for the Aid of Refugees. She taught a large Bible class, which comprised from one to three hundred soldiers. In 1869 she removed with her husband to California. Her first Bible class in San Francisco was in the Howard Presbyterian Church, where Dr. Scudder was filling the pulpit. From there she went to the Calvary Presbyterian Church, and still later opened: the class in the First Congregational Church. That class numbered over three-hundred members and embraced persons representing every sect, including even those of the Jewish and the Roman Catholic faith. While the credit of establishing the first free kindergarten in San Francisco is due to Prof. Felix Adler and a few of his friends, yet the credit of the extraordinary growth of the work is almost entirely due to Mrs. Cooper, who paid a visit to the Silver street free kindergarten in November, 1878, and from that moment became the leader of the kindergarten work and the friend of the training school for kindergarten teachers. The rapid growth of the free kindergarten system in California had its first impulse in six articles written by Mrs. Cooper for the San Francisco "Bulletin" in 1879. The first of these was entitled "The Kindergarten, a Remedy for Hoodlumism," and was of vital interest to the public, for just at that time ruffianism was so terrific that a vigilance committee was organized to protect the citizens. The second article was "The History of the Silver Street Free Kindergarten." That aroused immediate interest among philanthropic people. In the early part of 1878 there was not a free kindergarten on the western side of the Rocky Mountains; to-day there are sixty-five in San Francisco, and several others in progress of organization. Outside of San Francisco they extend from the extreme northern part of Washington to Lower California and New Mexico, and they have been formed in Oregon, Nevada and Colorado, and in almost every large city and town in California. In a recent report issued by Mrs. Cooper she attributes the rapid strides in that work in San Francisco to the fact that persons of large wealth have been induced to study the work for themselves, and have become convinced of its permanent and essential value to the State. The second free kindergarten in San Francisco was opened under the auspices of Mrs. Cooper's Bible class, in October, 1879. In 1882 Mrs. Leland Stanford, who had been an active helper in the work from the very first, dedicated a large sum for the establishment of free kindergartens, in San Francisco and in adjacent towns, in memory of her son. Then other memorial kindergartens were endowed. There are now (1892) thirty-two kindergartens under the care of Mrs. Cooper and her daughter, Miss Harriet Cooper. Over $300,000 have been given to Mrs. Cooper to carry on this great work in San Francisco, and over 10,000 little children have been trained in these schools. Her notable and historical trial for heresy in 1881 made her famous as a religious teacher and did much to increase the wide interest in her kindergarten work. Mrs. Cooper is a philanthropist and devotes all her time to benevolent work. She is a director of the Associated Charities, vice-president of the Pacific Coast Women's Press Association, an active member of the Century Club and the leader of one of the largest Bible classes in the country. She possesses great heroism, but is quiet, magnetic and exceedingly sensitive and sympathetic. She is one of the best-known and best-loved women on the Pacific Coast. She was elected a member of the Pan-Republic Congress, one of five women of the world who had that distinguished honor.

COPP, Mrs. Helen Rankin, sculptor, born in Atlanta, Logan county, IL, 4th August, 1853. She is descended from Scotch and German ancestors, who took a leading part in freeing America from the British yoke and from the curse of slavery. Her paternal grandfather, John Rankin, was one of the organizers of the Abolition movement. From her earliest childhood she dreamed of art. Stories and histories of artists were her favorite reading, and she tried to workout her dreams. It was weary labor, for the result was so far from her ideal. The few pictures the little country town afforded were but dreary disappointments. When she was five years old, her parents moved to Loda, IL, where she passed her childhood and early womanhood. At the age of eighteen she attended the opening of the Chicago Exposition and for the first time saw a work of art. She returned home with renewed hope to the work of finding a way in the dark. In 1874 she became the wife of W. H. Copp, of Wolfboro, NH, then engaged in the mercantile business in Loda. In 1884 they moved to Pullman, IL, with one son, leaving four sons lying in the little prairie cemetery. The years of working in the dark were ended. In 1888 Mrs. Copp entered the Art Institute of Chicago. There she soon discovered that sculpture was her forte. Abandoning all thoughts of painting, she plunged into the study of modeling and anatomy with a desperation born of the knowledge that half a lifetime was gone. Entering upon her work at an age when most artists begin to achieve success, she rapidly surmounted all difficulties, allowing herself no rest, even in vacation, and carrying off the honors of her class, until 1890, when she received the only medal ever given by the Art Institute for sculpture. Her instructor said that she had accomplished ten years' work in three. Mrs. Copp then established a studio in Chicago. She has modeled portraits of a number of prominent citizens of that city, besides many ideal works.

CORNELIUS, Mrs. Mary A., temperance reformer, born in Pontiac, MI, 25th September, 1829. Her maiden name was Mary A. Mann. In the veins of both her parents, who were of New England origin, flowed the blood of the Pilgrim Fathers. The child early developed the hereditary trait, a genius for leadership. Her first school composition, written when she was nine years of age, was a hit in the rural community where she lived, and was printed in the local newspaper. In 1850 she became the wife of Rev. S. Cornelius, D D., of Alexandria, VA. Her husband encouraged her in writing short articles for the press on religious and philanthropic subjects, but when, with the cares of motherhood and the responsibilities of her position as a pastor's wife upon her, she brought to his notice a story of thirty-nine long chapters which she had written, he protested against this draft upon her vitality. Although a semi-invalid for many years, she struggled heroically against her weakness and was, as she still is, a moving spirit in Christian and philanthropic enterprises. She was president of the Woman's Christian Temperance Union of Arkansas, in 1885. While leading an effort for prohibition in that State, her course aroused the hostility of the liquor interest. Her life was threatened by the desperate element in the capital of Arkansas, and personal violence was attempted. In spite of all, she persevered in her work. She edited a journal in the interest of the society about the time of her husband's death, in 1886. Her pen has never been quite idle, except since her bereavement. She assisted her husband when he was engaged in editorial work. Her poems, numerous prose articles and voluminous newspaper correspondence testify to her industry. Perhaps the best known of her writings are "Little Wolf," which has had a wide sale, and the poem, "Sweet Marie." With lately renewed health she has resumed literary work. She is now living in Topeka, Kans.

CORNELL, Mrs. Ellen Frances, born in Middleboro, MA, 20th July 1835. She is the daughter of George and Marcia Thompson Atwood, and the youngest of a family of nine children. She is a descendant in the seventh generation from John Atwood, Gentleman, of London, England, who came to Plymouth soon after the landing of the Pilgrims. The first mention of him in the old Colonial Records is made in 1633. Her maternal ancestor, John Thompson, from the north of England, came to Plymouth in May, 1622, in the third embarkation from England. In the troubles with the Indians, the people in the vicinity of his home chose him as their commander, and the Governor and Council of Plymouth gave him a general commission as lieutenant-commandant of the field and garrison and all posts of danger. Ellen attended the district school near her home and public and private schools in New Bedford, and later the academy in Middleboro. She became a teacher, and to that work she gave six years of her life. She became the wife, in February, 1859, of Mark Hollingsworth Cornell, of Bridgewater, MA. Since then they have resided in their pleasant home on the bank of the Taunton river, in one of the most beautiful spots in that region. For many years Mrs. Cornell was an invalid, confined to her home, and for seven years of that time unable to leave her bed. Her interest in the world about her, from which she was isolated, never wearied. The influence of her patient life was felt far beyond the confines of her own room. Her poems have been printed in various papers and magazines. Mrs. Cornell is a member of the New Church. Her summers are now passed in Edgartown, Martha's Vineyard, where she employs many hours of her time in adding to her already large collection of marine shells, which she has carefully classified.

CORONEL, Señora Mariana W. de, Indian curio collector, born in San Antonio, TX, in 1851. There she remained until eight years old, when her parents removed to Los Angeles, CA, and have there resided ever since. Her father, Nelson Williamson, is a hardy New

Englander from Maine, now ninety years old. Her mother is a woman of Spanish descent. Mrs. Coronel possesses the quiet disposition of her mother. She is the oldest of a family of six children. Having from infancy been familiar with the English and Spanish languages, she speaks them with equal fluency, and her knowledge of both has aided her materially while collecting her curios. She became the wife of Don Antonio F. Coronel, a native of Mexico and one of the most prominent participants in the early history of Los Angeles, in 1873. For many years, by travel in Mexico and California and by correspondence they have been collecting Indian and Mexican curiosities and have now one of the best private collections in Los Angeles. They are deeply interested in the mission Indians of California, having joined heart and hand with their friend, Helen Hunt Jackson, in aiding those unfortunates. Mrs. Coronel and her husband are active members of the Historical Society of California.

CORY, Mrs. Florence Elizabeth, industrial designer, born in Syracuse, NY, 4th June, 1851. She is a daughter of Johnson L. Hall. She comes of Revolutionary stock and traces her descent back through those on her father's side, who won distinction worthy of historical mention in the War of 1812, and more notably in the battles of Monmouth and Stony Point in the Revolution, to General Isaac Hall and to Col. Harry Hall. At the age of nineteen she became the wife of Hon. Henry W. Cory, of St. Paul, MN, but in two years returned with her only child, a girl, to reside with her parents. Her education was of that sort so commonly sufficient for the average society girl, but wholly inadequate to meet her great desire of becoming independent. In spite of the fact that she had loving parents and a home replete with all the comforts and luxuries that money and refinement bring, her longing to do for herself could not be conquered, and she was continually casting about for some occupation in which to find support and, possibly, distinction. Noticing how inartistic were the designs on most of the carpets, curtains and tapestries which met her eye, the question arose "why can I not make them better?" Then began her life-work, which

has placed her in the front rank of self-made women and won for her the enviable distinction of being the first practical woman designer in the United States, if not in the world. Mrs. Cory corresponded with leading carpet manufacturers, and they at once recognized the practicability of women designers, and from each she received encouragement and was advised to begin a course of instruction in Cooper Union, New York. That was in the spring, and she found she could not enter the institute till the following autumn. During the summer she employed her time constantly in studying the structure of fabrics by unraveling them and in making original designs, one of which was accepted by a prominent manufacturer, and she was the proud possessor of fifteen dollars, the first money she had earned. On entering Cooper Union in the fall, she found, much to her amazement, that her instructors, while they knew the principles of design and could teach them well, could not at that time teach any practical method of applying those principles to an industrial purpose. She began a course in drawing, of which she felt a great need, and occupied her afternoons in the particular study of carpet designing in the factory of E. S. Higgins, where six weeks of instruction had been offered free. Her improvement was rapid. She subsequently visited the representative factories of nearly every art industry in the United States and thoroughly familiarized herself with the technicalities of design and workings of machinery in each. She became an instructor in Cooper Union in the art she had herself come there to learn but a few months before. That position she was obliged to resign on account of ill health. After spending three years in the West, she returned to New York and established herself as a practical designer. In a short time she received more work than she could do. Much of her time was consumed by women who came to her for information and instruction, which she gave free. On account of the large number who applied to her for help, she set aside certain hours for receiving them, and finally was obliged to give whole afternoons to their service. That was the beginning of the institution now known as the School of Industrial Art and Technical Design for Women, to which for the last twelve years Mrs. Cory has devoted her entire time, attempting but little work not directly devoted to her pupils. By a system of home instruction Mrs. Cory has taught pupils in every

State and Territory in the United States, and several foreign countries. Mrs. Cory is a member of the society of the Daughters of the Revolution, of the Daughters of the American Revolution, and of the Daughters of 1812, and is president of the Society of Industrial Art for Women.

COTES, Mrs. Sara Jeannette Duncan, author and journalist, born in Brantford, Ontario, Canada. in 1862. She is most widely known by her maiden name, Sara Jeannette Duncan. Her father, Charles Duncan, is a merchant of Brantford and a man of wide information and keen intelligence. Her mother is a quick-witted Irish woman. As a child, Miss Duncan was an earnest reader. She received her education in the public schools and collegiate institute of her native town. She fitted herself for a public school-teacher and taught in the Brantford schools for a short time; the work was not congenial, however, and she soon relinquished it. She early began to write verse and prose, and after the usual discouragements she decided to make journalism a stepping-stone to literature. Her first newspaper work was in the year of the Cotton Centennial in New Orleans, whither she went to write descriptive letters for the Toronto "Globe," the Buffalo "Courier," the Memphis "Appeal" and other newspapers. After that she went to Washington, DC, and became a member of the editorial staff of the Washington "Post." Her newspaper experience, especially that in Washington, was of great service to her. Her "copy" was freely and even severely criticised by the editor of the "Post," with the result of improving her manner of writing. Leaving Washington, she joined the staff of the Toronto "Globe," and later that of the Montreal "Star," passing one season in Ottawa as the special correspondent of the "Star." She made a hit with her unconventional book of travels, entitled "A Social Departure; or How Orthodocia and I went Round the World by Ourselves." Her companion on that journey, whom she calls "Orthodocia," was Miss Lily Lewis, a young woman engaged in literary and journalistic work, a contributor to "Galignani" and several London journals. Her next book was "An American Girl in London." On her trip around the earth Miss Duncan met E. C. Cotes in Calcutta, India, and she became his wife within two years after their first meeting. Professor Cotes has a scientific appointment in connection with the Indian Museum, and has acquired considerable reputation in the field of his special research, Indian entomology. They make their home in Calcutta, India.

COUES, Mrs. Mary Emily Bennett, woman suffragist, born in New York City, 26th August, 1835. She was a daughter of Henry Silliman Bennett and Mary Emily Martin Bennett. On her father's side she is a collateral descendant of the famous Aaron Burr, cousin of Mr. Bennett, and is connected with the Silliman family of New Haven, CT, which includes the two Benjamins, father and son, both distinguished scientists. The maternal ancestry includes the name of Foote, honored in New England annals, and of Martin, borne by several officers of high rank in the English navy. Sir Henry Byam Martin, K.C.B., the second son of Admiral Sir Thomas Byam Martin, G.C.B., admiral of the fleet and vice-admiral of the United Kingdom, for many years comptroller of the navy and member of Parliament for Plymouth, who died 21st October, 1854, was Mrs. Bennett's cousin. The Martin family resided in Antigua, where they owned large estates, and Sir William Byam, who died in 1869, was president of the council of Antigua and colonel of the Antigua dragoons. The grandaunts of Mrs. Coues were the Misses Martin, Catherine, Penelope and Eliza, long known in New England for their devotion to education, whose historical school in Portland, ME, attracted pupils from far and wide. A strong character might be expected in a descendant of ancestry which included such marked individualities and developed such diverse tendencies, so it is no wonder that Mrs. Coues has taken a recognized position among those women who represent the advance thought of the day on all the great questions which affect their sex. The child was reared in all the rigor of the Presbyterian creed, which her mind rejected early, and the revolt of her young heart was final. Her education was completed under private tuition in London and Paris, the first of the twenty-four times she has crossed the ocean having been in the vessel that carried to England the news of the firing on Fort Sumter in 1861. Many of her earlier years were passed amid the gaieties of various European capitals, in strong contrast with the severity of her early training, an experience which served to broaden and strengthen her intellectual grasp. She became an accomplished musician, an art critic, a linguist and a brilliant society woman. In Dresden, in Saxony, 28th March, 1866, she became the wife of Joseph W. Bates, a leading merchant of Philadelphia, PA, who died in that city 27th March, 1886. She had no children. Mrs. Bates' twenty years of married life were divided between her homes in Yorkshire, England, and in Philadelphia. She was wealthy and could indulge her tastes for music and art. Her Philadelphia mansion was noted for the elegance and lavishness of its hospitality, its wonderful dinners and one of the finest private collections of paintings in this country. Since her marriage, in Boston, MA, 25th October, 1887, to the well-known scientist and writer, Dr. Elliott Coues, of Washington, DC, she has resided with her husband in their beautiful home on N street in that city, one of the most attractive literary, artistic and scientific centers of the national capital. She is in hearty sympathy with Dr. Coues' published views on the religious and social questions of the day, and her inspiration of one of his books is recognized in its dedication to his wife. Mrs. Coues is at present the secretary of the Woman's National Liberal Union and a prominent member of various other organizations for the promotion of enlightened and progressive thought among women, though she has thus far shrunk from taking the position of a public writer or speaker. Her attitude is that of the extreme wing of radical reform, now being agitated. Though at heart a deeply religious woman, Mrs. Coues has not found church communion necessary to her own spiritual aspirations. Among her dominant traits are a strong, intuitive sense of justice, a quick and tender sympathy for all who suffer wrongs and a never-failing indignation at all forms of conventional hypocrisy, intellectual repression and spiritual tyranny. No one appeals in vain to her sense of right and duty, and many are the recipients of her bounteous secret charities.

COUZINS, Miss Phœbe, lawyer, was born in St. Louis, MO, in 184– and has passed most of her life in that city. On her father's side her ancestry is French Huguenot, and on her mother's side English. She inherits her broad views of justice from both parents. Her mother, Mrs. Adaline Couzins,

was among the first to offer her services as volunteer aid to the Sanitary Commission in the Civil War, and Phœbe also was active in relieving the miseries of the wounded and sick soldiers. They served after many of the great battles of that conflict, and during those years the daughter was studying the question of prevention of war, and she came to the conclusion that woman, clothed with political powers, would be as powerful to prevent war, as, without such powers, she is to ameliorate its horrors and evils. In 1869 her ideas were crystallized in the Woman's Franchise Organization, which included some of the best and most intelligent women of St. Louis. Miss Couzins at that time began to think of entering some profession. Acting on the advice of Judge John M. Krum, she chose law and applied for admission to the Law School of Washington University, in St. Louis, in 1869. She had been educated in the public schools and high school of St. Louis, and the board of directors and the law faculty of the university were familiar with her career. Her application for admission was granted without a dissenting voice, thus giving the St. Louis university the honor of first opening a law-school to the women of the United States. Miss Couzins was an earnest student in the law-school, and she was graduated in 1871, and a public dinner was given to signalize the event. She did not enter largely into the practice of law, but she was one of the few who presented their cases to General Butler, when he was chairman of the judiciary committee of Congress in Washington. In 1876 she entered the lecture field as an advocate of woman suffrage, and her record was a brilliant one. She has been admitted to practice in all the courts of Missouri, in the United States District Court, and in the courts of Kansas and Utah. She has held positions of trust and honor. She was at one time United States Marshal for the Eastern District of Missouri, the first woman in the United States appointed to a federal executive office, receiving her commission from Justice Miller. Two governors of Missouri have appointed her commissioner for that State on the National Board of Charities and Correction. Superintendent of the Eleventh Census Robert P. Porter appointed her manager of the division of mortgage indebtedness for the city of St. Louis. She was appointed in July, 1890, a lady commissioner for Missouri on the World's Fair Board of Directors.

COYRIÈRE, Mrs. E. Miriam, business woman, born in London, England, when her parents were traveling and visiting relatives there. She comes of English ancestry, the Hopkins family on her father's side, who settled in New England and were prominent in the history of the Colonies, and on her mother's side the Archer family, at one time the owners of Fordham Manor, in Westchester county, NY. Lord John Archer received the letters patent on the estate in November, 1671. He was a descendant of Fulbert L'Archer, one of the companions of William the Conquerer. The manor was mortgaged in 1686 to Cornelius Van Steinwyck, a New York merchant, and he left it by will to the Dutch Church of New York. On her mother's side the families have been Episcopalians since the establishment of the Episcopal Church in England; on her father's side they have belonged to the same church for over one-hundred years. Mrs Coyrière's real name is Mrs. Carlos Pardo. She has been twice married. Her husband, Professor Carlos Pardo, is a writer on pedagogy. Both are members of the American Association of Science, and Mrs. Pardo, who has kept her business name, E. Miriam Coyrière, is interested in all the reform movements of the time. She is a member of the National Educational Association, of the Woman's Health Association and of other organizations. She inherits literary talent from her mother, who was both poet and artist. Her father, who was wealthy at the time of his marriage, was a talented and highly educated man, and he turned his attainments to account when his fortune was swept away. He was a fine linguist and an author. Mrs. Coyrière belongs to a family of six children. Her first marriage was unfortunate. Her husband failed, and her parents died and left three young sons to her and her sister's care. She soon set about the work of earning a livelihood for herself and her young charges. Aided by Peter Cooper, she became a teacher, after a course of study in Cooper Institute. To add to her labor, her first hus-

band became an invalid from paralysis. Her only son died in infancy. After teaching for a time, she learned the school furniture business. In 1880 she opened a teachers' agency, that has earned a world-wide reputation. She worked diligently to build it up and has succeeded. She supplies teachers for every grade of educational institution, from colleges down to district schools, and her patrons are in every State of the Union and in Canada, in Central America, Mexico and South America, and she has supplied teachers for European institutions. Her school furniture business has been a part of her work ever since she started in business for herself. In 1884 she displayed furniture and school apparatus at the International Congress in Rio de Janeiro, Brazil, where she won a diploma. Mrs. Coyrière has no living children, but her home life is exceptionally happy. She became the wife of Prof. Carlos Pardo in 1884, and their home is a center of intellectual activity.

CRABTREE, Miss Lotta, actor, born in New York City, 7th November, 1847. Her father was a bookseller in Nassau street, New York, for many years. In 1851 he went to California, where he engaged in gold-mining. His wife and daughter followed him in 1854. They lived in a little loghouse in the mining town, La Porte. Mr. Crabtree was only moderately successful in his search for gold. Lotta showed in childhood the talents which have made her famous. Her first appearance on the stage was in 1855, in an amateur performance in La Porte, in which she appeared as a singer. When she was seven years old, she took lessons in dancing, and she appeared as a singer and dancer in amateur entertainments, and she created a furore among the miners. At the end of one of the performances she was called before the curtain, and a shower of silver dollars and half-dollars greeted her. That event led her to become an actor, and shortly afterward she and her mother started on a tour of California. The bright little star everywhere won encouragement and reputation. She played the part of Gertrude, in the "Loan of a Lover," in Petaluma, in 1858. Her starring tour was made in 1860, and the troupe in which she and her mother played reaped a fortune. Lotta received countless presents, ranging from silver dollars and twenty-dollar gold-pieces up to sets of jewelry and diamond-studded watches. In her early tours she traveled in a suit of boy's clothes, for convenience in making horseback journeys among the mountains. In 1864 Lotta made her debut in New York City, in a spectacular play in Niblo's Garden. She made her first great success in "Little Nell and the Marchioness." She at once took a distinct and high rank as a star in eccentric comedy, and her singing, dancing and drollery, in plays written especially for her, made her one of the leading theatrical stars for years. Her rôles include the "Marchioness," "Topsy," "Sam Willoughby," "Musette," "Bob," "Firefly," "Zip," "Nitouche" and "The Little Detective." Of the last-named play, Lotta says: "I have played it season after season and year after year, until I am really ashamed to show my face in it upon the stage again. That play has always been a great hit, and it has brought me no end of money. We paid just twenty-five cents for it, the cost of the book from which it was adapted to me, and we have made thousands upon thousands out of it." Lotta has played successful engagements in England. She has always been accompanied by her mother, who has successfully managed her financial affairs. Lotta's earnings have been large, and her investments represent about a million dollars. During 1891 and 1892 she did not play, but it is not her intention to retire from the stage yet. Besides her dramatic talent, she possesses a decided talent for art. She has been a student and hard worker, and her example has been powerful in winning public respect for the stage and for actors.

CRAIG, Mrs. Charity Rusk, national president of the Woman's Relief Corps, was born in Morgan county, OH, about 1851, and went with her parents to Wisconsin when about three years of age. Her father is Jeremiah M. Rusk, ex-governor of Wisconsin and a member of President Harrison's cabinet. Her mother's maiden name was Mary Martin, the present wife of the secretary of agriculture being her step-mother. At the age of thirteen years Charity Rusk entered a Catholic school, St. Clare Academy, where she remained for one year. She then entered a private school in Madison, WI, and from that went to the University of Wisconsin, where she was graduated and afterward continued Latin and literature. She has had systematic studies every year since she left school, not neglecting them even during the four years spent in Washington, DC, when her father was a member of Congress, and she had a brilliant social career. In 1875 she became the wife of a classical student of the Wisconsin University, Elmer H. Craig. They spent a year in Milwaukee, WI, and a year in Boston, MA. Mr. Craig was connected with the United States Pension Department. Resigning his position in order to connect himself with the banking firm of Lindeman & Rusk, he moved to Viroqua, WI. where Mrs. Craig has since been the center of a coterie of distinguished people. In Viroqua is the Rusk homestead, which in summer is always sought by the Secretary of Agriculture and his family and more intimate friends. Mrs. Craig, after having long been quite prominently identified with various local charities and conspicuously interested in women's organizations, became a charter member of the Woman's Relief Corps, auxiliary to the Grand Army of the Republic. She was first president of the corps in Viroqua, then president of the State department, and was finally elected the national president. While serving as department president, she visited many places in the State for the purpose of awakening the interest of the Woman's Relief Corps and the G. A. R. in the Veterans' Home in Waupaca, WI. As national president she consolidated the work and introduced a new system of accounts, which was more successful. She was instrumental in extending the work into the new States, and laid the foundations for a wide increase of membership. She is a model presiding officer, conducting the deliberations of a large convention with grace and dignity. She admits that she likes to talk to bodies of women.

CRANE, Mrs. Mary Helen Peck, church and temperance worker, born in Wilkes Barre, PA, 10th April, 1827. She was the only daughter of Rev. George Peck, D. D., of the Methodist Episcopal Church, the well-known author and editor. She became the wife of the late Rev. Jonathan Townsley Crane, D. D., when twenty years of age, and was the mother of fourteen children. She was a devoted wife and mother and was energetic in assisting her husband in his work in the church and among the poor. Mrs. Crane was an ardent temperance worker and, as her children grew up, she devoted much time to the work of the Woman's Christian Temperance Union. Mrs. Crane delivered addresses on several occasions before the members of the New Jersey Legislature, when temperance bills were pending, and she greatly aided the men who were fighting to secure good laws. As the pioneer of press-work by women at the Ocean Grove Camp Meeting, she did valuable work, and her reports for the New York "Tribune" and the New York Associated Press, during the last ten years of the great religious and temperance gatherings at the noted Mecca of the Methodists, are models of their kind. For about ten years she was the State superintendent of press for New Jersey of the Woman's Christian Temperance Union. She wrote several leaflets that were of great value to the press-workers of the local unions. For over a half-century Mrs. Crane was an active member of the Methodist Episcopal Church. She led the life of a sincere Christian and died 7th December, 1891, after a short illness contracted at the National convention of the Woman's Christian Temperance Union in Boston. One daughter and six sons survive her.

CRANE, Mrs. Ogden, concert singer and musical educator, born in Brooklyn, NY, in 1850. She received her musical education in New York. She studied for six years under Antonio Barilli, and for five years under William Courtney. She adopted the pure Italian method and style of singing. Her voice is a dramatic soprano of wide range, and she is a successful singer. She has occupied many important positions as a member of the choirs in the South Congregational Church, Brooklyn, in St. Ann's Church, the Church of the Puritans and St. James's Methodist Episcopal Church, New York. She is well known on the concert stage, having traveled over nearly every state in the Union, and in 1890 made a tour through the South with her sisters, who are known as the Mundell Quartet. Her repertory of oratorios and standard concert pieces is very large, and during her career she has won for herself an enviable reputation. As an instructor she has been especially

successful; she has a large number of pupils, both professional and amateur, from all parts of the country. In conscientious work lies the secret of her success.

CRANE, Mrs. Sibylla Bailey, composer, born in Boston, MA, 30th July, 1851. She has always lived in that city with her parents. On the maternal side she is a descendant of Rev. Dr. Joseph Bellamy, the eminent theologian, and on the paternal side her ancestry runs back to the Mayflower Pilgrims. She became the wife of Rev. Oliver Crane, D.D., LL.D., in September, 1891. Mrs. Crane is deeply interested in the work of the philanthropists of Boston. She is an active member of the Women's Educational and Industrial Union, and an officer of the Beneficent Society whose members aid talented and needy students to pass the course of study in the New England Conservatory of Music. She is a worker in the church and is a member of the committee of the General Theological Library. She has always been a student of music, language and literature. Among her works as a composer are music for some of the poems of Bryant, Whittier and Longfellow. Her musical compositions have been sung by her in the prisons and hospitals which she has visited in her philanthropic work. She has traveled extensively in America and in Europe, and her impressions of Europe are recorded in her book, "Glimpses of the Old World." One of her most valuable papers is her history of music, which she prepared to read before the Home Club of Boston. That lecture covers the whole field of music, in its historical phases, from the early Egyptians down to the present. Mrs. Crane uses her noble voice and fine musical training with good effect in illustrating the music of the various nations, while delivering this lecture. She has given this and other lectures before many of the principal educational institutions of Massachusetts.

CRANMER, Mrs. Emma A., temperance reformer and woman suffragist, born in Mt. Vernon, WI, 2nd October, 1858. She is the daughter of Dr. J. L. Powers, was educated in Cornell College, and began to teach school when fifteen years old.

In 1880 she became the wife of D. N. Goodell, who died in 1882. Three years later she was united in marriage to Hon. S. H. Cranmer, and their home is in Aberdeen, SD. They have one child, a daughter, Frances Willard Cranmer. Mrs. Cranmer has been a member of the Methodist Episcopal Church since her early childhood, and is a class-leader in her church. She has written much for the press, both in prose and verse. She has lectured on literary subjects and on temperance in many of the cities and towns of the Northwest. As an orator she is eloquent and winning. She is in earnest worker in the white-ribbon movement, with which she has been connected for years, and is president of the South Dakota Woman's Christian Temperance Union. In equal suffrage she is profoundly interested, and is president of the South Dakota Equal Suffrage Association. She is a woman of strong convictions, and a cause must appeal to her judgment and sense of right in order to enlist her sympathy.

CRAWFORD, Mrs. Alice Arnold, poet, born in Fond du Lac, WI, 10th February, 1850. At an early age she gave promise of brilliancy of mind and facility of expression. Her youthful talent was carefully fostered and encouraged, both by a judicious mother and by her friends. Her father, a man of sterling qualities of mind and heart, died when she was but four years old. At sixteen she was graduated from the high school in Fond du Lac, with honors. For several years after her graduation she taught in the public school and gave lessons in music. At the same time she wrote for the papers of her city, in one of which she had a regular department, besides furnishing several continued stories. Her poems and short sketches were published by various periodicals. When the Grand Duke Alexis visited Milwaukee, WI, she was called upon and furnished the poem of welcome. In September, 1872, she became the wife of C. A. Crawford, a banker of Traverse City, MI, and that place was her happy home for two years before her death, which occurred in September, 1874. The year following an edition of her poems was issued in Chicago, and a second edition was published a few years later. Mrs. Crawford's whole life was in itself a poem. She left one child, a daughter, who inherits her mother's poetic temperament and bids fair to become as graceful a writer.

CRAWFORD, Mrs. John, newspaper correspondent, born near Syracuse, NY, 21st July, 1850. She is of German descent, her maiden name being Quackenbush. At an early age her family removed to Canada, and for several years resided in Consecon, Ont., where Miss Quackenbush attended a grammar school. She lived in Michigan for some time, and while there she was engaged in teaching. It was at that time she commenced to contribute to the literary press. In 1869 she returned to Canada, locating in Newtonville, Ontario. Writing for various Canadian and American newspapers was there a pleasant pastime. In 1871 she became the wife of John Crawford, of Clarke, Ontario. For a few years her literary efforts were rather desultory, owing to domestic cares. She has two children, a boy and girl. In 1887 an entire summer's illness afforded leisure for literary work, and since that time more or less writing for the press has occupied her time, and always under the assumed title, "Maude Moore." Her present residence is in Bowmanville, Ontario.

CRAWFORD, Mrs. Mary J., church organizer and worker, born in Great Valley, Cattaraugus county, NY, 15th April, 1843. Her maiden name was Mary Mudgett. She became the wife of William L. Crawford, 11th June, 1866. His business called him to Florida in 1883, and they built a home on the St. John river, in South Jacksonville, a suburb of Jacksonville. Their family consists of one son. Mrs. Crawford's time and means have been given to further the work of the Episcopal Church, of which she is a devoted member. As soon as they were settled in their Florida home, the need of a church was forced upon her attention. Services were held in the ferry waiting-room, and later services were held regularly in her home for several months. Mrs. Crawford at once started a project to secure a church. She opened a Sunday school with six or eight pupils and about as many teachers. In a short time the school grew, and it was necessary to rent a room for the work. Increased attendance followed. Mrs. Crawford circulated a subscription list and personally secured the money needed to erect a new church building. The new building was dedicated as All Saints Episcopal Church on Whitsunday, in 1888, Bishop Weed, of Florida, officiating. In the new and handsome structure the church has prospered greatly, largely through Mrs. Crawford's work. At present her home is in St. Augustine, FL, where she is an active member of Trinity Church, and the directress of the Ladies' Auxiliary Society of the parish.

CROLY, Mrs. Jennie Cunningham, pioneer woman journalist, was born in Market-Harborough, Leicestershire, England, 19th December, 1831. Her father was a Unitarian minister, descended from Scotch ancestors who left Scotland with James I and settled in England. Her mother belonged to an old country family. Her father, Rev. Joseph Howes Cunningham, brought his family to the United States when Jennie was about nine years old. He was a man of pronounced views, and he had made himself unpopular by preaching and lecturing on temperance in his native town. On account of his obnoxious temperance views his English neighbors once mobbed his house, and his children were assaulted on their way to school. He had visited the United States before settling here. Jennie inherited her father's traits of character. She was a precocious child and early showed her literary trend in little plays written in childhood. Her first production that was published appeared in the New York "Tribune." Her taste for journalism grew rapidly, and she at an early age took a position on the New York "Sunday Dispatch," at a salary of three dollars a week. Soon after she took a position on the New York "Sunday Times," at a salary of five dollars a week. That position she held for five years, doing general work in the line of items for women readers. She soon became a correspondent of the New Orleans "Delta" and the Richmond "Whig,"

an editorial writer on the "Democratic Review" and a regular contributor to the "Round Table." In 1856 she invented the duplicate system of correspondence and became one of the editors and the dramatic critic of the "Sunday Times." Her activity was remarkable. She became editor of the fashion department of "Frank Leslie's Magazine" and wrote the fashions for "Graham's Magazine." She aided in starting Madame Demorest's "Mirror of Fashions," a quarterly, which she wrote entirely for four years, and which was consolidated with the "Illustrated News" and became "Demorest's Illustrated Magazine." She edited it for twenty-seven years, and also started and controlled other minor publications for the same house. She introduced many novelties in New York journalism. Early in life she became the wife of David G. Croly, then city editor of the New York "Herald," on which paper she did much work. In 1860 her husband was chosen managing editor of the New York "World," just started, and Mrs. Croly took charge of the department relating to women, which she controlled until 1872, and during eight years of that time she did similar work for the New York "Times." When the "Daily Graphic" was started in New York, Mr. Croly became its editor, and Mrs. Croly transferred her services to that journal. During those busy years she corresponded for more than a score of prominent journals in different States, and she is still serving many of them in that capacity. Her work throughout has had the distinct aim of building up the intellectual status of women. Her ideas have taken form in the organization of women's clubs and societies. In March, 1868, Mrs. Croly, "Fanny Fern," Alice and Phœbe Cary, Mrs. Charlotte B. Wilbour, Miss Kate Field, Mrs. Henry M. Field, Mrs. Botta and other women met in Mrs. Croly's home in New York and started Sorosis, with twelve charter members. Alice Cary was chosen president, Mrs. Croly vice-president, Kate Field corresponding secretary, and Mrs. Wilbour treasurer and recording secretary. The New York Press Club invited Sorosis to a "Breakfast," at which the ladies had nothing to do but sit and eat. Sorosis, in return, invited the Press Club to a "Tea," and there the men had to sit and listen while the women did all the talking. The women were soon recognized, and Sorosis grew in numbers and influence. Alice Cary resigned the presidency at the end of the first year, and Mrs. Croly was unanimously elected in her place. She served fourteen years. She was among those calling woman's congress in New York, in 1856, and again in 1869. In 1887 she bought a half interest in "Godey's Lady's Book," and served as editor of that journal. She resigned that position and started a monthly publication, the "Cycle," in New York. That journal was consolidated with the "Home Magazine," and Mrs. Croly is at present the editor of that periodical. She was chosen president of the Women's Endowment Cattle Company, originated by Mrs. Newby. That company, incorporated under the laws of New Jersey, had a capital stock of $1,500,000 and controled 2,000,000 acres of grazing land in New Mexico, with thousands of head of cattle. Mrs. Croly has a pleasant home in New York City. Her family consists of one son and one daughter. She has contributed largely to scientific journals. She is a member of the New York Academy of Sciences, a member of the Goethe Club and vice-president of the Association for the Advancement of the Medical Education of Women. Her home has for years been a center of attraction for authors, artists, actors and cultured persons. Her writings would fill many volumes. Her published books are "Talks on Women's Topics" (1863), "For Better or Worse" (1875), "Three Manuals of Work" (1885–89). In nearly all of Mrs. Croly's literary correspondence she has used the pen-name, "Jenny June."

CROSBY, Fanny J., blind song-writer, born in 1823. For over a half-century she has been singing in her blindness, and her songs have gone around the earth, been tranlated into many languages and been sung in every land. Miss Crosby showed her talent for versification in childhood. At the age of eight years she composed verses that were remarkable in their way. She was educated in a school for the blind, and she became a teacher in the Institution for the Blind in New York City. While engaged there, she wrote the words for many of the songs composed by George F. Root, the well-known musician. Among these were some that became very widely known, including, "Hazel Dell," "Rosalie, the Prairie Flower," "Proud World, Good-bye, I'm Going Home," "Honeysuckle Glen" and "There's Music in the Air." She wrote the words for the successful cantatas, "The Pilgrim Fathers" and "The Flower Queen." Her most famous hymn, "Safe in the Arms of Jesus," was written in 1868. That hymn

is her favorite. In the same year she wrote that other famous hymn, "Pass Me Not, O Gentle Savior." Every year she has added new songs of remarkable power and taking qualities to her long list of productions. Her "Rescue the Perishing," "Jesus, Keep Me Near the Cross," and "Keep Thou My Way, O Lord," appeared in 1869. The last named song was set to music and used for years as the prayer-song in the Mayflower Mission connected with Plymouth Church, Brooklyn, NY. In 1871 she wrote "The Bright Forever," in 1873 "Close to Thee," in 1874 "O, Come to the Savior," "Like the Sound of Many Waters" and "Savior, More than Life to Me." In 1875 she wrote "I am Thine, O Lord," "So Near to the Kingdom," and "O, my Savior, Hear Me." She has always been known as Fanny J. Crosby, but her name since her marriage has been Van Alstyne. She lives in New York City. It is estimated that the hymns from her pen number over 2,500, and in addition to that wonderful total must be considered the many secular songs, cantatas and other lyrical productions which have appeared under her name or anonymously. One house has published 1,900 of her productions. No complete collection of her verses has yet been made.

CROSS, Mrs. Kate Smeed, social leader, born near Philadelphia, PA, 18th November, 1859. In 1869 she went with her parents to reside in Lawrence, Kans., where the next seven years were spent in school and studying in the University of Kansas. In 1876 she returned to Philadelphia and devoted herself industriously to the study of music, art and the great exhibition. In 1880 she returned to her Kansas home and in that year became the wife of Charles S. Cross, a banker and business man of Emporia, Kans., where in their charming home, "Elmwood," Mr. and Mrs. Cross, with their little daughter live and dispense hospitality. Nature has endowed Mrs. Cross with large gifts, and these gifts are ever made to administer generously to the welfare of those about her and to the help of every good cause. She is an efficient officer of nearly every art, musical and literary circle of Emporia and is a staunch church woman, a member of the Episcopal Church. Some of the finest classic musical entertainments given in Emporia have been given under her direction, she herself taking leading parts in such operas as the "Bohemian Girl" and showing herself possessed of histrionic ability.

CRUGER, Miss Mary, novelist, born in Oscawana, NY, 9th May, 1834. She belongs to the well-known Cruger family of English descent, whose members have always held distinguished positions in American society, since the days when Henry Cruger, who with Edmund Burke represented the City of Bristol in the British Parliament, zealously and ably advocated the cause of American independence. Miss Cruger is one of the children of the late Nicholas Cruger, of Westchester county, New York. Her father was educated in West Point and held the position of captain in the 4th Infantry of the regular army at the time of his marriage to Miss Eliza Kortright, daughter of Captain Kortright, of the British Army. He shortly afterward left the army and built a house in Oscawana, on the Hudson. There most of the children were born and grew up, till the death of both parents broke up the family circle. Shortly afterward Miss Cruger built a house near Montrose, NY, where she has since resided, and where most of her literary work has been accomplished. At her home, called "Wood Rest," she lives a unique and poetical life. Miss Cruger's first published work was "Hyperæsthesia" (New York, 1885). Her next book was called "A Den of Thieves, or the Lay-Reader of St. Marks" (New York, 1886). She then published her third novel, "The Vanderheyde Manor-House" (New York, 1887), which was followed by "How She Did It" (New York, 1888). "How She Did It" was a great success, and gave Miss Cruger a personal as well as an extended literary fame. "Brotherhood" (Boston, 1891) is her latest publication. Humanity is her watchword and inspiration. Tragic as must always be the result of such short-sighted struggles as those that occur between labor and capital, that story goes far toward solving a great problem.

CRUGER, Mrs. S. Van Rensselaer, novelist and social leader, born in Paris, France. She is a daughter of Thomas Wentworth Storrow, who spent the greater part of his life in France. The Wentworths were of New England. Her mother was a daughter of Daniel Paris, a well-known lawyer of Albany, NY, and for many years a member of the New York legislature. Mrs. Storrow was the favorite niece of Washington Irving, and a diamond, which he gave her when she was married in his Sunnyside home, is now in Mrs. Cruger's possession. Mrs. Cruger is the wife of Colonel S. Van Rensselaer Cruger, a member of one of the old Knickerbocker families of New York, and they make their home in that city and in a pleasant place called "Idlesse Farm" on Long Island. Mrs. Cruger has long been known as a social leader, and during the last three or four years she has won a most remarkable success as a novelist. She is a master of French, having spoken only that language until she was nine years of age, and, with her liberal education, her long residence abroad, and her experience in many spheres of life, she unites a distinctly literary talent that has enabled her to cast her stories in artistic form, while preserving in them a most intense humanity. Her novels have been published under the pen-name "Julien Gordon," and the critics, without exception, supposed "Julien Gordon" to be a man. Her novels are "A Diplomat's Diary," "A Successful Man," "Mademoiselle Réséda" and "A Puritan Pagan," all of which appeared as serials first and then in volumes. All have passed through many editions. She has written some poetry, but she has never published or even kept any of her verses.

CUINET, Miss Louise Adèle, doctor of dental surgery, born in Hoboken, NJ, 29th November, 1855. She is of French parentage. On the maternal side she is a descendant of the Huguenot Humberts, a family of local eminence in Neuchâtel, where they sought refuge in the sixteenth century. Upon her decision to adopt dentistry as a profession, Dr. Cuinet realized that, in addition to the ordinary obstacles presented to youth and inexperience, she might also encounter the prejudice which confronts every woman who ventures upon an innovation and threatens to invade a field considered the exclusive province of men. She therefore determined to equip herself with great thoroughness. With that view, after completing the course in one of the best New York schools, she studied two years with a prominent dentist in that city, preparatory to entering, in 1881, the Pennsylvania College of Dental Surgery. That institution graduated one woman about twenty-six years ago and then closed its doors against women for eight years, until Dr. Truman became dean. Dr. Cuinet was graduated in 1883, in high standing, taking one of the first places in a class of fifty-nine. She is the one woman belonging to the Second District Dental Society of New York, and the only one practicing in Brooklyn. With very engaging personal qualities she unites great skill and conscientious devotion to her work. These have won for her a high place in the estimation of professional experts, and the confidence and esteem of a large and increasing clientage. Her success in a vocation generally repugnant to feminine sensibilities represents extraordinary natural qualifications and great industry. She is a master of her profession in all its branches. Dr. Cuinet has always been distinguished by an ardent love of outdoor games and sports, in many of which she excels.

CULTON, Miss Jessie F., journalist, born in Henry, IL, 14th February, 1860. Her grandfather on her father's side was a native of Tennessee. On her mother's side she is descended from the Blanchards of Massachusetts. Mr. and Mrs. Culton moved to Chicago when Jessie was but a few months old, and there she grew up. She removed to Richmond, IN, in 1883, and took a position on the editorial staff of the "Register," in which capacity she served nearly a year, in the meantime doing reportorial work on the "Palladium" and "Item," daily papers of Richmond. In 1884 she went to California with her father, as Mr. Culton's health demanded a change of climate. They traveled extensively throughout the State, and settled in San Diego, where they built a pleasant home. She also has a home on a ranch in Garden Grove. Her duties as housekeeper prevent, to some extent, her journalistic work, but she contributes articles to St. Louis, Chicago and other eastern papers.

CUMINGS, Mrs. Elizabeth, see PIERCE, MRS. ELIZABETH CUMINGS.

CUMMINGS, Mrs. Alma Carrie, journalist, born in Columbia, NH, 21st March, 1857. Her father, Abner L. Day, was a farmer in moderate circumstances, and she had only the advantages in childhood of a common-school education. On 27th January, 1875, she became the wife of Edwin S. Cummings, at that time a compositor in the office of the "Northern Sentinel." A little later that paper was consolidated with the Colebrook "Weekly News," the result being the "News and Sentinel." Mr. Cummings in 1885 purchased the plant and, until his death, two years later, Mrs. Cummings went daily to the office and materially aided her husband in advancing the prosperity of the new paper. His sudden death left the business in what Mrs. Cummings aptly termed the "usual unsettled condition of a country newspaper office. Instead of disposing of the property at a sacrifice, she determined to hold it and, if possible, improve it, and in that endeavor she has succeeded far beyond her expectations. As editor and proprietor she has enlarged the circulation, increased the volume of news, secured more advertising, and in short has made the "News and Sentinel" a valuable paper for northern New Hampshire. Mrs. Cummings has two children, and to these and to her paper she devotes her life and energies.

CUMMINS, Mrs. Mary Stuart, educator, born in Jonesborough, TN, 31st May, 1854. Her maiden name was Mary Stuart Slemons. Her parents were strict Presbyterians of the old style, and the seven children were reared in that faith. Mary, the fourth child, was reared and educated to graduation at sixteen years of age in her native town. Ambitious to go beyond the academic course, she pushed her way, by her own efforts, to the attainment of a full diploma of the Augusta Female Seminary, Staunton, VA. Returning to

Tennessee in 1874, she began to teach in the high school in Knoxville, where as teacher and principal she remained until 1886, meanwhile, in 1877, having become the wife of W. F. Cummins, a merchant of that city. Mrs. Cummins found her greatest pleasure in the school-room, yet finding time to enter other fields of labor, as well as to enjoy social pleasures. A very large mission Sunday-school was a part of her work. She was the president of the Synodical Missionary Society and a State member of the executive board of Home Missions of New York for the Presbyterian Church. An effort was made to place her in charge of school interests in Mexico, but that did not seem to be compatible with her other duties. In 1886, partly for her husband's health and partly from the energetic spirit of both, Mr. and Mrs. Cummins accepted business engagements in Helena, Mont., where they now reside. Mrs. Cummins was teacher and principal in the Helena high school for five years. Since going to Montana she has received every token of a high appreciation of her religious character in the public work to which she has been called along that line. She was chosen by her co-laborers successively vice-president and president of the Montana State Teachers' Association. In temperance work she has taken a leading part and is now filling her second year as president of Montana Woman's Christian Temperance Union. In 1891, she was commissioned by Miss Willard as national organizer for the vacation months, to work in Montana, and she traveled over a large part of the State, organizing new unions. Partly as a result of that tour, the banner presented by Miss Willard for the largest percentage of gain in membership in the Western States was given to Montana in 1891. In September, 1891, Mrs. Cummins entered the Montana University, in Helena, as preceptress, in charge of the young ladies' department and professor of Latin and modern languages.

CUNNINGHAM, Mrs. Annie Sinclair, religious worker, born in the West Highlands, Scotland, 29th October, 1832. Her maiden name was Annie Campbell Fraser Sinclair. Her father, Rev. John C. Sinclair, a Presbyterian clergyman, was married in 1822 to Miss Mary Julia McLean, who was by close relationship allied to the noble houses of Duart and Lochbuy. There were nine children,

of whom Annie was the fifth. Only five of the number lived to mature age. While the children were young, the parents emigrated to Nova Scotia, and removed a few years later to Prince Edward's Island, where ten happy years were spent by her father in home missionary work. To secure a more liberal education for their children, the family went to Newburyport, MA, in 1852, where Annie was admitted to the girls' high school. Young as Annie was when the family left Scotland, she could read and speak two languages, Gaelic and English, though she had never been to school, except the home school in the manse. At the early age of eleven years she made a public profession of her faith and became a member of the church of which her father was the pastor. When her two brothers, the late Rev. James and Alexander Sinclair, were ready to study theology, choice was made of the Western Theological Seminary, in Allegheny, and the family removed to Pittsburgh, PA, in 1854. Four years later Annie became the wife of Rev. David Ayers Cunningham, who was at the time pastor of the Presbyterian Church, of Bridgewater, PA. There their only child was born and buried. In 1864 Dr. Cunningham was called to Philadelphia, where he was for twelve years a successful pastor. During those twelve years there came a period of great activity among the women of the various denominations. When the Woman's Foreign Missionary Society of the Presbyterian Church was organized in 1870 she was one of its founders, and is still one of its officers. The Woman's Christian Association of Philadelphia came into existence about the same time. Mrs. Cunningham was the first chairman of its nominating committee, and was thus intimately associated with Christian women of every name in the city. She was for a time an officer in the organization of the women of Philadelphia for the Centennial Exhibition of 1876. From her young womanhood to later years she has been a faithful and successful Bible-class teacher. In 1876 Dr. Cunningham accepted a call to the First Presbyterian Church of Wheeling, WV. New work was found there with capable women ready to be organized for Christian labor, and for fifteen years she has been the president of a missionary society which includes all the women and children of the thirty-nine churches in the Presbytery of Washington. For nearly ten years she has been one of the secretaries of the Chautauqua Missionary Institute, in which women of all denominations meet annually. She is also an enthusiastic admirer of the Chautauqua Literary and Scientific Circle, and completed the course of reading in 1888. She was chief officer of the Woman's Christian Association of Wheeling, and is the president of the West Virginia Home for Aged and Friendless Women. There is a great deal of work done which does not come under the public eye, and Mrs. Cunningham invariably insists that much of the activity in which she has had the privilege of engaging could not have been successfully carried on, but for the cooperation of him who has been for more than thirty years her husband and pastor.

CUNNINGHAM, Miss Susan J., educator, born in Harford county, MD, 23rd March, 1842. On her mother's side she is of Quaker blood. Her mother died in 1845, and Susan was left to the care of her grandparents. She attended a Friends' school until she was fifteen years old, when it was decided that she should prepare for the work of teaching. She was sent to a Friends' boarding school in Montgomery county, for a year, when family cares called her home, and she continued her studies in the school near by. At nineteen she became a teacher, and she has taught ever since, with the exception of two years, one of which she spent in the Friends' school in Leghorne, or Attleboro, and the other in Vassar College. She has spent her summer vacations in study. She studied in Harvard College observatory in the summers of 1874 and 1876, in Princeton observatory in 1881, in Williamstown in 1883 and 1884, under Prof. Safford, and in Cambridge, England, in 1877, in 1878, in 1879 and in 1882, under a private tutor. In 1887 she studied in the observatory in Cambridge, England, and in 1892 she spent the summer in the Greenwich, England, observatory. When Swarthmore College was established in Swarthmore, PA, in 1869, she was selected teacher of mathematics, Professor Smith now of Harvard being nominally professor. Professor Smith was called to Harvard at the close of the first year, since which time she has had entire charge of the department of pure mathematics,

having been made full professor in 1875. In late years she has had charge of the observatory, which was built with funds secured by her own exertions. She is a thoroughly successful educator, and her conduct of her departments shows that a woman can be quite as efficient as a man in the realm of mathematics and astronomy.

CUNNYNGHAM, Mrs. Elizabeth Litchfield, missionary and church worker, born in Abingdon, VA, 23rd February, 1831. Her maiden name was Elizabeth King Litchfield. Her parents were of old Virginia stock, true in all respects to the family history and traditions. Miss Litchfield received the best elementary training which the country could afford, and, when sufficiently advanced, was placed in Science Hill Academy, under the care of Mrs. Julia A. Tevis. While in that school she was converted and became an earnest and active Christian. After her return to Virginia she taught school, not from necessity, but of choice, her father having ample means. She felt it to be her duty to engage in some useful occupation, and she saw no position more promising than that of a teacher of young people. In March, 1851, she became the wife of Rev. W. G. E. Cunnyngham, a minister of the Methodist Episcopal Church, South, and in 1852 sailed from New York with her husband for Shanghai, China, as a missionary to the Chinese. She remained in the mission field nine years, when the failure of her health compelled her to return to her native land. During her stay in China she studied diligently, and with uncommon success, the Chinese language. She superintended native mission schools, instructed Chinese women and children orally, and translated into the local dialect tracts and small books, some of which have remained in use to the present time. A native woman, for years employed as a "Bible woman" by the mission in Shanghai, was brought to a knowledge of the gospel by Mrs. Cunnyngham's personal efforts. After she returned to America, she lost nothing of her missionary spirit, but labored as far as she had opportunity in the home work, doing all she could to awaken a deeper interest among her own people in the cause of foreign missions. When the Woman's

Board of Foreign Missions of the Methodist Episcopal Church, South, was organized, she was made one of the managers, a position she has held ever since. She was elected editor of leaflets by the board, and for six years discharged with acceptability the duties of that office. In addition to her labors in the missionary cause, she is an active Sunday-school teacher, an efficient helper in local church work, and a practical friend of the poor. She has traveled much. Her husband having been elected to one of the editorial chairs of the Methodist Episcopal Church, South, she removed to Nashville, TN, in 1875, and still resides in that city.

CURRAN, Mrs. Ida M., journalist and editor, was born in Waterbury, VT. When a mere child, her family removed to Boston and afterward to Woburn, MA. She early showed a marked talent for literary work, and at school won her highest standing in rhetoric and literature. This proficiency in composition gained for her one of the four class honors in the Woburn high school when she graduated. She contributed largely to the Grattan "Echo," and afterward became the wife of the publisher of the paper, F. P. Curran. Household duties compelled Mrs. Curran to withdraw for a time from literary labors, but in 1888 she once more became associated with newspaper work, her articles appearing in the Woburn "City Press," of which journal she assumed entire control in 1890. Mrs. Curran is a member of the New England Woman's Press Association. She is an accomplished violinist and an amateur actress. In addition to her newspaper duties, she presides over a charming home, and personally directs the education of her three children.

CURTIS, Mrs. Martha E. Sewall, woman suffragist, born in Burlington, MA, 18th May, 1858. She is descended from one of the oldest families of New England. Among her ancestors were Chief Justice Samuel Sewall, of witchcraft fame, and his son, Rev. Joseph Sewall, minister of the Old South Church, Boston. On her grandmother's side she is descended from Henry Dunster, first president of Harvard College. She was graduated from Cambridge high school in 1874, the youngest of her class. She subsequently pursued the study of various literary branches and accomplishments. For several years she was a teacher, and at one time was on the school committee of her native town. She became the wife of Thomas S. Curtis, 3rd July, 1879. They had two children, both of whom died in infancy. Her husband died 27th December, 1888. He fully sympathized with his wife in her literary and reformatory work. After her marriage she took a full course in elocution at the New England Conservatory and was graduated in 1883. She afterward spent a year in the study of oratory to fit herself for public speaking. A firm believer in the equality of the sexes, she began when quite young to work for the enfranchisement of women. Her first appearance as a public lecturer was in the meetings of the National Woman Suffrage Association in Boston and elsewhere. In 1889 she was appointed State lecturer of the Massachusetts Woman Suffrage Association, and in that capacity addressed many public meetings in different parts of the State. She has also done much work for the reform by contributing articles to the newspapers. She edits a weekly woman's column in the Woburn "News," and she is president of the Woburn Equal Suffrage League. She has been active in urging women to vote for the school committee, the only form of suffrage granted to them in Massachusetts. She is a thorough believer in temperance, but holds that the best way to obtain good laws is to put the ballot into the hands of women as well as men. From her grandfather, Rev. Samuel Sewall, a famous antiquarian of the past generation, she has inherited a taste for historical research. She has recently written a history of her own town for the "History of Middlesex County."

CUSHMAN, Miss Charlotte Saunders, actor, born in Boston, MA, 23rd July, 1816, died in Boston, 18th February, 1876. Miss Cushman was descended from two families of prominence in early New England. She was eighth in descent from Robert Cushman, the preacher who delivered the first sermon ever heard in New England. Her mother's ancestry ran back to the Puritan Babbits. The house in which Charlotte was born stood on the site of the present Cushman School, which was built in 1869. The school was named after her. Her early ambition was to become an operatic singer, and she made her début as a singer in Boston, in April, 1835, where she sang in a concert. After some experience as a singer in New Orleans, she decided to go on the dramatic stage. She at once began to study for the stage, and made her début as Lady Macbeth in New Orleans, in 1835. She made a good impression and played in a variety of characters, at first with no distinct preference for any particular line of drama, and finally settled on tragedy and Shakespearean rôles, in which she won her greatest fame. She was a charming comedian always, but her commanding talents drew her irresistibly to the higher walks of the profession. Her first appearance in New York City was in Lady Macbeth, 12th September, 1836, and she at once took a leading rank. After playing throughout the United States, always with growing power and reputation, she went to London, England, were she made her début in Bianca, 14th February, 1845. She returned to the United States in 1850, and played a second season in England in 1853. She played important engagements in the United States in 1857 and 1858, and again in 1860 and 1861. In addition to her stage work she won fame as a reader. She gave her first public reading in October, 1870, in New York. Her last appearance in New York was 7th November, 1874, and in Boston, 15th May, 1875. Her last appearance as a public reader was in Easton, PA, 2nd June, 1875. She was an ardent patriot, and during the Civil War she gave $8,267 to the Sanitary Commission. For over forty years her life was that of a great actor and a great-hearted woman of irreproachable character. She was buried in Mount Auburn, near Boston. She was a woman of intense emotional nature, an affectionate woman in private life, kind to a fault to the younger members of her profession, and generous in all ways to worthy causes. She had a voice of remarkable strength and flexibility, and her power over her audiences was sometimes appalling. Her famous female rôles included Lady Macbeth, Meg Merrilies, Nancy Sikes, Queen Katherine, Widow Melnotte, and many others, and she also played Romeo, Claude Melnotte, Hamlet, Cardinal Wolsey and other male rôles.

CUSTER, Mrs. Elizabeth Bacon, author, was born in Monroe, MI. She was married 9th February, 1864, to Major George A. Custer, afterward known as Major-General Custer. She accompanied her husband to the seat of war in 1864 and 1865, and after the close of the Civil War she accompanied him during his service in the West, going with him through all the perils of Indian warfare and all the discomforts of soldier life on the frontier. After her husband's death at the hands of the Indians, Mrs. Custer went to New York City, where she now makes her home. She has published two volumes on her life with her lamented husband in the West. The first of these was "Boots and Saddles, or Life in Dakota with Gen. Custer" (New York, 1885), and the second, "Tenting on the Plains, or Gen. Custer in Kansas and Texas" (New York, 1887). Both were successful volumes, and "Boots and Saddles" has gone well up toward its fiftieth thousand. Her style is racy, agreeable and different from that of any other author now before the public. She has written one novel. Besides her literary work, she has won a reputation as a lecturer on frontier life, in which rôle she has appeared in New York City and in the larger cities of the Eastern, Middle and Western States. Her lectures have been given principally before schools, and they have become very popular, so that her time is fully occupied.

DABBS, Mrs. Ellen Lawson, physician, born in her father's country home, five miles east from Mt. Enterprise, in Rusk county, TX, 25th April, 1853. She was reared in the country. Her father, Col. Henry M. Lawson, was a typical southern planter and a Georgian by birth, who settled in Texas in 1844 with his young wife and her first child. The mother came of a wealthy Georgia family, and, reared as she had been in luxury, with her husband she braved the dangers and privations of a pioneer's life. Colonel Lawson took a prominent part in early Texas politics. He represented his county for several years in the legislature. Ellen was the only girl in a family of eight children, of whom she was the fourth. She

attended the country schools until she was fourteen years old, and then her father sent her to Gilmer, TX. She attended school there for two years, and in that time made rapid progress in mathematics and the languages. She taught school as an assistant for six months, then went to Georgia, entered college and was graduated as valedictorian of her class from Furlow Masonic College, in Americus. After graduating, she returned to Texas and taught school and music for five years. In Galveston, TX, she met J. W. Dabbs, a merchant of Sulphur Springs, TX. In a year they were married. He was a widower with four children, all boys, and was struggling to get a foothold as a merchant. Mrs. Dabbs looked after his boys, did most of the housework, clerked in the store, bore five children in nine years, helped her husband to make a fortune, and, as his first wife's children came of age, she saw him deed over to them the property that she had made by work and economy. Feeling the need of some profession, she commenced the study of medicine. She read under the direction of Dr. E. P. Becton. She went north to Iowa and entered the College of Physicians and Surgeons in Keokuk, where she was graduated after two years of study. She then took a course in a school of midwifery in St. Louis, MO. She returned to Sulphur Springs, her old home, in 1890, and practiced there eighteen months. She owned an interest in a newspaper and did some editorial work. In 1891 she sold her interest in the paper and settled in Fort Worth, TX, with her four surviving children. There she has done some writing for the reform press. She was sent as a delegate to the Industrial Union held in St. Louis, in February, 1892. She was put on the committee on platforms and resolutions, and was appointed by the Industrial Convention as one of the committee of thirty to confer with the executive committee of the People's Party. She was disappointed because the People's Party failed to recognize woman in their platform. Knowing injustice under existing laws, she is a firm believer in equality before the law, and constantly pleads for the right of suffrage. She is an advocate of temperance and was sent as a delegate to the State Woman's Christian Temperance convention held in Dallas in May, 1892. She is the State chairman of the Woman's Southern Council.

DAHLGREN, Mrs. Madeleine Vinton, author, born in Gallipolis, OH, about 1835. She is the only daughter of Samuel F. Vinton, who served for a quarter of a century with much distinction as a Whig leader in Congress. Her maternal ancestors were French. At an early age she became the wife of Daniel Convers Goddard, who left her a widow with two children. On 2nd August, 1865, she became the wife of Admiral Dahlgren, and has three children of that marriage. Admiral Dahlgren died in 1870. As early as 1859 Mrs. Dahlgren contributed to the press, prose articles under the signature "Corinne," and, later, some fugitive poems. She also wrote under the pen-name "Cornelia." In 1859 her little volume, "Idealities" (Philadelphia), appeared, and this was her first work in book form. Since then she has found time to write upon a great variety of subjects. She has made several translations from the French, Spanish and Italian languages, notably Montalembert's brochure, "Pius IX.," the abstruse philosophical work of Donoso Cortes from the Spanish, and the monograph of the Marquis de Chambrun on "The Executive Power" (Lancaster, PA, 1874). These translations brought her many complimentary recognitions, among others a flattering letter from the illustrious Montalembert, an autograph letter from Pope Pius IX., the thanks of the Queen of Spain, and a complimentary notice from President Garfield. She is the author of a voluminous "Biography of Admiral Dahlgren," and a number of novels including "South-Mountain Magic" (Boston, 1882), "A Washington Winter" (Boston, 1883), "The Lost Name" (Boston, 1886), "Lights and Shadows of a Life" (Boston, 1887), "Divorced" (New York, 1887), "South Sea Sketches" (Boston), and a volume on "Etiquette of Social Life in Washington" (Philadelphia, 1881), "Thoughts on Female Suffrage" (Washton, 1871), and also of a great number of essays, articles, reviews and short stories written for papers and periodicals. Social questions and the live topics of the day have especially occupied her attention. Occasionally Mrs. Dahlgren has expressed herself in verse, and several of her efforts have found a place in anthologies of poets. Mrs. Dahlgren's estate is on South Mountain, MD, overlooking the battle-field. She is a woman of fine talents and a thorough scholar. Her writings show considerable versatility, and in the social circles of Washington, where her winters are spent, she is a literary authority. In 1870 and 1873 she actively opposed the movement for female suffrage, and drew up a petition to Congress, which was extensively signed, asking that the right to vote should not be extended to women. The Literary Society of Washington, of which she was one of the founders, held its meetings in her house for six years, and she was elected its vice-president. She was for some time president of the Ladies' Catholic Missionary Society of Washington, and has built the chapel of St. Joseph's of the Sacred Heart of Jesus, on South Mountain, MD.

DAILEY, Miss Charlotte Field, World's Columbian Exposition official, born in Providence, RI, 19th December, 1842. She was graduated from Mme. C. Mears' boarding school in New York City. The name Dailey dates back four generations in Rhode Island, and is found as early as 1680 in Easton, MA. Miss Dailey spent her first winter out of school with friends on the Island of Cuba, where her knowledge of the Spanish language added much to her enjoyment. In 1867 she went abroad with her parents to visit the Paris Exposition. She visited Italy, where her taste for art developed, and, after seeing Spain and the art treasures of that country, she discovered her ability to appreciate and recognize the great masters. Austria, Germany, Russia, Denmark, Sweden and England were visited, and, wherever time permitted, her musical studies were pursued under famous masters, such as Allari, of Rome, and San Giovanni, of Milan. Miss Dailey in her life at home was active in philanthropic work and in associations of artistic, dramatic, musical and literary character. The sudden death of her father, and with it the loss of fortune, made it necessary for her to support herself. Lessons in vocal music and lectures upon art were successfully used as a means to that end. Of late years she has fortunately not found it necessary to overtax her strength. She has spent her winters for the last seven years in Washington, DC. Her appointment to represent her State on the Board of Lady Managers of the World's Columbian Committee was followed by her appointment as secretary and treasurer of the Board of World's Fair Managers of Rhode Island. Mrs. Potter Palmer further assigned her to the chairmanship of fine arts, in oil-painting, water-colors and other departments.

DALL, Mrs. Caroline Wells, author, born in Boston, MA, 22nd June, 1822. She was a daughter of the late Mark Healey. She was educated thoroughly in private schools and academies, and she became a teacher. In 1840 she entered Miss English's school for young ladies, in Georgetown, DC, as vice principal. In 1844 she became the wife of Rev. Charles Henry Appleton Dall. She kept up her studies and literary work uninterruptedly. Her earlier literary productions were principally on reform subjects and the opening of new spheres of occupation to women. Her later productions have been purely literary and critical. In 1877 she received the degree of LL.D. from the Alfred University, Alfred, NY. Much of her activity has been in the cause of woman's rights. Her books are numerous and important. They include: "Essays and Sketches" (1849); "Historical Pictures Retouched" (1859); "Woman's Right to Labor" (1860); "Life of Dr. Marie Zakrewska" (1860); "Woman's Rights Under the Law" (1861); "Sunshine" (1864); "The College, the Market and the Court" (1867); "Egypt's Place in History (1868); "Patty Gray's Journey to the Cotton Islands" (3 vols., 1869 and 1870); "Romance of the Association" (1875); "My First Holiday" (1881); "What We Really Know About Shakespeare" (1885), and the "Life of Dr. Anandabai Joshee "(1888), all published in Boston. Mrs. Dall's works have found a wide sale and attracted the attention of critics everywhere. She has been an active member of the Social Science Association and has read many papers before that body. She was in 1854 associated with Paulina Wright Davis in the management of "Una," the woman's rights journal, in Boston. Her lectures were scholarly and profound. Her husband was a Unitarian clergyman and died 18th July, 1886, in Calcutta, British India, where he had been for many years a missionary.

DANA, Miss Olive Eliza, littérateur, born in Augusta, ME, 24th December, 1859. Her parents are James W. and Sarah Savage Dana. She is a direct descendant of Richard Dana, who came from England and settled in Cambridge, MA, about the year 1640. From one of his sons descended Miss Dana's father; from another, Richard H. Dana, the poet. She is also a direct descendant of the Rev. John Campbell, a graduate of the University of Edinburgh, who came to New England in 1717 and was for forty years pastor in Oxford, MA. Miss Dana was graduated from the Augusta high school in 1877, and has always lived in that city. Her first published article was a prose sketch, which was printed in 1877, and ever since its appearance she has been a prolific writer, sending out many poems, essays, stories and sketches. She has often been compelled by ill health to suspend literary work. Her poems have found a place in the "Magazine of Poetry" and other publications, and are always widely copied. Her prose work covers a wide range. Her short stories have appeared in the "Woman's Journal," "Union Signal," the "Morning Star," the "Christian Union," "Journal of Education," "New England Farmer," Portland "Transcript," "Golden Rule," the "Well Spring," "Zion's Advocate" and many other papers.

DANIELS, Mrs. Cora Linn, author, born in Lowell, MA, 17th March, 1852. She is descended from the Morrisons, hereditary judges in the Hebrides Islands since 1613, on her father's side. The family motto being translated, reads: "Long-headedness is better than riches." She is descended from the Ponds, on her mother's side, upon whom a coat-of-arms with the motto, "Fide et Amore," was conferred by Henry VIII, in 1509. Her grandfather, General Lucas Pond, was for many years a member of the Massachusetts Senate. Her great-uncle, Enoch Pond, D.D., was president of the Theological College in Bangor, ME. She was educated in the grammar school of Malden, MA. A private tutor took charge of her for two years. She was sent to Delacove Institute, near Philadelphia, and finished her studies in Dean Academy, Franklin, MA. At nineteen she became the wife of Joseph H. Daniels, of Franklin, a member of one of the historic families of the neighborhood. She has had no children. Her travels in her own country have been extensive. She has spent twenty winters in New York City, varied by trips to Washington, Bermuda and the West. Her literary life began with a poem published in the "Independent" in 1874. When William H. H. Murray conceived the idea of publishing the "Golden Rule," in Boston, he invited her to contribute a series of articles descriptive of prominent racehorses. That she did under the pen-name "Australia." The articles were attributed to Mr. Murray himself and were so successful that they immediately led to an engagement, and she became literary editor, remaining on the staff three years. She contributed much poetry to the paper under the pen-name "Lucrece," but afterward signed her own name, both to prose and poetry. Her poems were widely copied and sometimes translated into other languages, returning to this country by being retranslated for" Littell's Living Age." Becoming New York correspondent for the Hartford "Daily Times," her letters appeared regularly therein for ten years, touching upon every possible subject, but more particularly devoted to dramatic criticism, art and reviews of notable books. Among the reviews was a notice of Elihu Vedder's "Omar-Khayyám," which was reproduced in a pamphlet, which, being sent to Rome, was pronounced by Mr. Vedder the most comprehensive and excellent review that had been produced. Constantly contributing to a number of publications, her first novel, "Sardia" (Boston, 1891), was successful, and in future she will devote considerable time to fiction. The best work of her life, which she values beyond any possible novel, is a work treating of what might be designated "The Science of the Hereafter," or "The Philosophy of After Death," soon to be published. Despite travel and the life of cities, her existence has been one of mental solitude. She has never found companionship of thought and labor. She has collected a library of a thousand volumes during twenty years, but they have been packed in boxes for seventeen out of the twenty. What she has done has been done alone, without books at hand, and usual incentives to new thought gained through literary intercourse.

DANNELLY, Mrs. Elizabeth Otis, poet, born in Monticello, GA, 13th June, 1838. Her father,

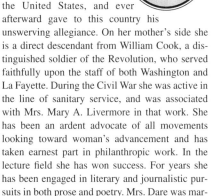

Jackson Marshall, is a native of Augusta, GA. On her mother's side she is descended from an old Huguenot family named Grinnell. Her grandfather, Peter Grinnell, was closely connected with Henry Grinnell, of Arctic Expedition fame, and was also a first cousin to Oliver Hazard Perry. Her grandmother was a daughter of Anthony Dyer, uncle of Elisha Dyer, Governor of Rhode Island. While quite young, her father moved to Oxford, GA, the seat of Emory College, where her early education was begun. At the age of twelve years she was sent to school in Charleston, SC, and from that city she entered the Madison Female College, Madison, GA, from which institution she was graduated 26th July, 1855. Immediately after receiving her diploma, Miss Otis went to New York City, where one year was spent in studying painting. Her father in the meantime had moved from Savannah to Madison, where she became the wife, 4th September, 1862, of Dr. F. Olin Dannelly, the son of Rev. James Dannelly, of South Carolina, the celebrated preacher-wit of that time. Dr. Dannelly was at the time of his marriage a surgeon in the Confederate army, stationed in Richmond, VA. Shortly after, he was ordered to Columbia, SC, where they continued to reside until the close of the war. About that time Mrs. Dannelly wrote her famous poem, "The Burning of Columbia," which was especially prized in the South and added to the popularity of her volume of poems, "Cactus, or Thorns and Blossoms" (New York, 1879). Soon after the close of the war Dr. Dannelly removed to Baltimore, MD, where he resumed the practice of medicine, in which profession he had attained distinction. During the years of her residence in Baltimore Mrs. Dannelly occupied a leading social position. She was a frequent contributor to many of the leading periodicals and magazines of that day. After living five years in that city, the family removed to Texas, where they settled in Waxahachie. After a few years in Texas, they returned to Baltimore, where Dr. Dannelly died. Mrs. Dannelly has had a life of varying fortune, from affluence to a moderate competence. In 1882 she returned to Texas with her six boys, again locating in Waxahachie, where she has since lived, the center of a large circle of friends. Although a busy mother, a painstaking and thrifty housekeeper, and giving much time to religious, charitable and temperance work, she has found time to add many graceful poems to her first volume, and to write a second volume, "Wayside Flowers" (Chicago, 1892). Within the past few years she has resumed her brush as a recreation.

DARE, Mrs. Ella, lecturer and journalist, born in West Batavia, Genesee county, NY, 1st May, 1842. Her maiden name was Ella Jones. Her father was born and reared in Point De Bute, New Brunswick, but came when a young man to the United States, and ever afterward gave to this country his unswerving allegiance. On her mother's side she is a direct descendant from William Cook, a distinguished soldier of the Revolution, who served faithfully upon the staff of both Washington and La Fayette. During the Civil War she was active in the line of sanitary service, and was associated with Mrs. Mary A. Livermore in that work. She has been an ardent advocate of all movements looking toward woman's advancement and has taken earnest part in philanthropic work. In the lecture field she has won success. For years she has been engaged in literary and journalistic pursuits in both prose and poetry. Mrs. Dare was married in 1872. She has no children, and therefore gives her life to her work, in which she is greatly aided by her husband's earnest sympathy. Her home is in Ridgeland, IL, a suburb of Chicago.

DARLING, Miss Alice O., poet, was born near Hanover, NH. She is the daughter of one of the California pioneer gold-hunters of 1849. Her father was a farmer's son, and his youth was spent on a farm in Croydon, NH, where he was born. His quest for gold in California was successful, and in 1855 he returned to New Hampshire and settled on a farm in the town of Lebanon. There he was married to Mary Ann Seavey. Several generations back his ancestry contained a drop of Indian blood, and to that fact Miss

Darling attributes many of her mental and physical characteristics. She has an Indian's love for the fields and forests, a deep and lasting remembrance of a kindness or an injury, and a decided distaste for crowds and great cities. Unlike most New Englanders, she would rather go round than through Boston, whose architectural beauties are to her "only impressive and oppressive." Notwithstanding the regular and arduous toil of farm life, Miss Darling has found time to do considerable literary work of no mean order. She published her first poems when she was seventeen years old. When she was twenty-two years old, she wrote for the Newport, NH, "Argus and Spectator," and later for the Boston "Traveller," the Boston "Record," the Boston "Globe," the Boston "Transcript," the Buffalo "Express," the Hanover "Gazette," and "Good Housekeeping."

DARLING, Mrs. Flora Adams, novelist, born in Lancaster, NH, in 1840. She is a member of the well-known Adams family, and inherits many traits of her ancestors. At an early age she became the wife of Col. Edward Irving Darling, a southerner, and they made their home in Louisiana. When the Civil War broke out, Colonel Darling went into the Confederate army. He was killed during the war, and Mrs. Darling was left a widow with one son, Edward Irving Darling, the musical composer. Mrs. Darling began to write industriously, and her works have brought her both fame and other rewards. She is the author of a number of books, the chief of which is "Mrs. Darling's Letters, or Memories of the Civil War" (1884). That book was written at the suggestion of Judge E. P. Norton, of New York City, who was her counsel in the "celebrated case" known as the Darling Claim, long pending in Congress and finally reaching the Court of Claims. That claim is founded on the fact that, while in custody of the New Orleans officials, her trunks were robbed of a casket of jewels and $25,000 worth of gold-bearing cotton bonds, that she never recovered, the authorities protesting that they were powerless to act upon the case. Mrs. Darling, after her return north, called on President Lincoln and stated her case, which he recognized as a just one, and manifested his intention to see it righted. His untimely death prevented,

and for the past twenty years it has been in litigation, supported by eminent counsel, who have no doubt that she will ultimately succeed in recovering not only principal and interest, but compensation for the hardships to which she was subjected. Losing her means through unfortunate investments, she was for a long time seriously ill, and her illness resulted in deafness and impaired vision. After recovering, she resumed her literary work, contributing to magazines and periodicals. Her books are "Mrs. Darling's Letters," "A Wayward Winning Woman" (1890), "The Bourbon Lily" (1890), "Was it a Just Verdict?" (1890), "A Social Diplomat" (1891), "From Two Points of View" (1892), and. "The Senator's Daughter" (1892). Her short stores are numerous. During the Civil War she was an intimate friend of Jefferson Davis and his family, and the acquaintance deepened into lifelong friendship. She assisted Mrs. Davis in collecting materials for the "Life of Jefferson Davis." For that purpose Mrs. Darling made a thorough examination of the official records of the War Department in Washington, DC. One of her most notable achievements is the organization of the society called "The Daughters of the Revolution," which she served as historian. The aims and purposes of the society are purely patriotic, and it intends to perpetuate the memories of the men and women who achieved or helped to achieve American Independence in the Revolution of 1776, by the acquisition or protection of historic spots and their indication by means of permanent tablets or monuments; to encourage historical research in relation to the American Revolution, and to publish the results; to cherish, maintain and extend the institutions of American freedom, to foster true patriotism and love of country, and to aid in securing for mankind all the blessings of liberty; and to aid in the work of inducing the United States Government to gather, compile and publish the authentic records of every officer, soldier, sailor, statesman or civilian who contributed to the cause of American Independence in the War of 1776. Recently she has edited the "Adams Magazine," published by her nephew, Francis A. Adams, which is the organ of the society. Mrs. Darling has received the college degrees of A.M. and A.B. in recognition of her literary work.

DAUVRAY, Helen, actor, born in San Francisco, CA, 24th February, 1859. Her family name is Gibson. Her childhood was spent in Virginia City, NV, and she made her first appearance on the stage in San Francisco, in 1864, playing Eva in "Uncle Tom's Cabin." She attracted a good deal of attention and became known as "Little Nell, the California Diamond." Junius Brutus Booth, Frank Mayo and Charles Thorne were members of the Uncle Tom Company in which she made her debut at the age of five. In 1865 she played the part of the Duke of York in "Richard III." Her next rôle was as the child in the "Scarlet Letter," with Matilda Heron as Hester Prynne. Helen afterward played in "Fidelia," "No Name" and "Katy Did," and she was a remarkably bright and successful actor. She appeared in New York City in June, 1870, playing in Wood's Museum in "Andy Blake" and "Popsy Wopsey." Returning to California, she sailed to Australia, where she played successfully. A successful investment in the Comstock mine made her wealthy, and she disappeared for a time from the stage. She went to Europe to complete her education. She studied vocal and instrumental music in Milan and French in Paris. She decided to play in French, before a French audience, in Paris, but had great difficulty to find a manager brave enough to back her. Finally, M. Gautier, of the Folies Dramatiques, introduced her to Paul Ferrier, the dramatist, who wrote "Nan, the Good-for-Nothing" for her. She appeared in that play 1st September, 1884, and scored a success. She broke down from overwork and returned to the United States. She made her re-entrance upon the American stage 27th April, 1885, in the title rôle of "Mona," in the Star Theater, New York City. Her next play was "One of Our Girls," in which she made a triumphant hit as Kate Stupley, an American girl in Paris. That play was the work of Bronson Howard. He then wrote for her "Met by Chance," in which she appeared 11th January, 1887, but it was soon withdrawn. On 7th March, 1887, she played in "Walda Lamar," and in April, 1887, in "The Love Chase." On 2nd June, 1890, she appeared in New York City in "The Whirlwind." She was married 12th October, 1887, in Philadelphia, PA, to John M. Ward.

DAVENPORT, Fanny Lily Gipsy, actor, born in London, England, 10th April, 1850. She is a daughter of the late Edward Loomis Davenport,

the well-known actor, who was born in Boston, MA, 15th November, 1814, and died in Canton, PA, 1st September, 1877. Her mother was a daughter of Frederick Vining, manager of the Haymarket Theater, London, England. Miss Vining became the wife of Mr. Davenport 8th January, 1849. Fanny was their first child. Mr. and Mrs. Davenport came to the United States, where both were for years favorite actors. Fanny was educated in the public schools in Boston, MA, where she made her début as the child in "Metamora." At the age of twelve years she appeared in New York, in Niblo's, in "Faint Heart Never Won Fair Lady," making her début in that city 14th February, 1862. She afterward played soubrette parts in Boston and Philadelphia, under Mrs. John Drew's management. Augustin Daly found her there, and he called her to New York, where she played Effie in "Saratoga," Lady Gay Spanker, Lady Teazle, Nancy Sykes, Leah, Fanny Ten Eyck and Mabel Renfrew. Encouraged by her evident success, she left Mr. Daly's company and formed a company of her own. She played "Olivia," in Philadelphia, and Miss Anna E. Dickinson's "An American Girl," both without success, when she conceived the idea of abandoning comedy and taking up tragedy. She induced Victorien Sardou, of Paris, to give her the American rights to "Fedora," "La Tosca" and "Cleopatra," and in those rôles she has won both fame and fortune in large degree. Her tours have been very successful, and the woman who was supposed to be merely a charming comedian has shown herself to be possessed of the very highest powers of tragedy. Miss Davenport, as she is known to the world, has been twice married. Her first husband was Edwin H. Price, an actor, to whom she was married 30th July, 1879. She secured a divorce from him in 1888. She was married in 1889 to Melbourne McDowell, the principal actor in her company. Recently Miss Davenport has given American theater-goers great pleasure in the magnificent staging and dressing of her plays. She has advanced to the extreme front rank in the most difficult of all histrionic fields, and comparison with the greatest actors cannot fail to show that she is one the most successful women who have ever lived before the footlights.

DAVIS, Mrs. Ida May, litterateur, born in Lafayette, IN, 22nd February, 1857. Her maiden name was Ida May De Puy. Her father was of French descent, and from him Mrs. Davis inherits her humor and vivacity. She was thoroughly educated, and her poetic inclinations and talents showed themselves at an early age. She has always been a facile versifier, and her thoughts naturally flow in rhyme. When she was seventeen years old, she began to publish poems, all of which were extensively copied and commended. Her productions have appeared in newspapers and magazines of the Central and Rocky Mountain States. She is a member of the Western Association of Writers, founded in 1886, and she has been conspicuous in the annals of that society, which she now serves as secretary. She is an artist of much talent and paints well. Her poems are mainly lyrical in form. She became the wife of Henry Clay Davis, of southern birth, in 1876. Mrs. Davis resides in Terre Haute, IN, where she is the center of a circle of literary and artistic persons. She is an ex-teacher and is a member of the board of education of Terre Haute, having been elected in 1891.

DAVIS, Mrs. Jessie Bartlett, prima donna contralto, born near Morris, Grundy county, IL, in 1860. Her maiden name was Jessie Fremont Bartlett. Her father was a farmer and a country schoolmaster. He possessed a remarkably good bass voice and had a knowledge of music. The family was a large one, and a sister about a year older, named Belle, as well as Jessie, gave early evidence of superior vocal gifts. Their father was very proud of their talents and instructed them as well as he could. Before they were twelve years of age they were noted as vocalists throughout their neighborhood. They appeared frequently in Morris and surrounding villages and cities in concert work, and they soon attracted the attention of traveling managers, one of whom succeeded in securing them for a tour of the western cities to sing in character duets. The older sister was of delicate constitution and died soon after that engagement was made. Jessie Bartlett then went to Chicago in search of fame and fortune, and was engaged by Caroline Richings, with whom she traveled one season. She was ambitious to perfect herself in her profession, and she soon returned to Chicago and devoted herself to the study of music, and at the same time held a good position in a church choir. During the "Pinafore" craze Manager Haverly persuaded her to become a member of his original Chicago Church Choir Company, and she assumed the rôle of Buttercup. That was the beginning of her career as an opera singer. Since that time, through her perseverance and indefatigable efforts, aided by her attractive personality, she has steadily progressed in her art, until she is one of the leading contralto singers of the United States. Her histrionic powers are not in the least inferior to her vocal ability. She is one of the best actors among the singers now on the American stage. She made her début in grand opera in New York City with Adelina Patti and the Mapleson Opera Company. Adelina Patti sang Marguerite and Jessie Bartlett Davis sang Siebel. Other grand operas in which she has won distinction are "The Huguenots," "Martha," "The Merry Wives of Windsor," "Il Trovatore," "Dinorah" and others. In comic opera she has probably a more complete repertoire than any other singer now before the public. For the last four years she has been the leading contralto of the Bostonians. Jessie Bartlett became the wife of William J. Davis, a Chicago theatrical manager, in 1880. Her home is in Chicago, with a summer residence in Crown Point, IN. Mr. Davis owns an extensive stock farm at that place. Her home life is very pleasant, and she divides her time into eight months of singing and four months of enjoying life in her city home or on the farm in Indiana. She is the mother of one son, eight years of age. Besides her musical and histrionic talents, Mrs. Davis has decided literary gifts. She is the author of "Only a Chorus Girl" and other attractive stories and a number of poems. She has composed the music for several songs.

DAVIS, Miss Minnie S., author and mental scientist, born in Baltimore, MD, 25th March, 1835. Her parents, Rev. S. A. and Mary Partridge Davis, were natives of Vermont, but moved to Baltimore soon after their marriage. In that city Mr. Davis was one of the earlier Universalist ministers.

When about six years of age, Minnie was thrown from a carriage and one of the wheels passed across her back. The shock of that accident was afterward supposed to be the cause of frequent illness and great delicacy of health. These circumstances kept the child by the mother's side, and the close companionship had a marked influence upon her future life, for the gifted mother became her constant instructor until her death in 1848. When seventeen years of age, Minnie entered the Green Mountain Institute, Woodstock, VT. When she was eighteen, she had completed a book, "Clinton Forest," which was afterward well received by the public. Miss Davis spent a year as a teacher. Writing claimed her attention, and soon "Marion Lester," another book, and perhaps her strongest and best was ready for the press, and was published in 1856. Three years later "Clinton Forest" was published, and later "Rosalie." She had been a frequent contributor to the "Trumpet," "Christian Freeman" and local papers, and a regular contributor to the "Ladies' Repository." Of the last, Miss Davis was for five years associate editor with Mrs. Sawyer and Mrs. Soulé. In 1863 she removed with her father's family to Hartford, CT. A few months after going into her new home she fell down stairs, and that was the beginning of long years of helplessness, suffering and partial blindness. All known means for her restoration had been tried, but, with only partial and temporary success. In 1885, when the wave of "Mental Healing" swept over the land and was accepted by those who were ready for the spiritual truth, Miss Davis was one of the first who recognized the reality of the philosophy. A friend visited her and offered to treat her according to the new method of healing. In four months the days of pain and the darkened room were but memories of the past. She then obtained the best teachers and studied with them the philosophy of healing, and went out in her turn to pass on the work, in which she has had unusual success. Teaching is evidently her forte, her lectures being clear, strong and logical. Miss Davis is interested in all the advanced movements of the day, in temperance, equal rights and everything that tends to the amelioration of the ills of humanity.

DAVIS, Miss Minta S. A., physician and surgeon, born in Johnstown, PA, 31st October, 1864, of Welsh and English parents. Her father died in her twelfth year, leaving her mother, a younger sister and herself dependent upon the exertions of two brothers. When seventeen years old she began to teach school, but she broke down physically at the end of the first term. Then followed a weary apprenticeship at anything that promised support, sewing, proof-reading, typesetting by day, and earnest work with her studies and writing at night. Her ill health turned her thoughts to the study of medicine. Her mother, a conservative English woman, looked coldly upon any divergence from the stereotyped work of woman. Her means were limited, but her brothers wished her to enter a profession, and she chose the study of medicine. At the request of two physicians, who had known the family for thirty years, her mother gave an unwilling consent. In 1887 she disposed of what property she had and put her all into a medical education. A few months later she entered the American Medical College in St. Louis, MO. Shortly before her graduation came the terrible flood of Johnstown, PA, and she hastened there to find her people and friends homeless. That calamity made serious inroads on her slender capital. The two physicians who were to help her were dead, but she finished her lectures and answered a call for physicians from the Northwest. She settled in Salem, OR, in June, 1890. By patience and industry she has established a fine practice, and was elected vice-president of the Oregon State Eclectic Medical Society.

DAVIS, Mrs. Mollie Evelyn Moore, poet and author, was born in Talladega, AL, in 1852. Her parents emigrating, she grew up on a Texas plantation. With her brother she learned not only to read, but to ride, shoot and swim, and received at home, under the supervision of a wise, book loving mother and a highly intellectual father, her mental training. Very early she began to write. Her first volume of poems, entitled "Minding the Gap" (Houston, Texas, 1867), was published before she was sixteen, and enlarged and corrected it has passed through five editions. Her later work has attracted critics at home and abroad. "Keren Happuch and I" is a series of sketches contributed to the New Orleans "Picayune." "In War Times at La Rose Blanche" was a collection of delightful stories (Boston, 1888). That mystic and beautiful prose poem, "The Song of the Opal," the already classical "Père Dagobèrt," "Throwing the Wanga," "The Center Figger," and "The 'Elephant's Track," were written for the Harpers, while many poems and sketches have been published in other periodicals. "Snaky Baked a Hoe-Cake," "Grief" and others, contributed to "Wide Awake" in 1876, were among the first, if not the very first, negro dialect stories which appeared in print. Certainly they preceded the furore for southern negro stories. In 1874 Miss Moore became the wife of Major Thomas E. Davis, of an excellent Virginia family, and now editor-in-chief of the New Orleans "Picayune," a gentleman, genial, refined and scholarly, who develops and cherishes what is best in his gifted wife. In 1880 Major and Mrs. Davis made their home in New Orleans, and every year their historic house in Royal street receives all the clever people in town, both French and American residents, while strangers find their way to the cozy drawing-room where General Jackson once discussed his plans of battle. With all her social cares she finds time for much reading and study and much unostentatious hospitality. Her domestic life is as complete as if her fingers were innocent of ink stains and her desk of publishers' proposals. She is an accomplished French scholar and also a lover and student of Spanish literature. She is president of the "Geographics," a select literary circle, and is a vice-president of the "Quarante," a large and fashionable club, also literary. In both those organizations she is recognized as a mental guide, philosopher and friend. She is a successful author and a magnetic woman, who draws about her the best representatives of southern society.

DAVIS, Mrs. Rebecca Harding, author, born in Washington, PA, 24th June, 1831. She was reared and educated in Wheeling, WV, where, in 1862, she became the wife of L. Clark Davis, at that time editorially connected with the Philadelphia "Inquirer," and a contributor to the prominent periodicals of the country. Mrs. Davis wrote from childhood, but her first successful bid for public notice was in 1861, when her "Life in the Iron Mills" was published in the "Atlantic Monthly." That story was afterward printed in book form and found a large sale. Her next work, "A Story of To-Day," appeared in the "Atlantic Monthly" and was republished as a book, under the title "Margaret Howth" (New York, 1861). After her marriage she went to Philadelphia, where she lived until 1869, when Mr. Davis became a member of the editorial staff of the New York "Tribune," and they took up their residence in that city. Mrs. Davis also contributed to the "Tribune." She was constantly writing, and short stories, sketches, essays and editorials without number flowed from her pen. Her other books are, "Waiting for the Verdict" (New York, 1867), "Dallas Galbraith" (Philadelphia, 1868), "The Captain's Story," "John Andross" (New York, 1874), "The Faded Leaf of History," and a number of novels, all of singular merit and attractiveness. Several years ago Mrs. Davis returned to Philadelphia, where her home now is. Her latest works include "Kitty's Chord" (Philadelphia, 1876), and "A Law Unto Herself" (Philadelphia, 1878), "Natasqua" (New York, 1886). Her son, Richard Harding Davis, one of the editors of "Harper's Weekly," has inherited her story-telling talent.

DAVIS, Mrs. Sarah Iliff, business woman and philanthropist, born in Oxford, Butter county, OH, 19th February, 1820. Her maiden name was Sarah A. Sausman. The family removed to Richmond, IN, in 1832. At the age of fifteen she united with the Methodist Episcopal Church, and was a teacher in the first Sabbath-school which was organized in the church in her town. She taught a private school for a time, and afterward learned the millinery business. At the age of eighteen she went into business for herself. She became the wife of John K. Iliff, 23rd February, 1841. Mr. Iliff was an excellent man of good family, an old-time Methodist, earnest and devout. Seven children were born to them, five sons and two daughters. Two sons died in infancy. Mrs. Iliff never gave up her business, but carried it steadily forward, assisting in the education of the children and the acquisition of a competency. Mr. Iliff died in 1867, after a long illness. Mrs. Iliff became the wife in 1870 of B. W. Davis, editor of the "Palladium" and postmaster of Richmond. He died in 1884. Mrs. Iliff Davis has marked executive ability. As early as 1844 she was a charter member and officer of the order of Daughters of Temperance. She was active in the Temple of Honor and the Good Templars. In 1861 the Woman's Aid Society of Union Chapel Methodist Episcopal Church, of which Mrs. Iliff was president from first to last, began sanitary work for the Union Army. It soon became auxiliary to the Indiana State Sanitary Commission. That society continued active work until the close of the war. Then her efforts were directed to giving entertainments to aid in establishing the State Soldiers' Orphans' Home. Later the Freedman's Aid Society claimed her attention. In 1868 she was appointed one of a committee of women by the Young Men's Christian Association of Richmond to organize a Home for Friendless Women. For twenty years she was in active work for the home, and for sixteen years she was president of its board of managers. In 1870 she was one of a committee of two women, appointed by the home management, to go before the county commissioners, asking that the home be legalized for the commitment of women prisoners. That request was granted. The same day these ladies attended the trial of a young woman, who received a sentence of imprisonment for two years, and who was committed to the home instead of the State penitentiary. They left the court-house in Centerville, taking the prisoner a distance of seven miles by railroad. That young woman served her time, working faithfully at domestic duties, and went out from the home to live an upright life. Afterward the managers of the home petitioned the city council to give them the keeping of all women prisoners. That was granted, and an addition was built to the home for a city and county prison. The action of the Wayne county officials was an initial step toward separate prisons for men and women, and toward establishing the Indiana State Reformatory for Women. Mrs. Iliff Davis is still actively engaged in business. As a writer her essays and reports show marked ability, and she has written poems and other contributions for the local press.

DAVIS, Miss Varina Anne, born in Richmond, VA, 27th June, 1864. She is more generally known as Winnie Davis, the second daughter of Jefferson Davis, President of the Southern Confederacy. She is endeared to the South as the "Daughter of the Confederacy." Shortly before the evacuation of Richmond, Mr. Davis sent his wife and daughter to Charlotte, NC, where they remained until he instructed them to go to Chester, SC. At Abbeville they heard the news of Lee's surrender, and Mrs. Davis and her children went on to Washington, GA, where Mr. Davis joined them and accompanied them to Macon. After Mr. Davis had been taken to Fortress Monroe, Mrs. Davis took her children to Savannah. After Mr. Davis returned to his family, they visited Canada, Cuba, various parts of the South, and Europe, and then settled in Memphis, TN, where Winnie remained till 1877. In that year she went to Carisruhe, Germany, where she remained until 1882. She next went to Paris, France, where she attended a boarding-school and was joined by her parents. Miss Davis studied drawing and the drama, and her experience convinced her that it is folly to send American children to Europe to be educated. Leaving Paris with her parents, they returned to New Orleans, LA, where in the following spring Miss Davis made her entrance into society at the Mardi Gras Ball. The family were invited to visit Alabama and were received with distinction. They extended their tour to Atlanta, GA, and there Governor Gordon presented Miss Davis to the people as "The Daughter of the Confederacy." She went to Paris, on the advice of her physicians, and was ill there at the time of her father's death. She has made her home with her mother in Beauvoir, Miss., the family residence since 1879. Miss Davis has recently shown literary talent of a high order and has contributed to a number of periodicals. She is an accomplished musician, a skilled linguist, a ready writer, and a most attractive type of the southern woman of intelligence, culture and refinement.

DAVIS, Mrs. Varina Howell, widow of Jefferson Davis, was born in Natchez, MS. She is a descendant of the famous Howell family, whose founder settled in New Jersey. Her grandfather, Gov. Richard Howell, was a Revolutionary officer, and her father, William Burr Howell, won high distinction under McDonough on Lake Champlain. Mrs. Davis's maternal grandfather, James Kempe, was an Irish gentleman, who came to Virginia after the Emmet rebellion. He was a man of large wealth and moved to Natchez, MS, when her mother was an infant. Col. Kempe organized and drilled the "Natchez troope," a company that fought through the Revolution. Mrs. Davis's uncle, Franklin Howell, was killed on the "President." Mr. Davis's marriage with Miss Howell took place 26th February, 1845. While the public life of the Davis family in many respects was one long storm, their private life was full of peace and sunshine. Few men have been happier in their domestic relations than Mr. Davis. Mrs. Davis has recently published memoirs of her husband, a work of great merit. She has the key of President Davis's career. She has written with the pen of truth and the ink of fact, for she, by loving ministrations and intellectual companionship, was his confidante through the memorable years of his life and greatly contributed to enable him more completely to achieve that career which has made his name immortal. The war record of Mrs. Davis is historical and cherished memory to those who watched her unfaltering devotion m the dark days, and when, overcome by misfortune, she met the inevitable like a true daughter of noble sires. The death of her husband ended a most remarkable chapter of national history and domestic devotion. Only two of Mr. Davis's children are now living, one the wife of Addison Hays, of Colorado, a woman of sterling and womanly characeristics, and the other affectionately known as Miss Winnie, "Daughter of the Confederacy." Mrs. Davis was recently elected honorary president general of the United States Daughters of 1812. She has her pleasant home in Beauvoir, MS.

DAVIS, Mrs. Virginia Meriwether, doctor of medicine, born in Memphis, TN, 18th April, 1862. She deserves a place in the muster roll of America's women as a representative of the present generation. A daughter of Lide Meriwether, heredity and education made simple to her the problem which had been complex to the generation before, and she took a personal independence naturally. This was without question due to the environment to which she was born. Shortly after becoming a widow, she went to New York to study medicine in the college of which Dr. Emily Blackwell was founder and dean. She was graduated in three years with the honors of her class, and she has since remained in New York to practice. Her medical work has been almost exclusively in connection with the New York Infant Asylum, where she has served as resident physician for four years. This city institution has the largest lying-in service conducted by women in the United States, and, to the credit of women be it said, the lowest mortality and sick rates of any lying-in wards in the world.

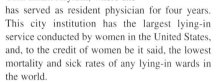

DAWES, Miss Anna Laurens, author, born in North Adams, MA, 14th May, 1851. She is the daughter of Hon. Henry L. Dawes, United States Senator from Massachusetts. She is of New England ancestry on both sides, her father having been born in Cummington, MA, and her mother, Electa Sanderson, in Ashfield, in the same State. She was educated in Maplewood Institute, Pittsfield, MA, and in Abbott Academy, Andover, MA. From her early years she has had the exceptional advantage of a life in Washington, her father's term of continuous service in Congress being almost unprecedented. She has known personally most of the noted men who have figured conspicuously in public life. Such a large experience, combined with a spirit of active inquiry, has caused her to be interested in a variety of enterprises and subjects of political and philanthropic character and to use her pen in their behalf. Her literary life had at the beginning a decided journalistic character. At intervals during the years from 1871 to 1882 she was the Washington correspondent of the "Congregationalist, "the Springfield "Republican," the "Christian Union," and had charge of a department of the "Berkshire Gazette," of Pittsfield, MA, in 1883. She has written book reviews for those papers as well as for the "American Hebrew" and the "Sunday School Times." Since 1874 she has contributed articles to the "Christian Union," the "Congregationalist," the "Independent" and the "Critic," and numerous articles to "Good Housekeeping," the "Andover Review," "America," "Lend a Hand," "Wide Awake," "Home Magazine," "Harper's Magazine," the "Century" and others. An article in "Wide Awake," The Hammer of the Gentiles," was republished in the series of the Magna Charta stories. One on A United States Prison, had the honor of being twice read in Congress, and afterward published in the "Congressional Record." An article on George Kennan in the "Century" has been translated into several languages. She has published a small volume, "The Modern Jew" (New York, 1884 and Boston, 1886), "How we are Governed" (Boston, 1885), and a "Biography of Charles Sumner" (New York, 1892). Miss Dawes is a trustee of Smith College, one of the Board of Managers for the World's Fair for the State of Massachusetts, and president of the Wednesday Morning Club, Pittsfield, MA, since its organization, in 1880. She is a vice-president of the National McAll Association, a manager of "Home Work," a charity organization in Pittsfield, and holds various offices in connection with the American Missionary Association, the work for Indians, and the National Conference of Charities and Correction. She is interested in and connected with several missionary and charitable societies, a member of a Working-Girl's Club, the Prison and Social Science Association and several alumnae associations and literary societies.

DAYTON, Mrs. Elizabeth, poet and author, born in Chertsey, Surry, England, 25th December, 1848. She is best known by her pen name, "Beth Day." When a child, she moved with her parents to Wisconsin, which has since been her home. Growing up in the intellectual atmosphere of a literary family, and endowed by nature with a peculiarly gifted and imaginative mind, she began early to exercise the poetic faculty. Although Mrs. Dayton's lot has been cast among what would seem to be uncongenial associations, she has the happy faculty of idealizing common things, and some of her best work has been wrought out of material that some might deem too coarse for a poet's uses. Although burdened with the cares and duties of a farmer's wife, she has

found time to send out many stories, sketches and poems, and has written for a number of years for the "Youth's Companion," Chicago "Inter-Ocean," "Godey's Lady's Book," "Demorest's Magazine," the "Weekly Wisconsin," "Home Magazine" and many other prominent periodicals. During the brief but brilliant career of "Our Continent," edited by judge Tourée, she was one of its contributors. She writes for juvenile magazines, in addition to her other literary work. Her home was for some years in a pleasant spot on Fox river, near Wrightstown, WI, but in the autumn of 1891 she removed to South Kaukauna, WI. Up to that date Mrs. Dayton's literary work had been but the recreation of a busy woman, but now, relieved of the cares and almost endless labor of farm life, she is devoting more time to her pen.

DECCA, Marie, operatic singer, was born in Georgetown, OH. She is the only daughter of the venerable judge Sanders Johnston, of Washington, DC, and a granddaughter of General Thomas Harney, of Mexican war fame. Of Scotch descent, she has the flexible qualities and the firmness of purpose which emphasize the character of that people, and, judging from her keen wit and remarkable gifts as a delineator of character, there is a vein of Irisn in her lineage. Much of her early life was spent in Maysville, Mason county, KY, and she enjoyed out-of-door pleasures with the intensity of healthy, happy girlhood. She was educated in the Sacred Heart Convent, New York, and later studied music in Philadelphia, PA. During her school years Marie had a preference and great fondness for the stage, and she would have made it her profession, had not her friends strongly opposed her. While studying in Philadelphia, she had the pleasure of seeing and hearing Madame Gerster, and that distinguished artist heard the young student sing in "Daughter of the Regiment." Gerster was delighted and exclaimed: "An Italian voice and an American girl!" That eminent artist advised the American girl to go to Paris and take a thorough course, and, risking all and braving everything, she went and was under the tuition of Madame Marchesi for four years. Out of a class of sixteen, "John," as the pupils called her, was the only one who finished the course. Madame Marchesi often said to her: "You have a well-fed voice, and it is good care, plenty of sleep and beefsteak, Marie, that gives you the advantage of all these extra half-hours." Some of the very strongest traits in the character of this artist are her persistent painstaking as an artist, her fearless devotion to principle, her undaunted bravery and integrity to herself and to her friends. Her devotion to the flag of the Union made her a subject of ridicule sometimes in other countries. It is well known that Madame Marchesi has neither admiration nor fondness for our "Stars and Stripes," and the nearest approach to a rupture between her and Marie Decca was the former's taunting remarks concerning the Red, White and Blue. Mlle. Decca always carries the American flag wherever she goes, and she would fight to shield it from insult. Her voice is a soprano of the most flexible and remarkable range, reaching F natural, with exquisite tone and strength. She made her début in Covent Garden, England, under the management of Col. Mapleson, as the Queen of Night in Mozart's "Magic Flute," and made an instant success. She sang three seasons with Her Majesty's Italian Opera and one season with Carl Rosa's English Opera Company. Her répertoire has a wide range, Italian, French, English, and includes "Lucia," "Sonnambula," "Dinorah," "Lakme," "Hamlet," "Linda," "Rigoletto," "Faust," "Fra Diavolo," "Il Barbiere," "Don Pasquale," "Daughter of the Regiment," "Marriage of Figaro," "Mignon," "Masked Ball," "Magic Flute," "Bohemian Girl," "Nordisa" and many others. Since Mlle. Decca's début in America she has won a place few American singers have ever attained. Her first appearance in Boston was a triumph, and the entire press was unanimous in enthusiastic admiration of her wonderful execution.

DE FERE, Mrs. A. Litsner, musician and voice-trainer, was born in Hungary. She was educated in Germany, and from her earliest youth displayed wonderful aptitude and taste for music and singing. When she was fourteen years old, she appeared in public for the first time, having been chosen to sing a solo part in a festival in Mainz, Germany. The success she achieved on that occasion was such that it was determined that she should pursue a musical career. She presented herself at the customary examination of the National Conservatory of Music, of Paris, and was at once admitted. After four years of study she won two second prizes for singing and opera, and the next year she obtained two first prizes also for singing and opera, which were unanimously awarded to her. A gold medal, yearly awarded to the best singer by the Académie des Beaux-Arts, was also bestowed upon her. Having completed her studies, she was engaged as prima donna in the opera of Paris, Lyon, Marseilles and Bordeaux. She sang in Belgium and Germany, and, having returned to her native country, she was received with enthusiasm at the National Opera of Pesth. Later she sang with great success in the West Indies, and finally went to New York, where she resolved to devote herself to the instruction of singing. She made a study of classical music and constantly sought to improve her method, which seeks the perfection of the vocal instrument and of the quality of the sound. She settled in New York in 1876 and taught vocal music there until 1883, when she removed to Brooklyn and formed her conservatory of music. In New York she taught in the schools of Mrs. Sylvanus Reed, of the Misses Charbonnier, of the Charliers and of Dr. and Mrs. Van Norman. Her home is now in Brooklyn, where she is firmly established. Mrs. De Fere combines the French and Italian methods of singing in her system. Her husband, Eugene De Fere, a graduate of the University of Paris, assists her in the conduct and management of the De Fere Conservatory. Mrs. De Fere has won the palm of "Officier d' Académie" in Paris, France, a distinction enjoyed by only one other woman in the United States, Madam Minnie Hauk.

DE JARNETTE, Mrs. Evelyn Magruder, author, born in Glenmore, Albemarle county, VA, 4th March, 1842. She is the third child of Benjamin Henry and Maria Minon Magruder. Her father was a prominent Virginia lawyer and legislator, and in 1864 was elected to the Confederate Congress. He was a great lover of good books and had a fine library. In the education of his ten children he took a lively interest and an active part. Her mother was from one of the leading families of Piedmont, VA. Evelyn May Magruder led in early childhood a free and happy country life, until boarding schools claimed her for several terms. Then she became an accomplished young lady of "before the war days in Virginia." She was frequently, during her father's connection with the General Assembly, a visitor to Richmond, where she enjoyed to the full the pleasant social gatherings of that city. In 1864 Miss Magruder became the wife of Captain Elliott H. De Jarnette, whose ancestral home, "Pine Forest." in Spottsylvania county, became her future abode. In the home of her childhood she had become impressed with a recognition of the heavy responsibilities of the ownership of slaves, and she had been the regular instructor of the young negroes on the plantation. Amid the cares attendant upon the mother of a family of eight children, she began her literary career, in 1870. "Frank Leslie's Magazine," the "Century," the "Atlantic Monthly," "Youths' Companion" and various newspapers have accepted her contributions. In both prose and poetry she has given to future generations a glimpse of her country's old-time life and customs. Among these are her "Old Vote for Young Master" and "Out on A' Scurgeon."

DELAND, Mrs. Margaret, poet and novelist, born in Pittsburgh, PA, 23rd February, 1857. Her maiden name was Margaret Campbell. She was reared in Pittsburgh, in the family of her uncle, Hon. Benjamin Campbell. When she was seventeen years of age, she went to Pelham Priory, a boarding school in New Rochelle, near New York, City. Afterward she entered the Cooper Institute and took the course in industrial design. A little later and she taught drawing and design in the Normal College of New York for a short time. In 1880 she became the wife of Lorin F. Deland and with her husband removed to Boston, MA, which city has since been her home. Mr. Deland is possessed of literary tastes and ability, and his critical interest is of much assistance to her in her work. Mrs. Deland began to write in 1884. Her introduction to the public was a curious incident. While walking one morning with Miss Lucy Derby in Boston, they stepped into a market to make some purchases. While they were waiting, Mrs Deland busied herself in writing several stanzas of rhyme on a piece of brown paper lying on the counter. Miss Derby read the verses with an exclamation of surprise and delight. The poem was the dainty and widely known "Succory." Miss Derby insisted on sending it to the editor of "Harper's Magazine." The result was that she began to publish. Several of her poems were sent to the same magazine without her knowledge. Others followed in the "Century" and other magazines. These were received with such favor that she collected her poems and had them published under the title of "The Old Garden and Other Verses" (Boston, 1886). Not yet conscious of her power, she issued only a limited edition, which was exhausted within a few days. Since then that volume has gone through six editions. Her next and greatest work was the celebrated novel, "John Ward, Preacher" (Boston, 1888), which passed through six editions in five months. She has since written a descriptive work, "Florida Days" (Boston, 1889), a second novel entitled "Sidney" (Boston, 1890), and short stories for the "Atlantic Monthly" and "Longman's Magazine."

DELETOMBE, Miss Alice S., poet, born in Gallipolis, OH, 2nd April, 1854. She is descended from an old French family long identified with the history of her native town. In early childhood Miss Deletombe displayed a talent for music, inherited from her mother, but delicacy of health prevented full development of that rich faculty, and the musical bent was turned into poetical channels, the eager soul finding that outlet of expression a silent solace through many sad years. Her sensitiveness is averse to criticism and publicity, a peculiarity which has ever been at war with her best interests. It is a remarkable fact that but few of her friends knew of her as a poet until recently, and that for over twenty years she has written for the mere pleasure of expressing her poetical thoughts, and not for any ulterior ambition or reputation. The admixture of French and German blood, she might say, "puts glamour into all I see." She has the French vivacity subdued by German sentiment, subtlety and harmony. The result is music and poetry. Some of her best poems were published for the first time in the "Magazine of Poetry" for January, 1891.

DEVOE, Mrs. Emma Smith, woman suffragist, born in Roseville, Warren county, IL, 22nd August, 1849. Her parents were strictly orthodox, her father having been a deacon in the Baptist Church for forty years. In early life Miss Smith moved with her parents to the village of Washington, Tazewell county, IL, where she lived till her marriage. In youth she developed a remarkable talent for music, which her parents employed every means in their power to culti- vate. At the age of nineteen years she was made a member of the faculty of Eureka College and placed in full charge of the department of music, which position she filled with honor to herself and credit to the institution. In 1879 Miss Smith became the wife of J. H. DeVoe, of Washington, IL, and soon after they moved to Huron, Dakota, where they lived till 1883, when they removed to Faulk county, Dakota, and founded the village that bears their name. About a year thereafter they returned again to Huron, where Mr. DeVoe engaged in mercantile business. During the summer of 1889, while filling the office of assistant State superin- tendent of franchise for the Woman's Christian Temperance Union of South Dakota, Mrs. DeVoe first attracted public notice and began to develop as a public speaker. In a convention in St. Lawrence, SD, in June of that year, she read an essay on "Constitutional Prohibition and How to Secure It," which was copied by various newspa- pers throughout the State and brought her before the reading public. During the following summer her fame spread over the entire State as a most forcible and logical public advocate of the equality of the sexes. A provision in the constitu- tion under which South Dakota was admitted into the Union required a vote of the people to strike out the word male in the clause describing the qualifications of an elector, and in consequence, at the first State election, a very spirited campaign was waged by the noble-minded women of the State, assisted by the officers of the National American Equal Suffrage Association, for the enfranchisement of their sex. Before the campaign had got fairly under way, Mrs. DeVoe's fitness for the work, coupled with her untiring energy, placed her in the front rank of the advocates of equal suf- frage. Her house in Huron was the birthplace of the State organization, and all friends of the cause she cherished found warm welcome there. Her home was the headquarters of the noted workers within the State, and also of the committee having the campaign in charge. She was made State lec- turer and a member of the executive board, and was constantly in the field from early spring till the close of the campaign. The State agricul- tural board placed her in charge of Woman's Day at the State fair, held in Aberdeen in September. That novel and entertaining feature of the fair origi- nated with Mrs. DeVoe, and the suc- cess of the enterprise was abundantly manifest in the increased attendance, the gate receipts being more than double that of any other day during the fair. The suffrage songs, composed by her husband, with which she embellished her lectures, had a very pleasing effect. Although the cause of equal suffrage was unsuccessful in South Dakota, the courage of Mrs. DeVoe was in no wise daunted, for immediately after election she commenced planning for future work and was the first publicly to adjure her co-workers to renewed efforts. In the spring of 1891 Mr. and Mrs. DeVoe removed from Huron to Harvey, IL, where they now reside. In their new home Mrs. DeVoe found many con- genial spirits and immediately organized an equal suffrage society, which through her efforts has grown to be the largest local suffrage society in the State. She is president of the local and also of the first Congressional district societies. In 1892 she lectured throughout Iowa in the interest of the Iowa State Equal Suffrage Association.

DEYO, Rev. Amanda, Universalist minister and peace advocate, born in Clinton, NY, 24th October, 1838. Her maiden name was Amanda Halstead. She was reared in the Society of Quak- ers, and for many years she was an active partici- pant in their meetings. At the age of fifteen she became a school-teacher. After teaching for some time she attended the Poughkeepsie, NY, Colle- giate Institute, from which she was graduated in 1857. In that year she became the wife of Charles B. Deyo, a farmer and a cultivated man of Huguenot descent. He has always aided his wife in her labors for the elevation of humanity. Their family consists of two daughters. Mrs. Deyo was present at one of the early anniversaries of the Universal Peace Union in New York City, where she met Lucretia Mott, Alfred H. Love and others of the friends of peace. There she made her mark as an advocate of the doctrines of that organization, and she has ever since been an earnest supporter of the cause. She has attended all the peace anniversaries throughout the country, has traveled extensively, spoken often and organized numerous peace societies. In 1888 she was called to the pastorate of the Universalist Church in Oxford, NY, having previously served as pastor of the Universalist Church in Poughkeepsie, NY. She is now the pastor of All Souls Universalist Church in Scranton, PA. She has always been so closely identified with the organizations devoted to the abolition of war that she is called the "Peacemaker." She was one of the delegates of the Universal Peace Union to the International Peace Congress and the Paris Exposition of 1889, and did some effective work in the peace cause. Her address to the congress was printed and distributed at the Exposition. She was also present and presented a paper in the Woman's Rights Congress in Paris. She represented the union in the Woman's Council held in Washington, DC, in March, 1888, and signalized the occasion by calling a grand peace meeting in the Church of Our Father, where many prominent women made addresses. In addition to her arduous work in the ministry for the last six years, preaching three times each Sabbath day and attending funerals and weddings, she has been an active worker in the temperance and prohibition cause, and at one time traveled and lectured for that interest and organized its work. That labor she still continues as opportunity will permit; but her great work is her effort to substitute peace for war and harmonize the difficulties constantly arising in families, neighborhoods and churches. By the efforts of herself and her husband, the Dutchess County Peace Society, one of the large and flourishing branches of the Universal Peace Union, was organized in 1875 and kept by them in active life until her ministerial duties made it necessary to turn over the work to others.

DIAZ, Mrs. Abby Morton, industrial reformer, born in Plymouth, MA, in 1821. She is descended from George Morton, one of the Plymouth Pilgrims. Her father, Ichabod Morton, was a prominent anti-slavery worker. Her early reccollections

are associated with anti-slavery meetings, and her first public work was as the secretary of a juvenile anti-slavery society, to whose funds each member aimed to contribute twenty-five cents weekly, a large sum in those days of scanty pence and simple living. To raise half her contribution she went without butter and knit garters to earn the other twelve. Educated in the public schools, she kept her influence at work, using for her homemade copybooks sheets of paper with the figure of a kneeling slave upon them. Among the men to whose utterances Abby Morton listened were Garrison and Horace Mann. She early began to put her thoughts on paper. While aiding in the work of her home, she found time to write prose and verse. She was the only daughter, and her five brothers made plenty of work for her. When the "community" ideas were started, her father seized upon them as promising realization of his hope for the practical recognition of the brotherhood of the race, and joined the celebrated Brook Farm Community, building a house and moving there with his family. A few weeks convinced him of the failure of the scheme, and he returned to Plymouth and resumed his business. Mrs. Diaz' married life was very brief, and she was left with two little sons to care for. When the boys were small, she cut and made their garments, taught a juvenile singing school, private and public schools, and was for one summer housekeeper at a summer resort on an island near Plymouth, where she did all the bread and cake making, because her cook was unsatisfactory. At one time she "put out" work for a large clothing house and in visiting the "lofts" where this was done she received harsh proofs of the poorly paid work of skillful women, who had no other recourse. In 1861 Mrs. Diaz sent a story to the "Atlantic Monthly," under an assumed name, and was delighted with her success when it was accepted and she received a check for forty dollars for it. From that time she took up her life work, to reach and help her fellows through her pen. Her stories for children, originally published in "Young Folks" and other magazines, have a wide fame, and series after series, beginning with "William Henry's Letters to His Grandmother," "Pink and Blue," "The Little Country Girl,"

"Farmer Hill's Diary," "The Schoolmaster's Story" and "Some Account of the Early Life of a Bachelor," were full of the subtle yet simple humor that imbues all Mrs. Diaz's writings. When Rev. Edward Eggleston became editor of "Hearth and Home," he was advised by William Dean Howells to write to Mrs. Diaz, and he did so, the correspondence resulting in the series of papers upon the household life of women which were feigned to have been found in "The Schoolmaster's Trunk." These and others are included in two volumes, "The Bybury Book" and "Domestic Problems." Her letters and articles on household and domestic difficulties caused her to be looked upon as one speaking with authority, and she was invited to lecture upon those questions. She read a paper in the Woman's Congress held in Philadelphia in 1876. The paper was entitled "The Development of Character in Schools," since published in the "Arena." She helped to organize the present Woman's Educational and Industrial Union of Boston. An important work of that association has been the impetus given to the legal protection of helpless women and girls from employers and advertisers who refuse to pay honestly earned wages, or by seductive printed promises wile from their victims money and hours of work, for which they elude payment by trickery. Mrs. Diaz is a profound believer in the "Science of the Higher Life," otherwise known as "Christian Science," and has tested its efficiency in healing and its power for spiritual good, and has written several pamphlets on the subject. Her latest work has been courses of talks on the questions of the day, including the ethics of nationalism, Christian socialism, progressive morality, life, or what is it to live? character work in homes and schools, human nature, competition, and another pamphlet of hers containing a series of papers on arbitration, first published in the "Independent." Mrs. Diaz now makes her home in Belmont, MA, with her oldest son. She has been unanimously re-elected president of the educational and industrial association every year since its organization.

DICKINSON, Miss Anna Elizabeth, orator, author, playwright, actor, reformer and philanthropist, born 28th October, 1842, in Philadelphia, PA. Her father, John Dickinson, died in 1844, leaving his family in straitened circumstances. Anna was sent to the Friends' free school, as her parents belonged to that society. Her early life was full of struggles against adverse conditions. She studied earnestly and read enthusiastically. Whenever she earned any money, she spent it for books. When she was only fourteen years old, she wrote an article on slavery for the "Liberator." She made her début as a public speaker in 1857, in a meeting for discussion held by the Progressive Friends, chiefly interested in the anti-slavery movement. One of the men delivered an insolent tirade against women, and Anna took up the cudgel in behalf of her sex and worsted her insulter. From that time she spoke frequently, generally on slavery and temperance. In 1859 and 1860 she taught school in Berks county, PA, and in 1861, from April to December, she was employed in the United States Mint in Philadelphia. She was dismissed from the Mint because, in a speech in West Chester, she said that the battle of Ball's Bluff "was lost, not through ignorance and incompetence, but through the treason of the commanding general (McClellan)." After dismissal she made a profession of lecturing, adding political subjects to her former ones. William Lloyd Garrison, who heard one of her addresses in Kennett, PA, named her "The Girl Orator," and invited her to speak in the Fraternity Course in Music Hall, Boston, MA, in 1862. She spoke on "The National Crisis." She attracted attention and was engaged to speak in New Hampshire, in Connecticut, in New York City and in Philadelphia. From that time till the end of the Civil War she spoke on war issues. In 1863 she was engaged to deliver a series of addresses, in the gubernatorial campaign, throughout the coal regions, as the male orators were afraid to enter those regions so soon after the draft riots. On 16th January, 1864, she spoke in Washington, DC, and donated the proceeds, over $1,000, to the Freedmen's Relief Society. She delivered many addresses in camps and hospitals. After the war-echoes ceased, she spoke from the lyceum platform chiefly, her lectures being on "Reconstruction" and "Woman's Work and Wages." In 1869 she visited Utah, and afterward she lectured on "Whited Sepulchres," referring to Mormonism. Her subsequent lectures were "Demagogues and Workingmen," "Joan of Arc," and "Between Us Be Truth," the last-named devoted to Missouri and Pennsylvania, in 1873, where obnoxious social evil bills were up for discussion. In 1876 Miss Dickinson decided to leave the lecture platform and go upon the stage. She made her début in "A Crown of Thorns," a play written by herself, and her reception was unfavorable. She next essayed Shakespearean tragic rôles, including Hamlet and others. She afterward gave dramatic readings, but the stage and the dramatic platform were not suited to her, and she returned to the lecture platform. She gave a number of brilliant lectures, "Platform and Stage," "For Yourself," and others. In 1880 she wrote a play, "The American Girl," for Fanny Davenport, which was moderately successful. Among Miss Dickinson's published works are "What Answer?" a novel (Boston, 1868), "A Paying Investment" (Boston, 1876), and "A Ragged Register of People, Places and Opinions" (New York, 1879). Among the plays written by her are "Aurelian," written for John McCullough, but never produced, as his failing powers prevented "A Crown of Thorns" and "The Test of Honor." After leaving the stage, in 1883, Miss Dickinson made her home with her family in Pittston, PA. In 1891 she again came before the public, through family difficulties and through a suit brought against the Republican managers of the Presidential campaign for services rendered by her in 1888. In 1892 she delivered a number of lectures. She has been under treatment for some time for failing health. Miss Dickinson in her younger days was a woman of singular powers of sarcasm, of judgment, of dissection of theories and motives, and of eloquence that can be understood only by those who have heard her on the platform. She has a strong, fine, intelligent face, self-possession, courage that enabled her to stand her ground when fired at by striking miners in Pennsylvania, and all the endowments of presence, voice, wit, pathos and intense dramatic fervor that go to make the great orator. Her work in each line was distinctly marked. In her school work, her novels, her sketches, her lectures, she was unique. Her plays contain passages of undisputed greatness, of poetic beauty and of sublime pathos. She acquired an ample fortune through her lectures, but she has given away the bulk of it in all kinds of charities.

DICKINSON, Miss Susan E., journalist, born near Reading PA, was reared and educated in Philadelphia. Her mother's family were among

the early settlers of Maryland. They were Quakers, who left England in 1660 and 1661 and settled on the eastern shore of the colony of Maryland. Her father's ancestors were of the same religious faith as her mother's, and were among the Maryland pioneers. About 1750 the Dickinsons moved into southern Pennsylvania. Miss Dickinson's father was a wholesale and retail dry-goods merchant in Philadelphia. He died and left a family of five young children, who were carefully reared by the mother. They were educated in the select schools of the Society of Friends in Philadelphia, and in the Westtown boarding-school in Chester county. Susan, at the age of seventeen, became a teacher in the public schools of Philadelphia. She began to write poetry at an early age. Her poems appeared first in the "Saturday Evening Post," the Boston "True Flag," and other journals, under the pen-names "Effie Evergreen," "Violet May" and "Ada Vernon." In 1872 she began to sign her own name to her productions. Her first book was a memoir of a young friend, written for the Presbyterian Board of Publication. Her first regular journalistic work was in the biographical or obituary department of the New York "Herald," to which she was a contributor from November, 1874, until 1881. From 1875 to 1878 she was a regular contributor to the New York "Daily Graphic." From 1875 to 1882 she was a correspondent from northeastern Pennsylvania to the Philadelphia "Press." She also wrote a good deal for the papers of Scranton and Wilkes-Barré, PA, and for the Boston "Evening Traveller." Other duties seriously interrupted her literary work for years, but she has never wholly given it up. Since June, 1891, she has been a member of the editorial staff of the Scranton "Truth." She contributes occasionally to other journals. Miss Dickinson has been a member of the Protestant Episcopal Church ever since she left school. She writes herself down a journalist, although her inclinations have always been toward purely literary work, and she has accomplished enough to justify the name "author." Domestic cares have hindered her in her work, but the Quaker courage born in her has carried her over obstacles that seemed insurmountable.

DICKLOW, Miss Adelaide Lynn, educator, born of French Catholic parents, in Orwell, VT, 6th March, 1859. At the age of fourteen she left the Catholic Church, and soon after united with the Baptist Church, of which she is now a member. As a girl she was bright and cheerful, fond of books and quick to learn. Her education was begun in the public schools of Orwell and Fair Haven, VT, where her parents resided. In 1874 she entered the State Normal School in Albany, NY, and from there she went to the Syracuse University, where she was graduated with honors. Miss Dicklow's parents being in humble circumstances, she had to work her own way from begining to end. After graduating she taught for two years and then entered the Woman's Medical College of Philadelphia, with the intention of taking up the practice of medicine. At the end of one year she was called to Kansas, and soon after the position of professor of modern languages in Ottawa University was offered to her, which she accepted. Miss Dicklow did not give up her studies at graduation but continued a close student and will receive the degree of Ph.D. from her alma mater.

DIEHL, Miss Cora Victoria, register of deeds, born in Laurelton, Union county, PA, 19th January, 1869. When eleven years old she moved with her parents to Great Bend, KS, where the family lived on a farm for five years. Her father, H. C. Diehl, having no son, shaped his daughter's education with the view of bringing her forward as a reformer. At the age of sixteen years she appeared at many public meetings of the Greenback party and delivered recitations. Her parents moved to Montrose, CO, where they lived a short time and then returned to Kansas. The daughter accompanied them and soon accepted a position in the office of the register of deeds in Great Bend. Later she was appointed deputy register, which position she filled for two years, when she resigned 1st January, 1890, to go to her parents in Oklahoma. Miss Diehl joined the Farmers' Alliance and, though but twenty-one years old, became a leader and speaker. She was unanimously nominated by the convention of the People's Party in session in Guthrie for register of deeds for Logan county and was afterward endorsed by the Democrats. She conducted an aggressive campaign and, accompanied by her father, stumped the county. Her speeches showed ability and earnestness, and she got the largest majority of any one on the ticket. She has the distinction of being the first woman to hold office in Oklahoma, and also is the youngest woman in the country to conduct a political campaign in her own behalf.

DIEUDONNÈ, Mrs. Florence Carpenter, littérateur, born in Stockbridge Falls, Madison county, NY, 25th September, 1850. In early life her parents removed to Oshkosh, WI, where her education was completed. In her writing as a school-girl was discerned exceptional excellence. After her marriage she resided for some years in Minnesota, and during that period published her first poems in the Oshkosh "Times" and "Peterson's Magazine." In 1878 she traveled extensively in Europe, and her descriptive letters, written for the papers of her own and other States, gained for her a reputation. "A Prehistoric Romanza" (Minneapolis, 1882), was the first poem she published in book form. She also wrote several cantatas, the most successful of which was "The Captive Butterfly," for which Prof. J. B. Carpenter composed the music. Her fondness for literary pursuits made her many social engagements burdensome, and her fondness for scientific and historical reading clashed with the attention which she felt it her first duty to give to her home, but by improving spare minutes during the last ten years she has written three prose works and many poems. Her descriptive style is vivid. She is a member of the Woman's National Press Association of Washington, DC, vice president of the Short Story Club and founder and president of the Parzelia Circle, a conversational and literary order. Mrs. Dieudonné now resides in Washington, DC.

DIGGS, Mrs. Annie Le Porte, politician and journalist, born in London, Ontario, Canada, 22nd Febuary, 1853. She became the wife of A. S. Diggs, of Lawrence, KS, in 1873. Their family consists of two daughters and one son. Mrs. Diggs traces her ancestry in a direct line to General John Stark, of Revolutionary fame. She has certainly inherited his fighting qualities. After her marriage she began her career in public as a journalist. She entered the field to fight for political and personal independence and equality. She lectured before literary, reformatory and religious assemblages very successfully. In religion she is a radical Unitarian. When the Alliance movement among the western farmers began, she entered the field and soon found herself at the front among those who were engineering that great industrial movement. During the political campaigns in Kansas and neighboring States she made many speeches. She was chosen by the People's Party to reply to the platform utterances of John J. Ingalls, to whose overthrow she contributed largely. She was elected national secretary of the National Citizens' Industrial Alliance, at the annual meeting of that organization in St. Louis, MO, 22nd Febuary, 1892. Mrs. Diggs is a clear, forcible writer, a strong, attractive orator, and a thinker and reasoner of unusual power. She has done considerable lecturing and preaching. In 1881 she addressed the annual convention of the Free Religious Association, in Boston, MA, on "Liberalism in the West." She has for years been a member of the Woman's Christian Temperance Union. Much of her journalistic work was done on the "Advocate," the organ of the Alliance, on which journal she served as the leading editorial writer. She has spent much time in Washington, DC, since the upheaval caused by the Alliance, and has done notable work in correspondence for the western newspapers. She is president of the Woman's Alliance of the District of Columbia.

DIGHT, Mrs. Mary A. G., physician, born in Portsmouth, OH, 7th November, 1860. She is the only daughter of Mary Y. Glidden and George Crawford. Her mother, who died 22nd April, 1891, was a woman of intelligence and refinement, inheriting from one of the cultured New England families the rare mental qualities which she transmitted to her daughter. Mrs. Crawford believed in the higher education of women and encouraged her daughter to pursue the profession of her choice, for which, by her natural abilities and her acquirements, she is qualified, and in which she is now actively engaged. Dr. Dight is a young woman of versatile talents. She is a fine musician, and a graduate of the New England Conservatory of Music, Boston. She speaks German fluently. She is a model housekeeper as well as mistress of the art of healing. She was graduated from the department of regular medicine and surgery of the University of Michigan, one of the youngest of the class of 1884. Returning to Ohio, she practiced a year and then went abroad and continued her studies in Paris and Vienna for two years. She returned to Portsmouth and was chosen president of the Hempstead Academy of Medicine. While a student in medicine, she made the acquaintance of Professor Charles F. Dight, M.D., at that time one of the medical faculty of the University of Michigan, who after a six year's professorship in the American Medical College in Beyrout, Syria, returned to America to marry her. As a lecturer Dr. Dight is pleasing and forcible. She is energetic in urging to efforts for social reforms and for the improvement of the race, by observing the laws of life, health and heredity. Her home is now in Faribault, Minn.

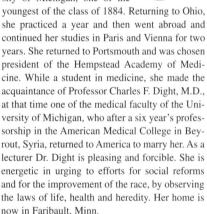

DILLAYE, Miss Blanche, artist, was born in Syracuse, NY. She is the daughter of the late Stephen Dillaye, of Syracuse, whose writings on paper money and the tariff won him an enviable reputation. From early childhood Miss Dillaye showed unusual talent from drawing and a genuine artistic appreciation of pictures. So marked was her ability and so strong her desire to be an artist, that she was allowed to devote a year to the study of drawing. About that time an opportunity to teach drawing in a young ladies' school in Philadelphia was opened to her, and she was thus enabled to pursue her art studies for several years in the Philadelphia Academy of Fine Arts. Her preference for black and white was the source of much concern to her in her early art days. She took one lesson of Stephen Ferrier in the technique of etching. It seemed so simple that she unhesitatingly sent in her name as a contributor to an exhibition to be held in the Academy of Fine Arts, and went so far as to order her frame. She knew little of the vicissitudes of the etcher, but she was on the way to learn, for, when the exhibition opened, her labor was represented only by an under bitten plate, an empty frame, the name in the catalogue of a never finished etching, and the knowledge that etching represents patient labor as well as inspiration. The same year Stephen Parrish came to her rescue, and by his counsel and assistance enabled her to work with insight and certainty. She has contributed to all of the leading exhibitions of this country. Her etchings have also been favorably received abroad. In the rage for etchings that has prevailed during the past few years Miss Dillaye has never condescended to degrade the art to popular uses, but has maintained that true painter-etcher's style which first brought her into notice. Her impressions are vivid and marked by a strong originality. Her ambition is not satisfied to travel in the single track of an etcher. Her studio on South Penn Square, Philadelphia, shows talent in various other directions. Her illustrations and manuscripts have found their way into several leading magazines.

DIX, Miss Dorothea L., philanthropist and army nurse, born in Hampden, ME, in 1802, and died in Trenton, NJ, 7th July, 1887. Her father, a Boston merchant, died in 1821, and Dorothea started a school for girls in that city. She became interested in the convicts in State prisons, visited them and worked to secure better treatment for them. Her school work and her philanthropic labors broke down her health in 1833, when she was prostrated by hemorrhages from the lungs. Having inherited a small fortune, she went to Europe for her health. The voyage benefited her, and in 1837

she returned to Boston and renewed her labors for the paupers, lunatics and prisoners, in which she was assisted by Rev. Dr. Channing. The condition of affairs in the East Cambridge almshouse aroused her indignation, and she set about to secure an improvement in the methods of caring for the insane paupers. She visited every State east of the Rocky Mountains, working with the legislatures to provide for the relief of the wretched inmates of the jails, prisons, almshouses and asylums. In Indiana, Illinois, North Carolina, New York and Pennsylvania she was especially successful in securing legislative action to establish State lunatic asylums. In January, 1843, she addressed to the Legislature of Massachusetts a memorial in behalf of the "insane persons confined within this Commonwealth, in cages, closets, cellars, stalls, pens; chained, naked, beaten with rods, and lashed into obedience!" The result was a great improvement. In twenty States she visited asylums, pointed out abuses and suggested reforms. She succeeded in founding thirty-two asylums in the United States, in Canada, Nova Scotia, Guernsey and Rome. She secured the changing of the lunacy laws of Scotland. She went to Europe, and there she visited Paris, Florence, Rome, Athens, Constantinople, Vienna, Moscow and St. Petersburg in search of her wards. Sensitive and refined, she encountered all kinds of men, penetrated into the most loathsome places and faced cruel sights, that she might render effectual service to men and women in whom the loss of reason had not extinguished the human nature, in which her religious soul always saw the work of God. The years between her return from Europe and the outbreak of the Civil War Miss Dix spent in confirming the strength of the asylums that had sprung from her labors. On 19th April, 1861, she went to do duty as a nurse in the Union army. During the war she was chief of the woman nurses, and to her is due the soldiers' monument at Fortress Monroe. She established a life-saving station on Sable Island, and, after the war, took up again her asylums, seeking their enlargement, improvement and maintenance. At eighty years of age a retreat was offered her in the Trenton asylum, which she was wont to call her "first-born" child. There, after five years of suffering, she died. Besides being the author of countless memorials to legislatures on the subject of lunatic asylums, Miss Dix wrote and published anonymously "The Garland of Flora" (Boston,

1829), "Conversations About Common Things," "Alice and Ruth," "Evening Hours" and other books for children, "Prisons and Prison Discipline" (Boston, 1845), and a great number of tracts for prisoners.

DIXON, Mrs. Mary J. Scarlett, physician, born in Robeson township, Berks county, PA, 23rd October, 1822. Her parents were members of the Society of Friends, and Mary was the youngest of seven children. Her father was a farmer. He died when she was about four years old, and a brother's death soon after left the mother with six children, on a farm not very productive, and with plenty of hard work, in which all the children did their full share. When the agitation against slavery loomed up in 1830, the family was the only one in the neighborhood that took an active part, and their house became the resort for anti-slavery lectures. When Mary was sixteen years old, her mother died. As soon as the estate was settled, she began to teach in country schools. After teaching a few years, she went to boarding-school for a year, and again taught for a time, and went again to boarding-school one term. Her thoughts were led toward medicine in early childhood. With the aim of becoming a physician, her teaching was to provide means. When in 1850 the Female Medical College of Pennsylvania, later changed to the Woman's Medical College of Pennsylvania, opened its doors to students, she received information from one of its professors that she was wanted. Duties to her oldest sister prevented her from entering until the autumn of 1855. She was graduated in 1857. Feeling that the time for study was too short, she took another course of lectures, better to fit her for general practice. During that course of lectures she took special pains to obtain practice among the poor, in order to build up the clinic at the college, not only for her own benefit, but for the general good of the college. During a part of 1858–59 she gave lectures on hygiene in country towns and villages. In the autumn of 1859 she was appointed demonstrator of anatomy in the Woman's Medical College and returned to Philadelphia to take the position. The hospitals in the city were not open to women physicians for instruction, and the college management felt it necessary to make some change for the better clinical instruction of the stu-

dents. Larger buildings were purchased for a woman's hospital, in which rooms could be utilized temporarily for college purposes. In the hospital Emeline H. Cleveland, M.D., was appointed resident physician and Dr. Scarlett assistant physician. There they built up a good clinic and outdoor practice, which, in addition to the hospital, afforded the students good opportunities for practical instruction. In 1862 she received the appointment of professor of anatomy in the college. After a few years, feeling she had undertaken too much, she resigned the position of demonstrator of anatomy. In 1865 she resigned the position of assistant physician in the hospital, to make a home for herself. In 1868 she returned to the hospital as resident physician, remaining there until 1871, when she returned to her home, at the same time being appointed visiting physician to the hospital. On 8th May, 1873, she became the wife of G. Washington Dixon, still retaining her professorship and engaged in active practice, along with her duties as professor of anatomy. In 1881 her connection with the college was discontinued. As glaucoma was troubling her, she placed herself under the care of a skilled ophthalmologist for the treatment of her eyes. She continued actively engaged until through diminished vision she was forced to hand over many patients to others. She still continues to treat some cases. She resides in Philadelphia.

DODD, Mrs. Anna Bowman, author, was born in Brooklyn, NY. She is a daughter of Stephen M. Blake. At the age of twelve years she began to write stories, and her subsequent education was supplemented by travel and study in Europe. One of her first efforts for the public was a translation of one of Théophile Gautier's works, which was published in the New York "Evening Post." She was engaged to contribute editorials and other articles to that journal. She wrote many short stories, essays and a series of articles on church music for "Harper's Magazine." She wrote a paper on the School of Philosophy in Concord. French and English journals copied it, and the author found her services and talents in growing demand. She was engaged by the Harpers to furnish an exhaustive article on the political leaders of France, to prepare which she went to Europe, in order to be able to study her subject on the ground. She was cordially received by scholars, who had read her articles on the Concord School. Before returning, she went to Rome and prepared a description of the carnival for "Harper's Magazine." Her first book was "Cathedral Days" (Boston, 1887), and her second "The Republic of the Future" (New York, 1887), both of which were successful. She has published one novel, "Glorinda" (Boston, 1888), and a book on Normandy, "In and Out of Three Normandy Inns" (New York, 1892). She is busy with domestic duties, but she is working always in the literary field. She has a charming home in New York. In 1883 she became the wife of Edward Williams Dodd, of Boston, but whose residence has been for several years in New York.

DODDS, Mrs. Susanna Way, physician, born in a log cabin in Randolph county, near Richmond, IN, 10th November, 1830. Her father was a lineal descendant of Henry Way, a Puritan, who emigrated from England to this country in 1630. Both father and mother were members of the Society of Friends. Their ancestors, who went west from Guilford, NC, were originally from Nantucket. Susanna was the eldest of thirteen children. The father was in moderate circumstances and could give them only a common-school education. The eldest daughter was ambitious, and early set her heart on going to college. To her great grief, she soon found that, with the exception of Oberlin, there was not a college in the land that would admit women. There were only ladies' seminaries. She therefore decided to go to Oxford Female Institute, which was then conducted by Rev. J. W. Scott, the father-in-law of President Benjamin Harrison. To do this, Miss Way began teaching in the common schools at a salary of eight dollars a month, and boarded herself. She was then seventeen years of age. By rigid economy she saved a small sum of money, and in her twenty-third year received her diploma from Dr. Scott's seminary. The much-coveted college course was not given up. The university in Ann Arbor was founded, and its doors were afterward thrown open to women. Antioch, with Horace Mann at its head admitted women and in the spring of 1856 Miss Way

entered the preparatory department of that college. Again her plans were frustrated. Sickness in her father's family called her home and also prevented her from earning money. The following year she became the wife of Andrew Dodd, a young Scotchman, whose liberal views were in harmony with her own. They made their home in Yellow Springs, OH, and Mrs. Dodds renewed her studies in Antioch, where she afterward graduated. She also completed a medical course, in 1864, in the New York Hygeio-Therapeutic College. Her husband at that time enlisted in the Federal army, and by exposure in the mountains of Virginia contracted a fatal disease. A short time before his death the family moved to St. Louis, MO, and in 1870 Dr. Dodds began to practice in that city. She was joined by her husband's sister, Dr. Mary Dodds, with whom she is still associated. As physicians they have done much for the physical redemption of women. Dr. Susanna Way Dodds is dean of the St. Louis Hygienic College of Physicians and Surgeons, and also a member of its faculty. She has written and published a work on dietetics, entitled "Health in the Household," and has contributed to a number of health journals and other papers.

DODGE, Miss Grace Hoadley, philanthropist and educational reformer, born in New York City, in 1856. With large wealth and high social position, Miss Dodge has devoted much of her time to works of charity in her native city. In 1886 she was appointed a school commissioner on the New York school board, in company with Mrs. Agnew. Her work in that position fully justified the new movement that called for women members of that board. On entering her new field of labor she said: "I came into the board of education with three distinct objects in view, to remember my oath of office, which means to sustain the manual of the board of education; to consider for the 200,000 children in the public schools what is wisest and best for them; to be loyal to the 4,000 teachers, and to think of myself as the especial representative of 3,500 women teachers." Immediately after appointment Miss Dodge and Mrs. Agnew made a study of the manual, of methods in this country and in others, of books, buildings, school furniture and apparatus, discipline and all that pertains to schools and teaching, and Miss Dodge gave to these duties almost her entire time, and accomplished an unprecedented amount of work. She visited, with more or less frequency, every day school in the city, 132 in number, and the thirty-nine evening schools, became acquainted as far as possible with every teacher and principal, studied the conditions and necessities of each school, and made careful notes for reports. The committees on which she served were those on auditing, on school books and courses of study, on school furniture, on sites and new schools, and on evening schools, and the reports which were made while she was a member of those committees were peculiarly interesting and important, and several of them have been the means of great and significant changes. When there are added to the duties already mentioned an attendance at school-board meetings twice a month, the sessions often lasting from four to eight o'clock, semi-weekly committee meetings, and a half day on Saturday, which Miss Dodge devotes to the reception of teachers in her private office in her home on Madison Avenue, when she hears their grievances and gives them advice, it will be understood that not only were the regular duties of the position onerous, but the gratuitous and self-imposed ones were far from light. It was due conspicuously to Miss Dodge's influence that, in spite of opposition, manual training has been introduced into the schools in part. She secured relief for certain over-crowded primary and grammar schools. She succeeded in having the school board continue the evening schools for girls, and she aided in correcting the plan of apportioning the salaries of teachers and of holding examinations for certificates. In every way the presence and work of Miss Dodge and Mrs. Agnew were a benefit to the cause of education in New York. Besides her regular school work, Miss Dodge has done a good deal of philanthropic and educational work in New York. Her charitable labor has been based not on theory, but on practical knowledge of the conditions of the working people, gained by personal contact with them. Of this the proofs are the large number of working girls' clubs, of which she is the founder, a movement of which she was the leader, and which has spread throughout the country, and the New York College for Training Teachers, of which she was the inaugurator. Observation convinced her that the needy should be helped to help themselves, and that was the origin of her interest in education, which dates back a considerable time before she was invited to serve on the board of education. She was an active member of the board of the State Charities Aid Association, and has been connected with hospitals, a training school for nurses, and is a trustee of the Medical College for Female Physicians.

DODGE, Miss Hannah P., educator, born on a farm in Littleton, MA, 6th February, 1821, where her girlhood was spent. She attended the public school and afterward spent several terms in a select school for young ladies. When she was seventeen years old, she began to teach a district school in a neighboring town. She next taught successfully in her own town. After teaching for some terms, she went to the Lawrence Academy in Groton, MA. She completed her education in the Townsend Female Seminary, in Townsend, MA. After graduating from that school, she was chosen a teacher in the institution. One year later she was chosen principal of the school, a position which she held for even years. She held the position of principal in the Oread Institute in Worcester, MA, for several years, traveled in Europe for a year and there studied modern languages and art. She has traveled much in her own country. After her sojourn in Europe, she took a desirable position in Dorchester, MA, where she successfully managed a young ladies' school for five years. Retiring from the school field, she purchased a pleasant home in Littleton, where her family had remained. In that town she was made a superintendent of schools, and served a number of years. She is president of the local Woman's Christian Temperance Union and one of the trustees of the public library, and is active in charitable work.

DODGE, Miss Mary Abigail, author, widely known by her pen-name, "Gail Hamilton," born in Hamilton, MA, in 1830. She received a thorough education, and in 1851 became instructor in physical science in the high school in Hartford, CT. She was next a governess in the family of Dr. Gamaliel Bailey, of Washington, DC, and was a regular contributor to his journal, the "National Era." In the years 1865 to 1867, inclusive, she was one of the editors of "Our Young Folks." After 1876 she lived principally in Washington. She contributed much to prominent magazines and newspapers, and the name "Gail Hamilton" attached to an essay is a guarantee that it is full of wit and aggressiveness. Her published volumes include "Country Living and Country Thinking" (1862), "Gala-Days" (1863), "A New Atmosphere" and "Stumbling Blocks" (1864), "Skirmishes and Sketches" (1865), "Red-Letter Days in Applethorpe" and "Summer Rest" (1866), "Wool-Gathering" (1867), "Woman's Wrongs, a CounterIrritant," (1868), "Battle of the Books" (1870), "Woman's Worth and Worthlessness" (1871), "Little Folk Life" (1872), "Child World" (2 vols., 1872 and 1873), "Twelve Miles from a Lemon" (1873), "Nursery Noonings" (1874), "Sermons to the Clergy" and "First Love is Best" (1875), "What Think Ye of Christ?" (1876), "Our Common-School System" (1880), "Divine Guidance, Memorial of Allen W. Dodge," (1881), "The Insuppressible Book" (1885), and "A Washington Bible Class" (1891). In 1877 she contributed to the New York "Tribune" a notable series of vigorous letters on civil service reform. Miss Dodge commands a terse, vigorous, direct style. She cuts through shams and deceits with an easy and convincing blow that leaves no room for doubt. Her essays cover almost every field of comment and criticism. She died in Hamilton, 17th August, 1896.

DODGE, Mrs. Mary Mapes, author and editor, born in New York City, 26th January, 1838. She is the daughter of Prof. James J. Mapes, the distinguished promoter of scientific farming in the United States. She was educated by private tutors, and early showed talents for drawing, modeling and musical and literary composition. At an early age she became the wife of William Dodge, a lawyer of New York City. He died in his prime, leaving Mrs. Dodge with two sons to care for. She turned to literature as a means to earn the money to educate her sons. She began to write short sketches for children, and soon brought out a volume of them, entitled "Irvington Stories," (New York, 1864), which was very successful. She next published "Hans Brinker, or the Silver Skates" (New York, 1865). With Donald G. Mitchell and Harriet Beecher Stowe, Mrs. Dodge

was one of the earliest editors of "Hearth and Home," and for several years she conducted the household and childrens' department of that journal. In 1873, when "St. Nicholas" was started, she became its editor, which position she still holds. Her "Hans Brinker" has been translated into Dutch, French, German, Russian and Italian, and was awarded a prize of 1,500 francs by the French Academy. Her other published volumes are "A Few Friends, and How They Amused Themselves" (Philadelphia, 1869), "Rhymes and Jingles" (New York, 1874), "Theophilus and Others" (New York, 1876), "Along the Way," poems (New York, 1879), and "Donald and Dorothy" (New York, 1883). She is the author of "Miss Maloney on the Chinese Question," published in "Scribner's Monthly" in 1870. She has a pleasant home in New York, which is a literary center. One of her sons died in 1881, and the other, James Mapes Dodge is a successful inventor and manufacturer, residing in Philadelphia, PA. Mrs. Dodge contributes to "Harper's Magazine," "Atlantic Monthly," the "Century" and other periodicals.

DODSON, Miss Caroline Matilda, physician, born near Keosauqua, IA, 17th December, 1845. Her father, Stiles Richard Dodson, was the son of Richard Dodson and Hannah Watson, being a descendant of Thomas and Mary Dodson, of whom the doctor's mother was also a descendant. Her mother, Mrs. Caroline Matilda Dodson, was the daughter of Stephen Harrison, and Mary Dodson. Miss Dodson's father and mother were natives of Huntington Valley, PA. On 28th July, 1836, they were united in marriage. The mother, Mrs. C. Matilda Dodson, was a woman of strong character and advanced thought. About six weeks after marriage they left Pennsylvania for the West and settled in Van Buren county, IA. Stiles R. Dodson died 28th October, 1847, leaving his widow with four daughters, the youngest not two years of age. That winter the mother taught school in her own house. In the spring of 1848 she returned with her family to her father's house in Pennsylvania. Caroline was baptized in November, 1857, and she was henceforth a laborer by the side of her mother, in the Baptist Church. Study at home under private teachers and at the district school supplemented the early lessons from the mother. At about twelve she was sent to an academy and normal institute. She began to teach in the winter of 1861. Returning at intervals to school, she followed the profession of teaching until the fall of 1871 when she matriculated at the Woman's Medical College of Pennsylvania, and entered upon the three year course just inaugurated. Dr. Ann Preston was then Dean. The summer of 1872 she spent in the Nurses' Training School of the Woman's Hospital of Philadelphia. The course required was completed and a certificate of the Training School for Nurses was given her. The summer of 1873 she spent in the same hospital as student in the wards and out practice. She received her diploma in March, 1874, and went to Ypsilanti, MI, for further study with Dr. Ruth A. Gerry, one of the first women to practice medicine. After a year spent in hospital and private practice with that worthy medical pioneer, she went to Rochester, NY, and there in connection with practice opened a drug store. In 1877, her mother having gone West again, she started for Iowa, going by the Hudson and Great Lakes. She lost a car load of valuables in the riot at Pittsburgh, PA. After her trip West she returned to Philadelphia and worked for a mere pittance. Among the offers that came finally was one from the Philadelphia Society for Organizing Charity, to act as superintendent of one of its districts, which position she filled for eight years. Realizing the need of a movement to educate the masses to a knowledge of self-care, she was prominent in having a call issued for a public meeting to be held in Association Hall, Philadelphia, 23rd July, 1890, and an organization was effected under the name of the National Woman's Health Association of America. The Association was chartered 1st November, 1890, and Dr. Dodson was elected first president.

DOE, Mrs. Mary L., woman suffragist, temperance reformer and business woman, born in Conneaut, OH, 27th July, 1836. Her maiden name was Thompson. Her immediate ancestors, the Thompsons and Harpers, emigrated from Vermont and settled in that portion of Ohio known as the Western Reserve. At nine years of age she was sent to the Conneaut Academy, then just completed. At fifteen she began to teach a country school for one dollar a week and "boarded around." Later she attended the State Normal School in Edinboro, PA. She signed the pledge under one of the original Washingtonians when but eight years old, and in 1853 she joined the Good Templars. In 1878 she became a member of the Michigan Grand Lodge of Good Templars, and held the office of grand vice-templar and of grand assistant secretary for several years. She has further shown her interest in temperance by joining the Woman's Christian Temperance Union and the various other temperance organizations in the towns where she has lived. In 1877 Mrs. Doe went to Saginaw, MI, where she at once made friends with the advocates of equal suffrage. In 1884, in a meeting called in Flint by equal suffragists of national prominence to organize a State suffrage association, Mrs. Doe was chosen president of the association. That office she held for six years. She has been active in securing many of the privileges granted to women by the Legislature of Michigan, and has spent much of her time with other equal suffragists in the State capital. Mrs. Doe changed her residence from Saginaw to Bay City in 1886, and opened a store for fancy goods.

DOLE, Mrs. Phebe Cobb Larry, poet, born in Gorham, ME, 28th November, 1835. Her great-grandfather, Dennis Larry, came from Ireland to fight in the French and Indian war, and afterward settled on land granted him in Gorham. Her mother was the great-granddaughter of Ezra Brown, one of the early settlers of Windham, ME, who was killed by the Indian chief Poland, during the last battle between the inhabitants of Windham and the Indians, 14th May, 1756. Her father, Joseph C. Larry, of Windham, was a blacksmith and farmer. She was educated in the common schools of her own town and in Gorham Seminary. Some of her early poetical productions fell into the hands of a well-known critic and scholar, who secured their publication in several Maine papers, much to the surprise of their youthful author. In 1853 she became the wife of Samuel T. Dole, of Windham. In 1860 Mrs. Dole began to write for the Portland "Transcript," the Kennebec "Journal," Hallowell "Gazette" and other Maine papers.

DONLEVY, Miss Alice, artist and writer on art, was born in Manchester, England. Miss Donlevy came to the United States in her infancy. She early showed a talent for drawing, and at ten years of age she exhibited water-color copies at the American Institute, and at thirteen she was admitted to the School of Design. For seven years she devoted her attention to wood-engraving for books and magazines, being one of the first workers in this art to introduce that original feature of American wood-engraving, the use of dots instead of lines for shades and shadows. Later engraving was given up for designing for decoration. Since childhood she has drawn with pen and ink for reproduction, her father, John J. Donlevy, having invented certain valuable reproductive processes. Original work once entered upon, she exhibited, while still very young, in the Academy of Design, and won prizes for general attainments. She received a second prize awarded by the Philadelphia Sketch Club for illumination. At the age of fourteen she wrote for the press. In 1867 she published a book on "Illumination," making all of the designs for its illustrations. Since that time she has written for the "Art Review" of Boston, the "Art Amateur," the "Art Interchange," "St. Nicholas," "Harper's Young People," "The Ladies' World," "Demorest's Magazine" and the "Chautauquan," and is now the art editor of Demorest's Magazine." In 1867 she was one of the nine professional women artists who founded the Ladies' Art Association of New York. Among new professions for women established by the association was that of painting on porcelain. In 1887 she was one of the committee of three to go to Albany and lay before the legislature plans of free art industrial instruction for talented, boys, girls and women, to be given during vacation seasons and on Saturday afternoons. The bill passed both houses. It was defeated later by eight votes when called up for reconsideration by Ray Hamilton. Probably the best work of Miss Donlevy has been the aid that she has given personally to promote the interests of struggling associations and individual artists by means of free lectures and free lessons, and also by giving the latter introduction by means of public receptions at which their works were exhibited.

DONNELLY, Miss Eleanor Cecilia, poet, born in Philadelphia, PA, 6th September, 1848. Her father was Dr. Philip Carroll Donnelly. Miss Donnelly

has been called "The morning star of Catholic song" in our land, for her poetic utterances, which form so valuable a contribution to the Catholic literature of the day, are of a lofty tone and great volume. When the Centennial of the Adoption of the Constitution was celebrated in Philadelphia, in 1887, an ode from her pen was read before the American Catholic Historical Society of that city. The first of Miss Donnelly's publications was a hymn to the Blessed Virgin, written at the age of nine. Though best known as a writer of poems, she has, besides producing many tales for secular magazines, made a number of meritorious contributions to Catholic fiction. In the spring of 1885 the Augustinian Fathers showed their appreciation of Miss Donnelly's gifts by procuring for her from Rome a golden reliquary ornamented with filigree work, which contains relics of the four illustrious members of their order. On 1st February, 1888, Pope Leo XIII manifested approval of her zeal and admiration for her powers by sending her his apostolic benediction. The "Jubilee Hymn" was translated into Italian and German. It was also set to music composed expressly for the words. Miss Donnelly's published works include: "Out of Sweet Solitude" (Philadelphia, 1874); "Domus Dei" (Philadelphia, 1875); "The Legend of the Best Beloved" (New York, 1880); "Crowned with Stars, Legends and Lyrics for the Children of Mary, and Other Poems" (Notre Dame, IN, 1881); "Hymns of the Sacred Heart, with Music" (Philadelphia, 1882); "Children of the Golden Sheaf, and Other Poems" (Philadelphia, 1884); "The Birthday Bouquet, Culled from the Shrines of the Saints and the Garden of the Poets" (New York, 1884); "Garland of Festival Songs" (New York, 1885); "Little Compliments of the Season, Original, Selected and Translated Verses" (New York, 1886); "A Memoir of Father Felix Joseph Barbelin, S. J." (Philadelphia, 1886); "The Conversion of St. Augustine, and Other Poems" (Philadelphia, 1887); "Liguori Leaflets" (Philadelphia, 1887), and "Poems" (Philadelphia, 1892).

DOOLITTLE, Mrs. Lucy Salisbury, philanthropist, born in Farmersville, Cattaraugus county, NY, 7th October, 1832. From infancy her

Hilda Clark.
From Photo by
Morrison, Chicago.

Maude Adams.
From Photo by
Morrison, Chicago.

Emma Dillman.
From Photo by
Hemperley, Philadelphia.

home was at Castile, NY. Not being satisfied with a common school education, at the age of twenty she went to Yellow Springs, OH, where she entered the preparatory department of Antioch College, and afterward took collegiate studies. In Antioch she became the wife of Myrick H. Doolittle, a graduate of the college and for awhile professor there. In 1863 she went to Washington, DC, at once entering into the work in the hospitals, and was thus engaged until the fall of 1865, a part of the time as volunteer nurse, and during the remainder as agent for the Sanitary Commission. Immediately after the war she became interested in the prisons and jails. It was her labor in them which brought to her a realization of the terrible condition of female convicts and convinced her of the need of suffrage for women, that they might have the power effectually to aid their suffering sisters of the lower classes. She was also at the same time conducting a sewing school for women and girls of the colored race, who had flocked to Washington at the close of the war. In that work, and also in that of the Freedmen's Bureau with which she was connected as agent, she saw so many homeless and friendless children

that her sympathies were aroused for them. She and her husband helped to organize the Industrial Home School for poor white children of the District of Columbia, now a flourishing institution supported by appropriations from Congress. In 1875 her energies were enlisted in work for poor colored children, and she became a member of the National Association for the Relief of Destitute Colored Women and Children, with which she has been connected ever since, being its efficient treasurer for nine years and working at other times on various committees. A comparatively new branch of that institution is a Home for Colored Foundlings, in which she at present takes an especial interest. In the associated charities and in the charitable work of the Unitarian Church she has done good service. In all of her work for the poor of Washington she has shown practical ability and a marked talent for business.

DORR, Mrs. Julia C. R., poet, born in Charleston, SC, 13th February, 1825. Her mother, Zulma De Lacy Thomas, was the daughter of French refugees who fled from San Domingo during the insurrection of the slaves near the close of the last century. The mother died during Mrs. Dorr's infancy, and her father, William Young Ripley, who was a merchant in Charleston, returned in 1830 to Vermont, his native state. There he engaged in business again, and devoted himself chiefly to the development of the Rutland marble quarries. There his daughter grew to womanhood, in a home of culture and refinement. When the poet was a little child, she began to write, but none of her poems were printed until she became a woman grown. In 1847 she became the wife of Hon. Seneca M. Dorr, of New York. Himself a man of wide culture, he gave to Mrs. Dorr the encouragement and stimulus which directed her to a literary life. In 1847 he sent one of Mrs. Dorr's poems, without her knowledge, to the "Union Magazine," and this was her first published poem. In 1848 her first published story, "Isabel Leslie," gained a one-hundred dollar prize offered by "Sartain's Magazine." In 1857 Mr. Dorr took up his residence in Rutland, VT, and since that date the author's pen has rarely been idle. Her work has constantly appeared in the best publications, and her books have followed each other at intervals until 1885, when her latest volume, "Afternoon Songs," appeared. Her books are: "Farmingdale" (New York, 1854), "Lanmere" (New York, 1855), "Sybil Huntington" (New York, 1869), "Poems" (Philadelphia, 1871), "Expiation" (Philadelphia, 1873), "Friar Anselmo and Other Poems" (New York, 1879), "The Legend of the Babouhka" (New York, 1881), "Daybreak" (New York, 1882), "Bermuda" (New York, 1884), "Afternoon Songs" (New York, 1885). In Mrs. Dorr's poems are found strength and melody, sweetness and sympathy, a thorough knowledge of poetic technique, and through all a high purpose which renders such work of lasting value. Her stories are particularly skillful in detail and plot, in the interpretation of the New England character. Her essays on practical themes of life and living have had a wide circulation and a large influence. A series of essays and letters published some years ago in a New England magazine and addressed to husbands and wives were collected and published without her consent by a Cincinnati publishing house. Mrs. Dorr's social influence in her own town is wide and strong, and from one who knows her well come these apppreciative words: "When summer days were long, and she

was bearing the burden and heat of the day as a young wife and mother, Mrs. Dorr's life was eminently quiet and secluded, her pen being almost her only link with the outside world. But with the autumn rest have come to her wider fields and broader activities. In and around her beautiful home, enriched with treasures from many lands, there has grown up a far-reaching intellectual life, of which she is the soul and center. She is loved and honored in her own town, and there hundreds of women, of all ranks, turn to her for help and inspiration. The year of Mr. Dorr's death, she became the leader of a band of women who founded the Rutland Free Library, the success of which has been so remarkable. Mrs. Dorr is still president of the association, and has given to the library, in memory of her husband, what is said to be the finest and most complete collection of books on political science to be found in New England, outside of Cambridge University." The character of Mrs. Dorr's personal influence is such as to leave a lasting impression upon the men and women of her time, and the quality of her work assures for her books a permanent place among the best achievements of literary workers in America.

DORSEY, Mrs. Anna Hanson, author, born in Georgetown, DC, 16th December, 1816. She is descended on her mother's side from the De Rastricks of Yorkshire, England, from the noble house of Vasa of Sweden, from the MacAlpine MacGregors and the Lingans. On her father's side she descends from the McKenneys. John Hanson became a distinguished colonist in Maryland, rose to the rank of colonel, and founded a race which stands second to none in the annals of the country. His grandsons, Samuel of Samuel and John Hanson, were two of the most earnest supporters of the cause of independence, the latter being one of the signers of the Articles of Federation. His great grandson, Daniel of St. Thomas Jenifer, signed the Constitution. His great-great-grandsons, Thomas Stone and John H. Stone, were respectively a signer of the Declaration of Independence and governor of Maryland. The Lingans were among the early colonists from Wales, and held positions of trust in Maryland as early as the reign of William and Mary. Their noblest representative, Gen. James Lingan, the brother of her grandfather, after brilliant Revolutionary services, was murdered by the same mob in Baltimore, in 1812, that wreaked its savagery on Light Horse Harry Lee and Musgrove, his comrades in arms. Mrs. Dorsey's grandfather, Nicholas Lingan, was educated in St. Omers, France, where his kinsman, barrister Charles Carroll, had been sent in his youth, and he was the first man in the District of Columbia to issue manumission papers. His objection to slavery extended down his line to his latest descendants. Mrs. Dorsey declined to answer "Uncle Tom's Cabin," because, as she said in response to the demand made on her by public and publishers, "with the exception of the burning of the slaves hinted at" (of which she had never heard an instance), "everything represented as the inevitable result of the system of slavery is true, however kind and considerate of the slaves the masters might be." She was brought up under the influence of the old emancipation party of the border States, who were conscientiously opposed to slavery, but never made themselves offensive to those who were not. Her father, Rev. William McKenney, belonged to an old Eastern Shore family, which has been represented in the Legislature, the courts and on the bench for generations. In politics her race were all Federalists and old-line Whigs, and she was an ardent Unionist during the Civil War. Her oldest brother was one of the last men in the Senate of Virginia to make a speech against secession. Her only son served in the Union Army and got his death-wound while planting the Stars and Stripes on the ramparts at Fort Hell. In 1837 she became the wife of Lorenzo Dorsey, of Baltimore, a son of judge Owen Dorsey. She and her husband are converts to the Catholic faith. She has devoted herself exclusively to Catholic light literature, of which she is the pioneer in this country, with the exception of two ringing war lyrics, "Men of the Land" and "They're Coming, Grandad," the latter dedicated to the loyal people of East Tennessee, who suffered such martyrdom for their fidelity to the old flag. She began her literary career by a touching little story called "The Student of Blenheim Forest," and this was followed rapidly by "Oriental Pearl," "Nora Brady's Vow," "Mona the Vestal," "Heiress of Carrigmona," "Tears on the Diadem," "Woodreve Manor," "The Young Countess," "Dummy," "Coaina, the Rose of the Algonquins," "Beth's Promise," "Warp and Woof," "Zoe's Daughter," "Old House at Gle-

naran," "Fate of the Dane," "Mad Penitent of Todi," "A Brave Girl," "Story of Manuel," "The Old Grey Rosary," "Ada's Trust," "Adrift," "Palms," and others. Her books have brought her the friendship of whole religious communities, prelates and authors, and across the seas the venerable Catholic Earl of Shrewsbury and Lady George Fullerton were among her warm admirers. "May Brooke" was the first Catholic book published in Edinburgh since the Reformation, and "Coaina" has been twice dramatized and translated into German and Hindustani. Pope Leo has twice sent her his special blessing, first by the Cardinal Archbishop James Gibbons, and the second time by her granddaughter, Miss Mohun, at a recent special audience. She has also received the gift of the Laetare medal from the University of Notre Dame for distinguished services rendered to literature, education and religion. Mrs. Dorsey is now an invalid, and is living with her children in Washington, DC.

DORSEY, Miss Ella Loraine, author, born in Washington, DC, in 185–. She is the youngest child of Mrs. Anna Hanson Dorsey, the pioneer of Catholic light literature in America. Born a few years before the breaking out of the Civil War, her early childhood was spent amid the stirring scenes of border life. The entire kin on both sides were in the Confederacy, with the exception of her father and her only brother, who received his death wound on the ramparts of "Fort Hell," where he had dashed up with the colors, caught from the color-bearer, and stood cheering his comrades to the charge. Miss Dorsey represents old and illustrious families of Maryland, counting among her kinsfolk and connections two signers of the Declaration of Independence, eight signers of the Act of the Maryland Convention of 26th July, 1776, two Presidents, seven Governors, thirty-six commissioned officers in the Continental Army, and a number of the young heroes of the famous old Maryland Line, who died on the field of honor at Long Island, Harlem Heights and Fort Washington. She began her literary career as a journalist and was for several years the "Vanity Fair" of the Washington "Critic," leaving that paper to take a special correspondence on the Chicago

"Tribune." John Boyle O'Reilly and the Rev. D. E. Hudson, editor of the "Ave Maria," urged her into magazine work: Her first three stories appeared almost simultaneously, "The Knickerbocker Ghost" and "The Tsar's Horses," in the "Catholic World," and "Back from the Frozen Pole," in "Harper's Magazine." "The Tsar's Horses" traveled round the world, its last reproduction being in New Zealand. It was attributed at first, because of its accuracy of detail, to Archibald Forbes, the war correspondent. Miss Dorsey's specialty is boys' stories. "Midshipman Bob" went through two editions in this country and England in its first year, and has been since translated into Italian. Scarcely second to it in popularity are "Saxty's Angel" and "The Two Tramps," while two poems printed in the "Cosmopolitan" have been received with marked favor. Miss Dorsey is the Russian translator in the Scientific Library of the Interior Department, Washington, DC. She is an enthusiastic member and officer of the Daughters of the American Revolution, and her latest work is "Three Months with Smallwood's Immortals," a sketch written for and read before the Washington branch of that society. Last year four sketches, "Women in the Patent Office," "Women in the Pension Office," and "Women in the Land Office," were prepared by her for the "Chautauquan." They attracted much attention and secured wide recognition for the brave ladies who toil at their department desks. Her home is on Washington Heights.

DORTCH, Miss Ellen J., newspaper editor and publisher, was born in Georgia, 25th January, 1868. She is descended from Virginia families on both sides, and her ancestors have figured conspicuously in affairs of state. Her father, James S. Dortch, who died in August, 1891, was for a quarter of a century a prominent lawyer. Miss Dortch received a thorough education, which, with her progressive and enterprising spirit, has enabled her to take high rank as a journalist. She became the owner and editor of the Carnesville, GA, "Tribune" in 1888, when the establishment consisted of one-hundred-fifty pounds of long primer type, mostly in "pi," a few cases of worn advertising type and a subscription book whose credit column had been conscientiously neglected. Now the old presses and worn type are replaced by new and improved ones, and the circulation of the paper has increased to thousands, and the

energetic, spirited woman who has been typo, editor and business manager, who has solicited and canvassed the district for subscribers, because she wasn't able to hire any one to do it for her, has the satisfaction of seeing her efforts crowned with a full measure of success. Beginning the work when only seventeen years old, she has fought the boycotters and Alliance opponents and overcome the southern prejudice against women who use their brain in making their way in the world. After working for two years, she went to Baltimore, MD, where she studied for two years in the Notre Dame school. She resumed her work on the "Tribune" in June, 1890.

DOUGHTY, Mrs. Eva Craig Graves, journalist, born in Warsaw, KY, 1st December, 1852. Her father, Judge Lorenzo Graves, was a politician and an able lawyer. Her mother was Virginia Hampton-Graves. Mrs. Doughty was educated in Oxford Female College, Oxford, OH, leaving her Kentucky home during the war years from 1860 to 1864, which years she passed in the college with her two other sisters. Prior to that she had been taught by private tutors. After a four-year course in Oxford, she entered the Academy of the Most Holy Rosary, in Louisville, KY, conducted by sisters of the Dominican order, where she studied nearly three years, and left just two months before she would have been graduated, to accompany a sister, whose husband was in the regular army, to a frontier post. On 24th May, 1874, she became the wife of John R. Doughty, then editor and proprietor of the Mt. Pleasant, MI, "Enterprise." She was at once installed as associate editor with her husband. Mrs. Doughty did regular newspaper work on that paper for fourteen years, keeping the office hours and doing anything connected with the office work, from proof-reading and type-setting to writing for any department of the paper where "copy" was called for. Subsequently Mr. Doughty sold the "Enterprise" and for three years engaged in business in Grand Rapids, MI, where the family removed. There Mrs. Doughty engaged in public work. She was elected president of the Grand Rapids Equal Suffrage Association, which position she resigned when the family removed to

Gladwin, MI. While in Grand Rapids Mrs. Doughty, Mrs. Etta S. Wilson, of the "Telegram-Herald," and Miss Fleming, connected with the "Leader," held the first meeting and planned the organization of the Michigan Women's Press Association, of Which Mrs. Doughty has remained an active member. In 1890 Mr. Doughty commenced the publication of the "Leader" in Gladwin, being the founder and owner of the plant. She was regularly engaged on that paper. Besides this she has ever been an active member of the Woman's Christian Temperance Union, having been secretary of the Eighth Congressional District for four years. She also belongs to the Good Templars and the Royal Templars. She has always engaged actively in Sunday-school work and is a member of the Presbyterian Church. She is a member of Golden Rod Lodge, Daughters of Rebecca. In addition to general newspaper work. Mrs. Doughty has been the special correspondent of several city daily papers and was for some time a contributor to the "Sunny South," writing short stories, sketches and an occasional poem. For several years she was the secretary of the Mt. Pleasant Library, Literary and Musical Association, an organization of which she was one of the founders. Having sold the Gladwin "Leader" in January, 1892, Mr. and Mrs. Doughty bought the "Post," of Port Austin, MI, in May of the same year, and Mrs. Doughty is now engaged daily as assistant editor of that paper. She has three children, two sons and a daughter.

DOUGLAS, Miss Alice May, poet and author, born in Bath, ME, 28th June, 1865. She still resides in her native city. She began her career as an author at the age of eleven years, when her first published article appeared among the children's productions of "St. Nicholas." The reading of "Little Women" at the age of thirteen marked an epoch in her life. She determined to be an author like Jo, and, like her, send for publication a composition from her pen to test her chances of authorship. Consequently she sent a poem pertaining to a little sister, who shortly before death was seen throwing kisses to God. The "Zion's Herald," to which the poem was sent, published it, and from that time Miss Douglas has been a constant contributor to the press. She is also engaged in editorial work on two monthly papers, the "Pacific Banner" and the "Acorn." Her first volume of poems was "Phlox" (Bath, ME, 1888). This was followed during the same year by a second volume, "May Flowers" (Bath, ME, 1888). Then she published "Gems Without Polish" (New York, 1890). She next wrote two juvenile books, one for boys and the other for girls, in the interest of the lend-a-hand clubs. Most of her books have first appeared as serials. Among them are "Jewel Gatherers," "Quaker John in the Civil War," "How the Little Cousins Formed a Museum," "The Peace-Makers" and "Self-exiled from Russia," a story of the Mennonites. Miss Douglas is State superintendent of the department of peace and arbitration of the Woman's Christian Temperance Union. She has also assisted the national peace department of that organization, by preparing much of its necessary literature and by founding a peace band for children, which has branches in Palestine and Australia.

DOUGLAS, Miss Amanda Minnie, author, born in New York City, 14th July, 1838. She was educated in the City Institute in New York. In 1853 she removed to Newark, NJ, where she took a course in reading with a private tutor. In childhood she was noted for her powers of story-telling, when she would tell her friends long tales, regular serials, that would continue for weeks. Much of her girlhood was taken up by sickness and family occupations. She was inventive, and one of her inventions, patented by herself, was a folding frame for a mosquito-net. She had no early dreams of becoming a great author. She knew Edgar Allen Poe and other conspicuous literary persons. After she had reached maturity, she began to write stories for publication, and she was immediately successful. Among her published books are "In Trust" (1866), "Claudia" (1867), "Stephan Dane" (1867), "Sydnie Adriance" (1868), "With Fate Against Him" (1870), "Kathie's Stories for Young People" (6 vols., 1870, and 1871), "Lucia, Her Problem" (1871), "Santa Claus Land" (1873), "Home Nook" (1873), "The Old Woman Who Lived in a Shoe" and "Seven Daughters" (1874), "Drifted Asunder" (1875), "Nelly Kinnaird's Kingdom" (1876), "From Hand to Mouth" (1877), "Hope Mills" (1879), "Lost in a Creat City" (1880), "Whom Kathie Married" (1883), "Floyd Grandon's

Honor" (1883), "Out of the Wreck" (1884), "A Woman's Inheritance" (1885), "Foes of Her Household" (1886), "The Fortunes of the Faradays (1887)", Modern Adam and Eve" (1888), "Osborne of the Arrochar" (1889), and "Heroes of the Crusade" (1889). Miss Douglas has suffered much from long illness, but she keeps up courage and refuses to be borne down by fate. She is a fluent talker and well informed on current events. She has done but little work for magazines and newspapers. Her works have been very popular. Her first book, "In Trust," sold 20,000 copies in a short time, but she had sold the copyright, and others reaped the benefit. She holds the copyrights of all her other books.

DOUGLAS, Mrs. Lavantia Densmore, temperance worker, born in Rochester, NY, 1st March, 1827. She was one of seven children. Her parents, Joel and Sophia Densmore, were very poor in all the externals of life, but they were very rich in honor and integrity, in industry, in energy and in aspiration. When Lavantia was about nine years old, her parents removed to Crawford county, PA, upon a farm. The father was unique in character, eccentric in person, in speech and in manners. The mother was of a bright, joyous, laughter-loving nature. Appreciating keenly their own lack of education, both parents strove to give their children the best educational opportunities possible. The sole luxury of their home was literature. They took the "Democratic Review," almost the only magazine then published in the United States, and such papers as the "National Era" and the "Boston Investigator." In 1853, when she was twenty-six years of age, she became the wife of Joshua Douglas, then just entering the profession of the law, and removed to Meadville, PA, where they have resided ever since. There her life was devoted to caring for her household, rearing her children and mingling somewhat in the social life of the place. In 1872 she made a visit to Europe. She arrived home from Europe on the 23rd of December, 1873, the day of the great Woman's Temperance Crusade. Meadville was aroused by the great spiritual outpouring, and the following March a mass meeting was called and a temperance organization

effected which, under one form or another, still exists. Mrs. Douglas very early identified herself with the movement, and has always been a most active and enthusiastic worker in the cause. She early became a member of the Woman's Christian Temperance Union, and for many years was president of the Meadville Union. Her ardent enthusiasm and untiring zeal have made her name in her own community a synonym for temperance. For a few years Mrs. Douglas has been obliged to retire from active efforts in the cause, owing to failing eye-sight. Cataracts formed on both her eyes, and during these later years she has walked in gathering darkness. The cataracts have been removed, but with only partial success.

DOW, Miss Cornelia M., philanthropist and temperance reformer, born in Portland, ME, 10th November, 1842. She is the youngest daughter of Neal Dow, of Portland, ME. Her mother, who died in 1883, was Maria Cornelia Durant Maynard, who was born in Boston, MA. Her daughter, Cornelia, was born in the house where she now lives with her father, who is in the eighty-eighth year of his age. Miss Dow possesses many of the characteristics of both mother and father. She excels as a careful home keeper, and yet is able to find a great deal of time for the world's work. For many years she was secretary of the Woman's Christian Association of Portland. She is the treasurer of the Home for Aged Women of Portland and also treasurer of the Temporary Home for Women and Children, a State institution situated in Deering, near Portland. The larger part of her time is given to works of temperance, which would seem the most natural thing for her to do. For years she has been officially connected with the Woman's Christian Temperance Union of Portland. She is president of the union in Cumberland county, one of the superintendents of the State union, as well as one of its most efficient vice-presidents. She is a member and a constant attendant of State Street Congregational Church in Portland.

DOW, Mrs. Mary E. H. G., financier, born in Dover, NH, 15th December, 1848. Her maiden name was Mary Edna Hill. She is a daughter of

Nathaniel Rogers Hill. She was educated partly in Dover. While she was yet a child, her parents removed to Boston, MA, and it was there she got the larger part of her schooling. When seventeen years of age, she was graduated with high honors from the Charlestown high school. For some years she was a successful assistant principal of the Rochester, NH, high school, and later went to St. Louis, MO, where for three years she was instructor in French and German in a female academy. When twenty-five years old, she was wooed and won by a wealthy resident of Dover, George F. Gray, part owner and editor of the Dover "Press," a Democratic weekly paper published there. They spent two years in Europe. Three children were born to them, and after a few years Mr. Gray died. Before her marriage she was correspondent for several newspapers, among them the Boston "Journal" and "Traveller," "New Hampshire Statesman," the Dover "Enquirer," and some southern papers. Five years after the death of her first husband she became the wife of Dr. Henry Dow, of Dover. They spent some time in England. Returning to Dover, Mrs. Dow began to attract attention as a financier. In January, 1888, she was elected president of the Dover Horse Railway, an event that caused much commotion in railway circles. She was perfectly familiar with the affairs of the road and had secured a majority of its stock. The story of this occurrence is interesting. The road had been a failing enterprise. The patrons found fault with the accommodations and the excessiveness of fares, and the stockholders growled at the excessiveness of expenses and the small receipts. For years it had paid but a small dividend. A Boston syndicate made overtures for possession of the whole stock, and with such success that the board of directors reached the point of voting to sell. Mrs. Dow was out of town during these negotiations, but returned as the sale was about to be consummated. She held a small amount of the stock, and was approached with an offer for it at something like one-third the price at which it had been bought. With characteristic promptness she at once decided that, if the stock was so low, and yet the Boston syndicate expected to make the road pay, any other able financier might reasonably indulge the same hope; that, if there were any profits to be obtained, they ought to be saved to Dover, and that she would try her own capabilities in the matter. Her attitude interrupted the syndicate's scheme, and for some weeks there

was a contest of wits to see who would get control of the most blocks. When the next meeting was called, it was supposed that the property would be transferred to the Boston party, but it transpired to every one's astonishment that Mrs. Dow was master of the situation; she had acquired more than half the stock. Her election to the presidency was certain. As her own votes would elect the directorate, that body would be necessarily of her own choice. Several among the Dover gentlemen, who desired to be on the board, said that they would not vote for a woman for president. It was simply preposterous and meant bankruptcy. But the matter presented itself to the ambitious gentlemen in this form: Agree to vote for Mrs. Dow, and you can hold office; otherwise you can not. They succumbed, but with chagrin and trepidation. Mrs. Dow at once demonstrated her ability to manage the road so as to make it a paying property. She did that to perfection, showing herself the equal of any male manager in the country.

DOWD, Miss Mary Alice, poet and educator, born in Frankford, Greenbrier county, WV, 16th December, 1855. Her parents were school-teachers of Puritan descent, their ancestors having landed in New England about the year 1630. In both families were found officers and privates of the Revolutionary army. On her father's side she is related to the well-known family of Field and the old English family of Dudley. She was the youngest of four children. Her early home was among the Berkshire Hills, whence her parents removed to Westfield, MA, a town noted for its schools. Alice was a delicate child, and her parents scarcely dared to hope that she would be spared to years of maturity. Shy and reserved, she early showed a great love of nature and a deep appreciation of all natural beauty. She was educated at home and in the public schools of Westfield. She was graduated from the English and classical departments of the high school, taking the two courses simultaneously. In the normal school she studied optionals with the prescribed branches and composed a class hymn sung at her graduation. Since that time she has been constantly employed as a teacher. During the past eleven years she has held her present position of first assistant in the high school of Stamford, CT. Of scholarly attainments, she has helped many young men to prepare for college. She has taken several courses in the Sauveur Summer School of Languages and has especially fitted herself to give instruction in German. In 1886 the greatest sorrow of her life came to her in the sudden death of her mother. She has published one volume of verse, "Vacation Verses" (Buffalo, 1891).

DOWNS, Mrs. Sallie Ward, social leader, is descended on the paternal side from Lord Ward, of England. Her maiden name was Ward. On her mother's side she is descended from the Fleurnoys, Huguenots, a prominent family. She is a resident of Louisville, KY, and has been a social leader in the society of the South and Southwest for many years. She is distinguished for her beauty of person, her charm of manners and her cultured intellect. Mrs. Downs has been married four times. She has traveled extensively in Europe, and was presented at various courts, and everywhere was admired for her graces of mind and person. She is a thoroughly educated woman, speaks French fluently and is a fine musician. In religion she is a Roman Catholic, a convert to that faith. She has one child, a son, John Hunt, of New York, who has won a reputation as a journalist. She is noted as a letter writer, and she has contributed to eastern journals. She is, despite her social prestige, a woman of democratic instincts. Her charities are numerous, large and entirely unostentatious. She has a fine and valuable collection of treasures, historical and religious, gathered from all parts of the world. Her husband, Major G. F. Downs, is a man of wealth, intellect and culture. They make their home in the Galt House, in Louisville, KY.

DRAKE, Mrs. Mary Eveline, minister of the gospel and church worker, born in Trenton, Oneida county, NY, 8th June, 1833. Her maiden name was Mary E. McArthur. Her father was of Scotch parentage, and her mother was English, a relative of Lady Gurney, better known as the celebrated Elizabeth Fry. From her parents she inherited that strong religious bent of character that has distinguished her life. When about six years of age, she removed with her parents to southern Michigan, where she received most of her common school and academic education. From there the family removed to the town of Geneseo, IL, where she spent her early married life, residing there most of the time for over twenty years. She joined her mother's church, the Congregational, and began that course of earnest personal effort for the conversion of others for which her nature peculiarly fitted her and in which she has been so successful. In addition to her work in prayer-meeting, Sunday school and young people's. Bible-classes, she was frequently called to assist evangelists by visiting and in revival meetings. During all that time she was active in all the various reforms and benevolences of the time. In war time she was especially active in the Women's Soldiers' Aid Society, going south as far as Memphis, and looking to the right distribution of the provisions sent to the hospitals there, and she was one of the leaders in the women's temperance crusade. She had the added care of her family, which she supported most of the time by the labor of her own hands. The natural result of such constant labors came in a severe attack of nervous prostration, which totally ended her work for a season. To secure full restoration, she went to reside for a time with her only living son, Gen. M. M. Marshall, then a railroad official in western Iowa. There she became the wife of Rev. A. J. Drake, of Dakota. A very few weeks of the bracing air of Dakota sufficed to restore her to perfect health and strength. She entered with her husband into the home missionary work, for which, by her zeal and his long experience, they were so well adapted. Mr. Drake was then laboring in Iroquois, a village at the junction of two railroads, where he had a small church of eight members worshiping in a schoolhouse. Though living for the first two years at DeSmet, sixteen miles away, they soon had other preaching stations and Sunday-schools in hand and preparations made for building a church in Iroquois. Mrs. Drake went east as far as Chicago and raised sufficient means to buy the lumber and push forward the work. Encouraged by her success, she was readily urged by her husband to take part in the public services, addressing

Sunday-schools, till she came very naturally to choose a subject or text and practically to preach the gospel. The wide extent of their field and the constant need of dividing their labors tended strongly to this. A very much needed rest and the kindness of an eastern friend enabled them to attend the anniversary of the American Home Missionary Society in Saratoga. On the way, by special invitation, she addressed the Woman's Home Missionary Union of Illinois in Moline. Being heard in that meeting by Dr. Clark, of the American Home Missionary Society, on arrival at Saratoga she was called to address the great congregation assembled there. She has since spoken in many of the large cities and churches of New England and other States. The result of these visits has been the raising of means sufficient, with what people on the ground could give, to build two other large churches in Esmond and Osceola, SD. She and her husband are caring for a field forty-five miles in length and fifteen miles in breadth, with five churches and Sunday-schools. They also publish a monthly paper, entitled the "Dakota Prairie Pioneer." At the earnest request of the leading ministers in the State she consented to ordination and the largest Congregational council ever assembled in South Dakota ordained her to the work of the ministry in December, 1890. That was one of the first ordinations of a woman to the ministry west of the Mississippi.

DRAKE, Mrs. Priscilla Holmes, woman suffragist, born in Ithaca, NY, 18th June, 1812. She is the youngest child of Judge Samuel Buell and Joanna Sturdevant, both of Cayuga county, NY. Judge Buell was a man of much intellectual vigor and marked attainments. He held several important offices in his State, and as senator served more than one term with De Witt Clinton, Martin Van Buren and others of distinction. Judge Buell removed with his family from New York to Marietta, OH, where he was held in great esteem. In the year 1831 his daughter became the wife of James P. Drake, a native of North Carolina, at Lawrenceburg, IN. He had held office under President Monroe and was then receiver of public moneys in Indianapolis, IN, appointed by President Jackson. While a resident of Posey county, he had been brought into intimate business and social relations with the New Harmony Community, under the Rapps, father and son, and when their possessions were transferred to the Scotch philanthropist,

Robert Owen, he naturally held the same relations with the Owen association. Those two communities, although striving in different ways to benefit humanity, had much to do with broadening his views and making his after-life tolerant and charitable, and probably had an influence in developing his young wife's interest in the laws relating to women. Their home was the center of happiness and progress, and it was only widening the circle of early associations to find therein a hearty welcome for David, Richard and Robert Dale Owen, the distinguished sons of Robert Owen. Colonel and Mrs. Drake worked with Robert Dale Owen during the Indiana Constitutional Convention of 1850 and 1851 to remove the legal disabilities of women. Before the sections were presented, which worked such benefit to women, they were discussed, line by line, in Mrs. Drake's parlor. She had an acute legal mind, and Mr. Owen was not slow to recognize her valuable aid in the construction of the important clauses. It was she who suggested a memorial to Robert Dale Owen from the many noble mothers who comprehended the scope of his work for women. When Lucy Stone delivered her first lecture in Indianapolis, Mrs. Drake was the only woman in attendance. She was also present at a notable meeting, shortly afterward, where Lucretia Mott presided. The acquaintance thus formed led to an interesting correspondence. Mrs. Drake was in possession of many valuable letters from distinguished men and women, addressed to herself and husband. In 1861 they removed to Alabama, near Huntsville, where they continued their interest and work in the cause of woman's suffrage. Mrs. Drake was left a widow in 1876 and died at her residence, 11th February, 1892. She was the mother of seven children, four of whom survive her and by inheritance and education are earnest supporters of the woman suffrage cause.

DREIER, Mrs. Christine Nielson, concert and oratorio singer, born in Madison, WI, 10th June, 1866. Her father's name is Andrew Nielson, and both parents were among the early Scandinavian immigrants to this country and settled in Chicago in 1851, afterward removing to Madison. Christine Nielson still retains her maiden name on the stage, although she became the wife, 4th June, 1891, of Otto Albert Dreier, since 1886 the Danish Vice-Consul in Chicago, where they make their home. The career of Christine Nielson thus far is a striking example of what energy and perseverance can do for a young woman of genius. Her first teacher, and the one to discover her capabilities, was Prof. T. A. Brand. She then studied with Mrs. Earl De Moe, herself a successful concert singer. Christine began to sing in public at the age of thirteen, attracting, at an orphan's home concert in Madison, the attention of those whose foresight discovered future fame for the young vocalist. She chose Chicago for her more advanced studies, and became the pupil of Mrs. Sara Hershey Eddy. She accompanied Mr. and Mrs. Eddy to Europe in 1889, and after singing with great success in London, Paris and Copenhagen, she spent a year or more in London as a pupil of George Henschel. Her voice is a contralto of wide range, and the comments of the American and foreign press have been highly complimentary, showing her to be possessed of unusual musical accomplishments.

DREW, Mrs. John, actor, born in London, England, 10th January, 1820. Her maiden name was Lane. Her father was an actor, and he placed the child on the stage in juvenile parts when she was eight years old. In 1828 she came to the United States with her mother and played in New York and Philadelphia. She made a tour of the West Indies and returned to the United States in 1832. In 1833 she played in a number of rôles in New York theaters. In 1834 she played the part of Julia in "The Hunchback" in the Boston Theater. In 1835, when fifteen years old, she played Lady Teazle in "The School for Scandal" in New Orleans. She won success from the beginning and was soon "leading lady" at a salary of twenty dollars a week. She became the wife of Henry Hunt, a veteran English opera singer, and from 1842 to 1846 she played at intervals in stock

companies in New York theaters, in burlesques, light comedies and domestic dramas. In 1847 she went to Chicago, Milwaukee, St. Louis, Mobile and New Orleans, playing always to good houses and increasing her reputation as a comedian. In 1848 she separated from Mr. Hunt and became the wife of George Mossop, a young Irish comedian of fine powers. He died in 1849, and in 1850 she became the wife of John Drew. In 1857 Mr. and Mrs. Drew made a successful tour of the United States. In 1861 Mrs. Drew assumed the sole management of the Arch-street Theater in Philadelphia, PA, which has since remained under her control. Mrs. Drew makes her home in Philadelphia. During the past few years she has played with Joseph Jefferson and William J. Florence. She has a large family of children, most of whom are connected with the stage. Although seventy-two years of age, Mrs. Drew retains the cheerful vivacity of her earlier years, and she is very popular with theater-goers. She excels in high-comedy parts.

DU BOSE, Mrs. Miriam Howard, woman suffragist, born in Russell county, AL, 28th November, 1862. She is a daughter of Ann Lindsay and Augustus Howard. Though born in Alabama, her life has been spent in and near Columbus, GA. At an early age she showed marked musical talent, playing simple melodies before she was tall enough to mount the piano stool unassisted. At fourteen years of age she began the study of music under a teacher in Columbus, and studied there about two years, which was the only instruction she received. At seventeen she applied for the organist's place in the First Presbyterian Church of Columbus, and held the position until her marriage. She was at that time the youngest organist in the State. She has composed several pieces of instrumental music. Her first piece "Rural Polka," was composed at the age of fifteen. She performs on the piano with brilliancy. Gifted in sketching, she has done some life-like work in that line. For the last three years, having been aroused to the work of woman's enfranchisement, she has worked for woman suffrage with heart, pen and purse. Her articles in its interest are earnest and convincing. She is vice-president of the Georgia

Woman Suffrage Association, and her busy brain and fingers have originated many schemes to fill the treasury of that organization. It was her generosity which made it possible for Georgia to send her first delegates to the twenty-fourth convention of the National American Woman Suffrage Association, held in Washington in January, 1892. The money donated was earned by her own hands. She has one son. Her home is in Greenville, GA.

DUDLEY, Mrs. Sarah Marie, business woman, born in Carlton, Barry county, MI. She is the youngest daughter of James T. and Catherine Lawhead, who went to Michigan, in the first years of their married life, from the State of New York, and settled in Carlton. She is of Scotch ancestry on her father's side, and pure American on that of her mother, back to and beyond the war for independence. At the early age of four years she was left an orphan and was adopted into the family of her uncle, Judge William McCauley, of Brighton, MI, who was at the time State Senator from that district. She received her education in the private and public schools of Brighton. At the age of fifteen she became the wife of Thomas Robert Dudley, from county of Kent, England, and moved to Detroit, MI, where, in 1876, her husband entered the mercantile business, in which he prospered so well that he retired from business, in 1889, with a competence. Mrs. Dudley has been successful in many ways. She proved herself a most excellent businesswoman. It was she who saw the business opening where her husband's fortune was made, and she has by judicious investments made another for herself. She works in pastel with the taste of a born artist. She is also an inventor, and the United States Patent Office holds proof of her ingenuity. But it is as an architect, designer and builder she has won her greatest success. Buying land in what proved one of the best locations in Detroit, she designed and built a graceful group of residences, among which is one of the most palatial stone mansions in the city. She took all the responsibility of planning, building and furnishing the money, and is the proud possessor of a handsome income from the rentals. She does much charitable work in an unostentatious way.

DUFOUR, Mrs. Amanda Louise Ruter, poet, born in Jeffersonville, IN, 26th February, 1822. She is the oldest daughter of Rev. Calvin W. Ruter, a pioneer Indiana preacher, and his wife, Harriet De Haas Ruter. Mr. Ruter was of Vermont and Puritan ancestry, and Mrs. Ruter of Virginia and Huguenot ancestry. Both were persons of marked character. Mr. Ruter was stationed in Jeffersonville when Louise was born. In her childhood school privileges were limited, and with her naturally delicate organization and the burden of household duties which devolved upon her as the oldest of five children, her attendance at school was often irregular. She was fond of books and had free access to her father's limited library. In 1842 she became the wife of Oliver Dufour, a descendant of an illustrious Swiss family, who immigrated to the United States early in the century. Mr. Dufour was elected to the Indiana Legislature in 1853, and in the same year received an appointment to a government position in Washington, to which place he removed with his family. He was a prominent member of the Independent Order of Odd Fellows, having been Grand Master of the State of Indiana, Grand Representative from that State and also from the District of Columbia for eight consecutive years. He died in November, 1891. Mrs. Dufour composed verses when too young to wield a pen, or even to read. Her peculiarly sensitive temperament long kept her talents from being appreciated. Having no confidence in her own abilities, she shrank from criticism. She is fond of writing for children, and has published many poems adapted to their comprehension. In 1848 Hon. Joseph A. Wright, then governor of the State, sent from Indiana, for the Washington monument, a block of marble, on which was inscribed the motto: "No North, No South, Nothing but the Union." This incident suggested to Mrs. Dufour her poem entitled "The Ark of the Union." It was first published in the Washington "Union," and was afterward, without her knowledge, set to music. Some months before the death of the scientist, Baron Von Humboldt, Mrs. Dufour wrote a poem on his distinction as "King of Science." An American in Berlin read the poem to the great man, who was then upon his death-bed, and it so pleased the Baron that he sent Mrs. Dufour the following message: "Tell that talented American lady, Mrs. Dufour, that I deem that poem the highest compliment that was ever paid to me by any person or from any clime." She has contributed to the "Ladies' Repository," the "Masonic Review," the "School Day Visitor," the "Republican," of Springfield, OH, the Louisville "Journal," whose editor was the talented author and poet, George D. Prentice, and the Louisville "Democrat."

DUNHAM, Mrs. Emma Bedelia, poet, born in Minot, now Auburn, ME, 31st August, 1826. She was the fourth child in the family of Capt. Joseph Smith Sargent and Ann Hoyt Sargent. She attended the district school, but it may be questioned whether she gained as much education within its walls as without. She moved with her parents to the city of Portland, ME, at the age of nine years. There she attended public and private schools and had the benefit of private teachers, and grew into the mature poet, story-writer and teacher. Her school education was finished in Westbrook Seminary. She now has a beautiful home in Deering, ME. Her library and collection of natural curiosities, the latter begun when she was about eleven years old, are used, like all her possessions, for doing good. She became the wife of Rufus Dunham, of Westbrook, now Deering, 25th August, 1845. She is the mother of three sons and two daughters. Four other children died young. She is still an enthusiastic writer and teacher. Children go to her school for the pleasure as well as instructon to be had there. Mrs. Dunham has had much influence, as a Christian, in the community in which she lives. At her suggestion, the Universalist Church, All Souls, was organized in 1881, she becoming one of the original members. She began to write when very young, and she fled from the shelter of one penname to that of another, dreading to have the public know her as an author, until, after years of success, she gained courage to use her own name. Her writings consist largely of poetry, but include also sketches on natural history, essays, letters of travel and stories for children. Some of her songs have been set to music. "Margaret, a Home Opera

in Six Acts," is one of the best of her poetic productions. It was brought out in 1875. Mrs. Dunham is a typical New England woman, who, in spite of her more than three-score years, is still young, enthusiastic and hopeful.

DUNHAM, Mrs. Marion Howard, born in Geauga county, OH, 6th December, 1842, passed the first part of her life upon a farm. She early decided to be a teacher, beginning her first district school at the age of fifteen, and taught in the public schools of Chicago, IL, from 1866 to 1873. In July, 1873, she became the wife of C. A. Dunham, an architect, of Burlington, IA, where they now live. In 1877 she entered upon temperance work with the inauguration of the red-ribbon movement, but, believing in more permanent methods, she was the prime mover in the organization of the local Woman's Christian Temperance Union, and has ever since been an active worker in that society. In 1883 she was elected State superintendent of the department of scientific temperance, and held the office four years, lecturing to institutes and general audiences on that subject much of the time. She procured the Iowa State law on that subject in February, 1886. When the Iowa State Temperance Union began to display its opposition to the National Union, she was rather slow to declare her position, which was always fully with the National, but she was soon forced to declare herself, and came to be considered rather a leader on the side of the minority. When the majority in the State Union seceded from the National Union, 16th October, 1890, she was elected president of those who remained auxiliary to that body. At the State convention in 1891 she was re-elected. She has spent a large part of her time in the field. She has always been a radical equal suffragist, and has spoken and written much on that subject. She is a Christian socialist, deeply interested in all reforms that promise to better the social system and the conditions of life for the multitudes.

DUNIWAY, Mrs. Abigail Scott, editor, born in Pleasant Grove, Tazewell county, IL, 22nd October, 1834. There she grew to girlhood. Her father removed to Oregon in 1852. Of a family noted for sturdy independence in word and deed, it is not strange that these inherent qualities, united with keen mental powers, have made her one of the most widely known women on the Pacific slope. She began her public career many years ago through necessity, an invalid husband and a large family leaving her no alternative. Nobly has she fulfilled the double trust of wife and mother. While Mrs. Duniway has been engaged in every sort of reputable literary toil, her life-work has been in the direction of the enfranchisement of women. While advocating woman suffrage she has undoubtedly traveled more miles by stage, rail, river and wagon, made more public speeches, endured more hardships, persecution and ridicule, and scored more victories than any of her distinguished cotemporaries of the East and middle West. The enfranchisement of the women of Washington Territory was the result of her efforts, and, had they listened to her counsel and kept aloof from the Prohibition fight of 1886, they would not have lost afterward, when the Territory became a State, the heritage of the ballot which she had secured for them at the cost of the best years of her life. As an extemporaneous speaker she is logical, sarcastic, witty, poetic and often eloquent. As a writer she is forceful and argumentative. Mrs. Duniway now fills the editorial chair of the "Pacific Empire," a new literary and progressive monthly magazine published in Portland, Ore., where she resides in a spacious home, the product of her own genius and industry.

DUNLAP, Miss Mary J., physician, born in Philadelphia, PA, in 1853. Dr. Dunlap is superintendent and physician in charge of the New Jersey State Institution for Feeble Minded Women. When a mature young woman, of practical education, with sound and healthy views of life, she made choice of the profession of medicine, not through any romantic aspirations after "a vocation in life," but as a vocation to which she proposed to devote all her energies. One year of preparatory reading preceded the regular college course of three years. Having been regularly graduated from the Woman's Medical College of Pennsylvania in 1886, an office was secured in Philadelphia, and it

was not long before the young doctor found her hands full. In a few months she was induced to make arrangements with Dr. Joseph Parrish, which made her his assistant in the treatment of nervous invalids in Burlington, NJ. This special training prepared her for her present responsible position. Dr. Dunlap's position in New Jersey is similar to that of Dr. Alice Bennett in Pennsylvania, being superintendent and physician in charge, with all the duties that the term implies. These two women furnish the only instances, at the present date, where women have full control of the medical department of institution work in connection with the superintendency.

DURGIN, Miss Harriet Thayer, artist, born in the town of Wilmington, MA, in 1848. She is the daughter of Rev. J. M. Durgin. Sprung from families who, leaving their homes for conscience's sake, sought New England's shores, and whose lives were freely given when they were needed in their country's defense, her father was a man of dauntless courage and remarkable

intellectual power. He was of the Baptist faith and a man of broad and liberal sentiments. An enthusiast in the anti-slavery movement, he entered the army in the late war and left behind him a brilliant military record. The mother, a woman of exalted character, fine intellect and lovely disposition, united two good New England names, as she was of the Braintree-Thayer family. One of a family of five children, Miss Durgin's youth was surrounded by those gentle and refining influences which are the lot of those born into the environment of a clergyman's household. She pursued her preparatory studies of life, not only in the training schools of those towns where her father's profession called him, but in a home where every influence was directed toward the upbuilding of a rich and well rounded character. She passed the concluding years of study in the New Hampton Institute, in New Hampshire. When it became necessary for Miss Durgin to assume the duties and responsibilities of life on her own account, she chose teaching as a stepping-stone to the realization of her dream, an art education. Finally the way opened to enter upon her favorite field of study, and in 1880 she joined her sister Lyle in Paris, France, where she entered the studio of Mme. de Cool, and later that of Francois Rivoire, where daily lessons were taken. Having in company with her sister established a little home, she found many famous artists who were glad to visit the cosy salon and give careful and valuable criticism. After seven years of study Miss Durgin returned to Boston, where she had many friends, and in company with her sister opened a studio in the most fashionable quarter of the city. Their rooms were soon frequented on reception days by admirers and lovers of art, and commissions have never been wanting to keep their brushes constantly employed. As a flower painter she stands among the foremost of American artists. A panel of tea-roses received special notice in the salon of 1886, and a group combining flowers and landscape in 1890 won much notice.

DURGIN, Miss Lyle, artist, was born in Wilmington, MA, in 1850. A sister of Harriet Thayer Durgin, she grew up as one with her, so far as environment and teaching were concerned. They drew the same life and inspiration from their home surroundings and studied in the same schools, and when their education was completed found themselves with the same inclination toward art. Lyle went to Paris in 1879 and became a pupil of Bonnat and Bastien Lepage. Later she entered the Julien Academy for more serious study in drawing, working enthusiastically, early and late, both in the school and in her own studio, supplementing her studio work by anatomical studies at the École de Médicine under M. Chicotôt. In summer time the sisters sketched in England, Switzerland and France, drawing fresh inspiration from nature and travel and taking home collections of sketches for their winter's work. Lyle chose figure painting in oil and portraiture as her special department of art. So earnestly did she study from 1879 to 1884 that the Salon received her paintings in the latter-named year, and again two years later, when she offered a painting of beauty, which won for her recognition as an artist of power. In 1886 the Misses Durgin returned to America and opened a studio in

Boston. Welcomed to the best society, in which they naturally found a home, the sisters began work, each in her own field of art. The first picture exhibited by Lyle in Boston was a portrait of a lady. Then followed in rapid succession one of Henry Sandham, a celebrated artist of Boston, and many others of persons of more or less distinction in the social and literary world. Receiving a commission for mural paintings for a church in Detroit, MI, she started early in 1890 for a prolonged course of travel in Italy, finally settling in Paris for the execution of those great original works, which were completed and placed in the church in December, 1891. They represent the four Evangelists and are of heroic size, filling the four compartments of the dome-shaped interior. They are painted after the manner of the middle time of the Venetian school, corresponding to the Byzantine character of the edifice. Although the ecclesiastical traditions of saints and church fathers allow of but little variation, her works are characterized by freshness, originality and strength unusual to find at the present day, and are worthy of more interest from the fact that this is a branch of painting which hitherto has been almost exclusively in the hands of men.

DURLEY, Mrs. Ella Hamilton, educator and journalist, was born in Butler county, PA. She is the oldest daughter of Mr. and Mrs. William Hamilton. In the spring of 1866 the family removed to Davis county, IA, where, in the most unpromising backwoods region, they made their home for a few years. It was in the rude log schoolhouse of that locality that the young girl acquired sufficient knowledge of the rudimentary branches to permit her to begin to teach at the age of sixteen. The loss of her father, whose ambition for his children was limitless, led her to make the attempt to carry out his oft-expressed wish that she should take a college course. To do so meant hard work and strenuous application, for every penny of the necessary expense had to be earned by herself. In the spring of 1878 she took the degree of B.A. in the State University of Iowa, and four years later she received the degree of M.A. After graduation Miss Hamilton accepted the principalship of the high school in Waterloo, IA, which she held for two years. She then went abroad to continue her studies, more especially in the German language and literature. She spent a year in European travel and study, features of which were the attendance upon a course of lectures in the Victoria Lyceum of Berlin, and an inspection of the school system of Germany and Italy. Upon her return the result of her observation was given to the public in the form of a lecture, which was widely delivered and well received. After a year spent in the Iowa State Library, Miss Hamilton decided to turn her attention to newspaper work. She became associate editor of the Des Moines "Mail and Times," which position she held over a year, when a tempting offer caused her to become editor-in-chief of the "Northwestern Journal of Education," where her success was very gratifying. Her later journalistic work has been in connection with the Des Moines "Daily News," upon which she served as reporter and editorial and special writer for several years. In 1884 Miss Hamilton was appointed a member of the State Education Board of Examiners for Iowa, which position she held until 1888, serving during the most of her time as secretary. In October, 1886, she became the wife of Preston B. Durley, business manager of the Des Moines "Daily News." Mrs. Durley's newspaper work was kept up uninterruptedly until the summer of 1890, when their home was gladdened by the birth of a son. At the present time she is president of the Des Moines Woman's Club, a large and prosperous literary society.

DURRELL, Mrs. Irene Clark, educator, born in Plymouth, NH, 17th May, 1852. Her father, Hiram Clark, is a man of steadfast evangelical faith. Her mother was an exemplary Christian. Until twelve years of age, her advantages were limited to ungraded country schools. She was a pupil for a time in the village grammar school and in the Plymouth Academy. Taking private lessons of her pastor in Latin and sciences, and studying by herself, she prepared to enter the State Normal School in Plymouth, where she completed the first course in 1872 and the second in 1873, teaching during summer vacations. In 1873 and 1874 she taught the grammar-school in West Lebanon, NH. In the fall of 1874 she became the teacher of the normal department in the New Hampshire Conference Seminary, and a student in the junior year in the classical course. She was graduated in 1876. She then taught in the State Normal School in Castleton, VT. On 23rd July, 1878 she became the wife of Rev. J. M. Durrell, D.D. As a Methodist minister's wife, in New Hampshire Conference, for thirteen years Mrs. Durrell has had marked success in leading young ladies into an active Christian life and interesting them in behalf of others. As an officer in the Woman's Foreign Missionary Society she has been an efficient organizer. For four years she was district secretary and was a delegate from the New England branch to the Evanston general executive committee meeting. With her husband, in 1882, she took an extended tour abroad. In the spring of 1891 her husband became president of the New Hampshire Conference Seminary and Female College, Tilton, NH, and Mrs. Durrell became the preceptress of that institution.

DUSSUCHAL, Miss Eugenie, musical educator, born in St. Louis, MO, 29th October, 1860. She is of French parents, and, with the exception of a short course of study in New York, received her school and musical education in her native city. Her father died when she was but four years of age, leaving herself and an older sister to be brought up by her mother, who was left in moderate circumstances. Eugenie showed her musical talent at an early age. The French citizens of St. Louis honored her by presenting her a gold medal after she sang the anthem "La Marseillaise," at the French Fête of 1890. She has a rich contralto voice, which has kept her in church positions and before the public since her fourteenth year. For a short time she traveled with an opera company and was most successful, but her family objected to her adopting the stage as a profession, and she returned to St. Louis. She was appointed public school music supervisor in the fall of 1890, a position that until then had been filled by men only.

DWYER, Miss Bessie Agnes, journalist, was born in Texas. She is the daughter of the late Judge Thomas A. and Annie C. Dwyer, of English descent. Miss Dwyer comes of a family renowned at home and abroad for uncommon gifts. Judge Dwyer left his native heath in youth, and his life

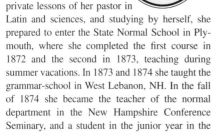

became part and parcel of the early history of Texas and the Rio Bravo. Six children blessed his home, and upon the youngest daughter, Bessie, alone fell the mantle of his literary powers and histrionic ability. As a child she dominated amateur circles in Texas as an acknowledged star, and she played a wide range of characters. Death abruptly removed Judge Dwyer, and his daughter found herself alone on the threshold of womanhood, minus a practical education and heir to naught but her father's mental gifts. The War of the Rebellion and other reverses dissipated a once generous fortune, and actual necessity faced the bereaved family. Casting to the winds the prejudices existing in the South against female occupation beyond the portals of home, Miss Dwyer accepted a position in the post-office department and held it six years. During that time vagrant poems and sketches from her pen were published. Waning strength necessitated change and rest, and in 1868 she resigned her position and visited her married sister at a remote army post in Arizona and later in New Mexico. Three years of rest restored her health, and she returned to civilization and entered journalism. Her sketches of army life and vivid word painting of scenes in two Territories and Old Mexico won notice at once. Her most remarkable works are two stories published in the Galveston "News," "Mr. Moore of Albuquerque" and "A Daughter of Eve." Miss Dwyer at present fills a position on the staff of the "National Economist," Washington, DC. She is a correspondent for some of the prominent southern journals. Her home is in San Antonio, TX.

DYE, Mrs. Mary Irene Clark, reformer, born in North Hadley, MA, 22nd March, 1837. Her parents were Philo Clark and Irene Hibbard. Her father moved his family to Wisconsin in Mary's infancy. When she was ten years of age, the family removed to Waukegan, IL. After removal to Illinois, she was under private tutors for two years, when she entered an academy. When she was sixteen years old, there came severe financial reverses, forcing her to abandon a plan for a full course in Mount Holyoke, MA. At that time, persuaded by a brother in charge of the village telegraph office, Mary learned telegraphy and assumed his place, having full care of the office for two years. There were but few women operators at that early day. Mrs. Dye is the only woman member of the Old Time Telegraphers' Association. She became the wife of Byron E. Dye in 1855. Of three children born to them, two survive, a daughter, and a son recently admitted to the bar. Mrs. Dye has been a widow many years and has lived in Chicago, IL, entering into the various lines of work which the conditions of a large city present to a benevolent and public-spirited woman. Since her children have outgrown her immediate care and concern, she has devoted her time almost exclusively to philanthropic and reformatory work. She was among the first to perceive the need of the Protective Agency for Women and Children, assisting in its establishment in 1886 and serving as secretary for the first three years, and is still an active member of its board of managers. As a charter member of the Illinois Woman's Press Association, she has great satisfaction in the work accomplished for pen-women through its efforts. She is a member of the Chicago Women's Club. With the Margaret Fuller Society, established for the study of political problems, Mrs. Dye did good work. Since the formation of the Moral Educational Society, in 1882, she has been its secretary. She was among the first of the Woman's Christian Temperance Union women to see and teach that the ballot power is an essential factor in the furtherance of temperance work. When the free kindergarten system was inaugurated, Mrs. Dye's pen did good service in the interest of that charity. The placing of matrons in police stations enlisted her sympathy, and her efforts contributed much to the granting of the demand. Her persistent work toward the establishment of the summer Saturday half-holiday is known to only two or three persons, and the same is true of that labor of love, extending over many months, creating a public sentiment that demanded seats for the shopgirls when not busy with customers. Mrs. Dye believes in individual work so far as practicable. In impromptu speeches she is fluent and forcible, and on topics connected with social purity, the obligations of marriage and parenthood she is impressively eloquent. As a speaker and writer on reform subjects she is dauntless in demanding a settlement of all questions on the platform of right and justice, manifesting the "no surrender" spirit of her ancestral relative, Ethan Allen. Religious as she is reformatory in her nature, Mrs. Dye seeks the highest estimate given to spiritual things.

DYER, Mrs. Clara L. Brown, artist, born in Cape Elizabeth, ME, 13th March, 1849. Her father was a popular sea captain. On many of his voyages he was accompanied by his daughter, then only a child. From her mother's family she inherited artistic talent. Several of her uncles were woodcarvers and excelled in decorative work. In December, 1870, she became the wife of Charles A. Dyer, then a successful business man of Portland, ME, now engaged in gold-mining in California. Her family consisted of a son and a daughter. The son survives, but the daughter died in childhood. Mrs. Dyer turned her attention to art and became very much interested, and her talent, so many years hidden, came to light. She soon became the most enthusiastic and persevering of students. She took a thorough course in an art school, under able instructors, drawing from the antique and from life. She has paid considerable attention to portrait painting. In landscape painting she is seen at her best. She has made many fine sketches of the scenery about Casco Bay, and she has added to her collection some excellent sketches of mountain and inland scenery. Some of her studies have been exhibited in Boston, Portland and other cities, and have been highly spoken of by critics, as well as the general public.

DYER, Mrs. Julia Knowlton, philanthropist, born in Deerfield, NH, in 1829. Her father was Joseph Knowlton, and her mother Susan Dearborn. Upon Bunker Hill Monument are inscribed the names of her mother's grandfather, Nathaniel Dearborn, and of her own grandfather, Thomas Knowlton. Julia Knowlton was one of six children. Her father served in the war of 1812, and his namesake, her brother, Joseph H. Knowlton, was a member of the secret expedition against Fort Beaufort, in the Civil War. After graduation in her eighteenth year, Miss Knowlton taught a year in the high school in Manchester, NH, where she was a successful instructor in French and English literature and higher mathematics. She became the wife, in her twenty-first year, of Micah Dyer, Jr., now a lawyer of Boston. Three children were born to them, two sons and a daughter, the latter dying in infancy. The two sons still live, Dr. William K. Dyer, of Boston, and Walter Dyer. Mrs. Dyer is connected prominently with twenty-four associations, only one of which, the Castilian Club, is purely literary. She is president of the Soldiers' Home in Massachusetts, president and founder of the Charity Club, a member of the executive boards of the Home for Intemperate Women, the Helping Hand Association, and president of the local branch of the Woman's Christian Temperance Union. For twenty-six years she has been a manager for the Home for Female Prisoners in Dedham, MA, and is a life member of the Bostonian Society. The association appoints a board of twenty-four women, two of whom visit the Soldiers's Home each month to look after the needs of the inmates. She is a member of the Methodist Church, but she attends regularly the services of her husband's choice, in the Church of the Unity, Boston, without comment, but without affecting her own faith in the slightest. Mrs. Dyer is so engaged in philanthropic work that she hardly thinks of herself as being a leader.

EAGLE, Mrs. Mary Kavanaugh, church worker and social leader, born in Madison county, KY, 4th February, 1854. She is the daughter of William K. Oldham and J. Kate Brown. Her father is the son of Kie Oldham and Polly Kavanaugh and a native and resident of Madison county. He is of English descent on his paternal and Irish on his maternal side. Both his father's and mother's families were early settlers of central Kentucky, and were among the most successful farmers and stockdealers in that section. That vocation he also followed with marked success for many years. Her mother, who died 11th July, 1880, was the daughter of Ira Brown and Frances Mullens, of Albemarle county, VA, and of Scotch-English extraction. Mrs. Eagle's early education was conducted mainly at home, under the watchful care of her mother, who selected the best of tutors and governesses for her three daughters. She was graduated in June, 1872, from Mrs. Julia A. Tevis's famous school, Science Hill, Shelbyville, KY. She united with the Viny Fork Missionary Baptist Church of Madison county, KY, in August, 1874, and has been a zealous church worker ever since. She became the wife of Governor Eagle 3rd January, 1882, and moved to his large cotton plantation in Lonoke county, AR, where he was engaged in farming. Governor Eagle being a devoted church man and a member of the same denomination, they soon united their efforts in upbuilding the interests of their church for home and foreign missions and for Christian and charitable work of various kinds, contributing liberally of their ample means to support those objects. Governor Eagle has stood at the head of his church work for many years, and Mrs. Eagle has been the leader of the woman's work of her denomination in her State for more than eight years. She has been president of the Woman's Central Committee on Missions since its organization in November, 1882, and is president of the Woman's Mission Union of Arkansas. Mrs. Eagle is her husband's most congenial companion and valued counselor, whether he is employing his time as a farmer, a churchman or a statesman. Their interests have ever been identical. In his political aspirations she has rendered him great assistance. She accompanied him in his canvass for the nomination for the office of governor in 1888. She accompanied him in his canvass with the representative of the Republican Union Labor Party, which immediately followed, and also in his canvass for re-election in 1890. Governor Eagle has entered upon his second term as governor, and since his inauguration the mansion has been famous for true southern hospitality. Governor Eagle has for many years been president of the Baptist State Convention and was speaker of the House of Representatives in 1885. This caused Mrs. Eagle to take an interest in parliamentary practice and to take up that study. She is now one of the best parliamentarians in the State and takes great interest in the proceedings of all deliberative bodies. As a member of the Board of Lady Managers of the Columbian Exposition she was appointed a member of many important committees.

EAMES, Emma Hayden, operatic singer, known in private life as Mrs. Julian Story, born in 1867, in China, where her father held a diplomatic post. Her parents were natives of Maine and residents of Boston, MA, where her father practiced law before going into the service of the government in Shanghai, China, where Emma was born. After the family returned to Boston, Emma began to study music under the tuition of her mother, who was a cultivated singer. After a thorough grounding in the preliminaries, Emma went to Paris, France, to study with Madame Marchesi. In 1888 she made her début in the Grand Opéra in Paris, after waiting in vain for a chance to appear under a contract for one year made with the Opéra Comique. She secured a cancellation of the contract with the Comique and prepared to sing in "Romeo et Juliette" in the Grand Opéra. Madame Patti sang in the title rôle twelve times, and then Emma Eames succeeded her. Following directly after the most famous singer of the age, Miss Eames won a brilliant triumph on her début, and at once was ranked by the French critics as one of the greatest singers and actors of the day. Her répertoire includes Juliette, Marguerite, Desdemona, Santuzza, Elsa, and other famous rôles, and in each of them her success has been marked. After her father's death her talents enabled her to maintain the fortunes of her family. She was married, 29th July, 1891, to Julian Story, in London, England. She is regard in Paris and London as one of the greatest singers of the age. Her latest triumph was won in the opera "Ascanio."

EAST, Mrs. Edward H., philanthropist, born in Bethesda, Williamson county, TN, 15th March, 1849. Her father, Rev. H. C. Horton, was a Virginian, her mother, Elizabeth Elliotte Kennedy, was a South Carolinian. Her grand parents came from England and Ireland and could boast a coat-of-arms on both sides of the house, but strong republican sentiments forbade a display of them. She came of Revolutionary stock. Lieutenant Kennedy fought under Gen. Francis Marion and was rewarded for bravery, having on one occasion, with only himself and one other, put to rout twelve Tories. Her father moved to Mississippi, where her girlhood was spent. She was educated in the Marshall Female Institue, under the management of Pres. Joseph E. Douglas. As a young lady she was popular with old and young. When the Mississippi & Tennessee R. R. was being built through Mississippi, the work had to stop for want of means when the road had been extended only fifty or sixty miles. A plan was suggested to get the men of the county together to raise a fund. A May Queen feast and a barbecue in the woods were chosen. The dark-eyed, rosy-cheeked little maiden, Tennie Horton, as she was called, only fourteen years old, was chosen queen, and she on that occasion made a railroad speech that brought thousands of dollars out of the pockets of that then wealthy people. She became the wife, when very young, of D. C. Ward, a merchant, who was killed in the war. During the war she was the only protection of her old parents, with the exception of a few faithful servants who remained with them. Her life has been one of great activity. In 1868 she became the wife of Judge East, a distinguished jurist, who sympathizes with and aids her in all her work. She is now and has been for several years in the Woman's Christian Temperance Union work. She is local president of the central union in Nashville, where she has for many years resided, and is also corresponding secretary of the State. She was appointed State chairman of the Southern Woman's Council. She has spent much time and money for the cause of temperance. In every reform movement she takes great interest. When the Prohibition amendment was before the people of Tennessee, she was active in the work to create a sentiment in its favor. A large tent, that had been provided in the city in which to conduct gospel services, she had moved to every part of the city for a month, and procured for each night able Prohibition speeches. She has been a delegate to every national convention since 1887. The poor of the city know her, for she never turns a deaf ear to their appeals nor sends them away empty-handed. She taught a night school for young men and boys for two years. She has written for several periodicals and been correspondent for newspapers.

She has now a book ready for the publisher. Being an active, busy woman, she finds but little time to write. She is the mother of five children, all living.

EASTMAN, Mrs. Elaine Goodale, poet, born in a country home called "Sky Farm," near South Egremont, MA, 9th October, 1863. Her mother, Mrs. D. H. R. Goodale, educated her and her sister Dora at home. Elaine at twelve years of age was a good Greek and Latin scholar, reading most of the classics with ease, and she was also familiar with French and German. She was a precocious child and never went to school, and in her isolated mountain home she grew to maturity, after astonishing the world with her poetical productions, written in the short-frock and mud-pie years of her youth. In 1878 Elaine published in conjunction with her eleven-year-old sister, Dora, a book of poems entitled "Apple Blossoms." A second volume, entitled "In Berkshire with the Wild Flowers," soon followed, and the fame of the Goodale sisters spread throughout the English speaking world. Their father, Henry Sterling Goodale, an experimental farmer, was devoted to poetry and literature, a good mathematician, a clever poet and a failure as a farmer. Financial reverses came to the family, and Elaine and her sister made an attempt to save the homestead by their literary work. In 1881 Elaine was attracted to the cause of the Indians, through some of the Indian students from the Carlisle and Hampton Institutes in Pennsylvania, who were spending the summer in the study of farming in the Berkshire Hills. She took a position as teacher in the Carlisle school, where she taught successfully. In 1885 she went with Senator Dawes on a trip through the Indian reservations, where she made a close study of the condition of the Indians. She then became a government teacher in White Pine Camp, on the Lower Brulé Indian Agency, in Dakota. In 1890 she was appointed superintendent of all the Indian schools in South Dakota, having her station in the Pine Ridge Agency. In that year she became acquainted with Dr. Charles A. Eastman, a full-blood Sioux Indian, known among the Indians as "Tawa Kanhdiota," or "Many Thunders," and became his wife, 18th June, 1891, in New York City. Dr. Eastman is a graduate of Dartmouth College. He is a man of marked intellectual power, and is engaged in the practice of medicine among his people. Mrs. Eastman is now living in the government house on the Pine Ridge Agency, devoting herself to her family and to the welfare of the wards of the nation. During several years past she has published little or nothing of importance.

EDDY, Mrs. Sara Hershey, musical educator, born in Lancaster county, PA. She is a daughter of the late Benjamin and Eliza-beth Hershey. She received her education and early musical training in Phila-delphia, where she sang in a church choir for sev-eral years. Bad training resulted in the ruin of her voice, and she turned her attention to the piano. In 1867 she went to Berlin, Germany, where she studied harmony, counterpoint, score-reading and piano-playing with Professor Stern, singing with Miss Jenny Mayer, declamation with Pro-fessor Schwartz, elocution and stage deportment with Berndahl, and, afterward, piano with Kullak and singing with Gustav Engel and Gotfried Weiss. She became familiar with the German lan-guage and literature, and after three years in Berlin she went to Milan, Italy, where for eighteen months she took vocal lessons with Gerli and the older Lamperti. There she learned the Italian lan-guage. She then went to London, England, where she studied oratorio and English singing with Madame Sainton-Dolby. She returned to the United States in October, 1871, and remained eighteen months in New York City, teaching pri-vate pupils and singing in concerts and churches. She was called to Pittsburgh, PA, as a teacher in the vocal department of the Female College. In 1873 she was placed in control of that department. In 1875 she went to Chicago and founded the Her-shey School of Musical Art with W. S. B. Mathews. Clarence Eddy afterward became the general musical director of the school, which was very successful. In July, 1879, Miss Hershey and Mr. Eddy were married. In 1885 the duties of the school became too exacting, and Mr. and Mrs. Eddy withdrew from it and became the instructors of private classes. Mrs. Eddy has been a promi-nent member of the Music Teachers' National Association. In 1887 she was elected to the board of examiners in the vocal department of the Amer-

ican College of Musicians. She has contributed a number of valuable articles to musical journals.

EDDY, Mrs. Sarah Stoddard, reformer, born in Hudson, NY, 24th February, 1831. Her grandfa-ther, Ashbel Stoddard, was among the first settlers of Hudson, who went from Nantucket and Provi-dence, RI, and were mostly of Quaker descent. He came of a severely orthodox family. Congrega-tional ministers were numerous on both his father's and on his mother's side, but he had become more liberal. He established a printing office, book-store and bindery in the central part of the new city and, on 7th April, 1785, issued the first number of the Hudson "Weekly Gazette." That was the pioneer newspaper of the Hudson valley and the oldest in the State. In 1824 he sold that political newspaper and published the "Rural Repository," a literary weekly which had a wide circulation. To the editing of that paper and to the printing establishment the father of Mrs. Eddy, William Bowles Stoddard, an only son, succeeded. Familiarity bred a reverence for books with a great love for them and a desire for their constant com-panionship. The mother of Mrs. Eddy was of a Holland Dutch family. She had literary taste and skill. Mrs. Eddy was educated in private schools in Hudson and in Clinton, NY. Her preference was for literary studies, the languages and compo-sition. In March, 1852, she became the wife of Rev. Richard Eddy, a Universalist clergyman of Rome, NY. After living in Rome two years, she removed to Buffalo, NY, then to Philadelphia, PA, and then to Canton, NY, where she lived until the beginning of the Civil War. Mr. Eddy was appointed chaplain of the 60th New York State Volunteers and, having gone to the front with his regiment, Mrs. Eddy wth her children went to live in Baltimore, MD, early in January, 1862, that her husband might more frequently see his family, and that she might find some way to be of service. She assisted in forming the aid associations in Balti-more and spent her days in the camps and the hos-pitals near the city. At the close of the war her husband became pastor of the First Universalist Church in Philadelphia, and, after living in that city for five years, she lived in Franklin, Gloucester, Col-lege Hill, Brookline and

Melrose, MA, and is now a resident of Boston. Mrs. Eddy is a member of the New England Women's Club, of the Women's Educational and Industrial Union, of the Woman Suffrage Association and of several purely literary clubs. She has organized several clubs in towns where she has lived, and presided over them for a time, and encourages women everywhere to band themselves together for study and mutual help. In literary matters she has done only fugitive work. She has three sons and two daughters, who have been educated to occupy honorable positions in life.

EDGAR, Mrs. Elizabeth, educator, born near the famous old Donegal Presbyterian Church of Lancaster county, PA, in 1842. She is the daughter of Rev. Thomas Marshall Boggs, of Washington, PA, and Amelia Jane Cunningham Boggs, of New London, PA. At the time of her birth, her father was a pastor, and continued pastor for fourteen years, up to the time of his death, of the Donegal Church, being also pastor of the Presbyterian Church in the neighboring town of Mount Joy, PA. She was educated in the Mount Joy Seminary, Rev. Nehemiah Dodge, principal, and on 7th July, 1870, became the wife of Rev. John Edgar, who had been pastor of the Mount Joy Presbyterian Church, but who, at the time of his marriage, had occupied a pastorate in New Bloomfield, PA. There Mr. and Mrs. Edgar remained thirteen years, having two sons born to them, James Marshall Edgar, in 1872, and John Boggs Edgar, in 1878. In 1883, Dr. and Mrs. Edgar removed to Chambersburg, PA, having been appointed respectively to the positions of president and lady principal of Wilson College for women, under the care of the Presbyterian Church. The work of Mrs. Edgar in that college is highly successful.

EDHOLM, Mrs. Mary G. Charlton, journalist, is official reporter of the World's Woman's Christian Temperance Union, secretary of the International Federation Woman's Press League, and has for years been pushing the temperance reform with a lead pencil. Her journalistic gift is the inheritance from her father, James B. Charlton, and her mother, Lucy Gow Charlton, who were both fine writers along reformatory lines, especially the abolition of slavery, the prohibition of the saloon and the ballot for women. During her sophomore year in college in Monmouth, IL, she wrote her exhibition essay on the subject, "Shall our Women Vote?" As a test she sent it for publication to the "Woman's Journal" of Boston, and it was published. Her marriage with E. O. L. Edholm, a journalist, developed still more her love for editorial and reportorial work, and for several years they traveled together extensively, and she thereby gained the knowledge and information which comes alone of travel. During those years her descriptive articles appeared in the New York "World," the Chicago "Tribune," St. Louis "Post-Dispatch," "Republican" and Chicago "Inter-Ocean" Both before and after the birth of her children she kept her pen busy. For years she was official reporter and superintendent of railroad rates of the California Woman's Christian Temperance Union, and annually wrote about two-hundred-fifty columns of original temperance matter for over two-hundred papers, including the San Francisco, Oakland, Portland, New Orleans, Boston and New York dailies, and the "Union Signal" and the New York "Voice." She conducted three Woman's Christian Temperance Union excursions across the Continent. Her promotion came through Frances E. Willard and Lady Henry Somerset, and she was unanimously elected official reporter of the World's Woman's Christian Temperance Union. Mrs. Edholm has for years been interested in the rescue of erring girls and has written hundreds of articles in defense of outraged womanhood, in such papers as the "Woman's Journal," the "Woman's Tribune," and the "California Illustrated Magazine," where her pen depicted the horrors of the slave traffic in Chinese women for immoral purposes. In evangelistic meetings in Oakland, CA, she met the millionaire evangelist, Charles N. Crittenton, the founder of Florence Missions for the rescue of erring girls, and at once entered into descriptive articles of Florence Mission work with such enthusiasm that Mr. Crittenton made her reporter of Florence Missions, thus honoring her as a champion of her sex and widening her field of journalism. The horrors of this traffic in girls and their redemption through Florence Missions Mrs. Edholm is now bringing out in book form. She is compiling a book of the life of Mrs. Emily Pitt Stevens, the Woman's Christian Temperance Union Demosthenes and national organizer. For years, Mrs. Edholm has resided in Oakland, CA, and has been active in Rev. Dr. Chapman's Church of that city.

EDWARDS, Miss Anna Cheney, educator, born in Northampton, MA, 31st July, 1835. Her father, Charles, was sixth in descent from Alexander Edwards, one of the early settlers of the town. Her mother, Ruth White, of Spencer, MA, was also of Puritan ancestry. Anna early showed a fondness for books and a predilection for teaching. She remembers making up her mind, on her first day of her attending school, at the age of four years, that she was to be a teacher. This was an inherited fondness, as her father and grandfather had successively taught the district school near the old Edwards homestead. Her great-grandfather, Nathaniel Edwards, is worthy of mention in these days of higher education for women, for his labors in the instruction of the girls of his neighborhood in vacations, because in his time they were not allowed to attend school with the boys during the regular terms. Miss Edwards' career as a teacher began at the age of sixteen, after she had passed through the public schools of Northampton, in an outer district of the town. After two years of experience she entered Mt. Holyoke Seminary, South Hadley, MA, in September, 1853. At the end of one year her studies were interrupted by three years more of teaching, after which she returned to the seminary and was graduated in July, 1859. She was recalled as assistant teacher the following year and has been a member of the Holyoke faculty most of the time since. She was absent at one period for about two years, her health being somewhat impaired, and from 1866 to 1868 she was principal of Lake Erie Seminary, Painesville, OH. She has spent eighteen months in travel in Europe, and in vacations she has taken separate trips to New Orleans, California, Alaska and various parts of the United States and Canada. She was appointed second associate principal of Mt. Holyoke Seminary in 1872, and first associate in 1883. A college charter having been obtained for that institution in 1888, she was made professor of theism and Christian evidences, and instructor of ancient literature. In scientific studies she shared the enthusiasm and the wide reading of Lydia W. Shattuck, the botanist, and became herself an earnest student and teacher of geology. She is identified with her alma mater in its religious character and work. For the use of her classes she printed in 1877 a volume of "Notes on Ancient Literature." She has given lectures to classes and to ladies' literary societies on a variety of topics. Her more public activities have been in the way of papers and addresses before the different associations of Holyoke alumnae and in connection with women's missionary meetings. Since 1876 she has been vice-president of the Hampshire County Branch of the Woman's Board of Missions. In 1888 the degree of Master of Arts was conferred upon her by Burlington University, Vermont.

EDWARDS, Mrs. Emma Atwood, educator, born in East Pittston, ME, 6th November, 1838. Her father, Rev. Charles Baker, a Methodist itinerant, was the chief promoter of education in the Maine Conference in that time, and fully alive to the importance of mental and moral training. Mrs. Edwards was graduated from the academy in Newbury, VT, in 1860. She engaged at once in teaching, and, while preceptress in Amenia Seminary, she became acquainted with her future husband, Rev. James T. Edwards, D.D., LL.D., who was at that time one of the professors in the seminary. Immediately after their marriage, in 1862, she became associated with him in teaching in East Greenwich Academy, Rhode Island, over which for six years he presided as principal. In 1870 Professor Edwards became principal of Chamberlain Institute, Randolph, NY, and Mrs. Edwards has been since that time associated with him as preceptress. Holding herself to the highest ideals of attainment possible, she is able to hold those under her charge to similar ideals, and thus confer upon them the greatest of benefits. Several thousand students have felt the molding influence of her elevated character.

EGGLESTON, Miss Allegra, artist, born in Stillwater, MN, 19th November, 1860. She is the second daughter of Edward Eggleston, the author, who came of a well-known Virginia family, with strains of Irish and Scotch in his descent. She inherited superior mental gifts from her father, combined with artistic qualities in her mother's family, which was of English origin. A delicate and high-strung child, she early showed a talent for drawing and modeling. One of her first works of art was an idol carved out of a piece of semi-decayed wood, when she was only six years of age. She drew constantly and modeled occasionally in clay, but she had no teaching until she was received into classes in Cooper Institute in October, 1875. She was under age, being not yet fifteen, but was accepted on account of remarkable promise. She did creditable work there for two years, after which she entered the studio of Wyatt Eaton, where she made rapid progress in painting from life. In 1879 she went to Europe in company with her father and family. While abroad she took two weeks' lessons under a Swiss wood-carver and astonished him by successfully carving the most difficult pieces as soon as she had learned the use of her tools. After her return home she occupied herself with wood-carving, painting also some portraits, which were exhibited in the annual exhibitions of the Society of American Artists. In 1882 she carved panels for a memorial mantel-piece in the editorial rooms of the "Century Magazine," on one of which was cut a portrait in bas-relief of Dr. J. G. Holland. That piece of work was destroyed by fire in 1888, and Miss Eggleston was called upon to replace it. Of late she has occupied herself much with book illustrations. Her father's novel, "The Graysons," is illustrated by her, while many of the pictures in his popular school histories, as well as in other school books, bear her signature. She has illustrated a life of Columbus, written by her sister, Mrs. Elizabeth Eggleston Seelye, and edited by their father. Miss Eggleston is versatile. She does many kinds of artistic decorative work for amusement. Among other things she models in leather, having executed the cover for the album containing autographs of distinguished American authors, which was presented to Mrs. Grover Cleveland as an acknowledgment of her interest in the copyright bill, by Edward Eggleston. Miss Eggleston spends the winter in New York and makes her home during the rest of the year at Lake George, where she has a studio in her father's picturesque stone library.

ELLIOTT, Mrs. Maud Howe, novelist, born in Boston, MA, 9th November, 1855. She is the youngest daughter of Julia Ward Howe, the poet, and of Dr. Samuel G. Howe, famous for his work in the Institute for the Blind in South Boston, MA. She was carefully educated under the supervision of her mother and drawn into literary activity by her intellectual environments. She traveled abroad and early saw much of the world in Rome, Paris and other European centers of art and literature. In her earlier years she wrote a good deal, but only for her own amusement. Her fear of ridicule and criticism kept her from publishing her first poems and novels. Her first published story appeared in "Frank Leslie's Weekly." She then began to write for newspapers in New York, and letters from Newport to the Boston "Evening Transcript." She became the wife, in 1887, of John Elliott, the English artist, and they made their home in Chicago, IL. Soon after her marriage her first book, "A Newport Aquarelle," was published anonymously. It was an instant success. Her next serious work was "The San Rosario Ranche," which appeared under her own name. After a visit to New Orleans she wrote her "Atalanta in the South," which scored a success. Her next book was "Mammon," which appeared in "Lippincott's Magazine." Her latest novel is "Phyllida." Among her miscellaneous works are a sketch of her mother in "Famous Women," "The Strike," a story published in the "Century," and a dramatic sketch entitled "Golden Meshes." Recently Mrs. Elliott has delivered lectures on "Cotemporaneous Literature," and has published a serial in the "Ladies' Home Journal." Among her productions is a play, "The Man Without a Shadow." Since her marriage, the greater part of her time has been passed in Chicago. Her summers she passes near Newport, RI, where her summer home, "Oak Glen," is situated. In Boston she spends her time with her mother. Her life is full of literary, artistic and social activities.

ELLSLER, Miss Effie, actor, born in Philadelphia, PA. She is a daughter of John A. Ellsler, the well-known actor and manager. Her mother also was an actor of merit. Effie's strongly marked talents are therefore an inheritance. She was early upon the stage. At the age of three years she made her début as the Genius of the Ring in "Aladdin." At the age of four years she played Eva in "Uncle Tom's Cabin," and she made a hit in that rôle. Soon after Effie's birth her parents settled in Cleveland, OH, where her father took the management of a theater. The child was called upon from time to time to play child parts. Her parents at first intended to train her for dancing, and Effie soon acquired remarkable agility in the preliminary training. She was sent for a number of years to the Ursuline Convent in Cleveland, where she received a very thorough education. She remained in that school until she was sixteen years old, at times leaving for a short space to assume child rôles in her father's theater. On one of those occasions she was cast as one of the witches in "Macbeth." The red-fire flash caused her to forget her lines, when she deliberately drew the book from her dress and read her words. At sixteen years of age she began the regular work of the stage, playing all sorts of parts from Juliet and Rosalind to a howler in a Roman mob. She made her first great success as Hazel in "Hazel Kirke," in the Madison Square Theater in New York City. She played in that rôle for three years, until her physician ordered her to discontinue it on account of the strain on her powers. During the past ten years she has traveled with her own company, presenting a variety of plays, most of them with great success. Her most successful play, aside from "Hazel Kirke," has been "Woman Against Woman." In 1891–92, in answer to countless requests, Miss Ellsler revived "Hazel Kirke," in which she again showed her great powers. She ranks among the foremost emotional actors of the United States.

ELMORE, Mrs. Lucie Ann Morrison, temperance reformer, born in Brandonville, Preston county, WV, 29th March, 1829, Her father was a Methodist clergyman, and she is an Episcopalian and a radical Woman's Christian Temperance Union woman. She is a pronounced friend of all oppressed people, and especially of the colored race in the United States. She is patriotic in the extreme. Her husband, who served as an officer in the Union Army through the Civil War, died in 1868, and her only child died in infancy. Mrs. Elmore is widely known as a philanthropist. She is an eloquent and convincing speaker on temperance, social purity and the evils of the tobacco habit. She has suffered financial reverses, but she has never given up her charitable work. Her home is in Englewood, NJ. Her chief literary works are her poems, one volume of which has passed through a large edition, and the popular story "Billy's Mother." She has held several important editorial positions, and her poems have been published in the leading magazines. A story now ready for the press is thought to bear in it promise of a great success, as it is the product of a ripe experience and close study of neighborhood influences for good and evil.

EMERSON, Mrs. Ellen Russell, author, born in New Sharon, ME, 16th January, 1837. Her father, Dr. Leonard White Russell, was a man of character and ability. He was a descendant of the Russells of Charlestown, MA. Dr. Russell had six children, the youngest of whom, Ellen, was born in the later years of his life. She early gave evidence of peculiarities of temperament, shy, dreamy and meditative, with an exceeding love for nature. At seventeen she was sent to Boston, where she entered the Mt. Vernon Seminary, in charge of Rev. Dr. Robert W. Cushman, under whose severe and stimulating guidance the student made rapid progress. There her literary work began to appear in fugitive poems and short essays. Her stay in the seminary was brought to an end by a severe attack of brain fever, caused by over study. In 1862 she became the wife of Edwin R. Emerson, then in the government service in Augusta, ME. Social duties demanded her attention, but gradually she returned to her study, and then began her interest in Indian history. A foundation was laid in systematic research for her book, "Indian Myths, or Legends and Traditions of the American Aborigines, Compared with Other Countries." In all her work she has the cordial interest and sympathy of her husband. Trips to the West, to Colorado and California, brought her in sympathy with the red race, whose history and genius she had studied so earnestly. In 1884 she sailed for Europe, where she worked among the records and monuments in the libraries and museums, using not only the note-book, but the sketch-book and brush of the painter as well. Wherever she went, the scholars of Europe recognized her ability and conscientious work, giving her unusual privileges in the pursuit of her researches and showing cordial interest in her labor. In Paris she was elected a member of the Société Americaine de France, the first woman to receive that honor. There she completed the object of her European visit, and returned to America to prepare for the publication of her recent work, "Masks, Heads and Faces, with Some Considerations Respecting the Rise and Development of Art." Mrs. Emerson usually spends her winters in Boston, and lives a quiet, studious life with her one daughter.

ENGLE, Mrs. Addie C. Strong, author, born in the town of Manchester, CT, 11th August, 1845. She traces her ancestry back to 1630, when John Strong, of some historic fame, came to this country from Taunton, England. Her girlhood years were spent in the picturesque town of South Manchester, and her later life, until 1882 in Meriden, CT. As a child she found her pen a recreation. Her talent for literary composition was inherited from her mother, who was Mary B. Keeney, whose ancestors were among the earlier settlers of South Manchester. When a girl of sixteen, she sent an article upon one of the terrible war years then just ended to "Zion's Herald," of Boston, in which it was printed as a leader, and she was engaged by its publisher to write a series of sketches for children. She

spent several years in teaching in South Manchester. In 1866 she became the wife of J. H. Bario, of Meriden. Two daughters of that marriage survive and share her home. For years she gave her best labors to the Order of the Eastern Star, in which she was honored by being called three years to fill the highest office in her native State. In the discharge of the duties pertaining to that position her executive ability and knowledge of jurisprudence won commendation as being "wonderful for a woman," a compliment she rather resented, as her pride and faith in the abilities of her sex are large. Her stories and poems have appeared for years in children's papers, the "Voice of Masonry," the "Churchman" and other periodicals. She has published many stories and poems. The odes used in the secret work of the Order of the Eastern Star and its beautiful memorial service were her contributions. In 1882 she became the wife of Rev. Willis D. Engle, of Indianapolis, an Episcopal clergyman, and removed to the Hoosier State. There she at once became identified, outside of church work, with local organizations of the Eastern Star, the Woman's Relief Corps, the McAll Mission and the King's Daughters, all of which received the hearty labors of her brain and pen. With her husband she commenced in 1889 the publication of a monthly illustrated magazine, the "Compass, Star and Vidette," in the interest of the Masonic, Eastern Star and Relief Corps Orders. The entire charge of the literary and children's departments fell upon her. In December, 1890, she ceased active participation in the work of the various societies to which she belonged, and joined the sadly increasing order of "Shut Ins." A fall the winter before had produced serious results. Nobly battling against heavy odds for nearly a year, nature finally succumbed, and congestion of the spine resulted. Still she keeps up her brain efforts, though in a lesser degree, and the incidents which came to her as she made in a hammock a short lake trip in the summer of 1892 were woven into a romance in the form of a serial, which was published. The injury to her eyes has impaired their appearance as well as their vision, and she wears glasses. Her Puritan ancestry shows plainly in some of her opinions, yet she is very liberal in her views and absorbed heart and soul in every great step toward progress and reform. She is a rapid talker, and when able to speak from the rostrum was an eloquent one.

ESMOND, Mrs. Rhoda Anna, philanthropist, born in Sempronius, NY, 22nd November, 1819. Her parents were Zadok Titus and Anna Hinkley Greenfield Titus, who were married in 1801. Zadok Titus was born in Stillwater, NY, and moved in 1795 to Sempronius, where he took up one-hundred-seventy-seven acres of wild land, which he converted into a beautiful farm, upon which he lived until his death, in 1836. Miss Titus' school-days, after leaving the district school, were spent for two years in Groton Academy and nearly a year in "Nine Partners Boarding School," Washington, NY. Here she met Joseph Esmond, a young Hicksite Friend, from Saratoga, NY, and became his wife 5th May, 1840. They resided in Saratoga two years and then went to Milan, Cayuga county, NY. In 1846 they moved to Fulton, and Mr. Esmond took up the study of law. What he read through the day was reviewed with Mrs. Esmond at night. That gave her much valuable legal knowledge and some acquaintance with the general rules of legal proceedings. In 1848 Mr. Esmond was admitted to the bar and practiced law in Fulton for twenty years. During those years Mrs. Esmond's health was very poor, but she was actively engaged in church work and often contributed articles to newspapers under the pen-name "Ruth." In 1872 Mr. Esmond moved with his family, consisting of his wife and three sons, to Syracuse, NY. When the influence of the Woman's Temperance Crusade of the West reached Syracuse, she helped to organize a woman's temperance society of four-hundred members. She was made a delegate to the first State Woman's Christian Temperance Union convention, held in Brooklyn, in February, 1875, with instructions to visit all of the coffee-houses and friendly inns in Brooklyn, New York and Poughkeepsie, to gather all the information possible for the purpose of formulating a plan for opening an inn in Syracuse. The inn was formally opened in July, 1875. As chairman of the inn committee she managed its affairs for nearly two years with remarkable success. Jealousies arose in the union, and Mrs. Esmond and thirty-two others resigned and formed a new union, called Syracuse Woman's Christian Temperance Union No. 2. Mrs. Esmond was elected president, but positively refused to act. In the first State Woman's Christian Temperance Union convention held in Brooklyn, in February, 1875, Mrs. Esmond was made chairman of the committee on resolutions and appointed one of a committee on "Memorial to the State Legislature." In the State's first annual convention held in Ilion, in October, 1875, she was made a member of the executive board. In its second annual convention in Syracuse, in 1876, she gave the address of welcome, was made chairman of the executive board, chosen a delegate to the National convention and made a member of the State committee on visitations. In 1877, in the State annual convention, she was made chairman of the finance committee and a member of the committee to revise the State constitution. In 1881 she was elected State superintendent of the department of unfermented wine. In 1887 she was elected a delegate to the National convention held in Nashville, but resigned. She was there appointed national superintendent of the department of unfermented wine. In 1888 she was delegate to the national convention, held in New York City. In 1889 she resigned the presidency of the local union, having held that office nearly six years. For the past four years her most earnest efforts and best thoughts have been given to the interest of her department work.

ESTY, Miss Alice May, operatic singer, born in Lowell, MA, 12th April, 1866. She is of purely American descent. Her great-great-grandfather on the maternal side fought under Washington. Her ancestors for generations have lived in New England. Early in life Miss Esty gave promise of great musical ability. As a child she possessed a wonderful soprano voce. At the early age of twelve she announced her intention to become a professional singer. Although from the outset she encountered difficulties that would have discouraged many of maturer years, she never wavered. She was fortunate in securing for her teacher Madame Millar, then Miss Clara Smart, with whom she studied for three years. Miss Esty's first engagement of importance in her native country was an extended tour through the United States with Madame Camilla Urso. That was followed by a very successful season in

Boston. The hard work of years began to tell, and Miss Esty after a severe attack of typhoid fever went to England for a change and rest. One of her numerous letters of introduction was to the head of the leading musical house in London. That gentleman expressed a wish to hear the latest singer from what has become recognized in England as the land of song, America. An appointment was made, and, as Miss Esty was singing, several gentlemen dropped in to listen. Among them were Edward Lloyd and Mr. N. Vert. These gentlemen were struck with her beautiful voice and excellent singing. Although only in search of health, Miss Esty received so many flattering offers from managers that she determined to settle in England for a few years. After a flying trip to Boston she returned to London, in March, 1891, and was in much demand for concerts during the season. She achieved a great success with Madame Adelina Patti in the Royal Albert Hall, and an equally successful appearance in a subsequent concert. She was well received in the best musical circles in England. An engagement with the Carl Rosa Grand Opera Company was entered upon in August, 1891. In seven months she learned the leading rôles in ten operas, singing to crowded houses on every occasion and never meeting an adverse criticism. During the winter of 1891–92 she filled concert engagements in Birmingham, Nottingham and other important musical centers in England. She has received flattering offers from Sir Charles Halle and other leading conductors. Miss Esty's voice is a pure soprano, of extended compass, powerful and sweet, she sings with warmth of expression as well as finished method, and her articulation is nearly perfection.

EVANS, Mrs. Lizzie P. E., novelist, born in Arlington, MA, 27th August, 1846. She is the youngest daughter of the late Captain Endor and Lydia Adams Estabrook, and a granddaughter of Deacon John Adams, who owned and occupied the Adams house, which was riddled with bullets when war swept through the quiet streets of West Cambridge, now Arlington, as the British soldiers, on their retreat from Concord and Lexington, erroneously supposed that the patriot, Samuel Adams, a cousin of Deacon John

Adams, was secreted within its walls. Lizzie Phelps Estabrook became the wife of Andrew Allison Evans of Boston, MA. He died in May, 1888. Mrs. Evans resides in Somerville, MA. Among her published works is the quaintly humorous book "Aunt Nabby," an entertaining picture of country life, customs, dialects and ideas. The book is a successful essay in laughing down the overdone conventionalities of fashionable life. Another of her successful books is "From Summer to Summer," an entertaining home story. Many short stories and sketches from her pen have been published under the pen-name "Esta Brooks."

EVE, Miss Maria Louise, poet, was born near Augusta, GA, about 1848. She is of old English ancestry. Her first literary success was a prize for the best essay awarded by "Scott's Magazine." She has since contributed, from time to time, articles on literary and other subjects to some of the prominent magazines and papers. In 1879 her poem "Conquered at Last" won the prize offered by the Mobile "News" for the best poem expressing the gratitude of the South to the North for aid in the yellow fever scourge of the preceding year. That poem was reproduced in nearly all of the papers and many of the magazines of the North, and also in some periodicals abroad. Its great popularity throughout the North, attested by the large number of letters received by her from soldiers and civilians, cultured and uncultured, was a complete surprise as well as a great gratification to her. In June, 1889, a short poem by her, entitled "A Briar Rose," won the prize offered by the Augusta "Chronicle." At the request of the secretary of the American Peace and Arbitration Society, in Boston, as a message of welcome to the English Peace Deputation to America in October, 1887, she wrote a poem, "The Lion and the Eagle." The underlying thought of the "Universal Peace," as found in one of her published poems, led the secretary to communicate with her in regard to it, and she has since written a number of poems bearing on the subject, which is perhaps the most practical work that she has done on any of the great lines of advancement and progress. Possessing that order of mind which crystallizes in thought rather than in action, she feels that anything she may hope to achieve must be chiefly through the channels of literary effort. Her writings are comparatively small in bulk, her endeavor being always toward force and directness, rather than expansiveness of thought.

EVERHARD, Mrs. Caroline McCullough, woman suffragist, born in Massillon, OH, 14th September, 1843, where she now resides. She received her early education in the public schools. Subsequently she spent a year in a private school for young women in Media, PA. Shortly after the close of her school days she became the wife of Captain Henry H. Everhard, who had returned from the war after three years of honorable service. The cares of home and family demanded her attention for several years, but, when her children were old enough for her to entrust their education to other hands, she resumed her literary pursuits. At an early age she began to investigate and reason for herself, and Goethe's words, "Open the Windows and Let in More Light," were the subject of her essay when she finished her course of study in the public schools. A natural consequence of her original and independent way of thinking was an unusual interest in woman's position in state and church, and she has done much to influence public sentiment in that respect in the community in which she has resided. Mrs. Everhard has been appointed to several positions of trust not usually filled by women, in all of which she has discharged her duties acceptably. In 1886 she was appointed by the Judge of the Court of Common Pleas to fill a vacancy caused by the death of her father, one of the trustees of the Charity Rotch School, an institution founded fifty years ago by the benevolent Quaker woman whose name it bears. That was the first instance in Ohio of the appointment of a woman to a place of trust that required a bond. She has been for several years a member of a board appointed by the court to visit the public institutions of the county, including the various jails, the county infirmary and the Children's Home. She has been a director of the Union National Bank of Massillon for a number of years. She entered actively into the ranks in 1888 and became more and more deeply engaged until May,

1891, when she was elected to fill the office of president of the Ohio Woman's Suffrage Association. She organized the Equal Rights Association of Canton, OH, and the one in her own city, and to her influence are due their prosperity and power for good in that portion of the State. From childhood she has been an ardent friend of dumb animals and has promoted the work of the Massillon Humane Society, of which she has been an efficient officer from its organization. Mrs. Everhard is an indefatigable worker. Her office necessarily imposes a large correspondence, to which she must give personal attention, and for many years she has made her influence felt through the medium of the press. Three children have blessed her married life.

EWING, Mrs. Catherine A. Fay, educator and philanthropist, born in Westboro, MA, 18th July, 1822. Her parents were in comfortable circumstances and, desiring a more liberal education for their children removed to Marietta, OH, in 1836, where they could have

the advantage of both college and female seminary. On her father's side Mrs. Ewing is descended from Huguenot ancestry. His mother was a woman of rare piety, and through her influence her twelve children became Christians in early life. Mrs. Ewing's mother was of Scotch descent, and in the long line of Christian ancestors there were many ministers and missionaries. All of her eleven children were devoted Christians. Two became ministers and two are deacons. Mrs. Ewing, from her eighteenth to her twentieth year, taught school in Ohio and then went as a missionary among the Choctaw Indians for ten years. Upon her return to Ohio, in 1857, she founded a home for destitute children, of which she had control for nine years. Through her efforts the Ohio Legislature passed a bill in Columbus, which entitled every county to establish a Children's Home. In 1866 she became the wife of A. S. D. Ewing. She has since devoted much time and labor to the children about her, teaching a large infant class in the Sabbath-school and also establishing a sewing-school. She is the author of a comprehensive historical report on the origin and growth of the children's home movement in Washington county, Ohio.

EWING, Mrs. Emma P., apostle of good cooking, born on a farm in Broome county, NY, in July, 1838. Since her marriage she has lived in Washington, DC, New York City, Chicago, IL, and other cities. In 1866 she became impressed with the belief that good food is an important factor in the development of the individual, morally, mentally and physically, and since then the leading aim of her life has been to improve the character of the everyday diet of the people by the introduction of better and more economical methods of cooking. Most of her culinary studies and experiments have been in that direction. In 1880 Mrs. Ewing organized a school of cookery in Chicago and conducted it in a highly satisfactory manner for three years, when she was appointed professor of domestic economy in the Iowa Agricultural College. That position she held until 1887, and then resigned to accept a similar one, at a largely-increased salary, in Purdue University, Indiana. In the fall of 1889 she resigned her professorship in Purdue University and went to Kansas City, MO, to organize and take charge of a school of household science; but before she had been there a year the calls upon her from all sections of the country for lectures and lessons upon culinary topics became so incessant and urgent that she resolved to leave the school. Placing it in other hands, she devoted her entire time and energies to itinerary work, preaching the gospel of good cookery to larger and more appreciative audiences than she could possibly reach in schools and colleges. Some idea of the amount of missionary work that is being done by her may be gathered from the fact that during 1891 she gave nearly two-hundred-fifty lectures and lessons on the preparation of food. For several summers Mrs. Ewing has been in charge of the School of Cookery at the Chautauqua Assembly, and every season she delivers a series of lectures there on household topics. Her popularity as a lecturer and teacher is such that her services are in constant demand, many of her engagements being made a year in advance. On all subjects pertaining to household science Mrs. Ewing is a leading authority. In addition to her other labors Mrs. Ewing has written two books, "Cooking and Castle Building" (1880) and "Cookery Manuals" (1886), and is now devoting her leisure time to the preparation of a text-book on cookery for schools and homes, to be entitled "The A B C of Cookery." Her home is in Rochester, NY.

EYSTER, Mrs. Nellie Blessing, author, was born in Frederick, MD. She is of good ancestry, with a commingling of Huguenot and Anglo-Saxon blood. On the maternal side she is a granddaughter of Captain George W. Ent, a commander at Fort McHenry in the war of 1812 and an intimate friend of Francis Scott Key. On the same side she is a kinswoman of famous old Barbara Frietchie. Abraham Blessing, Mrs. Eyster's father, who died in his early prime, when she was but ten years old, was a man of noble character, the youngest brother of George Blessing of Maryland, whose loyalty and patriotism, as displayed during the late Civil War, has won for him in history the title, "The Hero of the Highlands." The mother was a woman of unusual refinement and poetic taste, leaving as an inheritance to her five children the memory of a life of Christian rectitude and usefulness. The eldest of these five, Nellie, baptized Penelope, early gave promise of literary ability. When sixteen years old, she was wooed and won by her private tutor, David A. S. Eyster, a young lawyer of Harrisburg, PA. From the beginning of their acquaintance to Mr. Eyster's death, in 1886, he was her teacher, best friend and critic. Her family consists of one daughter, Mary, born a year after her marriage, and one son, Charles, several years later, who died at the age of ten, in 1872. Mrs. Eyster's first public work was in aid of the purchase of Mt. Vernon and she put forth earnest activity in the Sanitary Commission during the Civil War. Her first literary venture of any note was a series of children's books called the "Sunny Hour Library" (Philadelphia, four volumes, 1865–69). The success of these books gave fresh impetus to Mrs. Eyster's pen. She has written for many leading periodicals, "California Illustrated Magazine," the New York "Tribune," "Lutheran Observer," Harrisburg "Telegraph," "Our Young Folks," "St. Nicholas," "Wide Awake," "Harper's Magazine," the "Riverside Magazine," and others. She worked for a year with Gail Hamilton on "Wood's Household Magazine," editing the juvenile department. Mr. Eyster held a useful and remunerative post as financial clerk of the Pennsylvania State Board of Education. In 1872 and 1873 the death of her son and her mother caused her health to give way, and in 1876 the family removed to California, where, in San José, a delightful new home was made, and Mrs. Eyster rallied from her depression to take hold of religious and benevolent work once more. In Pennsylvania the family had been members of the English Lutheran Church, but in San José they became connected with the Presbyterian denomination, and Mrs. Eyster was linked with all its Christian and benevolent enterprises. Mrs. Eyster was made president of the San José Ladies' Benevolent Society, president of the Woman's Christian Temperance Union and secretary of the Woman's Missionary Society of the Presbyterian Church. Pecuniary reverses made her more than ever her husband's helper, and she taught literature and music in schools and homes with success. During those years her pen was never idle, and another book for children was written, "A Colonial Boy" (Boston, 1890). Ten years went by, and the sudden death of Mr. Eyster broke up the new home. Mrs. Eyster then went to San Francisco to live with her daughter, now Mrs. Scott Elder. Mrs. Eyster is state superintendent of juvenile work in the Woman's Christian Temperance Union, president of the California Women's Indian Association, and president of the Woman's Press Association of the Pacific Coast. None of these positions are sinecures, and all receive her supervision.

FAIRBANKS, Miss Constance, journalist, born in Dartmouth, Nova Scotia, 10th May, 1866. She belongs to an old provincial family nearly all of whose representatives have possessed more or less literary ability, and several of whom were long associated with the history of Nova Scotia. She is the second child and oldest daughter of L. P. Fairbanks, and is one of a family of nine children. Owing to delicate health when a child, Miss Fairbanks was able to attend school only in an irregular manner, but, being precocious and fond of the society of those older than herself, she gained much knowledge outside of the school-room. At the age of thirteen years she ceased to

have systematic instruction, and with patient determination she proceeded to carry on her education by means of careful reading. Finding it necessary to obtain employment, she became, in 1887, secretary to C. F. Fraser, the clever blind editor of the Halifax "Critic," and in that position gained a practical knowledge of the work which now occupies her attention. Gradually, as her ability to write became known, and as she developed a keen recognition of what was required by the public, Miss Fairbanks was placed in charge of various departments of the paper, until in June, 1890, the management of the editorial and certain other departments was virtually transferred to her and has since remained in her charge.

FAIRBANKS, Mrs. Elizabeth B., philanthropist, born in Elbridge, Onondaga county, NY, 17th October, 1831. Her father was Dr. Jared W. Wheeler, a physician of considerable prominence. Her mother's maiden name was Electa Brown, a Quakeress by birth and education, having received her school instruction at the "Hive," under the supervision of the Motts. From such parentage she naturally inherited clear perceptions, generous impulses and a sympathetic heart, combined with pure aims and unusual practical ability. Her maiden name was Wheeler. She was educated in the Monroe Collegiate Institute, founded by her uncle, Nathan Monroe, and in the Auburn Female Seminary. In 1857 she became the wife of John I. Fairbanks, of the firm of Ford & Fairbanks, booksellers in Milwaukee, WI, in which city they have ever since resided. Her benevolent work in that city commenced the first Sabbath after her arrival, and as her husband was a young deacon in the First Presbyterian Church, mission-school work claimed her early attention. She was one of the prime movers in various local charities, which have enlarged and broadened as time has advanced. She took to the State of Wisconsin the first plans for the organization of the present associated charities, and to her efforts is due in large measure the securing of the Wisconsin State Public School for Dependent Children. In 1880 she was appointed by the governor a member of the State Board of Charities and Reform, on which she served for a period of eleven years, being the only woman member. During that time the board became noted for its advanced views and methods of treating and caring for the chronic insane in the county asylums, a system pronounced by all who have investigated it superior to any other ever devised. By virtue of her official position and attention to its duties she soon became familiar with the condition and management of every institution in the State, winning friends wherever she went and becoming a welcome visitor and valued adviser both to officials and inmates, irrespective of nationality, religion or creed.

FAIRCHILD, Miss Maria Augusta, doctor of medicine, born in Newark, NJ, 7th June, 1834. Orphaned at the age of six years, she was left to the guardianship and care of her uncle, Dr. Stephen Fairchild, widely known as a philanthropist and temperance and medical reformer. He was surgeon in the army during the war of 1812, practiced allopathy a number of years and later adopted homeopathy, being foremost in its introduction into New Jersey. Augusta very early showed a strong preference for the study of anatomy, physiology, materia medica and even pathology. Both her uncle and his son, Dr. Van Wyck Fairchild, were amused and not a little pleased to observe the strong likings of the child, and they gave much encouragement in the directions so welcome to her. She unfolded rapidly under their instruction. She was often permitted to visit both their hospital and private patients, and there she learned to diagnose and prescribe with accuracy and skill. When she was sent to school, she found the work and surroundings distasteful, but she persevered in her studies and left school fitted to teach. For three years she forced herself to faithfulness in a work for which she had no liking beyond that of filling her position in the best possible way. Longing to become a physician, she read the names of a small band of women, medical pioneers, and encouragement came to her. At length the way was opened. Her health failed, and she was ill for months. In the very early stage of convalescence she felt the uprising of her unconquerable desire. With restored health she resolved to carry out her long cherished plan, and soon she found herself in the New York Hygeio-Therapeutic College, New York City, from which in 1860, three years later,

she was graduated. To be a woman doctor meant a great deal in those days. Immediately upon leaving college, Dr. Fairchild became associated with the late Dr. Trail, of New York, in both infirmary and outside practice. From the first she has given much attention to measures which elevate the standard of health among women. She was one of the earliest practitioners of the hygienic medical school, and probably there is no physician of that school now living who bears such unwavering testimony to the truths of its principles. During her thirty-two years of practice, in both acute and chronic ailments, she has never administered either alcohol or drugs. She is enthusiastic in whatever goes to make humanity better. In religion she is New Church, or Swedenborgian. As an author she has published "How to be Well" (New York, 1879), and her later work, entitled "Woman and Health" (1890). She contributes to various health journals and magazines, and has during all the years of her professional life occupied the lecture field as a champion for women, claiming that emancipation lies in the direction of obedience to the laws of health and total extinction of disease. She has lived in the West about twenty years, and is known as a leading physician, and proprietor of her own Health Institution in Quincy, IL. She is a careful hygienist, eats no meat, drinks only water, eats but one meal a day and wears neither corsets nor weighty clothing.

FALL, Mrs. Anna Christy, lawyer, born in Chelsea, MA, 23rd April, 1855. She acquired her early education in the public schools of that city, graduating from the high school in 1873. Six years later she entered the College of Liberal Arts of Boston University. There she was graduated in 1883 with the degree of Bachelor of Arts. She at once commenced a post-graduate course of study, and in 1884 received the degree of Master of Arts. The following September she became the wife of one of her class-mates, George Howard Fall, of Malden, MA, who was then teaching, but who immediately after marriage commenced the study of law. Five years later she began the study of law, having become deeply interested in it as a result of going into court and taking notes for her husband, who had meanwhile entered upon the practice of his profession in Boston, MA. In March, 1889, she entered the Boston University Law School. In

December, 1890, while still a student in the school, she took the examination for admission to the Boston bar, being the only woman among forty applicants. Twenty-eight of these, including Mrs. Fall, succeeded in passing and were sworn in before the Supreme Court of Massachusetts the following January. In June, 1891, Mrs. Fall graduated from the law school, taking the honor of magna cum laude. During the following autumn and winter she lectured in various parts of the State on the "Position of Women under the Massachusetts Law," and kindred subjects. She is now, although the mother of two children, engaged with her husband in the practice of law, and in November, 1891, won her first case before a jury, one of the ablest and most noted lawyers of Massachusetts being the principal counsel on the opposite side. That case was the first jury case in Massachusetts tried by a woman. Mrs. Fall is at present a member of the Maiden School Board.

FARMER, Mrs. Lydia Hoyt, author, was born in Cleveland, OH. Her family and ancestry include names prominent in the professions of law, theology and literature. Her father is the Hon. J. M. Hoyt, of Cleveland, OH. Her mother was Mary Ella Beebe, daughter of Alexander M. Beebe, LL. D. of New York. Her husband is the Hon. E. J. Farmer, of Cleveland, who is the author of several works on politics and finance, and is engaged in large mining enterprises in Colorado. Mrs. Farmer was thoroughly educated in music, art and literature. For the past ten years she has contributed to the leading newspapers and popular magazines. Her writings have been various, consisting of poems, essays, juvenile stories, historical sketches and novels. She is the author of "A Story Book of Science" (Boston, 1886), "Boys' Book of Famous Rulers" (New York, 1886), "Girls' Book of Famous Queens" (New York, 1887), "The Prince of the Flaming Star" (Boston, 1887), "The Life of La Fayette" (New York, 1888), "A Short History of the French Revolution" (New York, 1889), "A Knight of Faith" (New York, 1889), "A Moral Inheritance" (New York, 1890), and other works. Mrs. Farmer's books have received high commendation from the press, have had wide circulation throughout the country, and her "Knight of Faith," which is a strong religious novel, received flattering recognition from the Hon. William E. Gladstone, from whom Mrs. Farmer was the recipient of a personal note regarding her religious books. Her "Prince of the Flaming Star" is an operetta, and the words, music and illustrations are all of her production. Her "Moral Inheritance," is founded upon "Soul Heredity" and enters into rather novel fields in the realms of fiction. In her "Life of La Fayette" she had access to original files of newspapers, unique copies of works now out of print, and the private papers of the La Fayette family, and therefore has been able to incorporate in the book much that had been inaccessible to previous biographers. She has completed a historical novel, "The Doom of the Holy City: Christ and Caesar," founded on the destruction of Jerusalem, and the scenes are laid in that city and in Rome as they appeared in the first century. She is an indefatigable student, pursuing metaphysical and philosophical research with intense avidity. Her novels are always written for a high purpose, and their whole tendency and teaching are healthful and elevating. Mrs. Farmer has for years instructed Bible classes of young ladies, having devoted a large portion of her time to Biblical study. She has passed most of her life in Cleveland, having resided in that city from childhood, with the exception of five years spent in the City of New York.

FAWCETT, Mrs. Mary S., temperance reformer, born near Burlington, Ontario, Canada, 22nd February, 1829. In 1852 she became the wife of an older brother of Rev. D. V. Lucas, of the Montreal Methodist Conference. She was a worthy helpmate to her husband. Together they labored in church and Sabbath-school work and were equally useful in the neighborhood in which they resided. At the end of six years her husband lost his health. His death in 1862 left her alone and childless. For the next six years she devoted herself to the welfare of others, using her means as well as giving her time. She labored in the Sabbath-school and was most successful as a Bible class teacher. In 1868 she became the wife of Rev. M. Fawcett, an honored minister of the Toronto Methodist Conference, and for years shared with him the life of an itinerant. Four years of that time, from 1872 to 1876, he labored as a missionary in Manitoba, and, as the country was then comparatively new, there were hardships and privations to endure which are unknown in older countries. There, as elsewhere, Mrs. Fawcett found a field of labor. While in that distant province, she first read of the woman's Crusade, and her heart went out for the women engaged in it. About the time of their return, the first union in Canada was organized, and in a short time organizations sprang up in many of the towns and villages. She became interested, and from that time has been connected with it, first as corresponding secretary of the Ontario Woman's Christian Temperance Union, which office she filled for eight years, but, her husband being at the time in poor health, she refused office for a year. When his health was restored, she again took up the work and since then has filled the position of provincial and dominion president of the Canadian Woman's Christian Temperance Union. She is at present vice-president of the Provincial, but can not work as in former years. Her health began to fail in 1890 from overwork, and she is now obliged to rest.

FAY, Miss Amy, musician and author, born on a plantation on the Mississippi river, eighty miles from New Orleans, LA, 21st May, 1844. She is the daughter of Rev. Charles Fay, of Cambridge, MA, and Charlotte Emily Fay, a daughter of the late Bishop John Henry Hopkins, of the Protestant Episcopal Church of Vermont. Both families were musical, and Mrs. Fay was a pianist of remarkable gifts. The family consisted of six daughters and one son, and Amy was the third of the children, all of whom were singers and players. Amy showed remarkable musical talents at an early age. At the age of four years she played airs by ear and composed little airs, which she rendered on the piano. At five years of age she began to study regularly under her mother's tuition. The family removed to St. Albans, VT, in 1848. Amy studied Latin, Greek, French and German with her father, and music, drawing and composition with her mother. Her education was liberal and careful. Her mother died in 1856, and Amy went to live with her mar-

ried sister in Cambridge, MA. There she began the study of Bach with Prof. J. K. Paine, and piano with Otto Dressel, in the New England Conservatory of Music. She next studied piano technique with Prof. Pychowski, of New York. In 1869 she went to Europe. In Berlin she studied with Carl Tausig one year and with Prof. Kullak three years. In 1873 she went to Weimar and studied in Liszt's school. She studied again with Kullak and Deppe, and finished with a second course under Liszt. In 1875 she returned to the United States. She made her début in New York with the Mendelssohn Glee Club. She settled in Boston, where she gave a number of concerts, and was the first to add piano concerts to the programmes in the Worcester festivals. In 1878 she settled in Chicago, IL, where she now lives. Her concerts, styled "Piano Conversations," are very popular. Her principal literary work is her book, "Music Study in Germany," published on the suggestion of Henry Wadsworth Longfellow, and translated into German on the request of Liszt. It is a standard book in the United States, Germany and England. Miss Fay has been a successful piano teacher as well as concertist. She is the founder of the Artists' Concert Club, of Chicago, a club composed of musicians. She is one of the students whose names appear in Liszt's own roll of his best pupils.

FEARING, Miss Lillian Blanche, lawyer and poet, born in Davenport, IA, 27th November, 1863. She was educated partly in the Iowa College in Vinton, IA, and was graduated in 1884. In 1888 she removed to Chicago, IL, and entered as a student in the Union College of Law. She was graduated in the spring of 1890, the only woman in her class, and one of four students whose records were so nearly equal that the faculty of the college could not decide to whom the scholarship prize should be awarded. The difficulty was solved by the division of the prize between the four. Miss Fearing is thus far the only woman who has received a scholarship prize from that college. She is now practicing law in Chicago and achieving success in that arduous field of labor. She is the author of two volumes of verse, entitled "The Sleeping World, and other Poems"

(Chicago, 1887), and "In the City by the Lake" (Chicago, 1892). Her literary work shows merit of high order. Miss Fearing's success in life is nothing short of remarkable, when it is remembered that she is blind.

FELTON, Mrs. Rebecca Latimer, orator, born seventeen miles south of Atlanta, GA, 10th June, 1835. Her father was a native of Maryland, and her ancestry is a blending of English, Scotch and Irish. Governor Talbot of Georgia was a maternal relative. Mrs. Felton looks back upon her childhood as a time of surpassing freedom and happiness. She lived in the country, rode, romped, fished and was as free as air to come and go. Music has always been a passion with her, and as she developed it became an accomplishment and an art. She shared the first honor when she was graduated and was the youngest girl in her class. In her early education and through her college life she had the best and most thorough instruction to be had in the State. She became the wife of William H. Felton early in life, and after the war assisted her husband in a large school of nearly a hundred pupils. In 1874 her husband became a candidate for Congress, as an independent Democrat, removed from the sectionalism and ostracism of the regular organization, which dominated southern politics at that era. The wife became the helper of her husband and at once stepped to the front. Her pen was as ready as her brain, and the State gazed in wonder at the heroic work and indomitable perseverance of this remarkable woman. During the six years that her husband remained in Congress, she was his private secretary and general counselor. She intuitively comprehended his duties to his constituents and became so prompt and skillful in his work that it was hard to tell where her work ended and his began. His fame as a debater and student of public questions became national, and yet every printed speech passed through her hands, and his super-excellence as an orator and collector of statistical facts perhaps was largely due to her discriminating mind and thorough revision, as well as her inspiring sympathy and enthusiastic loyalty to his interests. During six years of Congressional life and six years in the State legislature her hand was on the helm of his political barque, and he took no important step without her aid and counsel. She traveled with him during campaigns and talked to the people in private, while he addressed them in public. Yet with all these efforts Mrs. Felton is an enthusiastic farmer and a regular contributor to farm journals. She keeps up the duties of a housekeeper as well as the duties of a wife and mother. Of her five children only one survives, and perhaps her distinguished domestic trait is her devotion to her only child and to her family. She makes frequent temperance addresses, her temperance work being as illustrious as her political life. She is the first southern woman who has been selected to deliver commencement addresses to female colleges. Her vindication by speech and in print of the maligned factory people of the South has endeared her to all fair-minded persons. She is treasured in the hearts of the laboring people. When she visits the factory towns, she is met by welcoming crowds. Two years ago, during a visit to the State capital, she was invited by the House of Representatives to occupy a seat beside the Speaker "as a woman in whom the State takes pride." As she was escorted down the aisle, the body stood to do her honor, and the speaker welcomed her "as the first woman ever so honored by the State." She is one of Georgia's lady managers of the World's Fair. When the board met to organize, Mrs. Felton was selected as their temporary president, and under her ruling, the permanent president, Mrs. Potter Palmer, was elected. Her later life has been one of continual triumph, and her struggle for truth, justice and reform is bearing sweet fruit in the reverence and love of her people. Of her early life she writes: "With a snow-white head and the sun declining to the West, I believe I can honestly say that a free, happy life in childhood is the best solace of old age." In appearance Mrs. Felton is distinguished and impressive, in speaking she is eloquent, and her ringing, sympathetic voice goes to the hearts of her hearers.

FENNER, Mrs. Mary Galentine, author, born in Rush, Monroe county, NY, 17th May, 1839. Her grandparents were among the first settlers of the Genesee Valley and traced their lineage back to sturdy Hollanders. From the time of reaching his majority, her father, John Galentine, occupied a prominent place in his native town. At a very early age Mrs. Fenner wrote for the "Rural New Yorker." She was educated in Genesee Wesleyan Seminary, Lima, NY, where she was graduated in 1861, one month before her marriage to Rev. F. D. Fenner, a graduate of Rochester University. Among her school essays are several written in blank verse, but she never gave the full expression of her thought in a satisfactory manner to herself until the revelation of her power of poesy came to her at a time of weakness and suffering. Her first published poem, "In Memoriam," dedicated to her mother on the anniversary of her father's death, in 1873, was written while she could not raise her head from her pillow. She then became a prolific versifier. Her home is now in North Manlius, NY, where, among people of her husband's parish, she finds her most delightful work. She has published one volume of poems.

FERREE, Mrs. Susan Frances Nelson, journalist and reformer, born in Mount Pleasant, IA, 14th January, 1844. She is a daughter of John S. Nelson, who was a lineal descendant of Thomas Nelson, the founder of Old York, VA, where his mansion still stands. His oldest son, William, was at one time president of the king's council. William's oldest son, Gen. Thomas Nelson, was the most illustrious of his race one of the signers of the Declaration of Independence, the war governor of Virginia, and a very brilliant member of that body of great men, who distinguished the country's early history. Mrs. Ferree is a fitting representative of her noble line of ancestors. Educated and refined, her influence is always on the side of kindness and right. At the age of one year she, with her parents removed to Keokuk, which was her home for many years. Her home at present is in Ottumwa, IA, where she is the center of a large and interesting family of children. Her husband is a successful business man of that city. Mrs Ferree is a great lover of poetry, of which she has written much, but she excels in journalism. Some of her newspaper correspondence from Washington, DC, is exceptionally fine. She is an untiring worker for temperance and for the advancement of woman. She is a member of the Order of the Eastern Star, Woman's Relief Corps, the Iowa Woman's Suffrage Assocation, and the local Woman's Christian Temperance Union, and a communicant of St. Mary's Episcopal Church, of Ottumwa.

FICKLEN, Mrs. Bessie Alexander, born near Frederickburg, VA, 10th November, 1861. Her maiden name was Bessie Mason Alexander. Her mother's maiden name was Mason. On her father's side she is of Scotch descent. Her great grandfather, a graduate of Edinburgh, emigrated from Scotland to America in Colonial days. He settled in Georgia and served as a surgeon in the War of the Revolution. Her father, Gen. E. P. Alexander, was educated at West Point, and, after completing the course of study there, entered the engineer corps of the United States army. On the breaking out of the Civil War he enlisted in the Confederate army and served with distinction as Longstreet's chief of artillery. Miss Alexander was graduated from the Columbia Female Institute, Columbia, TN. In 1886 she became the wife of John R. Ficklen, professor of history in the Tulane University, New Orleans, LA. On the opening of the art school in Sophie Newcomb College, in New Orleans, Mrs. Ficklen became a student there, showing special excellence in the direction of drawing and modeling. In the latter department she has done some good work, notably the head of a child, shown at the autumnal exhibition in 1891. In 1889 was published "Catterel, Ratterel, Doggerel," a set of satirical verses composed by General Alexander. The very clever illustrations which accompany these humorous verses are the work of Mrs. Ficklen. An essay of Mrs. Ficklen's, entitled "Dream-Poetry," appeared in "Scribners Magazine" in 1891.

FIELD, Miss Kate, journalist, lecturer and author, born in St. Louis, MO, in 1840. She was a daughter of the late Joseph M. Field, the well-known actor and dramatist. She was educated in seminaries in Massachusetts, and her education

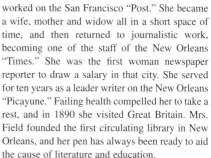

was broad and liberal, including thorough culture in music. After finishing her studies in the Massachusetts schools, she went to Florence, Italy, where she studied music and the modern languages. While living in Europe she corresponded for the New York "Tribune," the Philadelphia "Press" and the Chicago "Tribune," and contributed sketches for various periodicals. She studied music with Garcia and William Shakespeare. She became known in Europe as a woman of great powers of intellect and remarkable versatility.

Among her acquaintances was George Eliot, who took a strong fancy to the sparkling American girl. Returning to the United States, Miss Field, in 1874, made her début as an actor in Booth's Theater, New York City, where she won a fair success. Afterward she gave a variety song, dance and recitation. In 1882 and 1883 she was at the head of the Cooperative Dress Association in New York, which was abandoned for want of success. During the following years she lectured on Mormonism and Prohibition, as well as other current topics. In 1890 she went to Washington, DC, where she founded her successful journal, "Kate Field's Washington." Her published works are "Planchette's Diary" (New York, 1868), "Adelaide Ristori" (1868), "Mad On Purpose," a comedy (1868), "Pen Photographs from Charles Dickens's Readings" (Boston, 1868), "Haphazard" (1873), "Ten Days in Spain" (1875), and a "History of Bell's Telephone" (London, 1878). She was the author of an analysis of George Eliot's character and works, of dramatic criticisms without number, of a life of Fetcher, and of numerous political and economical essays. She spent much time and effort to secure an art congress in Washington, for the advancement of free art, with a governmental commission of art and architecture, and a national loan exhibition of paintings by American artista exclusively. Her widely regretted death occured in Honolulu, HI, 19th May, 1896, her remains being subsequently brought to this country and cremated.

FIELD, Mrs. Martha R., journalist, known by her pen-name of "Catherine Cole," born in New Orleans, LA, in 1856, where she passed her youth and received her education. She was a leader among the students in school, and soon after leaving the school-room she went into service on the "Picayune" of which journal her father was an editor. She did various work in New Orleans, and afterward worked on the San Francisco "Post." She became a wife, mother and widow all in a short space of time, and then returned to journalistic work, becoming one of the staff of the New Orleans "Times." She was the first woman newspaper reporter to draw a salary in that city. She served for ten years as a leader writer on the New Orleans "Picayune." Failing health compelled her to take a rest, and in 1890 she visited Great Britain. Mrs. Field founded the first circulating library in New Orleans, and her pen has always been ready to aid the cause of literature and education.

FIFIELD, Mrs. Stella A. Gaines, journalist, born in Paw Paw, MI, 1st June, 1845. Her family removed to Taylor Falls, MN, in 1861. She was liberally educated and was graduated from the Chicago Seminary, MN, in 1862. She taught school in Osceola, WI. In 1863 she became the wife of Hon. Samuel S. Fifield, ex-Lieutenant Governor of Wisconsin, who was then editing the Polk County "Press," the pioneer newspaper of the upper St. Croix valley. Mrs. Fifield at once associated herself with her husband in journalism. In 1872 she and her husband settled in Ashland, WI. She was chosen a member of the Wisconsin Board of Lady Managers of the Columbian Exposition.

FILLEY, Mrs. Mary A. Powers, woman suffragist and stock-farmer, born in Bristol, NH, 12th December, 1821. Her parents were Jonathan and Anne (Kendall) Powers. Left motherless at the age of thirteen, she undertook

the care of her younger brothers and sisters. At nineteen she made her home in Lansingburg, NY, and in 1851 became the wife of Edward A. Filley, of Lansingburg, and went to St. Louis, MO, to live. The passage of the law legalizing prostitution in St. Louis roused all the mother indignation in her, and she with other prominent ladies felt that they must do what lay in their power to secure the repeal of such a law. She worked vigorously with pen and petition, though against great odds, sparing no effort. The effort was crowned with success, and the law was repealed. Soon after Mrs. Filley removed to her country home in North Haverhill, NH. In 1880 she bought a large stock farm, which she has since conducted. It was a dairy farm, and though entirely new work to her, she learned the process of butter-making, found a market in Boston for her butter and made one year as much as 4,000 pounds. Finding the work too great a tax upon her strength, she sold the greater portion of her stock and turned the farm into a hay farm. In many ways she has made the moral atmosphere of those around her better for her having lived among them.

FILLMORE, Mrs. Abigail Powers, wife of President Fillmore, born in Stillwater, Saratoga county, NY, in March, 1798. Her father was Rev. Lemuel Powers, a well-known Baptist clergyman, a mail of Massachusetts ancestry. Abigail was a brilliant girl, and soon gained enough education to enable her to teach school. She taught and studied diligently, and acquired a remarkably wide and deep education. While living in Cayuga county she became acquainted with Millard Fillmore, then a youth, "bound out" to learn the trade of a clothier and fuller, but who was devoting every spare moment to books. He abandoned the trade to study law, and removed to Erie county to practice. In February, 1826, they were married in Moravia, NY. Mrs. Fillmore took an active interest in her husband's political and professional career. In 1828 he was elected to the State Legislature, and his success was largely due to the assistance of his wife. They were poor, but they made poverty respectable by their dignity and honesty. After serving three years in the State Legislature, Mr. Fillmore was elected to Congress. In 1830 they settled in Buffalo, NY, where prosperity smiled upon them. When her husband became President of the United States, she presided over the White House, but she had only recently been bereaved by the death of her sister, and she shrank from the social duties involved. Her daughter, Miss Mary Abigail Fillmore, relieved the mother of the onerous duties attached to her position. Under their regime the White House became a center of literary, artistic, musical and social attractions, somewhat unusual. Mrs. Fillmore died in Washington, 30th March, 1853.

FINLEY, Miss Martha, author, born in Chillicothe, OH, 26th April, 1828. She has lived many years in Maryland. Her father was Dr. James B. Finley, of Virginia, and her mother was Mary Brown, of Pennsylvania. The Finleys and Browns are of Scotch-Irish descent and have martyr blood in their veins. The name of their clan was Farquarharson, the Gaelic of Finley, and for many years Miss Finley used that name as her pen-name. In 1853 Miss Finley began her literary career by writing a newspaper story and a little book published by the Baptist Board of Publication. Between 1855 and 1870 she wrote more than twenty Sunday-school books and several series of juveniles, one series containing twelve books. These were followed by "Casella" (Philadelphia, 1869), "Peddler of LeGrave," "Old Fashioned Boy" (Philadelphia, 1871), and "Our Fred" (New York, 1874). It is through her "Elsie" and "Mildred" series that she has become popular as a writer for the young. Miss Finley's pen has not been employed in writing exclusively for the young. She has written three novels. "Wanted—A Pedigree" (Philadelphia, 1879), "Signing the Contract" (New York, 1879), and "Thorn in the Nest" (New York, 1886). Miss Finley resides in Elkton, Cecil county, MD.

FISHER, Miss Anna A., educator, born in Cambridge, NY, in 1858. She comes of New England parentage, and her early reading and education were well and wisely directed. As principal of Wyoming Seminary, Kingston, PA, she passed nine years of eminent usefulness, that left a marked impression upon that institution. She is

Katherine Grey.
From Photo by B. J. Falk, New York.

Amanda Fabris.
From Photo by Morrison, Chicago.

a graduate of Antioch College, from which institution she received her degree of A. M. She was a candidate for consideration as president of Barnard College. In the autumn of 1891 she was elected to the chair of literature in Denver University, CO, and is now lady principal.

FISHER, Mrs. Rebecca Jane Gilleland, philanthropist, born in Philadelphia, PA. Her father moved to Texas and joined the Texas army in 1838, but soon afterward both parents were killed by the Indians. Their orphaned daughter was cared for by friends and was educated in Rutersville College. In May, 1848, she became the wife of Rev. Orceneth Fisher, D. D. California, Oregon and Texas have been their special fields of labor. For forty-five years she has been actively engaged in church and charitable work. She has resided in Austin, Texas, for many years, and is a strong advocate and worker in the temperance and missionary causes.

FISKE, Miss Fidelia, missionary, born in Shelburne, MA, 1st May, 1816. She was the fourth daughter of Rufus and Hannah Woodward Fiske, and could look back through an unbroken line of godly ancestors to William Fiske, who came from Suffolk county, England, in 1637. Most of the time from 1833 to 1839, except for brief periods of study, she taught in the schools of her native town. In 1839 she entered Mt. Holyoke Seminary, and was graduated in 1842. Miss Lyon at once engaged her as a teacher. The next January a call came to the seminary for one to go to Persia with Dr. and Mrs. Perkins, to take charge of a school for Nestorian girls in Oroomiah. Miss Lyon laid the call before the school. Of the forty notes written in response, one of the shortest read: "If counted worthy, I should be willing to go. Fidelia Fiske." Already her services to the seminary seemed too valuable to be spared, but that point was soon yielded. Her widowed mother could not consent so readily. The same reason kept others from going, and a month later the question came back to Miss Fiske. "Then we will go and see your mother," said Miss Lyon, and within an hour they were on their way for a drive of thirty miles through the snowdrifts. It was ten days before Dr. Perkins was to sail. Roused from sleep by the midnight arrival, the mother knew at once their errand. Her consent was obtained. Miss Lyon returned to the seminary, and Miss Fiske followed, to find that the teachers and students had prepared a very good outfit for her. The next morning she was on the way to Boston. She sailed on Wednesday, 1st March, for Smyrna, and arrived in Oroomiah 14th June, 1843. Miss Fiske made arrangements for six boarding pupils, not knowing one whom she might expect besides day scholars. On the 16th October, the day appointed for the school to open, Mar Yohanan, a Nestorian bishop, who had visited America with Dr. Perkins, brought her two girls, one seven and the other ten years old, saying: "These are your daughters. Now you begin Mt. Holyoke in Persia." By spring she had six girls, wild and untutored. The school made steady progress, and in its fourth year it numbered over forty. Its first public examination in 1850 marked an era in the history of that Oriental nation and in the lives of its three graduates. The ten graduates of 1853 were between the ages of seventeen and nineteen. Miss Fiske's cares as mother, housekeeper and teacher so increased that Miss Rice went from Mt. Holyoke Seminary, in 1847, to be her assistant. When failing health forced her to leave for America, after fifteen fruitful years, there were ninety-three native women serving the Lord. Her influence in the mission and on Nestorian character is well set forth in the book entitled "Woman and Her Savior in Persia." The home voyage seemed to give a new lease of life, and her last five years were as useful as any that had preceded. Besides responding, as strength allowed, to the many urgent calls from the ladies' meetings for the story of her work in Persia, she spent many months in Mt. Holyoke Seminary, where her labors in the remarkable revivals of 1862–64 were a fitting close to her life's work. She died 26th July, 1864, in the home of her aged mother, in Shelburne. Her finely balanced mind, deep and delicate sensibilities, intuitive knowledge of human nature, and her discretion, all controlled by ardent Christian love, made her a power for good. Her career is described in the title chosen by her biographer: "Faith working by Love."

FISKE, Mrs. Minnie Maddern, actor, was born in New Orleans, the daughter of Thomas Davey and Minnie Maddern. Her father was a prominent theatrical manager of the South. Minnie Maddern made her debut in Little Rock, AR, at the age of three years as the Duke of York, in "Richard III." She played and traveled continuously until the age of fourteen, acting many of the leading juvenile parts, and occasionally old women's parts. Long before she wore long dresses off the stage she assumed them in the theater. When thirteen she assumed the part of Widow Melnotte with astonishing success. She played the round of child parts with Barry Sullivan, and later with Lucile Weston. Brief periods were spent by the young actress in French or convent schools in the cities of New Orleans, St. Louis, Montreal and Cincinnati. Becoming a star at the age of sixteen, she played until 1890, when she was married and retired from the stage for a time. She occasionally appeared for charity in New York during her retirement. Mrs. Fiske's repertoire includes "Marie Deloche," Ibsen's "A Doll's House;" an adaptation of Dumas' "La Femme de Claude," "Cesarine," and a one-act play by herself, "A Light from St. Agnes." Previous to her New York engagement Mrs. Fiske made a tour of the Southern cities in "The Right to Happiness." On 2nd March, 1897, Mrs. Fiske presented at the Fifth Avenue Theatre, New York City, for the first time on any stage, an adaptation by Lorimer Stoddard of Thomas Hardy's novel, "Tess, of the D'Urbervilles," appearing in the character of Tess.

FLETCHER, Miss Alice Cunningham, ethnologist, born in Boston, MA, in 1845. She received a thorough and liberal education. After studying the archaeological remains in the Ohio and Mississippi valleys she went, in 1881, to live among the Omaha Indians, in Nebraska, to make an investigation of their customs and traditions, under the auspices of the Peabody Museum of American Archaeology, of Harvard University. She became interested in the affairs of the Omahas and secured the passage of a law allotting lands to them. She was chosen to make the allotment in 1883 and 1884. She caused a number of the children of the Omahas to be sent to the Indian schools in Carlisle, PA, and Hampton, VA, and she raised large sums of money to defray the expenses of the education of other ambitious Indians. Under the auspices of the Woman's National Indian Association she established a system of loaning money to Indians who wished to buy land and build

homes of their own. Her scientific researches have been of great value, covering Indian traditions, customs, religions, moneys, music and ceremonies, and many ethnographic and archaeological subjects. In 1884 and 1885 she sent an exhibit of the industries of civilized Indians to the New Orleans Exhibition, prepared on request by the Indian Bureau. Her labors and lectures on that occasion won her a diploma of honor. In answer to a Senate resolution of 23rd February, 1885, she prepared her valuable book, "Indian Civilization and Education." In 1886 she was sent by the Commissioner of Education to visit Alaska and the Aleutian Islands, where she made a study of the conditions of the natives. In 1888 her reports were published in full. Acting for the government, she has allotted lands in severalty to the Winnebagoes, of Nebraska, and the Nez Percés, of Idaho. Her work in behalf of the Indians has been incessant and varied. She brought out the first Indian woman physician, Susan La Flesche, and induced other Indians to study law and other professions. Her work has been of the highest order, both scientific and philanthropic.

FLETCHER, Mrs. Lisa Anne, poet, born in Ashby, MA, 27th December, 1844. Her maiden name was Stewart. When she was two years old, her father died, and when she was sixteen, her mother died. There were no other children in the family. In 1864 she became the wife of Edwin S. Fletcher, of Manchester, NH, since which time her home has been in that city. From earliest childhood she has shown an almost equal fondness for music, painting and poetry. In 1865 she was stricken with diphtheria in its most malignant form, and since that time her life has been full of suffering, and these later years she has been an invalid. She is an example of what can be accomplished under great difficulties by firmness of spirit, force of will and a brave perseverance. All her work is done in a reclining position. She has a large correspondence, partly through the Shut-In Society. Thousands of letters have gone forth from her corner and fulfilled their mission of cheer and comfort. It is as an artist she excels. She is now painting a collection of wild flowers that grow about Manchester, and has already about one-hundred thirty kinds. With firm health she would doubtless have made a great name for herself, especially in painting wild flowers. In June, 1888, she allowed herself for the first time to write verse in earnest. Her poems have appeared in a large number of the best magazines and periodicals. Her love for birds amounts to a passion, and much that is interesting might be said of her studies of the wild birds from her window. A local secretary of the Audubon Society, she has done noble work in their behalf. A constant sufferer both physically and mentally, she yet accomplishes more work than many who are strong and well. Possessed of an intense love of beauty in every form, she deeply feels the fetters under which her spirit struggles, and longs for the freedom of larger opportunities.

FOLEY, Miss Margaret E., sculptor, born in New Hampshire, and died in Menan, in Austrian Tyrol, in 1887. Miss Foley was an entirely self-taught artist. She began her career in a small way, modeling in chalk and carving in wood. In youth she moved to Boston, MA, where she worked hard and suffered much privation, making a bare living at first by carving portraits and ideal heads in cameo. After working seven years in Boston, she went to Rome, Italy, where she passed the rest of her professional life in the company of Harriet Hosmer, Gibson, Story, Mrs. Jameson and William and Mary Howitt. In 1877 her health failed, and she accompanied Mr. and Mrs. Howitt to their home in Austrian Tyrol, where she died. Among the works she left are portrait busts of S. C. Hall, Charles Sumner and Theodore Parker, and medallions of William and Mary Howitt, Longfellow, Bryant and S. C. Hall. Her artistic work includes "The Albanese," a medallion, "Cleopatra," a bust, and statues of "Excelsior," "Jeremiah" and many others.

FOLTZ, Mrs. Clara Shortridge, orator and lawyer, born in New Lisbon, Henry county, IN, 16th July, 1849. Her father was the eloquent Christian preacher, Elias W. Shortridge. When seven years old, she removed with her parents to Mt. Pleasant, IA, where she attended, at intervals, Howe's Female Seminary for nearly three years. Leaving there she went to Mercer county, IL, and taught school six months, completing the term on her

birthday. The same year she was married. Household cares occupied her time for several years. In 1872, having removed to the Pacific coast, she began to write for the press and showed flashes of genius as a correspondent. Four years later she began the study of law, supporting herself and five children by her pen and occasional lectures. But women were not then allowed to practice law in the Golden State. In the winter of 1877–78 she went to Sacramento, the State capital, and secured the passage of an act opening the doors of the legal profession to women, and was the first to avail herself of the privileges of the new law, which she did in September, 1879, by being admitted to practice in the district court, and in December of the same year by admission to the supreme court of the State. During the year 1879 she applied for admission to the Hastings College of Law, which was refused. Acting on the theory that the law college was a part of the State University, to which men and women were alike entitled to admission under the law, she sued out a writ of mandate against the regents to compel them to admit her. Against the ablest counsel in the State she won her case, both in the district and in the supreme court. When the decision came at last, she was unable to avail herself of its benefits, having passed the student period and already acquired a promising practice. In the winter of 1880 she was made clerk of the judiciary committee of the assembly, and upon the adjournment of the legislature began the practice of law in San Francisco. The political campaign of 1882 gave opportunity for the first real display of her oratorical powers. She made a dozen or more speeches, and at once took rank among the leading orators of the coast, speaking in the campaigns of 1884, 1886 and 1888. In 1885 and again in 1887, as a respite from a laborious practice, she lectured a short time in the Eastern States under the auspices of the Slayton Lyceum Bureau. Upon her return from the East, Governor Bartlett appointed her trustee of the State Normal School, which place she filled for the full term. She settled in San Diego in 1887 and started the "Daily Bee," an eight-page paper, which she edited and managed with success until its consolidation with the "Union." Upon the sale of her paper she resumed practice in San Diego, and continued there until the fall of 1890, when she returned to San Francisco, where she now commands a large and growing practice. Her sunny temper, genial disposition, broad views, liberal sentiments, never failing charity and ready repartee make her a brilliant conversationalist. As a lawyer she stands prominent among the lawyers of the country. Her success has brought her into general favor and won for her the complimentary title, "The Portia of the Pacific."

FONDA, Mrs. Mary Alice, musician, linguist, and author, born 21st October, 1837. She is known by her pen-name, "Octavia Hensel." Her maiden name was Mary Alice Ives. She is descended from General Michael Jackson, of Newton, MA, who commanded a regiment of minute-men in the battle of Lexington. His son, Amasa Jackson, was the first president of the Union Bank of New York, in 1812. He was married to Mary Phelps, the only daughter and heiress of Oliver Phelps, of Boston, who with Nathaniel Gorham purchased in the interior of New York State from the Indians the tract of land now known as the Phelps and Gorham purchase. Mary Charlotte Jackson, the grandmother of Mrs. Fonda, was married to Ralph Olmstead, of New York. Their only child, the mother of Mrs. Fonda, Mary Phelps Olmstead, was married to George Russell Ives, of New York. Mrs. Fonda's childhood was most fortunate. Her parents were surrounded by literary people. Mrs. Fonda's early taste tended toward literature. In 1865 she became the wife of Rev. William Wood Seymour, at one time connected with Trinity Parish, New York. In 1886 her books on the festivals of the church, known as the "Cedar Grove Series," were published in New York, and have become standard. After Mr. Seymour's death his widow returned to her father's house, but his loss of property during the Civil War and his feeble health led her to go to Europe for study to become a vocal teacher. She never appeared on the stage, except for charitable objects, as her relatives were opposed to a professional life. Before she went to Europe, her "Life of Gottschalk" (Boston, 1870) was published. During her residence in Europe she corresponded for several journals, the "Home Journal" of New York, the San Francisco "Chronicle" and the St. Paul "Pioneer Press" of Minnesota. She held the position of musical instructor and English companion to the Archdukes and Archduchesses, children of the Archduke of Aus-

tria, Carl Salvator of Tuscany, and his wife, Princess Marie Immaculate of Naples. After the death of her father she returned to her home in the United States and taught music in New York and Philadelphia. In 1884 she brought out her papers on "The Rhinegold Trilogy" (Boston), which had been written in Vienna under the supervision of Liszt and Richard Wagner. After the death of her grandmother, in 1885, she opened a school of vocal music in Nashville, TN. She removed to Louisville, KY, in 1887, where she now resides. In the summer of 1888 she became the wife of Abraham G. Fonda, a descendant of the New York Fonda family, whose ancestor, Major Jelles Fonda, had purchased the Mohawk Valley land from the Phelps and Gorham estate, where the town of Fonda now stands. Mrs. Fonda is one of the most cultivated women in America. She speaks seven languages fluently, German, French, Spanish, Italian, Portuguese, Roumanian and Magyar dialects, while her musical abilities are marked. She plays the piano, harp, guitar and organ, and is the possessor of a fine voice. She has studied under the best European teachers. Her rare musical accomplishments have won the commendation of Liszt, Rubenstein and other masters. As a critic Mrs. Fonda has won renown. Her musical nature, her superior education, her thorough knowledge of the laws of theory and familiarity with the works of the great composers of the classic, romantic and Wagnerian schools, and the newer schools of harmony, give her a point of vantage above the ordinary. She is prominent among the Daughters of the American Revolution and has in her possession many rare Revolutionary relics. Her novel, "Imperia" (Buffalo, 1892), is a success.

FOOTE, Mrs. Mary Hallock, author and artist, born in Milton, NY, 19th November, 1847. Her maiden name was Hallock. She became the wife of Arthur D. Foote, a mining engineer, in 1876, and lived some years in the mining districts of Colorado and California, and afterward in Boisé City, ID. She studied art in the Cooper Institute, New York City, working there four winters under the instruction of Dr. Rimmer. She afterward studied with Frost Johnson and William Linton. Her artistic training ended with block-work with Linton. She has illustrated many books in black and white, and done much work for magazines. She has been particularly successful in her drawings of western and Mexican life and scenery. Many of her best detached illustrations have appeared in the "Century," "Scribner's Magazine," "St. Nicholas" and other periodicals. She is the author of "The Led Horse Claim" (Boston, 1883), "John Bodewin's Testimony" (Boston, 1886), and "The Last Assembly Ball" (1888). Her home is now in New York City.

FORD, Mrs. Miriam Chase, musician and journalist, born in Boston, MA, 20th September, 1866. Her parents are S. Warren Chase and Sarah Virginia Hulst. When she was three years old, her parents moved to Omaha, NE. Until her eleventh year she received instruction from her mother and private teachers. On the removal of her parents to Milwaukee, WI, she entered the Milwaukee College, where the artistic element in her soon found expression in some admirable crayons and freehand sketches. French was one of the studies in which she excelled. When fourteen years of age, she accompanied her grandmother, of Omaha, NE, to Europe. With eighteen months of travel and study on the Continent, with six months divided between Egypt, Palestine, Turkey and Greece, she gained knowledge and experience, perfected her French and learned some Italian, German and Spanish. The next two years she spent in Milwaukee College, during which time she began her vocal training under a German master. The family then returned to Omaha, and the next two winters she spent in New York City, studying under Errani. At that time she entered the literary field as special correspondent of the Omaha "World." The year 1886 found her again in Europe. She studied a year in Milan, under San Giovanni and Giovannini, and was a student for some time in the Paris Conservatory. Afterward she went to London to become a pupil of Randegger. There she remained but a short time. Having suffered in Milan from an attack of Roman fever, a severe illness necessitated her return home for rest. On leaving England she became engaged to Percival Boys Ford, of London, who traveled with her family to Omaha, where they were married in 1890. During her last long sojourn in Europe she was special correspondent of the Omaha "Bee." She has since written a good deal in the way of critiques, reminiscences and special articles. Mrs. Ford uses her voice in a public way only for the benefit of charity or some public enterprise.

FORNEY, Miss Tillie May, author and journalist, born in Washington, DC, in 1861. She is the youngest child of the eminent journalist, John W. Forney, founder and editor of the Philadelphia "Press," a man who wielded an acknowledged great political and social influence. This daughter, having inherited many of her distinguished father's tastes and ambitions, became his almost constant companion after leaving Miss Carr's celebrated academy on the Old-York-Road, PA. She had written for publication from early girlhood, and she then took up the task systematically and wrote regularly for prominent journals, besides acting frequently as her father's amanuensis, both in this country and in Europe. Under his experienced eye she received careful training for the work she preferred above all others. No accomplishment suitable to her sex was neglected in her education. She possesses a voice of unusual range and sweetness, and at that period it was her teacher's wish that all her interest should be centered on her musical talent, but it seemed impossible for her to drop her pen. She grows fonder of her literary duties, every year, and is a constant contributor to New York, Philadelphia and western dailies, besides writing regularly for several well-known magazines. She resides with her widowed mother in the old family residence, on South Washington Square, Philadelphia. She has been reared in a home of luxury, and the Forney library is one of the finest in Philadelphia. Mrs. John W. Forney is an accomplished lady of the old school, and she and her daughter are both social favorites, although each has aims and tasks that are preferred to those of fashionable life. Miss Forney's progress in literature, though rapid, is evidently but the promise of what she is yet to accomplish.

FOSTER, Mrs. J. Ellen Horton, temperance worker and lawyer, born in Lowell, MA, 3rd November, 1840. She is a daughter of Rev. Jotham Horton, a Methodist preacher. She was educated in Lima, NY, and removed to Clinton, IA, where, in 1869, she became the wife of E. C. Foster, a lawyer. Mrs. Foster studied law and was admitted to the bar of the Supreme Court of Iowa in 1872. She was the first woman to practice before that court. At first she practiced alone, but she afterward formed a partnership with her husband. She followed the legal profession for a number of years. She is widely known as "The Iowa Lawyer." In religion she is a Methodist. She joined the temperance workers when the crusade opened, and soon became prominent as a worker. Her home in Clinton was burned, presumably by the enemies of temperance. As a member of the Woman's Christian Temperance Union she was able to give most valuable service as superintendent of the legislative department. Her knowledge of law enabled her to direct wisely all the movement for the adoption of constitutional amendments in the various States, aimed to secure the prohibition of the sale and manufacture of alcoholic liquors. She has written a pamphlet on the legal bearings of the question. She has been exceedingly popular and successful as a lecturer. She is a pronounced suffragist, and she maintains that no organization has the right to pledge the influence of its members to any other organization for any purpose. Her views naturally led her to affiliate with the Non-Partisan League, and she served that body for several years as corresponding secretary, having her office in Boston, MA. She served her own State union as corresponding secretary and president for years. In 1887 she visited Europe, where she rested and studied the temperance question. In England she addressed great audiences. Returning to the United States, she took part in the International Council of Women in Washington. She has published a number of pamphlets and magazine articles on temperance. Her two daughters died in youth. Two sons make up her family. A part of each year she spends in Washington, DC.

FOSTER, Mrs. Susie E., author and philanthropist, born in Torbrook, Nova Scotia, Canada, 18th May, 1846. Her maiden name was Holland, and she was born and grew up on a farm. When she was twelve years old, she was sent away from home for better educational advantages. Two years later her mother's failing health made her presence at home necessary, and the routine of the school-room was never resumed. Her studies were continued at home, and her tastes were formed and her mind developed by a close perusal of the best authors. Both parents were of more than ordinary intellectual ability. Her grandfather Henderson was well known in educational circles. In his academy were trained men who became prominent in the religious and political history of Nova Scotia. Her father's father had been a member of the Provincial Parliament. The Hollands possessed literary and poetic ability, which was handed down to her. She became the wife of Mr. Foster when she was nineteen years of age. Brought up in the same faith, they pledged their allegiance in early years to God and Methodism. Three years after their marriage they joined the tide of migration westward, first to Illinois, and then to northwest Iowa. In the prairie homestead and later among a cultivated circle in town she contributed articles to the press. There the Woman's Christian Temperance Union won her to its great work. She served as corresponding secretary of the eleventh Congressional district during the stormy year that gave a prohibitory amendment to Iowa. She spent four years in Walla Walla, Wash., and her work continued along the lines of reform in local, county and State organizations. Going to Oregon for better educational advantages for their children, she was soon elected State corresponding secretary. Her pen is busy in the interests of the work, and while she sometimes is called upon to address an audience, she is not a ready speaker, and her thoughts find best expression through the medium of pen and paper. She has found, like other busy women, that her temperance work does not set her free from the claims of church and missionary effort, to which she gives much attention. Their home is in a suburb of Portland, near the university, where their daughter and son are students.

FOXWORTHY, Miss Alice S., educator, born in Mount Carmel, Fleming county, KY, 22nd December, 1852. Through her paternal grandmother, Mary Calvert Foxworthy, she is a lineal descendant of Cecil Calvert, Lord Baltimore, of Maryland. Her early education was received in the Stanford Academy, Stanford, KY, and there she began her career of teaching immediately after her graduation. In her native State she taught successfully in the Stanford Academy, the Catlettsburg High School and the East Kentucky Normal School. From the last mentioned position she was called to the responsible post of presiding teacher in the Tennessee Female College of Franklin, TN. She next received a call to the position of lady principal in the Nashville College for Young Ladies. Since 1884 Miss Foxworthy has occupied that position. Dr. G. W. F. Price, the president of that college, early invested her with full authority, leaving her to work out her ideas in the practical organization and management of the school. Miss Foxworthy's attainments are by no means insignificant. Her school training has been continued and extended by reading and study during the whole of her professional life. In 1890 the University of Nashville, Nashville, TN, conferred upon her the degree of M.A. Though the duties of principal have gradually withdrawn Miss Foxworthy from class-room work, her intimate acquaintance with each pupil under her care is not lessened. The Sabbath-school class of over one-hundred pupils and the flourishing missionary society which she has built up give her an opportunity for a strong influence in forming the characters under her charge. She is an original and impressive teacher of the Bible. Her religion is a religion of justice and unselfishness, her energy is inexhaustible, her perseverance indomitable. Her close observation, her keen and accurate judgment of men and things, and her long experience as a practical educator place her easily in the first rank in her profession.

FRACKLETON, Mrs. Susan Stuart, artist and inventor, born in Milwaukee, WI, in 1851. Her father's name was Goodrich. Her mother's maiden name was Mary Robinson, of Penn Yan, NY. Before her marriage to Richard G. Frackleton, this gifted young woman was a fellow-student with Carl Marr in the studio of Henry Vianden, in Milwaukee. Later she studied in New York City under the Harts, Mrs. Beers and Greatorex. She commenced china-painting in 1874, and in that field she has achieved great distinction in America and Europe. Mrs. Frackleton was the only woman in the country who exhibited in Philadelphia among the men, and her medals are numerous. She received the diploma awarded by the United States Potters' Association in 1889. Seeing the need of a portable gas-kiln for firing her artistic work, she invented and patented one. For her technical book, personal artistic work, colors and invention she has been honored by a special letter from the Queen of Italy. She has also been most flatteringly recognized and honored by the Academy of San Carlos, in the Mexican Republic. As an artist her admirable work has had court presentation in Rome at the request of the Queen. Mrs. Frackleton has written a very successful book on china painting. It is entitled "Tried by Fire" (New York, 1886). It has been accepted as a textbook in the library of the South Kensington Art Museum, and the thanks of the Lords of the Committee of Council on Education were tendered to the author. The volume and its results won the author four international medals. Over five-hundred women in America have been made self supporting by means of Mrs. Frackleton's skill in all that pertains to the ceramic art. She stands at the head of one of the most eminently successful china color and decorating works in the United States. In April, 1892, she was elected president of the National League of Mineral Painters. Her success in life she owes entirely to her own temperament and the full use of all the opportunities for developing her own genius.

FRAME, Mrs. Esther Gordon, minister and evangelist, born in Washington, IN, 10th July, 1840. Her maiden name was Gordon. Her father was born in Hamilton county, OH, and his ancestors came from the Scottish Highlands and were Scotch-Irish. In early life he resided in Centerville, IN, and there studied law. From Centerville he removed to Thorntown, IN, and in 1854 represented Boone county in the Indiana Legislature. In

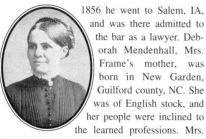

1856 he went to Salem, IA, and was there admitted to the bar as a lawyer. Deborah Mendenhall, Mrs. Frame's mother, was born in New Garden, Guilford county, NC. She was of English stock, and her people were inclined to the learned professions. Mrs. Frame was educated mostly among the Friends. In her school-days she often called her companions around her and preached to them with such effect that her juvenile audiences were brought to tears. She wove beautiful stories, to which her auditors listened with delight. In March, 1857, she became the wife of Nathan T. Frame, of Salem, IA. She has had three children, one of whom, a boy, died in infancy, and two daughters, Itasca M., and Hettie C. She was formerly a member of the Methodist Episcopal Church, but, feeling that she was called to preach and that the Methodists would not ordain her, she joined the Society of Friends and was ordained a minister by them. She began her ministry in New Garden Friends Meeting, in Indiana, 1869. If her home is now in Jamestown, OH, where she has lived since 1880. Her ministry has not been confined to her own denomination. For more than twenty years, with her husband, who is a minister, she has preached as an evangelist among all the principal churches of the United States.

FRANCIS, Miss Louise E., journalist, born in St. Helena, CA, 23rd April, 1869. Her teacher, noticing the marked love for books manifested by his pupil, "Still Water," as she was called, took pains to see that her thirst for reading was quenched only by good books and the master-spirits. She was educated in the public schools of her native town, graduating at the age of fourteen, the salutatorian of her class. She afterward attended a private academy for eighteen months, and subsequently finished her education in the State Normal School. Her forte was writing compositions, and her part in the school exercises was always to furnish one of her own articles. Her talent for writing grew, and when at the age of seventeen she went out in the world to make a living for herself; she naturally turned to an editor's office. She remained in the office of the "Santa Clara Valley," a monthly magazine, for three years, taking full charge of the household and young folks' departments, and adding an occasional literary note. She then rested for a year. Next she acted as correspondent for the San José "Daily Mercury" during the summer meetings of the Chautauqua Literary and Scientific Circle. Through that engagement she formed the acquaintance of T. A. Peckham, and with him went into partnership and started a newspaper in Monterey, called the "Enterprise." The, project did not prove a financial success, and after six months was discontinued. On 3rd April, 1891, a new "Enterprise" was started, this time in Castroville, of which Miss Francis was sole editor and proprietor. The new venture was successful, and Miss Francis is making her paper one of the brightest in the State. It is the official organ of the Pacific Coast Women's Press Association, and thus has a wider influence than the ordinary newspapers. Miss Francis was elected one of the delegates to the National Editorial Association, that met in California in May, 1892.

FRANK, Miss Rachel, author, born in San Francisco, CA, 10th April, 1866. She is more generally known as Ray Frank. She is of Jewish blood. Self-reliant from an early age, she entered upon the career of a school teacher when but fifteen years old, and, considering that her first field of labor was in the rough mining regions of Nevada, her success as an educator was remarkable. From childhood she gave evidence of literary and oratorical ability. Having a family of younger brothers and sisters dependent upon her, she patiently labored in a profession for which she had no real liking, and even gratuitously conducted evening classes for the benefit of young miners who were unable to attend the day school. In addition to her school work she contributed to various local and other papers and taught private classes in elocution with success. Her dramatic ability is undoubted, and she has had numerous inducements to adopt a stage career, but in this, as in all else, she has original ideas which have prevented her from accepting many good offers.

Deciding that journalism is a preparatory school for those wishing to engage in higher literary work, she became a regular and conscientious contributor to various periodicals on diverse subjects. In 1890 she accepted an offer of several journals to write up the great Northwest, and one of the features of the consequent trip was the organization of permanent congregations of her people. Her fame as a young woman of rare good sense and eloquence had preceded her, and her co-religionists conferred upon her the great honor of inviting her to address them on the eve of the Day of Atonement, the most sacred of all Hebrew festivals. She is probably the first woman in the history of the world who has ever preached to the Jews upon that day. The Jews, as a people, have ever been opposed to women occupying the pulpit, but in Miss Frank's case they have made an exception, believing that her sincere earnestness, natural eloquence and intense zeal peculiarly fit her for preaching. She is extremely liberal in her religious views, but possesses an intense interest in her people and their welfare. She has recently accepted the editorship of the "Pacific Coast Home Monthly," a journal of excellent standing. She has contributed to the New York "Messenger" "American Hebrew," Oakland "Times," "Jewish Times and Observer," "The Young California" and other periodicals in Tacoma, Seattle and San Francisco. One of her stories, "An Experience Extraordinary," has proved very popular. Miss Frank's home is in Oakland, CA, and her time is given up to teaching, preaching, housekeeping and journalism.

FRANKLIN, Miss Gertrude [Virginia H. Beatty], singer and musical educator, born in Baltimore, MD, of a wealthy and aristocratic family. She is a granddaughter of the late James Beatty, the millionaire, of Baltimore, and is also closely related to some of the oldest Maryland families. Miss Franklin early manifested musical gifts of an uncommon order, and while still young her education in music was begun. She soon gave promise of becoming a pianist of the first rank, but her tastes ran rather in a vocal than an instrumental direction, and, at the age of thirteen, prompted by her natural impulses and by the possession of a voice of sweetness and purity, she devoted her attention to singing. After pursuing her studies for a time in this country, she was at length induced by Signor Agramonte, with whom she had been studying, to go to Europe to complete her musical education. She went to London and became a pupil of Shakespeare, and then to Paris for two years, where she became a pupil of Madame Lagrange. She also studied with Professor Barbot, of the Conservatoire. Before leaving Paris, Miss Franklin appeared in a concert in the Salle Erard and achieved a flattering success, which was emphasized by immediate offers of concert engagements, and an offer from the Italian Opera management for a season of opera. Miss Franklin was in haste to reach London, where she made arrangements to study oratorio and English ballad music under Randegger, who was so pleased with her voice and method that he besought her to remain and make a career in England. Eager to return home after her prolonged absence, she declined that, and also an offer from Carl Rosa to join his English Opera Company. After her return to America she took an extended course of study under Madame Rudersdorff for oratorio and the more serious range of classical concert music.

Miss Franklin has appeared in New York, Boston and Brooklyn in symphony concerts, and in classical and other concerts in most of the leading cities in America with success. She has also sung with marked favor in London and Paris, where her artistic worth is perhaps still more appreciated than it is in her own country. Miss Franklin is in constant receipt of offers for opera and concert tours in Europe and America, but she objects to the fatigue and excitement of travel and does not appear before the public as often as she otherwise would. Being financially independent, she prefers the quiet of home and occasional appearances in important concerts. Miss Franklin is fully as successful as a teacher, as she has been as a singer.

FRAY, Mrs. Ellen Sulley, reformer, born in the parish of Calverton, Nottinghamshire, England, 2nd December, 1832. She is descended from both Huguenot and Danish ancestors. Her mother was a near relative of Lord Denman, Chief Justice of England, and from both sides of the house she inherited intellectual qualities. Her father was Richard Sulley, who married Elizabeth Denman in 1827, and of their six children Ellen was the third daughter. When she was but a child, Mr. Sulley moved with his family to the United States, and after some years located in Rochester, NY. During those early years of her life, while they were traveling from place to place, opportunities for education were limited so far as books were concerned. Her father thought that it mattered little, as all that girls needed was to write and read, with a little knowledge of arithmetic added. Ellen became a reader and a student of history. Her father was a well-known writer upon social and economical questions, and had distinguished himself at the time of the repeal of the Corn Laws in England. As a young girl Ellen heard such subjects discussed constantly and became deeply interested in all reforms of the day. In 1848 she first became roused upon the question of woman suffrage, through attendance upon a convention held in Rochester and presided over by Abigail Bush, with Lucretia Mott, Mrs. Stanton and others of the earlier agitators as speakers. That marked an epoch in her life. She had learned of woman's inferiority through the religious instruction which she had received, but henceforth she felt that something in it was wrong. She was advised by her Sunday-school teacher carefully to study and compare passages in the Old and New Testaments. That she did thoroughly, and became satisfied that Christ nowhere made any difference between the sexes. Henceforth her work lay in the direction thus given, and she has labored faithfully to promote political equality for woman and to advance her rights in the industrial fields. In 1853 she became the wife of F. M. Fray, and made her home in Toledo, OH, where she now lives. It was a happy union, lasting for twenty years, until the death of Mr. Fray. Her two children died in childhood, leaving her alone and free to devote herself to those things which she felt were of a character to help humanity. She has formed suffrage clubs in several different States and in Canada, and has been repeatedly a delegate to National councils, giving her time and money without stint. She has been foremost in testing woman's eligibility for various positions. In 1886 Mrs. Fray entered into a political canvass in Rochester to put a woman upon the board of managers of the State Industrial School. With Miss Mary Anthony, the sister of Susan, she worked for three weeks and gained the victory. Mrs. Fray is still full of vigor and energy in the cause to which she has given the best of herself for so many years. At present she is one of the district presidents of the Ohio Woman's Suffrage Association and a prominent member of several of the leading clubs, literary, social and economic, in Toledo.

FRAZIER, Mrs. Martha M., educator and temperance worker, born near Springfield, MA, 12th December, 1826. Her father's name was Albert Chaffee, and her mother's maiden name was Chloe Melinda Hyde. Her only memory of her mother was of being held to look at her as she lay in her coffin. Her father, being poor, took his young family west. They stopped in Washtenaw county, MI, and he was taken ill, as were the children also, of whom one died. Being discouraged, he gave his children to kind-hearted neighbors and disappeared. Martha was adopted into the family of John and Lois Thompson, and was always known by that name. When in her eighth year, the family moved to Illinois, twenty five miles west of Chicago, a country then nearly a wilderness. She had the same privileges as the rest of the family, but a few terms in a select school in Warrenville rounded out her educational career, and that was gained on promising the good man of the house that she would wear her home manufactured woolen dress, which promise she kept. Afterward, in teaching district school, she received in compensation one dollar per week and boarded around, then one dollar and fifty cents, and later two dollars and board herself, for which extravagance the board were censured. When nineteen years of age, while visiting a sister residing in Waukesha county, WI, she became acquainted with a young farmer, W. M. Frazier, whose wife she afterward became. She is an ardent lover of the church of her choice, and is an active sympathizer and helper in all modern reforms. She is an uncompromising advocate of prohibition, total abstinence and equal privilege and equal purity for men and women. She is a member of the school board and superintendent of scientific temperance instruction, and is president of the local Woman's Christian Temperance Union, and also president of the home library association in Mukwonago, WI.

FREEMAN, Mrs. Mattie A., freethinker and lecturer, born in Sturgis, St. Joseph county, MI, 9th August, 1839. Her ancestors were French and German, Americanized by generations of residence in the State of New York. Her father was a freethinker, her mother a close-communion Baptist. The mother tried to keep the children from what she considered the contamination of infidelity. They attended revivals and passed through all the usual experiences, but the daughter became an infidel in her early youth. Mrs. Freeman as a child learned rapidly. Her first public discussion was at the age of fourteen. An associate editor of a weekly newspaper had written an article on the inferiority of woman. Over a pen-name the school-girl replied to it. The controversy was kept up through several papers, the German student wondering, in the meantime, who it was that was making so effective an argument against him. He was thoroughly disgusted when he discovered that his opponent was a girl. At fifteen she taught her first school. It was a failure. She was yet in short dresses, and the "big" pupils refused to obey her. She endured it for six weeks, and then, disheartened and defeated, sent word to her father to take her home. About that time she heard Abby Kelly Foster speak on abolition, and the young girl's heart became filled with a burning hatred of slavery. Being invited soon after to take part in a public entertainment, she astonished all and offended some by giving a most radical anti-slavery speech. Her father was an old-time Whig and retained an intense admiration for Henry Clay. Even he was horrified to hear his young daughter, of whom he had been so proud, attack his dead pro-slavery idol. If her first attempt at teaching was a failure, the subsequent ones were crowned with success. She was hired to take charge of a winter school, receiving only one-third the pay that had been given to the male teachers, and had the credit of having had the best school ever taught in the district. Soon after the war, in a city in Illinois, whither she had gone from the East, a prominent so-called liberal minister preached a scathing sermon against women. Highly indignant, a committee of the suffrage association went to Mrs. Freeman and requested her to reply. At first she hesitated, but finally consented, and her lecture was a success. She has delivered many public lectures. After the Chicago fire Mrs. Freeman devoted herself to literary work, writing four years for a Chicago paper. She is the author of many serials, short stories and sketches. "Somebody's Ned," a story of prison reform, was published in 1880, and received many favorable notices. At that time Mrs. Freeman began her work in the Chicago Secular Union. To this for ten years she has devoted herself almost exclusively. She gave the first lecture on Henry George's "Progress and Poverty" ever delivered in Chicago. She is interested in the reform movement, and especially in woman's emancipation, which she is convinced underlies all other questions. Her last venture is the publication of the "Chicago Liberal." Her home is now in Chicago, and she is corresponding secretary of the American Secular Union.

FRÉMONT, Mrs. Jessie Benton, born in Virginia, in 1824. She is a daughter of the late Hon. Thomas Hart Benton, of Missouri, who was conspicuous as editor, soldier and statesman, and famous for thirty years in the United States Senate, from 1820 to 1851. During the long period of Col. Benton's public life Jessie Benton was an acknowledged belle of the old régime. She possessed all the qualities of her long and illustrious ancestry, illuminated by her father's record, and was the center of a circle of famous men and women. She became the wife of John Charles Frémont, the traveler and explorer, who was born in Savannah, GA, in 1813. Gen. Frémont is known to the world as the "Great Path Finder," and a "Grateful Republic" recognized his services. In 1849 he settled in California and was elected senator for that State. He received in 1856 the first nomination ever made by the Republican party for president. His wife was a prominent factor in that campaign. A major-general's commission was conferred in 1862, but General Frémont was more famous as explorer than as statesman or general. In 1878 he was appointed Governor of Arizona, where both he and Mrs. Frémont were very popular. Then closed the long and honorable public life of the Pioneer of the Pacific.

In all these public positions Mrs. Frémont won renown in her own right. As a writer she is brilliant, concise and at all times interesting. Her extensive acquaintance with the brightest intellects of the world enabled her to enter the field of literature fully equipped, and since the death of Gen. Frémont she finds pleasure in her pen. The memoirs of Mrs. Frémont will find a large circle of readers. She is now a resident of Los Angeles, CA, and lives with her daughter. Congress has recognized the services of "The Great Explorer" and given his widow a pension of two-thousand dollars per annum. Her published books are "Story of the Guard, a Chronicle of the War," with a German translation (Boston, 1863), a sketch of her father, Thomas H. Benton, prefixed to her husband's memoirs (1886), and "Souvenirs of my Time" (Boston, 1887). She is passing her days in quiet retirement.

FRENCH, Miss Alice, novelist, born in Andover, MA, 19th March, 1850. She is widely known by her pen-name, "Octave Thanet." She has lived in the West and South for many years. On both sides she is a descendant of the Puritans. She has Mayflower people and Revolutionary heroes, witch-hangers and modern rulers of Massachusetts among her ancestors, as well as godly ministers not a few, so that, as she has two centuries of unadulterated New England behind her, as she was educated there and goes there every summer, while she lives in the West and spends her winters in the South, she is so much of a composite that she says she hesitates to place herself. Two of her brothers were educated abroad, and one of them married one of the Irish Hamiltons. Her father was a manufacturer of agricultural implements. He was a loyal westerner, but he never lost his fondness for the East, going there regularly every summer. He was much more than a business man, being an enthusiastic lover of books and a connoisseur in the fine arts. Miss French began to write shortly after she was graduated from Abbot Academy, Andover, MA. The editors gave her the good advice to wait, and she waited several years, when she sent "A Communist's Wife" to the Harpers, who declined it, and she sent it to the Lippincotts,

who accepted it. Since that time she has always found a place for her works. The criticisms that editors offer she has found very valuable. Among her published works are "Knitters in the Sun" (Boston, 1887); "Otto the Knight" (Boston); "Expiation" (New York, 1890), and "We All" (New York). She has also edited "The Best Letters of Lady Mary Montagu" (Chicago). She is very fond of the Gallic models of style. She is interested in historical studies and the German philosophers. She likes all out-of-door sports and declares that she is a great deal better cook than a writer. It is a delight to her to arrange a dinner. She has a fad for collecting china. In politics she is a Democrat, a moderate free-trader and a firm believer in honest money. Miss French has a deep interest in English history and a great affection for England. She pursued her studies assiduously, going to original sources for her pictures of bygone times, and finding the most inspiration in the period which saw the rise of our present industrial system, the reign of Henry VIII and his children. Her pen-name was the result of chance. "Octave" was the name of her room-mate at school, and had the advantage of being suited to either sex. The word "Thanet" she saw written or printed on a passing freight-car. She prefers the Scotch to the French pronunciation of the word, although she regrets ever having used a pen-name.

FRISBY, Miss Almah J., physician, born in West Bend, WI, 8th July, 1857. Her father was Hon. Leander F. Frisby, a lawyer and at one time Attorney-General of the State of Wisconsin. Her mother's maiden name was Frances E. Rooker. They were originally from Ohio and New York. Almah Frisby was graduated from the University of Wisconsin in 1878, receiving the degree of B. S., and from the Boston University School of Medicine, in 1883, with the degree of M.D. She then located in Milwaukee, WI, and took up active practice, in which she was very successful. In the winter of 1886–87 she was resident physician in charge of the Women's Homeopathic Hospital, Philadelphia, PA. In the summer of 1887 she was homeopathic resident physician of the Hotel Kaaterskill in the Catskill mountains, after which she returned to Milwaukee and resumed local practice. Possessing keen insight, medical skill and deep womanly sympathy, she won in that city a large circle of friends in all walks of life. More especially did she interest herself in the dependent classes generally, who missed a valued benefactor when she was called to a chair in the University of Wisconsin and changed her field of labor. She is now preceptress of Ladies' Hall and professor of hygiene and sanitary science. Hundreds of young women yearly under her influence are enriched by her cultured mind and eminently noble and practical character.

FRISSELL, Miss Seraph, physician, born in Peru, MA, 20th August, 1840. She is a daughter of Augustus C. and Laura Mack Emmons Frissell. Her father and grandfather were captains of the State militia. Her great-grandfather, William Frissell, was a commissioned officer in the Revolutionary War and a pioneer settler in western Massachusetts. Her mother's father, Major Ichabod Emmons, was a relative of Dr. Nathaniel Emmons, and was one of the first settlers of Hinsdale, MA. Her grandfather, Col. David Mack, was the second white man to make a clearing in the town of Middlefield, MA, then a wilderness. The first eleven years of her life were spent within sight of Saddleback Mountain, the highest point of land in the State. As a child she was quiet and diffident, not mingling freely with her schoolmates, and with a deep reverence for religious things. After her father's death, which occurred when she was eleven years of age, the problem which confronted her mother was to gain a livelihood for herself and six children, Seraph being the third. Her twelfth year was spent with an aunt in western New York, during which time she decided she would rather earn her own living, if possible, than be dependent on relatives. Returning home, the next year and a half was devoted to school life and helping a neighbor in household work, thereby earning necessary clothing. When she was fifteen, her oldest sister decided to seek employment in a woolen mill, and Seraph accompanied her. The next six years were divided between a factory girl's life and school life. During those years she earned her living and, besides contributing a certain amount for benevolent and missionary purposes, saved enough for one year's expenses in Mt. Holyoke Seminary. The week she made her application for admit-

tance, the proposition was made to her to take up the study of medicine, but the goal toward which her eyes had been directed, even in childhood, and for which she had worked all those years, was within reach, and she was not to be dissuaded from carrying out her long cherished plan of obtaining an education. Hence she was found, in the fall of 1861, commencing her student life in that "Modern School of Prophets for Women," remaining one year. Then followed one year of teaching, and a second year in the seminary. After four years more of teaching, in the fall of 1868 she resumed her studies and was graduated in July 1869. The following three years were spent in teaching, during which time the question of taking up the study of medicine was often considered. It was in the fall of 1872 she left home to take her first course in the medical department of the University of Michigan. She received her medical diploma 24th March, 1875. The same spring found her attending clinics in New York City. In June, 1875, she went to Boston for hospital and dispensary work, remaining one year. In September, 1876, she opened her office in Pittsfield, MA, where for eight years she did pioneer work as a woman physician, gaining a good practice. In 1884 she removed to Springfield, MA, where she now resides. During the school years of 1890 and 1891 she was the physician in Mt. Holyoke College, keeping her office practice in Springfield. She was the first woman admitted to the Hampden Medical Society, which was in 1885, the law to admit women having been passed in 1884. A part of her professional success she attributes to not prescribing alcoholic stimulants. Dr. Frissell has held the office of president, secretary and treasurer of the local Woman's Christian Temperance Union, and is now county superintendent of the department of heredity and health. For years she has been identified with home and foreign missions, seven years having served as president of auxiliary to the Woman's Board of Missions.

FRY, Mrs. Elizabeth Turner, philanthropist, born in Trenton, TN, 22nd December, 1842, where she resided with her parents until the death of her father, James M. Turner. In 1852 her widowed mother, with five children,

among them Elizabeth, moved to Texas, settling in Bastrop. During the succeeding years of her life she attended school in different places, making one trip back to Tennessee, where she entered an academy for a term. Upon returning to Texas, she taught for a time in Bastrop, the remuneration going toward paying her tuition in special branches. In 1861, while on a visit to her sister, Mrs. O'Connor, who resided in Corpus Christi, she met, and one year later became the wife of, Lieut. A. J. Fry. The young couple moved to Seguin, where Mr. Fry engaged in general business on a large scale. Having accumulated a fortune, he moved with his family of three sons and one daughter to San Antonio. Mrs. Fry from her earliest youth possessed much religious reverence. She professed faith when but fifteen years old and joined the Methodist Church. For three years she faithfully followed its teachings, but, as she grew older and read more, she analyzed her feelings to find that the Christian Church opened the path. Accordingly she was baptized in that faith. She is a woman full of energy of spirit and mental endurance, which has been the secret of her success, both as a philanthropist and a Christian. She has taken an active and aggressive part in all temperance projects. In the Prohibition campaign in Texas, in 1889, she followed every line of defense and gained admiration for her pluck and willingness to express publicly her strongest views. Several years ago a bull-fight on Sunday was a public sport in San Antonio. The public and officers did not seem to suppress it, and finally Mrs. Fry decided to take the matter in hand. On a Sunday, when the fight had been announced and flyers were floating into every door, she determined to do what she could to prevent it from taking place, and accordingly circulated a flyer addressed "To All Mothers," setting forth the wickedness and degeneracy of such a sport, and the necessity of its suppression for the sake of husbands, sons and humanity. The bull-fight did not take place, and there has never been one on Sunday since that time in San Antonio. Being blessed with a goodly share of wealth, charity has flowed from her hands unrestrained. She is a prominent member of ten beneficent societies, and keeps up her voluminous correspondence without aid, besides distributing quantities of temperance and Christian literature. She is a woman suffragist from the foundation principle. Her sympathies were always with the Union and against slavery. She now holds a com-

mission as a lady manager from Texas to the World's Fair, besides being vice-president of the Queen Isabella Association. She was selected as a delegate to the national convention of the Women's Christian Temperance Union, in Boston, in 1891. With all these responsibilities, she attends to her many household duties.

FRY, Mrs. Emma V. Sheridan, actor and playwright, born in Painesville, OH, 1st October, 1864. Her mother was a niece of the well-known New England clergyman, Rev. Joseph W. Parker. Her father, General George A. Sheridan, made a fine record in the Army of the Cumberland during the late Civil war, and he has since won a national reputation as an orator. Emma has always been his friend, confidant and counselor, sharing his hopes, his disappointments and the joy of his successes. She is a graduate of Mrs. Hay's preparatory academy, Boston, MA, and of the Normal College in New York City. Choosing the stage as the field of her work, she went through a thorough course of study and training in the New York Lyceum School of Acting. She began at the bottom and in six seasons she rose to the front rank among American actors. She has filled many important rôles. In 1887 she played a notable engagement with Richard Mansfield in the Lyceum Theater, London, England. Returning to America, she played a round of leading Shakespearean parts through the country with Thomas Keene. In 1889 she became leading lady in the Boston Museum. At the close of her second and most successful season there her stage career was cut short by her marriage. She became the wife of Alfred Brooks Fry, Chief Engineer of the United States Treasury service, a member of the Loyal Legion and of the Order of the Cincinnati by heredity. During her stage experience Miss Sheridan had plied a busy pen and was well known as "Polly" in the "Dramatic Mirror," and by many articles, stories and verses published in the daily press, in magazines and in dramatic papers over her signature. Since her retirement from the stage Miss Sheridan, for she retains her signature, E. V. Sheridan, is devoting all her time to her pen, and she is in this second profession rapidly repeating the progress and notable success of her stage career. Miss Sheridan is quoted in her own country as an actor and a woman widely known, whose name has never been connected with scandal or notoriety. She is a member of the New England Woman's Press Association, and is president of the Alumni Association of the Lyceum School of Acting. On 23rd February, 1892, Richard Mansfield produced at the Garden Theatre, New York, a play by Miss Sheridan entitled, "£10,000 a Year," founded on Dr. Warren's famous book of the same name, and it won a flattering success.

FRY, Miss Laura Ann, artist, born in White county, IN, January 22nd, 1857. She is of English descent. Her father and grandfather are artistic designers and wood-carvers in Cincinnati, OH. Miss Fry, when still a child, was sent to the Art School in Cincinnati, to develop the talents for drawing and modeling which she had already displayed. She remained in the institution for twelve years, studying drawing under Professor Noble and modeling under Professor Rebisso. She then went to the Art Students' League in New York City. She learned the art of carving from her father and grandfather. One of her productions, a panel showing a bunch of lilies and dedicated to Mendelssohn, took the first prize, a hundred dollars in gold, when the Cincinnati women had offers of prizes for designs to decorate the organ screen of Music Hall. Miss Fry has made good use of her talents and training. She has had charge of the wood-carving school at Chautauqua Assembly for three years. The work done by her pupils there is quite equal to work done in the same line by the pupils of the best school in London. Miss Fry has worked much in china and pottery. She was one of the original members of the Cincinnati Ladies' Pottery Club, organized in April, 1878, to make original experiments and researches in the work of underglaze coloring and decorations. That club existed for ten years, and to it is due the credit of having set many good styles and methods, which have been meritorious enough to be adopted by the regular profession, and without credit acknowledged to the originators. Miss Fry's present home is on a farm in

Ohio, but most of her work has been done in Cincinnati. She has been connected with Purdue University, Lafayette, IN. Although she is the daughter of an Englishman, she is proud to call herself an American. She glories in being a Hoosier and in living in a land where she enjoys the privilege of doing the work for which her inclinations and talents best fit her.

FRYATT, Miss Frances Elizabeth, author and specialist in art as applied to the house, was born in New York City, but spent her girlhood in the country. In her childhood she wrote for pleasure and chiefly in verse, taking up literature as a life-work on the death of her father, Horatio N. Fryatt, who had written able articles on science, law and finance during the intervals of his busy life as a New York merchant. After the death of her father, the family removed to the city. She commenced to write for New York newspapers, the "Evening Post," the "Commercial Advertiser," the "Tribune" and the "Daily Graphic," a hue of work soon relinquished for the more congenial field of magazine literature. An article entitled "Lunar Lore and Portraiture," written for the "Popular Science Monthly" and published in August, 1881, involved extended reading and research. About 1879 she became a contributor to "Harper's Magazine," the "Independent," the "Churchman," the "Illustrated Christian Weekly," the "Art Age" and later to "Harper's Young People" and "Wide Awake." In 1881 she commenced the work which, carried up to the present day, has made her a specialist, writing articles for the "Art Interchange" on art applied to the house, including monographs on embroidery, glass painting and staining, wood-carving, painting on china, designing for carpets and wallpaper, schemes of exterior and interior coloring and decoration from architects' plans and sketches. She wrote all the answers to queries on house-furnishing and decoration published by the "Art Interchange" during the last ten years, as well as the answers to numberless queries on a great variety of subjects. In 1886 Miss Fryatt became editor-in-chief of the "Ladies' World," a monthly devoted to the home, conducting eight of its departments, and writing all the editorials and most of the technical articles up to the present day. Miss Fryatt had previously occupied the positions of assistant editor and art-editor of the "Manhattan Magazine" of New York.

FURBER, Miss Aurilla, poet, born in Cottage Grove, MN, 19th October, 1847. After a brief experience as a teacher, ill health forced her to a life of seclusion, which developed her poetic bent. She leads a retired life in her home in St. Paul, MN. Selections from her poems have been made for the "Magazine of Poetry" and "Women in Sacred Song." Her poem "Together" has been set to music by Richard Stahl. She has also written prose articles for the "Pioneer Press," "Church Work" and other papers. She has been identified with Woman's Christian Temperance work for years as an officer in local, county and district organizations.

FURMAN, Miss Myrtie E., professor of elocution, born in Mehoopany, PA, 8th November, 1860. Losing her sight in her fourteenth year, she went to Philadelphia and entered upon the seven-year course of study in the Educational Institution for the Blind. In a little more than four years she had finished the studies in that institution. She entered the National School of Elocution and Oratory in Philadelphia, from which she was graduated in two years with high honor, receiving a diploma, a silver medal and the degree of Bachelor of Oratory. A few days afterward, in June, 1884, she received a diploma and the highest honors awarded for scholarship from the Institution for the Blind, having finished the curriculum of studies in both educational institutions in less than the seven years usually given to the latter. Miss Furman enjoys the peculiar distinction of being the only blind graduate from the School of Elocution and Oratory, and it is believed that she is the only blind person in this country, or in the world, who ever accomplished a similar course of study

and physical training. For two years after her graduation she gave many successful elocutionary entertainments in various cities and towns of Pennsylvania and New York. In 1886 she accepted the position of professor of elocution in a young ladies' school in Ogontz, near Philadelphia. She remained there two years. For the past four years she has filled the chair of elocution in Swarthmore College.

FUSSELL, Miss Susan, educator, army nurse and philanthropist, born in Kennett Square, PA, 7th April, 1832, and died in Spiceland, IN, in 1889. She taught school from her fifteenth year until April, 1862, when she undertook to conduct the Memphis army hospital, and accomplished a wonderful work in the eight months she was in charge. She served in other hospitals in Tennessee and in Indiana, and at the close of the war became interested in soldiers' orphans' homes. The great work of her life was conducting such an institution at Knightstown, and subsequently at Spiceland, IN. Through her efforts the State legislature established at Knightstown a Home for Feeble Minded Children. Other homes of a similar character throughout this State are largely due to her influence.

GAGE, Mrs. Frances Dana, woman suffragist and author, born in Marietta, Washington county, OH, 12th October, 1808. Frances Dana Barker, as she was named, was educated at home, in a frontier log cabin. Her father was a farmer and a cooper, and she could make a good barrel and till a farm in her girlhood. In 1829 she became the wife of Mr. Gage, a lawyer practicing in McConnellsville, OH. They reared a family of eight children, and in spite of all her domestic distractions, Mrs. Gage read, wrote, thought and spoke on woman's rights, temperance and slavery. In 1851 she attended the woman's rights convention in Akron, OH, and was chosen president of the meeting. In 1853 she moved to St. Louis, MO, with her family. Her husband's health failed, and she took a position as assistant editor of an agricultural paper, published in Columbus, OH. Her four sons enlisted in the Union army, and she went in 1862 to Port Royal, to care for the sick and wounded soldiers. She spent thirteen months in Beaufort, Paris and Fernandina, ministering to soldiers and freedmen alike. She lectured throughout the North to soldiers' aid societies in advocacy

Beth Franklyn.
From Photo by Thors, San Francisco.

of the Sanitary Commission. She went without commission or salary to Memphis, Vicksburg and Natchez. After the war she lectured successfully on temperance. In 1867 she was made helpless by paralysis, which shut her from the world, being able only to talk, read and write. Under the pen-name "Aunt Fanny" she has written many juvenile stories, poems and social sketches. She has been a contributor to the "Saturday Visitor" and the New York "Independent." Her latest published works are a volume of poems and a temperance story, "Elsie Magoon."

GAGE, Mrs. Matilda Joslyn, woman suffragist, born in Cicero, NY, 24th March, 1826. She was largely educated at home, and at a later date she was sent to the Clinton, NY, Liberal Institute. She early stood upon the platform, giving her first lecture at the age of seventeen, before a literary society of her native village When eighteen, Matilda Joslyn became the wife of Henry H. Gage, a young merchant of her own town, and lived first in Syracuse, NY, afterward in Manlius, in the same county, and thence removing to Fayetteville, NY, where Mrs. Gage now resides. She early became interested in the subject of extended opportunities for woman, publicly taking part in the Syracuse convention of 1852, the youngest speaker present. The work of Mrs. Gage in the National Woman Suffragist Association is well known. From her pen have appeared many of the most able state papers of that body and addresses to the various political parties. As delegate from the National Woman's Suffrage Association in 1880, she was in attendance upon the Republican and Greenback nominating conventions in Chicago, and the Democratic convention in Cincinnati, preparing the address presented to each of those bodies and taking part in hearings before their committees. The widely circulated protest of the National Woman's Suffrage Association to the Men of the United States, previous to the celebration of the national centennial birthday, 4th July, 1876, was from her pen, as were also important portions of the Woman's Declaration of Rights presented by the National Woman's Suffrage Association in that celebration, Independence Hall, 4th July, 1876. From 1878 to 1881, Mrs. Gage published the "National Citizen," a paper devoted to woman's enfranchisement, in Syracuse, NY. Urged for many years by her colleagues to prepare a history of woman suffrage, Mrs. Gage, comprehending the vastness of the undertaking and the length of time and investigation required, refused, unless aided by others. During the summer of 1876 the plan of the work was formulated between herself and Miss Anthony and Mrs. Stanton, comprising three large octavo volumes, of one thousand pages each, containing engravings of the most noted workers for woman's enfranchisement. "The History of Woman Suffrage" (1881–87) is now to be found in the most prominent libraries of both Europe and America. In the closing chapter of volume one, Mrs. Gage included a slight resume of "Woman Church and State," a work she has still in hand. Several minor works have appeared from her pen. Among them are "Woman as Inventor" (1870), "Woman Rights Catechism" (1868), "Who Planned the Tennessee Campaign?" (1880), as well as occasional contributions to the magazines of the day. Among her most important speeches are "Centralization," "United States Voters," "Woman in the Early Christian Church" and "The Dangers of the Hour." Her resolutions in 1878 on the relations of woman and the church were too radical for the great body of woman suffragists, creating a vast amount of discussion and opposition within the National Woman Suffrage Association,

Louise Galloway.
From Photo by Baker, Columbus.

Katherine Florence.
From Photo by Morrison, Chicago.

Mrs. Minnie Maddern Fiske.
From Photo by Aime Dupont, New York.

Marie Graham.
From Photo by Baker, Columbus.

ultimately compelling her to what she deems her most important work, the formation of the Woman's National Liberal Union, of which she is president.

GAINES, Mrs. Myra Clark, heiress, born in New Orleans, LA, in 1805, and died in that city, 9th January, 1885. She was the daughter of Daniel Clark, a native of Sligo, Ireland. He emigrated from Ireland and settled in New Orleans. In 1796 he inherited a large property from an uncle. He died in New Orleans, 16th August, 1813, and his estate was disposed of under his will dated 20th May, 1811, giving the property to his mother, Mary Clark, then living in Germantown, PA. Myra Clark was his child by a secret marriage and was reared in a family by the name of Davis. After her marriage in 1832 to W. W. Whitney, of New York City she learned of her true parentage, and tried to regain the estate. Through a long period of litigation, extending over forty-two years, she recovered six million dollars of the thirty-five million, the valuation of the estate. She showed great magnanimity in refusing to dispossess four-hundred families occupying her lands. Mrs. Whitney became a widow, and in 1839 was married to Gen. Edmund Pendleton Gaines.

GALE, Mrs. Ada Iddings, author and educator, was born in Dayton, OH, and comes of a Quaker ancestry. Her education was received in Albion College. In her early childhood her literary inclining was apparent and received careful fostering from her father, Rev. Joseph T. Iddings, who was also largely her teacher. There yet remain fragments of her early fancy scrawled in a round childish hand. Her home is in Albion, MI. A woman of family, with numerous social demands upon her time, she yet sets apart certain hours of the day for research. As a student of English history and literature she has been painstaking and has gained a remarkable proficiency in these favorite branches of study. As a dramatic reader she is far above the ordinary, and as a teacher of dramatic art she excels. She has lectured on the "Attributes of Beauty" and has ready for publication two manuscripts, one a volume of verse, the other a seventeenth century romance. Owing to the care and education of her three children, it is with difficulty she has achieved work of any great length, but her endeavor is marked by eagerness and whole heartedness.

GALPIN, Mrs. Kate Tupper, educator, born in Brighton, IA, 3rd August, 1855. She is a sister of Mrs. Wilkes and Miss Tupper, whose lives are found elsewhere in this book. She lived during her girlhood on a farm near Brighton. As a child she was very frail, but the free and active life of her country home gave her robust health. Her first teacher was her mother, who taught school while her father was in the war. Her mother would go to school on horseback, with Kate behind her and a baby sister in her lap. Later she attended the village school until she was fifteen, when she was sent to the Iowa Agricultural College in Ames, where she was graduated in 1874. The vacations of the college were in the winter, and in the vacation following her sophomore year she had her first experience in teaching, in a district school three miles out of Des Moines, IA, where the family was then living. The next winter, when seventeen years of age, she was an assistant in a Baptist college in Des Moines, her earnings enabling her to pay most of her college expenses. As a student her especial delight was in oratory. In an oratorical contest, during her senior year, she was successful. over a number of young men who have since become well-known lawyers of the State, and in the intercollegiate contest which followed she received second honor among the representatives of all the colleges of the State. She has very marked dramatic ability, but this has been chiefly used by her in drilling students for the presentation of dramas. Her first schools after graduating were in Iowa. From 1875 to 1879 she taught in the Marshalltown, IA, high school, having held responsible positions in summer institutes in many parts of the State. In 1878 she taught an ungraded school in the little village of Beloit, IA, in order to be near her parents, who were living on a homestead in Dakota, and to have with her in the school her younger brother and sister. Later she taught for four years as principal. of the academic department of the Wisconsin Normal School in Whitewater. During the following three years she held positions in the high school of Portland, OR. Next she was called to the professorship of pedagogics in the State University of Nevada, with salary and authority the same as the men of the faculty. In 1890 she resigned her professorship in the university and received a call to the presidency of a prominent normal school, which she refused. That summer she became the wife of Cromwell Galpin, of Los Angeles, CA, consummating a somewhat romantic attachment of her college life. Since then she has rested from her profession, but has taught special classes in oratory in the University of Los Angeles. All the ambition, energy and ingenuity that made her so distinguished as a teacher are now expended with equal success in the management of her housekeeping and the care of her husband's children. She has one child, a daughter.

GANNETT, Mrs. Abbie M., author, born in North Brookfield, MA, 8th July, 1845. Her girlhood was passed in that town. Her love for the country and her early associations is shown in her dainty volume of poems, "The Old Farm Home" (Boston, 1888). She taught school a few years in Massachusetts, Michigan and St. Louis, MO. She became the wife of Captain Wyllys Gannett, of the latter place, a nephew of the distinguished Unitarian clergyman of Boston, and himself a writer of sketches of travel and sea stories. Captain Gannett served through the Civil War in the 24th Massachusetts and the 55th Massachusetts colored regiment. After living a few years in St. Louis, the Gannetts went to Boston, where they made their home for a short time. For many years they lived in Malden, MA. They have three children. Mrs. Gannett, while devoted to her home interests, has yet found time to do able outside work. She is well known in the womens' clubs as a reader of thoughtful essays on current themes. She has filled the Unitarian pulpit on a few occasions and has served on the Malden school board. Her essays, poems, sketches and stories have had a wide publication, many of them appearing in the leading magazines and periodicals. She is deeply interested in the welfare of women and their higher education. Her paper on "The Intellectuality of Women," printed in the "International Review" a few years ago, excited wide comment. Mrs. Gannett is philanthropical in her labors. She espoused the cause of the neglected Anna Ella Carroll with enthusiasm. By a series of articles in the Boston "Transcript" and other papers she has done as much as any one woman to bring her case to public notice. She joined the Woman's Relief Corps and attended the Grand Army of the Republic encampment in Minneapolis to advocate that lady's cause. She won recognition for her and was appointed chairman of a national relief committee to raise funds for Miss Carroll. The effort was successful. Not content with that, Mrs. Gannett visited Washington and argued Miss Carroll's case before the military committees of both Senate and House.

GARDENER, Mrs. Helen H., scientist and author, born near Winchester, VA, 21st January, 1853. Her father, the late Rev. A. G. Chenoweth, freed his inherited slaves and moved north with his family before the war. He saw the evils of slavery and determined that his children should not be educated where the atmosphere of race subjugation might taint them. Helen, the youngest of her father's family, was then less than one year old. She grew into young girlhood, little differing from other children of her surroundings and condition, and her school and college career did not vary much from that of girls whose environment and education were of a similar character. She was not remarkable, either as being the brightest or the dullest pupil of her classes. Her talent is not a result of scholastic training. Although books, from her babyhood, have been her friends, and she has eagerly absorbed from them all the information they could give, she has been and is a greedy student in a broader and deeper school than the colleges afford. She is a believer in the subtle law of heredity, and her own life is corroborative of that belief. She traces her paternal lineage back to Oliver Cromwell and her maternal to the Peels of England and Virginia. The first representative of her father's family in America was John Chenoweth of Baltimore county, MD, whose wife was Hannah Cromwell, whose mother was a daughter of Lord Baltimore. Her paternal grandmother was the daughter of Judge John Davenport, of Virginia, to whose family belongs the well-known southern writer, Richard M. Johnston, and she is a cousin of Gen. Strother (Porte Crayon). Her oldest brother, Col. Bernard Chenoweth, served with distinction during the war of the rebellion and was sent by President Grant as consul to Canton, China, where he died at the early age of thirty years. She did not choose literature or authorship as a profession, nor did a desire for fame induce her to write for the public. With her habit of close observation, rapid mental analysis and logical conclusion, she soon saw and appreciated the world-wide difference between the man and the woman as to advantages accorded by society to each in the struggle for existence and advancement. It seemed to her that the strong were made stronger by every aid society could give, and the weak were made weaker by almost every conceivable hindrance of custom and law. Her sense of right was shocked and she sought for the cause or causes for this manifest injustice. So she began to write because she had something to say to her fellow-creatures. For three or four years she simply wrote as she communed with herself. She was too diffident to let the public or even her friends, except one or two of the nearest, know what she wrote or that she wrote, and her first published article was sent by one of her most intimate friends to the press, against her desire. At length, when she was induced to send some of her writings for publication, she was so timid and distrustful of her own work that she used pseudonyms, generally masculine, and she rarely used the same name to more than one article. She was twenty-seven years old when the name of Helen H. Gardener was first given to her readers. She has devoted her life to the disenthrallment of women and thereby of humanity. Everything she has written has been done for the good of her sex and of humanity. She is a pronounced agnostic, not an atheist. She has generous hospitality for all honest opinions and principles. Her first book published, "Men, Women and Gods" (New York, was composed of a series of agnostic lectures, in which she called attention to the attitude of the Old and the New Testaments toward women, as interpreted by the adherents of the religions based upon those so-called sacred writings. She wrote other lectures in that direction, which were given to the public through the press and on the platform. She under-

took the study of anthropology in order that she might satisfy herself as to the correctness of the dictum of the doctors, generally accepted as indisputable, that woman is by nature man's inferior, having smaller brain and of inferior quality and less weight, and consequently having less mentality as less physical strength. Her investigations, in which she was aided by the leading alienists and anthropologists of America and Europe, caused her to discover the utter fallacy of the theory upon which this dictum, as to sex difference in brain, is based. Her work in that direction is the first scientific, basic work and the most thorough that has ever been done, and she settled beyond question the error of the assertion that there is any difference known to science, in brains, because of sex. She gave an epitome of her conclusions on that subject, a part of which was published in the "Popular Science Monthly," to the Woman's International Congress held in Washington, in 1888, in the form of a lecture on "Sex in Brain" (New York, 1888), and her paper was a revelation to all who heard it. It was favorably noticed and commented on by medical journals in this country and in Europe. Knowing that the general public does not read and would not understand essays and scientific articles, she concluded to incorporate some of her scientific and sociologic ideas and theories in stories. These stories appeared first in magazines. Their reception by the general public was immediately so cordial that a publisher brought out a number of them in a book entitled, "A Thoughtless Yes" (New York, 1890). They were read as interesting stories by the general reader, while the leading alienist in America wrote of them: "I have put the book in my scientific library, where I believe more works by the same able pen will appear later. I had believed there were but three persons in America able to do such work, and these are professional alienists." Her first novel, "Is This Your Son, My Lord?" (Boston, 1890), won extraordinary favor. Twenty-five-thousand copies were sold in the first five months, a success equaled by few other novels. All her vigor of thought and expression, her delicacy of wit, fine sense of humor and clever dramatic powers, so manifest in "A Thoughtless Yes," are equally marked in her volume of short stories, "Pushed by Unseen Hands" (New York, 1892). She has recently published a novel, "Pray You, Sir, Whose Daughter?" (Boston, 1892).

GARDNER, Miss Anna, anti-slavery agitator, born on the Island of Nantucket, 25th January, 1816. Her father, Oliver C. Gardner, was related to most of the prominent families in Nantucket, among whom were the Cartwrights, and through them Miss Gardner is descended from Peter Folger, the grandfather of Benjamin Franklin, and she is thus related to Lucretia Mott, Maria Mitchell and other distinguished men and women. Through her mother, Hannah Mackerel Gardner, she can claim descent from Tristram Coffin, the first magistrate of Nantucket. Seven generations of her ancestors lived in Nantucket. Miss Gardner's literary tastes and talents were inherited from her mother, who was known for her love of classical poetry. On her father's side, also, she received a literary strain, as the Cartwright family has produced poets in each generation. Slavery and its horrors were early forced upon Miss Gardner's attention. She became a student, a teacher, a lecturer and a worker in the cause of human liberty and equal rights. She was a regular reader of the "Liberator" when she was eighteen years old. In 1841 she was instrumental in calling an antislavery convention upon her native isle, which was largely attended. In that meeting Frederick Douglass made his first appearance as a public speaker. He had been exhorting in the Methodist Church and was unprepared for the call made upon him. Nevertheless, he responded and electrified his audience. Miss Gardner spent many years in teaching the freedmen in the South. Her work was done in North Carolina, South Carolina and Virginia. She returned to the North in 1878, and in Brooklyn, NY, she was injured by a carriage accident. The result was long weeks of suffering, a partial recovery, crutches and a return to her Nantucket home, where she is passing her days in serenity. She is still engaged in teaching those around her, and her pen is still active in the interests of truth and philanthropy. Besides her antislavery work, Miss Gardner has worked faithfully and potently in the cause of woman's rights. She lectured several times before the Nantucket Athenæum. In 1881 she published a volume of prose and verse, entitled "Harvest Gleanings." The work shows Miss Gardner's talents at their best.

GARFIELD, Mrs. Lucretia Rudolph, wife of James A. Garfield, twentieth President of the United States, born in Hiram, Portage county, OH, 19th April, 1832. She was the daughter of Zebulon Rudolph, a farmer. She received a classical education in Hiram, in a school in which her future husband was a teacher. She became the wife of James A. Garfield, 11th November, 1858, in Hiram, OH, where he was president of the college. Their family consisted of several children, one of whom, a daughter, died in infancy. The living children are four sons and one daughter. Her husband, after their marriage, was both college professor and a Campbellite preacher, often officiating in the churches of the sect of Disciples. His career is a matter of familiarity. When he was elected to the Presidency, Mrs. Garfield's public career began. Her occupancy of the White House was suddenly ended by the murder of her husband. During her reign in Washington she showed a great deal of force of character. She was in the most difficult position that any woman can hold in the United States, and she acquitted herself with tact and dignity. She was averse to publicity, discreet, retiring and reticent. The duties of her position broke her health, and she was taken to Long Branch to recover strength. While she was there, President Garfield, just starting from Washington to join her, was shot. Her devotion to him during the agonizing weeks that ended in his death, is historical. After his death Mrs. Garfield received a large amount of money presented to her by citizens of the country, and she made her home in Cleveland, OH. She visited Europe and lived for a time in Bournemouth, England. Returning to the United States, she settled in the Garfield homestead in Mentor, OH. Mrs. Garfield is passing her days in quiet retirement, doing good work for those about her in the unostentatious manner that distinguished her when she held the position of mistress of the White House. One of her philanthropic deeds was the donation of $10,000 to a university in Kansas, which took the name of her martyred husband. Her life has throughout been an illustration of American womanhood, wifehood and motherhood of the loftiest character.

GARNER, Miss Eliza A., educator, born in Union, SC, 23rd April, 1845. She is the daughter of G. W. Garner, Sr., the oldest child of a family of seven. She received her early education from her mother, and she subsequently attended a select school, two boarding schools and a State Normal School. Miss Garner, after finishing her studies, began to teach in the public school of her neighborhood. She taught successfully for twelve years. She was the first woman candidate for political office in South Carolina or in the South. In 1888 she announced herself a candidate for county school commissioner, with the proposition to the people that, if elected, she would use the salary of the office to lengthen the school term from three to six months and to supply the schools with books. A few conservatives and her own family prevented her election. The Democratic committee refused to print her ticktes or to allow them to be printed. She engaged the editor of the county paper to print her tickets, paying him in advance, and he printed them on inferior paper and in an unlawful shape, saying afterward that he had done so under the direction of the committee. When the votes were counted, her tickets were thrown out because of their unlawful shape. She was thus defeated. In 1890 she renewed her candidacy and her offer. She attended campaign meetings and read an address to the voters, but was again defeated in a similar way. Her opponent in 1890 was a former schoolmate. She returned to the work of teaching, only to receive a notification from him that the public money of the school district in which she was teaching had been appropriated to other schools. He requested her to close the school. She refused. She taught the school a full term and claimed her salary by law. Miss Garner's experience illustrates the disagreeable nature of the obstacles in the way of women in the South, who venture out of the beaten path.

GAUSE, Mrs. Nora Trueblood, humanitarian, born on a farm fifty-five miles north of Indianapolis, IN, 9th February, 1851. She is a daughter of Thomas E. and Sarah J. Trueblood. Her parents being members of the Society of Friends, well educated and of a progressive spirit, the daughter naturally championed the cause of the downtrodden. She early manifested a love for declamation and composition, and her first writings are remarkable for their emphatic denunciation of wrong and earnest pleadings for right. From 1868 to 1888 she served in the public schools of Indiana as a teacher. The succeeding five years, as far as lay in her power, were given to home and family, but, so successful was she in reaching the public that she was often called to the platform as a lecturer and organizer. In October, 1886, just one year from the date of her husband's death, she joined the humane workers of Chicago and spent the four succeeding months in writing for the "Humane Journal." In March, 1887, she began to organize societies for the prevention of cruelty, holding public meetings and doing whatever she could to awaken thought on the humane question. To say that her efforts have been attended with enthusiasm and success would be a mild statement, for thousands have been made to see the error of their ways by her convincing arguments and earnest appeals for better protection for all helpless life. She publishes occasional letters descriptive of her travels and work accomplished, and other articles in the "Humane Journal."

GAVITT, Mrs. Elmina M. Roys, physician, born in Fletcher, VT, 8th September, 1828. She is the second of eight children. She came of old Puritan stock, developing in her life that intense conscientiousness with regard to what she believes to be right, and that stern, uncompromising devotion to duty that characterized her New England ancestors. Her parents were to a great extent the instructors of their flock, both in religious and secular matters, for there were public schools but half of the year, and church privileges were few and far between. When Elmina was fourteen years old, business interests caused a removal of the family to Woonsocket, RI. For the next twelve years the shadow of ill-health stretched across her pathway, and the possibilities of life lay dormant. At last the door opened for her to begin what has proved a most successful occupation. Hoping to benefit herself by striving for what seemed then almost unattainable, and seeing no avenue open to American women which promised more usefulness than the profession of medicine, she entered the Woman's Medical College of Philadelphia, in 1862. In 1865 she was called to Clifton Springs, NY, as house physician in an institution there. Two years later she went to Rochester, MN, and commenced a general practice, winning from the first signal success, which has always since followed her. In 1869 she removed to Toledo, OH, where she has since lived. During that year she showed one of her most marked characteristics, self-sacrifice, by adopting a blind sister's six children, the youngest but two days old and the oldest but twelve years old. She bravely bore her burden and now has the satisfaction of seeing all those children prosperous and happy. In 1876 she became the wife of Rev. Elnathan Gavitt, an elder of the Methodist Episcopal Church, but her marriage did not cause her to give up her profession, in which she had come to stand among the first in the State. Mrs. Gavitt is a woman of strong individuality of character. She has absolute belief in the brotherhood of humanity, and for that reason her skill has been exercised for the poor and the rich alike. For her work she has a peculiar fitness, and it has brought her into the closest contact with suffering and sorrow, for which her sympathies never fail.

GEORGE, Mrs. Lydia A., army nurse and philanthropist, born in New Limerick, ME, 1st April, 1839. Her maiden name was Philpot, and she traces her ancestry back to English sources upon her father's side. In May, 1854, the family removed to Elk River, MN, where, in 1857, she became the wife of Charles H. Hancock, of that place. Two years after her marriage, having no children of her own, she took to her home an orphan girl, who remained with them until she was married. Later, she took a motherless boy, who remained with them five years. A devout Christian of non-sectarian spirit, she was earnest in the work of various missions carried on by different denominations. The fateful signal gun which boomed out over Fort Sumter found her superintending a Sabbath-school in Elk River. In August, 1862, her husband enlisted in Company A, Eighth Regiment, Minnesota Volunteer Infantry. She sought an interview with General Pope, then stationed in St Paul, and obtained permission to go with the regiment. The Indian outbreaks along the frontier at that time made it necessary for Minnesota troops to remain in the Northwest, and after the necessary drilling they were assigned by companies to their respective stations in the Sioux and Chippewa countries. Company A was ordered to the Chippewa Agency in September, and thither Mrs. Hancock soon followed. Arriving at the agency, she was assigned to a room in the agency building, which was the headquarters and also served as a hospital for the company. Work was awaiting her, for thirteen of the company were prostrated with measles, which rapidly spread until it attacked every man who had not previously had the disease In April, 1863, the company were ordered to Fort Ripley, and remained there two months. From Fort Ripley they went to the Sauk Valley. The winter following they were ordered to Fort Abercrombie, Dakota, in the Sioux country, where she remained until spring, having shared in all the vicissitudes of camp life on the frontier. Then her health demanded a rest. In Anoka, MN, in the fall of 1865, her husband was brought to her in the arms of his comrades, that she might once more look upon his face and minister to his last wants. Her interest in the soldier, his widow and his orphans did not cease with the close of the war. In June, 1885, she joined the Woman's Relief Corps, at the institution of Dudley P. Chase Corps, of Minneapolis, MN, of which organization she was chosen president. She served in that capacity for two years. On 11th January, 1887, she became the wife of Capt. J. W. George, Company G, Thirty-third Massachusetts Volunteers, one of the most prominent Grand Army men in Minnesota. Captain and Mrs. George worked hand in hand, and their voices were heard at many campfires and patriotic gatherings throughout the districts of the State, and pecuniary assistance was given by them to many enterprises for the assistance of needy comrades. Captain George organized William Downs Post, No. 68 in Minneapolis, and she was interested in the organization of an auxiliary corps, and in January, 1888, at the institution of William Downs Corps, she was elected president. She served in that capacity until she was called to serve the State as its department president. Her husband died in May, 1891. Mrs. George has served the Woman's Relief Corps in many capacities, both in the State councils and in national conventions. She is now actively engaged in temperance work.

GIBBONS, Mrs. Abby Hopper, philanthropist, born in Philadelphia, PA, 7th December, 1801. She was a daughter of Isaac T. Hopper, the Quaker philanthropist. She received a liberal education and taught in Philadelphia and New York City. In 1833 she became the wife of James Sloane Gibbons. In 1834 they settled in New York City. Mrs. Gibbons became at once prominent in charitable work. In 1845 she aided her father in organizing the Women's Prison Association, and the father and daughter cooperated in founding a home for discharged prisoners. Both were frequent visitors to the prisons in and around New York. The home was called the Isaac T. Hopper Home. For twelve years she was president of a German industrial school for street children. During the Civil War she worked in camp and hospital. In 1863, during the draft riots in New York, her house was one of the first to be sacked by the mob, as she had been conspicuous in anti-slavery agitation. After the war she founded a labor and aid association for soldiers' widows and orphans. In 1871 she aided, in founding the New York Infant Asylum. In 1873 she founded the New York Diet Kitchen. Her life was one of singular purity and exaltation. With all her charity for the criminals, she believed in the prevention of crime by reasonable methods. All the prominent philanthropies of New York bear the impress of her spirit and hand. Mrs. Gibbons died in New York City, 10th January, 1893.

GIBBS, Miss Eleanor Churchill, educator, was born in the plantation home of her parents, "Oak Shade," near Livingston, AL. Being descended from families pre-eminent for many generations for culture, refinement and talent, Miss Gibbs possesses these in a marked degree. The Revolutionary hero, Capt. Churchill Gibbs, of Virginia, was her grandfather. Through her mother she claims as her ancestor Rev. John Thomas, of Culpepper, VA. Her education was

given to her principally by her mother, a very brilliant woman. She pursued her studies also in Livingston College. Later she continued her studies in higher mathematics and science under Dr. Henry Tutwiler. In 1865 she accepted the position of assistant teacher in Livingston Academy, and as 1870 she was elected principal of the institution. In 1875 she resigned that position in order to take charge of high-school work in Selma, Ala. In 1887 she resigned to accept the position which she now fills as professor of English literature and history in Shorter College, Rome, GA. Miss Gibbs is an able, earnest, enthusiastic and successful teacher, and stands in the front rank in her chosen profession. She wields a strong and graceful pen and is a paid contributor to leading journals in Boston, Philadelphia, Chicago and elsewhere.

GIBSON, Mrs. Eva Katherine Clapp, author, born in Bradford, IL, 10th August, 1857. Her father removed from western Massachusetts and pre-empted a section of the best farming land in the State. There he built a log house of the frontier type, and in this his children were born. Miss Clapp's paternal grandmother was Lucy Lee, who was a direct descendant, on her father's side, from the famous Indian princess, Pocahontas. Her mother was Ann Ely, from Litchfield, CT, a direct descendant from Lady Alice Fenwick, a romantic figure in Colonial times, of Old Lyme, CT. Miss Clapp passed the first eleven years of her life under her mother's watchful care, on her father's farm. After her mother's death she lived with a married sister. She attended school in Amboy, in the Dover Academy, and subsequently in the Milwaukee Female College. While her studies were pursued in a desultory manner and at irregular intervals, she learned very rapidly and easily. When about sixteen years old, she visited for a time in the large eastern cities, and subsequently taught school in western Massachusetts. She commenced to write at an early age. Her first story, written when she was twenty years old, was a novel, entitled "Her Bright Future," drawn largely from life. Some thirty-thousand copies were sold. That was followed by "A Lucky Mishap" and "Mismated," which reached a sale of about ten-thousand copies, "A

Woman's Triumph," and a serial first published in one of the Chicago dailies as "Tragedies of Prairie Life," and subsequently published in book form as "A Dark Secret," She has written many short stories and sketches, and has done considerable editorial work. Her poems have had a wide circulation. They are to be published in book form, under the title, "Songs of Red Rose Land." She became the wife of Dr. C. B. Gibson, of Chicago, in 1892, and spent a year in Europe, where Mrs. Gibson made a special study of the literature of Germany and France.

GILBERT, Miss Linda, philanthropist, born in Rochester, NY, 13th May, 1847. She removed to Chicago, IL, with her parents when she was fifteen months old, and was educated in St. Mary's Convent, in that city. From an early period she regarded criminals with profound interest. At the age of eleven years she gave books from her grandfather's library to the prisoners in the jail of Cook county, IL. Her home was directly opposite. The first county jail library ever established she placed in that prison when she was seventeen years old. At the age of fifteen years she inherited a handsome fortune. After spending one-hundred-thousand dollars in philanthropy, the remainder was lost in a bank failure. After that her benevolent work was a continuous struggle. She entered into several business speculations to keep it alive, hoping that some rich man would leave it a legacy to place it on a permanent foundation. In all, she has established twenty-two libraries in six different States, each containing from two-thousand-five-hundred to three-thousand volumes. In Lincoln, NE, her library has been the means of educating eighteen or twenty native Indians, who were sentenced for long terms. She has procured employment for six-thousand ex-convicts, over five-hundred of whom she started as pedlars, furnishing them with an outfit worth from three to five dollars. Less than ten percent of that number have turned out unsatisfactorily. For her last thirteen years she constantly agitated the question of building an industrial and educational home to meet the wants of this class, who find it so impossible to secure employment after their release

from prison. Miss Gilbert felt that society more than the criminal is to-day responsible for crime. She was known as "The Prisoners' Friend." Miss Gilbert patented several devices, including a noiseless rail for railroads and a wire clothespin, and used these for the purpose of gaining money to carry on her philanthropic work. She died in Mt. Vernon, NY, 24th October, 1895.

GILBERT, Miss Ruby I., business woman, born in Junius, NY, 1st December, 1851. She has been for many years recording secretary of the Woman's Christian Temperance Union of Illinois and bookkeeper of the Woman's Temperance Publication Association, and is a most interesting and fit survival in the growing group of business women which this modern time has developed. Miss Gilbert handles from two to three hundred  thousand dollars a year, and has completely gained the confidence of all associated with her. She has the remarkable combination of a delicately poised conscience and a perfectly level head. Many persons might intend to be accurate as she is, but their intellectual make-up would render it impossible. Mathematical and ethical qualities must balance each other to produce such a result. Miss Gilbert was engaged in clerical work in Freeport, IL, when Miss Willard lectured there early in the crusade movement, and then first became especially interested in temperance work. The education of Miss Gilbert has been wholly in the public-schools, and in various relations that she has sustained she has received a diversified and thorough business training. In 1882 she came into association with Mrs. Mary B. Willard, who was at that time editor of the "Union Signal." She has since then sustained an intimate relation with Mrs. Willard, serving also as her legal business representative in this country after the American School for Girls was established in Berlin, Germany, in 1885. Miss Gilbert went to Illinois with her parents in 1855, and was reared in the town of Mendota, her father having been an itinerant minister in the pioneer days of the Baptist Church.

GILCHRIST, Mrs. Rosetta Luce, physician, author and poet, born in Ashtabula, OH. In youth

Pauline Hall.
From Photo Copyright, 1895,
by Morrison, Chicago.

Mary Hampton.
From Photo by Morrison, Chicago.

she was a student in the Mingsville, or Rexville, Academy, and later in Oberlin College. She taught in the Cleveland public schools, and after graduating from the Cleveland Homeopathic College, gained a lucrative practice in the medical profession. It seems evident to those who have read her "Apples of Sodom," "Margaret's Sacrifice," "Thistledew Papers," and numerous poems, which were written during the press of business or housekeeping affairs, that she would have attained a high place among American authors. She also possesses talent as an artist, and is a member of the Woman's National Press Association; also of the Cleveland Woman's Press Association, and president of the Ashtabula Equal Rights Club.

GILDER, Miss Jeannette Leonard, journalist, born in Flushing, NY, in 1849. Her father was a contributor to the journals in Philadelphia, and at one time he edited a literary monthly of his own. Jeannette published her first story, "Katie's Escapade," in the New York "Dispatch," when she was fourteen years old. At the age of seventeen she contributed to the Newark "Daily Advertiser," of which her brother was editor. He started a morning paper in Newark, and Jeannette contributed a column a day on "Breakfast-Table Talk." She soon advanced to dramatic and musical criticism. Since that year, 1869, she has been regularly and actively engaged in journalism. When her brother became assistant editor of "Scribner's Magazine," in New York City, he disposed of the Newark "Morning Register," but Miss Gilder continued for a time to serve it in every conceivable capacity. She became a correspondent of the New York "Tribune," and for a time served in a clerical position on "Scribner's Magazine." In 1875 she joined the staff of the New York "Herald" as a book reviewer. She also reported for that paper. In December, 1880, in conjunction with her brother, she started "The Critic." In addition to her work on her own paper, Miss Gilder has corresponded for a number of journals outside of New York. In 1876 she wrote a play, "Quits," which was brought out in the Chestnut Street Theatre, Philadelphia, by F. F. Mackey. She dramatized "A Wonderful Woman" for Rose Eytinge. She dramatized Dr. Holland's "Sevenoaks" for John T. Raymond. She wrote a comedy for Harry Becket, who died while preparing to produce it in England.

GILES, Miss Anne H., philanthropist, born in Prairie du Chien, WI, 1st August, 1860. She removed to Chicago in early life. Her father is William Alexander Giles, in pioneer days of Wisconsin a representative of the press. She was graduated from Smith College in 1882, taking the degree of A. B. From her childhood she was imbued with the missionary spirit, always attempting to help the poor and the suffering. As a teacher of the Chinese she was a special leader among church workers for a number of years. As

foreign corresponding secretary of the Woman's Presbyterian Board of Missions she has become widely known. Practically interested in the education of the freedmen, associated with various societies of Christian Endeavor, devoting all her time to benevolent work, and being a general financial contributor to home and foreign missions, she is recognized as one of the most earliest and useful daughters of philanthropy in Chicago. The story of the "Poacher's Daughter," which has gone through numerous editions, was translated by her for Sunday-school libraries.

GILES, Miss Ella A., author, was born in Dunkirk, near Madison, WI, 2nd February, 1851. She early showed musical talent. Her fine voice was carefully cultivated by Hans Balatka. She was quite distinguished as an oratorio and church singer when her health failed, and she was compelled to abandon what promised to be a successful career in music. During the isolation illness rendered necessary she wrote her first romance, "Bachelor Ben" (Chicago, 1875). It had a very wide sale, reaching the third edition in a few months and making its young author exceedingly popular throughout the Northwest. Her stories "Out from the Shadows" (1876) and "Maiden Rachel" (1879) followed with the same publishers. Meanwhile Miss Giles received many calls for lectures and achieved success in that field. In 1879 she became librarian of the public library in Madison and held the position for five years, doing at the same time much literary work. She has published one volume of poems entitled "Flowers of the Spirit" (Chicago, 1891). She has made a study of Scandinavian literature and is known for her scholarly sketches of Swedish and Norwegian writers. These sketches were translated into Swedish and Norwegian by different authors. She has written valuable articles on prison reform and ethical subjects, and now belongs to the Woman's Congress committee on journalism. Being deeply interested in liberal religious thought, she attended a course of lectures in the Meadville Theological School. She was on the staff of the Chicago "Times" for three years, still keeping her home on Lake Monona in Madison. She was the first woman to read a paper before the Wisconsin Academy of Science, Arts and Letters.

GILLESPIE, Miss Eliza Maria, religious devotee, known in the Roman Catholic Church as Mother Mary of St. Angela, born in Brownsville, PA, 21st February, 1824, the oldest daughter of John P. and Mary Myers Gillespie. The father died while the children were still young, and their mother removed to Lancaster, OH. Eliza Maria was placed in school with the Dominican Sisters in Somerset, Perry county, OH, and afterward with the Sisters of the Visitation, in Georgetown, DC, and graduated from that institution with the highest honors. The few years she spent in the world were marked by the most earnest work for the sick and distressed, especially the victims of the cholera in 1849. In 1853 she entered the Congregation of the Holy Cross, taking the name of Saint Angela, to be known as "Mother Angela." Almost immediately she sailed for Europe. She made her novitiate in France and took the vows of her religious profession at the hands of Rev. Father Moreau, the founder of the Congregation of the Holy Cross. In 1855 she returned to the United States and was made Superior of the Academy of St. Mary's, then in Bertrand, MI, to be removed the following summer to its present site, one mile from Notre Dame, South Bend, IN. From that time there stood forth from the ranks of the Sisters of the Holy Cross in the United States a personage so remarkable that even the leveling rule of religious profession could not lessen the charm of her individuality, one who, whether as Mother Superior or Mistress of Novius, or director of studies, or simply Sister Mary of St. Angela, carried into her obedience exaltation of purpose, swiftness of execution, grace, self-denial and oblivion of her brilliant place in the world. When the beat of drum, calling on the nation to arm her sons for the defence of the "Stars and Stripes," broke the still-

ness of seclusion in St. Mary's as well as Notre Dame, she heard and answered on the battlefield and in the hospital, commanding her trained nurses in the name of sweet charity. The war over, Mother Angela and her Sisters returned to St. Mary's to take up the old obedience, whatever it had been. The only thing to indicate their part in the national crisis was the spiked cannon, sent a few months after to Mother Angela and her community, as a recognition of their services, by the commander of the division in which they labored. From their return from the war, a new energy pervaded the ranks of the Sisters of the Holy Cross. Called for from the Atlantic to the Pacific, from the Northwest to Texas, asylums, hospitals, schools were opened and overlooked. She died 4th of March, 1887.

GILLETTE, Mrs. L. Fidelia Woolley, Universalist minister, born in Nelson, Madison County, NY, in 1827. She is the daughter of Rev. Edward Mott and Laura Smith Woolley. In 1847 her father removed to Michigan, where she was married, and where she has lived many years. Mrs. Gillette's literary work has continued since her sixteenth year under the pen-names "Lyra" and "Carrie Russell," and her own name. Her poems and prose articles have appeared in various papers and magazines. Her published works are her poems entitled "Pebbles from the Shore" (1879), "Editorials and Other Waifs" (New York, 1889), and a memoir of her father (Boston, 1855), who was a popular minister in the Universalist Church. Her missionary and pastoral work has been of several years' duration.

GLEASON, Mrs. Rachel Brooks, physician, born in the village of Winhall, VT, 27th November, 1820. No colleges were open for women during her girlhood, but she gave herself a fair collegiate education from college text-books studied at home. Her husband, Dr. Silas O. Gleason, when he became professor of hy-

giene in the Central Medical College in Rochester, succeeded in persuading the faculty and trustees to open the college doors to women. Mrs. Gleason studied with her husband and was graduated in medicine in 1851. She then practiced three years in a sanitarium in Glen Haven, NY, and one year in Ithaca, NY. She has been at the head of the Gleason Sanitarium in Elmira, NY, for forty years. Her book on home treatment for invalids, "Talks to My Patients" (New York, 1870), has run into its eighth edition. After her graduation in medicine she gave lectures on physiology and hygiene to women, assisted by the best models and charts to be had at the time. She was an advocate of dress reform and women's freedom from early girlhood. Mrs. Gleason was a strong anti-slavery worker before the Civil War, and has rendered constant assistance to Freedmen's schools ever since.

GOFF, Mrs. Harriet Newell Kneeland, temperance reformer and author, born in Watertown, NY, 10th October, 1828, of New England parentage. At sixteen she began to teach a public school in a country district, boarding among her pupils. During several years, teaching alternated with study, mainly in Grand River Institute, Ohio. At twenty-two she became the wife of Azro Goff, a young merchant and postmaster in the town of her residence. She entered the temperance lecture field in 1870, and has traveled throughout the United States, in Canada, New Brunswick, Nova Scotia, Newfoundland, England, Ireland, Scotland and Wales, speaking more or less extensively in all, and under various auspices. In 1872 she was delegated by three societies of Philadelphia, where she then resided, to attend the prohibition convention in Columbus, OH, and there she became the first woman ever placed upon a nominating committee to name candidates for the presidency and vice-presidency of the United States. To her presence and influence was due the incorporation of woman's suffrage into the platform of that party at that time. She published her first book, "Was It an Inheritance?" (Philadelphia, 1876), and early the next year became traveling correspondent of the New York "Witness," besides contributing to "Arthur's Home Maga-

zine," the "Sunday-school Times," the "Independent" and other journals. In 1880 she published her second book, of which she issued the sixth edition that year. Her third volume was "Who Cares?" (Philadelphia, 1887). Adhering to the British branch in the rupture of the Order of Good Templars, Mrs. Goff was in 1878 elected Right Worthy Grand Vice-Templar, and the following year was re-elected in Liverpool, England, over so popular a candidate as Mrs. Margaret Bright Lucas, on account of her acceptable and still desired services in the supervision and secretaryship of the order in America. She joined and lectured for the Woman's Temperance Crusade early in 1874 in several States, was a leader in the organization and work of the Woman's Temperance Association of Philadelphia, afterward rechristened the Woman's Christian Temperance Union. She was a delegate there from to the first national convention of the Woman's Christian Temperance Union in Cleveland, OH, and again from the New York State Union to the convention in Nashville, TN, in 1887. Her especial work from 1886 to 1892 was for the employment of police matrons in Brooklyn, NY, her place of residence for the past fourteen years, whence she removed to Washington, DC, in 1892. As committee of the New York State Union she endeavored to procure such amendments of an ineffective law as would place every arrested woman in the State in care of an officer of her own sex. For this she has labored with her usual diligence, drafting and circulating petitions, originating bills, interviewing mayors, commissioners, councilmen, committees of senate and assembly, and individual members of those bodies, and governors on behalf of the measure, and by personal observations in station-house cells and lodging-rooms, jails and courts, originated or substantiated her every argument. She is a believer in the cause of woman suffrage.

GOLDTHWAITE, Mrs. Lucy Virginia, author, born in Florence, AL. She is the youngest of her family. Her maiden name was Lucy Virginia Harmon. Her ancestors for generations were born and bred in Petersburg, VA, where her parents and their children, with the exception of Mrs. Goldthwaite, were reared. Her sister, called

"Lizzie of Woodlawn," for years was a writer for the Louisville "Journal." Woodlawn, the beautiful home where Mrs. Goldthwaite passed her childhood, may still be seen in Florence. Several little poems, written at five and six years of age by Miss Harmon, are still retained by relatives. Verses written at eight were published, with many sketches and poems at intervals in later years. Her most popular poem was on the death of Gen. Pat. Cleburn. For fifteen years the public have read nothing from the pen of Mrs. Goldthwaite, except at long intervals. During that time she was not idle, however, as she has numerous sketches and songs and several novels in manuscript. Her first novel, "Veta, a Story of the Blue and Gray," was published in "Sunny South," in 1890. Mrs. Goldthwaite has written many songs that have received public approval, and a tragedy for Lillian Lewis, which that actor pronounces exceptionally fine, and several other plays for leading actors. Mrs. Goldthwaite is a thorough scholar, a fine artist, a proficient linguist, and reads, writes and speaks fluently several languages. She has a high soprano voice of great sweetness and power. She was a pupil of the German composer, August Newmayer. She is happily married, and is the wife of George Goldthwaite, a prominent judge, an able lawyer, a nephew of ex-United States Supreme Court Judge, John A. Campbell, and son of ex-United States Senator, George Goldthwaite. Mrs. Goldthwaite resides at present in Leadville, CO.

GOOCH, Mrs. Fanny Chambers, author, is a native of Texas, where the greater part of her life has been spent. Through her book, "Face to Face with the Mexicans" (New York, 1888), she has become known to fame. The story of the inception, growth, publication and success of this book gives a luminous insight into the character of its author, and is at the same time an interesting illustration of the changed conditions of the modern American woman's life. Several years ago Mrs. Gooch removed with her family to the city of Saltillo, Mexico. She, who in her American home was famous as a housewife, went to Mexico almost entirely ignorant of the domestic manners of those most unyielding devotees of ancient custom, and set up her home among them, expecting to order her household affairs after the same comfortable fashion which made her home in Austin, Texas, a place of ease and plenty. The story of the disillusionment told in the opening chapters of her book is exquisitely ludicrous. To a woman less keenly alive to the humor of the situation it would have been less profitable as a lesson than it proved to the author. After a determined effort to force the immovable Mexican customs, she found herself compelled to yield to the inevitable. She might be compelled to do without a cooking-stove and to forego the delights of attending to her own marketing and shopping, but her genial soul demanded that, if foiled in her domestic plans, she would at least refuse to be shut out from social intercourse with the people among whom she found herself. That was hardly less difficult than to keep house in the American fashion with the help of Mexican servants and furniture. Her neighbors looked with small favor on Americans in general, having learned much to prejudice them against their brethren across the Rio Grande, and little in their favor. But here was an anomaly in the shape of an American, a woman full of the independent spirit of her people, but as full of sympathy and ready appreciation as the most courteous Latin. The result was that Mrs. Gooch obtained an insight into the innermost life and less superficial characteristics of our neighbors, which she afterward used in her book on Mexico so successfully as to give the work a peculiar value. Returning after some years to her former home in Austin, her descriptions of her Mexican experiences so entertained her friends that she was asked to prepare a series of articles on the subject for a Texas newspaper. Mrs. Gooch at once set to work. She soon found, however, an embarrassment of riches in the abundant material her memory supplied, and, abandoning her first intention, she decided to publish her work in book form. Her first intention had been to limit her book to he experiences in Saltillo, but the greatness of her overmastering idea soon proved that intention too narrow, and, putting aside her pen, she returned to Mexico, where she spent some time in its principal cities, mingling with its people in every station. She was fortunate in carrying on her new venture to have letters to the leading men and women of the Mexican capitol. When the literary portion of her work was complete, she went to New York and superintended the publication of the work. The book at once attracted the notice of the leading reviewers and became very successful. The year following the publication of "Face to Face with the Mexicans" Mrs. Gooch was married to Dr. D. T. Inglehart, of Austin, and has since devoted herself almost entirely to her extensive domestic and social duties. At present she has in contemplation another literary venture, the subject of which is to be Texas.

GOODALE, Miss Dora Read, poet, born in Mount Washington, Berkshire county, MA, 29th October, 1866. Her life and literary career have been intimately associated with those of her older sister, Elaine Goodale, now Mrs. Charles A. Eastman. The story of the childhood and remarkable literary achievements of Dora is similar to the story of Elaine's early life. At the age of six years Dora composed verses that are simply remarkable, in certain qualities of rhythm and insight, for so youthful an author. She was an earnest student, and she enthusiastically cooperated with her sister in publishing a monthly paper for the entertainment of the family. In conjunction with her sister she published "Apple Blossoms: Verses of Two Children," selected from their earliest work, (New York, 1878); "In Berkshire with the Wild Flowers" (1879), and "Verses from Sky Farm," an enlarged edition of the preceding volume (1880). Dora's verses are no less praiseworthy than those of her sister, and the achievements of these two remarkable girls, when the older was fifteen and the younger twelve years of age, set the critics of the world to work, and stirred them as critics had not been stirred by the work of virtual children since the time of Chatterton.

GOODRICH, Mrs. Mary Hopkins, originator of village improvement associations, born in Stockbridge, MA, in 1814. Her maiden name was Hopkins. She inherited the same intellectual qualities which marked her cousin, President Mark Hopkins, of Williamstown, with others of the name hardly less distinguished. She was born with a love of nature and a humanitarian spirit. She was left an orphan when barely two years old, and was brought up by older sisters. From the planting of a tree, when she was five years old, dates practically the beginning of the Village Improvement Association which has made of Stockbridge, MA, the most perfectly kept village in the United States. After an absence of many years in the South, she returned to find the village cemetery in a neglected state, and she resolved to attempt to remedy that and other unnecessary evils, and, as far as possible, by the aid of children. To interest them she had a tree planted for every child in town, to care for themselves, and that secured their interest in what was projected and begun for the rest of the village. A wretched street known as Poverty Lane, where some of them were then living, was thus gradually transformed into one of the prettiest streets in the village. A constitution was adopted on 5th September, 1853, and amended and enlarged in scope in 1878. Miss Hopkins became the wife of Hon. T. Z. Goodrich, whose interest in the work had been hardly less than her own, and who till his death never lost it. Mrs. Goodrich is not only the mother of every village improvement society in the United States, but the unwearying helper of every one who seeks to kindle this love in children, or to rouse interest in their elders.

GOODWIN, Mrs. H. B., novelist, was born in Chesterville, ME, but she has been a resident of Boston, MA, for many years. She is the daughter of the late Benjamin B. and Elizabeth Lowell Bradbury. Her school-life was spent mainly in Farmington Academy, under the tuition of Alexander H. Abbott. She was a successful teacher of girls in Bangor, ME, and afterward she was principal of the Charlestown Female Seminary. For the last fifteen years Mrs. Goodwin has been intimately associated with the educational work of Wellesley College. She is an active member of its board of trustees and of its executive committee, and has also written and read to the students of Wellesley many essays on art, the studies for which were made in the great art centers of Europe, where she traveled in England, France, Germany, Italy and Spain. Her first novel was "Madge" (New York, 1864), and was favorably received. Mrs. Goodwin regards it as the least worthy of her books, though it was written with as high an aim and as serious a purpose as any of its successors. Her second hook, "Sherbrooke" (New York, 1866), is a story of New England life. The success of that story was instantaneous. Her third book, "Dr. Howell's Family" (Boston, 1869), was written during months of great physical pain, and many readers regard it as the author's strongest work. "One Among Many" (Boston, 1884), added to the well-earned success of its author, and gave new evidence of her ability to represent real life. Another of her well-known stories is "Christine's Fortune" (Boston), a picture of German life. "Our Party of Four" (Boston, 1887), describes a tour in Spain. Perhaps to "Dorothy Gray" the highest praise is awarded by critics and literary friends.

GOODWIN, Mrs. Lavina Stella, author and educator, born in St. Johnsbury, VT, 4th February, 1833. Her maiden name was Tyler. When between fourteen and fifteen years old she taught a district school, and for a few years until her marriage was alternately teacher and pupil. Circumstances have developed Mrs. Goodwin's literary talent in the direction of versatility rather than specialty. After having conducted departments for women and children, and become favorably known as a writer of stories, at the beginning of 1869 she was made associate editor of the "Watchman," in especial charge of its family page, and the connection exists still, after an interval of service on the "Journal of Education." A season in California and Mexico tested her ability as a correspondent, and he was employed in that capacity in the Philadelphia Centennial and in the Paris Exposition of 1878, her published letters winning general admiration. She has produced a number of serials, one for a leading London journal. Two juvenile volumes from her pen have appeared, "Little Folks' Own" and "The Little Helper."

GORDON, Miss Anna A., author and temperance worker, born in Boston, MA, 21st July, 1853. Miss Gordon studied for years in the Newton high school and in Mount Holyoke Seminary. She went to Europe in 1875 and spent a year with her sister, Mrs. Alice Gordon Gulick, the founder of the College for Girls in San Sebastian, Spain. She was studying the organ in Boston, in 1877, when she was introduced to Miss Willard, who was holding meetings, on D. L. Moody's invitation, in connection with his Boston tabernacle. Miss Gordon was a member of the Congregational Church, and she became organist in Miss Willard's daily gospel meeting. Miss Willard promptly recognized her abilities, and for years these two zealous women have worked in the same field. Miss Gordon has served as Miss Willard's private secretary, as superintendent of juvenile work for the World's Woman's Christian Temperance Union, and as associate national superintendent of the same department. She has put her methods to the proof by conducting juvenile organizations for years in Evanston, IL, where she lives with Miss Willard and her mother in their "Rest Cottage" home. Miss Gordon is an excellent writer and has a charming gift of verse-writing, both humorous and pathetic. She also composes music that is in large request among white-ribboners. She has furnished to the children their "Marching Songs." She has prepared the "Songs of the Young Women's Christian Temperance Union" for the "Y's," and on invitation of the National Woman's Christian Temperance Union now has in hand a hymnal for that great society. Her book of "Questions Answered" is a complete manual of juvenile temperance work, and her "Prohibition Programme" is a delightful evening entertainment, by means of which the Band of Hope "puts money in its purse," while her droll "collection speech," in rhyme, has been used a thousand times. All of these have been given to the Women's Temperance Publishing House, Chicago. She has published a "White Ribbon Birth-day Book." Miss Gordon has traveled with Miss Willard an average of 10,000 miles a year, and in 1883 went with her to every State and Territory, making a trip of about 30,000 miles and assisting in twenty State and Territorial conventions.

GORDON, Miss Elizabeth P., temperance advocate, was born in Boston, MA, and is the third daughter of James M. Gordon. Miss Gordon was for seven years corresponding secretary of the Woman's Christian Temperance Union of Massachusetts, and is now one of its speakers and organizers. Reared in the most conservative manner in a Congregational church, Miss Gordon has made her experience in the thick of the fight and has become one of the acceptable speakers, writers, organizers and managers of the white ribbon work.

GORDON, Mrs. Laura De Force, lawyer and journalist, was born in 1840. Her first ambition was in the line of journalism, and in that she soon succeeded, becoming, in 1873, the editor and publisher of the "Daily Leader" of Stockton, CA, which she afterward continued as the "Daily Democrat" in Oakland, CA. While attending the session of the California legislature, in 1887, for the purpose of reporting its proceedings for her paper, Mrs. Gordon assisted in the preparation of a bill asking the legislature to allow the admission of women to the bar. That bill was known as The Woman Lawyer's Bill." When it was presented to the legislature a long and acrimonious debate took place, in which Mrs. Gordon bore a spirited and brilliant part, and the bill was finally passed. At the same session the legislature founded the Hastings College of Law. Mrs. Gordon decided to become a lawyer, and, when that institution was opened, she applied for admission, but was excluded. Together with Mrs. Foltz, another law student, she brought a writ of mandamus, which was successful, and a year later both women were admitted. Mrs. Gordon was a diligent student, and in 1879 was admitted to the bar. She immediately began the practice of her profession in San Francisco, where she remained for five years. She was admitted to the bar of the United States Supreme Court, 3rd February, 1887, being the second woman allowed to plead before that high court. She is now located in Stockton, CA.

GORDON, Mrs. S. Anna, physician and author, born in Charlemont, MA, 9th January, 1832. On her father's side she is a descendant of John Steele, who founded the colony of Connecticut and established the town, now city, of Hartford. Among the distinguished persons in her family lineage was Noah Webster. She early removed with her parents to New York, where she was reared and took the first year of a college course of study, which was afterward completed in Illinois. She was married in Wisconsin in 1858, to W. A. Gordon, M.D., of Wausau. Some years previous she had charge of the ladies' department in Rock River Seminary, and subsequently the same position was twice tendered her in Ripon College. The principalship of the State Normal School of Wisconsin, which was soon to be opened, had been tendered her through the governor of the State, and was awaiting her acceptance. She attended teachers' institutes, wherever held throughout the State, for the purpose of agitating the subject of a normal school, until the desire became an object accomplished. After her marriage she immediately commenced the study of medicine with her husband, attended a partial course of lectures, and was called upon by the people to assist him in an overburdening practice. In 1859 and 1860 they were connected with the Smithsonian Institution, taking meteorological notes and making collections for the same. She filled an engagement of one year as associate editor on the "Central Wisconsin," and then joined her husband in Louisville, KY, where he was stationed most of the time during the Civil War. She was a weekly contributor to the literary columns of the Louisville "Sunday Journal" during the war. She has been a member of the Dante Society since its organization, and in 1882 and 1883 was State editor for the Missouri Woman's Christian Temperance Union on the Chicago "Signal." During a residence in Denver, CO, she was the first person to suggest the demand for the newsboys' home there, which she had the opportunity of aiding in establishing. She was also assistant superintendent of Chinese work in that city for some time. She is the author of a book entitled "Camping in Colorado," and several papers and poems that have entered into other collections. In medicine she is a homoeopathist. She was graduated in 1889 with honors from the Hahnemann Medical College of Chicago. Her home is now in Hannibal, MO.

GORTON, Mrs. Cynthia M. R., poet and author, born in Great Barrington, Berkshire county, MA, 27th February, 1826. Her father, Samuel Roberts, died when she was but one year old. At fourteen years of age she was left an orphan, and soon after began the supreme struggle of her life, to relieve the darkness that subsequently folded its sable wings about her. When her sight began to fail she was a pupil in Mrs. Willard's Seminary, Troy, NY, where she lived with her widowed mother. Not until the death of her mother, and she

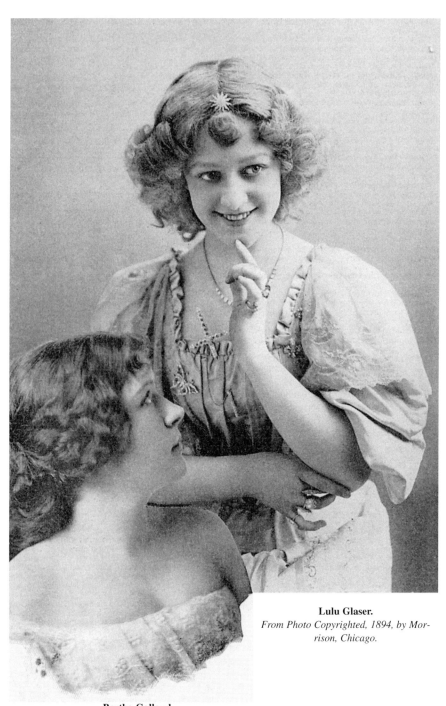

Lulu Glaser.
From Photo Copyrighted, 1894, by Morrison, Chicago.

Bertha Gallaud.
From Photo Copyrighted, 1896, by B. J. Falk, New York.

began to realize the stern fact that she was alone in the world, did she yield herself to that grief which, combined with arduous application to study, produced severe inflammation in her eyes, aggravated by shedding tears. She was thereafter unable to resume her studies, her fondest hope, and the anxious desire of her sympathizing friend and teacher, Mrs. Willard. At twenty-one years of age Miss Roberts became the wife of Fred Gorton, a prosperous paper manufacturer. Six years after, during a most painful and lingering illness, the pall of darkness encompassed her, and she was blind. With the return of physical strength the natural powers of her mind became active and prolific. One of her first efforts was the successful rehearsal of an original poem, entitled "Adolphus and Olivia, or a Tale of Kansas." That she performed with great acceptance to her audience. Her oratorical powers were unusual, and her remarkable memory enabled her to recite for one-and-a-half hours a poem of historical and tragic interest. For the last twenty years Mrs. Gorton has lectured many times before large and enthusiastic audiences. She has written many serials, stories and poems for the Detroit "Christian Herald" and other papers and periodicals. For the last fifteen years she has proved herself an expert with the type-writer. Being a member of the Shut-in Band, this accomplishment has enabled her to extend her efforts in blessing the lives of others, by sending loving words and sympathy to many lonely hearts. Her home is in Fenton, MI. During her long literary career she has become widely known as "Ida Glenwood," this being her chosen pen-name. She has also been called "The Sweet Singer" and "The Blind Bard of Michigan."

GOUGAR, Mrs. Helen M., orator and woman suffragist, born in Litchfield, MI, 18th July, 1843. From her earliest years Mrs. Gougar has been an intense and unflinching enthusiast for the right. At forty years of age her hair was prematurely whitened by a bitter and hard-fought attempt to weaken her power, in political circles, by defamation, but, the battle over and her enemies completely vanquished, she goes on unflinchingly and contests heroically for what she believes to be the right and patriotic course to a higher civilization. In this battle she decided forever the right of women to take an active part in political warfare without being compelled to endure defamation. As a speaker she is earnest, easy, dignified and at times impassionedly eloquent, wholly without affectation or oratorical display. She speaks without manuscript or notes, rapidly and convincingly. Her special work in reforms is in legal and political lines, and constitutional law and statistics she quotes with marvelous familiarity, when speaking in public. She has been repeatedly called upon to address special committees in Congress, also the legislatures of Indiana, Illinois, Nebraska, Iowa, New York, Wisconsin and Kansas. She recognizes the historical fact that popular governments are overthrown by corrupt municipalities. She believes that the "home vote" is the only power that can control the proletariat mob of large cities, and this causes her to espouse woman suffrage on the platform and with a forcible pen. Mrs. Gougar is the author of the law granting municipal suffrage to the women of Kansas, and the adoption of the measure was largely due to her efforts. She proved the correctness of her theory by redeeming Leavenworth, the largest city in the State at that time, from slum rule by the votes of women. The success which has attended that law, in the interest of political honor and the exaltation of public service, is well known. As a writer she is concise, direct and fluent. She was for many years a contributor to the "Inter-Ocean" and is still held in high esteem by the management of that Republican organ, notwithstanding her radical Prohibition party affiliation. As a businesswoman she is thorough, prompt and systematic; as a companion, cheerful, witty, voluble. In her domestic life she is happy and fortunate, the wife of a man of wealth, education and refinement, a successful lawyer, respected and beloved by all who know him, and whose affectionate sympathy, self-poise and financial independence have sustained her in the aggressive methods peculiar to her public work. Their home in Lafayette, IN, is one of unusual elegance and comfort. Although childless, both she and her husband are fond of children and young people, and they are seldom without a youthful guest in the house, the children of her five sisters, or other relatives or friends, and sometimes a waif of charity, who share the cheery hospitality of their elegant surroundings.

GOULD, Miss Elizabeth Porter, critic and author, born in Manchester-by-the-sea, MA, 8th June, 1848. She is the daughter of John A. and Elizabeth C. Gould, and is descended from generations of worthy Essex county people, including the famous schoolmaster, Ezekiel Cheever. Had she never given to the public any other work than her "Gems from Walt Whitman" (Philadelphia, 1889), she would be entitled to a lasting place in the literary world. No word said of the poet has brought a deeper expression of thanks from him than the essay in the book on his life among the soldiers. Her essays on education during the past ten years have been valuable additions to the educational thought of the day. One, "John Adams as a Schoolmaster," published in pamphlet form, attracted the notice of the leading educators of the country. Through the courtesy of Charles Francis Adams, who called it a most thorough piece of historical work, it has been placed in the leading libraries of the land. Another, "Daniel Webster as a Schoolmaster," with other articles on that great statesman, gave her an honorary membership in the Webster Historical Society. Those on "Robert College" and "Bulgaria under Alexander," the former the only full account of that American institution on the Bosphorus ever written, brought her most complimentary words from the ex-Prince himself. Others, such as, "Friedrich Froebel," "School Life in China," "The Steele Orphanage in Chattanooga" and "The Woman Problem," have become authority on those subjects. The versatility of Miss Gould's mind, as well as her conscientious research, are seen in articles published in the Chicago "Law Times," the New York "Critic," "Literary World," "Independent," "Christian Union," "New England Magazine," "Woman's Journal," and other periodicals. Her article in the "Century," in 1889, on Pundita Ramabai, was but an outline of the lecture which, with those on Abigail Adams, Hannah Adams, Mary Somerville and Caroline Herschel, has brought her as an interesting lecturer before the chief woman's clubs in Boston and vicinity. Besides having inspired clubs in the city of her long residence, Chelsea, MA, she has been, and still is, an intellectual power among the society women of Boston, Brookline, Newton and other places, by her "Talks on Current Events." Besides her unique work in private circles, Miss Gould, as an officer in philanthropic organizations in Boston and Chelsea, has struck important chords for more efficient work, especially in the line of reform. Her brochure, "How I became a Woman Suffragist," is a book of personal experience. She has written poetry, a volume of her verse, "Stray Pebbles from the Shores of Thought" (Boston, 1892), having been recently published. She has a novel ready for the press.

GOULD, Miss Ellen M., philanthropist, born at The Hope, near Providence, RI, 7th January, 1848. Her father, Daniel Gould, was born in Middletown, RI, where his ancestors settled in 1637. Her mother, an Earle, descended from the Chases, who were the earliest settlers of Nantucket, was born in Providence. Both parents are of unmixed English lineage, and both are by birth and education Quakers. The father of Ellen is the eighth in the direct line of descent who has borne the name of Daniel Gould. In 1852 the family removed to Providence, where they remained till 1857, when they made a final remove to Davenport, IA. During the stormy decades in the middle of the century, Mr. and Mrs. Gould took an active part in the progressive movements of the time, especially the abolition of slavery. Their three daughters have inherited a like interest in the philanthropic efforts of the present. This has been especially the case with Ellen. Although naturally of a strong literary bent, a systematic training in that direction was rendered impossible by delicate health in early youth and by the imperative nature of home duties. Yet, so eager has been her thirst for knowledge and so persistent her efforts in making the most of every opportunity for self improvement offered, that no one but herself can discover any deficiency. She has contributed short stories to children's magazines, and has also contributed able papers to the various societies of which she is a member. Her sympathies were enlisted during the Civil War in a Soldier's Aid Society. She was the only young girl member, and she was sent as a delegate to one of the large sanitary fairs. She has been a member of the Unitarian Church of Davenport from its first organization and at a critical period in its history did much to restore its prosperity. Always an advocate of woman suffrage, she has done all in her power to promote its interests. With the help of a friend she organized the first and only suffrage association in Davenport. She has been for many years a member of the Library Association and also of the Academy of Science, but circumstances have hindered her from taking an active part in the work of either. She organized a literary club for young women, which had a very successful course for six years. It was called the Bric-a-Brac Society, and it aided in a very substantial way several important enterprises. She has been a most energetic member of the Ladies' Benevolent Society, and also of the Association for the Advancement of Women, and of the Ramabai Association. For six years she was directress of an industrial school for poor children, having worked as a teacher for two years. After a careful personal examination of the working of such schools in the East, she was able, with the aid of others, to systematize and give to the school such plans that few changes have since been necessary. In 1887, with the aid of a generous friend, she organized a cooking school, which proved so successful that in the following year it was incorporated into the public school system. To the two last mentioned enterprises she has given much time and strength gratuitously. Circumstances in her home have obliged her of late to give up all public work with the exception of that connected with the church, called the Post-Office Mission, the duties of which can be performed quietly at home. In this mission she has been a pioneer worker.

GOWER, Mrs. Lillian Norton, opera singer, widely known by her stage-name, "Lillian Nordica," born in Farmington, ME, in 18—. When she was five years old, her parents removed to Boston, MA, where she studied in the New England Conservatory of Music. After graduating she made an extensive concert tour of the United States, singing with the Händel and Haydn Society and with Theodore Thomas's Orchestra. She visited Europe with Gilmore's Band, and there won distinction as a singer. She decided to remain in Europe and to prepare for an operatic career. She studied in Milan with San Giovanni. In six weeks she learned ten operas completely. She sang in opera in Brescia, Aquila and Genoa. In St. Petersburg, Russia, she won her first great triumph as Filina in "Mignon." In 1881 she went to Paris. She made her début in that city as Marguerite in Gounod's "Faust," where she scored one of the most brilliant triumphs on record. Mrs. Gower is not only a great singer, but a great actor as well. She sang in Her Majesty's Theater, in London, England, for three years. She returned to the United States with the reputation of one of the great queens of the lyric stage. She has a repertory of forty grand operas at her command. She became the wife, in London, of Mr. Gower, a man of wealth. Her husband disappeared in a tragic manner. He made a balloon ascension from Paris, and balloon and men were never heard from afterward. Mrs. Norton's latest triumphs have been won in Covent Garden, London.

GOZA, Miss Anne, humorist, born in Hatchett Creek, AL, 4th July, 1872. Her home has always been in her native town, excepting the time spent in school. Although one of the very youngest of the rising writers of the South, Miss Goza has already acquired a wide reputation as a writer of humorous and dialect stories. She has chosen the dialect of the people of the Alabama mountains, and she has made skillful use of that peculiarly interesting jargon. She is a regular contributor to the Burlington "Hawkeye," the Atlanta "Sunny South," the Cleveland "Plain Dealer," the New Orleans "Times Democrat," and many other prominent journals. Her success has been marked and remarkable. She is a prolific writer, and in the quaint people around her she has abundant material for her future work. She is distinctly original, and her sketches record much that will be of interest to the future students of American folk-lore. She has published one volume, "The Fall of Queen Prudence."

GRANBERY, Miss Virginia, artist, born in Norfolk, VA. When she was a child, her parents moved to New York, where they have resided ever since. She early showed a fondness for drawing, but, as there was no drawing taught in the schools, she did not have the benefit of instruction. She learned to copy engravings and made several drawings from casts, without a teacher. After she was grown, she went to the Cooper Institute for a short time, spending a part of each day under the instruction of A. F. Bellows in his studio, where she worked in colors. She studied in the Academy of Design school in the antique, portrait and life classes, and received honorable mention for a drawing. She began to paint fruits and flowers from nature, many of which have been chromoed by Prang, of Boston. From 1871 to 1882 she was teacher of the art department of the Packer Institute, Brooklyn. NY. On entering the Packer Institute she received the same salary as her predecessor, but at the end of the first year her method had doubled the number of pupils, and she had offers from other large schools that wished to secure her services. The board of trustees decided to increase her salary fifty per cent, and also gave her a further substantial recognition of their appreciation of her services in a check for a handsome amount, accompanied by a very complimentary letter. The department increased so that an assistant was necessary. After eleven years of work she broke down under the constant demand on her strength, and was obliged to send in her resignation. She and her sisters were among the very few women artists whose work was accepted with that of the men to be exhibited in the Centennial of 1876, in Philadelphia. Recently she has devoted herself principally to portraits. She is very successful in painting small pictures of children. She has shown pictures in all the principal exhibitions thoughout the United States.

GRANGER, Miss Lottie E., educator and school officer, born near Granville, OH, 28th January, 1858. Her father, Sylvester Granger, was of New England descent, and her mother, Elizabeth Walrath, of German origin. Village and country schools afforded sufficient tuition to Miss Granger to enable her to begin teaching at the age of sixteen years. For three consecutive summers she followed teaching, when her desire to add to her education had become so great that she made for herself a way to gratify this ambition. Through the cooperation of the president of Shepardson College, then Young Ladies' Institute, she was enabled to complete a classical course of study in that excellent institution, deserving a medal for her brave and sterling character as well as a diploma for her mental proficiency. She was graduated in 1880, and spent the following year in Kansas, and the next five years in Shenandoah, IA, occupied with the duties of the school-room. In 1886, having been elected to the office of county superintendent of the public schools of Page county, she held the position for six years, and by the excellence of her work made for herself a name that is State-wide among educators. At the annual meeting of the Iowa State Teachers' Association, held in Des Moines in 1888, she was unanimously elected president, being the second woman ever chosen to fill that honorable place during the thirty-five years of the organization. She has also been a member of the Educational Council, which is the senate of the teachers' association. From its organization she has served on the board of managers of the Iowa State Teachers' Reading Circle. She is an active Sunday-school and temperance worker, is a Chautauqua graduate, a ready speaker, a forcible writer and of magnetic presence on the platform. Declining a fourth term of service as county superintendent, Miss Granger, never being satisfied with present attainments, will pursue a post-graduate course of study in the Chicago University. Since her election to office, her home has been in Clarinda, IA, where she is a member of the household of Mr. and Mrs. Edwin Henshaw. The names of Mrs. Henshaw and Miss Granger are almost synonymous in Page county as an ardent friendship has taken them together into every township where political canvass, school visitation and temperance work have made their interests common. Being of an unassuming disposition, Miss Granger seldom passes, on chance acquaintance, at her true worth. A close observer, however, will discover beneath her unpretentiousness an equipoise of character, a cool decisive judgment, a penetrating eye and an activity of thought.

GRANT, Mrs. Julia Dent, wife of General Ulysses S. Grant, the eighteenth President of the United States, born in St. Louis, MO, 26th January, 1826. She is a daughter of Frederick and Ellen Wrenshall Dent. Her grandfather, Capt. George Dent, led the forlorn hope in Fort Montgomery, when it was stormed by Mad Anthony Wayne. On her mother's side she is descended from John Wrenshall, an English Puritan who settled in Philadelphia, PA. She began to attend Miss Moreau's boarding-school in 1836, and she remained in that school until 1844. Returning home in that year, she met Lieutenant U. S. Grant, then stationed in Jefferson Barracks, in St. Louis. She became his wife 22nd August, 1848. They lived in Detroit, MI, until 1852 and then went to Sackett's Harbor, NY, where Captain Grant was stationed. When Captain Grant was ordered to California, Mrs. Grant returned to St. Louis, her health not being strong enough to endure so great a change of climate. During the Civil War she remained much of the time near her husband. She was with him in City Point in the winter of 1864 and 1865, and she accompanied him to Washington when he returned with his victorious army. She for eight years filled the arduous position of mistress of the White House in a most charming manner. Her régime was marked by dignity, simplicity and home-like ways that endeared her to all who came into contact with her. She accompanied her husband around the earth. After General Grant's death, Congress voted her a pension of $5,000 a year. Her family consists of three children, Frederick Dent Grant, Ulysses S. Grant, Jr., and Mrs. Nellie Sartoris. She now lives in New York City, occupied much of the time with literary labors.

GRASER, Miss Hulda Regina, customhouse broker, born in Montreal, Canada, 23rd June, 1869. In 1870 the family removed to Chicago, IL, where, in the great fire of 1871, they lost all their property and nearly lost their lives. Her father, Ernst G. Graser, was a native of St. Gallen, Switzerland, where he was born in 1842. He came to America in 1867 and settled in Montreal. Her mother was a resident of Zurich, Switzerland. After the loss of their home and property in Chicago, the family went to Cincinnati, OH, where they began life anew. Mr. Graser, who was a thoroughly educated man and could speak several languages well, secured employment with the government. He also gave private instruction in foreign languages. He remained in the custom-house ten years, after which time, in 1882, he opened what is called a customs brokerage business, and one year prior to his death, which occurred in 1884, he took into partnership with him his older daughter, styling the firm E. & M. Graser. After his death the daughter continued the business until her marriage, in 1885, to Dr. E. H. Rothe, when she sold it. Hulda, the younger daughter, was educated in the Cincinnati free schools, and in 1885 she was employed as clerk and then as cashier in a wholesale and retail notion house. She afterward studied stenography, did some reporting and helped on the senatorial investigation, in the above capacity, and in the fall of 1886, when seventeen years old, opened a new office as customs broker and forwarder, her sister's successor having sold out to her present competitor. In 1887, about five months after she commenced, there was a decision by the department, on the strength of false representations made to the department, prohibiting brokers or their clerks from getting any information from customs officials without an order from the different importers, thus making her beginning doubly hard. That necessitated her calling upon every importer in the city, securing his signature to a petition asking for any and all information regarding each firm's importations. In 1890, in connection with brokerage, she took up an agency for tin-plates, and she handles large quantities of that article. The greater amount of tin-plates arriving at Cincinnati between January and July, 1891, went through her office, and her undertaking has proved very successful. She occupies a unique position, and her success in that arduous line of work is another demonstration of the truth that women can conduct business that exacts great care, sound judgment, originality and untiring industry.

GRAVES, Mrs. Adelia C., educator and author, born in Kingsville, OH, 17th March, 1821. She is the wife of Dr. Z. C. Graves, a noted educator both north and south, founder and for forty years president of Mary Sharp College, in Winchester, TN. She is the daughter of Dr. Daniel M. Spencer and Manan T. Cook, and a niece of P. R. Spencer, the originator of the Spencerian system of penmanship. The mother of Mrs. Graves was a woman of fine intellect. Her people were wealthy and cultured, all the men having for generations had the benefit of collegiate education. Her father especially excelled in the Greek and Latin languages. Perhaps one of the most critical linguists of the time was his youthful granddaughter. For years she taught classes of young men in languages in the Kingsville Academy, who desired her instructions in preference to all others. Many of them have since attained positions as lawyers, ministers, physicians, presidents and professors of colleges. The present president of Beyrout College, in Syria, Asia Minor, was for some time a student with her, especially in the Latin language. Mrs. Graves may be said to have inherited the poetic temperament from both sides of the house. The Mary Sharp College under Dr. Graves' presidency acquired a national reputation, and he avers that its success was owing quite as much to her wise counsels and management as to his own efforts. There were few positions in the college she did not, at some time, occupy, save that of mathematics. For thirty-two years she was matron and professor of rhetoric, belles-lettres, elocution and English composition, at different times, as need be, teaching French, ancient history and ancient geography, English literature, or whatever else was required. The published works of Mrs. Graves are "Seclusaval, or the Arts of Romanism" (Memphis, TN, 1870), a work written to deter Protestants from sending children to Catholic schools, and "Jephtha's Daughter," a drama, (Memphis, 1867). Besides these are two prize stories. Twelve or thirteen small volumes were also compiled from the Southern Child's Book, at the request of the Southern Baptist Sabbath School Union, for the use of Sabbath-schools. Mrs. Graves for years edited and wrote for that publication. She wrote the "Old Testament Catechism in Rhyme" (Nashville, TN, 1859), on request of the same society, for the use of the colored people while still slaves, for which she received twenty cents a line, they, her employers,

saying, they knew of no one else that could do it. Her unpublished poems are numerous. Mrs. Graves has found a place in "Woman in Sacred Song," and "Southland Poets," and she is mentioned in the "Successful Men of Tennessee" for her extraordinary financial ability, having managed a business of fifteen-thousand to twenty-thousand dollars per year for years at a time, most successfully.

GRAVES, Miss Mary H., Unitarian minister, born in North Reading, MA, 12th September, 1839. Her parents were Eben Graves and Hannah M. Campbell Graves. Her maternal ancestors, the Campbells and Moores, were descendants of the Scotch-Irish settlers of Londonderry, NH. Mary was graduated from the State Normal School, Salem, MA, in February, 1860 She taught in the public schools of her native town and of South Danvers, now Peabody, MA. She was inclined to literature and wrote for the "Ladies' Repository and other journals. She took a theological course of study under Rev. Olympia Brown in Weymouth, MA, and in Bridgeport, CT, preaching occasionally in the neighboring towns. In the summer of 1869 she supplied the pulpit of the Universalist Church in North Reading, MA. In the summer of 1870 she preached in Earlville, IL. On December, 14th, 1871, she was regularly ordained as pastor of the Unitarian Church in Mansfield, MA, having already preached one year for that society. In 1882 she had pastoral charge of the Unitarian Society in Baraboo, WI. She has done some missionary work in the West, mainly in Illinois and adjoining States. In 1885 and 1886, while living in Chicago, she assisted in the conduct of "Manford's Magazine," acting as literary editor. For one year she was secretary of the Women's Western Unitarian Conference. At present her strength is not sufficient to allow her to do the full work of the ministry, and she is devoting herself to literary work. She contributes occasionally to the "Christian Register," the "Commonwealth," the Boston "Transcript," the "Leader" and other journals.

GRAY, Mrs. Jennie T., temperance worker, born in Pilot Grove, IA, 16th September, 1857. Her father, Stephen Townsend, was of English descent. Her mother was of Welsh and English descent. She was reared in the faith of the Quaker Church. From her father she inherited literary taste and ability, and from her mother a fearless firmness for the right. She always showed an intense love for books and at an early age made herself acquainted with a large number of the best authors. From Iowa her father removed with his family in the spring of 1865 to Fountain City, IN, near the place of his nativity, where the remainder of her childhood was spent. She and her older sisters identified themselves early in life with the temperance cause, and they are still active, enthusiastic workers in the Woman's Christian Temperance Union. She became the wife of Dr. C. F. Gray, of Winchester, IN, 18th December, 1878. Her husband not only encourages her in every good word and work, but supplies with lavish hand all the financial assistance which she may feel called upon to bestow in any good cause. She consecrated herself wholly to Christian work in the spring of 1889, and since then she has been led into more active service in the line of temperance. At present she is president of the Woman's Christian Temperance Union of Randolph county, IN. In all her travels from ocean to ocean and gulf to lakes she has tried to carry the strongest possible influence for temperance, often finding suitable occasions for advocating her theme in a modest but convincing way.

GRAY, Mrs. Mary Tenney, editorial writer and philanthropist, born in Brookdale, Liberty township, Susquehanna county, PA, 19th June, 1833, and became a citizen of Kansas by adoption. Her fitness as a leader in the struggles and labors of the new State was the result of a thorough training in her father's theological library, supplemented by a course of study in the Ingalls Seminary, Binghamton, NY, and continued in a Pennsylvania seminary. After she was graduated, she was for several years preceptress in Binghamton Academy. On the editorial staff of the New York

"Teacher" for two years her influence was felt among the teachers of the State. After she became the wife of Judge Barzillai Gray in 1859, and her removal to Wyandotte, Kansas Territory, and afterward to Leavenworth, she entered upon many enterprises in the line of charities, church extension, the upbuilding of State and county expositions, and was a prominent mover in the Centennial exhibit for Kansas in Philadelphia in 1876. She was a contributor or correspondent to the leading magazines and papers of Kansas and to the eastern press. The orphan asylum in Leavenworth was debtor to the appeals of her pen for recognition and assistance. The "Home Record," of the same city, was an outgrowth and exponent of her deep and abiding interest in the welfare and elevation of women. The compilation of the Kansas "Home Cook Book," for the benefit of the Home for the Friendless, was and is still a source of financial strength to the institution, more than ten-thousand copies having been sold. She has been for twenty years one of the officers of the board of control for the Home. As editor of the home department of the "Kansas Farmer" for some years she showed both sympathy and interest in a class who by force of circumstances are largely debarred from intellectual pursuits. As one of the original founders and first president of the Social Science Club of Kansas and Western Missouri, she has given an impetus to intellectual culture in those localities, and through skill, tact and personal influence has seen the organization grow from a small number to a membership of five-hundred of the brightest women of the two States. To these labors have been added scientific attainments unusual among women, and artistic work of much merit.

GREATOREX, Mrs. Eliza, artist, born in Manor Hamilton, Ireland, 25th December, 1819. She was the daughter of Rev. James Calcott Pratt, who removed to New York in 1840. Eliza became the wife, in 1849, of Henry Wellington Greatorex, the musician. After marriage she studied art with William H. Witherspoon and James Hart, in New York, with Emile Lambinet, in Paris, and with the instructors in the Pinakothek, in Munich. In 1879 she studied etching with C. H. Toussaint. She visited Europe in 1861 and 1870, spending several years, studying in Italy and Germany. In 1868 she was made a member of the National Academy of Design, in New York City. She was the first woman member of that organization, and she was the first woman to belong to the Artists' Fund Society, of New York. Her reputation as an artist rests largely on her pen-and-ink sketches, many of which have appeared in book form, filling four large volumes. She has painted many notable pictures in oil. Her work is of a singularly great quality. Her home is in New York City. Her two daughters have inherited her artistic talents.

GREEN, Anna Katharine, see ROHLFS, ANNA KATHARINE GREEN.

GREEN, Mrs. Julia Boynton,
poet, born in South Byron, Genesee county, NY, 25th May, 1861. When she was fifteen years old, she and her older sister entered Ingham University, in LeRoy, NY, where they remained a year as students. Another year was spent by both in preparation for Wellesley College. After entering that institution, they were called home on account of domestic bereavement. Their interrupted course of study was continued for several years, chiefly in Nyack-on-the-Hudson, and Miss Boynton afterward passed two winters in New York in the study of art, for which she has marked talent. She spent a season in London, England, and in 1888 she was preparing for an extended tour in Europe, when she was called home by the illness of her mother. Since then both her parents have died. In June, 1890, Miss Boynton became the wife of Levi Worthington Green, and after a six-months' tour in Europe they made their home in Rochester, NY. Necessarily, her literary work has been seriously disturbed by so many changes and diversions, but Mrs. Green has found time to write some strikingly excellent poetry. Most of her work has appeared in local journals and in the Boston "Transcript." She has published one volume of poems, "Lines and Interlines" (New York, 1887).

GREEN, Mrs. Mary E., physician, born in Machias, NY, 6th August, 1844. Both her parents were of New England stock. They moved to Michigan, when she was very young, and with limited means they were obliged to endure all the hardships of pioneer life. As there were no brothers in the family, little Mary worked both indoors and outdoors, preferring the latter, until, the little house being built and a few acres about it cleared, she was allowed to think about education. She went to a neighbor's, several miles distant, where she worked for her board and began to attend school At fourteen years of age she passed the required examination and began to teach, her salary being two dollars a week, with the privilege of boarding round. She was soon able to enter Olivet College. There she earned her own way, chiefly by doing housework, and partially so in Oberlin College, which she attended later. While yet in her teens, she realized the necessity of choosing some life work for herself, and as she desired to pursue the study of medicine, she quietly determined to do so. Undaunted by the criticism of her friends, in 1865, after one year's study with a physician, Miss Green entered the New York Medical College. She was soon chosen assistant in the chemical laboratory, and besides that work, every evening found her, knife in hand, making the dissections to be used on the following day by the demonstrator of anatomy. She entered Bellevue Hospital and remained there, in spite of the hisses and insults which the students felt in duty bound to offer any of the "weaker" sex who presumed to cross their pathway. Miss Green's thorough womanliness, as much as her stronger qualities, won her cause. On account of its hospital advantages, the next year she entered the Woman's Medical College in Philadelphia, and for two years was an interne of the hospital. In 1868 she was graduated from that college with honor, her thesis being entitled "Medical Jurisprudence." Two years before graduation Dr. Green became the wife of her cousin, Alonzo Green, then a practicing lawyer in New York, whither she went in 1868 and engaged in active practice. Outside of office hours Dr. Green's time was occupied with charitable work, as she was visiting physician to the Midnight Mission, the Five Points Mission, Dr. Blackwell's Infirmary and the Prison Home for Women. By personal effort she organized and built up a large dispensary for women and children in a neglected quarter of the city, which was so successful that, after the first year in which over two-thousand patients were cared for, it received State and city support. Dr. Green's consulting physicians and surgeons were the most eminent in the city. In 1870 she delivered part of a course of lectures on medical subjects in connection with Dr. Elizabeth Blackwell, Dr. Willard Parker and others. The year after her graduation Dr. Green's name was presented for membership to the New York Medical Society, and after a stormy discussion she was admitted, being the first woman in America to win that opportunity for broader work. Soon after, she became a member of the Medico-Legal Society. Wishing to pursue a higher course in the study of chemistry, she applied for admission to Columbia College, but her request was not granted. She entered upon a course of evening lectures given by Professor Chandler in the College of Pharmacy, and, although she could not graduate, as she was a woman, the coveted knowledge was gained. During those years of constant mental and physical work Dr. Green became the mother of two children. She removed in 1873 to Charlotte, MI, where she now resides. There three more little ones came into her family. Several years ago she took up wood-carving in Cincinnati. While in New York, she attended the Cooper Institute lectures regularly, and was otherwise interested in both literary and art work. Dr. Green has been twice elected health officer of the city in which she lives, and has three times been elected delegate to the American Medical Association by the State Medical Society.

GREENE, Mrs. Belle C., author, born in Pittsfield, VT, 17th March, 1844. Her maiden name was Colton, and her descent is a mixture of American, English and Indian. One of her ancestors on her father's side married an Indian princess belonging to a Massachusetts tribe, and settled in that State. Her mother, Lucy Baker, came from Puritan stock. She died at the age of forty-seven, leaving her husband and a family of six girls. Isabel, who was next to the youngest, was but four years old at the time. She was taken into the family of a distant relative living in a New Hampshire country town, where she was reared and educated in strictest orthodox ways. In 1868 she became the wife of M. B. V. Greene, of

Nashua, NH, where she has since made her home. It was not till the year 1881 that Mrs. Greene began her literary work in earnest. She sent a short story and a humorous sketch to her friend, Mrs. Phelps-Ward, then Miss Phelps, asking for advice and encouragement. Miss Phelps replied with characteristic honesty and kindness that Mrs. Greene's voice was doubtless her one great gift, and, as mortals were seldom blest with two, she advised her to stick to music, but added, since she must give an opinion, that she considered the humorous sketch better than the story. Upon this scanty encouragement Mrs. Greene offered the humorous sketch to "Godey's Lady's Book," and it was accepted. She continued to furnish sketches for a year or more, and concluded her work for the magazine by writing her first story proper, a novelette, afterward published in book form under the title "A New England Idyl." "Adventures of an Old Maid," a second book, was a collection of humorous sketches published first in the magazines, and has had a sale of over seventy-five-thousand copies. Her religious novel, "A New England Conscience," attracted wide comment. Though severely denounced by some of the critics, it was regarded by others as a masterpiece of condensed thought and realistic character drawing. In 1887–88 Mrs. Greene made an extended tour of southern California and the Pacific Coast, and during her stay of several months in Los Angeles and San Diego she contributed to the newspapers a series of humorous sketches founded upon the phases of the boom, which added greatly to her reputation as a humorous writer. These last mentioned articles constitute her only newspaper work, with the exception of the "Mill Papers," regarding the operatives in the cotton-mills, written for the Boston "Transcript" in 1883 and 1884. Mrs. Greene's success thus far has been largely as a short-story writer. Her family consists of her husband and one son.

GREENE, Miss Frances Nimmo, educator, born in Tuscaloosa, AL, in the late sixties. She is known to the public as "Dixie." She is descended through her father from an old South Carolina family, and through her mother from the best Virginia stock. Her mother's family have been literary in taste for several generations. Miss. Greene received her education in Tuscaloosa Female College, where she made an excellent record for earnestness and intelligence. Since leaving school she has made teaching her profession. While teaching in a mining town in north Alabama, she first conceived the idea of writing sketches for publication. Her first attempt, "Yankees in Dixie," was promptly accepted by the Philadelphia "Times." Since that time she has contributed to that paper many letters on southern affairs. She also writes for the Birmingham "Age Herald" and other southern papers. She has directed her efforts as a writer toward bringing about a better state of feeling between the sections by giving the people of the North a correct understanding of the negro and his condition, and also of the temper of the southern whites. Besides writing in prose, she sometimes writes verse, but has published only one poem.

GREENE, Mrs. Louisa Morton, reformer and author, born in Ashburnham, MA, 23rd May, 1819. She is a descendant from sturdy New England ancestors. Her father, Henry Willard, blacksmith and farmer, removed from Vermont and settled in Ashburnham in the early years of the present century. Bereft of both parents in early childhood, she was deprived of schooling and thrown upon her own resources at the age of thirteen years. She obtained employment in a woolen factory in Dedharn, MA, and worked for several years for the pittance of one to two dollars per week and board, working fourteen hours a day. There, upon the heads of bobbins, she learned to write. Notwithstanding her long hours of labor, she found time for constant improvement by reading and study. Her habits of strict economy enabled her to save a portion of her wages, and at the age of seventeen she had one-hundred-fifty dollars in the bank. Then came her first revolt against the injustice shown to women in industrial pursuits. Gross discrimination in the matter of wages was made, simply on the ground of sex. Called upon at one time to take a man's place at a spindle, she performed her duties with greater dispatch and to the acknowledged satis-

faction of her employer. When pay-day came around and she demanded the same compensation that the man had been securing, her request was received with amazement. The plucky young girl stood her ground and refused to return to the spindle unless paid at the same rate as the man whose place she was filling. She was promptly dismissed from the factory, to be recalled a few weeks later at increased wages. In 1840 she taught school near Portsmouth, NH. There she formed the acquaintance of Jonas Greene, of Maine, becoming his wife in 1841. Mr. Greene subsequently became a prominent politician, representing his district in each branch of the State legislature for several successive terms. His success in life he ascribed largely to the coöperation and support of his prudent, intelligent and broadminded wife. Removing with her husband to the then somewhat sparsely settled Oxford county, ME, a new and active life opened for her. While performing faithfully her duties, she found time to enter vigorously into the philanthropic and reform work of the times. Early becoming a convert to the "Water Cure" system of treating the sick, she familiarized herself with it and soon developed a remarkable ability for the care and treatment of the sick. Physicians and medicines were unknown in her household, and her skill was in demand in the community. In 1850 Mrs. Greene began to espouse the anti-slavery cause. She, with a few kindred spirits, gathered the country women together and organized anti-slavery societies. Literature was distributed, "Uncle Tom's Cabin" was read far and near, and many stirring articles from her pen appeared in the local papers, and sentiment against the system was rapidly created. During the Civil War Mrs. Greene's patriotic labors were untiring. When hospital supplies were called for, she spent much time in collecting, preparing and forwarding them. Mrs. Greene's newspaper contributions for years covered a wide range of subjects. The temperance and suffrage causes were early championed by her and have ever commanded her best service of pen and voice. In 1869 she removed with her family to Manassas, VA, where her husband died in 1873. With advancing years, Mrs. Greene has withdrawn largely from active philanthropic work.

GREENE, Miss Mary A., lawyer, born in Warwick, RI, 14th June, 1857. She is a lineal descendant of Roger Williams, and also of John Greene, the founder of the famous Greene family of Rhode Island, prominent in the military and civic affairs of the State and the nation. Her Revolutionary ancestor, Colonel Christopher Greene, the gallant defender of Red Bank on the Delaware, was a cousin of General Nathaniel Greene. Miss Greene began the study of law in 1885, in order to be able to manage her own business affairs and to assist other women to do the same. She took the full course of three years in the Boston University Law School, graduating in 1888 with the degree of Bachelor of Laws, magna cam laude, being the third woman to graduate from the school. She was at once admitted to the Suffolk bar, in Boston, becoming thus the second woman member of the Massachusetts bar. After practicing eighteen months in Boston, she returned to her native State. She now resides in Providence, where she is engaged in the work of writing and lecturing upon legal topics. Always frail in constitution, Miss Greene found herself unable to endure the strain of court practice, although she was successful in that line of work. For that reason she has never applied for admission to the Rhode Island bar, her standing at the Boston bar being sufficient for the kind of work she is at present doing. She is a regular lecturer upon business law for women in Lasell Seminary, Auburnbale, MA, the first girls' school to give systematic instruction in principles of law. Among her literary productions are a translation from the French of Dr. Louis Frank's essay, "The Woman Lawyer," which appeared in the Chicago "Law Times," and the original articles: "Privileged Communications in the Suits between Husband and Wife," in the "American Law Review"; "The Right of American Women to Vote and Hold Public Office," in the Boston "Evening Traveller"; "A Woman Lawyer," and a series of articles upon "Practical Points of Every-Day Law," in the "Chautauquan." Miss Greene is firmly impressed with the importance to all women of a practical knowledge of the principals of business law, and in all her professional work she endeavors to educate her hearers and readers in those most necessary matters. As a public speaker she is very successful. She always speaks without notes and with great fluency and felicity.

At the fortieth anniversary of the first woman's rights convention, celebrated in Boston in January, 1891, Miss Greene was invited to speak for "Women in Law" as the representative of that profession. She is not, however, identified in any way with the woman suffrage movement, possessing, as she does, that spirit of conservatism mingled with independence which has always characterized the people of Rhode Island. She believes that her mission is to educate women to an intelligent use of the rights they possess, and that to others may be left the work of demanding further rights for her sex.

GREENLEAF, Mrs. Jean Brooks, woman suffragist, born in Bernardston, Franklin county, MA, 1st October, 1832. She is the daughter of John Brooks, M.D., and Mary Bascom Brooks. Dr. Brooks was a man of decided opinions, a liberal in both religion and politics, and had the courage of his convictions. His ideas were advanced, for his time, with regard to the training of his daughters for lives of usefulness and independence, and the cultivation of a habit of independent thought on matters of vital interest. Mrs. Brooks, a devoted mother, was very domestic in her taste, caring well for her household, and, although an invalid, actively alive in alleviating the wants of those less fortunate in life than herself. Jean was the youngest of the six children of Dr. Brooks who lived to advanced years. Her school life was limited to a few years in the public schools and academy of her native village, supplemented by two terms in Melrose Seminary, in West Brattleboro, VT. At the age of seventeen years the confirmed invalidism of her mother necessitated the ending of school life, and from that time until her marriage, three years later, she assumed largely the cares and duties of her father's household. Her interests in the rights and wrongs of woman was early awakened while listening to the spirited remonstrance of a widowed aunt, Mrs. Willard, against paying taxes upon property that she had acquired by her own exertions, when she had no representation at the polls, while a miserable drunkard in the neighborhood, who was supported by his wife and daughters, and who owned no property, was allowed to vote in opposition to what both she and the wife and daughters of the drunkard believed to be for the best interests of the community. Since 1862, the year of Mrs. Greenleaf's marriage to Halbert S. Greenleaf, her life has been passed quietly at home. Her husband has given both military and civil service to his country, having commanded the 52nd Massachusetts Volunteers in the late war for the Union, and is now serving his second term as member of Congress. He is in full sympathy with his wife in her views respecting the enfranchisement of women. The changes brought about by the war made a residence in Louisiana necessary for a few years, but for the last twenty-four years, Rochester, NY, has been the home of their adoption. The cause of woman suffrage is most dear to Mrs. Greenleaf. For its sake she is ready and happy to make all needful sacrifice. For the past three years she has been president of the Woman's Political Club of Rochester, and in December, 1890, was elected to succeed Mrs. Lillie Devereux Blake as the president of the New York State Woman's Suffrage Association.

GREENWOOD, Miss Elizabeth W., temperance reformer, born in Brooklyn, NY, in 1849. Her father was a lawyer. She was converted at the age of fourteen and turned from a fashionable life to her books and to philanthropic work. She was educated in Brooklyn Heights Seminary and was graduated in 1869. She took a post-graduate course and spent some time as a teacher in that school, giving instruction in the higher branches and weekly lectures to the junior and senior classes. When the Woman's Temperance Crusade opened, she enlisted at once. Her peculiar talents fitted her for good work for temperance, and she has been conspicuous in the white ribbon movement throughout the State and the nation. When scientific temperance instruction in the New York schools was being provided for, Miss Greenwood did important work with the legislature, as State superintendent of that department. She served as national superintendent of juvenile work. She has for years served as president of the Woman's Christian Temperance Union on the Hill in Brooklyn, as superintendent of its juvenile work, and as lecturer and evangelist. She spends her summers in the Berkshire Hills, MA, where she preaches on Sundays to large audiences. In 1888 she was made superintendent of the evangelistic department of the National Woman's Christian

Temperance Union. In 1889 she visited Europe, and there she continued her reform efforts.

GREENWOOD, Grace, see LIPPINCOTT, MRS. SARA JANE.

GREGORY, Mrs. Elizabeth Goadby, author, born in London, England, 25th April, 1834. She came to the United States when young. She is the only daughter of the late Dr. Henry Goadby, F. L. S., author of "Animal and Vegetable Physiology," and well known in the scientific world thirty years ago through his valuable original work in the field of microscopical investigation. Elizabeth Goadby became the wife, in 1855, of John Gregory, a civil engineer and author in Milwaukee, WI. She has since resided in that city, and was for eleven years a teacher in the Milwaukee public schools. Her name has been familiar in newspaper literature of the Northwest since 1861, when she first began to write for the press. She has written on industrial and social topics. As a translator of French and German, in the department of fiction and biography, she has done some excellent work. She has raised to manhood a family of three sons, two of whom are still living.

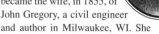

GREGORY, Mrs. Mary Rogers, artist, born in Apalachicola, FL, 6th May, 1846. Her maiden name was Mary Bland Rogers. Her father, Charles Rogers, was a prominent cotton merchant of Columbus, GA. Her paternal ancestors were distinguished Revolutionary heroes. Among them were the celebrated Platt family of Dutchess county, New York. One of them, Zephadiah Platt, was the first Senator elected by the State of New York to the first Congress of the United States. Another, Richard Platt, was aid-de-camp to General Montgomery at the fall of Quebec. On her mother's side she belongs to the Virginia families of Bland and Spottswood, and she is closely connected with the family of the artist Rembrandt Peele. She became the wife, at an early age, of Dr. John R. Gregory, of a well known Tallahassee, Fla., family. Mrs. Gregory is one of the most distinguished artists of the South. She has painted many portraits of prominent men and women. Among her best-known works are portraits of Hon. Ben. H. Hill, Judge James Jackson, Henry Grady and Mary E. Bryan. The legislature of Georgia paid her the high honor of appointing her to paint the full-length portraits of Hon. Alex. Stephens and Hon. Herschel V. Johnson. These pictures adorn the walls of the new capitol in Atlanta. She holds a life membership in the Academy of Fine Arts in Philadelphia, where she studied for several years. She also worked in Cooper Institute and has had training under several noted European artists.

GREW, Miss Mary, anti-slavery agitator and preacher, born in Hartford, CT, 1st September, 1813. Her childhood and early youth were spent there. In 1834 she removed to Boston, MA, and afterward to Philadelphia, PA, where she still resides. The principal work of her life has been performed in the interest of our colored population. By inheritance and training she was a radical Abolitionist. When the Boston Female Anti-Slavery Society was organized, she became a member of it. On her removal to Philadelphia she joined the Female Anti-Slavery Society of that city, became its corresponding secretary, and wrote its annual reports until 1870, when the society disbanded. She was a member of the Woman's Anti-Slavery Convention in 1838, which held its sessions in Pennsylvania Hall, surrounded by a furious mob, which destroyed the building by fire a few hours after the convention adjourned. Her public speaking was for many years confined to anti-slavery platforms almost exclusively. That cause demanded much of its advocates during the years when their number was few and the name of Abolitionist was counted odious in church and state. After slavery was abolished and the fifteenth amendment of the United States Constitution was ratified, she devoted her energies and time to other reforms, especially to the enfranchisement of women. She became a member of a Unitarian Church, in which there were no distinctions based upon sex. There she commenced the work of occasional preaching. She found the pulpits of Unitarian churches freely opened to her, and in northern New England also the pulpits of Freewill Baptists, Methodists and Congregational churches. She was one of the founders of the New Century Club, of Philadelphia. She was also one of the founders of the Pennsylvania Woman Suffrage Association, and is still its president.

GRIFFITH, Mrs. Eva Kinney, journalist and temperance worker, born in Whitewater, WI, 8th November, 1852. She is a daughter of Francis Kinney and Sophronia Goodrich Kinney. She was educated in the Whitewater State Normal School and as graduated in the class of 1871. She entered journalism and wrote for the Detroit "Free Press," "Pomeroy's Democrat," the Educational Weekly," the Cincinnati "Saturday Night" and many other journals. Overwork broke her health in 1878, and she was not able to resume her pen to any great extent until 1883. In 1879 she went to Kansas for her health. In 1880 she became the wife of Charles E. Griffith, and they moved to St. Louis, MO. The marriage proved a mistake. They separated, and Mrs. Griffith returned to Whitewater and entered the temperance field. She was made lecturer and organizer of the Wisconsin Woman's Christian Temperance Union for seven years. Her illustrated lectures won her the name of "Wisconsin Chalk Talker." She wrote temperance lessons and poems for the "Temperance Banner" and the "Union Signal." She has published a temperance novel, "A Woman's Evangel" (Chicago, 1892), and a volume named "Chalk Talk Hand-Book" (1887). In 1889 she published the "True Ideal," a journal devoted to social purity and faith studies. In 1891 she removed to Chicago, IL, where she became a special writer for the "Daily News-Record" and afterward society editor of the Chicago "Times." She is a regular contributor to the "Union Signal," writing the semi-monthly "Queen's Garden" for that journal.

GRIFFITH, Mrs. Mary Lillian, philanthropist and author, born in Germantown, Philadelphia, PA, 5th October, 1854, and died in Tamaqua, PA, in March, 1884. She was the only daughter of Thomas and Mary Thurlby. As a child she was devoted and conscientious. She attended the grammar-schools, and was graduated from the Normal School of Philadelphia. She accepted a position as teacher, and for herself and pupils pursued her ideals of highest culture. On 12th October, 1875, she became the wife of Rev. T. M. Griffith, pastor of the Cumberland Street Methodist Episcopal Church, of Philadelphia. She entered with zeal into work that appealed on every side to her sympathetic heart. In 1877 she was appointed secretary of the Ladies' and Pastors' Christian Union, a benevolent organization designed to call out the women of the churches to work among the people. She became deeply interested in moral educational work. Her tract, "Wifehood," which she printed and circulated privately, was so highly appreciated that, to meet the demand for it, another edition of a thousand copies was printed. The Moral Educational Society published a third edition, and the organ of that society, the "Alpha," gave it to the world with her name appended. She organized a local Woman's Christian Temperance Union, speaking and writing in behalf of that organization and other reform movements. Her articles attracted the attention of Miss Frances E. Willard, who urged her to take the national superintendency of the branch of work now known as "Heredity" in that society, which was then in the process of development. She accepted the arduous task and wrote a series of twelve papers, some in tract form, doing all that work in addition to her labors as a pastor's wife. Early in life she was led to adopt advanced opinions in relation to the position and rights of women. She was often impelled to speak and write in behalf of her sex. That, together with her moral educational work, brought out antagonism. A pamphlet entitled "An Open Letter," a most pathetic and powerful plea for unselfishness and purity in the marriage relation, excited hostility and criticism. She was interested in the woman's branch of the Society for Prevention of Cruelty to Animals. Her religious life was remarkable for fervor, activity and consecration. She was often called upon to address public assemblies on Christian themes. A series of six religious tracts she wrote at the request of Rev. Dr. John H. Vincent, which were published by the Tract Society of the Methodist Episcopal Church. When the General Conference of that church met, she wrote,

published and sent to each member of that body an eight-page pamphlet entitled, "The Position of Women in the Methodist Episcopal Church." Another on "License and Ordination of Women," which she had prepared for the next meeting of that chief legislative body, was sent when the hand that had written and the head that had planned were at rest.

GRIMKÉ, Miss Sarah Moore, reformer, born in Charleston, SC, 6th November, 1792, died in Hyde Park, NY, 23rd December, 1873. She was a daughter of the famous jurist, John Faucheraud Grimké. After her father's death, in 1819, Sarah and her sister, Angelina, freed their slaves and left their home. They could not endure the scenes connected with slavery, and they sought more congenial surroundings. Sarah went to Philadelphia, PA, in 1821. She became a prominent anti-slavery and woman's rights advocate. She lectured in New England, and then made her home with her sister, who had become the wife of Theodore D. Weld and was living in Belleville, NJ. Sarah taught in Mr. Weld's school. Among her published works are "An Epistle to the Clergy of the Southern States," an anti-slavery document, in 1828; "Letters on the Condition of Woman and the Equality of the Sexes" (Boston, 1838), and a translation of Lamartine's "Joan of Arc" (1867). She was a woman of great force and directness of character.

GRINNELL, Mrs. Katherine Van Allen, (Adasha) religious worker, born in Pillar Point, Jefferson county, NY, 20th April, 1839. Her maiden name was Katherine Van Allen, and her father was the owner of a fine estate near Sackett's Harbor. About the time of her birth a great religious revival swept over the country. Her parents came under its influence and joined the Methodist Episcopal Church. Their home thereafter was the home of the Methodist preacher and a center of active work for building up the interests of the town. At the age of fourteen years she became a member of the church. At fifteen she was sent to Falley Seminary. Her preceptress was Miss Rachel C. Newman, and the young student owed much to the influence of that noble woman. In 1864 she became the wife of Graham

G. Grinnell, a deacon in the Presbyterian Church in Adams, NY, and united with that church, frankly asserting her inability to accept its doctrines as she understood them, engaging to acquaint herself with them and to come into harmony with them if possible. As the years passed, her spiritual life deepened and her sympathy with dogmatic teachings grew less. In 1871, just before the great fire, the family removed to Chicago, IL. Soon after she took up seriously spiritualistic study and has written much upon that subject. Whatever success she may have achieved has been the result of the sincerity and spirit of absolute self-renunciation with which she strove to find the truth of things. Mrs. Grinnell is now living in Mayfair, Cook county, IL, devoting her time to the propagation of her exalted theories.

GRISHAM, Mrs. Sadie Park, educator and officeholder, born in Litchfield Township, near Athens, Bradford county, PA, 22d July, 1859. Mrs. Grisham is a direct descendant of Josiah and Thomas Park, and is the daughter of J. P. and Jane A. Park. She spent the first ten years of her life in her native place. In 1870 her father removed with his family to Kansas and settled on Middle creek, in Chase county, where he still resides. Sadie spent the greater part of her time in the common schools until 1876, at which time she went to the State Normal School in Emporia, KS, graduating in 1882. She then engaged in school teaching, until December, 1882, when she became the wife of Thomas H. Grisham, a lawyer of Cottonwood Falls, KS, who was at that time the prosecuting attorney of Chase county. In 1886 Mrs. Grisham accepted and still retains a position in the public schools of Cottonwood Falls. In 1890 she was employed as principal, with a corps of seven teachers. In the spring of 1889 she was elected a member of the common council of Cottonwood Falls. She was made president of the council and chairman of the committee on streets and alleys. Mrs. Grisham is an industrious worker in all educational matters.

GRISWOLD, Mrs. Frances Irene Burge, author, born in Wickford, RI, 28th April, 1826.

She is a daughter of Rev. L. Burp and Elizabeth Frances Shaw. Mrs. Griswold inherited from her father, many of those traits of character most clearly manifest in her writings. He was a man of lofty purposes, broad sympathies and tender Christian piety. The child grew to womanhood beneath the historic shades of St. Paul's Narragansett Church, of which her father was for twenty years the rector. Mrs. Griswold began to publish her literary work in 1853, and, though thirty-two volumes have already been published, besides innumerable fugitive articles for newspapers and other periodicals, her fruitful pen is not yet idle. Perhaps the most widely known of her books are the "Bishop and Nanette" series, which, as a carefully prepared exposition of the Book of Common Prayer, have long been in use in advanced classes of Episcopal Sunday schools; "Sister Eleanor's Brood," a story of the lights and shadows of a country clergyman's family life, in which the gentle, optimistic nature of the author works in its best vein, and which is understood to figure, under a thin veil of fiction, the actual experience of her mother, and the third book, "Asleep," to whose pages so many have turned for comfort in bereavement. Mrs. Griswold is an ardent Episcopalian and the church has been from her earliest youth a spur to her glowing imagination and the outlet of her abundant energy. Her Christmas and Easter poems represent her most finished poetic work. She has been twice married. After the death of her first husband, Allen N. Smith, of Stockbridge, MA, she became the wife of her distant kinsman, Judge Elias Griswold, of Maryland. Judge Griswold passed the latter days of his life in Brooklyn, NY, the home through many years of Mrs. Griswold's family, where she still resides. Mrs. Griswold descended, on her father's side, from the Mucklestons of Muckleston Manor, Oswestry, and on her mother's side, from the Brentons of Hammersmith, England. Most of her books were written under the name of F. Burge Smith.

GRISWOLD, Mrs. Hattie Tyng, author and poet, born in Boston, MA, 26th January, 1842. Her father was Rev. Dudley Tyng, a Universalist minister. Her mother's maiden name was Sarah

Haines. Both parents were typical New Englanders. They were Universalists, converted by Hosea Ballou, in Boston, in early life, and abolitionists, even at that period of the great national conflict. Mrs. Griswold's unusual inheritance of the poetic gift and intense practicality combined may be traced as a cross between her father's ideality and her mother's Puritanical attention to actual details. The childhood days of Hattie Tyng were spent in Maine and Michigan until she was eleven years of age, when she went to Wisconsin, which State has been her home ever since. In 1863 she became the wife of Eugene Sherwood Griswold and in Columbus, WI, their three daughters have been reared. When the "Home Journal" of New York was under the control of N. P. Willis, and the "Knickerbocker" the leading magazine of the country, Hattie Tyng, a mere girl, was a contributor to both. In 1874 she published her first volume of poems, "Apple Blossoms" (Chicago). Her other books are "Home Life of Great Authors" (Chicago, 1877), "Waiting on Destiny" (Boston, 1889), and "Lucille and Her Friends" (Chicago, 1890). None of the women poets of America have written anything more widely known or popular of its class than Mrs. Griswold's short poem, "Under the Daisies." Much of the work of her later years has been in the field of practical philanthropy as well as literature. She has been actively interested in associated charities, temperance and all efforts looking toward the amelioration of suffering and reform of evils. She was a delegate from Wisconsin to the National Conference of Charities in St. Paul, and has read papers that attracted much attention in various Unitarian conferences and in State associations.

GROENEVELT, Mrs. Sara, littérateur, was born on the "Bon Dieu," a cotton plantation of her uncle, F. G. Bartlett, which was romantically situated on a bend of the Red river called Bon Dieu, near Natchitoches, LA. She is a daughter of Dr. Sylvanus Bartlett, of Maine, and Julia Finch Gresham, of Kentucky. Mrs. Groenevelt is a cousin of the late Washington journalist, Ben. Perley Poore. At the age of fifteen she was graduated from the girl's high school of New Orleans. A few years later she became the wife of Eduard Groenevelt, a descendant of the old Dutch noble, Baron Arnold de Groenevelt, of Netherland fame. Shortly after her marriage she accompanied her husband to Europe, where she spent several years, completing her musical education under the careful guidance of Moscheles, Reinecke and other masters. She was the only lady solo-player at the Haupt-Prüfung of the Leipzig Conservatory of Music, held in the Gewandhaus, 2nd May, 1867, where she played with success Moscheles' Concerto for piano, accompanied by the famous Gewandhaus Orchestra, Moscheles himself leading. Mrs. Groenevelt has written under various pen-names, and her poems have received recognition from the "Times-Democrat," of her own State, and also from the Chicago "Current," for which latter she wrote under the pen-name "Stanley M. Bartlett." Her home is now in New Orleans, LA.

GRUBB, Mrs. Sophronia Farrington Naylor, temperance worker, born in Woodsfield, OH, 28th November, 1834. Her father and mother were persons of force, character and intellect. Her educational training was directly under the care of her father. When seventeen years old, she was graduated from the Illinois Conference College, in Jacksonville, and at nineteen she was put in charge of the woman's department of Chaddock College, Quincy, IL. In 1856 she became the wife of Armstead Otey Grubb, of St. Louis, MO. In the home they made she was engrossed until 1861, the beginning of the Civil War, when she and her family returned to Quincy. In the emergencies of wartime began to be manifest the ability, energy and enthusiasm that have distinguished her through life. Devoted to her country and humanity, she served them for four years, as those who, without compensation, gave time and strength in loving help in hospital, camp and field. At times she helped bring up the sick and wounded from southern swamps and fields. Again, surgeons and nurses being scarce, she was one of the women of nerve in requisition for surgical operations. Meanwhile the needs of the colored people were forced on her attention. Many of them, as refugees, went to Mr. Grubb's office, asking assistance, and were sent by him on to his home, with directions that their wants were to be supplied. The work became so heavy a drain on time, strength and sympathy, that Mrs. Grubb called a public meeting, and with her sister, Mrs. Shields, and with others, organized a Freedman's Aid Society. In the three years following they cared and provided for over three-thousand destitute negroes. At the close of the war Mr. and Mrs. Grubb returned to St. Louis. When her sons grew to manhood, the dangers surrounding them growing out of the liquor traffic led Mrs. Grubb to a deep interest in the struggle of the home against the saloon. She saw there a conflict as great, and needs as pressing as in the Civil War, and she gradually concentrated upon it all her powers. In 1882 she was elected national superintendent of the work among foreigners, one of the most onerous of the forty departments of the national organization of the Woman's Christian Temperance Union. By her effort and interest she has brought that department up to be thoroughly organized, wide-reaching and flourishing. She publishes leaflets and tracts on all the phases, economic, moral, social and evangelistic, of the temperance question in seventeen languages, at the rate of fifty editions of ten-thousand each per year. These are distributed all over the United States. She established a missionary department in Castle Garden, New York City, through which instructions in the duties and obligations of American citizenship are afforded to immigrants in their own tongues as they land. She has also recently been made president of the Kansas Woman's Christian Temperance Union. Her home is now in Lawrence, KS.

GUINEY, Miss Louise Imogen, poet and essayist, born in Boston, MA, 17th January, 1861. She is of Irish descent, with a blending of French blood. From her father, Gen. P. R. Guiney, a brave soldier of the Union, who was also an excellent lawyer, his only child inherits her dauntless spirit and her critical faculty. Her education, both in private and public schools, and later in the Convent of the Sacred Heart, in Providence, RI, was supplemented by constant affectionate study of English literature, which developed into fuller expression her inborn talent for writing. Beginning with fugitive essays and verse, which at once attracted attention, and were received from the first by such periodicals as "Harpers' Magazine" and the "Atlantic Monthly," she had made for herself an early and honorable place among literary people at the appearance of her first volume. That was a book of poems, entitled "Songs at the Start" (Boston, 1884), and was folowed by "Goose-Quill Papers" (Boston, 1885), a collection of prose sketches, "The White Sail and Other Poems" (Boston, 1887), and "Brownies and Bogies," a book of fairy lore, compiled from "Wide Awake" (Boston, 1888). She has also published "Monsieur Henri, A Foot Note to French History" (New York, 1892), a concise and romantic memoir of Henri de la Rochejaquelein, the brilliant young hero of La Vendée. The quality of Miss Guiney's work is of such subtle and delicate beauty as to be difficult of classification. Her original thought has felicity of form and is brightened by a wit which reminds one of her favorite authors in the golden age of 17th Century English. Her poetry, always interesting, is dominated, sometimes over-strongly, by peculiarities of phrasing, but ranges at its best from tender and pure sentiment to a splendid concentration of dramatic force. Both forms bear mark of conscientious and studious revision. Miss Guiney is a lover of nature, fond of all out-door sports, an adept with canoe and bicycle, and able to walk any distance without fatigue. Her poetic gift is in the heroic vein. She is an excellent scholar and has so much of the classic spirit that she has won the sobriquet of the "Sunny Young Greek."

GULICK, Mrs. Alice Gordon, mssionary, was born in Boston, MA, and graduated in Mt. Holyoke College, where she afterward taught. After becoming the wife of Rev. William Gulick, of the famous missionary Gulick family, she went to Spain, twenty years ago, where she has wrought efficiently with her husband, not only in the regular work of the mission, but has been the chief force in establishing a college for young women in San Sebastian, the chief watering place of the kingdom. Mrs. Gulick is now raising funds to erect a first-class college building, to be called the

Isabella College, where American ideas will be set forth. She is an unusually fine writer and speaker. She has four children, who are being educated in this country.

She is the president of the Woman's Christian Temperance Union of Spain.

GUSTAFSON, Mrs. Zadel Barnes, author and poet, born in Middletown, CT, 9th March, 1841. Her maiden name was Zadel Barnes. She wrote a good deal in her youth, but not till 1871 did she win general notice through "The Voice of Christmas Past," a tribute to Dickens, published in "Harper's Magazine." In 1873, "Where is the Child?" published in the same magazine, increased her reputation. She has contributed much to "Harper's Magazine," the Springfield "Republican," the "Home Journal" and the "Independent." She has also been a contributor to "The Magazine of Poetry." In 1878 she published a volume of verse, entitled "Meg, a Pastoral," which drew the attention of Whittier, Whipple and Longfellow. Besides her exquisite poems, Mrs. Gustafson has written many short stories of high merit. Among these are "Karin," "Laquelle" and others. In 1880 Mr. and Mrs. Gustafson went to London, England, where they remained until 1889. There she formed many literary acquaintances and saw much of life. They saw in London sights that stirred in their hearts the impulse to a crusade against drink. The result was "The Foundation of Death, a Study of the Drink Question," written jointly, and pronounced by thinkers in all countries to be one of the most effective and the best considered work ever published on the subject. Its sales in England and South Africa, India, the far East and Australia have been very large. Her home in the United States is in New York City, but she spends much time in London, England.

GUTELIUS, Mrs. Jean Harrower, artist and business woman, born in Perthshire, Scotland, 24th March, 1846. Her maiden name was Jean Harrower Reid, and her parents were honorable and Christian persons, whose lives were models of inspiration for their daughter. The Reid family came to the United States just before the Civil War broke out, and Jean saw her brother, Tom Chalmers Reid, and other relatives enter the Union army. Her brother died in the army at the early age of seventeen years. Connellsville, PA, her home, was the center of great business activity and pleasant social life between the years 1865 and 1875, and Miss Reid was fitted by nature to enjoy the animated life that came to her in those years. In 1874 she became the wife of N. P. Gutelius, a son of the Rev. Samuel Gutelius, a well known clergyman of the German Reformed Church. During two years she traveled with her husband over the United States. In 1878 she found herself alone in the world, with her infant daughter to care for. For several years she managed her father's home and attended her delicate mother, and in 1884 she began to study painting with S. Kilpatrick, who had a summer class in Connellsville. She was encouraged by the praise and advice of Frank Millet, to whom she submitted specimens of her work for criticism, and who introduced her to prominent and influential New York friends. She worked and painted industriously, and in 1886, at the suggestion of her teacher, Frank Fowler, she entered into the competition for the Cassel's prize in landscape painting, and received the first prize. Her mother died in that year, and Mrs. Gutelius took her head for a model, sending a photograph of the drawing to a magazine for illustration. The picture was seen by Marion Harland and Mrs. M. C. Hungerford, who at once wrote to secure it for an article on "Beautiful Old Age," which was published in the "Home Maker" of September, 1890. Her paintings found a ready sale in Pittsburgh, and her brush was seldom idle. She assisted her aged father in the management of his book-store, soon mastering all the details of the business. The father died on 9th April, 1891, at the age of seventysix years, leaving Mrs. Gutelius alone in the management of the concern. She is now dividing her time between the care of her daughter, the details of her business and the delight of the successful artist at her easel.

GUZMAN, Madame Marie Ester, social leader, born in Baltimore, MD. She is the wife of Señor Don Horacio Guzman, minister from Nicaragua to the United States. Her grandfather, Hon. Samuel Ewing, belonged to the old Maryland family of that name. He was a member of the bar and a life-long resident of Philadelphia, PA. Her father, Rev. Charles Henry Ewing, was a theologian. He married a Miss Page, of Virginia, and. was also a resident of Philadelphia. Although Madame Guzman was born in Baltimore, while her parents were temporarily residing there, her early life was spent in Philadelphia, except the time she spent in Boston, studying the languages and music. The death of her mother occurred in her girlhood, and much responsibility rested on her in presiding over her father's household. While Señor Guzman was in this country, in 1873, attending the Jefferson College in Philadelphia, as a medical student, Miss Ewing met him. Señor Guzman was graduated, and after two years of acquaintance their marriage took place, and Dr. Guzman took his bride to Granada. His father, one of the former presidents of Granada, was an active politican, but Dr. Guzman, always devoted to medical science, built up a large and extensive practice in Granada and became a recognized leader in literature as well as medical science. Madame Guzman is a good musician, sings well, and is devoted to her home. She has studied every phase of life and character in Granada. Dr. Guzrnan was a delegate to the International Congress, and is one of the directors in the Nicaragua Ship Canal project. Madame Guzman is very fond of company and entertains a good deal. She has no children.

HAENSLER, Mrs. Arminta Victoria Scott, physician, born in Kinsman, OH, 27th July, 1842. Her maiden name was Scott, and her parents were of Scotch-American extraction. Her father, a teacher, married one of his pupils. Of this union Mrs. Haensler is the third child. She had more trials during her childhood than at any time since, owing to her parents' belief in and practice of "good wholesome restraint" and her own intense dislike of being curbed or controlled. She became converted in her eleventh year, and then earnestly began to control herself. At that early age she showed a quick mind, an excellent memory and fine mathematical powers. She entered Kinsman Academy at fourteen years of age,

doing domestic service in the family of a Presbyterian minister for her hoard. She made rapid progress in study and began to teach when she was eighteen years old. Her attention was turned to medicine by reading a newspaper article concerning Elizabeth Blackwell and her trials in securing a medical education. Miss Scott then determined to be a physician in some large city, and thenceforth all her energies were spent in earning the money and preparing herself for the medical profession. She taught for six years. At the age of twenty-four she entered Farmington Seminary, and a year later she went to Oberlin College. There she helped in household work as an equivalent for her board. After some months she went to the Ladies' Hall, where, during the rest of the course, she taught both private pupils and college classes. As soon as she had earned the degree of A.B., she received the offer of an excellent position, not only as teacher, but as reviewer, editor and reporter. She was true to her aim and entered the Woman's Medical College of Pennsylvania, from which, in 1875, she received the degree of M.D. Since then Dr. Scott has practiced in Philadelphia and at different times has held the positions of resident physician of the Mission Hospital, gynaecologist to the Stockton Sanitarium, consulting gynæcologist to the Pennsylvania Asylum for the Insane, consulting physician to the Woman's Christian Association, lecturer to the Woman's Christian Association, lecturer to the working Women's Club, member of the Philadelphia Clinical Society, member of the Philadelphia Electro-Therapeutic Society, member of the Alumni Association of the Woman's Medical College of Pennsylvania, resident physician to the Franklin Reformatory Home for Women, physician to the Hospital and Dispensary for Women and Children, and lecturer before the National Woman's Health Association of America. Dr. Scott is the author of a lecture on Alaska, which country is among the many she has visited, and is the author of several articles on medical topics. On 13th November, 1890, she became the wife of Franz Joseph Haensler, M.D., of Philadelphia.

HAGER, Mrs. Lucie Caroline, author, born in Littleton, MA, 29th December, 1853. Her parents were Robert Dunn Gilson and Lydia, Gilson. There were nine children in the family, of whom Mrs. Hager was the youngest. Heavy and peculiar trials attended her childhood, yet these circumstances deepened and intensified her poetical nature, while the more practical side of her character was strongly developed. She had a thirst for knowledge and used all available means to satisfy it. Her education was acquired in adverse circumstances. Having entered the normal school in Framingham, MA, in 1875, she was recalled to her home during the first weeks of the school year, and her studies were exchanged for days of patient watching with the sick, or such employment as she could obtain near her home. Her first poems appeared at that time. She met the daily ills of life with courage and lifted herself above them, seeking out what good she could find. With such private instruction as her country home afforded, she took up her studies with earnest purpose. She became a successful teacher of country schools and a bookkeeper. In October, 1882, she became the wife of Simon B. Hager. She has one child, a boy. Most of her poems have appeared over the name Lucie C. Gilson. She has written a number of short prose stories. Her estimate of her own work is modest. She has recently written and published a very interesting history of the town in which she resides, entitled "Boxborough: A New England Town and its People."

HAHR, Miss Emma, pianist, composer and musical educator, was born in Fayetteville, NC. She is of Swedish parentage on the paternal side, and oil the maternal of French Huguenot extraction. Her father, Franz Josef Hahr, was a Swedish general whose ancestors had for generations held prominent places at court. He was both musical composer and artist. He gave Emma the choice of music or painting. She turned to music. The groundwork of her musical education was laid by her father. After his death she was sent to Germany, where she had the peculiar good fortune to be received into the home of Karl Klinworth as a private pupil. That led to another privilege, the happiest that could have fallen to the ambitious young genius, that of becoming a pupil of Liszt. She studied under the great master at Weimar the summer before he died. In him she found her ideal guide. One of the highest of the many honors conferred upon her on her return to America was an invitation to appear in concert in the Music Teachers' National Association in Philadelphia. Then followed a series of triumphs throughout the South. There was but one verdict, from the press, from critical audiences, from rival artists: A musical genius of rarest type. Though Miss Hahr has made Atlanta, GA, her home for several years, where she has been perhaps a more potent factor than any other in awakening and developing musical interest throughout the South, being a teacher of teachers, it is, however, her intention to accept one of the many calls she has received to go on a concert tour through America. In all her labors, as teacher and on the concert stage, she has never ceased to be a student, and she has found time for much earnest composition. Her "Lullaby" and "Good-Night Song" are perhaps her best known contributions to the music of America. She has also composed the music for two ballads, a "Song" from Browning's "Pippa Passes," and Orelia Key Bell's "Lady in the Moon." Besides these, there are yet many studies which have met the enthusiastic endorsement of the judges, but which the composer modestly withholds until she shall have more fully tested her strength with less ambitious efforts.

HALL, Miss Lucy M., physician, was born among the rugged hills of northern Vermont. She carries in her veins some of the best blood of New England, certain strains of which can be traced back to a titled ancestry in the Old World. Her education was begun in her native State, continued in Milton College, Wisconsin, and in the Dearborn Seminary, Chicago, IL, from which she was graduated. She taught successfully for a few years, but soon after the death of her mother and father she was persuaded by the family physician to begin the study of medicine. In the spring of 1878 Dr. Hall was graduated with distinction from the medical department of the University of Michigan, Ann Arbor. She continued her medical observations in the hospitals and clinics of New York City, and later in those of London, England, where in St. Thomas Hospital she was the first woman ever received at its bedside clinics. In Dresden, Germany, she was house physician in the Royal Lying-in and Gynæcological Hospital, under Prof. F. Winckel. From there she was called back to America, where she was appointed by Gov. Talbot, of Massachusetts, to the responsible position of physician to the State Reformatory for Women in Sherborn. Connected with the prison was a hospital of one-hundred-fifty beds, likely to be filled from a body of from three to four hundred inmates, bringing with them all the ills and diseases following the train of ignorance, vice and crime. "Four years later," writes Clara Barton, "it became my privilege, as superintendent of that prison, to observe how that duty was discharged by its resident physician. Perfect system prevailed. No prisoner could enter upon her term without a careful diagnosis of her physical condition and administration of the needful treatment. If any trace of mental trouble manifested itself, the case was closely watched and tenderly cared for. The most difficult surgical operations were performed, not only without loss of life, but with marked success. The control of the doctor over her patients, and these included from time to time nearly every inmate, was simply marvelous, and her influence throughout the entire institution not less remarkable. Among all classes she moved as one born to command, that most successful of all command, the secret of which lies in tact, conscious ability and sympathy with mankind. So long as that prison remains a success, so long will the influence of Dr. Hall's early administration and example for good be felt there." After nearly five years of service there, she was appointed superintendent by acclamation of the governor and his council. Though grateful for the honor, she declined the position, as its acceptance would necessitate the giving up of her medical work. Soon after that she formed a partnership with her distinguished colleague, Dr. Eliza M. Mosher, and together they began to practice in the city of Brooklyn, NY, where they still reside. In the autumn of 1884 they were appointed associate professors of physiology and hygiene and physicians to Vassar College, resigning in 1887, very much to the regret of all concerned. During the same year, upon the occasion of the semi-centennial commencement of the University of Michigan, Dr. Hall, as first vice president of the Department of Medicine and Surgery, was called upon to preside at the meeting of that body. As her colleagues many of the most eminent physicians and professors of the land were present. Afterward one of them remarked: "I had predicted that fifty years after the admission of women a scene like this might occur. My prophecy has been anticipated by more than thirty years." As a writer Dr. Hall has contributed many articles upon health topics to the best magazines and other periodicals of the day. Her writings are characterized by a strength of thought, knowledge of her subject and a certain vividness of expression which holds the attention of the reader. Dr. Hall is a member of the Kings County Medical Society, of Brooklyn; of the Pathological Society; of the New York Medico-Legal Society, of which she has been treasurer; of the New York Academy of Anthropology; of the American Social Science Association, of which she is also vice-president, and a large number of other organizations, both in New York and Brooklyn. In the fall of 1887 she was appointed central committee delegate to the fourth International Conference of the Red Cross, of Geneva, held in Carlsruhe, Germany. By invitation she was a guest at the court of their Royal Highnesses, the Grand Duke and Grand Duchess of Baden. The latter will be remembered as the only daughter of the revered old Kaiser William and Empress Augusta. That high conference brought Dr. Hall into contact with very many of the most noted personages of the European courts, and that for a series of royal occasions and a length of time sufficient to challenge the scrutiny of the most critical. She passed not only unscathed, but with the highest commendations, everywhere doing honor to America and to American womanhood. Her elegance of bearing was a subject of personal remark. The respect of Her Royal Highness, the Grand Duchess, was marked and thoughtfully manifested by the appreciative gifts bestowed as tokens of remembrance. Dr. Hall became the wife of Robert George Brown, of New York, on 29th December, 1891.

HALL, Mrs. Margaret Thompson, educator and newspaper correspondent, born in Dayton, OH, 28th March, 1854. Great care was taken with her early education by her father, the late Dr. Thompson, who was a member of the Medical Board in Nashville, TN, during the latter part of the Civil War. As a child she showed a keen desire for learning, and at the age of fifteen she was graduated, but continued her studies under Prof. A. Reily, D.D., of Michigan. Being a natural musician, she accompanied her father through central Ohio on his recruiting expeditions for the Union Army. After the war, with her widowed mother and gallant brother, Capt. J. A. Thompson, she settled in Iowa, and then took up her vocation as a teacher, continuing her labors there and in Illinois until her marriage to J. Charles Hall, the publisher of the "Pacific Veteran" of San Francisco, CA. She was the associate editor of that paper as long as it continued publication. She also organized and formed a department of the Loyal Ladies' League, and was publicly decorated for her services to the Grand Army of the Republic by the late General Sullivan. From time to time her little sketches and letters have appeared in different papers, among which are the "National Tribune," of Washington, DC, the "American Tribune," the "Golden Gate" and Healdsburg "Enterprise," of California. Literary work of varied kinds has been her occupation for the last two years.

HALL, Miss Mary, lawyer, born in Marlborough, CT, in 185–. She was the oldest daughter of Gustavus Ezra Hall, of Marlborough. The original Hall ancestor was John Hall, of Coventry, Warwickshire, England, who came to this country with Governor Winthrop in 1630.

Miss Hall was graduated in the Wesleyan Academy, Wilbraham, MA, in 1866, and taught in that institution for several years, later filling the chair of mathematics in Lasell Seminary. During a summer vacation in July, 1877, she began her legal studies. In 1879 Miss Hall was appointed a commissioner of the Superior Court. It was the first time that such an honorable appointment had been given to a woman in Connecticut. In March, 1882, Miss Hall formally applied for admission to the bar, having passed her examinations with credit. The affair made a sensation. She took her examination in an open court-room, and not under the most favorable circumstances, but went through the ordeal with credit. The question of her eligibility was submitted to the Supreme Court, and in July, 1882, a decision was rendered in her favor. She took her attorney's oath 3rd October, 1882, and was also made a notary public in the same year. In 1890 Miss Hall began a rescue work for street boys that so increased until it attracted the attention of gentlemen of wealth and influence, who contributed of their means, until now it stands upon a firm foundation. The Hartford Female Seminary building was purchased and fitted up at a cost of more than $25,000. In 1890 the number enrolled was 846, and the largest attendance at any one time was 500.

HALL, Miss Pauline, opera singer, born in Cincinnati, OH, in 1862. In private life she is known by her family name, Schmitgall. Her first venture on the stage was made with the Alice Oates Company, in 1879, in which she appeared in the chorus and in minor parts. In 1882 Miss Hall went to New York City, where she has made her permanent home. In New York she made her debut as Venus with "Orpheus and Eurydice," and then she first attracted general attention. Her most notable success was in "Erminie," which ran for three years. Miss Hall has traveled with a company of her own, in the double rôle of star and manager. She has acquired a large fortune.

HALL, Mrs. Sarah C., physician, born on a farm in Madison county, NY, 15th August, 1832. Her maiden name was Larkin. She taught previous to and after her marriage in 1893. Her preparatory studies were made while caring for her two children and doing all her own house-work and sewing, and in 1867 she entered the Woman's Medical College of Pennsylvania, from which she was graduated in 1870. She was one of the class which, in November, 1869, was hissed by the male students at the first Pennsylvania hospital clinic to which women were admitted, ignored by the lecturers, and followed and almost mobbed on the streets. The mere mention of such an occurrence now serves to show the advance of public opinion, but even at the time it caused a reaction in favor of women in medicine. In 1870 Dr. Hall went with her family to Fort Scott, KS, where they now reside. She was one of the very first regularly qualified women physicians to practice in that state. She has long been a member of the State Medical Society, holds the position of medical examiner to several insurance orders of standing, and lately became a member of the American Medical Association. Although necessarily making her profession her chief task, Dr. Hall is an active member of the. Eastern Star and Woman's Relief Corps, in both of which she has held high office. After moving to Kansas she was at first identified with suffrage work in her own city, after ward with both State and National Associations.

HALL, Mrs. Sarah Elizabeth, educator, was born in New York City. She is the third daughter of John George Heybeck, and began to teach when very young. After graduating from the Saturday Normal School, the only institution in those days for the improvement of teachers in New York City, she received a State certificate, the highest honor conferred on teachers of the public schools. After teaching about three years in the lower part of the city, she was appointed, in 1858, to grammar-school No. 35, under Thomas Hunter, which for many years was known as the best boys' school of the city, and there she acquired the particular esteem of the principal. It was her influence in that school that induced the principal to abolish corporal punishment and to rule by moral suasion. When the Normal College was established, in February, 1870, she accepted the position of assistant to the president in preference to that of principal of a grammar-school which was offered her. In the past twenty-two years' service in the Normal College she has filled her place with zeal and executive ability.

HAMILTON, Miss Anna J., educator and journalist, born in Louisville, KY, 20th April, 1860. She is descended on the maternal side from the old Kentucky family of Caldwells, and on the paternal side from the Hamiltons, of Pennsylvania. She inherits the marked intellectual traits which distinguished her ancestors. She was educated in the public schools of Louisville and was graduated from the girls' high school. She is now occupying a commercial chair in the Normal School, which she fills with success. She is known as an enthusiastic educator. She is a member of the Filson Club, which is the State historical club, and is a member of the Daughters of the Revolution. She is a writer of both prose and poetry. Her poems have been published in the local journals and in various periodicals. Much of her time has been given to editorial work. For a year she edited the children's column in a prominent educational journal, and wrote many entertaining lesson stories for the children. She is one of the editors for Kentucky on "A Woman of the Century" and is engaged in editorial work on the "National Encyclopedia of America." She is a member of the library committee from Kentucky for the World's Fair. The committee purpose to establish a woman's library, and she will collect and contribute all the volumes written by the women of Kentucky.

HAMM, Miss Margherita Arlina, journalist, born in Montreal, Canada, 29th, April, 1871. She is a descendant from a long line of scholarly ancestors. Among her forefathers were literary men, theologians and soldiers. She has in her veins the best blood of southern France. Her maternal grandfather was Rev. Harold Jean Spencer, a prominent Episcopal clergyman, who was the author of several widely known pamphlets of the controversial order. Her paternal grandfather was General Pierre Hamm, a leader in the Liberal party in Montreal, Canada. Miss Hamm was only thirteen years old when she began to write for the newspapers. She found her first regular position on the Boston "Herald," and for four years she did all kinds of work on that journal. She then went to New York and joined the staff of the "World." Among her notable work was her interview with Mr. Cleveland on the tariff question, in 1889, which was cabled to

Edna Wallace Hopper.
From Photo by Morrison, Chicago.

Virginia Harned.
From Photo by Schloss, New York.

the London, England, "Times." Another well-known achievement was her Bar Harbor interview with Mr. Blaine. She has done much "special" work for most of the New York dailies and at the same time corresponded for a number of western journals. She conducted the woman's department of the "United Press Literary Budget." Besides her prose work, covering everything in the line of daily journalism, Miss Hamm is a writer of much graceful verse, and her poems have appeared in "Current Literature," "Youth's Companion," "New England Magazine" and other leading periodicals. Her work is noted for its clear-cut, scholarly character, and there is nothing in the line of journalism that is not within the easy command of her pen Wherever and whenever brought into direct rivalry with male journalists, she has shown her ability to do the work far better than most of the men, and as well as the best of them. In political work she has been very successful.

HAMMER, Mrs. Anna Maria Nichols, temperance worker, born in Pottsville, PA, 14th September, 1840. Her father was Alfred Lawton, one of the pioneers of the coal region. On both sides of the house Mrs. Hammer is descended from Revolutionary stock. Her mother's great-grandfather was Michael Hillegas, the confidential friend of Washington and the first Continental Treasurer of the United States. Mrs. Hammer's great grandfathers, General Francis and General William Nichols, distinguished themselves in the Revolutionary War, as did also her great-grandfather Lawton, who was a surgeon in the army and for many years was surgeon at West Point. Her grandfather Nichols was an officer in the war of 1812. Anna was educated in Philadelphia, Pottsville and Wilkes-Barré, PA. In the former city she became the wife of William A. Hammer, and returned with him to Schuylkill County. After several years they removed to Newark, NJ. There a great spiritual awakening came to her, followed by her entrance into temperance work as a member of the Woman's Christian Temperance Union, very soon after the inauguration of that movement. Her national connection with the work has been as superintendent of three departments, work among

the reformed, juvenile work and her present work, social or parlor work. She is also vice-president of the Woman's Christian Temperance Union for the State of Pennsylvania. Mrs. Hammer ranks high as a clear, forceful and ready speaker. At present her home is in Philadelphia, where her husband is in charge of the Reformed Episcopal Theological Seminary. She is a cultured woman of strong individuality, an earnest expounder of the work in Bible readings, and greatly interested in the instruction and training of the young.

HAMMOND, Mrs. Loretta Mann, physician, born in Rome, MI, 4th April, 1842. Her parents were Daniel and Anna Stoddard Mann. Her mother came from the Stoddards, of Litchfield, CT, a family of preachers, teachers and editors. Her father is descended from the Pilgrims of the Mayflower, and from the same Plymouth progenitor came the Hon. Horace Mann. Early in life Loretta showed tendencies toward her later study. At the age of nine she decided to study medicine, but in that she received no sympathy. Her father, though intelligent and valuing education in a man, was prejudiced against the education of women. When she was fourteen, she walked three miles, went before the school board, and on examination received a first-grade certificate. The first intimation her parents had of her ambition in that direction was when she walked in with the document in her hand. After that she had an hour a day for study, and her father began to say that they might as well let Loretta get an education, as she was so queer no man would ever want to marry her. At sixteen she was sent to Hillsdale College, and she never heard any more laments that she was a girl. After finishing the preparatory and junior years, she decided to study medicine. To be self-supporting, she learned printing, in Peru, IN, and was an object of curiosity and remark for doing work out of woman's sphere. She began to set type in Hillsdale, MI, at the sum of twelve cents per thousand, but her wages increased until, as compositor and reporter in Kalamazoo, she received the same wages as a man. While there, on invitation, she joined the State Typographical Union, the only woman in that body. Later she was the only female compositor in Philadelphia, PA. The Typographical Union there did not admit women, but, being national, her card from Michigan had to be recognized. The book firm of Carey & Baird employed her at men's wages, despite the protests of their employés. There she earned the money for her medical course, graduating in 1872 from the Woman's Medical College of Pennsylvania. She soon after went to California and, during her eight years of practice, introduced to the profession a new remedy, California laurel. She wrote copious articles for the "Therapeutic Gazette," of Detroit, which were copied into the London journals, and the medicine was sampled all over America and England, before the manufacturers knew they were dealing with a woman. While in California she became the wife of Dr. W. M. Hammond, of Kansas City, MO. Removing thence, they became proprietors and physicians of the "Fountain of Health," a mineral spring resort, where they now reside. One child, a daughter, Pansy, blesses their home. As a physician Dr. Hammond is hopeful, cheerful, painstaking and foreseeing. She believes stimulants are neither curative nor nutrient, but benumbing to the nerve centers, which is incipient death. She never gives morphine as a sedative. She was always an advocate of physical culture and while in college often walked twelve miles before breakfast, without fatigue. As a child, as soon as she knew the inequalities of human conditions, she was an active abolitionist and a woman suffragist. She has allied herself with the Socialist Labor Party movement and, although a capitalist, sympathizes with the laboring classes. With all her positiveness, she never antagonizes.

HAMMOND, Mrs. Mary Virginia Spitler, World's Fair Manager, born in Rensselaer, Jasper county, IN, 12th March, 1847, where she has always resided. She is a member of the Board of World's Fair Managers of Indiana, a member of the committee on machinery and manufactures, and secretary of the committee on woman's work.

Her father, Col. George W. Spitler, was a pioneer settler and prominent citizen of Jasper County, and during his life held many positions of trust and honor. The rudiments of her education were obtained in the common schools in her native town. She attended the seminary in Crawfordsville, IN, under the superintendency of Miss Catherine Merill, and then spent a year near the early home of her father and mother, in Virginia. She next became a student in St. Mary's Academy, near South Bend, IN, then under the charge of Mother Angela. She was graduated in that institution with the highest honors of her class. Her husband, Hon. Edwin P. Hammond, was in the Union service during the Civil War, before its close becoming Lieutenant Colonel and Commandant of the 87th Indiana Volunteers. He is an ex-judge of the supreme court of his State and is now serving his third term as judge of the thirtieth circuit. Their family consists of five children, four daughters and a son. She is a typical representative of the intelligent cultured Hoosier wife and matron. Her heart is always open for charitable work and deeds of benevolence. She takes great interest in the work of the World's Fair. Her acquaintance with general literature is broad.

HANAFORD, Rev. Phebe Anne, Universalist minister and author, born in Nantucket, MA, 6th May, 1829. Her father, George V. Coffin, was a merchant and ship-owner. Phebe was reared in the doctrines and discipline of the Society of Friends. She was educated in

the schools of her native town. From childhood she was ambitious to become a preacher. With advancing years her religious belief changed. She joined the Baptist Church first, and afterward became a member of the Universalist Church. In 1849 she became the wife of Joseph H. Hanaford, a teacher. Her domestic and literary pursuits for a time kept her ministerial ambitions in check. She taught for several years in Massachusetts schools. From 1866 to 1868 she edited the "Ladies' Repository" and the "Myrtle." In 1865, while visiting in Nantucket, she preached twice in the schoolhouse in Siasconset, at the request of her father. In 1866 she was invited to preach in South Canton, MA, as a substitute for Rev. Olympia Brown. Miss Brown urged her to enter the ministry, and in 1868 she was ordained in Hingham, MA. Her long ministerial career has been uniformly successful. She preached and lectured throughout New England and the Western and Middle States. She was the first woman to serve as chaplain in a State legislature, serving in the Connecticut House and Senate in 1870 and 1872. She has had pastoral charges in Hingham and Waltham, MA, New Haven, CT, and Jersey City, NJ. In 1887 she was pastor of the Church of the Holy Spirit in New Haven, CT. She was conspicuous in temperance work, serving as grand chaplain of the Good Templars. In 1867 she represented her State grand lodge in the right worthy lodge in Detroit, MI. Her literary work includes poems, essays, addresses and stories. Her published books are: "Lucretia the Quakeress" (1853); "Leonette, or Truth Sought and Found" (1857); "The Best of Books, and its History" (1857); "Abraham Lincoln" (1865); "Frank Nelson, the Runaway Boy" (1865); "The Soldier's Daughter" (1866); "The Captive Boy of Tierra del Fuego" (1867); "Field, Gunboat, Hospital and Prison" (1867); "The Young Captain" (1868); "George Peabody" (1870); "From Shore to Shore and Other Poems" (1870); "Charles Dickens" (1870); "Women of the Century" (1877), and "Ordination Book" (1887). She is the mother of several children. One son is a clergyman. Her life has been full of hard, earnest, conscientious and exalting work.

HANNA, Miss Sarah Jackson, musical educator, born on her father's sugar plantation, near New Orleans, LA, 4th December, 1847. She is the oldest daughter of James Jackson Hanna and Ellen Cooper. Her father was born in Ireland. The family comes of Scotch-Irish lineage of noble birth the mother of James Jackson Hanna belonged to the same Scotch-Irish stock. She, and her brothers and sisters, after being actively interested in the Irish rebellion of 1803, sought refuge in the United States. Coming to this country in 1810, they settled in Tennessee, and then went to the rich cotton belt of Florence, AL. From there Mrs. Hanna, the grandmother of Miss Sarah Hanna removed to southwestern Louisiana, where she devoted all her energies to the culture of sugar, in which she succeeded, leaving a valuable property to her heirs. On her mother's side Miss Hanna is the granddaughter of Dr. Thomas Cooper, a native of Manchester, England. He was a distinguished scientist and man of letters, and for

many years before and at the time of his death president of South Carolina College, in Columbia, SC. In 1860 Miss Hanna resided in New Orleans. Having shown in early childhood unusual musical talent, her father gave her every advantage. The last few years of her student life she spent under the instruction of Madame Francoise Lacquer. Her father's fortune having been swept away by war and lost in litigation, when he died, in 1867, she resolved to support herself as a teacher of the piano. She first went to Florence, Ala. Later, she accepted a position in Ward's Seminary, Nashville, TN. There she met Thomas B. Binyon, to whom she was married in 1870. They went to Atlanta, GA, where she has since resided. Later domestic and financial troubles compelled her to adopt again the teaching of music as a profession, which she has followed since, uninterruptedly and with marked success. For three years she was organist of St. Luke's Cathedral, organizing the first surpliced choir in Atlanta. Her health failing, she resigned that position and devoted herself exclusively to teaching. In 1885, by permission of the Superior Court of Fulton county, GA, she resumed her maiden name.

HAPGOOD, Miss Isabel F., translator and author, born in Boston, MA, 2nd November, 1850. She lived in Worcester, MA, until 1880, when she became a resident of Boston. Miss Hapgood received a liberal education, and her talent for language has been developed to a remarkable degree. She has utilized her knowledge of the leading modern languages in the translation of standard authors' works into English. She is known wherever English is spoken by her work in Russian literature. Her "Epic Songs of Russia" is a standard classic and the only rendering of those productions in English that has ever been made. Her translations from the Russian include the works of Tolstoi, Gogol, Verestchagin and many others of the highest grade. She has written for various magazines a number of valuable articles on Russian subjects. Her translations of Victor Hugo's "Les Misérables," "Les Travailleurs de la Mer," "Notre Dame" and "L' Homme qui Rit" are pronounced the standards by the critics. She has translated many works, prose and verse, long and short, from the French, the Spanish and the Italian languages, with which she is perfectly familiar. Besides her work in translations, She has written much signed and unsigned critical work and articles in publications of the highest order in the United States. She is an industrious worker. Her home is now in New York City.

HARBERT, Mrs. Elizabeth Boynton, author, lecturer and reformer, born in Crawfordsville, IN, 15th April, 1843. She is a daughter of William H. Boynton, formerly of Nashua, NH. Her mother was Abigail Sweetser, a native of Boston. Elizabeth was educated in the female seminary in Oxford, OH, and in the Terre Haute Female College, graduating from the latter institution with honors in 1862. She published her first book, "The Golden Fleece," in 1867, and delivered her first lecture in Crawfordsville in 1869. She became the wife, in 1870, of Capt. W. S. Harbert, a brave soldier and now a successful lawyer. After their marriage they lived in Des Moines, IA, and there Mrs. Harbert published her second book, entitled "Out of Her Sphere." While living in Des Moines, Mrs. Harbert took an active part in the woman suffrage movement. She succeeded in inducing the Republicans of Iowa to put into their State platform a purely woman's plank, winning the members of the committee appointed to prepare a platform for the State convention by her earnest and dignified presentation of the claims of woman. Thus Mrs. Harbert earned the distinction of being the first women to design a woman's plank and secure its adoption by a great political party in a great State. In the winter of 1874 Mr. and Mrs. Harbert removed to Chicago, and soon afterward they made their home in the suburb of that city called Evanston, where they now live. Mrs. Harbert was engaged to edit the woman's department of the Chicago "Inter-Ocean." She held that arduous position for eight years, and her name was made a household word throughout the West. Their family consists of one son and two daughters. Mrs. Harbert is an earnest worker in the cause of woman suffrage and is interested deeply in philanthropic and charitable enterprises. For two years she served as president of the Social Science Association of Illinois, an organization formed "to suggest plans for the advancement of industrial, intellectual, social, educational and philanthropic interests, to the end that there maybe better

homes, schools, churches, charities, laws, and better service for humanity and God." She served as vice president of the Woman's Suffrage Association of Indiana, as president of the Woman's Suffrage Association of Iowa, and twelve years as president of the Illinois Woman's Suffrage Association. She has been one of the board of managers of the Girl's Industrial School in South Evanston. She is connected with the association for the advancement of women known as the Woman's Congress. She is president of the Woman's Club, of Evanston. Notwithstanding all the work implied in filling so many important offices, she finds her greatest pleasure in her pleasant home and her interesting family. Besides their Evanston home, they have a summer cottage in Geneva Lake, Wisconsin, where they pass the summers. Mrs. Harbert is versatile to a rare degree. Her love of nature finds expression in music and poetry, and her interest in the unfortunate members of the community shows in her many charitable and philanthropic works. Throughout her career she has been self-forgetful in her desire to do for others. Her pen and voice have been ready to render praise and encouragement, and her eyes have been closed to ingratitude on the part of those for whom she has unselfishly labored, that a better spirit of cooperation might spring up among womankind. The crowning excellence and most prominent characteristic of Mrs. Harbert is her deep sense of patriotism. As a writer she is pointed, vigorous, convincing. She has now in press a third book, entitled "Amore."

HARBY, Mrs. Lee C., author, born in Charleston, SC, 7th September, 1849. She is a descendant of two families well-known in the South for the number of distinguished soldiers and authors they have produced, the Harbys and Cohens. The Harbys were soldiers in the Revolution, in which contest both of Mrs. Harby's great-grandfathers fought. Her father-in-law, L. C. Harby, who is also her granduncle, was a midshipman in the war of 1812, served in the Mexican war and in several other minor wars. At the outbreak of the late Civil War, in 1861, he held the rank of captain in the United States navy, but resigned and espoused the Confederate cause and served with distinction during the four years of that war. His son, J. D. Harby, the husband of Mrs. Harby, served in the same army. Mrs. Harby's maiden name was Cohen. She is a daughter of Marx E. Cohen, a native of Charleston and a graduate of the University of Glasgow, Scotland. Her mother was Miss Armida Harby, a great-granddaughter of Solomon Harby who was a grandson of Sir Clement Harby of the Harbys of Adston, an old English family; her father, Isaac Harby, of Charleston, SC, was distinguished as a critic, essayist and dramatist, and his grand-daughter, Mrs. Lee C. Harby, has inherited his literary talent. Mr. Cohen's family numbered six children, of whom Mrs. Harby was the fifth. Her early life was passed amid romantic city and plantation surroundings, which developed the vien of poetical thought in her nature. She was never a regular student in school, but was educated mainly by her scholarly father and her greataunt, a refined and cultured woman, and their training was such as to turn her to literature at an early age. Arrived at maturity, she became the wife of her second cousin, I. D. Harby. They made their home in Galveston, TX, and while living in that city Mrs. Harby published one of her first important compositions,"Christmas Before the War" (1873). In 1879 Mrs. Harby removed to Houston, TX. In 1880 she became known as a poet of superior powers through a poem of welcome to the Texas Press Association, which met in Houston in the spring of that year. The larger portion of her historical work deals with the interesting subject of Texas. Besides her historical work, she has contributed to leading periodicals a series of poems, essays and stories, all of which have found wide favor. Among other societies of which Mrs. Harby is a member is Sorosis, which elected her to membership while she was yet a resident of the South. She now resides in New York City.

HARPER, Mrs. Ida A., journalist, was born in Indiana, of New England parentage. She showed in childhood a remarkable memory and marked literary talent. Her education was almost wholly received in private schools, although she was graduated in the public high school. She entered the State University in Bloomington, but was married before completing the course. For a number of years after marriage she did a considerable amount of writing. Her work was of a character that always commanded excellent pay. For a dozen years she conducted a department in the Terre Haute "Saturday Evening Mail," that discussed all of the questions of the day and was widely copied. During that time Mrs. Harper traveled extensively and corresponded for a large number of papers, including the "Christian Union," "Western Christian Advocate," "Advance," Chicago "Inter Ocean," Chicago 'Times," the Detroit "Free Press," the Toledo "Blade," the Boston "Traveller," the Cleveland "Leader," the Indianapolis "Journal" and the Terre Haute "Gazette and Express." For the past ten years she has edited a woman's department in the "Locomotive Firemen's Magazine." In 1889 she decided to make literature a profession. She was at once invited to an editorial position on the Terre Haute "Evening News." In a short time she was made managing editor by the directors, one of the first instances on record of a woman occupying the position of managing editor on a political daily paper. She carried the paper through the hottest municipal campaign ever known in that city, making up an independent ticket from the best men on the other tickets. She wrote every line of the editorials and dictated the policy of the paper throughout the canvass, and every man on the ticket was elected. At the end of a year she was called to a place on the editorial staff of the Indianapolis "News," which she has filled for two years, going to her office regularly each morning.

HARRELL, Mrs. Sarah Carmichael, educator and reformer, born in Brookville, IN, 8th January, 1844. Her maiden name was Sarah Carmichael. In 1859 she began to teach in the public schools of Indiana, and for twelve years was remarkably successful, being the first woman teacher to receive equal wages with male teachers in southeast Indiana. Mrs. Harrell entered the primary class in Brookville College when eight years of age, and while still in the intermediate class she left college to take charge of her first school. Under various pen-names she has written articles on floriculture,

Caroline Lavinia Scott Harrison.

Ethel Hillyer Harris.

Minnie Hauk.

Constance Cary Harrison.
From Photo Copyrighted, 1895, by B. J. Falk, New York.

educational items and letters of travel. She became the wife, in 1872, of Hon. S. S. Harrell, a successful lawyer, now serving his fourth term in the State legislature. Her family consists of two daughters. She was appointed one of the Board of World's Fair Managers of Indiana by Gov. Hovey. She is a member and the secretary of the educational committee and one of the committee on woman's work. Her greatest work is the origination and carrying to a successful completion of the plan known as the "Penny School Collection Fund of Indiana," to be used in the educational exhibit in the Columbian Exposition. Besides these positions, she is superintendent of scientific temperance instruction for Indiana, and is preparing to secure the enactment of a law to regulate the study of temperance in the public schools.

HARRIS, Mrs. Ethel Hillyer, author, was born and reared in Rome, GA. She was educated in Shorter College. She graduated after taking the full course, including music, Latin and French. Her love for Rome, her "hill-girt city," is one of her strongest characteristics, and her enthusiastic devotion to her native land is deep-rooted. A daughter of Dr. Eben Hillyer and a granddaughter of Judge Junius Hillyer, she comes from one of the best families in the State. Her grandfather served five years in Congress, and was the friend of such men as Stephens, Toombs, Hill and Cobb. Mrs. Harris is a niece of Judge George Hillyer, of Atlanta, a prominent member of the Georgia bar. On her grandmother's side she is a lineal descendant of Lyman Hall and George Walton, two of the signers of the Declaration of Independence, and consequently she is a "Daughter of the Revolution." She became the wife of T. W. Hamilton Harris, a young lawyer, of Cartersville, GA. Mrs. Harris has contributed to some of the leading papers of the country, and many of her negro dialect and pathetic sketches have been praised by eminent critics. Her friends number a charming coterie of literary people, who honor and appreciate all that comes from her pen, and in society she ever finds a warm welcome.

HARRISON, Mrs. Anna Symmes, wife of William Henry Harrison, the ninth president of the United States, was born near Morristown, NJ, 25th July, 1775, and died near North Bend, OH, 25th February, 1864. She was a daughter of John Cleve Symmes. She received a thorough educa-tion and was a woman of marked mental powers along many lines. She became General Harrison's wife 22nd November, 1795, without the consent of her father. The marriage was performed during Mr. Symmes' absence from home. The father was soon reconciled to the marriage. During her husband's illustrious career as soldier, as secretary of the Northwest Territory, as territorial delegate in Congress, as governor of the Territory of Indiana, as a leader in the war of 1812 and 1813, as commissioner to the Indians, as a member of the House of Representatives, as a United States Senator, as a minister to the United States of Columbia, as county court and State official in Indiana, and finally as President of the United States, Mrs. Harrison was his helper and guide. She was well informed on political affairs. Her husband was inaugurated President 4th March, 1841, and died on the 4th of the next month. Mrs. Harrison had remained in North Bend, OH, on account of sickness, and was unable to attend him in his last hours. She remained in North Bend until 1855, when she went to the home of her son. Her children were John Scott Harrison, born in 1804 and died in 1878, and Lucy B. Harrison, afterward Mrs. David K. Este, born in Richmond, VA, and died in 1826. Her grandson, Benjamin Harrison, born in 1833, was elected President of the United States in 1888.

HARRISON, Mrs. Caroline Lavinia Scott, wife of Benjamin Harrison, twenty-third President of the United States, was born in Oxford, OH, 1st October, 1832. She was the daughter of Rev. John Witherspoon Scott and Mary Neal Scott. She was educated in the Female Institute of Oxford, where her father was a professor and teacher. Carrie Scott became the wife of Benjamin Harrison, a rising young lawyer and former fellow-pupil, in Oxford, 20th October, 1853. In 1854 they removed to Indianapolis, IN, and began house-keeping in a very modest way, while Mr. Harrison devoted himself to the practice of the law in such a vigorous and manly fashion as soon to attract the attention of the bar in the community. Two children were the offspring of their union, Russell B. and Mary Scott Harrison, now Mrs. McKee. Mrs. Harrison was always a home-loving woman, of a decidedly domestic turn, and noted for her perfect housekeeping. Well born and educated, she kept pace with her husband intellectually, and took an intelligent interest in all that pertained to his business or success in life. After her husband's inauguration as President and her installation as mistress, the White House underwent a thorough course of repairs, such as it never experienced before, notable as were several of its former occupants for good housekeeping. The results were very gratifying, and greatly enhanced the convenience and comfort of the household. Mrs. Harrison left the record of a warm advocate of the extension of the family part of the executive building, which have long since ceased to equal the residence of wealthy representative citizens in Washington and other places. She came of good Revolutionary stock, and was the first president chosen to preside over the Society of the Daughters of the American Revolution, which she did with much grace and dignity. Mrs. Harrison's administration is remembered for her patronage of art. While not highly gifted with artistic ability herself, she was capable of very clever work in both water color and on china, and several struggling young artists owe much of their success to her patronage. She was not fond of public and official social life, its responsibilities being somewhat onerous to her, but enjoyed the society of her friends. In religion she was a Presbyterian. She was quietly interested in all that tended to build up the interests of the Church of the Covenant, where the family worshiped. Mrs. Harrison's character can be summed up in a few words. She was a well-born, well-educated woman of the domestic type, who numbered among her chosen friends many persons distinguished for literary ability, or high personal character. In the White House, where she had seemed to feel the responsibility of her station more than she was uplifted by its honors and privileges, she died, 25th October, 1892. Her widowed niece, Mrs. Dimmick, became ex-President Harrison's second wife.

HARRISON, Mrs. Constance Cary, author, born in Vaucluse, Fairfax county, VA, in 1835. She comes of an old Virginian family, related to the Fairfaxes and to Thomas Jefferson. After the close of the war Miss Cary went to Europe with her mother, and returned in 1867, becoming the wife of Burton Harrison, a lawyer of Virginia. Several years after their marriage they removed to New York, where they now live. In 1876 Mrs. Harrison published her first magazine story, "A Little Centennial Lady." Her published books are "Golden Rod" (New York, 1880); "Helen of Troy" (1881); "Woman's Handiwork in Modern Homes" (1881); "Old Fashioned Fairy Book" (1885), and "Bric-a-Brac Stories" (1886). She has written more recently "Flower de Hundred," a curious history of a Virginia family and plantation since 1650. She is the author of "My Lord Fairfax, of Greenway Court, in Virginia," and of "The Home and Haunts of Washington." She has produced several plays, chiefly adaptations from the French. In 1890 her anonymous story, "The Anglomaniacs," appeared in the "Century Magazine," and the authorship was not revealed until the story was published in book form. That story won for her recognition abroad, and she is now ranked among the leading novelists of the day. Her home in New York City is a social and literary center.

HASKELL, Miss Harriet Newell, educator, born in Waldborough, ME, 14th January, 1835. Her father was Bela B. Haskell, a banker and shipbuilder and a conspicuous citizen of Lincoln county. He served two terms in the Maine legislature and was collector of customs of his district under President Taylor. Miss Haskell was educated in Castleton Collegiate Seminary, Vermont, and Mount Holyoke Seminary, Massachusetts, from which school she was graduated with honor in 1855. An unlimited capacity for fun is one of Miss Haskell's prominent traits, and is one of the points in which her nature touches that of a school-girl, making her relation to them one of unbounded sympathy. She has never lost this characteristic in all the serious responsibilities of her life, and therefore she holds the very key to the school-girl's heart. She is a fine scholar, an able critic and also preeminently a Christian woman. Her first experience in teaching was in Boston, in the Franklin school. Afterward she was principal of the high school in her own town, and later in Castleton Collegiate School. It was while in that school the Rev. Truman Post, D.D., president of the board of trustees of Monticello Seminary, wrote to a friend in Maine, asking him if he could recommend to him a woman to take the the then vacant place of principal of Monticello, who was a scholar and a Christian, a woman of good business capacity and a good educator as well. The friend replied that there was only one such woman in the world, and that was Miss Haskell, of Castleton College, but that she could not be removed from the State of Vermont. After three years of solicitation, Miss Haskell became principal of Monticello, in 1868. The last years of her father's life were passed with her in the seminary. He died in 1887. The Monticello Seminary was destroyed by fire in November, 1888, just as the institution was beginning its second half-century. Through Miss Haskell's energetic efforts a temporary building was put up, and the school was re-opened with eighty-nine of the one hundred and thirty young women who were in the institution when the fire came. In less than two years the present fine buildings were erected. The cornerstone of the new building was laid on 10th June, 1889. The Post Library was given by friends of Dr. Post, of St. Louis, MO, who was for thirty-six years the president of the board of trustees of the seminary. The Eleanor Irwin Reid Memorial Chapel was given by William H. Reid, of Chicago, IL, in memory of his wife. The new seminary was opened in 1890, with one hundred and fifty students, and is now in successful operation, equipped with every modern appliance, and managed by Miss Haskell, whose ideas dominate the institution in every detail.

HASWIN, Mrs. Frances R., musician, composer, poet and actor, born in Ripon, WI, 14th May, 1852. She is descended from a notable ancestry. Gen. Isaac Clark, the Indian fighter and Revolutionary officer, of Vermont, was her great-grandfather. Her grandfather, Major Satterlee Clark, was graduated in the first West Point class in 1807. Her father, Col. Temple Clark, was a gallant officer in the Civil War. Her mother, now Mrs. Annie Starr, born Strong, was descended from noted New England Puritans. Mrs. Haswin's education was directed by her mother, a woman of marked characteristics in many ways, and from whom she inherits sterling traits of character as well as her love of the ideal. She was a proud spirited, sensitive girl, and showed her strong talent in music and histrionics at a very early age. She has composed and published music of a superior order,

both vocal and instrumental. She has written many poems, both tender and heroic, all possessing a strong virility of touch, that have been widely copied and admired. She is the wife of Carl A. Haswin, a man of broad culture, and a gifted and well-known actor. With him she has appeared in most of the prominent theaters of the United States, playing successfully leading rôles in his support. With all her talent and versatility, Mrs. Haswin is a woman of domestic tastes, which find full play in her ideal married life. Her home is in Holly Beach, NJ.

HATCH, Mrs. Mary R. P., poet and story writer, born in the town of Stratford, NH, 19th June, 1848. She is the daughter of Charles G. and Mary Blake Platt. Her ancestors were English. The Blakes settled in Dorchester, MA, in 1620, and the Platts in Stratford, CT, the families presenting a long line of illustrious names, from Admiral Blake, the naval hero, to Senator Platt, who managed the Copyright Bill in Congress. The list includes the Blakes, Judsons and McLellans, of literary fame. Mrs. Hatch's life has been spent in the Connecticut valley. In childhood she possessed a quiet manner and a sensitive disposition, was a close observer and a student of nature. She early developed scholarly and literary tastes. At the age of fifteen she left the common schools and attended the academy in Lancaster, eighteen miles from her home. There she studied the higher mathematics, rhetoric, Latin and French, and there her ability as a writer was discovered and recognized. From that time she contributed sketches on various subjects for the county papers, and articles under her pen-name, "Mabel Percy," from time to time appeared in the Portland "Transcript," "Peterson's Magazine," "Saturday Evening Post" and other papers and periodicals. Since then, under her true name, she has written for "Zion's Herald," Springfield "Republican," Chicago "Inter-Ocean," the "Writer," the "Epoch," "Frank Leslie's Illustrated Newspaper," and others. After leaving school she became the wife of Antipas M. Hatch. Their family consists of two sons, and as the wife of an extensive farmer she has been a busy woman. Her management of her home has left her some time to devote to literature, and her versatility has enabled her to do creditable work in the wide realm of short stories, dialect sketches, essays and poems, grave and gay, society verses and verses in dialect. "The Bank Tragedy," published serially in the Portland "Transcript" and issued in book form, was a great success. Other stories from her pen are "Quicksands," "The Missing Man" and "A Psychical Study."

HAUK, Minnie, operatic singer, born in New York City, 16th November, 1852. Her father, Professor Hauk, was a German, and her mother was an American. She maintains her maiden name on the stage. In private life she is known as the wife of Chevalier Ernst Von Hesse-Wartegg, the well-known traveler, to whom she was married in 1881. When she was a child her parents moved to the West, settling in Kansas, near Leavenworth. They made their home in New Orleans, LA, in 1855, where they lived during the Civil War. Minnie early showed her musical talent and inclination. A wealthy friend made it possible for her to receive a thorough musical education. Her first public appearance was in a charity concert in New Orleans, in 1865. In 1867 she went to New York City, where she sang in the choir in Christ Church and studied with Errani. In 1868 she made her debut as Amina in "La Sonnambula," in New York City, and her success was complete. She won the critics and the public, and ever since that year she has ranked among the most popular of American singers. She made a successful tour of the United States, and then went to London, England, where she sang with brilliant success in Covent Garden, in October, 1868. In 1869 she sang in the Grand Opera, Vienna, and she repeated her triumphs in Moscow, Berlin, Brussels and Paris for several successive seasons. In Brussels, 2nd January, 1878, she created her famous rôle of Carmen. She studied with Richard Wagner, learning two rôles, Elsa and Senta, from him. Her repertory is an extensive one. She is both a superb singer and a powerful actor. Her impersonations have the force and truth of life. Madame Hauk is as happy in her domestic life as she is successful in her profession.

HAVEN, Mrs. Mary Emerson, educator, born in Norfolk, CT, 22nd November, 1819, where her father, Rev. Ralph Emerson, subsequently professor in Andover Seminary, was then pastor. He was a relative of Ralph Waldo Emerson, and many of the family were noted educators. Her uncle, Joseph Emerson, was celebrated as a pioneer in female education, having given a life-long inspiration to such pupils as Mary Lyon and Miss Z. P. Grant, which resulted in their founding such institutions as those in Ipswich and Mt. Holyoke. Mary was educated in her uncle's school and in Ipswich, Andover and Boston. She became the wife of Rev. Joseph Haven, D.D., LL.D., pastor successively in Ashland and Brookline, MA, and afterward professor, first in Amherst College, and then called to the chair of systematic theology in the Chicago Theological Seminary. He was the author of text-books on "Mental and Moral Philosophy," standard in various colleges and schools in this and other countries. Mrs. Haven's position has given her large acquaintance with the literary world. Since her husband's death, in 1874, she has continued to reside in Chicago and has carried on work for the intellectual upbuilding in social life, for which she is admirably fitted by education, experience and extensive travel in this and foreign countries. She has been president of various clubs, of the Haven Class in English literature, of art and history classes, of the "Athena" and of the "Heliades," or Daughters of the Sun, who are following his course around the world, studying all lands he shines upon. Mrs. Haven is a member of the Fortnightly of Chicago, the Woman's Board of Missions of the Interior, and of other associations. Her daughter, Miss Elizabeth Haven, was a teacher in Rockford Female Seminary. Another daughter, Mrs. Alice Haven Danforth, is the wife of Rev. J. R. Danforth, D.D. A third daughter, Miss Ada Haven, has been a missionary under the American Board of Foreign Missions in Pekin, China, since 1879. Mrs. Haven resides with her son, Joseph Haven, a physician, in Chicago.

HAWES, Miss Charlotte W., composer, lecturer and musical educator, born in Wrentham, MA. She comes of old Puritan stock, her ancestors on the father's side having settled in Massachusetts in 1635. A large part of her early education was received in a good and cultivated home. She was the oldest daughter of a large family and became a close companion of her father, from whom she inherited her musical gift. She had her preliminary musical training in Boston and New York, continuing her studies in Germany, in Berlin and Dresden, under the direction of the father of Robert and Clara Schumann. During her stay in Dresden she formed the acquaintance of many eminent musicians, among them the famous Liszt. In 1877 she returned to Boston, where she has since made her home. She holds a high place as a composer of music, a musical lecturer and critic, and a teacher of music. She is well versed in the literature of music. One of her popular achievements in the double rôle of composer and poet is her song, "God Bless the Soldier," written for the National Encampment in Boston in August, 1890, and dedicated to the Grand Army of the Republic. During the week of the encampment it was often played by the bands in the processions. Others of her popular songs are "Cradle Song," "Greeting," and "Nannie's Sailor Lad." She has filled engagements as a musical lecturer throughout the United States. In 1878 she was publicly invited by a number of men and women most distinguished in Boston's musical, literary and social circles to repeat the course consisting of "Nature's Music," "National Music, Hymns and Ballads," "The Influence of Music," and "Liszt." Miss Hawes is a frequent contributor of critical and biographical sketches to musical publications. She is the editor of "Famous Themes of Great Composers," which has gone through four editions. She is a prolific and successful composer, a faithful interpreter of the music of the great masters, a true poet, and a keen, though kindly, critic.

HAWES, Mrs. Flora Harrod, postmaster, born in Salem, IN, in 1863, where she was educated. Her maiden name was Flora New Harrod. She is a daughter of the late Dr. Sandford H. Harrod, a physician well known throughout southern Indiana. The Harrods, after whom Harrodsburg, KY, was named, went to that State with the pioneer, Daniel Boone. Miss Harrod, at an early age, became the wife of Professor Edgar P. Hawes, of Louisville, KY. After a brief married life, her husband died, and she was left upon her own resources. She turned to teaching, and became a successful instructor in elocution, an art in which she excelled and had earned the honors in her school-days. She applied to President Harrison for the post-office in Hot Springs, AR, going in person to urge her own appointment. She received the commission 16th August. 1889, took charge of the office 15th September, 1889, and was confirmed by the Senate 19th December of the same year. Mrs. Hawes receives a salary of $2,600 a year and has a force of thirteen employés, four of whom are women. As postmaster, she is a rigid disciplinarian, and she keeps the business of her office in the most satisfactory shape in every department. She is the youngest woman in the United States holding so important a position, and her office is the second largest one in the Union controlled by a woman. Her administration has been thoroughly satisfactory and successful.

HAWES, Miss Franc P., artist, was born near Chicago, IL. She spent the larger portion of her life in the East, and returned to Chicago in 1886, where she now resides. She comes of good ancestry and claims descent from Queen Anne of England. She is a daughter of John Hughes Hawes, a Virginian, and is related to the Lees and other noted Virginian families. The first wife of Mr. Hawes was a cousin of Jefferson Davis. He was a benevolent, liberal, public-spirited man, and a lawyer by profession. His second wife, the mother of Miss Franc, was a native of Cincinnati, OH, and from her the daughter inherited her artistic talents. Miss Hawes, both as woman and artist, is a person of marked individuality. She has been an artist from her infancy. In childhood she painted whatever she saw, and frequently what her imagination saw. There are treasured still in her family several quaint landscapes and animal studies, painted by the eight-year-old girl before she had had a lesson, either in painting or drawing. The first landscape she painted under the eye of a teacher illustrates her singular gifts. It was scarcely "laid in" before the teacher was called away on some errand. He was gone three hours, and at last returned, with apologies for his absence, but they were unuttered, because in amazement he saw the picture finished, and finished so well that he had no suggestion to make, and it was never touched afterward. One artist, to whom she went for lessons, set her at work in drawing from the cast, but she declined to do that; her wish was to paint directly from nature, and she required instruction only in the intricacies of coloring. She has an intense earnestness, combined with a natural woman's gift of understanding without analysis. From a delicate watercolor of Venetian landscape with local color and atmosphere to a study of lions, her range is seen. A striking characteristic possessed by Miss Hawes is her memory. An idea once worked out never leaves her remembrance. While she prefers landscape, with an occasional excursion into the field of still life, as evidenced by her lion pictures, she yet has done a great deal in decorative work. She has received orders from Marshall Field, of Chicago, and others, receiving $5,000 for a single commission. Many of her tapestries and screens are exquisite, and all of them show originality and artistic merit. Though she has given the greater part of her life to art, she is distinguished for achievements in other fields. She has been a contributor to various publications in the East, furnishing articles on philosophical subjects which show much research. She has also acquired an enviable reputation as an organizer of clubs for philanthropical and literary study.

HAWKS, Mrs. Annie Sherwood, poet and hymn writer, born in Hoosick, NY, 28th May, 1835. Her maiden name was Sherwood. Her ancestry on her father's side was English, and on her mother's side, remotely, Holland Dutch. She was never graduated from any school, but she always had a passion for books and read widely. In her fourteenth year her genius began to find expression in verse. The first poem which she published appeared in a Troy, NY, newspaper. That poem at once attracted attention and was followed by others which were printed in various local papers. Miss Sherwood became the wife, in 1859, of Charles Hial Hawks, a resident of

Hoosck. Mr. Hawks was a man of culture and intelligence, and he understood and appreciated his wife. In January, 1865, Mr. and Mrs. Hawks removed to Brooklyn, NY, in which city Mrs. Hawks still makes her home. Her husband died there in 1888. They had three children, one of whom, a daughter, is now living. Mrs. Hawks has always been identified with the Baptist denomination. In 1868 her pastor and friend, Rev. Dr. Robert Lowry, requested her to turn her attention to hymn writing. She did so, and wrote, among many others, "In the Valley," "Good Night," and "Why Weepest Thou?" In 1872 the hymn by which she is most widely known, "I Need Thee Every Hour," was written. Dr. Lowry sets all her hymns to music. Though Mrs. Hawks is chiefly known as a writer of hymns, she has by no means put her best work into them alone. She has written many noble poems.

HAWLEY, Mrs. Frances Mallette, poet and author, born in Bridgeport, CT, 30th January, 1843. Her father, Prof. Rich, was a well known teacher of vocal music. Frances possessed the gift of music in a remarkable degree. From the time she could speak plainly, she delighted in telling stories to her young companions. On 1st September, 1864, she became the wife of Wheeler Hawley, in Bridgeport, CT, where she has resided since. Mrs. Hawley has a family of three sons and one young daughter. A fourth and youngest son died in youth. Her later stories and poems show deepening and widening powers.

HAYES, Mrs. Lucy Ware Webb, wife of Rutherford B. Hayes, the nineteenth President of the United States, born in Chillicothe, OH, 28th August, 1831, and died in Fremont, OH, 25th June, 1879. She was the daughter of Dr. James Webb and Maria Cook Webb, and the granddaughter of Judge Isaac Cook, of Connecticut. She was educated in the Wesleyan Female Seminary, in Cincinnati, OH, and was graduated in 1852. She became the wife of Mr. Hayes in 1853. Her husband and all her brothers served in the Union army during the Civil War, and her home was the shelter of soldiers sick and wounded. She spent two winters in camp in Virginia with her husband, and also served in the hospital for soldiers in Frederick City, MD. While her husband was a member of Congress from Ohio and Governor of that State, Mrs. Hayes actively promoted State charities. She was one of the organizers of the Ohio Soldiers' and Sailors' Orphans' Home, and served on its board of directors until it was made a State institution. She became mistress of the White House when Mr. Hayes was inaugurated, in March, 1877, and she presided throughout his term of office. Her régime was a decided departure from all former ones. While performing her duties in the most queenly manner and in accordance with every proper demand of the situation, she made the White House a religious and temperance home. She was a woman in whom the religious and moral elements predominated. While she presided in the White House, she would not permit wine to be served on the table. The innovation called down upon her much censure from certain quarters, but her action was highly commended by all temperance workers. At the close of her term in the White House she received a large album and other testimonials of approval from prominent persons. Retiring from the White House in 1881, Mr. and Mrs. Hayes returned to their home in Fremont, OH. Mrs. Hayes became deeply interested in the Woman's Relief Corps. She served for several years as president of the Woman's Home Missionary Society of the Methodist Episcopal Church. She was elected an honorary member of the Society of the Army of West Virginia, in recognition of her services to the soldiers during the Civil War. Mrs. Hayes was a woman of broad mind, liberal culture, exalted views and strong and positive character.

HAYNES, Miss Lorenza, minister, born in Waltham, MA, 15th April, 1820. She is a direct descendant on the paternal side of Walter Haynes, who came from England with his family in 1638. The next year he bought of Cato, an Indian, for the sum of five pounds, a tract of land, now the town of Sudbury, near Boston. Lorenza is of the seventh generation, all of whom, including her father's family, except herself, were born in Sudbury. The maternal side is descended from the Scotch. From childhood Lorenza showed an unusual interest in books, and, born in a town which had a library and an annual course of lectures, she became a constant reader and student. Miss Haynes passed through the grades of the public schools, and then attended the Waltham Academy of Louis Smith. She taught one of the public schools in her native town for nearly two years, but love of study was so strong that she went for a time to the old academy in Leicester, MA. Afterward she taught a public school for six years in the city of Lowell, and there made the acquaintance of Margaret Foley, a cameo cutter. Then began a friendship which continued for nearly thirty years and ended only at the death of Miss Foley, who had become an eminent sculptor in Rome. Miss Haynes. afterward held the position of lady principal in the Academy in Chester, NH. She subsequently established a young ladies' seminary in Rochester, NY. After four years of intense labor she was compelled to return to her home for rest and restoration. Passing through many years of invalidism, she then accepted the position of librarian of the public library which Waltham was to establish, having entire charge of the cataloguing and work of organizing the library. After six-and-a-half years of service, she resigned her office in order to enter the Universalist Theological school of St. Lawrence University, Canton, NY. Frequently, while librarian, she has been upon the platform as a lecturer. For a year before leaving the library she read and studied under the direction of Rev. Olympia Brown, who wished her at once to take charge of a parish which was open to her. Miss Haynes was not willing to enter the work less equipped theologically than young men graduates. Two months before her course of study was finished in Canton, she received a call from the Universalist Church in Hallowell, ME, to become its pastor when she left Canton. She had never preached before the society. She accepted the call, and was there ordained on 10th February, 1875. She officiated as chaplain in the House of Representatives and also in the Senate, in Augusta, ME. This was the first instance of a woman acting in that capacity in that State. She was chaplain for two terms in the National Soldiers' Home near Augusta, the first woman who had filled that place, and had an invitation for a third term, when she resigned her pastorate in Hallowell for one in Marlborough, MA. While preaching in the latter place she was invited by Post 4, Grand Army of the Republic, to make some remarks in the exercises of Memorial Day, 1876. The following year she was unanimously invited to deliver the oration of the day. It was the first time a woman in Massachusetts had filled that position. Miss Haynes has been settled over parishes in Fairfield, ME, Rockport, MA, and Skowhegan, ME. She has often found her labors exceedingly arduous, especially during Maine winters, preaching sometimes in two or three places the same day. She has ridden ten and twelve miles in an open sleigh, with the mercury below zero, to officiate at a funeral. She left her parish in Fairfield, ME, in 1883, for a European tour. She has been from its organization a member and first vice-president of the Woman's Ministerial Conference. Miss Haynes has been a worker in various reformatory societies. She has always been a woman suffragist. She has often spoken upon platforms and before legislative committees in the State Houses of Massachusetts and Maine. Greatly to the regret of her society as of herself, in 1889, she was obliged to leave her last pastorate, which was in Skowhegan, ME, on account of over-worked eyes. Having previously bought herself a home in Waltham, but a few rods from the family homestead, where her only sister resides, she became the occupant of her cottage in July, 1889, where she now resides.

HAYWARD, Mrs. Mary E. Smith, business woman, born in Franklin, PA, 9th July, 1849. Her maiden name was Mary E. Smith. When she was twelve years old, her father died. Her mother's determined efforts secured for her a good education. Imbued with the desire of being a useful member of the commonwealth, and endowed with natural abilities for a practical business life, she, after a season of teaching, entered into the oil and mercantile business till 1885, when she removed to Dawes county, NE, then but sparsely settled, and took up some land claims. When the town of Chadron was located, she

was one of the first to go into business there. She has been very successful. Tender toward all life, though her business includes a large millinery department, she never sells a bird or wing. On 29th December, 1887, she became the wife of W. F. Hayward. For years she has been one of the most prominent woman suffragists of Nebraska and has been identified with all humane work and reforms. She believes the church is responsible for the subservient condition of women. She is an agnostic and believes in "one world at a time." Mrs. Hayward is an embodiment of energy, push, perseverance and industry; and a fair example of woman's ability to succeed in practical life. She is a State member of the Nebraska Woman Suffrage Association.

HAZARD, Mrs. Rebecca N., philanthropist and woman suffragist, born in Woodsfield, OH, 10th November, 1826. With her parents, at an early age, she removed to Cincinnati, OH, and thence to Quincy, IL, where, in 1844, she became the wife of William T. Hazard, of Newport, RI. Five children were born to this union. In 1850 the family removed to St. Louis, MO. For many years domestic affairs claimed the attention of Mrs. Hazard, but, being deeply imbued with religious principles, the wants and woes of humanity everywhere manifested received a share of her activities. In 1854 she united with other women, in establishing an Industrial Home for Girls in St. Louis. For five years she was on the board of managers of that institution, which has sheltered thousands of homeless children. At the breaking out of the war Mrs. Hazard, who was an ardent Unionist, engaged in hospital work, giving all the time she could spare from her family to the care of sick and wounded soldiers. She helped to organize the Union Aid Society and served as a member of the executive committee in the great Western Sanitary Fair. Finding that large numbers of negro women and children were by the exigencies of war helplessly stranded in the city, Mrs. Hazard sought means for their relief. They were in a deplorable condition, and, as the supplies contributed to the soldiers could not be used for them, she organized a society known as the Freedmen's Aid Society, for their special benefit. At the close of the war that society was merged in an orphan asylum. Closely following that work came the establishment of a home for fallen women, promoted and managed chiefly by the same workers. It was maintained under great difficulties for some years, and was finally abandoned. Deeply impressed with the disabilities under which women labor in being deprived of political rights, Mrs. Hazard with a few other earnest women met one May day in 1867, and formed the Woman Suffrage Association of Missouri, the first society bearing the name, and having for its sole object the ballot for woman. To this cause Mrs. Hazard gave devoted service for many years, filling the various offices of the association, and also serving one term as president of the American Woman Suffrage Association. In 1870 the city of St. Louis, falling under evil counsels, framed into law man's lowest thought concerning woman. Realizing the danger to good morals, Mrs. Hazard at once engaged in the conflict for the overthrow of that iniquity, a conflict more distasteful than any she had ever been called to share. Victory was with the right, and the law was repealed by the Missouri Legislature in 1874, one member only voting against repeal. The call for the formation of the association for the advancement of women, known as the Woman's Congress, was signed by Mrs. Hazard, and she has ever since been a member of that body, contributing at various times to its sessions the following papers: "Home Studies for Women," "Business Opportunities for Women," and "Crime and its Punishment." Mrs. Hazard is a member of the Woman's Christian Temperance Union and of the American Akadêmê, a philosophical society having headquarters in Jacksonville, IL. Since the death of her husband, in 1879, she has practically retired from public work, but at her home in Kirkwood, a suburb of St. Louis, a class of women meets each week for study and mutual improvement. As a result of these studies Mrs. Hazard has published two papers on the "Divina Commedia." She has also written a volume on the war period in St. Louis, not yet published, and her contributions to local and other papers have been numerous.

HAZELRIGG, Mrs. Clara H., author, educator and reformer, born in Council Grove, KS, 23rd November, 1861. She is the youngest living daughter of Col. H. J. Espy. Her mother was Melora E. Cook, teacher in the schools of Sandusky, OH. Her father was apprenticed to learn a trade, but ran away at the age of thirteen to become a soldier. For more than ten years he was a member of the standing army of the United States. He served with distinction in the Mexican war and was Colonel of the 68th Indiana Volunteers during the Civil War. Wounded several times, carried off the field of Chickamauga for dead, his injuries caused his death shortly after the close of the war, and his four children were left orphans, their mother having died several years before his decease. With an only sister, Clara returned to Indiana, where she had resided during the war, and remained there until after her marriage. At the time of her birth Kansas was undergoing her early struggles for freedom, and the spirit of the times stamped itself on the mind of the child. From the age of eleven she supported herself. Fitting herself for teaching, she began to teach when a young girl, and that occupation she has followed almost without cessation for sixteen years. When twelve years old, she wrote for the press, but, being of a sensitive, retiring disposition, she shrank from public criticism and seldom wrote over her own name. In 1877 she became the wife of W. A. Hazelrigg, of Greensburg, IN. They have one child, a girl. They removed to Kansas in 1884, and Mrs. Hazelrigg has taught every year since. She is principal of one of the city schools in El Dorado. She has traveled much during her vacations, and writes constantly during the entire year for the press. She has written for many prominent periodicals in various States. She is the editor of a department in a prominent Chicago paper, and is a regular contributor to the Topeka "Lancet." She has labored in the silver-medal work for the Woman's Christian Temperance Union and in the public work of the Woman's Relief Corps. An active member of the Christian Church since childhood, her work has always been with young people, with whom she is very popular.

HEAD, Mrs. Ozella Shields, author, born in Macon, GA, 19th October, 1869. Her maiden name was Shields. She was reared and educated in Atlanta, GA, and she is a thorough Georgian in heart as well as by birth. Her taste for literature and her talent for production were shown in childhood, when she wrote a number of love stories. Her first published work, a sensational love story of thirty chapters, was "Sundered Hearts," published in the Philadelphia "Saturday Night," when Miss Shields was eighteen years old. Her next works were "Verona's Mistake" and "A Sinless Crime," published in the same journal. Other stories followed in quick succession. In 1889 she brought out her "Izma" through a New York house. In November, 1889, she became the wife of Daliel B. Head, of Greenville, Miss., and her home is now in that town.

HEARNE, Miss Mercedes Leigh, actor, was born in Atlanta, GA, 20th March, 1867. She is widely known by her stage name, Mercedes Leigh, which she chose when she began her professional career. Miss Leigh was born into the changed conditions that followed the Civil War in the South, and her early life was full of the echoes of the great struggle. She was educated in a private school in Philadelphia, PA. At an early age she developed marked dramatic talent, which was carefully cultivated. Her histrionic powers and her emotional nature fitted her for stage work. She went to England, and while there achieved a brilliant success in London drawing-rooms as a damatic reader. The critics abroad gave her high rank, and at home she has repeated her successes an even greater scale. Besides her dramatic talents, Miss Leigh is the possessor of poetic talent of a fine order. Her work in verse bears every mark of culture. Her home is now in New York.

HEATON, Mrs. Eliza Putnam, journalist and editor, born in Danvers, MA, 8th August, 1860. She is the daughter of the late Rev. James W. Putnam, a Universalist minister. She comes from Revolutionary ancestry. She was in youth a delicate girl and attended school irregularly. In 1882 she was graduated from the Boston University with the first honors of her class. In that year she became the wife of John L. Heaton, then associate editor of the Brooklyn "Daily Times." Her newspaper work as an occasional contributor to the columns of that paper began almost immediately. In 1886 she took an office desk and position upon the editorial staff of the "Times." For four years her pen was busy in nearly every department of the paper, her work appearing mostly on the editorial page and in the special sheets of the Saturday edition, and ranging from politics to illustrated city sketches, for which her camera furnished the pictures. She handled the exchange editor's scissors and did a vast deal of descriptive writing and interviewing. Almost coincident with her engagement upon the "Times" was her entrance into the syndicate field. Through a prominent syndicate publishing firm of New York she sent out an average of three New York letters per week, illustrated from photographs taken by herself, and dealing with men, women and current topics of the day. In September, 1888, she took passage from Liverpool to New York in the steerage of the Cunarder "Aurania," for the purpose of studying life among the emigrants. She not only landed with her fellow-travelers at Castle Garden, but accompanied them as far west as Chicago in an emigrant train. When the New York "Recorder" was started in 1891, she undertook a task never before attempted by any New York daily, to run a daily news page dealing with women's movements. The experiment was successful and had become recognized as the unique and especially attractive feature of the paper, when she resigned her charge to join her husband on the Providence "News," which he established in September of that year. From the first issue of the new daily Mr. and Mrs. Heaton were associated as joint-editors, and during a long and critical illness, into which Mr. Heaton fell at the end of the first few weeks of its existence, Mrs. Heaton was for months sole responsible editor. She has one child, a boy of eight years. She is a member of Sorosis and other women's clubs.

HEINSOHN, Mrs. Dora Henninges, opera singer, born in Mansfield, OH, 2nd August, 1861. Mrs. Heinsohn comes from a very musical family. She began her studies when but seven years old, both vocal and instrumental, with her father, R. E. Henninges. She sang in concerts and operettas at fourteen, and her advancement was so rapid that she soon entered the Cincinnati College of Music, where she advanced to the highest position among vocal pupils, attracting not only the attention of the faculty, but also of persons generally interested in music. Her teachers up to that time had been Signor La Villa and Signor Stefanone. Later she became a pupil of Max Maretzek, under whose guidance she began to study Italian opera. Her first appearance in opera, after having sung many times in oratorios and concerts under Theodore Thomas, was under Mapleson, when she appeared as Leonora in Beethoven's "Fidelio." Soon after, she went to Paris, where she became a pupil of Mme. Lagrange, under whose direction she completed her studies. After her return to this country, Miss Henninges appeared in German opera in the Metropolitan Opera House, New York, and in many concerts, both in the East and the West. She possesses a powerful dramatic soprano voice, which she uses with intelligence. Her repertory is a large one, consisting of hundreds of songs and dozens of operatic rôles. In 1888 Miss Henninges became the wife of G. W. Heinsohn, of Cleveland, OH, and has ince been devoting her time to teaching and to church and concert singing in St. Louis, MO.

HELM, Miss Lucinda Barbour, author, born in Helm Place, near Elizabethtown, KY, 23rd December, 1839. She is the granddaughter of Ben. Hardin, the satirist, humorist and jurist of Kentucky, and the daughter of John L. Helm, twice governor of Kentucky. He was the first governor after the Civil War. Her paternal grandfather, Thomas Helm, went to Kentucky in Revolutionary times and settled near Elizabethtown. That place, known as Helm Place, is still in the possession of the family. Her mother, Lucinda B. Hardin, the oldest daughter of Ben. Hardin, was a woman of culture. She early trained her children to a love for books. Miss Helm inherited from her mother a love for

reading and a deep religious faith. At an early age she commenced to write poetry and prose under the pen-name "Lucile." When she was eighteen years old, she published a strong article on the "Divinity of the Savior." During the Civil War she wrote sketches for the English papers, which were received very favorably and were widely copied in England. While George D. Prentice was editor of the Louisville "Journal," she wrote many sketches for that paper. She afterward wrote short stories for the "Courier" and the "Courier Journal," and articles in the "Christian Advocate." She has published one volume, "Gerard: The Call of the Church Bell" (Nashville, TN, 1884). Miss Helm has written many leaflets for both home and foreign missions, which have been widely circulated. In May, 1886, the General Conference of the Methodist Episcopal Church South authorized the Board of Church Extension to organize the woman's organization known as the Woman's Department of Church Extension, until 1890, when it received a more definite title, Woman's Parsonage and Home Mission Society. Miss Helm was made the general secretary, and to her endeavors is due much of its success. The society, hoping to enlarge its power of good, decided to publish a paper, "Our Homes." Miss Helm was made the editor, and its success is assured. Miss Helm is also a member of the Woman's Foreign Missionary Society and of the International Christian Workers' Association.

HENDERSON, Mrs. Augusta A. Fox, social leader, born near Tiffin City, OH, 17th May, 1843. She is the daughter of Alonzo H. Fox and Caroline A. Brownell, originally of New York, now of California. Mr. Fox was a successful "Forty-niner" and removed to Iowa with his family in 1853. Mrs. Henderson was a student in the Upper Iowa University, where she met her future husband, David B. Henderson, the able and brilliant representative of the 3rd District of Iowa since 1883. In 1866 she became Mr. Henderson's wife in West Union, the home of her parents. From there they went to Dubuque, where they now live. Alive to all the interests of the day and their ever increasing demands for attention, she has the qualities of mind and heart, a true sympathy, clear

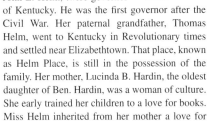

discernment and sound decision, that belong to those whom fate and fortune call out as leaders.

HENDERSON, Mrs. Frances Cox, linguist, traveler, author and philanthropist, born in Philadelphia, PA, 21st July, 1820. She was educated abroad and spent twenty-one years in Europe, excepting Russia, associating always with persons speaking the language of the country. Her talent for languages was shown early by her translating, at the age of fourteen, from English into French two books, which were published in Paris by a well-known bookseller. In 1882 she published her "Epitome of Modern European Literature," comprising translations from nineteen European languages, the Swedish, Hungarian, Italian, Russian, Slovack, Spanish, Dutch, German, Polish, Czeck, Flemish, Portuguese, French, Croatian, Danish, Serbian, Slavonian, Norwegian and Roumanian. The first edition, published in 1881, of this work contained only seventeen translations. In its preparation she did not receive the slightest assistance. She has written numbers of short stories for periodicals, among others, sketches of southern life as it was before the abolition of slavery, but the "Epitome" is the only work to which she has ever affixed her name. Very much of her writing has been for purposes of immediate use, to awaken interest in local needs, or for household purposes, in aid of progressive opinions, especially those which affect the status of woman. She claims to be the first person who understood that the Bible is the stronghold of "woman's rights." In 1848, when the two or three who dared to speak in favor of women were tempted to renounce their belief in revelation, she wrote to the leaders of the movement, proving to them that they would be forsaking their surest stronghold. Mrs. Henderson is a pronounced advocate of female suffrage, though she is not a platform speaker and takes no public part in their meetings. Like many others unknown to the public, she keeps up a guerrilla warfare as opportunity offers. She has published, at various times, very pronounced views upon the scattered race of the Hebrews, with ingenious arguments to sustain the position which she takes. She gives a generous portion of her time as well as means to looking after the welfare and comfort of those in her vicinity who are in need of any kind of help. Her affiliations are with the Episcopal Church. Mrs. Henderson is the widow of Gen. James Pinckney Henderson, U. S. A. Gen. Henderson is best remembered as the first Governor of Texas, after the admission of that State to the Union in 1845.

HENDRICKS, Mrs. Eliza C. Morgan, social leader and philanthropist, born near North Bend, a suburb of Cincinnati, OH, 22nd November, 1823. She is the widow of the late Vice-President Thomas A. Hendricks. Her father was Hon. Isaac Morgan. The love of nature, which is one of Mrs. Hendricks' characteristics, was fostered by her early surroundings. The large and attractive homestead, in which she first saw the light, adjoined that of Gen. William Henry Harrison, and both dwellings were noted for their fine outlook. Mrs. Hendricks is connected with some of the leading families of Cincinnati, and it was in that city she made her début in the social world. She was married 26th September, 1845, and since that time she has resided in Indiana. Her first Hoosier home was in Shelbyville, in which place her husband was then engaged in the practice of law. They removed to Indianapolis in 1860, where he practiced for some years as a member of the law firm of Hendricks, Hord & Hendricks. Mrs. Hendricks was fond of domestic life and was the administrator of the household, saving her husband from all unnecessary annoyance or responsibility, and in many other ways was she his true help-meet. Her husband depended much upon her judgment. Often, while an occupant of the gubernatorial chair, when perplexed over applications for the pardon of criminals, did he call her into the conference, in order to avail himself of her intuitive perception of the merits of the case Mrs. Hendricks' love of nature leads her to spend much time in the culture of flowers, in which she has much success. She has a great penchant for pets. Her fondness for horses led to that close observation of them which made her a good judge of their qualities, and it was she, not her husband, who always selected the carriage horses. A few years after her marriage, her only child, a bright and beautiful boy, died. Mrs. Hendricks was not only the light of her husband's home life, but, wherever his official duties called him, he was accompanied by her, and when he twice visited the Old World, in quest of health, she was his faithful companion. The great sorrow of her life was his death, which occurred in November, 1884. Since that event she has sought assuagement for grief and loneliness in a quickening of activities, especially in the lines of charity. Her most prominent philanthropic work was her persevering efforts, with other earnest women, to establish a "Prison for Women and Reform School for Girls." In answer to earnest and persistent solicitation on their part, the State Legislature made an appropriation, and in 1883 the building was erected. That institution has, from its beginning, been under the entire control and management of women. For some years it was the only one of its kind in the country. Mrs. Hendricks has, from its beginning, been the president of its board of managers. Before her marriage she connected herself with the Methodist Church. Her husband, the son of an elder in the Presbyterian Church, was strongly Calvinistic in faith. They both had a leaning toward the Episcopal form of worship, and together they entered that communion. Mrs. Hendricks is now living in Indianapolis.

HENRY, Mrs. Josephine Kirby Williamson, woman suffragist, born in Newport, KY, 22nd February, 1846. After receiving a liberal education she became the wife, in 1868, of Captain William Henry, a Confederate soldier, a distinguished scholar and one of the most noted educators in the South. Their only child, Frederick Williamson Henry, who was killed in the terrible railroad disaster in Crete, IL, inherited the genius of his mother and the talent of his father. Mrs. Henry enjoys the distinction of being the leader in her State of the most advanced political and social reform party in the country, the Equal Rights or Woman Suffrage party. She knows human nature and history well enough to realize that "human virtue demands her champions and martyrs." With courage, zeal and industry Mrs. Henry has for years been struggling with "supreme prejudice and sublime mediocrity "in her efforts to awaken in the breasts of her countrymen a sentiment of justice toward women, and in her countrywomen a sense of the dignity of true womanhood. What she has already accomplished marks an advance in the political and social history, not only of Kentucky, but of the Southern States. She is the only woman in the South who ever ran for a State office. She was a candidate of the Prohibition party of Kentucky, in 1890, for clerk of the Court of Appeals, receiving nearly five-thousand votes, and that in a State where, perhaps, the popular prejudice is stronger against "Woman's Rights" than in any other in the Union. She has spoken before the legislature and the constitutional convention and has addressed large audiences all over the State on woman's suffrage. Although she is physically frail and delicate, she can address a public meeting for an hour or more with the force of true eloquence and with happy touches of humor and quiet sarcasm. She is a woman of literary talent. She has written several poems of merit, and her prose is clear, bold and incisive. Over three hundred articles of hers on the subject of "Married Women's Property Rights" have been published. Her leaflet on "Kentucky Women and the Constitution" and her editorials in the "Clarion," published in Versailles, attracted general attention and were copied into papers all over the country. She is superintendent of legislative and petition work of the Kentucky Equal Rights Association. She is an accomplished musician and pianist. As a vocalist she has achieved success. Her home is in Versailles, KY.

HENRY, Mrs. Sarepta M. I., evangelist, temperance reformer, poet and author, born in Albion, PA, 4th November, 1839. Her father, Rev. H. Nelson Irish, was a Methodist clergyman of the old style. He was preaching in Albion at the time of the daughter's birth. In 1841 he was sent to Illinois as a missionary, where he did heroic pioneer work and where he ended his days. In 1859 Miss Irish entered the Rock River Seminary, in Mt. Morris, IL, when she had for her pastor Rev. J. H. Vincent, then just coming into his life work. Recognition had been given to her literary ability, and during her school days she won many honors in composition. On 7th March, 1861, Miss Irish became the wife of James W. Henry, of East Homer, NY. The Civil War broke in upon the plans of the young couple and left Mrs. Henry, in 1871, a soldier's widow. The trio of children born from this union are just such as would be expected from so true a marriage. Mary, an alumna of the Northwestern University in Evanston, IL, is already a writer of acknowledged ability in both prose and verse, and at the national convention of the Woman's Christian Temperance Union in New York, in 1888, she was elected to the position of superintendent of the press department. Alfred, the oldest son, is a faithful and eloquent clergyman, and Arthur is an author. Mrs. Henry was among the first to join the crusade against rum. From the beginning of the organization of the Woman's Christian Temperance Union she has been associated with the national body as superintendent of evangelical work and as evangelist. The result of her seven years of service in gospel temperance in Rockford, IL, would alone suffice to crown the labors of any ordinary life-time. A partial record of this work is found in her book "Pledge and Cross." Her published books number fourteen, of which two, "Victoria," written during the first year of her daughter's life, and "Marble Cross," are poems. The prose works are "After the Truth," in four volumes, "Pledge and Cross," "Voice of the Home and its Legend," "Mabel's Work," "One More Chance," "Beforehand," "Afterward," "Unanswered Prayer," and "Frances Raymond's Investment." Mrs. Henry has long occupied pulpits among all denominations throughout the land. Through her evangelistic work saloons have been closed, churches built and hundreds converted. Her home is now in Evanston, Illinois.

HENSCHEL, Mrs. Lillian Bailey, vocalist, born in Columbus, OH, 17th January, 1860. Her musical talent manifested itself very early in life, as, when she was fifteen months old, she plainly showed her choice of different tunes, crying and refusing to sleep if her mother sang one song, and at once remaining quiet when she heard another air. At the age of eighteen months the little one could sing the different tunes she had been accustomed to hear. From that point her whole life has been devoted to the study of music. She began to take piano lessons at the age of seven. Her mother, who was also a singer and had received vocal instruction in Boston, MA, from the best teachers of her time, directed the daughter's vocal studies. At the age of fifteen the family removed to Boston, and she continued her studies with her uncle, Charles Hayden, a well-known vocal teacher. Later she became a pupil of Madame Rudersdorf, with whom she studied two years. In 1876 Lillian Bailey made her first public appearance in one of B. J. Lang's concerts, given in Boston, meeting with success. After her début she continued to be a favorite singer in Boston, and her services were in constant demand during the concert season, until, in 1877, she went to Paris to study with Madame Viardot, with whom she remained for some time. In the spring of 1878 she went to London, where she made her first appearance in England with the London Philharmonic Society. In that concert she sang for the first time one of those duets with Mr. Henschel, which have since become so famous. She returned to America in the autumn of 1880 and became the wife of George Henschel, the musician, in the spring of 1881. They remained in Boston three years, Mr. Henschel having charge of the Boston Symphony Orchestra. They removed to London in 1884, which is now their permanent home. There Mr. Henschel holds the position of a leading musician. Mrs. Henschel's fame as a singer is worldwide, as she has been heard in all the principal cities of Europe. At the time of the Ohio Centennial, held in Columbus, she was represented as being one of the celebrated women of that State. Mr. and Mrs. Henschel receive their friends with great hospitality in their beautiful home. Many a homesick American, having located in London to study music with Mr. Henschel, has found in these successful musicians true friends and helpers, who were ready and willing to dissipate the feeling of unrest and to assist in showing the way onward to success.

HERRICK, Mrs. Christine Terhune, author and editor, born in Newark, NJ, 13th June, 1859, where her father was settled as pastor of a Dutch Reformed Church. Her mother is the well-known author, "Marion Harland." In 1876 she went abroad with her parents and spent two years in some of the principal cities of Europe, acquiring a knowledge of foreign languages and continuing an education which had been previously carried on under private teachers at home. After returning to this country, Miss Terhune lived for several years in Springfield, MA, perfecting herself in English literature, Anglo-Saxon and philology. Her ambition was to teach her favorite branches, and for a time she had a class in a private school for girls. About that time she met and became the wife of James Frederick Herrick, a member of the editorial staff of the Springfield "Republican." Early in her married life Mrs. Herrick began to write on home topics, developing the talent which has made her so well known. She has contributed to many leading periodicals and newspapers, and has published five books, four of them on home topics, and the other a compilation of correspondence between the late Duke of Wellington and a young woman known as "Miss J." At present Mrs. Herrick lives in New York. She edits the woman's page of the New York "Recorder." Her husband is connected with another metropolitan daily newspaper. While kept very busy by her literary engagements, she does not neglect her household cares, the precepts which she teaches finding practical illustration in her pretty and well-regulated home. She has had four children, and two little boys survive. The rapidity and ease with which Mrs. Herrick turns off her literary work enables her to pay some attention to the obligations and pleasures of society. She is as clever a talker as she is a writer, and is an active member of Sorosis. Her health is unusually good and her activity and good spirits unfailing. She spends her summers in her country home, "Outlook," among the hills of northern New Jersey.

HERSOM, Mrs. Jane Lord, physician, born in Sanford, ME, 6th August, 1840. Her father and mother were of good English descent. She was educated in Springvale, ME, whither the family had removed. She began to teach before she was sixteen, going to school in the fall and winter and teaching in the summer. In 1865, when twenty five years of age, she became the wife of Dr. N. A. Hersom. He took his bride to Farmington, NH, where they settled. In 1862 Dr. Hersom had entered the army as an assistant surgeon, was promoted to first surgeon, and afterward had charge of a field hospital. After the war he began a laborious country practice. His strength soon gave way so as to necessitate a vacation of five years. He then resumed work and established himself in Portland, ME, where he soon acquired a practice which demanded all his time and energies. In 1881 Dr. Hersom went abroad for needed rest and died in Dublin, Ireland, one week after landing. Mrs. Hersom had read medical works to her husband during his sickness, and, enjoying them, continued to read when the need was past. Her husband had been aware of her special fitness, and had often told her she would make a fine physician. The knowledge of his confidence in her abilities acted as a stimulus, and with characteristic energy she began her studies with Prof. S. H. Weeks, of Portland, ME. In 1883 she entered the Woman's Medical College in Philadelphia. After her graduation from that institution she began work in Portland, planning only for a small office practice. Her desires have been far more than realized. She has had a large and increasing practice from the first. She was elected physician of the Temporary Home for Women and Children, in Portland, which position she held for four years, until she was obliged to resign in order to attend properly to her other duties. She is a member of the American Medical Association, the State and County Medical Societies and also of the Practitioner's Club, of which she was elected president for 1892. She is an active member of the Woman's Suffrage Association. She became a woman suffragist through her experience as a student and physician. One of her children died in infancy, and one daughter is living.

HEWITT, Mrs. Emma Churchman, author and journalist, born in New Orleans, LA, 1st February, 1850. At three years of age she moved north with her parents, who settled on a farm in Rahway, NJ, afterward moving to Burlington, NJ, and later to Camden, in the same State, where she resided until several years ago, when she moved to West Philadelphia, PA. She comes of a long line of cultured and educated people, and is a direct descendant of old John Churchman, who was prominent in the sect of Friends in his day. Mrs. Hewitt is a fluent French scholar, with a knowledge of several other modern languages. She began to write short stories at such a very early age that it has been quaintly remarked that she was "born with a pen in her hand." In 1884 she became a journalist and engaged with the "Daily Evening Reporter" of Burlington, NJ, where she labored until its change of management. In 1885, at the solicitation of the publisher of the "Ladies' Home Journal," she began a series of articles with the unique title "Scribbler's Letters to Gustavus Adolphus." The next year she received a call from the same publisher to the associate-editorship of the journal, which position she filled for four years. Notwithstanding her arduous and exacting work while occupying the editor's chair, she contributed regularly sketches, short stories and articles on domestic topics to at least a dozen other periodicals. Her "Ease in Conversation" first appeared in the "Ladies' Home Journal" under the title of "Mildred's Conversation Class." These articles have been published in book form (Philadelphia, 1887), and the volume, entitled "Ease in Conversation," has gone into its third edition, and her "Hints to Ballad Singers" (Philadelphia, 1889) has had an extended sale. Her chief literary work is the "Queen of Home," (Philadelphia, 1889) treating in an exhaustive and masterly manner subjects of household interest from attic to cellar. She has contributed from time to time to the Philadelphia "Press," the "Christian-at-Work," the "Sunday-School Times," the "Weekly Wisconsin," the "Housekeeper," the "Ladies' Home Journal," "Babyhood," the "Home Guard," "Golden Days," "Our Girls and Boys," "Our Young Men," "Wide Awake," "Munyon's Illustrated World," "Lippincott's Magazine," and a number of others. She is a regular contributor to several English home magazines and has lately completed a series of papers on household topics for a London periodical. Mrs. Hewitt has a son, a young man of eighteen years, and a daughter in her sixteenth year. About two years ago Mrs. Hewitt severed her connection with the "Ladies'

Home Journal" and accepted a position on the editorial staff of the "Home Magazine," published in Washington, DC, which she was obliged to resign on account of the death of her sister, which compelled her to live in Philadelphia. She is now connected with "Leisure Hours," a monthly publication in Philadelphia.

HIBBARD, Mrs. Grace, author, born in a suburb of Boston, MA, and there received her education. She is the daughter of the late Dr. Porter, a Massachusetts clergyman, and a descendant of an old English family. Her early life was spent in New England, where, at her father's knee, when still a child, she learned the Hebrew and Greek alphabets long before she learned the English. At an early

age she was graduated from a young ladies' college near Boston. Soon after she graduated her father removed to Chicago, where after a short time he died. Mrs. Hibbard has spent the last few years in Colorado and California, and she has made a number of trips to Mexico, where she studied the Mexican character, which she has portrayed in her writings. Her first literary work appeared in the Springfield, MA, "Republican," and since then she has been a contributor to many of the leading magazines and papers of America. In short stories and ballads she excels. One short sketch, "Bummer and Lazarus," a story of San Francisco, was translated into the German and printed in one of the leading papers published in the German language. She has contributed to "Belford's Magazine," the San Francisco "Morning Call" and other journals. About three years ago she became the wife, in Colorado Springs, CO, of Dr. Hibbard, of Denver, CO, and now lives in the last named city.

HIBLER, Mrs. Nellie, musical educator, born in Utica, NY, 10th September, 1858. Her parents, Mr. and Mrs. John R. Owen, are Welsh, and members of families of culture. Nellie from her early childhood was noted for her love of music. When quite young, she was graduated from the Utica advanced school and entered the academy. When in her sixteenth year, she accompanied her parents to Wales, and for three years they lived in the town of Aberystwyth. There Nellie received a scholarship for piano and harmony. By extraordinary diligence she was graduated in two-and-a-half years instead of three. She received the title Associate in Music of the University College of Wales. While abroad, her studies were under the direction of Dr. Parry, the famous Welsh composer. Not long after her graduation she returned with her parents to Utica, where she was for a time the organist of the South Street Methodist Episcopal Church. Afterward the family moved to Parker's Landing, PA, where the daughter sang in the Presbyterian Church. She gathered a large class in music, which she taught with much success until she became the wife of Mr. Hibler, of Parker's Landing, who was then teller of the Exchange Bank. In less than three years after her marriage her husband and infant son died, within a few days of each other. Again she took up her profession and concluded to make a specialty of voice culture. She has been instructed by some of the best teachers in America. In Bradford, PA, where she now resides, she was a leading soprano for two years in the Presbyterian Church, and for two more years the leader of the choir. Owing to the increased number of her private students, she resigned her position as a leader. She often sings in concerts and some of her compositions have been lately published.

HICKMAN, Mrs. Mary Catharine, journalist, born in Hanover, Columbiana county, OH, 7th November, 1838. Her father, David Arter, was of German descent and was remarkable for energy and force of character. Her mother was a woman of much natural refinement and great gentleness and kindness of disposition. She was the daughter of Henry Laffer, distinguished in his day as a general, judge and legislator. Mrs. Hickman was endowed with fine natural ability and maintained a high rank in all her classes as a school-girl, although delicate health interfered somewhat with her early studies. In 1857 she was graduated from the Cleveland Female Seminary, and a year later became the wife of Rev. S. M. Hickman, a minister of the Methodist Episcopal Church. For several years the cares of a growing family and participation in her husband's labors prevented Mrs. Hickman from exercising to any great extent her gift for literary work. During the last twelve years she has resumed the use of the pen, contributing frequently to the Cleveland "Leader" and other papers. Possessing strong moral convictions and wide sympathies, Mrs. Hickman has made a study of social and humanitarian problems, and has generally chosen to write on subjects connected with some phase of reform, in which she has become especially interested. She has been prominently connected with temperance and missionary societies since their first organization, and much of her work has been that of an outspoken champion of those two great movements. She is an active member of the Ohio Woman's Press Association. Although keeping in touch with all the great questions of the day, she has not allowed other interests to interfere with those nearest her own home. Of her six children, four are living, two sons and two daughters. For sixteen years past she has lived in or near Cleveland, OH.

HICKS, Mrs. Mary Dana, art educator, born in Syracuse, NY, 7th October, 1862. Her father was Major Dana and her mother Agnes A. J. Dana. Mr. Dana died in 1882. Mrs. Dana still lives. Mrs. Hicks received a very thorough and advanced education. Her husband was Charles S. Hicks, of Syracuse. Her married life was brief. Her husband was drowned. Mrs. Hicks rallied from the shock and sorrow that came upon her, and, with the thought of her child's education in mind, renewed her interest in educational matters. She entered the high school of Syracuse as art teacher, and finally took the supervision of such teaching in all the schools of the city. She was largely instrumental in founding the Social Art Club of Syracuse. Mrs. Hicks appeared before the Woman's Congress in 1875 and 1876, urging that the subject of art education should be promoted by associations for study similar to the Social Art Club and Portfolio Club of Syracuse, and that public exhibitions, loan exhibitions and museums should be established. She urged the matter through art and educational journals. The fame of her work went beyond her city, and in 1879 she was called to Boston to assist in the Prang art educational work in the public schools. Mrs. Hicks brought to the art educational movement exceptional qualifications for directorship. She had received not only a fine technical art training, but she had also made a thorough study of the history and literature of art. On the educational and practical side her preparation has been no less broad and strong. As the art educational movement has developed throughout the country during the past twelve years, Mrs. Hicks has been recognized as one of the leaders. She is deeply interested in the kindergarten and industrial movements in education, and has done much to bring them into harmony with art teaching in the public schools. She is a fine speaker. She is one of the pioneers in summer-school teaching, being one of the faculty with Col. Francis W. Parker in Martha's Vineyard in 1883. At the present time Mrs. Hicks is director of the Prang Normal Art Classes in Boston, MA, and associate author and editor of the Prang art educational publications.

HIGGINSON, Mrs. Ella Rhoads, poet and author, was born in a log cabin near Council Grove, KS, in 1862. Her maiden name was Ella Rhoads. In 1864 her family moved westward over the plains to Oregon, where she has spent most of her life. Her educational advantages were limited to a grammar-school course and a short season in the Oregon City Seminary. In 1886 she became the wife of Russell C. Higginson, a druggist, and their home is in Sehome, on Bellingham Bay, Puget Sound, Washington. Mrs. Higginson edited a woman's department in the "West Shore" for several years, and she also contributes to a number of eastern periodicals and journals. In her girlhood she wrote several love stories, but she did not seriously attempt literature until 1888. In that year she sent a poem to the Boston "Courier," which attracted general attention and was widely copied. She had published a number of poems in the "West Shore," but the Boston incident was her first

important incentive to higher effort. Since that date she has written and published many remarkable poems, and she now ranks with the foremost of the younger singers of the United States.

HILES, Mrs. Osia Joslyn, philanthropist and poet, born near Batavia, NY, 13th February, 1832. Her father's name was Joslyn, and his family were originally Bostonians and related to the Breckenridges of Kentucky. Her mother was a Sprague, a first cousin of President Fillmore. During the childhood of Osia Joslyn her father removed to Erie county, NY. At the age of nineteen she went to Illinois, where, two years later, she became the wife of John Hiles, a man of English birth and highly cultured family. Since 1854 she has lived in Milwaukee, WI, and has been conspicuously associated with all its larger philanthropies. One of the first was the Home for the Friendless, of which she was an incorporator and whose constitution she helped to frame. She was one of the prime movers and the heaviest worker in the establishing of the Wisconsin Humane Society. The flourishing Woman's Club of Wisconsin, in Milwaukee, has had more original matter in the form of essays from the pen of Mrs. Hiles than from any other member. She has for sometime been its first vice president and the president of the ladies' art and science class. One of the first stock companies of women for revenue owes its existence to Mrs. Hiles. It was she who originated and propounded to the club the idea of a stock company of women for the building of a permanent woman's club home, which building idea was afterward extended by the stock company facilities for revenue other than that derived from the club. Although all members of the club, the company is entirely distinct from it. She was one of the active incorporators of the Wisconsin Training School for Nurses, and has several times been a delegate to the National Conference of Charities and Reforms. In the mind of the public generally she is most clearly recognized as an agitator of the wrongs of the Indians. At first she gave her time to the Mission Indian work in California, personally visiting nearly every reservation and Mexican land grant in southern California. Twice she went to the Interior Department and to the President in the interest of the Indians. She plead their cause in the East and assisted in sending legal help for their protection. Mrs. Hiles, being a woman of wealth, as been able to put money as well as zeal into her philanthropic work. When the Wisconsin Indian Association was formed, she was made secretary. Its labors were largely legislative, and Mrs. Hiles used her influence in helping to defeat some obnoxious bills, in originating and pushing some beneficent ones, and in creating harmony of action with branches in other States. The fact that for twelve years, while her son was completing preparatory and college courses, Mrs. Hiles did all the outside work of her deceased husband's extensive estate, has given her considerable prominence as a successful business woman. Yet, with all the record of her practical philanthropies and financial responsibilities, she is essentially a literary woman and a poet. She has published in various periodicals. From the time she was an infant up to the present, Mrs. Hiles has been a sufferer physically, scarcely knowing a well day. Again and again she has been very near death's door, and yet the amount of work she has done and the good she has accomplished in various fields make her career remarkable in the history of public-spirited women. She has traveled extensively, both in America and Europe. She is a lover of art, of nature and of humanity. She is a woman of great personal magnetism and thoroughly conversant with the field of ancient and modern literature, as well as of occult science. Her two homes in Pewaukee and Milwaukee are in summer and winter centers of generous hospitality and centers of art. She is earnestly interested in all measures for the progress of her sex in high and womanly lines.

HILL, Mrs. Agnes Leonard, author, was born in Louisville, KY. Her father, Dr. Oliver Langdon Leonard, was a native of Springfield, MA, his mother belonging to the well-known Langdon family. He was locally prominent, forty years ago, for his scholastic attainments and literary ability. He was president of the Masonic College in La Grange, KY, just before the Civil War, and afterward president of Henry Female College, New Castle, KY. In the latter college Mrs. Hill was graduated in 1862, and the following year she went to Chicago, where she became the wife, in the autumn of 1868, of Dr. S. E. Scanland, a native of Kentucky, who died about two years after marriage. On 15th May, 1872, Mrs. Agnes Leonard Scanland became the wife of Samuel Howe Hill, of Bangor, ME. Mrs. Hill's mother was a native of Kentucky, and was born of Virginian parentage. In her veins flowed the blood of the Howards and Percys. She died in Louisville, leaving three children. Placed in boarding-school at an early age, and having no home duties in her youth, Mrs. Hill developed literary tastes and habits. She wrote verses at the age of eight years, and George D. Prentice, then editor of the Louisville "Journal," began to publish her verses when she was only thirteen years of age. Mrs. Hill has done editorial work for the Chicago "Tribune," "Times," "News" and the Leadville "Dispatch," edited by her brother, Percy Allan Leonard. She has three volumes of poetry and a novel, "The Specter of Gray Gulch," a story of Colorado, about ready for publication. Her last work published is "Hints On How to Talk." In her early girlhood she published three books, but does not consider any of them worthy of preservation. She was the founder of "Western Society," a weekly paper started in Denver, CO, in December, 1888, afterward changed to "Home and Society." Mrs. Hill's lectures in Denver University and other places have been both profitable and congenial work. She has four children, three daughters and a son, all of whom have manifested literary ability.

HILL, Mrs. Eliza Trask, woman suffragist and journalist, born in Warren, MA, 10th May, 1840. She is the youngest daughter of Rev. George Trask and Ruth Freeman Packard. On her father's side she is of Scotch ancestry. Her mother was a daughter of Rev. Asa Packard, of Lancaster, and granddaughter of Col. Josiah Quincy, of Quincy, MA. Mrs. Hill inherits from both father and mother the spirit of reform, her father having been well known as a temperance, anti-slavery and anti-tobacco reformer. During the Civil War Mrs. Hill's great love of country led her to obtain, by subscription, and present a flag to the Fifteenth Massachusetts Regiment. Her presentation speech was so filled with the fire of patriotism that it produced a marked effect and was widely quoted. For ten years she was a teacher. In June, 1867, she became the wife of John Lang Hill, of Boston. She is the mother of two sons and a daughter. She was one of the first to join the Woman's Christian Temperance Union, and has served in an official capacity in that body from its beginning. She is now connected with the prison and jail department. She has labored earnestly for the redemption of abandoned women, but, believing that preventive is more effectual than reformatory work, she has identified herself with the societies that care for and help the working girls. Since 1879, when the right of school suffrage was granted to the women of Massachusetts, she has been actively engaged in politics, having worked for the Prohibition party. Her services as an advocate of the Australian ballot system were in great demand. During the public school agitation in Boston in 1888, when twenty-thousand women rescued the public schools from mismanagement, Mrs. Hill was among the leaders of the movement, making plans for the campaign, helping to rally the women, and by her addresses arousing both men and women. She is now, and has been for several years, the president of the ward and city committee of independent women voters, a recognized powerful political organization. The need of a party organ was felt, and Mrs. Hill, unaided at first, began the publication, in Boston, of a weekly newspaper, which is now cared for by a stock company of women. Mrs. Hill is editor of the paper, which is called the "Woman's Voice and Public School Champion."

HINMAN, Miss Ida, litteratéur and journalist, was born in Keokuk, IA. Sir Edward Hinman, the progenitor of the family in America, was an officer of the body-guard of Charles I of England. After the king's death, having risked all for royalty, he came to America and settled in Connecticut. He was the father of two sons, from the oldest of whom Miss Hinman's family is descended. Her father, B. B. Hinman, was for years a suc-cessful merchant in Keokuk. Her mother, who before marriage was Miss Ellen E. Fithian, is a woman of rare strength of character. Ida, the fourth child, was the first to live to maturity. She has two younger sisters, Ella and Carrie. Miss Hinman is a graduate of the Iowa Wesleyan University, Mount Pleasant, and early in life she showed a decided tendency toward literary pursuits, which, when financial difficulties overtook the family, she utilized with profit and success. She has contributed for a number of years to many periodicals, including "Harper's Magazine," leading religious journals and prominent newspapers. For five seasons she had charge of the Washington, DC, correspondence of a large New York paper, doing an incredible amount of work. She spent a part of the year 1891 in Europe, writing for a number of American periodicals. Among the questions that her editors desired her to investigate were the socialist movement in Germany, the principles of the sub-treasury system in England, and the impetus that the temperance movement has received in Germany. Though not strong, Miss Hinman can do a large amount of work in her profession.

HIRSCHBERG, Mrs. Alice, artist, born in England, 12th February, 1856. Her maiden name was Kerr-Nelson, and she belonged to an old county family, whose pedigree in Burke's Landed Gentry dates back to Richard Nelson, who flourished in 1377. Miss Kerr-Nelson was educated without particular attention to her artistic talents. At the age of twenty-two she sent her first picture, a water-color, to the Royal Academy. It was rejected, but it found a purchaser. She decided to follow her inclinations. Without preliminary study from cast or life she went to Heatherly's art-school in London. There she began to paint heads and costumed figures, which she sold in country exhibitions in England. In the school she met Carl Hirschberg, and became his wife in 1882. They went to Paris and studied two years, but Mrs. Hirschherg says she owes more to her husband's teaching than to the slight criticisms of Raphael Collin, who visited the women's class once a week. She exhibited some of her work in the Salon of 1884. In 1884 Mr. and Mrs. Hirschberg came to the United

States. She exhibited the next year in the collection of the Water-Color Society, and is a regular contributor to its exhibitions. Her family consists of three sons. Her principal pictures are: "The Lace Maker," "Vieille Normande," "An Interested Spectator," "Aunt Phœbe," "Maggie Tulliver," "The Trysting Place," "Sunday Afternoon," "At Meeting," "Beach Plum Gatherers," "Look, then, into Thine Own Heart and Write," "A Lesson," "Music," "Hide and Seek." Her home and studio are in Morristown, NJ.

HITCHCOCK, Mrs. Mary Antoinette, temperance reformer, born in the town of Rodman, Jefferson county, NY, 28th April, 1834. She is the only daughter of Lorenzo Dow and Urrilla Barnes. When she was eleven years old, her parents moved to Wisconsin, then a new country with poor educational facilities in that part of the State where they settled. Much of her instruction was received at home, under the care of a governess. At sixteen years of age she began to teach, and her efforts were attended with success. In 1852 she became the wife of Alfred Hitchcock, but for some time after continued to teach. In 1857 her husband was ordained to the ministry and became not only an earnest teacher of the gospel, but a fearless advocate of temperance reform. When the Civil War cloud hung over the country, they were living in Kansas, having moved to that State in 1859. Being imbued by nature and training with the most ultra Union and anti-slavery sentiments, she was all enthusiasm for the cause and the soldier, ready to lend her aid in every possible way. At that time many of the leaders passed through their town to Osawatomie to form the Republican Party, and she housed and fed fifty of them in one night, among them Horace Greeley, and spent the hours of the night in preparing their food for the next day. As first assistant and county superintendent of schools she and her husband divided Phillips county, KS, into school districts and started a number of schools. Afterward removing to Fremont, NE, where her husband accepted a pastorate, she became an enthusiastic member of the Woman's Christian Temperance Union, and, impressed with the idea that a State organization was necessary for

its lasting influence, she was in 1874 the projector of the movement that resulted in the State organization. She refused the presidency at that time, on account of her husband's health. The next few years, deprived by death of husband and father, she entered still more actively into the work and became district president and vice-president-at-large of the State. Called to Sioux City, IA, on account of the death of her cousin, George C. Haddock, the circumstances of whose untimely end caused general indignation and horror, she there, over his lifeless form, promised the sorrow-stricken wife to devote the remainder of her life to the eradication of the terrible alcohol evil. Since accepting the State presidency in 1888 she has traveled continually over the State, organizing unions and attending conventions. Though not calling herself a lecturer, she has delivered many earnest talks. She has one son and one daughter. Her home is in Fremont, NE.

HOBART, Mrs. Fannie Tuttle, the wife of the Vice-President of the United States, was born in Patterson, NJ. She is a daughter of judge Socrates Tuttle, with whom Mr. Hobart studied law, and they were married 21st July, 1869. Mrs. Hobart, on hearing of Mr. Hobart's nomination, telegraphed back to him the devoted words of Ruth, "Whither thou goest I will go." She has always lived in the city of her birth, with whose leading philanthropies she has been connected. She is president of the Old Woman's Home, a promoter of the Woman's Exchange, and a prominent worker in the Presbyterian church. All her life she has proven an excellent home-maker and home-keeper, and their home is famed for its hospitality. Of their two children, a son called Garret A. Hobart, Jr., is yet in his teens; but their daughter, Miss Fannie, a young woman of great promise, died in her twentieth year, of diphtheria, while the family were touring through Italy in 1895, and was buried at Lake Como. In appearance Mrs. Hobart is of medium height, with dark hair and blue eyes, and possesses a stately dignity of presence. Her cheery, wholesome nature and gentle ways win friends and admirably fit her for the position of prominence she must fill at the nation's capital.

HOBART, Mrs. Sarah Dyer, poet and author, born in Otsego, WI, 20th September, 1845. Her parents were among the earliest settlers in that part of the State, and her early life was that of a pioneer. Her parents were intelligent and ambitious for her, and gave her all the assistance in their power, and she did the rest for herself. She became a well-educated person. She commenced her literary career at the age of eighteen, and has been a contributor to the periodical press ever since. Her poems soon made her name well known, and her sketches added to her popularity. In 1866 she became the wife of Colonel M. C. Hobart, who had just returned from the war. Three children grace their pleasant home on Fountain Prairie, in Wisconsin. Mrs. Hobart now stands among the acknowledged poets of the country. Her sonnets are perhaps her best work. Her poems have not yet been gathered in a volume.

HODGIN, Mrs. Emily Caroline Chandler, temperance reformer, born in Williamsport, IN, 12th April, 1838. Her father, Hon. Robert A. Chandler, who was of German descent, emigrated from New York to western Indiana while it was yet a wilderness. Mr. Chandler was a self-made man, a scholarly lawyer. He accumulated a competence and reared a large family. The mother was a member of the Dodd family, of Orange, NJ, and was a cultured Christian lady. Mrs. Hodin had the advantage of the best schools of Williamsport and her father's large library. Accepting her father's doctrine that every one should learn to be self-supporting, she early taught school, and paid her own way through the Illinois Normal University, graduating in 1867, making a record as a strong student, especially in mathematics. After graduating she became the wife of her classmate, Cyrus W. Hodgin, and settled in Richmond, IN. There two years later, a daughter, her only child, was born. In 1872 she removed to Terre Haute, where for many years her husband was a teacher in the State Normal School. It was there Mrs. Hodgin entered the field of work that has since chiefly occupied her time and best thought. She was one of the leaders in the temperance crusade in the city, and was

a delegate to the convention in Cleveland, OH, where the crusading spirit was crystallized by the organization of the Woman's Christian Temperance Union. After that she began the work of organizing the forces in neighboring parts of the State. In 1878 the strain upon her strength induced nervous exhaustion, from which she found relief by a six-months retirement in the sanitarium in Dansville, NY. In 1883 she returned to Richmond, and has since been devoting much of her time to furthering the work of the Woman's Christian Temperance Union. She is president of the Woman's Christian Temperance Union in her own county, is secretary of the State Suffrage Association, and is one of the trustees of the Hadley Industrial Home for the education of poor girls. In addition to these lines of work, she received in 1886 the Chautauqua diploma for a four-years course of study, and recently completed a course of biblical and theological study in Earlham College. She is a member of the Society of Friends and avails herself of the freedom accorded to the women of that church to "speak in meeting."

HODGKINS, Miss Louise Manning, author and educator, born in Ipswich, MA, 5th August, 1846. Descended from a line of soldiers reaching back to Revolutionary times, it was not strange that Miss Hodgkins brought courage, faithfulness, fortitude and enthusiasm to the work of life. Her education was begun in the Ipswich Seminary under Mrs. Eunice P. Cowles, continued in Pennington Seminary, NJ, and in Wilbraham, MA, where she was graduated in 1870. In 1876 she received the degree of A.M., from Lawrence College, Appleton, WI, where she began her career as a teacher, rising to the position of lady principal while yet in her twenties. In 1876 she was elected professor of English literature in Wellesley College, with leave of absence abroad for study. In 1877 she entered actively upon her duties. She served the college till June, 1891, making in the meantime two visits to Europe. Although well known as a brilliant and original teacher, Prof. Hodgkins was called the "Poet-Professor" in Wellesley. During her term of service she contributed poems, stories and educational articles to magazines and periodicals. Her chief service to literature was associated closely with her work and is well known under the title of "A Guide to the Study of Nineteenth Century Literature," and three books in the "English Classics" series. Miss Hodgkins resigned her professorship in Wellesley in order to give more leisure to the literary work that is pressing upon her. She adds frequently to her programme lectures on literary themes. With leisure for writing and a mind to do it, her contributions to literature are increasing. Her present residence is in Auburndale, MA.

HOEL, Mrs. Libbie Beach, philanthropist, born in Livingston county, IL, 11th March, 1858. She is of a family of educators. Her parents were estimable people, who were generally known as leaders in reform movements. She received a seminary education and entered the teacher's profession, performing her work acceptably for five years before her marriage, in 1882. In one year she was a wife, a mother and a childless widow, but she bravely took up the teacher's life again, until 1890, when she accepted the position of superintendent of the Home for the Friendless, in Lincoln, NE, to which office she brought the qualities for success. Her strong, firm character is softened by womanly gentleness; she is not easily daunted in her undertakings, and is systematic and wise in judgment. She was sent by the Governor of the State as a delegate to the National Convention of Charities held in Indianapolis in May, 1891, and went as a delegate to the same convention held in Denver in June, 1892. The press of the State has only praise for her as a woman and business manager. She is well known and influential in temperance affairs and other reform movements, and has always affiliated with the progressive elements. Mrs. Hoel is a musician, and for years made music a large part of her life-work. As a singer, she excels.

HOFFMAN, Mrs. Clara Cleghorn, temperance worker, born in De Kalb, NY, 18th January, 1831. She is the eleventh child in a family of thirteen children, seven daughters and six sons. She is the daughter of Humphrey Cleghorn, a sturdy Scotchman of strong intellectual convictions and indomitable courage and will power. He was an abolitionist and a conductor on the famous "underground railroad" in the anti-slavery days. Her mother was Olive Burnham, daughter of Major Elisha Burnham, who bore an honorable part in the Revolutionary War. She had the good fortune to be reared in the country, where she developed the fine physique that has carried her through many hardships. In 1861 she became the wife of Dr. Goswin Hoffman, a cultured German physician. For twelve years she was principal of Lathrop School in Kansas City, MO. In 1882 she was appointed, by the general officers of the National Woman's Christian Temperance Union, president of the Missouri Woman's Christian Temperance Union, Miss Willard having visited Kansas City to look over the ground and having learned of the mental powers and vigorous executive talents of Mrs. Hoffman, her success as a teacher, her remarkable voice and elocutionary training, and her earnest Christianity. Headquarters were established in Kansas City, and Mrs. Hoffman is now a national organizer.

HOFFMAN, Mrs. Sophia Curtiss, philanthropist, born in Sheffield, Berkshire county, MA, in 1825. She is active in the Woman's Congress, and the Association for the Advancement of Women, and has been a member of Sorosis for many years. Her name appears in the list of incorporators of the Chapin Home, a benevolent institution greatly esteemed in that city. In fact, it is to Mrs. Hoffman the inception of the home came as a sort of inspiration, and she gave at various times thousands of dollars to promote its beneficent aims. Mrs. Hannaford, in her book, "Daughters of America," after referring to Mrs. Hoffman as the founder of the Chapin Home, says: "In her early life, an invalid aunt, by her own suffering with a sense of dependence, impressed upon Mrs. Hoffman's mind the importance of a home where aged women who had been accustomed to the comforts of a competence in earlier days could feel independent, at the same time that they were

Mrs. Caroline Miskel-Hoyt.
From Photo Copyright, 1894, by Morrison, Chicago.

The Hengler Sisters.   **Mrs. Caroline Miskel-Hoyt.**
From Photo by Morrison, Chicago.   *From Photo Copyright, 1895, by Schloss, New York.*

made comfortable; and she promised this relative that, if ever the means were in her possession, she would seek to establish such a retreat." The Chapin Home was the outgrowth of that experience. While in Europe she visited many such homes in Great Britain and on the Continent, that she might study their methods and develop a plan for a self-sustaining and permanent institution. Mrs. Hoffman has proved herself also the friend of struggling genius, for it was in her residence on Fifth Avenue that the charming operatic favorite, Emma Abbott, was introduced to the public of New York and secured a choir position.

HOGUE, Mrs. Lydia Evans, educator, born in Crawford county, PA, near Meadville, 14th April, 1856. Her maiden name was Evans. Mrs. Hogue's mother, Mary Kemble Evans, was a native of East Liverpool, OH, of English descent and a relative of Mad Anthony Wayne. At eleven years of age she was sent to Cattaraugus county, NY, where she was graduated in gymnastics at the age of thirteen, and pursued piano music and literary and scientific studies, and afterward entered the Pennsylvania State Normal School in Edinburgh, where she was graduated in 1875. After graduation she began to teach in Grandintown. The next year she was called to the high school of Tidioute, PA, where she taught for eight years. In 1885 she was elected preceptress of the high school of Oil City, which place she resigned in 1886 to become the wife of Prof. S. F. Hogue and the preceptress of Defiance College, with Dr. Hogue as president. In 1888 and 1889 they laid the foundation of Redstone Academy, in Uniontown, PA. In 1890 they accepted the presidency and preceptorship of Monongahela College, in Jefferson, PA. Mrs. Hogue was graduated in the first class of the Chautauqua Literary and Scientific Circle, in 1882, and attended the lectures, and has taken the degrees B.E.D., M.E.D., and A.M.

HOLCOMBE, Mrs. Elizabeth J., physician, was born 19th August, 1827. She is related on the side of her maternal grandmother to Elias Hicks, the founder of the Unitarian branch of the Society of Friends. After graduating from the State Normal School in Albany, NY, she became the wife of Dr. J. W. Justin. After his early death, to provide for her children she filled the position of preceptress in the union free school and academy in Newark, NY, for fourteen years. In 1864 she became the wife of Rev. Chester Holcombe, the father of the Hon. Chester Holcombe, late secretary of legation to China. After the death of her second husband, and at the age of forty, she began in earnest the professional study of medicine. After her graduation from the Woman's Medical College in Philadelphia, she was appointed resident physician to the Woman's Hospital, filling, at the same time, the position of lecturer in the training school for nurses. There she remained three years. She then entered upon a private practice in Syracuse, NY. Soon after that her son, Dr. Joel Justin, joined her, having graduated from the University of Pennsylvania and acquired, as the result of a post-graduate course, the degree of Ph.D. For a time he, too, practiced medicine, being connected with the College of Physicians and Surgeons, in Syracuse University, first as instructor in chemistry and afterward as professor of medical jurisprudence. He has since become widely known as the inventor of the Justin dynamite shell, and has surrendered his medical practice to become president of the company which bears his name. Mrs. Holcombe has made her home in Syracuse for the last seventeen years.

HOLLEY, Miss Marietta, humorist, was born in a pleasant country place between the two villages, Adams and Pierrepont Manor, NY. Her country home stands now in that place, where five generations of the Holleys have resided. The Holleys went to Jefferson county from Connecticut. Her maternal grandfather, "Old Squire Taber," as he was called, went to Pierrepont Manor from Rhode Island. Miss Holley commenced to write at an early age, both verses and sketches, which she used to hide jealously from every eye. Her first appearance in print was in a newspaper published in Adams. Her first pen-name was "Jemyma." The editor of that paper encouraged the young aspirant with some timely praise, as did Charles J. Peterson, for whom she wrote later. The editors of the "Christian Union" published what they called "a sweet little poem" from her pen. She wrote also for the "Independent" and several other weekly and monthly journals. Her articles at that time were mostly poems, and were widely copied in this country and in Europe. It was in a dialect sketch written for "Peterson's Magazine" that she first adopted the pen-name "Josiah Allen's Wife." That name and "Jemyma" were a sort of protest against the too musical pen-names of literary aspirants. Those articles attracted the attention of Elijah Bliss, president of the American Publishing Company, of Hartford, CT. Against the protest of his company, he brought out Miss Holley's work. He urged her to write a book for him, which she did, and it was an immediate success, and was republished at once in England and Canada. The name of that book was "My Opinions and Betsy Bobbet's" (Hartford, 1872). Her next book, "Samantha at the Centennial," appeared in 1877. "The Wayward Pardner" appeared in 1880. "Miss Richard's Boy," a book of stories not in dialect, was published in 1882. These books were brought out by the American Publishing Company, and the same firm published an illustrated poem of hers called "The Mormon Wife." Miss Holley has also written "Sweet Cicely, or Josiah Allen's Wife as a Politician," (New York, 1885); "Samantha at Saratoga" (Philadelphia, 1887); a book of "Poems" (New York, 1887), and "Samantha Amongst the Brethern," in 1891. Miss Holley's work appeals to all classes of society. Her readers are scattered over the entire world and include men and women of every station and grade. Her books are widely read in Europe.

HOLLISTER, Mrs. Lillian, temperance and church worker, born in Oakland county, MI, 8th September, 1853. Her father, Phineas Bates, was a well-to-do farmer, a native of New York. He was a deacon in the Baptist Church and an. earnest anti-slavery man. Lillian was one of a family of six children. She was well educated, and at the age of fifteen was a normal and high school graduate. She at once began to teach. In 1872 she became the wife of Daniel W. Hollister. They lived on a farm until 1881. Mrs. Hollister was active in Sunday-school work and served as superintendent. In 1881 she moved to Detroit, MI, her present home. There she continued her musical and literary studies. She associated herself with the Methodist Episcopal Church and the Woman's Christian Temperance Union. In church work she took a leading part, acting as president of the Ladies' Aid Society of the Simpson Methodist Episcopal Church and as conference secretary of the Woman's Home Missionary Society. She is a member of the Sunday-school normal class of the Chautauqua Circle, the Deaconess Board and various philanthropic and charity societies. In the Woman's Christian Temperance Union she was for two years secretary, then vice-president and then president, in which office, for six successive years, she has received the compliment of a unanimous re-election each year. Recognizing the commanding influence of woman in advancing the interests of the church and of all humanitarian institutions, she has been slow to favor woman in politics, but has of late become a convert to the principle of the woman suffrage movement. In addition to her extensive local work in Detroit, she holds the office of State superintendent of the Young Woman's Christian Temperance Union. Her trained executive talents are manifested throughout the State in organizing new unions and in the prosperity they show under her care. As a parliamentarian, there are but few presiding officers who excel her in maintaining harmony and expediting the business of meetings. With her, life is too short to be spent in sheer idleness, and she is therefore as much the student to-day as when a school-girl. She has one son, about seventeen years old.

HOLMES, Mrs. Georgiana Klingle, poet, born in Philadelphia, PA. Through her mother, Mary Hunt Morris, who became the wife of George Franklin Mingle, M.D., she is a member of the historic Morris family, of Morrisania, and is the wife of Benjamin Proctor Holmes, of New York City. She was educated in Philadelphia. Her father's ancestry is found in Upper Saxony. Hans George Klingle, her great-grandfa-

ther, came to this country in the ship "Restoration" with his son, 9th October, 1747, and settled in Pennsylvania. At the breaking out of the Revolutionary War her grandfather, George, resided in Chestnut Hill. Dr. Klingle was a man of literary and scientific reputation. From early childhood Georgiana contributed to periodicals of the different cities. Her taste ran in a groove not often entered by young authors, children's stories with a moral to leave an impression. She is an artist of merit, but writing is the passion of her life. She has written no long list of books, but the heartfelt poetry of "George Klingle" has touched many hearts. Her collection of poems entitled "Make Thy Way Mine" (New York, 1876) was made after repeated letters from interested strangers in different parts of the country. That collection was followed by "In the Name of the King" (New York, 1888), and another volume is ready for publication. Being interested in philanthropic work, she founded Arthur's Home For Destitute Boys, in Summit, NJ, in memory of her son, who died at the age of nine years, his unselfish savings being the germ of the institution.

HOLMES, Mrs. Jennie Florella, temperance worker, born on a farm in Jersey county, IL, 26th February, 1842. Her maiden name was Hurd. Her early years were spent in her native place. In 1859 she commenced the collegiate course of study in Lombard University, Galesburg, IL, one of the few educational institutions that then gave equal opportunities to both sexes. At the beginning of the Civil War in 1861 she, like many others, cast aside the student's mantle and entered active life, teaching and, being a staunch Unionist, giving good service to the Soldiers' Aid Society of Jerseyville. In 1866 she became the wife of Charles A. Holmes, of Jefferson, WI, who had served three years as captain in the 29th Wisconsin Regiment. With her husband and two daughters she removed to Tecumseh, NE, in September, 1871. Earnest and untiring in her advocacy of the temperance cause and of equal political rights for both sexes, she immediately allied herself with these elements in Nebraska, and in the winter of 1881 she became a member of the first woman's suffrage conven-

tion held in the State, and labored for the amendment submitted at that session of the legislature. She was chairman of the executive committee of the State Suffrage Society from 1881 to 1884. In 1884 she was elected president of the State Woman's Christian Temperance Union, which office she held for three years. She was elected delegate-at-large from Nebraska to the National Prohibition Party Convention, held in Indianapolis in 1888. In her ardent love for the cause she considered this the crowning honor of her laborious life. She was an active member of the Woman's Relief Corps, and was sent a delegate to the Woman's Relief Corps convention held in Milwaukee in 1889. She was warmly interested in educational affairs in her own little city, as well as abroad. She was made a member of the school board in 1891. Mrs. Holmes had a family of eight children, four of whom are living. She died in her home in Tecumseh, 20th March, 1892.

HOLMES, Miss Mary Emilie, educator and scientist, born in Chester, OH, 10th April, 1850. She is the only daughter and only surviving child of Rev. Mead and Mrs. Mary D. A. Holmes. On the paternal side of Scotch-Irish and Holland descent, and on the maternal of Huguenot and New England stock, she inherited a nature active, persistent, thorough, with a special bent toward original investigation in science, literature and religion. In addition to performing efficiently the duties of a Presbyterian clergyman's wife in a large parish, her mother was for many years principal of a seminary for young ladies and gentlemen. As a child, little Mary's associations were almost entirely with those greatly her senior in years. Never remembering the time when she could not read readily, she early picked up, by listening to recitations and also to her older and only brother studying aloud at home, many things far beyond her full comprehension at the time, but which, later, proved of great value. Thus at eight years of age she was perfectly familiar with Greek, Latin and French conjugations and declensions and could parse and translate quite well. At five years she had read the entire Bible through aloud to her mother, receiving there for, from her father, a beautiful canary. A special delight of her life has ever been to have many pets about the home, not so much to train, though they must all live peaceably together, and generally in freedom, outdoors and in, but for psychological study. Among these were several species of squirrels, gophers, chipmunks, guinea pigs, coons, woodchucks, cats, dogs, a bear, foxes, robins, thrushes, mocking-birds, a parrot and an eagle, with some amphibians. All these, being nicely tamed, developed many characteristics which have formed the basis of her carefully prepared zoological articles. With her fifth birthday she began the regular study of music, ever since a delight, and commenced systematically to study natural history, and to prepare a herbarium, analyzing mainly by Gray's "How Plants Grow." This collection, still existing in part, was the nucleus of what is now one of the finest and largest private herbariums in Illinois. Always encouraged to take examinations with those much older, primarily to keep her pleasantly occupied, and to try for county school certificates, at thirteen years of age she was triumphant, having won one-hundred per cent in each of the eight subjects then required. This certificate is a much-prized trophy. At eleven years of age she became organist in Sunday-school, and soon after in church, a position almost continuously held from that date. A favorite pastime for several years, commencing with her eighth year, was regularly editing, alternately with an older friend, in single copy, a hand-written weekly paper, "The Planetary World," copiously but neatly illustrated, with advertisements, the sanctum being movable, on the various planets and stars. Each gave everything she could imagine or learn pertaining to the orbs, and the objects supposably within sight or reach, including "news from earth." At the age of fourteen she was prepared for an advanced place in the junior year of Rockford Seminary, where she was graduated. She was also the first student to receive the full A.B. Teaching several years, holding the department of natural science in the seminary, after a thorough and exhaustive examination in Michigan University, she received the degree of A.M., and in 1888, on an original scientific thesis, with copious illustrations from nature, "The Morphology of the Carinæ on the Septa of Rugose Corals," an acknowledged authority in England and Germany, she received the degree of Ph.D. from the University. Still later, on the score of "original investigation and discovery," she was elected a Fellow of the Geological Society of America, a distinction as yet conferred upon no other woman. In her delightful home several rooms are devoted to natural history, ornithology, zoology, conchology, geology, mineralogy and botany, in many thousand specimens, chiefly of her own collecting or exchange, and all scientifically arranged. While delighting in literary or scientific pursuits, she imbibed the missionary spirit, home and foreign, of her mother. On this line of humanity and piety she exerts her noblest energies. From early girlhood she has presided over a thriving mission band. For seven years she has been president of the Presbyterian Home Missionary Society, Freeport Presbytery, and for five years has been chairman of the Synodical Committee on Freedmen, Synod of Illinois, since their organization. She is now engaged with the Freedmen's Board of the Presbyterian Church North, in planning a literary and industrial school for colored girls, the "Mary Holmes Seminary," in Jackson, MS, to be a memorial of her mother and a power in uplifting an unfortunate race. A prompt and sprightly newspaper correspondent, chiefly scientific and missionary, her articles are always welcome, often passing from the editor's sanctum to the compositor without reading. Her home is in Rockford, IL.

HOLMES, Mrs. Mary Emma, woman suffragist, born on a farm in Peoria county, IL, 3rd August, 1839. She is descended from Puritan stock. Her father, Capt. Ira Smith, was born in Hampden, ME, 5th January, 1806. Her mother, Sarah Jenkins Smith, was a native of Thomaston, ME, and was born 20th November, 1813. Her father enlisted in a man-of-war at the age of seventeen. It was the custom, in those days, to deal out "grog" daily to the sailors. This troubled him, and he attempted to give away his allowance or to throw it overboard, but was stopped by the officer in charge. He appealed to the captain, and was allowed to receive two dollars and fifty cents per month instead of the rum. Mr. Smith soon became the master of a merchant vessel. He hung out his sign, which said that he would not allow "grog" except in cases of sickness, and wanted only men who would be willing to go without it. His vessel was the first one that sailed out of Boston with temperance regulations. His men were so faithful that other captains soon followed his example. This reformatory spirit was born in his daughter. Mrs. Holmes was educated in Peoria, IL, where she lived during her girlhood. Her father vas a man of means, but she was a teacher in the Peoria public schools for six years. She taught in the poorest part of the city, from choice, and did missionary work at the same time. At the age of twenty-six she became the wife of Rev. David E. Holmes, and moved to his field of labor in Berlin, WI. The failure of her husband's health during the first year of their married life made a change of business necessary, and both Mr. and Mrs. Holmes taught in the Berlin high school for six years. They were chosen members of the faculty of the Normal School in Oshkosh, WI, and began their labors there with much promise of usefulness; but another failure of health on the part of her husband made a change to a business life a necessity. Within a year they removed to their present home, in Galva, IL, where her husband has been successful as a lumber merchant, Mrs. Holmes keeping the books for several years. They have one son, Edward, born in 1874, and an adopted daughter, Emma Holland. Although Mrs. Holmes was always a reformer, the last fifteen years have been crowded unusually full of public work. She was for several years president of the county societies for temperance and suffrage. Then she was superintendent of the franchise department for the Illinois Woman's Christian Temperance Union for several years. These positions she resigned after she became president of the Equal Suffrage Association of Illinois. After being president of the State five years, she resigned to rest, but at the end of one year of rest she again accepted the presidency in the annual meeting in November, 1890. By virtue of this office she is also vice-president of the National American Suffrage Association. Mrs. Holmes excels in executive ability and as a presiding officer. She is the treasurer of a fund contributed to obtain a marble portrait bust of Susan B. Anthony, to be exhibited in the World's Fair, in Chicago, in 1893. Mrs. Holmes is also a member of the "government reform" committee of the woman's branch of the World's Congress Auxiliary, and also represents the National American Suffrage Association in the World's Fair as the committee from Illinois. She belongs to the liberal

wing of the Congregational Church and is an active member, having been clerk in the Galva church for many years. She teaches a Sunday-school class of a hundred men and women and a society of two-hundred-fifty children, called "Careful Builders." A free public library in her own home has been provided for these charges. She has written a good deal in a local way, and also for educational journals, all through her active life.

HOLMES, Mrs. Mary Jane, novelist, was born in Brookfield, MA. Her father was Preston Hawes, a man of intellect and a deep thinker. The Rev. Dr. Joel Hawes, one of the celebrated New England divines, was her father's older brother, and Mrs. Holmes seems to have largely partaken of the intellectual force, faith in human nature and insight into the moving springs and desires of the human heart, which were a family characteristic and made her uncle's preaching so potent, searching and fruitful. From her mother she inherited her romance, poetry and love of the beautiful. She is described as a precocious and sensitive child, more fond of her own companionship and dreaming out the pictures and fancies that came into her active mind than of associating with other children. Her imagination, the creative faculty, was alive almost in infancy, and at her earliest remembrance her little brain was buzzing with germs of what have since become her mental offspring. She went to school at three years of age and studied grammar at six. She was a quick student, and at the age of thirteen she was installed as the teacher of a district school a few miles from home. There she had a varied experience as the little "schoolmarm" with blue eyes and the golden hair, at whom the older boys looked first with contempt and later with still more embarrassing admiration and devotion. She was possessed with an inspiration to write, and saw her first article in print at fifteen. She became the wife of Daniel Holmes, a young lawyer of Richmond, NY, and the union has proved an ideal marriage. Their home is in Brockport, NY, a flourishing town near Rochester. She has no children but is very fond of young people, especially girls, often giving them parlor talks upon art and other subjects connected with her foreign travels, which have taken her over most of the Old World. As an author she has had a most happy career, with none of the trials which fall to the lot of so many writers, and her publishers have always been her friends. Appleton published her first book. G. W. Carleton has been her publisher for the past twenty years, but has recently sold out to the partner, Mr. Dillingham, who now has all her books. An estimate and comparison from the statistics of a wholesale bookstore, which supplies the trade of the upper half of the Mississippi Valley, show that, next to E. P. Roe's works, Mrs. Holmes' novels are the most popular of any American author. It is a fact that more than one-million copies of her books have been sold, and their popularity shows no sign of waning. A number of libraries find it necessary to keep twenty and thirty sets of her books on their shelves. Her success as an author is said by some to be the result of her powers of description; others assert that it is her naturalness, her clear, concise English and her faculty to hold the reader's sympathy from the beginning to the end; while others attribute it to the fact that mothers are willing their young daughters should read her books, knowing there is nothing in them but what is pure and elevating. The following is a list of some of her books: "Tempest and Sunshine" (1854), "English Orphans" (1855), "Homestead on the Hillside" (1855), "Lena Rivers" (1856), "Meadow Brook" (1857), "Dora Deane" 1858), "Cousin Maude" (1860), "Marian Gray" (1863), "Hugh Worthington" (1864), "Cameron Pride" (1867), "Rose Mather" (1868), "Ethelyn's Mistake" (1869), "Edna Browning" (1872), "Mildred" (1877), "Forest House" (1879), "Daisy Thornton," "Queenie Hetherton" (1883), "Christmas Stories" (1884), "Bessie's Fortune" (1885), "Gretchen" (1887), "Marguerite" (1891), and in the recent past she has written a series of articles for different journals. The popularity of her books is shown in the fact that several of them, recently issued in paper covers, have each sold to the number of fifty-thousand copies. Most of her novels are distinctively American, with an occasional digression to Europe, where she has spent a great deal of time.

HOOKER, Mrs. Isabella Beecher, lecturer and woman suffragist, born in Litchfield, CT, 22nd February, 1822. She is the youngest of the four daughters of Dr. Lyman Beecher, the illustrious preacher of New England. She was the first child of the second wife of Dr. Beecher, and her brothers, Thomas K. and James C. Beecher, filled that wonderful family of eleven children, eight of whom were the children of the first wife. Individually and collectively the Beecher family is justly considered the most remarkable in the United States, each member of it being the possessor of commanding talent, great energy and force of character, and varied gifts of the highest order. Isabella inherited her personal beauty from her mother, and her great intellectuality came to her from her father. Isabella Beecher became the wife of John Hooker, of Hartford, CT, in 1841. Mr. Hooker is a lawyer and has achieved distinction in his profession. He is a descendant, in the sixth generation, of Thomas Hooker, who founded the city of Hartford, and who was the pastor of the First Congregational Church there. Thomas Hooker was a man of note in his day, a famous theologian, an earnest patriot, an enlightened statesman and a person of the highest character. He formulated the first written constitution of Connecticut, which afterward served as a model for the Constitution of the United States, of other States of the Union, and of various republics in South America. John Hooker has served as Reporter of the Supreme Court of Connecticut since his appointment in January, 1858. His work covers thirty-seven volumes of reports, and these reports have made him known throughout the legal circles of the country. In his early manhood he refused a seat on the bench of the Supreme Court. After his marriage he lived ten years in Farmington. In 1851 the family moved to Hartford, where they have lived ever since, and are near neighbors to Mrs. Hooker's sister, Harriet Beecher Stowe. Mrs. Hooker kept pace intellectually with her husband, accompanying him in his theological researches and speculations, learning from him much of his profession, and making a study of the basis and evolution of the laws that govern the United States. She has always been an earnest and profound student of social, political and religious questions, and, when she adopted the idea that women should be allowed to vote, as a fundamental right, she at once, in characteristic style, began to do what she could to bring about the great reform. She considered woman suffrage the greatest movement in the world's history, claiming that the ballot would give woman every social and intellectual, as well as political, advantage. She wrote and lectured, studied and expounded the doctrine of free suffrage. For more than thirty years she has been at the front of this and other reform movements, and has gone cheerful and undeterred through years of that ridicule and abuse that fall to the lot of earnest agitators and reformers. During several seasons she held a series of afternoon talks in Boston, New York and Washington, and in these assemblages she has discussed political economy and other topics. Her lectures on legislation and jurisprudence have done much to educate the people upon the relations of the individual to the commonwealth and to the nation. In late years she and her husband have made a close and exhaustive study of Spiritualism and have become believers in it. Several years ago she published a book entitled "Womanhood—Its Sanctities and Fidelities," which treated of the marriage relation and of the education of children to lives of purity, in a courageous, yet delicate way, and attracted wide attention. It brought to her many earnest expressions of gratitude from intelligent mothers. One of her most striking productions was a tract entitled "A Mother's Letter to a Daughter," published in "Putnam's Magazine." This was an effective argument upon the reform that has absorbed her energies for so many years, the enfranchisement of woman. For many years she held the office of vice-president for Connecticut in the National Woman Suffrage Association, and in the yearly conventions of that organization in Washington, DC, she has delivered a number of able and brilliant addresses. In the International Council of Women, in 1888, in the session devoted to "Political Condition," she delivered an address on "The Constitutional Rights of Women of the United States," a masterly, exhaustive and unanswerable presentation of the subject. In 1878 she took a leading part and acted as spokesman before a committee of Congress appointed upon a petition, referred to the committee, asking for legislation in favor of the enfranchisement of woman. One of her most recent efforts in behalf of woman was in the Republican National Convention in Chicago, where, in company with Miss Susan B. Anthony, she prepared an open letter

reviewing the work of woman, claiming that she had earned recognition, and ending with a powerful plea that the convention would include women in the term "citizens." Mrs. Hooker's long life has been one of ceaseless toil, heroic endurance of undeserved abuse, and exalted effort. She has been singularly fortunate in her domestic relations. Her family numbered three children. Her son, Dr. Edward Beecher Hooker, is a successful homeopathic physician in Hartford. One daughter, Mrs. John C. Day, has been living abroad for several years with her, husband and children. Her third child, Mrs. Mary Hooker Burton, died several years ago. Mr. and Mrs. Hooker celebrated their golden wedding on August 5th, 1891. The celebration took place in the City Mission Hall, in Hartford. On that occasion Senator Joseph R. Hawley acted as master of ceremonies. The whole city turned out to honor the venerable couple, whose fame shed a luster on the place they call home. Many prominent persons attended the reception. The judges of the Supreme Court of Connecticut went in a body to tender their respects. The National American Woman's Suffrage Association was represented by Susan B. Anthony, Mrs. Mary Seymour Howell, Mrs. Rachel Foster Avery, Miss Sara Winthrop Smith, Mrs. Caroline Gilkey Rogers, Miss Phebe Cousins and many others. The Board of Lady Managers of the World's Columbian Exposition, of which Mrs. Hooker is a member, was represented by one of its vice-presidents and other well-known women from various States. Two of her brothers, Rev. Edward Beecher and Rev. Thomas K. Beecher, were present. Other guests were Hon. William M. Evarts, Judge Nathaniel Shipman and wife, William Lloyd Garrison, Rev. Charles E. Stowe, a son of Harriet Beecher Stowe, Mrs. Frank Osborne, Regent of the Daughters of the Revolution for Illinois, and scores of other men and women of note in politics, art, journalism, religion and literature.

HOOPER, Mrs. Lucy Hamilton, poet and journalist, born in Philadelphia, PA, 20th January, 1835. She was the daughter of a well-known merchant of that city. Her maiden name was Jones. She became the wife, in

1854, of Robert E. Hooper, a native of Philadelphia, and resided in that city until a few years ago. Her first poems, written at a very early age, were published in "Godey's Lady's Book." In 1864 appeared a small collection of her poems, published by Mr. Leypoldt, the first hundred copies of the edition being presented by the author to the Great Central Fair for the benefit of the sanitary commission, which was then in progress in Philadelphia. In 1868 was begun the publication of "Lippincott's Magazine," to which Mrs. Hooper became a constant contributor. She assumed the functions of assistant editor of that periodical, a post which she retained till her visit to Europe, in 1870. In 1871 a second collection of her poems was published, including most of those that had been printed in the first volume, with important additions. Though born to great wealth, Mrs. Hooper found herself finally compelled by the consequence of a commercial crisis to adopt, as a profession, those literary pursuits which had hitherto formed her favorite recreation. She went to Europe in 1874 to become the Paris correspondent of several prominent American newspapers. Her efforts in that direction were crowned with success. She became a regular contributor to the "Daily Evening Telegraph," of Philadelphia, an engagement of sixteen years' duration, and of the "Post-Dispatch," of St. Louis. She was the author of a translation of Alphonse Daudet's novel, "The Nabob," which was published by special agreement with M. Daudet. An original novel, called "Under the Tricolor," and a four-act drama, entitled "Helen's Inheritance," were among her latest literary works of important character. The latter was first produced in June, 1888, in a French version, in the Théatre d' Application, in Paris, Miss Nettie Hooper playing the part of the heroine. She sustained the rôle when the piece was brought out by A. M. Palmer in the Madison Square Theater, in New York, in December, 1889. The drama has been played under another title, "Inherited," throughout the United States for several seasons. For some years Mrs. Hooper made her home in Paris, where she died 31st August, 1893. She had never missed a weekly letter in the "Philadelphia Telegraph" during eighteen years.

HOSMER, Miss Harriet G., sculptor, born in Watertown, MA, 9th October, 1830. Her father was a physician. Her mother and sister died of consumption, and Harriet was led to live an outdoor life. Her genius for modeling in clay showed itself in her youth, when in a clay-pit near her home she spent her time in modeling horses, dogs and other forms. She received a fair education and took lessons in art in Boston. With her father she studied anatomy, and afterward went to St. Louis, MO, where she took a course of study in the medical college. In 1851 she executed her first important work, an ideal head of "Hesper." In 1852 she went to Rome, Italy, with her father and her friend, Charlotte Cushman. There she was a pupil with Gibson. She at once produced two ideal heads, "Daphne" and "Medusa," which were exhibited in Boston in 1853. In 1855 she produced her first full-length marble figure, "Œnone." Her other productions include "Will-o'-the-Wisp," "Puck," "Sleeping Faun," "Waking Faun," "Zenobia," a statue of Marie Sophia, Queen of the Sicilies, and other famous figures. Her "Beatrice Cenci" and her bronze statue of Thomas H. Benton are both in St. Louis, MO. Miss Hosmer's work has received the highest favor. Her commissions have brought her fortune as well as fame. Among her European patrons are the Prince of Wales, the church authorities in Rome, Lady Manan Alford, Earl Brownlow and others. Most of her best work is owned in St. Louis, where she has spent much of her time. Besides her talent in sculpture, Miss Hosmer has shown marked talent in poetical composition and in prose articles on sculpture, which she has treated in a philosophical way in the "Atlantic Monthly." Her works are numerous, and each one is an evidence of her greatness as a sculptor. She executed a statue of Queen Isabella for the Colombian Exposition.

HOUGHTON, Mrs. Alice, broker, born in Montreal, Canada, 18th August, 1849. Her father, Frederick Ide, an architect, moved in 1853 to Mondovi, WI, with his family. Alice was the fourth in a family of five daughters. She received a liberal education and was noted for her strong powers of mind. In 1864 she became the wife of Horace E. Houghton, an attorney of Mondovi. After suffering financial losses Mr. and Mrs. Houghton removed to Spokane, WA, where they have lived since. Her business talents led her into active business life, and she became the head of the successful real estate, insurance and investment brokerage house, Mrs. Alice Houghton & Co., in 1888. Her management has been very practical and progressive, and her house is known throughout the State. She is a safe and sound financier. Her business methods are good, and her tact and energy have enabled her to compete with the active men of her State in the arduous field of brokerage. She is a cultured and refined woman. Her family consists of two children. She has large social connections and is president of the Sorosis of Spokane. She has taken an active and conspicuous part in preparing various novel displays for the Columbian Exposition, being the lady manager and superintendent of the woman's department of her State.

HOUGHTON, Mrs. Mary Hayes, journalist, born in Penfield, Lorain county, OH, 26th March, 1837. Her maiden name was Hayes. Her parents were Western Reserve pioneers from New England, whose ancestry was Norman-French. She was the oldest daughter of a large family. She was in childhood of a nervous temperament, slight in figure, active, energetic, with a strong memory, an omnivorous reader, and always a student. Her school-life was interrupted by ill-health, but her reading and study went on, covering a large range in history, philosophy and literature. In the Civil War and its excitements her family had full share. There was prodigal expenditure of strength and sympathy, resulting in broken health, but no abatement of industry. She became the wife of J. W. Houghton, A.M., M.D., in 1874. Two years after, he became proprietor of the Wellington, OH, "Enterprise," in which, with his wife as editorial assistant, they continued nine years, when it was sold on account of failing health. From the age of eighteen years Mrs. Houghton had written more or less for publication, chiefly upon current topics, and her connection with the press served to give variety, breadth and finish to her composition. She has the journalistic faculty and

reportorial instinct in a marked degree, selecting, discarding, condensing, revising and editing with swift judgment. The bulk of her literary work has been anonymously written, and some of it has been widely copied. Impelled by anxiety for an overtasked and frail husband, the wife became familiar with his many lines of business, private, professional and official, and with many years of efficient service proves that "woman's work" may cover a wide range without impairing her womanliness, her taste for domestic life or her skill in feminine accomplishments. With organizations religious, reformatory and literary, she is actively identified, and she cooperates with all that will elevate humanity. She is president of a woman's club which for years has done excellent work, and is also a member of the Ohio Woman's Press Club. An enthusiastic student of sociology, she aids the aspiring and arouses all who know her to higher ambitions and more exalted views of the real purposes of life. Her home is in Wellington, OH, and her energies and sympathies are now chiefly occupied in repeating earlier experience, comforting bereaved old age and caring for motherless childhood, in which labor of love her nature finds large compensations.

HOUSH, Mrs. Esther T., temperance worker and author, was born in Ross county, Ohio. She is descended from Scotch and English ancestors. Her grandfather was Col. Robert Stewart, of Ohio, whose home was a station on the "underground railroad." Her grandmother was the first one of the family to sign the Washingtonian pledge. Her father was a Congregational minister. Her mother, Mrs. Margaretta Stewart, was a cultured and refined woman. Esther was the second child in a family of eight, and her early days were full of cares and work. She received a liberal education, and studied her Greek and Latin while busy with the work of the home. In childhood she became a believer in woman's rights. She was married at an early age. She has one living child. One other died in childhood. Her son. Frank, was the publisher of the "Woman's Magazine," commenced in Louisville, KY, in 1877, and continued in Brattleboro, VT, until 1890. Mrs Housh did all the editorial work on that periodical. She became prominent in temperance work. In 1883 she was sent from Brattleboro as a delegate to the State convention in West Randolph. She was invited to attend the national convention in Detroit, MI, and there she was elected national press superintendent of the Woman's Christian Temperance Union. She held that position until 1888. She instituted the "National Bulletin," which averaged eighty-thousand copies a year. She wrote special reports and numerous leaflets, some of which reached a sale of two-hundred-thousand copies. In the national conventions in Nashville and New York she furnished a report to a thousand selected papers of high standing. In 1885 she was elected State secretary of the Vermont Woman's Christian Temperance Union, and she has ever since had editorial charge of "Our Home Guards," the State organ. In 1877 she was elected State president of Vermont. In 1890 and 1891, in Boston, MA, she edited the "Household," which had been removed from Brattleboro. In 1891 she returned to Vermont. She is a dignified presiding officer, and her work has been of a most valuable character. Besides her prose works, she has written a number of poems of merit. Her home is now in Brattleboro.

HOWARD, Mrs. Belle, dramatic reader, born in Center county, PA, 27th August, 1857. She is the only daughter of Samuel and Mary S. Gill. With her parents, at the age of eight years, she removed to Emporia, KS, where she was placed in the model department of the State Normal School, and remained a student in that institution for ten years. At the age of eighteen years she began to teach, and not many months later contracted an unfortunate marriage, and at the end of three years, with her two infant children, she launched upon the world alone. Among other duties the care of an invalid mother fell to her lot. After years of struggles she failed in health and was forced to abandon labor of all kinds. After two years of rest she gained strength enough to take up again life's duties, and with her twelve-year-old daughter, May Belle, began to give musical and elocutionary entertainments. Mrs. Howard inherited from her father musical

talent of a high order, and literary talent from her mother. Her musical studies have gone hand in hand with her literary work. She gave lessons in music with her school-teaching. After seven years of successful work in the public schools of Lyon county, in the vicinity of Emporia, Mrs. Howard removed with her family to El Dorado, KS, teaching in the El Dorado city schools with marked success for a period of three years. Her work was of the character that imbued her pupils with life's lofty purposes. She resigned her position there to devote her energies exclusively to musical and literary work, and organized a prosperous music school at her home. When Garfield University was opened in Wichita, KS, she moved there from El Dorado for further study and development for herself and children. She obtained a position in the Wichita schools with a salary sufficient to meet all her expenses, tuition in the University and support of her family. Many painful experiences came to her, accompanied by the serious and protracted illness of her mother, herself, and lastly of her son, but she persevered in the work of her life's effort and ambition. Her daughter became at the same time a violinist, elocutionist and vocalist of marked skill. Twenty-five years of Mrs. Howard's life have been spent in the schoolroom, as student and teacher. She now lives in Wichita with her daughter May Belle and son Guello P., a bright lad of fifteen years. She is connected with the Mozart Conservatory of Music and the Western School of Elocution and Oratory. Her entertainments are generally given in churches, and she is assisted by her daughter.

HOWARD, Blanche Willis, see TEUFFEL, MME. BLANCHE WILLIS HOWARD VON.

HOWARD, Mrs. Elmira Y., physician, born in Shelby, Richland county, OH, 3rd May, 1841. Her mother's family were people of education and refinement, of old Puritan stock. Stephen Marvin, her maternal grandfather, was born in Connecticut. His wife was Sarah Burr Sherwood, daughter of Deborah Burr, a second cousin of Aaron Burr. From her grandmother Dr. Howard inherited her taste for medical studies. Dr. Howard's father's family were Virginians. She

is one of several children. In 1859 she became the wife of Jerome B. Howard, an artist. Her husband was a son of Nathan Howard, of Stephentown, NY, and a brother of Judge Howard, of New York, the author of "Howard's Reports." Jerome B. Howard, as an artist, was connected with the State Normal School, of New York. When the Civil War broke out, he volunteered. Until then Dr. Howard's life had been calm and uneventful. Three children were born to her, two boys and a girl. Her husband was past the age of forty-five when he volunteered. He was taken prisoner by Mosby and died in Andersonville prison. Left a widow at the age of twenty-three years, with three helpless children, and wholly unprepared for the battle of life, her position was painful. Finally she decided to study medicine. Her parents demurred, but Mrs. Howard was firm. Her little girl was a cripple, and the study of medicine was suggested by that fact. At the age of twenty-seven she went to New York. She entered the New York Medical College for Women and was graduated. She was induced to move to Cincinnati, OH, in 1870, and she opened there an office for practice, the first woman in that city to take such a responsibility. She was heartily welcomed and endorsed by the medical fraternity, and her efforts were soon appreciated. Her first year's practice brought her a mere living. The second year she doubled it, and the third year trebled her income. Her health failed through over-taxation, and in 1873–74 she went to Europe, and studied in the Vienna Hospital nine months. While absent, she was a correspondent of the Cincinnati "Commercial-Gazette." Dr. Howard studied both allopathy and homeopathy, but is a homeopathic practitioner, and has built up a fine practice. She is very charitable.

HOWARD, Miss Mary M., musician and musical educator, born in Batavia, NY. She received her musical education in New York, with S. B. Mills and William H. Sherwood for piano teachers and Frederick Archer and S. P. Warren as organ teachers. She began her career as church organist at fifteen years of age, and she has never been abroad. She is exclusively an American product. She taught three years in the New York State Institute for the Blind, in Batavia, and for

two years was at the head of the musical department of Howard College, Fayette, MO. For one year she held the position of director of the Batavia Philharmonic Club, an organization numbering eighty members. In 1887 she went to Buffalo, NY, and took the position of organist in the First Presbyterian Church, which she has retained ever since. She is the only woman who has ever held the place of organist in that church. In 1888 she opened in Buffalo a school of music, which has been the first institution of that kind to succeed in that city.

HOWE, Mrs. Emeline Harriet, poet, born in West Hickory, Forest county, PA, 2nd January, 1844. Her maiden name was Siggins, of Scotch-Irish extraction. Her grandparents were people of the best type and were among the pioneer settlers in that part of the country. Her father's farm had been the favorite camping-ground of the Indians in early times. Her father was a lover of poets, and often, on his return from rafting lumber to Pittsburgh, brought to his forest home the choicest literature of ancient and modern times. Surrounded by the beautiful in nature, the companionship of her loved books and constant association with her father had a refining effect on the youthful mind of Miss Siggins. She grew up with a love of the grand and beautiful in nature, art and literature, inspiring her at an early age to write verses for publication. In the twenty-third year of her life she became the wife of Capt. W. C. Howe, who served his country gallantly in the Civil War. Their home is in the city of Franklin, PA. Mrs. Howe is the mother of five sons, and her home is the domain of her power. Writing poems has been only an incident in her active life, although her published ones would make a volume. She is a graduate of the first class of the Chautauqua Literary and Scientific Circle, and her poem "From Height to Height," written on the motto of her class, was read at Chautauqua. She is a woman of studious habits, extensive knowledge and of refined tastes, an earnest worker in the ranks of the Woman's Christian Temperance Union and active in missionary society work.

HOWE, Mrs. Julia Ward, poet, author and philanthropist, born in New York City, 27th May, 1819. Her parents were Samuel Ward and Julia Cutler Ward. Her ancestors included the Huguenot Marions, of South Carolina, Governor Samuel Ward, of Rhode Island, and Roger Williams, the apostle of religious tolerance. Her mother died in 1824. Her father, a successful banker, gave her every advantage of education. She was instructed at home by able teachers; her education including music, German, Greek and French. She became the wife of Dr. Samuel G. Howe in 1843. They went abroad and remained a year, and her first child was born in Rome, Italy. Her father died in 1829, and Mrs. Howe became a Unitarian in religion after rallying from the sorrow caused by his death. In youth she had shown her literary trend. At seventeen she published a review of Lamartine's "Jocelyn," an essay on the minor poems of Goethe and Schiller, and a number of original poems. Her marriage interrupted her literary work for a time. In 1850 she went to Europe, and passed the winter in Rome with her two youngest children. In the fall of 1851 she returned to Boston. In 1852 and 1853 she published her first volume of poems, "Passion Flowers," which attracted much attention. In 1853 she published her "Words for the Hour" and a blank verse drama, which was produced in Wallack's Theater, in New York City, and later in Boston. Her interest in the anti-slavery question dated from 1851. Her third volume, "Later Lyrics," included her "Battle Hymn of the Republic," which was written in Washington, DC, in the fall of 1861. Her book, "A Trip to Cuba," written after her visit to Cuba in 1857, is a prohibited volume on that island. Her prominence during the Civil War was due to her celebrated patriotic songs. Her "John Brown" song was the most popular. It at once became known throughout the country and was sung everywhere. In 1867, with her husband, Mrs. Howe visited Greece, where they won the gratitude of the Greeks for their aid in their struggle for national independence. Her book, "From the Oak to the Olive," was written after her visit to Greece. She has been a profound student of philosophy, and has written numerous essays on philosophical themes. In 1868 she joined the woman suffrage movement. In 1869, before a legislative committee in Boston, she made her first suffrage speech. She has been officially connected from the beginning with the New England, the American. and other woman suffrage organizations. Her husband died in 1876, and since that year she has preached, lectured, written and traveled much in all parts of the United States. Her lectures included "Is Polite Society Polite?" "Greece Revisited," and "Reminiscences of Longfellow and Emerson." In 1872 she went to England to lecture on arbitration as a means for settling national and international disputes. In London she held a series of Sunday evening services, devoted to "The Mission of Christianity in Relation to the Pacification of the World." In 1872 she attended, as a delegate, the Congress for Prison Reform held in London. Returning to the United States, she instituted the Women's Peace Festival, which meets on 22nd June each year. Several years ago she went to Europe and spent over two years in travel in England, France, Italy and Palestine. In Paris she was one of the presiding officers of the Woman's Rights Congress in 1878. She lectured in Paris and Athens on the work of the women's associations in America. In Boston she aided to organize the Woman's Club and the Ladies' Saturday Morning Club. In Newport she aided to form the Town and Country Club. She has served as president of the Association for the Advancement of Women for several years. She maintains her connection with these organizations, and is an active promoter of their interests. She is still a vigorous, active woman. In the clubs which she has formed, the members study Latin, French, German, literature, botany, political economy and many other branches. Her life has been and still is one round of ceaseless activity. Her home is in Boston, MA.

HOWELL, Mrs. Mary Seymour, lecturer and woman suffragist, born in Mount Morris, NY, 29th August, 1844. She is the only daughter of Norman and Frances Metcalf Seymour and a lineal descendant of the Seymour family, well known in English history through the Puritan representative, Richard Seymour, who settled in Hartford, CT, in 1639. She received a

classical education and has devoted much time to the higher educational interests of New York. Under the care of lecture bureaus she has delivered many historical and literary lectures and has done much work for the cause of temperance. Ten years ago she became interested in securing suffrage for women, and has addressed audiences in many of the cities and villages of the North and West, as well as in New England and her own State. She has repeatedly plead the cause of women before committees of State legislatures and of Congress. Mrs. Howell is the only woman ever asked to speak before the House of Representatives of Connecticut. In 1890 she delivered the address to the graduating class of South Dakota College. Her addresses are enlivened with anecdotes and through them all runs a vein of sentiment. She a very magnetic orator. Her speeches have always been received with enthusiasm, and the press has spoken of her in terms of highest praise. She is broad in thought, liberal in spirit, holding justice as her guide in all the relations of life. She was appointed in 1891, by Mrs. Elizabeth Cady Stanton, the president of the National American Woman Suffrage Association, to represent that body in the National Council of Women in Washington. Mrs. Howell's home is in Albany, NY. She is the wife of George Roger Howell, of the State Library. Mrs. Howell's only child, Seymour Howell, a young man of great promise and lofty integrity, died a junior in Harvard University, 9th March, 1891.

HOWLAND, Miss Emily, educator, philanthropist and reformer, born in Sherwood, NY, 20th November, 1827. Her ancestors on both sides were members of the Society of Friends, and she was reared according to the strict requirements of that sect regarding speech, dress and conduct. Her father was a Garrisonian Abolitionist. Her home was open to the anti-slavery lecturer, and as a station on the underground railroad for the fugitive slave. Besides the writings of friends, the weekly visits of the "Liberator," the "North Star," the "Philanthropist" and the "Anti-Slavery Standard" furnished the literature of the family. A free school for colored girls in Washington, DC, which had attracted attention, both friendly and hostile, needed a teacher. Impelled to work, she offered herself for the position, and in the fall of 1857, without the approval of her friends, she took the conduct of that school and taught with interest and profit until the spring of 1859. In 1863, just after the Proclamation of Emancipation, she returned to Washington and worked among the freed people, crowded into rude barracks, which had been built and used for cavalry horses. After the war Miss Howland's father bought a tract near the mouth of the Potomac, and early in 1867 a few families of freedmen settled on the land. It is now nearly all divided into small farms and owned by the colored people. She opened a school at once, and has supplied it with teachers from that time to the present. Her interest in education has not been limited to the colored race. In 1882 she erected a handsome school-house for the children of her native place, and equipped it with complete physical and chemical apparatus. She has also helped many young people to a professional education. In 1890 she was made a director of the First National Bank of Aurora, one of the first women to fill such a position in the country. She is connected with the Wimodaughsis Club, the Cayuga County Woman Suffrage Society and the Sherwood Ramabai Circle; is a prominent worker in the local equal rights club and the Woman's Christian Temperance Union, and has the settling of several estates.

HOXIE, Mrs. Vinnie Ream, sculptor, born in Madison, WI, 23rd September, 1847. Her father, Robert L. Ream, was register of deeds in Madison at the time of her birth. Her mother was of Scotch descent, and her name was Lavinia McDonald. When fifteen years of age Vinnie, in two hours, modeled a medallion of an Indian chief so cleverly as to at once attract the attention of Thaddeus Stevens, Hon. John Wentworth and other members of Congress, who insisted upon her studying art. In six months she had modeled such striking likenesses of Reverdy Johnson, Frank P. Blair, General Grant, Parson Brownlow, Senator Voorhees, General Albert Pike and Senator Sherman, that she was taken to President Lin-

Isabel Irving.
From Photo by Morrison, Chicago.

coln, who sat to her for his likeness. When he was assassinated, six months later, Congress gave her a commission to make a life size statue of Abraham Lincoln, which stands in marble in the United States Capitol. She received fifteen-thousand dollars for that work. After finishing the model she took it to Italy to be transferred to marble, and lived in Rome three years with her parents. There she made many ideal works, and among them a statue of "Miriam," a copy of which she sold to Mrs. Larner, of Philadelphia, for three-thousand dollars. Her "Indian Girl" was put in bronze and sold, and Vinnie also made another marble bust of Lincoln, for Cornell University, and a bust in marble of Mayor Powell, of Brooklyn, NY, which now stands in the city hall of that city. She made a likeness of Mr. Rice, of Maine, in marble, and also put into marble the two fair daughters of Mr. Clark. Congress then appropriated twenty-five-thousand dollars for a bronze statue of Admiral Farragut, and, competing with William Story, Ward, Launt Thompson and many distinguished sculptors, Vinnie Ream won the

order. While in Paris, Gustave Dore gave Vinnie a painting by his own hand, inscribed "Offered to Miss Vinnie Ream, on the part of her affectionate colleague, Gustave Dore." Spurgeon sat in his Tabernacle to her for his likeness, and in Munich, Kaulbach, the great painter, sat to her. In Rome Cardinal Antonelli sat to her for his likeness, and presented her three stone cameos, set in pearls, one very large and exquisitely beautiful, representing the head of Christ. On the inside of the frame was a beautiful inscription to the artist. Liszt sat to Miss Vinnie for his medallion, and gave her many handsome souvenirs. Returning to the United States, her statue of Lincoln was unveiled in the rotunda of the Capitol with many imposing ceremonies, Senator Cullum, of Illinois, and Senator Carpenter, of Wisconsin, being the speakers. When Miss Vinnie received the order for the statue of Farragut, she worked on the model in the ordnance building of the navy yard, and that statue was cast from the metal of the propeller of the Hartford, his flag-ship. Before the model was finished, she was introduced to Lieutenant Hoxie, a young engineer officer, by General Sherman, and they became engaged and married with the warm approval of General Sherman and Mrs. Farragut. General Sherman gave the bride away, and the wedding was one of the most imposing ever seen in Washington. Lieutenant Hoxie built for themselves a most artistic home on Farragut Square, and hopes to spend his declining years there, when the distant day of his retirement comes. When the statue of Farragut was unveiled, Senator Voorhees, President Garfield and Horace Maynard spoke. Captain Hoxie is now stationed in the engineering post of Willets Point, New York harbor. Mrs. Hoxie, at the earnest request of her husband, now models only for love and not for money. In later years she has developed talent both as a poet and a musician.

HUDSON, Mrs. Mary Clemmer, journalist and poet, born in Utica, NY, in 1840, and died 18th August, 1884. Her ancestors on both sides came from famous families. Abraham Clemmer, her father, a native of Pennsylvania, was of Huguenot descent, and Margaret Kneale, her mother, was a descendant of the Crams, a well-known

family of the Isle of Man, who trace a direct line back to 1600. Her principal education was received in the Westfield Academy, in Westfield, NY. Married at seventeen, she resided in Massachusetts, Minnesota, New York and, during the war, in Harper's Ferry, VA, where she witnessed and afterward very vividly described in her novel, "Erena," the contest which took place there. When but a school-girl she formed a strong liking for Alice Cary and her poetry, and when she went to New York she readily found her way to the home and heart of that noble woman, with whom she formed a lasting friendship and to whom she afterward paid high tribute in her work, "Memorial of Alice and Phœbe Cary," which she called her work of love. Miss Clemmer tried novel-writing, and her first work to receive attention was "Erena: A Woman's Right." "Then His Two Wives" appeared in "Every Saturday," Boston. Among her literary works which received special attention was "Ten Years in Washington" (Hartford, 1870). In 1882 her poems were collected and published under the title, "A Volume of Poems." From 1866 to 1869 Miss Clemmer resided in Washington, doing regular work in the way of letters from Washington for the New York "Independent." In 1869 she engaged for three years' work on the Brooklyn "Daily Union," and for the third year's work of that engagement she received a salary of five-thousand dollars, the largest sum ever paid to a newspaper woman for one year's labor up to that time. In 1872 she resumed her work on the New York "Independent." In January, 1879, while in Washington, she received a serious injury from a carriage accident, and she suffered intensely, getting but little relief during the remaining six years which she lived. On 19th June, 1883, she became the wife of Edmund Hudson, the journalist, and they immediately went to Europe, but she was brought home to die the next year.

HUGHES, Mrs. Caroline, business woman and philanthropist, was born in Phelps, Ontario county, NY. Her ancestors were of English descent and were among the early settlers of New England. When her education was completed, she took a position as teacher of mathematics

and other branches in the Mississippi State Female College. Afterward she had charge of the collegiate department of the Huntsville Female College, Alabama, as the colleague of its president. After several years passed in the South, she returned to Chicago and engaged on her own account in the real estate business. She was the first woman who began to operate in real estate in Chicago, buying and selling for herself and for others. Her record in public life is notable in connection with her exposition work, having represented the woman's department for the State of Illinois, in the Centennial Exposition in Philadelphia, in 1876, and the World's Exposition in New Orleans, in 1884 and 1885. She was married in 1878 and was left a widow in 1888. As an active philanthropist, she stands among the first women of Chicago. She was one of the incorporators of the Illinois Industrial School for Girls and its first secretary. In real estate Mrs. Hughes transacts a large business, and her office is a great rendezvous for women investors. Though Mrs. Hughes has become a conspicuous figure in the world of business and has achieved marked success in an occupation unusual for her sex, she is thoroughly gentle and feminine, always keeping herself in the background as much as possible, while pushing her ventures in the most enterprising manner.

HUGHES, Mrs. Kate Duval, author and inventor, born in Philadelphia, PA, 15th June, 1837. She is of French descent. Her maiden name was Duval. Her parents were wealthy, and she received a thorough education. Her marriage proved an unfortunate one, and the loss of her fortune threw her upon her own resources. She spent several years in Europe, and after her return to the United States she settled in Washington, DC, where she secured a position in one of the governmental departments. She has shown her versatility in inventing two mechanical contrivances for locking windows, both of which have been patented. Mrs. Hughes is in religion a Roman Catholic, and her three books, "Little Pearls" (New York, 1876), "The Mysterious Castle" (Baltimore, 1878), and "The Fair Maid of Connaught" (New York, 1889), are religious in character. About three years ago she discovered the art of extracting the essential oil of frankincense as used by the ancients. This she has introduced into an ointment for skin diseases, which has been used in many hospitals.

HUGHES, Mrs. Marietta E., physician, was born in Southern Michigan. She was educated in an academical school in Three Rivers, MI, and the State Normal School in Ypsilanti. She taught successfully in the high school in Three Rivers for several years. After pursuing a thorough preparatory course with a preceptor, she took the regular course in the medical department of the University of Michigan in 1874 and 1875. She afterward entered the Hahnemann Medical College, in Chicago, IL, and was graduated with high honors in that institution in the centennial class. A prize was awarded her for passing the best examination in gynæcology. After her graduation, she at once took up active practice in her native State. Soon after graduating she became the wife of a classmate, Dr. C. A. Hughes. Leaving Detroit, MI, in 1889, Dr. Hughes went to Spokane, WA, sine which time she and her husband, with whom she is associated in business have been steadily establishing themselves in the confidence of the people.

HUGHES, Mrs. Nina Vera B., author, was born in Paris, Canada. She was reared and educated in the United States, living in New York State and in Boston principally. Her present work is entirely professional and instructive along the lines of ethical and metaphysical culture. Among her best known works are "Twelve Simple Lessons in Metaphysics," "Practical Home Thoughts," "Truth for Youth," "Office, In and Out," "Lecture-Room Talks," and "Guide to Health." Her home is now in Washington, DC.

HULING, Miss Caroline Augusta, journalist, philanthropist and reformer, born in Saratoga Springs, NY, in April, 1856. Her father, Edmund J. Huling, was a native of that county, and was an editor and publisher in the famous watering-place for a half-century. Through her mother she is related to "Fanny Fern," N. P. Willis, and the brothers Prime, so long connected with the New York "Observer," who were cousins. Under the tuition of her father she began active journalistic work when but twelve years old, starting with society reporting in the ball-rooms of that gay spa. She was educated in the public schools, and made special study of music and languages. She became a Good Templar in 1874 and was prominent in the work, holding several offices in the lodges. When the Woman's Christian Temperance Union was organized, she was one of the first to don the white ribbon, which she still wears. She was one of the first executive board of the Humane Society and secretary of the local Woman Suffrage Society. She became associate editor of the Saratoga "Sentinel" with her father, and had special superintendence of his book-bindery. She was also correspondent of many city papers during the summer. Ex-President Cleveland, then Governor of New York, made her a notary public, which was at that time a decided innovation and created a precedent. In 1884, wishing for a broader field, she removed to Chicago, taking up the same lines of work, but devoting most of her time to the cause of woman's enfranchisement. She was for two years secretary of the Cook County Equal Suffrage Association, for two years superintendent of press work of the State society. Since the formation of the Illinois Woman's Press Association, in 1885, Miss Huling's name has been on its membership roll, and for several years she was one of its executive board. In 1890 she represented the association in the National Editorial Association, and was unanimously elected assistant recording secretary of that body. She took great interest in the formation of the Illinois Woman's Alliance, in October, 1888, and as elected president, serving two years without opposition, and declining election the third year in order to devote herself to a working woman's club, of which she was also president. From October, 1887, to November, 1888, she edited and published an eight-page semi-monthly periodical called "Justitia, a Court for the Unrepresented," in which she had a small pecuniary interest. It was the organ of the Illinois Equal Suffrage Association, and devoted to the advancement of women, social purity and other reforms. In 1884 she made several addresses for the Prohibition party, and is known as a superior parliamentarian. In the fall of 1891 Miss Huling aided in the organization of the Woman's Baking Company, and became its secretary. The philanthropic features of the plan appealed to her sympathies, and she relinquished her professional work in a great measure to aid her sisters, the company aiming to provide a good investment for small savings and an avenue of employment for many women. She is, however, doing editorial work on several publications, and has two or three books under way.

HUMPHREY, Miss Maud, artist, born in Rochester, NY, 30th March, 1868. From early childhood she showed a fondness for sketching. She began her first studies when she was twelve years old, in Rochester, under the tuition of Rev. J. H. Dennis, in a free evening school which met twice a week. After two winters of instruction, during which time she took a few lessons in oils, her eyes failed, and for two years she was unable to use them, even to read. At sixteen she began to illustrate some children's magazines and books. The following winter she went to New York City to study in the Art Students' League. Her studies were occasionally interrupted by commissions for illustrating. Returning to Rochester, she took two terms of instruction in water-colors, which is the only water-color instruction she received. Each winter found her in New York, trying to find time from her illustrating to study in the League, but about two months each winter was all she ever secured. In the summer of 1888 she painted a child's head for a friend, who took the picture to F. A. Stokes Co., to be framed. Mr. Stokes asked permission to correspond with Miss Humphrey, with regard to doing a book for him, which led to the successive years of work for that firm, for the past two years of which the firm had contracts for the sole control of her color work. Although best known as a child painter, she has done considerable work with older subjects, much of it in black and white, and she has lately begun to work for exhibitions in New York and some of the larger cities. The studies of children are done partly from little professional models and partly from her little friends. She works rapidly, catching a little at a time from the children while at play, as a rule. Her home is now in New York.

HUMPHREYS, Mrs. Sarah Gibson, author and woman suffragist, born in southwestern Louisiana, on a sugar plantation, 17th May, 1830. Her father, Hon. Tobias Gibson, was a man of education and advanced ideas. Her mother was Louisiana Breckenridge Hart, of Kentucky, a woman of masculine intellect, unusual culture and great force of character. Until she was fourteen, Mrs. Humphreys' education was supervised by her parents, although the most accomplished teachers were employed to instruct her. At fourteen she was sent to the school of Miss Margaret Mercer, of Loudoun county, Virginia. For three years she studied in the French school of Charles Picot in Philadelphia. Her mother died soon after her return from school, and she assumed the charge of her father's summer home in Lexington, KY, as well as the winter plantation home in Louisiana, and took the place of her mother in the care and control of six brothers younger than herself, and an infant sister. Two years later she became the wife of Jos. A. Humphreys, of Kentucky, a gentleman of culture and refinement. He died during the war, leaving her with a family of little children to bring up and a large estate to manage unaided. Since her children have been grown and she has been in a measure relieved of financial responsibilities, Mrs. Humphreys has been able to follow her inclination in literary pursuits and the cause of the emancipation of woman. Her first literary work was a novel, which she wrote when only thirteen, and which was never published. During the last ten years she has contributed stories, essays, letters and sketches to various magazines and papers north and south, always over a penname. One of her contributions to "Bedford's Magazine" was the "Negro Libertines in the South." The most original of Mrs. Humphrey's literary productions is an article read before the Convention of the Kentucky Equal Rights Association on "Man and Woman in the Bible and in Nature," in which she advanced the theory of the sexual duality of God, of the Adam made in His image. Mrs. Humphreys has served on a board of road directors, a unique office for a woman.

HUNT, Mrs. Augusta Merrill, philanthropist, born in Portland, ME, 6th June, 1842. She was the youngest daughter of George S. and Ellen Merrill Barston, of Portland, ME. In 1863 she became the wife of George S. Hunt, a prominent and successful merchant of Portland. She has been actively identified with many of the prominent charitable organizations of Portland, notably that of the Portland Fraternity, the Associated Charities, a Home for Aged Women, the Woman's Christian Temperance Union and the Woman's Suffrage Association. For seven years she has been the president of the Ladies' History Club, the first literary society organized by the women of Portland, which was originated in 1874. She became, in 1876, the first president of the Woman's Christian Temperance Union of her home city. Under her direction the coffee-house, diet kitchen and diet mission and the flower mission were successfully organized and carried forward. In 1878 the society became auxiliary to the National Woman's Christian Temperance Union. She has three times held the position of national superintendent in the Woman's Christian Temperance Union, the last department being that of higher education. In 1890 she was obliged to resign that position on account of ill health. In 1884 she was appointed by the governor of Maine as a member of the Reform School Committee.

HUNT, Mrs. Mary H., temperance reformer, born in Litchfield, CT, 4th July, 18—. She was well educated and undertook the professorship of natural science in a leading educational institution in Baltimore, MD, where she

remained until the next step in her true education, the development that comes with wifehood and motherhood, began. Then, in the home life, the study of the highest need of her own son, led to the study of the needs and the problem of supply for the highest needs of all the young. She studied carefully the sentimental, religious and legal phases of the temperance reform, and became convinced that, if the nation were to be saved, it must be by the wide dissemination of actual knowledge concerning the nature and effects of alcohol upon the body, the mind and the soul of man. She felt she must reach the child through the medium of the public school. To reach the public school, with authority to teach, she must have behind her the power of the law, and her plan of operation must include direct attack upen legislation, and to secure any influence over legislation there must be a demand from the people. Mrs. Hunt laid her plan before the National Woman's Christian Temperance Union, who created an educational department, of which she became the national superintendent. By an appeal to the American Medical Association, in their annual national meeting in 1882 she secured a series of resolutions from that body concerning the evil nature and effects of alcoholic beverages. These resolutions have been the text for her successful appeals before legislative bodies and committees State and National, in this and other lands. She superintends this work in the Woman's Christian Temperance Union of the world, and is bringing all Christian nations to see the need of compulsory temperance education. Her work meant years of journeying from state to state, addressing audiences. It meant victory in the thirty-five States, with more to follow, and in all the Territories, in the national military and naval academies, in all Indian and colored schools under national control, covering in all more than twelve-million school children. It meant the creation of a new school literature, the revision of the old text-books and the actual creation of new ones covering the entire courses of instruction concerning the welfare of the body, a work that was carried on until there has been published under Mrs. Hunt's auspices many series of text-books on this topic.

HUNTINGTON, Miss Agnes, operatic singer, born in Michigan in 18—. She was reared and educated mainly in New York City. Her musical talents were shown early. In 1880 her family decided

Marie Engle.
Copyright, 1895, by Aime Dupont, New York.

May Irwin.   **Barbara Huntley.**
From Photo by Chickering, Boston.   *From Photo by Morrison, Chicago.*

that she should follow a career of her own choosing. She hesitated to choose between music and art, for both were attractive to her, and she finally decided to become an operatic singer. She went to Dresden in 1880, where she studied four years with Lamperti. She made her début as a singer in one of the Gewandhaus concerts in Leipzig. While in Dresden she sang in concerts, and during her vacations she sang in other German cities and in Paris and London. In 1885 she returned to the United States and sang in concert, opera and oratorio. After making a tour of the principal cities, she joined the Boston Ideal Opera Company, and with that company she sang successfully for several seasons. Many offers of engagements were made to her by English and German managers. In 1889 she went to London, England, under the management of the late Carl Rosa, having signed for a season of concert, oratorio and light opera. There she created the rôle of Paul Jones in Planquette's opera of that name, and in it she made a great hit. Originally put on for a short run, "Paul Jones" remained on the boards during three-hundred-forty-six nights in the Prince of Wales Theater, and at every performance the house was crowded. A dispute with her managers led her to leave the company, and she returned to the United States. Here she repeated her triumphs. Miss Huntington is tall, fair and of commanding presence. Her voice is a pure, clear, strong and thoroughly cultivated contralto. In London her social successes are quite as great as her professional ones. Among her intimate friends there are the Baroness Burdett-Coutts, the Duchess of Westminster and other prominent personages. She makes her home in New York, but is arranging to manage a theater in London. A series of new operas, written for her, will be produced there.

HUNTLEY, Mrs. Florence, journalist, author and humorist, was born in Alliance, OH, and was graduated in the Methodist Female College, Delaware, OH. She became known to the public as the wife of the late Stanley Huntley, of New York, the author of a series of remarkably humorous sketches in which Mr. and Mrs. Spoopendyke are the characters. She met Mr. Huntley, and the were married in Bismarck, Dakota, in 1879, at which time he was editor of the Bismarck "Tribune." They returned East in 1880. She suggested to her talented husband, who was a special writer on the Brooklyn "Eagle," the sketches which made him famous. They were used, at her suggestion, in his special department under the title of "Salad." This department was always written by Mr. Huntley on Friday. Mrs. Huntley was often said to be the author of the "Spoopendyke" sketches, but she disposes of the assertion by her acknowledgment that she wrote but one of them. She adopted the style employed by her husband, who was too ill to write or even to read a sketch, and the production went over the country as her husband's. While suggesting subjects to him, the work was done by him. Her husband was an invalid for two years before his death. Mrs. Huntley tells the story of her own entrance into the literary field as follows: "The people who laughed over the humorous things he continued to write would have felt tears burning in their hearts, if they could have seen this frail, delicate, nervous man, racked with pain and burning with fever, sitting bravely at his desk writing jokes to pay our board bills. Now and then, when I could not bear to see him working thus, I prevailed on him to let me do it for him. In this way I wrote considerable for the 'Salad' column, but it was always supposed at the office that I had acted as his amanuensis. Once, when driven by necessity, he agreed, against his inclination, to write a serial story for a New York young folks' paper. Three weeks after the beginning of 'Daddy Hoppler,' Mr. Huntley broke down completely and was ordered to sea by the physician. An increasing board bill and an unfinished contract stared us in the face and nerved me to the rashness of writing the next installment, for which I received twenty dollars. This encouraged me. At the end of five weeks Mr. Huntley returned, considerably improved, and found me with bills all paid and a new serial underway, and the gifted editor apparently none the wiser." Since that time Mrs. Huntley has written much in various lines, and her productions are in constant demand. Mr. Huntley died in July, 1886. Her first journalistic work after Mr. Huntley's death was that of political correspondent of the Minneapolis "Tribune" from Dakota Territory, in 1887. She then accepted an editorial position on that paper, doing regular social and political editorial, with the humorous paragraphing. She next accepted a position on the Washington, DC, "Post," and remained there a year, having charge of a woman's page and regular editorial and Humorous paragraphs. She then took charge of the political correspondence of the Hutchinson, Kans., "News," a daily giving support to Ingalls in his last Senatorial fight. Besides this, she did much miscellaneous work for many papers, stories for the "National Tribune," specials for the New York and Chicago papers, and tariff papers for the "Economist." She has published one novel," The Dream Child" (Boston, 1892). She has recently published two original Spoopendyke papers, and has been asked by the editor of a Chicago daily to resume the work. Mrs. Huntley makes her home in Washington, DC.

HUNTLEY, Mrs. Mary Sutton, church worker, born in La Rue county, KY, 30th November, 1852. When she was yet an infant, her parents removed in 1853 to Iowa, and from there to Pawnee county, NE, in 1857, where she grew to womanhood and where she still makes her home. She inherited from her father rare conversational powers and a winning address, and from her mother a courageous character and fidelity. She was for some time engaged as a teacher in the public schools. She was married in 1874. Since her eighteenth year she has been an enthusiastic worker in religious affairs. She has served as chairman and county organizer of Sunday-school associations and has conducted institutes, conventions and normal drills, and delivered many public addresses. Without regard to creed, she has striven to promote the general growth of a true and broad Christianity. Her work has been very rich in results. She has been a frequent contributor of poems, essays and various articles to different papers and periodicals and was for four years editor of a little paper in the interest of juvenile temperance. She is interested in and allied with all advanced reforms and educational movements. Mrs. Huntley has been the mother of three sons, two of whom are living.

HURD, Miss Helen Marr, poet, born in Harmony, ME, 2nd February, 1839. Her father, Isaiah Hurd, 2nd, was the son of Jeremiah and Nancy Hurd, who went from New Hampshire and settled in Harmony at the time of its incorporation. When Isaiah grew to manhood, he settled in that town, where he always lived. He and his wife, Mary, a daughter of John and Hannah Page, were people of intelligence. Before Helen was eleven years old, she had learned nearly the whole of the Bible. As soon as she could read, she manifested a preference for poetry, and when but eleven years old, she had written many disconnected bits of rhyme. On her thirteenth birthday she wrote a little poem, and others soon followed. Between the years of thirteen and eighteen she composed two stories in verse and several other short poems, which are not in print. A very great impediment to her studies was severe myopia. Her greatest bereavement was the death of her father, when she was but sixteen years of age, leaving her mother, who was in feeble health, with the care of a large family, and throwing Helen upon her own resources for further advancement in her studies beyond the common school. Her perseverance overcame both difficulties to such an extent as to make her studies and readings quite ample, and in the normal class she prepared herself for teaching. The trouble with he eyes had made teaching impossible, and thus poem after poem followed in quick succession. Miss Hurd had hoarded her rhymes, making no effort to come before the public until, one plan after another of her life having failed, she began to believe that she should not bury her talent. She has published a large volume, her "Poetical Works" (Boston, 1887), illustrated by Miss Allie Collins, and has ready for publication another volume of poems, a novel and a history of Hallowell, which she hopes to complete soon. Miss Hurd has taken an active interest in the temperance cause and other movements that concern humanity. Her home is now in Athens, ME.

HURLBUT, Miss Harriette Persis, artist, born in Racine, WI, 26th February, 1862. She is a daughter of the late Henry H. Hurlbut, the author of several works, among them "Chicago Antiquities" and

"Hurlbut Genealogy." Through her mother, Harriet E. Sykes Hurlbut, she traces her ancestry back to four of the Mayflower pilgrims, among them Priscilla Mullins and her husband, John Alden. The line of descent through their daughter, Ruth, includes the names of Deacon Samuel Bass, his daughter, Mary Bass Bowditch, Abigail Bowditch, Jeremiah Pratt and Harriette Partridge Pratt, who married Dr. Royal S. Sykes, of Dorset, VT, and was the grandmother of Miss Hurlbut. With her family Harriette moved to Chicago in the winter of 1873, and has resided in that city ever since. Miss Hurlbut possessed parents of marked superiority, whose constant companionship she enjoyed, as the youngest child and only daughter, until the death of both occurred within the past two years. Her father was a man of literary tastes and pursuits, especially devoted to the graver works of learning and research. He loved history, personal and impersonal, and cultivated it with unfailing enthusiasm. Mrs. Hurlbut possessed many graces of mind and strength of character. The daughter partakes more of the traits of her father, his fondness for matters historical and genealogical. From this tendency it comes that even her art is not to her an inspiration, and what success has been achieved has been due to hard work. She was graduated from Park Institute, Chicago, in June, 1880. An early fondness for drawing turned her attention to art, and she entered the studio of Professor P. Baumgras, with whom she pursued her studies in sketching and oil painting almost continuously for eight years. Her first venture was in connection with Mrs. Mary B. Baumgras. Together they opened a studio in Chicago. Miss Hurlbut's best known picture is the life-size portrait of Samuel Champlain, which forms part of the Chicago Historical Society's collection. Always of a serious cast of mind, Miss Hurlbut passes her life in retirement, with her brother, in the paternal home in Chicago, where she is devoting herself at present to the completion of a family record-book, which her father began long ago.

HUSSEY, Mrs. Cornelia Collins, philanthropist, born in New York in 1827. Her maiden name was Collins. She is a member of the Society of Friends, to which sect her family have belonged for several generations. In early years she was in sympathy with the anti-slavery movement, and before reaching her majority became a manager of the Colored Orphan Asylum in her native city. In 1851 Miss Collins became the wife of William H. Hussey, of New Bedford, a man of similar tendencies with herself. About that time she became acquainted with Dr. Elizabeth Blackwell, who had just settled in medical practice in New York. Dr. Blackwell became Mrs. Hussey's medical adviser, and some years afterward, in cooperation with her and several other ladies and gentlemen, among whom was the late Cyrus W. Field, she formed a body of trustees for the New York Infirmary for Women and Children. The purpose of that society was to give poor women medical treatment at the hands of their own sex. From that hospital was developed in the course of time a medical college for women. Later Mrs. Hussey's only daughter studied her profession first in the college and then in the infirmary. The family moved to Orange, NJ. As her children grew up, Mrs. Hussey took an active interest in the woman suffrage agitation, and became a member of the executive committee of the American Suffrage Association, and subsequently, on the request of Miss Anthony, she was made vice-president for New Jersey of the National Suffrage Association. She retained those positions during a number of years. In 1876 efforts were made in several large cities to permit the licensing of the social evil, and Mrs. Hussey, always interested in efforts for social purity, was chosen secretary of the committee formed to oppose such evil legislation. When that work had been brought to a successful termination, Mrs. Hussey became interested in the claim of Miss Anna Ella Carroll for a government pension, on account of services rendered during the war and her plans of the Tennessee campaign. Through her efforts considerable sums of money were raised by private subscription, and articles were published in some of the leading magazines on the work of Miss Carroll. During the last twenty years Mrs. Hussey has contributed numerous articles to the "Woman's Journal" and various other reform periodicals, as well as to the papers of her State.

ILIOHAN, Mrs. Henrica, woman suffragist, born in Vorden, Province of Gelderland, Kingdom of the Netherlands, 3rd May, 1850. Her maiden name was Weenink. Her parents were in good circumstances, her father being a successful architect and builder. The love of liberty and independence seemed to have been instilled into her from birth, and when but a child her eyes were opened to the different education of boys and girls. She showed a taste and aptitude for the carpenter's trade, and her father's workshop had a fascination for her. When she was eight years of age, she could plane a board as well as an older brother. The workmen would often send her home crying by saying she was a girl and therefore could never be a carpenter. She remembers that this happened when she was so young that to her consciousness the only difference lay in dress, and she would earnestly beg her mother to dress her in her brother's clothes, so that she might become a carpenter. The disability of sex became of more and more importance as she thought and studied upon it. She was but eighteen years of age when her mother died. In 1870 her father sailed with his three children for America, arriving in Albany, NY, in May. She was fortunate in being the object of one woman's considerate kindness and patience, in her efforts to learn the English language. In trying to read English she noticed for the first time an article on woman suffrage in the Albany "Journal," in 1871, when Mrs. Lillie Devereaux Blake addressed the assembly and asked the question: "Whom do you think, gentleman of the committee, to be most competent to cast a ballot, the mother who comes from the fireside, or the husband that comes from the corner saloon?" This was to the young discoverer a javelin that struck home, and she made inquiries why women did not and could not vote. Very much interested, she read all that was accessible on the subject, and when, in 1877, the first Woman Suffrage Society of Albany was organized, she became an earnest member. With the remembrance of woman's share in the brave deeds recorded in Dutch history, she gained in courage and enthusiasm and began to express herself publicly. Her first appearance on the lecture platform was a triumph. Encouraged by many, she gained in experience and became one of the acknowledged leaders of the society. She was elected four times a delegate from the society to the annual convention in New York City, and worked during the sessions of the legislature to obtain the consideration of that body. Mrs. Iliohan has also done some good work in translation. "The Religion of Common Sense," from the German of Prof. L. Ulich, is a sample of her ability in that direction. In 1887 she removed, with her family, to Humphrey, NE, where she has since lived. Since she has been identified with Nebraska and with subjects of reform in that State, she has endeared herself to the leaders and the public.

IMMEN, Mrs. Loraine, elocutionist and club leader, born in Mount Clemens, MI, 3rd August, 1840. Her mother's maiden name was Cook, and her ancestors were related to Captain Cook, the famous navigator. Her father, E. G. Pratt, was a native of Massachusetts, who settled in Michigan in the pioneer days, making his home in Mount Clemens. He was conspicuous in every movement that had for its object the development of the community and the State. The two daughters of the Pratt family enjoyed the advantages of a thorough education. Loraine became a teacher at the age of fourteen years, and she succeeded well in the arduous work of the school-room. She taught in Mount Clemens until 1860, when she became the wife of Frederick Immen. She continued her studies after marriage, and in 1880 she was graduated and received the first honor in a senior class contest of the National School of Elocution and Oratory in Philadelphia, PA. Returning to her home, she gave a public reading in the Mount Clemens opera house, giving the proceeds of the entertainment for the beginning of a fund to purchase a town clock. Appearing as a lecturer in Grand Rapids, her subject was "Paris," and the proceeds she gave to aid in erecting the soldier's monumental fountain in that city. Later, while in London, she gave readings and was made a life fellow of the Society of Science, Letters and Art. In Grand Rapids she has been connected with the St. Cecilia Society and the Ladies' Literary Club since their institution, and in 1890 she was president of the latter club, a society that numbers over five-hundred members. She is the founder of the Shakespeare Club and has been its president from the beginning. Besides her work in literary, elocutionary and social lines, she is an earliest worker in the Sunday school, where her success has been quite as marked as in the other fields. Mrs. Immen is a most enthusiastic club woman. She is warmhearted, generous, interested in all the great events of the day, and particularly alive to the doings of women in all fields of effort that are now open to them. The Ladies' Literary Club, in Grand Rapids, is a monument to her enthusiasm, her industry and her executive ability, In 1887 she and the other leaders of the club purchased a site for a club-house, and a beautiful building was finished and dedicated in January, 1888. It is now the center of intellectual activity among the women of Grand Rapids, and it has become a fountain of art, literature, history, science and education.

INGALLS, Mrs. Eliza B., temperance worker, born on a farm in St. Louis county, MO, where the early years of her life were spent. In 1880 she became the wife of Fred H. Ingalls, a successful merchant in St. Louis, MO. She has been an active temperance worker since she was a child, having joined the order of Good Templars when only fourteen years of age. She is superintendent of the narcotic department of the National Woman's Christian Temperance Union. Her special mission is the eradication of tobacco in all forms. She is assisted in her work by State superintendents, and the results are shown by the enactment of laws in nearly every State in the Union prohibiting the sale of tobacco to minors. Mrs. Ingalls is young and gifted with great executive ability. Her pleasant manner and untiring persistence bring success to all her undertakings. She receives frequent invitations to lecture, but never leaves home for that purpose. Her husband is in sympathy with her work and gives her liberal financial aid.

INGHAM, Mrs. Mary Bigelow, author and religious worker, born in Mansfield, OH, 10th March, 1832. Her parents, of Revolutionary ancestry, were from Vermont. Her father, Rev. John Janes, was a pioneer clergyman in Ohio and Michigan, and her mother, Hannah Brown, was one of the founders of the Methodist Episcopal Church in Ann Arbor, MI. Having attended Norwalk Seminary and Baldwin Institute, Miss Janes, when eighteen years old, went to Cleveland, OH, as a teacher in the public schools, and soon became the head of primary instruction in that city. During a portion of the six years spent there she boarded and studied in the family of Madame Pierre Gollier, learning to speak the French language fluently. Appointed professor of French and belles-lettres in the Ohio Wesleyan College for young ladies, in Delaware, OH, she applied herself to the study of German, adding thereto Spanish and Italian, and received from her alma mater the honorary degree of M.L.A. On 22nd March, 1866, she became the wife of W. A. Ingham, and removed to Cleveland, OH. In 1870 she was chosen to inaugurate in northern Ohio the work of the Woman's Foreign Missionary Society. She presided over and addressed the first public meeting ever held in the city of Cleveland conducted exclusively by religious women. Afterward she addressed large audiences in the various cities of Ohio, in Baltimore, Washington, Buffalo, New York, New Haven and Minneapolis, upon the needs of the women of foreign lands. In March, 1874, being in charge of the praying band of her own city, she led for six weeks a very successful temperance crusade and was among the most active of Cleveland women in establishing inns, reading-rooms and chapels. She became chairman of the Pearl street inn, which for seven years did a great work in the evangelization of the masses in the ninth, tenth and eleventh wards of Cleveland. She was one of the original committee in Chautauqua, NY, that projected in August, 1874, the National Woman's Christian Temperance Union. That organizing convention met in her city 18th, 19th and 20th November, 1874. Writing has always been a favorite pastime with Mrs. Ingham. At ten years of age her first article was published in the Norwalk "Reflector." While in Delaware, encouraged by Professor W. G. Williams, she wrote her first story, for which he gave her the subject, "Something to Come Home To," receiving for it fifteen dollars from the "Ladies' Repository." That was followed by other articles. For the Cleveland "Leader" she has written letters from both sides of the ocean that have inspired more than one young person to cultivate the "best gifts." Her letters from Florida in 1882 contained very accurate descriptions of natural scenery in the land of flowers. In 1880, at the request of the management of the "Leader," she began, in a series of articles covering three years' space, the "History of Woman's Work in Cleveland since 1830." She included, besides the founding of the four great churches and a review of the principal charities, sketches under the title of the "Women of Cleveland." Her pen-name was "Anne Hathaway." In 1884 she wrote the history of the pioneer Methodist Episcopal Churches of Cleveland. In 1890 Mrs. Ingham wrote her famous Flag Festival, the third edition being adapted to Discovery Day. She is one of the founders of the Western Reserve School of Design and a charter member of the order of the Daughters of the American Revolution, and also of the Cleveland Sorosis, modeled upon that of New York. All that helps woman to advance is to her a delight, and it is part of her life-work to forward culture either in home or public life.

IRELAND, Mrs. Mary E., author, born in the village of Brick Meeting House, now called Calvert, Cecil county, MD, 9th January, 1834. She is a daughter of the late Joseph and Harriet Haines. In the old homestead of her parents she grew to womanhood, became the wife of John M. Ireland, of Kent county, in the same State, and lived there for several years, when they removed to Baltimore, where Mr. Ireland was engaged in business. They now reside in Washington, DC. They are the parents of three children, one of whom died in infancy. The others, a son and daughter, are now grown to man's and woman's estate. Mrs. Ireland was educated in the ladies' seminary of Jamaica, Long Island, and has talent for music and painting. In the last few years literary work, particularly translating from the German, has been her favorite pastime. She has written several serials and many short stories, which have been published in different magazines, two of them taking prizes. One of her first sketches was "The Defoe Family in America," published in "Scribner's Magazine" in 1876, which was widely copied into other periodicals. Her first book was a collection of her short published stories, which she wove into a continuous narrative, entitled "Timothy: His Neighbors and Friends." Her translations published in book form are: "Red Carl," treating of the labor question, "Lenchen's Brother," "Platzbacker of Plauen," "The Block House on the Shore," "Era Stark" and "Betty's Decision."

ISAAC, Mrs. Hannah M. Underhill, evangelist, born in Chappaqua, NY, 27th September, 1833. Her maiden name was Underhill. Her ancestors for many generations were members of the orthodox Friends Society in which her parents were members and elders. Her education was received principally in the Friends' boarding schools in Dutchess county, NY, and Westtown, PA. For four years after leaving school she taught in her native town, and later carried on a private school at home. She spent several winters with friends and relatives in New York City, where she entered society with the same ardor that characterizes all her efforts. During one of these winters of pleasure there came to her a deep sense of her responsibility. This strong conviction so wrought upon her mind that, in the summer of 1861, she determined to renounce the worldly life she had been leading. She was converted, and for some time that life satisfied her, and then there came a conviction for a deeper work of grace, and five years after conversion she entered into the rest of faith. At once there came what she believed to be a call to preach the gospel. She was an invalid for three years, and on recovering her health she began to do evangelistic work. For six years she was connected with Miss Elizabeth Loder in mission work in the village of Cornwall, NY. Miss Loder owned a chapel, and together these women worked for the saving of souls. Sailors, boatmen and laborers went to their meetings, and many were converted. When the temperance crusade came, Miss Underhill at once joined in the work of the Woman's

Christian Temperance Union, entering a union in Brooklyn. In 1880 she organized a society in Cornwall, which now is one of the most prominent of the local organizations in Orange county, NY. For some years past she has given her time entirely to evangelistic work. Her services are in frequent demand by ministers in revival work. She became the wife of William Isaac, of Cornwall, in March, 1886. Her pleasant home is in that town.

IVES, Miss Alice Emma, dramatist and journalist, born in Detroit, MI, where she lived until September, 1890, when she removed with her mother to New York, which is now her home. Her literary bent was early shown. Before she knew how to form the script letters, she printed the verses which she composed. When about seventeen years of age, she wrote her first story, which was promptly accepted by Frank Leslie. So severe was she in judging her work that, instead of being elated at her success, she was appalled at what seemed to her an unwarrantable presumption, and never sent another line to a publisher for ten years. Miss Ives' father died when she was two years old, and she very early felt the necessity of earning her own bread, and after a time that of two others. With her strong imaginative nature rebelling against the uncongenial task, she taught school till her health broke down under the strain. Then she began to send poems and stories to the press. Compiling books, writing plays, magazine articles, dramatic criticisms, and, in short, all-around news-paper work, have since been her work. Her magazine article, "The Domestic Purse-Strings," in the "Forum," September, 1890, was copied and commented on in column editorials, from London and New York to San Francisco. The production of Miss Ives' play, "Lorine," in Palmer's Theater, New York, was successful.

IVES, Mrs. Florence C., journalist, born in New York City, 10th March, 1854. She is a daughter of the distinguished artist, Frank B. Carpenter. Soon after her graduation from Rutgers' Female College, she became the wife of Albert C. Ives, a brilliant young journalist of New York, at that time stationed in London, England, where their home for several years was one of the centers of attraction for cultivated Americans and Englishmen. They lived for several years in a like manner in Paris, France. In 1882, during a year spent in America, a son was born to them. In 1887, after her return to New York City, Mrs. Ives became a general worker on the "Press," and finally literary editor, which place she held as long as her connection with the paper lasted. In 1891 she widened her field, her articles on topics of important and permanent interest appearing in the "Sun," the "Tribune," "The World," the "Herald" and other journals. She became editor of the woman's department of the "Metropolitan and Rural Home." With the opening of executive work for the World's Fair, she was put in charge of all the press work sent out by the general board of lady managers to the New York papers.

JACK, Mrs. Annie L., horticulturist, born in Northamptonshire, England, 1st January, 1839. Her maiden name was Annie L. Hayr, a name well known to readers of the "Waverley Magazine," to which periodical she contributed many articles. In 1852 she came to America and was at once sent to Mrs. Willard's seminary in Troy, NY. One of her first published productions was a school composition, an allegory, which Mrs. Willard caused to be published in the Troy "Daily Times." Before she was sixteen years old, she passed the required examination and gained a position as first-assistant teacher in the city free schools. After a time she moved to Canada, and became the wife of Mr. Jack, a Scotch fruit-grower, a man of sterling worth. Mrs. Jack found congenial surroundings and employment on their fruit farm, called "Hillside," which is beautifully situated on the Chateauguay river, and where she has reared eleven children. Mrs. Jack is a recognized authority on horticultural subjects. She has won several prizes in competition in the "Rural New Yorker" and other periodicals. Her oldest son developed a taste for botany and entomology, and he is now on the staff of the Harvard Arboretum and a regular contributor to the columns of the New York "Garden and Forest." Another son has developed a talent for scientific writing. The family are noted for clear and wholesome thinking, and the genius of both parents is seen reflected in each member. Mrs. Jack's literary friends and acquaintances are chiefly Americans. Her success in horticulture attracted the attention of the venerable John Greenleaf Whittier, who in a letter to her wrote: "Many women desire to do these things, but do not know how to succeed as thou hast done." Her library contains many fruit and farm books, but not all her work is given to the tempting grapes, strawberries, raspberries, apples and other fruits to whose culture she has given so much attention. During all the busy years of her farm life she has found time to write poems and short stories by the score. One series of stories, showing the fields of work that are open to women, attracted much attention, and it resulted in an order from "Harper's Young People" for an article on that subject from her pen. To the Montreal "Witness," over the pen-name "Loyal Janet," she contributed a series of Scotch articles that hit upon social topics. Mrs. Jack's management of her home has shown that it is possible to make a farm-house a home of comfort, refinement and luxury, with art, music, flowers and education quite as much at command as in the crowded towns. In Hillside all the Scotch and English home traditions are preserved, and the accomplished mistress has made the country farm-house one of the landmarks of the Dominion of Canada.

JACKSON, Mrs. Helen Maria Fiske, author, poet and philanthropist, born in Amherst, MA, 18th October, 1831, and died in San Francisco, CA, 12th August, 1885. She was the daughter of Professor Nathan W. Fiske, of Amherst College. She was educated in the female seminary in Ipswich, MA. In 1852 she became the wife of Captain Edward B. Hunt, of the United States Navy. She lived with him in various military posts until his death, in October, 1863. In 1866 she removed to Newport, RI, where she lived until 1872. Her children died, and she was left desolate. Alone in the world, she turned to literature. In early life she had published some verses in a Boston newspaper, and aside from that she had shown no signs of literary development up to 1865. In that year she began to contribute poems to the New York "Nation." Then she sent poems and prose articles to the New York "Independent" and the "Hearth and Home." She signed the initials "H. H." to her work, and its quality attracted wide and critical attention. In 1873 and 1874 she lived in Colorado for her health. In 1875 she became the wife of William S. Jackson, a merchant of Colorado Springs. In that town she made her home until her death. She traveled in New Mexico and California, and spent one winter in New York City, gathering facts for her book in behalf of the Indians, "A Century of Dishonor," which was published in 1881. Her Indian novel, "Ramona," was published in 1884; a copy of which, at her own expense, was sent each member of Congress. The Government appointed her a special commissioner to investigate mission Indians in California. That novel is her most powerful work, written virtually under inspiration. Her interest in the Indians was profound, and she instituted important reforms in the treatment of the Red Men by the Government. Her other published works are "Verses by H. H." (1870, enlarged in 1874), "Bits of Travel" (1873), "Bits of Talk About Home Matters" (1873), "Sonnets and Lyrics" (1876), several juvenile books and two novels in the "No Name" series, "Mercy Philbrick's Choice" (1876) and "Hetty's Strange History" (1877), "Mammy Tittleback's Stories" (1881), and "The Hunter Cats of Connorloa" (1884). A series of powerful stories published under the pen-name "Saxe Holme" has been attributed to her, but there has been no proof published that she was "Saxe Holme." She left an unfinished novel, "Zeph," a work in a vein different from all her other works. "Glimpses of Three Coasts" (1886), "Sonnets and Lyrics" (1886), and "Between Whiles" (1887) were published posthumously. She was injured in June, 1884, receiving a bad fracture of her leg. She was taken to California, to a place that proved to be malarious, and while confined and suffering there, a cancerous affection developed. The complications of injuries and diseases resulted in her death. Her remains were temporarily interred in San Francisco, and afterward were removed to Colorado and buried near the summit of Mount Jackson, one of the Cheyenne peaks named in her honor, only four miles from Colorado Springs, but the vandalisms of tourists

Mrs Garret A. Hobart.
From Photo by Davis and Sanford,
New York.

Mrs. William McKinley.
From Photo by Courtney,
Canton, Ohio.

Mrs. John Sherman.
From Photo by F. B. Johnston
Washington.

made it necessary to remove the body to Evergreen Cemetery in Colorado Springs.

JACKSON, Mrs. Katharine Johnson, physician, born near Sturbridge, MA, 7th April, 1841. Attendance in the district school alternated with home studies until the age of sixteen, when she spent a year in a select school in Hopedale, MA. Afterward, under a private tutor, she prepared for the high-school course in Hartford, CT, where she was subsequently engaged as a teacher. From both parents she inherited refined and cultivated tastes and a fondness for books, which has made her an eager and faithful student. Her father, the Hon. Emerson Johnson, has been a member of both the House of Representatives and Senate of Massachusetts. Dr. Jackson has always enjoyed active physical exercise, especially housework. To be self-supporting she studied stenography at home, and was probably among the first women to adopt that profession. Her acquaintance with the Jackson Sanatorium, in Dansville, NY, where she was destined to find her life-work, began in the year 1861, when she became private secretary to Dr. James C. Jackson, who was at that time conducting his institution under the name of "Our Home on the Hillside." It was during the two-and-a-half years which she spent there that the acquaintance with Dr. Jackson's son, James H. Jackson, ripened into a mutual affection, which resulted in their marriage on 13th September, 1864. After the lapse of a few years, during which time their only child, James Arthur Jackson, was born, she and her husband went to New York for a medical course, he in Bellevue and she in the Woman's Medical College of the New York Infirmary. She was graduated in 1877 as the valedictorian of her class, and at once assumed professional duties and responsibilities in the institution, which she, as much as any one individual, has helped to make a home and haven of rest for the sick and suffering. Her nature is rarely well poised, sympathetic and hopeful, and it is often observed by strangers that the experiences of professional life have in no wise lessened the womanly grace and charm which are her peculiar attributes. From her New England ancestry she has inherited a catholic religious spirit, which

expresses itself in an unwavering trust in the Infinite Love and faith in the inherent goodness of human nature. The secret of her influence is in her single-minded devotion to the work of helping all who need help, whether physical or spiritual. To her nothing is common or trivial. Though she has a heartfelt interest in all progressive social movements which tend to alleviate suffering, uplift humanity or insure the progress of women, her time is so fully occupied as to afford little opportunity for public expression of her sentiments, except through her writings. While she is progressive, she is never aggressive. Her presence, like her spoken or written word, radiates peace. She is an able and accomplished writer and an attractive and persuasive speaker, her talks upon health and kindred topics being among the most practical and valuable instructions given to the patients in the Jackson Sanatorium. As a successful physician, a devoted wife, mother, daughter and friend, Dr. Jackson is an inspiring type of the nineteenth century woman.

JACKSON, Miss Lily Irene, sculptor, artist and designer, born in Parkersburg, WV, which has always been her home. She is recognized as an artist of merit. She has studied in New York, and some of her work has been highly praised by art critics and has sold for good prices. Several of her paintings are to find place in the art exhibit in the World's Fair in 1893. It is in painting she excels, although in sculpture her work has elicited the commendation of leading artists. Miss Jackson is descended from one of the most noted families of the South. Her father, Hon. John J. Jackson, has for over a quarter of a century been Federal District Judge in West Virginia. Her grandfather, General Jackson, was in his day possessed of all those lofty virtues that went to make up a typical southern gentleman of the old school. She is closely related to the great "Stonewall" Jackson, and is a niece of ex-Governor I. B. Jackson, all of Parkersburg. This noted family holds for itself a high standing in the community in which they live. For nearly a century Parkersburg has been their home. Miss Jackson, by her attainments, keeps fresh in the memory of a large society circle the charm of the belles and beauties of her name of the old régime. She is a member of the Board of Lady Managers of the World's Fair, and represents West Virginia in that body. She is indefatigable in her work.

JACOBI, Dr. Mary Putnam, physician, born in London, England, 31st August, 1842. She is a daughter of George P. Putnam, the well-known publisher, and her parents returned to America during her early childhood. She studied in the Woman's Medical College in Philadelphia, PA, afterward taking the course in the New York College of Pharmacy, of which institution she was the first woman graduate. In 1866 she went to Paris, France, where she was the first woman to be admitted to the Ecole de Medecin, from which she graduated in 1871, receiving the second prize, a bronze medal for her thesis. During the siege of Paris she corresponded for the New York "Medical Journal." Her return to New York marked the opening of a new epoch in the history of women physicians in this country, for she established a claim to be received on equal terms with men in medical societies. In 1872 she read a paper on "Pyæmia and Septicemia" before the Medical Journal Association, which was the first medical paper read in public in America by a woman and led to her admission to the County Medical Society. In 1873 she became the wife of Dr. Abraham Jacobi, a native of Hartum, Westphalia, Germany, who studied in the universities of Greifswald, Bonn and Gottingen, and, having become involved in the German revolutionary movement, was imprisoned. He came to the United States and settled in New York, where he holds high rank in the medical fraternity. Three children were born to them. After her marriage she retained her maiden name with that of her husband, hence is known as Dr. Putnam-Jacobi. She was for twelve years dispensary physician in the Mount Sinai Hospital in New York City. For the first sixteen years of her professional life she held the chair of therapeutics and materia medica in the Woman's Medical College of the New York Infirmary, and later was professor in the New York post-graduate medical school. In 1874 Dr. Putnam-Jacobi founded the Association for the Advancement of the Medical Education of Women, and has been its president from the beginning. She has written much on medical and scientific subjects. She is the author of "The Question of Rest During Menstruation," an essay which won the Boylston prize in Harvard University in 1876; "The Value of Life" (New York, 1879); "Cold Pack and Anæmia" (1880); "Studies in Endometritis" in the "American Journal of Obstetrics" (1885); the articles on "Infantile Paralysis," published in 1873, was the first systematic study on that subject in America, and "Pseudo-Muscular Hypertrophy" appeared in "Pepper's Archives of Medicine," and "Hysteria, and Other Essays" (1888). She is interested in many reforms and charities. Her knowledge of medicine and all its allied sciences is profound and accurate. Her home is in New York City, where she has acquired an extensive practice. She stands in the front rank in her profession.

JAMES, Mrs. Annie Laurie Wilson, journalist, born in Louisville, KY, 5th November, 1862. She attended Wellesley College for five years and taught several years in a high school, resigning to assist her father as confidential clerk of his extensive business of stock-breeding. In 1888 she was sent to California on a business trip. While in San Francisco she met the owners of the "Breeder and Sportsman," who offered her a lucrative position as assistant editor and business manager of that journal. She accepted their offer, and for eight months filled the arduous position to the satisfaction of all concerned, making good use of her varied and intimate knowledge of the trotter and the thoroughbred. She became the wife of R. B. James in 1889, and lives on their ranch in Baker County, OR. Her knowledge of the pedigrees of the famous horses of the United States is full, accurate and remarkable. Among other work she has given much time to a thorough and systematic compilation of horse pedigrees, in which statistics play a prominent part. Aside from that, she is a student of the problems of heredity in horses, on which subject she has no superiors. She is a fluent, direct and luminous writer, and her position as an authority on the horse is unique.

JANES, Mrs. Martha Waldron, minister, born in Northfield, MI, 9th June, 1832. Her father, Leonard T. Waldron, was a native of Massachusetts. In 1830 he went to Michigan, bought a farm, married and became a successful farmer. He was an enthusiastic advocate of the free-school system and worked and voted for it, after he had paid for his own children's education. His ancestors came from Holland and settled in New Holland, now Harlem, NY, in 1816. Her mother, Nancy Bennett, was a gentle woman and a good housewife. She was a native of New York. Martha is the oldest of seven children. Her opportunities for knowledge were limited by the impossibility of obtaining it in that new country, but all her powers were used in the effort to possess all there was to be given. All her school advantages were secured by doing housework at one dollar a week and saving the money to pay her tuition in a select school for one term. At the age of thirteen she was converted and joined the Free Baptist Church. She took part in public meetings, and both prayed and exhorted, because she felt that she must, and, as at that early day a woman's voice had not been heard in the frontier churches, she earned the reputation of being crazy. On 12th October, 1852, she became the wife of John A. Sober, a young minister, fully abreast of the times in the many reforms that agitated the public mind. He died 19th November, 1864, leaving her with two children, the older eleven years old and the younger four. She was in poor health. The conviction that she ought to preach the gospel dates almost to the time of her conversion. Her duty and ability to enter that untried and forbidden field were long recognized by the church and conference to which she belonged, and she was encouraged to do what the church felt was her duty. In 1860, after much thought, she began to preach, and her work in the pulpit was crowned with success. On 23rd May, 1867, she was again married. Her second husband is Rev. II. H. Janes. In June, 1868, she was ordained, being the first woman ordained in the conference. She has administered all the rites of the church except immersion, which she has never felt called to do. She has had the care of a church as its pastor on several occasions, and has traveled quite extensively under the auspices of the conference as evangelist. Her public work outside the church has not been very extensive. She was district superintendent of franchise of the Woman's Suffrage Association, during which time she edited a suffrage column in seventeen weekly papers. She also held meetings in the interest of that reform. Her temperance work dates back to 1879. She was county president of Clay county, Ia, and organized every township in that county.

JARNETTE, Mrs. Evelyn Magruder, see DE JARNETTE, MRS. EVELYN MAGRUDER.

JEFFERIS, Mrs. Marea Wood, poet, born in Providence, RI. She is a direct descendant of Elder William Brewster, of Mayflower fame. Her father, Dr. J. F. B. Flagg, was the author of a book on anæsthetics written about forty years ago, and to him belongs the credit of making practical in the United States the use of anæsthetics in the practice of medicine. Her paternal grandfather, Dr. Josiah Foster Flagg, was a pioneer in the practice of dental surgery in this country. Mrs. Jefferis received a thorough education and showed literary talent early, although she published but few of the poems of earlier years. She has been twice married. Her first husband was Thomas Wood, a leading iron manufacturer of Pennsylvania. One son by her first marriage, William Brewster Wood, survives. Her second husband is Professor William Walter Jefferis, the well-known scientist and mineralogist. She has published one volume of verse, entitled "Faded, and Other Poems" (Philadelphia, 1891), which she brought out at her own expense, and the proceeds of the sale of which she devoted to charity. It is a volume in memory of her, daughter, who died young, and who was greatly interested in charitable work among the sick and poor children of Philadelphia. Mrs. Jefferis has done much charitable work. She has resided in Philadelphia since her early childhood.

JEFFERSON, Mrs. Martha Wayles, wife of Thomas Jefferson, third President of the United States, born 19th October, 1748, in Charles City county, VA, and died 6th September, 1782, in Monticello, the President's country home, near Charlottesville, VA. She was the daughter of John Wayles, a wealthy lawyer. She received a thorough education and was a woman of strong intellectual powers, great refinement and many accomplishments. She was married at an early age to Bathurst Skelton, who died and left her a widow before she was twenty years old. Her hand was sought by many prominent men, among whom was Thomas Jefferson, the successful suitor. They were married 1st January, 1772, and set out for Monticello. Five children were born to them. In 1781 Mrs. Jefferson's health failed, and her husband refused a European mission in order to be with her. Her fifth child was born in May, 1782, and she died in the following autumn. Her husband's devotion to her partook of the romantic. Two of their children died in infancy. Mrs. Jefferson was a woman of mark in her time.

JEFFERY, Mrs. Isadore Gilbert, poet, born in Waukegan, IL, in 184–, where her parents lived for a time. For many years their home was in Chicago, IL, where her father had extensive business interests. She is of English parentage. In a letter to a friend Mrs. Jeffery says: "Those who knew my sainted parents will accentuate the utmost words of praise a loving daughter's heart could prompt. Noble and true in every possible relation, their record in life is a priceless inheritance to their children. They made a perfect home for fifty years, and when Mother was taken suddenly away in 1878, Father, then a hale and hearty man of unshaken intellect, said he couldn't live without her, and died within the year. No briefest notice of me would seem anything to me, that contained no reference to the parents who were my confidants, in all things up to the day of their departure." Although she has written ever since girlhood for a large number of papers and periodicals, Mrs. Jeffery has never published a book. She writes for the joy of it, and would do so always, if there never were a dollar's return there from. She became the wife, in 1878, of M. J. Jeffery then superintendent of the American District Telegraph and Telephone Service of Chicago. One morning, about two years

after their marriage, while driving to business, he was injured in the tunnel by a runaway team, and brought home to a time of suffering that forbade any active life for three years. When he finally began to get about on crutches, the faithful wife, who had watched and waited beside him so long, accepted the responsible position of stenographer in the office of the Chicago "Advance," which she occupied for nearly six years, to the praise and satisfaction of all concerned. The home of Mr. and Mrs. Jeffery is a childless one, though both are intensely fond of children.

JEFFREY, Mrs. Rosa Vertner, poet and novelist, born in Natchez, MS, in 1828. Her maiden name was Griffith, and her father was a cultured and literary man, a writer of both prose and verse. He died in 1853. Rosa's mother died and left her an orphan at

the age of nine months. The child was placed in the care of her maternal aunt, who adopted her and gave her name. Rosa Vertner passed her childhood in Burlington, MS, with her adopted parents. In 1838 her parents removed to Kentucky and settled in Lexington, that they might superintend her education. She received a thorough education in a seminary in that town, and became a polished scholar and an intelligent student of history and literature. In 1845 she became the wife of Claude M. Johnson, a wealthy citizen of Lexington. Mrs. Johnson at once became a leader in society, not only in Lexington, but in Washington and other cities. In 1861 Mr. Johnson died. Mrs. Johnson removed to Rochester, NY, where she remained during the Civil War. In 1863 she became the wife of Alexander Jeffrey. While living in Rochester, she published her first book, a novel, "Woodburn," which was sent out from New York in 1864. She was the first southern woman whose literary work attracted attention throughout the United States. At the age of fifteen she wrote her well-known "Legend of the Opal." In 1857 she published a volume of verse, "Poems by Rosa," and at once she became known as an author of merit. Her volume of poems, "Daisy Dare and Baby Power," was published in Philadelphia, in 1871. Her third volume of poetry, "The Crimson Hand, and Other Poems," was published in 1881.

Her novel, "Marsh," was brought out in 1884. Among her literary productions are several dramas of a high order of merit.

JENKINS, Mrs. Frances C., evangelist and temperance worker, born in Newcastle, IN, 13th April, 1826. Her maiden name was Wiles. Her father was of Welsh descent, her mother came from a refined English family. Both parents were educators, and her home was always a school. Books and study were ever her delight. She was married young, and consequently did not possess a finished education, but her study did not cease when she was married. The bent of her mind was toward medicine and theology. So well informed did she become in medicine and nursing that for twenty-five years she took almost entire charge of the health of her family of nine children. For several years after her marriage she devoted herself exclusively to home-making and her family, but she was finally led to broaden her circle of usefulness. She took up church work in her own church, the Friends, or Quakers. She became so efficient in church work of various kinds and so devoted a Bible student that the Society recognized her ability and at twenty-six years of age recorded her a minister of the gospel. The Friends Society was at that time the only orthodox one to recognize women as ministers. Her public work became a prominent feature of her life, yet she never lost sight of, or interest in, her home. She was especially successful as an evangelist and temperance worker. She was among the first crusaders against the liquor traffic. As a result of her work many saloons were closed in the town where she lived, and many surrounding towns received a like benefit. The proprietors of numerous saloons gave up saloon-keeping and engaged permanently in honorable business for bread winning. For several years she was one of the vice-presidents of the Illinois Woman's Christian Temperance Union. She went to England early in January, 1888, where she remained fifteen months, engaged in evangelical and temperance work. She was very successful. She is engaged most of the time in work along that line. Her home is now in Kansas City, MO.

JENKINS, Mrs. Therese A., woman suffragist, born in Fayette, Lafayette county, WI, in 1853. She is a daughter of the late Peter Parkinson, one of the pioneers of Wisconsin, who fought in the Black Hawk War and won military honors. Miss Parkinson became the wife of James F. Jenkins, a wealthy merchant of Cheyenne, WY, in which city they reside. She is a thoroughly educated woman, and her writings are clear and forcible. Since 1887 she has labored to secure equal rights and justice for all citizens. She was one of the orators of the day when Wyoming's admission to statehood was celebrated, and her address on that occasion was powerful and brilliant. She has done much journalistic work. In April, 1889, she contributed to the "Popular Science Monthly" a striking paper entitled, "The Mental Force of Woman," in reply to Professor Cope's article on "The Relation of the Sexes to the Government," in a preceding number of that journal. She has contributed a number of graceful poems to the Denver "Times" and other journals. She is now the regular Wyoming correspondent of the Omaha "Central West," "Woman's Tribune" and the "Union Signal." She is active in church work and is a member of the Woman's Relief Corps and of the Woman's Christian Temperance Union, in both of which she is earnestly interested. She was sent as an alternate to the Republican national convention in Minneapolis, MN, in 1892. Her family consists of three children. Her life is a busy one, and she is a recognized power in Wyoming among those who are interested in purifying and elevating society, and in bringing about the absolute recognition of the equality of the sexes before the law.

JEWETT, Miss Sarah Orne, author, born in South Berwick, ME, 3rd September, 1849. She is the daughter of Dr. Theodore H. Jewett, a well-known physician, who died in 1878. She received a thorough education in the Berwick academy. She began to publish stories at an early age. In 1869 she contributed a story to the

"Atlantic Monthly." She traveled extensively in the United States, in Canada and in Europe. She spends her time in South Berwick, ME, and in Boston, MA. She used the pen-name "Alice Eliot" in her first years of authorship, but now her full name is appended to all her productions. Her stories relate mainly to New England, and many of them have a great historical value. Her published volumes include "Deephaven" (1877), "Play-Days" (1878), "Old Friends and New" (1880), "Country By-Ways" (1881), "The Mate of the Daylight" (1883), "A Country Doctor" (1884), "A Marsh Island" (1885), "A White Heron "(1886), "The Story of the Normans" (1887), "The King of the Folly Island, and Other People" (1888), and "Betty Leicester" (1889). Miss Jewett is now engaged on several important works.

JOHNS, Mrs. Laura M., woman suffragist, born near Lewiston, PA, 18th December, 1849. She was a teacher in that State and in Illinois. Her maiden name was Mitchell. As a child she had a passion for books, was thoughtful beyond her years, and her parents encouraged in their daughter the tendencies which developed her powers to write and speak. In her marriage to J. B. Johns, which occurred in Lewiston, PA, 14th January, 1873, she found a companion who believed in and advocated the industrial, social and political equality of women. Her first active advocacy of the suffrage question began in the fall of 1884. The then secretary of the Kansas Equal Suffrage Association, Mrs. Bertha H. Ellsworth, of Lincoln, while circulating petitions for municipal suffrage for women, enlisted her active cooperation in the work, which culminated in the passage of the bill granting municipal suffrage to the women of Kansas, in 1887. Mrs. Johns was residing in Salina, KS, where she still lives, when her lifework brought her into public notice in the field in which she has so ably championed the cause of woman. A strong woman suffrage organization was formed in Salina, of which Mrs. Johns was the leading spirit. Columns for the publication of suffrage matter were secured in the newspapers, and Mrs. Johns took charge of those departments. The tact and force with which she has used those and all other instrumentalities to

bring out, cultivate and utilize suffrage sentiment have helped to gain great victories for woman suffrage in Kansas and in the nation. With the idea of pushing the agitation and of massing the forces to secure municipal suffrage she arranged for a long series of congressional conventions in Kansas, beginning in Leavenworth in 1886. Mrs. Johns worked in the legislative sessions of 1885, 1886 and 1887 in the interest of the municipal woman suffrage bill, and there displayed the tact which has later marked her work and made much of its success. In her legislative work she had the support of her husband. Since the bill became a law, her constant effort has been to make it and the public sentiment created serve as a steppingstone to full enfranchisement, and to induce other States to give a wise and just recognition to the rights of their women citizens. She has spoken effectively in public on this question in Pennsylvania, OH, New York, Massachusetts, Missouri, Rhode Island and the District of Columbia. She took an active part in the woman suffrage amendment campaign in South Dakota. She visited the Territory of Arizona in the interest of the recognition of woman's claim to the ballot in the proposed State constitution framed in Phoenix in September, 1891. Recognition of her services has come in six elections to the presidency of the State Suffrage Association. Her last work consisted of thirty great conventions beginning in Kansas City, in February, 1892, and held in various important cities of the State. In those conventions she had as speakers Rev. Anna H. Shaw, Mrs. Clara H. Hoffman, Miss Florence Balgarnie and Mrs. Mary Seymour Howell. As workers and speakers from the ranks in Kansas there were Mrs. Johnston, Mrs. Belleville-Brown, Mrs. Shelby-Boyd, Mrs. Denton and Mrs. Hopkins. Mrs. Johns was enabled to lift the financial burden of this great undertaking by the generous gift of $1,000 from Mrs. Rachel Foster-Avery, of Philadelphia. Although she has given time, service and money to this cause and received little in return, save the gratitude and esteem of thinking people, it is not because she prefers the care, labor, responsibility and unrest involved in this work to the quiet home-life she must often forego for its sake. Her cozy home is a marvel of good taste and comfort.

JOHNSON, Mrs. Carrie Ashton, editor and author, born in Durand, IL, 24th August, 1863. Her maiden name was Ashton. When she was fifteen years old, her parents moved to Rockford, IL, where she attended the high school and private schools for several years. Then she took a course in the business college and was graduated there. She is an active member of the Young Woman's Christian Temperance Union and of the Equal Suffrage Association. She has been State secretary of the Illinois Equal Suffrage Association for the past three years. Four years ago she published "Glimpses of Sunshine," a volume of sketches and quotations on suffrage work and workers. She is a contributor to the "Cottage Hearth," the "Housewife," "Table Talk," the "Ladies' Home Companion," the "Household," the "Housekeeper," the "Modern Priscilla," "Godey's Magazine," "Home Magazine," the "Decorator and Furnisher," "Interior Decorator," and other journals. She writes mainly on domestic topics, interior decorations, suffrage and temperance subjects. She was for more than three years in charge of the woman's department of the "Farmer's Voice," of Chicago, called "The Bureau for Better Halves," and is now conducting a like page for the "Spectator," a family magazine published in Rockford. She became the wife, 27th November, 1889, of Harry M. Johnson, managing editor of the Rockford "Morning Star." Their home is in Rockford.

JOHNSON, Mrs. Electa Amanda, philanthropist, born in the town of Arcadia, Wayne county, NY, 13th November, 1838. Her maiden name was Wright. Her father was of revolutionary stock, and her mother, born Kipp, was of an old Knickerbocker family. While she was still a child, her parents moved west and settled near Madison, WI. She attended the common schools of the neighborhood and finished her school life in the high school in Madison. After that she became a successful teacher in that city. In 1860 she became the wife of D. H. Johnson, a lawyer of Prairie du Chien, WI. In 1862 she and her husband settled in Milwaukee, where he is now a circuit

judge, and where they have ever since resided. Her attention was early directed to works of charity and reform. She was one of the founders of the Wisconsin Industrial School for Girls, was for many years its secretary, and is now an active member of its board of managers. It commenced operations as a small local charity in Milwaukee and has grown to be a great State institution. Mrs. Johnson has been several times commissioned by the Governor of Wisconsin to represent the State in the national conferences of charities and reforms, and in that capacity has participated in their deliberations in Washington, Louisville, St. Louis, Madison and San Francisco. She has interested herself in the associated charities of Milwaukee. Her views of public charity strongly favor efforts to aid and encourage the unfortunate to become self-supporting and self-respecting, in preference to mere almsgiving. She recognizes the necessity of immediate pecuniary assistance in urgent cases, but deprecates that method of relief, when it can be avoided, as the cheapest, laziest and least beneficial of all forms of charity. A close and thoughtful student of all forms and schemes of relief and repression, she has little faith in any plan for the immediate wholesale redemption of the criminal and improvident classes, but hopes and strives for their gradual diminution through the judicious and unselfish organized efforts of good men and women. She is an active member and was for two years corresponding secretary of the Women's Club of Wisconsin. She is not a professional literary woman, but her pen has been busy in the preparation of short articles and brief stories for publication, and numerous papers read before the societies, conferences, clubs and classes with which she has been affiliated.

JOHNSON, Mrs. Eliza McCardle, wife of Andrew Johnson, seventeenth President of the United States, born in Leesburg, Washington county, TN, 4th October, 1810 and died in Home, Greene county, TN, 15th January, 1876. She was the only daughter of her widowed mother, and her early life was passed in Greenville, TN. Her education was thorough for that day and place, and she enriched her mind by a wide course of reading. Miss McCardle was a young woman of great personal beauty and refinement, when, in 1826, Andrew Johnson, just out of his apprenticeship, arrived in Greenville. They became acquainted and were married on 27th May, 1826.

Mr. Johnson had had only the most meager education. He had never attended school a day. Feeling the need of education, he at once set to work to remedy the defect in his training, and in that work he was greatly aided by his cultured wife, who devoted herself solely to him and contributed materially to his success in life. Mr. Johnson entered politics. He was elected to the State legislature, and in 1861 he was in the United States Senate. In that year Mrs. Johnson spent several months in Washington. On account of impaired health she returned to Greenville, and on 24th April, 1862, she was ordered to pass beyond the Confederate lines within thirty-six hours. Too ill to obey the order, she remained in Greenville all summer. In September, 1862, she went with her children to Nashville, to join her husband. The excitement of the journey broke her health still further. When her husband became President, she was a confirmed invalid. She was not able to appear in society in Washington, and she was glad to leave the White House and return to Greenville. The duties of mistress of the White House fell upon her daughter, Mrs. Martha Patterson. Another daughter, Mrs. Mary Stover, was a member of the White House household during a part of President Johnson's term of office.

JOHNSON, Miss E. Pauline, poet, born in the family residence, "Chiefswood," on the Six Nation Indian Reserve, Brant county, Ontario, Canada, ten miles east of Brantford, her present home. Her father, George Henry Martin Johnson, Owanonsyshon (The Man With the Big House), was head chief of the Mohawks. Her mother, Emily S. Howells, an English woman, was born in Bristol, England. Miss Johnson's paternal grandfather was the distinguished John Sakayenkwaeaghton (Disappearing Mist) Johnson, usually called John Smoke Johnson, a pure Mohawk of the Wolf clan and speaker of the Six Nation Council for forty years; he fought for the British through the War of 1812-15, and was noted for his bravery. The name of his paternal great-grandfather was Tekahionwake, but when christening him "Jacob," in Niagara, Sir William Johnson, who was present, suggested they christen him Johnson also, after himself; hence

the family name now used as surname. Miss Johnson was educated at home by governesses and afterward in the Brantford Model School. She is an earnest member of the Church of England, and was christened Pauline, after the favorite sister of Napoleon Bonaparte, who was Chief Johnson's greatest hero. It is an interesting fact that, with her birth-claim to the name of a Mohawk Indian, she possesses an uncommon gift of felicitous prose as well as an acknowledged genius of verse. Her first verses appeared in the "Gems of Poetry" New York. She is a constant contributor to various Canadian papers, the "Week," "Saturday Night" and the "Globe," also prose articles in the "Boston Transcript." She has been very successful on the platform.

JOHNSON, Mrs. Sallie M. Mills, author, born in Sandusky, OH, 6th March, 1862. She is a granddaughter of judge Isaac Mills, of New Haven, CT. Her father is Gen. William H. Mills, of Sandusky. Her husband is C. C. Johnson. Mrs. Johnson was educated in New York City, and her attainments are varied. She is widely known as the author of "Palm Branches," and numerous other books from her pen have found large circles of readers. She has traveled much in the United States and in Europe. Her compositions in verse are of a fine order. She is a skilled musician, and, while studying in Weimar, received a signal compliment from Liszt. Her home is now in Denver, CO, where she owns much valuable real estate. She is a woman of great versatility, and shines equally in society, in literature, in music and in the more prosaic business affairs in which she is largely interested.

JOHNSTON, Mrs. Adelia Antoinette Field, educator, born in Lafayette, OH, 5th February, 1837. When eleven years old, she was sent to a good academy, and at fourteen she taught a country summer school. In 1856 she was graduated from Oberlin, and went to Tennessee as principal of Black Oak Grove Seminary. She returned to Ohio in the autumn of 1859, and became the wife of James W. Johnston, a graduate of Oberlin, and a teacher by profession. He died in the first year of the war, just as he was entering active service. Mrs. Johnston again became a teacher, and was for three years principal of an academy in Kinsman, OH. She then devoted a year to the study of Latin under the direction of Dr. Samuel Taylor, in Andover, MA, and taught three years in Scituate, R. I. In 1869 Mrs. Johnston went to Germany for two years of study, giving her attention to the German language and European history. On her return to America she was called to her present position of principal of the woman's department in Oberlin College. In addition to the regular duties of her office, she has taught one hour a day in the college, in the meantime continuing her historical studies. She has made three additional visits to Europe, and since 1890 has held the chair of mediæval history in Oberlin College.

JOHNSTON, Mrs. Harriet Lane, niece of James Buchanan, fifteenth President of the United States, and mistress of the White House during his incumbency, born in Mercersburg, PA, in 1833. She was a daughter of Elliott T. Lane and Jane Buchanan Lane. Her ancestry was English on her father's side and Scotch-Irish on her mother's side. Her maternal grandfather, James Buchanan, emigrated in 1783 from the north of Ireland and settled in Mercersburg, PA. In 1788 he was married to Elizabeth Speer, a wealthy farmer's daughter. Their oldest son was President James Buchanan. Their second child, Jane, was the mother of Harriet Lane. The daughter was left motherless in her seventh year, and her illustrious uncle took her into his care. She went with him to his home in Lancaster, PA. There she attended a day school. She was a frolicsome, generous, open-hearted child. She was next sent to school in Charlestown, VA, where, with her sister, she studied for three years. After leaving that school she went to the Roman Catholic convent school in Georgetown, DC. There she was liberally educated, her tastes running mainly to history, astronomy and mythology. She developed into a stately and beautiful woman. She had a clear, ringing voice, blue eyes and golden hair. She accompanied her uncle to England in 1853, and in London she presided over the embassy. Queen Victoria became a warm friend of the young American girl, and through her wish Miss Lane was ranked among the ladies of the diplomatic corps as Mr. Buchanan's wife would have ranked, had he been a married man. With her uncle she

traveled extensively in Europe. When Mr. Buchanan became President, Miss Lane was installed as mistress of the White House. Her régime was marked by grace and dignity. During the difficult years of President Buchanan's term of office Miss Lane's position was one of exceeding delicacy, but she ever maintained her self-poise and appeared as the true and honorable woman. In 1863 she was confirmed in the Episcopal Church in Oxford, Philadelphia, of which one of her uncles was rector. In January, 1866 she became the wife of Henry Elliott Johnston, a member of one of the distinguished families of Maryland. After marriage they traveled in Cuba. They made their home in Baltimore, MD. Her married life has been an ideal one. Her husband died some years ago, and she makes her home in Baltimore and Wheatlands. Her two sons died early.

JOHNSTON, Mrs. Maria I., author and editor, born in Fredericksbnrg, VA, 3rd May, 1835. Her father, Judge Richard Barnett, of that city, moved to Vicksburg, Miss., while she was still young. There she became the wife of C. L. Buck, who died in the first year of the war, leaving her with three children. She was in Vicksburg during its forty days' siege and made that experience the subject of her first novel. Although that book had a wide local sale, she dates her literary success from the subsequent publication of an article entitled "Gallantry, North and South," which appeared in the "Planters' Journal" and was copied in several other papers. At that time her literary work embraced contributions to the New Orleans "Picayune," "Times-Democrat," and later, articles to the Boston "Woman's Journal." After the war she became the wife of Dr. W. R. Johnston and lived on a Mississippi plantation. By the use of her pen, when she was widowed the second time, Mrs. Johnston was able to support herself. Her children were well educated and have taken positions of eminent social rank in life. Both daughters have married well and her son, after graduating in Yale, became a member of the Montana bar and was made Judge of the circuit court, Helena. Mrs. Johnston has written many stories both, long and short. In editing the St. Louis "Spectator," a literary weekly paper for family reading, Mrs. Johnston covers a broad field in literature, both general and personal. In her stories she deals for the most part with life in the West and South. The conditions caused by war and slavery are considered. In 1883 Mrs. Johnston wrote a strong reply to Dr. Hammond's criticisms of woman politicians in the "North American Review." Her reply was printed in the New Orleans "Picayune" and was copied throughout the United States. Her essay on "Froude's Character of Mary Stuart" was published as a serial in the "Inland Journal of Education," and will be published in book form. Her novel, "Jane," was issued in 1892. Mrs. Johnston resided in Madison parish, LA, from 1881 to 1887. During that time she was connected with the Cotton Planters' Association and wrote constantly in the interest of the New Orleans Centennial and Cotton Exposition. In 1886 appeared "The Freedwoman" from her pen. It was an earnest appeal to the matrons of the South, in behalf of their whilom slaves and foster sisters. Mrs. Johnston is an earnest advocate of full legal and political rights for her sex and has written extensively on that subject. She now resides in St. Louis, MO, where she is president of the St. Louis Writers' Club, and chairman of the press committee of the St. Louis branch of the World's Fair Commission.

JOHNSTON, Miss Marie Decca, see DECCA, MARIE.

JONES, Miss Amanda T., poet and inventor, born in Bloomfield, NY, 19th October, 1835. She is descended from Puritan, Huguenot, Quaker and Methodist ancestors, all thoroughly Americanized. Her forefathers were among the patriots of the Revolution. Miss Jones wrote a number of war poems during the Civil War. These were published, with others, in book form. Ill health for a number of years made it impossible for her to keep up her literary work. Some of her poems appeared in "Scribner's Magazine" when Dr. Holland was in charge; others have been published in the "Century," "Our Continent" and other journals. Some years ago she published a volume of verse entitled "A Prairie Idyl and Other Poems." Miss Jones is the inventor of improved processes for canning food, which are pronounced superior to any heretofore used. Business cares connected with their introduction have drawn her away from literary work. Her home is now in Chicago, IL.

JONES, Miss Harriet B., physician, born in Ebensburgh, PA, 3rd June, 1856. Her ancestors on both sides were Welsh. Her father emigrated from Wales when a boy. The family removed from Pennsylvania to Terra Alta, WV, in June, 1863. There Harriet dwelt during her childhood. At an early age she entered the Wheeling Female College, from which she was graduated 3rd June, 1875. Music and art were important features of her education.

After leaving school, she was not content to remain at home. She realized the need of more female physicians, and proposed to take up the study of medicine. This idea did not exactly meet the approval of her parents and friends; but when they saw her determination, all opposition was withdrawn, and, instead, assistance and encouragement were rendered. She went to Baltimore to pursue her studies, and was graduated with honors from the Woman's Medical College, 1st May, 1884. Dr. Jones commenced to practice in Wheeling in September, 1885, having spent some time in travel. In August, 1887, she was elected assistant superintendent of the State Hospital for the Insane in Weston, WV. Desiring to make a specialty of nervous diseases, she accepted that position and rendered faithful and efficient service until April, 1892, when she returned to Wheeling and established a private sanitarium for women's and nervous diseases, which institution is now in a prosperous condition. Besides her professional work, she is interested in every movement tending to promote morality, temperance and religion. Her work in Weston in the temperance cause was successful. There she organized a White Cross League, beginning with five, and the membership increased to thirty-three, including boys from fifteen to twenty years of age. The organization is still in existence and doing good work. When she went to Wheeling, she immediately resumed that work there, and is leader of a band of twenty-four members. Recognizing her ability as a leader, the

Woman's Christian Temperance Union unanimously elected Dr. Jones to be their president, as did also the Union Chautauqua Circles of Wheeling. Her knowledge of the needs of her sex, together with the earnest solicitations of her friends, have induced her upon several occasions to speak in public. Dr. Jones spends her days in alleviating suffering, dispensing charities and encouraging literary culture.

JONES, Mrs. Irma Theoda, philanthropist, born in Victory, NY, 11th March, 1845. Her maiden name was Andrews. Her ancestors were among the pioneers of western New York, 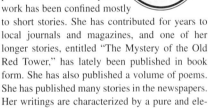 with a strong mixture of German blood on the father's side. In 1849 her father, a physician, removed his family to Rockford, IL. Miss Anna P. Sill had just then opened her female seminary, to which a primary department was attached, wherein the child of five years began her studies. The study of languages was her specialty. After teaching a year, in July, 1863, Mrs. Jones removed to Lansing, MI, where her uncle, John A. Kerr, held the position of State printer. In May, 1865, she became the wife of Nelson B. Jones, a prominent and public-spirited citizen of Lansing, where they have since resided. Four sons and one daughter enliven the home. One daughter died in infancy. Though at intervals from her girlhood Mrs. Jones has been a contributor to various newspapers, her most influential work has been in connection with the Lansing Woman's Club, of which she was one of the originators and president from 1885 to 1887, and also with the Woman's Christian Temperance Union in the days following the crusade movement, with the rise of the Young Woman's Christian Association and with the Lansing Industrial Aid Society, of which she has been president for the past thirteen years. The last-named society has for its object the permanent uplifting of the poor, and maintains a weekly school for teaching sewing, cooking and practical lessons in domestic economy to the children of the needy. The mother of Mrs. Jones, Mrs. N. Andrews, a woman of remarkable executive ability, is matron of the industrial school. Mrs. Jones has given time and effort freely to that work

for the unfortunate. In her Christian faith she is zealous, and the earnestness of her religious life characterizes her work in every field. In 1892 she became editor of the literary club department of the "Mid Continent," a monthly magazine published in Lansing.

JONES, Mrs. Jennie E., poet and storywriter, born in Dansville, NY, 17th May, 1833, and is now a resident of Hornellsville, NY. In her early years she displayed a talent for literary work, and she has always been in sympathy with the movements for the advancement of women in the United States. She has written much, in both prose and verse. Her prose work has been confined mostly to short stories. She has contributed for years to local journals and magazines, and one of her longer stories, entitled "The Mystery of the Old Red Tower," has lately been published in book form. She has also published a volume of poems. She has published many stories in the newspapers. Her writings are characterized by a pure and elevating tone.

JONES, Mrs. May C., Baptist minister, born in Sutton, NH. 5th November, 1842. She was the daughter of an English physician. Her mother was a descendant of the Scotch Covenanters, and her fearless, outspoken defense of the truth proclaims her a fit representative of such an ancestry. At the age of thirteen Miss Jones began to teach school, which occupation she followed until her marriage. In 1867 she moved with her husband to the Pacific coast, spending over ten years in California. In 1880 she removed to Seattle, WA, where she preached her first sermon in August of the same year, since which time she has been engaged in the gospel ministry. She was licensed to preach by the First Baptist Church of Seattle, and acted as supply in the absence of the regular pastor. Afterward the council, with representatives of other churches composing the Baptist Association of Puget Sound and British Columbia, ordained her on 9th July, 1882, and she became the permanent pastor of the First Baptist Church of Seattle. She has rare gifts as an evangelist and has been very successful as a pastor. Her last pastorate was with the First Baptist Church of Spokane, the second largest church in the State of Washington. That position she held four years, baptizing and performing the marriage ceremony and such other duties as devolve upon the pastor of a large and rapidly growing church. On 1st January, 1892, she resigned the charge to devote herself to the care of her invalid husband, who has since died. At the present time she is engaged in evangelistic work, accompanied by her talented daughter, a sweet singer, in which work they are much sought after and are very successful. Mrs. Jones is the founder of Grace Seminary, a flourishing school in the city of Centralia, Wash. She has organized several churches and erected two houses of worship. She has a flexible voice of marvelous power and sweetness. She speaks rapidly and fluently, with a style peculiar to herself. Added to these gifts is a deep undercurrent of spiritual life.

JORDAN, Mrs. Cornelia Jane Matthews, poet, born in Lynchhurg, VA, in 1830. Her parents were Edwin Matthews and Emily Goggin Matthews. She was born to wealth, and received all the advantages of liberal education and polished society. Her mother died in 1834, and Cornelia and two younger sisters were sent to the home of their grandmother in Bedford county. In 1842 she was placed in the school of the Sisters of the Visitation, in Georgetown, DC. In school she led her mates in all literary exercises. Her poetical productions were numerous and excellent. In 1851 she became the wife of F. H. Jordan, a lawyer of Luray, VA, where she made her home. During the first years of her married life she wrote a great deal. A collection of her poems was published in Richmond, VA, in 1860 with the title, "Flowers of Hope and Memory." During the Civil War she

wrote many stirring lyrics. A volume of these, entitled "Corinth, and Other Poems," was published after the surrender. The little volume was seized by the military commander in Richmond and suppressed as seditious. In 1867 she published "Richmond: Her Glory and Her Graves," in a volume with some shorter lyrics. She has contributed many poems to magazines and newspapers. Her best-known war poems are The Battle of Manassas," "The Death of Jackson" and "An Appeal for Jefferson Davis."

JORDAN, Miss Elizabeth Garver, journalist, born in Milwaukee, WI, 9th May, 1867. Her father was William F. Jordan and her mother, who was Spanish, had for her maiden name Margarita G. Garver. The childhood of Elizabeth Garver Jordan was spent in Milwaukee, and her career as a journalist began while she was a resident of that city. Under her own name she contributed to the Milwaukee "Evening Wisconsin," the St. Paul "Globe," "Texas Siftings," and Chicago

papers. The publishers of "Peck's Sun," then recognizing the cleverness of her work, offered her a place on that paper, and she edited its woman's page for two years. In 1888 she went to Chicago and became an all-round reporter. While on the staff of the Chicago "Tribune" she filled several notable assignments, not the least of which was her report of the terrible Chatsworth disaster. She went to the scene of the accident and remained several days, helping in the heartrending work of caring for the injured and the dead. The courage which sustained her in that test stood her in good stead later on, when she took up her work in New York. She went to that city in May, 1890, at the invitation of Col. Cockerill, then editor-in-chief of the New York "World." Her fine credentials gained for her immediate recognition among her fellow-workers. Miss Jordan accepted the same class of assignments that were given to her brother reporters and filled them with equal success. She developed a special talent for interviewing and has interviewed a large number of the most noted men and women of the day, succeeding when others failed. In the New York tenement houses she has done a work that entitled her to be known as a practical philanthropist. In September, 1890, the "World" began the publication of its series, "True Stories of the News," each story being the recital of some tragic, humorous or dramatic event of the day before, and which was of strong human interest. Miss Jordan wrote the majority of these stories, and the work of gathering them took her into the hospitals, the morgue, the police courts, and the great east-side tenements of New York. She became known to the city officials, who took a special interest in her stories and never missed a chance to give her a good news "pointer." At the time of the Koch lymph agitation she spent a night in the Charity Hospital on Blackwell's Island, at the death-bed of a consumptive, that she might write the story of the last struggle of a patient with that dread disease. The woman patient died at 3 a. m., holding fast the young journalist's hand. The story was finished three hours later. Among her frequent out-of-town assignments was one to Harper's Ferry, where she saw and talked with eye-witnesses of John Brown's famous raid in 1859. She obtained interviews with the man who tended the bridge on that eventful night, and with others, who made the report of her trip not only interesting, but of actual historical value. Later she made a most perilous trip into the Virginia and Tennessee mountains, traveling on horseback through almost impenetrable forests, fording rivers and climbing gorges, her only companion being a negro guide, and her only defense a Spanish stiletto to use in case of treachery. During that trip she visited a lonely milling camp in the mountains, where no other woman ever set foot. She slept in the cabins of the mountaineers by night, visited the camps of moonshiners and wrote numerous "Sunday World" mountain stories afterward, which were widely copied. She was promoted to the editorial staff of the "World," and has since edited the woman's and child's pages. In April, 1892, she was appointed assistant editor of the "Sunday World." She enjoys the distinction of being the youngest woman editor on the staff of any New York newspaper. She was referred to by a prominent journalist as "the best newspaper man in New York." The strongest point in her character is firmness, and the quality which has contributed greatly to her journalistic success is quiet courage, which prompts her to accept unquestioningly whatever is given her to do, regardless of dangers involved. She has no higher ambition than to shine in journalism, though she is an accomplished musician and linguist, and possesses broad social culture.

JUCH, Miss Emma Johanna Antonia, operatic singer, born in Vienna, Austria-Hungary, 4th July, 1863. Her father, Justin Juch, was a music professor. He was a native of Vienna, but had become a citizen of the United States. In Detroit, MI, he was married to Miss Augusta Hahn. Emma was born during a visit made by her parents in Vienna. When she was six months old, her parents returned to the United States and made their home in New York City. Emma was a precocious child. She passed through the public school course and was graduated in the Normal in 1879. Her father recognized her musical talents, but did not encourage her to cultivate them, as he was opposed to her entering the professional field. She inherited her fine voice from her French-Hanoverian mother, and decided to pursue her musical studies in secret. She studied for three years with Madame Murio-Celli, and made her début in a concert in Chickering Hall. Her father was among her auditors, and he listened to her singing with surprise. Her triumph was perfect. Her father then encouraged her to pursue the study of music, and for two years she was subjected to the severest discipline. Her pure, strong soprano voice gained in power and flexibility. In May, 1881, Colonel Mapleson engaged her to sing leading soprano rôles in Her Majesty's Grand Italian Opera in London, England. There she made her début as Filina in "Mignon" and won a brilliant triumph, in June, 1881. She then appeared as Violetta in "Traviata," as Queen of Night in "Magic Flute," as Martha in "Martha," as Marguerite in "Faust," as the queen in "Les Huguenots," and as Isabella in "Robert le Diable." She sang during three seasons under Colonel Mapleson's management. When her contract lapsed, she refused to renew it. William Steinway, of New York City, introduced her to Theodore Thomas, and she accepted from his manager an offer to share the work of Nilsson and Materna on the tour of the Wagnerian artists, Materna, Scaria and Winkelmann. Miss Juch sang alternate nights with Nilsson as Elsa in "Lohengrin." She won a series of triumphs on that tour. When the American Opera Company was formed, she was the first artist engaged. Many tempting offers were made to her, but she decided to remain with the American Opera Company. During three seasons with that company she sang in six rôles and one-hundred-sixty-four times. The operas presented were "Magic Flute, "Lohengrin," "The Flying Dutchman," Gluck's "Orpheus," Rubinstein's "Nero," and Gounod's "Faust." During the past four or five years she has been constantly before the public in festivals, orchestral symphonic concerts and the German choral societies, and in the Emma Juch Grand English Opera Company. The Aschenbroedel Verein of professional orchestral musicians recently conferred upon her the unusual compliment of honorary membership, in return for her services given in aid of the society's sick fund. Miss Juch possesses a fine stage presence, a powerful and cultured voice. Her fine singing is coupled with equally fine acting. Her home is in New York City.

JUDSON, Miss Jennie S., author, born in Paris, IL, 31st July, 1859, but spent the early years of her life in Mississippi and Alabama. With the members of her father's family, she has been a resident since 1875 of Paris. Her grandfather, Gen. M. K. Alexander, was one of the pioneers of Illinois. Miss Judson's education was obtained mainly in the Mount Auburn Institute, Cincinnati, OH. Soon after her graduation she began to write. For four years she wrote with her father as her sole reader. In 1882 she offered a poem, "Fire Opal," to "Our Continent," and it was accepted. From that time she became a regular contributor to that magazine, publishing in it her first prose composition which saw the light. Making next a trial in juvenile work, she found a ready place for it in "Our Little Ones," and soon became a regular writer for that magazine, with an occasional sketch in "Wide Awake." Then her work began to appear in the "Golden Argosy," "Our Youth" and other juvenile periodicals. She then offered manuscript to the "Current" and "Literary Life" of Chicago, and in a short time became identified with them. In the South her name came before the people in poems and sketches copied by the New Orleans and other papers. Lately she has done much syndicate work in the leading papers of the United States. A series of Southern sketches, illustrated, which recently appeared in this way, has been successful. She excels in society verses. The

"Century" has published some of her work in its bric-a-brac columns. Miss Judson is now slowly emerging from a long period of invalidism, which has clouded the best years of her life. She is a member of the Western Association of Writers.

KAHN, Mrs. Ruth Ward, author, born in Jackson, MI, 4th August, 1870. Her father, Judge Ward, had been a leading lawyer in that city, serving as district attorney and as judge of the probate court of Michigan. Miss Ward early showed her literary tastes and talents. She became a contributor to local newspapers and school magazines. She was educated in the Michigan University, Ann Arbor, where she was graduated with honors and the degree of B.A., in 1889. On 17th May, 1890, she became the wife of Dr. Lee Kahn, in Leadville, CO. On their return from the South Sea Islands she published in the "Popular Science News" a noted paper on "Hawaiian Ant Life." She contributes to the Denver "Commonwealth," and "Rocky Mountain News," to the "American Israelite," of Cincinnati, New Orleans "Picayune," Elmira "Telegram," and the St. Louis "Jewish Voice." She has recently brought out an epic poem, "Gertrude," and a novel, "The Story of Judith." Mrs. Kahn is widely known in all fields she has occupied. She is one of the youngest members of the Incorporated Society of Authors, of London, England, which society she joined in 1890. She is an honorary member of the Authors' and Artists' Club, Kansas City, MO, and of the Woman's National Press Association. She is an artist of marked talent. Her home is in Leadville, CO.

KEATING, Mrs. Josephine E., literary critic, musician and music teacher, born in Nashville, TN, and was educated in the Atheneum in Columbia. From that institution she was graduated with distinction in vocal and instrumental music. She was first in all her other classes. She has been a student ever since her school-days and has an intimate acquaintance with modern French and English literature. As the literary editor of the Memphis "Appeal" first, and later of the Memphis "Commercial," she made this evident. At the beginning of her career she gave much attention to music and its history and to that of the persons most distinguished as executants or professors of it. She became a brilliant singer. After many signal triumphs in the field of her first endeavor, in Nashville, Baton Rouge, LA, and Memphis, TN, where she sang altogether for charitable and patriotic purposes, teaching music, vocal, piano, harp and guitar, for the support of her family during the war, she turned to literature, of which she had always been a student. She became well known to publishers and literary people throughout the country as a discerning and discriminating critic. In the midst of all her tasks, many of them profound, Mrs. Keating found time to be a devoted wife and mother, to supervise the education of her children and to be a counselors and helper of her husband, Col. J. M. Keating, a journalist. A busy woman, she is nevertheless a diligent reader. Mrs. Keating is a born letterwriter, and for eight years was New York correspondent of the Memphis "Appeal." During her connection with that journal she wrote many musical criticisms of value and several sketches of notable musical and theatrical people. She also made many valuable translations from the French, which were well received.

KEEZER, Mrs. Martha Moulton Whittemore, author, born in West Roxbury, MA, 26th April, 1870. Her maiden name was Whittemore. She was the second daughter in a family of eight children. Her youth was spent on a country estate. She passed through the grammar and high schools rapidly, and at the age of sixteen years entered Cornell University, although her age was less by a year than the regulations in that institution provide for. She studied there two years, when she left school to begin a career in journalism. Her first contributions were published in the "Woman's Journal." Her work soon extended to daily papers and to a number of periodicals, including "Youth's Companion," the "Household," the "Home Magazine" and the "Woman's Illustrated World." Her articles were mainly in the educational line, but she also wrote juvenile articles for the "Young Idea" and other journals. She is now planning wider work. Her home since her marriage has been in Dorchester, MA.

KEISTER, Mrs. Lillie Resler, church worker and organizer, born in Mt. Pleasant, PA, 15th May, 1851. She was the first of seven children born to Rev. and Mrs. J. B. Resler. Her father died in March, 1891. The father, with only a small salary, moved to Westerville, OH, to give his children the benefit of Otterbein University, as soon as Lillie was ready to enter, which was in 1866. She was graduated with the class of 1872. Being the oldest of the children, she early became a worker and planner in the home, and the useful home-girl became the school-girl, the school-teacher and the professor's wife, and broader fields for helpful planning opened before her in home, school and church. The early death, in 1880, of her husband, Rev. George Keister, professor of Hebrew in Union Biblical Seminary, Dayton, OH, opened the way to broader usefulness in church work. The church of her choice, the United Brethren in Christ, organized the Woman's Missionary Association in 1875, of which she was corresponding secretary for the first year. The work of the society grew and, in 1881, it called for the full time of one woman as its corresponding secretary and to establish and edit its organ, the "Woman's Evangel." Mrs. Keister was the available woman well qualified for the responsible position. She was unanimously elected, and up to the present she has filled the place with success. She is a woman of marked executive ability. Besides the work on the paper, much of her time is given to public addresses. She is an excellent traveler. One year she traveled in association work over 12,000 miles in the United States. Twice she has been on short trips abroad, first in 1884, when the illness of her sister studying in Germany called her thither, and again in 1888, when she was one of two delegates sent by the Woman's Missionary Association to the World's Missionary Conference in London, England.

KEITH, Miss Eliza D., journalist, was born in San Francisco, CA, where her grandfather was an "Argonaut of '49" and a prominent public officer. Under the pen-name "Di Vernon" she has acted as special writer for the "Alta Californian," San Francisco "Chronicle," "Examiner" and "Call," as well as the "News Letter"; is special correspondent of the San Francisco "Recorder-Union," and writes also for the "Journalist," "Good Housekeeping" and many other periodicals. She is an enthusiastic member of the Society for the Prevention of Cruelty to Animals, and in 1891 she received the bronze medal of the San Francisco Society for the Prevention of Cruelty to Animals, in recognition of service rendered to the cause of humane education by voice and pen. In 1890 she was elected life member of the Golden Gate Kindergarten Association for similar reasons.

KELLER, Mrs. Elizabeth Catharine, physician and surgeon, born in a small town near Gettysburg, PA, 4th April, 1837. In 1857 she became the wife of Matthias McComsey, of Lancaster, PA, and within two years was a mother and a widow. In 1860 she was appointed superintendent of the Lancaster Orphans' Home, where, during seven years, she had charge of the hundreds of children who were provided for in that institution. She was not only the mother and teacher of the children, but she was their physician, treating the various diseases incident to childhood with success. In 1867 she became the wife of George L. Keller, and went to Philadelphia, PA, to live. Thrown among medical women there in connection with the Woman's Hospital, her natural taste for medical work assumed definite shape, and with the approval of her husband she entered the Woman's Medical College of Pennsylvania in the fall of 1868, graduating in March, 1871. After graduation she almost immediately opened a dispensary and hospital. During the year following graduation, she was appointed successor to Dr. Ann Preston on the board of attending physicians of the Woman's Hospital of Philadelphia, a position which she held until 1875, when she was appointed resident physician of the New England Hospital in Boston. In 1877 she entered upon private practice in Jamaica Plain, one of the suburbs of Boston, where she is still in practice. In 1890 she was elected a member of the Boston school board.

KELLEY, Miss Ella Maynard, telegraph operator, born in Fremont, OH, 13th December, 1859. She received a good education in the public schools of that town, and learned telegraphy in Lindsey, OH. She has won a unique rank as the foremost woman in active telegraphy in the United States. She began telegraphy at the age of fourteen years. When a girl at that age, she had charge of a night office in Oak Harbor, on the Lake Shore Railroad, and worked all night alone. After working four years at railroad telegraphing, in which she was responsible for the running of trains, she was engaged in commercial telegraphy in Atlantic City, NJ, in Detroit, MI, in Washington, DC, and in the Western Union office in Columbus, OH. For the past three years she has been in charge of the first wire of the Associated Press circuit. She is the first woman who used the typewriter in the telegraphic service.

KELLOGG, Clara Louise, operatic singer, born in Sumterville, SC, 12th July, 1842. She is the daughter of the well-known inventor, George Kellogg. Her childhood was spent in Birmingham, CT. She received a good education and showed her musical talents at an early age. At the age of nine months she could hum a tune correctly, and the quickness and accuracy of her ear astonished the musicians. Her mother, a clairvoyant doctor, was a fine musician, and Clara, the only child, inherited her talents. In 1856 the family removed to New York City, where Clara began her musical studies in earnest, with a view to a professional career. She studied both the French and Italian methods of singing. In 1860 she made her debut in the Academy of Music, New York, as Gilda in "Rigoletto," winning a modest triumph. In 1864 she won the public by her Marguerite in Gounod's "Faust," which has stood as the greatest impersonation of that rôle ever seen on the stage. After brilliant successes in this country, Miss Kellogg went to London, Eng., and appeared in Her Majesty's Theater. She sang in the Handel Festival in the Crystal Palace in the same year. In 1868 she returned to the United States and made a concert-tour with Max Strakosch. In 1869 she again sang in Italian opera in New York City, appearing for three consecutive seasons, and always drawing crowded houses. She then organized an opera company to sing in English. The organization was a success during 1874 and 1875. In one winter Miss Kellogg sang one-hundred-twenty-five nights. In 1876 she organized an Italian opera company, and appeared as Aida and Carmen. After the dissolution of that company she left the operatic stage and sang in concert throughout the country for several years. In 1880 she accepted an operatic engagement in Austria, where she sang in Italian with a company of German singers. She extended her tour to Russia and sang in St. Petersburg. Her list of grand operas included forty-five. She is most closely identified with "Faust," "Crispino," "Traviata," "Aida" and "Carmen." Her voice in youth was a high soprano, with a range from C to E flat. With age it lost some of the highest notes, but gained greatly in power and richness. She was the first American artist to win recognition in Europe. She has amassed a large fortune. Her latest appearance was on a concert tour in 1889. She became the wife of Carl Strakosch several years ago and is now living in retirement.

KEMP, Mrs. Agnes Nininger, physician, born in Harrisburg, PA, 4th November, 1823. She is a daughter of Anthony Nininger, who was a native of Alsatia, France. While but a mere girl in years, she became the wife of Col. William Saunders, and was brought into intimate association with Lucretia Mott, William Lloyd Garrison, Abbey Kelly Foster and Ralph Waldo Emerson and others of like spirit. She invited successively to Harrisburg those sturdy pioneers and helped them to sow the seed of patriotism in the conservative capital of Pennsylvania. After a few years, being widowed, she went to Philadelphia, entered the

Woman's Medical College, and was graduated in 1879, being the first woman in Dauphin county to begin there the practice of medicine and the first one to be received into the medical society of that county. Her second marriage, to Joseph Kemp, of Hollidaysburg, PA, occurred in 1860 When the Woman's Christian Temperance Union became a national organization, she was active in establishing a local union in Harrisburg.

KENDRICK, Mrs. Ella Bagnell, temperance worker, born within a stone's cast of Plymouth Rock, 24th May, 1849. She is the daughter of Richard W. and Harriet S. Allen Bagnell. She was educated in the public schools, and graduated from the Plymouth high school at the age of sixteen. In 1870 she became the wife of Henry H. Kendrick, and in the following year removed to Meriden, CT. She was among the most zealous and active members of the Meriden Scientific Association, being especially interested in plants and plant life. She was at the same time an efficient member of the Woman's Christian Temperance Union, being always an earnest advocate of temperance reform. Her home in Meriden was a museum of antiques and curios, together with various objects of natural history, stones and plants. She was formerly secretary of the Meriden Prohibition Club, also secretary for New Haven county, and in the latter capacity was an active director of the party work in the campaign of 1890. In 1891 she removed from Meriden to Hartford, where her husband became business manager of the "New England Home," one of the leading Prohibition newspapers of the country, and Mrs. Kendrick became associate editor. She is assistant secretary of the Hartford Prohibition Club and State superintendent of Demorest Medal Contests.

KEPLEY, Mrs. Ada Miser, attorney-at-law, temperance agitator and minister, born in Somerset, OH, 11th February, 1847. She is of Scotch-Irish and German ancestry. Among her ancestors was William Temple Coles, who came to the colonies in the ship that brought General Braddock. Mr. Coles had been educated for the English Church, but, instead of taking holy orders, he turned his face toward the land of promise. He settled near Salisbury, in North Carolina. His only son, William Temple Coles, Jr., was a captain in the Revolutionary War. His only daughter, Henrietta, was one of the pioneer Methodists of America, and settled in Bedford, PA. She was known as "Mother Fishburn." She collected the money and secured the site for the first Methodist Episcopal Church in that town, and in the new structure now occupying the site is a stained-glass window commemorating her and her daughter, Elizabeth Fishburn. The Temples trace their lineage directly to Sir William Temple. The family were intense haters of the institution of slavery. William Temple Coles, Sr., even refused to have a slave in his house, and brought over white servants from England. In Mrs. Kepley this intense hatred of slavery has taken the form of hatred for the bodily slavery of alcoholic drink. She is best known for her work for the abolition of alcoholic drinking and of the laws that perpetuate the evil habit. In 1867 she became the wife of Henry B. Kepley, a well-known attorney of Effingham, IL. She became interested in law and began the study of the profession in her husband's office. She studied during 1868 and 1869, and was graduated in the Union College of Law, in Chicago, in 1870. She is a member of the bar. She has been identified with the National Woman's Christian Temperance Union, and also with the Illinois State branch of that organization. She is the editor of the "Friend of Home," a flourishing monthly established seven years ago. In its pages she expounds the law, demands its enforcement, declares for new laws and suggests ways to secure them. Her work has been positive and well directed. She has made a specialty of exposing the hidden roots of the liquor traffic in her town and county, and the readers of the "Friend of Home" know who are the grantors, grantees, petitioners and bondmen for dram-shops. She has made a specialty of children's and young people's work in her county, and achieved a high position in that line in 1890. She and her husband erected and support "The Temple," in Effingham, a beautiful building, which is headquarters for the Woman's Christian

Temperance Union, prohibition and general reform work. Mrs. Kepley's ancestors were Episcopalians, Catholics and Methodists in religion, from which combination she is, by a natural process, a Unitarian in belief, and 24th July, 1892, she was ordained a minister of that denomination in Shelbyville, IL. She is a vice-president of the Federated Clubs of this state.

KEYSOR, Mrs. Jennie Ellis, educator, born in Austin, MN, 2nd March, 1860. She was a high-school graduate of 1878, and began to teach in a district school, riding nearly four miles on horseback daily and utilizing the long ride in the study of English literature. She was graduated from the Winona Normal School in 1879, and was appointed to a position in the Austin school in the same year. After two years in the normal she completed in Wellesley College her course in English literature, history and Anglo-Saxon. She again occupied a position in the Winona normal, having charge of the department of English literature and rhetoric. She resigned to become the wife of William W. Keysor, an attorney of Omaha and at present one of the district judges. She has been for years a writer for the "Popular Educator" and a frequent contributor to other periodicals.

KIDD, Mrs. Lucy Ann, educator, born in Nelson county, KY, 11th June, 1839. Her maiden name was Lucy Ann Thornton. Her father, Willis Stretcher Thornton, was a descendant of an old English family, resident in Virginia since the time of the Pretender. The old ancestral home,"Hunter's Rest," is still owned by some member of the family. Lucy received a collegiate education in Georgetown, KY. In her seventeenth year she became the wife of a southern physician, who died, leaving his estate heavily encumbered. She accepted a position in a college in Brookhaven, MS, and two years after bought an interest in the school. Nine years later she was elected president of North Texas Female College, in

Sherman, TX, a position she still holds. Mrs. Kidd is the first woman south of Mason and Dixon's line who has held such a position. Her administrative ability is marked in the popularity and numbers of this school within three years after she assumed the presidency.

KIMBALL, Miss Corinne, actor, born in Boston, MA, 25th December, 1873. She is widely known by her stage-name, "Corinne." She is the daughter of Mrs. Jennie Kimball, actor and theatrical manager. Originally her mother had not the slightest intention of placing her on the stage. It was led up to by a combination of circumstances. In 1876 a grand baby show was held in Horticultural Hall, in Boston, and Corinne was one of the infants placed on exhibition. She created marked sensation, caused not only by her great personal beauty, but also by her ability to sing and dance prettily at the age of three. She received the prize medals and diploma. The attention she attracted caused her mother to accept an engagement for her to appear in Sunday-evening concerts in conjunction with Brown's Brigade Band. Her success in these concerts determined her mother to keep her on the stage. She next appeared in the Boston Museum as Little Buttercup, in a juvenile production of "Pinafore." Her mother became her manager and has so continued ever since. Judging her from her past successes, Mrs. Kimball placed her in comic opera. She sang in "The Mascotte," "Olivette," "Princess of Trebizonde," "Chimes of Normandy" and "Mikado." She played the principal parts in all of these, and memorized not only her own rôle, but the entire operas, so as to be able to prompt every part from beginning to end. Then Mrs. Kimball, thinking to save Corinne's voice, from her twelfth to sixteenth year put her in burlesque. Her success in that line of work was much greater than expected, and consequently she has remained in burlesque. In "Arcadia" she first established herself; in "Monte Cristo, Jr.," she attracted attention and won the title of "Queen of the Stage" in the New York "Morning Journal" voting contest over the heads of prominent actors.

KIMBALL, Miss Grace, actress, who made her debut playing a maid's part in "A Possible Case" with the J. M. Hill Co. Subsequent engagements included Miranda, in "The Tempest," at McVickers' Theater, Chicago, and Agnes in "Dr. Jekyll and Mr. Hyde," with Richard Mansfield. She then played the *ingenue* parts with Nat C. Goodwin and afterward signed with Charles Frohman, creating the parts of Olive Corey in "Giles Corey, Yeoman," and the School Mistress in "Squirrel Inn." For three years she supported E. H. Southern, during which time she played Fanny Hadden in "Captain Letterblair," Clara Dexter in "Master of Woodbarrow," Eleanor in "Lord Chumley," Rose in "The Highest Bidder," besides creating the parts of Betty Lindley in "Sheridan," Madge in "A Way to Win a Woman," Joan in the "Victoria Cross," and Princess Flavia in the "Prisoner of Zenda." Miss Kimball's more recent appearance has been at the Garden Theater, New York, in "Heart's-Ease" and in Hooley's Theater, Chicago, in "Never Again."

KIMBALL, Miss Harriet McEwen, poet, born in Portsmouth, NH, 2nd November, 1834. She is a daughter of the late Dr. David Kimball, a refined and scholarly man. Miss Kimball has been interested in charitable work throughout her life, and a Cottage Hospital in Portsmouth is one of the monuments that attest her philanthropy. Her first volume of verse was published in 1867. In 1874 she published her "Swallow Flights of Song," and in 1879 "The Blessed Company of All Faithful People." In 1889 her poems were brought out in a full and complete edition. Most of her poems are religious in character. Many of them are hymns, and they are found in all church collections of late date. Her devotional poems are models of their kind, and her work is considered unique in its rather difficult field. She lives in Portsmouth, devoted to her literary work and her religious and philanthropic interests.

KIMBALL, Mrs. Jennie, actor and theatrical manager, born in New Orleans, LA, 23rd June, 1851. Her first appearance in public was as Obeda in "Bluebeard," in the Boston Theater, in 1865,

Margaret Mather.
From Elite Photo, San Francisco.

Grace Kimball.
From Photo by Morrison, Chicago.

under H. C. Jarrett's management. After devoting a year to the study of music and the drama, she was engaged by Manager Whitman for leading soubrette business in the Continental Theater, Boston, in 1868, appearing as Cinderella in Byron's burlesque, and Stalacta in "The Black Crook," which ran the entire season. She afterward played a star engagement with him in the West, appearing as Oberon in "A Midsummer Night's Dream," and singing the title rôle in "The Grand Duchess" in Buffalo, Louisville, Chicago, St. Louis and other western cities, winning unqualified approbation. After concluding her engagement with Mr. Whitman, she returned to the East and traveled through New England as prima donna of the Florence Burlesque Opera Company, until she was engaged by John Brougham for his New York company, in 1869, and opened 1st March in Brougham's Fifth Avenue Theater, now the Madion Square, in the operetta of "Jenny Lind," afterward playing Kate O' Brien in "Perfection," and other musical comedies. In 1872 she was especially engaged in the Union Square Theater, under the management of Sheridan Shook, as stock star, playing all the leading parts in the burlesque, "Ernani," "The Field of the Cloth of Gold," "Bad Dickey," "Black-Eyed Susan," "Aladdin," "The Invisible Prince" and others, and remaining there two seasons. After Little Corinne made her success as Little Buttercup in "Pinafore," in the Boston Theater, Jennie Kimball retired from the profession, in order to devote her whole time and attention to Corinne's professional advancement. She has occasionally reappeared with her, singing the Countess in, Olivette" and the Queen in "Arcadia." In 1881 Mrs. "Kimball commenced her career as a manager, organizing an opera company of juveniles, of which Corinne was the star. They continued uninterruptedly successful until the interference of the Society for the Prevention of Cruelty to Children, of New York City. After the celebrated trial, which gave Mrs. Kimball and her daughter, Corinne, such notoriety, they opened in the Bijou Opera House, 31st December, 1881, and played four weeks, thence continuing throughout the United States and Canada, winning marked success. Mrs. Kimball has had an interest

in several theaters. She has a capacity for work that is marvelous. She has, by her energy and executive ability, brought Corinne to the front rank as a star. She personally engages all the people, makes contracts, books her attractions and supervises every rehearsal. All details as to costumes, scenery and music receive her attention. The greater portion of her advertising matter she writes herself, and she is as much at home in a printing-office as she is in the costumer's or in the scenic artist's studio.

KIMBALL, Mrs. Maria Porter, see BRACE, MISS MARIA PORTER.

KING, Madame Julie Rive, piano virtuoso, born in Cincinnati, OH, 31st October, 1857. Her maiden name was Rive. Her mother, Madame Caroline Rive, was a cultured musician, a fine singer, a finished pianist, and a teacher of long experience. At an early age Julie was trained in piano playing, and at thirteen years of age her remarkable precocity was shown in concerts, when she played Liszt's "Don Juan." She early and easily mastered the preliminary studies, and went to New York City, where she studied with Mason and Mills, and also with Francis Korbay and Pruckner. Returning to Cincinnati, she appeared in concerts and created a furore. In 1873 she went to Europe and entered the classes of Liszt, after studying in Dresden with Blossman. She played in public in Leipzig and other cities, and was at once ranked with the great pianists of the day. In Leipzig she studied with Reinecke. In 1874 she appeared with the Euterpe Orchestra in Leipzig. She won brilliant triumphs in all the musical centers of Europe. She was recalled to the United States by the sudden death of her father in a railway collision. Shortly afterward she was married to Frank H. King. She played in concerts in all the larger cities and established a reputation as one of the great pianists of the United States. In 1879 she made her home in New York City, and there she has lived ever since. In 1884 her health broke under the strain of public performances, and after recovering her strength she devoted her time to teaching and composition. She has composed scores of successful pieces.

Her numerous tours have taken her from Massachusetts to California. She has played in more than two-hundred concerts with Theodore Thomas. Her memory is flawless. Her repertory includes over three-hundred of the most elaborate concert compositions.

KINNEY, Mrs. Narcissa Edith White, temperance worker, born in Grove City, PA, 24th July, 1854. She is Scotch-Irish through ancestry. Her mother's maiden name was Wallace, and family records show that she was a direct descendant of Adam Wallace, who was burned in Scotland for his religion, and whose faith and death are recorded in Fox's "Book of Martyrs." At his death his two sons, David and Moses Wallace, fled to the north of Ireland, whence Narcissa's grandfather, Hugh Wallace, emigrated to America in 1796. Her father's ancestor, Walter White, was also burned during Queen Mary's reign, and the record is in Fox's "Book of Martyrs," and four of her faraway grandfathers, two on each side of the house, fought side by side in the battle of the Boyne. Her maiden name was Narcissa Edith White. She was reared in a conservative church, the United Presbyterian. Rarely endowed as a teacher, having entered the profession before she was fifteen years old, it was natural enough that she should be recalled to her alma mater as an instructor in the training department. She was also chosen at the same time superintendent of Edinboro Union School, New Erie, PA. Later she was engaged as a county institute instructor. Not until the fall of 1880 did she find her place in the white-ribbon rank. She brought to the work the discipline of a thoroughly drilled student and successful teacher. Her first relation to the Woman's Christian Temperance Union was as president of the local union in her town, Grove City, and next of her own county, Mercer, where she built up the work in a systematic fashion. Next she was made superintendent of normal temperance instruction for her State, and did an immense amount of thorough, effective work by lecturing, writing and pledging legislators to the hygiene bill after her arguments had won them to her view of the situation. Next to Mrs. Hunt, Miss White was probably the ablest specialist in that department, having studied it carefully and attended the school of Col. Parker, of Quincy fame, to learn the best method of teaching hygiene to the young. In the autumn of 1884 Miss White was sent by the National Woman's Christian Temperance Union to assist the Woman's Christian Temperance Union of Washington Territory in securing from the legislature the enactment of temperance laws. Under the persuasive eloquence and wise leadership of Miss White the most stringent scientific temperance law ever enacted was passed by a unanimous vote of both houses. Also, in spite of the bitter opposition of the liquor traffic, a local-option bill was passed, submitting to the vote of the people in the following June the prohibition of the liquor traffic in each precinct. Miss White assisted in that campaign and had the gratification of seeing prohibition approved by a majority vote of all the citizens, both men and women, of the Territory. In 1888 Miss White became the wife of M. J. Kinney, of Astoria, OR. In 1890 she was prostrated by the death of her infant. She recovered her health, and in 1891 she undertook the work of organizing a Chautauqua Association for the State of Oregon, in which she succeeded. She served as secretary of the association. Her husband, who owns a popular temperance seaside resort, gave the association grounds and an auditorium that cost two-thousand-five-hundred dollars. The first meeting of the new Chautauqua Assembly of Oregon was held in August, 1891. Mrs. Kinney has liberally supported the Chautauqua movement in Oregon, having contributed about six-thousand dollars to the work. She retains her interest in that and all other reform work.

KIPP, Mrs. Josephine, author, born in Brooklyn, NY, 27th March, 1845. Her father, Ten Eyck Sutphen, for many years a prominent New York merchant, was descended from an old Dutch family of colonial times, who originally came from the city of Zutphen, where traditions of the "Counts of Zutphen" still exist. In Mrs. Kipp's early childhood she developed a passion for music, which led her to devote to the art every moment that could be spared from more prosaic studies. After spending several years in a French school, and afterward attending Packer

Institute, Brooklyn NY, at sixteen years of age she removed with her parents to New York City, where she was graduated from Rutgers' College, having had also the advantage of Prof. Samuel Jackson's training in music. In October, 1870, she became the wife of Rev. P. E. Kipp, of Passaic, NJ. The first five years of their married life were spent in Fishkill, NY, where their two children were born. Surrounded by parishioners and busied with domestic cares and the duties which fill the life of a minister's wife, Mrs. Kipp accomplished little literary work. Ill health prevented all effort for a time, and, her husband's strength also failing, the family spent a winter in Bermuda. Recuperated by their sojourn there, husband and wife returned to work in Brooklyn, NY, but after three years of service they were compelled to seek rest and strength in European travel. They next settled in Schenectady, NY, whence they removed in 1887 to their present home in Cleveland, OH. During these frequent periods of enforced idleness Mrs. Kipp's pen was her great resource. A musical book by her remains incomplete, on account of a serious ocular trouble. Many of her articles have appeared in religious journals and in magazines of the day. When health has permitted, Mrs. Kipp has given most entertaining and instructive parlor lectures upon historical subjects.

KIRK, Mrs. Ellen Olney, novelist, born in Southington, CT, 6th November, 1842. Her maiden name was Ellen Warner Olney. She removed with her parents a few years after her birth to Stratford-on-the-Sound, an old Connecticut town. Her father, Jesse Olney, who for some time held the office of State comptroller, was widely known as the author of a number of text-books, especially of a "Geography and Atlas," published in 1828, which passed through nearly a hundred editions and was long a standard work in American schools. Her mother is a sister of the late A. S. Barnes, the New York publisher. Mrs. Kirk had from her childhood a passionate love for literature, and in writing she obeyed an imperative instinct, but with little desire for an audience, she made no precocious attempts to reach the public, and it was not until after the death of her father, in 1872, that she took

up systematic literary work, and her first published novel was "Love in Idleness," which appeared as a serial in "Lippincott's Magazine," during the summer of 1876. Another and more thoughtful novel, "Through Winding Ways," followed in the same periodical. In 1879 Miss Olney became the wife of John Foster Kirk, author of the "History of Charles the Bold," and at that time editor of "Lippincott's Magazine." Since her first appearance in print, writing has been with her a daily and regular work. She is an industrious worker. Since her marriage she has resided in Germantown, a suburb of Philadelphia. Two of her books have their scenes laid in that region, "Sons and Daughters" (Boston, 1887), with its inimitable Shakespeare Club and its picture of the pleasures and perplexities of youth, and "A Midsummer Madness" (Boston, 1884). The full expression of Mrs. Kirk's talent is to be looked for in her novels of New York life, which not only deal with the motives which actuate men and women of that town, but offer free play for her clear and accurate characterization, her humor and her brilliant comedy. The first of these was "A Lesson in Love" (Boston, 1881). "The Story of Margaret Kent" (Boston, 1886) is now in its fortieth edition. This was an adaptation to a different phase of life of the situation in "Better Times," one of Mrs. Kirk's early tales, which gives its title to the volume of short stories published in 1887. Her other novels are "Queen Money" (Boston, 1888), "A Daughter of Eve" (Boston, 1889), "Walfred" (Boston, 1890) "Narden's Choosing" (Philadelphia, 1891), and "Cyphers" (Boston, 1891).

KNAPP, Mrs. Phœbe Palmer, musician and author, born in New York, NY, 8th March, 1839. She is the daughter of Dr. Walter C. and Phœbe Palmer, of New York City. Her mother was eminent as a religious author and teacher. It has been estimated that forty-thousand souls were converted through their labors. Their home was a home of prayer and song. Mrs. Knapp early showed musical ability, both in singing and in composition. She became the wife of Joseph F. Knapp in 1855. In her new relation opportunity was furnished for the development of her gifts. Her husband was the superintendent of South Second Street Methodist Episcopal Sunday-school, and later of the St. John's Methodist Episcopal Sunday-school, of Brooklyn, NY. Under their labors those schools became famous. She wrote much of the music sung by the schools. Her first book was entitled "Notes of Joy" (New York, 1869). It contained one-hundred original pieces written by Mrs. Knapp, and had a wide circulation and great popularity. She is also the author of the cantata, "The Prince of Peace," and many popular songs. Her organ is her favorite companion. She writes music, not as a profession, but as an inspiration.

KNOWLES, Miss Ella L., lawyer, born in New Hampshire, in 1870. She received a collegiate education and was graduated in Bates College, Lewiston, ME. In her school-days she was noted for her elocutionary powers, and she often gave dramatic entertainments and acted in amateur theatrical organizations. She received her degree of A.M. in June, 1888, from Bates College, and after hesitating between school-teaching and law as a profession, she decided to study law. She at once entered the office of Judge Burnharn, of Manchester, NH. In 1889 she went to Iowa, where she taught classes in French and German in a seminary for a short time. She next went to Salt Lake City, UT, where she took a position as teacher. While there, she received an offer of a larger salary to return to the Iowa University, in which she had taught. She had seen enough of the Rocky Mountains and of the people of that region to make her willing to remain in the West. She went to Helena, MT, and there was invited to take a position as teacher in the central school. Not long after reaching Helena, she decided to finish her law course, and she entered a law office. During her first year in Helena she served as secretary of a lumber company. While studying law she acted as collector, and then took up attachment and criminal cases, and she received several divorce cases, which she handed over to her principal, Mr. Kinsley. In 1889 she was admitted to practice before the Supreme Court of Montana. She at once formed a law partnership with Mr. Kinsley, and they are doing a large business. On 18th April,

1890, she was admitted to practice before the District Court of the United States, and on 28th April, of the same year, she received credentials that enabled her to practice before the Circuit Court of the United States. In 1888 she was appointed a notary public by Governor Leslie, and she was the first woman to hold such an office in Montana. In 1892 she was nominated for Attorney General of Montana by the Alliance party. She is a woman of tact, courage, enterprise and perseverance. Her profession yields her a good income. Her home is in Helena.

KNOX, Mrs. Adeline Trafton, author, born in Saccarappa, ME, 8th February, 1845. She is the daughter of Rev. Mark Trafton, a talented and well-known Methodist clergyman of New England. Much of her life was passed in the towns and cities of New England. She lived two years in Albany, NY, where her father held a pastorate at the beginning of the Civil War, and two years in Washington, DC, while he was serving his term as a member of the House of Representatives. During this latter period Miss Trafton was for a while a pupil in the Wesleyan Female College, in Wilmington, Del. In 1868 she began her literary career by publishing a few stories and sketches, under a fictitious name in the Springfield, MA, "Republican." These were so well received that, in 1872 after spending six months in Europe, she gathered a series of foreign letters, which had appeared in the same paper, into a book under the title of "An American Girl Abroad" (Boston, 1872). This was a success. She next tried a novelette, "Katherine Earle" (Boston, 1874), having run as a serial through "Scribner's Monthly." She had already contributed a number of striking short stories to the columns of that magazine. A year or two later followed a more ambitious novel, "His Inheritance" (Boston, 1878), which also ran as a serial through "Scribner's Monthly." Subsequently ill health compelled her to lay aside her pen, which she has never resumed, except to bring out, through the columns of the "Christian Union," in 1889, a novelette treating of social questions, which was afterward republished in book-form under the title of "Dorothy's Experience." In 1889 Miss Trafton became the wife of Samuel Knox Jr., a lawyer, of St. Louis, MO, son of Hon. Samuel Knox, a distinguished advocate of that city. Her residence is divided between New England and the West.

KNOX, Mrs. Janette Hill, temperance reformer, born in Londonderry, VT, 24th January, 1845. She is the daughter of Rev. Lewis Hill, of the Vermont Conference of the Methodist Episcopal Church. Her mother's maiden name was Olive Marsh. The daughter was reared with that care and judicious instruction characteristic of the quiet New England clerical home. Her earlier education was received in the schools of the various towns to which her father's itinerant assignments took the family, together with two years of seminary life, when she was graduated as valedictorian of her class from Montpelier Seminary, in 1869. In 1871 she became the wife of Rev. M. V. B. Knox, and in 1873, after the death of their only child, they removed to Kansas. There she pursued additional studies, taking the degree of A.B., from Baker University, and together with her husband was four years on the faculty of that college. She went to Boston University in 1877 for special studies in her department of English literature and modern languages, and received the degree of A.M., with her husband, from the School of All Sciences in 1879. Their duties then took them to the New Hampshire Conference of the Methodist Episcopal Church, where they have since been at work. In 1881 she was elected president of the State Woman's Christian Temperance Union. The responsibilities connected with that office drew her out from the quieter duties of home to perform those demanded by her new work. Her executive ability has been developed during the years since her election to the office. Her manner of presiding in the numerous meetings of various kinds, especially in the annual conventions, elicits hearty commendation. The steady and successful growth of the Woman's Christian Temperance Union of New Hampshire during these years, and the high position the New Hampshire Union takes, attest her success. Her re-election year by year has been practically unanimous. She has attended every

one of the national conventions since taking the State presidency. In addition to keeping house and heartily aiding her husband in the church work, she fills the duties of the State presidency, and lectures before temperance gatherings, missionary meetings in Chautauqua Assemblies, teachers' conventions and elsewhere. She also exercises her literary talents in writing for the press.

KOLLOCK, Miss Florence E., Universalist minister, born in Waukesha, WI, 19th January, 1848. Her father was William E. Kollock, and her mother's maiden name was Ann Margaret Hunter, a native of England. Miss Kollock received her collegiate education in the Wisconsin State University, and her theological training in St. Lawrence University, Canton, NY. In the former institution she was by her fellow-students considered a girl of much natural brightness and originality, while great earnestness characterized her actions. She was credited most for possessing attributes of cheerfulness, amiability, affection and perseverance. None thought of her in connection with a special calling or profession. She was from the first "pure womanly," as she is to-day. With a man's commanding forces she has all the distinctly feminine graces. Her first settlement, in 1875, was in Waverly, IA, a missionary point. After getting the work well started there she located in Blue Island, IL, and in conjunction took another missionary field in charge, Englewood, IL. The work grew so rapidly in the latter place that in 1879 she removed there and has remained ever since. Her first congregation in Englewood numbered fifteen, who met in Masonic Hall. Soon a church was built, which was outgrown as the years went on, and in 1889 the present large and beautiful church was erected. Now this, too, is inadequate to the demands made upon it, and plans have been proposed for increasing the seating capacity. Miss Kollock's ability as an organizer is felt everywhere, in the flourishing Sunday school, numbering over three-hundred, which ranks high in regular attendance and enthusiasm, and in the various other branches of church work, which is reduced to a system. In all her undertakings she has been remarkably successful. To her fine intellectual qualities and her deep spiritual insight is added a personal magnetism which greatly increases her power. She is strong, tender and brave always in standing for the right, however unpopular it may be. In her preaching and work she is practical and humanitarian. In 1885, when a vacation of three or four months was given to Miss Kollock, she spent the most of it in founding a church in Pasadena, CA, which is now the strongest Universalist Church on the Pacific Coast. In all reformatory and educational matters she is greatly interested. The woman suffrage movement, the temperance cause and the free kindergarten work have all been helped by her.

KROUT, Miss Mary H., poet, author, educator and journalist, born in Crawfordsville, IN, 3rd November, 1852. She was reared and educated there amid surroundings calculated to develop her gifts and fit her for the literary career which she entered upon in childhood. Her family for generations have been people of ability. Her maternal grandfather was for many years the State geologist of Indiana and professor of natural science in Butler University. Her mother inherited his talent in a marked degree. Her father is a man of the broadest culture. Her first verses were written when she was eight years old, and her first published verses appeared in the Crawfordsville "Journal," two years later. "Little Brown Hands," by the authorship of which she is best known, was written at the age of fifteen, and was accepted by "Our Young Folks," while Miss Larcom was its editor. The poem was written in the summer of 1867, during an interval snatched from exacting household duties, every member of the family but herself being ill. Miss Krout taught in the public schools of Crawfordsville for eight years, devoting her time outside of school to her literary work. She went to Indianapolis to accept a position in the schools there, in the fall of 1883. She resigned at the expiration of five months to take an editorial position on the Crawfordsville "Journal," which she held for three years. She was subsequently connected with the Peoria "Saturday Evening Call," the "Interior," the Chicago "Journal" and the Terre Haute "Express." In con-

nection with her regular editorial duties she did special work for magazines and syndicates. In April, 1888, she became connected with the Chicago "Inter-Ocean" and early in July was sent to Indianapolis as the political correspondent and confidential representative of that paper. She now holds an editorial position on that journal, having charge of a department known as the "Woman's Kingdom." She has a good deal of artistic ability and is a good musician.

KURT, Miss Katherine, homeopathic physician, born in Wooster, Wayne county, OH, 19th December, 1852. She is the eighth of a family of twelve children, and the first born on American soil. Her father and mother were natives of Switzerland. The father was a weaver and found it hard to keep so large a family. Upon the death of the mother, when Katherine was eight years of age, all the children but one or two of the older ones were placed in the homes of friends. The father was opposed to having any of the children legally adopted by his friends, but he placed Katherine in a family where, for a number of years, she had a home, with the privilege of attending school a few months in each year, and there was laid the foundation of the structure which, as she grew older, developed her native strength of mind. She performed the duties of her station, treading unmurmuringly the appointed way of life. When about nineteen years old, she began to teach in the public schools of her native county, and she saved enough to allow her to enter an academy, that she might better prepare herself for teaching, which, at that time, was her only aim. While in the academy in Lodi, OH, the idea of being a physician was first suggested to her, and from that time on she worked, studying and teaching, with a definite aim in view. In the spring of 1877 she entered Buchtel College, Akron, OH, as a special student. There she remained about three years, working her own way, the third year being an assistant teacher in the preparatory department. During the latter part of her course in Buchtel College, she also began the study of medicine under the preceptorship of a physician in Akron, and in the fall of 1880 she entered the Hahnemann Medical College of

Chicago, from which institution she was graduated on 23rd February, 1882, ranked among the first of a class of one- hundred-one members, having spent one term as assistant in the Chicago Surgical Institute. She then went to Akron, OH, and opened an office in June, 1882. In less than ten years she has secured an established, lucrative practice, has freed herself from all debts and has some paying investments. In religion Dr. Kurt is a Universalist. She is active in church work and for a number of years has been a faithful and earnest teacher in Sunday-school. Her work has been on the side of philanthropic and reformatory movements. She is an advocate for the higher education of woman and a firm believer in suffrage for woman. Politically she sympathizes with the Prohibition party. For several years she has been the State superintendent of heredity in the Ohio Woman's Christian Temperance Union.

LA FETRA, Mrs. Sarah Doan, temperance worker, born in Sabina, OH, 11th June, 1843. She is the fourth daughter of Rev. Timothy and Mary Ann Custis Doan. Her mother was of the famous Virginia Custis family. In the formative period of life and character religious truths made a deep and lasting impression on her plastic mind, and at sixteen she was converted and became a member of the Methodist Episcopal Church. She and her entire family are now members of the Metropolitan Methodist Episcopal Church of Washington. When a girl, Mrs. La Fetra improved the opportunities for study in the public schools where she resided, and prepared herself for teaching in the normal school of Professor Holbrook in Lebanon, OH. She taught in a graded school in Fayette county, OH, for several years before she became the wife of George H. La Fetra, of Warren county, OH, in 1867. Mr. La Fetra had spent three years in the army, in the 39th Ohio Volunteers, and afterward accepted a position under his cousin, Hon. James Harlan, then Secretary of the Interior Department. Three sons were born to Mr. and Mrs. La Fetra. The youngest died in infancy; the other two are young men of lofty Christian character, and both are prohibitionists and anti-tobacconists. Mrs. La Fetra was elected president of the Woman's Chris-

tian Temperance Union of the District of Columbia in October, 1885, having been a member of the union since its origin, in 1876. Her mother and sister were among the leaders of the Ohio crusade. Under her leadership the Washington auxiliary has grown to be a recognized power. The work of the union is far-reaching in its influences and embraces various fields of Christian endeavor. It has one home under its patronage, the "Hope and Help Mission," for poor unfortunate women, inebriates, opium-eaters and incapables of all conditions. The society is on a safe financial basis and has an executive committee composed of over thirty leading women of the various denominations. Mrs. La Fetra is a practical business woman and has fought the rum traffic in a sure and substantial way, by successfully managing a temperance hotel and café in the very heart of the city of Washington for many years. Her efficient management of that house involves a principle and is a practical demonstration that liquors are not necessary to make a hotel successful, financially and otherwise. She is a woman suffragist, although not identified with the organization.

LA FOLLETTE, Mrs. Belle Case, social leader, born in Summit, Juneau county, WI, 21st April, 1859. Her father's name was Anson Case. Her mother's maiden name was Mary Nesbitt. Belle Case spent her childhood in Baraboo, WI. She was educated in the

public schools and in the State University, from which she was graduated in 1879. She was conspicuously bright, and won the Lewis prize for the best commencement oration. Her perfect health was proved by the fact that she attended school and was a close student for eight consecutive years, including her university course, without losing a recitation. She became the wife in 1881 of her classmate, Robert M. La Follette, a lawyer. She became interested in his work, which led to her enter the Wisconsin Law School in 1883, and from which she was graduated in 1885. She was the first woman to receive a diploma from that institution. During the same year Mr. La Follette was elected to Congress, which necessitated their removal to Washington, and Mrs. La Follette has done no practical professional work. In meeting the social obligations incident to her husband's official position, held for six years, she found no time for anything else. While not the most profitable life imaginable, Mrs. La Follette yet found it far from vain or meaningless. She saw women greet one another in drawing-rooms in much the same spirit as men meet in the Senate Chamber and House of Representatives, and her Washington experience resulted in enlarged views touching the opportunities and possibilities offered women, called into the official circle from all parts of the United States, not only for broad social development, but also for wholesome and effective, though indirect, influences upon the life and thought of the nation. On the banks of Lake Monona, in Madison, WI, the present home of Mrs. La Follette is delightfully located. She has proved herself a most worthy and inspiring sharer of the honors, trials and responsibilities of her distinguished husband's professional and political life. Devoted to him and to the education of their young daughter, Flora, she is today not only one of the most prominent, but one of the most quietly contented, of Wisconsin's progressive women.

LA GRANGE, Miss Magdalene Isadora, poet, born in Gulderland, NY, 17th September, 1864, which is now her home. Her family is of Huguenot origin. The ancestral home, "Elmwood," has been in the possession of the family for over two-hundred years. Miss La Grange was educated in the Albany Female College, Albany, NY. She studied for three years with Prof. William P. Morgan. She began at an early age to write prose articles for the press. Some of her early poems were published and met such favor that she was led to make a study of poetical composition. Her songs are of the plaintive kind, religious and subjective in tone. She has issued one volume, "Songs of the Helderberg" (1892).

LAMB, Mrs. Martha Joanna, historian, born in Plainfield, MA, 13th August, 1829 was long a resident of New York City, where she earned her reputation of the leading woman historian of the nineteenth century, and will long be remembered as a middle-aged woman, a good talker and a most industrious worker in the historic and literary field. Recognition of her genius was prompt and full. She was elected to honorary membership in twenty-seven historical and learned societies in this country and Europe, and a life-member of the American Historical Association and a fellow of the Clarendon Historical Association of Edinburgh, Scotland. She held her precedence by the high character and importance of the subjects to which her abilities were devoted. Her position as editor of the "Magazine of American History" was one of great responsibility, which she filled acceptably for eleven consecutive years. The name this periodical has won, of being the best distinctively historical magazine in the world, and its growth while Mrs. Lamb occupied the editorial chair, tell very forcibly that she not only loved facts, but knew perfectly well how to use them. Her father was Arvin Nash, and her mother, Lucinda Vinton, of Huguenot descent. Mrs. Lamb was the granddaughter of Jacob Nash, a Revolutionary soldier, of an old English family of whom was the Rev. Treadway Nash, D.D., the historian, and his wife, Joanna Reade, (of the same family as Charles Reade) whose ancestors came to America in the Mayflower. She comes of such stock as she describes in her article, "Historic Homes on Golden Hills." Much of her early life was spent in Goshen, MA, and part of her school life in Northampton and Easthampton. She was a bright, healthy, animated girl, full of energy and with faith in her own ability to perform any feat. She developed precocious talents at an early age, and wrote poetry and stories before she was ten years old. She was in her happiest mood when among the books of her father's library, and eagerly devoured all the historical works she found there, and scandalized her family and amused her friends by innocently borrowing precious volumes from the neighbors. A distinguished teacher developed her taste for mathematics, in which she became an enthusiast, and at one time for a brief period, occupied the important chair of mathematics in a polytechnic institute, and, was invited to revise and edit a mathematical work for the higher classes in polytechnic schools. She became the wife, in 1852, of Charles A. Lamb and resided in Chicago, IL, from 1857 to 1866, where she was prominent in many notable charities. She was one of the founders of two that are still in existence. In 1863 she was made secretary of the first sanitary fair in the country, the success of which is said to have been largely due to her executive ability, and she was prominently concerned in the second sanitary fair, held in Chicago at the close of the war. After 1866 she resided in New York City and devoted herself to historical and literary productions. Her fine mathematical training enabled her, in 1879, to prepare for Harpers the notable paper translating to unlearned readers the mysteries and work of the Coast Survey. Many of Mrs. Lamb's magazine articles are sufficiently important and elaborate to form separate volumes. Her distinguishing work, which occupied fifteen years of continuous and skillful labor in its preparation, is the "History of the City of New York," in two octavo volumes (New York, 1876–1881), pronounced by competent authorities the best history ever written of any great city in the world. Mrs. Lamb also wrote and published "The Play School Studies," 4 vols. (Boston, 1869) ; "Aunt Mattie's Library," 4 vols. (Boston, 1871); "Spicy," a novel that chronicled the great Chicago fire in imperishable colors, (New York, 1873); "Lyme, A Chapter of American Genealogy," "Newark," a complete sketch of that city, and the "Tombs of Old Trinity," ("Harper's Magazine," 1876); "State and Society in Washington," ("Harper's Magazine," 1878); "The Coast Survey," ("Harper's Magazine," 1879); "The Homes of America" (New York, 1879); "Memorial of Dr. J. D. Russ," the philanthropist, (New York, 1880); "The Christmas Owl" (New York, 1881); "The Christmas Basket" (New York, 1882); "Snow and Sunshine" (New York, 1882); "The American Life Saving Service," ("Harper's Magazine," 1882); "Historical Sketch of New York," for tenth census, (1883); "Wall Street in History" (New York, 1883); "Unsuccessful Candidates for the Presidency of the Nation," "The Van Rensselaer Manor" ("Magazine of American History," 1884); "The Framers of the Constitution," "The Manor of Gardiner's Island," "Sketch of Major-General John A. Dix" ("Magazine of American History," 1885); "The Van Cortlandt Manor House," "Historic Homes in Lafayette Place," "The Founder, Presidents and Homes of the New York Historical Society" ("Magazine of American History," 1886); "The

Historic Homes of our Presidents," "Historic Homes on Golden Hills," "The Manor of Shelter Island" ("Magazine of American History," 1887); "Foundation of Civil Government beyond the Ohio River, 1788–1888," "The Inauguration of Washington in 1789," written by special request of the New York Historical Society ("Magazine of American History," 1888); "Historic Homes and Landmarks in New York," three papers, "The Story of the Washington Centennial" ("Magazine of American History," 1889); "America's Congress of Historical Scholars," "Our South American Neighbors," "American Outgrowths of Continental Europe," "The Golden Age of Colonial New York" ("Magazine of American History," 1890); "Formative Influences," ("The Forum," 1890); "William H. Seward, a Great Public Character," "Glimpses of the Railroad in History," "The Royal Society of Canada," "Some Interesting Facts about Electricity," "A Group of Columbus Portraits," "Judge Charles Johnson McCurdy" ("Magazine of American History," 1891); "The Walters Collection of Art Treasures," "Progression of Steam Navigation, 1807–1892," ("Magazine of American History." 1892). Aside from these prominent papers mentioned, Mrs. Lamb has written upwards of two hundred historic articles, essays and short stories for weekly and monthly periodicals. Her greatest achievement, however, was her "History of the City of New York," a work that has become a standard for all time. Mrs. Lamb died in New York City, 3d January, 1893.

LAMSON, Miss Lucy Stedman, business woman and educator, born in Albany, NY, 19th June, 1857. Her father, Homer B. Lamson, was a lawyer of note, who died in 1876. Her mother, Caroline Francis Brayton Lamson, was a woman of culture and died at an early age, leaving three children, Lucy S., Hattie B. and William Ford. Miss Lamson was educated in a private school and in the public schools of Albany. She was a student of the Albany high school for one year and attended the Adams Collegiate Institute, Adams, NY, four years, where she was graduated in 1874. Since that time she has taught in the public schools of Adams, Cape Vincent,

Albany and Brooklyn, NY, and Tacoma, Wash. In 1886 she was graduated from the State Normal School in Albany, NY, and in the following year she studied with special teachers in New York City. In September, 1888, she accepted a position in the Annie Wright Seminary, Tacoma, Wash. During 1888 and 1889 much excitement prevailed in regard to land speculations, and Miss Lamson, not being in possession of funds, borrowed them and purchased city lots, which she sold at a profit. In March, 1889, she filed a timber claim and a pre-emption in Skamania county, Wash., and in June, in the beginning of the summer vacation, she moved her household goods to her pre-emption, and, accompanied by a young Norwegian woman, commenced the six months' residence required by the government to obtain the title to the land. The claim was situated nine miles above Cape Horn, Washougal river, a branch of the Columbia. Having complied with the law and gained possession of the timber claim and pre-emption, Miss Lamson sold both at an advantage and invested the proceeds in real estate. In September, 1890, she accepted a position in the Tacoma high school. She has charge of one-hundred sixty pupils in vocal music, elocution and physical culture, and instructs the city teachers, one-hundred-ten in all, in music and gymnastics. In the fall of 1890 she built a small house in the northern part of the town, which she makes her home.

LANGE, Mrs. Mary T., journalist born in Boston, MA, 25th September, 1848. Her maiden name was Nash. She is of French-Irish descent on the maternal side and Puritan on the paternal. She lost her mother at the age of fourteen and two years later her father was killed in the battle of Winchester, in Virginia. Her early education was obtained in the public schools, but, later, she attended the school of Dr. Arnold, in Boston, and it was through that distinguished French scholar that she was induced to make her first venture in literature. Her first publication was a short story entitled "Uncle Ben's Court-ship," which appeared in the Boston "Wide World," in 1865. A year later, in company with her brother and sister, she sailed for Europe, for the purpose of studying the languages and music, remaining three years in Italy for the latter purpose. After five years study and travel from France to Egypt, she found herself in Ems, the famous watering-place, when war was declared with France. She immediately proceeded to Paris, to join her brother who was attending school in that city, and remained with him through that memorable siege, witnessing all the horrors of the Commune. During that time, she was not idle, but, acted as correspondent for the New York "Herald," and her letters attracted widespread attention. The siege lasted five months and during that time Miss Nash and her young brother suffered many privations. While the Palace of the Tuilleries was burning, she secured many private, imperial documents, being allowed to pass the Commune Guards, by reason of a red cloak which she constantly wore during the Commune and which they would salute, saying: "Passez Citoyenne!" At that time she contracted a romantic and unhappy marriage, but was free in less than a year. She returned, in 1877, to America, where she became the wife, in 1878, of H. Julius Lange the son of the distinguished lawyer, Ludwig Lange, of Hanover, Germany. Four children were born of this union, two of whom are living. That marriage was a happy one and the great grief of Mrs. Lange's life was the death of her husband, which occurred recently after a long period of suffering. Mrs. Lange is now engaged in writing her reminiscences of the siege of Paris. She made the acquaintance of many distinguished people during her long stay abroad, among whom were the Countess Rapp, Countess Ratazzi, Gambetta, Victor Hugo, Verdinois, the poet-journalist, and Alexander Dumas, who dedicated to her a special autograph-poem.

LANGWORTHY, Mrs. Elizabeth, public benefactor, born in Orleans county, NY, 22nd October, 1837. At twelve years of age she removed with her parents to the West. Her father was of Holland descent and one of the heirs to the Trinity Church property in New York. Her mother was of French descent. Her grandfather was a well-known soldier of the Revolutionary War. She received a liberal education, which was completed in Hamlin University, Red Wing, MN. From childhood she showed a love for the best in literature and art. In 1858 she became the wife of Stephen C. Langworthy, of Dubuque, IA, an influential citizen, whose family was among the early pioneers. In 1861 Mr. and Mrs. Langworthy settled in Monticello, IA, where for fifteen years she divided her time between family duties and public work. There she was instrumental in founding a fine public library, and was an efficient leader in sanitary improvements. They removed to Seward, NE, in 1876, and there she still maintains her interest in public affairs. She was for years a member of the school board and superintendent of the art department in State fairs. She has served as president of many influential societies for improvement, local and foreign, and is at present president of the Seward History and Art Club. She is a member of the Board of Associated Charities of Nebraska. She is a member of the Board of Lady Managers of the World's Columbian Exposition. It was at her suggestion Mrs. Potter Palmer granted to the women of Nebraska the honor of contributing the hammer with which she drove the last nail in the Woman's Building. To her labors is due the raising of the fund for that purpose. She was an observant visitor to the Centennials in Philadelphia and New Orleans, and therefore was better qualified for acting as one of the Board of Managers for 1893. Mrs. Langworthy has reared six children, four sons and two daughters. One of the daughters died recently.

LANKTON, Mrs. Freeda M., physician, born in Oriskany, NY, 10th August, 1852. She grew to womanhood in Rome, NY. Her father was a Baptist clergyman of ability. Her mother was a woman of mental and spiritual strength. Being a delicate child, she received mostly private instruction. Much of her time was spent in her father's study, with the companionship of his extensive library or as a listener to scientific and religious discussions. Her early inclinations foretold her mission in life. As a child she was especially fond of administering to cats, dogs and dolls, indiscriminately, the medicines of her compounding and took delight in nursing the sick and in reading on such subjects. When fifteen years of age, an inflammation of the optic nerve, caused by over-

study and night-reading, forced her into complete rest. Grief for her mother's death aggravated the inflammation, and for three years she was unable to study. Her college course was relinquished, and she depended entirely for information upon the reading of others. As her vision improved, she persevered in study and again visited the sick. She was married in 1870. Later, overwork and anxiety for others reduced her to an invalid's life for three years. During that time medical study was her amusement, and the old longing developed into a purpose, encouraged by her husband, to devote her life to the relief of suffering. She had charge, for some time, of the "Open Door," a home for fallen women, in Omaha, NE. She is one of the King's Daughters, and her purpose is usefulness. She now resides in Omaha.

LANZA, Marquise Clara, author, born in Fort Riley, a military post in Kansas, where her father, Dr. W. A. Hammond, the celebrated physician and specialist, then in the service of the government, was stationed, 12th February, 1858. Her father removed to New York City when she was seven years old, and she has lived in that city ever since, with the exception of several protracted visits to Europe. She was educated in a French school in New York, and, after finishing her course there, studied in Paris and Dresden. Her training and reading cover a wide range. In 1877 she became the wife of the Marquis de Lanza, of Palermo, Sicily. Her family consists of three sons. Although she has written from her early girlhood, her literary career did not begin until her first novel, "Mr. Perkins' Daughter," was published in 1884. That was followed by "A Righteous Apostate" (1886), and by a collection of short stories, "Tales of Eccentric Life" (1887), "Basil Morton's Transgression" (1890), "A Modern Marriage" (1891), and "A Golden Pilgrimage" (1892). She has written much for the magazines, and at one time occupied herself exclusively with journalism. She is an accomplished mandolinist, and occasionally performs in charitable entertainments. She is the center of a circle of clever people in New York City.

LARCOM, Miss Lucy, poet and author, born in Beverly, MA, in 1826. Her father was a sea captain, who died while she was a child, and her mother, taking with her this daughter and two or three others of her younger children, removed to

Lowell, MA. The year 1835 found Lucy, a girl of about ten years, in one of the Lowell grammar schools, where her education went on until it became necessary for her to earn her living, which she began to do very early as an operative in a cotton factory. In her "Idyl of Work" and also in "A New England Girlhood" Miss Larcom has described her early life. In the "Idyl" the mill life of forty or fifty years ago is portrayed, and, in following the career of some of those bright spirits, watching their success in their varied pathways through life, it is very pleasant to know that the culture, the self-sacrifice and the effort begun in that hard school have developed characters so noble and prepared them so well for their appointed life-work. Her biographer writes: "My first recollection of Miss Larcom is as a precocious writer of verse in the Lowell 'Casket,' and that the editor in his notice of them said 'they were written under the inspiration of the nurses 'a misprint, of course, for muses; although, as the author was only ten or twelve years old at that time, the mistake was not so very far wrong. That was not Miss Larcom's first attempt at verse-making, for she began to write while a child of seven in the attic of her early home in Beverly." Miss Larcom's first work as a Lowell operative was in a spinning-room, doffing and replacing the bobbins, after which she tended a spinning-frame and then a dressing-frame, beside pleasant windows looking toward the river. Later she was employed in a "cloth-room," a more agreeable working-place, on account of its fewer hours of confinement, its cleanliness and the absence of machinery. The last two years of her Lowell life, which covered in all a period of about ten years, were spent in that room, not in measuring cloth, but as book-keeper, recording the number of pieces and bales. There she pursued her studies in intervals of leisure. Some text-books in mathematics, grammar, English or German literature usually lay open on her desk, awaiting a spare moment. The Lowell "Offering," a magazine "Whose editors and contributors were "female operatives in the Lowell Mills," was published in 1842, and soon after Miss Larcom became one of its corps of writers. One of her first poems was entitled "The River," and many of her verses and

essays both grave and gay, may be found in its bound volumes. Some of those Lowell "Offering" essays appeared afterward in a little volume called "Similitudes." That was her first published work. In time Lucy Larcom's name found an honored place among the women poets of America. Latterly her writings assumed a deeply religious tone, in which the faith of her whole life found complete expression. Among her earlier and best-known poems are "Hannah Binding Shoes," and "The Rose Enthroned," Miss Larcom's earliest contribution to the "Atlantic Monthly," when the poet Lowell was its editor, a poem that in the absence of signature was attributed to Emerson by one reviewer; also "A Loyal Woman's No," which is a patriotic lyric and attracted considerable attention during the Civil War. It is such poems as those, with her "Childhood Songs," which will give the name of Lucy Larcom high rank. During much of her earlier life Miss Larcom was teacher in some of the principal young women's seminaries of her native State. While "Our Young Folks" was published, she was connected with it, part of the time as associate, and part of the time as leading editor. She wrote at length of her own youthful working-days in Lowell in an article published in the "Atlantic Monthly," about 1881, entitled "Among Lowell Mill Girls." In her late years she turned her attention more to prose writing. "A New England Girlhood" described the first twenty to twenty-five years of her own life. Miss Larcom was always inclined to write on religious themes, and made two volumes of compilations from the world's great religious thinkers, "Breathings of the Better Life" (Boston, 1866) and Beckonings" (Boston, 1886). Her last two books, "As it is in Heaven" (Boston, 1891) and "The Unseen Friend" (Boston, 1892), embodied much of her own thought on matters concerning the spiritual life. She died in Boston, MA, 17th April, 1893.

LARRABEE, Mrs. Anna Matilda, social leader, born in Ledyard, CT, 13th August, 1842. She was the oldest child of Gustavus Adolphus Appelman and Prudence Anna Appelman. Her father's family is of German lineage. Her grandfather, John Frederick Appelman, was the son of a Lutheran minister stationed in Wolgast, near the city of Stettin. He arrived in the United States in 1805, and shortly afterward took up his residence in Mystic, CT, engaging in the fishing business and ship-rigging. His son, Gustavus, early followed the sea, and was, while still a very young man, placed in command of a whaler, upon which he made a number of long and successful voyages. Mrs. Appelman, the mother of Mrs. Larrabee, was the daughter of Erastus and Nancy Williams, of Ledyard, CT. Mr. Williams was in succession judge of New London county and member of both houses of the legislature in his native State. Captain Appelman, tired of a sailor's life, in 1854 abandoned the sea and removed with his family to the West to engage in farming. He settled on a farm near the village of Clermont, IA. The educational facilities which the new community offered to the children were rather meager, but home tuition supplemented the curriculum of the village school. At the age of fourteen years Anna was sent East to enter the academy in Mystic, CT. She remained in that institution two years, pursuing her studies with unusual vigor. After her return to Clermont, she was placed in charge of the village school, which had an enrollment of over seventy pupils, but the young teacher proved equal to her task. On 12th September, 1861, she became the wife of William Larrabee. Their family numbers three sons and four daughters. Mrs. Larrabee is the constant companion of her husband, sharing his reading at the fireside and accompanying him in his travels and political campaigns. There can be no doubt that to her fascinating manners, pleasant address and nice perception is due much of Governor Larrabee's popularity and political success. Her home, which, since her marriage, has been continually in Clermont, is a temple of hospitality. While Mrs. Larrabee is averse to frivolous pleasures, she possesses all the graces of a true hostess and leader in refined society. She forms positive opinions upon all questions agitating the public mind, but is always a lenient critic and a merciful judge. Though not a member of any religious denomination, she is deeply religious in her nature. She is interested in Sunday-school and temperance work, yet her innate love of humanity expends itself chiefly in those words of kindness and deeds of charity which shun public applause and find their reward solely in an approving conscience.

LATHRAP, Mrs. Mary Torrans, poet, preacher and temperance reformer, born on a farm near Jackson, MI, in April, 1838. Her maiden name was Mary Torrans. Her parents were Scotch Irish Presbyterians. Miss Torrans' childhood was passed in Marshall, MI, where she was educated in the public schools. She was a literary child, and at the age of fourteen contributed to local papers under the pen-name "Lena." She was converted in her tenth year, but did not join the church until she was nearly eighteen years old. From 1862 to 1864 she taught in the Detroit public schools. In 1864 she became the wife of C. C. Lathrap, then assistant surgeon of the Ninth Michigan Cavalry. In 1865 they removed to Jackson, MI, where they now reside. Mrs. Lathrap there joined the Methodist Episcopal Church, of which her husband was a member, and in the classroom began first to exercise her gifts of speech in the services. In 1871 she was licensed to preach the gospel and began in the Congregational church in Michigan Center. Her sermons aroused the people, and for years she labored as an evangelist, many thousands being converted by her ministry. She took an active part in the Woman's crusade, was one of the founders of the Woman's Christian Temperance Union, and has been president of the State union of Michigan since 1882. Her work has been largely devoted to that organization for the past eight years. She has labored in various States and was a strong helper in securing the scientific-instruction law, and in the Michigan, Nebraska and Dakota amendment campaigns. In 1878 she secured the passage of a bill in the Michigan legislature appropriating thirty-thousand dollars for the establishment of the Girls' Industrial Home, a reformatory school, located in Adrian. In 1890 she was a member of the Woman's Council in Washington, DC. Her evangelistic and platform work has taken the best part of her life and effort, but her literary work entitles her to consideration. Her poems are meritorious productions, and she has written enough to fill a large volume. During the years of her great activity in evangelistic and temperance work her literary impulses were overshadowed by the great moral work in which she was engaged. Recently she has written more. Her memorial odes to

Garfield and Gough have been widely quoted, as have also many other of her poems. Her lectures have always been successful, and she is equally at home on the temperance platform, on the lecture platform, in the pulpit or at the author's desk. Her oratory caused her to be styled "The Daniel Webster of Prohibition," a name well suited to her.

LATHROP, Miss Clarissa Caldwell, reformer, was born in Rochester, NY, and died in Saratoga, NY, 11th September, 1892. She was a daughter of the late Gen. William E. Lathrop, a Brigadier General of the National Guard. Soon after her graduation from the Rochester academy she became a teacher, which, owing to her father's failure in business, became a means of support to her family as well as to herself. She continued to teach successfully until her unlawful imprisonment in the Utica insane asylum. Her strange experience was the consummation of the scheme of a secret enemy to put her out of existence by a poison, pronounced by medical authority to be aconite, when her life was saved on two occasions by the care of two friends. She took some tea to a chemist for analysis, as she was desirous of obtaining reliable proof before making open charges against any one, and at the instigation of a doctor who was in sympathy with the plot to kidnap her, she went to Utica to consult Dr. Grey. Instead of seeing Dr. Grey upon her arrival, she was incarcerated with the insane, without the commitment papers required by law, and kept a close prisoner for twenty-six months. At last she managed to communicate with James B. Silkman, a New York lawyer, who had been forcibly carried off and imprisoned in the same insane asylum. He obtained a writ of habeas corpus at once, and in December, 1882, Judge Barnard of the Supreme Court pronounced her sane and unlawfully incarcerated. Immediately upon her restoration to freedom she went before the legislature, and stated her experience and the necessity for reform in that direction. After making another fruitless effort the succeeding year, she found herself homeless and penniless, and dependent upon a cousin's generosity for shelter and support, and was forced to begin life anew under the most dis-

heartening circumstances. She collected money for a charitable society on a commission, spending her evenings in studying stenography and typewriting, after a hard day's toil. She soon started a business of her own and was successful as a court stenographer. Ten years after her release she wrote her book, "A Secret Institution," which is a history of her own life. The interest her book created led to the formation of the Lunacy Law Reform League in 1889, a national organization having its headquarters in New York City, of which she was secretary and national organizer.

LATHROP, Mrs. Rose Hawthorne, poet and author, born in Lenox, MA, 20th May, 1851. Her mother was Mrs. Sophia Peabody Hawthorne, a native of Salem, MA. Her father was the famous Nathaniel Hawthorne. The family is of English descent, and the name was originally spelled "Hathorne." The head of the American branch of the family was William Hathorne, of Wilton, Wiltshire, England, who emigrated with Winthrop and landed in Salem Bay MA, on 12th June, 1630. He had a grant of land in Dorchester and lived there until 1636, when he accepted a grant of land in Salem and made his home upon it. He served as legislator and soldier. The Hathornes became noted in every department of colonial life. The daughter, Rose, early showed the Hawthorne bent toward literature. She soon became a contributor of stories, essays and poems to the "Princeton Review," "Scribner's Magazine," "St. Nicholas," "Wide Awake," the Harper periodicals and other publications. She has published several volumes of poems, "Along the Shore," and others. Her husband is George Parsons Lathrop, the author. Since her marriage her home life and literary work have absorbed her time. Mr. and Mrs. Lathrop were received into the Roman Catholic Church on 19th March, 1891, by Rev. Alfred Young, of the Paulist Fathers, in New York City, and were confirmed by Archbishop Corrigan, on 21st March.

LATIMER, Mrs. Elizabeth Wormeley, author, born in London, England, 26th July, 1822. Her maiden name was Mary Elizabeth Wormeley. Her parents were Rear Admiral Ralph Randolph Wormeley, of the English navy, and Caroline Preble, of Boston, MA. In 1842 Miss Wormeley spent the winter in Boston as the guest of the family of George Ticknor, and in the cultured society of that city she derived much encouragement for her fancy for literature. Her first appearance in print was in the appendix to Prescott's "Conquest of Mexico," for which she had translated an ancient Mexican poem. Returning to London, in 1843, she published her first novel and began to contribute to magazines. The family moved to the United States, making their home in Boston and Newport, RI. Admiral Wormeley died suddenly at Utica, NY, on his way to Niagara Falls, in 1852. On 14th June, 1856, Miss Wormeley became the wife of Randolph Brandt Latimer. Her pen has been a prolific one. Her books, published in England and the United States, are numerous. Among the most popular are "Amabel" (London and New York, 1853); "Our Cousin Veronica" (New York, 1856); "Salvage" (Boston, 1880); "My Wife and My Wife's Sister" (Boston, 1881); "Princess Amelie" (Boston, 1883); "A Chain of Errors" (Philadelphia, 1890; "France in the XIXth Century" (Chicago, 1892). Mrs. Latimer is now living in Howard county, Maryland.

LAUDER, Mrs. Maria Elise Turner, author, born in St. Armand, Province of Quebec, Canada. Her late husband, A. W. Lauder, was for several years a member of the Ontario Legislature and a prominent barrister in Toronto. She studied in Oberlin University, OH, as women were not then admitted to the University of Toronto. She studied theology two years under Rev. Charles Finney, D. D., of that institution. During the year of her sojourn in Rome, she was presented at the royal court to their majesties, Umberto Primo and Queen Margherita, and Was honored with private audiences with the queen, and invitations, both in the Quirinal palace and the palace of Capo-di-Monte, in Naples. One of Mrs. Lauder's books," Legends and Tales of the Harz Mountains"

(London, 1881), is dedicated to Queen Margherita, and the Queen presented her her royal portrait with her autograph. She was presented, with her son, at the papal court to the venerable Pope Leo Tredici. She has also published "My

First Visit to England" (1865), "In Europe" (Toronto, 1877), and many literary articles and poems have been published over a pen-name. She is prominent in all works of benevolence and is engaged in literary work. Her home is in Toronto, Ontario, Canada.

LAWLESS, Mrs. Margaret Wynne, poet, born in Adrian, MI, 14th July, 1847, and there passed her childhood and youth. In 1873 she became the wife of Dr. James T. Lawless, a practicing physician in Toledo, OH, which city is still their home. Her life has been a busy one, for she is the mother of eight sons. Mrs. Lawless is not a prolific writer, but her name is not a strange one in many of the leading magazines and papers of the country, such as "Lippincott's Magazine," "Frank Leslie's Magazine," the "Catholic World," and the "Travelers' Record," of Hartford, CT.

LAWSON, Miss Louise, sculptor, born in Cincinnati, OH. Her father, Prof. Lawson, was a Kentuckian by birth and was graduated from the Transylvania College, Lexington. He was married young, and after the birth of several children went to Europe to take a course of medical study, leaving his wife to edit his medical journal, the "Lancet," during his absence, and to look after the little family. Mrs. Lawson filled the editorial chair satisfactorily, for she was familiar with medical literature. All the children of the family, except Louise, died young, and the mother early followed them. Louise became the companion of her father. He never sent her to school, but took charge of her education himself, teaching her just as he would a boy, Latin and Greek, physiology and anatomy, in the most unconventional way. He aroused her enthusiasm for art, through his teaching in regard to the beauty and dignity of the human form. She lived out of doors all summer long, in their countryseat near the city. There she developed the physique which has carried her through studies that would have broken down a girl educated according to common standards. She one day awoke to the fact that only in art could the impulses of her mind find expression. She has always regarded what people call genius as the

Helen Keating.　　　　**Clara Lanza.**　　　　**Roselle Knott.**
From Photo by,　　　　*From Photo by*　　　　*From Photo by*
Baker Columbus.　　　*Sarony, New York.*　　*B. J. Falk, New York.*

ability to labor with great patience for the desired results. She spent fourteen years in training, the first two years in the Art School in Cincinnati, three in the School of Design in Boston, three years in the Cooper Union, New York, three in study in Paris, and three in modeling in Rome. Miss Lawson went to Rome a stranger. When she arrived in that famous city, she put up in a hotel, but soon took a studio near Villa Ludi Visi, a beautiful estate with extensive grounds. Her fame came about in an unusual manner. She employed many living models, and they, recognizing her genius, had so much to say of the charming American in other studios that one day she awoke to find herself famous, almost without introduction or presentation outside of a limited circle. She soon after was the recipient of public recognition, the medal from the president of the Raphael Academie Di Belle Arti, as a compliment to her genius, her "Ayacanora" placing her at once among the great modern sculptors. Returning to the United States, she settled in New York and opened a studio. Among Miss Lawson's finest pieces are "The Origin of the Harp," "Il Pastore," "The Rhodian Boy," and a statue of the late Congressman S. S. Cox, of New York. Her work is marked by the highest artistic excellence. Many of the subjects of her work as a sculptor are American in origin.

LAWSON, Mrs. Mary J., author, born in Maroon Hall, Preston, near Halifax, Nova Scotia, in 1828. Her maiden name was Mary J. Katzmann. In 1868 she became the wife of William Lawson. She had one daughter, who survives her. She died in 1890, lamented by a wide circle who admired and loved her for her talents, character and devotion to duty. Her father, Conrad C. Katzmann, lieutenant in the 60th, or King's German Legion, was a native of Hanover, Germany. Her mother, Martha Prescott, was a granddaughter of Dr. Jonathan Prescott, who at the close of the Revolutionary War went to Nova Scotia with the Loyalists. He was of the same family as the historian Prescott. Under the initials "M. J. K.," which after her marriage became "M. J. K. L.," she began to write and to publish in the local press verses that attracted the attention of an

unusually brilliant literary circle then in Halifax. Joseph Howe, writer and statesman, encouraged her to devote herself to literature as the best way of serving the country and humanity, and in 1852 and 1853 she edited and wrote for the "Provincial Magazine." Great facility of expression enabled her to supply any demand at brief notice, and her energy and determination to carry through whatsoever she undertook kept the magazine in existence for two years, when for lack of support it had to be discontinued. Whenever a good cause was in need, she came to its help with pen and heart. Blessed with a strong constitution, there was almost no work of brain or hand from which she shrank. Strongly attached to the Church of England, and of a profoundly religious nature, she never wearied in self-sacrificing labors in its cause or the cause of the poor and suffering.

LAWTON, Mrs. Henrietta Beebe, musician and educator, born in New York, NY, 2nd December, 1844. Her father was William H. Beebe, the well-known hatter, who was conspicuous for his espousal of the cause of the workingman. Henrietta was a musical child. Her fine voice was early discovered, and she received a very liberal and thorough training. At the age of fourteen she was already a successful church-choir singer, and for thirty years she sang in the most prominent choirs in New York City. At the age of sixteen years she sang in Haydn's "Creation" in Cooper Institute, under the direction of Professor Charles A. Guilmette, her first teacher. She was successful throughout her career before the public. She did a notable work in English music, both sacred and secular. For fifteen years she was connected with the English Glee Club of New York City. She has visited Europe four times. In 1867 she went to Milan, Italy, to study with Perini and to perfect herself in the Italian method of singing. In 1881 she went to London, England, where she studied a year with Sir Julius Benedict, Sir Michael Costa, Joseph Bamby, Fred. Cowen, and others of the best English musicians. The climate of London proved uncongenial to her, and she was obliged to give up her plan of permanent residence in that city. Among her English friends was Jenny Lind

Goldschmidt. In 1886 Miss Beebe became the wife of William H. Lawton, the distinguished tenor. Since her marriage she has made her home in New York. She is now employed by Mrs. Jeannette M. Thurber in the National Conservatory of Music in New York City. She is devoting her time entirely to the teaching of oratorio and secular English music.

LAZARUS, Miss Emma, a poet and author, born in New York, NY, 22nd July, 1849, and died there 19th November, 1887 She was a member of a Jewish family of prominence. She was noted in childhood for her quickness and intelligence. She received a  liberal education under private tutors, and her attainments included Hebrew, Greek, Latin and modern languages. She read widely on religious, philosophical and scientific subjects, and was a profound thinker. Her literary bent displayed itself in poetry at an early age. In 1867 she published her volume, "Poems and Translations," and at once attracted attention by the remarkable character of her work. In 1871 she published "Admetus, and Other Poems," and the volume drew friendly notice from critics on both sides of the Atlantic. In 1874 she published her first important prose work, "Alide, an Episode of Gothe's Life." She contributed original poems and translations from Heinrich Heine's works to "Scribner's Magazine." In 1881 she published her translations, "Poems and Ballads of Hein," and in 1882 her "Songs of a Semite." She wrote for the "Century" a number of striking essays on Jewish topics, among which were "Was the Earl of Beaconsfield a Representative Jew?" and "Russian Christianity versus Modern Judaism." Her work includes critical articles on Salvini, Emerson and others. In the winter of 1882, when many Russian Jews were flocking to New York City to escape Russian persecution, Miss Lazarus published in the "American Hebrew," a series of articles solving the question of occupation for the incomers. Her plan involved industrial and technical education, and the project was carried out along that line. In 1882 she wrote her "In Exile," "The Crowing of the Red Cock" and "The Banner of the Jew." In 1887 she published her last orig-

inal work, a series of prose poems of remarkable beauty. Among her many translations are poems from the mediaeval Jewish authors, Judah Halévy, Ibn Gabirol and Moses Ben Ezra. Some of these translations have been incorporated in the rituals of many American Hebrew synagogues. She was a woman of marked poetic talent, and many of her verses are aflame with genius and sublime fervor.

LEADER, Mrs. Olive Moorman, temperance reformer, born in Columbus, OH, 28th July, 1852. In her early childhood her parents moved to Iowa, but she returned to her native State to finish her education. As a child her ambition was to become an educator,  and all her energies were directed to that end. For thirteen years she was a successful teacher. She became the wife, in 1880, of J. B. Leader, and removed to Seward, NE. She was identified with school work in Seward, Lincoln and Plattsmouth successively, and, removing to Omaha, she began, in connection with the Woman's Christian Temperance Union, active work in the temperance cause. She introduced the systematic visiting of the Douglas county jails. She was one of the first workers among the Chinese, being first State superintendent of that department. In 1887, removing to Dakota Territory, she labored indefatigably for its admission as a prohibition State. During her three years' residence in Dakota she was State superintendent of miners' and foreign work in the Woman's Christian Temperance Union. In 1889 she returned to Nebraska and settled in Chadron, her present home. She has been for two years superintendent of soldiers' work in Nebraska, and has been for twelve years identified with the suffrage cause. She is an adherent of Christian Science and a strong believer in its efficacy, having, as she firmly believes, been personally benefited thereby.

LEAVITT, Mrs. Mary Clement, missionary temperance organizer, born in Boston, MA. She comes from an old New England family prominent in the early days of the Colonies. She was educated in Boston and, after completing her studies, conducted a successful private school in that city, continuing the work until her children were grown up. She had been prominent in temperance work for years, and was elected president of the Woman's Christian Temperance Union of Boston and national organizer of the society. In 1883 she accepted from the president of the National Woman's Christian Temperance Union, Miss Willard, a roving commission as a pioneer for the World's Woman's Christian Temperance Union, which was organized in that year. Since then Mrs. Leavitt's work has been without a parallel in the records of labor in foreign missions. She commenced with a canvass of the Pacific-coast States, and, when volunteers were asked for, she was the first one to answer the call to go abroad in the interests of the new organization. The association offered to pay her expenses, and $1,000 had been subscribed toward the funds, but she decided not to accept it. She said: "I'm going on God's mission, and He will carry me through." She bought her ocean ticket with her own money, and in 1883 sailed from California for the Sandwich Islands. In Honolulu the Christians and white-ribboners aided her in every way, and after organizing the Sandwich Islands she went on to Australia, where she established the new order firmly. In 1884 the local unions raised $2,613 for her, but she would receive money only in emergencies, and the amount forwarded to her was only $1,670. Leaving Australia, she visited other countries. During the eight years of her remarkable missionary tour she visited the following countries: Hawaiian Islands, New Zealand, Australia, Tasmania, Japan, China, Siam, Straits Settlements, Singapore and Malay Peninsula, Burmah, Hindoostan, Ceylon, Mauritius, Madagascar, Natal, Orange Free State, Cape Colony, England, Ireland, Scotland, Wales, Congo Free State, Old Calabar, Sierra Lione, Madeira, Spain, France, Holland, Norway, Sweden, Finland, Denmark, Germany, Italy, Greece, Egypt, Syria and Turkey. She organized eighty-six Woman's Christian Temperance Unions, twenty- four men's temperance societies, mostly in Japan. India and Madagascar, and twenty-three branches of the White Cross, held over one-thousand-six-hundred meetings, traveled nearly one-hundred-thousand miles, and had the services of two-hundred-twenty-nine interpreters in forty-seven languages. Her expenses were paid with money donated to her in the places she visited. She returned to the United States in 1891. Since her return she has published a pamphlet, "The Liquor Traffic in Western Africa." Her next missionary tour was made in Mexico, Central America and South America. She is corresponding secretary of the World's Woman's Christian Temperance Union. During her great tour of the world she never in seven years saw a face she knew, and only occasional letters from her enabled the home workers to know where she was laboring.

LEGGETT, Miss Mary Lydia, minister, born in Semproius, Cayuga county, NY, 23rd April, 1852. She is the daughter of Rev. William Leggett and Frelove Frost Leggett. She was educated in Monticello Seminary, Godfrey, IL. In temperament she is a 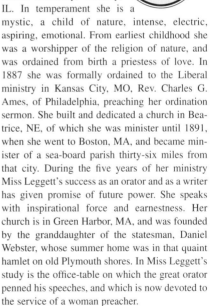 mystic, a child of nature, intense, electric, aspiring, emotional. From earliest childhood she was a worshipper of the religion of nature, and was ordained from birth a priestess of love. In 1887 she was formally ordained to the Liberal ministry in Kansas City, MO, Rev. Charles G. Ames, of Philadelphia, preaching her ordination sermon. She built and dedicated a church in Beatrice, NE, of which she was minister until 1891, when she went to Boston, MA, and became minister of a sea-board parish thirty-six miles from that city. During the five years of her ministry Miss Leggett's success as an orator and as a writer has given promise of future power. She speaks with inspirational force and earnestness. Her church is in Green Harbor, MA, and was founded by the granddaughter of the statesman, Daniel Webster, whose summer home was in that quaint hamlet on old Plymouth shores. In Miss Leggett's study is the office-table on which the great orator penned his speeches, and which is now devoted to the service of a woman preacher.

LEIGH, Miss Mercedes, see HEARNE, MISS MERCEDES LEIGH.

LELAND, Mrs. Caroline Weaver, educator and philanthropist, born in Sandusky county, OH, 19th

October, 1840. When she was three years old, her parents, Jacob and Charlotte H. Weaver, who were of German origin, removed to Branch county, MI. They were interested in all the issues of the day, particularly those of a political character. From them Caroline inherited her love of study, from her earliest years manifesting a desire to learn of the great world lying beyond her little horizon. Her mother, during the father's absence, took an axe, and with her oldest son, a lad of ten or twelve years, marked a path through dense woods by blazing the trees, that her two sons and three daughters might attend the district school, two miles from home. These children hungered and thirsted for knowledge. Caroline was not ashamed to do any honorable thing to realize the dream of her life, a college education. She was unable to accomplish it in her earlier years. She taught several years before she became the wife of Warren Leland, in 1882. He was of the family known to the traveling public through their palatial hotels. He lost his life in the service of his country in 1865. Mrs. Leland then took a classical course in Hillsdale College teaching two years in the Latin department while pursuing her studies. After graduation she accepted and filled the position of preceptress in the city high school, having charge of the department of languages and history. For years she has been an earnest Sunday-school worker, and at the present time is superintendent of the First Presbyterian Sunday-school of Hillsdale. Her strong literary mind leads her to give profound study to any subject which interests her. Her voice and pen are ready in the cause of reform. She is a writer of ability, her efforts usually taking the form of essays or orations written for some special occasion, and she has, in rare instances, written in verse. She early developed a talent for oratory. She has a dignified presence and a deep, impressive voice. The Grand Army of the Republic require her frequent service in the way of speeches, toasts and addresses, and to their interests she in turn is thoroughly devoted. Mrs. Leland is one of the force of World's Fair workers. Notwithstanding the numerous demands on her time and strength, she does a surprising amount of charitable work. She has built a beautiful home, styled "Green Gables," where she dispenses a charming hospitality.

LEONARD, Mrs. Anna Byford, sanitary reformer, born in Mount Vernon, IN, 31st July, 1843. She is a daughter of the eminent physician and surgeon, William H. Byford, of Chicago, IL, whose long professional career and devotion to the cause of woman in medicine have done much to advance them in that profession. He was the founder and president of the Woman's Medical College of Chicago. In 1889 Mrs. Leonard was appointed sanitary inspector, being the first woman who ever held that position, and was enabled to carry out many of the needed reforms. It was through her instrumentality, aided by the other five women on the force, that the eight-hour law was enforced, providing that children under fourteen years of age should not work more than eight hours a day. That was enforced in all dry-goods stores. Through her endeavors seats were placed in the stores and factories, and the employers were instructed that the girls were to be allowed to sit when not occupied with their duties. She was enabled to accomplish this through the fact that the physicians and women of Chicago were ready to sustain her, and the other fact that her position as a sanitary inspector of the health department made her an officer of the police force, thus giving her authority for any work she found necessary to do. As a result of this eight-hour law, schools have been established in some of the stores from eight to ten a.m., giving the younger children, who would spend that time on the street, two hours of solid schooling, and many a girl, who could not write her name, is now cashier in the store where she commenced her work as an ignorant cash-girl. In 1891 Mrs. Leonard was made president of the Woman's Canning and Preserving Company, which, after one short year from its organization, she left with a factory, four stories and basement, with a working capital of $40,000. Mrs. Leonard is an artist of ability, having studied abroad and traveled extensively. She is a close observer of character.

LEONARD, Mrs. Cynthia H. Van Name, philanthropist and author, born in Buffalo, NY, 14th February, 1828. She was an old-fashioned, matter-of-fact child, noted for her remarkable memory. She received her first prize for literary work when a schoolgirl of fourteen. She was a pioneer in many of the fields of labor invaded by the women of this century. She was the first saleswoman to stand behind a counter, and was a member of the first woman's social and literary club in her city. She was a fine contralto singer and a good performer on both violin and guitar. In 1852 she became the wife of Charles E. Leonard, connected with the Buffalo "Express." Later Mr. Leonard took a position on the "Commercial Advertiser" in Detroit, MI, and in 1856 removed to Clinton, IA, where he published the "Herald." Mrs. Leonard took an active part in all projects for the establishment of schools and temporary churches in the rapidly-growing town of Clinton. When the war-cry rang through the land, she was among the foremost in sanitary work, assisting in the opening of the first soldiers' home in Iowa. She made her "maiden speech" in Keokuk, IA, when it was proposed to withdraw from the general sanitary commission and work exclusively for Iowa. In 1863 Mr. Leonard sold the "Herald" and established a printing house in Chicago, where Mrs. Leonard at once gravitated to her own field of labor. She was made part of the management of the Washington House, and chairman of an extensive fair for the Freedman's Aid Commission, when all the Ladies' Loyal Leagues of the Northwest lent a helping hand. She was organizer and president of a woman's club, which held meetings each week, and subsequently, when Alice Cary was president and Celia Burley secretary of the New York Sorosis, it was arranged that the club be called the Chicago Sorosis, and for which was published a weekly paper by Mesdames Leonard and Waterman. At a woman suffrage meeting in Farwell Hall, in 1874, Mrs. Leonard advanced the idea of high license. On one occasion Mrs. Leonard was informed that the common council of Chicago intended to pass an ordinance to license houses of ill-fame. Before eight o'clock that night, with her allies she was at the place of meeting with a carefully prepared petition, which caused the prompt defeat of the measure. After the great fire in Chicago many of the "unfortunates" were shelterless and were constantly arrested for walking the streets. Mrs. Leonard made daily appeals through the press, and finally called a meeting in her home, the result of which was the establishment of the Good Samaritan Society, and at the second meeting a shelter was opened. At the third session a house of forty rooms was offered by a wealthy German, and great good was accomplished among those forlorn women, homes being secured for many and reforms instituted among them. In a book published by Mrs. Leonard, entitled "Lena Rouden, or the Rebel Spy," is a description of the Chicago fire. Mrs. Leonard was for many years a member of the Chicago Philosophical Society. She has contributed articles of merit to newspapers and magazines, and has been largely occupied for some time on a work entitled "Failing Footprints, or the last of the League of the Iroquois." In 1877 Mrs. Leonard took her daughter Helen (Miss Lillian Russell) to New York City to pursue her musical studies. She organized in New York the Science of Life Club. Lillian Russell's success has justified her mother's expectations. Mrs. Leonard's five daughters are gifted musically and artistically.

LE PLONGEON, Mrs. Alice D., archæologist, born in London, England, 21st December, 1851. Her maiden name was Dixon. Her father was born in London and was one of a large family. Medicine, the church, literature and art were the callings of the family, more particularly art. Mrs. Le Plongeon's mother was Sophia Cook, of Byfleet, in the very Saxon county of Surrey, and in her girlhood was called the "Lily of Byfleet." Mrs. Le Plongeon did not receive the high-school education now granted to girls, but only the usual English schooling and smattering of accomplishments. Her father was a very fine reader, and he trained her in that art. As a girl she was gay-hearted, restless, ambitious and fond of music. At seventeen she wished to become a singer and actress, but her parents did not encourage that wish. When nineteen years old, she became acquainted with Dr. Le Plongeon, who had journeyed from San Francisco, CA, to London for the purpose of studying ancient Mexican and other manuscripts preserved in the British Museum. In listening to his enthusiastic accounts of travels and discoveries in Peru she became imbued with a desire to visit unfamiliar places and seek for unknown things. After marriage she accompanied Dr. Le Plongeon to the wilds of Yucatan. Their work there is known all over the world. Eleven years were passed by them in the study of the grand ruins existing in that country. It is difficult to speak of Mrs. Le Plongeon apart from her learned husband, for, as she says, she is but his pupil in archæology. She has toiled by his side and endured many hardships and dangers. The work among the ruins was laborious, not only in the matter of exploring and excavating, but in making hundreds of photographs, in surveying and making molds, by means of which the old palaces of Yucatan can be built in any part of the world. Their greatest achievement has been the discovery of an alphabet, by which the American hiero-glyphics may be read, something which had before been considered quite impossible. She is the only woman who has devoted her time and means to ancient American history, and that should certainly be sufficient to Americanize her. Brooklyn, L. I., has been her place of residence since her return from Yucatan. She has written for several magazines and papers and has published a small volume, "Here and There in Yucatan "(New York, 1886), which has a good sale. A larger work, "Yucatan, Its Ancient Palaces and Modern Cities," is not yet in print. With the object of making ancient America known to modern Americans, she took to the lecture platform, and seldom fails to arouse the enthusiasm of her hearers. In recogni-tion of her labors the Geographical Society of Paris asked for her portrait to place in its album of celebrated travelers. Hitherto she has always refused to give her biography for publication, saying that she considers her work only begun, for she hopes to do much more. Socially, Mrs. Le Plongeon is a favorite, and she takes a lively interest in all the questions of the day.

LEPROHON, Mrs. Rosanna Eleanor, poet and novelist, born in Montreal, Canada, November 9th, 1832. Her maiden name was Rosanna Eleanor Mullins. She was educated in the convent of the Congregation of Notre Dame, in her native city. Long before her education was completed,

she had given evidence of no common literary ability. She was fourteen years old, when she made her earliest essay in verse and prose. Before she had passed beyond the years and scenes of girlhood, she had already won a reputation as a writer of considerable promise, and while John Lovell conducted the "Literary Garland," Miss Mullins was one of his leading contributors. She continued to write for that magazine until lack of financial success com-pelled its enterprising proprietor to suspend its publication. In 1851 Miss Mullins became the wife of Dr. J. L. Leprohon, a member of one of the most distinguished Canadian families. She was a frequent contributor to the Boston "Pilot" and to several of the Montreal journals. She wrote year after year the "Newsboys' Address" for the "True Witness," the "Daily News" and other newspa-pers. The "Journal of Education," the "Canadian Illustrated News," the "Saturday Reader," the "Hearthstone" and other periodicals in Canada and elsewhere were always glad to number Mrs. Leprohon's productions among their features. Although a poet of merit, it was as a writer of fic-tion she won her most marked popular successes. Four of her most elaborate tales were translated into French. These are "Ida Beresford" (1857), "The Manor House of Villerai" (1859), "An-toinette de Mirecourt" (1872), and "Armand Durand" (1870). Besides these, she wrote "Flo-rence Fitz Harding" (1869), "Eva Huntington" (1864), "Clarence Fitz Clarence" (1860), and "Eveleen O'Donnell" (1865), all published in Montreal.

LESLIE, Mrs. Frank, business woman and pub-lisher, born in New Orleans, LA, in 1851. Her maiden name was Miriam Florence Folline, and she is a French Creole. She was reared in opu-lence and received a broad education, including all the accomplishments with many solid and useful attainments. She wrote much in youth and was already known in the world of letters, when she became the wife of Frank

Leslie, the New York publisher. Mr. Leslie was an Englishman. His name was Henry Carter. He was born 29th March, 1821, in Ipswich, England, and died 10th January, 1880 in New York, NY. The name "Frank Leslie" was a pen-name he used in sketches published by him in the London "Illustrated News." In 1848 he came to the United States, assumed the name "Frank Leslie" by a legislative act, and engaged in literature and publication. Miss Folline went to Cincinnati during the Civil War, and finally to New York City. She was engaged in literary work there. One of the editors of Leslie's "Lady's Magazine" was sick and in poverty, and Miss Folline volunteered to do her work for her and give her the salary. The invalid died, and Miss Folline was induced to retain the position. In a short time she became the wife of Mr. Leslie, and their life was an ideally happy one. Her experience and talents enabled her to assist him greatly in the management of the many art publications of his house and she learned all the details of the great business concern, of which she is now the head. During their married life Mr. and Mrs. Leslie made their summer home in "Interlaken Villa," Saratoga Springs, NY, and there they entertained Emperor Dom Pedro, of Brazil, and the Empress. Many other notable people were their guests, and in New York City Mrs. Leslie was, as she still is, one of the leaders of society. In 1877 the panic embarrassed Mr. Leslie, and he was compelled to make an assignment. Arrangements were made to pay off all claims in three years. A tumor developed in a vital part, and he knew that his fate was sealed. He said to his wife: "Go to my office, sit in my place, and do my work until my debts are paid." She undertook the task without hesitation, and she accomplished it with ease. Her husband's will was contested, and the debts amounted to $300,000, but she took hold of affairs and brought success out of what seemed chaos. She adopted the name Frank Leslie in June, 1881, by legal process. She is now sole owner and manager of the great publishing house. One of her published volumes is "From Gotham to the Golden Gate," published in 1877. She has spent her summers in Europe for many years. In 1890 she became the wife, in New York City, of William C. Kingsbury Wilde, an English gentleman, whom she met in London. Her hand had been sought by a number of titled men in Europe, but her choice went with her heart to Mr. Wilde. In European society she shone brilliantly.

Her command of French, Spanish and Italian enabled her to enter the most cultured circles, and her personal and intellectual graces made her the center of attraction wherever she went. Mrs. Leslie is one of the most successful business women of the country. Her home is in New York City, and she is in full control of the business she has built up to so remarkable a success.

LE VALLEY, Mrs. Laura A. Woodin, lawyer, born in Granville, NY, and was the only daughter of Daniel and Sarah Palmer Woodin. Her girlhood was spent in Romeo, MI, where she attended an institute of that place, and afterward she became a student in Falley Seminary, Fulton, NY. She made a specialty of music, and entered Sherwood's Musical Academy, Lyons, NY, from which she was graduated. She soon gained the reputation of a thorough instructor in instrumental music. Finding her services in demand in her father's office, she was appointed a notary public, and assisted him for several years, especially in the prosecution of United States claims. During that time she had much business experience and began the study of stenography. She commenced to study law, and, encouraged by her father, entered the law department of the University of Michigan in the fall of 1880, from which she was graduated in the class of 1882. She was a faithful student, made rapid progress, and had barely entered upon the work of the senior year, when she applied for admission to the bar, stood a rigid examination in open court, and was admitted to practice before the supreme court of Michigan on November 12th, 1881. In the law school she first met her future husband, D. W. LeValley, from the State of New York, then a senior in the law department in the class of 1881. Mr. LeValley opened an office in Saginaw, MI, where they have resided since their marriage, on December 28th, 1882. For five years after her marriage she gave close attention to office work, her husband attending to matters in court, and they have built up a profitable business. Since the birth of her daughter, Florence E., the nature of her employment has been somewhat changed. She is now the mother of two daughters. Since her marriage she, and her husband who is the author of the historical chart entitled "The Royal Family of England," have spent nearly all their spare time in reading, chiefly history. Mrs. LeValley is a member of the Congregational Church, and for years was an active worker in the Sunday-school of that denomination.

LEWING, Miss Adele, pianist, born in Hanover. Germany, 6th August, 1868. She was educated in classic music by her grandfather, A. C. Prell, first violoncellist in the Hanover Royal Orchestra, a former pupil of Bernhard Romberg, and in the modern school of piano-playing by J. Moeller, a pupil of Ignaz Moscheles. At the age of fourteen years she made her first public appearance. Later she became the student of Prof. Dr. Carl Reinecke and Dr. S. Jadassohn, in Leipzig, studying also harmony with the latter. Reinecke selected Miss Lewing to play the master's sonata in B flat, for piano and violoncello, in the Mendolssohn celebration, and she was also chosen to play the F minor suite by Handel in a concert in honor of the King of Saxony. April 30th, 1884, Miss Lewing played Beethoven's G major concerto, with orchestra, on her first appearance in the public examination in the old Leipzig Gewandhaus-saal. May 10th, 1884, Reinecke selected Miss Lewing to play his quintet, op. 82, in another concert. In her last public examination concert she played Beethoven's E flat concerto, with orchestra, and graduated from the Leipzig Royal Conservatory "with high honors." She came unheralded to America, formed a class of piano pupils in Chicago, and gave her first public concert in that city, 7th December, 1888, in Weber Music Hall. Since then she has played before the Artists' Club, in the Haymarket concerts and numerous others. June 27th, 1889, she played before the Indiana State Music Teachers' Association. July 5th, 1889, she played in the thirteenth meeting of the Music Teachers' National Association, in Philadelphia PA, and in August of the same year she gave a series of piano recitals in the Elberon Casino, New Jersey. Her concert tour to Boston, Philadelphia, St. Louis and other cities took place in the early part of May 1890. Not only is she an artistic performer, but she is a composer as well. In her

youth she displayed literary talent, which took form in poetry, but her long and earnest study of music has kept her from developing her talents in literary and other directions. She is winning success as a composer, teacher and performer and a woman who has a message for the world. She now resides in Boston, MA.

LEWIS, Miss Graceanna, naturalist, born on a farm belonging to her parents, John and Esther Lewis, of West Vincent township, near Kimberton, Chester county, PA, 3rd August, 1821. Both parents were descended from the Quakers. Her father was the fifth in descent from Henry Lewis, of Narberth, Pembrokeshire, Wales, who came to this country about the beginning of 1682 and settled in what is now Delaware county, at first in Uplands, now Chester, and later in Haverford, with a winter residence in the city of Philadelphia. He was one of the friends and companions of William Penn, and was a man of education and influence. A number of his descendants have been among the educators of their generation. On his mother's side, through the Meredith family of Radnorshire, Wales, he was the ninth in descent from David Vaughan, who lived about the time of the discovery of America. In accordance with a mode peculiarly Welsh, his son took the name of Evan David; his son that of William Evan; his son that of Meredith William; and his son that of Hugh Meredith. This Hugh was a Cavallier, and with him the name of Meredith was retained for that of the family. His son, Simon, born 1663, was among the early colonists of Pennsylvania, and settled in West Vincent, purchasing a tract of land held in the family until recently. Here the five children of John and Esther Lewis were born. Her mother was the oldest child of Bartholomew Fussell, sr., and Rebecca Bond Fussell, his wife. The former was a minister in the Society of Friends and was of English descent. The latter was of mingled English, French and Hollandish blood. The father of Graceanna died, leaving a wife and four daughters. Graceanna was then not three years old. Before her marriage the mother had been a successful teacher, at first of her own brothers and sisters, and later of large and flourishing schools. She was eminently fitted for the task of educating her children. After twenty-four years of widowhood she died, leaving her oldest and youngest daughters with Graceanna in the home known as "Sunnyside." Graceanna had always been fond of natural history. She studied for the love of it in prosperity, and it became her consolation in sorrow. In the field of natural history her most important work has been the preparation of a "Chart of the Class of Birds"; a "Chart of the Animal Kingdom"; a "Chart of the Vegetable Kingdom"; a "Chart of Geology, with Special References to Palaeontology"; "Microscopic Studies, including Frost Crystals and the Plumage of Birds, as well as the Lower Forms of Animal and Vegetable Life, with Studies in Forestry with original Paintings of Forest Leaves;" "Water-color Paintings of Wild Flowers," and illustrations for lectures on plants and animals. In 1869 she printed a small pamphlet, showing the relation of birds in the animal kingdom. That pamphlet was the result of long studies, both in her home on the old farm and with the benefit of the library and the collection of the Academy of Natural Sciences, Philadelphia, under the direction of John Cassin, one of the leading ornithologists of the world. It was the germ of her later and improved charts. She was delighted to find that her views, which she had reached from general considerations, were sustained by anatomical research of the highest order. In 1876 she exhibited in the Centennial Exposition, a wax model along with her chart of the Animal Kingdom. Here Prof. Huxley and other prominent naturalists found opportunity of examining her productions, and they were highly commended. Fortified by the encouragement of the best zoologists of England and America, her confidence was now assured, and she was ready to apply the same principles to the construction of a "Chart of the Vegetable Kingdom." By 1880, she had outlined the latter, and had completed it by 1885. Since then, all her charts are revised in accordance with the progress of scientific knowledge. Prof. Maria Mitchell, then of Vassar College, elected president of the fourth congress of the Association for the Advancement of Women, having urged Miss Lewis to prepare a scientific paper for reading before the meeting, the latter responded by choosing for her subject "The Development of the Animal Kingdom." Prof. Mitchell published that paper in pamphlet form, and circulated it widely amongst scientists. In

1870 Miss Lewis was elected a member of the Academy of Natural Sciences, Philadelphia. She is at present an honorary member of the Rochester Academy of Science, Rochester, NY; of the Philosophical Society of West Chester, Chester County, PA; of the New Century Club of Philadelphia; of the Women's Anthropological Society of America, Washington, DC; and recently, has been elected a life member of the Delaware County Institute of Science, in Media, where she now resides. Miss Lewis continues to lead a busy life, and in addition to her scientific studies, finds time for many diverse social duties. At home, she is secretary of the Media Woman's Christian Temperance Union, secretary of the Media Woman Suffrage Association, secretary of the Delaware County Forestry Association, superintendent of scientific temperance instruction of the Delaware County Woman's Christian Temperance Union, and chief of the cultural department of the Media Flower Mission.

LEWIS, Miss Ida, heroine and life-saver, born in Newport, RI, in 1841. Her father, Captain Hosea Lewis, was keeper of the Lime Rock lighthouse in the Newport harbor, and she became in early youth a skilled swimmer and oarsman. Much of her time was spent in the boat which was the only means of communication between the lighthouse and the mainland. Her free outdoor life gave her great strength and powers of endurance, and she was at home on the water, in calm or storm. Her first notable deed in life-saving was in 1859, when she rescued four men, whose boat had capsized in the harbor. Since that event she has saved many lives. Her fame as a heroine grew, and thousands of visitors thronged her humble home to make her acquaintance. Captain Lewis became a paralytic, and Ida was made custodian-for-life of the Lime Rock lighthouse. The appointment was conferred upon her in 1879 by General Sherman, who paid her a signal compliment for her bravery. In July, 1880, the Secretary of the Treasury, William Windom, awarded the gold lifesaving medal to her, and she is the only woman in America who has received that tribute. Besides these, she has received three silver medals, one from the State of Rhode Island, one from the Humane Society of Massachusetts, and a third from the New York Life Saving Association. In the Custom House in Newport, in 1869, before hundreds of its citizens, Miss Lewis received from General Grant the lifeboat "Rescue," which she now has. It was a gift from the people of the city in recognition of her acts of bravery. For it James Fisk, jr., ordered a boat-house built. Mr. Fisk sent the heroine a silk flag, painted by Mrs. McFarland, of New York. After being made a member of Sorosis, Miss Lewis received from that body a brooch. It is a large gold S, with a band of blue enamel around it. Across is the name of the club in Greek letters, and engraved on the main part of the pin, "Sorosis to Ida Lewis, the Heroine." From the two soldiers from the fort, whom she rescued, she received a gold watch, and from the officers and men a silver teapot worth $150 Presents of all sorts, from large sums of money to oatmeal and maple-sugar, have flowed in to her from all parts of the country. She retains and is known by her maiden name, but she was married, in 1870, to William H. Wilson, of Black Rock, CT.

LINCOLN, Mrs. Martha D., author and journalist, widely known by her pen-name, "Bessie Beech," born near Richfield Springs, NY, in 1838. She was educated in Whitestown Seminary, NY. When she was sixteen years old she began her literary career in numerous contributions to the Dover, NH, "Morning Star," now published in Boston, MA. She became the wife of H. M. Lincoln, a medical student of Canandaigua, NY, in 1858. Soon after her marriage she became a regular contributor to "Moore's Rural New Yorker," the "Morning Star" and the "Northern Christian Advocate." Her husband's health became impaired, and in 1871 they moved to Washington, DC, to secure a warmer climate. The financial crisis of 1871 and 1872 wrecked his fortune. Then Mrs. Lincoln took up journalistic work in earnest. She became the correspondent of the old "Daily Chronicle," the "Republican," the "Union," the "Republic," and several Sunday journals, and retained her connection with papers outside of Washington. In January, 1878, she contributed to the New York "Times" a description of President Hayes' silver wedding, and, 20th June, 1878, she described the Hastings-Platt wedding in the White House for the New York "Tribune." She corresponded for the New York "Sun" and the Jamestown "Daily Journal"

during the same year. She reported for the Cleveland "Plain Dealer" and the New York "Tribune" and "Sun." The amount of work she turned out was remarkable. On 10th July, 1882, she, with two other journalists in Washington, organized the Woman's National Press Association, the first chartered woman's press organization in the world. She became its first secretary, and afterward for several years served the organization as president. With all her journalistic work she is domestic in her taste and an excellent housekeeper. Her literary work includes some superior verse. Much of her best work is included in her "Beech Leaves," which are being illustrated for publication, and her late work, "Central Figures in American Science." She is doing a great amount of literary work, as biographical sketches of famous women, illustrated articles and poems for children. In 1891 she was appointed delegate to the International Peace Congress, in Rome, Italy, and again, in 1892, delegate to the Peace Congress, in Berne, Switzerland. The same year she was elected president of the American Society of Authors, for Washington, DC. Mr. and Mrs. Lincoln have a delightful home in Washington, where they have resided since 1870. Their only child, a son, recently married, has, as Mrs. Lincoln says, given her the latest and grandest title, that of "Grandma," which has been one of her coveted honors.

LINCOLN, Mrs. Mary Todd, wife of Abraham Lincoln, sixteenth President of the United States, born in Lexington, KY, 12th December, 1818, and died in Springfield, IL, 16th July, 1882. She was the daughter of Robert S. Todd, whose family were among the influential pioneers of Kentucky and Illinois. Her ancestors on both sides were conspicuous for patriotism and intelligence. She was reared in comfort and received a thorough education. She went to Springfield, IL, in 1840, to make her home with her sister, Mrs. Ninian W. Edwards. There she was wooed by Abraham Lincoln, then a prominent lawyer, and they were married on 4th November, 1842. They began life in a humble way. When Mr. Lincoln was sent to Congress, in 1847, Mrs. Lincoln remained in Springfield with her children. Her family were divided by the Civil War, and the division caused Mrs. Lincoln much sorrow, as she was devoted to the Union cause throughout the struggle. During the war she spent much time in the camps and hospitals in and around Washington. Her life as mistress of the White House was eventful from beginning to end, and she was subjected to much hostile criticism, most of which was based upon ignorance of her true character. She was conscious of and sensitive to criticism, and her life was embittered by it. She never recovered from the shock received when her husband was shot while sitting beside her. After leaving the White House she lived in retirement. She traveled in Europe for months, and lived for some years with her son, Robert T. Lincoln, in Chicago. Two of her sons, William Wallace Lincoln and Thomas Lincoln, died before her. The assassination of her husband intensified some of her mental peculiarities, and those near her feared that her intellect was shattered by that appalling event. She died of paralysis, in the home of her sister, Mrs. Edwards, in Springfield, IL.

LINN, Mrs. Edith Willis, poet, born in New York, NY, 19th February, 1865. She is a daughter of Dr. Frederic L. H. Willis, who is a member of the family of the late N. P. Willis, and who formerly practiced medicine in New York. Her mother is Love M. Willis, who was quite well known some years ago as a writer of juvenile stories. Both parents are inclined to literature, and the daughter inherited a double share of the literary gift. When Edith was six years old, the family went to Glenora, on Seneca Lake, for the summers, and to Boston, MA, for the winters. In Boston she was educated in private schools until she was eighteen years old, after which her education was conducted by private tutors. In 1886 she became the wife of Dr. S. H. Linn. She has two sons. She has traveled in Europe and through the United States since her marriage. Since her eleventh year she has preserved all her compositions, and the number is nearly four-hundred. She has written very little in prose, a few short stories descriptive of nature. Mrs. Linn is proficient in French, German and English literature and music. She has contributed to the "Christian Register," the "Cottage Hearth," the "Christian Union," the Boston "Transcript," "Godey's Lady's Book," "Peterson's Magazine," the "New Moon," the "Century" and other promi-

nent periodicals. She has published one volume of "Poems" (Buffalo, 1891). Her home is in Rochester, NY.

LINTON, Miss Laura A., scientist, born on a farm near Alliance, OH, 8th April, 1853. She is the daughter of Joseph Wildman Linton and Christiana Craven Beans. On her father's side she is descended from English Quakers, and on her mother's side from one of the  old Dutch families of eastern Pennsylvania. Her girlhood, up to the age of fifteen, was passed on farms in Ohio, Pennsylvania and New Jersey. In 1868 her parents settled on a farm in Minnesota, and she entered the Winona Normal School and was graduated from that institution in 1872. Later she entered the State University in Minneapolis, from which she was graduated in the class of 1879, with the degree of B.S. After graduation she taught two years in the high school in Lake City, MN. She assisted Prof. S. F. Peckham in the preparation of the monograph on petroleum for the reports of the Tenth Census of the United States. She accepted the professorship of natural and physical sciences in Lombard University, in Galesburg, IL, and afterward assumed charge of the physical sciences in the central high school of Minneapolis, MN. When an undergraduate, she completed an analysis of a new variety of Thomsonite, found on the north shore of Lake Superior, that Profs. Peckham and Hall named "Lintonite," as a reward for her successful efforts. She is a member of the American Association for the Advancement of Science, and of the Association for the Advancement of Women. She was State chairman of electricity for the World's Fair.

LIPPINCOTT, Miss C. H., pioneer seedswoman, born in Mt. Holly, Burlington county, NJ, 6th September, 1860. Growing up in a quiet home-life, she went to Minneapolis in 1887 from Philadelphia. Living all her life among flowers and plants, she readily adopted the idea of entering the seed business, suggested by a brother, a seed producer, who foresaw the possibilities in seed-dealing for a woman of enterprise. Acting upon her brother's advice, she invested her money in a flower-seed house, issuing her first circular in 1891, receiving in answer some six-thousand orders. The next year she was able to close her book with twenty-thousand orders. Nerve to advertise extensively, which amounts to an annual outlay of twenty-seven-thousand dollars, and strict attention to filling her orders intelligently and to the satisfaction of her customers, has increased her business to one of the most extensive in the country. That day is past when an upstairs room, with her family as helpers, included the entire plant, to-day a force of clerks attend to all business detail in a two-story brick building, which contains all the modern improvements to insure rapid and correct work on orders which are sent to every corner of the world. A woman's finer taste is displayed in the dainty catalogues she brings out in the highest style of the printer's art, which are acknowledged to be the most artistic published pertaining to seeds. This combination of art and floriculture comes of Miss Lippincott's theory that there is a vein of refinement in any one who plants a seed or cares for a flower or plant. The plan of stating the number of seeds contained in each packet is original with this bright woman, an innovation that has compelled all the prominent seed houses to follow suit and state the quantity their packets contain.

LIPPINCOTT, Mrs. Esther J. Trimble, educator and reformer, born near Kimberton, PA, 2nd March, 1838, and died in Wilmington, Del., 2nd June, 1888. Her parents were Joseph and Rebecca Fussell Trimble. She became an instructor in Swathmore College, Pennsylvania, and later became a professor of literature in the normal school of West Chester, PA. Her married life with Isaac H. Lippincott, of Woodstown, NJ, lasted but a brief period, as he died at the end of two years. After she became a widow she visited Europe in pursuance of her studies. As an author she was successful in the preparation of a "Chart of General Literature," a "Hand-Book of English and American Literature" and a "Short Course of Literature." In every effort for homes for invalids she

was in special sympathy, and before her death left a substantial token of her interest in the founding of several such homes for invalids in Philadelphia. Mrs. Lippincott was laid to rest in the Friends' Burial Ground, in Merion, near to her father and mother.

LIPPINCOTT, Mrs. Sara Jane, author, widely known by her pen-name, "Grace Greenwood," born in Pompey, Onondaga county, NY, 23rd September, 1823. She is a daughter of Dr. Thaddeus Clarke and was reared in Rochester. NY. In 1842 she went with her father to New Brighton, PA. She received a good education in public and private schools. In 1853 she became the wife of Leander K. Lippincott, of Philadelphia, PA. She began to write verses in childhood under her own name. In 1844 she published some prose articles in the New York "Mirror," using for the first time her now famous pen-name, "Grace Greenwood." She had a liking for journalism, which she satisfied by editing the "Little Pilgrim"; a Philadelphia juvenile monthly, for several years. She contributed for years to "Hearth and Home," the "Atlantic Monthly," "Harper's Magazine," the New York "Independent," New York "Times" and "Tribune" and California journals, and the English "Household Words" and "All the Year Round." She was one of the first women newspaper correspondents in the United States, and her Washington correspondence inaugurated a new feature of journalism. Her published works include "Greenwood Leaves" (1850); "History of My Pets" (1850); "Poems" (1851); "Recollections of My Childhood" (1851); "Haps and Mishaps of a Tour in Europe" (1854); "Merrie England" (1855); "Forest Tragedy, and Other Tales" (1856); "Stories and Legends of Travel" (1858); "History for Children" (1858); "Stories from Famous Ballads" (1860); "Stories of Many Lands" (1867); "Stories and Sights in France and Italy" (1868); "Records of Five Years" (1868); "New Life in New Lands" (1873) and "Victoria, Queen of England" (1883). The last named work was brought out in New York and London simultaneously. She has spent much time abroad. During the Civil War she read and lectured to the soldiers in the camps and hospitals, and President Lincoln called her "Grace Greenwood, the patriot." She is interested in all questions of the day that relate to the progress of women. She has one daughter. Her home is in Washington, DC, but she spends much time in New York City.

LITCHFIELD, Miss Grace Denio, novelist and poet, born in New York City, 19th November, 1849. She is the youngest daughter of Edwin Clark Litchfield and Grace Hill Hubbard Litchfield, both of whom died some years ago. Miss Litchfield's home was in Brooklyn, NY, but much of her life has been passed in Europe. When she returned to the United States from a European trip, in 1888, she made her home in Washington DC, where she has built a house on Massachusetts avenue. She has written almost constantly, both in prose and verse, since early childhood, and in spite of much ill health. She did not begin to publish until 1882. Since that year her verses and stories have appeared in the "Century," the "Atlantic Monthly," the "St. Nicholas," the "Wide Awake" and the New York "Independent." All her novels were written during the six years she spent in Europe. The first of these, "The Knight of the Black Forest," was written on the spot where the scene is laid, in 1882, and published in 1884–85, first appearing as a serial in the "Century." Her first published work in book form, "Only an Incident," was written two months later, and was brought out in February, 1884. "Criss-Cross," written in 1883, was published in August, 1885. "A Hard-Won Victory" was begun in 1883, laid aside a year on account of illness, finished in 1886 and published in 1888. A fifth book, a reprint of short stories, under the title of "Little Venice," appeared in September, 1890. Her sixth and last book, "Little He and She," a child's story, written in the spring of 1888, was published in November, 1890. Miss Litchfield was in Mentone, on the Riviera, when that portion of Italy was visited by the earthquake of 23rd February, 1887, and narrowly escaped death under the falling walls of her residence. Miss Litchfield is an industrious worker, and her wide circle of readers expects much from her in future.

LITTLE, Mrs. Sarah F. Cowles, educator, born in Oberlin, OH, 6th March, 1838. Her father was Rev. Henry Cowles, D.D., a professor in Oberlin Theological Seminary, and an eminent scholar, author and divine. He was born in Litchfield county, Connecticut, and was descended from an old New England family of English origin. Her mother, Alice Welch, was a woman of superior attainments and character, and for several years the principal of the ladies' department of Oberlin College. She was the daughter of Dr. Benjamin Welch, of Norfolk, CT. Her five brothers were physicians and have made the name of "Dr. Welch" widely known throughout western New England. Sarah F. was the second daughter and fourth child of those parents. As her home was under the very shadow of the college in Oberlin, her opportunities for education were excellent. She was graduated in the classical course in 1859, with the degree of B.A., followed by that of M.A. within a few years. Miss Cowles commenced teaching at the age of fifteen years in a district school near her home. She taught during several college vacations, and was also employed as a teacher in the preparatory department of the college during the later years of her course. After graduation she taught with success for two years in the public schools of Columbus, OH, and in the fall of 1861 went to Janesville, WI, to serve as principal teacher in the Wisconsin School for the Blind, of which Thomas H. Little was the superintendent. Mr. Little was a graduate of Bowdoin College, in Brunswick, ME, and had been a teacher in the institutions for the blind in Ohio and Louisiana. He had made a special study of that branch of education and was admirably fitted for his post of responsibility by natural endowments, by training and by experience. On 14th July, 1862, Miss Cowles became the wife of Mr. Little, and thenceforth actively participated in all his labors for the blind with hearty sympathy and earnest helpfulness. She continued to teach regularly for a time after her marriage, and at intervals thereafter, being always ready to supplement any lack in any department of the school. In Mr. Little's absence or illness he was in the habit of delegating his duties to his wife. When Mr. Little's death occurred, 4th February, 1875, after a week's illness, Mrs. Little was at once chosen by the board of trustees as his successor. There was no woman in the United States in charge of so important a public institution as the Wisconsin School for the Blind, but Mrs. Little's experience and her executive tact fully justified such an innovation. She was thoroughly identified with the work and had proved herself competent for leadership in it. The main building of the institution had been destroyed by fire in 1874, and to the difficulty of carrying on the school work in small and inconvenient quarters was added the supervision of the erection of the enlarged new building. The work was done upon plans made under Mr. Little's direction, with which Mrs. Little was already familiar, and no detail escaped her watchful eye. During the time of her superintendency, the Wisconsin School for the Blind was one of the best managed institutions of the kind in the country, and Mrs. Little was everywhere recognized as a leader in educational circles. She continued at the head of the school until August, 1891, leaving it at the close of thirty years of active service, more than sixteen of them as superintendent. The school had grown from an enrollment of thirty to one of ninety pupils. All the buildings were left in good condition and had been improved and enlarged until little remained to be desired for convenience or durability. Mrs. Little brought to her work strength of mind such as few possess, coupled with rare executive ability and a gentle, womanly sympathy. To those qualities and to her absolute fidelity and practical wisdom in managing every department of the complex work entrusted to her is due the fact that no breath of scandal ever came near the institution, and no difficulties ever arose requiring the intervention of the advisory board, a thing which could not be said of any other institution in Wisconsin, or perhaps in the country. Her care of the blind pupils had in it a large element of maternal tenderness, and the school was really a large family, at once a place of careful instruction and thorough discipline, and yet a real home. Besides her interest in educational lines, she has always taken an active part in Christian work of all kinds. Wherever she is, her influence is felt for good. In the church her loyalty and zeal and her thorough consecration are a constant inspiration. She is a thorough Bible student, and has for years been a successful teacher of a large Bible class for adults, bringing to that work not only a scholarly mind and a quick insight into spiritual things, but a warm heart stored with the riches of years of experience. On leaving the school it was natural that she should turn to some form of Christian work, and that her mother-heart should seek again the care of children who must be separated from home and parents. One of her own four daughters was doing missionary work in a distant land, and thus the way was prepared for her to have a natural and deep interest in the Oberlin Home for Missionary Children, from the very beginning of the plans for its establishment, and at the opening, in 1892, she was ready to take a place at its head. There are gathered children from distant mission fields, sent by their parents, that in the home-land they may receive an education removed from the influences of heathen surroundings.

LIVERMORE, Mrs. Mary Ashton Rice, was born in Boston, MA, 19th December, 1821. Her father, Timothy Rice, who was of Welsh descent, served in the United States Navy during the war of 1812–15. Her mother, Zebiah Vose Glover Ashton, born in Boston, was the daughter of Captain Nathaniel Ashton, of London, England. Mrs. Livermore was placed in the public schools of Boston at an early age and was graduated at fourteen, receiving one of the six medals distributed for good scholarship. There were then no high normal or Latin schools for girls, and their admission to college was not even suggested. She was sent to the female seminary in Charlestown, MA, now Boston, where she completed the four-year course in two, when she was elected a member of the faculty, as teacher of Latin and French. While teaching, she continued her studies in Latin, Greek and metaphysics under tutors, resigning her position at the close of the second year to take charge of a family school on a plantation in southern Virginia, where she remained nearly three years. As there were between four and five hundred slaves on the estate, Mrs. Livermore was brought face to face with the institution of slavery and witnessed deeds of barbarism as tragic as any described in "Uncle Tom's Cabin." She returned to the North a radical Abolitionist, and thenceforth entered the lists against slavery and every form of oppression. She taught a school of her own in Duxbury, MA, for the next three years, the ages of her pupils ranging from fourteen to twenty years. It was in reality the high school of the town, and was so counted when she relinquished it, in 1845, to become the wife of Rev. D. P. Livermore, a Universalist minister settled in Fall River, MA. The tastes, habits of study and aims of the young couple were similar, and Mrs. Livermore drifted inevitably into literary work. She called the young parishioners of her husband into reading and study clubs, which she conducted, wrote hymns and songs for church hymnals and Sunday-school singing-books, and stories, sketches and poems for the "Galaxy," "Ladies' Repository," New York "Tribune" and "National Era." She was identified with the Washingtonian Temperance Reform before her marriage, was on the editorial staff of a juvenile temperance paper, and organized a Cold Water Army of fifteen-hundred boys and girls, for whom she wrote temperance stories which she read to them and which were afterward published in book form under the title, "The Children's Army" (Boston, 1844). She wrote two prize stories in 1848, one for a State temperance organization, entitled, "Thirty Years too Late," illustrating the Washingtonian movement, and the other, for a church publishing house, entitled, "A Mental Transformation," elucidating a phase of religious belief. The former was republished in England, where it had a large circulation, has been translated into several languages by missionaries, and was republished in Boston in 1876. In 1857 the Livermores removed to Chicago, IL, where Mr. Livermore became proprietor and editor of a weekly religious paper, the organ of the Universalist denomination in the Northwest, and Mrs. Livermore became his associate editor. For the next twelve years her labors were herculean. She wrote for every department of the paper, except the theological, and in her husband's frequent absence from home, necessitated by church work, she had charge of the entire establishment, paper, printing-office and publishing house included. She continued to furnish stories, sketches and letters to eastern periodicals, gave herself to church and Sunday-school work, was untiring in her labors for the Home of the Friendless, assisted in the establishment of the Home for Aged Women and the Hospital for Women and Children, and was actively identified with the charitable work of the city. She performed much reportorial work in those days, and at the first nomination of Abraham Lincoln for the Presidency, in the Chicago Wigwam, in 1860, she was the only woman reporter who had a place among a hundred or more men reporters. All the while she was her

own housekeeper, directing her servants herself and giving personal supervision to the education and training of her children. A collection of her stories, written during those busy days, was published under the title, "Pen-Pictures" (Chicago, 1863). The great uprising among men at the opening of the Civil War, in 1861, was paralleled by a similar uprising among women, and in a few months there were hundreds of women's organizations formed throughout the North for the relief of sick and wounded soldiers and the care of soldiers' families. Out of the chaos of benevolent efforts evolved by the times, the United States Sanitary Commission was born. Mrs. Livermore, with her friend, Mrs. Jane C. Hoge, was identified with relief work for the soldiers from the beginning, and at the instance of Rev. Dr. Henry W. Bellows, president of the commission, they were elected associate members of the United States Sanitary Commission, with headquarters in Chicago, and the two friends worked together till the end of the war. Mrs. Livermore resigned all positions save that on her husband's paper, secured a governess for her children, and put aside all demands upon her time for those of the commission. She organized Soldiers' Aid Societies, delivered public addresses to stimulate supplies and donations of money in the principal towns and cities of the Northwest, wrote letters by the hundreds, personally and by amanuenses, and answered all that she received, wrote the circulars, bulletins and monthly reports of the commission, made trips to the front with sanitary stores, to whose distribution she gave personal attention, brought back large numbers of individual soldiers who were discharged that they might die at home, and whom she accompanied in person, or by proxy, to their several destinations, assisted to plan, organize and conduct colossal Sanitary Fairs, and wrote a history of them at their close, detailed women nurses for the hospitals, by order of Secretary Stanton, and accompanied them to their posts; in short, the story of women's work during the war has never been told and can never be understood save by those connected with it. Mrs. Livermore has published her reminiscences of those crucial days in a large volume, entitled "My Story of the War" (Hartford, CT, 1888), which has reached a sale of between fifty-thousand and sixty-thousand copies. The war over, Mrs. Livermore resumed the former tenor of her life, and took up again the philanthropic and literary work which she had temporarily relinquished. The woman suffrage movement, which had been inaugurated twelve years before the war, by Lucretia Mott and Mrs. Cady Stanton, and which had been suspended during the absorbing activities of the war, was then resuscitated, and Mrs. Livermore identified herself with it. She had kept the columns of her husband's paper ablaze with demands for the opening of colleges and professional schools to woman, for the repeal of unjust laws that blocked her progress, and for an enlargement of her industrial opportunities, that she might become self-supporting, but she had believed this might be accomplished without making her a voter. Her experiences during the war taught her differently. She very soon made arrangements for a woman suffrage convention in Chicago, where never before had one been held. The leading clergymen of the city took part in it, prominent advocates of the cause from various parts of the country were present, and it proved a notable success. The Illinois Woman Suffrage Association was organized and Mrs. Livermore was elected its first president. In January, 1869, she established a woman suffrage paper, "The Agitator," at her own cost and risk, which espoused the temperance reform as well as that of woman suffrage. In January, 1870, the "Woman's Journal" was established in Boston by a joint-stock company, for the advocacy of woman suffrage, and Mrs. Livermore received an invitation to become its editor-in-chief, which she accepted, merging her own paper in the new advocate. Her husband disposed of his paper and entire establishment in Chicago, the family returned to the East, and have since resided in Meirose, MA. For two years Mrs. Livermore edited the "Woman's Journal," when she resigned all editorial work to give her time more entirely to the lecture field. For twenty-five years she has been conspicuous on the lecture platform and has been heard in the lyceum courses of the country year after year in nearly every State of the Union, as well as in England and Scotland. She chooses a wide range of topics, and her lectures are biographical, historical, political, religious, reformatory and sociological. One volume of her lectures has been published, entitled "What shall we do with our Daughters? and Other Lectures" (Boston, 1883), and another is soon to follow. She has traveled extensively in the United States, literally from ocean to ocean, and from Canada to the Gulf of Mexico. In company with her husband, she has made two visits to Europe, where she was much instructed by intercourse with liberal and progressive people. Her pen has not been idle during these last twenty years, and her articles have appeared in the "North American Review," the "Arena," the "Chautauquan," the "Independent," the "Youth's Companion," the "Christian Advocate," "Woman's Journal" and other periodicals. She is much interested in politics and has twice been sent by the Republicans of her own town as delegate to the Massachusetts State Republican Convention, charged with the presentation of temperance and woman suffrage resolutions, which have been accepted and incorporated into the party platform. She is identified with the Woman's Christian Temperance Union, and for ten years was president of the Massachusetts Woman's Christian Temperance Union. She was president of the Woman's Congress during the first two years of its organization, has served as president of the American Woman's Suffrage Association, is president of the Beneficent Society of the New England Conservatory of Music, which assists promising and needy students in the prosecution of their musical studies, is identified with the National Women's Council, which holds triennial meetings, is connected with the Chautauqua movement, in which she is much interested, is a life-member of the Boston Woman's Educational and Industrial Union, and holds memberships in the Woman's Relief Corps, the Ladies' Aid Society of the Massachusetts Soldiers' Home, the Massachusetts Woman's Indian Association, the Massachusetts Prison Association, the American Psychical Society and several literary clubs. In religion she is a Unitarian, but cares more for life and character than for sect or creed. She is a believer in Nationalism, and regards Socialism, as expounded in America, as "applied Christianity." Notwithstanding her many years of hard service, she is still in vigorous health. Happy in her home, and in the society of her husband, children and grandchildren, she keeps at work with voice and pen.

LOCKWOOD, Mrs. Belva Ann, barrister-at-law, born in Royalton, Niagara county, NY, 24th October, 1830. Her parents' name was Bennett. They were farmers in moderate circumstances. Belva was educated at first in the district school and later in the academy of her native town. At fourteen years of age she taught the district school in summer and attended school in winter, continuing that occupation until eighteen years of age, when she became the wife of a young farmer in the neighborhood, Uriah H. McNall, who died in April, 1853, leaving one daughter, now Mrs. Lura M. Ormes, Mrs. Lockwood's principal assistant in her law office. As Belva A. McNall she entered Genesee College, in Lima, NY, in 1853, and was graduated therefrom with honor, taking her degree of A.B. on 27th June, 1857. She was immediately elected preceptress of Lockport union school, incorporated as an academy, and containing six-hundred male and female students. She assisted in the preparation of a three-year course of study and introduced declamation and gymnastics for the young ladies, conducting the classes herself. She was also professor of the higher mathematics, logic, rhetoric and botany. She continued filling that position with efficiency and success for four years, when she resigned to become preceptress of the Gainesville Female Seminary, and later she became the proprietor of McNall Seminary, in Oswego, NY. At the close of the Civil War Mrs. McNall removed to Washington, DC, and for seven years had charge of Union League Hall, teaching for a time, and meanwhile taking up the study of law. On the 11th of March, 1868, she became the wife of Rev. Ezekiel Lockwood, a Baptist minister, who during the war was chaplain of the Second DC. Regiment. Dr. Lockwood died in Washington, DC, 23rd April, 1877. Jessie B. Lockwood, the only child of their union, had died before him. Mrs. Lockwood took her second degree of A. M. in Syracuse University, NY, with which Genesee College had previously been incorporated, in 1870, at the request of the faculty of that institution. In May, 1873, she was graduated from the National University Law School, Washington, DC, and took her degree of D.C.L. After a spirited controversy about the admission of women to the bar, she was, on 23rd September, 1873, admitted to the bar of the supreme court, the highest court in the District. She at once entered into the active practice of her profession, which she still continues after nineteen years of successful work. For about thirteen years of that time Mrs. Lockwood was in court every court-day and engaged in pleading cases in person before the court. In 1875 she applied for admission to the Court of Claims. Her admission was refused on

the ground, first, that she was a woman, and, second, that she was a married woman. The contest was a bitter one, but sharp, short and decisive. In 1876 Mrs. Lockwood's admission to the bar of the United States Supreme Court was moved. That motion was also refused on the ground that there were no English precedents for the admission of women to the bar. It was in vain that she pleaded that Queens Eleanor and Elizabeth had both been Supreme Chancellors of the Realm, and that at the Assizes of Appleby, Ann, Countess of Pembroke, sat with the judges on the bench. Nothing daunted, she drafted a bill admitting women to the bar of the United States Supreme Court, secured its introduction into both Houses of Congress, and after three years of effort aroused influence and public sentiment enough to secure its passage in January, 1879. On the 3rd of March of that year, on the motion of Hon. A. G. Riddle, Mrs. Lockwood was admitted to the bar of that august tribunal, the first woman upon whom the honor was conferred. Of that court she remains a member in good standing. Nine other women have since been admitted under the act to this, the highest court in the United States. After the passage of the act, Mrs. Lockwood was notified that she could then be admitted to the Court of Claims, and she was so admitted on motion of Hon. Thomas J. Durant, 6th March, 1879, and has before that court a very active practice. There is now no Federal Court in the United States before which she may not plead. From the date of her first admission to the bar she has had a large and paying practice, but for the last four years she has confined her energies more especially to claims against the government. She often makes an argument for the passage of a bill before the committee of the Senate and House of the United States Congress. In 1870 she secured the passage of a bill, by the aid of Hon. S. M. Arnell, of Tennessee, and other friends, giving to the women employees of the government, of whom there are many thousands, equal pay for equal work with men. At another time she secured the passage of a bill appropriating $50,000 for the payment of bounties to sailors and mariners, heretofore a neglected class. During Garfield's administration, in 1881, Mrs. Lockwood made application for appointment as Minister to Brazil. The negotiations were terminated by the unfortunate death of the President, to whom voluminous petitions had been presented by her friends. In the summer of 1884 Mrs. Lockwood was nominated for the Presidency by the Equal Rights party in San Francisco, CA, and in 1888 was renominated by the same party in Des Moines, IA, and in both cases made a canvass that awakened the people of the United States to the consideration of the right of suffrage for women. The popularity given to her by these bold movements has called her very largely to the lecture platform and into newspaper correspondence during the last six years. Mrs. Lockwood is interested not only in equal rights for men and women, but in temperance and labor reforms, the control of railroads and telegraphs by the government, and in the settlement of all difficulties, national and international, by arbitration instead of war. In the summer of 1889, in company with Rev. Amanda Deyo, Mrs. Lockwood represented the Universal Peace Union in the Paris Exposition and was their delegate to the International Congress of Peace in that city, which opened its sessions in the Salle of the Trocadéro, under the patronage of the French government. She made one of the opening speeches and later presented a paper in the French language on international arbitration, which was well received. In the summer of 1890 she again represented the Universal Peace Union in the International Congress in London, in Westminster Town Hall, in which she presented a paper on "Disarmament." Before returning to the United States, Mrs. Lockwood took a course of university extension lectures in the University of Oxford. She was elected for the third time to represent the Universal Peace Union, of which she is corresponding secretary, in the International Congress of Peace held in November, 1891, in Rome. Her subject in that gathering was "The Establishment of an International Bureau of Peace." Mrs. Lockwood is assistant editor of the "Peacemaker," a monthly magazine published in Philadelphia, and is the general delegate of the Woman's National Press Association. She is also chairman of the committee for the International Federation of Women's Press Clubs. Mrs. Lockwood has always been a student and is deeply interested in the rapidly-growing sentiment for university extension in this country.

LOGAN, Mrs. Celia, journalist and dramatist, born in Philadelphia, PA, in 1840. She was in girlhood a writer of graceful verse. When she arrived at the age of maturity she went to London, England, where for some years she filled a highly responsible position in a large publishing house as a critical reader of submitted manuscripts and a corrector and amender of those accepted for publication. The works she examined were chiefly fiction, but there were also many scientific works upon which she sat in judgment. While in London, and subsequently during several years' residence in France and Italy, Mrs. Logan was a regular correspondent of the Boston "Saturday Evening Gazette" and the "Golden Era" of San Francisco. She also won considerable fame as a writer of short stories for the magazines of England and the United States. After the Civil War she returned to this country. She lived in Washington, DC, writing stories and corresponding for several journals. At length she became associate editor of Don Piatt's paper, "The Capital." As is the case of hundreds of other journalistic writers, it has been her fortune to do much of her best work in an impersonal way. In addition to her original writing, she has done much work as a translator from the French and Italian. Curiously enough, her first efforts in that field were made in converting American war news from English into Latin. She lived in Milan, Italy, during the Civil War. The facilities of the Milanese press for obtaining American war news were then much below what was demanded by the importance of the occasion. Mrs. Logan was known as one of the literati, and as it was understood that she regularly received news from her own country concerning the struggle, the directors of the Milanese press appealed to her for aid. Not then being sufficiently acquainted with Italian to translate into that language, and English being a sealed book to Milanese journalists, a compromise suggested by her was tried and proved to be a happy solution of the difficulty. She first put the American war news into Latin, and then the journalists turned the Latin into Italian. Another important branch of Mrs. Logan's literary work has been the rewriting, adapting and translating of plays. As in the case of her editorial work, much of the credit of what she has done in that direction has gone to others, who have won fame and fortune by her literary and dramatic talent. One of her works, the drama "An American

Marriage," has been eminently successful. Her intimate relations with the stage have given her unusual advantages for critical judgment upon it and literary work pertaining to it. She contributed to the "Sunday Dispatch" a few years ago a long series of articles under the title, "These Our Actors," which attracted much comment. Her first original play was entitled "Rose." It was produced in San Francisco by Lewis Morrison and his wife, and played by them throughout the country. The next was a comedy called "The Odd Trick," in which William Mestayer made his first appearance as a star. In her third play Fay Templeton as a child made a great hit. The Villas starred in her drama of "The Homestead," and it is a fact that within the past few years there has been no time when this author has not had a play on the boards somewhere. Her successful rearrangements and adaptations from the French are "Gaston Cadol, or A Son of the Soil," used as a star piece by Frederick Warde, "The Sphinx," "Miss Multon," "Froment Jeune," by Daudet, and a "Marriage In High Life." Her original novels are entitled "Her Strange Fate" and "Sarz, A Story of the Stage." Her latest work is upon the subject of corpulence, called "How to Reduce Your Weight, or to Increase It." For several years past she has lived in New York City. She became the wife while living in France, of Miner K. Kellogg, an artist, and she was married a second time, to James H. Connelly, an author.

LOGAN, Mrs. Mary Cunningham, editor, born in Petersburg, (now Sturgeon) MO, 15th August, 1838. The family moved to Illinois when she was a child. She was educated in St. Vincent, a Catholic academy in Morganfield, KY. Her father was a captain of volunteers in the Mexican War, and John A. Logan was in the same regiment. He and the captain became warm friends, and their friendship continued through life. Mrs. Logan was the oldest of thirteen children, and the large family, with the modest circumstances of her father, compelled her early acquaintance with the cares and responsibilities of life. Her father was appointed land register during President Pierce's administration, and his daughter Mary acted as his clerk. It was then she and John A.

Logan met and formed an attachment which resulted in marriage. He was thirteen years her senior. It was a union that proved to be mutually helpful and happy. Mr. Logan was then an ambitious young lawyer, the prosecuting attorney for the third judicial circuit of Illinois, residing in the town of Benton. Mrs. Logan identified her interests with those of her husband and in many ways she contributed to his many successes in the political world. While treading the paths of obscurity and comparative poverty with him cheerfully, she acted as his confidential adviser and amanuensis. Even when the war broke out, she did not hold him back, but entered with enthusiasm into his career and bore the brunt of calumny for his sake, with the burden of family life devolving upon her, for he organized his regiment in a hostile community. She followed him to many a well-fought field and endured the privations of camp life, as thousands of other patriotic women did, without murmur, only too glad to share her husband's perils or to minister to the sick and wounded of his regiment for the sake of being near him. When the war was over, Gen. Logan was elected to Congress, and later to the United States Senate. In the political and social life of Washington Mrs. Logan's talent for filling high positions with ease and grace made her famous. General Logan owed much of his success in life to this devoted, tactful and talented woman, who steadily grew in honor in the estimation of the public, as did her husband. It was a terrible blow when the strong man, of whom she was so proud, was struck down with disease, and the mortal put on the immortal. To a woman of Mrs. Logan's ambitions, to say nothing of her strong affection for her husband and her activity, that stroke was appalling, and she nearly sank under it, but for the sake of the son and daughter left she rallied, and recovered her health and power to live, through change of scene and a trip to Europe, chaperoning the Misses Pullman. On her return Mrs. Logan received the offer of the position of editor of the "Home Magazine," published in Washington, which position she has continued to fill acceptably ever since. The family residence, "Calumet Place," Washington, in which Gen. Logan died, was then a new and long-desired home, but unpaid for. Friends of the General in Chicago voluntarily raised a handsome fund and put it at Mrs. Logan's disposal. The first thing she did was to secure the homestead, and in it devoted what was once the studio of an artist and former owner to a "Memorial Hall," where now all the General's books, army uniforms, portraits, busts, presents and souvenirs of life are gathered. They form a most interesting collection. During the past few years honors seem to have been showered upon Mrs. Logan in full measure. During the Templar Triennial Conclave in the capital city, in October, 1889, the Knights Templar carried out a programme planned by the General, who was one of their number. They were received in Mrs. Logan's home, where thousands paid their respects, leaving bushels of cards and miles of badges, mementoes of the visit. President Harrison appointed Mrs. Logan one of the women commissioners of the District of Columbia to the Columbian Exposition, to be held in Chicago in 1893, a business that has occupied much of her attention and her peculiar executive ability since, both as to work and with her pen. She has found time to carry out successfully the plans of the greatest charity in Washington, the Garfield Hospital, having been president of the board nine years, during which time the charitable people associated with her have built up one of the best hospitals east of the Alleghanies. There is no woman of to-day with more personal influence on the public than Mrs. Logan. Other women may be more brilliant, of broader culture, of greater ability in many lines, but she possesses the qualities that take hold of the popular heart. As wife and mother no name shines with brighter luster, especially with the men and women who compose the Grand Army of the Republic and the Woman's Relief Corps, in which order she is regarded as the one whom all delight to honor, both for the name she bears as Gen. Logan's wife, and for her own sake. The honors conferred upon her in Minneapolis in many respects have never been equaled in this or any other country.

LONGSHORE, Mrs. Hannah E., physician, born in Montgomery county, MD, 30th May, 1819. For the past forty years she has been a conspicuous figure in Philadelphia, PA. In the early part of that time she was notable because she dared to practice medicine in opposition to public sentiment, and without question it may be said that she plowed the ground, and, by her practical work, prepared the way for the hosts of women doctors who have followed. Her father and mother, Samuel and Paulina Myers, were natives of Bucks county, PA, and members of the Society of Friends. From her second till her thirteenth year the family resided in Washington, DC, where she attended a private school. Her parents, not wishing to raise a family of children under the demoralizing influences of slavery, then prevalent in the South, moved to Columbiana county, OH, settling upon a farm. To her the pursuit of knowledge was always a keen delight. As a child she enjoyed the study of anatomy, dissecting small animals with great interest and precision. As a young woman her great ambition was to enter Oberlin College. At twenty-two years of age she became the wife of Thomas E. Longshore, and returned with him to his home, near Philadelphia, where the following few years were devoted to domestic duties. Eight years later Mrs. Longshore read medicine with her brother-in-law, Prof. Joseph S. Longshore, in addition to taking care of her two children and home. Prof. Longshore was deeply interested in the medical education of women, and was one of the leading spirits and active workers in securing the charter and opening the Female Medical College of Pennsylvania, in Philadelphia, now the Woman's Medical College. His pupil availed herself of that opportunity and became a member of the first class, graduating at the close of the second session, in 1850. She was appointed demonstrator of anatomy in the following session of the college. As a means of bringing herself before the public in a professional way, she prepared and delivered several courses of popular lectures on physiology and hygiene. That was an innovation and aroused considerable discussion. Lucretia Mott presided at the opening lecture. During the first year after graduation Dr. Longshore was called to see a woman ill with dropsy, who had been given up by the doctors to die. One, a leading physician, staked his medical reputation that the case would terminate fatally. To the surprise of all interested, the patient recovered under the care of "that woman." That was a triumph, and the story spread among the friends of the family and brought the young doctor many patients. The story of the difficulties and criticisms that met Dr. Longshore in every direction in the early years of her practice seems like fiction. Who would believe to-day that she found it almost impossible to procure medicines, that druggists would not fill her prescriptions, saying "a woman could not be trusted to prescribe drugs; she could not know enough to give the proper dose"; that men doctors persecuted her and would not consult with a woman? The doctor's sign on her door, the first one seen in Philadelphia, called forth ridicule. People stopped on the pavement in front of her house and read the name aloud with annoying comments. She drove her own horse, which was contrary to custom and sure proof of her strong-mindedness. Nothing is so successful as success. As time passed, all these obstacles faded away, and Dr. Longshore followed the usual course of general practitioners. At the zenith of her practice she visited, was consulted by and prescribed for great numbers, and, with few exceptions, had more patients than any other of the leading physicians. To-day, at the age of seventy-two, she is full of activity and able to attend to a large practice. During her professional career she has been confined to her home by sickness but twice, and has taken but few short vacations. She is a splendid illustration of what a congenial occupation and out-door exercise will do in developing the physical power of women. Professionally and socially she has always been actuated by high motives. She is noted for honesty of opinion and fearless truthfulness. While her surroundings indicate material prosperity, no suffering woman has been refused attendance because of her inability to pay for service. In connection with her practice she has given attention to minor surgery, and in the reduction of dislocations has been most successful. She is frequently called upon as a medical expert, and in a recent case her testimony given in the form of an object lesson, was so explicit that the judge remarked: "This is a revelation and will cause a new era in expert testimony." The home-life of Dr. Longshore has been of the most happy kind.

LOOP, Mrs. Jennette Shephard Harrison, artist, born in New Haven, CT, 5th March, 1840. She is descended on her father's side from Rev. John Davenport and Oliver Wolcott, of Connecticut, and on her mother's side from Nathaniel Lynde, one of the first settlers of Saybrook and the founder of the first Yale College. Nathaniel Lynde was a grandson of Kenelm, Earl

of Digby. She began her art studies under Professor Bail in her native city, and later entered the studio of Henry A. Loop, becoming his wife in 1864. With him she spent two years of study in Rome, Venice and Paris. Most of her professional life has been passed in New York City. In 1875 she was elected an associate of the National Academy of Design, and has exhibited in nearly all of its exhibitions since. Many prominent people of New Haven have portraits by her, and her portraits of New York people have given her a wide reputation. She has produced a number of ideal pictures. She has four daughters, three of whom are studying music and painting. Her home is in New York.

LORD, Mrs. Elizabeth W. Russell, educator and philanthropist, born in Kirtland, OH, 28th April, 1819. She is the oldest child of Alpheus C. and Elizabeth Conant Russell. Her parents, natives of Massachusetts, were among the early settlers of the Western Reserve. Both had been teachers in New England, and Mr. Russell continued for some years to teach school in the winters, carrying on his farm at the same time. After some terms in the district school, Elizabeth was for several years a pupil of Rev. Truman Coe, pastor of the Congregational Church in Kirtland. In the spring of 1838 Mr. Russell sent his daughter to Oberlin. About that time the Western Reserve Teachers' Seminary was established in Kirtland, with Mr. Russell as one of its board of trustees. During the succeeding years Miss Russell divided her time between that seminary and Oberlin College, until 21st July, 1842, when in Oberlin she became the wife of Asa D. Lord, MD, and with him returned to Kirtland to share his work as teacher in the seminary. In 1847 Dr. Lord was induced to go to Columbus, OH, there to establish a system of graded schools, the first of the kind in the State. When the high school was opened, a little later, Mrs. Lord was its first principal. In the summer of 1856 Dr. Lord assumed charge of the Ohio Institution for the Education of the Blind, remaining there until 1868 when he went to Batavia, NY, to organize the new State Institution for the Blind. During the nineteen years Dr. Lord was superintendent of the institutions for the blind in Ohio and New York, Mrs. Lord was to her husband a helpmeet, serving also as a faithful and earnest teacher of the blind. She has probably taught more blind persons to read than any other one teacher in this country, and probably more than any other in the world. Her success in teaching adult blind persons to read was especially remarkable. In March, 1875, after a very brief illness, Dr. Lord died, and the board of trustees unanimously elected Mrs. Lord to succeed her husband as superintendent in the institution. Mrs. Lord performed the duties of that important office until the fall of 1877, when she no longer deemed it best to act as superintendent. Her resignation was reluctantly accepted, on condition that she remain in the institution. After a few months spent in the home of her only child, Mrs. Henry Fisk Tarbox, of Batavia, NY, Mrs. Lord returned to the institution and spent five more years in labors for the blind. Mrs. Lord had been accustomed from early childhood to the active life begun in the home of a hardy pioneer. Still in full vigor of health, in full possession of every faculty, and desirous of filling all her days with usefulness, she was ready to respond to a call to serve as assistant principal of the woman's department of Oberlin College. She entered upon the duties of that office, which she now holds, in the summer of 1884. She has given liberally of her means to charitable and educational institutions. Her largest gift was that of ten-thousand dollars to Oberlin College in 1890, which, with additions from other sources, builds "Lord Cottage" for the accommodation of young women.

LOTHROP, Mrs. Harriett M., author, born in New Haven, CT, 22nd June, 1844. She is best known as "Margaret Sidney." She was the daughter of Sidney Mason Stone and Harriett Mulford Stone. Her parents were from New England and connected with some of the most distinguished of the Puritan families. Mrs. Lothrop was educated in the old classic town, and, during his lifetime and till the daughter's marriage, her father's house was the center for his friends, men of letters. It may well be said that Mrs. Lothrop was reared in an atmosphere of books, having likewise the advantage of a polite education. Her genius for writing began to develop very early. At the outset she adopted the pen-name which has gained her wide popularity. All her writings have wide circulation, but the work by which her reputation was effectually established is "Five Little Peppers," and the two succeeding "Pepper" volumes. The vivacity of thought and energy of expression at once revealed the earnest, impassioned writer for young folks, whose influence has exercised a remarkable sway. Mrs. Lothrop has written many books, and always struck the keynote of a worthy purpose. In "A New Departure for Girls" (Boston, 1886), she was the first to write a book for girls who are left without means of support, who are wholly unprepared to earn money, that should make them see their opportunities in the simple home-training they have received. Consequently her book has been the basis for those practical attempts to help girls, such as advising them to open mending bureaus and the like, while the countless letters from all over the country attest the success of her efforts. In October, 1881, she became the wife of Daniel Lothrop, publisher, founder of the D. Lothrop Company. Their married life was eminently happy; it was an ideal union in all things. Mr. Lothrop was a man of cultivated tastes and fine literary attainments. During the ensuing ten years their summer home was the "Wayside," in Concord, MA, the home of Nathaniel Hawthorne, where Mrs. Lothrop now resides. The historic house and grounds were purchased by Mr. Lothrop, early in their married life, as a gift to his wife. Their winters were passed either in travel or their Boston home, where Mr. Lothrop died, 18th March, 1892. Mrs. Lothrop has one daughter, Margaret, born 27th July, 1884, to whom and to the undeveloped plans and interests which she looks upon as the last request of her husband, and to her writings, she purposes henceforth to devote her time and interest. In domestic knowledge and the performance of household duties, Mrs. Lothrop shows as ready acquaintance and as much skill as though these alone formed her pursuits. She is a typical American woman, with that religious fiber of New England that is the very bone and sinew of our Republic. Besides the books named above, she is the author of "Polly Pepper's Chicken-Pie" (Boston, 1880), "Phronsie's New Shoes" (Boston, 1880), "Miss Scarrett" (Boston, 1881), "So as by Fire" (Boston, 1881), "Judith Pettibone" (Boston, 1881), "Half a Year in

Brockton" (Boston, 1881), "How They Went to Europe" (Boston, 1884), "The Golden West" (Boston, 1886), and "Old Concord, Her Highways and Byways" (Boston, 1888). Her stories are very numerous, and many of them are to be found in "Our Little Men and Women," "Pansy," "Babyland," "Wide Awake" and other periodicals.

LOUD, Miss Hulda Barker, editor and publisher, born in East Abington, now Rockland, MA, 13th September, 1844. She attended the public schools of that town until she was seventeen years of age. At eighteen she began to teach school in her native place, and taught there most of the time until 1886, retaining for thirteen years the highest position held by a woman in that town, and receiving the highest salary, her salary always being the same as that of a man in the same grade of work. That was owing to her constant agitation of the question of equal rights with her school committee. In 1884 a new paper was started in her town, and she was asked by the publisher to take the editorial chair. She consented and named the paper the Rockland "Independent," of which she has always been editor-in-chief. In 1889 she bought the business, job-printing and publishing, and is now sole proprietor. That paper she has always made the vehicle of reformatory principles, social and political. In 1889, when it became her own property, she announced in the opening number that she had bought the business to help save the world; that it was not a business venture in any sense of the word; that the business would always be in charge of a foreman; that she desired a medium through which she could convey her best thought to the world, unhampered by worldly interests. She represented the Knights of Labor in the Woman's International Council, held in Washington in 1887, and her address was received with enthusiasm. At that time she spoke also before the Knights of Labor and Anti-Poverty Society of Washington. She has frequently spoken on the labor and woman-suffrage platform with success. She prefers home life, and her newspaper work is more congenial. She served three years on the school board of her town, and for many years she has addressed town-meetings, without question of

her right from any of the citizens. In the spring of 1891 she adopted two boys, relatives, and, besides carrying on her paper and business, she does the work of her household. Her adopted children are governed wholly without force of any kind. She is an apostle of the new mental science, though recognizing the claims of her body. She may always be found at home, except for a few hours in the afternoon, which she spends in her office. She lives away from the village, in a retired spot, on her mother's farm, where she has built a house of her own. She boasts that she has never known a day of sickness in her life, and that through sheer force of will, as she has many hereditary weaknesses. Although she works from sixteen to eighteen hours a day, she was never physically or mentally stronger in her life than now.

LOUGHEAD, Mrs. Flora Haines, author, whose maiden name was Flora Haines, born in Milwaukee, WI, 12th July, 1855. Both her parents were natives of Maine. She attended school in Columbus, WI, and in Lincoln, IL, graduating from Lincoln University in June, 1872, with the degree of A.B. Her literary career has been a quickly successful one. When fifteen years old, and a very busy school-girl, the desire came over her to write a story. She wrote it by stealth and sent it to the "Aldine." The editor, Richard Henry Stoddard, returned the manuscript to her, suggesting that she would do well to try her story in the Harper and Appleton periodicals, as the "Aldine" had accepted manuscript enough for two or three years. The manuscript and letter went to the bottom of her trunk and were hidden there for years. She came to a serious and care-laden womanhood before she began to see the encouragement the editor's words contained and to appreciate their consideration. She began to write stories in earnest in 1883. Mrs. Loughead's newspaper work began in 1873 on the Chicago "Inter-Ocean." In 1874 and 1875 she was on several of the Denver newspapers. While there, she became acquainted with Helen Hunt Jackson, who was afterward one of her most intimate friends. During Mrs. Jackson's fatal illness Mrs. Loughead was in daily attendance to the end. Between 1878 and 1882, and again from 1884 to 1886, she supported herself by writing for the San Francisco dailies on space-work. She published a number of excellent short stories in the "Ingleside," the "San Franciscan," the "Argonaut," "Drake's Magazine," the Chicago "Current" and the "Overland Monthly." She now does a good deal for the syndicates, has occasional correspondence in the New York "Post," and works upon her books. The first volume she published was a valuable work upon "The Libraries of California" (San Francisco, 1878). It is now out of print and marked "rare" in catalogues. Her first novel, "The Man Who Was Guilty," after giving her some local reputation, was taken up by a Boston house in 1886, and has had a steady sale ever since. She wrote, in 1886, a practical "Hand-Book of Natural Science," which the "San Franciscan" issued. In 1889 she published a housekeeper's book on "Quick Cooking." She has written a California story, "The Abandoned Claim," published in 1891 and has edited a volume of "Hebrew Folk-Lore Tales." She became the wife of John Loughead in February, 1886. She is the mother of five children. Her home is in Santa Barbara, CA.

LOWE, Mrs. Martha Perry, poet, born in Keene, NH, 21st November, 1829. Her parents were Gen. Justus Perry and Hannah Wood. At the age of fifteen years she was sent to the famous school of Madame Sedgwick, in Lenox, MA. After her graduation she spent a winter in Boston in the study of music. A few years later she passed a winter in the West Indies, and the next year she visited in Madrid, Spain, with her brother, who was a member of the Spanish Legation, and who married Carolina Coronado, the poet laureate of Spain. In 1857 Miss Perry became the wife of Rev. Charles Lowe, a prominent clergyman in the Unitarian denomination of New England. After her marriage she published her first volume of poems, "The Olive and the Pine." The first part is devoted to Spain, and the latter to New England. A few years later she published another volume, "Love in Spain," which is a dramatic poem. The book also contains poems on the Civil War and on miscellaneous subjects. In 1874 her husband died. In 1884 she published his

memoirs, a book not only full of interesting incidents of his life, but containing a vivid history of the liberal church of that period. In 1861 her "Chief Joseph" appeared, a metrical version of the eloquent speech of Chief Joseph before the council of white men, in order to awaken sympathy for the Indian cause. Her last publication was issued in 1891. Mrs. Lowe has constantly contributed to newspapers and periodicals, and has been frequently invited to read poems on public occasions. She has always taken an active part in the cause of woman suffrage and temperance. Her children are two daughters, happily married, who reside near their mother in Somerville, MA.

LOWMAN, Mrs. Mary D., municipal officer, born in Indiana county, PA, 27th January, 1842. Her maiden name was McGaha. She resided on a farm until she had fitted herself for teaching. She was a successful teacher for a number of years. In April, 1866, she became the wife of George W. Lowman, and they went to Kansas. Being deeply, interested in the condition of the colored race so recently emancipated, she became a teacher among them for three years. Her health becoming impaired, she then applied herself for some years to domestic affairs. She was an earnest worker in the cause of Christianity. Early in life she identified herself with the Presbyterian Church, and has remained loyal to its interests. She served in 1885 as deputy register of deeds in Oskaloosa, where she has resided for many years. In 1888 the women of Oskaloosa, feeling that the municipal affairs of their city might be improved, decided to put in the field a ticket composed entirely of women, with Mary D. Lowman for mayor. The move created much excitement. When the result was declared, it was found that Mrs. Lowman had been elected mayor, with a common council of women, by no small majority. They served for two years, being reelected in 1889, and an examination of the records of the city will show how faithfully they executed the trust. When their administration began, they found an empty treasury and the city in debt. At the end of the year they had made many public improvements, and there was money in the treasury, showing conclusively that a woman's ideas of economy may extend beyond the domestic side of life. They closed the business houses that were wont to open their doors on the Sabbath, and many other reforms were brought about under her administration. She was not the first woman mayor in Kansas, but she was the first with a full council of women. She has two children, a son and a daughter.

LOZIER, Mrs. Jennie de la Montagnie, physician and president of Sorosis, was born in New York, and has been a lifelong resident of that city. Her father was William de la Montagnie, Jr. Her ancestors were Dutch and Huguenot French, who settled there as early as 1633. She was born and reared in the old seventh ward of New York, then the best portion of the city. She was thoroughly educated, and was a graduate of Rutgers' Female Institute, now Rutgers' Female College, of which she is a trustee, and which, in 1891, conferred upon her the degree of Doctor of Science. Her education was liberal, including languages and science. After her graduation she traveled in the West Indies. When she was nineteen years old, she began to teach, and several years later became instructor in languages and literature in Hillsdale College, Hillsdale, MI. She was afterward chosen vice-principal of the woman's department of that college. Returning to New York in 1872, she became the wife of Dr. A. W. Lozier, the only son of Dr. Clemence S. Lozier, who had been her lifelong friend. The young college professor became the head of a family at once, as her husband was a widower with two children. She became interested in medicine through her mother-in-law, Dr. Clemence S. Lozier, who was the founder and for twenty-five years the dean of the New York Medical College and Hospital for Women. The young wife studied in that college was graduated MD after her first and only child was born, and was made professor of physiology in the institution. She also served on the hospital staff. After twelve years of faithful service Mrs. Lozier retired from the profession and devoted herself to domestic, social and educational interests. Just before her retirement she was invited by Sorosis to address that club on "Physical Culture." She was soon made a member of Sorosis, and at once became prominent in its councils. She is a forceful speaker, clear-brained, broad-minded and thoroughly cultured. In Sorosis she has served as chairman of the committee on science, as chairman of the committee on philanthropy and as corresponding secretary. She was elected president in 1891, and was reelected in 1892. In 1892 she was sent as a delegate to the biennial council of the Federation of Women's Clubs, held in Chicago 11th, 12th and 13th of May, and she read an able paper on the "Educational Influence of Women's Clubs." Her activities have been numerous. In 1889 she was sent by the New York Medical College and Hospital for Women as a delegate to the International Homeopathic Congress in Paris. She there presented a paper, in French, on the medical education of women in the United States, which was printed in full in the transactions of that congress. She is the president of two other important clubs, The Emerson, a club of men and women belonging to Rev. Dr. Heber Newton's church, of which she is a member, and The Avon, a fortnightly drawing-room club. She is a member of the science committee of the Association for the Advancement of Women, and is also a member of the Patria Club. She has read papers of great merit before various literary and reform associations in and near New York City. Her family consists of two sons and one daughter. Their summers are spent in their summer home on the great South Bay, Long Island, in a pleasantly situated villa named "Windhurst." Her husband, Dr. Lozier, gave up his practice some time ago, and is now engaged in the real-estate and building business in New York. Their winter home, in Seventy-eighth street, New York, is an ideal one in all its appointments and associations. Mrs. Lozier is strongly inclined to scientific study and investigation, but she is also a student of literature and art. She speaks for the liberal and thorough education of women, not only in art and music, but also in chemistry, social economics, psychology, pedagogy and physiology. Her influence as a clubwoman has been widely felt, and as president of Sorosis she occupies a commanding position in the new field of social, literary and general culture opened to women by the clubs.

LUKENS, Miss Anna, physician, born in Philadelphia, PA, 29th October, 1844, of Quaker parents. The family lived in Plymouth, PA, from

1855 to 1870. Anna was educated in the Friends' Seminary, Philadelphia, and began the study of medicine with Dr. Hiram Corson, of Montgomery county, PA, in 1867. She was graduated in the Woman's Medical College of Pennsylvania on 13th March, 1870. She attended clinics in the Pennsylvania Hospital on that memorable day in November, 1869, when students from the Woman's Medical College were first admitted. Hisses and groans were given during the lecture. Miss Anna E. Broomall and Miss Anna Lukens led the line as the women passed out of the hospital grounds amid the jeers and insults of the male students, who followed them for some distance, throwing stones and mud at them. She was elected a member of Montgomery County Medical Society, in Morristown, PA, in the spring of 1870, soon after graduation. The society had never before elected a woman. It was done through the efforts of Dr. Hiram Comon, the brave champion of women physicians for more than forty years. Dr. Lukens was the youngest member of her class and was graduated with the highest vote that had been awarded in the college in many years. During the spring and summer of 1870, after graduation, she was engaged in the special study of pharmacy, attending a course of lectures given to a few women by Prof. Edward Parrish in the Philadelphia College of Pharmacy, in connection with practical work in Prof. Parrish's private laboratory. In October, 1870, she entered the Woman's Hospital of Philadelphia for six months' experience as interne. In the fall of 1871 she began to teach in the college as instructor in the chair of physiology. During the winter of 1871 and 1872, when Prof. Preston's health failed, she gave a number of lectures for her on physiology and took charge of her office practice which was continued at Prof. Preston's request for some months after the death of the latter, in April, 1872. During the spring of 1872 she taught pharmacy in the college by lectures and practical demonstrations in the dispensary of the Woman's Hospital. She was the first woman to apply for admission to the Philadelphia College of Pharmacy, to take the regular course with a view to graduation. Application was made in the spring of 1872. Several of the professors were favorable and expressed much cordiality, but thought such an innovation would be met by the students in a manner that would

make it very unpleasant for a woman attending alone. Hearing of more liberality in the New York College of Pharmacy, where one woman was already studying, she began a course of lectures there in October, 1872, with the hope of receiving the diploma of that school. It was expected at that time that a professorship in pharmacy would be established in the Woman's Medical College in Philadelphia, and Dr. Lukens was invited to prepare for it. During the winter of 1872 and 1873 she took a course in analytical chemistry in the laboratory of Dr. Walz, of New York, working five hours a day, and attending lectures on pharmacy in the evening. She was forced to discontinue these lectures on account of eye troubles. In the spring of 1873 she was appointed attending physician to the Western Dispensary for Women and Children, the only dispensary on the west side under the charge of woman physicians. At the same time she was appointed attending physician to the Isaac T. Hopper Home, of the Women's Prison Association. She continued the work in the Western Dispensary until the winter of 1877, paying the rent for some months after the appropriation failed, in order to keep up the work. She was elected a member of the New York County Medical Society in 1873. She had some private practice in New York City until 1877, when she was appointed assistant physician in the Nursery and Child's Hospital, Staten Island, with entire charge of the pharmaceutical department. Soon after she was elected a member of the Richmond County Medical Society. In February, 1880, she was appointed resident physician in the Nursery and Child's Hospital, which office she held until December, 1884. She was a member of the Staten Island Clinical Society, for which she prepared and read two papers, one on Omphalitis, and one on Noma Pudendi, both of which were published in the New York "Medical Journal." The paper on Omphalitis was copied in the London "Lancet" and noticed by the "British Medical Journal." In May, 1884, she went to Europe, carrying a letter of recommendation from the New York State Board of Health, the first ever given to a woman, which secured her admission to the principal hospitals for the study of diseases of children. In December, 1884, she entered upon private practice in New York City. She was elected consulting physician to the Nursery and Child's Hospital,

Staten Island, and elected a fellow of the New York State Medical Association. She was present at the organization of the New York Committee for the Prevention of State Regulation of Vice, in 1876, and was appointed one of the vice-presidents, which office she still holds. She was elected a member of Sorosis in 1889. The work done in the various positions which Dr. Lukens has filled since she graduated has all been distinguished for its unfailing thoroughness. Her executive ability in hospital administration has been of a high standard and marked with the same methodical order that has characterized her whole career in life.

LUMMIS, Mrs. Dorothea, physician, born in Chillicothe, OH, 9th November, 1860. Her parents were Josiah H. Rhodes, of old Pennsylvania Dutch stock, and Sarah Crosby Swift, of New England Puritan stock. Several brothers and a sister of the young Dorothea died in infancy. In 1868 the family moved to Portsmouth, OH. Dorothea entered the Portsmouth Female College, and at the age of sixteen years was graduated as B.A. and was the salutatorian of her class. Two years later she went to Philadelphia, PA, and entered Mme. Emma Seiler's conservatory of music. She remained two years, learning some music and hearing a great deal of the best in concert and opera, and reading indiscriminately and superficially everything that was found on the shelves of the Public Library, that looked interesting. Later she went to Boston, MA, and studied music under James O'Neil of the New England Conservatory of Music. In 1880 she became the wife of Charles F. Lummis, the well-known writer. In 1881 she entered the medical school of Boston University, and graduated with honors in 1884. During the last year of her college life she served as resident physician in the New England Conservatory of Music. In 1885 she removed to Los Angeles, where she began to practice medicine. She has been highly successful in her practice. She has obtained prompt recognition from her fellow physicians, and has served as president and secretary of the County Medical Society, and as corresponding secretary of the Southern California Medical Society. She served as dramatic editor of the Los Angeles "Times," and

she is now the musical editor and critic of that journal. In her practice she found much cruelty and neglect among the children, chiefly of the Mexicans, and among animals. She at once set about the formation of a humane society, and brought the cases of neglect and cruelty into the courts, making the society at once a power. In her vacation tours she has visited many of the Indian pueblos in New Mexico, and has made a collection of arrow-heads, Navajo silver and blankets, Acoma pottery, baskets and other curios of that country. Besides her professional labors, Dr. Lummis has done some notable literary work. She has contributed to "Kate Field's Washington," "Puck," "Judge," "Life," "Woman's Cycle," the "Home-Maker," the San Francisco "Argonaut" and the "Californian." She is a member of the Pacific Coast Press Association, and has contributed many important papers to the various medical journals of standing in the United States.

LUTZ, Mrs. Adelia Armstrong, artist and art-teacher, born in Knoxville, TN, 25th June, 1859. She is full of ambition for herself and the people of her native city, and for that reason, besides devoting herself to training a large class of pupils, she opens her private gallery and studio to visitors. She is a daughter of Robert Houston Armstrong, a lawyer and an amateur artist of note. Mrs. Lutz from her childhood breathed an atmosphere of refinement and culture. Her fondness for the pencil was developed early. Her general education was received in Augusta Seminary, Staunton, VA, and in the Southern Home School, in Baltimore, MD. In both schools her art study was prominent. Afterward she was a pupil in painting under the best masters. She worked nearly a year in the Pennsylvania Academy of Fine Arts and supplemented that course by study in the Corcoran Gallery in Washington, DC. The mother of two children, a devoted wife and the mistress of a beautiful home, "Westwood," she finds her enthusiasm for artwork in no wise abated. Her studio contains many pictures that are worthy. Her husband warmly seconds all her efforts as artist and teacher. Notwithstanding her home cares and the claims of society, she finds time for the labor of her life. She has been the recipient of various prizes and medals.

LYNDE, Mrs. Mary Elizabeth Blanchard, philanthropist, born in Truxton, Cortland county, NY, 4th December, 1819. Her father was Azariel Blanchard. Her mother was Elizabeth Babcock, a native of South Kingston, RI. She was educated principally in the Albany Female Academy, where she was graduated in 1839, taking the first prize medal for composition, which was presented by the governor of the State, Hon. William H. Seward. Mrs. Lynde has spent most of her married life in Milwaukee, WI. She is the widow of the eminent lawyer, Hon. William Pitt Lynde. She was appointed a member of the Wisconsin State Board of Charities and Reforms, while Governor Lucius Fairchild was in office. She was the first woman to hold such a position, and she filled it with great honor to herself and benefit to the dependent classes. She has spoken much in public, chiefly before legislative committees in behalf of charitable institutions, but also before State conventions of charities. She read papers in the meetings of the Association for the Advancement of Women in Chicago and Boston, and her ideas were so practical and forcible as to attract unusual attention. She is at present engaged in looking after the general interests of the Girls' Industrial School in Milwaukee, and she is more especially prominent in connection with the World's Columbian Exposition.

LYON, Miss Anne Bozeman, author, born in Mobile, AL, 25th February, 1860. Her father's people were English and Welsh. He was connected with some of the leading families of Virginia, among them the Temples, the Pendietons and the Strothers. "Porte Crayon," General Strother of the Union Army, the noted artist and descriptive writer, was his cousin. Mr. Lyon was a man of remarkable influence and was noted for his learning and marvelous memory. His name was Thomas T. A. Lyon. Miss Lyon's mother was Mary Coffee Heard, a descendant of two illustrious Georgia families. Anne is the oldest of ten children, six of whom are living. Her father died in 1888. In early youth she resided in Mobile and in the swamp country of the Mississippi, where her father was constructing a railroad. She always had the best instructors. Her favorite studies were French, history and mythology. She read poetry with a passionate love and a clear perception. Her associations have always been congenial and conducive to her art. Miss Lyon's successes have been in poetry, short sketches and novels. Her poetry is particularly pleasing. She has contributed to many well-known papers. "No Saint" (Louisville), her first novel, made an immediate name for itself. It is well written. "At Sterling's Camp," her second novel, maintains the author's standards. She excels in descriptive work.

LYON, Miss Mary, educator, born in Buckland, MA, 28th February, 1797. From long-lived ancestors, prominent for six generations in New England in all activities of church and State, she inherited a sound mind in a sound body and sterling qualities of character. From the common school she went to the academies in Ashfield and Amherst, MA, and had been for seven years teaching successfully in the schools of Buckland and vicinity, when her thirst for knowledge led her, in 1821, to Rev. Joseph Emerson's seminary in Byfield, MA. At that time it was generally thought that the common elements of education were sufficient for women, and that more learning tended to make them less useful. Mr. Emerson believed in a higher education for women and taught that it should be sought and used as a means of usefulness. After two terms under his teachings, Miss Lyon was assistant principal for three years in the academy in Ashfield, a position never before occupied by a woman. For the next ten years she was associated with a former pupil and assistant of Mr. Emerson, Miss Grant, in an academy for girls in Derry, NH. During the winter, when that school was closed, owing to the severity of the climate, she taught a school of her own in Ashland or Buckland, and subsequently in Ipswich, MA. The six diplomas given their graduates in Derry in November, 1824, on completing a three-year course of study, were the first, so far as known, ever conferred on young women. Under more favorable auspices in Ipswich their marked success and the call from all parts of the Union for their graduates as teachers warranted the desire to perpetuate their school, and they pleaded for endowment, urging that it was as necessary for the permanence of a seminary for young women as of a college for young men. The public was apathetic, and their appeals were fruitless. Failing in that effort, Miss Lyon left Ipswich, in 1834, after much and close study of the problem, with the distinct purpose of founding a permanent institution designed to train young women for the highest usefulness. Her aim was not the benefit of woman primarily, but the good of the world through woman. She laid her plan before a few gentlemen in Ipswich, invited together for the purpose, 6th September, 1834. They appointed a committee to act till trustees should be incorporated. The committee issued circulars and delegated Rev. Roswell Hawks to solicit funds. Miss Lyon's aims were pronounced visionary and impracticable. Her motives were misunderstood and misinterpreted. Many people had no faith in appeals for free gifts, a low salary for teachers was disapproved, and the domestic feature, regarded unadvisable by many, was ridiculed by others. Miss Lyon never doubted that the object would eventually commend itself to the common-sense of New England. She often went with Mr. Hawks from town to town, though at great cost of feeling, for she knew she was misjudged. The peculiar features of her plan became the means of its success. Within two months she collected from the women of Ipswich and vicinity nearly $1,000. What Ipswich Seminary did for her in the eastern part of the State, the Buckland school did in the western. She obtained the aid of a few men of wealth, but, instead of depending on a few large gifts, chose to gain the intelligent interest of the many with their smaller sums. On 11th February, 1836, the Governor of Massachusetts signed the charter incorporating Mount Holyoke Seminary, and on 3rd October the corner-stone was laid for a building to accommodate eighty students and their teachers. It was only half the size of the original plan, but was all that funds would then allow. As fast as money was received, it was used upon the building, and for furnishings Miss Lyon appealed to benevolent women. Sewing-societies in different towns gave each a bed and bedding or money for furniture and apparatus. After three years of labors and anxieties the school opened on 8th November, 1837. The house was not wholly finished nor fully furnished, but it was filled with eager students, who

knew that twice their number were as eagerly waiting to take their places. Miss Lyon's threefold plan was then put to the third test. Her wondrous powers of invention were never called into more frequent or more successful use than in so adjusting her time-tables that literary and domestic departments should not interfere. Such was her skill in systematizing the work and in organizing her forces, every student giving an hour a day, that all the details of household cares were faithfully provided for, and without infringing on schoolwork. That feature of the plan, least understood and most ridiculed, was not introduced to teach housework. It was first thought of as one means of lessening outlay. It did contribute to that end, and for sixteen years the annual charge for board and tuition was only $60. But in its usefulness for creating a home atmosphere, for developing a spirit of self-help and of willing cooperation, and for cultivating other traits essential to making any home a happy one, Miss Lyon saw reasons in its favor so much stronger, even before it was put to test, that she seldom alluded to its economy, and afterward often said: "If dollars and cents alone were concerned, we would drop it at once; the department is too complicated and requires too much care to be continued, were it not for its great advantages." Besides organizing and overseeing all the departments, she gave systematic religious instruction, matured a course of study and taught several branches herself. She was versatile and enthusiastic in the class-room and out of it. Her personal influence permeated the family. She was uniformly cheerful and often humorous. Her voice was sweet and strong. She was of full figure, pure pink-and-white complexion, with clear blue eyes, wavy, light brown hair and a face that varied with every shade of feeling. Of the first year's students, four entered the senior and thirty-four the middle class. Their zeal for the seminary and that of their teachers were scarcely inferior to Miss Lyon's. Before the school opened, many feared that students could not be obtained without easier terms of admission, for the preparation required was in advance of what had generally been regarded as a finished education for girls. That fear was never realized, though the requirements were steadily increased. Nearly two-hundred were refused the first year, and four-hundred the second for want of room. In the fourth year the building was enlarged and its capacity doubled; yet applicants greatly exceeded accommodations. The three-year course of study was begun with the intention of extending it to four, and Miss Lyon continued to urge the change. But public opinion upon woman's education was such for many years that "the trustees," says the seminary journal, "are still afraid to venture it." It was made in 1862. She designed to include Latin and French and wished time for Greek and Hebrew, but, because the views of the community would not allow it sooner, she waited ten years before Latin had a place in the required course. Yet there were classes in Latin and in French almost from the first. For eleven-and-a-half years she was spared to perfect her plans, simplifying each department and reducing its details to such order that others could take them in charge. Her successors continued her progressive work. It contributed to the change in public opinion that created colleges for women, and a new charter in 1888 granted full college powers to Mount Holyoke Seminary and College. From the first the seminary had a decidedly religious, though not sectarian, character. Miss Lyon lived to see not less than eleven special revivals and nearly five-hundred hopeful conversions there. Hundreds of her pupils became home-missionaries or teachers in the West and South. Nearly seventy were connected with foreign missions. Miss Lyon never would accept from the institution more than a salary of $200 and a home within its walls, and nearly half that salary she gave to missions. She died 5th March, 1849. Late in February she was suffering with a severe cold and nervous headache, when she learned of a fatal turn in the illness of a student. Regardless of herself, she went to the sufferer with words of comfort and help. Her own illness was brief and attended with delirium. The marble above her grave bears the sentence from one of her last talks with her school: "There is nothing in the universe that I fear, but that I shall not know my duty, or shall fail to do it."

McAVOY, Miss Emma, author and lecturer, born in Cincinnati, OH, 23rd October, 1841. She is a daughter of Daniel and Mary B. McAvoy. Her father, a Scotch-Irishman, was born in Belfast, Ireland. He was one of the pioneers of Cincinnati. He was a horticulturist and a lover of nature. The Cincinnati Art Museum now stands on the site of the McAvoy homestead. Emma McAvoy was graduated as a gold-medalist from the Woodward high school in 1858. For a number of years she was known as one of the grammar-teachers of Cincinnati. Her reputation as a teacher secured for her early in 1870 the principalship of one of the largest schools in Kansas City, MO. Illness in her family caused her to return to Cincinnati. She then gave her time to literary pursuits. She was one of the first women who presented parlor lectures on literature in the West. The subject of her first lecture was "The Sonnet." "The Ode" was her second presentation to the public. A series of lectures on literature completed her course. Her success in her native city led her to try a new field. In 1880 she started on a literary tour in the West. Her afternoon and evening "literaries" were given in almost every city of note from Cincinnati to Laramie, Wyo. She will publish her aids and helps to the study of English literature in book form. The prolonged illness and recent death of her mother interrupted her literary pursuits.

McCABE, Mrs. Harriet Calista Clark, philanthropist, born in Sidney Plains, Delaware county, NY. Her parents were devout members of the Methodist Church. Calista was reared on a farm. Until the age of twelve she was educated either in the district school or by private governess. She became a fluent French scholar before she was ten years of age, and delighted in the scientific study of plants. When she was twelve years of age, her parents removed to Elmira, NY, where she passed several years in school. She taught seven years in Dickinson Seminary, Williamsport, PA, at the end of which time she became the wife of L. D. McCabe, professor of mathematics and afterward of philosophy in the Ohio Wesleyan University, Delaware, OH. Her conversion occurred at the age of twenty. She has been engaged in the various women's societies in the church since that time. In April, 1874, she wrote the constitution of the Woman's Christian Temperance

Union of Ohio, which was the first union organized. That constitution was accepted by the organizing committee, which represented the State and which proposed the name, "Woman's Christian Temperance Union." The State convention met in June in Springfield, OH, and ratified the convention and accepted the name. The convention was held in the Evangelical Lutheran Church of Springfield, but the William Street Methodist Episcopal Church, Delaware, OH, claims the honor of having the organizing work done and the name of the great organization given within its walls. The National Union, organized in the fall following in Cleveland, OH, accepted the constitution of the Ohio union, with the requisite modifications. It also accepted the name which it now bears. After serving the Ohio union for five years, she withdrew to enjoy her home and respite from public assemblies, to which she is not inclined. After some time she yielded to earnest persuasion to aid in the National Woman's Indian Association, and then in the Woman's Home Missionary Society of her own church. She now edits "Woman's Home Missions," the official organ of that society, is one of its vice-presidents, and also secretary of its Indian bureau.

McCABE, Miss Lida Rose, author and journalist, born in Columbus, OH, of Irish parents. She showed an early inclination for literary work, and at eighteen years of age she was a contributor to the Cincinnati "Commercial-Gazette." Since then her pen has been busy in newspaper and magazine work and more ambitious ventures in book-making. A little volume of historic sketches, with the title "Don't You Remember?" dealing with early events in her home, Columbus, and the Scioto valley, OH, was successful. When her "Social and Literary Recollections of W. D. Howells" appeared in "Lippincott's Magazine," the reviewer referred to the writer as "Mr. L. R. McCabe," her initials only being given. For some time those initials covered her identity and won a hearing from those who failed to detect "only a woman" in her robust, graceful style. In 1889, in the Paris Exposition, she did her first work for the American Press Association, and her letters were favorably received from the start. Her first intention was to spend a few months abroad and then return to her home, to engage in literary work. A love of Paris and its wonderful possibilities, and a desire to become familiar with the French language, kept her there for more than a year. She has written for several Ohio papers since she was thirteen years old, her later communication, with widening circles of readers, being through the American Press Association, McClure's Syndicate, Harper's publications, "St. Nicholas," "Frank Leslie's Magazine," "Popular Science Monthly," "Lippincott's Magazine," the "Cosmopolitan" and the "Christian Union." She has been a contributor to Chicago, Washington and New York papers, and since making her home in New York she has written for the "Tribune," "Herald," "World" and "Commercial Advertiser." She has succeeded in New York. She is on the sunny side of the twenties, thoroughly up in the theory and the execution of art, music and literature.

McCLAIN, Mrs. Louise Bowman, author, born in Madison, IN, 9th August, 1841. She was educated in the common schools of that city, graduating from the high school when but little more than fourteen years of age. While in those days she exhibited remarkable facility in the stiff, formal lessons of the text-books, her mind and heart were fast developing along another line wholly independent of the discipline of the school-room, and at an early age she had shown a great fondness for poetry. That fondness was partly inherited and partly due to the inspiring scenes amid which she grew up. Her mother, Emily Huntley Bowman, who was a cousin of Lydia Huntley Sigourney, was herself a poet of more than ordinary ability. Her father, Elijah Goodell Bowman, was a man of strong mental powers and wide and diversified knowledge, and to his careful and healthful pruning is due much of the symmetry which her work possesses. Mrs. McClain has never published a book, but her poems, sketches and stories have appeared in various papers and magazines of Indiana and other States. Her work is of a high order, pure, refined and elevating. She is the wife of Rev. T. B. McClain, of the Methodist Episcopal Church.

McCOMAS, Mrs. Alice Moore, author, editor, lecturer and reformer, born in Paris, IL, 18th June, 1850. Her father, the late Gen. Jesse H. Moore, scholar, clergyman, soldier and statesman, who died while serving his government as United States Consul in Callao, Peru, was at the time of her birth, president of the Paris academy. He came of an old Virginia family whose ancestors were noted for their valor and love of country in the wars of 1776 and 1812. Her mother, a native of Kentucky, was a daughter of one of Kentucky's prominent families, which gave to the world the famous clergyman, William H. Thompson, and John W. Thompson the celebrated Indiana jurist. From both sides of her family she inherited literary taste. From the age of eight years she had her own opinions on social and religious questions, and often astonished her elders with profound questionings, which brought upon her the name of "peculiar," and her aggressiveness as she became older, in clinging to those opinions, even when very unpopular, added to that the opprobrium, "self-willed and headstrong." During the Civil War, in which nearly all her male relatives and friends, including the man whose wife she afterward became, had enlisted for the defense of the Union, she commenced the study of politics. At that time she read of the woman's rights movement. While she had not the courage openly to advocate a thing hooted at and pronounced "unwomanly" by many in her circle, her nature rebelled against the inequality of the sexes. In school she traded compositions for worked-out mathematical problems, averaging many terms from six to ten compositions weekly on as many different subjects, changing her style so as to escape detection. At fifteen her ambition was to achieve something, and her main solace was in writing stories and poems, many of which were destroyed as soon as written. Her education was finished in the Convent of St. Mary, near Terre Haute, IN. In 1871 she was united in marriage to Charles C. McComas, a young lawyer, and for the next five years she devoted herself to the duties of wife, mother and housekeeper. Financial disaster consequent on the panic of 1876 swept away home and property. Her husband, believing that he could quickly retrieve his lost fortune in a new country, emigrated to Kansas, where his wife and family, consisting of two daughters, joined him in 1877. She there resumed the half-forgotten joys of authorship, which brought her a neat little income, but she concealed her identity under a pen-name, which she still uses for fiction and poetry. After her removal to Los Angeles, CA, in 1887, she began to write over her own name. She has edited, with occasional interruptions for the past three years, a woman's department in the Los Angeles "Evening Express." During 1891 and 1892 she filled the position of vice-president of the Woman Suffrage Association, first vice-president of the Ladies' Annex to the Los Angeles Chamber of Commerce, and member of the board of directors of the Woman's Industrial Union. She secured the promise of a land donation for a public park in her neighborhood on condition that the city would improve it, and took the matter before the city council, urging that body in a stirring speech to accept the gift, and by diligent and persistent work finally securing an appropriation of ten-thousand dollars. She occasionally addresses a public audience.

McCRACKEN, Mrs. Annie Virginia, author, born in Charleston, SC, 13th October, 1868. She is known in the literary world as "Alma Vivian Mylo." Her maiden name was McLaughlin. Miss McLaughlin's education was begun in Charleston, and she was graduated from the Academy of the Visitation, Frederick, MD. She became a widow in less than a year after her marriage. Returning to her old home in South Carolina, she first wrote for diversion. On every side she received encouragement for her work. In January, 1892, Mrs. McCracken became contributing editor to the "Lyceum Magazine," Asheville, NC. In May, 1892, she issued, as editor and proprietor, a handsomely illustrated monthly, the "Pine Forest Echo." In addition to its literary features, it is designed to describe the beautiful historical environs of the famous health resort, Summerville, SC, her home. She has written short stories, notably for the "Old Homestead," of Savannah, GA, for the "Sunny South," "Peterson's Magazine," the "St. Louis Magazine" and the "American Household."

McCULLOCH, Mrs. Catharine Waugh, lawyer, born in Ransomville, Niagara county, NY, 4th June, 1862. In 1867 her parents removed to Winnebago county, IL, where she lived on a farm until she entered the Rockford Seminary, where she graduated, in 1882, and afterward took a post-graduate course. She was graduated from the Union College of Law, Chicago, IL, and was admitted to the bar in 1886. She practiced law in Rockford, IL, from that time until her marriage, on 30th May, 1890, with a former classmate in the Union College of Law, Frank H. McCulloch. since which time both have been engaged in the practice of law in Chicago, under the firm name McCulloch & McCulloch. In February, 1892, she addressed both senate and house of representatives in Illinois, in committees of the whole, on the suffrage question.

MACE, Mrs. Frances Laughton, poet, born in Orono, ME, 15th January, 1836. Her maiden name was Laughton. In 1837 her family moved to Foxcroft, ME, where Frances was reared and educated. She studied in the academy in that town. She was a bright, active, intelligent girl, and at the age of ten years was studying Latin and other advanced branches. At the age of twelve years she wrote verses that were published, and her talents in that line were cultivated and developed. The family moved to Bangor, ME, and there she was graduated in the high school and took a course in German and music with private teachers. She published poems in the New York "Journal of Commerce." At the age of eighteen she published her famous hymn, "Only Waiting," in the Waterville "Mail." Others attempted to claim the authorship of that hymn, but she proved her right to it, beyond all doubt, in 1878, after it had been rated as a classic. In 1855 she became the wife of Benjamin F. Mace, a lawyer of Bangor, remaining in that city until 1885, when they removed to San José, CA, where they now reside. Four of the eight children born to them died. When the latest born had entered its second year, her fountain

of poetry, which had run mostly underground during twenty years, sprang up afresh, and "Israfil" was written, appearing with illustrations in "Harper's Magazine," winning for her quick recognition and advancing her toward the front rank of singers. Since then her poems have found place in the leading magazines and journals. In 1883 she published a collection of poems in a volume entitled "Legends, Lyrics and Sonnets," soon followed by a second edition, enlarged and extended. In 1888, a volume of her latest work was published with the title "Under Pine and Palm," adding to her reputation.

McELROY, Mrs. Mary Arthur, sister of Chester Arthur, twenty-first President of the United States, and mistress of the White House during his term of office, born in Greenwich, Washington county, NY, in 1842. She is the youngest child of the late Rev. William Arthur. She was educated in private schools and completed her education in Mrs. Emma Willard's Female Seminary, in Troy, NY. Her attainments and accomplishments are far beyond the standards usually set for young women, and her strong intellectual powers enabled her to gain a thorough knowledge of every subject which she took up. She became the wife, in 1861, of John E. McElroy, of Albany, NY, and her home has been in that city continuously, excepting during her brother's term of office as President. When Chester A. Arthur became President of the United States, after the assassination of President James A. Garfield, he was a widower, and he invited Mrs. McElroy to serve as mistress of the White House. She did so, and her regime in Washington was distinguished by its refinement and its pleasant affableness. Mrs. McElroy is a woman of commanding and attractive person, and no administration was ever more marked for social elegance than was that of President Arthur. After his term ended she returned to her home in Albany, where she is still living.

MacGAHAN, Mrs. Barbara, author and journalist, born in the government of Tula, Russia, 26th April, N.S., 1852, where the estate of her father, Nicholas Elagin, was situated. She was educated at home with tutors and then placed

Leotta.
From Photo by Morrison, Chicago.

Clara Lipman.
From Photo by B. J. Falk, New York.

Norah Lamison.
From Photo by Morrison, Chicago.

in the girls' gymnasia in the city of Tula, where she came under the influence of the directors and teachers of that establishment, men who were collaborators of Count Tolstoi in his school work in Yassnaya Poliana. For several years after graduating she led a worldly and luxurious life. In the fall of 1871, after the conclusion of the Franco-Prussian War, she was staying with her sister in Yalta, in the Crimea, where the Russian Court was at the time. There she made the acquaintance of Januarius A. MacGahan, an American, native of the State of Ohio, war correspondent of the New York "Herald," whom she married in 1873. Since then Mrs. MacGahan has led a very migratory life, following her husband to Roumania, where she remained throughout the Russo-Turkish War in the rear of the army, accompanied by her three-year-old son, watching the care of the wounded, and at work receiving her husband's dispatches written for the "Daily News," of London. She carried his instructions as to the translating and telegraphing of the dispatches and the regulation of the movements of his couriers. As during the Carlist War, so also from the rear of the Russian army, Mrs. MacGahan was writing news-letters about the campaign, and had them published under her husband's name, in St. Petersburg's most influential liberal paper, the "Golos." Then began her own journalistic career, to which she gave herself up altogether on the death of her husband, at the close of the Russo-Turkish War. Having received an offer of a position in the editorial rooms of the "Golos," she filled it for nearly two years, and at the same time wrote articles for Russian periodicals, letters from St. Petersburg for the New York "Herald," and filled in that city the position of regular correspondent to the Sidney "Herald," Australia. In 1880 Mrs. MacGahan was sent by the "Golos" as special correspondent of that paper to the United States, with orders to witness and write up the presidential campaign of that year. She continued in the employ of the same paper in America until the "Golos" was suppressed by the Russian censor. Mrs. McGahan returned to Russia early in 1883. It was the year of the coronation of Alexander III and she engaged to supply news-letters from Russia to the New York "Times" and the Brooklyn "Eagle." During her stay in Russia in that year she entered into an arrangement with the "Novosti" of St. Petersburg and the "Russkya Viedomosti" of Moscow, the leading liberal papers of Russia, and returned in

the capacity of correspondent to those papers, to the United States, where she has lived ever since, still continuing to be the resident correspondent of the latter paper. In 1882 she became regularly associated with the leading liberal magazine of Russia, the "Messenger of Europe." Since the first part of 1890 she has written regular monthly articles on American life for the St. Petersburg magazine, the "Northern Messenger." She wrote for publication in Russia over her own signature, with the exception of some works of fiction, published in the "Messenger of Europe," under the pen-name "Paul Kashirin." While living in America Mrs. MacGahan has frequently contributed letters to the syndicate "American Press Association," the New York "Herald," the New York "Times" and the New York "Tribune." She wrote articles for the "Youth's Companion," "Lippincott's Magazine," and her novel, "Xenia Repunina," written in English, was published in New York and London (1890). Mrs. MacGahan considers her home in America, where her only child, Paul MacGahan, is being brought up, and where her husband's remains rest in his native State, OH, to which they were brought over in 1884 from Constantinople by the Federal government, at the request of the Ohio legislature.

McGEE, Miss Alice G., lawyer, born in Warren county, PA, 10th February, 1869. Her father, Joseph A. McGee, has long been prominently identified with the petroleum industry, having been one of the pioneers of that work in 1860. Most of her life was passed on a farm. She was graduated in the Warren high school in 1886. She took a course of training in the Boston School of Oratory, and taught one term in a district school. In 1887 she decided to study law, and on 16th February of that year she registered as a law student with Messrs. Wetmore, Noyes & Hinckley, in Warren, PA, where she had been serving as librarian in the public library. She was admitted to the bar on 13th May, 1890. Since her admission she has practiced law successfully in Warren. She was the second woman in Pennsylvania to be admitted to the bar. The first was Mrs. Carrie Kilgore, of Philadelphia. Miss McGee is equally successful as counselor and pleader.

McHENRY, Mrs. Mary Sears, a president of the National Woman's Relief Corps, born in New Boston, MA, 30th December, 1834. She is a daughter of David G. Sears and Olive Deming Sears. She received a liberal education in the female seminary in Rockford, IL, and became the wife of William A. McHenry on 28th January, 1864, while he was home on a veteran's furlough, after serving three years in the Union Army. Mr. McHenry returned to Washington and joined his command. Mrs. McHenry accepted the position of deputy treasurer of Crawford county, IA, in the office of her husband's brother, who was treasurer of that county. When Mr. McHenry returned from the war, he settled in Denison, IA, where he has resided ever since. She has been in the work of the Woman's Relief Corps from the first. She was in the Denver convention, where the Woman's Relief Corps was organized, and soon after her return a corps was instituted in Denison. She has served with acceptability as corps, department and national president, and in various other offices.

McKINLEY, Mrs. Ida Saxton, wife of William McKinley, twenty-fourth President of the United States, born in Canton, OH, 8th June, 1847. The families of her parents were among the pioneers of Ohio, and her grandfather, John Saxton, established the Canton "Repository," one of the oldest newspapers in the State. She inherited a cheerful, bright temperament from her mother, which has been the foundation of a womanly life under the drawback of ill health, and from her father practical ability and good judgment in all the affairs of the world. Her delicacy of constitution made it necessary to shorten her school days, and she left the young ladies' school in Media, PA, at the age of sixteen years. Her practical father believed in a business education for young women, something unusual in those days, and she spent some time in a bank as his assistant. A six-month tour abroad completed her education, and upon her return she began a social life, which resulted in her marriage to Major McKinley on the 25th January, 1871. Although delicate from her earliest years, invalidism did not make Mrs. McKinley its victim until after her marriage. Though she has been unfitted for active participation in the social enjoyments which Washington life affords, she has been in the highest sense of the word a happy woman, a more than ordinarily happy married life, in the friendship of those who know her worth, and in the performance of charitable works, unknown to any except the recipients and members of her own family. Those who know her best say she has been an inspiration to her husband in his political career, his most faithful constituent and adviser, and proud of his success. After four years' residence at Columbus, OH, Governor and Mrs. McKinley returned in January, 1896, to Canton. A magazine article in 1891 described Mrs. McKinley under the heading, "Unknown Wives of Well-known Men." The presidential campaign of 1896 made this characterization obsolete, and since 4th March, 1897, she has been the honored mistress of the executive mansion at Washington. In consequence of her delicate health Mrs. McKinley cannot respond to every social demand her position levies, and will be in a great measure relieved by Mrs. Hobart, the Vice-President's wife, who will preside when necessary at affairs of state. Both are women of refinement and tact.

McKINNEY, Mrs. Jane Amy, educator and philanthropist, born in Vermont, 25th October, 1832. She still retains her family name, Amy. Mrs. McKinney's family moved to northern Ohio in 1835, and settled in Mentor. Jane was educated in the Western Reserve Seminary and in Oberlin. She was married in 1856 and went with her husband to Winneshiek county, IA, where her home was until 1888, when she removed to Chicago, IL, where she now resides. Since the age of fifteen she has been engaged in educational and philanthropic work almost continuously. In Iowa she was actively engaged in temperance work and in the advocacy of woman suffrage. She has served a term of four years by election of the legislature as trustee of the hospital for the insane in Independence, IA. She is president of the Cook County Equal Suffrage Association. Recently she has taken up kindergarten work, and has for two years served as supervisor of the Chicago Kindergarten Training School. She is a woman of distinct individuality.

McKINNEY, Mrs. Kate Slaughter, author and poet, born in London, KY, 6th February, 1857, is familiar to the public by her pen-name,"Katydid."

She was graduated in Daughters' College, Harrodsburg, KY, and soon after became the wife of James I. McKinney. She has written verses since she was fifteen years of age. The first were published in the "Courier-Journal," from which they found a way into the leading newspapers and magazines. Her Kentucky home stands out with frequency in the pages of her published volume. "Katydid's Poems." She has a lyric gift, and her poems have a melody and sweetness. Mrs. McKinney gets her inspiration from the trees and the flowers and the brooks, which are to her the open books of Nature. She has the faculty of singing with ease and naturalness on these subjects nearest her heart.

McMANUS, Miss Emily Julian, poet, born in Bath, Ontario, 30th December, 1865. She is of Irish extraction on both her father's and mother's side. She grew up an imaginative child, fond of the companionship of books, especially books of poetry. Her father, a man of scholarly tastes, encouraged the love of literature in his daughter. Miss McManus obtained her early education in the public school of her native town, and later, in the Kingston Collegiate Institute and in the Ottawa Normal School. In the latter she was fitted to be a public-school teacher. Having taught for a period with marked success, she entered in 1888 the arts department of Queen's University, Kingston, Ontario. Miss McManus has con-

tributed poems to the Kingston "Whig," the Toronto "Globe," the "Irish Canadian," the "Educational Journal," "Queen's College Journal" and the Toronto "Week." Mr. W. D. Lighthall, of Montreal, the compiler of an anthology of Canadian poetry, entitled "Songs of the Great Dominion," which was published in London, England, makes special mention of Miss McManus' poem, "Manitoba," in his introduction to that work.

McMURDO, Mrs. Katharine Albert, social leader, was born in the "Beckwith Homestead," the beautiful home in Palmyra, NY, of her grand-father, Col. George Beckwith. Her maiden name was Katharine Albert Welles. Her youth was chiefly spent in New York City, where her parents, Albert, the historical and genealogical writer, and Katharine Welles, resided, and where she became the wife of. Col. Edward McMurdo, a brilliant Kentuckian, who fought for the Union throughout the Civil War. In 1881 they took up their residence in London, where Col. McMurdo engaged in such important and far-reaching enterprises as to make his name a familiar one throughout the financial world. He was one of the earliest to recognize the commercial and financial possibilities of South Africa, and his investments and enterprises in that country gave him almost the importance and power of a potentate. Their mansion in Charles street, Berkeley Square, a survival of the time of William III, into which they had introduced many modern comforts and luxuries, became the center of a generous hospitality, where scholarly, agreeable people, distinguished in letters, art or science, men notable for civil or military services, or for lineage and position, found congenial association. Ever a devoted student of the best books, with a mind enriched by extensive travel, a residence in foreign capitals, and acquaintance with intelligent society, with a brilliant conversational gift, and a fascinating personality, she soon won a host of devoted friends. The happy home in Mayfair received an awful shock in 1889, when Col. McMurdo died, without a moment's warning, from the bursting of a blood-vessel in the brain. The Portuguese government took advantage of that event, and seized the Delagoa Bay Railway, an important line traversing the Portuguese territory in southeast Africa, from Delagoa Bay on the coast to the Transvaal frontier, which Col. McMurdo had built under a concession direct from the king of Portugal, and which from its unique position gave the man whose courage and enterprise had prompted its construction a power sufficient to arouse the envy of the Portuguese government and people. The seizure was made under the flimsy pretext of a technical breach of contract, and was such a high-handed outrage that the English and American governments took prompt action to protect the interests of Mrs. McMurdo and those associated with her husband in the ownership of the railway. Portugal admitted its liability and joined with the United States and British governments in asking the Swiss parliament to appoint a commission from the leading jurists to enquire and determine the amount of idemnity to be paid for the railway and the valuable rights conferred by the concession. That being one of the interesting diplomatic incidents of the day, with four governments officially concerned, Mrs. McMurdo was thrust into a prominence perhaps repugnant to one of her retiring disposition. The tribunal will conclude its labors in 1892, in accordance with the terms of the protocol under which is sitting. In all her business with the State Department, with diplomatic and other officials, her great dignity, composure, ability and good sense have commanded respect and admiration. Her engagement to Frederic Courtland Penfield was formally announced, and their marriage was celebrated in the fall of 1892. Mr. Penfield is an American gentleman who has lived many years abroad and who is widely known in diplomatic, literary and social circles. He was for several years United States vice-consul-general to Great Britain. It is probable that, after her marriage, Mrs. McMurdo will divide her time between Europe and America.

McPHERSON, Mrs. Lydia Starr, poet, author and journalist, born in Warnock, Belmont county, OH. Her father was William F. Starr, and her mother was Sarah Lucas Starr, a woman of English descent. The family moved from Belmont county to Licking county when Lydia was three years old. They settled near the present town of Jersey. Lydia early showed poetical tastes and talents. She was precocious in her studies, learning everything but mathematics, with ease and rapidity. When she was twelve years old the family removed to Van Buren county, IA, where they settled on a claim near the Des Moines river. There she grew to womanhood. At the age of seventeen she became teacher of a select school in Ashland, IA. She taught successfully and received a salary of one dollar a week, with board among the patrons of the school. In her twenty first year she became the wife of D. Hunter, and they settled in Keosauqua, IA. Five children were born to them, of whom three sons and one daughter are now living. Widowed in early life, she placed her sons in printing-

offices to learn a trade and earn a living. They are now editors and publishers of newspapers. In 1874 Mrs. Hunter moved to the South, where she became the wife of Granville McPherson, editor of the "Oklahoma Star," published in Caddo, Indian Territory. Mrs. McPherson's taste for literary work there found exercise. She worked on her husband's journal as editor-in-chief until 1876, when she established the "International News" in Caddo. She did the literary work, while her two sons did the printing. Mr. McPherson had aroused hostility by his conduct of the "Star," and he was threatened with personal injury. He left Caddo and went to Blanco, TX, where he died. Mrs. McPherson wearied of life among the tribes in Indian Territory. In 1877 she removed to Whitesboro, TX. There she started the "Whitesboro Democrat," which was the first paper published in Texas by a woman. In 1879 the "Democrat" was moved to Sherman, TX, where it is still published as a daily and weekly. The daily is now in its twelfth year and has long been the official paper of the city as well as the county organ. She has, with the aid of her sons, made it a paying and influential journal. Mrs. McPherson was chosen honorary commissioner to the New Orleans Exposition from her county. In 1881 she joined the State Press Association of Texas and was elected corresponding secretary. In March, 1886, she was elected a delegate to the World's Press Association, which met in Cincinnati, OH. In the same month she was appointed postmaster of Sherman, which office she filled successfully for four years. Besides all her journalistic work, her society associations and her relations in numerous fields of work and influence, she has written much for publication. Her poetical productions are numerous. They have been widely quoted, and have been collected into a volume entitled "Reullura" (Buffalo, 1892). She has a number of books now in manuscript, one of which is a novel entitled "Phlegethon." She has traveled much in the United States. She spent four months of 1890 in Oregon, Nevada, Utah and neighboring States, and furnished letters of travel for Oregon journals. She is one of the busiest women of the age and country in which she lives.

MADISON, Mrs. Dorothy Payne, commonly called Dolly Madison, wife of James Madison, fourth President of the United States, born in

North Carolina, 20th May, 1772, and died in Washington, DC, 12th July, 1849. She was a granddaughter of John Payne, an Englishman, who removed from England to Virginia early in the eighteenth century. His wife was Anna Fleming, a granddaughter of Sir Thomas Fleming, one of the pioneers of Jamestown, VA. His son, the second John Payne, Dorothy's father, was married to Mary Coles, a first-cousin to Patrick Henry. Dorothy was reared as a Quaker. In 1791 she became the wife of John Todd, a lawyer of Pennsylvania, who was a member of the Society of Friends. Mr. Todd died in 1793, in Philadelphia, PA, during the yellow-fever scourge. In September, 1794, Mrs. Todd became the wife of James Madison, and their union was a cause of joy to President Washington and his wife, both of whom were warm friends of Mr. and Mrs. Madison. Their long married life was one of unclouded happiness. Mrs. Madison's extraordinary personal beauty, her brilliant intellect and her great social powers made her the model mistress of the White House during the two terms of her husband as President. She was a conspicuous figure in society, and her knowledge of politics and diplomacy was extensive, and her brilliant management of society contributed powerfully to the success of President Madison's administration. During all the stirring scenes of that period, including the sacking of Washington by the British, she bore herself always with dignity and courage. After the close of President Madison's second term of office they removed from Washington to his estate in Montpelier, VA, where they passed their lives in quiet retirement. Her life was embittered by the misconduct of her son, Payne Todd. Mrs. Madison left the manuscript of her book, "Memoirs and Letters," a most interesting volume, which was published in Boston in 1887.

MALLORY, Mrs. Lucy A., editor, born in Roseburg, Douglas county, OR, 14th February, 1846. Her father, Aaron Rose, settled in Oregon early in the forties, and the city of Roseburg was named for him. He was one of the first white settlers at a time when the country was an unbroken wilderness. The wife and mother died in giving birth to Lucy. Though reared among Indians and surrounded constantly in early life by the wildest aspects of nature, she was always a vegetarian. Soon after reaching the years of womanhood she became the wife of Rufus Mallory, who afterward represented the State in Congress, and who is now one of the most successful lawyers in the Pacific Northwest, and is the senior member of the extensive law firm to which Senator Dolph belongs. She accompanied her husband to Washington. Not long after their return to Salem, which at that time was their home, an incident occurred which brought out the spirit of the woman. In 1874 the old slavery prejudice was so strong in Oregon that some forty-five negro and mulatto children were prevented from attending the Salem public schools and kept from all chance of acquiring an education, as no white teachers could be found who would condescend to teach them. A public fund was set apart for them, but no one came forward to labor for it. Mrs. Mallory volunteered to instruct the dusky children, in the face of sneers and ridicule. Her course shamed the people into a sense of duty, and within three years the children were admitted into the white schools and classes, when all friction and opposition disappeared. Mrs. Mallory, having no immediate use for the public money which she drew for her work, let it remain in the bank. In 1886 she used the fund for the purchase of a printing plant, and soon after started her monthly magazine, the "World's Advanced Thought," with Judge H. N. Maguire for assistant editor. The latter recently retired from editorial connection, on account of the pressure of other business affairs, but still contributes to its pages, while Mrs. Mallory, who was always the proprietor, has full control. Her magazine circulates among advanced thinkers and workers in every portion of the civilized world. Count Tolstoi, of Russia, takes it. Her work, like that of her husband, is in Portland, but their home, where they rest nights and Sundays, is on their ranch or fruit farm, four miles out in the suburbs of the city.

MANNING, Mrs. Jessie Wilson, author and lecturer, born in Mount Pleasant, IA, 26th October, 1855. Her maiden name was Wilson. She spent her childhood and received her education in Mount Pleasant. Immediately after graduation in the Iowa Wesleyan University, in 1874, Miss Wilson entered the field of platform work, and was for five years an able and eloquent speaker on literary subjects and for the cause of temperance. In the fall of 1889 all her private ambitions and public work were changed by her marriage to Eli Manning, of Chariton, IA, prominent in business and political circles in that State. Since her marriage Mrs. Manning has devoted herself to her home and family of three sons. Her first book, published in 1887, called the "Passion of Life," is her most ambitious work and has achieved a moderate success. She has written a large number of articles for the Iowa press, among them a series of literary criticism, and poems, and essays for magazines, besides stories under a pen-name. Her Chariton home is a social and literary center.

MANVILLE, Mrs. Helen Adelia, poet, born in New Berlin, NY, 3rd August, 1839. Her father was Col. Artemus Wood. She inherited literary talent from her mother, several members of whose family won local celebrity, and who were connected with the Carys, from whom Alice and Phebe were descended, and also the house of Douglas, whose distinguished representative was Stephen. Accompanying her father as Helen Wood, she removed to the West at an early day, where she became Mrs. Manville, and has since lived in La Crosse, WI. For many years her pen-name was "Nellie A. Mann," under which she contributed to leading periodicals. Renouncing her pen-name, she assumed her own, and in 1875 published a collection of her poems entitled, "Heart Echoes," which contains but a small portion of her verse. She has one child, Marion, a poet of decided gifts. Mother and daughter possess unusual beauty. They are both high-minded, refined and essentially feminine. Mrs. Manville's life has been one of complete self-abnegation. She is wholly devoted to family and friends, while yet doing excellent literary work.

MARBLE, Mrs. Callie Bonney, author, was born in Peoria, IL, where her father, Hon. C. C. Bonney, was a young lawyer just beginning prac-

tice. He shortly afterward removed to Chicago, IL, where he has since resided. Mrs. Marble is of Anglo-Norman origin and is descended from the noble De Bon family, who figured in the days of William the Conqueror. Afterward the spelling of the name became De Bonaye, and later assumed its present form. She attended the best schools in Chicago, and afterward was graduated from the Chestnut Street Seminary for young ladies, then located in Philadelphia, PA, but since removed to Ogontz, PA. While purely feminine in every respect, she yet inherits from her legal ancestry a mental strength that is very decided, though not masculine. She has published two prose works, "Wit and Wisdom of Bulwer" and "Wisdom and Eloquence of Webster." She is a proficient French scholar and has made translations of many of Victor Hugo's shorter works. Her first writing for periodicals was a story, which was printed serially in a Chicago Masonic magazine. Since its appearance she has written poems, sketches and stories for a great number of periodicals. She has written the words of a number of songs that have been set to music by F. Nicholls Crouch, the composer of "Kathleen Mavourneen," Eben H. Bailey and W. H. Doane. She has written two operettas, one set to music by Mr. Bailey, and the other by Mr. Doane, and has dramatized the "Rienzi" of Bulwer, an author who holds a very warm place in her affections. She has been in delicate health for many years. Although Mrs. Marble did not begin to write until 1882, and much of her work has been done while in bed or on her lounge, she has accomplished a great deal, and has gained a recognition that is general and gratifying. Several years ago she became the wife of Earl Marble, the well-known editor, art and dramatic critic, and author, and they now reside in Chicago.

MARBLE, Mrs. Ella M. S., journalist and educator, born in Gorham, ME, 10th August, 1850. Left motherless at nine years of age, she was her father's housekeeper at twelve, and that position she filled until she was seventeen, attending the village school during that time. A natural aptness for study fitted her for teaching, and she taught and attended school alternately until she was married, in 1870. She has two children, a son and daughter. Losing none of her interest in educational matters, she joined the Society for the Encouragement of Study at Home, conducted by a number of educated Cambridge women, supplementing her studies by contributions to the leading papers and magazines of Maine and Massachusetts. In 1873 she accepted the editorial management of the juvenile department of a Maine paper. Failing health put a stop to her literary work for a time, and in search of health she moved to the West, spending five years in Kansas and Minnesota, devoting herself almost exclusively to philanthropic and educational work. She held at one time the offices of president of the Minnesota State Suffrage Association, president of the Minneapolis Suffrage Association, seven offices in the Woman's Christian Temperance Union and secretary of the White Cross movement. She was also secretary and director of a maternity hospital, which she did much toward starting. She was one of the founders of the immense Woman's Christian Temperance Union Coffee Palace in Minneapolis. Receiving, in 1888, a flattering offer from a Washington daily newspaper, she moved to the Capital to take a position upon the editorial staff. She contributed also Washington letters to eastern and western papers. Failing health caused her to abandon all literary work and engage in something more active, and she turned her attention to physical culture for women. She established, in 1889, the first women's gymnasium ever opened in Washington, DC. She also established in connection with it an emporium for healthful dress, and found great pleasure in the fact that she had surrounded herself with two-hundred-fifty women and children who, as teachers, pupils and sewing-girls, were all looking to her to guide them toward health. In 1890, and again in 1891, she was made president of the District of Columbia Woman's Suffrage Association. She was several times called by the national officers to address the committees of the House and Senate. As a public speaker she was effective. Her wide experience in philanthropic work caused her to be called frequently to fill pulpits of both orthodox and liberal churches. In 1891, having made her school of physical culture a social and financial success, she sold it

and accepted the financial agency of Wimodaughsis, the national woman's club. From girlhood she has taken an active interest in any movement calculated to advance the interests of women.

MARK, Miss Nellie V., physician, born in Cashtown, PA, near Gettysburg, 21st July, 1857. Whether or not her advent into the world at a time when the aphorism, "All men are born free and equal," was on everybody's tongue, developed in her a belief that woman shares in the term "man," and a residence at the most susceptible age on the scene and at the time of the greatest battle ever fought in defense of that idea, inspired the desire to aid the suffering, suffice it to say that Dr. Mark can not remember the time when she was not a suffragist and a doctor. She was always making salves and ointments for lame horses and dogs. Only one cat and no chickens died under her care. The account of those early days is brief: "Smart child, but very bad!" In July, 1875, Dr. Mark was graduated from the Lutherville Seminary, Maryland, and in 1883 she returned to make an address before the alumni on "Woman Suffrage and its Workers." Three years later she delivered another on "Woman in the Medical Profession," which the faculty had printed in pamphlet form for distribution, and she was elected president of the Alumni Association. After her graduation she studied under the professors in Gettysburg for several years, during which time she was under allopathic treatment in that place and in Baltimore for inherited rheumatism, which affected her eyes. Experiencing no improvement, she tried homeopathy in Philadelphia, and, being benefited, read medicine with her physician, Dr. Anna M. Marshall, for about a year. In 1881 Dr. Mark began a course of study in the Boston University School of Medicine, and was graduated in 1884. She settled in Baltimore and has built up a large and remunerative practice. Dr. Mark is a bright, breezy writer and debater on all subjects, and has been kept busy, in addition to her practice, with addresses and discussions in medical and suffragist conventions. She has given health lectures to working girls' clubs. She is superintendent of the scientific-instruction department of the Baltimore Woman's

Christian Temperance Union. She holds the position of director for Maryland, and auditor, in the Association for the Advancement of Women. In the meeting of that society in Detroit, in 1887, she read a paper on "Women as Guardians of the Public Health." She also read a paper on "La Grippe" in the last meeting, 16th October, in Grand Rapids, MI, and was on the programme in November, 1892, in Memphis, TN, for one on "The Effect of Immigration upon the Health of the Nation." Dr. Mark is a practical refutation of the idea that a professional woman must vacate her own sphere, and be of necessity an inefficient housekeeper. With youth and talents at her command, much may be expected from her in her chosen life-work and in any cause which she may espouse.

MARKSCHEFFEL, Mrs. Louise, journalist, born in Toledo, OH, in 1857. Her mother's father was the president of one of the Cantons of Switzerland, and was descended from royalty. His daughter fell in love and eloped with Caspar Weber, a teacher in a Swiss university. The young couple came to the United States, finally fixing their home in Toledo, OH. There, in a strange land, after a hand-to-hand struggle with poverty during those earlier years, Mrs. Weber gave up her life in bringing Louise, the youngest of nine children, into the world. When but two weeks old, the little Louise was taken by her father's brother, George Weber, and his wife, to be brought up by them as their own child. She attended the public schools and showed great aptness as a scholar, but at the early age of fifteen her school career was brought to a close by her betrothal and marriage to Carl Markscheffel, a prosperous business-man of large property. That occurred 15th October, 1872. Four years later her son Carlos was born. Mr. Markscheffel died in August, 1892, after a long and painful illness. Mrs. Markscheffel began her regular literary work several years ago, when continued misfortunes had caused Mr. Markscheffel's loss of fortune and bereft him of health and ambition. She became the literary and society editor of the Toledo "Sunday Journal." Her work immediately became a marked feature of the "Journal." She created social columns that are absolutely unique, and delightful even to those

who care nothing for the news details. Her leaders sparkle with bright comments upon things in general, with witty sayings, mingled with pathetic incidents, while underneath runs a current of kindly thought that can only come from a truly womanly spirit. She is an excellent dramatic, musical and literary critic. In the intervals of her arduous labors, she occasionally finds time to contribute short stories and sketches to eastern papers.

MARLOWE, Miss Julia, actor, born in the Lake district of England, in the village of Coldbeck, in 1865. She was christened Sarah May Frost. Though Brough was a family name, there was a well-known English actor named Fannie Brough, she decided, when she went on the stage, to take the name Julia Marlowe. In 1872 her family came to the United

States and settled in Kansas, but finally removed to Cincinnati, where Julia Marlowe had five years' schooling. Her education was thoroughly American, received in the public schools of America, and she wishes to be known and classed as an American actor. In 1874, when Julia was nine years old, she played as Sir Joseph Porter in "Pinafore" with her younger sister, Alice. Then came the children's parts in Rip Van Winkle. In 1879 she went on a tour in a company with Miss Dowe, and during that tour saw much of Shakespearean characters. One day the Romeo page of the company was sick, and the youthful Julia, after proving that she knew every line of "Romeo and Juliet," was permitted to play the page's part. She did it in such a way as to suggest great possibilities, and for the next four years she studied in retirement with Miss Dowe. She studied school branches and elocution, with all the stage "business," and soon was ready to begin regular work before the public. She played in New England towns with great success, and on 20th October, 1887, she made her debut in New York City as Parthenia in a matinee performance of "Ingomar." She won a triumph at once. All the critics were favorable. Soon afterward she appeared as Viola in "Twelfth Night," and her success led her to enter the ranks as a star. She made a tour, appearing in "Ingomar," "Romeo and

Juliet," "Twelfth Night," "As You Like It," "The Lady of Lyons," "Pygmalion and Galatea" and "The Hunchback." While her first tour was not wholly successful financially, it introduced her to the public and paved a way for her brilliant triumphs of the past eight years. She has steadily worked her way to the front rank, and to-day she is considered one of the leading actors. In 1890 over-work brought on a serious illness in Philadelphia, PA, and she was long ill in the home of Col. Alexander K. McClure, of the Philadelphia "Times." Since her recovery she has continued her successes in the principal cities of the country. She is a woman of slight form, with a beautiful and expressive face, and in her rôles she appears true to life without visible effort. Her art is of that high, sure and true sort which hides itself and makes the portrayal natural. Her marriage occurred in 1894, to Robert Taber, her leading man, a young tragedian of great promise and histrionic power. Together they have managed their own company and accomplished great reforms in the selection of the people and talent of their support. Nothing but the highest art is selected, and, above all, only the chaste and moral appear in their rôles, and the same high standard is required of the players selected to interpret those rôles. Since her marriage Mrs. Taber has retained, for stage purposes, her maiden name, Julia Marlowe, which has now become synonymous with her famous rôle of Juliet. In fact, Mr. and Mrs. Taber have created for themselves an unsurpassed fame as interpreters of "Romeo and Juliet," and are so recognized on the American stage. During the winter of 1896–97 Mr. and Mrs. Taber surprised their most confident friends in the skill they displayed outside the purely classic drama in the title rôles of the popular historic play, "For Bonnie Prince Charlie." The Tabers have located their home in Vermont, a few miles from Burlington, where Mr. Taber's family resides on the old farm homestead. Thither the actors turn their footsteps when a little leisure is granted them in their busy career, though of the year 1897 their three months' vacation was spent abroad. Duse predicts that with Julia Marlowe rests the hope of classic drama in America.

MARSH, Mrs. Alice Esty, see ESTY, MISS ALICE MAY.

MARSHALL, Miss Joanna, poet, born in Harford county, MD, 14th August, 1822. There were

published her first attempt at song-writing. Her early life was spent mainly in Baltimore, MD, where her family lived for many years. In her childhood home she received her first schooling from her father, Thomas Marshall. Having directed the elements of her education aright, he permitted her to browse at will in his well-stocked library. Joanna received her literary bent from her father. No slave ever toiled on her father's homestead, freedmen tilled his lands, and women disenslaved performed the household services. Her mother, Sarah Marshall, belonged to the Montgomery family, one of the oldest and most prominent of Maryland. In their Fairmount home in Cincinnati, OH, for many years have lived the Marshall sisters. The three sisters shared the home of their married sister, Mrs. Louis F. Lannay. Miss Marshall possesses a pleasing personality. Her love of flowers she shares with her love of poesy. Endowed with a deep religious feeling, she aims to make her life Christ-like. Her pen is always ready with contributions to Christian literature. A deep spirituality pervades her later poems. The late years of Miss Marshall's life are filled with peace. Her pen is not so busy as in her earlier days, but her later productions have been her very best.

MATHER, Margaret, actor, born in Tilbury, near Montreal, Canada, in 1862. She is of Scotch descent. In 1868 her family left Canada and settled in Detroit, MI. Margaret went to New York City to live with one of her brothers, who offered to educate her. She passed through the public schools, and her brother died in 1880, leaving her dependent upon herself for a living. Having become inspired with the desire to go on the stage, she studied with George Edgar. She made her début as Cordelia in "King Lear," and she soon attracted the attention of Manager J. M. Hill, who made a contract with her for a six-year engagement. She at once went under instruction, and for twenty-one months she received the best of training in every line of stage business from dancing to elocution. She opened her career with Mr. Hill, as Juliet, 28th August, 1882, in McVicker's Theater, in Chicago, and her success was instantaneous. She then played in the principal cities, and in 1885, on 16th October, appeared in the Union Square Theater, in New York City, in her famous rôle of Juliet. Her season of seventeen weeks was played to crowded houses. She has worked and studied diligently, and her repertory includes Rosalind, Imogen, Lady Macbeth, Leah, Julia, Lady Gay Spanker, Peg Woffington, Mary Stuart, Gilbert's Gretchen, Pauline, Juliana, Barbier's Joan of Arc, Nance Oldfield, Constance and Medea. She is constantly adding new attractions to her list, and her artistic growth is substantial. While playing under Mr. Hill's management she became the wife, in 1887, of Emil Haberkorn, the leader of the Union Square Theater orchestra. Soon after her marriage she severed her relations with her manager, and since then she has been playing with a company of her own.

MATHER, Mrs. Sarah Ann, philanthropist, born in the town of Chester, MA, 20th March, 1820. She is the wife of the Rev. James Mather, an honored member of the New England Southern Conference of the Methodist Episcopal Church. She is of Puritan ancestry, and traces her descent through eight generations born in this country. The father and mother of Mrs. Mather commenced their conjugal life on a farm among the hills of Hampden county, MA, where they reared a family of eight children in rural plenty. The three daughters were converted in their youth through the labors of the Methodist ministry, and found their way to the Wesleyan Academy in Wilbraham, MA, during the presidencies of Rev. Drs. Adams and Allyn, where they were noted for love of order and scholarship. The second daughter, Sarah A. Babcock, after leaving the academy, engaged in teaching, and continued her studies in modern languages and literature. In her course as teacher, she became preceptress and instructor in the art department in the New England Southern Conference Seminary, East Greenwich, RI, and subsequently principal of the ladies' department and professor of modern languages in the Wesleyan College, Leoni, MI. After the close of the war, and before the United States troops were withdrawn from the South, she went among the freedmen as a missionary. With characteristic energy and devotion to whatever line of labor absorbed her for the time, she brought all her powers to bear upon this work, sacrificing health, bestowing labor without measure, and, at the risk of loss, invested all her available means in the work of establishing a normal and training school for colored youth in Camden, SC. In the prosecution of that work for the colored youth, she became a public speaker in their behalf, much against her natural inclination, and, before she was fully conscious of the transformation going on within her, lost herself in their cause. An entire failure of health became imminent, and she left the work to others, but resumed it again on the organization of the Woman's Home Missionary Society of the Methodist Episcopal Church, becoming one of its conference secretaries and organizers. Through her efforts, a model home and training school in Camden, SC, has been established. Buildings have been erected and purchased, which will accommodate fifty pupils, and the school is sustained by the Woman's Home Missionary Society of the Methodist Episcopal Church. Of her works as an author, "Itinerant Side" (New York), was her first venture. This was favorably received and went through many editions. "Little Jack Fee," a serial; "Young Life" (Cincinnati), and "Hidden Treasure" (New York) followed. The cares of a parsonage and the requirements of local church work, the secretaryship of a conference society and a general care of the model home in Camden, SC, forced her to lay down her pen, which she did with great reluctance. Now, in the comparative quiet of a retired minister's life in Hyde Park, MA, and released from the duties of a burdensome secretaryship, she resumes the delightful literary recreation of former days. With speech and pen, she is now endeavoring to revive the lost art of Systematic Beneficence.

MEE, Mrs. Cassie Ward, labor champion, born in Kingston, Ontario, Canada, 16th October, 1848. Her parents and ancestors belonged to the Society of Friends, many of whom were and are prominent and accredited ministers of the society. She was educated and followed teaching for several years in her native city. She came with her husband, Charles Mee, to the United States and settled in Cortland, NY, in 1882, where the family now reside. She has gained considerable prominence by her writings. Several years ago she first appeared on the public platform in the cause of temperance. She is a member of the Order of Rebecca, and in 1886 she became a member of Peter Cooper Assembly, No. 3,172, Knights of Labor of Cortland. In August, 1885, she first spoke on the labor question, and her speeches gave her prominence as an advocate of labor. On 12th August, 1886, she addressed ten-thousand people on Boston Common. She received a splendid illuminated address from the Knights of Labor of Kingston, Canada, in token of their appreciation of an address made by her in that city, 14th March, 1887. She has lectured extensively among the miners of Pennsylvania. She is an earnest and powerful speaker and a great admirer of the principles of the Knights of Labor. Her work is the education of the members of that powerful organization.

MEECH, Mrs. Jeannette Du Bois, evangelist and industrial educator, born in Frankford, PA, in 1835. Her father, Gideon Du Bois, was descended from the French-Huguenots. He was a deacon in the Baptist Church for nearly half a century. Her mother, Annie Grant, was a Scotch woman and came to this country when a girl. She is still living. Jeannette learned to read when she was four years old. The first public school in Frankford was built opposite to her home, in 1840, and she attended it as soon as it was opened. She went through all the departments, and afterward was graduated from the Philadelphia Normal School. She then commenced to teach in the Frankford school, and taught there eight years, resigning her position in 1880. In 1861 she became the wife of Rev. W. W. Meech, then pastor of the Baptist Church, in Burlington, NJ. In 1869, during her husband's pastorate in Jersey Shore, PA, she opened a free industrial school in the parsonage, with one-hundred scholars, boys and girls. The boys were taught to sew and knit, as well as the girls. She provided all the material and utensils and sold the work when it was finished. In 1870 her husband was chosen superintendent of the Maryland State Industrial School for Girls. There she had an opportunity to develop her ideas. The materials were provided, and they taught cooking, canning and housekeeping as well as sewing, reading, writing, drawing, arithmetic and music. Her husband lost his health, and they were obliged to give up the work. They went to Vineland, NJ, in search of health in 1873, and have lived there ever since. Her oldest daughter was an invalid and could not be sent to school at that time, and Mrs. Meech invited a few of the neighbor's children to make a class in her home, that she might have companionship for her daughter in her studies. She continued that "Cottage Seminary" till the daughter was able to go from home to school, and then she started an "Industrial Society," composed mainly of scholars from the Vineland high school, in 1875. The boys were taught to make a variety of articles in wood and wire work. The girls cut and made garments and fancy articles. In 1887 Mrs. Meech was appointed by the trustees of the Vineland high school to introduce there and to superintend the department of manual education. This plan was only partially carried out. Mrs. Meech was converted in 1850 and became a member of the Baptist Church in her fifteenth year. During the Civil War her husband was a hospital chaplain. She was with him in Louisville, and while there helped in a mission school in the suburbs. He was afterward stationed in Bowling Green, KY, and there she had a Sunday-school class in the convalescent ward of the hospital. While they were in the industrial school in Maryland, she had to conduct the religious meetings with the girls, on account of her husband's loss of voice. A remarkable revival began in the school and all but four of the girls became Christians. After moving to Vineland, Mrs. Meech started a Sunday-school in Vineland Center, in the face of obstacles, and conducted it for ten years, serving as superintendent, collecting a library and training teachers for the work. Many of the pupils were converted, and the school became known far and wide. In connection with her Sunday-school work she organized a society for missionary information in 1877. A correspondence was opened with missionaries in China, and she set to work to study up the customs and religions of China, Japan and India, in order to interest her scholars in the work in those countries. They always had a full house on missionary Sunday. Her lectures have been given by request in a number of churches, school-houses and conventions. One young lady, a member of one of her societies, is now a missionary in Japan. Mr. Meech has been pastor of the South Vineland Baptist Church for seventeen years. During his vacations Mrs. Meech frequently filled his place. She addressed an audience for the first time in Meadville, PA, in 1867, in a Sunday-school convention. In 1890, in company with Mrs. Ives, of Philadelphia, she commenced a series of cottage prayer meetings in Holly Beach, NJ. They visited from house to house, talking with unconverted people and inviting them to the meetings. The religious interest was great. Since then she has frequently held Sunday evening services in the Holly Beach Church, which is Presbyterian in denomination, and which years ago refused her the use of their church for a missionary lecture, because she was a woman. In March, 1891, the South Vineland Baptist Church granted her a license to preach. Since receiving that license, she has held a number of meetings on Sunday evenings in Wildwood Beach, NJ, and in Atlantic City, NJ. She held aloof from temperance societies till about three years ago. As the church did so little, and the evil increased so fast, she joined the Woman's Christian Temperance Union in 1889. She was made county superintendent of narcotics the first year. Two years ago she received an appointment as national lecturer for the Woman's Christian Temperance Union in the department of narcotics. She edited the Holly Beach "Herald" in 1885, but could not continue it for want of means. She has been engaged in business as a florist and art store-keeper for some years.

MELVILLE, Mrs. Velma Caldwell, writer of prose and poetry, born in Greenwood, Vernon county, WI, 1st July, 1858. Her father was William A. Caldwell. Her mother's maiden name was Artlissa Jordan. They were originally from Ohio, removing to Wisconsin in 1855. The call of war, which, at the age of five years, forever severed Velma from a father's love and care, explains the intensely patriotic spirit of all her writings. He perished in the frightful mine before Petersburg.

When twenty years of age Velma Caldwell became the wife of James Melville, C.E., a graduate of the Wisconsin State University, since well known as an educator and a prohibitionist. Her productions in verse and prose have appeared extensively in the St. Louis "Observer," "St. Louis Magazine," "Housekeeper," "Ladies' Home Journal," "Daughters of America," Chicago "Inter-Ocean," "Advocate and Guardian," "Weekly Wisconsin," "Midland School Journal," Chicago "Ledger," "West Shore Magazine" and many other publications. She is at present editing the "Home Circle and Youth's Department" of the "Practical Farmer" of Philadelphia, PA, and the "Health and Home Department" in the "Wisconsin Farmer" of Madison, WI. She is a devoted follower of Henry Bergh, and with her pen delights to "speak for those who can not speak for themselves." For ten years past her home has been in Poynette, WI, but she has recently removed to Sun Prairie, WI, where her husband is principal of the high school. She has been one of the most voluminous writers in current publications that the central West has produced. She is always felicitous in her choice of subjects, and her work has been very remunerative.

MERIWETHER, Mrs. Lide, author and lecturer, born in Columbus, OH, 16th October, 1829. Mrs. Meriwether's parents resided in Accomack county, Virginia, and it was during a temporary sojourn in Columbus their daughter was born. Her mother dying a few days after her birth, Lide was sent to her paternal grandparents in Pennsylvania. Setting forth in her seventeeth year to earn her own living, she and her only sister, L. Virginia Smith, who afterward as L. Virginia French became one of the best known of Southern authors, went as teachers to the Southwest. Almost ten years after that practical declaration of independence, an act requiring much more hardihood forty years ago than now, Lide Smith was married and settled in the neighborhood of Memphis, TN, where, with the exception of a few years, she has since remained. There she lived through the war, passing through the quickening experiences of four years on the picket line with three young children. After the war she led a simple home life, devoted to husband and children, to the needs of neighbors and to personal charities, of which she has had a large and varied assortment. Though a reader and living in a rather literary atmosphere, she scarcely began to write until forty years old, nor to speak, a work for which she is even better fitted, till she was over fifty. The duties which came to her hand she did in a broad and simple way, while the thought of another work, which must be sought out was growing and her convictions were ripening. Then, when, as she says, most women are only waiting to die, their children reared and the tasks of the spirit largely ended, began for her a life of larger thought and activity. While many of her poems are imaginative, her prose has been written with a strong and obvious purpose. Her first literary venture, after a number of fugitive publications, was a collection of sketches, which came out under the name of "Soundings" (Memphis, 1872), a book whose object was to plead the cause of the so-called fallen women, a cause which both by her precepts and practice the author has for years maintained. In 1883 she published, as a memorial of her sister, who died in 1881, a volume of poems, "One or Two" (St. Louis), her sister's and her own alternating. But Mrs. Meriwether's real call to public work came less than ten years ago from a friend in Arkansas, who demanded that she should go and help in a Woman's Christian Temperance Union convention. She went and found, to her surprise, that she could speak, and she has been speaking with growing power and eloquence ever since. Almost immediately after going into the field she was elected president of the Woman's Christian Temperance Union of Tennessee, a post which she has continued to fill by the unanimous vote of its members. Under her leadership and remarkable executive ability the union has grown greatly in size and undertakings and has seen stirring times, having gone through the arduous fight for constitutional prohibition, in which they came much nearer victory than they had anticipated. From her interest in the temperance work naturally grew up a still more ardent interest in woman suffrage, of which league also, she has become State president, and to which she has devoted her ablest efforts. On both subjects Mrs. Meriwether is a fine speaker. It was her breadth of character which won her instant recognition, in her first notable speech before the National Woman Suffrage Convention, as being of the same stuff as the old leaders of the movement.

MERRICK, Mrs. Caroline Elizabeth, author and temperance worker, born on Cottage Hall Plantation, East Feliciana parish, LA, 24th November, 1825. Her father was Capt. David Thomas, who belonged to a prominent South Carolina family. She was thoroughly and liberally educated by governesses at home, and at an early age she became the wife of Edwin T. Merrick, an eminent jurist, chief justice of the Supreme Court of Louisiana for ten years before the Civil War, and reelected under the Confederacy. Their family consisted of two sons and two daughters. Mrs. Merrick devoted the first twenty years of her wedded life to maternal duties. While pondering deeply on the manifold responsibilities motherhood involves, she was led to look long and anxiously into the evils as well as the benefits of society. Having an original mind, she reasoned out vexed problems for herself and refused to accept theories simply because they were conventional. At that time the temperance cause was being widely agitated in the South, and, though its reception on the whole was a cold one, here and there women favored the movement. She became at once president of a local union, and for the last ten years has filled the position of State president for Louisiana. She has written extensively on the subject, but her chief talent is in impromptu speaking. She is a very successful platform orator, holding an audience by the force of her wit and keen sarcasm. Again her sympathies were aroused upon the question of woman suffrage, and for years she stood comparatively alone in her ardent championship of the cause. She was the first woman of Louisiana to speak publicly in behalf of her sex. She addressed the State convention in 1879, and assisted to secure an article in the Constitution making all women over twenty-one years of age eligible to hold office in connection with the public schools. It required considerable moral courage to side with a movement so cruelly derided in the South, but, supported by her husband, she has always worked for the emancipation of women with an eloquent and fluent pen, defining the legal status of woman in Louisiana, and is a valued correspondent of several leading woman's journals. In 1888 she represented Louisiana in the Woman's International Council in Washington, DC, and also in the Woman's Suffrage Association, which immediately afterward held a convention in the same city. She has always taken an active part in the charitable and philanthropic movements of New Orleans. For twelve years she was secretary of St. Anna's Asylum for Aged and Destitute Women and Children. She has been president of the Ladies' Sanitary and Benevolent Association, president of the Woman's Foreign Missionary Society, and in a recent meeting of the societies for the formation of a woman's league of Louisiana she was unanimously elected president. She has published a series of stories and sketches of the colored people of the South, which have been widely copied. Those stories show that she possesses literary ability of no mean order. She has written some poems that show a good degree of poetic feeling and talent. No collection of her literary productions has been published. She is living in New Orleans.

MERRICK, Mrs. Sarah Newcomb, educator and business woman, born in Charlottetown, Prince Edward Island, Canada, 9th May, 1844. She is a descendant of Elder Brewster, of Pilgrim Father fame, and counts among her ancestors some of the most notable New England names. She is a member of the Daughters of the Revolution by virtue of her great-grandfather, Simon Newcomb, having, with others, instigated rebellion in Nova Scotia. The rebellion was quelled soon after Mr. Newcomb's untimely death in 1776. Forty-one of his kinsmen, amply avenged his death by taking an active part in the war in the New England and other States. From such ancestry one could but suppose Mrs. Merrick to have inherited good physical and mental strength and great power of endurance. In her earliest childhood she played at teaching, and when barely nine years of age offered her services, in earnest sincerity, to a missionary, as a teacher for the Mic-Mac Indians of Nova Scotia. She was left an orphan at the age of seven, and then arose great obstacles in the way of her obtaining the education she so much craved, which should fit her for her coveted profession. In 1860 she reached the United States, and the following year entered the public schools of Boston, and, through the financial assistance of her oldest

brother, remained there till 1867, when she was graduated in the Girls' High and Normal School. Her steps were immediately turned southward. Her first teaching was done in Manassas, VA. There she not only labored throughout the week, but on Sunday afternoon gathered all the children of the town together and gave them scripture lessons, illustrated on the blackboard. That drew the attention of a Baltimore clergyman, who attended the meeting one day, and he strongly urged her to leave teaching and take up divinity, assuring her of a license from the Baltimore Synod. She declined, and resolved that nothing should allure her from her chosen field. Hearing of Texas as a wide and new ground for teachers, she next resolved to go there. Having thus resolved, no tales of wild Indians and wilder desperadoes could deter her. In September, 1872, she was appointed principal of a public school in San Antonio, and held that position with but little interruption for eighteen years. Even marriage did not wean her from the school-room. She was for over two years a paid contributor to the "Texas School Journal," and it is through her work that San Antonio has long borne the reputation of having the best primary schools in the State. Writer's cramp attacked her right hand about ten years ago. That was another agent trying to draw her from the school-room, but she taught her left hand to write, while she was in the meantime perfecting her invention of a pen-holder to fit on the finger like a thimble, leaving the hand free and thus avoiding cramp. Her investments in realty in San Antonio have proved profitable, and Mrs. Merrick is looked upon as a good business woman. She is president of the Business Woman's Association, lately formed in that city. Having retired from active work in the school-room, she intends to continue her work in the cause of education through her pen.

MERRILL, Miss Helen Maud, littérateur, born in Bangor, ME, 5th May, 1865. From 1881 to 1887 she lived in Bucksport, in the same State. In 1889 she removed to Portland, ME, where she still resides. There she soon became connected with several literary associations. She early showed a talent for composition, and since

1882 she has been a contributor, both in prose and verse, to the newspaper press. Her humorous sketches over the pen-name "Samantha Spriggins" had extensive reading. In 1885 she wrote a poem on the death of Gen. Grant, which was forwarded to his widow, and a grateful acknowledgment was received by the author in return. Her memorial odes and songs written for the anniversaries of the Grand Army of the Republic always find appreciation. In a recently-published work on the poets of her native State she has honorable mention. She has not yet collected her work in book-form, nor has she been in haste with her contributions to magazines and newspapers. Delicate in her childhood, she was tenderly and constantly cared for by her affectionate mother, who, doing her own thinking on all the most important themes pertaining to both man and womankind, encouraged her daughter to do the same. Early in life Miss Merrill was led to take herself into her own keeping, resolved on an honorable, useful and womanly life.

MERRILL, Miss Margaret Manton, journalist, born in England in 1859. She spent thirty-five years of her life in Minnesota, Colorado and California. Her father was the Rt. Rev. William E. Merrill, who for forty years was one of the foremost educators of the Northwest. Her mother was a grandniece of Sir Arthur Wellesley, Duke of Wellington, and her grandmother on the maternal side was second-cousin to "Royal Charlie" of Scotland. In spite of her lineage, Miss Merrill was very proud of the fact that she was an American woman. Entering Canton College at the age of fourteen, she remained there a year, and then continued her studies in the University of Minnesota, from which institution she was graduated, being chosen by her class as the valedictorian. The succeeding fall, when just eighteen years old, she began her career as teacher, which vocation she continued successfully for two years. Her taste for literary work led her to the journalistic field, when she was barely twenty years old. Going to Denver, she purchased the "Colorado Temperance Gazette," which was then the only temperance paper in that State. The venture was not a success, on account

of the doings of a partner, and also because the anti-temperance spirit was at that time too strong in Colorado for the prosperity of a paper wholly devoted to that cause. Later, during the temperance campaigns in Kansas and Iowa, she did very excellent service as a lecturer and organizer. She was especially fortunate in her labors among children. In 1887 she went to New York City to do regular newspaper work. When the Woman's Press Club of New York was organized, she was one of the charter members, and was elected the club's first secretary. She was a club journalist of Sorosis, and a very active member of that club. While later upon the staff of the New York "Herald" she was the only woman employed in that capacity by that great journal. In addition she did syndicate and miscellaneous work, being especially successful as a writer of children's stories. During her vacations she became an extensive traveler, at various times visiting almost every habitable portion of the globe. At the time of the famine in South Dakota, in 1889, she went through nineteen destitute counties in midwinter, visiting the homes of the people, and bringing back to her paper correct accounts of the condition of affairs there. The result was that large contributions were sent from the East, and many were relieved from want. During 1890 she visited the Yellow-stone Park and wrote accounts for papers in the West and in England, which attracted attention. While in California she wrote a poem entitled "The Faro Dealer's Story," which gained for her considerable local fame. She died in New York City, 19th June, 1893.

MESSENGER, Mrs. Lillian Rozell, poet, was born in Ballard county, KY. Her parents were Virginians. Her paternal grandfather came from Nice, France, during the Napoleonic War and settled in Virginia. Her maternal ancestors were of English descent. Her father was a gifted physician, fond of poetry and music. Lillian's early education was varied, and her free country life made her familiar with nature. From reading poetry, she early began to make it. At the age of sixteen she began to publish her poetical productions, and her pen has never been idle for any great length of time since then. Her father died while she

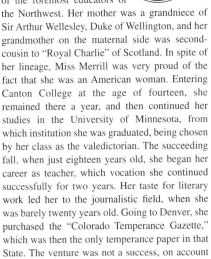

was in college. After Dr. Rozell's death Lillian did not return to school. When a little more than sixteen years of age, she became the wife of North A. Messenger, a native of Tuscumbia, AL, an editor and a man of means. His father had been an editor for forty years before him. Their wedded life was brief, only lasting four years, when Mr. Messenger died. She was left with one son, whom she raised and educated. He is a journalist. After her husband's death she made her home in Washington, DC. She has published four volumes of verse. Most of her work is cast on a high plane, and all of it bears the stamp of genius. She is now nearly forty years old, and is actively engaged in literary pursuits. She has always been very fond of music and painting, and has acquired knowledge of both arts. She has given some dramatic recitals, and is said by critics to possess dramatic talents of a high order.

MEYER, Mrs. Annie Nathan, author and worker for the advancement of women, born in New York, NY, in 1867. Her maiden name was Annie Nathan. She belongs to a prominent Jewish family and is a cousin of the late Emma Lazarus. She was educated at home in her childhood and afterward entered the School for Women, a branch at that time of Columbia College. She became the wife of Dr. Alfred Meyer, before she had finished her school course, and withdrew from her class. She was one of the first to enter the woman's course in Columbia College, in 1885, and her efforts and those of others resulted in the founding of Barnard College, affiliated with Columbia College, receiving full official sanction and recognition. She is now one of the trustees. She is the editor of "Woman's Work in America," a volume containing the result of three years of earnest work and research. Mrs. Meyer is opposed to woman suffrage, unless the franchise be restricted by laws providing for an educational qualification. It is her theory that legislation should follow in the footsteps of education. She is a gifted woman, a poet and essayist, but most of her activities have been expended on philanthropic, reform and charitable work. Her home is in New York City.

MICHEL, Mrs. Nettie Leila, editor, born in Oswego, NY, 26th September, 1863. Her father was Mortimer A. Champion, a descendant of the Tifft family, of Connecticut, early settlers of this country. Her mother was Cecelia Penny Cham-

pion a descendant of the Clark family, of central New York. She received her early education in the public schools of Syracuse, NY, and later in the public schools of Oswego. She was married 29th March, 1882, but her wedded life was of brief duration, extending over a period of less than one year. Being obliged to support herself she went out as an advertising agent for a large wholesale house of Chicago, IL, and was the first woman in this country to fill such a position. She then became a drummer, visiting the drug trade in the interests of an Eastern supply house. She was one of the first, if not the first, women sent out as an agent for staple articles and occasioned no little comment, traveling from place to place with her sample trunk. Her territory embraced the States of New York, New Jersey, Pennsylvania and Michigan. As a drummer she was very successful, but left the road at the end of two years. She then took a course in stenography in Prof. Warner's school in Elmira, NY, in 1888, and was graduated in three months, one of the best qualified students sent out by that school during a term of twenty-five years. In the fall of 1888 she entered the office of the "Magazine of Poetry," in Buffalo, NY, and took charge of the correspondence as an expert stenographer. The following year she became the business manager of the magazine, a position she resigned in 1891 to become its editor. Mrs. Michel is interested in all movements for the advancement of women, and she has represented business interests in various conventions throughout the country. She is a member of St. John's Episcopal Church, Buffalo, of the King's Daughters, and of the Woman's National Press Association.

MILLAR, Mme. Clara Smart, singer and musical educator, born in McConnell's Grove, near Freeport, IL, in 1852. She was the daughter of Porter M. Smart and Sarah E. Stowell Smart. The family moved to Boston, MA, and Clara entered the New England Conservatory of Music in that city. She studied for four years under the direction of L. W. Wheeler, and was graduated in 1870. She at once began her work with enthusiasm, and won success as a vocalist, making a specialty of church music as a leading member of quartette choirs connected with the prominent churches of Boston and vicinity. In 1874 she became the special pupil of Madame Rudersdorf, who urged her to make a specialty of teaching. Clara studied faithfully, and following her teacher's advice, became the exponent of the Rudersdorf system in Boston, where now, in 1892, she holds the first rank as teacher of musical vocalism. Miss Smart made a decided success in 1876 in oratorio, appearing in Music Hall with Titiens. She went to Milan, Italy, where she was so fortunate as to enjoy the teaching of San Giovanni. Returning to Boston, she again took a class of pupils, and now nearly all her time is occupied with the duties of her arduous profession, giving ninety-six lessons a week. She became the wife, in 1891, of William Millar, a business man of Boston.

MILLER, Mrs. Addie Dickman, born in West Union, IA, 26th July, 1859. Her maiden name was Dickman. In 1863 her parents moved to a farm near that town, where her youthful years were passed in quiet. Her schooling from her seventh to her fourteenth year was limited to a few months each year. She was the oldest of nine children. From her refined and educated mother she learned music and inherited literary tastes. From her public-spirited father she imbibed a taste for discussing current questions of public interest. She became a teacher in her fifteenth year, and continued in that profession for eight years, teaching during vacations and studying in the Western College of Iowa. In that institution she completed a Latin and scientific course in 1881, and took the chair of history and literature in Avalon College, Missouri. At the close of her first term in that institution she became the wife of Prof. G. M. Miller, a fellow-student and graduate of the Iowa College, who was professor of ancient languages in Avalon College. During the next two years she taught German and acted as supernumerary to the faculty of Avalon. In 1883 Professor Miller accepted the presidency of Philomath College, in Philomath, OR. In that college

Mrs. Miller taught German and acted as superintendent of the young women's department, giving the students practical lectures on the questions of the day. Mrs. Miller and her husband identified themselves with the temperance movement, and Professor Miller served as president of the Oregon Temperance Alliance. In 1886, having been nominated for Congress, he lectured in various towns in the State, and while he was gone Mrs. Miller performed his work in the college. Leaving Philomath they went to Portland, OR, where Mr. Miller began to practice as an attorney-at-law. Mrs. Miller gave up teaching and has devoted herself to the work of the Woman's Christian Temperance Union. While caring for her three children, she found time to serve for two years as president of the Portland Woman's Christian Temperance Union, arraying the motherhood of the city against the evil of intemperance. She is a most enthusiastic worker. Besides her platform work she for years edited the woman's department in the "West Shore," a Portland periodical. She has also published "Letters to Our Girls" in an eastern magazine, a series of articles containing many valuable thoughts for the young women to whom they were addressed. In 1890 Mrs. Miller and her family removed to Woodbridge, CA. While living there, her practical nature found expression in the invention of a dish-washing machine. Her life is still devoted to moral and charitable work.

MILLER, Mrs. Annie Jenness, dress-reformer, born in New Hampshire, 28th January, 1859. She was educated in Boston, MA. Her maiden name was Annie Jenness, and she traces her ancestry back to that illustrious stock which produced Wendell Phillips and Oliver Wendell Holmes. She is the most prominent of all the leaders in the movement for reform in the matter of woman's dress. Before her marriage she had won considerable fame in Massachusetts as a woman of letters. She is a young and beautiful woman, highly cultured, who has taken up with energy and with a great deal of taste and good judgment the question of dress reform, or "the principles of correct and artistic dressing." She has lectured in all of the leading cities of the United States, to crowded houses, and has been well received, being invited over and over again to the same places. She now lives in Washington, DC. She is one of the owners of a magazine published in New York and devoted to the aesthetics of physical development and artistic designs for dresses, containing articles by the best writers on all topics of interest to women. She has presented her ideas on dress to large assemblies, and her influence is widely acknowledged. All the progressive and reformatory movements of the day appeal to her and have her sympathy and support. She is the author of "Physical Beauty" and of "Mother and Babe," the latter a work which furnishes information and patterns upon improved plans for mother's and baby's wardrobe. Mrs. Miller's ultimate hope is to establish at the national capitol an institution for physical development and the highest art of self-culture, which shall be under the control of able students of anatomy, chemistry and physical science.

MILLER, Mrs. Dora Richards, author and educator, was born in the Island of St. Thomas, Danish West Indies. Her father, Richard Richards, was from Liverpool, England, and her mother's family also was of English descent, through Hezekiah Huntington, of Connecticut. He was her grandfather and belonged to the same family from which came Samuel Huntington, signer of the Declaration of Independence. The death of her father while she was yet an infant caused her to be taken to the home of her Huntington grandmother, in the neighboring island of Santa Cruz. Hurricanes and earthquakes were among her experiences there, and not long before she left the island a negro insurrection took place, which resulted in the emancipation of the slaves in all the Danish Islands. Her mother, with the other children, had removed to New Orleans, LA, but it was not until after her mother's death, when she was about fourteen, she joined there her unknown brothers and sisters, to reside in the family of a married sister. She was graduated with distinction, her school-girl essays having for several years attracted attention, and the editors of a New Orleans paper invited her to contribute to their journal. She had prepared herself for the profession of

a teacher and undertaken the support and education of a young brother, and thought it best to give all her powers to that work. A few years later, when that and other duties were accomplished, she became the wife, in 1862, of Anderson Miller, a lawyer from Mississippi, and they went to Arkansas to reside. Troubles resulting from the war caused a break-up and those Journeyings in the Confederacy, culminating in the siege of Vicksburg, which are recounted in her articles published in the "Century," entitled "Diary of a Union Woman in the Siege of Vicksburg" and "Diary of a Union Woman in the South." Her husband died soon after the close of the war, leaving her with two infant sons. She took up more earnestly than ever public-school work, rising steadily from grade to grade, till she was appointed to the chair of science in the girls' high school of New Orleans. During those busy years she was using her pen in the local papers, without name, on school subjects. In 1886 her "War Diary" was published in the "Century." Those articles attracted great attention. In 1889 she wrote, in collaboration with George W. Cable, "The Haunted House on Royal Street," being science teacher in the high school held in that building when it was invaded by the White League. She was correspondent for the Austin, TX, "Statesman" during the second Cotton Exposition. She was assistant editor of a paper published in Houston, TX, and has written for "Lippincott's Magazine," the "Louisiana Journal of Education," the "Practical Housekeeper" and other journals.

MILLER, Mrs. Elizabeth, physician, born on the banks of the Detroit river, near the town of Detroit, MI, 2nd July, 1836, of Scotch parents. She was the youngest of six sisters. The pre-natal influences there received from her mother, who always had a kind word and a piece of bread and meat for the dusky woodman, infused into the child's nature a friendly regard and large sympathy for the Indian. This mother was a rigid prohibitionist, even in those far-away days, and no one ever received from her a drink stronger than coffee. Dr. Miller's heart has rebelled against the cruel wrong perpetrated upon the Indian. Any work for the betterment and uplifting of the Indian has found a ready endorsement by her. While yet quite young, her parents removed to the city of New York, where she spent her girlhood years.

Those were the happiest years of her life, and still, when the family concluded to return to Detroit, she responded joyfully, so sweet was the memory of green fields, wild flowers and free birds singing their happy songs in the great forests. In her seventh year she received a fall, which injured her spine and cast a shadow over every hope and ambition of her life, and which in later years has been the cause of much suffering and disability. A few terms in a young womans' boarding-school proved to be all she could accomplish in school work. Environed with frailty and other adverse circumstances, there was little to be done but simply to wait, but in her waiting there was the planting of a better heart garden than could have been accomplished by any other process. In her seventeenth year she was so desirous of becoming educated, that she might devote her life to foreign mission work, it was in a measure decided to have her attend Albion Seminary, MI, when she was taken quite ill and forced to yield to an apparent decree. After serious consideration and mental struggle she resolved upon a course of home study and selfculture. For this she took as a foundation the Bible with the helps received from eminent biblical writers, such as Boardman, Tupper, Thomas à Kempis, Pollok and many others, becoming familiar with her chosen authors through their spiritually-inspiring influences, giving also attention to higher studies. At the age of twenty-two years she was married. In 1862, under the first three-year call, her husband entered the army. In 1863, in answer to a telegram, she went to Jefferson Barracks, MO, to nurse her husband, who was seriously injured while on detached service, in charge of sick and wounded from the fields of Corinth. It was during her stay in that general hospital that Mrs. Miller began the study of medicine, which she pursued until 1866, when she attended her first course of lectures in the allopathic college in Boston, MA. She was graduated in 1870 in the Homeopathic College, Cleveland, OH. Her impelling motive in obtaining a medical education was her own health. From girlhood Dr. Miller was peculiarly gifted to heal the sick, making her first and marvelous cure, when fifteen years of age, of a critical case of hernia. She reduced the displacement per-

fectly while waiting for the family physician, Dr. M. P. Stewart, of Detroit. It was the only case known to him reduced in that way. He pronounced it one of the most wonderful cures known to medical science. The patient is still living. The experiences and victories of Dr. Miller furnish the women of to-day another example of self-sustaining heroism not found in every walk in life, for hers has been a life of heroic endeavor. Dr. Miller is living in Muncie, IN, surrounded by a large circle of friends and acquaintances, still engaged in professional work, both medical and literary.

MILLER, Mrs. Emily Huntington, author and educator, born in Brooklyn, CT, 22nd October, 1833. She received a liberal education and was graduated in Oberlin College, Oberlin, OH. In 1860 she became the wife of John E. Miller. Of their children, three sons are living. Their only daughter died in infancy. Mr. Miller was a teacher for many years. He was the principal of the academy in Granville, IL, and afterward professor of Greek and Latin in the Northwestern College, then located in Plainfield, IL. He was always an earnest Sunday-school and Young Men's Christian Association worker. In connection with Alfred L. Sewell he published the "Little Corporal," which, after the great fire in Chicago, was merged with "St. Nicholas." Mr. and Mrs. Miller moved from Evanston, IL, to St. Paul, MN, where Mr. Miller died in 1882. Mrs. Miller had shown her literary ability in her school-days. While yet a mere girl, she published a number of sketches and stories, which attracted general attention. She has ever since been a constant and prolific contributor of sketches, short stories, serials, poems and miscellaneous articles to newspapers and magazines. She earned a reputation by her work on the "Little Corporal." She has given much time and work to Sunday-school and missionary interests. She has been connected with the Chautauqua Literary and Scientific Circle from its commencement, and has been president of the Chautauqua Woman's Club for four years. Recently she was elected president of the Woman's College of the Northwestern University, in Evanston, IL, where she now resides. Her published literary work includes fifteen volumes, some of which have been republished in England, and all of which have found wide circles of readers. Her poetical productions are very numerous and excellent. Over a hundred of her poems have been set to music. Her life is full of activity along moral lines, and she still labors for good with all the earnestness and vigor of youth. In her varied career she has been equally successful as writer, educator, temperance-worker and journalist.

MILLER, Mrs. Frances M., author, born in the north of Ireland, 30th June, 1846. In 1849 her parents came to the United States and settled in Pennsylvania. In 1869 her family moved to California. There Frances was married. Mrs. Milne was educated mainly at home. From her thirteenth to her sixteenth year she went to a public school. Her training was quite thorough, and her reading covered a wide range of authors. She began to write, in both prose and verse, in early life, and her work soon attracted attention. She has published poems in the San Francisco "Star" and many other prominent Pacific-coast journals. For some years she has made her home in San Luis Obispo, CA. In 1883 she became interested in the single-tax movement, and many of her songs were written in the interest of that movement. She has made a profound study of economic and political questions and with pen and voice she has aided in extending the discussion of the relations of progress and poverty, and of individuals and society. Since the publication of her earliest productions in the Cincinnati "Christian Standard," she has written and published much. In 1872 she issued a book, a story for young people. She has written a number of poems, essays and sketches over the pen-name "Margaret Frances." In all her work on reform she has used her own name in full.

MILLER, Mrs. Mary A., editor, born in Allegheny City, PA, in 18—. She is the second daughter of David Davis, deceased, a highly-respected citizen of Allegheny. Her school-days, till the age of seventeen, were spent in the schools of her native city, her higher education being received in the Allegheny College for Young Ladies, in the same town. Choosing the profes-

sion of teacher, she taught for five years, until she became the wife of William Miller, of Allegheny. Her first public literary work was done in 1858, being poems and short stories, the latter of which were continued with more or less intermission, under a pen-name, until 1874, when the death of her husband and the business cares consequent caused an interruption. Her natural timidity, in her early efforts, caused her frequently to change her pen-name, so that it often occurred in the household that her stories were read without a suspicion of the author's presence. Her first literary work over her own name was in 1878, being a series of letters descriptive of a western trip from Pittsburgh, PA, to Montana by rail and stage, from Montana to Utah, and from Utah to New Mexico. Since that time her name has appeared as missionary editor of the woman's department in the "Methodist Recorder," published in Pittsburgh, and since 1885 as editor and publisher of the "Woman's Missionary Record," organ of the Woman's Foreign Missionary Society of the Methodist Protestant Church. She has served very efficiently as corresponding secretary of the society for six years, has represented the society in a number of the annual conferences of the church, in two general conferences and in 1888 was a delegate to the World's Missionary Conference in London, England.

MILLER, Mrs. Minnie Willis Baines, author, born in Lebanon, NH, 8th January, 1845. The first years of her life were spent on New England soil. Ohio has been her home during the greater portion of her life, and there all her literary work has been accomplished. Her maiden name was Minnie Willis. She has been twice married. Her first husband was Evan Franklin Baines, and the name of her present husband, to whom she was married 18th February, 1892, is Leroy Edgar Miller. Her literary career was commenced early. Her taste for composition in both poetry and prose was a feature of her character in childhood. Her writing, during many years of her life, was without any fixed purpose, save that of indulging her own inclination and entertaining others. The loss of her children, Florence May Baines and

Frank Willis Baines, within three years of each other, caused her to devote herself largely to strictly religious literature. Her best-known works of that character are "The Silent Land" (Cincinnati, 1890), "His Cousin, The Doctor" (Cincinnati, 1891), and "The Pilgrim's Vision" (Cincinnati, 1892). She has been a regular contributor to various religious newspapers, writing often over her own name, and oftener perhaps behind an editorial "we" or a pen-name. She is the first president of the Springfield Woman's Pioneer Press Club, a literary association formed of women who write for the press. During the crusade throughout Ohio and the western States against the liquor-traffic some years ago, and also in the popular temperance movement known as the "Murphy Work," she was an active, earnest participant, lecturing extensively and successfully in her own and other States. Her home is in Springfield, OH.

MILLER, Mrs. Olive Thorne, author, naturalist and humanitarian, born in Auburn, NY, 25th June, 1831. She was married at an early age. Her husband is descended from a sterling New England family and Mrs. Miller said that with them "the dish-cloth was mightier than the pen," at least so far as women were concerned. In her youth it was the custom of the time to disapprove a woman's ambition to give play to her talents, and Mrs. Miller allowed herself to be guided by those about her. When her four children had grown up, she began to write for young people, but about twelve years ago she became interested in birds and wrote of their habits for an older audience and since then she has mainly confined herself to that field of work. She lived in Chicago, IL, for twenty years after her marriage and it was in that city she made her appearance as an author. Her talents are of a high order, and her field was practically unoccupied, so that she was soon able to get a hearing. Among her productions are "Little Folks in Feathers and Furs" (New York, 1879); "Queer Pets at Marcy's"(New York, 1880); "Little People of Asia" (New York, 1883); "Bird Ways" (Boston, 1885), and "In Nesting Time" (Boston, 1888). She became known as a specialist on birds, but she has done much other literary work, including descriptive work for children, articles upon natural history and various kinds of manufactures for the children's magazines, and a series of papers on "Our Daughters at Home" for "Harper's Bazaar," in which her decided views in the training of children and of the bad effect of much that goes by that name found expression. She loves all birds and nature devotedly. Her articles have appeared in the "Atlantic Monthly," "Harper's Magazine," "Harper's Bazaar" and other journals. Among the birds she has studied with exhaustive care are several species of thrush, the kingbird, the catbird, the red-wing blackbird, the bluebird, the Baltimore oriole, the mocking-bird, the English sparrow, the golden-wing woodpecker, the thrasher or brown thrush, the Virginia cardinal, the scarlet tanager and the rose-breasted grosbeak, all of which are described in her volumes, "In Nesting Time" and "Bird Ways." Her "Little Brothers of the Air" (Boston, 1892) contained studies of the bobolink, the junco, the redstart and other birds. In the summer she studies the birds out of doors, and in her winter home in Brooklyn, NY, she has a room given up entirely to her pets, and there she studies their habits in confinement. She devotes herself absolutely to birds out of doors through the nesting months of June and July, taking copious notes of everything she sees and thinks. Through August and September she works up her notes into magazine and newspaper articles, working undisturbed from morning till night. The rest of the year she gives to her family, her clubs and club friends, to the observation of pet birds in her room and to literary work pursued in a more leisurely and less exacting fashion than during her busy period. She has consistently and persistently opposed the wearing of birds and bird-wings on women's bonnets, and one of her pointed articles on that custom, which appeared in the "Chautauquan," was the means of stirring up a great deal of interest in the matter. With all her affection for her birds, she is very fond of society, and in Brooklyn, where she has been living thirteen years, her benevolent face is frequently seen in social assemblages. She is a member of the Brooklyn Woman's Club, of Sorosis, of the Meridian Club, and of the Seidl Society. She is a member of the Women's Unitarian League, although she is not a Unitarian and attends the New Church, or Swedenborgian. Her views are broad, liberal and exalted. She recognizes the great educational value of women's clubs and believes that those organizations are working a revolution among women. She has published a book on the subject, "The Woman's Club," (New York, 1891). Although she is now a grandmother, she preserves her freshness of disposition and her mental activity unimpaired. The name by which she is so widely known is neither her own name nor wholly a pen-name. Years ago, when she was writing about the making of pianos, jewelry, lead pencils and various things for the old "Our Young Folks," she had a pen-name, "Olive Thorne." As her work grew in quantity, she found it extremely inconvenient to have two names, and she compounded her pen-name and her husband's name into Olive Thorne Miller, by which she is now known everywhere outside her own family.

MILNE, Mrs. Frances M., author, born in the north of Ireland, 30th June, 1846. In 1849 her parents came to the United States and settled in Pennsylvania. In 1869 her family moved to California. There Frances was married. Mrs. Milne was educated mainly at home. From her thirteenth to her sixteenth year she went to a public school. Her training was quite thorough, and her reading covered a wide range of authors. She began to write, in both prose and verse, in early life, and her work soon attracted attention. She has published poems in the San Francisco "Star" and many other prominent Pacific-coast journals. For some years she has made her home in San Luis Obispo, CA. In 1883 she became interested in the single-tax movement, and many of her songs were written in the interest of that movement. She has made a profound study of economic and political questions and with pen and voice she has aided in extending the discussion of the relations of progress and poverty, and of individuals and society. Since the publication of her earliest productions in the Cincinnati "Christian Standard," she has written and published much. In 1872 she issued a book, a story for young people. She has written a number of poems, essays and sketches over the pen-name "Margaret Frances." In all her work on reform she has used her own name in full.

MIMS, Mrs. Sue Harper, social leader and Christian Scientist, born in Brandon, MS, 17th May, 1842. She is the daughter of the late Col. William C. Harper and Mrs. Mary C. Harper. Her father was a lawyer of great learning and distinguished ability. Her mother, eminent for her physical beauty and mental power, is living still, over eighty years of age, in the comfortable old homestead where Mrs. Mims was born. The town of Brandon, now lapsed into age and inaction, was once a center of affluence and was noted for its beautiful and intellectual women. Miss Harper, dowered with every charm of person, spirit and heart, had the added advantage of thorough study and extensive travel and was as much admired in her girlhood as she is now in her perfected bloom. She became the wife of Maj. Livingston Mims in 1866. Maj. Mims is a leader in social and business circles, a gentleman of aristocratic lineage and culture. He was for several years president of the Capitol City Club in Atlanta and during his reign President and Mrs. Cleveland were entertained by the club. In his elegant home, "Heartsease," he and his wife receive their friends with courtly and graceful hospitality. They are prominent for their scholarly attainments and accomplishments. Their home is a gathering place for the literary, artistic and musical people of the city. Mrs. Mims' influence has always been for intellectual and ethical culture, and nothing affords her or her husband greater happiness than to know that hers has been a character at all times essentially uplifting. She is at once a leader and a follower of Christian Science. In the South she has been one of its prime movers and teachers. Nor is it only on this subject that she has so charmingly conversed and contributed forceful and interesting articles. Her critiques on various books and authors from time to time have met warm approval. Her time, her means, her powers of heart and soul are spent in doing good. She is a most approachable and sympathetic woman. The humblest laboring woman, the saddest sin-sick outcast can to her freely and be made to feel the absolute sisterhood that abides forever.

MINER, Miss Jean Pond, sculptor, born in Menasha, WI, 8th July, 1866. Her father is Rev. H. A. Miner, a Congregationalist clergyman. Her mother's maiden name was Harriet Pond Rice. Miss Miner in early life removed to Madison, WI, with her parents. She attended the high school and was known among her mates as an artist in embryo, although she had not shown her gifts as a sculptor. After two years as a special student in Downer College, Fox Lake, WI, she went to Chicago and began her art studies. In the Art Institute she first found that her power lay in clay-modeling. After working only three months she took the second honors of the institution. Soon after, because of her ability, she was sought as an instructor, and at the end of the year she accepted a position as student teacher. Her statue "Hope" was among those that met very, favorable recognition. It will be placed in the McCowen Oral School, in Englewood, IL. Portrait busts of Miss Miner's have been solicited by the American Artists' Association and conspicuously exhibited. In her ideal work the heads of "Hypatia," George Eliot's "Dorothea," "Christiphin," "Ioni" and others, which have been shown in various Chicago art exhibitions, have attracted attention. The woman's art club known as The Palette Club has recognized her later work and conferred upon her the honor of active membership. Her figure "Wisconsin" is more than locally celebrated. Her group especially prepared for the World's Fair is called "Leave-Taking." Her representations of childlife take high rank in collections.

MITCHELL, Miss Maria, astronomer, born in Nantucket, MA, 1st August, 1818, and died in Lynn, MA, in 1889. She was the daughter of William Mitchell, the well-known astronomer, from whom she inherited her scientific tastes. In childhood she showed remarkable talent for mathematics and astronomy, and at an early age assisted her father in his investigations, while studying with him. She studied afterward with Prof. Charles Pierce and assisted him in the summer school in Nantucket. For many years she was librarian of the Nantucket Athenæum. She was a regular student of astronomy and made many discoveries of comets and fine studies of nebulae. On 1st October, 1847, she discovered a small comet, and on that occasion she received a gold medal

from the King of Denmark and a copper medal from the Republic of San Marino, Italy. When the "American Nautical Almanac" was established, she became a leading contributor to its pages, and her work on that periodical was continued until after she was chosen astronomer in Vassar College, Poughkeepsie, NY. In 1858 she visited the chief observatories in Europe, and while abroad she formed the acquaintance of Sir John Herschel, Sir George B. Airy, Le Verrier and Humboldt. Returning to the United States, she received a superb gift, a large telescope, from the women of the country, headed by Miss Elizabeth

Peabody, of Boston, MA. In 1865 she began her work as professor of astronomy in Vassar College, which she continued until 1888, when failing health compelled her to resign. The trustees were not willing to accept her resignation, but gave her a leave of absence. Besides her work as a teacher, she made a specialty of the study of sun-spots and of the satellites of Saturn and Jupiter. She received the degree of LL.D. from Hanover College in 1852 and from Columbia College in 1887. She belonged to numerous scientific societies. She became a member of the American Association for the Advancement of Science in 1850, and was made a fellow in 1874. She was the first woman elected to the American Academy of Arts and Sciences. She was prominent in the councils of the Association for the Advancement of Women, serving as president of that society in the convention in Syracuse, NY, in 1875, and in Philadelphia, PA, in 1876. She wrote much, but her published works were restricted to scientific papers.

MITCHELL, Miss Marion Juliet, poet, born in Buffalo, NY, 4th September, 1836. Her father was Dr. John Mitchell, who died in 1885. Her mother died in 1888. She went with her parents to Wisconsin, and the family settled in Janesville, which was then a small village. One of the best of her earlier poems, "My Grandmother's Home," is a memorial of several happy

Sadie Martinot.
From Photo by Sarony, New York.

Fannie Johnston.
From Photo by Morrison, Chicago.

Jean Mawson.
From Photo by Baker, Columbus.

years which she passed in childhood with her grandparents, Hon. Isaac Lacey and wife, near Rochester, NY. She attended school in Rochester, and went afterward to the Ingham Collegiate Institute, in Le Roy, NY. She finished with a thorough course in Mrs. Willard's seminary, in Troy, NY. She inherited literary tastes from her parents. Most of her poetic work is of recent date and shows matured powers of imagination and expression. She is quiet and domestic in her tastes, and cares little for what is generally termed society. She is surrounded by a circle of congenial friends, and her life is passed in good works and the delights of literature.

MITCHELL, Mrs. Martha Reed, well known in charity, art and society circles at home and abroad, born in Westford, MA, March, 1818. Her parents were Seth and Rhoda Reed. Her childhood was full of sunshine and hope. Beloved by all on account of her happy, loving disposition, she returned in full the affection bestowed upon her and thought only of the world as beautiful, and of mankind as good and true. She was one of a large family, and in early years learned the lessons of unselfishness and thoughtfulness of others, characteristics that in a marked degree have remained prominent through her life. At thirteen years of age she attended Miss Fisk's school in Keene, NH, and at seventeen went to Mrs. Emma Willard's seminary in Troy, NY, where the happiest days of her life were passed. In 1838 she was forced to renounce a tempting offer of a trip to Europe, and to bid farewell to all her beloved companions, to go with her parents to the wilds of Wisconsin. No vestibuled trains in those days transported passengers across the continent. Instead of hours, weeks were necessary for such a journey. Through the Erie Canal and by the chain of great lakes the family wended their way, and after three weeks of anxiety and trouble they touched the shores of Wisconsin at Milwaukee, their objective point. Wisconsin was then a Territory. Milwaukee was a village of five-hundred souls. Forests covered the area where now stands a city of 250,000 inhabitants. Indians with their wigwams occupied the sites now graced by magnificent buildings devoted to religion, education, art and commerce. In 1841 Martha Reed became the wife of Alexander Mitchell, a young Scotchman. Early in the forties she helped organize what is now known as the Protestant Orphan Asylum, and was its first treasurer. As the years rolled by, children were born to Mr. and Mrs. Mitchell, and great wealth rewarded their zeal, but neither prosperity nor popularity ever deprived Mrs. Mitchell of her love of God or love for her fellow-man. In all institutions where support or home comforts were extended to unfortunate women, Mrs. Mitchell was ever ready with advice and assistance. For years after leaving Milwaukee she supported a mission kindergarten, where, daily, nearly a hundred children from the lowest grades of society were taught to be self-respecting and self-sustaining men and women. In 1858 Mrs. Mitchell was elected vice-regent of the Mount Vernon Association for Wisconsin. Art and artists are indebted to her for her liberal patronage. She has visited many European countries and traveled extensively in America. Soon after the Civil War, while visiting Florida, she found the spot where health and the pleasures of a home could be combined. A tract of land was purchased on the St. Johns river three miles from Jacksonville, and with her indomitable will and energy, aided by ample means, Mrs. Mitchell in a few years converted a sandy waste into a luxurious garden. She has there brought to perfection the tropical fruit-bearing trees. Among her rare trees are the camphor and cinnamon from Ceylon and the tea plant from China. Her list of bamboos includes the sacred tree of India and five varieties of cane. The family of flowers embraces all the well-known varieties of the temperate zone and the tropics. Prominent among her charities in Florida stands St. Luke's hospital. After the death of her husband, which occurred on 19th April, 1887, Mrs. Mitchell bade farewell to Milwaukee and located her summer resting-place on the St. Lawrence, in the vicinity of the Thousand Islands.

MODJESKA, Mme. Helena,  actor, born in Cracow, Poland, 12th October, 1844. Her maiden name was Helcia Opido. She is a daughter of Michael Opido, a cultured musician, a teacher in Cracow. In childhood and youth she felt a longing for the stage, but her parents would not permit her to become an actor. At an early age she became the wife of Mr. Modrzejewski, now abbreviated to "Modjeska," and she then was permitted to carry out her wish to go on the stage. Helena appeared successfully in a charity performance in Bochnia, Austrian Poland, and her husband was so impressed by her talents that he organized a company, and they traveled through Galacia, playing in the towns with considerable success. During the last part of 1862 she played a three-month engagement in the government theater in Lemberg. She next managed a theater for herself in Czernowice, taking the prominent rôles and assisted by her younger sister and two half-brothers. In 1865 she returned to Cracow, and her reputation at once made her leading lady in the chief theater in that city. Her fame spread to France and Germany, and she received invitations to play in other countries. Alexander Dumas, fils, invited her to go to Paris to play the rôle of Marguerite Gautier in his "Dame aux Camelias," but she preferred to remain on the Polish stage. Her husband died, and in September, 1868, she became the wife of Charles Bozenta Chlapowski, a Polish count. In 1869 they settled in Warsaw, where Madame Modjeska played the principal parts in the standard dramas of Shakespeare, Goethe, Schiller and Moliere, as well as in new Polish dramas. They remained in Warsaw until 1876. Her repertory in her native language included two-hun-dred-eighty-four plays. Failing health and discontent under the Russian censorship induced her to leave the stage, and she and her husband came to the United States in 1876. With the aim of founding a Polish colony, they settled on a ranch near Los Angeles, CA. In the spring of 1877 she went to San Francisco to study English, and after four months of study she was able to appear as Adrienne Lecouvreur in the California Theater. Her success was instant, and she at once entered upon her remarkably brilliant American career. She has made many tours of the United States and a few short tours in Poland, and has played several seasons in London and the English provinces. Her repertory on the American stage includes twenty-five rôles. She has literary talent of a fine order, and among her achievements are successful adaptations of "As You Like It" and "Twelfth Night" for the Polish stage. In common with all patriotic Poles, Madame Modjeska burns with indignation over the tyranny exercised by Russia over Poland.

Both Madam Modjeska and her husband are natur-alized citizens of the United States.

MONROE, Mrs. Elizabeth Kortright, wife of James Monroe, fifth President of the United States, born in New York, NY, in 1768, and died in Loudoun county, VA, in 1830. She was the daughter of Capt. Lawrence Kortright, of the British Army, who settled in New York City in 1783. Elizabeth was one of a family of five children, one son and four daughters. She was thoroughly educated, and was a belle in the society of the metropolis. She became the wife of James Monroe in 1789. He was then a Senator. After marriage they settled in Philadelphia, PA, whither the seat of government had been moved. In 1794 he was appointed minister to France, and his wife accompanied him to Paris. He went abroad again in 1803, and while there Mrs. Monroe secured the release of Madame de La Fayette from the prison of La Force, where she was imprisoned under a sentence of death by decapitation. Her life has been left almost completely without mention by the chroniclers of her time. After their return from the first mission to France, Mr. Monroe was made Governor of Virginia, and Mrs. Monroe aided him greatly by her administration of social affairs in the Capital. She accompanied him to England when he was sent as minister to that country. When he became President, in 1817, Mrs. Monroe took her place as mistress of the White House, and she filled it with grace, tact and dignity. Although she performed carefully all the duties implied in her position, she preferred a quiet home to the splendor of public life. Her health was delicate during the last years she spent in the White House. After President Monroe's retirement they lived on his estate in Loudoun county, VA. The two daughters of the family were married, and the old home, "Oak Hill," was a quiet retreat. Mrs. Monroe died suddenly, in 1830, and her husband died 4th July, 1831.

MONROE, Mrs. Harriet Earhart, lecturer and educator, born in Indiana, PA, 21st August, 1842. She is the daughter of Rev. David Earhart and Mary W. Earhart, of Atchison, KS. When the Civil War broke out she was teaching in Kansas, and then she went to Clinton, IA, where she taught until peace was restored. She returned to Kansas and in 1865 was married. In 1870, thrown upon her own resources, she opened a private school in Atchison, KS, which grew rapidly into a collegiate institute. In 1885 her health failed and she was compelled to give up the school, and until 1887 served as correspondent for a number of western journals. She then decided to enter the lecture field. In that line of effort she has succeeded in a remarkable degree. Her lectures are on religious, artistic, war, temperance, personal, economic and historical topics. Her first book, "Past Thirty," was published in 1878. Her "Art of Conversation" (New York, 1889) found an extraordinar sale. In the preparation of her lectures she has repeatedly visited Europe. Her permanent home is in Philadelphia, PA.

MONTGOMERY, Mrs. Carrie Frances Judd, church worker and poet, born in Buffalo, NY, 8th April, 1858. Her father was Orvan Kellogg Judd, and her mother was Emily Sweetland. Her first paid efforts were made at fifteen, when she wrote for "Demorest's Young America." The Buffalo "Courier" next published her poems. At eighteen she published a small volume of poems. About that time, while attending the normal school, she was injured by a fall, and she became a helpless invalid. A full account of her sickness and wonderful restoration may be found in a book which she has since published, called "The Prayer of Faith," which has had a wide circulation. Ever since her healing, in 1878, she has labored in Christian work. She has written books and many tracts and published a journal called "Triumphs of Faith." She has established a "Faith Rest," a home where sick and weary ones may stay a brief time for Christian counsel, free of charge. It is sustained by voluntary contributions in answer to prayer. Two years ago she became the wife of George Simpson Montgomery, of San Francisco, CA, and having heard, as they believe, a special call from God, joined the Salvation Army on Thanksgiving Day, 1891. Not entering as officers, they will remain in their home in Beulah, near Oakland, CA.

MOODY, Mrs. Helen Watterson, journalist, was born in Cleveland, OH. Her maiden name was Watterson. She was one of the four young women who competed with men in the University of Wooster, where she was graduated with high honors in 1883. Her newspaper work was begun as soon as she left college, in the offices of the Cleveland "Leader" and "Sun." At the end of two years she was invited to return to her alma mater as assistant professor of rhetoric and English, and she accepted the position, remaining until she was called, in 1889, to the staff of the New York "Evening Sun." From that time until she left the "Sun," on the occasion of her marriage, in 1891, her identity was merged in that of the "Woman About Town," a title created for her, under which she wrote, in a semi-editorial manner, a column every day. Her husband, Winfield S. Moody, jr., is also a journalist, and she still appears under her pen-name, "Helen Watterson."

MOODY, Mrs. Mary Blair, physician, born in Barker, Broome county, NY, 8th August, 1837. Her parents were Asa Edson Blair and Caroline Pease, well-known to readers of magazine poetry twenty-five years ago under her nom de plume "Waif Woodland." She taught in public schools, in the Five Points House of Industry in New York, founded by her uncle, and in a female seminary, at the same time prosecuting her own studies. In 1860 she married, and became the mother of seven children. Soon after her marriage she commenced a course of study in the Philadelphia Woman's Medical College, but failing health and the cares of a growing family prevented its completion. In 1876 she graduated with honors from the Buffalo Medical College and has been engaged since then in active and successful practice. She was the first woman to receive a diploma from the Buffalo college. She is a member of the National Medical Association, the American Association for the Advancement of Science, the American Microscopical Association, the

American Association for the Advancement of Women and other organizations. Her home is now in Fair Haven Heights, CT.

MOORE, Mrs. Aubertine Woodward, musical critic, translator and lecturer, born near Philadelphia, PA, 27th September, 1841. Her maiden name was Annie Aubertine Woodward. Mrs. Moore began at an early age to produce literary work, after acquiring a wide education, including a course of music under Carl Gaetner, the well-known artist and composer. She wrote under the pen-name "Auber Forestier," and her work attracted attention immediately. She contributed to the Philadelphia papers a series of letters on the resources of California. She published translations of several novels from the German, including "The Sphinx," by Robert Byr, in 1871; "Above Tempest and Tide," by Sophie Verena, in 1873, and "Struggle for Existence," by Robert Byr, in 1873. She translated Victor Cherbuliez's "Samuel Brohl and Company," which appeared as number one of Appleton's series of "Foreign Authors." Then followed in rapid succession stories, sketches, translations of poetry for music, and original songs. She became interested in the "Niebelungen Lied," and in 1877 she published "Echoes from Mist-Land," or, more fully, "The Niebelungen Lay Revealed to Lovers of Romance and Chivalry," which is a prose version of the famous poem. Hers was the first American translation of that work. That was the first American edition of the Niebelungen Lied, and the book was favorably received in the United States, in England and in Germany. In 1879 she went to Madison, WI, to extend her studies in Scandinavian literature, under the direction of Prof. R. B. Anderson, and soon brought out a translation of Kristofer Janson's "Spell-Bound Fiddler." She then assisted Prof. Anderson in the translation of Bjornson's novels, and George Brandes' "Eminent Authors," and became a pioneer in the translation of "The Norway Music Album," a valuable collection of Norwegian folk-songs, dances, national airs and recent compositions for the pianoforte and solo singing. In December, 1887, Miss Woodward became the wife of Samuel H. Moore. She has read papers before women's clubs, schools of philosophy, literary societies, editorial conventions and Unitarian conferences. She is authority on the music, history and literature of the Scandinavians, and a collection of her writings in that field would form the most valuable compendium of Scandinavian lore to be found in the English language. She has done valuable work in making Americans familiar with Norwegian literature and music in her "Evenings with the Music and Poetry of Norway," which she initiated in Concord, MA, while visiting relatives in that historic town. Reading the songs and playing the airs upon the piano, she aroused an intense interest in her auditors, and was invited to give similar "evenings" before numerous clubs and art societies, including the Woman's Club, of Boston, Sorosis, of New York, and others in the East and West. As a translator of the poetry of Norwegian, French and German writers she is unexcelled. Her translation of Göthe's "Erl King" is called by Prof. William T. Harris "by all odds the finest ever made." Her translations of some of the poems of "Carmen Sylva," the Queen of Roumania, have been widely read, and the queen sent her an autograph letter acknowledging the merit of her translations. Mrs. Moore in all her work shows the greatest thoroughness. Everything she does is well done.

MOORE, Mrs. Clara Jessup, poet, novelist and philanthropist, born in Philadelphia, PA, 16th February, 1824. Her ancestry is distinguished. Her mother's family name is found in Domesday Book, compiled in 1081. From Ernald de Moseley descended the families of Maudesley, Moseley and Mosley, in the counties of York, Lancaster and Staffordshire, in England, and the families of that name in Virginia, Massachusetts and other States in the Union. The first of her mother's family who came to America was John Mosley, who settled in Dorchester, MA, in 1630, and died in 1661. His son, John Joseph Mosley, born in Boston in 1638, married Miss Mary Newbury and settled in Westfield, MA. He was a lieutenant in King Philip's war and held a number of military and other offices. His son John and his descendants filled many offices in Westfield, serving as magistrates and army officers. Many of the prominent men in those pioneer days were among Mrs. Moore's ancestors. Her father was lineally descended from John Jessup, who settled on Long Island in 1635. Mrs. Moore's home education was carefully superintended by competent teachers, the late Mrs. Gov. Ellsworth of Kentucky, having been among them. She next went through a course of study in Westfield Academy, and completed her studies in New Haven, CT, in the school of Mrs. Merrick and her sister, Mrs. Bingham, where she studied for three years. She became the wife of Bloomfield Haines Moore, of Philadelphia, PA, on 27th October, 1842. The marriage occurred in the old country home of her father, in a glen of the Hampshire hills, bordering on Berkshire, in western Massachusetts. Up to the time of her marriage Mrs. Moore had displayed but little talent for or tendency toward literary work. After her marriage she took up her pen as a means of filling her leisure hours, and her immediate success made her home in Philadelphia the resort of literary people, among whom were some of the most gifted authors of the day. In 1855 she was widely known as a writer of both prose and poetry, and her name was included in Hart's "Female Prose Writers of America," published in that year. One of Mrs. Moore's early stories, "The Estranged Hearts," received the first prize out of four-hundred stories offered. George H. Boker and Dr. Reynell Coates were on the committee. Several novelettes, "The Adopted," "Compensation," "The Fulfilled Prophecy," "Emma Dudley's Secret" and "Renunciation," next bore off prizes from numerous competitors. Those were followed by an anonymous romance called "The Hasty Marriage." One of Mrs. Moore's stories was published in London with much success, and was copied here as an English production. The London "Daily News," under the heading "Who Reads an American Book?" wrote of the "ingenious heart picturings of Clara Moreton." Up to that time Mrs. Moore had shielded herself from publicity under that pen-name. Her next story, "The Houses of Huntley and Raymond," was published without any name, as was "Mabel's Mission," her last story before the breaking out of the Civil War, which took her from her literary pursuits, giving her other work to do as corresponding secretary of the Woman's Pennsylvania Branch of the United States Sanitary Commission. Mrs. Moore, who was nominated by Dr. Bellows, of New York, as president, declined the nomination, naming Mrs. Grier, who was elected, and whose rare executive ability, as shown in the fulfillment of the duties devolving upon her while holding that office, did credit to Mrs. Moore's discernment of Mrs. Grier's capacities. Mrs. Moore projected and aided in founding the Union Temporary Home for Children in Philadelphia, and she aided potently in establishing the women's branch of the Sanitary Commission. She also created and organized the Special Relief Committee which took such an active part in the hospital work during the Civil War, knowing no difference between the soldiers of the North and the soldiers of the South in its objects of aid, laying aside all feeling of sectional animosity and administering, with the hands of christian charity, alike to the suffering wearers of "the blue and the gray." In the organization of the committees of women for the great Sanitary Commission Fair, by which over one-million dollars was realized in Philadelphia, the entire responsibility devolved upon Mrs. George Putt and herself. Mrs. Moore resumed the companionship of her pen after the war. She has always given the proceeds of her books to works of charity. When her pen-name was no longer a shield to her, she published without any signature until her anonymous paper on "Reasonable and Unreasonable Points of Etiquette," which title was changed by the editor to "Unsettled Points of Etiquette," published in "Lippincott's Magazine," in March, 1873, drew down upon her a storm of personal abuse, such as would not have been poured out, had her name accompanied the essay. Mrs. Moore, who holds the same ideas as Herbert Spencer concerning a life regulated by spendthrifts and idlers, dandies and silly women, did not submit to being held up as a "leader of fashion," but, overcoming her sensitiveness and rising out of it into the independence that was natural to her, and which had been held in check by her shrinking from publicity, she now boldly entered the ranks of authors and gave to the public two volumes under her own name. In 1873 she published a revised edition of the "Young Lady's Friend," continuing her work in behalf of the young. In 1875 she collected in one volume some of her verses with the title "Miscellaneous Poems, Stories for Children, The Warden's Tale and Three Eras in a Life." Those poems met no adverse criticism. In 1876 she published her romance, "On Dangerous Ground," which has reached a seventh edition, and has been translated into the Swedish and French languages. It is eminently a book for women. Mrs. Moore also wrote "Master Jacky's Holidays," which went through over twenty editions, and "Frank and Fanny," another book for children. Her many charitable works are known the country over, but it is not generally known that she is bound by a promise never to give when asked. Often her life is burdened by requests to give, which are useless. She has spent much time abroad, and her house in London, England, was a resort for literary and scientific men. Interested in all things scientific, Mrs. Moore has been a supporter of Keely, the inventor, and her support has been of the substantial kind, enabling- him to pursue his investigations of the force which he liberated by dissociating the supposed simple elements of water. She has been a widow since 1878. She maintains her interest in everything that pertains to the elevation of men and women. Her latest literary work is "Social Ethics and Society Dutie', University Education for Women" (Boston, 1892).

MOORE, Miss Henrietta G., Universalist minister and temperance worker, was born in Newark, OH. Her ancestry is mixed English, Irish and Scotch, and she inherits the best qualities of each of the mingled strains. Many of her ancestors were prominent persons in the three kingdoms. Reginald Moore, a nephew of Queen Elizabeth, was Secretary of State and Lord Chief Justice of England under her, and was by King James raised to the peerage and created Earl of Drogheda. His brother came to the colony of New York under a large land grant from Charles II, and, marrying the sister of Governor Nichols, established the family in America. Dr. Moore, first bishop of the Protestant Episcopal Church, Dr. Moore, president of the Columbia Theological Seminary, and President Moore, of Columbia College, are of the immediate descendants. Her mother's family was of the Murrays and the house of McCarter, of Scotland. Upon both sides were furnished revolutionar patriots, and all were conspicuous pioneer Baptists. Henrietta was a delicate child, but the outdoor life she led after her parents removed to Morrow, OH, on the Miami river, gave her strength and health. She was educated in both public and private schools, and when she was fifteen years old she began to teach school, family troubles in financial ways

making self-support a necessity. She was a successful teacher. She early became interested in the temperance crusade movement. Her vigorous work in the crusade brought her at once to the front. She enforced the gospel plea in the work, but she stood also for the enforcement of the existing law, which was practically prohibitory. She aroused the enmity of those devoted to the liquor interest, and circumstances rendered it expedient that she should prosecute a leading and influential man for libelous charges in reference to the work. She was ably defended through a wearisome and long-drawn trial by leading lawyers, who, however, had no sympathy with any temperance move, but, with all the odds heavily against her, she triumphantly won her case. That experience proved a wonderful educator, bringing her by rapid steps to ground gained much more slowly by her coadjutors. She learned that law alone was powerless, that behind it must be an enforcing power, and thus she was a pioneer in recognition of and cooperation with the party pledged to the destruction of the liquor traffic. While still engaged in teaching, Miss Moore was made corresponding secretary of the Ohio Woman's Christian Temperance Union, and soon her services as national organizer were called for, and she gave up school work. She was one of the first women to brave the difficulties of travel in the Territories, enduring long and wearisome journeys on railroad lines, and going the second time beyond the Sierras. She has labored in every State and Territory with one exception. Her home is in Springfield, OH, and her mother is with her there. She was in youth trained under Presbyterian influences, but her faith is with the Universalist Church, in which she has held a minister's license for some years. On 4th June, 1891, she was regularly ordained to the ministry in that church, in the Ohio Universalist Convention in Columbus. She is still laboring earnestly in the ranks of the Woman's Christian Temperance Union.

MOORE, Mrs. Marguerite, orator and patriot, born in Waterford, Ireland, 7th July, 1849. She is an American by adoption and Irish by descent, birth and education. In 1881 she sprang into a foremost place in the politics of her native land. Parnell and the rest of the national and local leaders were in prison, and the existence of the great organization they had built up was imperiled. The sister of Charles Stewart Parnell called the women of Ireland to help in the struggle. Mrs. Moore's patriotism, sympathy for the suffering and eloquence made of her an invaluable auxiliary. She threw herself into the struggle, which had for its aim the fixing of the Irish tenant farmer in his holding and the succoring of the tenants already evicted. She traveled through Ireland, teaching the doctrine of the Land League and bringing help to the victims of landlord tyranny. In all the large cities of England and Scotland she addressed crowded meetings. After twelve months of hard toil she was arrested and sentenced to six months' imprisonment in Tullamore jail, Kings county, Ireland. In the summer of 1882, when Mr. Parnell and his followers were released from prison, the women returned into their hands the trust they had so faithfully guarded. Two years afterward Mrs. Moore, accompanied by her family of four girls and two boys, came to the United States. Here she has gained a reputation as a speaker on social matters, woman suffrage, labor question and land reform. Any good cause finds in her an able platform advocate. Her pen is ready in defense of the oppressed. She takes deep interest in American politics, as a believer in the single-tax doctrines. She took a prominent part in the New York election campaigns of 1886–87, addressing two or three meetings each evening. She is a vice-president of the Universal Peace Union, a member of the New York Woman's Press Club, treasurer and secretary of the Parnell Branch of the Irish National League, and prominent in the literary society of New York City.

MOORE, Miss Sarah Wool, artist, born in Plattsburg, NY, 3rd May, 1846. She was graduated from the Packer Collegiate Institute in 1865, after which she spent some years in teaching. From 1875 to 1884 she traveled in Europe, and for five years she was engaged in the special study of painting under Prof. Eisenmenger, director of the academy of fine arts, Vienna. Returning to the United States in 1884, she was placed in charge of the art department of the State University in Lincoln, NE, and was appointed lecturer on the history of art and teacher of drawing and painting, a position she held with credit and honor until June, 1892, when she resigned to enjoy a period of rest and special study. Her art talks are not only interesting in the historical sense, but in stimulating a perception of the beautiful. Much of the quickening and development of artistic taste and expression in Nebraska is due to her efforts. She is a woman of quiet presence, modest and sensitive.

MOORE, Mrs. Susanne Vandegrift, editor and publisher, born in Bucks county, PA, 15th May, 1848. She was educated in a female seminary in Philadelphia, PA. She taught for several years after graduation in private and public schools. In 1877 she was married, and with her husband moved to St. Louis, MO, where she has since resided. She became a regular contributor to the St. Louis "Spectator," and contributed to the woman's department of the New York "World." Thrown upon her own resources, she began in 1889 the publication of an illustrated weekly journal, "St. Louis Life," of which she is editor and owner. The venture has been successful, and she now has a comfortable income from it. Her work is of a character that attracts and holds readers, and her sprightly journal is a fixture in St. Louis. She has found a way to demonstrate the capacity of woman to cultivate one of the arduous fields of labor, generally supposed to demand the services of men only.

MOOTS, Mrs. Cornelia Moore Chilison, temperance evangelist, born in Flushing, MI, 14th October, 1843. Mrs. Moots' parents were of New England lineage. Her father, Calvin C. C. Chillson, was a temperance advocate and was said to be a descendant of the Whites, who came over in the Mayflower. Her mother was a typical Green Mountain girl, a granddaughter of James Wilcox, a minute man of the Revolution, and the second man to enter Fort Ticonderoga at the time of its capture by Ethan Allen. Mrs. Moots' parents moved to Michigan in 1836. Abigail Chillson, the grandmother, then a widow, went with them. The new settlements were without preachers, and her grandmother Chillson, an ardent Methodist, often supplied the itinerary by preaching in the log school-houses and cabins of the early pioneers. Mrs. Moots' father was a stanch anti-slavery man, a member of the underground railroad, and the Chillson home was often the refuge of the slave seeking liberty across the line. He died 3rd May, 1864. Her mother is still living and has more than a local reputation for deeds of charity and her care of homeless children. Self-reliant, persevering, fond of books and of a highly religious temperament, those prominent characteristics in early life forecast something of Miss Chillson's future. She began to teach school at the age of fifteen and continued in that employment until she entered Albion College, in the fall of 1865. Her college career was cut short in the junior exhibition of her class, in the close of the winter term of 1869. She thought the president of the college overstepped his jurisdiction in criticising and dictating the style of dress she was to wear on that occasion. She left her seat on the platform, and, accompanied by one of the professors, left the hall, never to return as a student, although later, in 1882, the college awarded her a full diploma with the degree of A.B. She returned home and was immediately employed as a teacher in the Bay City high school, where she remained until she became the wife of William Moots, a merchant of West Bay City, MI, in 1870. Household cares and the education of her little daughter, with occasional demands upon her to fill vacant pulpits, by the clergy of her own and other denominations, absorbed her time, until the death of Mr. Moots in 1880. As a Bible student she had always desired to visit historic lands, and that desire was granted in 1881. A trip through the principal countries of the continent was followed by a tour through the Holy Land and Egypt. The entire journey through Palestine was made on horseback. Always active in church, a new field opened to her as a temperance worker, and she turned her forces into the broad channel of temperance reform. She is now serving her third term as State evangelist in the Woman's Christian Temperance Union. She is radical in her views on temperance, admission of women to the Methodist Episcopal General Conference and equal suffrage, and believes in the same standard of morals for men and women. Before an audience she is an easy speaker, and is both persuasive and argumentative.

MORELAND, Miss Mary L., Congregational minister, born in Westfield, MA, 23rd December, 1859. On her father's side she is of Scotch ancestry, and on the maternal side she is of good lineage. She commenced her school-days at the age of six years. The family removed to New Ipswich, NH, where they lived six years. While there, at the age of fourteen, she entered Appleton Academy. She was graduated with the high record of scholarship. She was converted at the age of fourteen and joined the Baptist Church. Soon after her graduation the family removed to Fitchburg, MA. There she became a member of the First Baptist Church. About that time she began her temperance work. She was among the first of Massachusetts young women to take the white ribbon in the Woman's Christian Temperance Union, and, although a girl of sixteen she was upon the platform a successful lecturer. After her graduation in Appleton Academy she taught school several terms. Soon after she went to Fitchburg, Dr. Vincent went with his Chautauqua Assembly to Lake View, Framingham, MA. She attended the assembly for six consecutive years and laid foundation for the study of the Word, to which she added the normal courses in the Bible and also took the four years in the Chautauqua Literary and Scientific Circle, class of 1884. While in the assembly she collected the materials for her books, "Which, Right or Wrong?" (Boston), and "The School on the Hill." During the four years in which she was taking the Chautauqua course, editing the above books and contributing many short articles to different papers, she was constantly invited to address public meetings. She studied theology two winters in the home of Rev. Mr. Chick. In 1882 she had occupied the pulpit a number of times, but had not then thought that she was called to ministerial work. In the fall of 1885 she went to Illinois on a visit to her sister, intending to labor in the West in the cause of temperance. She became interested in revival work, in which she has been eminently successful. Her first revival was through a meeting held in the interest of the Woman's Christian Temperance Union. The most remarkable of those revivals was that which occurred in February and March, 1889, in Sharon and Spring Hill. There were more than one-hundred conversions and a church was organized. Her first call to settle as pastor was in the summer of 1888, in the Keithburg circuit, Illinois conference, by Elder Smith, of the United Brethren Church. She declined to accept the invitation. At that time Rev. E. M. Baxter, of the Dixon district, urged her to preach the gospel, and Rev. Louis Curtis, elder of that district, requested her to spend the time which she could spare from revival work in Eldena, Lee county. She began her labors, and they gave her a unanimous call, but, being a Methodist Church, according to the discipline, she could only be a stated supply. A few months later she received an invitation to supply the pulpit of the First Congregational Church of Wyanet, IL. The church prospered, and the people desired that Miss Moreland should be ordained and installed as their pastor. After much persuasion and deliberation she consented. A council of six ministers and the same number of delegates from the adjacent churches convened in Wyanet, 19th July, 1889. It was one of few instances in which a woman has been called to the ministry in the Congregational Church in this country. After a rigid examination the council retired and voted unanimously to proceed to the ordination. She is now a successful preacher.

MORGAN, Miss Anne Eugenia Felicia, professor of philosophy, born in Oberlin, OH, 3rd October, 1845. Her father, Rev. John Morgan, D.D., was one of the earliest professors in Oberlin College. Called to the chair of New Testament literature and exegesis upon the opening of the theological seminary, in 1835, he retained his official connection with the college during forty-five years, and was always one of the leading spirits in the institution. Miss Morgan's mother was of a New Haven family, named Leonard. The daughter treasures a ticket admitting Miss Elizabeth Mary Leonard to Prof. Silliman's lectures in chemistry in Yale College. The Leonard family removed to Oberlin in 1837. There Miss Leonard entered upon the college course, but in her sophomore year she became the wife of Prof. John Morgan. Had she completed the academic course, she would have been the first woman in this country to

receive the bachelor's degree. Miss Anne Eugenia Morgan was graduated from Oberlin in 1866. Throughout her collegiate course she was distinguished for brilliant scholarship, notably in the classics. The appointment to write the Greek oration was assigned to her as an honor in her junior year. Her humorous imagination declared that distinction of being the earliest woman to receive that college honor to be chiefly due to her mother, since her mother's wisdom in preferring the highest home achievements before the distinction of being the first woman in the bachelor's degree had prepared her daughter in time to strive for classical scholarship in that historic epoch. Inheriting from her father a mind essentially philosophical, she was always in close sympathy with his thinking and, after graduation, pursued theological studies in his classes. She received the degree of M.A. from Oberlin in 1869. Later on she was for three years in New York and Newark, NJ, conducting classes in philosophy and literature and devoting considerable attention to music, studying harmony with her brother, the distinguished musician, John Paul Morgan, at that time director of the music in Trinity Church, NY. In those years there came to her mind many revelations of the philosophy to be discovered through embodiments of human thought and life in literature and music. Her vivid interest in the philosophical aspects of language and art led her to pursue studies in Europe for fifteen months before she returned, in 1875, to teach Greek and Latin in Oberlin. In 1877 she accepted an appointment to teach in the classical department in Vassar College. That work was undertaken in her characteristically philosophical way, always seeking explanations beyond the forms of language in the laws of the mind-effort that formed them. In 1878 she was appointed to the professorship of philosophy in Wellesley College, and that appointment she retains at the present time. A philosopher of rare ability, uniting a poet's insight with keen logic, Prof. Morgan is developing a system of thought of marked originality and power. As an instructor, she leads students to do their own thinking, aiming rather to teach philosophizing than to impose upon her classes any dogma of human opinion. The influence of her personality is an inestimable power for good. Herself a splendid example of symmetrical christian character, she offers to all who come in contact with her a strong fellowship toward high ideals and earnestness of life. She possesses charming social qualities, drawing about her a large circle of listeners to conversations which are full of thought and sympathy, and in occasional public addresses manifesting her vivid interest in the great social movements. In 1887 Prof. Morgan published a small volume entitled "Scripture Studies in the Origin and Destiny of Man," consisting of scripture selections systematically presented in the lines of interpretation in which she has conthcted successive Bible classes. Her little book entitled "The White Lady" is a study of the ideal conception of human conduct in great records of thought. The book is a presentation of lecture outlines and of notes on the philosophical interpretation of literature.

MORGAN, Miss Maria, widely known as "Middy Morgan," journalist and authority on horses and cattle, born in Cork, Ireland, 22nd November, 1828, and died in Jersey City, NJ, 1st June, 1892. She was a daughter of Anthony Morgan, a landed proprietor, and one of a large family of children. She received a thorough education and became an expert horsewoman. Her father died in 1865, the oldest son succeeded to the estate, and the other children were left dependent. Maria and a younger sister went to Rome, Italy. There Maria went to the court of Victor Emanuel, king of Italy, by whom she was engaged to select the horses for his Horse Guards and have entire supervision of his stables. That place she filled with credit and to the complete satisfaction of the king. After five years spent in the service of the king she decided to come to the United States. On parting from the king of Italy, he gave her his ring from his finger, a pin from his bosom and a handsome watch of great value. The watch was heavily set with jewels, and the case bore his initials set with diamonds. When she came to America, she bore letters of introduction to Horace Greeley, James Gordon Bennett and Henry J. Raymond. For the "Tribune," the "Herald" and the "Times" she wrote more or less, and recently she did the live-stock reporting for the "Times," the "Herald," the "Turf, Field and Farm" and the "Live-Stock Reporter." In addition she wrote the pedigrees and the racing articles for the "American Agriculturist." Weekly letters were also sent to Chicago and Albany papers. Miss Morgan was six feet two inches tall. She wore

heavy, high-laced walking boots, and a clinging woolen skirt. Her hat was always plain and conspicuous for its oddity. All her clothes were bought in Europe. She walked with a limp, for a horse once crushed one of her feet by stepping on it. She was proud and self-contained and never made an effort to gain new friends, but a friend once acquired she never lost. She frequently attended the races and bet moderately at times, as her judgment of horses was exceptionally good. The "copy" which she wrote was difficult to read, and special compositors on the "Times" set it. She lived in Robinvale, NJ, and took care of the Pennsylvania Railroad station in that place, for which she received house rent and free transportation. In her absence she employed a woman to sell tickets for her. In the last eighteen years of her life she made three trips to Europe, but never visited her family near Cork. Her first trip was made on a cattle-boat, and after her return she wrote a series of articles on the treatment of cattle on ocean steamers, which resulted in kinder treatment for the cattle. When Victor Emanuel died, she had a mourning chain made for his watch and wore the watch and ring for one year, taking them from the safe deposit company, where she always kept them. Soon after coming to America she adopted a German boy, but he displeased her by his marriage, and she never recognized him again. She made the acquaintance of William H. Vanderbilt, by whose advice she made several fortunate investments in New York Central Railroad stock. Other investments equally fortunate increased her savings to fully $100,000. She intended to retire when she was sixty-five years old, and a house which she had been building for ten years on Staten Island was nearly completed. The cost was over $20,000. It is entirely fire-proof, three stories high, and has one room on each floor. The floor is tiled and the wainscoting is of California redwood; the second story is finished in inlaid wood brought from different parts of the world; the third floor is finished in ash. The dining-room is finished in inlaid shells. Her sister Jane did most of the decorating. A chimney and fireplace are situated in the center of the house, the chimney running through each floor.

MORGAN, Miss Maud, harpist, born in New York, NY, 22nd November, 1864. She is a daughter of the famous organist, George Washbourne Morgan, who was born 9th April, 1822, in

Gloucester, England, and settled in New York City in 1853. Maud received a liberal education, with particular care to develop her musical gifts, which were early displayed. She took a long and thorough musical course with her father, and afterward studied the harp with Alfred Toulmin. She made her début as a harpist in 1875, in a concert with Ole Bull. She played in concerts with her father, and has made tours of the United States with prominent musical organizations. She is ranked among the most famous harpists of the century.

MORRIS, Miss Clara, actor, born in Cleveland, OH, 17th March, 1850. Her mother was a native of Ohio, and her father was born in Canada. He died while Clara was an infant. The mother broke down under the effort to sustain her family, and Clara went to live with strangers, earning her living by caring for younger children. She was engaged by Mr. Ellsler, the theatrical manager, to do miscellaneous child work about his theater. She was then only eleven years old. In the theater she attracted attention by her intensity in every part which fell to her, and she gradually worked her way well up toward the rank of leading lady. In the winter of 1868–69 she went to Cincinnati, OH, where she played a successful season, and at its close went to New York City, where many brilliant and popular women were holding the leading places. She accepted an offer of forty dollars a week from Augustin Daly. She made her début as Anne Sylvester in "Man and Wife," as the result of an accident to Agnes Ethel, whose place she took at a notice of only a few hours. She was suffering with the malady that has made her life a continued agony, but she committed the part, appeared, and won one of the most notable triumphs of the American stage. She lived down the critics, who acknowledged her power and criticised her crudeness, and one emotional rôle after another was added to her list. The public thronged the houses wherever she played. She appeared as Jezebel, Fanny, Cora, Alixe,

Camille, Miss Multon, Mercy Merrick, Marguerite Gauthier, Denise, Renée and many other of the most exacting emotional characters, and in each and all she is finished, powerful, impassioned and perfect. Her own sufferings from her incurable spinal malady are thought to intensify her emotional powers. Her power over her audiences is something almost incredible, and specialists have even gone so far as to assert that she studied her maniac rôle, Cora, in the wards of an insane asylum. She retains her maiden name, Miss Clara Morris, although she became the wife, in 1874, of Frederick C. Harriott, of New York City. Despite her invalidism she is a woman of genial temper. She has amassed a fortune and owns a beautiful country home, "The Pines," in Riverdale, on the Hudson. She has traveled in Europe, and during a tour of Great Britain she published a description of her journey in the New York "Graphic." Her literary style is crisp, clear and telling. During the past few years she has limited her presentations to "Camille," "Miss Multon," "The New Magdalen," "Article 47" and "Renée." In person she is a delicate woman, fair-haired, white-skinned, strong-featured, with gray eyes of remarkable powers of expression. She has always been a devoted daughter to her invalid mother.

MORRIS, Miss Ellen Douglas, temperance worker, born in Petersburg, IL, 9th March, 1846. Her father was a Kentuckian, a descendant of the Virginia families, Deakins and Morris. Her mother was of German descent from Wagoner and Wurtzbaugh. Mr. Morris was an intimate personal friend of Abraham Lincoln. He received an offer of a position under the great martyr's administration, but declined. He early espoused the cause of the oppressed and was always interested in public welfare. Miss Morris was educated in a seminary for girls under direction of the Presbyterian Church of Petersburg. She afterward attended the public schools and was finally graduated from Rockford Seminary, IL. From 1872 to 1885 she taught in the public schools of Illinois and Missouri, but left the school-room for work in the wider educational field of the Woman's Christian Temperance Union. In Savannah, MO, where she attended the fourth district convention of the Woman's Christian Temperance Union, the local union was dying because it had no leader. She had attended that convention to look on. Reared according to the straightest sect of the Presbyterians, she never dreamed of opening her mouth in the church. The State president believed she saw a latent power and reserve force in the quiet looker-on, and said to the local union, "Make that woman your president." After great entreaty on their part, and great quaking on hers, that was done. The next year saw her president of the district, which she quickly made the banner district of the State. When a State secretary was needed, Miss Morris was almost unanimously chosen and installed at headquarters. Her success in every position she held may be attributed to the careful attention she gives to details and the exact faithfulness of her service. She makes her home in Kansas City, MO.

MORRIS, Mrs. Esther, justice, born in Spencer, Wyoming county, NY, in 1813. She comes of a long line of English ancestry. Her early years were spent amid the struggles of pioneer life following the Revolution. Daniel McQuigg, her grandfather, fought on the side of the American colonies and afterward served as a captain under General Sullivan in the expedition that drove the Indians out of western New York. Under his commission her father was entitled to a farm, which he located near Owego, NY, and was one of the first twelve settlers of Tioga county. Esther's efforts to better the condition of women arose from no sudden conversion. Left an orphan at eleven years of age, she was early thrown upon her own resources. For a number of years she carried on successfully a millinery business in Owego. Before her marriage, at the age of twenty-eight, she had acquired a competence. She became the wife of Artemus Slack, a civil engineer by profession, and at that time engaged in the construction of the Erie Railroad. He died several years thereafter, leaving his wife a large tract of land in Illinois, where he had been engaged as a chief engineer in building the Illinois Central Railroad. With an infant in her arms, she removed to the West. During the settlement of that estate she fully realized the injustice of the property laws in their relation to women. In the long conflict with slavery she was an early and earnest worker. In 1845 she

became the wife of John Morris, a merchant of Peru, IL, and for more than twenty years resided in that place, rearing her family and being an earnest helper in the church, schools and other good works. In 1869 she joined her husband and three sons in South Pass, WY, and there she administered justice in a little court that became famous throughout the world. During her term of office, which covered a period of one year, Judge Morris tried about fifty cases, and no decision of hers was ever reversed by a higher court on appeal. She became a widow in 1876, since which time she has resided in Wyoming, where her three sons are prominently identified with the growth and progress of the new State. She is justly regarded as the mother of woman suffrage in Wyoming, having inaugurated the movement there. She was the first woman who ever administered the office of justice of the peace. It has been sometimes said that the law giving equal rights to women in Wyoming was passed as a joke and as a means of advertising the new Territory of Wyoming, but Colonel Bright, who is now a resident of Washington, asserts that it was no joking matter with him, that he favored it because he believed it was right. The condition of Wyoming at that time is of interest. With an area greater than all of the New England States combined, Wyoming, in 1869, had a population of less than ten-thousand, mostly scattered in small frontier villages along the line of the newly-constructed Union Pacific Railroad. The northern portion of the Territory was given over to roving tribes of wild Indians, with here and there a few mining camps held by adventurous gold-seekers. Several hundreds of those miners had penetrated into the country known as the Sweetwater mines, the chief town of which was South Pass City, and contained about two-thousand people. There Governor Campbell commissioned Mrs. Morris to hold the office of justice of the peace.

MORSE, Miss Alice Cordelia, artist, born in Hammondsville, Jefferson county, OH, 1st June, 1862. She removed with her parents to Brooklyn, NY, two years later, where she has since resided. She traces her origin back on her father's side to the time of Edward III, of England. She is descended from Samuel Morse, one of seven brothers who came to America between 1635 and

1644, and settled in Dedham, MA. Her ancestors on her mother's side, Perkins by name, were among the early settlers of Connecticut. Seven of her great-grandfather's brothers lost their lives in the assault on Fort Griswold by Benedict Arnold. Her great-grandfather, Caleb Perkins, afterward removed to Susquehanna county, PA, which was then a wilderness. Being a sturdy, fearless child, of great perseverance and determination, she was sent to school at the age of five years. After a common-school education she took her first lesson in drawing in an evening class started by the Christian Endeavor Society of Dr. Eggleston's Church. Her drawing at that time has been described by a friend as conspicuously bad. Evidently no flash of inspiration revealed her genius in her first attempt to immortalize a model. That little class of crude young people builded better than it knew, for a number of its members are to-day doing creditable work among the competitors in New York art circles. Miss Morse submitted a drawing from that class to the Woman's Art School, Cooper Union, and was admitted to a four years' course, which she completed. Entering the studio of John LaFarge, the foremost artist of stained-glass designing in this country, she studied and painted, with great assiduity under his supervision. Later, she sent a study of a head, painted on glass, to Louis C. Tiffany & Company, and went into the Tiffany studio to paint glass and study designing, and accomplished much in the time devoted to her work there. Having been the successful contestant in several designs for book covers, and the awakened aesthetic sense of the public requiring beauty, taste and some fitness to the subject in the covering of a book, she then decided to take up that field of designing. She made many covers of holiday editions and fine books for the Harper, Scribner, Putnam, Cassell, Dodd, Mead & Company and other publishing firms. That, with glass designing, a window in the Beecher Memorial Church of Brooklyn testifying to her skill, has made her name familiar to the designing fraternity, and the annual exhibits of her work in the New York Architectural League have called forth high praise from the press. She won the silver medal in the life class in Cooper Institute in 1891, and is now studying with a view to combine illustration with designing. She is a very clear, original thinker, with an earnestness relieved by a piquant sense of humor, a fine critical estimate of literary style and a directness of purpose and energy which promise well for her future career.

MORSE, Mrs. Rebecca A., club leader, born on Manhattan Island, NY, on the Gen. Rutgers estate, in 1821. She is a descendant of the well-known Holland-Dutch family, the Bogerts, one of the pioneer families of New York. She received the educational training usual among the substantial families of those days. She became the wife of Prof. M. Morse in 1853. She was known as a correspondent in New York City for newspapers and magazines in 1846. Her work consisted of notes on society, descriptions of costumes, art notes, art gossip from studios, and similar features of metropolitan life. She wrote under the pen-names "Ruth Moza," "R. A. Kidder" or the initials "R. A. K." In youth she imbibed the principles of the anti-slavery agitators, and she was always the fearless advocate of the colored people. In the home of her sister, Mrs. M. E. Winchester, which was headquarters then for woman suffragists, Mrs. Morse met Elizabeth Cady Stanton, Susan B. Anthony and other leaders. During twenty-five years she has spent her summers in Nantucket, where she has a home. She was one of the earliest members of Sorosis, and was vice-president for several terms. She has filled other offices in that society. She was one of the originators of the Woman's Congress, and has always been an earnest worker for the advancement of women. She founded the Sorosis of Nantucket. Her residence is in New York City.

MORTIMER, Miss Mary, educator, born in Trowbridge, Wiltshire, England, 2nd December, 1816, and died in Milwaukee, WI, 14th July, 1877. Her parents came to the United States when she was five years old. When she was twelve, her father and mother died within a single week. Her education was received in the Geneva, NY, Seminary, where she completed her course of study in 1839. She then taught for several years in Geneva

Seminary, in Brockport Collegiate Institute, and in Le Roy Seminary, now known as Ingham University. In 1848 she went to the new State of Wisconsin on a visit, and in 1849 she taught a private school in Ottawa, IL. Miss Catherine Beecher, then on an educational tour in the West, became acquainted with her very remarkable power as a teacher, met her in Ottawa, laid great educational plans before her, and persuaded her to take up work as a helper in the carrying out of those plans. She began the work in 1850, in Milwaukee, WI, in a school which Miss Beecher had adopted and adapted to her plans, afterward named Milwaukee College. Remarkable success was attained by the faculty of that school, among whom Miss Mortimer was foremost. She spent four-and-a-half years, from 1859 to 1863, in the Baraboo Seminary, Wisconsin, there graduating three classes from a course identical with that of Milwaukee College, and, after a time spent in Boston, MA, returned to Milwaukee College, in 1866, where she was principal until her resignation, in 1874. In 1871 she traveled extensively in Europe. Her home, "Willow Glen," in the suburbs of Milwaukee, was in her later years an ideal retreat. She gave courses of lectures on art and history to classes of women in Milwaukee and Baraboo, WI, in Elmira, NY, Auburndale, MA, and St. Louis, MO. She was instrumental in founding an industrial school for girls in Milwaukee, and she was a leading spirit in originating the Woman's Club of Milwaukee. Her chief monument is Milwaukee College, to which she devoted the prime of her life. The Mary Mortimer Library in Milwaukee College and her Memoir by Mrs. M. B. Norton are among the tributes of pupils to the life and character of that remarkable woman.

MORTON, Mrs. Anna Livingston Street, wife of ex-Vice-President Levi P. Morton, born in Poughkeepsie, NY, 18th May, 1846. Her father was a lawyer, William I. Street, a brother of the poet, Alfred B. Street. Her mother was Miss Susan Kearney, a cousin of General Phil Kearney. Miss Street was a pupil in Madame Richards' select school in New York City. She became the wife of Hon. Levi P. Morton, in New York City, in 1873. She is a most happy wife and the mother of five daughters, Edith, Lina, Helen, Alice and Mary, all accomplished young women. In person Mrs. Morton is one of the most attractive women that has ever graced society in Washington. She is domestic in her tastes and takes deep interest in the education of her daughters. She is fond of reading and is a highly cultivated French scholar. Observation and travel have refined her taste in both art and literature. While Mr. Morton was the vice-president they made Washington their home, and the residence on Scott Circle dispensed a cordial hospitality during the social season. The house was perfect in all its appointments and was always thronged with visitors on reception days. Mrs. Morton's taste in dress is very simple as to style and cut, but rich and in harmony throughout. Of vice-presidents Mr. Morton was the first to become a householder in Washington since Mr. Colfax's regime. During those winters, regularly, one of the finest receptions was given by them, to meet the President and Mrs. Harrison, besides many other receptions and dinners, which included as guests the notable officials and distinguished citizens of the nation's capital. Mrs. Morton has enjoyed unusual advantages socially all her married life, and has spent much time abroad. The American colony in Paris were proud of her refined manners and the elegant hospitality of the American legation when Mr. Morton was minister plenipotentiary to France. In the rooms of the Washington home there were many works of art and choice souvenirs. One of these is a life-size portrait of Mrs. Morton, in a crimson dress, by Bonnat. With honors, happy home life and promising children, Mrs. Morton is to be called one of the happiest of women, and she looks it. Her greeting to even the humblest of strangers crossing her threshold is always as gracious as to the most elegant of her visitors, and therein lies the secret of her popularity, her kindness of heart and gentleness of manner to all.

MORTON, Miss Eliza Happy, author and educator, born in Westbrook, ME, 15th July, 1852. She is the only daughter of William and Hannah Eliza Morton. Her parents were teachers in their earlier years, and she inherited a taste in that direction. She was educated in

Westbrook Seminary and began to teach at the age of sixteen. While teaching, she was impressed with the fact that many of the old methods of instruction were not productive of the best results, and she began at once to write articles for educational journals, advocating reforms, at the same time putting into practice the principles she advanced and securing remarkable results in her work. Her first article for the press was a prose sketch entitled "The Study of Geography." She taught in various parts of her own State. In 1879 she was called to the entire charge of geographical science in Battle Creek College, MI. The idea of preparing a series of geographies gradually assumed shape in her mind, while her name was constantly appearing in print in publications east and west. In 1880 she published a volume of verse entitled "Still Waters" (Portland, ME), which was well received. Many of her best poetical productions have been written since that date. As a writer of hymns noted for their religious fervor she is well known. They have been set to music by some of the best composers, and the evangelist, D. L. Moody, has used many of them in his revival work with telling effect. Among those published in sheet form, the most popular are "The Songs My Mother Sang" and "In the Cleft of the Rock." After three years of earnest work in Battle Creek College Miss Morton withdrew and began to gather material for her geographies. Hundreds of books were examined, leading schools were visited and prominent educators in America and Europe were interviewed as to the best methods of teaching the science. In 1888 her "Elementary Geography" was completed. It was published in Philadelphia as "Potters' New Elementary Geography, by Eliza H. Morton." It had a wide sale, and an immediate call was made for an advanced book, which was written under the pressure of poor health, but with the most painstaking care and research. The higher book was also successful. As a practical educational reformer Miss Morton has won public esteem. Her home is in North Deering, ME. She now has several important literary works under way.

MORTON, Miss Martha, author and playwright, born in New York, NY, in 1865. Her parents are English, and in 1875 she was taken to their native town in England, where she lived and studied for several years in an artistic atmosphere. Her early studies included a thorough course in English literature, and she became a profound student of dramatic form and style in composition. Her studies of the English classics were earnest and wide, and her own literary tastes and ambitions soon began to take form. Returning to New York City, she made her first effort in dramatic composition, a fine dramatization of George Eliot's "Daniel Deronda." Her effort was encouraged by the late John Gilbert. She then devoted herself to study and composition for several years. One of her plays was put upon the boards by Clara Morris, and it still holds a place in the repertory of that great actor. In 1881, when the subject of high-pressure living was occupying public attention, she wrote her now famous play, "The Merchant." She presented the manuscript to a number of New York managers, who read it and returned it to her labeled "unavailable." Discouraged by repeated rejections, she put away the manuscript, and only when her family suggested to her that she compete for a prize offered by the New York "World" for the best play sent within a given time, did she draw it forth from her desk. Carrying the manuscript downtown one day, she absent-mindedly left it on the counter of a shop, walked off and forgot the entire incident, until reminded of the approaching competition. The manuscript was recovered after much difficulty, won the first prize, and, after production in a matinee performance, was again threatened with oblivion. By accident the play was finally purchased, but another delay of twelve months occurred before it earned real success. Miss Morton is a profound student, is ardently ambitious, works for pure love of the profession, and is keenly critical of her own work. She composes very slowly and her fastidious taste involves an immense amount of labor. She is writing new dramas to place on the boards and has work laid out for several years to come. She is the author of "Geoffrey Middleton, Gentleman," an American play that has run successfully in New York City and other towns. Among her patrons is William H. Crane, the comedian. She has set up a high standard in her work and she labors diligently to reach it in every case. She is the youngest woman who ever became a successful playwright. She has a pleasant home in New York

City, and her pecuniary returns from her work have given her abundant leisure to devote to her forthcoming plays.

MOTT, Mrs. Luceretia, reformer, born on Nantucket Island, MA, 3rd January, 1793, and died near Philadelphia, PA, 11th November, 1880. Her father, Capt. Thomas Coffin, was a descendant of one of the original purchasers of Nantucket Island. In 1804 her parents removed to Boston, MA. She was educated in a school in which her future husband, James Mott, was a teacher. She made rapid progress, and in her fifteenth year she began to teach in the same school. In 1809 she went to Philadelphia, whither her parents had gone, and there, in 1811, she became the wife of Mr. Mott. In 1817 she took charge of a small school in Philadelphia. In 1818 she became a minister in the Society of Friends. Her discourses were noted for clearness, refinement and eloquence. When the split occurred in the Society of Friends, in 1827, she adhered to the Hicksite party. From childhood she was interested in the movement against slavery, and she was an active worker in that cause until emancipation. In 1833 she aided to form the American Anti-Slavery Society in Philadelphia. Later, she was active in forming female anti-slavery societies. In 1840 she went to London, England, as a delegate from the American Anti-Slavery Society to the World's Anti-Slavery Convention. It was decided not to admit women delegates, but she was cordially received and made many telling addresses. The exclusion of women from the convention led to the establishment of woman's-rights journals in France and England, and to the movement in the United States, in which she took a leading part. She was one of the four women who, in 1848, called the convention in Seneca Falls, NY, and thereafter she devoted much time and effort to the agitation for improving the legal and political status of women in the United States. She was deeply interested in the welfare of the colored people, and held frequent meetings in their behalf. For several years she was president of the Pennsylvania Peace Society. During her ministerial tours in New England, New York, Pennsylvania, Virginia, Maryland, Ohio and Indiana, she often denounced slavery from the pulpit. She was actively interested in the Free Religious Association movement in Boston, in 1868, and in the Woman's Medical College in Philadelphia. She was the mother of several children. One of her granddaughters. Anna Davis Hallowell, edited the "Life" of Mrs. Mott and her husband, which was published in Boston in 1884. Lucretia Mott was a slight, dark-haired, dark-eyed woman, of gentle and refined manners and of great force of character. She was a pioneer woman in the cause of woman, and the women of to-day owe much of their advancement to her efforts to gain equality for the sexes in every way.

MOULTON, Mrs. Louise Chandler, poet and author, born in Pomfret, CT, 5th April, 1835, and was chiefly educated there. After the publication of her first book, a girlish miscellany called "This, That and the Other" (Boston, 1854), which sold wonderfully, she passed one school-year in Mrs. Willard's Female Seminary, Troy, NY. During her first long vacation from the seminary she became the wife of the well-known Boston journalist, William U. Moulton. Almost immediately the young author set to work on a novel, "Juno Clifford" (New York, 1855), issued anonymously, and on a collection of stories, which owed to its fantastic title, "My Third Book" (1859), the partial obscurity which befell it. In 1873 Roberts Brothers brought out her "Bed-time Stories," and have ever since been Mrs. Moulton's publishers. Their catalogue numbers five volumes of her tales for children, two volumes of narrative sketches and studies, "Some Women's Hearts" (1874), and "Miss Eyre from Boston," memories of foreign travel, entitled "Random Rambles" (1881), a book of essays on social subjects, "Ourselves and Our Neighbors" (1887), and two volumes of poems. The earliest of those, which came out in 1877, was reprinted, with some notable additions, under its original English title of "Swallow-Flights," in 1892. At the close of 1889, Messrs. Roberts, in America, and Messrs. Macmillan, in England, published "In the Garden of Dreams," of which one-thousand copies were sold in twelve days, and which is now nearing its fifth edition. Since the death of Philip Bourke

Marston, in 1887, Mrs. Moulton has edited two volumes of his verses, "Garden Secrets" and "A Last Harvest," and she is now engaged in editing his poetical work as a whole. Mrs. VIoulton's leisure, in the intervals of her many books, has been devoted often to magazines and newspapers. From 1870 to 1876 she was the Boston literary correspondent of the New York "Tribune," and for nearly five years she wrote a weekly letter on bookish topics for the Boston "Sunday Herald," the series closing in December, 1891. During all those busy years her residence has been in Boston, and sixteen consecutive summers and autumns have been passed in Europe. In London, especially, she is thoroughly at home, and lives there surrounded by friends and friendly critics, who heartily value both her winning personality and her exquisite art. Mrs. Moulton, to whom all circumstances are kind and whom success has never spoiled, is an enviable figure among American women of letters. Full of appreciation for the great bygone names of honor, she reaps a certain reward in enjoying now the friendship of such immortals as Mr. Hardy, Mr. Meredith, Mr. Whittier, Mr. Swinburne and Mr. Walter Pater. The very best of her gifts is the tolerant and gracious nature which puts upon every mind, high or low, its noblest interpretation. She has been all her life much sought and greatly beloved. Many young writers have looked to her, and not in vain, for encouragement and sympathy, and may almost be ranked as her children, along with the sole daughter, who is in a home of her own, far away. Mrs. Moulton's literary reputation rests, and ought to rest, upon her poetry. It is of uneven quality, and it has a narrow range, but it securely utters its own soul, and with truly impassioned beauty. Occupied entirely with emotions, reveries and thoughts of things, rather than with things themselves, it yields, in our objective national air, a note of mysterious melancholy. It has for its main characteristic a querulous, but not rebellious sorrow, expressed with consummate ease and melody. Few can detect in such golden numbers the price paid for the victory of song, how much of toil, patience and artistic anxiety lie at the root of what sounds and shows so naturally fair. Mrs. Moultonis in herself two phenomena: the dedicated and conscientious poet, and the poet whose wares are marketable and even popular. Whatever sensitive strength is in her work at all, concentrates itself in her sonnets, steadily pacing on to some solemn close. Not a few critics have placed those sonnets at the head of their kind in America.

MOUNTCASTLE, Miss Clara H.,
artist, author and elocutionist, born in the town of Clinton, Province of Ontario, Canada, 26th November, 1837, where she has passed her busy life. Her parents were English born, of mixed Scotch and Irish descent. Her early years were passed on her

father's farm where she cultivated the acquaintance of nature in all her moods, early evincing a taste for poetry and painting that the hardships incident to a home of limited means could not subdue. Later she studied painting in Toronto. She has taken prizes in all the provincial exhibitions and is very proficient in pencil drawing. As a teacher she is very successful. In 1882 a Toronto firm published "The Mission of Love," a volume of poems by Miss Mountcastle, which has been very favorably received. She then wrote "A Mystery," a novelette, which was purchased and published by the same firm. It had a good sale. Her style is clear, chaste and forcible. Miss Mountcastle was recently elected an honorary member of the Trinity Historical Society, Dallas, Texas. Her first important painting, "Spoils of the Sable," was exhibited in the Royal Canadian Academy, and it brought her instant recognition. Other fine pictures have extended her reputation. Her poems and prose works have been very popular throughout Canada and in the United States. Her platform work has included the rendition of her own essays and poems. She is a forcible and dramatic reader, a versatile author, and an artist of strong, varied powers.

MOWRY, Miss Martha H., physician, born in Providence, RI, 7th June, 1818. Her parents were Thomas and Martha Harris Mowry. Her father was a merchant in Providence. Her mother died in August, 1818, and her father in June, 1872. The young Martha was reared by her father's sister, Miss Amey Mowry, a cultured woman of literary tastes, who inspired her young niece with a fondness for literature, science and study. Martha attended the schools of Miss Sterry and Miss Chace, in Providence, and in 1825 she was sent to Mrs. Walker's academy. In 1827 she became a student in the Friends' Yearly Meeting Boarding School, in Providence, where she remained until 1831. She next went to Miss Latham's select boardingschool, and later to Miss Winsor's young ladies' boarding-school. While in that school, over exercise brought on an attack of heart weakness, which troubled her for over four years, forcing her to leave school. During that enforced quiet she studied various branches, such as mathematics, Latin, Greek and Hebrew. She also read extensively, and especially the works of the ancient philosophers. After her health was restored, she studied in the Green Street Select School, in Providence. After leaving the school she kept up her studies, with increasing interest in languages and oriental literature. In 1844 she decided to take up the study of medicine. At that time no woman had been or could be admitted to a medical college, and she studied with Drs. Briggs, Fowler, Fabyan, Maurau and De Bonnerville. In the winter of 1849–50 she was requested to take charge of a medical college for women in Boston, MA. She spent some months in close study, to fit herself for work, and under the instruction of able and experienced physicians, such as Dr. Cornell, Dr. Page, Dr. Gregory and others, she soon became proficient. Dr. Page established a school in Providence, where Miss Mowry took a course in electropathy and received a diploma. She afterward lectured before physiological societies in neighboring towns. In 1851 her services were recognized by the Providence Physiological Society, which presented her a silver cup as a token of their respect and confidence. In 1853 she received a diploma as M.D. from an allopathic medical school in Philadelphia, PA, after examination by a committee of physicians who visited her in Providence. She was in the same year appointed professor of obstetrics and diseases of women and children in the Women's Medical College of Pennsylvania, an institution then only three or four years old. She accepted the call and went to Philadelphia. Among her auditors, when she was introduced and delivered her first address, were Mrs. Maria Child and Mrs. Lucretia Mott. Her work in the college was pleasant and successful, but her father desired to have her with him, and she returned to Providence. In that city she was called into regular practice, and for nearly forty years she has been an active physician. Since 1880 she has limited her work somewhat, and since 1882 she has refrained from answering night calls. Dr. Mowry always felt a deep interest in all educational matters. She has been interested in woman suffrage, and appeared in a convention held in Worcester, MA, where she was introduced by Mrs. Mott. She is a trustee of the Woman's Educational and Industrial Union of Providence, a member of the Rhode Island Woman's Club, and vice-president for her State of the Association for the Advancement of Women. Dr. Mowry has had a remarkable career, and her greatest achievement has been in aiding the opening up of one of the most important fields of professional and scientific work for the women of the United States.

MUMAUGH, Mrs. Frances Miller, artist, born in Newark, NY, 11th July, 1860. She is a descendant of an old Lutheran family from Saxony. Her childhood was passed in the Genesee Valley. When a mere child her artistic faculty attracted the attention of her teachers. She was educated in the public schools, but without instruction in her special line, in which she continued to show development. In 1879 she became the wife of John E. Mumaugh, of Omaha, NE, where they afterward resided, and which is now her home. She was soon identified with western art and artists. Broad in her ideas, she was not a follower of any particular school, but absorbed truth and beauty wherever interpreted, and sought for herself nature's inspirations. Thrown on her own resources in 1885, with a two-year-old daughter to care for, this delicate woman, strengthened to the test and faltering not in devotion to her art, won her way unaided to a recognized supremacy among western artists. With the exception of a course of study in water-color under Jules Guerin, of Chicago, and a summer course in oil with Dwight Frederick Boyden, of Paris, her progress is due almost entirely to her own efforts. She is an artist of exceptional merit and promise. She delights in landscapes, in which line she is always successful. As a teacher she excels; her classes are always full. She has conducted the art department in Long Pine Chautauqua for four years, and one season in Fremont, NE. She has been one of the board of directors of the Western Art Association since its organization, in 1888.

MURDOCH, Miss Marion, minister, born in Garnavillo, IA, 9th October, 1849. She is one of the successful woman ministers of Iowa, where most of the active work of her life has been done. Her father, Judge Samuel Murdoch, is the only living member of the Territorial legislature of Iowa. He has been a member of the State legislature and judge of the district court, and is well known throughout the State. Her mother is a woman of strong individuality, and now, at seventy-two years of age, is a woman of great mental activity and excellent physical powers. The daughter inherited many of the vigorous mental traits of her parents. Her early life was spent in outdoor pursuits, developing in her that love of nature and desire for a life of freedom for women, which is one of her strongest characteristics. She was educated in the Northwestern Ladies' College, Evanston, IL, and in the University of Wisconsin, Madison. She was graduated in the Boston University School of Oratory, then under the leadership of Prof. Monroe, and afterward spent several years in teaching in Dubuque, IA, and Omaha, NE. During that time she was engaged in institute work each summer, thus gaining a wide acquaintance and reputation in her own State. On deciding to take up the ministry she at once entered the School of Liberal Theology in Meadville, PA, in 1882. She graduated and took her degree B.D., from the same school in 1885. Her active labor in the ministry began while she was still in the theological school. She occupied pulpits constantly during the vacations, and occasionally during the school year. Immediately after completing her theological course she was called to Unity Church, Humboldt, IA, and remained there five years. Under her management it became the largest church in the place. It is growing and vigorous, full of enthusiasm for the cause it represents, and active in all benevolent enterprises. It stands as a worthy monument of the years of labor

she has bestowed upon it. She was minister of the First Unitarian Church in Kalamazoo, MI, for one year, following which time she returned to Meadville Theological School and took a year of post-graduate work. She has now (1892) gone abroad to take a year's course of lectures in Oxford, England. From the first her ministry has been successful. Her fine training under Prof. Monroe developed a naturally rich, powerful and sympathetic voice, making her a very attractive and eloquent speaker. Her pulpit manners are simple, natural and reverent. Miss Murdoch is essentially a reformer, preaching upon questions of social, political and moral reform in a spirit at once zealous and tolerant. While decided in conviction, she is liberal and generous to opponents of her views. She is very popular and active in the social life of her church and greatly loved by her people. In clubs and study-classes she rouses men and women to active thought, being especially fitted to lead Shakespeare classes by her years of study with Prof. Hudson in Boston.

MURFREE, Miss Mary Noailles, novelist, born in Grantlands, near Murfreesborough, TN, in 1850. She is widely known by her pen-name, "Charles Egbert Craddock." She is the great-granddaughter of Colonel Hardy Murfree, of Revolutionary fame, and her family have long been distinguished in the South. Her father was a brilliant lawyer before the Civil War, and a literary man. Mary was carefully educated. She was made lame in childhood by a stroke of paralysis, and, debarred from the active sports of youth, she became a student and reader. The Civil War reduced the fortunes of her family. After the conflict was ended, they removed to St. Louis, MO, where they now reside. Mary began to busy herself in writing stories of life in the Tennessee mountains, where she had in youth been familiar with the people. She chose a masculine pen-name and sent her first productions to the "Atlantic Monthly." They were published, and at once inquiries were made concerning "Charles Egbert Craddock." She concealed her identity for several years. Her works have been very popular. They include "In the Tennessee Mountains," a volume of sketches (Boston,

1884), "Where the Battle was Fought" (1884), "Down the Ravine" (1885), "The Prophet of the Great Smoky Mountain" (1885), "In the Clouds" (1886), "The Story of Keedon Bluffs" (1887), and "The Despot of Broomsedge Cove" (1888). She has contributed much matter to the leading magazines of the day. Her work was supposed to be that of a man, from her pen-name and from the firm, distinct style of her writing. She is a student of humanity, and her portraitures of the Tennessee mountaineers have very great value aside from the entertainment they furnish to the careless reader.

MURPHY, Mrs. Claudia Quigley, journalist, born in Toledo, OH, 28th March, 1863. She is descended from one of the pioneer settlers of the Maumee valley. Her father is Edward Quigley, and his wife was Eliza Sidley, whose home was in Geauga county, OH. The newly-married couple settled in Toledo, OH. When five years old, Claudia's school education began in the Ursuline Convent of the Sacred Heart, in her native city. She continued her studies there until 1881, when she commenced the study of medicine with Dr. E. M. Roys Gavitt, the leading- woman physician of Toledo and one of the foremost in the State. Mrs. Murphy entered into that work with energy and enthusiasm, but at the end of a year's hard toil her eyes gave out, and she was compelled to abandon labor in that direction. In 1883 she became the wife of M. H. Murphy and continued to make her home in Toledo. Five years later her newspaper work was begun as the Toledo correspondent of the "Catholic Knight," of Cleveland, OH, in which position she showed the qualities necessary for success in that field of action. Her next step was into the place of managing editor of the Grand Rapids edition of the "Michigan Catholic," with headquarters in that city. During her stay there she, with two other enterprising women, began the work, of organizing the Michigan Woman's Press Association, of which she was elected recording secretary, a position she held until her removal from the State. In the fall of 1890 she went upon the staff of the Toledo "Commercial," resigning after doing efficient work in order to enter upon a broader field of action. She

next became the editor and publisher of the "Woman's Recorder," a bright paper devoted to the interests of women in all directions, and a power in urging the political equality of women with men. She is a very clear and incisive writer. Her courage and energy are inexhaustible, and these are added to a quick brain and ready pen. She was, in December, 1891, the Ohio president of the International Press League, president of the Toledo Political Equality Club, secretary of the Isabella Congressional Directory, and an active worker in the Woman's Suffrage Association of her own city, one of the oldest and most efficient societies in the State of Ohio.

NASH, Mrs. Clara Holmes Hapgood, lawyer, born in Fitchburg, MA, 15th January, 1839. She is the daughter of John and Mary Ann Hosmer Hapgood, the former dying in 1867, the latter in 1890. Her mother was of the same race of Hosmers as Harriet Hosmer, the noted sculptor, and Abner Hosmer, who fell with Capt. Isaac Davis in defense of the old North Bridge in Concord, MA. On her father's side she is related to Prof. Henry Durant, the founder of Oakland College, California, of which he was first president, elected in 1870. Clara was the fifth child in a family of eight children. She early showed an aptitude for study and was always fond of school and books, but, on account of ill health in early life, was unable to attend school continuously. During her protracted illness she frequently wrote in verse as a pastime. After recovery, by most persevering effort, she succeeded in obtaining a liberal education, acquainting herself with several languages and the higher mathematics. She was a student in Pierce Academy, Middleboro, MA, and in the Appleton Academy, New Ipswich, NH, and graduated from the advanced class in the State Normal School, Framingham, MA, after which she was a teacher in the high schools of the State in Marlborough and Danvers. On 1st January, 1869, she became the wife of Frederick Cushing Nash, a rising young lawyer of Maine. Soon after her marriage she commenced the study of law, and in October, 1872, she was admitted to the bar of the supreme judicial court of Maine, being the first woman admitted to the bar in New England. A partnership was formed with her husband, and they practiced in Washington county and afterward in Portland, ME. They have one son, Frederick Hapgood Nash, who was graduated in the Concord high school, Concord, MA, in 1891, and is now in Harvard College. Mrs. Nash's home is now in West Acton, MA.

NASH, Mrs. Mary Louise, educator, born in Panama, NY, 16th July, 1826. She is of old Puritan stock, embracing many historical characters notable in early New England history. With a love of books and literary pursuits, she gave early indication of talent for literary work. She was married, when quite young, to a southern gentleman, a professor engaged in teaching, and her talents were turned into that channel. For a number of years she filled the position of lady principal in various southern colleges. After the Civil War she, with her husband, established in Sherman, TX, the Sherman Institute, a chartered school for girls, where she still presides as principal. Amid all the duties of her profession she has kept up her love of literary pursuits. She is the author of serials, descriptive sketches and humorous pieces, which have appeared in various newspapers and periodicals. For some time she has published a school monthly. She has won a reputation as a scientist, especially in the departments of botany and geology. She conducts a flourishing literary society, an Agassiz chapter, and supervises a Young Woman's Christian Association. She is a graduate of the Chautauqua Literary and Scientific Circles class of 1890. She is studying Spanish and reading Spanish history and literature at the age of sixty-five. She has one son, A. Q. Nash, who has won reputation as a chemist and civil engineer.

NASON, Mrs. Emma Huntington, poet and author, born in Hallowell, ME, 6th August, 1845. She is the daughter of Samuel W. Huntington, whose ancestors came from Norwich, England, to Massachusetts in 1633. Her mother was Sally Mayo, a direct descendant of Rev. John Mayo, the Puritan divine, who was one of the founders of the town of Barnstable, Cape Cod, and the first pastor of the Second Church in Boston. Mrs. Nason's early days were passed in Hallowell Academy, where she distinguished herself as a student, excelling in mathematics and the languages. In 1865 she was graduated from the collegiate course of the Maine Wesleyan Seminary, in Kent's Hill, and spent the two following years in teaching French and mathematics. In 1870 she became the wife of Charles H. Nason, a business man of Augusta, ME, and a man of refined and cultivated tastes, and they now reside in that city. At an early age Mrs. Nason began to contribute stories, translations and verses to several periodicals, using a pen-name. "The Tower," the first poem published under her true name, appeared in the "Atlantic Monthly" in May, 1874. It quickly won recognition and praise from literary critics. Since that time Mrs. Nason has written chiefly for children in the columns of the best juvenile magazines and papers. Occasionally, poems for children of a larger growth have appeared over her signature in leading periodicals. She has also written a valuable series of art papers and many interesting household articles, as well as short stories and translations from the German. She has published one book of poems, "White Sails" (Boston, 1888). Her verses entitled "Body and Soul," which appeared in the "Century" for July, 1892, have been ranked among the best poems published in this country in recent years. Mrs. Nason devotes much time to literature, art and music, in each of which she excels.

NAVARRO, Mme. Antonio, see ANDERSON, MARY.

NEBLETT, Mrs. Ann Viola, temperance worker, born in Hamburg, SC, 5th March, 1842. Six months after her birth her parents returned to their home in Augusta, GA. Mrs. Neblett is a descendant of two old Virginia families, the Ligons, of Amelia county, and the Christians, of the Peninsula, who were originally from the Isle of Wight. Her maternal great-grandfather was a captain in the Revolutionary War and served with distinction. Her grandmother was a Methodist preacher's wife, class-leader and Bible-reader. Mrs. Neblett's girlhood and early woman-hood were passed in a quiet home in Augusta. The abolition of slavery and its enforcement at the close of the Civil War reduced her grandmother, her mother and herself to poverty, and, but for the aid rendered by a devoted former slave, they would have suffered for food in the dark days of 1865. In February, 1867, she became the wife of James M. Neblett, of Virginia, a successful busi-ness man. They made their home in Augusta till the fall of 1879, since which time they have re-sided in Greenville, SC, where she has been an indefatigable Woman's Christian Temperance Union worker, showing great energy and execu-tive ability. She was the first woman in her State to declare herself for woman suffrage, over her own signature, in the public prints, which was an act of heroism and might have meant social ostracism in the conservative South. After years of study and mature thought on theological ques-tions, she takes broader and more liberal views concerning the Bible and its teachings, and is in accord with the advanced religious thought of the present time. Having been reared amid slavery, seeing its downfall and observing the negro since 1865, she believes that the elevation of the negro must come by the education of the heart, the head and the hand. Her husband died 28th December, 1891, after a long illness. He had sustained and encouraged her in her charitable work throughout their married life.

NEVADA, Mme. Emma Wixon, operatic singer, born in Nevada City, CA, in 1861. Her maiden name was Emma Wixon, and in private life she is known as Mrs. Palmer. Her stage-name, by which she is known to the world, is taken from the name of her native town. Emma Wixon received a fair education in the seminary in Oakland, CA. Her musical gifts were early shown, and she received a sound preparatory training in both vocal and instrumental music. She studied in Austin, TX, and in San Francisco, CA. Having decided to study for an operatic career, she went to Europe in March, 1877. She studied in Vienna with Marchesi for three years. In order to accept the first rôles offered to her she was compelled to learn them anew in German. She learned four operas in German in four weeks, and overwork injured her health, in consequence of which she was forced to cancel her engagement. She remained ill for six months, and after recovering she accepted an offer from Colonel Mapleson to sing in Italian opera in London, England, and in 1880 she made her triumphant début in "La Son-nambula." She was at once ranked with the queens of the operatic stage, and in that year she sang to great houses in Trieste and Florence. She was rec-ognized as a star of the first magnitude. Her suc-cess in all the European cities was uninterrupted. She repeated her triumphs in Paris, in the Opéra Comique and the Italian Opera in a concert tour and an operatic tour in the United States, in a tour in Portugal, in a tour in Spain, and in a remarkably successful season in Italy. She has a soprano voice of great range, flexibility, purity and sweetness. She is an intensely dramatic singer, and her reper-tory includes all the standard operas.

NEWELL, Mrs. Harriet Atwood, pioneer mis-sionary worker, born in Haverhill, MA, in 1792. Her maiden name was Harriet Atwood. She was educated in the academy in Bradford. While in school, she became deeply religious and decided to devote her life to the foreign missionary cause. At an early age she became the wife of Rev. Samuel J. Newell. She was the first woman sent out to India as a missionary, leaving her native country in her eighteenth year. They were ordered away from India by the government, and she and her husband decided to try to establish a mission on the Isle of France. Their long trip to India and then to the Isle of France kept them nearly a year on shipboard, and her health was failing when they landed, in 1811. Within a month she died. Her husband was one of the five men who, in 1810, were selected by the Board of Com-missioners for Foreign Missions to go to India. Her career was pathetic.

NEWELL, Mrs. Laura Emeline, songwriter, born in New Marlborough, MA, 5th February, 1854. She is a daughter of Edward A. Pixley and Anna Laura Pixley. Her mother died when Laura was only a few days old, and the child was adopted by her aunt, Mrs. E. H. Emerson, of New York City. Her home is in Zeandale, KS. Her husband is an architect and builder, and he works at his trade. Her family consists of six children, and in spite of her onerous domestic cares Mrs. Newell has been and now is a most prolific writer of songs and poems. She began to write poetry at an early age, publishing when she was fourteen years old. Many of her early productions appeared in local papers. Her first attempt to enter a broader field was made in "Arthur's Magazine." Several of her songs were set to music and published by eastern houses, and since their appearance she has devoted herself mainly to the writing of songs for sacred or secular music. During the past decade she has written over two-thousand poems and songs, which have been published. Besides those, she has written enough verse to fill a volume, which she is keeping for future publication. In the year 1890 several hundreds of her productions were published in various forms. She writes in all veins, but her particular liking is for sacred songs. Her work as a professional song-writer is very exacting, but she has a peculiar combination of talents that enables her to do quickly and well whatever is required of her. Of late she is composing music to a limited extent. She also adapts words to music for composers. In 1891 a Chicago house published a children's day service of hers, entitled "Gems for His Crown," over eighteen-thousand copies of which were readily sold. In 1892 the same firm accepted three services of hers, "Grateful Offerings to Our King," a children's day service, "Harvest Sheaves," for Thanksgiving or harvest home exercises, and "The Prince of Peace," a Christmas service.

NEWMAN, Mrs. Angelia F., church worker and lecturer, born in Montpelier, VT, 4th December, 1837. Her maiden name was Angelia Louise French Thurston. When she was ten years old, her mother died, and when she was fifteen years old, her father removed to Madison, WI. She studied in the academy in Montpelier, and afterward in Lawrence University, in Appleton, WI. She taught in Montpelier at the age of fourteen years, and later in Madison. She was married in 1856, and her hus-

band, Frank Kilgore, of Madison, died within a year after marriage. She afterward became the wife of D. Newman, a dry goods merchant of Beaver Dam, WI, and on 5th August, 1859, moved to that town. She has two children of that marriage, a son and a daughter. From 1862 to 1875 she was an invalid, afflicted with pulmonary weakness. In August, 1871, she removed to Lincoln, NE, when, as she believes, health was restored to her in answer to prayer. From December, 1871, until May, 1879, when she resigned, she held the position of western secretary of the Woman's Foreign Missionary Society, lecturing on missions throughout the West and serving on the editorial staff of the "Heathen Woman's Friend," published in Boston, MA. Her attention being drawn to the condition of the Mormon women, in 1883, at the request of Bishop Wiley, of the Methodist Episcopal Church, she went to Cincinnati, OH, and presented the Mormon problem to the National Home Missionary Society. She was elected western secretary of the society, and a Mormon bureau was created, to push missionary work in Utah, of which she was made secretary. She acted as chairman of a committee appointed to consider the plan of founding a home for Mormon women, who wish to escape from polygamy, to be sustained by the society. She returned home to proceed to Utah in behalf of the society. In a public meeting called in Lincoln she fell from a platform and was seriously injured, and her plans were frustrated. During the interval the Utah gentiles formed a "Home" association, and on her recovery, Mrs. Newman went as an unsalaried philanthropist to Washington to represent the interests of the Utah gentiles in the Forty-ninth, Fiftieth and Fifty-first Congresses. She prepared three elaborate arguments on the Mormon problem, one of which she delivered before the Congressional committees. The other two were introduced by Senator Edmunds to the United States Senate, and thousands of copies of each of those three papers were ordered printed by the Senate for Congressional use. Mrs. Newman also secured appropriations of eighty-thousand dollars for the association. A splendid structure in Salt Lake City, filled with polygamous women and children, attests the value of her work. In Nebraska Mrs. Newman has served as State superintendent of prison and flower mission work for the

Woman's Christian Temperance Union for twelve years. In 1886 a department of Mormon work was created by the national body, and she was elected its superintendent. In 1889 she became a member of the lecture bureau of the same organization. In the cities of every northern and several of the southern States she has spoken from pulpit and platform on temperance, Mormonism and social purity. She has long been a contributor to religious and secular journals. In 1878 her "Heathen at Home," a monogram, was published and had large sale. "Iphigenia," another work, was recently published, and at this writing other books are engaging her thought. From 1883 to 1892 she was annually commissioned by the successive governors of the State as delegate to the National Conference of Charities and Corrections. In 1888 she was elected a delegate to the Quadrennial General Conference of the Methodist Episcopal Church, which held its session in New York City, the first woman ever elected to a seat in that august body. In January, 1890, on the way to Salt Lake, she met with an accident which held her life in jeopardy for two-and-one-half years, from which she is now slowly convalescing.

NEWPORT, Mrs. Elfreda Louise, Universalist minister, born in Muncie, IN, 8th September, 1866. Her maiden name was Shaffer. Her father is a tradesman and mechanic. Her mother is esteemed as a singer and elocutionist of local reputation in the present home of the family, in Iola, KS. Her paternal grandfather was a preacher in the German Evangelical Association. Elfreda Louise attended the public schools of Muncie and was graduated from the high school in 1883. She attended normal classes and obtained a certificate for teaching, but, desiring to become an artist, she entered a photograph gallery, as an apprentice, in the fall of 1883. A stronger purpose soon supplanted that. From her early childhood she had been deeply intent upon becoming a preacher. Her favorite pastime had been to gather the chickens into her father's workshop and to preach to them, playing at church. In the winter of 1883 she had a deep religious experience. Encouraged by her pastor and aided by the Universalist Church, of which she was a member, she entered the divinity school of Lombard University, in Galesburg, IL, in September, 1884. There she was graduated 20th June, 1888, with the degree of B.D. During two years of that course she aided herself financially by singing in a church quartette choir as contralto. In June, 1886, she preached her first sermon in Muncie, IN. In June, 1887, she began to preach in Swan Creek, IL, twice a month. In October, 1887, she engaged to preach also in Marseilles, IL, filling those appointments alternately until May, 1888. After her graduation she settled in Marseilles. There she was ordained to the ministry of the Universalist Church, 21st September, 1888, and there she remained as pastor for two years, receiving many new members, performing every church ordinance, and declining a call to a mission in Chicago and calls to important city charges. Resigning her place in Marseilles, Miss Shaffer became the wife of Nathan G. Newport, a merchant of Wauponsee, IL, 15th October, 1890. She became the pastor of churches in both Wauponsee and Verona, and soon a new church was erected in the former place through her efforts. Mrs. Newport is a pleasing and impressive preacher. She is an energetic worker in all things that tend to the upbuilding of the church.

NICHOLLS, Mrs. Rhoda Holmes, artist, was born in Coventry, England. Her maiden name was Rhoda Carlton Marian Holmes. The first ten years of her life were passed in Littlehampton, Sussex, where her father was vicar of the parish. The family then moved to Hertfordshire, where her youth was passed in quiet. She showed no talent for art in childhood, and entered the Bloomsbury School of Art in London merely to acquire the usual accomplishments. She there tried for the Queen's scholarship prize of £40 a year for three successive years, and to her surprise she won it and received the unusual compliment of a gift of £10 from the Queen, to whom her drawings had been sent for examination. Then Miss Holmes began to study for a career. At the end of a year she went to Rome, Italy, where she studied the human figure with Cammerano and landscape with Vertuni, and attended the evening classes of the Circolo Artistico. In the winter of 1881 she enjoyed special privileges. In Rome she exhibited her works and received personal compliments from Queen Margherita. From Rome she went to South Africa, near Port Elizabeth, where she and her mother remained a year among the Kaffirs and ostriches of the Karoo desert. She made many studies of Kaffirs, of desert scenes, and of tame and wild animals. In Venice she became acquainted with Burr H. Nicholls, who is an American, and they were married the next year in England. They came to the United States in the spring of 1884 and settled in New York City. Mrs. Nicholls at once began to exhibit her work in the exhibitions of the Society of American Artists, and she has been a successful contributor ever since. In 1885 she won a silver medal in Boston, MA, and in 1886 she won a gold medal from the American Art Association for her picture in oil, "Those Evening Bells." Every year she has added new laurels to her wreath. As a water-color artist she excels. She has been elected vice-president of the New York Water-Color Club. Her range of subjects is very wide, and in every line she succeeds. Besides her water-color work, she has done much work in oils.

NICHOLS, Mrs. Josephine Ralston, lecturer and temperance reformer, born in Maysville, KY, in 1838. She was attracted to the temperance movement by an address delivered in Maysville by Lucretia Mott. When it became the custom to have women represented in the popular lecture courses in her city, her fellow townsmen, recognizing her abilities and the readiness with which she served every good cause, appealed to her to help out the funds of the lecture association, and she prepared and delivered a lecture on "Boys." Her own two boys at home provided her with material for observation, and her motherly heart suggested innumerable witty, graphic and helpful comments for the boys themselves and all their well-wishers. It proved popular. Her literary productions were free from fault, and her natural style soon won a high place for her among platform speakers. That led to the preparation of other lectures, one on "Girls," and another on "Men." She was drawn into the movement started by the Woman's Christian Temperance Union, and she added to her list of lectures a number devoted to temperance. Among those

were "Woman's Relations to Intemperance," "The Orphans of the Liquor Traffic" and others. The scientific aspects of the work received her special attention. A lecture on "Beer, Wine and Cider" was often called for, and proved so helpful that at last she consented to have the first part of it published by the Woman's Temperance Publication Association. She is a strong advocate of woman suffrage and has delivered several lectures in its favor. Her greatest triumphs have been won in her special department as superintendent of the exposition department of the World's Woman's Christian Temperance Union, and of the National Woman's Christian Temperance Union work, of which she has been superintendent since 1883. She has enabled the women in State and county fairs throughout the land to aid in making them places of order, beauty and sobriety. In many cases they have entirely banished the sale of intoxicants, either by direct appeal to the managers or by securing the sole privileges of serving refreshments. In all cases, banners and mottoes were displayed, and cards, leaflets, papers and other literature given away, and very often books, cards and pamphlets sold. So general has been the satisfaction that several States have passed laws prohibiting the sale of intoxicating drinks on or near the fair grounds. All that practical work has largely been the result of Mrs. Nichols' use of her knowledge of such affairs. One of the most successful means of extending and illustrating that knowledge was the way in which she handled her work in the World's Fair in New Orleans. She obtained favors from the management. She secured from the State and national departments the preparation and loan of banners and shields with which to decorate the booth. She made that booth a place of rest and refreshment, furnishing freely the best water to be had on the grounds. She secured the donation and the distribution of immense quantities of temperance literature in tongues to suit the foreign visitors. She continued the work the second year, and closed up the account with a handsome balance in the treasury. The Woman's Christian Temperance Union of the State of Indiana made her its president in 1885. The State work thrives under her leadership, although her health has been so poor for some time that she has been able to go out but little. She went to Europe in 1889 and remained a year. She spent six months in the Universal Exposition, arranging and superintending the exhibits of the National Woman's Christian Temperance Union of the United States, and of the World's Christian Temperance Union. Returning to the United States she prepared illustrated lectures on Rome and Paris, which were very successful. She will perform a valuable work for the same two societies in the Columbian Exposition in Chicago in 1893. She is now in the popular lecture field, as well as the special philanthropic field. She lives in Indianapolis, IN, surrounded by a family of children and filling a prominent position in society.

NICHOLS, Mrs. Minerva Parker, architect, born in Chicago, IL, 14th May, 1863. She is a descendant of John Doane, who landed in Plymouth in 1630 and took an active part in the government of the Colony. Mrs. Nichols' grandfather, an architect, Seth A. Doane, went to Chicago, when they were treating with Indians, and settled there. Her mother was actively engaged and interested in her father's labors, and early developed a marked talent for mechanical and artistic work. Her father, John W. Doane a rising young lawyer, died in Murfreesborough, TN, during the Civil War, having gone out to service with the Illinois volunteers. Mrs. Nichols possesses the sturdy strength of character of her Puritan ancestors, inheriting a natural bent for her work, and encouraged and fostered by the interest of her mother, she has devoted her entire time to the cultivation of that one talent, and her work has been crowned with as much success as can be expected from so young a member of a profession, in which success comes only after years of patient study and experience. She has devoted several years to careful study in the best technical schools. She studied modeling under John Boyle and finally entered an architect's office as draughtsman, working for several years. She has devoted most of her time to domestic architecture, feeling that specialists in architecture, as in medicine, are most assured of success. She built, however, the Woman's New Century Club, in Philadelphia, PA, a departure from strictly domestic architecture. It is a four-story structure, in Italian Renaissance style. She is very deeply interested in the present development of America architecture, and devotes her life and interest as earnestly to the emancipation of archi-

tecture as her ancestors labored for the freedom of the colonies from England, or for the emancipation of the slaves in the South. Her husband is Reverend William J. Nichols, of Cambridge, MA, a Unitarian clergyman located in Philadelphia, PA. They were married on 22nd December, 1891. Her marriage will not interfere with her work as an architect. Besides her practical work in designing houses, she has delivered in the School of Design in Philadelphia a course of lectures for women on historic ornament and classic architecture. Among other important commissions received by her was one for the designing of the international clubhouse, called the Queen Isabella Pavilion, in Chicago, for the World's Columbian Exposition, in 1893. In connection with that building there was a hall, used as the social headquarters for women in the exposition grounds. She has had many obstacles to overcome, the chief of which was the difficulty in obtaining the technical and architectural training necessary to enable her to do her work well. She believes that architects should be licensed. Among the very first of women to enter the field of architecture, she was surprised to find that her sex was no drawback. Encouragement was freely given to her by other architects, and builders, contractors and mechanics were ready to carry out her designs. Her success is shown in the beautiful homes built on her designs in Johnstown, Radnor, Overbrook, Berwyn, Lansdowne, Moore's Station, Philadelphia and other Pennsylvania cities and towns.

NICHOLSON, Mrs. Eliza J., editor and business woman, born near Pearlington, Hancock county, MS, in 1849, and died 15th February, 1896. She was well known in literary circles by the pen-name "Pearl Rivers," and as the successful owner and manager of the New Orleans "Picayune." In her short life she accomplished a wonderful work. She was perhaps the only woman in the world who was the head of a great daily political newspaper, shaping its course, suggesting its enterprises, and actually holding in her hands the reins of its government. Mrs. Nicholson was Eliza J. Poitevent, born of a fine old Huguenot family, whose descendants settled in Mississippi. Her childhood and girl-life were spent in a rambling old country house, near the brown waters of Pearl river. She was the only child on the place, a lonesome child with the heart of a poet, and she took to the beautiful southern woods and made them her sanctuary. She was a born poet, and it was not long before she found her voice and began to sing. She became a contributor to the New York "Home Journal" and other papers of high standing under the pen-name "Pearl Rivers." She was the poet laureate of the bird and flower world of the South. Her first published article was accepted by John W. Overall, now literary editor of the New York "Mercury," from whom she received the confirmation of her own hope that she was born to be a writer. While still living in the country the free, luxurious life of the daughter of a wealthy southern gentleman, Miss Poitevent received an invitation from the editor of the "Picayune" to go to New Orleans as the literary editor of his paper. A newspaper woman was then unheard of in the South, and it is pleasant to know that the foremost woman editor of the South was also the pioneer woman journalist of the South. Miss Poitevent went on the staff of the "Picayune" with a salary of twenty-five dollars a week. The work suited her and she suited the work, and she found herself possessed of the journalistic faculty. After a time she became the wife of Col. A. M. Holbrook, the owner of the "Picayune." When her husband died, she was left with nothing in the world but a big, unwieldy newspaper, almost swamped in a sea of debt. The idea of turning her back on that new duty did not occur to the new owner. She gathered about her a brilliant staff of writers, went faithfully and patiently to her "desk's dead wood," worked early and late, was both economical and enterprising, and, after years of struggle, won her battle and made her paper a foremost power in the South. To those in her employ she was always kind and courteous, and her staff honored and esteemed her and worked for her with enthusiasm. In 1873 she became the wife of George Nicholson, then business manager of the paper and now part proprietor. Mrs. Niholson personally shaped the policy of her paper up to the hour of her death. In their hospitable home the gentle poet's proudest poems were her two little boys. She had published a volume of poems, "Lyrics by Pearl Rivers" (Philadelphia, 1873), and two poems, "Hagar" and "Lear," 1895.

NIERIKER, Mrs. May Alcott, artist, born in Concord, MA, in 1840, and died in 1879. She was a daughter of A. Bronson Alcott. Early showing a decided talent for art, she was trained in that direction in the Boston School of Design, in Krug's studio, in Paris, and by S. Tuckerman, Dr. Rimmer, Hunt, Vautier, Johnston, Muller and other well-known artists. She spent her life in Boston and London, and after her marriage to Ernest Nieriker she lived in Paris, France. Her work included oil and water colors of high merit, and her copies of Turner's paintings are greatly prized in London, where they are now given to students to work from in their lessons. Her work was exhibited in all the principal American and European galleries. She was at the height of her powers at the time of her death.

NIXON, Mrs. Jennie Caldwell, educator, born in Shelbyville, TN, 3rd March, 1839. Descended on her mother's side from the English Northcotes and Loudons, she received from her father the vigorous blood of the Campbells and Caldwells of Scotland. Reared in ease and affluence on the fine old family estate, she exhibited at an early age a marked fondness for books. Her education was interrupted by her early marriage, which took place in New Orleans, but the following year, spent in foreign travel, did much to quicken her intellectual growth by developing her natural taste for art and cultivating that high poetic instinct which is one of the leading characteristics of her mind. Recalled to America by the war, which swept away her inheritance, and widowed shortly afterward, she determined to adopt teaching as a profession. Though already possessed of an unusual degree of culture, she again went abroad, with her two little children, and courageously devoted herself to hard study for several years in France and Germany, in order to acquire a more thorough knowledge of general literature before attempting to teach her own. On her return she entered at once upon her chosen career, varying its arduous duties by lectures to literary clubs and by the use of her pen in purely literary work. In the World's Industrial and Cotton Centennial Exposition, held in New Orleans in 1884–85, she represented Louisiana in the department for woman's work, and in the followng year she was appointed president of the same department in the North, Central and South American Exposition. When the Sophie Newcomb Memorial College for young women was founded, in New Orleans, in 1887, she was invited to the chair of English literature, a position which she continues to fill with great ability. Of late years she has contributed to leading periodicals many articles on the topics of the day, essays in lighter vein, fiction and verse. Of special note is her scholarly set of lectures entitled "Immortal Lovers," which were delivered before the Woman's Club of New Orleans. Her style, though forcible and vivid, is at the same time singularly flexible and graceful. As a poet she shows that tender sympathy with Nature which is the poet's greatest charm. To her other gifts she adds the homely grace of the good housewife. Strangers and residents in New Orleans will not soon forget "The Cabin," abandoned since the marriage of her children, that "little home innocent of bric-a-brac," described by Maud Howe in her "Atalanta in the South," where choicest spirits were wont to assemble and where the genius of hospitality brooded in the air. The frank, liberal, high-souled nature of the poet-teacher reflects itself into the lives of all.

NOBLE, Mrs. Edna Chaffee, elocutionist, born in Rochester, VT, 12th August, 1846. She spent her childhood in happy, healthful living until the age of fourteen, when she went to the Green Mountain Institute, Woodstock, VT, where she studied for four years. After a year of study there she was allowed to teach classes, and she has been connected with schools in one way or another ever since. She first taught in district schools, where she "boarded around," and later was preceptress of an academy in West Randolph, VT, teaching higher English, French and Latin. She was the first woman to teach the village school in her native town, where she surprised the unbelieving villagers by showing as much ability as her predecessors. When the committee came to hire her and asked her terms, she replied: "The same you have paid the gentleman whose place you wish me to fill, unless there is more work to do, under which circumstances I shall require more pay." The committee thought they could not give a woman a man's wages, hut she remained firm, and at length they engaged her for one term, but kept her two years. Her first study in elocution was with Mr. and Mrs. J. E. Frobisher, when she was fifteen years old. They gave her careful instruction and developed her extraordinary talent, but forty-eight weeks in a year devoted to teaching left little time for the pursuit of art, and she would never, perhaps, have taken it up again, had it not been for one of those accidents which, though apparently most unfortunate, often turn the current of life into broader and deeper channels. After five years of annoyance and suffering from loss of voice, she resolved to study elocution again as a means of cure. For that purpose she placed herself under the guidance of Prof. Moses True Brown, of Boston, regaining through his instruction both voice and health and making rapid advancement in the art of expression. On Prof. Brown's recommendation she was invited to take the chair of oratory in St. Lawrence University, where she taught until her marriage to Dr. Henry S. Noble. Probably the most important step ever taken by her was the opening of the Training School of Elocution and English Literature in Detroit, MI, in 1878. Previous efforts of others in the same direction had ended in failure. Her venture proved to be a fortunate one. In speaking of it she seems surprised that people should wonder at the undertaking. She says: "If it is noteworthy to be the first woman to do a thing, why, I suppose I am the first in this particular field of establishing schools of elocution, but I didn't mean to be. I simply did it then, because it was the next thing to be done." She might now be a rich woman in this world's goods, but for her lavish giving, for she has earned a fortune; but she has a wealth of love and gratitude and is content. She once said: "As I have no children, I have tried to show the good God that I knew my place was to look after a few who had no mothers." "Speaking pieces" is but a small part of that which is learned by her pupils. Both art and literature are taught broadly, and, more than that, she exercises a wonderfully refining and elevating influence over the hundreds of pupils of both sexes who enter her school. She is a mother to every girl who comes to her, and has been so in a very practical way to many who were bereft of the benefits of a home. Mrs. Mary A. Livermore, who once visited her school, said to Mrs. Noble: "The strength of your school lies in the fact that you loved it into life." Mrs. Noble has never been content with simply doing well. She has studied with eminent teachers, at home and abroad, and has used every means for strengthening and perfecting her work, which now stands an acknowledged power in the educational world. Aside from her work in the one school, her personality has been felt in the schools which she has founded in Grand Rapids, MI, Buffalo, NY, Indianapolis, IN, and London, England, as well as by the thousands who have heard her as a reader and lecturer. She teaches from October to May each year in the Detroit school, and during May and June visits the Chaffee-Noble School of Expression in London. August she spends in "Lily Lodge," her summer home in the Adirondacks.

NOBLES, Miss Catharine, club woman, born in New Orleans, LA. She is a daughter of the late Charles H. Nobles, a native of Providence, RI, who moved to New Orleans in early life. He married a woman belonging to a patriotic Irish family, and the daughter inherited literary inclinations and talents from both parents. Miss Nobles' humanitarian views are inherited from her father, who was one of the founders of the Howard Association of New Orleans, and was an officer of that body until his death, in 1869. He rendered valuable assistance in the various epidemics that fell upon New Orleans and the adjoining country in the years 1837 up to 1867. The daughter was educated mainly in St. Simeon's school, in New Orleans. Her love of literature was displayed early in life. Over her own name and also anonymously she has contributed, to both nothern and southern journals, sketches, as well as articles devoted to the general advancement of women. She has been prominent in club life in New Orleans and has become widely known as a club woman. She served as secretary of the Woman's Club of New Orleans and of the Women's League of Louisiana. In 1889 she was one of the two southern women who attended the March convention of Sorosis in New York. The other southern representative was a delegate from Tennessee. In that convention Miss Nobles presented a comprehensive report of the work done by the New Orleans Woman's Club. In the general federation of woman's clubs, held in Chicago, May, 1892, Miss Nobles was elected one of the board of directors of that national body of women, to serve for the ensuing two years. Her life is devoted to the advancement of women in every possible way.

NORRAIKOW, Countess Ella, author, born in Toronto, Canada, 9th November, 1853. She was educated in St. John, New Brunswick, and when quite young became the wife of a son of Hon. A. McL. Seely, a prominent statesman of the Dominion of Canada. Soon after her marriage she went abroad, and has spent many years in travel, having crossed the Atlantic Ocean eighteen times. She has resided in London, England, and in many cities on the Continent, chiefly in Germany and Belgium. She has visited the various cities of India and other parts of the Orient, afterward returning to the West and spending some months in traveling through South America. After the death of her husband she took up her residence in New York City, where, in 1887, she became the wife of Count Norraikow, a Russian nobleman. She has since made a deep study of the methods of government that prevail in her husband's native land, where the Count was a distinguished lawyer, but because of his political opinions he has been an exile for many years. To "Lippincott's Magazine," the "Cosmopolitan Magazine," the New York "Ledger," the "Independent," the Harper publications, the "Youth's Companion" and various other leading periodicals of the United States the Countess has contributed many articles on the political and social conditions of the Russian Empire. In collaboration,with her husband she has translated several volumes of Count Tolstoi's short stories, which are being issued by a New York publishing house. She is now at work upon a book on "Nihilism and the Secret Police," which, it is said, will be one of the most impartial and accurate expositions of those subjects yet published.

NORTHROP, Mrs. Celestia Joslin, vocalist, born in Hamilton, NY, 8th September, 1856. Her father, Willard C. Joslin, was at the time of his death the oldest choir-leader in the United States, having acted in that capacity in the Baptist Church of Hamilton for forty-three years. His daughter inherited her father's musical talent and assisted him for many years as the soprano of the choir. She was graduated in June, 1876, from the Hamilton Female Seminary, leading her class in vocal culture and the fine arts. In August, 1877, she became the wife of Rev. Stephen A. Northrop, who began that year his first pastorate in Fenton, MI. He remained there for over five years, with a success which attracted the attention of the First Baptist Church of Fort Wayne, IN, which gave him a call, and where for ten years he has been at the head of one of the largest churches in the West. During those fifteen years Mrs. Northrop has been by his side, contributing largely to his popularity and favor with the people. Her ability as a singer has made her services are in constant demand by the Baptist denomination.

NORTON, Mrs. Della, Whitney, poet, author and Christian Scientist, born in Fort Edward, NY, 1st January, 1840. She was educated mainly in Fort Edward Academy. Before her twelfth year she was a regular contributor, as Miss Della E. Whitney, to several Boston and New York papers and magazines. The Boston "Cultivator" published her first literary efforts. Afterward she contributed to many leading periodicals. The International Sunday-School Association a few years ago offered prizes for the best hymns on the lessons for the year. Mrs. Norton wrote fifty-nine hymns in about ten days, which were accepted, and among eight-hundred competitors she won three first prizes. In January, 1874, she became the wife of H. B. Norton, of Rochester, NY. Madame Parepa Rosa, the Italian prima donna, sent her manager on a journey of five-hundred miles to request of Mrs. Norton a song for concert purposes, when Mrs. Norton wrote the humorous poem, "Do Not Slam the Gate," which has since been sung and published the world over.

NORTON, Mrs. Minerva Brace, educator and author, born in Rochester, NY, 7th January, 1837. Her father, Harvey Brace, moved to Michigan, and, when she was nine years old, to Janesville, WI, where her youth was spent. Her education was received in the schools of Janesville, in Milwaukee College, and in Baraboo Seminary, where she was graduated in 1861. She first taught and afterward became assistant editor of the "Little Corporal" in Chicago, in 1966, and has since done considerable editorial work. She became the wife of Rev. Smith Norton, 18th April, 1867, and she has devoted most of the years of her married life to domestic and parish duties, varied by teaching, from 1871 to 1874, in the College for Women, Evanston, IL, and as principal of the ladies' department of Ripon College, from 1874 to 1876. She traveled from 1886 to 1888 over Europe, and in 1890 she was again abroad. She was a secretary of the Woman's Board of Missions, Boston, MA, in 1876 and 1877, and has since spent three years with her husband in home missionary work in Dakota. She has used her pen much in benevolent work and has published many articles in leading periodicals. Her home is now in Beloit, WI. She is the author of "In and Around Berlin" (Chicago, 1889), and, jointly with her husband, of "Service in the King's Guards" (Boston, 1891).

NORTON, Miss Morilla M., specialist in French literature, born in Ogden, NY, 22nd September, 1865. Miss Norton received her education through study at home and in some of the best private schools of Boston, MA. She spent the five years 1886 to 1891 in Europe. She has taken extended courses in the Sorbonne and College de France in English literature, in Italian history and art, and the political history of Europe, but has devoted most of her time and energies to a study of the French poets, philosophers, moralists, dramatists, critics and novelists, from the earliest times to the present. She speaks French with ease and purity. Her home is with her parents in Beloit, WI. Since her return, in 1891, to her native land, she has devoted herself to the preparation of courses of lectures on French literature, which she delivers before literary clubs and classes.

NOURSE, Mrs. Laura A. Sunderlin, poet, born in Independence, Allegany county, NY, 9th April, 1836. In 1855 she became the wife of Dr. Samuel Sunderlin, of Potter county, PA. In 1881 they removed to Calamus, IA, where they lived until her husband's death, in 1886. Mrs. Sunderlin in 1888 became the wife of Dr. William Nourse, of Moline, IL, and her home is now in that city. In childhood her poetical talents manifested themselves strongly, and some of her earliest verses were printed in the "Christian Ambassador," of Auburn, NY. In 1876 she published a volume of her prose and verse, "Pencilings from Immortality." She was a regular contributor to a number of newspapers. Between 1881 and 1886 she contributed a series of important articles on the science of life in the "Liberal Free Press," published in Wheatland, IA. She has published an important long poem, entitled "Lyric of Life" (Buffalo, 1892).

NOWELL, Mrs. Mildred E., author and journalist, born in Spartanburg, SC, 15th February, 1849. After several years of married life, finding herself confronted by trials and reverses of fortune, thrown upon her own resources for the support of herself and two invalid children, she was forced to lay aside for a time her congenial literary pursuits. She taught large classes in French, her pupils very creditably performing French plays in public, and during many years she has successfully taught music. Her love for literary pursuits has remained unabated during the years in which she has had so little time to spare for it, contributing in a somewhat desultory way to periodicals and magazines under assumed names.

OBERHOLTZER, Mrs. Sara Louisa Vickers, poet and economist, born in Uwchland, PA, 20th May, 1841. She is a daughter of Paxson and Ann T. Vickers, cultured Quakers of the time, and her early educational opportunities were good. Her education was received in Thomas' boarding-school and in the Millersville State Normal School. She began to write for newspapers and magazines at the age of eighteen. Ill health interfered with a medical course of study, for which she had prepared. In 1862 she became the wife of John Oberholtzer, a worthy and able man. They resided in Chester county until 1883, since which time their winter home is in Norristown, PA, and their summer residence in Longport, NJ. Mrs. Oberholtzer is a person of various talents. Her published books are "Violet Lee and Other Poems" (Philadelphia, 1873); "Come for Arbutus and Other Wild Bloom" (Philadelphia, 1882); "Hope's Heart Bells" (Philadelphia, 1883); "Daisies of Verse" (Philadelphia, 1886), and "Souvenirs of Occasions" (Philadelphia, 1892), consisting mainly of poems read by the author on public occasions. A number of poems have been set to music by different composers. Among those best known are "The Bayard Taylor Burial Ode," sung as Pennsylvania's tribute to her dead poet at his funeral service in Longwood, 15th March, 1889, and "Under the Flowers," a Decoration ode. She is listed in catalogues of naturalists and has one of the finest private collections of Australian bird-skins and eggs in the United States. Interested in the uplifting of humanity, she has always given her close attention to the introduction of school savings-banks into the public schools since 1889. Her "How to Institute School Savings-Banks," "A Plea for Economic Teaching" and other leaflet literature on the subject have broad circulation. She has been elected world's and national superintendent of that work for the Woman's Christian Temperance Union. She has aided in instituting the university extension movement.

O'DONNELL, Miss Jessie Fremont, author, was born in Lowville, NY. Miss O'Donnell studied in the Lowville Academy and later spent several years in Temple Grove Seminary, Saratoga Springs. Being care-free she divided

Charlotte Behrens-Mantell.
From Photo by Morrison, Chicago.
Clara McChesney.
From Photo by B. J. Falk, New York.

Amalia Kussner.
From Photo by Schloss, New York.
Julia Mackey.
From Photo by Baker, Columbus.

her time between horseback-riding and the pursuit of studies which she chose for her pleasure. She began to write of what she beheld and what she felt in her daily life, and she has developed an extraordinary gift of imagery. While she was writing in an irregular way, she learned the art of printing, working at the case in her native village and in Minneapolis, MN, and writing occasional editorials. Her first poems were published in the Boston "Transcript." In 1887 she published a volume of poems entitled "Heart Lyrics" (New York). The strong originality and musical quality shown in those poems won appreciation. The reception of her book was so assuring that she decided to pursue literary work systematically. Since that time she has accomplished much work. She has chosen largely historical subjects for her poems, which have been published in various magazines. In December, 1890, after patient preparation, she published "Love Poems of Three Centuries" in the Knickerbocker Nugget Series. She is also a very successful writer of prose. Her story, "A Soul from Pudge's Corners" was first issued serially in the "Ladies' Home Journal." Her series of essays entitled "Horseback Sketches" (New York, 1891) has been one of her pleasantest and most successful works. They were written for "Outing" and were issued in that periodical through 1891 and 1892. She is achieving a marked success in the lecture field with her "Three Centuries of English Love Song," an outgrowth of her editorial work on the "Love Poems."

O'DONNELL, Mrs. Martha B., temperance worker, born in Virgil, Cortland county, NY, 5th February, 1837. Her maiden name was received by adoption into the family of Zalmon P. Barnum, her mother having died when she was four years of age. She was educated in New York Central College, McGrawville, NY, a college founded by Gerrit Smith, which recognized the same right of education for women and colored people that belonged to men. At the age of nineteen years Martha Barnum became the wife of Charles F. Dickinson, editor of the Olean, NY, "Times." Their family consisted of two daughters and one son. The son died in infancy. Having long been identified with the Independent

Order of Good Templars, she began in 1868 the publication of the "Golden Rule," a monthly magazine, in the interest of the order. In 1869 she was elected one of the board of managers of the grand lodge of the State of New York. In 1870 she was elected grand vice-templar, and was reëlected in 1871. Her husband died in June, 1871. For two years she edited the two publications which fell to her charge, but declining health and overwork compelled her to dispose of them. At her first attendance in the right worthy grand lodge of the nation she was elected right grand vice-templar. Interested deeply in the children, she was the moving spirit in securing the adoption of the "Triple Pledge" for the children's society connected with the order. Upon the adoption of the ritual containing that pledge she was elected chief superintendent of that department of work by the right worthy grand lodge. She had charge of introducing the juvenile work in all the known world. During the first year she succeeded in securing the introduction and adoption of the ritual in Africa, India, Australia, England, Ireland, Wales and Scotland, and also in every State in the Union. She was reelected four successive years. In 1873 she became the wife of Hon. John O'Donnell, one of the leading temperance men of the State. Her activity in temperance work has led her to visit Europe, as well as many parts of the United States, and always with success. She is now grand vice-templar of the order of Good Templars and president of the Woman's Christian Temperance Union of her county. Her home is in Lowville, NY.

O'DONNELL, Miss Nellie, educator, born in Chillicothe, OH, 2nd June, 1867. Both her parents were natives of Massachusetts. Her father was born in Auburndale and her mother in Brookline. She removed with them to Memphis, TN, while yet a child. She was educated in St. Agnes Academy, where she was graduated 17th June, 1885. In the following year she was an applicant for a position as a teacher in the public schools, stood the necessary examination and was appointed. In 1887 she was advanced to the grade of principal and took charge of a school in the thirteenth district, and has been connected with the county schools ever since. After two years in that capacity she was elected superintendent of public schools in Shelby county, TN. She was reëlected in 1891. She has been remarkably successful. She has extended the average school-term from seven to nine months; has established sixteen high schools, eleven for white children and five for black; holds normal training-schools for teachers during each summer vacation, one for the white and one for the colored teachers, and holds monthly institutes during the months when the schools are in session. She is devoted to her profession. She believes in technical training and continued study. She demands from the teachers under her the same fidelity to duty that she exhibits. When she first assumed the duties of superintendent, she found but one-hundred-forty-eight schools open in the county; now there are two-hundred-seventeen. She introduced the higher mathematics and book-keeping, rhetoric, higher English, civil government, natural philosophy, physiology and the history of Tennessee as studies in the high schools. She added vocal music as a study in all the schools. She is a strict disciplinarian and a fine example of conscientiousness to duty.

OHL, Mrs. Maude Andrews, poet and journalist, born in Taliaferro county, GA, 29th December, 1862, in the home of her great-grandfather, Joshua Morgan. Her maiden name was Maude Andrews. In infancy she went with her parents to Washington, GA, where she spent the years of her childhood in the home of her grandfather, Judge Andrews. She received a liberal education and early showed her bent toward literature. Her first newspaper work was a series of letters from New York City to the Atlanta "Constitution," which at once won her reputation as a young writer of much promise. Her work has included society sketches, art and dramatic criticism, and brilliant essays on social subjects, reforms, and public charities. She became the wife, at an early age, of J. K. Ohl, and both are now members of the staff of the "Constitution," in Atlanta, where they have made their home. They have one daughter. Mrs. Ohl has published poems in the "Magazine of Poetry" and in various journals. Her poems are widely copied. Her work in

every line reveals the earnestness and conscientiousness that are her characteristics. Her life is full of domestic, literary and social activities, and her career has aided powerfully in opening up new fields of work for the intelligent and cultured women of the Southern States.

O'KEEFFE, Miss Katharine A., educator and lecturer, born in Kilkenny, Ireland. Her parents came to the United States in her infancy and settled in Methuen, MA, removing later to Lawrence. Katharine attended for several years the school of the Sisters of Notre Dame, and later she took the course in the Lawrence high school, graduating with the highest honors of her class in 1873. She has taught in the Lawrence high school since 1875, and now fills the position of teacher of history, rhetoric and elocution. At an early age she manifested unusual cleverness in recitations, and, from the beginning of her career as a teacher, a forcible and lucid way of setting forth her subject. She is, probably, the first Irish-American woman, at least in New England, to venture in the rôle of lecturer. She began to come into prominence in the old Land League days, and made her first public appearance in Boston at the time of a visit to that city of the lamented poet and patriot, Fanny Parnell. She has since made a satisfactory development as a lecturer, gaining steadily in strength and versatility, as well as in popularity. Among her lectures are "A Trip to Ireland," "Landmarks of English History," "Mary, Queen of Scots," "An Evening With Longfellow," "An Evening With Moore," "Catholic and Irish Pages of American History," "An Evening With Milton," "An Evening With Dante," "History of the United States," "The Passion Play," and "Scenes and Events in the Life and Writings of John Boyle O'Reilly." Some of those lectures have been given before large audiences in the cities and towns of New England. In 1892 she delivered the Memorial Day oration before the Grand Army of the Republic in Newburyport, MA. She was one of the evening lecturers in the Catholic Summer School, New London, CT, in the summer of 1892. She is patriotic and public-spirited. She has a keen sense of humor, dramatic instinct and a self-possession not common in women. She has found time to do some excellent work as an original writer and compiler, and has published a "Longfellow Night" and a series of school readings. She furnishes local correspondence to the "Sacred Heart Review," of Boston and Cambridge, and is an associate member of the New England Woman's Press Association.

OLDHAM, Mrs. Marie Augusta, missionary worker, born in Sattara, Western India, in November, 1857. Her maiden name was Marie Augusta Mulligan. Her father was from Belfast, Ireland, and an officer in the British army on service in India. Her mother was born in India and was of the old "Butler" stock, also of Ireland. Her mother was early left a widow, with three daughters and one son to care for. Although accustomed to the ease and luxury of Anglo Indian life, she was yet a woman of clear judgment and energy, and she saw that, to raise her family for usefulness, her life of ease must cease. She opened a dressmaking and millinery establishment and was enabled to give her children a practical idea of life and a fair education, and to make them more self-reliant than Anglo-Indian children are wont to be. When Marie was fifteen years of age, a great change in the family life was caused by the advent, in Poona, of William Taylor, the American evangelist, now Bishop of Africa. Her oldest sister, Lizzie, became the wife of A. Christie, a government surveyor, who one day announced that a long-bearded, fine-spoken American was holding very extraordinary services in the Free Kirk. The family were all rigid Episcopalians, but curiosity was too strong for their prejudices, and to the Free Kirk they went. They had never before heard such pungent and direct presentations of gospel truths. When, at the close of the service, the evangelist requested all who there determined from that time to become followers of Christ, to rise to their feet, Marie was the first to respond, followed by her sister and her brother-in-law. A new trend was given to the whole inner life of the family. Marie became an earnest working member of the Methodist Episcopal Church. In 1875 she became the wife of William F. Oldham, at that time an active layman in the church, who had been led to his religious life by hearing a few words of testimony spoken

by Miss Mulligan, in a meeting which he had entered through curiosity. She went to Bangalore, South India, with her husband, who was a government surveyor. While there her sympathies induced her to open a girls' school, which she did, unaided, conducting it alone until help was furnished her. In 1879 an American college for his life work. Mrs. Oldham heroically consented to four years of separation from her husband, while she in the meantime should support herself in India. In one year she was, largely through the kindness of the ladies of the Methodist Episcopal Church, in Meadville, PA, enabled to join her husband in Allegheny College. After spending two years in the college, she entered Boston University as a sophomore. While there her health was menaced, and after a season of rest she entered Mount Holyoke Seminary, South Hadley, MA. Leaving that school in the spring of 1884, she, in the same year, sailed with her husband to India, where they hoped to live and work. She visited her mother and friends a few weeks, holding herself in readiness to go wherever her husband might he sent. Bishop Thoburn, presiding over the India missionary work, appointed him to the South India conference in the fall of 1884, to go to Singapore in far-off Malaysia and plant there a self-supporting mission. The Bishop, seeing the delicate-looking little wife of his newly-appointed missionary standing with her mother and sisters, asked her if she wished the appointment changed. She, though remembering the five years of separation from her home and friends, and looking at the long one in prospect in the distant mission field fourteen days journey by sea and land, answered: "Dr. Thoburn, if my husband has been appointed to open a new foreign mission in Singapore, we will go and open it." Arriving there, she was an inspiration in all branches of the work. She assisted and encouraged her husband in his work among the boys and men. She taught in the boys' school, opened the work among women, and was appointed first president of the Woman's Christian Temperance Union in Malaysia, where with Mrs. Mary Leavitt she organized the work. She, with ladies of her union, was deeply interested in the welfare of English, American and German sailors, visiting the saloons and persuading them to attend gospel and temperance meetings. To reach the women of the different nationalities with a more direct and efficient agency became her aim. Two English women who, like herself, were then in mission work, gave their aid, and by their untiring efforts a permanent mission was established among the women of that beautiful island. America, through the women of Minnesota, furnished the money, and Australia supplied the missionary, Miss Sophia Blackmore. After years of incessant labor, the Oldhams, not only to recruit their health, but in the interest of missions, returned to America, coming by way of China and Japan. Mrs. Oldham, though busy with her husband in a large church in Pittsburgh, PA, is in much demand on the platform to plead for the work among women in the foreign mission fields. She has written much in behalf of that work and is a contributor to the "Gospel in All Lands" and other missionary periodicals.

OLIVER, Mrs. Grace Atkinson, author, born in Boston, MA, 24th September, 1844. She is the daughter of a well-known merchant of Boston, James L. Little. In 1869 she became the wife of John Harvard Ellis, a talented young lawyer, the son of Rev. Dr. George E. Ellis, of Boston. Her husband died about a year after their marriage. That was a sad event for Mrs. Ellis. In order to divert her mind from her trouble, she was advised by Rev. Dr. E. E. Hale to write for his magazine, "Old and New." That was her first literary work, which was succeeded from time to time by contributions to the "Atlantic Monthly," "Galaxy" and "Scribner's Magazine." She was for some years a regular contributor to the Boston "Transcript" on book notices, and she wrote also for the "Daily Advertiser." In 1873 she wrote the "Life of Mrs. Barbauld," which is an interesting work and well received by the public. In 1874 Mrs. Ellis spent a season in London, England, where she enjoyed the best literary society of that metropolis. While in England she met some members of the family of Maria Edgeworth. They suggested to her the writing of the life of Miss Edgeworth. That book was published in the famous "Old Corner Bookstore," in Boston, in 1882. In 1879 she became the wife of Dr. Joseph P. Oliver, a physician of Boston. Subsequently she wrote a memoir, of the revered Dean Stanley, which book was brought out both in Boston and London. In the winter of 1883-84 she edited three volumes of selections from Anne and Jane Taylor, Mrs. Barbauld and Miss Edgeworth. Mrs. Oliver is at present engaged upon a work of great value and importance, upon which she is bestowing her usual labor and painstaking. The subject will relate to the lives and reminiscences of some Colonial American women. She has also been engaged recently upon the "Browning Concordance," edited by Dr. J. W. Rolfe, and soon to be published. Her reputation as a writer is established. Mrs. Oliver is a woman of unselfish and generous impulses. Blessed with a competency, she is always ready with time and means to do even more than her part in every good cause. She is a kindly, public-spirited woman. In the year 1889, after the death of her father, Mrs. Oliver bought and fitted up a house in Salem, where she moved in the last month of the year. In that place had lived in the time of the Revolution her great-grandfather, Col. David Mason, a noted man, who figured in "Leslie's Retreat," at the North Bridge, in February, 1775. Colonel Mason was, it is said, a correspondent of Dr. Franklin, and gave in Salem, as early as 1774, the first advertised public lecture on the subject of electricity. In 1890 Mrs. Oliver bought a small piece of land on the cove known as Doliver's Cove, which is the earliest settled part of the historic town of Marblehead. The old wharf, known to the antiquary as Valpey's, she has raised and made into a terrace with stone walls. This exceedingly picturesque spot is now her new summer home. Mrs. Oliver is an associate member of the New England Woman's Press Association, a member of the New England Woman's Club, of the North Shore Club, in Lynn, and of the Thought and Work Club, in Salem, of which she is a vice-president. She is a member of the Essex Institute, in Salem, and other organizations.

OLIVER, Mrs. Martha Capps, poet, born in Jacksonville, IL, 27th August, 1845. Her father, Joseph Capps, was the son of a Kentucky slaveowner, a kind master, but so strong was the son's abhorrence of wrongs of any nature, that he refused to profit by what he thought was an inhuman institution, and sought a free State in which to establish himself in business. He located in Jacksonville, IL. There he was married to Miss Sarah A. H. Reid, a woman of christian character. Miss Capps was educated in the Illinois Female College, where she took high rank in her studies, early showing a talent for composition. From her father she inherited an aptitude for versification and a temperament which was quick to receive impressions. Soon after her graduation she became the wife of William A. Oliver. Some of her verses soon found their way into print. They met with such appreciation that she finally began to write for publication. A number of her poems have been used in England for illustrated booklets. As a writer she has been quite as kindly received there as in America. In collaboration with Ida Scott Taylor, she has recently published several juvenile books in verse, entitled "The Story of Columbus," "In Slavery Days" and "The Far West." She has also given some attention to sacred song and hymn writing. Mrs. Oliver is skilled in all the arts of home-making and is an active, efficient church member and worker.

OLMSTED, Mrs. Elizabeth Martha, poet, born in Caledona, NY, 31st December, 1825. Her ancestral stock was from Pittsfield, MA. Her father, Oliver Allen, belonged to the family of Ethan Allen. She was educated carefully and liberally. She was a child of strong mental powers and inquiring mind. Her poetic trend was apparent in childhood, and in her youth she wrote poems of much merit. She became the wife, in February, 1853, of John R. Olmsted, of Le Roy, NY, and she has ever since resided in that town. The Olmsteds are descended from the first settlers of Hartford, CT, and pioneers of the Genesee valley. Mrs. Olmsted has contributed to the New York "Independent" and other papers. During the Civil War she wrote many spirited war lyrics, among which are the well-known "Our Boys Going to the War" and "The Clarion." Her poem, "The Upas," first appeared in the "Independent" of 16th January, 1862. She has published a number of sonnets of great excellence. Her productions are characterized by moral tone, fine diction and polish.

ORFF, Mrs. Annie L. Y., editor and publisher, was born in Albany, NY. She is a niece of the well-known artists John and William Hart, of New York City, and has inherited in an eminent degree their artistic tastes and talents.  She passed the early part of her life in her native city, where she had a happy girlhood, with no thought of care. She became the wife, at the age of eighteen, of Mr. Swart, a business man of ability and with him she removed to St. Louis, MO. After a brief married life, she was left a widow, dependent upon her own exertions and with no experience of the world or its ways. There existed, at that time, a railroad guide, a small publication which its owner was desirous of converting into a weekly issue that would be of service to the traveling public, giving exact tables of the twelve railroads culminating in St. Louis. The first step necessary to be taken was to secure a successful canvasser for its subscription list and to solicit advertising matter. That canvasser Mrs. Swart became, and through sheer courage and endurance she made a success of her first venture, and was retained on the publication for a few years in the capacity of canvasser until, seeing a better prospect in becoming the owner of the guide, she bought out its proprietor. The success of that venture, together with the business knowledge so gained, induced her to establish a chaperone bureau for the purpose of supplying female guides to strangers of their own sex in the city. From that idea grew the publication of a magazine called the "Chaperone," which is now one of the finest periodicals in the West. Shortly after the inauguration of the "Chaperone" Mrs. Swart became the wife of Mr. Orff who is associated with her in the publication of the magazine. In addition to her business ability, Mrs. Orff is also a highly cultured woman, discussing politics, art and science, with masterly diction ad comprehensive learning. She is, in an unostentatious manner, a very charitable woman. She is lady manager for the World's Fair.

ORMSBY, Mrs. Mary Frost, author, journalist and philanthropist, born in Albany, NY, about 1852. She comes of Irish-Protestant stock. Her maiden name was Mary Louise Frost. Her family connections included many distinguished persons, among whom were Robert Fulton and two uncles, Judge Wright, of New York, and Gen. D. M. Frost, of St. Louis, MO. Miss Frost was educated in Vassar College. At an early age she became the wife of Rev. D. C. Ormsby. Finding herself unjustly deprived of her patrimony, she at once decided to put her accomplishments to practical use. Against the wishes of her relatives, she opened in New York City a private school for young women, known as the Seabury Institute, which she has managed successfully from the start. She has been a Sunday-school worker for years, and from her class she formed a society of young men, who are regular temperance-workers. She has been active in reforms and movements on social and philanthropic lines. Her invalid mother lived with her and aided her in all her work until her death, 30th July, 1892. Mrs. Ormsby is a member of Sorosis. She is a member of the Society of American Authors, and of the Woman's National Press Association; she is an officer and member of the Pan-Republic Congress and Human Freedom League; she is a member of the executive committee of the Universal Peace Union and is one of the building committee which has in charge the erection of the first peace temple in America, to be built in Mystic, CT. She was in 1891 the delegate from the United States to the Universal Peace Congress in Rome, Italy. She made a speech there and presented the flag of peace sent from this country. While engaged in investigating the condition of the homeless, she was brought into contact with the advanced economic thinkers of the day. She became a convert to the single-tax doctrine. In the Peace Congress in Mystic, CT, she declared against all the old-time theories for bringing about permanent peace, and said that war would be abolished only when injustice is abolished and all have an equal right to the use of land. She made her first appearance as a speaker in public in the first National Peace Congress in Washington, where she recited a poem. She is a writer of short stories and a contributor of timely articles to various publications. As a correspondent of the "Breakfast Table," she is best known.

ORUM, Miss Julia Anna, educator, born in Philadelphia, PA, 28th October, 1844. She is principal of the Philadelphia School of Elocution and of the Mountain Lake Park Summer School of Elocution. One of her maternal ancestors, Leonard Keyser, was burned at the stake for his faith, in 1527. Another of that stanch Holland family, Dirck Keyser, settled in Germantown, PA, in 1688, and helped to establish a school there under Francis David Pastorius. One of her paternal ancestors, Bartholomew Longstreth, of Yorkshire, England, was disinherited for becoming a Quaker and came to America in 1698. Miss Orum was graduated with honor from the Philadelphia Normal School, when she was twenty years of age. Having chosen the teaching of elocution as her profession, she studied for several years with the veteran tragedian, James B. Roberts. Becoming a personal believer in the Lord Jesus Christ, she determined to use her talent and culture, as far as possible, to help those who teach or preach. Large numbers of ministers and teachers have been under her instruction. Many a young woman, whose voice had given out under the severe strain of contant school-room reiterations, has been saved from pulmonary and throat diseases by Miss Orum's teaching. Men with faulty vocal habits have been kept in the pulpit by her voice-culture and have delivery of sermons. Her method is that taught by the English tragedian, James Fennell; principles, rather than rules; the analysis of sense the basis of delivery; naturalness the height of art. For years she has been connected as instructor in elocution with the Young Men's Christian Association of Philadelphia and Germantown. She taught with marked success in several private schools, until she established an institution of her own, in 1885. All who come under her influence feel the power of her enthusiastic love for her art. Though she has given due attention to the higher styles of secular literature, she makes Bible-teaching the climax of elocutionary training. Her Bible-readings are largely attended. They are wonderfully graphic and realistic and bring out in a marked degree the strength and beauty of the sacred text. Her lectures are rich in illustration and remarkable for their clearness. Her receptions are large and brilliant gatherings. She declines all invitations to appear before public audiences, except as a teacher or Bible-reader. She has always been actively engaged in the philanthropic and benevolent work of the church, particularly its home missions.

OSGOOD, Miss Marion, violinist, composer and orchestra conductor, was born in Chelsea, MA. She comes of an artistic and musical family. Her late father was associated as a teacher with Lowell Mason, and her mother, Mrs. Mary A. Osgood, is an author and music composer. It is claimed that Miss Osgood's was the first fully organized professional orchestra of the best class, composed exclusively of women, that has done public service in America, and perhaps in the world. That orchestra, called by her name, consisting of brass and wood-winds and tympani, as well as strings, has won brilliant success, season after season, in social circles and upon the concert platform, and has secured praises from the most exacting metropolitan critics. Her example has been widely imitated, both with and without some measure of success, and to-day professional orchestra-playing by women upon brass, woodwind, strings and tympani is an established feature of American musical life. Miss Osgood is not desirous of being known to fame mainly as an orchestral conductor. She is giving more and more of her time to solo playing, to musical composition and to teaching, and she already ranks among the first of women violinists in this country. Among her many published works are a "Fantaisie Caprice," an album of descriptive pieces for violin and piano, and the song "Loving and Loved." She is arranging for an extended trip through the West as a violin soloist during 1892 and 1893. She teaches in Boston, and her home is in a residential suburb of that city.

OSSOLI, Mme. Sarah Margaret Fuller, educator and philosopher, born in Cambridge, MA, 23rd May, 1810, lost at sea 15th July, 1850. She received a broad education and early felt a deep interest in social questions. She learned French, German and the classics, and her associates in Cambridge were persons of culture, experience and advanced ideas. In 1833 the family removed to Groton, MA, where she gave lessons to private classes in languages and other studies. Her father, Timothy Fuller, died of cholera, 26th September, 1835, and his death threw the family upon Margaret for support, and her plans for a trip to Europe were abandoned. In 1836 she went to Boston, where she taught Latin and French in A. Bronson Alcott's school, and taught private classes of girls in French, German and Italian. In 1837 she became a teacher in a private school in Providence, RI, which was organized on Mr. Alcott's plan. She translated many works from the German and other languages. In 1839 she removed to Jamaica Plain, MA, and took a house on her own responsibility, to make a home for the family. The next year they returned to Cambridge. In 1839 she instituted in Boston her conversational class, which was continued for several years. She did much writing on subjects connected with her educational work. In 1840 she became the editor of "The Dial," which she managed for two years. Her contributions to the journal were numerous. Several volumes of translations from the German were brought out by her. In 1843 she went on a western tour with James Freeman Clarke and his artist-sister, and her first original work, "Summer on the Lakes," was the result of that trip. In 1844 she removed to New York City, where for two years she furnished literary criticisms for the "Tribune." In 1846 she published her volume, "Papers on Literature and Art." After twenty months of life in New York she went to Europe. She met in Italy, in 1847, Giovani Angelo, Marquis Ossoli, a man younger than she and of less intellectual culture, but a simple and noble man, who had given up his rank and station in the cause of the Roman Republic. They were married in 1847. Their son, Angelo Philip Eugene Ossoli, was born in Rieti, 5th September, 1848. After the fall of the republic it was necessary for them to leave Rome, and Madame Ossoli, desiring to print in America her history of the Italian struggle, suggested their return to the United States. They sailed on the barque "Elizabeth" from Leghorn, 17th May, 1850. The trip was a disastrous one. Capt. Hasty died of the small-pox and was buried off Gibraltar. Mme. Ossoli's infant son was attacked by the disease on 11th June, but recovered. On 15th July the "Elizabeth" made the New Jersey coast at noon, and during a fog the vessel ran upon Fire Island and was wrecked. Madame Ossoli refused to be separated from her husband, and all three were drowned. The body of their child was found on the beach and was buried in the sand by the sailors, to be afterward removed to Mount Auburn Cemetery, near Boston. The bodies of Marquis and Madame Ossoli were never found. Madame Ossoli was one of the most remarkable women of the century, and her death in middle life ended a career that promised much for humanity.

OTIS, Mrs. Eliza A., poet and journalist, was born in Walpole, NH. Her maiden name was Wetherby. She is a graduate of Castleton Seminary, Vermont. She early developed a strong love for poetry, and her first productions were written when she was about ten years old. Her first published poem appeared in the "Congregationalist" when she was sixteen. After her graduation she visited Ohio, where she met and became the wife of Harrison Gray Otis. After the war Mrs. Otis and her husband lived for some years in Washington, DC. In 1876 they removed to California, where Colonel Otis assumed the conduct of the Santa Barbara "Press," which he continued for several years. In 1879 he accepted the position of United States Treasury Agent in charge of the Seal Islands of Alaska, which position he resigned in 1882. One year Mrs. Otis spent with her husband in St. Paul's Island, and then they returned to Santa Barbara. Having disposed of his interest in the "Press," Colonel Otis purchased a share in the Los Angeles "Times," of which he now owns a controlling interest; holds the position of president and general manager of the "Times-Mirror" company, and is editor-in-chief of the "Times." Mrs. Otis is connected with the paper as a member of its staff, and also has her special departments, among the most popular of which are "Woman and Home" and "Our Boys and Girls." As a prose-writer she is fluent and graceful. Her choice is in the domain of poetry. She has published one volume, "Echoes from Elf Land" (Los Angeles, 1890). Her home is in Los Angeles.

OVERSTOLZ, Mrs. Philippine E. Von, musician, linguist and artist, was born in St. Louis, MO. At the age of eight years she won medals and other premiums for pencil-drawings and several studies in oil, and she continued to win premiums offered to young artists until her thirteenth year. The study of vocal music was next taken up. In instrumental music she commanded a knowledge of harp, piano, organ, violin, mandolin and banjo, and her proficiency was marked. In late years her talent for modeling has been displayed, and without any instruction she has achieved success. In her husband Mrs. Overstolz ever found help and encouragement in both art and literature. One of his legacies to her was a large library and a very fine collection of paintings, valued at one-hundred-thousand dollars, which has been widely exhibited in large fairs and expositions.

OWEN, Mrs. Ella Seaver, artist and decorator, born in Williamstown, VT, 26th February, 1852. Her father, Asahel Bingham Seaver, born and brought up in Williamstown, was a descendant of Robert Seaver, an Englishman, who came to America in the seventeenth century. Her mother, whose maiden name was Aurelia Adams, was also of English descent. Mrs. Owen is one of two children. Her brother, Harlan Page Seaver, lives in Springfield, MA. When she was an infant, her father moved to Burlington, VT, where he was a successful teacher in the public schools for many years. From early childhood she was fond of pencil and color-box, and, as she grew older, she had the best instruction in drawing and painting the town afforded. Fond of study, she was ambitious to receive a college education and prepared in the high school, studying Greek. When, in 1872, the University of Vermont, in Burlington, opened its doors to women, she was ready to enter, and was graduated in 1876, taking the degree of A.B. After teaching a few terms in the Clark Institution for the Deaf, in Northampton, MA, she decided to go to the

Cooper Union Art School, in New York. Before that move she had decorated small articles, which had begun to find sale at home. It was in the beginning of the decorative craze, when the term "hand-painted" was expected to sell anything to which it could be applied. She looked about and found such inartistic things on sale in the stores in New York that she offered some of her work, and was gratified to have it readily taken and more ordered. She found herself able, besides spending four hours a day pursuing her studies in the art school, to earn enough by decorative work to pay her expenses and graduate from the normal designing-class in May, 1880. A part of the time she was a member of the sketch-class in the Art Student's League and took lessons in china-painting in the school now called the Osgood Art School. In August, 1880, she became the wife of Frank Allen Owen, a chemist, born and reared in Burlington, VT. She continued her art and sent work to the women's exchanges, and with those societies had much profitable experience. She taught painting in her own and neighboring towns, having had, in all, several hundreds of pupils. In 1881 she became interested in china-firing. From the time she left the art-school she worked constantly in oils and water-colors. In 1886, having acquired a large number of studies and receiving many calls to rent them, she decided to classify them and to send out price-lists, offering to rent studies and send them by mail anywhere in the United States and Canada. That venture proved successful. She has had calls from every State in the Union. She now makes her home in Burlington. Her mother lives with her. She has a family of three children.

OWEN, Miss Mary Alicia, folk-lore student and author, born in St. Joseph, MO, 29th January, 1858. She is the daughter of the late James A. Owen, the lawyer and writer on finance, and Agnes Jeannette, his wife. From an early age she manifested a fondness for literary pursuits, but it is only within the last ten years that that fondness has induced her to choose letters as a profession. She began with the writing of modest verses and ballads, followed by newspaper correspondence, book-reviewing, and finally by work as literary editor of a weekly paper. After several years of successful newspaper work, she turned her attention to the writing of short stories, and, under the pen-name "Julia Scott," as well as her own name, contributed to nearly all of the leading periodicals, "Frank Leslie's Illustrated Newspaper," "Peterson's Magazine," the "Overland Monthly" and the "Century." For the last few years she has chiefly devoted herself to the collection of the curious and romantic myths and legends of the Mississippi Valley. Her most notable success has been the discovery of Voodoo stories and ritual. Her papers on that subject were read before the American Folk-Lore Society, in its annual meeting in Philadelphia, before the Boston Folk-Lore Society, and in the International Folk-Lore Congress in London, England. Her book of folk-tales appeared simultaneously in America and England. She is at present engaged on "A Primer of Voodoo Magic," for the English Folk-Lore Society, and "The Myths of the Rubber Devil," for the Chicago Folk-Lore Society. Her home is in St. Joseph, MO.

OWLER, Mrs. Martha Tracy, journalist, was born in Boston, MA. Her name is familiar to the readers of the Boston "Herald" and other publications. A granddaughter of one of the most distinguished literary divines of New England, Rev. Joseph Tracy, she inherits intellectual tastes and a fondness for scholarly pursuits. When a child, it was her delight to clamber to an upper room in the house of her guardian and there amuse herself by the hour in writing stories, which showed a wonderful power of imagination. A foundation was laid for her present literary work by her experience as principal for two or three years of some of the large schools in and around Boston. Desirous of a wider field of action, where she could devote her talents to the labors of writing, she accepted a position on the Malden, MA, "Mirror," where her contributions attracted the attention of the city editor of the Boston "Herald." Called to the staff of that journal, her powers of composition were fully brought into play, and she was soon recognized as a valuable auxiliary on the great daily. In the summer of 1890 she was sent by the paper on a European mission, and her description of the "Passion Play" and her letters from various parts of France, Great Britian and Ireland were widely read. She spent the year 1892 abroad in the interests of the "Herald," in Brittany, Alsace Lorraine, Italy and the Scandinavian peninsula. She was accompanied to Europe by her only son, Charles, a boy of twelve years. Mrs. Owler is the author of an art biography soon to be published, which will show that she has talent in another field, that of art-criticism.

PALMER, Mrs. Alice Freeman, educator, born in Colesville, Broome county, NY, 21st February, 1855. Her maiden name was Alice Elvira Freeman. Her parents were farmers, and her youth was passed on a farm. She was the oldest of a family of four children. Her father was a delicate man unsuited for farm life. His tastes ran to medicine, and he studied with a neighboring village physician, and finally took the course in the medical college in Albany, NY, graduating in 1866. While he was in college, Mrs. Freeman managed the farm. When Alice was ten years old, the family moved into Windsor, and Dr. Freeman began to practice there. Alice studied diligently and prepared to take the course in Vassar, but changed her plans, and in 1872 went to the University of Michigan, where she was graduated after a four-year course. While in Ann Arbor she organized the Students' Christian Association, in which male and female students met on equal terms. In 1879 she was engaged as professor of history in Wellesley College. In 1881 she became acting president of that college, and in 1882 she accepted the presidency, which she filled until 1888. She has since been a member of the Massachusetts Board of Education, trustee of Wellesley College, president of the Massachusetts Home Missionary Association, president of the Association of Collegiate Alumna, president of the Woman's Educational Association, Massachusetts commissioner of education to the World's Fair and member of many important educational and benevolent committees. She has lectured on educational and other subjects. In 1882 the University of Michigan conferred upon her the degree of Ph.D., and in 1887

she received the degree of Doctor of Letters from Columbia College. In 1887 she resigned all active duties and became the wife of Prof. George Herbert Palmer, of Harvard University. Her home is in Cambridge, MA.

PALMER, Mrs. Anna Campbell, author, born in Elmira, NY, 3rd February, 1854. Her maiden name was Anna Campbell. She has passed her life, except four years of childhood, in Ithaca, NY, in the beautiful Chemung Valley. She was an author while yet a mere child. When she was ten years old, she published a poem in the Ithaca "Journal." At the age of fourteen she was left an orphan, and in 1870 she became a teacher in the Elmira public schools. She taught successfully for a number of years. In September, 1880, she became the wife of George Archibald Palmer. Her family consists of two daughters. In her early years she wrote under a number of pen-names, but after her marriage she chose to be known as "Mrs. George Archibald," and that name has appeared with all her productions since that date. She has written much and well. Some of her best work has appeared in the "Magazine of Poetry." Her published works are "The Summerville Prize" (New York, 1890); a book for girls, "Little Brown Seed" (New York, 1891); "Lady Gay" (Boston, 1891); "Lady Gay and Her Sister" (Chicago, 1891), and "Verses from a Mother's Corner" (Elmira, NY). She has a fifth volume in press. Mrs. Palmer's life is quiet and her tastes domestic.

PALMER, Mrs. Bertha Honoré, social leader and president of the ladies' board of managers of the Columbian Exposition in Chicago, was born in Louisville, KY. Her maiden name was Bertha Honoré. Her early years were passed in Louisville, where she received a solid education. She afterward took the course in the convent school in Georgetown, DC. Shortly after graduating, in 1871, she became the wife of Potter Palmer, the Chicago millionaire, and since her marriage she has been the recognized leader of fashion in that city. She has shown her literary talent in essays on social subjects, one of which is "Some Tendencies of Modern Luxury." She is an accomplished linguist and musician and a woman of marked business and executive capacity. She is a member of the Fortnightly Club, of Chicago. She was chosen president of the board of lady managers of the exposition of 1893, and she went to Europe in 1891 on a mission in the interest of the exposition. She succeeded in interesting many of the prominent women of Europe in the fair, and much of the success of the woman's department is due to her work. Mrs. Palmer is a tall, slight, dark-haired and dark-eyed woman, of decided personal and intellectual charms, and a woman of mark in every way. She is a skillful parliamentarian and a dignified presiding officer. Her home is a marvel of artistic luxury.

PALMER, Mrs. Fanny Purdy, author, born in New York, NY, 11th July, 1839. She is the only child of Henry and Mary Catherine Sharp Purdy, descended on her father's side from Capt. Purdy, of the British army, who was killed in the battle of White Plains, and a member of whose family was among the early settlers of Westchester county, NY. On the maternal side Mrs. Palmer comes of the Sharps, a family of Scotch origin settled in Albany, NY, about 1750, and having descendants for four generations residing in New York City. Of a high intellectual order, her mind encompasses a wide field of literary and executive ability. With the advantage of a good early education, acquired in part in the Convent of the Sacred Heart, Buffalo, NY, and later in Packer Institute, Brooklyn, NY, she has been trained to the development of faculties and characteristics that render her a marked type of the American woman of to-day, who combines literary tastes and social activities with a domestic sovereignty that is pronounced in its energy. Her literary bent was early indicated by contributions to the "Home Journal" over the penname of "Florio," and to "Putnam's Magazine" and "Peterson's Magazine." On William October, 1862, she became the wife of Dr. William H. Palmer, Surgeon of the Third New York Cavalry,

and accompanied him to the seat of war, there continuing her literary work, during the fourstirring years which ensued, by short stories and poems for Harper's periodicals and the "Galaxy," and letters to various newspapers from North Carolina and Virginia. In 1867 Dr. and Mrs. Palmer located in Providence, RI, where they have since resided. During those years she has been continuously identified with all the prominent measures for the advancement of women and with many philanthropic and educational movements. From 1876 to 1884 she served as a member of the Providence school committee. For several years she was secretary of the Rhode Island Woman Suffrage Association. For the year 1891–92 she was president of the Woman's Educational and Industrial Union, and from 1884 to 1892 president of the Rhode Island Women's Club and a director of the General Federation of Women's Clubs. Mrs. Palmer's public work has been accompanied by habits of systematic private study and of professional literary employment involving regular work on one or two weekly newspapers. She is a moving spirit in various parlor clubs and reading circles, and her own reading, especially in philosophy and history, has given her mental discipline and a wide range of culture. She speaks readily and understands the duties of a presiding officer. She has taken special interest in popularizing the study of American history, having herself prepared and given a series of "Familiar Talks on American History" as a branch of the educational work of the Women's Educational and Industrial Union. She is one of the managers of the Providence Free Kindergarten Association, and, being keenly alive to the importance of the higher education of women, is secretary of a society organized to secure for women the educational privileges of Brown University. By the recent action of Brown (June, 1892) all of its examinations and degrees have been opened to women. She is the author of a volume of entertaining short stories, "A Dead Level and Other Episodes" (Buffalo, 1892). She is at present preparing a collection of her poems for the press. She has two children, a son and a daughter, the latter a student in Bryn Mawr College.

PALMER, Mrs. Hannah Borden, temperance reformer, born in Battle Creek, MI, 8th October, 1843. Her father is a Presbyterian clergyman. On her mother's side she is descended from Hollanders, who were among the first settlers of Manhattan Island. She is the oldest of a family of eight children and her youth was full of work and care. At the age of sixteen she entered Albion College, in Albion, MI, and after a three-year course of study took the degree of M.A. After her graduation she began to teach in the union school in Lapeer, MI. In November, 1864, she became the wife of Dr. Elmore Palmer, then surgeon of the Twenty-ninth Michigan Volunteer Infantry. She accompanied him to the front with his regiment, camping with them until the muster-out in September, 1865. After that home duties and the care of her children occupied her time until the crusade began. She was elected president of the Woman's Christian Temperance Union, of Dexter, MI, under whose guidance and auspices were organized a public library and reading-room. In 1881, after the death of all her children, she removed to Colorado. There she opened a private school, which she conducted with success until her removal to Buffalo, NY. Mainly through her efforts, a lodge of Good Templars was organized in Boulder, CO, she being its presiding officer for five successive terms. Her love for children induced her to organize a Band of Hope, which soon grew to nearly two-hundred members. During that time she became a member of the Woman's Christian Temperance Union of that city and soon received the gavel. In the spring of 1886 business led her husband to Buffalo, NY, in the practice of his profession. Seeing in the Royal Templars what she believed to be a fruitful source of great good, she united with that order, serving as chaplain, vice-councilor and select councilor. After three years as select councilor of Advance Council No. 25 she declined reëlection. Her council sent her as its representative to the Grand Council in February, 1890. On her first introduction into that body she was made chairman of the committee on temperance work and was elected grand vice-councilor, being the first woman to hold that position in the jurisdiction of New York. In the subsequent sessions of the Grand Council in February, 1891, and February, 1892, she was reelected grand vice-councilor, being the only person ever reëlected to that office.

PAPPENHEIM, Mme. Eugenie, opera singer, born in Vienna, Austria, 15th February, 1853. She is the daughter of the late Albert Pappenheim, a well-known merchant of that city, and is a sister-in-law of the famous actor, Chevalier Adolf von Sonnenthal. Madame Pappenheim is a dramatic prima donna and the possessor of a voice of great compass and rare quality. She has a worldwide reputation, having filled engagements in most of the great musical centers of Europe, North America and South America. Her musical talent was developed at an early age, and she made her debut as Valentine in the "Huguenots," in Linz, Austria, when seventeen years of age. She came to the United States in 1875, under the management of Adolf Neuendorf, in company with the tenor, Theodor Wachtel, and sang in 1876 during the Centennial Exhibition in Philadelphia and also at the opening of the new Music Hall in Cincinnati. She was for a number of years a star in Colonel Mapleson's company, and appeared in concerts and in the great musical festivals in Worcester, Boston, New York and other large cities in the East and West. The United States is especially indebted to her for advancing the ideas of Wagner. She was the first to create Senta in "The Flying Dutchman," and Walküre, without being an absolute disciple of that great composer, for she was equally successful in the rôles of Italian and French operas. In 1888 she retired from public life and has since devoted her time to vocal instruction in New York City. What the stage has lost, the coming generations will profit by her teachings. Although established for a few years only, she is already recognized as one of the most successful vocal instructors in the United States, and some of her pupils are rising stars on the operatic and concert stage.

PARKER, Miss Alice, lawyer, born in Lowell, MA, 21st April, 1864. She attended the public schools and was graduated from the high school in Lowell. She entered the Boston Latin school, which she left to take up the study of medicine. Her father is the well-known Dr. Hiram Parker, of Lowell, and it was natural that her tastes should run in that direction. On her father's death, being left an only daughter with a widowed mother and

in possession of a considerable estate, she felt the
necessity for educating
herself to a pursuit where
she could eventually
manage her affairs. Not
being in very robust
health, she went in 1885 to
California, where, regaining
her health, she entered upon a
course of law studies. She continued her studies
under the tuition of a prominent lawyer in that
State. She applied for admission to the supreme
court of California in the July term of 1888, and in
a class of nineteen applicants took the first place
and was admitted without consultation by the full
bench in open court, a distinction seldom shown
by that rigid tribunal. Equipped with a thorough
theoretical knowledge of law, she began at once to
enter into the practice, preparing briefs for
lawyers and searching for precedents and authorities among the thousands of volumes of reported
cases from the highest tribunals of England and
America. As she was getting into active practice,
her mother's health required her to return to the
East. She was admitted to the Massachusetts bar
in 1890 and entered into active practice in Boston,
retaining her residence in Lowell and also having
her evening office and a special day each week for
Lowell clients. She is a general practitioner and
tries or argues a case irrespective of any specialty,
though probate business has come to her in large
portions by reason, no doubt, of her series of
learned and highly interesting articles published
in the "Home Journal," of Boston, under the title
of "Law for my Sisters." Those contain expositions of the law of marriage, widows, breach of
promise, wife's necessaries, life insurance on
divorce, sham marriages and names. When completed, they will he published in book form. They
have been largely quoted by the press and entitle
the author to a place among the popular law-
writers. Miss Parker devotes her time solely to her
profession. Though she does not enter into the
spirit cf becoming a public reformer for suffrage
and woman's rights, she assists with her talents
and labor any object having in view the amelioration of her sex. She is the author of many amendments before the Massachusetts legislature affecting property rights of women, and she has made it
her task to procure such legislation at each session
as will accomplish that end.

PARKER, Miss Helen Almena, dramatic reader
and impersonator, was born near Salem, OR. She
is from Puritanic German and Scotch ancestry,
and is a near relative of Commodore Oliver H.
Perry. Her family is one of
patriots. One of her grandfathers went entirely through
the Revolutionary War.
Her father and his only
brother enlisted in the
Union service in the
rebellion. Miss Parker's
parents are both natives of
New York State. They are

well known to reformers, much
of the best years of their lives having been spent
in active work in the temperance cause. The
mother was one of the leaders in the crusade, and
the history of that movement written by her has
had a large circulation. She is widely known as a
philanthropist; she organized the first "Home for
the Friendless" society in Nebraska and was for
many years State president of the same. Through
her efforts an appropriation was made by the
Nebraska Legislature and a home was established
in Lincoln. Miss Parker's education was begun in
Holy Angels' Academy, Logansport, IN. Later she
removed with her parents to Lincoln, NE, where,
after taking a high-school course, she entered the
Nebraska State University. During her second
year in the university she was chosen to represent
that institution in a literary contest with Doane
College, in Crete, NE. She won the laurels and
determined to make oratory a study. She entered
the special course in oratory in Northwestern University, Evanston, IL, from which she was graduated in 1885. Immediately after graduating she
entered upon her work as teacher and reader. After
a successful year in the Nebraska Wesleyan University she was called to a position in Cotner University, Lincoln, where she still fills the chair of
professor of oratory and dramatic art.

PARKHURST, Mrs. Emelie Tracy Y. Swett,
poet and author, born in San Francisco, Cal, 9th
March, 1863, and died there 21st April, 1892. She
was the daughter of Professor John Swett, a
prominent educator of California, known as "The
Father of Pacific Coast Education" and the author
of many excellent educational works, which have
been in wide use in the United States, England,
France, Norway, Sweden, Denmark and Australia.

Both Professor Swett and his wife were inclined to literature. Emelie was educated in the public schools of San Francisco, ending with the normal school. She made specialties of French and music and was proficient in art and designing. She went, after graduation, to Europe and spent some time in France. Returning to California, she taught vocal and instrumental music in a female seminary in Eureka. She became the wife of John W. Parkhurst, of the Bank of California, in 1889. Her literary career was begun in her youth, when she wrote a prize Christmas story for the San Francisco "Chronicle." She was then fourteen years old. She served for a time as private secretary to a San Francisco publisher, and while in that position she wrote and published much in prose and verse. She contributed to eastern papers, to the San Francisco papers and to the "Overland Magazine." She collected materials for a book on the best literary work of the Pacific coast. Soon after her marriage she organized the Pacific Coast Literary Bureau, and out of it grew the Pacific Coast Woman's Press Association, and she served as corresponding secretary of the latter organization. She contributed to the "Magazine of Poetry," the "California Illustrated Magazine" and many other high-class periodicals. She wrote much in the editorial line, and her literary work includes everything from Greek, French and German translations to the production of finished poems of high merit. She wrote a biography of Charles Edward de Villers in French and English. She dramatized Helen Hunt Jackson's Indian novel, "Ramona." Her life was crowded full of work.

PARTON, Mrs. Sara Payson Willis, author, born in Portland, ME, 9th July, 1811, and died in Brooklyn, NY, 10th October, 1872. She was a daughter of Nathaniel and Sara Willis. She received the name Grata Payson, after the mother of Edward Payson, the preacher, but she afterward took the name of her mother, Sara. The family removed to Boston in 1817, where her father for many years edited "The Recorder," a religious journal, and the "Youth's Companion." Sara was a brilliant and affectionate child. She was educated in the Boston public schools, and afterward

became a student in Catherine Beecher's seminary in Hartford, CT. She received a thorough training, that did much to develop her literary talent. In 1837 she became the wife of Charles H. Eldredge, a Boston bank cashier. In 1846 Mr. Eldredge died, leaving Mrs. Eldredge, with two children, in straitened circumstances. She tried to support herself and children by sewing, but the work prostrated her. She sought vainly to get a position as teacher in the public schools. After repeated discouragements, she, in 1851, thought of using her literary talent. She wrote a series of short, crisp, sparkling articles, which she sold to Boston newspapers at a half-dollar apiece. They at once attracted attention and were widely copied. Her pen-name, "Fanny Fern," soon became popular, and her "Fern Leaves," as the sketches were entitled, brought her offers for better pay from New York publishers. She brought out a volume of "Fern Leaves," of which eighty-thousand copies were sold in a few weeks. In 1854 she removed to New York City, and there she formed her literary connection with Robert Bonner's "New York Ledger," which was continued for sixteen years. In New York she became acquainted with James Parton, the author, who was assisting her brother, Nathaniel P. Willis, in conducting the "Home Journal." In 1856 she became Mr. Parton's wife. Their tastes were similar, and their union proved a happy one. She was a prolific writer. Her works include: "Fern Leaves from Fanny's Portfolio" (Auburn, 1853, followed by a second series, New York, 1854); "Little Ferns for Fanny's Little Friends" (1854); "Ruth Hall," a novel based on the pathetic incidents of her own life (1854); "Fresh Leaves" (1855); "Rose Clark," a novel (1857); "A New Story-Book for Children" (1864); "Folly as it Flies" (1868); "The Play-Day Book" (1869); "Ginger-Snaps" (1870), and "Caper-Sauce, a Volume of Chit-Chat" (1872). Most of her books were republished in London, England, and a London publisher in 1855 brought out a volume entitled "Life and Beauties of Fanny Fern." Her husband published, in 1872, "Fanny Fern: A Memorial Volume," containing selections from her writings and a memoir. Her style is unique. She wrote satire and sarcasm so that it attracted those who were portrayed. She had wit, humor and pathos. With mature years and experience her productions took on a philosophical tone and became more polished. Her books have been sold by the hundreds of thousands, and many of them are still in demand. She was especially successful in juvenile literature, and "Fanny Fern" was the most widely known and popular pen-name of the last forty years.

PATTERSON, Mrs. Minnie Ward, poet and author, was born in Niles, MI. Her youth was passed in that town. Her maiden name was Ward. Her father was a teacher and a man of some literary and forensic ability, and her mother was a woman of decidedly poetic taste. Minnie Ward's naturally poetic temperament found exactly the food it craved in her surroundings, and many of her early school compositions displayed much of both the spirit and art of poetry. Before she reached womanhood, both her parents died, and she was left to the care of strangers and almost wholly to the guidance of her own immature judgment. She appreciated the value of education and by teaching school, taking a few pupils in music and painting and filling every spare moment with writing, she managed to save enough to take a course of study, graduating with honor from Hillsdale College at the age of twenty years, and afterward received from her alma mater the degree of A.M. Soon after leaving school, she opened a studio in Chicago, and while there was a frequent contributor to the "Sunday Times," usually over the signature of "Zinober Green." While on a sketching tour along the Upper Mississippi, during the summer of 1867, she became the wife of John C. Patterson, a former class-mate in Hillsdale, and a graduate of the law school in Albany, NY, who has since become a prominent member of the Michigan bar and has been twice elected to the Senate of that State. They reside in Marshall, MI. Mrs. Patterson has never been a profuse writer of poetry, but what she has written bears the impress of a clear, well-disciplined mind, earnestness of purpose and intensity of feeling, and her poems have appeared in the Boston "Transcript," "Youth's Companion," "Wide Awake," "Peterson's Magazine," the "Free Press" and the "Tribune" of Detroit, the "Times" and the "Journal" of Chicago, and various other periodicals. Her only published volume of poems is entitled "Pebbles from Old Pathways." Not long after the appearance of that book she became greatly interested in the Norse languages and literature, and her next work of importance was the translation of three

volumes of "The Surgeon's Stories" from the Swedish, entitled respectively "Times of Frederick I," "Times of Linnæus," and "Times of Alchemy." Besides those volumes from the Swedish, she has translated many folklore tales from the Norwegian, which first appeared in the Detroit "Free Press" and "Demorest's Magazine," as well as some novelettes by living Scandinavian writers. She has now an unpublished novel and an original epic poem. During 1889 she had a series of articles running in the Detroit "Sunday Free Press," entitled "Myths and Traditions of the North," which give an outline of Norse mythology intermingled with quaint original remarks and sparkling wit. Besides the above mentioned and similar work, she is the author of words and music of a half-dozen songs of much sweetness and depth of feeling.

PATTERSON, Mrs. Virginia Sharpe, author, born in Delaware, OH, in September, 1841. Authorship and journalism were family professions. Her father, Hon. George W. Sharpe, published and edited a paper when a boy of seventeen, and for many years edited the "Citizen," in Frederick, MD. He was distinguished as being the youngest member of the Senate of Maryland, and furnished stenographic reports regularly to the Washington and New York papers, an accomplishment unusual in 1828. He was married to Caroline, daughter of Capt. Nicholas Snyder, of Baltimore, a woman of great force of character. They soon removed to Delaware, OH. Their two sons were authors. Mrs. Patterson's education was acquired rather by reading than study, as, up to the age of fourteen, she had but few school-days. Her father instructed her at home. His choice library was her delight, and through it was developed that taste for higher literature which characterized her as a child. Language and rhetoric she acquired unconsciously from constant companionship with her father in his office duties. After his death she was put in school, and for three years attended the Delaware Female Seminary, where she was recognized as a clever essayist. Her first published articles appeared when living in

Bellefontaine, OH, about six years after her marriage, in the old Cincinnati "Gazette," and were widely copied. At the same time she wrote a series of satires entitled "The Girl of the Period" for the Bellefontaine "Examiner." A eulogistic notice from the late Dr. J. G. Holland decided Mrs. Patterson to publish them in book form. It appeared under the pen-name "Garry Gaines," in 1878. Under that pen-name she has contributed to various journals for many years. At that time she was invited to take the editorial chair of a Chicago weekly, but ill health compelled her to decline. For months she was an inmate of a Cincinnati hospital, stricken with a malady from which she has never fully recovered. Notwithstanding almost constant invalidism since 1881, against obstacles that would have crushed one who loved letters less, she has done much mental work. In 1889 she was made vice-president of the Ohio Woman's Press Club. A year later she founded the Woman's Club of Bellefontaine, OH, inaugurated the magazine exchange, and later organized the Monday Club of Kokomo, IN, where she now resides. In 1888 she originated and copyrighted an entertainment called "Merchant's Carnival, or Business-Men's Jubilee." which has been popular, and has been given with great success in all parts of the United States and Canada.

PATTI, Mme. Adelina, prima donna, born in Madrid, Spain, 19th February, 1843. Her maiden name was Adelina Juaña Maria Clorinda Patti. Her father was Salvatore Patti, a Sicilian operatic tenor, who came to the United States in 1848, and died in Paris, France, in 1859. Her mother, known by her stage-name, Signora Barilli, was a native of Rome, Italy, and a well-known singer. She sang the title rôle in "Norma" on the night before the birth of Adelina. The mother was twice married, and her first husband was Sig. Barilli. The Patti family removed to the United States in 1844 and settled in New York City. Adelina's great musical talent and her remarkably fine voice were early discovered by her family, and in infancy she was put under training. She learned the rudiments of music from her step-brother, Sig. Barilli, and her brother-in-law, Maurice Strakosch. She could sing before she could talk well, and at four years of age she sang many operatic airs correctly. When seven years old, she sang

"Casta Diva" and "Una Voce" in a concert in New York City. In 1852 she made her début as a concert-singer, in a tour in Canada with Ole Bull and Strakosch. In 1854 she sang again in New York City, and she then went with Gottschalk, the pianist, to the West Indies. She thus earned the money to complete her musical education, and she studied for five years. She made her début in Italian opera in New York City, 24th November, 1859, in "Lucia." Her success was instantaneous and unparalleled. She sang in other standard rôles and at once went to the front as a star. She sang first in London, England, in "La Sonnambula," 14th May, 1861, and she carried the city by storm. She made her first appearance in Paris 6th November, 1862, and during the next two years she sang in Holland, Belgium, Austria and Prussia, winning everywhere a most unprecedented series of triumphs. After 1864 she sang in the Italiens in Paris, and went to London, Baden, Brussels and St. Petersburg. In St. Petersburg, in 1870, the Czar bestowed upon her the Order of Merit and the title of "First Singer of the Court." She sang in Rome and returned to Paris in 1874. From 1861 to 1880 she sang every season in the Covent Garden concerts in London, in the Handel festivals, and in concert-tours through the British provinces. In 1881 and 1882 she sang in concerts in the United States. She sang in opera in this country in the seasons of 1882–83, of 1884–85, and of 1886–87. In December, 1887, she started on an extensive tour of the United States, Mexico and South America. Her career has been one of unbroken successes. Her earnings have amounted to millions. She was married 29th July, 1868, to Marquis de Caux, a French nobleman. The wedding took place in London, England. The marriage proved uncongenial, and she separated from her husband. In 1885 she obtained a divorce from him, and in 1886 she was married to Ernesto Nicolini, an Italian tenor-singer. Her second union has been an ideal one. She has a fine estate, called "Craig-y-Nos," in the Swansea valley, Wales, where she lives in regal fashion. She has there a private theater, costing $30,000, in which she entertains her visitors. In person Madame Patti-Nicolini is rather small. She has dark eyes and black hair, and a very mobile face. She has never been a great actor, but all other deficiencies were lost in the peerless art of her singing. Her voice is a soprano, formerly of a wide range, but now showing wear in the upper ranges. She has a faultless ear for music and is said never to have sung a false note. On the stage she is arch and winning, and even now she sings with consummate art. Her repertory includes about one-hundred operas.

PATTON, Mrs. Abby Hutchinson, singer and poet, born in Milford, NH, 29th August, 1829. She was widely known as Abby Hutchinson, being the fourth daughter and the sixteenth and youngest child of Jesse and Mary Leavitt Hutchinson, of good old Pilgrim stock. Thirteen of those children lived to adult age, and their gift of song made the Hutchinson name famous. Mrs. Patton came from a long line of musical ancestors, pricipally on the maternal side. Her mother sang mostly psalms and hymns, and the first words Abby learned to sing were the sacred songs taught her by her mother, while she stood at her spinning-wheel. When four years of age, Abby could sing alto, which seemed to the family a wonderful performance. A little later she went to the district school with her sister and young brothers. There she acquired the simple English branches of study. In 1839 she made her first appearance as a singer in her native town. On that occasion the parents and their thirteen children took part. In 1841, with her three younger brothers, Judson, John and Asa, she began her concert career. The quartette sang in autumn and winter, and the brothers devoted the spring and summer to the management of their farms, while the sister pursued her studies in the academy. In May, 1843, the Hutchinson family first visited New York City. Their simple dress and manners and the harmony of their voices took the New Yorkers by storm. The press was loud in their praise, and the people crowded their concerts. The Hutchinsons, imbued with the love of liberty, soon joined heart and hand with the Abolitionists, and in their concerts sang ringing songs of freedom. This roused the ire of their pro-slavery hearers to such an extent that they would demonstrate their disapproval by yells and hisses and sometimes with threats of personal injury to the singers, but the presence of Abby held the riotous spirit in check. With her sweet voice and charming manners she would go forward and sing "The Slave's Appeal" with such effect that the mob would become peaceful. Those singers were all gifted as

song-writers and music-composers. In August, 1845, Abby went with her brothers, Jesse, Judson, John and Asa, to England. They found warm friends in William and Mary Howitt, Douglas Jerrold, Charles Dickens, Macready, Harriet Martineau, Hartly Coleridge, Mrs. Tom Hood, Eliza Cook, Samuel Rogers, Hon. Mrs. Norton, George Thompson, Richard Cobden, John Bright and many others. Charles Dickens gave the family an evening reception in his home. Mr. Hogarth, the father of Mrs. Dickens and the critic of the Italian opera, after hearing the family sing, took them by the hands and said that he never before had heard such fine harmony. At their opening concert many prominent literary and musical people were present. After one year of singing in Great Britain the family returned to America and renewed their concerts in their native land. On 28th February, 1849, Abby Hutchinson became the wife of Ludlow Patton, a banker and broker in New York City, and an active member of the New York Stock Exchange. After her marriage Mrs. Patton sang with her brothers on special occasions. At the outbreak of the rebellion, in 1861, Mrs. Patton joined with her brothers in singing the songs of freedom and patriotism. In April, 1873, Mr. Patton retired from business with a competency. For the next ten years Mr. and Mrs. Patton traveled for pleasure through Europe, Asia, Africa and all portions of their own country. During her travels Mrs. Patton was a frequent contributor to various American newspapers. She composed music to several poems, among which the best known are "Kind Words Can Never Die" and Alfred Tennyson's "Ring Out, Wild Bells." In 1891 she published a volume entitled "A Handful of Pebbles," consisting of her poems, interspersed with paragraphs and proverbs, containing the essence of her happy philosophy. She was always interested in the education of women and by tongue and pen aided the movement for woman suffrage. Her summers were spent in the old homestead where she was born, and her winters in travel or in the city of New York. Mrs. Patton died in New York City, 25th November, 1892.

PEABODY, Miss Elizabeth Palmer, educator, born in Billerica, MA, 16th May, 1804. She was the daughter of Nathaniel Peabody, a well-known physician. Her sister Sophia became the wife of

Nathaniel Hawthorne, and her sister Mary the wife of Horace Mann. Elizabeth was the oldest of a family of six children. She was a precocious child. She received a liberal and varied education, including the complete mastery of ten languages. At the age of sixty she learned Polish, because of her interest in the struggle of Poland for liberty. In early womanhood she put her attainments to use in a private school, which she taught in her home. In 1849 the family removed to Boston, where she opened a school. Her theory was that "education should have character for its first aim and knowledge for its second." She succeeded Margaret Fuller as teacher of history in Mr. Alcott's school. Her personal acquaintances included Channing, Emerson, Thoreau and other prominent men of the time. Identified with all the great movements of the day, she was especially prominent among the agitators who demanded the abolition of slavery. She was an attendant in the meetings of the Transcendental Club. She advocated female suffrage and higher education for women, and aided Horace Mann in founding a deaf-mute school. Her later years were spent in Jamaica Plain, MA, she being partially blind from cataracts on her eyes. Her literary productions include "Æsthetic Papers" (Boston, 1849); "Crimes of the House of Austria" (edited, New York, 1852); "The Polish-American System of Chronology" (Boston, 1852); "Kindergarten in Italy" in the "United States Bureau of Education Circular" (1872); a revised edition of Mary Mann's "Guide to the Kindergarten and Intermediate Class, and Moral Culture of Infancy" (New York, 1877); "Reminiscences of Dr. Channing" (Boston, 1880); "Letters to Kindergartners" (1886), and "Last Evening with Allston, and Other Papers" (1887). During her last years she wrote some, but her loss of sight and the increasing infirmities of great age tended to make literary effort difficult. Her intention to write her autobiography was frustrated. She was one of the most conspicuous persons in the famous literary and educational circles of Boston, and the last to pass away of the persons who wrought so well for freedom, for light and for morality. Miss Peabody died in Jamaica Plain, Boston, 3rd June, 1894.

PEATTIE, Mrs. Elia Wilkinson, author and journalist, born in Kalamazoo, MI, 15th January, 1862. Before she was ten years old, her father removed with his family to Chicago, IL, where Mrs. Peattie grew to womanhood, was married, and spent most of her life. Very little of her education was acquired in the usual way. As a child she attended the public schools, but her sensitive originality unfitted her to follow patiently the slow progress of regular instruction. At the age of fourteen years she left school, never to return. Judged by all ordinary rules, that was a mistake. Whether her peculiar mind would have been better trained in the schools than by the process of self-culture to which she has subjected it can never be known. From childhood she had an intuitive perception of things far beyond her learning and years. She was always a student, not merely of what she found in the books, but of principles. Her tastes led her to read with eagerness upon the profoundest subjects, so that, before she was twenty, she was familiar with English and German philosophy as well as with that of the ancients, and had her own, doubtless crude, but positive, views upon the subject of which they treated. She has always been an earnest student of history, more especially of those phases of it that throw light upon social problems. She has read widely in fiction, having the rare gift of scanning a book and gleaning all that there is of value in it in an hour. Her marriage, in 1833, to Robert Burns Peattie, a journalist of Chicago, was most fortunate. Nothing could have prevented her entering upon her career as a writer, but a happy marriage, with one who sympathized with her ambitions and who was also able to give her much important assistance in the details of authorship, was to her a most important event. From that time she has been an indefatigable worker. She began by writing short stories for the newspapers, taking several prizes, before securing any regular employment. A Christmas story published in the Chicago "Tribune" in 1885 was referred to editorially by that journal as "one of the most remarkable stories of the season," and as "worthy to rank with the tales of the best-known authors of the day." Her first regular engagement was as a reporter on the Chicago "Tribune," where she worked side by side, night and day, with men. She afterward held a similar position on the Chicago "Daily News." Since 1889 she has been in Omaha, and is now chief editorial writer on the

"World-Herald." As a working journalist she has shown great versatility Stories, historical sketches, literary criticisms, political editorials and dramatic reviews from her pen follow one another or appear side by side in the same edition of the paper. Although her regular work has been that of a journalist, she has accomplished more outside of such regular employment than most literary people who have no other occupation. She has been a frequent contributor to the leading magazines and literary journals of the country, including the "Century," "Lippincott's Magazine," "Cosmopolitan Magazine," "St. Nicholas," "Wide Awake," "The American," "America," "Harper's Weekly," San Francisco "Argonaut" and a score of lesser periodicals. In 1888 she was employed by Chicago publishers to write a young people's history of the United States. That she did under the title of "The Story of America," producing in four months a volume of over seven-hundred pages, in which the leading events of American history are woven together in a charming style and with dramatic skill and effect. One of the most remarkable things about that work is that she dictated the whole of it, keeping two stenographers busy in taking and writing out what she gave them. In 1889 she wrote "The Judge," a novel, for which she received a nine-hundred-dollar prize from the Detroit "Free Press." That story has since been published in book form. In the fall of 1889 she was employed by the Northern Pacific Railroad to go to Alaska and write up that country. That she did, traveling alone from Duluth to Alaska and back. As a result of that trip she wrote a widely-circulated guidebook, entitled "A Trip Through Wonderland." She has also published "With Scrip and Staff" (New York, 1891), a tale of the children's crusade. In addition to her literary work, Mrs. Peattie is a model housekeeper. She has three children.

PECK, Miss Annie Smith, archæologist, educator and lecturer, born in Providence, RI, 19th October, 1850. She is of good old New England stock, a descendant on her mother's side of Roger Williams, on her father's of Joseph Peck, who came to this country in 1638. In England the line may be traced back to the tenth century through an old Saxon family of the English gentry, a copy of whose coat-of-arms and crest may be seen in the Peck

genealogy. Her home was of the rather severe New England type, but from early childhood Annie was allowed to engage in boyish sports with her three brothers. She has always had an unusual fondness for physical exercise, with an especial love of mountain climbing, and thus preserves a healthful buoyancy of spirits not always found in those of studious habits. She attended the public schools in Providence and was always the youngest, often the best, scholar in her class. While teaching in a high school in Michigan, the opportunities afforded to women by the Michigan University were brought to her attention. Her naturally ambitious temperament led her to seek a career which should give scope to her talents, and she determined to secure a college education similar to that received by her brothers. Resigning her position as preceptress, to prepare for college, she entered the University of Michigan without conditions the next September, having accomplished two years' work in seven months. She was graduated in 1878, second to none in her class, having distinguished herself in every branch of study, whether literary or scientific. After graduation Miss Peck again engaged in teaching, spending two years as professor of Latin in Purdue University. In 1881 she took her master's degree, mainly for work in Greek. Going abroad in 1884, she spent several months in the study of music and German in Hanover, some months in Italy, devoting her time especially to the antiquities, and the summer in Switzerland in mountain climbing. In 1885 and 1886 she pursued the regular course of study in the American School of Classical Studies in Athens, Greece, of which Prof. Frederick D. Allen, of Harvard, was then director. She traveled extensively in Greece and visited Sicily, Troy and Constantinople. Immediately after her return home she occupied the chair of Latin in Smith College, but of late has devoted herself to public lecturing on Greek archaeology and travel. Her lectures have attracted wide notice and have received hearty commendation both from distinguished scholars and from the press. In her few spare moments she is planning to write a book within the range of her archæological studies. Her course has been strictly of her own determination, receiving but the negative approval of those from whom cordial sympathy might have been expected, except for the encouragement and assistance rendered by her oldest brother, Dr. George B. Peck, of Providence, RI. In religion Miss Peck is a good orthodox Baptist, but has, like her renowned progenitor, broad views of life and sympathy with those of other creeds or none. In addition to her more solid acquirements, she possesses numerous and varied accomplishments, which are all characterized by skill and exactness. She is a profound classical scholar, a distinguished archaeologist and an accomplished musician. Her home is still in Providence, though most of her time is spent elsewhere.

PECKHAM, Mrs. Lucy Creemer, physician, born in Milford, CT, 27th March, 1842. Her father, Joshua R. Gore, was a native of Hamden, CT, and his parents and grandparents were Connecticut people. Her ancestors on the maternal side were among the first settlers of the old town of Milford. Her mother's name was Mary Smith. Lucy was the oldest of four children, and when she was about seven years of age, the family removed to New Haven, and the children were all educated in the public schools of that city. The girls were brought up to be self-reliant and helpful. From eighteen to twenty-three Lucy helped toward the well-being of the family by the use of her needle. In 1865 she became the wife of Charles N. Creemer, of New York, who died in 1878. She gained entrance to the New Haven School for Nurses, in the hospital, and faithfully discharged the duties of nurse until she was graduated. In August, 1880, she was sent to Pittsfield to take charge of the hospital called the "House of Mercy." There she remained two years. As the work opened before her, she realized that deeper and more thorough knowledge of medical science would give her a still larger scope. She resolved to enter college and pursue the regular curriculum. In 1882 she matriculated in the Woman's Medical College of Philadelphia, and was graduated in 1885. Since that year she has practiced medicine in her old home, New Haven, CT. In August, 1889, she was married a second time. On the suggestion of her husband, John A. Peckham, who is in full sympathy with all her work, she selected from poems which she had written and published at intervals during many years, about forty, and had them published in book form, with the title "Sea Moss" (Buffalo, 1891). Dr. Peckham is a practical woman and has had marked success in whatever she has undertaken. Her poems are the outcome of inspirations, and they have been put into form as they have sung themselves to her during the busy hours of the day or night.

PEEKE, Mrs. Margaret Bloodgood, author, born near Saratoga Springs, NY, 8th April, 1838. Most of her youthful days were spent in the city of New York. At her father's death she was but twelve years of age. Her mother's brother, Chancellor Erastus C. Benedict, of New York, charged himself with her education and became in many ways her counselor and guide. At the age of sixteen years she was already a contributor to magazines and periodicals. At the age of twenty-two years she became the wife of Rev. George H. Peeke, now of Sandusky, OH. For fifteen years she attended only to family and parish duties, and the cherished thought of a literary life was abandoned. At length leisure came in an unexpected way. Long continued ill health gave truce to outer cares without damping the ardor of the spirit. Her pen was resumed, and songs and stories found their way to various periodicals. Mrs. Peeke was for a time associate editor of the "Alliance," of Chicago. Her letters drew attention to her favorite summer-resort in the Cumberland mountains, and a little pamphlet entitled "Pomona" was her reply to many requests for information. A serial story, "The Madonna of the Mountains," and other serial sketches, breathe the pure air and primitive human sympathies of that region. Her college novel, called "Antrobus," written while her son was in college in New England, was purchased by the Detroit "Free Press" and published as a serial in 1892, preparatory to a more permanent book form. Her later time has been devoted to a work connected with the pygmies of America and the origin of the race. That was issued under the title "Born of Flame" (Philadelphia, 1892). She is an enthusiastic lover of the Bible and teaches it with ease and success that fill her classes to overflowing.

PEIRCE, Miss Frances Eliz-abeth, elocutionist and educator, born on her father's place, Bellevue, eighty miles from Detroit, MI, 11th August, 1857. She is the only child of Dr. James L. and Rachel M. Peirce. When she was nineteen months old, her parents removed to Fallsington, PA. Her father's health failed from overwork in his profession, and they sought a home in Philadelphia, PA, when she was in her seventh year. Her early education was entirely under her father's care, and, while thorough, it was in some ways very peculiar. She learned her letters from the labels upon her father's medicines and could read their Latin-names before she could read English. Miss Peirce never entered a school-room before her thirteenth year, when she was sent to the University School, which was under the care of the University of Pennsylvania. After studying there for two and one-half years, and being number one in her classes the entire time after the first six months, her desire and taste for elocution attracted the attention of the late Prof. J. W. Shoemaker. He induced her parents to place her under his instruction, and she received from him more than ordinary care and attention, graduating in 1878 from the National School of Elocution and Oratory, of which he was president. She then accepted the position of lecturer on vocal technique in that institution, that department having been organized especially for her, but at the end of three years, her own teaching having increased so rapidly, she was compelled to relinquish all outside work and devote herself to a school of elocution which she had opened in Philadelphia. In 1880 she established the Mt. Vernon Institute of Elocution and Languages in that city, erecting a building to suit her purposes. In 1884 the institute received a perpetual charter from the State. By dint of persistent effort and "hold-on-ativeness," as she expresses it, she has raised the school to its present high standing among the educational institutions of the country. A board of five directors constitutes the management of the school, and with if is also connected the Mt. Vernon Institute Association, consisting of fifty-four members, twenty-five of whom form an advisory board. As a teacher she is preeminently fitted for her position, possessing as she does the innate faculty of discovering the capabilities and possibilities of her pupils, and of being able to adapt remedies to their faults, wherewith most quickly to overcome bad habits of delivery. Owing to her constant practice of physical exercises, Miss Peirce enjoys the best of health, and in the twelve years of her teaching has never once, through sickness, failed to fulfill her duties. All that she undertakes is pervaded by a high and noble purpose and firm resolution, and her niche in the world has been ably filled.

PERKINS, Mrs. Sarah Maria Clinton, temperance worker, born in Otsego, near Cooperstown, NY, 23rd April, 1824. She is the seventh child of Joel and Mary Clinton. On her father's side she is connected with De Witt Clinton, who was a cousin of her grandfather. On her mother's side she is descended from the Mathewson family, so well known in the early history of Rhode Island and Connecticut. Her mother was the daughter of a Puritan of the strictest type, and trained her daughter according to the good old-fashioned rules which came over in the Mayflower. Sarah early showed a fondness for books and for study, and eagerly read everything that came in her way. Misfortune came to the family. The dollars were few, and sickness brought its attendant evils. Her father died, when she was ten years of age, and the mother and children united their efforts to keep the wolf from the door. Books were never given up by the little student. She learned the multiplication table by cutting it out of an old book and pinning it to the head of her bedstead, and studying it early in the morning, when first she awoke. Picking up bits of knowledge in the intervals of work, she progressed so well that, when eighteen years of age, she was teaching a district school in her own neighborhood. At the age of fifteen years she examined the evidences of christianity and sought for a brilliant conversion, but never found it in any remarkable way. Like a little child she consecrated herself to the Master, after a long struggle of doubt bordering on despair. At twenty-three years of age she became the wife of Rev. Owen Perkins, of Savoy, MA. The years passed pleasantly in a little parsonage home, visiting the sick, comforting the mourners, teaching in the Sabbath-schools and keeping a most hospitable home. Her student-life was continued. She read history, studied French and German and took care of three daughters, who came to them and found a happy home-welcome. The two younger daughters graduated from Vassar College as the valedictorians of their respective classes. The oldest was finely educated in a New England seminary. After years of earnest toil Mr. Perkins' health failed, and for fifteen years he was an invalid. Then the wife came to his assistance in the pulpit, writing sermons and preaching them to his people. She also went on the platform as a lecturer. She gave literary and temperance lectures before the crusade. Since the death of Mr. Perkins, 30th October, 1880, Mrs. Perkins has given nearly her whole time to temperance work. She has succeeded well as a public speaker. She also advocates woman suffrage. She is now editor of a paper, "A True Republic," which is becoming justly popular. She is the author of six or seven Sabbath-school books, most of them published in Boston. Her home is now in Cleveland, OH. She is at present the president of the Literary Guild of Cleveland and the Ramabai Missionary Circle, and superintendent of infirmary work for the Ohio Woman's Christian Temperance Union. In the temperance work she has been sent by the national society to Kansas, Texas and the Indian Territory, and many new unions and a revival of interest were the result of those missionary visits. Besides her own children, Mrs. Perkins has assisted nine orphans to secure an education, and they are now self-reliant men and women, who are grateful for her early assistance. At the death of Mr. Perkins, one-half of his large library was given to his native town, to start a free library in that sparsely settled region.

PERLEY, Miss Mary Elizabeth, educator and poet, born in Lempster, NH, 2nd July, 1863. She was educated in the public schools of her native State and in the New Hampshire Conference Seminary, Tilton, NH, after which she became a teacher in the public schools. A few years later she studied in Europe to fit herself to teach modern languages. She is now a teacher of French and German in the New Hampshire Conference Seminary. At an early age she began to contribute poems to the press. Sketches of her life and poems from her pen appear in several compilations. She is known as a graceful and finished poet.

PERRY, Miss Carlotta, born in Union City, MI, 21st October, 1848. Her father's name was William Reuben Perry. He was a descendant of English Quakers, who came to America in early colonial days. He was a man of sterling mental and moral qualities, a lover of books and especially zealous in the cause of education. Her mother's maiden name was Louisa M. Kimball. She was of Scotch ancestry. It was she who gave to Carlotta the gift of song. The death of her father, when she was eight years of age, and her childhood sorrow were the theme of her first verses. She has been represented again and again in all the leading magazines and papers of the country. She has written a great deal for the Harper publications and has had many stories and poems in "Lippincott's Magazine." There are few standard publications for the youth in which her name is not familiar. In 1880 she moved with her mother from Watertown, WI, to Milwaukee, WI. Three years later her mother died, and thus was severed a companionship that the long years had made peculiarly close and tender. Since that time Miss Perry has given herself more entirely than ever before to literary work, though she has been from early days a voluminous writer of prose and poetry. The recognition she has always received and the prompt acceptance of her manuscripts have united to give constant encouragement and inspiration. Her only book thus far is a volume of poems, published in 1889. There are selections from her pen in perhaps a dozen different volumes, notably Kate Sanborn's "Wit and Humor of American Women," Jessie O'Donnell's "Love Songs of Three Centuries," Higginson's collections of "American Sonnets," and in numerous religious, elocutionary and juvenile works. Miss Perry is now living in Chicago, IL, and is engaged in miscellaneous literary labors, chiefly devoting her versatile genius to prose fiction. She belongs to the Chicago Woman's Press League and is a member of a World's Fair committee on poetry and imaginative literature.

PERRY, Miss Nora, poet, born in Massachusetts, in 1841. Her parents removed to Providence, RI, in her childhood, and her father was engaged in mercantile business there. She was educated at home and in private schools. She received a varied and liberal training in many lines, and her literary talent was predominant always. At the age of eighteen she began to write for publication. Her first serial story, "Rosalind Newcomb," was published in "Harper's Magazine" in 1859. She went to Boston, which was long her home. There she became the correspondent of the Chicago "Tribune" and the Providence "Journal." She contributed many stories and poems to the magazines of the day. Her published books are "After the Ball, and Other Poems" (Boston, 1874 and 1879), "The Tragedy of the Unexpected, and Other Stories" (1880), "Book of Love Stories" (1881), "For a Woman" (1885), "New Songs and Ballads" (1886), "Flock of Girls" (1887), "Youngest Miss Lorton, and Other Stories" (1889), "Brave Girls" (1889), and "Her Lover's Friends, and Other Poems." Her most popular poem is "After the Ball," which has been many times republished under the title "Maud and Madge." Her work shows high thinking and careful polish. She died in Dudley, MA, 13th May, 1896.

PETERS, Mrs. Alice E. H., church and temperance worker, born in Dayton, OH, 13th March, 1845. Her father, Lewis Heckler, was an enterprising and successful man of business. From the date of his death, on her seventh birthday, misfortunes came in rapid succession. In her fourteenth year the family removed to Columbus, OH, and Alice undertook the herculean task of providing for the necessities oilier loved ones. Inexperienced and without previous training, she found few occupations open to girls, but desperation prepared her to meet every emergency, and she managed to keep the wolf from the door with the help of a sewing-machine. Hard and unjust were the experiences she encountered. Sometimes the purse was so low that she met all her obligations by under-

going the most rigid self-denial; not one dishonorable act or discourtesy marred her conduct to others during the four years of struggle. She had a fine sense of justice and an insatiable longing for knowledge. There being no public library, Alice often burned the "midnight oil," poring over her Bible and books procured from the Sundayschool. Biographies of the Wesleys and Fletchers made a deep impression on her mind. At the age of eighteen she became the wife of Oscar G. Peters, a christian gentleman, twenty-one years old. Together they economized to secure capital. Mr. Peters was then chief clerk in the Commissary Department. While her husband was stationed in Cleveland, Mrs. Peters took an active interest in the Sanitary Commission, making garments and scraping lint. In Fort Leavenworth she gathered one-hundred-fifty neglected children together and taught them unaided every Sabbath for eleven months, the length of time she remained there. Returning to Columbus in 1866, Mr. Peters engaged in the grocery business for ten years. A daughter was born to them in 1868, but died in 1869. That great bereavement has been an abiding sorrow. A year later their only son was born. When he was three years of age, his mother entrusted him daily to the care of her sister-in-law and devoted her energies to the temperance crusade for eleven weeks, speaking and praying in saloons and on the street. She has contributed by pen and means to furthering the Woman's Christian Temperance Union movement since its inception. Identifying herself with the Methodist Episcopal Church in her fifteenth year, Mrs. Peters became a charter member of both foreign and home missionary societies. The woman suffrage cause enlisted her active sympathy many years ago. She has delivered lectures on the subject and in every way in her power advanced its principles, being a member of the national executive board. For seven years her efforts have been given to the work of the Woman's Relief Corps. Through journalistic writing and poems Mrs. Peters has voiced the philanthropic and reform methods she advocates. Her diction is fluent and graceful, yet incisive, her address forceful and magnetic, her presence stately; her private life is the embodiment of persevering adherence to an exalted ideal. Deprived of text-book education, she has become through ceaseless endeavor a woman of broad general information and rare culture. By rigid application to systematic study, prescribed in the

Chautauqua course, she graduated in 1887 with nine seals on her diploma. Mr. Peters with his brother and a friend organized a large manufacturing company, which has become a business enterprise of worldwide reputation, and made it possible for Mr. and Mrs. Peters to further their philanthropic endeavors.

PETTET, Mrs. Isabella M., physician, born in Holstein, Germany, 6th June, 1848. She came to the United States in 1868, locating in Milwaukee, WI, where she became engaged in voluntary mission work connected with the Methodist Church. She went to

New York City in 1874, afterward connecting herself with the Mariner's Church of the New York Port Society, where she remained for three years. She commenced the study of medicine in 1878 and was graduated with honors in 1881 in the New York Medical College and Hospital for Women. She has an office in her residence in East Fifteenth street, a private dispensary in East Twenty-third street and an office in Newark, NJ, visiting the latter place two days in the week. She is a member of the New York County Medical Society, and is on the medical staff of the New York Medical College and Hospital for Women.

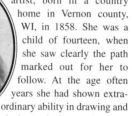

PHILLIPS, Mrs. L. Vance, artist, born in a country home in Vernon county, WI, in 1858. She was a child of fourteen, when she saw clearly the path marked out for her to follow. At the age often years she had shown extraordinary ability in drawing and was looked upon by her teachers as a child of talent. Thrown on her own resources at the age of fourteen, she not only supported herself, but, without other aid than her own courageous and determined spirit, she succeeded in obtaining a good education in the art to which she was devoted, as well as in other branches. She studied under the best teachers in Chicago, Cincinnati and New York. Limited always to her

own earnings, she has progressed steadily and won an enviable fame. Not only in the State of Nebraska, but in the art centers of the country, her work has received high praise, and the art magazines do her honor in their reviews of the Chicago yearly exhibits. In china-decorating, her specialty, she excels, also in figure-painting. Nebraska probably owes as much to her as to any one person for the present high plane art has attained within its borders. The four cities in which she has resided, Hastings, Grand Island, Kearney and Omaha, have felt her vivifying influence and breathe a more elevated atmosphere of art. She is the mother of one child, a daughter.

PHILLIPS, Miss Maude Gillette, author, born in Springfield, MA, 9th August, 1860. On the paternal side she comes from one of the oldest Dutch families in New York State, and still holding in possession the spacious house built by Peter Phillips, who came to this country two-hundred years and purchased his land of an Indian chief. Through her mother she is descended from General Eaton, of Revolutionary fame. Her mother's father traced his ancestry back to France. Miss

Phillips' home has always been in Springfield. In 1878 she entered the sophomore class of Wellesley College and was graduated in 1881. Her literary work consists of miscellaneous articles published in various periodicals, some of them under pennames, in the line of criticism and fiction. She has published a "Popular Manual of English Literature" (New York, 1885). That work has been characterized as the best of its kind now extant. It is carried out upon a philosophic system, that recognizes all literature as a unit based upon national and international influences. A characteristic feature is its colored charts, providing ocular summaries of the cotemporary civilians, authors, scientists, philosophers and artists of each age in Great Britain, France, Germany, Italy and Spain. A recent article has classified Miss Phillips as one of the most discriminating literary critics of the day. Though fond of books, she is anything but bookish. In short, she seems to be more a woman of the world than a scholar or author.

PIATT, Mrs. Sarah Morgan Bryan, poet, born in Lexington, KY, 11th August, 1836. Her grandfather, Morgan Bryan, a relative of Daniel Boone, was one of the earliest settlers of the state of Kentucky. He emigrated from North Carolina with Boone's party, and his "station" near Lexington, known still as "Bryan's Station," was one of the principal points of attack by the Indians who invaded Kentucky from the Northwest in August, 1782, having been besieged by them for several days before the celebrated battle of the Blue Lick. Mrs. Piatt's early childhood was passed near Versailles, in Woodford county, where her mother, a lovely and beautiful woman, whose maiden name was Mary Spiers, and who was related to the Stocktons, Simpsons and other early Kentucky families, died in her young womanhood, leaving her oldest child, Sarah, only eight years of age. Later she and a younger sister were placed by their father with an aunt, Mrs. Boone, in New Castle, where she went to school and was graduated in the Henry Female College. The loss of her mother, with various consequent influences, lent to a very sensitive nature a hue of sadness not easy to outgrow, and observable, though often in company with playful and humorous elements, in her writings early and late. It was in her young girlhood, in New Castle, her poetic temperament first manifested itself in the composition of verse. She had always been an eager reader of books, and had especial fondness for Shelley, Coleridge and Byron, among modern English poets, though she also read Moore, Scott, Mrs. Hemans and the others of their period. Some of her early verses, which often recalled and suggested such models, were shown by intimate friends to George D. Prentice, then editor of the "Louisville Journal," and he praised them highly, recognizing what seemed to him extraordinary poetic genius and confidently predicting the highest distinction for their author as an American poet. He wrote to her: "I now say emphatically to you again . . . that, if you are entirely true to yourself, and if your life be spared, you will, in the maturity of your powers, be the first poet of your sex in the United States. I say this not as what I think, but what I know." Her early published poems, appearing in the "Louisville Journal" and the "New York Ledger," were widely read and appreciated, and were perhaps more popular than her later and far better and more individual work. On 18th June, 1861, she became the wife of John James Piatt, and went with her husband to reside in Washington, DC. They remained in that city, where Mr. Piatt was in governmental employment, until 1867, seeing somewhat of the great events of the time. In July, 1867, they removed to Ohio, where, soon after, they made their home on a part of the old estate of Gen. W. H. Harrison, in North Bend, a few miles below Cincinnati, on the Ohio River. That home they left only for brief periods until they went to reside abroad. It is the place most endeared to Mrs. Piatt by love and sorrow, for there several of her children were born and two of them are buried. It was after her marriage Mrs. Piatt's more individual characteristics as a poet distinctly manifested themselves, especially the quick dramatic element seen in so many of her best poems, and the remarkable sympathy with and knowledge of child life, which Prof. Robertson has recognized in his volume entitled "The Children of the Poets" (London, 1886). The first volume in which her poems appeared was a joint volume by herself and husband, entitled, "The Nests at Washington, and Other Poems" (New York, 1864). Her next volume was "A Woman's Poems" (Boston, 1871), appearing without the author's name on the title page. That was followed by "A Voyage to the Fortunate Isles," etc. (1874); "That New World," etc. (1876); "Poems in Company with Children" (1877); and "Dramatic Persons and Moods" (1878). All the last-mentioned volumes were published in Boston. At the same time Mrs. Piatt has contributed to the various American magazines, the "Atlantic Monthly," "Scribner's Monthly," the "Century," "Harper's Magazine," and "St. Nicholas." In 1882 Mrs. Piatt accompanied her husband to Ireland, where he went as Consul of the United States to Cork, and has since that time resided in Queenstown. Since going to Ireland Mrs. Piatt, who perhaps has some remote Irish traces in her blood, as her maiden name might be held to indicate, has published "An Irish Garland" (Edinburgh, 1884); a volume of her "Selected Poems" (London, 1885); "In Primrose Time: a New Irish Garland" (London, 1886); "The Witch in the Glass, and Other Poems" (London, 1889), and "An Irish Wild-Flower" (London, 1891). The first, third and last of the volumes just mentioned contained pieces suggested by her experiences in

Ireland. A little joint volume by herself and husband, "The Children Out-of-Doors: a Book of Verses by Two in One House," was also published (Edinburgh, 1884), and all of those later volumes were issued simultaneously in the United States. Mrs. Piatt's foreign critics have been, perhaps, more generous in their appreciation than even those of America.

PICKEN, Mrs. Lillian Hoxie, educator, born in Clarksville, Mercer county, PA, 24th December, 1856. Her family moved to Michigan, and in that State she received a normal and university education. After graduation she taught for twenty years,  her work covering all the grades of schools, including six years in the Kansas State Normal School. She has been an instructor in twenty-three normal institutes, and she was conductor of the majority of them, has contributed to educational and literary periodicals for many years and has been identified with the educational interests of Kansas for eighteen years. She had that instinctive love for the work of teaching which is marked in all successful educators. In 1886 she became the wife of W. S. Picken, and her home is now in Iola, KS.

PICKETT, Mrs. Lasell Carbell, author, born in Chuckatuck, Nansemond county, VA, in 1848. She became the wife of Gen. George E. Pickett on 15th September, 1863, a short time after his famous charge at Gettysburg and the three-day conflict which linked his name to the line of heroes crowned with national homage. At the time of her marriage, Mrs. Pickett was a beautiful girl of fifteen. Her trousseau was smuggled across the lines in bales of hay, and the girlish bride-to-be, taking her fate in her own hands, donned the garb of an old country woman, who sold vegetables to the soldiers, and through strategy reached the camp of General Pickett, who was eagerly waiting for his young bride. From the day of her marriage she shared every phase of army life in camp and in battle, by the side of the hero whom she worshiped. When the war was over, an effort was made to take from General Pickett the privileges given him by the Grant-Lee cartel, and General and Mrs. Pickett went to Canada. Without money and far from friends, it was for the heroic woman to show her indomitable courage. She obtained a professorship in belles-lettres and took care of her family, until General Grant insisted that the cartel should be honored, and the General and his family returned to their home. General Grant then tendered General Pickett the position of Marshal of Virginia, but he chose to accept a situation in an insurance company in Norfolk, with a large salary. Then gladness and peace came to the wife and mother, but only for a little while, and she was left a heartbroken widow with the care of an orphaned son. Again her courage shone out. The sympathy of the South was aroused, and a subscription was started with eight-thousand dollars from one State, and pledges of thousands more from the devoted comrades of her dead hero. Hearing of that plan to put her above the anxiety of temporal want, Mrs. Pickett resolutely declined to accept financial aid, and soon secured a small government position sufficient to support herself and son. In 1891, after recovering from a distressing accident, she was threatened with total blindness. As with one heart, the South gave her assurances of sympathy and support, and messages flashed over the wires that she had only to command Pickett's old comrades, and they would rally to her aid. To her belongs the honor of uniting the Blue and the Gray in fraternal bonds. She has been the messenger of peace, trying to reconcile the two factions and bridge over the chasm once so broad and deep. No woman to-day is more widely known and honored than Mrs. Pickett. Beautiful still, attracting by her grace and dignity the worthy and illustrious of all circles; gifted with intellect and known as an author, though only by her pen-name, she commands admiration everywhere. With health broken and the almost total loss of her sight, she retains her position in the clerical service of the government, in Washington, and honestly earns her own living, when she could have been heir to the liberality of the South.

PIER, Miss Caroline Hamilton, lawyer, born in Fond du Lac, WI, 18th September, 1870. She was educated in the public schools of that city and was

Miss Harriet Pier.   Miss Caroline Pier.

Mrs. Kate Pier.
Miss Kate H. Pier.
The Pier Family of Lawyers.
From Photos by Small, Milwaukee.

graduated in the classical course of the high school, after studying music and perfecting herself in various womanly accomplishments, until ready to enter the law school of the Wisconsin University. That she did in 1889, finishing the course in 1891 and receiving the degree of LL.B. She belongs to the firm in Milwaukee, WI, of which her mother and two sisters are the other members. She is paying special attention to admiralty and maritime law and will make it a specialty. The women of Wisconsin should certainly appreciate the fact that their legislature has been far ahead of those of very many States in granting privileges to, or rather, declaring the rights of women. That Caroline H. Pier will follow in the footsteps of her mother and sister in helping to liberalize the code still more is a very natural belief on the part of those who have watched the remarkable career of the legal quartette thus far.

PIER, Miss Harriet Hamilton, lawyer, born in Fond du Lac, WI, 26th April, 1872. She is the third daughter of Mr. and Mrs. C. K. Pier, and a sister of Kate H. and Caroline H. Pier. All the daughters of Mrs. Pier have received her maiden name, Hamilton. Harriet was educated in the public schools of Fond du Lac, Madison and Milwaukee, and was graduated from the Milwaukee high school in 1889. She entered the law department of the Wisconsin University soon after, and at the end of two years she took her degree of LL.B. With her sister she is now studying the Polish language, all having practical knowledge of the German. The Pier family cannot fail to be known in future as the family of woman lawyers.

PIER, Mrs. Kate, court commissioner, born in St. Albans, VT, 22nd June, 1845. Her father was John Hamilton, and her mother's maiden name was Mary Meekin. Both parents were of Scotch-Irish descent. Kate Hamilton was educated in the public schools of Fond du Lac, WI, and she taught there for about three years. She became the wife of C. K. Pier, of Fond du Lac, in 1866. Her father died in 1870, and since that time her mother has lived with her, thus making it possible for Mrs. Pier to accomplish what no other woman in America, or in the world, has done. She has made a lawyer of herself and lawyers of her three daughters. Misses Kate H. Pier, Caroline H. Pier and Harriet H. Pier, with herself, constitute a law firm now practicing in Milwaukee, WI. Mrs. Pier

began business life by assuming the charge of her mother's and her own share of a large estate left by her father. Her success therein brought others to her for assistance in their own affairs, and so, from a general real estate business, in which there was naturally more or less legal work continually, Mrs. Pier, under the advice of her friends, entered upon the profession of law, in which she pays now and has always paid special attention to real estate and probate law. In addition to the three daughters of her own, Mrs. Pier has brought up two nephews from their infancy, being assisted by her mother in the care of the large family. She greatly desired that her daughters should begin business life under her personal supervision. She had started alone and knew what pioneer business undertakings meant for a woman. She wished her girls to benefit by her experience. As it was a new venture for girls to enter law schools, she desired to take the course with her oldest. Mrs. Pier and Kate therefore began their legal studies together in the law department of the Wisconsin State University, in 1866. It was a unique precedent and brought the talented pair immediately into public notice. Their companionship was evidently so pleasant, their manners were so perfect and their aims so high and womanly, that they met with general kindness and pronounced courtesy. In May, 1892, Mrs. Pier received a distinguished appointment; she was made court commissioner.

PIER, Miss Kate Hamilton, lawyer, born in Fond du Lac, WI, 11th December, 1868. Her father's name was C. K. Pier, a lawyer by profession. He was the first white child born in Fond du Lac county, in 1841, and Kate, the oldest of three daughters, was born on the same farm. Her mother's maiden name was Kate Hamilton. Both her parents' families were originally from Vermont. During the childhood and early school life of Kate H. Pier, as she is known (her mother being also a lawyer and distinguished as Kate Pier, without the initial), she lived on the homestead farm just outside the limits of Fond du Lac. She attended the German and English academy, where she learned the German language, which has enabled her so successfully to practice law in Milwaukee, WI. Later she went to the public schools and was graduated from the Fond du Lac high school in 1886, just twenty-five years after her mother had graduated from the same institution. A university course was then much desired, and

Kate would have entered upon it well prepared for special honors, but her mother's anxiety to be with her and to have her begin business life under her personal supervision led to their both entering the law department of the Wisconsin State University in September, 1886. Both mother and daughter accomplished the two-year course in one year by taking the work of the junior and senior classes simultaneously. Kate H. Pier therefore received the degree of LL.B. in 1887. She was very popular with the faculty and students, and was elected vice-president of the senior class. After receiving her degree she returned to Fond du Lac for one year, where she did some law business, but also spent much time in perfecting her knowledge of German and stenography. In 1888 she removed with her parents to Milwaukee and went into the law department of the Wisconsin Central Railroad for a year. Since that time she has been in general practice and has steadily gained in reputation for remarkable intellectual vigor and solid legal acquirements. She won her first victory in the Supreme Court of Wisconsin in September, 1889. In 1894 she was admitted to practice before the Supreme Court of the United States. She also practices before the Federal and State Courts of the Districts. From the bench and bar of Wisconsin she receives every mark of courtesy and respect. She has done some very praiseworthy legislative work, spending many weeks in looking after bills in the interest of women.

PIERCE, Mrs. Elizabeth Cumings, poet and author, born in Fulton, NY, in 1850. She comes of good American ancestry. Her grandfather, Levi Cumings, served with some distinction in the War of 1812, and three of her great-grandfathers served their country in the Revolution. Roger Williams, the founder of Providence, was an ancestor upon her father's side, and her mother, whose maiden name was Harriet Hartwell Perkins, had in her veins the blood of Samuel Gorton, even more than the ardent Roger the champion of religious liberty; the inventor, Joseph Jenckes; John Crandall, who was sent to jail for holding Baptist meetings, and Edward Wanton, who, from being an assistant in Quaker persecutions, turned Quaker preacher himself, and, in his descendants, furnished Newport colony with four governors, one of whom was the great-grandfather of Elizabeth.

As a child, Mrs. Pierce loved books and, as she phrases it, "all outdoors." She says she was remarkable for nothing, save fleetness of foot. There were plenty of books in her home, but she counted that day lost which was spent entirely indoors. The grass, the flowers, the birds, the insects, even the snow and the rain were her intimates. At about the age of eight she began her literary work by writing a dialogue, which she taught her little schoolmates during recess. The teacher, overhearing the performance, asked Elizabeth where she found it. "I made it up," was the reply. Whereupon the teacher accused the small author of falsifying and proceeded to exorcise the evil demon by means of a rose branch well furnished with thorns. The dots of blood upon her frock, where the thorns had impressed their exhortation to truthfulness, made no impression upon Elizabeth's spirit. After due apology to the parents, the teacher made the dialogue the chief feature of the "last day of school." Curiously enough, in spite of that early suggestion of future possibilities, the bugbear of Elizabeth's boarding-school days was composition-writing. In 1869 she became the wife of Rev. George Ross Pierce, a man of much culture and refinement. About 1876, over her maiden name, she began to write stories for children, which appeared in "Wide-Awake," the "Independent" and "St. Nicholas." Later, she began to write essays, under the pseudonym "Rev. Uriah Xerxes Buttles, D.D.," for the "Christian Union," and in those have appeared many shrewd and, at times, somewhat biting comments upon matters and things. A curious incident of that part of her work has been that what was pure fiction has been taken by people, of whose existence she never heard, for pure fact, or, more correctly, a description of performances in which they have taken part. Mrs. Pierce's stories, verses and essays have appeared not only in the publications noted, but also in "Harper's Weekly," "Lippincott's Magazine" and on one occasion the "Scientific Monthly." Her only long stories are "The Tribulations of Ebenezer Meeker," published in "Belford's Magazine" for May, 1889, and "The Story of an Artist," in "Music." In 1891 she published a juvenile serial, "Matilda Archambeau Van Dorn," in "Wide Awake," and she had a serial in "Little Men and Women" for 1892.

PIERCE, Mrs. Jane Means Appleton, wife of Franklin Pierce, the fourteenth President of the United States, born in Hampton, NH, 12th March, 1806, and died in Andover, MA, 2nd December, 1863. Her father, Rev. Jesse Appleton, D.D., became the president of Bowdoin College one year after her birth. Miss Appleton received a liberal education and was reared in an atmosphere of refined christian influences. She was a bright child, but her health was never strong, and she grew more and more delicate and nervous as she advanced to womanhood. In 1834 she became the wife of Hon. Franklin Pierce, then of Hillsborough and a member of the House of Representatives in Washington. Three sons were born to them, two of whom died in early youth. The youngest, Benjamin, was killed 6th January, 1853, in a railroad accident near Lawrence, MA. His death, which happened in the presence of his parents, shocked Mrs. Pierce so that she never fully recovered her health. In 1838 they removed to Concord, NH, where both are buried. Mrs. Pierce's illness kept Mr. Pierce from accepting various honors that were tendered to him by President Polk. When she went to the White House as mistress, she was in an exhausted condition, but she bore up well under the onerous duties of her position. In 1857 she went with her husband to the island of Madeira, where they remained for six months. In 1857 and 1858 they traveled in Portugal, Spain, France, Italy, Switzerland, England and Germany. Of her reign in the White House it may be said that her administration was characterized by refinement and exaltation. Politics she never liked. All her instincts were in the line of the good and the lovely in life. She was respected and admired by her cotemporaries.

PITBLADO, Mrs. Euphemia Wilson, was born in Edinburgh, Scotland. Her, father was a lawyer and was of the same family as Prof. John Wilson, better known as "Christopher North." Her mother was a near relative of Dr. Dick, the christian philosopher and astronomer. She received her education in Edinburgh and in Winnington Hall, near the old city of Chester, England. In that college all the students were obliged to study French and converse in it during school

hours, that they might speak it fluently. She received there a thorough musical and vocal education and the opportunity of hearing classical music. Afterward, in this country, she got up, and often participated in, concerts, and at one time was leader of a choir. Mrs. Pitblado was a student in the Chautauqua school for several years. She also studied drawing and painting, but had not much time for the development of that talent. Her home in Edinburgh having been broken up after the death of her father, she came to America to live with her oldest sister, the wife of a Presbyterian minister. Here she became the wife of Rev. C. B. Pitblado, D.D., of the Methodist Episcopal Church. She had previously become a member of that church and was greatly interested in its services, especially those in which women might speak, having been deprived of that privilege in the Presbyterian Church, the church of her father. She engaged with her husband in evangelistic work, and has led his meetings and supplied his pulpit. She helped in the inquiry meetings of the Boston Tabernacle, in response to a call from Rev. D. L. Moody for such christian workers. When the woman's crusade was inaugurated, she was ready to work with the Woman's Christian Temperance Union, and has been an active member ever since of that organization. While her husband was pastor of a church in Manchester, NH, a great temperance wave passed through the State, and Mrs. Pitblado was invited to give temperance addresses in many towns and villages, and she organized the Woman's Christian Temperance Union of Nashua, NH, with about sixty members. She always believed in the right of a sister with her brother to equal opportunities for education and work, and to that end she has advocated the advancement of women in every department of life. In their behalf she has spoken before conventions of the Woman's Christian Temperance Union, woman's suffrage associations, woman's foreign missionary societies and before the legislature in the capitol in Hartford, CT, and she has been sent a delegate to the annual Woman's Christian Temperance Union convention in New York, the annual Woman's Foreign Missionary Society in Lowell and Boston, MA, and to the National Woman Suffrage Association in Washington, DC. She has contributed articles from time to time to several papers on that and other related topics, besides giving addresses before clubs and societies. She is a member of the executive committee of the New England Woman Suffrage Association and an honorary member of the Campello, MA, League, of which she was the first president. She is a member of the National American Woman Suffrage Association. She is a charter member of the Woman's Educational and Industrial Union of Providence, RI, where her husband was at one time stationed. She has had five children, two only of whom are living.

PITTSINGER, Mrs. Eliza A., poet, born in Westhampton, MA, 18th March, 1837. Her father was of German descent, and a most humane man. Her mother was of Anglo-Saxon birth and blended unusual personal attractions with a nature bold and aspiring. At the age of sixteen Eliza was the teacher of a school in her native State, and she afterward occupied a position as proof reader and reviewer in a large stereotype establishment in Boston. She went to California, where she soon became known by her stirring war-songs and poems written during the Civil War. Her pen has kept pace with the march of thought that leaves its marks upon the present age. She writes wholly from inspiration. Her heart is filled with philanthropy and abhorrence of oppression. Freedom and justice to all is her motto. She accepts the theory of reincarnation, embodiments in the material form, and the varied experiences thereby obtained, to prepare it for its immortal destiny. That idea is embodied in a number of her most remarkable poems. She was chosen the poet for the fortieth anniversary celebration of the raising of the first American flag in California. She wrote a stirring poem for the four-hundredth anniversary of the birth of Martin Luther, which was recited by herself and others on that occasion. Her poems are varied and numerous. With the exception of eight years spent in the northern Atlantic States, she has lived in San Francisco since the days of the war. Her home is with her only sister, Mrs. Ingram Holcomb, who is known among her friends as a woman of sterling qualities.

PLIMPTON, Mrs. Hannah R. Cope, Woman's Relief Corps worker, born in Hanover, OH, 30th June, 1841. She is in a direct line of descendants from Oliver Cope, a Quaker, who came to America with William Penn in 1662. Her father, Nathan Cope, and mother, Elizabeth Taylor, were reared in West Chester, PA. After their marriage, in 1833, they emigrated to the "Far West," to eastern Ohio, Columbiana county, where their daughter Hannah was born, in the town of Hanover. In 1856 Mr. Cope moved to Cincinnati, OH, to give his children better educational advantages. In a few years Miss Cope became one of the teachers in the public schools of that city, teaching for four years in Mt. Auburn. It was during that time, in the spring of 1862, after the battle of Shiloh, when the wounded soldiers were sent up the Ohio river to Cincinnati, and a call was made for volunteers to help take care of them, that she, with her mother, responded and did what they could in ministering to the needs of the sick and afflicted ones, providing many delicacies and such things as were needed in a hastily-improvised hospital. Finally the old orphan asylum was secured and fitted up as comfortably as possible, and called the Washington Park Military Hospital. Many of the convalescent soldiers were entertained in the home of Miss Cope. After the close of the war she became the wife of Mr. Silas W. Plimpton, Jr., of Providence, RI, and moved to Caldwell county, MO, residing there nine years, and moving from there to her present home in Denison, IA. She has always taken an active part in church and temperance work, having served as treasurer and secretary in various societies, and as secretary of the local Woman's Christian Temperance Union for fifteen years. At the institution of John A. Logan Corps No. 56, in March, 1885, in Denison, with Mrs. McHenry as its president, Mrs. Plimpton was her secretary. The following year Mrs. McHenry was elected department president, and Mrs. Plimpton served as department secretary. The next year she was department instituting and installing officer, and in 1889, during Mrs. Stocking's administration as department president of Iowa, she was department secretary, working again with Mrs. McHenry, who was department treasurer. In December, 1889, Mrs. McHenry was elected conductor of John A. Logan Corps No. 56, and Mrs. Plimpton was her assistant. They both served in that capacity until the National convention, held in Boston, 5th August, 1890, when she was appointed national secretary of the Woman's Relief Corps. In the fall of 1891 she was elected matron of the National Woman's Relief Corps Home, in Madison, Lake county, OH.

PLOWMAN, Mrs. Idora M., author, born near Talladega, AL, in 1843. She is known by her pen-name "Betsy Hamilton." She is a daughter of the late Gen. William B. McClellan and of Mrs. Martha Roby McClellan. Her father traced the lineage of his family to William Wallace, of Scotland. He was a graduate of West Point, and before the Civil War held the office of Brigadier-General, commanding the militia troops of the counties of Talladega, Clay and Randolph, AL. While quite young, Idora Elizabeth McClellan, became the wife of a brilliant young lawyer, Albert W. Plowman, of Talladega. Mr. Plowman died suddenly a few years after marriage. Recently Mrs. Plowman became the wife, in Atlanta, GA, of Capt. M. V. Moore, of the editorial staff of the Atlanta "Constitution." Their home is in Auburn, AL. "Betsy Hamilton" is the author of innumerable dialect sketches depicting the humorous side of life, life as seen by herself on the old time plantations, and in the backwoods among the class denominated as Southern "Crackers." Her first sketch," "Betsy's Trip to Town," written in 1872, was printed in a Talladega paper. The article revealed at once the fine and wonderful genius of its author. She was afterward regularly engaged for a number of years on the great southern weekly, "Sunny South," and on the "Constitution," papers published in Atlanta, GA. Her articles were entitled "The Backwoods," "Familiar Letters," and "Betsy Hamilton to Her Cousin Saleny." At the personal request of Mr. Conant, the editor of "Harper's Weekly," several of her sketches went to that paper, and were illustrated as they appeared in its columns. The late Henry W. Grady was her warm personal friend and aided much in bringing her talent before the world. Her articles have been copied in some of the European papers. While the "Betsy Hamilton Sketches" have given their author a wide fame and deserved popularity, doubtless her highest and most popular achievements have been reached in her public recitations and impersonations upon the stage of the characters she has so vividly portrayed. Her acting is to the very life; it has been pronounced of the very highest and most superb order, one writer calling her the "Joe Jefferson" among women.

PLUMB, Mrs. L. H., financier, born in Sand Lake, NY, 23rd June, 1841. She has lived in Illinois since 1870.Her husband died in 1882, and after his death she took charge of his estate. She was elected vice-president of the Union National Bank of Streator, IL, of which her husband had been president for years. She is a woman of liberal education, sound business judgment, great tact and wide experience in practical affairs. She is interested in temperance work. Her work in that reform began in 1877. She was one of the charter members of the Woman's Temperance Publishing Association. She was one of the charter members and originators of the temperance hospital in Chicago, IL. Since 1890, while retaining her business interests in Streator, she has made her home in Wheaton, IL, in order to superintend the education of her four children, who are attending school there. Mrs. Plumb is as successful a home-maker as she is a business woman and financier.

PLUNKETT, Mrs. Harriette M, sanitary reformer, born in Hadley, MA, 6th February, 1826. Her maiden name was Harriette Merrick Hodge. The town, though a community of farmers, had the unusual and perpetual advantage of an endowed school, Hopkins Academy, which early in the century was a famous fitting school, and even after its prestige as such was eclipsed by Andover and Exeter, it still afforded exceptional opportunities to the daughters of the town, who could better be spared from breadwinning toil than the sons. There Miss

Hodge obtained her early education, alternating her attendance in school with terms of teaching in the district schools in her own and adjoining towns, till, in 1845, desiring to improve herself still farther, she became a pupil of the Young Ladies' Institute of Pittsfield, MA, at that time one of the leading schools in the country. There, in 1846, she was graduated, being one of the first class who received diplomas. She taught in the school a year, and then became the wife of Hon. Thomas F. Plunkett. Theirs proved a remarkably happy union, which lasted twenty-eight years, till his death in 1875, during which time she was principally absorbed in domestic duties and the care of a large family. In 1869 he had a very important share in the establishment of the Massachusetts State Board of Health, the first State board established in this country. Mrs. Plunkett became greatly interested in sanitary matters through her husband's influence, and was especially anxious to awaken in the women of America an interest in the theory and practice of household sanitation. She was convinced that, if the women of the country would inform themselves of what is needed, and see that it is put in practice, there would be a great gain in the saving and lengthening of life and in making it more effective and happy while it lasts. To promote that cause she wrote many newspaper articles, and in 1885 published a valuable book "Women, Plumbers and Doctors," containing practical directions for securing a healthful home, and she probably would have continued to fulfill what seemed a mission to her, had not a great calamity befallen her only son, Dr. Edward L. Plunkett. In his twenty-first year, while studying to become a mechanical engineer, he became totally blind. After the first shock and grief were passed, he resolved to study medicine and enrolled himself as a member of the College of Physicians and Surgeons of New York, his mother becoming his reader and constant assistant. Through the use of pictures and models, she was enabled to make herself his intelligent helper, and by taking a five-year course instead of the usual three, he was graduated with honor and at once set about the instruction of medical undergraduates in the capacity of "coach" or "quiz-master," a work to which he brought great enthusiasm and indomitable will, and in which he had achieved notable success, when, in 1890, after a week's illness, he died. The work to which Mrs. Plunkett

had dedicated herself having thus fallen from her hands, she at once resumed her pen and returned to sanitary subjects, though at the same time producing other articles, political, educational and aesthetic, for various magazines and journals. One on the increasing longevity of the human race, entitled "Our Grandfather Died Too Soon," in the "Popular Science Monthly," attracted wide attention. Her leaning toward the prevention and healing of disease is ever conspicuous, and she is probably most widely known in connection with the establishment and growth of a cottage hospital in Pittsfield, MA, called "The House of Mercy," started in 1874, of which she is president. It was the first one of its class, to be supported by current contributions from all religious denominations, in this country. She belongs to the great army of working optimists.

POLK, Mrs. Sarah Childress,
wife of James K. Polk, eleventh Governor of Tennessee and eleventh President of the United States, born in Murfreesboro, TN, 4th September, 1803, and died in Nashville, TN, 16th August, 1891. She was the daughter of Joel and Elizabeth Childress of Rutherford county, TN. She was educated in the Moravian Seminary, Salem, NC, and on 1st January, 1824, she became the wife of Mr. Polk, then a member of the legislature of Tennessee, of which during the previous session he had been clerk. They took up their residence in Columbia, Maury county, where Mr. Polk had for some time practiced law. The following year he was elected to Congress, and she accompanied him to the National Capital. There she became noted for her quick sympathy, ready tact and graceful manners, for a lovely and inspiring womanhood, and for her devotion to her husband, whose ambition in political life she seconded. Theirs was a union of heart and life, full of strength and blessing to both, growing in tenderness and devotion. Mrs. Polk stamped herself on the social life of Washington and impressed all with whom she was brought into contact as being a woman of deep piety and profound convictions, a noble character made up of strength, individuality and gentleness, clinging love and single-hearted devotion to her husband,

relatives and friends. Her experience in the National Capital prepared her for the duties that devolved upon her as the wife of the governor of the State in 1839. In Nashville she became at once the social leader. She was as successful as Mr. Polk was, though he was then declared to be one of the most statesmanlike, prudent, thoughtful and conscientious of the governors of Tennessee. After a brief season of rest from official cares he was elected President of the United States. In 1845 they again became residents of Washington. During his term of office Mrs. Polk achieved her greatest successes as a social leader. As the mistress of the White House she set an example of American simplicity that has become one of the traditions of the presidential mansion. Gentle, dignified, courteous, approachable and bright, she was esteemed equally by the high and the lowly. Well-informed, thoughtful, vivacious, her conversation had a charm for all, while she kept strictly within the sphere of a true and noble womanhood. In domestic life she did not neglect the little duties of the household, while she kept in sympathy with her husband's deeper cares. She banished dancing from the President's mansion and wine from the table, except at the State dinners, and it was all done so kindly that none were offended. Upon the close of his term they journeyed homeward by way of New Orleans and the Mississippi river, stopping in Memphis for a day or two. There the ex-president in a speech to his friends predicted the greatness of our country and stated it to be his intention to cross the Atlantic, accompanied by his wife, and pass a year in foreign travel before settling down in the home he had purchased in Nashville. A few days after his arrival in Nashville, Mr. Polk was seized with cholera and survived but a little while. He died generally regretted. His widow since then and until her death lived faithfully devoted to the memory of her dead. She gave herself with earnest purpose to the work of making others happy. She was a center of social attention in the city, and with gracious tact and unfailing kindness she made her circle bright. Having no children of her own, she took a little niece, two years old, and reared her with motherly care. From her she received the dutiful and loving devotion of a daughter, and her age was gladdened by the voices of children and children's children gathering about that daughter and her child.

POLLARD, Miss Josephine, poet and author, born in New York, NY, 17th October, 1834, and died there 15th August, 1892. Her father was a native of New Braintree, MA. While he was a child, the family removed to Cazenovia, NY. On reaching his majority he went to New York City to make his fortune, and succeeded in a few years, by his own efforts, in becoming one of the leading architects in the metropolis. Miss Pollard's mother was of good old Puritan stock, well educated, and a woman of noble impulses. At an early age Josephine gave evidence of poetic talent, and, while a pupil in Springler Institute, she wrote a poem descriptive of Cole's pictures, the "Voyage of Life," which were then on public exhibition. That was her first published poem. In school, composition day was her delight, and her efforts were nearly always in rhyme. She wrote many verses and songs, that have been widely sung. In person she was never strong, the frail body often hindering her in her good work. Many of her poems appeared in the Harper periodicals and in the New York "Ledger." She was a frequent contributor to those periodicals. She wrote many stories, among them the "Gypsy Books." Her later works were written in words of one syllable, "Our Hero, Gen. Grant," "Life of Christopher Columbus," "The Bible for Young People" and "The Wonderful Story of Jesus." When the Sorosis Club was organized, she was one of its charter members. Owing to her continued ill health, she felt constrained to withdraw. She remained in warm sympathy with the club and was always interested in its welfare.

POLLOCK, Mrs. Louise, pioneer kindergartner, born in Erfurt, Prussia, 29th October, 1832. Her father, Frederick Wilhelm Plessner, was an officer in the Prussian army. Retiring from active service and pensioned by Emperor Wilhelm, he devoted the rest of his life to literary labors. His history, German and French grammars, arithmetic and geometry were used as text-books in the Prussian military schools. He took special delight in directing the education of his youngest daughter, Louise, who at an early age showed a marked preference for literary pursuits. On her way to Paris, where she was sent at the age of sixteen to complete her knowledge of French, she made the acquaintance of George H. Pollock, of Boston, MA, whose wife she became about two years later in London. Even at that time she was interested in books treating of the subjects of infant training, hygiene and physiology. In 1859, with five children constituting their family, Mrs. Pollock was first made acquainted with the kindergarten philosophy, by receiving from her German relatives a copy of everything that had been published upon the subject up to that time. Her first work as an educator was in her own family. Her husband being overtaken by illness and financial reverses, Mrs. Pollock began to turn her ability to pecuniary account, and commenced her literary work in earnest. Executing a commission from Mr. Sharland, of Boston, she selected seventy songs from the German for which she wrote the words. Then she translated four medical works for Dio Lewis, and a number of historical stories, besides writing for several periodicals. In 1861 her "Child's Story Book" was published. Among the kindergarten works received from Germany was a copy of Lena Morgenstern's "Paradise of Childhood," which she translated in 1862 into English. Adopting the system in her own family, she became so enthusiastic on the subject that she sent her daughter Susan to Berlin, where she took the teacher's training in the kindergarten seminary there. In 1862, upon the request of Nathaniel T. Allen, principal of the English and classical school in West Newton, MA, Mrs. Pollock opened a kindergarten in connection therewith, the first pure kindergarten in America. During 1863 she wrote four lengthy articles on the kindergarten, which were published in the "Friend of Progress" in New York. Those were among the earliest contributions to kindergarten literature in this country. In 1874 Mrs. Pollock visited Berlin for the purpose of studying the kindergarten system in operation there. Upon her return to America in October, 1874, the family removed to the city of Washington, where her Le Droit Park Kindergarten was opened, and her series of lectures to mothers was commenced. Her sixty hygienic and fifty-six educational rules, which she wrote in connection with those lectures, were first published in the "New England Journal of Education." Other works from her pen are the "National Kindergarten Manual" (Boston, 1889), "National Kindergarten Songs and Plays" (Boston, 1880), and her latest song-book, "Cheerful Echoes" (Boston, 1888). She continues to write for educational papers. In 1880, through President Garfield, who was a patron of her daughter's school, she presented a memorial to Congress, asking an appropriation to found a free National Kindergarten Normal School in Washington. That was signed by all the chief educators of this country, but was unsuccessful. Nothing daunted, she presented another memorial to Congress the next year through Senator Harris, of Tennessee, and the succeeding year one by Senator Ingalls, of Kansas, but without success. Then she turned from Congress to providence, and with better success, for, after giving a very profitable entertainment on 12th February, 1883, the Pensoara Free Kindergarten, with the motto, "Inasmuch as ye have done it to the least of these, ye have done it unto me," was opened. In order to raise the necessary funds for its continuance, a subscription list was started at the suggestion of Mrs. Rutherford B. Hayes, who, during her life, was a regular subscriber. That list has had the names of all the Presidents with their cabinets, and the school has been maintained by subscriptions ever since. In connection with that kindergarten Mrs. Pollock has a nursery maids' training class in the care of young children. In Buffalo, San Francisco, Boston, Chicago and other places, nursery maids' training schools have lately been opened upon somewhat the same plan. Mrs. Pollock is the principal, with her daughter, of the National Kindergarten and Kindergarten Normal Institute, for the training of teachers, over a hundred of whom are filling honorable positions throughout the country.

POMEROY, Mrs. Genie Clark, author, born in Iowa City, IA, in April, 1867. Her father, Rush Clark, when a young man, was an Iowa pioneer. Both parents were college graduates. Her mother was a teacher. The mother yielded her young life that her child might live. Mr. Clark again married in a few years, and to this union several children were born, of which two are now living. When Genie Clark was eleven years old she went to Washington, DC, to be with her father during his second term in Congress. After his death in 1879, she returned to her former home and lived with her guardian at his country seat near Iowa City. Two years were afterward spent in Schellsburgh, PA, with relatives. At the age of fourteen she was fitted in the public schools of Iowa City for the University, from which, after the freshman year, she was sent to Callanan College, in Des Moines, where she studied two years. There she met and became the wife of Carl H. Pomeroy, a son of the president of the college. After their marriage Mr. Pomeroy took the chair of history in the college, and Mrs. Pomeroy remained as a pupil. Both afterward returned to Iowa City and entered school, the one in the post-graduate law department, and the other in the collegiate. In 1888 they moved to Seattle, Wash., and afterward to Hoquiam, in the same State. In Seattle Mrs. Pomeroy for the first time made literature a matter of business as well as pleasure, contributing to the "Press" "Washington Magazine," "Woman's Journal" of Boston, "Pacific Christian Advocate," "Time," "West Shore," and other publications. Mrs. Pomeroy writes bright and strong stories, sketches and essays, but it is chiefly as a poet she is known. Her verse is delicate, fanciful and pure. She is an omnivorous reader.

POND, Mrs. Nella Brown, dramatic reader, born in Springfield, MA, 7th May, 1858. Her maiden name was Nella Frank Brown. She is an accomplished reader and stands in the front rank of the women of America who have made their mark upon the platform. Her father, Dr. Enoch Brown, was an eminent physician of Springfield some years, and afterward moved to New York, where he died, while Mrs. Pond was quite young. The family then went to Middletown, CT, and finally became permanent residents of Boston. It was there Mrs. Pond's natural dramatic talent became known to a few friends, who induced her to become a member of the Park Dramatic Company, an amateur organization of great excellence. She appeared for the first time as Margaret Elmore in "Love's Sacrifice" and achieved an instantaneous success. She remained with the company during that season, and her great dramatic talent secure for her a widespread popularity and won recognition from prominent professionals. She received numerous flattering offers from managers of leading metropolitan theaters, but refused them all, having conscientious scruples against going on the stage. Mrs. Thomas Barry, then leading lady of the Boston Theater, became greatly interested in her and advised that she appear upon the lyceum platform as a reader, prophesying that she would soon become celebrated. Through Mrs. Barry's exertions an engagement was effected with the Redpath Lyceum Bureau, and Mrs. Pond at once assumed a position and gained a popularity which successive seasons have only served to intensify. In 1880 she became the wife of Ozias W. Pond, of Boston, the well-known manager of musical and literary celebrities. Her husband died in February, 1892. Her home is in Boston, MA.

POOLE, Mrs. Hester Martha, author, artist and critic, was born in western Vermont, about 1843. Her maiden name was Hester M. Hunt. She inherited poetical and literary tastes, which were developed by study and travel. At an early age she wrote poems and stories, which were often published. After she became the wife of C. O. Poole, and while taking an extended tour through Europe, she furnished a series of letters to daily papers in New York City, in which was begun her first regular contributions to the press. Interrupted for some time by domestic duties, her contributions were resumed in the "Continent" and "Manhattan" magazines. Those consisted chiefly of illustrated articles upon the arts of decoration, and have been followed in various publications by a large number of critical and descriptive essays upon those and similar topics. Her series of articles applied to the house has appeared in the "Home Maker," another in "Good Housekeeping," and a large number of her illustrated articles appeared from time to time in the "Decorator and Furnisher" of New York. In them have been furnished original schemes for house decoration, which have been widely copied. Another series, "From Attic to Cellar," was furnished to the "Home Magazine," and a still longer series, "The Philosophy of Living," was contributed by Mrs. Poole to "Good Housekeeping." In spite of her fondness for art, all her tastes incline her rather to studies of a nature purely literary, ethical or reformatory. Upon one or another of those topics she has frequently given conversations or lectures in drawing-rooms. In those fields also her papers have found acceptance with the "Chautauquan," the "Arena," the "Union Signal," the "Ladies' Home Journal" and many others. During several years she edited with success a column upon "Woman and the Household" in a weekly newspaper of a high character, and also wrote leading editorials for journals on ethics and reform. Her last book, entitled "Fruits and How to Use Them" (New York, 1891), is unique and has attained a large circulation. Mrs. Poole is known as an enthusiastic worker and advocate for the advancement of women, with their higher education. She has been almost from the beginning an officer of Sorosis, is a member of the New York Woman's Press Club, and believes that the progress of humanity depends upon the unfolding of a noble womanhood. Some of Mrs. Poole's verses, always tender and graceful, are to be found in "Harper's Encyclopædia of Poetry." Her present residence is in Metuchen, NJ.

POPE, Mrs. Cora Scott Pond, born in Sheboygan, WI, 2nd March, 1856. She is a second cousin on her father's side of General Winfield Scott. Her father was born in Calais, ME, and her mother in St. John, New Brunswick. After marriage they went immediately to the West, settling first in Sheboygan, in 1850, and then moved to Two Rivers, Wabasha, MN, Chippewa Falls, and finally settled in Eau Claire, WI. Miss Pond was the third in a family of eight children, three girls and five boys. She attended the public schools regularly and added to her already robust constitution by outdoor games, until she was fifteen years old. She could run as fast as the boys, who were invariably her playmates. There were no books or libraries in the town, and from fifteen to twenty-one years of age she devoted herself to music and social interests. She desired above all things to finish her education in the University of Wisconsin. Her father was a successful inventor of machinery and booms for milling and logging pur-

poses. Her mother was indefatigable in her care of the children. The question of expense was a crucial one, with so large a family to support, but it was decided that her wish should be gratified and, in her twenty-second year, Miss Pond entered the State University. She was unable to interest herself particularly in mathematics or the languages, but whatever related to the English and to history, literature, rhetoric and oratory was especially attractive. She decided to fit herself as a teacher of oratory and, not wishing to finish any prescribed course in the university, after studying there three years, she set out for Boston alone in 1880, one of the first young women in her city, in those days, to go away from home, and adopt a profession. She entered the department of oratory of the New England Conservatory of Music. In 1883 she was graduated first in her class. For one year afterward she taught with her professor in the conservatory. While there, she was much interested in woman's work at the polls, in woman suffrage and temperance, and because of special work done alone in the hardest ward of the city, where no woman had ever labored before, she was invited by Mrs. Lucy Stone to help them organize the State for woman suffrage. Miss Pond had intended to teach for ten years and then go West and take up the work for women, but she decided to accept the proposition. She continued the work and organized eighty-seven woman suffrage leagues in Massachusetts, more than had ever been organized before, arranged lectures, spoke in the meetings and raised money to carry on the State work for six years. Although engaged in that work, she was interested in every reform. Her first great effort in raising money was in 1887, when she organized a woman suffrage bazaar. It was held in Music Hall, Boston, for one week. Over six-thousand dollars were cleared. After that most of her time was spent in raising money for State work. While teaching in the conservatory, Miss Pond arranged five-minute sketches from Dickens, Shakespeare and other authors, and presented them with her scholars to the public in the conservatory. In 1889 she arranged national historical events in the same way to raise money for the State work. The inventive mind of her father showed itself in that. The pictures for dramatic expression arranged themselves, in one evening, spontaneously in her mind. She called it "The National Pageant" and copyrighted her programme. The idea was not at first received with enthusiasm by some of the prominent women of Boston. Two only stood by her and said "Go on." "The National Pageant" was given in Hollis Street Theater, 9th May, 1889. The house was crowded at two dollars per ticket. It was a grand success. Over one-thousand dollars were cleared at one matinée performance. Miss Pond decided to give up her State work, devote herself to "The National Pageant" and give it for various societies of women to help them raise money to carry on their work. Seconded by Mrs. Mary A. Livermore, who had always been to her as a godmother in her Boston work, and by a prominent business woman of Boston, Miss Amanda M. Lougee, Miss Pond made her venture and carried it into the large cities of the country, and has given one performance each month since then for local societies, and raised many thousands of dollars for charitable purposes. She gave it in Chicago, in the Auditorium, the first historical work given after the decision by Congress to hold the Columbian Exposition in that city. In one night six-thousand-two-hundred-fifty dollars were cleared. While in Chicago, Miss Pond met a man of excellent business ability, John T. Pope, who assisted her in the pageant for over a year. They were married 29th December, 1891, and make their home in Chicago.

POPE, Mrs. Marion Manville, poet and author, born in La Crosse, WI, 13th July, 1859. She is the daughter of Mrs. Helen A. Manville, the well-known author, of La Crosse. Marion was an active, intelligent and precocious child. In her early childhood she wrote verses in great numbers, and most of her work was surprisingly good to come from the pen of one so young. Some of those earlier productions she included with later ones in her first published book, "Over the Divide" (Philadelphia, 1888). The volume has passed through several editions, and the critics of high repute have received it favorably. Many of the poems contained in the book are much read by dramatic readers. Miss Manville became the wife on 22nd September, 1891, of Charles A. Pope, of Valparaiso, Chili, and her permanent home will be in that city. She traveled after marriage in Cuba and Mexico. Mrs. Pope is a woman of liberal educa-

tion and varied talents and accomplishments. She is a dramatic reader, a pupil of the Lyceum School in New York City. She is an artist of merit, and her work includes crayon, oils and pen and ink. She models well, and some of her heads are genuinely artistic. She is a social favorite and delights in society. Her poems have found wide currency, but she believes that her best work is her prose fiction. Her love for children has led her to write for them, and in their behalf she has contributed both prose and verse to "St. Nicholas," "Wide Awake," "Our Little Ones," "The Nursery," "Babyhood" and other periodicals devoted to the young. Her work shows, not only true poetic gifts, but also that other indispensable thing, careful thinking and proper attention to form, without which no author can do work that will endure. Her poems are clear-cut and finely polished.

PORTER, Mrs. Alice Hobbins, journalist, born in Staffordshire, England, 9th February, 1854. She is a daughter of Joseph Hobbins, M.D., Fellow of the Royal College of Physicians and Surgeons, and of Sarah Badger Jackson, of Newton, MA, a descendant on her father's side of the famous Jackson family, which gave forty of its men, including Gen. Michael Jackson, the friend of Washington, to the Revolutionary War, and on her mother's side from the Russell family, of Rhode Island. Jonathan Russell, her grand-uncle, was one of the commissioners who negotiated the concluding treaty with Great Britain in Ghent, and later was minister plenipotentiary to Sweden. His wife was educated in the school of Madame Campan, in St. Germain, and received a gold medal from Napoleon I, in 1807, for her skill in drawing and painting. She afterward painted under Benjamin West, who gave her his palette of colors which, with some drawings presented to her by Verney, are still preserved in the family. Mrs. Porter's early life was spent in Madison, WI. In 1877 she went to Chicago and made her first venture in journalism as correspondent for the Milwaukee "Sentinel" and the Cincinnati "Enquirer," contributing frequently to the Chicago "Times" and "News," and to the Wisconsin "State Journal." She became a member of the "Inter-Ocean" staff and was promoted successively to religious editor, dramatic editor, and finally as writer of special articles. In 1879 she went to New York as correspondent for several western newspapers, and while there was regularly on the staff of the New York "Graphic," and a frequent contributor to the New York "Sun," and occasionally to the "Herald" and "World." She contributed to "Harper's Magazine" and "Bradstreet's," and wrote the prize sketch in a Christmas number of the "Spirit of the Times," which was entirely made up of contributions from the eight best-known women correspondents of America. Later she visited Europe, twice as correspondent for New York and western papers, and after she became the wife of Robert P. Porter, journalist and statistician, she accompanied him on his industrial investigations abroad. She wrote a series of letters for a syndicate, embracing thirty of the principal journals of the country, and special letters to the New York "World," Philadelphia "Press," "National Tribune," and other papers, most of which were reprinted in England. Up to the time of her marriage she wrote principally under the pen-name "Cress." When Mr. Porter founded the New York "Press," in 1887, Mrs. Porter joined the editorial staff and contributed special articles, which attracted wide-spread attention. She edited Mr. Porter's letters and essays on the condition of the working classes abroad. During Mr. Porter's residence in Washington as superintendent of census, Mrs. Porter has been occupied with family cares and social obligations, and has written only in aid of working women, educational projects and in behalf of suffering children. She has recently assumed the editorship of a paper in eastern Tennessee, in the development of which part of the country Mr. Porter is greatly interested.

PORTER, Mrs. Florence Collins, temperance worker, born in Caribou, ME, 14th August, 1853. Her father, Hon. Samuel W. Collins, was one of the early pioneers of Aroostook county. Her early surroundings were those incidental to a new country. In November, 1873, she became the wife of Charles W. Porter, a Congregational clergyman. Besides the pastorate in Caribou, her husband has also a church in Old Town and Winthrop, their present home. Her interests have been longer identified with Caribou, for not only were her girlhood days spent there, but ten years also of her

married life. At about fifteen years of age she began to write for the newspapers and periodicals. Since then she has done more or less journalistic work and has also contributed short sketches and stories to various publications. During the last five years she has been interested in public temperance reform, with good success as a lecturer. She first came into public work upon the platform through her husband's encouragement, influence and cooperation. At the formation of the Nonpartisan Woman's Christian Temperance Union, in Cleveland, OH, in 1889, she was chosen national secretary of literature and press-work. In that capacity she is now actively engaged, with plenty of work to do and widening possibilities.

PORTER, Miss Rose, religious novelist, was born in New York, NY. Her father, David Collins Porter, was a wealthy New Yorker. He died in 1845, while Rose was an infant. Her mother was a cultured woman, the daughter of an English army officer. Miss Porter's early years were spent in New York and in their summer home in Catskill-on-the-Hudson. She was educated in New York, with the exception of a year abroad. After completing her education, she and her mother made their home in New Haven, CT. The mother died several years ago, and Miss Porter has kept her home in New Haven, where, with her servants, she lives in English style. Her books have a large sale. Her first success was "Summer Drift-Wood for the Winter Fire." Notwithstanding the fact that she has been an invalid for years, her pen has been busy and prolific, and illness has not been sufficient to break her courageous spirit or to check the operations of her bright, active, well-stored mind. Her work is all of the moral order, but she is by no means a sickly sentimentalist. Her books are healthful intone. As a writer of quiet religious romance she stands in the first rank. Fastidious critics in both secular and religious papers commend her work for its evident and successful mission to the world, graceful style and pure English. She has published thirty-three or more volumes.

POST, Mrs. Amalia Barney Simons, woman suffragist, born in Johnson, Lamoille county, VT,

30th January, 1836. Her ancestors were prominent in early American history, one of them, Thomas Chittenden, being the first Governor of Vermont, and several were officers in the Revolutionary War and in the American army and navy in the War of 1812. Mrs. Post is the daughter of William Simons and Amalia Barney, of Johnson. Both parents were of sterling integrity and patriotism, and of great strength of character. Miss Simons, in Chicago, 1864, became the wife of Morton E. Post, and with her husband crossed the plains in 1866, settling in Denver, CO, and moving to Cheyenne, WY, in 1867, where they have since lived. Her life in Wyoming, has been closely identified with the story of obtaining and maintaining equal political rights for Wyoming women, and to her, perhaps more than to any other individual, is due the fact that the women of Wyoming to-day the right of suffrage. In 1869 the first legislature of Wyoming Territory granted to women the right to vote. The movement was an experimental one, and few expected that the women of the Territory would avail themselves of the privileges granted by the law. That the movement was a success and became a permanent feature of Wyoming's political history was due to the dignified and wise use of its privileges by the educated and cultured women of the Territory. Without lessening the respect in which they were held, Mrs. Post and other prominent women quietly assumed their political privileges and duties. Mrs. Post was for four years a member of the Territorial Central Committee of the Republican party. Several times she served on juries, and she was foreman of a jury composed of six men and six women, before which the first legal conviction for murder was had in the Territory. In 1871 she was a delegate to the Woman's National Convention in Washington, DC, and before an audience of five-thousand people in Lincoln Hall she told of woman's emancipation in Wyoming. In the fall of 1871 the Wyoming legislature repealed the act granting suffrage to women. Mrs. Post, by a personal appeal to Governor Campbell, induced him to veto the bill. To Mrs. Post he said: "I came here opposed to woman suffrage, but the eagerness and fidelity with which you and your friends have per-

formed political duties, when called upon to act, has convinced me that you deserve to enjoy those rights." A determined effort was made to pass the bill over the governor's veto. A canvass of the members had shown that the necessary two-thirds majority would probably be secured, though by the narrow margin of one vote. With political sagacity equal to that of any man, Mrs. Post decided to secure that one vote. By an earnest appeal to one of the best educated members, she won him to its support, and, upon the final ballot being taken upon the proposal to pass the bill over the governor's veto, that man, Senator Foster, voted "No," and woman suffrage became a permanency in Wyoming. From 1880 until 1884 Mrs. Post, whose husband was delegate to Congress from Wyoming during that time, resided in Washington, DC. By her social tact and sterling womanly qualities she made many friends for the cause of woman suffrage among those who were inclined to believe that only the forward or immodest of the sex desired suffrage. For the past twenty years she has been a vice-president of the National Woman Suffrage Association. In 1890, after equal rights to Wyoming women had been secured irrevocably by the constitution adopted by the people of the new State, Mrs. Post was made president of the committees having in charge the statehood celebration. On that occasion a copy of the State constitution was presented to the women of the State by Judge M. C. Brown, who had been president of the constitutional convention which adopted it. Mrs. Post received the book on behalf of the women of the State.

POST, Mrs. Caroline Lathrop, poet and author, born in Ashford, CT, in 1824. Her ancestry runs back to the New England Puritans. In her youth her family removed to Hartford, CT. After her marriage she lived for some years in Pittsfield, MA, after which she lived in Springfield, IL, for twenty-five years. In that town she did the greater and the better part of her work. She has written verse since her childhood days. At the age of seven years she was a rhymer, and at the age of twelve she was the possessor of a mass of manuscript of her own making. She had concealed her practice of rhyming and was so mortified, when her older sister discovered her work, that she thrust her productions into the fire. She continued to write verses all through her school-days, and in 1846 her poems were being published in the "Sunday Magazine," the "Advance," the "Golden Rule," "Life and Light," the "Floral World" and many other periodicals. She has written in prose a series of leaflets for the Woman's Board of Missions. She has been an unobtrusive and diligent worker in various lines. Her husband, C. R. Post, to whom she was married in 1862, was a business man in Springfield. He has encouraged her in all her good works. They have three sons, two of whom are engaged in business in Fort Worth, TX, where Mrs. Post now makes her home. She has of late years done some writing, but she no longer wields her pen regularly.

POST, Miss Sarah E., physician, born in Cambria, WI, 2nd November, 1853. She studied in the Milwaukee schools and was graduated from the high school in that city in 1874. She then entered the training school for nurses connected with Bellevue Hospital, in New York City, from which she was graduated in 1876, later becoming a student in the Woman's Medical College, New York Infirmary, from which she was graduated in 1882. Dr. Post has practiced in medicine in New York City, has been represented in medical literature, and in 1885 founded "The Nightingale," the first paper in the world published exclusively in the interests of nursing.

POTTER, Mrs. Cora Urquhart, actor, was born in New Orleans, LA. Her maiden name was Cora Urquhart. Her father was a wealthy cotton-planter, and Cora in childhood lived a life of the typical southern kind, surrounded by wealth and refined

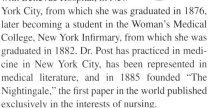

associates. In her school-days she showed a talent for recitation, and she was early engaged in amateur theatricals and in elocutionary entertainments. She became the wife of James Brown Potter, of New York City, a man of wealth and high social standing in the metropolis. After her marriage she took a prominent part in New York society, and soon became famous locally as a reciter and emotional actor. In 1887 she went to Europe to study, and soon announced to her family and friends her intention to adopt the stage as a profession. In the Haymarket Theater, London, England, she made her debut as Anne Sylvester in Wilkie Collins' "Man and Wife." The English critics praised her work. In June, 1887, she played Faustine de Bressier in "Civil War," and Inez in "Loyal Love," in the London Gaiety Theater. She made her first professional appearance in New York City, 31st October, 1887, in the Fifth Avenue Theater. In 1888 she brought out "Cleopatra" in a superb style, and in that rôle she eclipsed all her former successes. In 1890 she went to Australia on a professional tour, and was very well received. In 1891 she went to India and was enthusiastically received. Mrs. Potter is a handsome woman, and her stage work is characterized by great earnestness, directness, simplicity and intense dramatic force.

POTTER, Miss Jennie O'Neill, actor and dramatic reader, born in Wisconsin, in 1867. She made her debut in Minneapolis, MN, meeting immediately with decided success. Before she had been long out her talent attracted the attention of Major Pond, under whose direction she subsequently undertook her first tour throughout the Eastern States. Many in Washington remember her performances, which led to her becoming a favorite in Washington society, introduced by Mrs. Senator Dolph, and particularly and very cordially patronized by the Postmaster-General. In London, bearing letters of introduction from a number of the most prominent social leaders and press men in the United States, she was warmly welcomed, and during her first season became a general favorite in the circles where she was invited to give her readings.

POTTS, Mrs. Anna M. Longshore, physician and medical lecturer, born in Attleboro, now Langhorne, Bucks county, PA, 16th April, 1829. She was one of the class of eight brave young

Pennsylvania Quaker girls graduating from the Woman's Medical College of Pennsylvania, in Philadelphia, in 1852. That college was the first one ever chartered wherein a woman could earn and secure a medical degree. The commencement exercises on that memorable occasion were marked by the hoots of the male medical students, by the groans of the established medical practitioners, and by the faint applause of the friends of the brave girls. It is pleasant to record that each member of that pioneer class has won an enviable position in the profession and in the scientific world. Mrs. Potts, whose maiden name was Anna M. Longshore, was twenty-two years old when she was graduated. She was without means at her graduation, yet she soon established a lucrative practice in Philadelphia. Her health became somewhat impaired, and she moved to Langhorne, PA, in 1857, where she became the wife of Lambert Potts, one of the merchants there. A few years later, Dr. Longshore, now Dr. Longshore Potts, moved to Adrian, MI, where she speedily rose to a high position in her profession. She became imbued with the belief that a physician's most sacred duty is to prevent rather than cure disease, and to that end she gave many private lectures to her patients. Her addresses were so favorably received that she concluded to devote all her time to them. She commenced first in small towns. The first city of any consequence which she visited as a lecturer was San Francisco, where she appeared in 1881. She then visited the principal coast towns, north as far as Seattle and south to San Diego, CA. In May, 1883, she sailed with her party, then consisting of seven, for New Zealand, where, from Auckland to Invercargal, the largest houses were packed to listen to the words of wisdom that she so eloquently uttered. In November, 1883, she stood before an audience of four-thousand-five-hundred people in the exhibition building, Sydney, New South Wales, where she was introduced by Charles A. Kahlothen, United States Consul. She received a greeting there which was repeated in Melbourne, Brisbane and the larger interior towns of the colonies. In November, 1884, she sailed for London, England, where she delivered her first lecture in the large

St. James Hall, on the night of 17th February, 1885. She spent nearly three years in the United Kingdom, lecturing in all the chief provincial cities and repeating her lectures in London at frequent intervals. In October, 1887, she returned to America, making her first appearance in Tremont Temple, Boston. She then appeared in Chickering Hall, in New York, and from there went to California, lecturing only in the large cities. Just five years from the time she sailed for the Antipodes, she stood before an audience in the Baldwin Theater, San Francisco, CA, that packed that building to the roof. In January, 1890, the close of her lectures in the Grand Opera House, Indianapolis, IN, was marked by an unusual scene of enthusiasm. Dr. Longshore-Potts has made a fortune and has demonstrated the possibility of delivering popular medical lectures free from any trace of chicanery.

POWELL, Miss Maud, virtuoso violinist, born in Aurora, IL, in 1867. Her father, Professor Powell, was principal of the public schools in Aurora, and she received a thorough education. Her musical trend was early visible, and in childhood she readily played by ear all the airs she heard on the violin, her favorite instrument. While still a child, she began the systematic study of the violin with Professor William Lewis. She studied with him for seven years, and in 1881 she accompanied him to Europe, where she studied one year in Leipzig with Schradick, and afterward with Danckler, in Paris, and with Joachim, in Berlin. She returned to the United States and made her debut in Chicago, IL, with the Thomas orchestra, in June, 1886. She won an instant success, and she has played on several concert tours through the country. She is everywhere greeted by full houses. Her playing is marked by repose, a full tone and fine technique. She excels in all the difficult work usually done by virtuosos, and she is master of all the finer and more soulful qualities that alone distinguish the true artist from the merely skillful technician.

PRATT, Miss Hannah T., evangelist, born in Brooks, ME, 12th July, 1854. She is the daughter of Joseph H. and Martha E. Pratt, prominent in the Society of Friends. Miss Pratt is a born preacher. When six years old she felt impressed to preach the gospel. When eleven years old, in a public audience, she was much wrought upon for service, but she did not yield until she was four-teen years of age. At a large convention in New-port, RI, for the first time she addressed a public audience. Miss Pratt was educated in the common schools and in the Friends' College in Providence, RI. When nineteen years of age she stepped into public fields, laboring for a time in temperance work with the Woman's Christian Temperance Union in New Hampshire. Through her lectures before that organization and the Young Men's Reform Club her fame spread, and calls were made for her to lecture in various parts of the State. In 1876 she went to New York City and addressed large audiences. In 1885 she accompa-nied Mrs. Hoag, of Canada, on an evangelistic tour in New England and New York, having marked success. The following spring she accept-ed a pastorate in Vermont, which she held two years. In 1886 she was engaged in gospel work in Ohio, Iowa and Indiana, preaching to large audiences with remarkable effect. In 1887 she was ordained by the Friends' Church and received credentials of their high esteem to labor with all denominations and in any field. In 1888 she returned to Augusta, ME, with her aged parents. In the opera house of that city she conducted one of the most remarkable revivals ever known in the State. Having organized several churches in Maine and New York, she traveled more extensively in the States and Provinces. On 23rd Jannary, 1889, she accepted a call to officiate as chaplain in the Senate Chamber of Augusta, ME, an honor never before conferred upon a woman.

PRESTON, Miss Ann, physician, born in West Grove, PA, in December, 1813, and died in Philadelphia, 18th April, 1872. She was the daughter of Amos and Margaret Preston, both of the Society of Friends. She studied for some time in a West Chester boarding-school, and was an industrious reader. She studied Latin after reaching an age of maturity. She was in particular an ardent opponent of slavery. In 1838 she attended the meeting held in Philadelphia for the dedication of Pennsylvania Hall, a building erected for and devoted to free discussions. That building was burned by a mob, and one of her most striking poems, "The Burning of Pennsylvania Hall," was inspired by the conflagration, which she witnessed. She did much to help the fugitives from the slave States, and was also a pioneer temperance worker. In 1848 she pub-lished a volume of poems, enti-tled "Cousin Ann's Stories," some of which have been widely known. When the Woman's Medical College of Pennsylvania was opened in the fall of 1850, Miss Preston was among the first applicants for admission. She was graduated in the first com-mencement of the college, at the close of the ses-sion of 1851 and 1852. She remained as a student after graduation, and in the spring of 1852 she was called to the vacant chair of physiology and hygiene in the college, which she finally accepted. She lectured in New York, Baltimore, Philadel-phia and many other towns on hygiene, and every-where she drew large audiences. Her winters were passed in Philadelphia, lecturing in the college. Miss Preston and her associates obtained a charter and raised funds to establish a hospital in connec-tion with the college, and when it was opened she was appointed a member of its board of managers, its corresponding secretary and its consulting physician, offices which she held until the time of her death. In 1862 Dr. Preston was prostrated by overwork. Recovering her health, she resumed her lectures in the college. The Woman's Hospital gave the college a new impetus. In 1866 Dr. Pre-ston was elected dean of the faculty. In 1867 she wrote her famous reply to a preamble and resolu-tions adopted by the Philadelphia County Medical Society, to the effect that they would neither offer encouragement to women in becoming physicians nor meet them in consultation. In 1867 she was elected a member of the board of corporators of the college. In 1871 she was a second time afflicted with articular rheumatism. The last work of her life was the preparation of the annual announcement for the college session of 1872 and 1873. During the twenty years of her medical practice she saw the sentiment toward women physicians become more liberal and they were admitted to hospital clinics with men.

PRESTON, Mrs. Margaret Junkin, poet, born in Philadelphia, PA, in 1825. She is a daughter of

Florence Roberts Morrison.
From Photo by Morrison, Chicago.

Minnie Murray.   **Blanche Massey.**
From Photo by Baker, Columbus.   *From Photo Copyrighted, 1895, by Morrison, Chicago.*

the late Dr. George Junkin, who at the outbreak of the war was president of Washington College in Lexington, VA. He died in 1868. In her young womanhood she became the wife of Col. Preston, connected with the Virginia Military Institute. She began to write verses when a child. Her first published work appeared in "Sartain's Magazine" in 1849 and 1850. In 1856 she published her novel, "Silverwood, a Book of Memories." She sympathized with the South in the Civil War, and many of her fugitive poems, printed before the war in southern journals breathed her spirit of resistance to the North. In 1865 she published a volume of verse, "Beechenbrook," devoted to the Civil War, and containing her "Slain in Battle" and "Stonewall Jackson's Grave," with many other lyrics on the war. In 1870 she published a second volume of verse, "Old Songs and New," which contains the most admirable of her productions. She has contributed art-poems to a number of leading magazines, and her ballads are particularly fine pieces of work. She was one of the most prominent contributors to the "Southern Literary Messenger." Her attainments are varied, and she has made excellent translations from both ancient and modern languages. Her recent publications are "Cartoons" (Boston, 1875), "For Love's Sake: Poems of Faith and Comfort" (New York, 1886), "Colonial Ballads, Sonnets and Other Verse" (Boston, 1887), "A Handful of Monographs, Continental and English" (New York, 1887).

PRITCHARD, Mrs. Esther Tuttle, minister and editor, born in Morrow county, OH, 26th January, 1840. She comes from along line of Quaker ancestry, and her ministerial ability is inherited from both parents. Her father, Daniel Wood, was an able preacher, and there were a number in her mother's family. A gay girl, strong-willed and ambitious, it was not until the discipline of sorrow brought a full surrender to Christ, that she yielded to what was manifestly her vocation. In early womanhood she became the wife of Lucius V.

Tuttle, a volunteer in the Civil War, who had survived the horrors of a long imprisonment in Libby, Tuscaloosa and Salisbury to devote the remainder of his life to the profession of teaching. He died in 1881, and in 1884 Mrs. Tuttle was chosen by the Woman's Foreign Missionary Boards of her church to edit the "Friend's Missionary Advocate," and took up her headquarters in Chicago, IL. Shortly after her removal to that city she became the wife of Calvin W. Pritchard, editor of the "Christian Worker." She became the proprietor of the "Missionary Advocate" in 1886, and continued to edit and publish the paper with a marked degree of success until the autumn of 1890, when it passed by gift from her hands to the Woman's Foreign Missionary Union of Friends. For the last two years she has been actively engaged as teacher of the English Bible in the Chicago training school for city, home and foreign missions, besides acting as superintendent of the systematic-giving department of the National Woman's Christian Temperance Union. Her talents would compass far more, but frail health imposes limitations upon her work. Her present home is in Western Springs, IL.

PROCTOR, Mrs. Mary Virginia, journalist and philanthropist, born in a quaint old homestead on a farm in Rappahannock county, VA, 2nd May, 1854. Her maiden name was Mary Virginia Swindler. In 1858 her parents removed to Greene county, OH, and settled upon a farm, where Mary grew

to womanhood, receiving such educational advantages as the rural schools of the time could offer. When scarcely fifteen years of age, she engaged in teaching neighborhood schools, but, after a period of such labor covering two years, feeling the necessity of a broader education, she entered the Xenia Female College, a Methodist institution, where in eighteen months she was graduated. After her graduation she was engaged as a teacher in the Ohio Soldiers' and Sailors' Orphan Home, in Xenia. In her capacity as teacher she served in that institution until 1879. At the time of her incumbency Thomas Meigher Proctor was engaged in editing the "Home Weekly," a paper devoted to the interests of the institution. He was a man of fine abilities and has been connected with many of the leading daily journals of the country. Their acquaintance ended in marriage on 27th November, 1879, in the Home. After the marriage Mr. Proctor continued the management of the "Home Weekly" for nearly a year, when they removed to Wilmington, OH, where he became the editor and proprietor of the "Clinton County Democrat." In Wilmington their only child, Merrill Anne Proctor, was born. They continued to live in Wilmington until 1883, and during that time Mrs. Proctor contributed many articles to the "Democrat." In 1883 they removed to Lebanon, OH, where they commenced the lucrative and successful management of the "Lebanon Patriot." In no small degree its prosperity must be attributed to the foresight, prudence and executive ability of Mrs. Proctor. Mr. Proctor died 13th July, 1891. In her widowhood and with the care and nurture of her child solely upon her, Mrs. Proctor was broken, but not dismayed. She assumed the management of the paper. It has grown in literary excellence. In addition to the labor she expends upon the paper, she is a regular contributor to the Cincinnati "Enquirer," and furnishes many articles to other dailies and magazines. She has been honored by two governors of Ohio with appointments as visitor to the Home where she taught the youth informer days. At present she is president of the board of visitors. Two judges have appointed her a visitor to the charitable and correctional institutions of Warren county. She united with the Methodist Episcopal Church in early life and a part of her time is devoted to its cause.

PROSSER, Miss Anna Weed, evangelist, born in Albany, NY, 15th October, 1846. At the age of seven years she removed to Buffalo, NY, where she has since resided. Reared in a luxurious home, she sought no higher ambition than the applause and favor of the world of fashion in which she moved. As early as four years of age she can recall deep stirrings of conscience at times and heart-longings after God. Left without even the instruction of the Sabbath-school, she grew up in entire ignorance of God's Word. At the age of fifteen she voluntarily entered the Sabbath-school of the Presbyterian Church in the neighborhood. Leaving school very young, she began the usual career of a "society" girl. Gradually her health failed under the incessant strain, until at last she was taken with a congestive chill,

which was followed by a serious illness. She was carried to her room, and ten weary years of invalidism followed. Two of those years she spent in bed, and for five years she was carried up and down stairs. One disease followed another, until finally, all physicians failing, she was removed from home on a mattress, too low to realize much that was passing around her. When every human hope had fled and death seemed inevitable, she was led, in March, 1876, to a Christian woman of great faith, who pointed her to Christ as the sinner's only hope. Then and there, realizing herself for the first time a perishing sinner, she cast herself upon His mercy and was healed of her iniquities and her diseases. Awakening thus to the "newness of life," in a double sense, in Christ, in gratitude and joy she dedicated her life unreservedly to His service. In a few weeks she was able, in answer to prayer, without the use of medicine of any kind, to walk three miles without injury, and returned to her own home, a walking miracle in the eyes of all who knew her. Declaring to all whom she met the work wrought in her body and soul, she met incredulous looks from many, and soon also with bitter opposition in her attempts to carry on a work for the fallen. She took up a city mission work under the Woman's Christian Temperance Union, where she labored with interest and joy for several years. Feeling led to open a mission of her own, her steps were directed to the old Canal Street Mission in Buffalo, of which she undertook the charge, assisted by her Bible-class of reformed men. Many diamonds were gathered out of the mire and filth of that most frightful locality. The musical talent, which had formerly been used for the applause of the world, she then dedicated to God alone, and it has since become the most prominent feature of her work. About ten years having been spent in ministry among the fallen, many calls having come from churches all over the land, among them several invitations to assume the pastorate of a church, she entered general evangelistic work, and is at present the president of the Buffalo Branch of the National Christian Alliance. It is composed of members of various evangelical churches. She now lives in Kenmore, a suburb of Buffalo.

PRUIT, Mrs. Willie Franklin, poet, born in Tennessee, in 1865. Her maiden name was Franklin. Her parents moved to Texas at the close of the Civil War, while she was an infant, and the larger part of her life has been spent in that State. She belongs to one of the oldest and most aristocratic families of Tennessee. She received a liberal and thorough education. While in school, she displayed unusual intellectual powers. She began to write verses when she was a child, and at the age of thirteen years she contributed to the local press. Most of her poems have been published under the pen-name "Aylmer Ney." Her reputation extends throughout the South. In 1887 Miss Franklin became the wife of Drew Pruit, a lawyer, of Fort Worth, TX, in which city she resides. Her family consists of one son. She is a very energetic woman and takes great interest in her city. She is engaged in charitable and public enterprises. She is vice-president of the Woman's Humane Association of Fort Worth, and through her exertions the city has a number of handsome drinking fountains for man and beast. She is a member of the Texas board of lady managers of the World's Fair Exhibit Association, and she works actively and intelligently in its interests.

PUGH, Miss Esther, temperance reformer, was born in Cincinnati, OH. Her father and mother were Quakers of the strictest sort. Mr. Pugh was for many years a journalist in Cincinnati, publisher of the "Chronicle," and was famous for his strict integrity. Esther received a fine education. She early became interested in moral reforms, and soon became prominent in the temperance movement. She was one of the leaders in the Crusade, and she joined the Woman's Christian Temperance Union in its first meetings. She was elected treasurer of the National Woman's Christian Temperance Union, and has served in that capacity for years. She was an officer of the Cincinnati union from the beginning, and she has given the best years of her life to the work. She was publisher and editor of "Our Union" for years. Her management has repeatedly aided the national order in passing through financial difficulties. She is a clear and forcible orator, and her addresses are marked by thought and wisdom. She has traveled in temperance work through the United States and Canada, lecturing and organizing unions by the score. She calls herself "The watch-dog of the treasury," and her co-workers call her "Esther, our Treasure." Her home is in Evanston, IL, and she is busy in the good work.

PULLEN, Mrs. Sue Vesta, poet and author, born near Coesse, IN, 7th September, 1861, where she passed her childhood days. She is the youngest daughter of Luke and Susanna L. Tousley. In 1878 she became the wife of James C. Pullen, who died in 1889. At the age of eleven years she began to write for the press. Mrs. Pullen was not a prolific writer. Her first productions appeared in the county or State papers, but later she found many channels for her work. At the age of sixteen years she received prizes for her sketches in prose. Her first poems in the Chicago "Tribune" and other leading papers were published under her full name, but notoriety proved annoying, and she wrote under different pen-names, finally adopting that of "Clyde St. Claire," and wrote under it exclusively. She is an artist and can paint her poetic fancies as well on canvas as in words. Her best poems and sketches were written during a stay in Wisconsin, and were extensively copied. Mrs. Pullen has published one volume of poems, "Idle Hours." Her home is now in Coesse, IN.

PUTNAM, Mrs. Sarah A. Brock, author, was born in Madison, Madison county, VA. She is known in literature by her maiden name, Sallie A. Brock. She is a daughter of the late Ansalem and Elizabeth Beverley Buckner Brock. Her ancestry includes many names prominent in the colonial and Revolutionary history of her native State. Her education was conducted privately, under the supervision of her father, a man of literary culture, through whose personal instruction she was grounded in grammatical

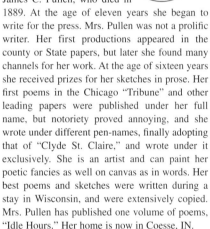

construction and analysis of the English language. She studied with a tutor, a graduate of Harvard University, who lived four years in the family. It was not until after the termination of the Civil War, the death of her mother, and the breaking up of her home in Richmond, that Miss Brock had any experience of life outside of Virginia. During the summer of 1865 she visited New York City, and was induced, by the acceptance of articles for the press, to devote herself to literature. Her first book, "Richmond During the War," a record of personal experience and observations in the Confederate capital, was published in 1867, simultaneously in New York and London. Its favorable acceptation encouraged her to make a compilation of the war poetry of the South, a volume entitled "The Southern Amaranth" (New York). In that work a number of her earlier poems are inserted. At the request of Rev. A. T. Twing, secretary and general agent of the domestic department of the board of missions of the Protestant Episcopal Church, she prepared a catechetical history of the missions of that society in the United States. It was issued as a serial under the title "The Domestic Missionary Catechism." In the autumn of 1869, under the escort of Bishop Lynch, of Charleston, SC, Miss Brock crossed the Atlantic and, spending a short time in England, joined friends in Paris and traveled with them in France, Switzerland, Italy, Austria and Germany. A portion of the winter and the following spring she spent in Rome, during the session of the last œcumenical council. She was presented at the Papal Court and to His Holiness, Pope Pius IX. While abroad, she wrote letters for several periodicals with which she was connected. On her return to America Miss Brock was engaged for "Frank Leslie's Lady's Journal," a connection which was continued uninterruptedly for more than ten years. For five years she was connected with "Frank Leslie's Lady's Magazine." Her contributions to the New York "Home Journal" cover a period of more than fifteen years. She has been associated with other periodicals of New York, the Sacramento "Journal," and a magazine of Baltimore. She was one of two women contributors to Appleton's "Picturesque America." A descriptive and critical article by her pen from Richmond for the "Home Journal," entitled "Fine Arts in Richmond," was copied in "Il Cosmopolita," a journal of Rome, printed in the Italian, English, French and Spanish languages. Her "Kenneth, My King"

a novel published in New York and London, a romance of life in Virginia previous to the late war, is a faithful transcript of the conditions which then existed. She has a work on the poets and poetry of America in preparation, which has occupied her leisure hours for several years. She has two other volumes in manuscript and material for a third book. Her numerous contributions to magazines and other periodicals comprise editorials, descriptive articles, letters, essays, extended and short stories, critiques and poems. Her poems number over two-hundred, and some of them have been widely copied. Her favorite metrical structure is the sonnet. On 11th January, 1882, Miss Brock became the wife of Rev. Richard F. Putnam, then of New York, and for the last few years rector of Trinity Church, Lime Rock, CT. In December, 1891, Rev. and Mrs. Putnam crossed the Atlantic, and while abroad traveled in England, France, Italy, Egypt, Palestine and other portions of Syria, Turkey in Asia, Turkey in Europe, and Greece, returning through Italy, Switzerland, France and Belgium. Since her marriage Mrs. Putnam's literary work has been diminished, but not discontinued, and each month finds her in the city of New York, planning the editorials and other articles to be written in the quiet rectory.

QUINTON, Mrs. Amelia Stone, president of the Women's National Indian Association, was born near Syracuse, NY. She comes of English ancestry and is directly descended from both Pilgrim and Puritan New England stock. Her childhood and girlhood were passed in Homer, NY, the nearly life-long home of her parents, Jacob Thompson Stone and Mary Bennett Stone. Her father was a man of noble nature, of great conscientiousness and of musical gifts, while her mother was endowed with energy, executive ability and courage. Of her three brothers one is a publisher, one a southern planter, and one a lawyer. A prominent admixture in early times was with the Adamses, four brothers and sisters of one ancestral family having married four sisters and brothers of one Adams family. The son of one of those was the father of Samuel Adams, the distinguished patriot. Another member of one of those families was aunt to John Adams, the second

President of the United States, and great-aunt to John Quincy Adams, the sixth President. Mrs. Quinton early finished the usual curriculum of study pursued in female seminaries, having special aptitude for mathematics, composition and music, and while yet in her teens was invited to become the preceptress of an academy near Syracuse. She spent a year as teacher in a Georgia seminary, after which she became the wife of Rev. James F. Swanson, an able christian minister of that State. Under the enervating climate a period of invalidism followed, and soon after her recovery her husband died, and she decided to return to the North, where after teaching for a year in the Chestnut Street Seminary of Philadelphia, PA, she turned to the religious and philanthropic work to which she has given the best years of her life. At first that volunteer service was among the poor and degraded of New York City, where she had weekly engagements in various institutions. One day of the week was spent in the prison, the almshouse, or the workhouse, and another in some infirmary or reformatory for women. One service was a weekly Bible-class for sailors briefly on shore. During the first temperance crusade in Brooklyn she joined the band of workers. Very soon she was invited to go out and represent the work, to organize unions, and, a little later, was elected by the State Woman's Christian Temperance Union as State organizer. That service was continued till, much worn, she went to Europe for a year's rest. After a few months on the continent, she was drawn into temperance work in England and addressed drawing-room and church meetings in London and other cities. On the voyage to England she met Professor Richard Quinton, a native of London and a lecturer in institutions there on historical and astronomical subjects, and a year later they were married in London, where they continued to reside for some months. She returned to America in the autumn of 1878, and Philadelphia, where Prof. Quinton resumed his lecturing, again became her home. In April, 1879, her friend, Miss Mary L. Bonney, became deeply stirred on the subject of national wrongs to Indians, and the missionary society over which she presided sought to circulate a petition on the subject. The anniversary occasion on which the attempt was made was already overcrowded with topics, and the petition was therefore not presented or read. A few weeks later Miss Bonney presented the facts she had collected to

her friend, Mrs. Quinton, whose heart and conscience at once responded, "Something must be done." Mrs. Quinton had had large experience in christian work and knew how to bring a cause before the people. The two formed their plan of action. Miss Bonney agreed to supply the means needed for printing, and Mrs. Quinton to plan and work as God opened the way, and she studied in libraries, prepared literature and petitions and circulated them through the sympathizers and helpers she gained in many States. The first petition was enlarged and she prepared a leaflet of facts and special appeal, and sent those out widely to leading citizens, and to women in many kinds of christian and philanthropic work, and the returns, from thirteen States, prepared by her in a roll three-hundred feet long, were presented to Congress in February, 1880. At the end of that year that committee of two had become a committee of eight and held its first meeting, when Mrs. Quinton reported her nearly two years' work and was elected secretary of the committee. Three months later Miss Bonner was elected chairman, and, in June, 1881, the constitution written by Mrs. Quinton was adopted, and the society that day elected an executive board, nominated at her request by the pastors of the churches, and became the Indian Treaty-keeping and Protective Association. Mrs. Quinton then began the work of wider organization and secured thirteen associate committees in five States before the close of the year. In the memorial letter which she wrote to accompany the petition of 1881, she made an earnest plea that Congress would win Indians into voluntary citizenship by making that to their interest, rather than by the coercion of acts of Congress. In her petition-form for January, 1882, universal Indian education, lands in severalty and the full rights of citizenship for Indians were prayed for. At that date the society had sixteen State committees, all of which she revisited and reorganized as permanent auxiliaries. A memorable discussion in the Senate over that third petition, which represented a hundred-thousand citizens, was eloquently closed by Senator Dawes. To-day the association, now the Women's National Indian Association, has branches, officers or helpers in forty States of the Union, and more than twenty missions in Indian tribes have been originated or established by it since 1884, and during 1891 its missionary work was done in fifteen tribes. When Miss Bonney retired from the presidency of the association, November, 1884, Mrs. Mary Lowe Dickinson was elected to the office, filling it for three years, when Mrs. Quinton, till then doing the work of general secretary, was unanimously elected president, and still holds the office. Of late years attaining full health, Mrs. Quinton, though somewhat past fifty, is at her best, and still continues her public addresses, many hundreds of which she has given in her visits to nearly every State and Territory, and on her last tour of many months, extending entirely around the United States, she bore a government commission and did service also on behalf of Indian education.

RAGSDALE, Miss Lulah, poet, novelist and actor, born in "Cedar Hall," the family residence, near Brookhaven, MS, 5th February, 1866. She is a genuine southerner. Her father was a Georgian. Her mother was a member of the Hooker family. One of her ancestors was Nathaniel Hooker, a pilgrim father, whose immediate descendants settled in Virginia. Her mother, a gifted woman, supervised her early education and selected her books. She was graduated from Whitworth College. She began early in life to study two arts, the art of poesy and the Thespian art. She believes that poetry is constitutional, and she fed on works of poetry and romance. Her poems have appeared in the leading southern papers. Her stories and novelettes have won her fame. As an actor, she has succeeded so well that she will adopt the theatrical profession. She has written for many northern magazines, as well as weekly and daily papers. The twin loves of her life, the drama and poetry, have made their impress upon her with equal strength. In her acting she is always poetical, in her poetry always dramatic. Strength, delicacy and a romantic intensity characterize all her work.

RALSTON, Mrs. Harriet Newell, poet, born in Waverly, NY, 21st October, 1828. She is the daughter of Rev. Aaron Jackson. Her youth was passed in New York, Massachusetts and Illinois, and her education was received in the institutions of learning in the first two named States. Upon her removal to Quincy, IL, she formed the acquaintance of Hon. James H. Ralston, whose wife she became shortly afterward. Judge Ralston was a leading man in Illinois and held various important offices in that State. After serving as an officer in the Mexican War, he turned his attention again to the practice of law, settling in the then new State of California. On their wedding day judge and Mrs. Ralston set out from New York for the Pacific coast, enjoying on the way the tropical beauties of the Nicaraguan Isthmus. Following the death of Judge Ralston, his widow left her home in Austin, Nev., for the East, eventually settling in Washington, DC, where her son is at present a professor of law in the National Law University of that city. Mrs. Ralston has written many fine poems, which, although never collected in the form of a volume, have been published and widely copied by the press. She is the author of "Fatherless Joe," "Decoration Day," "The Spectral Feast," "The Queen's Jewels," and "The White Cross of Savoy," for which poem King Humbert of Italy sent her a letter of thanks and appreciation. Her poems are very numerous, among which may be specially mentioned "The Queen's Jewels," written for the occasion of a banquet given by the Woman's National Press Association of Washington, DC., of which she is a member, to the delegates of the Pan-American Congress assembled in that city, and for which poem she has received many acknowledgments from the representatives of Central and South American governments. She still takes an active interest in philanthropic and social movements tending to ameliorate the conditions of individuals and of society at large.

RAMBAUT, Mrs. Mary L. Bonney, educator, born in Hamilton, Madison county, NY, 8th June, 1816. Her father was a farmer in good circumstances, a man of integrity, of sound judgment, of special military power and of strong influence. Her mother, a teacher before her marriage, was always cheerful and kind, interested in everything that concerned human weal, and especially in educational, moral and religious movements. Religion and an education were prominent in their thoughts and directed in the training of the son and the daughter. To the latter was given the benefit of several years of valuable instruction in the female academy in Hamilton, and the superior course of study under Mrs. Emma Willard in Troy Seminary, then the highest institution for young ladies in this country. Her committal to a christian life expressed itself by union with the Episcopal Church, and subsequently, owing to a change of view with regard to the subject of baptism, with the Baptist Church. The important discipline of sorrow came to her in the loss of her loved and honored father. Through teaching in Jersey City, NJ, New York City, De Ruyter, NY, Troy Seminary, Beaufort and Robertville, SC, Providence, RI, and Philadelphia, PA, she reached 1850 with wide observation and tried and developed powers. Then, in order to give a home to her mother, she decided to establish a school of her own, and, inviting Miss Harriette A. Dillaye, a teacher in Troy Seminary and a friend of earlier days, to join her, they founded the Chestnut Street Seminary, located for thirty-three years in Philadelphia, and enlarged in 1883 into the Ogontz School for Young Ladies, in Ogontz, PA. Thus was she for nearly forty years before the world as an independent educator, putting her maturest thoughts and her life-force into thousands of rich young lives, and reaching with her influence the various States and Territories of the Union and Canada. To an unusual degree she taught her pupils to think, and how to think. With clear perceptions, logical processes and conclusions reached in such a way that they could be firmly held and vigorously pushed, she not only impressed her own strong nature on her pupils, but equipped them with her methods, to go out into the world as independent thinkers and actors. It has been her pleasure, from the financial success granted by a kind providence, to secure to one white young man and four colored men all their school preparation for the christian ministry, and to dispense largely in many other directions. With very great sensitiveness to wrong and quick benevolence, it is not surprising that her sympathy has been roused for the "Wards of the Nation." She says: "Seeing from newspapers that Senator Vest, of Missouri, had been pressing Congress for thirteen years to open the Oklahoma lands to settlement by whites amazed me. A senator, I said, urging that injustice! A moral wrong upon our Government! It took hold of me. I talked about it to one and another. One day my friend, Mrs. A. S. Quinton, visited me in my room. I told her the story and of my deep feeling. Her heart and conscience were stirred. We talked and wondered at the enormity of the wrong proposed by Senator Vest, and that Congress had listened. Then and there we pledged ourselves to do what we could to awaken the conscience of Congress and of the people. I was to secure the money, and Mrs. Quinton was to plan and to work." Seven-thousand copies of a petition protesting against contemplated encroachments of white settlers upon the Indian Territory, and a request to guard the Indians in the enjoyment of all the rights which have been guaranteed them on the faith of the nation, with a leaflet appeal to accompany it, were circulated during the summer in fifteen States by that volunteer committee of two and those whom they interested, and the result in the autumn was a petition roll, three-hundred feet long, containing the signatures of thousands of citizens. That memorial was carried to the White House, 14th February, 1880, by Miss Bonney and two women, whom she invited to accompany her. It was presented by Judge Kelly in the House of Representatives the twentieth of that month, with the memorial letter written by Miss Bonney, the central thought of which was the binding obligation of treaties. Thus was begun what finally resluted in the Woman's National Indian Association. During the first four years Miss Bonney's gifts amounted to nearly fourteen-hundred dollars. She became the first president of the society, and continues its beloved honorary president, with undiminished devotion to the great cause of justice to the native Indian Americans. While in London, in 1880, as a delegate to the World's Missionary Conference, Miss Bonney became the wife of Rev. Thomas Rambaut, D.D., LL.D., a friend of many years and a delegate to the same conference, who has since died. God is helping in a precious way to round her character and her life, as in her attractive home in Hamilton, the home of her childhood, she uses her remaining strength in ministries to others.

RAMSEY, Mrs. Lulu A., temperance worker, was born near Fort Wayne, IN. Her father, Rev. John Stoner was a prominent clergyman of the

Methodist Episcopal Church. At an early age she entered the Methodist Episcopal College in Fort Wayne, where her education was mainly acquired. Immediately after her graduation she began to teach school. In 1886 she became the wife of Samuel A. Ramsey, LL.B., a lawyer of Pittsburgh, PA. They settled in Woonsocket, South Dakota, where they are at present living. Mr. Ramsey was one of the delegates to the constitutional convention of South Dakota in 1889, and holds the position of Commissioner of the World's Fair from his State. Mrs. Ramsey has been identified from the first with the most prominent workers of the place, whose aim is social reform or intellectual advancement. She is an accomplished woman, a musician of no common grade, gifted in painting and a fine elocutionist. The citizens of Woonsocket placed her upon the city board of education, and she was chosen president. Broad in her aims and charities and a firm believer in woman's power and influence, she chose the Woman's Christian Temperance Union as the field wherein to exert her energies and benevolences. She has been for years president of the local union, has taken an active part in the work of her district, for which she fills the office of corresponding secretary, and which selected her as its representative in the national convention in Boston, in November, 1892. Her ambition is to place before girls and boys, who are desirous of obtaining a liberal education, an opportunity to pursue their ambition, by founding for them an industrial school, which shall be so broad and practical in its aims and methods that each pupil will be self-supporting while there, and will leave the institution as master of some occupation. It is her desire to make the school the especial charge of the National Woman's Christian Temperance Union. Her philanthropic interests are many and varied.

RANSFORD, Mrs. Nettie, general grand matron of the Order of the Eastern Star, born in Little Falls, NY, 6th November, 1838. Her parents were from Scotland. She was reared and educated in Little Falls. After graduating, in 1857, she went to the West and settled in Nebraska. She taught school in Omaha and Fort Calhoun. In the latter place, on 25th April, 1858, she became the wife of William P. Ransford. In 1862 they moved to Laporte, IN, and in 1870 they made their home in Indianapolis, where they now reside. Mrs. Ransford joined the Episcopal Church in Laporte. She was one of the first women to join the Order of the Eastern Star, soon after that society was organized in 1872. She joined Queen Esther Chapter, No. 3, and entered enthusiastically into the work. In 1874 she was elected worthy matron, and was reelected in 1875 and 1876, and again in 1884, in which capacity she is still serving. She was an interested visitor at the organization of the grand chapter of Indiana, in 1874, and of the general grand chapter in 1876. She became a member of the grand chapter in 1875, was chairman of the committee on correspondence reported in 1878, and was elected grand matron in 1879 and 1880, and again in 1883. While filling that high office, she was an active officer, making numerous official visits. She was a member of the general grand chapter in Chicago, in 1878 and 1880, and in San Francisco in 1883. She was always in requisition for service in the order. She was elected most worthy general grand matron in the session of the general grand chapter, held in Indianapolis in September, 1889, and was the first general grand matron to serve under the changed constitution, making that officer the executive during the vacation of the general grand chapter. Her duties are such as an officer of so large and influential a body would naturally be called upon to perform, and cause her to travel throughout the entire general grand jurisdiction. She is now a member of the Woman's Relief Corps, serving as delegate to its various grand conventions, national and State, and in the department convention of 1890, in Boston, took a prominent part. As chairman of the reception committee in Detroit, she rendered excellent service to the corps. Of the two children born to her, one died in infancy and the other in young womanhood. Mrs. Ransford, as the highest officer in the branch of the Freemasonic fraternity devoted to the wives of the members, has distinguished herself in many ways that only members of the society can understand.

RATHBUN, Mrs. Harriet M., author and business woman, born in Port Jefferson, Suffolk county, NY, 18th May, 1840. Her maiden name was Harriet M. Lee. She was the youngest of a family of twelve children. Her father died in 1842, and the large family were left in the mother's care and dependent upon their own exertions, as those who should have been friends, through persuasion and misrepresentation, wrested from the widow all her property. At fourteen years of age the studious little girl began to teach in Bellport, NY, while attending the village academy a portion of the year. At the beginning of the Civil War she resigned her position in the Brooklyn public schools, in order to be an assistant in a publishing house in New York City. Near the close of the rebellion Miss Lee became the wife of Captain E. H. Fales, of the 131st Regiment New York Volunteers. At the end of the war Capt. Fales purchased the magazine named "Merry's Museum," founded by Peter Parley. Disease contracted in the army blasted all his hopes of personal success, but the business was not allowed to suffer. With energy extraordinary Mrs. Fales came to the front, and with the help of a literary friend, during the decline of her husband, lasting more than a year, she assumed charge of both the departments, editorial and publishing. Finally, with the hope of prolonging his life, the business was allowed to pass into other hands, while Capt. and Mrs. Fales, with their babe, sought a milder climate in the West. Writing done by the wife, which she could not have secured in her own name, appeared under that of her husband, and procured for his last moments most grateful luxuries. At last husband and child were laid at rest, in 1868, and Mrs. Fales returned alone to New York City. Again she entered a publishing house, and at a salary which would have been paid to a man holding the same position. She was probably one of the first women in the metropolis to receive her just dues. It was while faithfully fulfilling her duties there, she met Milton Rathbun, now of Mt. Vernon. NY, whose wife she became in 1873. Soon after, she began to write for the weekly press, and at various times has contributed tales, sketches, essays and articles on ethics to a variety of weekly journals. She is favorably known on local platforms as a speaker upon temperance and ethics. She is noted for incessant activity benevolence and cheerfulness; and is interested in every phase of woman's work and in all sensible reformatory movements. She has a family of two sons, the older a student in Harvard University.

RAY, Mrs. Rachel Beasley, poet and author, born in Anderson county, Kentucky, 31st January, 1849. She is known to the literary world as "Mattie M'Intosh." She is the fifth daughter of Judge Elisha Beasley and Almeda Penney, who reared eight girls, of whom "Kate Carrington" is the youngest. When she was an infant, her parents moved to Hickman county and settled in the town of Clinton. Judge Beasley gave his children every educational advantage within his reach, and the consequence was that the eight daughters became teachers. At the age of sixteen years Mrs. Ray was left an orphan by the death of her mother, her father having died two years before. A few months later she entered Clinton Seminary, KY, as both student and teacher. For fourteen years she was almost constantly employed in educational work, either as teacher or student, and often as both. She spent every spare moment during that time in writing stories, poems and practical articles. Her last school work was done in Clinton College, where she acted in the capacity of both student and teacher. She became the wife of E. R. Ray, of Hickman county, KY, on 10th October, 1878. In the summer of 1880 Mrs. Ray had an attack of rheumatic fever, from which her recovery was so slow that a change of climate became necessary, and her husband took her to Eureka Springs, a health resort in Arkansas. There she improved sufficiently in a short time to resume her usual duties, and the family settled there permanently. For many years she has indulged her fondness for the pen by contributing largely to different weeklies and periodicals. "The Ruined Home," a continued story, published in 1889, in a St. Louis weekly, gives her views on the use of alcoholic drinks. She is a member of the Baptist Church. Her husband is a Baptist and fills the office of deacon in that church. The "Leaves from the Deacon's Wife's

Scrap Book," from her pen, which have been so well received by the public, are original and humorously written sketches from her daily life. She strongly favors woman's advancement and is a staunch advocate of temperance. Judge Ray is a lawyer and real estate agent with extensive business, and Mrs. Ray is his secretary. She writes daily at a desk in his office, and in his absence has entire charge of his business. In addition to her usual literary engagements, office work and superintending her home, she edits three Woman's Christian Temperance Union columns each week in the papers of her own city.

RAYMOND, Mrs. Annie Louise Cary, contralto singer, born in Wayne, Kennebec county, ME, 22nd October, 1842. Her parents were Dr. Nelson Howard Cary and Maria Stockbridge Cary. She was the youngest in a family of six children. She received a good common-school education in her native town, and finished with a course in the female seminary in Gorham, ME, where she was graduated in 1862. Her musical talents were shown in childhood, and at the age of fifteen years her promise was so marked that she was sent to Boston to study vocal music. She remained in Boston for six years, studying with Lyman W. Wheeler and singing in various churches. She went to Milan, Italy, in 1866, and studied with Giovanni Corsi until 1868. She then went to Copenhagen, where she made her début in an Italian opera company. In the first months of 1868 she sang successfully in Copenhagen, Gothenburg and Christiania. During the summer of 1868 she studied in Baden-Baden with Madame Viardot-Garcia, and in the fall of that year she began an engagement in Italian opera in Stockholm, with Ferdinand Strakosch. After two months she was engaged to sing in the royal Swedish opera, and sang in Italian with a Swedish support. In the summer of 1869 she studied in Paris with Signor Bottesini, and in the autumn of that year she sang in Italian opera in Brussels. There she signed with Max and Maurice Strakosch for a three-year engagement in the United States. In the winter of 1869–70 she studied in Paris, and in the spring she sang in London, England, in the Drury Lane Theater. In 1870 she returned to the United States. She made her début in Steinway Hall, New York City, in a concert, with Nilsson, Brignoli and Vieuxtemps. She then for several years sang frequently and with brilliant success in opera and concert,

appearing with Carlotta Patti, Mario, Albani and others. In the winter of 1875–76 she sang in St. Petersburg and Moscow, and a year later she repeated her Russian tour. In the seasons of 1877–78 and 1878–79 she sang in the United States, in opera with Clara Louise Kellogg and Marie Roze. From 1880 to 1882 she sang in opera with the Mapleson company and in numerous concerts and festivals, including a tour in Sweden. She sang in the New York, Boston, Cincinnati, Chicago and Worcester festivals, and with the Brooklyn Philharmonic Society. Her voice is a pure contralto, of remarkable strength, great range and exceeding sweetness. Her dramatic powers are of the highest order. Her professional life has been a series of successes from beginning to end. She became the wife, 29th June, 1882, of Charles Monson Raymond, of New York City. Since her marriage she has never sung in public. Her only service in song has been in assisting her church choir and in charitable entertainments. She is ranked with the greatest contraltos of the century.

RAYMOND, Mrs. Carrie Isabelle Rice, musician and educator, born in South Valley, NY, 12th July, 1857. Her parents removed to Iowa when she was quite young. Her love of music displayed itself very early in life, and at the time when most children delight in amusement, she was happy in practicing her music. At ten years of age she was sufficiently far advanced to play the cabinet organ in church, having had the benefit of such instruction as the small town afforded. At fourteen years of age she began to play on the pipe-organ. Her progress and the real talent she displayed warranted the desire for better instruction than the West then afforded. She went to Brooklyn, NY, and placed herself under the instruction of Professor Lasar. While with him she paid particular attention to the piano and organ. At the close of her stay in Brooklyn she went to Washington, DC, and there began her career as a teacher and organist, in both of which she has been successful. Very few women can manipulate an organ with the ease and skill shown by Mrs. Raymond. Perfect master of her instrument, her fine musical nature and cultivated taste find little difficulty in correctly rendering the works of the great masters. In 1877 she became the wife of P. V. M. Raymond, and in 1885 settled in Lincoln, NE. Soon after that she drew together a little company of musicians for the purpose of doing chorus work. In doing that she encountered many obstacles, but by perseverance and ability as a musical director she overcame them. She spared neither time nor effort in her work, and she was at length rewarded in knowing that her chorus was considered one of the best drilled in the West. In 1887 she organized an annual musical festival, during which some of the great masterpieces were to be performed. Among those already given are Handel's "Messiah" and "Judas Maccabaeus," Haydn's "Creation" and "Spring," Mendelssohn's "Elijah" and "Lobgesang," Spohr's "Last Judgment," Gaul's "Holy City," Gounod's "Messe Solennelle" and Gade's "Crusaders." She was in the habit of drilling and preparing the chorus for the festivals and then handing over the baton to an imported director, but in May, 1891, the members of the chorus prevailed upon her to conduct the music in the festival. The works given on that occasion were Haydn's "Creation," with full chorus and orchestra and Gade's "Crusaders," quite sufficient to test her ability as a director. Success crowned her efforts. That was undoubtedly the first instance in the history of music where a woman filled that position in the rendition of an oratorio. In the December following she conducted Mendelssohn's "Lobgesang" with marked success. In May, 1892, the "Messiah," Cowen's "Sleeping Beauty" and a miscellaneous concert were given. The work of the orchestra in those concerts was especially commented upon. An attractive feature of the miscellaneous programmes has been a chorus of one-hundred-fifty misses, which is under the complete control of Mrs. Raymond's magnetic personality and always charms the audience. In July, 1892, she was director of music in the Crete, NE, Chautauqua Assembly, during which a number of successful concerts were given.

RAYMOND, Mrs. Emma Marcy, musical composer, born in New York, NY, 6th March, 1856. She is the daughter of Dr. Erastus Egerton Marcy, of New York City. She showed a remarkable aptitude for music at a very early age, having composed her first song before the completion of her fifth year. She inherits her musical talents from her parents, both of whom are gifted amateurs. She

was reared in an atmosphere of music, and had the advantage of studying under the best teachers who visited this country. She studied the piano with Gottschalk and Raccoman, vocal music with Ronconi, and counterpoint and harmony with the best German masters. Her musical sympathies are almost entirely with the Italian and French schools. Being a firm believer in the gift of free and spontaneous melody, she believes that, where human emotions are to be portrayed in music, the proper means to use in such portrayal is the human voice, and she leaves to the instruments the task of accompanying. She is a prolific writer and is equally at home in the composition of a waltz, a ballad, an operetta or a sacred song. Her opera "Dovetta" was produced in New York in 1889. She is the author of several pieces sung by Patti, and her productions cover the entire field of music.

RAYNER, Mrs. Emily C., author and journalist, born in Boston, MA, 8th March, 1847. She is the only daughter of the late Stephen Bartlett and Eliza Cook Hodgdon, and is of Puritan descent. She was graduated from Ipswich Seminary, Massachusetts, in 1865, and in 1866 became the wife of Thomas J. Rayner, second son of Thomas Lyle and Eunice L. Rayner, of Boston. Since her marriage Mrs. Rayner has resided in New York City. She was at an early age a contributor to various papers and magazines, but not until 1880 did she join the ranks of the professional writers. Always fond of social life, for which she is, by vaious accomplishments, particularly adapted, she has enjoyed an intimate association with many prominent Americans, including the late Samuel J. Tilden. Some of the brightest glimpses of the private life and noble character of that statesman can be obtained from her journals, which are a daily record, in many uniform volumes, not only of her own life, but of the important events of the social, dramatic, political, religious and literary world. Those journals are profusely illustrated and are of great value, since the daily record is unbroken for a period of over twenty years. They will probably find a resting place in some public library, as their versatile author has no children to inherit them. She is now in editorial charge of important departments in several leading magazines. Perseverance and power of concentration, joined with inherited ability, have led to her success.

READ, Mrs. Elizabeth C. Bunnell, journalist and woman suffragist, born on a farm in Dewitt township, near Syracuse, NY, on Christmas eve, 1834, the fifth child in a family of four boys and five girls. her father, Edmund Harger Bunnell, was born in Connecticut, the son of Nathan Bunnell and Currence Twitchell, his wife. Her mother was Betsey Ann Ashley, daughter of Dr. John Ashley, of Catskill, NY, and his wife, Elizabeth Johnstone, of the Johnstones of colonial fame.

Her paternal grandfather was a soldier of 1812, and his father was a Revolutionary hero. One of her brothers, Nathan Bunnell, enlisted at the age of seeventeen, in Company A, Twentieth Indiana Infantry, was wounded at Gaines' Mill, taken prisoner, and died in Libby prison, Richmond, VA, 12th July, 1862. When Elizabeth was fourteen years old, her parents removed from New York to Indiana, where within six weeks after their arrival, her mother died. Business ventures proved unfortunate, and the family circle was soon broken. Before she was sixteen, Miss Bunnell began to teach school. Having an opportunity to learn the printing business, she determined to do so, and found the occupation congenial, though laborious. She served an apprenticeship of two years, and then accepted the foremanship of a weekly paper and job office in Peru, IN. That post she filled four years. At the end of that time, in January, 1861, she commenced the publication of a semi-monthly journal called the "Mayflower," devoted to literature, temperance and equal rights. That paper had a subscription list reaching into all the States and Territories. On 4th March, 1863, she became the wife of Dr. S. G. A. Read. In 1865 she removed with him to Algona, IA, where they now live. There she began the publication of a weekly county paper, the "Upper Des Moines," repre-

senting the itnerests of the upper Des Moines valley, which at that time had no other newspaper. She commenced to write for the press when about twenty, and has continued as a contributor to several different jourants. A series of articles in the status of women in the Methodist Church, led to their more just recognition in subsequent episcopal addresses. In church membership Mrs. Read is a Methodist, and in religious sympathy and fellowship belongs to the church universal. She is deeply interested in all social and moral problems. The unfortuante and criminal classes have always enlisted her most sympathetic atention. She is now associate editor of the "Woman's Standard," of Des Moines, IA, a journal devoted to equal rights, temperance and literature. She was vice-president of the Indiana State Woman Suffrage Society, while residing there, adn has been president of the Iowa State Society, and one of the original members and promoters of the Woman's Congress. She has lectured occasionally on temperance, education and suffrage. She is generally known in literature as Mrs. Lizzie B. Read.

READ, Miss Jane Maria, poet and artist, born in Barnstable, MA, 4th October, 1853. Her father, Rev. William Read, is a Baptist clergyman. She comes from old colonial families on both sides, and her ancestors were among the early English pioneers. Until six years of age her home was in Massachusetts. In 1859 her parents moved to the sea-coast of Maine, where they lived till 1865, at that time returning to Massachusetts. Her parents noted her literary trend and developed and shaped it so far as lay in their power. She studied in the Coburn Classical Institute, in Waterville, ME, for several years. Her poetic tendencies were intensified by reading. She began to publish her poems in 1874 in various magazines and newspapers, and in 1887 she published a volume of verse entitled "Between the Centuries, and Other Poems." Much of her poetry is of the introspective kind, with a strong element of the religious and the sentimental. She has contributed, among others, to the "Magazine of Poetry." Besides her meritorious poetical work, she is an artist of marked talent, and makes a specialty of portraits and animal pictures in oil colors. She received her art training in Boston, MA, from prominent artists and instructors. She is a woman of broad views, liberal culture and versatility. Her home is now in Coldbrook Springs, MA, where her father is in charge of a church.

REED, Mrs. Caroline Keating, pianist, was born in Nashville, TN, and reared and educated in Memphis, where her father, Col. J. M. Keating, was the half owner and managing editor of the "Appeal." Early in her childhood she displayed her fondness for music, in which art her mother was proficient, the leading amateur singer in the city, a pianist and harpist. As soon as she could comprehend the value of notes and lay hold of the simplest exercises, her mother began to train her. She became the pupil of a local teacher, Emile Levy, and went forward very rapidly. Her parents determined that her earnestness should be seconded by the very best teachers in the United States, and she was sent in 1877 to New York, where, under S. B. Mills, she made great progress, but still more under Madame Carreno. She also took lessons from the pianist, Mrs. Agnes Morgan. She subsequently studied under Richard Hoffman and under Joseffy. She studied harmony and thorough bass with Mr. Nichols. To those lessons she added later on the study of ensemble music as a preparation for orchestral works, under the guidance of leading members of the New York Philharmonic Club. During the two last years of her stay in New York, she played in several concerts in that city and its vicinity. As an artist, she was recognized by the musicians of New York and the musical critics of the press. In January of 1884 she returned home. Before entering upon her successful professional career, she gave several concerts in Memphis and surrounding cities. The following year she became a regular teacher of the piano-forte and singing, having been fitted for the latter branch of her art by three years of study under Errani. She is very practical in her philanthropy, and since first forming her class, which has always averaged forty pupils, has never been without one or more whom she taught free of charge. For two or three years she gave lessons gratuitously to six pupils, who were unable to pay

anything. She has contributed frequently to charitable purposes, either by concerts or with her earnings. Since her marriage in 1891 she has continued to teach. She is at present engaged in preparing a primer on technique for beginners. Mrs. Reed is broad and progressive in her views of life, especially those concerning women and women's work. When a mere child, she was wont to declare her determination to earn her living when she grew up. In stepping out from the conventional life of a society belle and conscientiously following the voluntary course she marked out for herself, she was a new departure from the old order of things among the favored young girls of the South. Thoroughly devoted to her art and in love with her vocation as a teacher, she stands among the best instructors of music in the country. She has no patience with triflers, and no money could induce her to waste time on pupils who are not as earnest and willing to work as she is herself. Though young, she has accomplished much and will maintain the high position she has so honestly won.

REED, Mrs. Florence Campbell, author, born in Door Creek, WI, 17th January, 1860. Her father's name is Harvey Campbell, and her mother's maiden name was Melissa D. Reynolds. The mother was a woman of fine taste and culture, and was known as an author in her early days. She excelled in story-telling, and her improvised tales to amuse her children are remembered vividly by her daughters. Many of them afterward found their way into the "Little Pilgrim" and other papers. A part of the childhood of Florence Campbell was spent in Lone Rock, WI, her father having abandoned farming for the mercantile business. She clerked for him during vacation, being familiar with ledgers, bills and prices of everything when she had to climb on a stool to reach the desk. Receiving a certificate at a teachers' examination when only twelve years old, she planned to enter the field of pedagogics, and did so when she had scarcely more than reached her teens. She soon ceased to teach and entered the State University, the youngest student in that institution. She taught in various schools, most of the time as principal, for ten years. Her work was in Wisconsin, Iowa and Kansas. She wrote a cantata, "Guardian Spirits," which met a favorable reception. Having given some time to the study of elocution and voice-training, she traveled in Wisconsin, Iowa and Illinois and brought out the cantata herself among school children. It was very successful, but her health failed, and she was compelled to give up so arduous an undertaking. Her record is one of hard work and many disappointments and discouragements. She has written stories, essays and poems, read proof, and done reporting, been her own seamstress and done housework, given entertainments as a reader, and battled bravely with many adverse circumstances. Her first book, "Jack's Afire" (Chicago, 1887), a novel, found a wide sale, and some of her poems have been extensively copied on both sides of the ocean. She has written for a great many periodicals, eastern and western. She became the wife of Myron D. Reed, and they now reside in Madison, WI. She is doing her literary work parenthetically, as any home-maker must, but her husband being a poet, she finds perfect sympathy in all her ambitions and coöperation in her most congenial labors.

REESE, Miss Lizette Wood-worth, poet, born in a country place near Baltimore, MD, 9th January, 1856. Her parents were French and German, and her blood has a dash of Welsh from her father's side. Her parents moved to Pittsburgh, PA, when she was a child. They lived in that city only six months, when they removed to Baltimore, MD, where they have resided ever since. Miss Reese was able to read when she was five years old, and she read in childhood everything that came in her way, history, essays, novels, poems and religious biography. At the age of eight years she was reading Dickens and Thackeray. Her education was conducted on a broad plan. She began to versify early, and her work showed unusual merit, even in her first attempts. She published a volume of verse, "A Branch of May," in 1887, and the most conspicuous critics and authors gave it a cordial reception. She is not a prolific writer. She is a deliberate worker, and her best work comes out at the rate of only three or four poems a year. Some of her most notable verses have appeared in "The Magazine of Poetry." She has recently published a second volume of poems, "A Handful of Lavender" (Boston 1891). She is a teacher by profession and lives in Baltimore.

REESE, Mrs. Mary Bynon, temperance worker, born in Pittsburgh, PA, 27th June, 1832, of Welsh parents. While she was a child, the family removed to Wheeling, WV, where Miss Bynon had the advantages of a good seminary. Graduating in 1847, she  became identified with the public schools of the Old Dominion, and for a time was one of three teachers in the only free school in the State, the Third Ward public school of Wheeling. That school was soon followed by others, in two of which she was employed. While yet a school-girl, she gave promise of poetic talent and wrote frequently for local papers. She was for many years a contributor to "Clark's School Visitor." After she became the wife of John G. Reese, she removed to Steubenville, OH, where the greater part of her life has been spent. During the Civil War her time was devoted to alleviating the sufferings of Union soldiers. Her pen was busy, and her best thought was woven into song for the encouragement of the Boys in Blue. She was poet laureate in her city, and New Year addresses, anniversary odes and corner-stone poems were always making demands upon her mind and pen. Just before the breaking out of the Ohio crusade, she removed with her family to Alliance, OH. She led the women of her city in that movement. While lecturing in Pittsburgh and visiting saloons with the representative women of the place, she was arrested and, with thirty-three others, incarcerated in the city jail, an event which roused the indignation of the best people and made countless friends for temperance. After the organization of the Woman's Christian Temperance Union she was identified with the State work of Ohio, as lecturer, organizer and evangelist. She was the first national superintendent of the department of narcotics. In 1886 she was made one of the national organizers and sent to the north Pacific coast, where her work has been very successful. The Puget Sound country fascinated her completely, and, after a stay of nine months in the northwest, she removed in 1887 to Washington, where she resides in Chautauqua, on Vashon island, a few miles from Seattle, which she makes her head-quarters, as State and national organizer.

REHAN, Miss Ada C., actor, born in Limerick, Ireland, 22nd April, 1859. Her name is Crehan, but the name was accidentally spelled "Ada C. Rehan" in a telegraphic dispatch, and she kept the name as a stage-name. Her parents brought their family to the United States in 1864, and settled in Brooklyn, NY. Ada studied in the common schools until she was fourteen years old, when she made her appearance as an actor in Oliver Doud Byron's "Across the Continent." The company was playing in Newark, NJ, and Ada took the place of one of the actors who was sick. Her family decided to have her study for the stage. In 1874 she played in New York City in "Thoroughbred," not attracting attention. She then played in support of Edwin Booth, Adelaide Neilson, John McCul-lough, Mrs. D. P. Bowers, John T. Raymond and Lawrence Barrett, playing Ophelia, Desdemona, Celia, Olivia and other Shakespearean rôles. In 1878, while playing in "Katherine and Petruchio" in Albany, Augustin Daly met her and invited her to join his company. In 1879 she made her first essay in Daly's Theater, as Nelly Beers in "Love's Young Dream," and as Lu Ten Eyck in "Divorce." She at once took the position of leading lady, which she held for a number of years. In 1888 the Daly company went to London, England, where they achieved one of the most remarkable suc-cesses on record. Miss Rehan is piquant, charming and original in all her stage work. Her repertory includes most of the standard comedies, and her sparkle is bright and constant. She ranks as one of the most intelligent and talented comedians of the age. Although her best work has been done in comedy, she is capable of more serious work. Her home is in New York City.

REINERTSEN, Mrs. Emma May Alexander, writer of prose sketches, born in Buffalo, NY, 6th January, 1853. Her pen-name is "Gale Forest." Her father's name was Squire Alexander. Her mother's maiden name was Henrietta E. Sherman. Mrs. Reinertsen is the wife of Robert C. Reinertsen, a prominent civil engineer of Milwaukee, WI. As "Gale Forest" she has more than a local reputa-tion. Her sketches are bright with womanly wit and con-densed wisdom, and she has aptly been called the Fanny Fern of the West, a title which gives a clear idea of her literary style. She has a beautiful home, and two bright boys make up her family. One of the foremost literary women of the age, meeting her in her Milwaukee home, pronounced her the most perfect wife she knew, and deep, indeed, must be the conjugal allegiance of so gifted a writer as "Gale Forest," when she acknowledges that immortal fame would be less desirable on her part than doing the nearest home duty and taking pleasure in the doing. To a friend she once wrote: "To have happiness is to have the best of life, and I know I have as much of that as ever falls to the lot of woman." Her attitude is not one of expectancy as regards applause or recogni-tion of her writings, for she admits that nothing surprises her more than occasional infallible evi-dence that some of her oldest sketches are still going the rounds of the newspapers. She has been a contributor to the Cincinnati "Times," Chicago "Tribune," "Christian Union," "Good Cheer," and the Milwaukee "Wisconsin," "Sentinel" and "Telegraph." She wrote also for the "Milwaukee Monthly," which was at one time quite a popular magazine. One of her best sketches, "A Forbidden Topic," was incorporated in the book entitled "Brave Men and Women." In telling what the women of Wisconsin have done, it will not do to omit a pleasant mention of "Gale Forest," who, as a writer of decidedly meritorious, though not voluminous, prose sketches, occupies a sunny little niche by herself.

RENFREW, Miss Carrie, poet and biographer, was born in Marseilles, IL. She is a daughter of the late Silvester Renfrew, one of the pioneer set-tlers of Hastings, NE, who died in 1888. She is one of a family of five children. She was carefully educated and reared in a refined and cultured atmosphere. She received all the educational advantages of her native town, and she has supplemented her school course with a wide course in reading. In childhood she was a thinker, a dreamer and a philosopher with a poetic turn of mind, but she did not "lisp in numbers." She waited until reason was ready to go hand in hand with rhyme, and then she began to write verses. She had not studied the art of rhyming, and some of her first productions showed the crudity to be expected where there was a lack of training in modes of expression. In spite of all drawbacks of that kind, she wrote well enough to attract attention, and her maturer work leaves nothing to be desired in the matter of form. In 1885 she became a contributor to the Chicago "Inter-Ocean," the "Woman's Tribune" and other prominent journals. In 1890 she began to contribute to the "Magazine of Poetry," and her poems have found wide currency. Her prose work includes a large number of biographies of prominent Nebraska women for this volume. She has written much in verse, and her work shows steady advancement in quality. She stands among the foremost of the literary women in Nebraska.

RÉNO, Mrs. Itti Kinney, novelist and social leader, born in Nashville, TN, 17th May, 1862. She is the daughter of Col. George S. Kinney, of Nashville. She was a high-strung, imaginative child, remarkably bright and precocious, and while still very young she was sent to a convent in Kentucky, where she remained until her education was completed. She was graduated with first honors, and her valedictory was delivered by the embryo author in the form of an original poem. Her début in the great world was marked by the brilliance that wealth and social influence confer, and soon she became one of the belles of Tennessee's capital. She became the wife, in May, 1885, of Robert Ross Réno, only child of the late M.A. Réno, Major of the Seventh United States Cavalry, famous for the gallant defense of his men during two days and nights of horror, from the

overwhelming force of Sioux, who the day before had massacred Custer's entire battalion. Through his mother Mr. Réno is related to some of the oldest families in Pennsylvania, and, though possessed of private wealth, he has expectations of a brilliant fortune, being one of the heirs of old Philippe François Rénault (anglicized Réno), who came over with Lafayette, and who left an estate valued now at $200,000,000. For several years after her marriage Mrs. Réno led the life of a young woman of fashion and elegance. In the summer of 1889 she began to write a romance, entirely for self-amusement, with never a thought of publication. She kept her work a secret till its completion, and then she laughingly gave it to her mother for criticism. Her parents insisted on publication, but Mrs. Réno declined. Finally her father won her consent to submit her manuscript to his friend, Hon. Henry Watterson, and to abide by his decision. Mr. Watterson read and pronounced it "a genuine southern love story, full of the fragrance of southern flowers and instinct with the rich, warm blood of southern youth." He gave the young author some letters to eastern publishers, and her first novel, "Miss Breckenridge, a Daughter of Dixie" (Philadelphia, 1890), was published. It proved successful, and within a few months it had passed through five editions. Her second book, "An Exceptional Case" (Philadelphia, 1891), is one of great force and power, and it has also proved a success. Mrs. Reno lives in luxurious surroundings in a sumptuous home on Capitol Hill. She will henceforth devote her life to literature.

RHODES, Mrs. Laura Andrews, musician and opera singer, born in Casey, IL, 1st October, 1854. She is the second oldest daughter of Rev. J. R. and Delilah Andrews, the parents of the Andrews family, of which the well-known Andrews Opera Company is mainly composed. She possesses in a remarkable degree the musical ability which is the heritage of the Andrews family. She has a lyric soprano voice of great purity, richness and compass. Among her instructors were Prof. W. N. Burritt, of Chicago, Prof. Lowenthal, of the Paris Conservatory, and Madam Corani, of the Conservatory of

Milan. She began her stage career with the Andrews Concert Company at the age of seventeen. Soon after, she became the wife of F. B. Rhodes, a druggist, who, at one of their entertainments, became enamored of her voice and speedily thereafter of herself. They were married within six months after the first meeting. Since their marriage Mr. Rhodes has been connected with the opera company from time to time as business manager. When, a few years later, the Andrews family organized as the Andrews Swiss Bell Ringers, Mrs. Rhodes was the soprano bell ringer, becoming famous in that capacity. When the present Andrews Opera Company was organized Mrs. Rhodes took the leading rôles and for years was their prima donna, scoring success everywhere and winning applause in nearly every State in the Union. In 1890 the constant strain of daily singing and the weariness of incessant travel brought on a severe attack of nervous prostration, from which she made a very tardy recovery. Although thus compelled to abandon the stage for a time, she has not been idle, but has been busily engaged in vocal teaching and in special solo work in the various Chautauqua assemblies of the Northwest.

RICE, Mrs. Alice May Bates, soprano singer, born in Boston, MA, 14th September, 1868. Her parents were both well known in the musical profession, and her ancestors on both sides were musical for a number of generations. Mrs. Rice's father possessed a baritone voice of rare quality and held positions in quartette choirs, musical societies and clubs in and around Boston, until a few years before his death, in 1886. Her mother was a thoroughly cultured and earnest teacher of music. Mrs. Rice was nurtured in an atmosphere of music and was a singer by birth as well as by tuition. Her début in Chickering Hall, Boston, in September, 1883, was a brilliant event. During her first season she appeared in several operas, which Charles R. Adams, with whom she studied rendition, brought out, assuming the prima donna rôles in "Martha," "Figaro," "Maritana," "La Sonnambula," "La Filie du Régiment," "Faust," and "Lucia di Lammermoor." She was the prima donna, subsequently, of the Maritana

Opera Company and appeared with them for several seasons in the leading cities in New England and Canada. She sang in many concerts for the Philharmonic Orchestra of Boston and for Seidl's New York Orchestra. She has held positions in quartette choirs in Lowell and Worcester, MA, and in her own city, leaving a lucrative one for her recent tour with Remenyi, with whom she traveled through the South and West for one-hundred-fifty concerts in seven months. She exemplifies the opinion of many that an American girl can be educated and achieve success without European study, believing it better that young girl students should have the influence of home and the protection of parents.

RICH, Mrs. Helen Hinsdale, poet, born in a pioneer log cabin on her father's farm in Antwerp, Jefferson county, NY, 18th June, 1827. On her father's side she is akin to Emma Willard. She is known as "The Poet of the Adirondacks." She ran away to school one frosty morning at the age of four, and her life from that time was centered in books and the beautiful in nature. Few of the first were allowed to her, but she reveled in forest and stream, rock and meadow. At twelve years of age she wrote verses. She led her classes in the academy and won prizes in composition. She attended a single term. She became proficient in botany at the age of thirteen in the woods on the farm. She was obliged to read all debates in Congress aloud to her father, and the speeches of Henry Clay and Daniel Webster made her an ardent patriot and politician. Her poetry has appeared in the Springfield "Republican," Boston "Transcript," the "Overland Monthly" and other prominent journals. She has published one volume of her poems, "A Dream of the Adirondacks, and Other Poems" (New York, 1884), which was compiled by Charles G. Whiting, who is preparing another volume for a Boston house. She was the first woman of northern New York to embrace woman suffrage. For two seasons she gave lectures for the Union cause in the Civil War. She has always been a defender of woman's right to assist in making the laws that govern her. She has carried out her ideas of woman's ability and need of personal achievement, self-support and self-reliance

612   RICH, Mrs. Helen Hinsdale

in the rearing of her daughter. Her "Madame de Stael" has the endorsement of eminent scholars as a literary lecture. Her "Grand Armies" is a brilliant Memorial Day address. She excels in poems of the affections. Mr. Whiting has said in his introduction to her volume: "Her works have a distinctive literary quality, which all can appreciate, but few can express. She is one of the best interpreters of mother-love in this country. Her 'Justice in Leadville,' in the style of Bret Harte, is pronounced by the London 'Spectator' to be worthy of that poet or of John Hay." That highly dramatic poem and "Little Phil" are included in nearly all the works of elocution of the present day. She became the wife, at the age of twenty, of a man of scholarly tastes and fine ability, who cordially sympathizes with her ambitions and cherished sentiments. Her culture has been gained by the devotion of hours seized from the engrossing domestic cares of a busy and faithful wife and mother. Her home is in Chicago, IL.

RICHARDS, Mrs. Ellen Henrietta, educator and chemist, born in Dunstable, MA, 3rd December, 1842. She received a thorough education and was graduated from Vassar College in 1870. She then took a scientific course in the Massachusetts Institute of Technology, Boston, where she was graduated in 1873. She remained in that institution as resident graduate, and in 1875 she became the wife of Professor Robert Hallowell Richards, the metallurgist. In 1878 she was elected instructor in chemistry and mineralogy in the woman's laboratory of the institute. In 1885 she was made instructor in sanitary chemistry. She has done a great deal of original work in the latter branch, her researches covering the field thoroughly. She has done much to develop the love of scientific studies among women. Her chosen field is the application of chemical knowledge and principles to the conduct of the home, and she is the pioneer in teaching that subject to the women of the United States. She is the first woman to be elected a member of the American Institute of Mining Engineers. She is a member of many scientific associations. Among her published works are: "Chemistry of Cooking and Cleaning" (Boston, 1882), "Food Materials and Their Adulterations" (1885), and "First Lessons in Minerals" (1885). In 1887 she, with Marion Talbot, edited "Home Sanitation." She is a profound student and a clear thinker, and her work is without equal in its line.

RICHARDSON, Mrs. Hester Dorsey, author, born in Baltimore, MD, 9th January, 1862. She is the daughter of James L. Dorsey and Sarah A. W. Dorsey, both representatives of Maryland's old colonial families. Hester Crawford Dorsey, the best known of three literary sisters, made her first appearance in the Sunday papers of her native city. She wrote in verse a year or more, before turning her attention to prose writings. Not a few of her poems attracted favorable comment and found their way into various exchanges. In 1886 she wrote "Dethroned," a poem narrating the fate of Emperor Maximilian of Mexico, a copy of which, handsomely engrossed, was presented to Francis Joseph, of Austria, to whom it was dedicated. The emperor accepted the dedication in a letter of thanks to the author. Then Miss Dorsey, at the request of the Baltimore "American," began a series of articles on ethical and sociological subjects, to which she signed the pen-name "Selene." Those "Selene Letters" at once attracted wide attention and excited controversy in literary circles. While her prose writings did much toward improving the hospital service in Baltimore, and a pungent letter from her pen helped to rescue the now prosperous Mercantile Library from an untimely end, her name will not always be associated with those institutions, but she has been a benefactor to the women of Baltimore in a way which will not allow her soon to be forgotten. In organizing the Woman's Literary Club of Baltimore, two years ago, she laid the firm foundation of a controlling force in the intellectual and social life of her native city. The club is over a hundred strong, including among its members many of the best known writers of the day. In January, 1891, she became the wife of Albert L. Richardson, a journalist of experience and ability. The Woman's Literary Club tendered its founder a brilliant reception a week after her marriage. Mrs. Richardson resigned the first vice-presidency of the club upon her removal to New York, where she has lived since her marriage, holding now but an honorary membership. She is still devoting herself wholly to literary work. She has appeared several times in "Lippincott's Magazine," and is now giving her attention to short stories. She is earnest in her purpose and has a grasp of subjects which makes her a force on the printed page.

RICHMOND, Mrs. Euphemia Johnson, author, born near Mount Upton, NY, in 1825. Her maiden name was Guernsey. Her father, Dr. J. Guernsey, was a native of New Hampshire. Her mother was a Miss Putnam, a daughter of Dr. E. Putnam, a relative of the Revolutionary hero. On both sides her ancestors were professional and literary people. Miss Guernsey became Mrs. Richmond in early womanhood. She received good schooling and became an omnivorous reader. Her first poem and prose sketches were published in the Cincinnati "Ladies' Repository." She contributed poems to the New York "Tribune" under her pen-name, "Effie Johnson." One of her early stories, "The McAllisters," was a temperance history, and was very successful. She published "The Jeweled Serpent," "Harry the Prodigal," "The Fatal Dower," "Alice Grant," "Rose Clifton," "Woman First and Last" (in two volumes), "Drifting and Anchored," "The Two Paths," "Hope Raymond," "Aunt Chloe" and an "Illustrated Scripture Primer" for the use of colored children in the South. She is now living in Mount Upton, NY.

RICHMOND, Miss Lizzie R., business woman and insurance agent, born in Lacon, IL, 19th November, 1850. Her mother's family is of old New England stock. When she started as an insurance agent, in Peoria, IL, a business woman was hardly heard of in the place. It was uphill and hard work, but she succeeded in spite of all predictions to the contrary, and is recognized as one of the most successful business managers in Peoria.

RICKER, Mrs. Marrilla M., lawyer and political writer, born in New Durham, NH, 18th March, 1840. Her maiden name was Young. She graduated from Colby Academy, New London, in 1861. For several years thereafter she taught, and became the wife of John Ricker, a farmer, in May, 1863. He died in 1868, in Dover, NH. In 1872 Mrs. Ricker went abroad and spent two years on the continent. After close application to the law for three years, under a tutor, she was, 12th May, 1882, admitted to the bar of the supreme court of the District of Columbia. On 11th May, 1891, she was, on motion of Miss Emma M. Gillett, admitted to the bar of the United States Supreme Court. Soon after her admission to the bar, in 1882, she was appointed by President Arthur a notary public for the District of Columbia, and in 1884 by the judges of the District supreme court, a United States commissioner and an examiner in chancery, both of which offices she continues to exercise. She has long been known as the "Prisoner's Friend," from her constant habit of visiting prisons to befriend those confined. She was one of the assistant counsellors in the famous Star Route cases. Her legal work has been almost invariably on the side of criminals and for the oppressed. She was one of the electors for New Hampshire on the equal rights ticket on which Belva A. Lockwood ran for president in 1884. She opened the New Hampshire bar to women in July, 1890, her petition having been filed in December, 1889. She went to California in 1887 and worked for the Republican ticket in 1888. She visited Iowa in 1892 in the interests of the Republican party.

RIGGS, Mrs. Anna Rankin, temperance reformer, was born in Cynthiana, KY. Her parents removed to Illinois when she was two years of age. Her maiden name was Anna Rankin. She united with the white-ribbon army, in whose ranks she has won so many honors. When she went to Oregon, Portland had no home for destitute women and girls. In 1887 the Portland "Union," under the auspices of Mrs. Riggs and a few noble women, opened an industrial home. The institution was kept afloat by great exertions and personal sacrifice, until it was merged into a refuge home and incorporated under the laws of the State. She has been president of the Oregon Woman's Christian Temperance Union. In 1891 she started the "Oregon White Ribbon," which has been a success. A prominent feature of her

Charlotte Neilson.
From Photo by Morrison, Chicago.
Alice Nixon.
From Photo by Morrison, Chicago.

May Merrick.
From Photo by Morrison, Chicago.

work in this State has been a school of methods which has proved an inspiration to the local unions in their department work. She has also represented Oregon at conventions and been president of the International Chautauqua Association for the Northwest Coast. She has been a christian from early womanhood, is a member of Grace Methodist Episcopal Church, one of a corps of teachers who are making its Sabbath-school a success. She is a talented speaker. Her home is in her brother's elegant residence on Portland Heights, Portland. Mr. and Mrs. Riggs are childless, but they have adopted three orphan children.

RIPLEY, Mrs. Martha George, physician, born in Lowell, VT, 30th November, 1843. She was the oldest of five children. Her paternal ancestors came over in the Mayflower. Her maternal grandfather was Scotch, and served in the Revolutionary War. Her mother, Esther A. George, a woman of fine intellectual powers, became the wife of Francis Rogers. One of the first to be interested in the anti-slavery movement, she was also a pioneer in the temperance cause. Dr. Ripley's father was a man of character and ability. Mr. and Mrs. Rogers left Vermont, when Martha was eleven months old, and settled in northwestern Iowa. There she grew up. Hungry for knowledge, she availed herself of every advantage the country offered, and acquired a substantial education. When the war of the rebellion broke out, her deepest interests were enlisted in the struggle. Too young to go as a hospital nurse, she found an outlet for her sympathies and activities in work for the United States Sanitary Commission. Endowed with a natural aptitude for teaching, she worked several years in the school-room. June 25th, 1867, she became the wife of William W. Ripley. Soon after their marriage Mr. and Mrs. Ripley removed to Massachusetts, where they lived for thirteen years. The science of medicine had always been a subject of deep interest to her. Even before she thought of obtaining a thorough education, she devoted much time to that study. Mr. Ripley's health becoming impaired by close application to business, his wife felt a new desire for proficiency in medical science, and in 1880 entered the Boston University

School of Medicine. At her graduation in 1883 she was pronounced by the faculty one of the most thorough medical students who had ever received a diploma from the university. Soon after, she settled in Minneapolis, MN. There her medical knowledge and skill have brought her reputation and an extensive and lucrative practice. In her large practice she very soon saw the need of a temporary home for a certain class of patients. Maternity Hospital, founded by her, and for several months carried on by her unaided efforts, has risen in response to that need. Her work in its behalf has continued earnest and constant. She is now attendant physician of the institution and one of its board of directors. A born reformer, her zeal for human rights has grown more ardent with years. Deeply interested in the enfranchisement of woman and in temperance, she has done valiant service for both causes, devoting to them all the time not required by family and professional duties. The center of a happy home, where three young daughters are growing up to inherit her health of body and of mind as well as her earnest, progressive spirit, she proves that in devotion to outside interests she has not forgotten the more sacred ones of her own household. Elected president of the Minnesota Woman Suffrage Association in 1883, she served in that capacity for six years. An earnest advocate of that cause, and an effective speaker and writer, she has done good work in helping to bring many unjust laws into harmony with the higher civilization of the present day and the golden rule of christianity.

RIPLEY, Miss Mary A., author, lecturer and educator, born in Windham, CT, 11th January, 1831. She is the daughter of John Huntington Ripley and Eliza L. Spalding Ripley. The Huntington family is prominent in New England. One of its members, Samuel Huntington, signed the Declaration of Independence and the Articles of Confederation. Miss Ripley is, on her mother's side, of Huguenot ancestry, and is descended from the French family, D'Aubigné, anglicized into Dabney, a well-known Boston name, which is well distributed throughout the country. Miss Ripley, in early childhood, showed studious and literary tastes, and commenced to write stories when very young. She was educated in the country district-schools of western New York, and in the free city-schools of Buffalo, NY. She taught school in Buffalo for many years. Her contributions to the press have been, principally, poems, vacation-letters, terse communications on live questions, and brief, common-sense essays, which have attracted much attention and exerted a wide influence. In 1867 an unpretending volume of poems bearing her name was published, and, later, a small book entitled "Parsing Lessons" for school-room use was issued. That was followed by "Household Service," published under the auspices of the Woman's Educational and Industrial Union of Buffalo. With Miss Ripley the conscience of the teacher has been stronger than the inspiration of the poet. Had she given herself less to her pupils and more to literature, she would assuredly have taken a high place among the poets of our country. Her poems are characterized by vigor and sweetness. She was for twenty-seven years a teacher in the Buffalo high school. It was in the management of boys that she had the most marked success. The respect with which she is regarded by men in every walk of life is evidence that she made a lasting impression upon them as a teacher. Her clear-cut distinctions between what is true and what is false, and her abhorrence of merely mechanical work, gave her a unique position in the educational history of Buffalo. She resigned her position in the Buffalo high school on account of temporary failure of health. When restored physically, she entered the lecture-field, where she finds useful and congenial employment. Her present home is in Kearney, NE, where she is active in every good word and work. Her decided individuality has made her a potent force in whatever sphere she has entered. She now holds the responsible position of State superintendent of scientific temperance instruction in public schools and colleges for Nebraska. Her duty is to energize the teaching of the State schools on that line.

RITCHIE, Mrs. Anna Cora Mowatt, author and actor, born in Bordeaux, France, in 1819, and died in London, England, 28th July, 1870. She was the daughter of Samuel Gouverneur Ogden, a New York merchant, who was living temporarily in France at the time of her birth. She was the tenth in a family of seventeen children. She lived near Bordeaux until 1826, when the family returned to New York City. Cora entered school. At the age of fourteen she won the affection of James Mowatt, a young lawyer,who persuaded her to marry him that he might superintend her studies. Her parents approved the engagement, and stipulated that the union should be postponed until she was seventeen years old. The young lovers were secretly married, and the parents soon forgave them. For two years Mrs. Mowatt studied diligently, and in 1836 she published her "Pelayo, or the Cavern of Covadonga," under the name "Isabel." That poetical romance elicited adverse criticism, and she replied to her critics in 'Reviewers Reviewed," a satirical effusion, in 1837. Her health became impaired, and she went to Europe to recuperate. There, in 1840, she wrote her drama, "Gulzara, the Persian Slave," which was played after her return to New York City. Mr. Mowatt suffered financial reverses, and Mrs. Mowatt gave a series of dramatic readings in Boston, New York and Providence in 1841. Ill health forced her to leave the stage. Mr. Mowatt entered business as a publisher, and she returned to literature. Under the pen-name "Helen Berkley" she wrote a series of stories for the magazines that were widely read, translated into German and republished in London. Her play, "Fashion, a Comedy," was a success in New York and Boston, and, when her husband failed a second time in business, she decided to go on the stage. On 13th June, 1845, she appeared as Pauline in "The Lady of Lyons," and was successful. In 1847 she wrote another play, "Armand, or the Peer and the Peasant," which was well received. She then went to England, in company with Edward L. Davenport, and on 5th January, 1848, she made her début in London in "The Hunchback." She returned to New York in 1851. Her husband died in that year. She remained on the stage until 3rd June, 1854. On 7th June, 1854, she became the wife of William F. Ritchie, of Richmond, VA. In 1860 she was recalled to New York to attend her father in his last illness. Her health was impaired, and after her father's death she went to Europe, where she spent the time with relatives in Paris, Rome and Florence. Her second husband died in 1868, and she went again to England, where she remained till her death. Her other works include: "The Fortune Hunter," a novel (1842); "Evelyn, or a Heart Unmasked: a Tale of Domestic Life" (two volumes, Philadelphia, 1845, and London, 1850); "The Autobiography of an Actress: or Eight Years on the Stage" (Boston, 1854); "Mimic Life: or Before and Behind the Curtain" (1855); "Twin Roses" (1857); "Fairy Fingers, a Novel" (New York, 1865); "The Mute Singer, a Novel" (1866), and "The Clergyman's Wife, and Other Sketches" (1867).

RITTENHOUSE, Mrs. Laura Jacinta, temperance worker, author and poet, born in a pleasant home on the forest-crowned hills in Pulaski county, IL, near the Ohio river, 30th April, 1841. She is a daughter of Dr. Daniel Arter. From her parents she inherited her tastes and talent for literature. Her education was received in the schools of the sparsely settled country, but she supplemented her deficient schooling by earnest self-culture and wide reading. She became the wife, on 31st December, 1863, of Wood Rittenhouse, a prominent business man and honored citizen of Cairo, IL. Their family numbers one daughter and four sons. The daughter is a promising writer, who recently won $1,000 for an original story, and who is also president of the Young Woman's Christian Temperance Union of Cairo. Of the sons, the oldest is an electrician, the second a physician, the third a business man, the fourth a high-school boy, and all are energetic and industrious, total abstainers and free from the use of tobacco or narcotics of any kind. After her marriage, for many years, Mrs. Rittenhouse was able to spare but little time for literary work, but during the past three or four years she has been a frequent contributor to magazines and newspapers. Her best work is done in her short stories. She is a skillful maker of plots, and all her stories are carefully wrought out to their logical ending. Her warmest interest has for years been given to the work of the Woman's Christian Temperance Union, and for that body and its great cause she has toiled and written unceasingly. She was the first president of the Woman's Christian Temperance Union of Cairo, serving in that office for many years. She was elected district president of that organization for

four consecutive years, and for the past five years she has served as district treasurer. She was secretary of the Social Science Association in Cairo so long as it was in existence. She served as secretary of the Centennial Association in Cairo, and also as secretary of the Cairo Protestant Orphan Asylum, besides acting as manager of the asylum for many years. She served a year as secretary of the Cairo Women's Library Club. For three years she was president of the Presbyterian Woman's Aid Society in Cairo. She was one of the vice-presidents of the Red Cross Society in Cairo. Her life is a busy one, and her latest work in literary fields gives promise of valuable results.

ROACH, Miss Aurelia, educator, born in Atlanta GA, 10th March, 1865. Her father, Dr. E. J. Roach, was a physician, a native of Maryland, who removed to Georgia several years before the Civil War. His ancestors were among the earliest settlers of Somerset county, MD, and the original land-grants are still in the family. During the war Dr. Roach was surgeon of the 18th Georgia Regiment. After the war he returned to Atlanta, where he achieved distinction in his profession and served the public in several offices. Her mother was a daughter of A. Weldon Mitchell, one of the early settlers of Atlanta, and at one time one of its wealthiest citizens. Her great-great-grandfather on the maternal side served as lieutenant in a Georgia regiment in the Revolutionary War. Miss Roach was graduated with distinction from the girls' high school of Atlanta in June, 1882. The two years succeeding her graduation she spent in the study of French and German, with which languages she was already familiar, having studied them since early childhood. In 1884 she was appointed a teacher in one of the public schools. Beginning with the lowest grade, she was promoted until she had reached the fifth grade, when she left the school to travel in Europe. She made a northern tour, visiting Norway, Sweden, Russia and Denmark. During her sojourn in Europe in 1889 she acted as a special correspondent for the Atlanta "Constitution." In her absence she was elected to a position in the girls' high school, which she held until

1891, when she again went abroad. On her return to Atlanta she became principal of the Crew street school, one of the largest in the city. She has won distinction by her narrative and descriptive powers, and she has shown a capacity for a higher range of original and philosophic thought.

ROBERTS, Mrs. Ada Palmer, poet, born in North East, Dutchess county, NY. 14th February, 1852. Her father, Elijah Palmer, was a scholarly lawyer, who had poetical talent. His satirical poems, many of which were impromptu, did much to make him popular as a lawyer. From her father Mrs. Roberts inherited poetical talent. From him she received most of her early education, as her delicate health would not permit her to be a regular attendant in school. When she was sixteen years old, her education was sufficient for her to teach a private school, her pupils having been her former playmates. She was married 31st January, 1878, and household duties, maternal cares and recurring ill health have kept her from doing regular literary work. Her poetical productions have not been intended for publication, but have come from her love of writing. She has published but few poems, and some of them have found a place in prominent periodicals, the "Youth's Companion," the New York "Christian Weekly" and others. Mrs. Roberts' home is in Oxford, CT.

ROBERTSON, Mrs. Georgia Trowbridge, educator and author, born in Solon, OH, 2nd August, 1852. The ancestry of Mrs. Robertson's mother, Lavinia Phelps Bissel, reaches back to the Guelphs. That of her father, Henry Trowbridge, is recorded in the "Herald's Visitation" as holding Trowbridge Castle, Devonshire, in the time of Edward First in the thirteenth century. The name Trowbridge is also frequently found in Revolutionary annals. During her girlhood Mrs. Robertson imbibed much of the honest, earnest thought of the New England settlers, among whom her early years were spent. At fifteen

she became a teacher in the Ledge district of Twinsburgh, OH, and two years later passed to wider fields of action, teaching in the graded schools and attending Hiram College. During her life as student and teacher she published various essays and poems. Her writings trended from the first in the direction of ethics, philosophy and nature. In 1875 she became the wife of George A. Robertson, an alumnus of Hiram College and a well-known journalist of Cleveland, OH. For several years she was an invalid. She recovered her health and is again at work, thinking and writing in the line of social and divine science. She is actively connected with the Ohio Woman's Press Association and various historical, literary, art and social organizations in her city. Her work is sometimes anonymous, but is known over her signature, "Marcia."

ROBINSON, Mrs. Abbie C. B., editor and political writer, born in Woonsocket, RI, 18th September, 1828. Her father was George C. Ballou, a cousin of Rev. Hosea Ballou and of President Garfield's mother. Her mother's maiden name was Ruth Eliza Aldrich. She was a woman of ideas quite in advance of her time, brought up, as her ancestors had been, under the Quaker system of repression. The daughter inherited from both parents most desirable qualities of devotion, courage and mental strength. She was educated in her native town and in New England boarding-schools. She studied music in Boston and spent three years in Warren Seminary, RI. She took the regular course in the institute in Pittsfield, MA. In 1854 she became the wife of Charles D. Robinson, of Green Bay, WI. He was the editor of the Green Bay "Advocate" and for many years one of the controlling minds of Wisconsin in all matters of public polity. He was at one time Secretary of State. Mrs. Robinson was as famous for political wisdom as her husband. Of her newspaper career it is somewhat difficult to write, since her public work was so closely interwoven with her private experiences during the very sorrowful and troublous period of her connection with the "Advocate." She went into the office of that paper by the usual route, the desire to help her husband, in the early part of 1882, as Colonel Robinson's health was failing rapidly. Gradually the sick man's duties fell to his devoted wife, and before long she assumed charge of them all, taking the place in the office while she performed her own duties at home, doubly increased by the care of a dying husband. Her lot was rendered infinitely harder by other troubles, which harassed and hampered her almost beyond endurance. After three years of editorial management of the "Advocate," she was placed in a position to assume control of the whole establishment connected with the paper, including not only the business management, but also a job department, a bindery and store. That position she held for four years, during which time Colonel Robinson died. Then came the inevitable result, nervous prostration, an attempt again to take up the work, then her final retirement from the paper in 1888. Under all these trying conditions she won for herself an enviable reputation as a woman of much force and ability, always animated by the highest, purest motives, and as an easy, graceful, cultured writer. She was also a good deal of a politician, with original Republican tendencies, though the "Advocate" was and is a Democratic paper. The story of her having brought out a Republican issue of the paper, when it was once put under her charge during Colonel Robinson's editorship, is a standard joke, and is periodically repeated in the State papers. The stand taken by the "Advocate" during the labor strikes and riots in Milwaukee, in 1881, is said to have saved the Democratic party in Wisconsin from making a serious mistake.

ROBINSON, Miss Frannie Ruth, author and educator, born in Carbondale, PA, 30th September, 1847. In 1859 her parents took up their residence in Albany, NY, and there the formative years of her life were passed. She was graduated at the age of seventeen years from the Albany Female Academy, and later received the degree of A.M. from Rutgers' College, New York. Among the influences which quickened her early ambitions, she recognizes three: First, the impulses received from a small circle of men and women, some of whom were very much older than herself; second, the impetus given to youthful

ambitions by a class of young people in the alumnæ of the female academy, and third, the lift into a rarer air which was hers, happily through many seasons, when Emerson and Phillips, Curtis and Beecher, Chapin and Holmes went to the capital city at the bidding of the lyceum. She began to write early. Most of her published poems appeared in "Harper's Magazine" in the years between 1870 and 1880, during which time she wrote occasionally for the "Contributor's Club" of the "Atlantic Monthly." Her poem, "A Quaker's Christmas Eve," was copied in almost every city in the Union. Albany twice paid her the honor of asking for her verse, once for the services of the first Decoration Day, and again when an ode was to be written for the ceremony of laying the corner-stone of the capitol. In 1879 she began to teach, and since then she has written little for publication. A poem on Emerson, published after his death in the "Journal of Philosophy," is considered one of her best. Two of her sonnets found place in the collection of "Representative American Sonnets," made in 1890 by Mr. Crandall. She is at present preceptress of Ferry Hall Seminary, the woman's department of Lake Forest University, Lake Forest, IL, a position she has held since 1888. She is a member of the Woman's Educational Auxiliary of the Columbian Exposition.

ROBINSON, Mrs. Harriet Hanson, author, born in Boston, MA, 8th February, 1825. Her maiden name was Harriet Jane Hanson. Her ancestry is thoroughly New England and her lineage may be traced in direct line to Thomas Hanson and Nicholas Browne, early settlers of New England. Nicholas Browne was a member of "The Great and General Court" of Massachusetts in 1655, in 1656 and in 1661. Her grandfather, Seth Ingersoll Browne, was in the Revolutionary army and a non-commissioned officer in the battle of Bunker Hill. Miss Hanson's father died while she was a child. In 1832 her widowed mother moved with her family to Lowell, MA, where they lived for some years on the Tremont Corporation. Her early years were full of toil, but she studied and educated herself, and showed literary talent in her girlhood. In 1848 she became the wife of William S.

Robinson, at that time the editor of the Boston "Daily Whig," and afterward famous as "Warrington" in the Springfield "Republican" and in the New York "Tribune." He was for eleven years clerk of the Massachusetts House of Representatives. He died 11th March, 1876. Their family consisted of four children. Three of them are still living, and two of them, daughters, are mentioned elsewhere in this book. Mrs. Robinson's first attempt at writing for the press was made while she was yet an operative in the Lowell mills. Her verses appeared in the newspapers and annuals of the time, and in the "Lowell Offering," that unique factory girls' magazine. During her early married life she was too deeply engaged in helping a reformer-journalist to earn his daily bread to use her pen in verse-making. Later in life she resumed her literary work, and since then she has been a contributor inverse and prose to many newspapers and periodicals. Her sonnets are among the best of her poetical contributions. Her first published work was "Warrington Pen Portraits" (Boston, 1877), a memoir of her husband, with selections from his writings. She wrote "Massachusetts in the Woman Suffrage Movement," a history (Boston, 1881), "Captain Mary Miller," a drama (Boston, 1887), "Early Factory Labor in New England" (Boston, 1883), and she has in preparation a book which will illustrate that phase in the life of the New England working girls. Her best literary achievement is her latest, "The New Pandora," (New York. 1889). That dramatic poem is modern in all its suggestions, and puts the possibilities of humanity on a noble upward plane. She is very deeply interested in all the movements which tend to the advancement of women, and she uses her voice and pen freely in their behalf. She was one of those to speak before the select committee on woman suffrage when it was formed in Congress. She presented a memorial to Congress in December, 1889, through Senator Dawes, asking for a removal of her political disabilities and that she might be invested with full power to exercise her right to self-government at the ballot-box. Senator Dawes then presented a bill to the same effect in the Senate, which was read twice and referred. A hearing was refused by the select committee on woman suffrage, and there the matter rests. The woman's club movement has always had her support. She is one of the original promoters of the General Federation of Women's Clubs, an organization numbering at least two-hundred women's clubs, representing more than thirty-thousand members in all parts of the United States, and she was the member for Massachusetts on its first advisory board. Her home is now in Malden, MA.

ROBINSON, Mrs. Jane Bancroft, author and educator, born in West Stockbridge, MA, 24th December, 1847. She is descended on her mother's side from an old Dutch family of New York City, and on her father's side from early English settlers in New Jersey. Her father, Rev. George C. Bancroft, was for over fifty years a member of the Methodist Episcopal Church. Mrs. Robinson was graduated in 1871 from the Troy seminary for girls, founded by Mrs. Emma Willard. In 1872 she was graduated from the State Normal School in Albany, NY, and immediately thereafter was appointed preceptress of Fort Edward Collegiate Institute, Fort Edward, NY, where she remained until 1876. During the years from 1870 to 1876 colleges for women were being established, and the doors of colleges hitherto open only to men were thrown open to women. Urged by her far-sighted mother, she determined to take a college course. While in Fort Edward, she took private lessons in advanced studies, and in the fall of 1876 entered Syracuse University as a member of the senior class, and was graduated from that institution in 1877. Immediately thereafter she was invited to become the dean of the Woman's College of the Northwestern University in Evanston, IL, and professor of the French language and literature, a position previously occupied by Miss Frances Willard and Mrs. Ellen Soulé Carhart. In addition to the arduous work of the position, she diligently pursued her studies in French history, with a view to taking a higher degree, and she received from Syracuse University, upon examination, the degree of Ph.M. in 1880, and of Ph.D. in 1883. Her thesis for the latter degree was a treatise on the parliament of Paris and other parliaments of France, and the research and study therein displayed won her at once a fine reputation. Many of the leading historical students in the United States and England sent her appreciative letters. In 1885 she resigned her position in the Northwestern

University to pursue historical studies as a fellow of history in Bryn Mawr College. In 1886 she went to Europe, matriculated in the University of Zürich and remained there one year, devoting herself to the study of political and constitutional history. The following year she went to Paris and became a student in the Sorbonne, continuing her researches in history. She was also received as a student in the École des Hautes Études, being the first woman to hear lectures in the literary department of that school. Her stay abroad was diversified by travel and writing. She contributed to various papers and periodicals. Visiting London before her return to the United States, she became deeply interested in the deaconess work as illustrated in different institutions there and studied it carefully. She returned to the United States, convinced that that social and religious movement might prove a great agency in the uplifting of the poor and the degraded of her native land. Her wide information and executive ability were at once pressed into service for developing deaconess work in the United States, where it had already gained a foothold. At the invitation of its officers, she in 1888 took full charge of the department of deaconess work in the Woman's Home Missionary Society of the Methodist Episcopal Church. She has visited most of the large cities of the United States, speaking in behalf of the deaconess cause, and interesting the women of different Protestant churches by means of parlor meetings and public lectures. She is a logical and fluent speaker as well as a writer of marked talent. In 1889 she published her most important work, entitled "Deaconesses in Europe and their Lessons for America," which is now in its third edition and is the leading authority in this country upon the subject. She is now the secretary of the Bureau for Deaconess Work of the Woman's Home Missionary Society. She is a life member of the American Historical Association and of the American Economic Association. She is connected with many philanthropic and social organizations. In 1891 she became the wife of Hon. George O. Robinson, of Detroit, MI, widely known in philanthropic and legal circles.

ROBINSON, Mrs. Leora Bettison, author, born in Little Rock, AR, 8th June, 1840. Her parents, Dr. Joseph R. Bettison and Ann Eliza Cathcart, moved to Louisville, KY, before she was a year old. The Bettisons are of distinguished Huguenot lineage, being descended from Pierre Robért, of South Carolina. Mrs. Bettison's family belong to the Cathcarts, of Glasgow, Scotland, who, before coming to America in the seventeeth century, had settled in Antrim county, Ireland. Dr. Bettison was a surgeon in the Confederate army. Leora was the sixth of eleven children. In her classes, always the genius during her school-days, her writings attracted attention, and many of her early efforts were published in the local papers. On 29th June, 1864, she became the wife of Prof. Norman Robinson, a graduate of Rochester University. To that union was born one child, Jeannette Cathcart. Prof. and Mrs. Robinson established in Louisville a flourishing school, named Holyoke Academy.

During that time she wrote her earliest books, "Than" (New York, 1877), a sequel to "The House With Spectacles,"and "Patsy" (New York 1878). Owing to an accumulation of business interests in Florida, Prof. Robinson moved to that State in 1880, where he now holds the office of State chemist and resides in the capital, Tallahassee. Mrs. Robinson has there done the best literary work of her life. It is conceded, that by her contributions to the press and her pamphlet, "Living in Florida," she has done more to induce immigration to the State than any other agency has accomplished. She is a member of the Baptist Church.

ROBY, Mrs. Ida Hall, pharmacist, born in Fairport, NY, 8th March, 1857. Her parents removed to Michigan when she was a child, and she was educated mainly in that State. Her father was a noted educator, a man of brilliant intellect and sterling character. He was a professor in the high school in Battle Creek, MI, and served as superintendent of schools in Kalamazoo county, in the same State. He died one year before his daughter, Ida, was graduated from the Illinois College of Pharmacy, a department in the Northwestern University, in Evanston, IL. She was thus thrown upon her own resources at an early age, and, having a natural fondness for chemistry, which was intensified by study and work in a drug house for several years, she started a pharmacy in Chicago. She attended the college on alternate days, and is the first woman to graduate from the pharmaceutical department of that institution. She is by natural instinct a chemist, and she has won a unique reputation as a successful woman in a line of business generally left to men to handle. Her model pharmacy on Forest avenue, in Chicago, is one of the features of that great city.

ROBY, Mrs. Lelia P., philanthropist and founder of the Ladies of the Grand Army of the Republic, born in Boston, MA, 25th December, 1848. Her father and grandfather were clergymen and antislavery agitators. She is descended from Priscilla Mullens and John Alden, of the Mayflower colony. Among her ancestors were many Revolutionary heroes. She has always felt a deep interest in the soldiers who fought in the Civil War. She is a regent of the Daughters of the Revolution. On 12th June, 1886, in Chicago, IL, where she lives, she founded the order of the Ladies of the Grand Army of the Republic, which started with twenty-five members, and now numbers about 15,000 mothers, wives, sisters and daughters of soldiers and sailors who served in the war of 1861–65. The members of that order are pledged to assist the Grand Army of the Republic in works of charity, to extend needful aid to members in sickness and distress, to aid sick soldiers, sailors and marines, to look after soldiers' orphan's homes, to see that the children obtain proper situations when they leave the homes, to watch the schools, and see to it that the children receive proper education in the history of the country and in patriotism. She has secured many pensions for soldiers and in countless ways worked for the good of the survivors of the war. Her activities cover a wide range. She was one of four women selected by the board of education of Chicago to represent them before the legislature of the State to help pass the compulsory education bill. It was passed, for a large majority of the legislators were old soldiers, and the fact that Mrs. Roby was their friend made voting for a measure she advocated a pleasant duty. She is the only woman member of the Lincoln Guard of Honor of Springfield, IL, and an honorary member of the Lincoln Guard of Honor of California, an honor conferred on her "for her many acts of devotion to his memory," through

Gen. Sherman. She is a member of the Chicago Academy of Science, she is president of the South Side Study Club of Chicago, vice-president of the Woman's National Press Association of Washington for Illinois, a member of the Nineteenth Illinois Veteran Volunteer Infantry, of the Society for the Advancement of Women, and of the American Society of Authors. She has the care and oversight of supplying the soldiers' homes with books, magazines and periodicals; she visits the homes in various parts of the country and looks after the comfort of the old soldiers, and if there is special legislation needed to right their wrongs or give them additional comforts, she goes to the State legislatures or to Washington to secure such enactment. Through her efforts Memorial Day was set apart in the schools for the reading of histories or stories of the war, and preparing for Memorial Day itself. She never tires in her work, and her husband and two sons are enthusiastic in the work also. She is the wife of General Edward Roby, a constitutional lawyer of Chicago. She does a good deal of literary work under the pen-name "Miles Standish." She is preparing for publication a large volume entitled "Heart Beats of the Republic." She is a model home-maker, a connoisseur in architecture and art, a fine linguist, thoroughly educated, and a well-read lawyer.

ROGÉ, Mme. Charlotte Fiske Bates, author, critic and educator, born in New York, 30th November, 1838. Her father died during her infancy, and her home from her eighth year almost to the time of her marriage was with her mother and family in Cambridge, MA. There Mme. Rogé attended the public schools, and there for twenty-five years was engaged in private teaching. She began to write at eighteen, and her first paid efforts appeared several years later in "Our Young Folks." She has ever since contributed more or less to the periodicals, and has much in manuscript awaiting publication, but only one volume of her verse has been issued, "Risk, and Other Poems" (Boston, 1879). Nine of the French translations in the book she made for Longfellow's "Poems of Places," in whose preparation she aided considerably. She edited two delightful compilations from his own works, and to his memory was dedicated her anthology of British and American verse, "The Cambridge Book of Poetry and Song" (New York, 1882). She has given some admirable lectures and readings from her own writings, which are in many veins of thought. Nowhere is she happier than in the humorous epigram. The ethic fun which she can put into twenty words, no other writer can surpass. She has done much for good causes, especially for those connected with her art, and once at least was a successful organizer. Alone and under difficulties she carried out the authors' reading in Sanders' Theater, Cambridge, which added a loyal emphasis and a considerable sum to the Longfellow memorial fund. It was in her native city that she taught last, and there an attack of pneumonia proved nearly fatal. The physicians expecting her death, the report of its occurrence was circulated by the press, and, though the error was speedily and publicly corrected, it crept into Cassell's late publication, "Younger American Poets," whose preface regrets her loss. On 4th June, 1891, Miss Bates, who still keeps her maiden name in literature, became the wife of M. Edouard Rogé, of New York, where she is now living. In December, 1891, she was appointed an honorary and corresponding member of the advisory council on literary congresses, woman's branch of the W.C.A., in the Chicago Exposition. She has a broad mind, open to the most advanced ideas of the epoch. She is a poet, divining well the moods and needs of the human heart. She is a christian, eager above all to help and uplift men through her genius.

ROGERS, Mrs. Effie Louise Hoffman, educator, born in Jackson, OH, 13th May, 1855. She is the only daughter of Dr. D. A. and Emily Smith Hoffman. When a small child, she went to Iowa with her parents, who settled in Oskaloosa. She received her education in the public schools. In the fall of 1869 she entered college and was graduated 19th June, 1872, in Mount Pleasant, IA. Returning home, she gave her time to music and literary work. She wrote for several papers and magazines. In 1877 she entered a conservatory of music and became proficient in the art. At the close of that year she began to teach music and continued for a number of years. On 28th April, 1880, she became the wife of J. F. Rogers, cashier of the Cloud County Bank, Concordia, KS. He was a man of unusual business ability as well as a

man of fine literary attainments. The first two years of her married life were spent in Concordia, where her time was devoted to church and society work. There she gathered around her the young girls of the town and entered with all her heart into the work of helping them into a higher literary and religious life. Each Saturday afternoon found her home filled with girls, who spent an hour in Bible reading and study. In December, 1882, she moved with her husband to Great Bend, KS, where he organized the Barton County Bank. The March following, their first child, a daughter, was born. In August, 1883, Mr. Rogers, after three days' illness, died. Mrs. Rogers at once returned to her former home in Iowa, where in August her second child, a son, was born. He lived only two months. In 1885 she made an extended trip through the Southern States. She achieved considerable fame as a newspaper writer at that time. In the fall of 1885 she became city editor of the "Oskaloosa Times," a Democratic newspaper. That position she held for eighteen months. She next entered the "Globe" office, and there remained for nearly two years. She then began the publication of the "P.E.O. Record, "a secret society journal. That magazine she edited and published for two years, but, owing to increasing demands upon her time, was obliged to give it up. She was president of the Iowa Grand Chapter P.E.O. Sisterhood three years. Under her supervision the organization grew and prospered. In 1890 she was elected national grand chapter president of that sisterhood. She has ever been interested in all work connected with woman's advancement. She is a member of the Woman's Christian Temperance Union and has been, since its organization, holding important offices in that society. In 1889 she was elected county superintendent of the public schools of Mahaska county, IA. She is the first woman ever elected to that office in that county. She was reelected in 1891 with an increased majority. Under her supervision the county schools are taking high rank, and education in all lines is being advanced. She also served as member of the school board, vice-president of the State teachers' association, and president of the Woman's Round Table. In 1891 her name was mentioned for State Superintendent of Public Instruction. She refused at once to allow her name to be presented to the Democratic convention. She is a member of the executive council of the educational department of the Columbian Exposition of 1893. She is a member of the Presbyterian Church and interested in the Young People's Society of Christian Endeavor. She is at present editor of the "Schoolmaster," an educational journal published in Des Moines, IA.

ROGERS, Mrs. Emma Winner, author, is a native of Plainfield, NJ. On both sides she has the advantage of good ancestry. She is the daughter of Rev. John Ogden Winner, and the granddaughter of Rev. Isaac Winner, D.D., both being clergymen of the Methodist Episcopal Church and natives of New Jersey. On the maternal side she is the granddaughter and great-granddaughter of Moses Taylor, and Moses Taylor, second, during their lives successful business men of New York City. She received her early education in private schools in Jersey City, NJ, graduating from Pennington Seminary, Pennington, NJ, and later from the University of Michigan. For six years she was the corresponding secretary of the Woman's Home Missionary Society of Detroit Conference, and is now the honorary president of the Rock River Conference Woman's Home Missionary Society. She is connected with the woman's work of the Columbia Exposition, as the chairman of the committee on municipal order, of the World's Congress Auxiliary. She is a member of the Chicago Fortnightly Club. She is specially interested in literary work in the line of social science and political economy, and has been a contributor on those subjects to various papers and periodicals. She has written a monograph entitled "Deaconesses in Early and Modern Church," which exhibits diligent research and marked historical and literary ability. While yet young, she became the wife of Henry Wade Rogers, of Buffalo, NY, afterward dean of the law school of the University of Michigan, and now the president of Northwestern University, Evanston, IL. She is a woman of marked ability, especially endowed with the logical faculty and with the power of dispassionate judgment. She is a type of the younger college woman, who, with the advantage of the wider training of the higher education, brings her disciplined faculties to bear with equally good effect upon the amenities of social life and the philanthropic and economic questions of the day. As the wife of the president of a great university, her influence upon the young men and women connected with it is marked and advantageous. While she is still a young woman, she has already left an impress upon the life of her times that is both salutary and permanent.

ROGERS, Mrs. Mary Fletcher, author, was born in Louisville, KY. She is a member of the well-known Fletcher family of New England. Her ancestor, Robert Fletcher, emigrated from England and settled in Massachusetts in 1630. The family has given to the world such women as Grace Webster, Hannah Emerson, Valinda Young, Elizabeth Trumbull, Julia Fletcher, known as "George Fleming," and others distinguished in the varied walks of literary, religious or scientific life. Mrs. Rogers is a versatile and graceful writer, though she has never aimed at book-making. Of late years her time has been largely given to benevolent work. She is an official member of the American Humane Association and a director in the Association for the Advancement of Women. She holds various offices in the smaller organizations in her city. She is recognized as a woman of strong character, impressing those with whom she comes in contact that the latent forces of her nature, if called into controversial effort, are capable of strong and untiring resistance. Ever ready to oppose wrong, the suffering and needy find in her a champion and a friend. Taking active interest in all the reforms that are for the elevation of mankind everywhere, she is in every sense a representative woman of the day.

ROHLFS, Mrs. Anna Katharine Green, poet and novelist, born in Brooklyn, NY, 11th November, 1846. Her maiden name was the pen-name by which she is known throughout the world. She is the daughter of a lawyer, and from him she inherits the legal turn of mind shown in her famous novel "The Leavenworth Case" (New York, 1878), and in other productions. In childhood she wrote innumerable poems and stories. Her family removed to Buffalo, NY, when she was a child, and in that city she was educated and reared, until she was old enough to enter Ripley Female College, in Poultney, VT. Soon after her graduation she published her novel, "The Leavenworth Case," which at once attracted the attention of the literary world. Her successes brought her many invitations from publishers to furnish them books, and she was so busy with her novels that her poetical ambitions, which were her chief ones, were temporarily held in check. Notwithstanding the call for prose works from her pen, she published in 1882 a volume of verse, "The Defense of the Bride, and Other Poems," and in 1886 she brought out a second volume of poetry, a drama, entitled "Risifi's Daughter." After living in Buffalo for some years, the family returned to Brooklyn, NY. On 25th November, 1884, she became the wife of Charles Rohlfs, formerly an actor. Since their marriage they have lived most of the time in Buffalo. They have three children. Her published works include, besides those already mentioned, "The Sword of Damocles" (1881), "Hand and Ring" (1883), "X. Y. Z." (1883), "A Strange Disappearance "(1885), "The Mill Mystery" (1886), "7 to 12" (1887), "Behind Closed Doors" (1888), "The Forsaken Inn" (1890), "A Matter of Millions" (1890), "The Old Stone House" (1891), "Cynthia Wakeham's Money" (1892) and has dramatized her first novel. Her "Leavenworth Case" is used in Yale College as a text-book, to show the fallacy of circumstantial evidence, and it is the subject of many comments by famous lawyers, to whom it appeals by its mastery of legal points. Her stories have been republished throughout the world, in various languages, and the sales of her books have reached enormous proportions. She has visited Europe, where she supervised the translation of some of her books into the German language. She is a prolific author, but all her work is well done.

ROLLINS, Mrs. Alice Wellington, author, born in Boston, MA, 12th June, 1847. She is a daughter of Ambrose Wellington, who taught her at home until she was fourteen years old. She then studied in different schools in Boston, and finished with a year of study in Europe. In 1876 she became the wife of Daniel M. Rollins, of New York City. They have one son. Mrs. Rollins has traveled much in Europe, Brazil, Alaska and the United States. For seven years from its commencement she contributed reviews every week to the New York "Critic." She has been a frequent contributor to the "Christian Union," the "Independent," "Lippincott's Magazine," the "North American Review," the "Century," the "Cosmopolitan Magazine," the "Forum," "St. Nicholas," "Wide Awake" and "Harper's Young People," "Bazar," "Weekly" and "Magazine." Her published books are: "The Ring of Amethyst," poems (New York, 1878); "The Story of a Ranch" (1885); "All Sorts of Children" (1886); "The Three Tetons" (1887), and "From Palm to Glacier." Her essays on tenement-house life in New York City are crystallized in the form of a novel, "Uncle Tom's Tenement." She has read papers on that subject before various societies and clubs, and has done much to show up the evils of the tenement system in New York City. Her home is a center of culture and refinement.

ROLLSTON, Mrs. Adelaide Day, poet and author, was born near Paducah, KY. Her earliest years were spent in the country, in the midst of a landscape of quiet pastoral beauty. Her father was a physician of good standing. At the age of twelve years her talent for writing verse began to manifest itself in brief poems published in the local press. Later, several appeared in the defunct "Saturday Star-Journal," of New York. She was educated in St. Mary's Academy, in Paducah, to which city her parents had removed when she was twelve years old, and where she still lives. After the conclusion of her school-life she continued her contributions to the neighboring press, and frequently verses over her name appeared in the "Courier-Journal" of Louisville. They attracted little or no attention, until she found a friend and helper in the veteran of the Kentucky press, Col. H. M. McCarty. In 1877 she began to contribute to the "Current," and since then she has won wide recognition as a contributor to "Once a Week," "Youth's Companion," "Godey's Lady's Book" and other eastern periodicals.

ROSE, Mrs. Ellen Alida, practical agriculturist, born in Champion, NY, 17th June, 1843. On 5th December, 1861, she became the wife of Alfred Rose. In 1862 they moved to Wisconsin, where her life has been spent on a farm near Brodhead. In 1873, near her home in Brodhead, she joined the Grange, and for seventeen years was an active member of that organization, holding many offices, among them county secretary and a member of the State committee on woman's work. As a result of her efforts, assisted by two or three other members, a Grange store was organized, which has been in successful operation many years and saved to the farmers of Green county many thousands of dollars. In 1888, when speculation in wheat produced hard times, Mrs. Rose prepared and presented to her Grange the following resolutions: "Whereas, our boards of trade have become mere pool-rooms for the enrichment of their members, and whereas, by their manipulations of the markets they unsettle the values and nullify the law of supply and demand, so that producers do not receive legitimate prices for what they produce; and, whereas, by 'cornering' the markets they are enabled to force up the prices of the necessaries of life, to the great distress and often starvation of the poor; therefore, resolved, that we demand immediate action by Congress, and the passage of such laws as shall forever prohibit gambling in the necessaries of life." They were unanimously adopted and forwarded through county and State Granges to the National Grange, where they were adopted and placed in the hands of the legislative committee of the Grange in Washington, where they have been urged upon Congress with such force that the Anti-Option Bill in Congress was the result. She is now a prominent member of the Patrons of Industry, being one of the executive committee of the State Asso-

ciation, and by voice and pen is doing much to educate the famers in the prominent reforms of the day, of which the advancement of women is one which claims her first interest. From her earliest recollection she has been an advocate of woman suffrage, although she did not join any organization until 1886, when she became a member of the Wisconsin Woman's Suffrage Association and was instrumental in forming a local club, becoming its first president. In 1887 she assisted in organizing a county association and was appointed county organizer. In 1888 she was appointed district president, which office she still holds.

ROSE, Mrs. Martha Parmelee, journalist, reformer and philanthropist, born in Norton, OH, 5th March, 1834. Her father, Theodore Hudson Parmelee, went to Ohio in 1813 with the colony that founded Western Reserve College, then located in Hudson, OH. Educated under Lyman Beecher, he was too liberal to be an adherent of Calvin, and he accepted the views of Oberlin, which opened its college doors to the negro and to woman. In 1847 his widow removed to that village, and Martha, the youngest, from twelve years of age to womanhood heard the thrilling sermons of Charles G. Finney. She was graduated in 1855, and, when teaching in a seminary in Pennsylvania, became the wife of William G. Rose, a member of the legislature of that State, an editor and lawyer. In the oil development of 1864 he acquired a competency and removed to Cleveland, OH. Mrs. Rose, interested in the benevolent work of Cleveland, found that those who asked for aid often labored for wealthy firms, whose business was suspended in the winter, and that such idleness was the cause of pauperism and crime. During her husband's first term as mayor of Cleveland she investigated the reports of destitution among the Bohemians of her own city. She made it one object of her life to see for herself the sufferings of sewing women, and brought to light the frauds and extortion practiced upon them. A lecture by the sculptor, McDonald, of New York, gave an account of the manual training-schools of France and Sweden. Mrs. Rose reviewed the report of the Royal Commission of England for the daily press and sent copies of it to business men. Other lectures followed, and a manual training-school was established in Cleveland. She has written a book, not yet published, "The Story of a Life; or, Pauperism in America." She has written on the labor question and kindred topics, and has reported numerous lectures and sermons on those subjects. She reviewed Mrs. Field's "How to Help the Poor," and some of its suggestions were used by the Associated Charities of Cleveland. She helped to form the Woman's Employment Society which gave out garments to be made at reasonable prices and sold to home missions and centers of merchandise. Mrs. Rose is president of the new Cleveland Sorosis, carrying forward the enterprise with vigor and grace. She is a patron of art. She has reared a family.

ROSEWALD, Mrs. Julie, vocalist, born in Stuttgart, Germany, 7th March, 1850. She is a member of the highly musical family named Eichberg, of which Julius Eichberg, of Boston, MA, is also a member. Julie was educated in the Stuttgart Conservatory and in the Royal Theater School in the same city. It was a high honor for her to enter the Royal Theater School, as but two candidates were selected annually by the king, and they were, of course, chosen from the most promising and advanced students in the conservatory. After she had finished her studies in Stuttgart, she came to the United States, to make her home with her sister, an excellent pianist. She met J. H. Rosewald, of Baltimore, MD, the well-known solo violinist and composer, and became his wife in 1869. After her marriage she returned to Europe and continued her studies under Marie Von Marra, in Frankfort, Germany. She returned to the United States in company with Franz Abt, under an engagement to interpret his songs during his concert tour in the principal American cities. In 1875 she entered the operatic field. She made her début in Toronto, Canada, as "Marguerite." She scored a success. She traveled as prima donna with the Caroline Richings Opera Company and with the Clara Louise Kellogg English Opera Company. She and her husband went to Europe again, and while there they filled engagements in Berlin, Vienna, Rotterdam, Prague and Cologne. Returning to the United States after a successful tour, Mrs. Rosewald accepted an engagement as prima donna with the Emma Abbott Opera Company, of which her husband was musical director. She earned a brilliant reputation. In 1884 she withdrew from the stage and settled with her husband in San Francisco, CA, where they now live. She has become a most successful vocal teacher. She has an extensive list of musical compositions in her mastery, and she speaks, reads and writes English, German, French and Italian with ease and elegancy, and has sung operas in those four languages. As a vocal teacher she exercises a strong influence on general musical culture of the metropolis of the Pacific coast.

ROSS, Mrs. Virginia Evelyn, author, born in Galena, IL, 1st February, 1857. Her maiden name was Conlee. She is the youngest of twelve children. She comes of a hardy pioneer class of genuine Americans. She removed with her parents, who are still living, to Charles City, IA, in 1864, but the restless spirit of the pioneer settler carried them to Johnson County, NE, in 1869, where Virginia passed the greater part of her early life. She there became the wife of T. J. Ross, in 1879. She had received only the rudiments of a text-book education, but her talent sprang into activity, like the crystal flow from a mountain spring. Not being possessed of a strong physical body, she has taxed herself severely. She is a model housekeeper, wife and mother, and has found time, with all her home and society duties, to execute some beautiful paintings. Her series of articles entitled "To Brides, Past, Present and Future," and "Hints to Husbands," has been extensively copied. Her literary work has been so far confined to newspapers and magazines, and her publishers have kept their demand for material far ahead of her ability to produce. Her numerous poems show a high order of talent. Her home is in Omaha, NE.

ROTHWELL, Mrs. Annie, poet, born in London, England, in 1837. Her father, Daniel Fowler, is an artist of wide reputation, who won the only medal given for water-color work to

American artists in the Philadelphia Centennial Exhibition in 1876. Miss Fowler removed with her family to Canada, when she was four years old. They settled in Kingston, Ontario, where most of her life was passed. She was well educated, and spent three years in England. She was married at an early age. She wrote verses in her first years, but none of her childish productions have been published. She contributed many short prose stories to American, Canadian and English magazines, and some of her best poems have appeared in the "Magazine of Poetry." She has published four novels, "Alice Gray" (1873), "Edge Tools" (1880), "Requital" (1886), and "Loved I Not Honor More" (1887). During the Riel Rebellion in Canada, in 1885, she wrote a number of poems on that incident that attracted wide notice. Much of her best work has been published in the United States. She was married young, but was early left a widow. Her home is now in Kingston.

ROUTT, Mrs. Eliza Franklin, social leader, born in Springfield, IL, in 1842, of Kentucky ancestry. Her grandfather, Colonel William F. Elkin, was one of the famous "Long Nine" that represented Sangamon county, IL, in the legislative session of 1836–37. They averaged six feet in stature. Abraham Lincoln was one of those stalwarts, whose efforts that year secured the location of the capital for their county. Her father, Franklin Pickrell, also a Kentuckian, was of a family as noted for generous physical proportions as for their kindness of heart. The ancestral traits are marked in Mrs. Routt. Left an orphan in babyhood, Col. Elkin's home welcomed the grandchild. Orphanage doubtless accounts in some measure for the self-reliance and determination that have characterized her life. In a day when it was uncommon in the West, she secured an excellent education, which the family patrimony enabled her to supplement by travel and study abroad. When Colonel John L. Routt, the second assistant

Postmaster-General, in 1874, wedded his bride in her uncle's home in Decatur, IL, he took back to the national capital a talented, cultured woman, a desirable addition in every way to the society of Washington. In 1875 Colonel Routt went to Colorado as Territorial Governor under President Grant's appointment. In 1876 Colorado became a State and made him her first governor. In 1891 he was again the incumbent of the office. Their home has been in Denver for sixteen years. That Mrs. Routt has added strength and luster to her husband's administrations is recognized in the State, while culture, character, position and wealth have made her socially preeminent. The influence of herself and her associates has been a chief factor in developing the remarkably refined, almost unique, character of Denver's "best society" today. A devout member of the Christian Church, she has ever been generous in its support, generous in charity and always ready to recognize worth and "make friends with it" in any station of life. Still in the vigor of life, with a remarkably large and happy experience of the world's honors and advantages, rest from undue effort in calm anticipation of the future, with a husband honored and exalted in the State he has done so much to mold and direct, with a daughter glowing in the inherited grace of the family, she now delights to keep up her studies and fellowship with the more serious women of the day, who recognize it as a duty to be intelligent and useful.

RUDE, Mrs. Ellen Sergeant, author and poet, born in Sodus, NY, 17th March, 1838. Her paternal grandmother was a Harkness, and her maternal grandmother was one of the pioneer women of the West. Both were women of superior intellect and force of character. Her mother died while she was an infant, and the daughter was reared under the tender care of her father, William Sergeant, who is still living, at the age of eighty-six. She passed through the public schools of Sodus, and afterward took a course of study in Genesee College, in Lima, NY. She became the wife of Benton C. Rude, a graduate of that institution, in 1859. She had always shown literary talent, and in college her compositions attracted notice for their excellence and finish.

She has written much, both in prose and verse, for publication. Her sketches in the "Rural New Yorker" and "Arthur's Home Magazine" first brought her into notice. She won a prize for a temperance story from the "Temperance Patriot." The "Sunday-school Advocate" and "Well-Spring" have published many of her stories for children. As a temperance advocate she has done excellent service. She was the first woman chosen to the office of Worthy Chief Templar by the order of Good Templars of New York State. She made her first public address in the State lodge of Good Templars in Rochester, and was immediately placed on the board of managers of that order. She was made a member of the board of managers of the first State Woman's Christian Temperance Union, established in Syracuse, and was one of a committee sent from that convention to appeal to the Albany legislature for temperance laws. As a lecturer she was decidedly successful, but, in spite of the earnest solicitation of friends, she resigned the field to devote herself to domestic life. For a few years she lived in St. Augustine, FL, during which time she published a volume of poems entitled "Magnolia Leaves" (Buffalo, 1890). Some of the choicest poems of the "Arbor Day Manual" are from her pen. She has contributed to the "Magazine of Poetry" and now expends her literary work on poems and short stories. She lives in Duluth, MN, where her husband and only son are engaged in the law.

RUGGLES, Miss Theo Alice, sculptor, born in Brookline, MA, 27th January, 1871. As a child she took delight in modeling in clay, expressing an admiration for form and beauty that attracted the attention of her parents to her talent. At the age of fourteen she modeled a "Reclining Horse" in snow in the door-yard of her home, and crowds of visitors went out to Brookline from Boston to see the wonderful work of the little girl. In 1886 she was placed under the instruction of Henry Hudson Kitson, the sculptor. In the autumn of 1887 she went to Paris, France, with her mother, where she remained during the following three years, working and studying under the guidance of Mr. Kitson, pursuing at the same time the study of drawing under Dagnan-Bouveret, Blanc

and Courtois. Her first work, a bust of an Italian child, made in Boston, was exhibited, together with a bust of "A Shepherd Lad," in the Paris Salon of 1888, where each succeeding year during her stay her work was readily accepted. In the International Exposition of 1889 she received honorable mention for a life-sized statue of a boy, entitled "Aux Bords de l'Oise," and the same honor was accorded to her in the Paris Salon of 1890 for her "Young Orpheus." She had the distinction of being the youngest sculptor to whom any award had ever been granted. She has won two medals from the Massachusetts Charitable Mechanics' Exposition of Boston, in which city she continues her art work. She is the daughter of C. W. Ruggles, a well-known business man of Boston, and she lives with her parents in the Back Bay. She is descended from an old English family, who settled in America in the seventeenth century. An industrious, unpretentious worker, quiet, swift, modest, she has the character of a true artist.

RUNCIE, Mrs. Constance Faunt Le Roy, poet, pianist and musical composer, born in Indianapolis, IN, 15th January, 1836. She is a daughter of Robert Henry Faunt Le Roy and Jane Dale Owen Faunt Le Roy. On the maternal side she is a granddaughter of Robert Owen, the great advocate of coöperative associations. Her maternal great-grandfather was David Dale, Lord-Provost of Glasgow, Scotland. Her father was a member of the well-known Faunt Le Roy family of eastern Virginia. Her mother was born in Scotland and educated in London, where she received, in addition to her scientific and literary attainments, a thorough training on piano and harp and acquired facility in drawing and painting. Her father died while attending to his coast survey duties, in the Gulf of Mexico, during the winter of 1849. In 1852 Mrs. Faunt Le Roy, in order to develop still further the talents of her children by giving them the advantages of modern languages, German literature and art, took them to Germany and remained there six years. Miss Faunt Le Roy's environment was highly favorable. Her home was in New Harmony, IN, the winter quarters of the officers connected with several geological surveys, and the town possessed an extensive public library and had occasional lectures, besides being the residence of her four uncles, all devoted to science or literature. On 9th April, 1861, she became the wife of Rev. James Runcie, D.D., a prominent clergyman of the Protestant Episcopal Church. They lived in Madison from 1861 to 1871, and then went to St. Joseph, MO, where Mr. Runcie has since served as rector of Christ Church. Their family consists of two sons and two daughters. Mrs. Runcie has been a prolific author. She has published a number of volumes, among which are "Divinely Led," in which she portrays the religious struggles through which she passed in her early years; "Poems, Dramatic and Lyric," "Woman's Work," "Felix Mendelssohn," "Children's Stories and Fables" and "A Burning Question." Besides her literary work she has done much in music. She is a talented pianist and ranks among the foremost performers on the piano. As a composer she has done notable work. Acting on a suggestion by Annie Louise Cary, she published a number of songs, which at once became popular. Among those are: "Hear Us, O, Hear Us," "Round the Throne," "Silence of the Sea," "Merry Life," "Tone Poems," "Take My Soul, O Lord," "I Never Told Him," "Dove of Peace," "I Hold My Heart So Still," "My Spirit Rests" and others. Mrs. Runcie edited a church paper for six years. She served as vice-president of the Social Science Club of Kansas and Western Missouri, organized the now oldest literary woman's club in Indiana, and also served on the committee to draft the constitution for the present flourishing woman's club, of San Francisco, CA. She has lectured successfully on subjects connected with general culture among women. She is chairman of the committee on music and the drama to represent St. Joseph in the World's Columbian Exposition in 1893. She writes concerted pieces. Some of her music is orchestrated. She has written also for the violin. She has been for thirty-four years a successful Sunday-school teacher, illustrating her lessons with free-hand drawings on the blackboard. Her two most dramatic poems, "Anselmo the Priest" and "Zaira, a Tale of Siberia," are used constantly in the field of elocution. In a concert tendered her in Kansas City, every number on the programme was her own musical or poetical composition.

RUPRECHT, Mrs. Jenny Terrill, author, born in Liverpool, OH, 23rd May, 1840. She is of New England parentage. Her early years were spent on a farm, whose picturesque beauty fostered her love of nature. She received less encouragement to cultivate her early talent for writing, perhaps, than she would have done, had not her parents feared that writing, with the ordinary routine of study, would prove too great a strain on the child's sensitive mental organization. After a brief experience as a schoolteacher, Miss Terrill became the wife of Charles Ruprecht, a native of Baden, Germany. For many years her home has been in Cleveland, OH. While she has contributed largely to the local press, many of her poems and sketches have appeared in eastern and other magazines and papers. Some of them have been published over a fictitious name. She has written numerous juvenile stories and poems, which she will soon publish in book-form, illustrated by her daughter, also a volume entitled "Home Rhymes." She has long been engaged in christian work. The neglected quarters of Cleveland, crowded with the increasing foreign element, have been the scenes of her busiest years of mission work. Her warmest sympathies are enlisted by little children. Many have become members of the Sunday-school, organized and put under her supervision more than nine years ago, superintendent of which she still is. She is a member of the Ohio Woman's Press Association, of the Cleveland Sorosis and other literary and social organizations.

RUSSELL, Mrs. Elizabeth Augusta S., philanthropist and reformer, born in Mason, NH, 3rd October, 1832. She was educated in the common schools and in the academy in New Ipswich, NH. She was trained in habits of industry, morals and the severe theologies of the day, after the belief of the Congregationalists. Her father and mother were Yankees, the father from Rindge, NH, and the mother from Ashburnham, MA. Mrs. Russell was married in Worcester, MA, and all her married life was spent in Ashburnham in the same State. There her husband and many of her people are buried. When the war began, she was teaching a school in Florence, AL. During the first fight at Big Bethel she returned to the North. A few months after, at the time of the first battle of Bull Run, she took charge of the New England Soldiers' Relief Association in New York City, and was not mustered out until the close of the war. During those years in the hospital she did not content herself with a superficial knowledge. She visited Washington to study hospital methods. After the close of the war she was actively engaged in the Freedmen's Bureau. She had entire charge of the colored orphan asylum in New Orleans. Later she spent four years in Togus Springs, Augusta, ME, where she was matron of the Soldiers' Home. She then took up hotel work. She took charge of the Continental Hotel in Philadelphia, PA, and remained there eight years. After seven months abroad she spent two years in charge of the Grand Union Hotel, in Saratoga Springs, NY. Afterward she was in Manhattan Beach, the Oriental on Long Island, the Neil house, Columbus, OH, and the West Hotel, Minneapolis, MN. Then she went into the white-ribbon work and took charge of the Woman's Christian Temperance Union Coffee House in Minneapolis, MN, a little unpretentious structure and a business that every one said would be a failure. The women of the Central Woman's Christian Temperance Union realize that it was through the untiring energy and ceaseless endeavor of their manager, that the large restaurant and boarding-house has been brought to its present standing among hotels, a restaurant that furnishes from sixteen-hundred to two-thousand meals per day. She was made superintendent of coffee-house work for the National Woman's Christian Temperance Union in its convention in 1891. She will have charge of the World's Fair Temperance Hotel, located in Harvey, IL, during the exposition. Mrs. Russell's great energy gives form promptly and successfully to all her philanthropic conceptions.

RUSSELL, Lillian, operatic singer, born in Clinton, IA, 4th December, 1862. Her maiden name was Helen Louise, and she is the fourth daughter of Charles E. and Cynthia H. Leonard. In 1865 the family removed to Chicago, IL, where, fortunately for Nellie, music was taught in the primary schools. Coming from a long line of musical people, the child gave early promise of her bril-

liant artistic career. When six years of age, she imitated closely her older sisters on the piano in the music of the old masters. At seven she was placed under her first instructor, Professor Nathan Dye, famous for his success in teaching juveniles, and he laid the foundation of her musical career. At the commencement exercises of the Sacred Heart School, when she was nine years old, Nellie personated a stolen child, in which rôle she sang, danced and played the tambourine so well that the Lady Superior remarked to Mrs. Leonard: "She will one day be a grand prima donna." At ten she was quite proficient on the violin, and at fifteen she sang in the choir of St. John's Church. Prof. Gill was her instructor in church music. At one of his recitals she sang "Let Me Dream Again," and received complimentary mention. She next studied under Carl Woolfson, who expected to make of her an oratorio singer. In one of his concerts she sang "Hast Thou Ever Seen the Land?" from "Mignon," and the comments which followed in the daily press brought Madame Schoenburg to Mrs. Leonard to secure Nellie as her pupil for operatic training. Nellie was studying painting under Madame St. John, and she felt unwilling to assume the added expense of vocal culture. Madame Schoenburg adjusted the matter by an exchange that was satisfactory to all concerned. Some of Nellie's paintings were transferred to Madame Schoenburg's apartments, and the musical work was successfully carried forward. After Lillian learned the premier part in four operas, Mrs. Leonard decided to go to New York, and later to Europe, to prepare her daughter for the operatic stage. When the "Pinafore" craze was at its height, Ed. Rice engaged Nellie, and soon afterward she became the wife of Harry Braham, leader of the orchestra. She next appeared in San Francisco with the Willie Edouin Company, afterward returning to New York. It chanced that in the parlor of a mutual friend Mr. Pastor heard her sing the "Kerry Dance." He said at its close: "I would give forty dollars per week if you would sing that on my stage." The following week "Lillian Russell" began her engagement under Mr. Pastor's management and christening. At the end of a month Mr. Pastor put on the "Pirates of Penzance," somewhat abbreviated and slightly burlesqued. Miss Russell had the part of "Mabel." Among other managers who heard that opera was Manager Mapleson, who was greatly pleased with the youthful prima donna. At the end of the season Mr. Pastor reëngaged Miss Russell for the coming year. Meanwhile John McCall wanted her for the "Snake Charmer." Mr. Pastor released Miss Russell for part of the season, and in one week she prepared herself for the new rôle, which proved a great success. Her next appearance was in Mr. Pastor's new Fourteenth Street Theater, in "Billee Taylor," and she achieved another success. In the Bijou the next season in "Patience" she sang to crowded houses, giving eight performances weekly. In December Miss Russell's strength failed, and a long and severe illness followed. Its tedium was relieved by the kindly attention of her friends, many of whom, both women and men, she had never met personally. Reporters called daily. One cadaverous young man called regularly at midnight to ascertain if it would be safe to publish the "obituary" he had prepared. Toward spring Miss Russell began to mend, and when she was able to sing, a concert was arranged for her in what is now the Broadway Theater. On that occasion she was received with great enthusiasm. She next appeared in the Casino in the "Princess of Trebizond." Under a most unfortunate management Miss Russell made a trip to England and a brief tour through France, Belgium and some portions of Holland. Returning to New York, she sang a full season in the Casino. She next made a tour which included the principal cities of the northern States. She returned again to the Casino. With each new opera came opportunity for the display of her versatility. Mr. French is her present manager and partner in the Lillian Russell Opera Company. Her "La Cigale" had a run of one-hundred nights in New York, and was enthusiastically received in Boston and in Chicago. Miss Russell is ambitious for herself and for her company. She has had her full share of the trials which nearly all successful actors expect at the hands of newspaper writers, who delight in sensationalism at whatever cost. Her home is in West Forty-third street, New York. She is generous to a fault, a devoted daughter, a loving sister and a worshipful mother to her little daughter, who gives promise of having inherited her mother's talents.

RUTHERFORD, Miss Mildred, author and educator, born in Athens, GA, 16th July, 1852. She is the third daughter of Williams Rutherford, professor of mathematics in the University of Georgia, and Laura Cobb, the sister of Gens. Howell and Thomas R. R. Cobb. She was educatd in the Lucy Cobb Institute, Athens, GA, graduating when sixteen years of age. She was made principal of the school in 1881 and still holds that position. During her experience she has sent forth one-hundred-thirty-seven of her pupils as teachers. After teaching English literature for ten years, she determined to prepare her lectures to be used by other teachers and pupils. The result was "English Authors" (Atlanta, GA, 1889). In three months the third edition was called for, and the reception of that book induced the author to prepare a series of text-books, "American Authors," "French and German Authors" and "Classic Authors," for the use of her pupils in Lucy Cobb Institute and pupils elsewhere. So impressed was she with the importance of having the Bible taught in the public schools, that she prepared, in 1890, the questions on Bible history, which she had been using for many years in her school, in such form that it could be used by the common schools without offending any religious faith, "Bible Questions on Old Testament History" (Atlanta, 1890).

RYAN, Mrs. Marah Ellis, author and actor, born in Butler county, PA, 27th February, 1860. She comes of a pioneer family on both sides. Her blood is mingled Huguenot, English, German and Scotch-Irish, with a dash of Quaker gray. She is most thoroughly American. Her maiden name was Martin. Her literary talent developed early, and her first poems and stories appeared in the "Waverly Magazine," over the pen-name "Ellis Martin." She became the wife, in 1883, of the late Sam Erwin Ryan, the comedian, and went upon the stage. After five successful years before the footlights she took up the study of art. Her literary and artistic work combined proved too much for her strength, and she confined her work to literature. Much of her best work was written or conceived during her theatrical life. Since 1890 she has lived near Fayette Springs, Fayette county, PA, in a forest area described in her "Pagan of the Alleghenies" (Chicago, 1891). There she finds health and recreation in the practical management of her farm. While she was on the stage, she had a strong liking for rôles of the marked "character" order, such as old people of the witchy, grotesque sort, and that peculiarity may be noted with distinctness in her stories, in which the characters are strongly drawn on the lines indicated. She is now self-exiled from the stage and from art, and in her mountain home devotes her energies to literature. Her other novels are "Merze" (Chicago, 1889), first issued as a serial in the "Current"; "On Love's Domains" (1890); "Told in the Hills" (1891), and "Squaw Elouise" (1892).

SABIN, Miss Ella Clara, educator, born in Sun Prairie, WI, 29th November, 1850. Her father was Samuel Henry Sabin, originally from Ohio, and her mother's maiden name was Adelia Bordine. In childhood Ella Sabine was the intimate companion of Ella Wheeler Wilcox and Clara Bewick Colby, their country homes being in the same locality, near Windsor, WI. The three were unusually bright girls and, in their several lines, have attained distinction. Ella Sabin attended the Wisconsin State University and was afterward principal of one of the ward schools in Madison, WI. In 1874 she went to Portland, OR. In 1878 she became principal of the North school, the first woman principal in the Northwest. An enlightened board gave her equal pay with men in the same position. In 1888 she was elected superintendent of the city schools of Portland and served three years. Called to the presidency of Downer College, Fox Lake, WI, in 1891, she declined to reapply, though she left Portland when at the height of popularity. She has traveled extensively in Europe and is a woman of broad culture as well as liberal learning.

SAFFORD, Mary Jane, physician and surgeon, born in Boston, MA, in 18–, and died in 1891. She was a woman of marked mental powers. She received a good education and studied medicine in New York City, graduating in 1867. She went to Vienna and studied in the university. She and her classmate, Josephine K. Henry, M.D., of Versailles, KY, were the first women allowed to matriculate in that institution. She studied in Vienna a year, and then went to northern Germany, where she studied surgery and practiced. While in Germany, she performed the operation of ovariotomy, probably the first ever performed by a woman. She returned to Boston, where she practiced and served as instructor in the Boston University. She was one of the first women to serve on the Boston school committee. She lectured on dress-reform and hygiene, and was active in reform work. Her health failed, and she made her home in Florida during the last years of her life. She adopted two girls, who constituted her family.

SAGE, Miss Florence Eleanor, pianist, born in Terre Haute, IN, 3rd March, 1858. Her father is of English descent and a native of the State of New York. Her mother is of French and German extraction and was born in Ohio. Both families are made up of cultured and intelligent persons. Miss Sage early displayed her musical gifts. At the age of four years she played upon the guitar, rendering by ear the melodies she heard. At the age of eight years she began to study the piano, and at eleven she was so far advanced as to be able to play difficult selections from classic authors in concerts. She is distinguished for her ability to read music at sight, having no superior in that respect in the country. She studied in New York City under the leading masters, and her progress was exceedingly rapid. In 1875 she played in concerts in New York and other eastern cities. After completing her studies in New York she removed to Chicago, IL, where, in the season of 1884 and 1885, she inaugurated a series of historical piano recitals, the second of the kind ever given in this country, and the first to be given by a woman. She was very successful in Chicago, and she gave other series in other cities with equally gratifying results. Her piano playing is marked by skill in technique, delicate touch, refined expression and soulful interpretation. Her repertory includes compositions in all styles, from those of the earliest masters down to those of cotemporaneous composers. She is a woman of liberal education. She speaks six modern languages fluently and has read widely. Her literary work includes translations from the literature of Hungary. She lived in Chicago from 1880 to 1887, and since the latter year she has made her home in St. Louis, MO.

ST. JOHN, Mrs. Cynthia Morgan, Wordsworthian, born in Ithaca, NY, 11th October, 1852. She is the only daughter of Dr. E. J. Morgan, a successful homeopathic physician, and Anne Bruyn Morgan. Her maternal grandfather was judge A. D. W. Bruyn. From early girlhood Mrs. St. John showed a passionate love of nature and a devotion for the poetry of Wordsworth. She also possessed the gift of composition and wrote for children's papers before the age of fourteen. On 25th June, 1883, she became the wife of Henry A. St. John, a former civil engineer, now a resident of Ithaca, NY. Her one pre-eminent interest in a literary way has been Wordsworthian. She was a member of the English Wordsworth Society and a contributor to its meetings. She has collected the largest Wordsworth library in this country, and probably the largest in the world. The library contains all the regular editions, the complete American editions of the poetry, autograph letters, prints, portraits, sketches and relics associated with the poet. In 1883 Mrs. St. John, with her husband, visited the English Lake Region and saw every place associated with Wordsworth from his cradle to his grave, and alluded to in his poems. One result of that visit was a "Wordsworth Floral Album," the flowers, ferns and grasses in which were gathered by her own hand. The chief fruit of her life-long study of the poet has been her "Wordsworth for the Young" (1891).

SANBORN, Miss Kate, author, lecturer and farmer, is a native of New Hampshire, the daughter of Professor Sanborn, who held the chair of Latin and English Literature at Dartmouth College for nearly fifty years. Miss Sanborn is descended from the eminent Revolutionary hero, Captain Ebenezer Webster, and is a grand-niece of Daniel Webster. Her inherent lit-

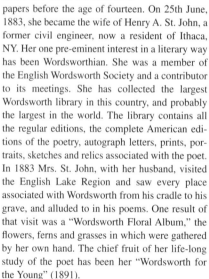

erary talent was developed by a severe course of instruction and mental discipline under her father, who privately instructed her in the regular college course. At eleven she was a regular contributor to the "Wellspring," and at seventeen supported herself by her pen. She became an instructor in elocution at Packer Institute, Brooklyn, and filled for five years the chair of English Literature at Smith College. The idea of discussing current events, now so prevalent in literary clubs, is said to have originated with her as a method used to instruct pupils in the affairs of the day. "Adopting an Abandoned Farm" and "Abandoning an Adopted Farm" are witty records of her original theories regarding farming, put into practice upon an abandoned farm she bought a few miles distant from Boston. Other books have been, "Home Pictures of English Poets," "A Truthful Woman in Southern California," "Vanity and Insanity, Shadows of Genius," "Purple and Gold," "Grandmother's Garden." Her latest book, "My Literary Zoo," treats of the animal friends of many noted people. Miss Sanborn has devoted considerable time to lecturing, and is in great demand before women's clubs. The organization and promotion of the society of the Daughters of New Hampshire is due to her enthusiasm and energy, of which she has been the presiding head from the beginning. Her latest enterprise has been in this direction, the publication of a valuable historical work on New Hampshire. Few women are so versatile and can lay claim to superiority in so many lines of work as Miss Sanborn, who is a teacher, reviewer, compiler, essayist, lecturer, author, farmer, and, above all, famed for her cooking and housekeeping.

SANDERS, Mrs. Sue A. Pike, formerly a national president of the Woman's Relief Corps, born in Casco, ME, 25th March, 1842. She was educated in the State Normal University, of Normal, IL, and was a teacher in the public schools of Bloomington, IL, up to the time of her marriage. She was secretary of the Soldier's Aid Society, of Bloomington, IL, during the war, and corresponding secretary for the sanitary commission branch of that city. She became the wife of James T. Sanders, of Jacksonville, IL, in 1867. She became a member of the Order of Good Templars when fifteen years of age, and took an active part in advancing its principles. When eighteen years old she was elected to the highest office in that order for women in her State. She became a member of the Woman's Relief Corps in December, 1885, and became the first president of her corps. In February, 1886, she represented the corps in department convention of Illinois, where she was elected department treasurer of the order and delegate-at-large to the California convention, where she went in August. On her return she published a journal of her travels. In February, 1887, she was elected department president of her State, and ruled with an economy and dignity that placed the order foremost among the States of the Union. In February, 1888, she was made department counselor of the Illinois Woman's Relief Corps and a member of the national pension committee, in which she served two years. In the Milwaukee convention she presented the recommendation for the adoption of the present site of the National Woman's Relief Corps Home in Madison, OH. She recommended the certificate of service for the army nurses of the late war, and was afterward appointed by the national president to prepare a design for the same, which was adopted and issued by the national order. She was one of the board of incorporators of the National Woman's Relief Corps Home. In 1890 and 1891 she served as national instituting and installing officer. In the national convention in Detroit, MI, in August, 1891, she was elected national president of the Woman's Relief Corps, Auxiliary to the Grand Army of the Republic, the largest charitable organization on earth. During her teaching experience she was located in a Copperhead community. Notwithstanding the sentiment that surrounded her, she kept a little Stars and Stripes hanging over her desk. One day she returned to her school-room to find it broken from its staff and lying upon the floor. She gathered it up and nailed it to the wall. It hung there the rest of the term. That was the first flag-raising in a public school. Ever since that day she has advocated the placing of an American flag in every school-house and church of the land, and her idea has been made popular all over the country.

SANDERSON, Miss Sybil, opera singer, born in Sacramento, CA, in 1865. She is the oldest daughter of the late judge S. W. Sanderson, chief-justice of the supreme court of California. She passed her youth in Sacramento. In 1884 she went with her mother to Europe. She studied for a year in the Paris Conservatoire, and then returned in 1885 to Sacramento. Miss Sanderson went to Paris the third time and renewed her studies with Massenet, who predicted a brilliant career for her. She made here debut as Manon, in the opera of that name, in Amsterdam, 6th February, 1888. Massenet selected her to create the rôle of Esclarmonde, and in the first year she sang that opera one-hundred times to crowded houses. On 8th November, 1890, she made her debut in Massenet's "Mignon" in Brussels. In 1891 she appeared in London, England. Miss Sanderson has a pure soprano voice, reaching from E flat to G in alto. Her debut in Paris was made on 16th May, 1889, when she astonished the music lovers and critics with her rendition of the florid music in "Esclarmonde," which was written for her by Massenet. She ranks with the greatest singers of the age, and is a favorite with the American public.

SANDES, Mrs. Margaret Isabelle, industrial reformer, born in Glasgow, Scotland, 21st May, 1849, of an old and wealthy Scotch family. Her parents came to this country when she was quite young, and finally settled in Milwaukee, WI. At the age of sixteen years she became the wife of Henry R. Sandes, late Adjutant of the 3rd Wisconsin cavalry, and in 1867 settled in Chicago, IL. She never engaged in public work until she became identified with the Woman's Relief Corps auxiliary to the Grand Army of the Republic, of which her husband is a prominent member. She held the position of president of Woman's Relief Corps No. 23 for four successive terms, and has been department inspector, department junior vice-president, and served on the department executive board and as national aid in the same order. She was one of the original nine women appointed by the local directory of the World's Fair, and acted as secretary of that committee until the national commissioners convened, and she went to Washington with the mayor and other influential citizens to aid in securing the site for Chicago. She was appointed alternate lady manager of the World's Columbian Commission. Her position as secretary of the Illinois Industrial School for Girls consumes much of her time, and she is thoroughly devoted to the work of caring for and bettering the condition of the dependent girls. Her home is in Ravenswood, a suburb of Chicago, where she is Matron of Chapter No. 190 of the Order of the Eastern Star.

SANGSTER, Mrs. Margaret Elizabeth, author and editor, born in New Rochelle, NY, 22nd February, 1838. Her maiden name was Margaret Elizabeth Munson. In 1858 she became the wife of George Sangster. Her literary productions were numerous, and she was a regular contributor to many of the leading periodicals. She gradually drifted into editorial work, and in 1871 she became the editor of "Hearth and Home." In 1873 she took an editorial position on the "Christian at Work," which she held for six years. In 1879 she joined the staff of the "Christian Intelligencer," and served as assistant editor until 1888. In 1882 she added to her work the editing of "Harper's Young People," then starting. In 1890 she became the editor of "Harper's Bazar," which position she now fills. During all her busy years she has written poems of high order. Her miscellaneous work includes stories, sketches, essays, editorial comment, criticisms and everything else implied in the important journalistic positions she has held. Her published books are "Manual of Missions of the Reformed Church in America" (New York, 1878); "Poems of the Household" (Boston, 1883); "Home Fairies and Heart Flowers" (New York, 1887), and a series of Sunday-school books.

SARTAIN, Miss Emily, artist, and principal of the School of Design for Women, in Philadelphia, PA, born in that city 17th March, 1841. She is a daughter of John Sartain, the well-known engraver. She early showed an artistic temperament, and her father instructed her in the art of engraving. She studied from 1864 till 1872 in the Pennsylvania Academy, with Christian

Schuessele. In 1872 she went to Paris, France, where she studied till 1875 with Evariste Luminais. Her style in engraving is a combination of line, which she learned from her father, and mezzotint, which she learned from her other instructors. Her work includes framing prints and many portraits for the illustration of books. In oil painting her principal work is portraiture, with a small number of genre pictures. In the Centennial Exposition of 1876 her "Record" won a medal. In 1881 and 1883 she won the "Mary Smith Prize" in the Philadelphia Academy. From November, 1881, till February, 1883, she edited the art department of "Our Continent." In 1886 she was chosen principal of the Philadelphia School of Design for Women, which position she now holds.

SAUNDERS, Mrs. Mary A., business woman, born in Brooklyn, NY, 14th January, 1849. Her father, Dr. Edward R. Percy, settled in Lawrence, KS, ceased to practice medicine and took up the study of the growth and culture of the grape and the manufacture of wine. Mary A. Percy became the wife of A. M. Saunders, and was left a widow with a baby after two years of married life. Being too independent to rely upon her father for support, he not being in prosperous circumstances, she began to support herself. She was hindered in her endeavors to earn a livelihood on account of her infant, and after receiving instruction on the pipe-organ, in the hope of obtaining a position as organist in one of the churches in Lawrence, and making several efforts to obtain music pupils, she at last accepted the invitation so oft repeated by letter from her husband's relatives, who were Nova Scotians, and with her baby started on a week's trip to reach an unfamiliar land. She found a hearty welcome on her arrival, and succeeded in obtaining a pleasant means of livelihood by teaching both vocal and instrumental music. After two years of that life she concluded to leave her little girl with her relatives and returned to her native city, New York, to continue the study of music. At that time her attention was drawn to a new invention, the typewriter. She was introduced to G. W. N. Yost, the inventor of typewriters, and received a promise from him that, as soon as she could write on the typewriter at the rate of sixty words per minute, he would employ her as an exhibitor and sales-woman. In three weeks she accomplished the task required, and was engaged in January, 1875, by the Typewriter Company. She is one of the first women who dared to step out and travel down town for the purpose of earning a livelihood in the walks generally presumed to belong to the sterner sex. The typewriter offered her a field and business which seemed to suit her exactly, and to-day, out of the three first typists, she is the only woman remaining in the business. She assisted in arranging the first keyboard of the Remington typewriter, which is now, with slight alterations, used as the key-board on all typewriters. After a few months of experience in the office in business methods, she took a position as general agent. She traveled all over the West, and sold and inaugu-rated the use of the first typewriters in St. Louis, Cincinnati, Chicago, Indianapolis, Detroit and other cities. After three years she decided she would prefer to settle in New York, and she obtained the position of corresponding clerk in the Brooklyn Life Insurance Company. She then studied stenography. When the head bookkeeper died about two years later, she applied for the vacancy, which was given to her at an advanced salary, and she not only attended to all the corre-spondence and bookkeeping, but examined all the policies and had charge of the real-estate accounts. After nearly thirteen years her failing health warned her that a change was necessary. In the spring of 1891 the Yost Typewriter Company, Limited, of London, England, was about being formed, and they offered her a fine position with them in London as manager and saleswoman, under a contract for a year. She accepted and sailed from New York in April, 1891, accompanied by her daughter. Her position as manager of a school enrolling more than a hundred pupils gave her ample scope to carry out her life-long scheme of aiding women to be self-supporting in the higher walks of life. She has had the pleasure of obtaining positions for some sixty young men and women. At the expiration of her contract she decided to return to New York and undertake the management of the company's office in that city. As a slight mark of their appreciation of her efforts in their behalf, a reception was given to her the evening before her departure. An overture, "The Yost," especially arranged for the occasion, and other musical selections followed. The chief feature of the evening was the presentation of a beautiful dia-mond brooch, as a farewell token of respect and esteem, from pupils and members of the staff. She will now carry on the same line of work in New York that was so entirely satisfactory in London, and will use the same methods of teaching.

SAVAGE, Mrs. Minnie Stebbins, known also under her pen-name, "Marion Lisle," writer of poetry and prose, born in the town of Porter, WI, 25th March, 1850. Her father was Harrison Stebbins, a well-to-do farmer and an influential man in Rock county, a man of integrity and solid worth. Her mother's maiden name was Mary Bassett. She was a woman of much mental strength and nobility of character. Both had a taste for literature. Both were of New England stock. The childhood and early womanhood of Minnie Steb-bins were passed in a pleasant country homestead, full of light and life. Imperfect health and conse-quent leisure, good books and pictures, a piano and standard periodicals may be counted among the influences that helped to mold her. She has written both poetry and prose, more of the former than the latter, for the "Woman's Journal," the "Woman's Tribune," the "Christian Register," "Unity," the Chicago "Inter-Ocean," the "Weekly Wisconsin" and other journals. She became the wife of Edwin Parker Savage in 1876, and since that time has lived in Cooksville, WI. She has been long identified with the temperance work of the State. Both in emanations from her pen and in practical personal efforts she has manifested her belief in a widening future for women. She is also active in Unitarian Church work. It is as a poet she deserves special mention.

SAWYER, Mrs. Lucy Sargent, missionary worker, born in Belfast, ME, 3rd April, 1840. Her maiden name was Sargent. Her remote ancestors were among the earliest set-tlers of Gloucester, MA. Her grandfather, John Sargent, went from Bev-erly, MA, to what was then called the District of Maine, before 1778, and took up a large tract of land, on a part of which members of the family still reside. He was a charter member of the Congregational Church in Belfast, ME. Lucy was thoroughly educated in the best academic institutions in the State. In March, 1862, she became the wife of James E. C. Sawyer, a young clergyman, and in the following July accompanied him to his first charge in Machias, ME. Mr. Sawyer's pastorates have since been some of the most prominent in the Methodist Episcopal denomination. In the large city churches to which he has been called for twenty-five years past, the varied gifts, intellectual brilliancy and spiritual devotion of his wife have made her admired and revered. Their home has ever been the happy resort of great numbers of young people. By the General Conference of the Methodist Episcopal Church, which met in Omaha in May, 1892, Dr. Sawyer was elected editor of the "Northern Christian Advocate," published in Syracuse, NY. Their home is now in that city. Mrs. Sawyer has been especially active in missionary work. While in Providence, RI, she organized the Woman's Foreign Missionary Society of the Methodist Episcopal churches of that city, directly after the beginning of the Woman's Foreign Missionary Society in Boston. The Providence organization was for several years known as the Providence Branch. When the women of the denomination entered upon the organization of a home missionary society, Mrs. Sawyer, then residing in Albany, NY, was elected first president of the Troy Conference Home Missionary Society, and to the wisdom and energy with which she laid the foundations the remarkable growth and prosperity of the society in that conference are largely due. In all reformatory and philanthropic movements she is greatly interested, and she is a generous and zealous patron of many of those organizations by which the christian womanhood of our day is elevating the lowly, enlightening the ignorant, comforting the poor and afflicted, and saving the lost.

SAXON, Mrs. Elizabeth Lyle, woman suffragist, born in Greenville, TN, in December, 1832. She was left motherless at two years of age, and from her father she received her early training. Fortunately he was a man of liberal culture, who entertained advanced views respecting the development and sphere of women. Elizabeth was permitted to grow up naturally, much as a boy would have done, roaming the fields as the chosen companion of her father. Mr. Lyle seems to have recognized that his daughter was a child of unusual endowment, and to have endeavored to foster her peculiar genius. Certain it is that his love of literature and his habits of close observation of nature became prominent characteristics of the daughter. When but sixteen years of age, she became the wife of Lydell Saxon, of South Carolina. Their life was passed largely in Alabama until after the war, when the family removed to New Orleans, LA. Circumstances compelled Mrs. Saxon's absence from her home for twelve years. During that time much of her public work was done. She lived three years on a government claim in Washington Territory to regain lost health, but is now again in New Orleans. Seven children were the fruit of their union, four of whom still live. Of a legal turn of mind, Mrs. Saxon became early interested in the study of constitutional questions. She seems to have inherited a liberty-loving spirit and to have always had an instinctive hatred for every form of slavery. Her father died a prisoner of war in Memphis, TN, and on his death-bed exacted from her a solemn promise "never to cease working for unfortunate women, so long as her life should last." She has devoted herself to the social and legal enfranchisement of her sex. For years she has been in demand as a lecturer on gospel temperance, universal suffrage, social purity and kindred topics. Her keen, logical and yet poetic and impassioned style of oratory fairly takes her audiences by storm and has won for her a national reputation as a public speaker. As a writer she has won an enviable reputation, her poems, stories and prose sketches being published in leading periodicals, both north and south. Her genius seems to be versatile in its nature. She is an elegant home-maker, brilliant conversationalist, an eloquent speaker and an active philanthropist, but it is as a woman working for the most degraded and downtrodden of her sex she is to be held in lasting and grateful remembrance by the women of the nation.

SCHAFFER, Miss Margaret Eliza, insurance agent, born near Riverton, IA, 2nd April, 1869.

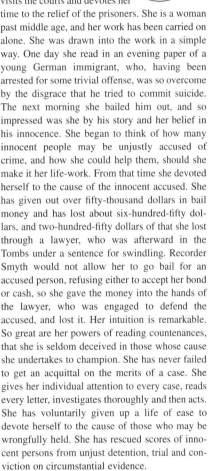

Her father was of German parentage, born in Pennsylvania, and while yet a child moved with his parents to Fulton county, IL. At the early age of seventeen he began to teach school. At the breaking out of the Civil War he entered the Union service. His musical ability was soon recognized, and he was made fife-major and brigade leader during his march with Sherman. On his return he was married to Emma Wadsworth, a young woman of literary tastes. They bought a home in Fremont county, IA, where in the following year Margaret was born. Until twelve years of age she studied under private tutors. In 1880 her father embarked in the mercantile business in Malvern, IA. Entering school there, she pursued her studies diligently, at the same time taking lessons in music of Prof. Willey, a graduate of the Leipzig Conservatory of Music. Later she entered the Corning Academy, IA. After leaving the academy, she successfully followed her musical profession till in May, 1890, when the subject of life insurance was brought to her attention. In that line she found a work that was at once uncrowded, pleasant and remunerative. She entered the work with the true missionary spirit. Her task has been to educate the women to urge their husbands to insure, because it means to them contentment and, in the majority of cases, increased comfort and protection against want in case of financial reverses in the husband's business, or declining health. She was one of the first of the few women to venture in that work, and it is claimed she was the first to open an office of her own and make a special department for the insurance of women. On 1st January, 1892, she connected herself with the National Life of Vermont, in Omaha, NE, after having worked in Omaha a year in another company. The National laid aside the prejudice against admitting women on equal terms with men.

SCHAFFNER, Mrs. Ernestine, "The Prisoner's Friend," is a citizen of New York City. She is the possessor of wealth, that enables her to indulge her charitable leanings in a substantial way. She has always felt a deep interest in the criminal and downtrodden people of her city, and since 1885 she has done remarkable work in behalf of pris-

oners of both sexes, who are under arrest or serving sentences in the city prisons. She has an office at No. 21 Center street, near one of the prisons. Over the door is the legend: "Free Advice to the Poor and to the Innocent Accused." She visits the courts and devotes her time to the relief of the prisoners. She is a woman past middle age, and her work has been carried on alone. She was drawn into the work in a simple way. One day she read in an evening paper of a young German immigrant, who, having been arrested for some trivial offense, was so overcome by the disgrace that he tried to commit suicide. The next morning she bailed him out, and so impressed was she by his story and her belief in his innocence. She began to think of how many innocent people may be unjustly accused of crime, and how she could help them, should she make it her life-work. From that time she devoted herself to the cause of the innocent accused. She has given out over fifty-thousand dollars in bail money and has lost about six-hundred-fifty dollars, and two-hundred-fifty dollars of that she lost through a lawyer, who was afterward in the Tombs under a sentence for swindling. Recorder Smyth would not allow her to go bail for an accused person, refusing either to accept her bond or cash, so she gave the money into the hands of the lawyer, who was engaged to defend the accused, and lost it. Her intuition is remarkable. So great are her powers of reading countenances, that she is seldom deceived in those whose cause she undertakes to champion. She has never failed to get an acquittal on the merits of a case. She gives her individual attention to every case, reads every letter, investigates thoroughly and then acts. She has voluntarily given up a life of ease to devote herself to the cause of those who may be wrongfully held. She has rescued scores of innocent persons from unjust detention, trial and conviction on circumstantial evidence.

SCOTT, Mrs. Emily Maria, artist, born in Springwater, NY, 27th August, 1832. Her maiden name was Spafard, and her ancestry on both her father's and mother's side is purely English. Her father's family came from Yorkshire, England, in the early Colonial days, with Rev. Ezekiel Rogers, and their history is connected with the struggles and privations of those early settlers. Her father was a man of sterling virtues. At an early age he left New England for western New York, where he built a home and reared a large family. From him she has derived the qualities which have enabled her to overcome serious obstacles. Educated in Ann Arbor, MI, and married at an early age, she went with her husband, a young lawyer, to Iowa, but, his death occurring soon after, she removed to New York City with the purpose of making a place for herself among the thousand other struggling women. After studying in the Academy of Design, she went abroad for two years, copying in the galleries and continuing her studies in Rome, Florence and Paris. Since that time she has made many more trips and in Holland, France and England has lingered for months to obtain all the helps possible from those sources. She entered with enthusiasm into all the avenues for the advancement of art and was one of the organizers of the New York Water Color Club, and has been its recording secretary since its incorporation. Her unselfishness has made her career as a teacher remarkable, and she has helped many a young girl over the rough places until they were self supporting. Mrs. Scott is an accomplished linguist and has fine literary tastes.

SCOTT, Miss Mary, temperance reformer and editor, born in Ottawa, Canada, then called Bytown, 17th August, 1851. Her mother's family were among the pioneers of the place. Her childhood was that of a romping girl. She owes much to the influence of such teachers as Abbie M. Harmon, of Ottawa, and Annie M. McIntosh, of Montreal. While a school-girl in Montreal, she attended the revival services of Lord Cecil, and a light shone upon her path which brightened all her afterlife. She has been a Sabbath-school teacher for many years. She is engaged in other church work, and is a member of St. Andrew's Presbyterian Church. In 1882 she joined the Woman's Christian Temperance Union. She heard Miss Willard in Boston, in 1877, for the first time, but did not listen very attentively, as a woman speaking on the temperance question on a public platform was not at all to her taste. She attended the annual meeting of the Ottawa Woman's Christian Temperance Union, when Sir Leonard Tilley presided as chairman. She was struck with the earnestness of the women, the reasonableness of the cause and the evident power of the Holy Spirit in it, and that day she cast her lot with that organization. She was immediately put on a committee, and she has filled many offices, especially in connection with the work of the young women. In January, 1889, she became editor and proprietor of the "Woman's Journal," the organ of the Dominion Woman's Christian Temperance Union. Her literary work has been confined to stories and descriptions of travel for Canadian papers. She is an earnest advocate for the prohibition of the liquor traffic and uses all the weapons at her command. Her home is in Ottawa.

SCOTT, Mrs. Mary Sophia, business woman, born in Freeport, IL, 17th October, 1838. Her father, Orestes H. Wright, was a native of Vermont. Her mother, Mary M. Atkinson, was born in Durham, England. Her father settled in Freeport and began business as a merchant. Mary was the first female child born in that city. Her father died in early manhood, having laid the foundation for a competence for his family. In 1863 Miss Wright became the wife of Col. John Scott, of Nevada, IA, when he was servng in the army, and where she now lives. She soon after collected his motherless children and made a home for them. Her busy life in Iowa began in the fall of 1864. In 1875 she was invited by the executive council to collect and exhibit the work of Iowa women in the Centennial Exposition in Philadelphia. In 1884 she was invited to take entire charge of a similar exhibit in the New Orleans Cotton Centennial Exposition. That she accomplished under many disadvantages. She is eminently domestic in her tastes and a model homekeeper. Probably the most useful and important work of her life was the publication of her book on "Indian Corn as Human Food" (1891).

She is at present the president of the Iowa Woman's Monument Association, the object of which is to encourage the erection of a suitable memorial by the State to commemorate the valor of the Iowa soldiers in the war for the suppression of the Great Rebellion.

SCRANTON, Miss Lida, social leader, born in Scranton, PA, 20th July, 1868. She is the only daughter of Congressman Scranton, of the 11th Congressional District of Pennsylvania. She made her début in Washington during her father's second term in Congress, in 1884 and 1885. She is descended on both sides of the house from families of historic renown. Her father belongs to the celebrated Scrantons, of Connecticut, who settled in Guilford in the latter part of the seventeenth century. Her mother was the daughter of General A. N. Meylert, who was associated with all the early industries of Pennsylvania, and the granddaughter of Meylert, who was an intimate friend of Napoleon I, and fought on his staff as volunteer aid during the temporary illness of D'Abrantes in the battle of Friedland. Miss Scranton has inherited all the noble qualities of her ancestors, which make her a general favorite. Her eyes are dark brown in color. Her hair is tinged with a shade of gold in the sunlight. She is vivacious in manner, intelligent and witty. She is a fine horsewoman. A great deal of attention has been paid to her musical education, and she sings and plays exquisitely, having a rich contralto voice.

SEARING, Miss Florence E., orchestra leader, born near Mobile, AL, 16th October, 1868. She has made New Orleans, LA, her home since childhood. Her father was R. B. Searing, of New York, her mother, Miss Sibley, of Alabama. In 1887 she offered her professional services as pianist for teas, dances and receptions, and by reason of her attractive presence, marked talent and winning manners she soon held a monopoly of the business in all the fashionable gatherings of New Orleans. She was so pretty and so evidently to the manner born that society people were pleased to have her appear as an ornamental adjunct to their entertainments. Her music, they discovered, was selected with exceeding care, fragments culled from light operas that had failed in Paris, but had dancing gems worth retaining. She avoided all hackneyed airs, often getting new waltzes from Europe before their publication in this country. She conceived the idea of forming a string-band, and to that end added one violin, then another, afterward a bass, and next a clarionet, until now a full orchestra of many pieces is admirably trained under her leadership.

SEARING, Mrs. Laura Catherine Redden, author, born in Somerset county, MD, 9th February, 1840. Her maiden name was Laura Catherine Redden. She was made deaf, when ten years of age, by a severe attack of cerebro-spinal meningitis. She lost the power of speech with hearing, but she retained her memory of sounds and her understanding of rhythm. She began in youth to write verses and contributed both in verse and prose to the press. She was irregularly educated. Her parents removed to St. Louis, MO, where she attended the State institution for the deaf and dumb. In 1860 she adopted the pen-name "Howard Glyndon" and became a regular writer on the St. Louis "Republican." That journal sent her to Washington, DC, as a correspondent during the Civil War. In 1865 she went to Europe, where she remained until 1868, perfecting herself in German, French, Spanish and Italian. During her stay in Europe she was a regular correspondent of the New York "Times." Returning to New York City in 1868, she joined the staff of the "Mail," on which she remained until 1876, when she became the wife of Edward W. Searing, a lawyer. During her eight years of service on the "Mail" she studied articulation with Alexander Graham Bell and other teachers, and learned to speak easily and naturally. In 1886 her health failed, and she and her husband removed to California, where she now lives. In addition to her voluminous newspaper and magazine work, she has published "Notable Men of the Thirty-Seventh Congress," a pamphlet (1862); "Idyls of Battle, and Poems of the Rebellion" (1864); "A Little Boy's Story," translated from the French (1869), and "Sounds from Secret Chambers" (1874).

SEAWELL, Miss Molly Elliot, author, was born in a country-house in Gloucester county, VA. Her early education was irregular in the extreme. She was not allowed to read a novel until she was seventeen years old. She read history and encyclopædias, Shakespeare, Shelley and Byron, and went to school at intervals, to learn the common branches. She learned to ride, to dance and to conduct a household. After the death of her father the family made their home in Norfolk, VA, and there Miss Seawell began to devote herself to literature. She visited Europe, and on her return wrote a story, which was published in "Lippincott's Magazine." She then became a contributor to a number of leading periodicals, using five different pen-names to conceal her identity. In 1888 she began to use her own name. She removed with her family to Washington, DC, where for a time she wrote political correspondence for the New York dailies. Her first novel, "Hale Weston," was written for "Lippincott's Magazine" in 1887. It was translated into German and had a large sale. Her next book was "The Berkeleys and Their Neighbors," in 1888, and her most successful book. "Throckmorton," appeared in 1889. It has passed through a number of editions. Another of her books is "Little Jarvis." She contributed to the "Youth's Companion" a story that won a prize of five-hundred dollars. Her books are pictures of life in Virginia before the Civil War. She is fond of society, and her home in Washington is a resort of well-known people.

SEDGWICK, Miss Catherine Maria, author, born in Stockbridge, MA, 28th December, 1789, and died near Roxbury, MA, 31st July, 1867. She was a daughter of Theodore Sedgwick, the well-known lawyer of Boston, MA. She received a thorough education. Her father died in Boston, 24th January, 1813, and she started the private school for young women, which she continued for fifty years. Her brothers encouraged her to make use of her literary talents. Her first novel, "A New England Tale," was published anonymously in New York, in 1822. It was favorably received, and she next brought out "Redwood" (two volumes, 1824), also anonymously. It was reprinted in England and translated into French and three other European languages. The French translator attributed the work to James Fenimore Cooper. She then published "The Traveler" (1825); "Hope Leslie, or Early Times in Massachusetts" (two volumes, 1827); "Clarence, a Tale of Our Own Times" (two volumes, Philadelphia, 1830); "Home" (1836), and "The Linwoods, or Sixty Years Since in America" (two volumes, 1835). In 1835 she issued her collection of "Sketches and Tales," which had been published in various magazines. Her other works include: "The Poor Man and the Rich Poor Man" (New York, 1836); "Live and Let Live" (1837); "A Love-Token for Children" and "Means and Ends, or Self-Training" (1838). In 1839 she went to Europe, where she remained a year. Her travels were described in "Letters from Abroad to Kindred at Home," which were published in two volumes in 1841. In that year she published "Historical Sketches of the Old Painters" and biographies of the sisters "Lucretia and Margaret Davidson," followed by "Wilton Harvey, and Other Tales" (1845); "Morals of Manners" (1846); "Facts and Fancies" (1848), and "Married or Single?" (1857). In addition to her school and novel work, she edited and contributed to literary periodicals and wrote for the annuals. Her work in these lines fills several large volumes.

SEELYE, Mrs. Elizabeth Eggleston, author, born in St. Paul, MN, 15th December, 1858. She is a daughter of Edward Eggleston, the novelist, and she comes of a line that has produced students, writers and professional men of mark for several generations. Her mother was of English parentage and of a family with talent for graphic art. Mrs. Seelye early showed the "book hunger" that has characterized members of her family, but, on account of her delicate health, her parents were obliged to restrain her eagerness for study. In 1866 the family removed to Evanston, IL, where her father had built in his own grounds one of the earliest kindergartens in America, that his children, of whom Elizabeth was the oldest, might be trained correctly from the start. After the removal of the family to Brooklyn. NY, in 1870, Elizabeth attended Packer Institute for a short time, but the methods of teaching that prevailed did not satisfy her parents, and she and her sister were taught mainly at home by private teachers. She also attended for some years the classes in French and German in the Brooklyn Mercantile Library, and was the only child in classes of adults. She early became an eager reader of the best books, especially in English and French. In the midst of her cares as the mother of a family, she reads works of philosophy, natural science and political economy with the keenest relish. Her study of the literature of the Middle English period enabled her to supply the editor of the "Century Dictionary" with five-hundred new words and definitions. In 1877 she became the wife of Elwyn Seelye, and she has since that time lived on or near Lake George, NY. She has written four of the five volumes in the Famous American Indian Series, "Tecumseh" (New York, 1878); "Pocahontas" (New York, 1879); "Brant and Red Jacket" (New York, 1879), and "Montezuma" (New York, 1880). Mrs. Seelye has also published "The Story of Columbus" (New York, 1892), illustrated by her sister, Allegra Eggleston.

SEGUR, Mrs. Rosa L., woman suffragist, born in Hessa, near Cassel, Germany, 30th January, 1833. When she was five years old her parents made the journey to America, settling first in Detroit, MI, but finally, in 1840, selecting Toledo, OH, for a permanent home. Before she had completed her sixteenth year, she was a successful teacher in the same school. In 1851 she became the wife of Daniel Segur, whose encouragement of her literary efforts was constant. Three years before marriage she had begun to write short stories and sketches for the Toledo "Blade," which won public favor. She has been from the first a stanch supporter of movements in favor of woman suffrage. To her belongs much of the credit for obtaining the repeal of obnoxious laws in regard to the status of women in the State of Ohio.

SELINGER, Mrs. Emily Harris McGary, artist, born in Wilmington, NC, in 1854. She is a descendant on her father's side of Flora McDonald. She finished the high-school course in Providence, studied with private tutors, and ended with a course in the Cooper Institute School of Design in New York City. In her nineteenth year she taught in southern schools, acting as instructor in painting, drawing, elocution, botany, French and Latin for seven years in various institutions. While teaching in Louisville, KY, she read a paper on "Art Education" before a gathering of five-hundred teachers, which resulted in the establishment of a normal art-school in that city, of which she was principal. In 1882 she became the wife of Jean Paul Selinger, the artist. From 1882 to 1885 they traveled in Europe, studying in Italy, and while abroad Mrs. Selinger corresponded for the Boston "Transcript." She became a student of flower-painting, and earned the title "Emily Selinger, the Rose Painter." Returning to the United States, Mr. and Mrs. Selinger settled in Boston, MA, where they now live.

SERRANO, Mme. Emelia Benic, opera singer, was born in Vienna, Austria-Hungary. Her maiden name was Benic. She studied under Prof. Simm, of the Conservatory of Prague. She finished the course in singing there and then took a course with Lewy Richard in Vienna. She then went to Italy to study the Italian language with Bona. She made her debut in Vienna, in concert, with Prof. Richard, and won quick recognition. Berger, the German impresario, engaged her to sing in opera, and in Kiev she made her operatic debut, singing in Russian the rôle of Marguerite in Gounod's "Faust," and the soprano part in Glinko's "Life for the Czar." In Moscow she sang in "Faust" with brilliant success, which she repeated in St. Petersburg and Odessa. She then returned to Vienna and became prima donna of the German Opera Company in the Ring Theater. She next made a successful tour in South America, and then went to Central America. In Bogota, Colombia, she founded the Conservatory of St. Cecelia. The climate in that country did not agree with her, and she came to the United States with

Senor Serrano, to whom she was married 3rd May, 1884, in Caracas. She is now living in New York City, where she is giving instruction in vocal music, and winning new laurels teaching and developing the voice.

SEVERANCE, Mrs. Caroline Maria Seymour, re-former, born in Canandaigua, NY, 12th January, 1820. Her father, Orson Seymour, was of an old Connecticut family. She received excellent educational advantages in her youth, taught awhile and was married, 27th August, 1840, to J. C. Severance, a Cleveland banker, and commenced housekeeping at once in Cleveland. They remained there until 1855, when they removed to Boston, MA, for the education of their children. The impulse which first took her into public effort came from a visit with the famous Hutchinson Family, to the first Ohio convention for the discussion of the political and educational disabilities of women, held in Akron, OH, over which convention "Aunt Fanny" Gage presided. That meeting she reported with much enthusiasm for the Cleveland dailies, and that led to book-reviews and similar work for them, and occasional bits of rhyme. It led also to the request from the newly-formed Ohio Suffrage Association for a memorial to the legislature, which she was asked to present before it. Her interest in that pressing question drew her later into a little campaigning with "Aunt Fanny" in Ohio and Indiana, and into calling a convention, with her, in Cleveland, during a Republican rally there in 1848. She next attended the Women's Convention in Syracuse, NY, and another later, in New York City, where she was invited by Wendell Phillips. Her paper, "Humanity: a Definition and a Plea," was given to an immense audience in Cleveland, was repeated in the Parker Fraternity Lecture Course, in Tremont Temple, Boston, soon after her removal there in 1855, and was in both places the first lecture by a woman in those popular lecture courses of the time. She was elected an officer of the Parker Fraternity Lecture Course, Boston, the first and only woman officer in it, and was pressed into repeating before it her Cleveland paper, when Mrs. Elizabeth Cady Stanton, whom she had proposed, had failed to appear. She was active in organizing and served upon the board of the New England Women's Hospital. She aided in organizing the New England Women's Club, of which she was first president. She was active in the organization and work of the Woman's Congress, before which she read in 1882 a paper on the "Chinese Question," a paper written in the light of her years of experience in California. She was active in the organization and work of the Moral Education Association of Boston, and in the Woman's Educational and Industrial Union. She removed with her husband to southern California in 1875, in the wish to make a home for the two sons already there for its climate, and with a longing for its more quiet life. She has been president of the Channing Club of Unity Church, Los Angeles, and one of its board of trustees; is president of the Free Kindergarten Association, through which nine kindergartens have been made a part of the public school system of that city; is president of the flourishing Friday Morning Club of two-hundred women members and of a promising Women's Exchange, and is serving on the board of the city free library. She is the mother of five children, four of whom lived to maturity, and three of whom still live. Her home is still in Los Angeles, the center of a circle of relatives and of their later-formed friends.

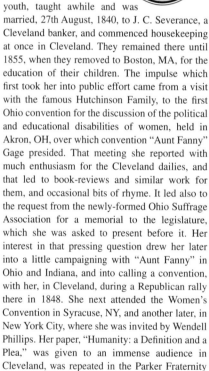

SEVERANCE, Mrs. Juliet H., physician, born in the town of De Ruyter, NY, 1st July, 1833. Her father, Walter F. Worth, was a native of Nantucket, a Quaker, and a cousin of Lucretia Mott. She became interested in woman's rights, anti-slavery, temperance and religious subjects, and soon won fame as an orator in convention, for her arguments and enthusiasm for the cause. Her delicate health in girlhood led her to the study of hygienic methods of treatment, which resulted in making her strong and vigorous. She studied medicine for three years with a physician, and then went to New York, where she took the regular college course and graduated with the title of M.D. in 1858. She had kept up her interest in woman's rights and became an advocate of the abolition of the death penalty. Settling in De Witt, IA, she began to practice medicine, having to meet the assaults of the "regulars," who joined in a crusade against her. She soon won her way to success. She had, while in college, met a spiritualistic medium, whose tests of the return of spirits were so strong and convincing as to upset her religious views. She began to read Liberal literature, beginning with Paine's "Age of Reason," which at once took her outside of the church. She studied Darwin, Huxley and other authors, and embraced the theory of evolution. She wrote and published a volume entitled "Evolution in Earth and Spirit Life," which has passed through several editions. In 1862 she moved to Whitewater, WI, where she soon gained a large practice. In 1863 she began to lecture on social freedom, attracting attention by the courage of her views on marriage. In 1865, in a medical convention in Minneapolis, MN, she, as chairman of the committee on resolutions, introduced a clause favoring magnetism as a therapeutical agent, which caused great excitement among the regulars. In 1868, in Sterling, IL, Dr. Severance delivered a Fourth of July oration, said to be the best ever delivered by a woman, in which she advocated the adoption of a Sixteenth Amendment to the Constitution, which was designed to enfranchise women. In 1869 she removed to Milwaukee, WI, still continuing her practice with enlarged opportunities. In 1878 she attended a State convention of Spiritualists and was chosen president, an office which she held four years. Her address on "Industrial Problems," delivered then, was pronounced a revolutionary document. Dr. Severance is a thorough parliamentarian, and has served as president of State associations of Spiritualists in Illinois, Wisconsin and Minnesota. In 1880 she was elected first vice-president of the Liberal League in place of Colonel Robert G. Ingersoll, who resigned. In that position she often relieved the president, the venerable Elizur Wright, from his arduous duties. She served as Master Workman of the Knights of Labor for three years, and Progressive Assembly was noted under her charge for its educational work. She has served three years as president of the Liberal Club, of Milwaukee. She has been prominent in political agitations, having served in three presidential nominating conventions of the Labor party. In the convention which formed the Union Labor party in 1888, in Cincinnati, OH, she introduced the woman-suffrage plank. All her public work has not kept her from being a model mother and housekeeper. Her family consists of three children by her first husband. Two of those, Lillian

Stillman and F. W. Stillman, are on the stage and are well-known in theatrical circles. The third, B. D. Stillman, is a well-known musician. Dr. Severance is a radical of the radicals. In religion she is a Free Thinker of the Spiritualistic school. Politically, she believes in individualism against nationalism, and she is especially interested in the emancipation of woman from every form of serfdom, in church, State or home. In 1891 she removed to Chicago, IL, where she now resides.

SEWALL, Mrs. May Wright, educator and woman suffragist, was born in Milwaukee, WI. She is descended on both sides from old New England stock, on the father's side from the Montagues, of Massachusetts, and on the mother's side from the Bracketts, of New Hampshire. Her father, Philander Wright, was one of the early settlers of Milwaukee. Miss Wright entered the Northwestern University, in Evanston, IL, and was graduated in 1866. She received the master's degree in 1871. After an experience of some years in the common schools of Michigan, she accepted the position of principal of the Plainwell high school, and later was principal of the high school in Franklin, IN. From that position she was called to the Indianapolis high school as teacher of German, and was subsequently engaged to work in English literature. That was in the year 1874, and since that date she has resided in Indianapolis. In 1872 she became the wife of Edwin W. Thompson, of Paw Paw, MI, a teacher by profession, but an invalid. Mr. Thompson died in 1875. In 1880 Mrs. Thompson resigned her position in the Indianapolis high school, receiving the unprecedented compliment of a special vote of thanks from the school board for her conspicuously successful work. In October of the same year she became the wife of Theodore L. Sewall, a graduate of Harvard, who had opened a classical school for boys in Indianapolis in 1876. In 1883 Mr. and Mrs. Sewall opened a classical school for girls, making the course identical with the requirements of the Harvard examinations for women. A private school for girls which made Latin, Greek and mathematics through trigonometry a part of its regular course was then a novelty in the West,

Rena Prockett.
From Photo by Baker, Columbus.

Anne O'Neill.
From Photo by B. J. Falk, New York.

Marie Prescott.
From Photo by B. J. Falk, New York.

Isadore Rush.
From Photo by Morrison, Chicago.

Madeline Lucette Ryley.
From Photo by B. J. Falk, New York.

but the immediate success of the girls' classical school showed that the public was quick to appreciate thorough work in the education of girls. The labor of carrying on two separate schools and a large boarding department becoming too great for one management, Mr. Sewall disposed of the boys' school in 1889, and since that time Mr. and Mrs. Sewall have given their whole attention to the school for girls. The school now has an annual enrollment of one-hundred-ninety pupils, including thirty in the boarding department. It has graduates in all the prominent colleges for women. About the time of her removal to Indianapolis, Mrs. Sewall became prominent in various lines of woman's work. Her varied powers found employment in the organization of literary, social and reform movements. She soon became known as a lecturer and as a delegate to conventions called in the interest of the higher education of women and the promotion of the cause of woman's equality before the law. She inherited a passion for human liberty in all its phases, and she can not remember the time when she did not feel that men and women were not treated alike, and that the discrimination was in favor of men. One of her earliest griefs was that she could not enter Yale College, as her father had done. Her lifework has been founded on the conviction that all avenues of culture and usefulness should be open to women, and that, when that result is obtained, the law of natural selection may safely be trusted to draw women to those employments, and only those, for which they are best fitted. She edited for two years a woman's column in the Indianapolis "Times," and she has written largely in the line of newspaper correspondence. She has prepared countless circulars, calls, programmes of work and constitutions, and carries at all times a very heavy personal correspondence. She is the author of the Indiana chapter in the "History of Woman Suffrage" edited by Miss Anthony, Mrs. Stanton and Mrs. Gage and of the "Report on Woman's Industries in Indiana" for the educational department of the New Orleans Exposition; of the chapter on the "Work of Women in Education in the Western States" in "Woman's Work in America," and of many slighter essays. Her first public appearance in reform work, outside of local efforts, was as a delegate from the Indianapolis Equal Suffrage Society to the Jubilee Convention in Rochester NY, in 1878. Since that time she has been one of the mainstays of the cause of woman's advancement and has enjoyed the fullest confidence and the unqualified support of its leaders. Her writings and addresses are characterized by directness, simplicity and strength. Her extemporaneous addresses are marked by the same closeness of reasoning, clearness and power as her written ones, and they display a never-failing tact. She is conspicuously successful also as a presiding officer, a position in which she has had a long and varied experience. Her work in various organizations has been so extensive that its scope can hardly be indicated in a brief notice. She early organized conversation clubs and history classes in Indianapolis. She was one of the founders of the Indianapolis Equal Suffrage Society, the Indiana National Woman Suffrage Association, the Indianapolis Art Association, the International Council of Women, the National Council of Women, the Indianapolis Woman's Club, the Indianapolis Propylæum, the Indianapolis Ramabai Circle, the Indianapolis Contemporary Club, the Western Association of Collegiate Alumnæ and the Indiana University Extension Association, and she has held high offices in each. She was for seven years chairman of the executive committee of the National Woman Suffrage Association, is a member of Sorosis, the Association for the Advancement of Women, the American Historical Association and the Executive Board of the Federation of Women's Clubs. At the present time she holds the office of president in the following organizations: The Indianapolis Cotemporary Club, the Indianapolis Ramabai Circle, the Indianapolis Propylæum, and the Woman's National Council of the United States. She is now a member-at-large of the Indiana Board of Commissioners of the World's Fair, by appointment of Gov. Hovey. She has delivered addresses before most of the organizations above named, and also before committees of the Indiana legislature, committees of the United States Senate, the National Teachers' Association, the educational section of the New Orleans Exposition, high schools and colleges in all parts of the country, and the Century Club of Philadelphia; and she has appeared in many lecture courses. She always has more invitations to speak than she can accept. The work done by her in the lines indicated has been the work of her spare time. Her profession is teaching, and to that she gives the ordinary working hours of the day. Her special work for several years has been in English literature and rhetoric, and in addition to that class-room work several hours daily of her time are given to the details of supervision in the Girls' Classical School, an institution which is her special pride. The girls in that school are taught to dress plainly and comfortably, to which end they wear a school uniform, to practice gymnastics daily in the spacious and well-equipped school-gymnasium, and to believe that all departments of knowledge are worthy of their attention and of right ought to be open to them. In addition to all those occupations, she attends to every detail of her housekeeping and has the oversight of the large boarding department of the school. To keep in hand that mass of heterogeneous work evidently implies the possession of great executive ability, good health and endless industry. The home of Mr. and Mrs. Sèwall is ordered on the basis of the largest hospitality. Aside from the ordinary uses of social intercourse, it has entertained many a well-known guest, and literary "tramps" from all quarters have slept under its roof, including Baroness Gripenberg, from Finland, Pundita Ramabai, from India, and others from all parts between, as an inspection of its "tramp" register shows. Mr. and Mrs. Sewall have been abroad during three summers. In 1889 Mrs. Sewall was the delegate from the National Woman Suffrage Association and from the Woman's National Council of the United States to the International Congress of Women, assembled in Paris by the French Government, in connection with the Exposition Universelle. In that congress she responded for America, when the roll of nations was called, and later in the session gave one of the principal addresses, her subject being "The National Woman's Council of the United States." Her response for America, which was delivered in the French language, was highly praised for its aptness and eloquence by M. Jules Simon, who presided over the session.

SEYMOUR, Miss Mary F., law reporter, business woman and journalist, born in Aurora, IL. Her father was a lawyer in Galena, a man well read in his profession, a fine linguist, and a student and writer on scientific subjects. Her mother was a broad-minded, philanthropic woman, possessing great executive ability. Mary, the oldest daughter, inherited the best traits of both parents. She was a born

scribbler and, when she was eight years old, she began to write poems and stories. When she was eleven, a little drama she had written was acted by the children in the village school. She was educated in a boarding-school. While she was still young, her father, acting as counselor for a large company, started for California. While crossing the Isthmus, he was attacked by yellow fever and died. The family returned to the East. Miss Seymour secured a school in New York City, where she taught until the confinement affected her health, and she was forced to resign. For a long time she was confined to her bed in New England, where she had been sent for a change of climate. Surrounded by books, she busied herself with her pen. She wrote stories for children, many of them of an instructive character, and a series of "talks" which appeared under the head of "Table Talk of Grandmother Greyleigh," and other more substantial work. The editor of one of the periodicals to which she had been contributing, offered her a regular position on the staff of a new paper he was starting, which has since become well known. She has always used a pen-name. Recovering health, she accepted a position in a New Jersey school. She was soon again forced to give up work, and in the enforced confinement she took up the study of stenography. She went to work in New York City, and was soon earning a large salary. She felt that women should be permitted to fill any position for which they had the capacity, and she decided to do anything in her power to help them. Opening an office for typewriting, she engaged two competent young women who understood the use of the machine. As the business increased, there was work for more women, but no women who understood the work. At first tuition was free, but, as the expenses and pupils increased, a regular school was opened, which continues to flourish under the name of The Union School of Stenography. The office work increased until six separate offices were running successfully. Her tastes all tended to journalistic work, and, as her other enterprises reached their full fruition, she gave way to her natural bent and commenced the publication of a magazine devoted to the interest of women, the "Business Woman's Journal." After the first year a publishing company, composed entirely of women, was formed with the name of The Mary F. Seymour Publishing Company, Miss Seymour acting as editor of the magazine and as president of the company. The "Journal" was something new in the line of periodicals and was warmly received. In October, 1892, the magazine was enlarged and appeared under the name of the "American Woman's Journal and The Business Woman's Journal." In the spirit of self-help, and to prove the ability of women to manage large enterprises, all the stock of the company has been kept in the hands of women, and with very satisfactory results. When Miss Seymour was appointed Commissioner of Deeds for New Jersey, an appeal to the legislature was necessary to repeal the law to make it possible for a woman to be appointed to such an office. She was also a commissioner for the United States for the Court of Claims and a notary public of New York county, NY. Besides her interest in woman suffrage, she gave considerable attention to all branches of reform. She was vice-president-at-large of the American Society of Authors. Miss Seymour died in New York City, 21st March, 1893.

SHAFER, Miss Helen Almira, educator, born in Newark, NJ, 23rd September, 1839. Her father was a clergyman of the Congregational Church. She was a child of marked intellectual powers, and she received a thorough and liberal education. She studied in the seminary in Albion, NY, and afterward entered Oberlin College, where she was graduated in 1863. After leaving Oberlin, she taught in a school for young women in New Jersey, and for some years she was in charge of the advanced classes of the school. In 1865 she became the teacher of mathematics in the public high school in St. Louis, MO, where she remained till 1875, attracting wide notice by her superior methods of preparing pupils, by the study of algebra, for work in higher analytical mathematics. Professor W. T. Harris, superintendent of the schools of St. Louis, ranked her as the most able and successful teacher in her chosen line in the country. She inspired the students to do their best in all their work, and she was one of the most potent educational forces in St. Louis. In 1877 she was called to Wellesley College as professor of mathematics. She filled that chair admirably until 1888, when she was elected

president of Wellesley. In 1878 Oberlin College conferred on her the degree of A.M., and in 1893 that of LL.D. As professor of mathematics her work showed even greater results than she achieved in St. Louis. Her methods have been widely imitated in other schools, and their success is in every case a confirmation of their merit. As president of Wellesley College she manifested executive capacity and a faculty for business quite as marked as her talents in purely pedagogical work. She was visibly advancing the standing of Wellesley, and every year adding new proof that she was one of the most prominent and successful college administrators when stricken by death, 20th January, 1894.

SHARKEY, Mrs. Emma Augusta, journalist and story-writer, born in Rochester, NY, 15th September, 1858. She is known to the literary world as "Mrs. E. Burke Collins." Her father, W. S. Brown, was a successful business man in that city. Her mother, an accomplished lady, was the only sister of Hon. Frederic Whiting, of Great Barrington, MA, whose published genealogy traces the family back six-hundred years. Conspicuous among her ancestors was the famous Capt. John Mason, whose valor saved from hostile savages the first settlers of Connecticut. In early childhood Mrs. Sharkey lost her most excellent mother, who died in mid-life, of consumption. Her lack of physical vigor precluded her from joining in the sports of other children, and, being much alone, her thoughts turned in upon themselves, and she was called a dreamy child. Yet she enjoyed companionship, and often attracted a circle of little friends, who would sit around her for hours, listening to her stories, improvised as rapidly as her tongue could give them utterance. That rapidity of thought and facility of expression are characteristic of her maturer years. She begins a sketch of one or more columns and usually finishes it at one sitting. With increasing years her health grew better, so that she entered school, but at the age of fifteen years left it and became the wife of E. Burke Collins, a rising young lawyer of Rochester, and soon after they sought the mild climate of Louisiana. There she gained perfect health. Within a year after her arrival in Louisiana, by an accident, she was suddenly made a widow, among comparative strangers, and left almost alone in the world. Up to that time she had never known a want that wealth could supply, but after the first shock and her grief had subsided, she saw that a struggle for subsistence was before her. From her childhood she had written stories and poems for amusement, and given many of them to the local press without thought of remuneration. She then decided that the pen, which she had previously used for pastime, should be a weapon to keep the wolf from her door. She conceived and executed the daring scheme of starting a purely literary journal in New Orleans. It was a most unpropitious time and place for such an enterprise. A few months convinced the young journalist of that fact, and she discontinued it before her finances were exhausted. Though that journalistic venture was a large pecuniary loss to her, yet it gave her such prestige that applications to become a regular contributor poured in from different publishers, and her literary success was assured. The amount of literary work that she accomplishes in a given time is wonderful. Now, and for ten years past, she has received a larger salary for her work than any other literary person in the far South, and larger than any official of her State. She became the wife, in 1884, of Robert R. Sharkey, a Mississippi cotton planter, who is the nephew and sole male descendant of the late Governor Sharkey, of Mississippi, who was United States Senator for several terms and judge in the United States Supreme Court. Mr. and Mrs. Sharkey spend their summers in their country residence, known as "Hillside," near Tangipahoa, LA. Their winters are passed in their home in the sixth district of the city of New Orleans. Mrs. Sharkey has written several quite successful novels, chiefly representing life in the South, more especially the pine woods of Louisiana, hitherto an almost untrodden field in literature.

SHATTUCK, Mrs. Harriette Robinson, author and writer on parliamentary law, born in Lowell. MA, 4th December, 1850. She is the oldest child of William S. and Harriet H. Robinson. She was educated in the Malden, MA, public schools

and had the advantage of several years of literary training under the supervision of Theodore D. Weld, of Boston. Since then she has continued to be a student on various subjects, philosophy and politics being the chief ones of late years. Soon after leaving school, she began to write stories for children and articles for the newspapers on different subjects, mainly relating to women, and, until 1878, when she became the wife of Sidney D. Shattuck, of Malden, she was clerk in the office of the American Social Science Association in Boston. During the five or six years of the Concord Summer School of Philosophy, she wrote letters for the Boston "Transcript," in which the philosophy of the various great teachers, such as Plato, Hegel, Dante and Goethe, was carefully elucidated and made available to the general public. "The Story of Dante's Divine Comedy" (New York, 1887) is the outcome of those letters from the Concord school. Her other books are "Our Mutual Friend" (Boston, 1880), a dramatization from Dickens and "Little Folks East and West" (Boston, 1891), a book of children's tales. She was for ten years president of the National Woman Suffrage Association of Massachusetts, and is now president of the Boston Political Class, which she has conducted for seven years, and in which the science of government and the political topics of the day are considered. She is the founder of "The Old and New" of Malden, MA, one of the oldest woman's clubs in the country. She is interested in all movements for the advancement of women, especially in the cause of woman's political enfranchisement. She made her first speech for suffrage in Rochester, in 1878. She has since spoken before committees of Congress and of the Massachusetts legislature, and in many conventions in Washington and elsewhere. She was the presiding officer over one of the sessions of the first International Council of Women, held in Washington, DC, in 1888. She is a quiet speaker and makes no attempts at oratory. Her best work has been done in writing, rather than in public speaking, unless we include in this term the teaching of politics and of parliamentary law, with the art of presiding and conducting public meetings. When her father was clerk of the Massachusetts House of Representatives, she was his assistant, being the first and only woman to hold such a position in that State (1871–72). Her most popular book is the "Woman's Manual of Parliamentary Law" (Boston, 1891), a work that is a recognized standard.

SHATTUCK, Miss Lydia White, educator, born in East Landaff, now Easton, NH, 10th June, 1822, The Shattuck family was prominent in early New England days. Her Grandfather Shattuck went from eastern Massachusetts to New Hampshire in 1798. Her father was Timothy Shattuck, who was married on 28th January, 1812, to Betsey Fletcher, of Acton, MA. Lydia was their fifth child, and the first of their children to reach maturity. She grew up on a farm in the Berkshire Hills. In her youth she was an artist and a poet. At the age of fifteen she began to teach school, and after teaching eighteen terms she went to South Hadley, MA, where she studied for a time. She next went to Haverhill, where she attended the academy for one term. She then taught in Center Harbor, NH. She entered Mount Holyoke in 1848, and paid her own way through that school. She was graduated in 1851 and was engaged to remain in the seminary as a teacher. She was scientific in her tastes and made specialties of botany and chemistry. In 1887 she visited the Hawaiian Islands and made a study of the flora there. She was connected with the Penikese Island summer school in 1873. In 1869 she traveled in Europe. In 1876 she made an exhibition in the Centennial Exposition. Her whole life was spent in research and teaching. She died in South Hadley on 2nd November, 1889.

SHAW, Mrs. Anna H., woman suffragist, born in Newcastle-on-Tyne, England, 14th February, 1847. She is descended from a family of English Unitarians. Her grandmother refused to pay tithes to the Church of England, and year after year allowed her goods to be seized and sold for taxes. She sat in the door, knitting and denouncing the law, while the sale went on in the street. Her granddaughter inherited from that heroic ancestor her sense of the injustice of taxation without representation. Her parents came to America when she was four years old, and after living for years in Massachusetts they moved to the then unsettled part of Michigan, where the young girl encountered all the hardships of pioneer life. She was a lively child. Those pioneer days were an aspiration to her. Thirsting for learning and cut off from all school privileges, she took advantage of every book and paper that fell in her way. At fifteen years of age she began to teach. She was a teacher for five years. When about twenty-four years old, she became a convert to Methodism and joined the church. Her ability as a speaker was soon recognized. In 1873 the district conference of the Methodist Church in her locality voted unanimously to grant her a local preacher's license. It was renewed annually for eight years. In 1872 she entered the Albion College, MI, and in 1875 she entered the theological department of the Boston University, from which she was graduated with honor in 1878. Throughout her college course she supported herself. While in the theological school, she was worn with hard work, studying on week days and preaching on Sundays. A wealthy and philanthropic woman offered to pay her the price of a sermon every Sunday during the remainder of her second year, if she would refrain from preaching and take the day for rest. That help was accepted. Afterward, when Miss Shaw was earning a salary, she wished to return the money, but was bidden to pass it on to aid in the education of some other struggling girl, which she did. She often says now that, when she was preaching those Sundays while in college, she never knew whether she was going to be paid with a bouquet or a greenback. During the last year of her theological course she was pastor of the Methodist Episcopal Church of Hingham, MA. Her second pastorate was in East Dennis, on Cape Cod, where she remained seven years. A pastorless Congregational Church in Dennis asked her to supply their pulpit until they secured a minister, and they were so well satisfied with her labors that they made no further effort to obtain a pastor. For six years she preached twice every Sunday, in her own church in the morning, and in the afternoon in the Congregational Church. During her pastorate in East Dennis she applied to the New England Methodist Episcopal Conference for ordination, but, though she passed the best examination of any candidate that year, ordination was refused to her on account of her sex. The case was appealed to the general conference in Cincinnati, in 1880, and the refusal was confirmed. Miss Shaw then applied for ordination to the Methodist Protestant Church and received it on 12th October, 1880, being the first woman to be ordained in that denomination. She supplemented her theological course with one in medicine, taking the degree of M.D. in the Boston University. That course was taken during her pastorate. Becoming more and more interested in practical reform, she finally resigned her position in East Dennis and became lecturer for the Massachusetts Woman Suffrage Association. After entering the general lecture field and becoming widely and favorably known as an eloquent speaker on reform topics, she was appointed national superintendent of franchise in the Woman's Christian Temperance Union. In the Women's International Council in Washington, in 1888, she preached the opening sermon. Soon after, at the urgent request of leading suffragists, she resigned her office in the National Woman's Christian Temperance Union and accepted that of national lecturer for the National American Woman Suffrage Association, of which, in 1892 she was elected vice-president-at-large. She is president of Wimodaughsis, a woman's national club, of Washington, DC. Her old parishioners sometime reproach her for no longer devoting herself to preaching the gospel, but she replies that in advocating the enfranchisement of women, the temperance movement and other reforms, she is teaching applied christianity, and that she has exchanged the pulpit, where she preached twice a week, for the platform, where she preaches every day and often three times on Sunday. To use her own expression, she can not remember the time when it was not her desire and purpose to devote her life to the uplifting of women. She is one of the most eloquent, witty and popular speakers in the lecture field. She is possessed of the most remarkable personal magnetism, a fine voice and power of pointed argument. Much of her strength and force of thought and expression are believed to result from the experiences of her pioneer life in Michigan, and her power of moving audiences from the touch with humanity which came to her while practicing medicine in the city of Boston, during her studies to be a physician. She is believed to be the first woman to have the double distinction of the titles of "Rev." and "M.D." Her family were opposed to her studying for the ministry, on the ground that she would be a disgrace to them if she persisted in such an unheardof course. Her success has effectually reconciled them to that disgrace. Dr. Shaw has spoken before many State legislatures and several times before committees of congress in both houses. Among her most popular characteristics as a speaker are her keen sense of humor and ready wit, often enabling her to carry her points where logic alone would fail.

SHAW, Miss Annie C., artist, born in West Troy, NY, 16th September, 1852. She studied art in Chicago, IL, with H. C. Ford, and was elected an associate of the Chicago Academy of Design in 1873, and an academician in 1876, being the first woman to receive those distinctions from that institution. She has studied from nature in the Adirondack Mountains, on the coast of Maine, and in the picturesque parts of Massachusetts, for many summers. She has produced a large number of fine pictures, some of the best-known of which are: "On the Calumet" (1874); "Willow Island" and "Keene Valley, NY" (1875); "Ebb Tide on the Coast of Maine" (1876); "Head of a Jersey Bull" (1877); "Returning from the Fair" (1878); "In the Rye-Field" and "Road to the Creek" (1880); "Close of a Summer Day" (1882); "July Day" and "In the Clearing" (1883); "Fall Ploughing," "Ashen Days" and "The Cornfield" (1884), and "The Russet Year" (1885). Her "Illinois Prairie" was shown in the Centennial Exposition in 1876.

SHAW, Mrs. Cornelia Dean, woman suffragist and philanthropist, born in Tremont, IL, 18th February, 1845. Her father, George W. Dean, was a native of Boston and a direct descendant of Carver, the first governor of Massachusetts. Her mother was born in New York City. After her parents had resided there a number of years, having a family of nine children, her father moved west with his family and settled in Tremont. Two more children were added to the family after removal to their new home, the youngest of whom was Cornelia. Miss Dean early showed a talent for music. She was able to sing a tune before she could speak distinctly, and when only a few years old to play well by ear on the piano. At the age of three years her family removed to Chicago, her father dying a few years after, and her mother following him to the grave when Miss Dean was fourteen years of age. She then found a home with a married sister. Most of her education was received in the public schools of Chicago, and at the age of seventeen she attended the Northwestern Female College, in Evanston. At the beginning of the war she left school, returning to her sister's home in Chicago, where, on 8th June, 1869, she became the wife of Daniel C. Shaw, of Chicago. The second year after their marriage they removed to Toledo, OH, where her husband became the senior partner of a prominent business house. She is an active member of the Central Congregational Church and a leader in its missionary work. She is ever alert in all movements for the enfranchisement of women, a sincere believer in the rights of women, a tower of strength to the Toledo Woman Suffrage Association, attending its State and national conventions, secretary of the Ramabai Circle, one of the congressional committee of the seventh Ohio district of the Queen Isabella Association, an energetic worker in the Newsboys' Home, a member of the day nursery, and devotes much time to other public and private work of a benevolent kind. She has still found time to give to her art work. With wealth to gratify her taste, she is devoted to the improvement of humanity.

SHAW, Miss Emma, author and traveler, born in Thompson, CT, 3rd September, 1846. She was educated in a private school until 1862, when she became a teacher of country schools. She taught until 1872, when she made her home in Providence, RI. There she became a teacher, and she has risen to a high position. In 1881 she began her literary work. She went in that year on a trip to the Northwest, for the purpose of regaining her strength. Her tour of the Great Lakes and the Mississippi she made the subject of a series of brilliant sketches in the Providence "Press." She made other trips in the following years, and each time she described her journeys in an entertaining manner. In 1884 she published a series of illustrated articles in the "Journal of Education," continuing from February till June, after which she visited Alaska, and she has delivered a lecture on that country before clubs and lyceums. In 1885 she revisited Alaska, returning via the Yellowstone National Park. She traveled in the West extensively in 1886-87, and in 1888 she extended her journeys into Canada, penetrating the Hudson Bay Company's country, where no other reporter had ventured. Her articles on that, as well as her wanderings for the next five years, have made her name well known to the readers of the Boston "Transcript." The years 1889, 1891 and 1892 found her exploring unfrequented nooks in British America and the Queen Charlotte Islands. In 1890 she visited all the Hawaiian Islands, the wonders of which furnished material for a long series of articles as well as for several illustrated lectures of exceeding interest. Her lectures were entitled "Up the Saskatchewan," "Through Hawaii with a Kodak" and "From Ocean to Ocean." She published her first poem, "New Year's Eve," in 1883. She has since then written much in verse.

SHEARDOWN, Mrs. Annie Fillmore, singer and musical educator, born in Franklin, CT, 8th June, 1859. She is descended from five New England Colonist families, the English Fillmores, Hydes, Pembers and Palmers, and the French Fargos. As those families settled early in America, she can call herself purely American. Her mother's family were all musical, and from her earliest childhood her desire was to sing. She began her studies when she was between eight and nine years of age, first with a pupil of Bassini. She afterward took lessons from the late C. R. Hayden, of Boston, and others. Her intention at first was to become an oratorio singer, but after she became a student under the late Emma Seiler, in Philadelphia, she decided to study the voice, with the intention of becoming a teacher. After three years with Mrs. Seiler, she took a position as soprano in Christ Church in Norwich, CT. After filling her engagement, she became the wife of Dr. T. W. Sheardown, son of the late Hon. S. B. Sheardown, of Winona, MN. After marriage she continued to sing and teach for the love of it. Five years later, owing to marital troubles, she separated from Dr. Sheardown and took up teaching as a profession. In 1882 she studied six months with George Sweet, of New York, taking lessons, listening to his lectures and studying his method of imparting. She studied with other teachers, and in 1891 she made a most valuable discovery relative to the voice, finding the voice to be an exact science, a principle to be demonstrated, with laws as unalterable as those of mathematics. She is the first person to note this great fact. She has always felt there was something wrong in all methods, and now, looking at the voice as a principle, she is able to demonstrate where the error lies. A lengthy article from her pen, entitled "The Philosophy of the Voice in Singing," setting forth a few of her discoveries, appeared in "Werner's Voice Magazine" for April, 1892. She has lived in nine States of the Union, and is now permanently located in Atlanta. GA.

SHELDON, Mrs. Mary French, translator, traveler and author, born in Pittsburgh, PA, in 1846. She is a great-great-granddaughter of Sir Isaac Newton, and her ancestry includes many notable men and women. Her maiden name was Mary French. Her father was a machinist and engineer of ability and high standing in Pittsburgh. Her mother was Mrs. Elizabeth French, the well-known spiritualist and faith healer, who died in 1890. Miss Mary French was married in early life to her first husband, Mr. Byrne, from whom she was divorced in 1868. Her second husband was E. F. Sheldon, who died in the summer of 1892. Mrs. Sheldon received a fine education. She is a musician and a linguist. She has published one novel and a translation of Flaubert's "Salammbo" from the French. She was educated as a physician, but has not practiced. In 1890 she determined to travel in central Africa, to study the women and children in their primitive state. She was the first white woman to reach Mount Kilima-Njaro. She traveled with one female attendant and a small body of Africans. She carried a camera and secured many interesting views, which she published in her interesting volume on Africa, "Sultan to Sultan." Her home is in New York City.

SHELLEY, Mrs. Mary Jane, temperance and missionary worker, born in Weedsport, NY, 20th May, 1832. Her maiden name was Wright. Her father was pastor of the Methodist Episcopal Church in Weedsport. They removed to Illinois in 1843, where her father died in 1846. She received religious training under Bishop Peck, of New York, and was one of his special charges. She became the wife of Rev. L. Shelley, whose ancestral home was in Shelley Islands, eastern Pennsylvania. They removed to Iowa, where her influence for good was felt in her husband's work. Though naturally timid, retiring and adverse to publicity, she responded willingly when Bishop Peck called her forth to special work in the interest of reform and religious affairs. With spirit and determination she began her public work at the age of forty-seven. She was for five years vice-president of the first Nebraska district for the Woman's Christian Temperance Union.

SHERIDAN, Miss Emma V., see FRY, MRS. EMMA V. SHERIDAN.

SHERMAN, Mrs. Eleanor Boyle Ewing, social leader, born in Lancaster, OH, 4th October, 1824, and died in New York City, 28th November, 1888. Descended from a long line of Scotch and Irish ancestors, she inherited from them the strength of will and persevering determination which characterized her actions, and also her Catholic faith. Her father, Thomas Ewing, was one of the most eminent lawyers of his day, twice a Senator of the United States and twice a member of a President's cabinet. Her mother, Maria Boyle, was a gentle, lovely woman, who devoted her life to her husband and children. Surrounded from infancy as Eleanor Ewing was by all the charms and graces of a refined and elegant home, it is not strange that she developed into a woman of unusual brilliancy. Her mind was clear and analytical. When a boy of nine years, William Tecumseh Sherman was adopted, out of love for his family, by Mr. Ewing. Unconsciously the child's admiration for the lad grew into the pure devotion of the maiden, and at seventeen Eleanor was engaged to her soldier lover. They were married 1st May, 1850, in Washington, where her father was a member of President Taylor's cabinet. The wedding was a military one. One or two stations completed her experience of army life at that time, and when her husband resigned from the army and accepted a position in a bank in California, in 1853, she went with him. They returned to the East in

1857. During the Civil War, when her husband and brothers were fighting for the Union, she waited and watched with an anxious heart, powerless to do anything but pray for the success of the cause dear to every loyal soul. When the newspapers raised the cry against her husband, she made a long and weary journey to Washington, saw President Lincoln, convinced him that matters had been misrepresented to him, and, as a result of her endeavors, her husband was placed over another command. Again, at the close of the war, when General Sherman was abused on all sides for his terms in the Johnston Treaty, she defended him by word and pen. After the war the family resided in St. Louis, MO, where her life was devoted to the service of the poor. In 1869 her husband's promotion to the command of the United States Army took her to Washington, where her position gave her ample opportunities for exercising her benevolence in aiding charities, great and small. The Aloysius Aid Society was organized by her and inaugurated by a grand charity fair, of which she was the leader. That home still exists and flourishes under the charge of the good Sisters. Her aim in Washington was not social success, but simply to fulfill her duties as the wife of the general of the army. Her great pleasure was to help those who came to Washington without friends. While in Washington, 1st October, 1874, her oldest daughter, Minnie, became the wife of Lieut. Thomas William Fitch, post assistant engineer, United States Navy. Her son, Thomas Ewing Sherman, entered the order of the Society of Jesus in May, 1879, and was ordained 7th July, 1889. Her daughter, Eleanor, during their last residence in St. Louis, became the wife of Lieut. Alexander Montgomery Thackara, United States Navy, 5th May, 1880. Her oldest son, Willie, "Our Little Sargeant," as he was proudly called by the battalion under his father's command, died in Memphis, 3rd October, 1863. An infant son, Charles Celestine, died 4th December, 1864, near the convent of St. Mary's, over which presided that cousin to whom Mrs. Sherman was so deeply attached, Mother Angela. Born in the same year, from their childhood they had been united in works of mercy. Mary Elizabeth Sherman is the daughter on whom her mother leaned during her last years. Philemon Tecumseh Sherman is a member of the New York bar. Rachel Ewing Sherman became the wife, 30th December, 1891, of Dr. Paul Thorndike. Mrs. Sherman was buried in the cemetery, in St. Louis, where her children have been laid, and where her brave husband now rests beside her.

SHERMAN, Mrs. Margaret Stewart, wife of Hon. John Sherman, Secretary of State under President McKinley's administration, was the only child of Judge Stewart, of Mansfield, OH. She was well educated with a course at Granville, OH, and afterward at Patapsco Institute near Baltimore. On 31st December, 1848, she was married to Mr. Sherman, then a young lawyer on the first rounds of the ladder of official prominence. During President Hayes' term her husband was Secretary of the Treasury, and she again enters cabinet circles with an intimate knowledge of all the social demands the position requires.

SHERMAN, Miss Marrietta R., musical educator and orchestral conductor, born in Lowell, MA, 5th July, 1862. She showed a strong liking and talent for music, and at the age of seven years she began the regular study of the art. With her parents she removed to Boston, and at the age of nine commenced the study of the piano and organ. After a short course on the piano, she began the study of the violin, with William Shultz, formerly first violin of the Mendelssohn Club. She afterward studied with Eichberg and Charles N. Allen, being with the latter for ten years. She is at present one of the faculty of Wellesley College of Music, besides which she has about fifty private pupils. It is as leader of the Beacon Orchestral Club she is best known, and the remarkable success attained by that popular organization is the best testimonial to her talents and ability as a leader and teacher. That club contains fifty young women, many of whom belong to the most prominent families of Boston. It was organized, with a small membership, in 1881, and has grown to its present size under Miss Sherman's training and direction. The players present a striking appearance in costumes of white silk, with gold cord trimmings, and they have won success during the past two seasons, having played in New York for the Frank Leslie's Doll's Fair, for the Woman's Charity Club in Music Hall, Boston, and for many weddings and receptions given by society people. Their repertory is very extensive, and embraces both popular and classical music, with solos by the different instrumentalists. The opinion of the press in the various towns and cities where the club has appeared is that it is justly entitled to the claim that "it is the finest ladies' orchestra in the world." During the summer months Miss Sherman divides the club and furnishes music in the various hotels. She makes her headquarters in the Hoffman House, Boston.

SHERWOOD, Mrs. Emily Lee, author and journalist, born in Madison, IN, in 1843, where she spent her early girlhood. Her father, Monroe Wells Lee, was born in Ohio, and her mother was from Massachusetts. Mr. Lee, who was an  architect and builder, died when his daughter was ten years old. Miss Lee's early education was received in a private school, and later she took the educational course in the public and high schools of her native town. At the age of sixteen she entered the office of her brother, Manderville G. Lee, who published the "Herald and Era," a religious weekly paper in Indianapolis, IN. There she did whatever work she found to be done in the editorial rooms of a family newspaper, conducting the children's department and acquiring day by day a knowledge and discipline in business methods and newspaper work that fitted her for the labors of journalism and literature which she has performed so creditably. After four years she became the wife of Henry Lee Sherwood, a young attorney of Indianapolis. Some years ago Captain and Mrs. Sherwood went to Washington, and they now reside in a suburban home upon Anacostia Heights. Mrs. Sherwood sent out letters, stories and miscellaneous articles to various publications, some of which were the Indianapolis "Daily Commercial," "Star in the West," "Forney's Sunday Chronicle," "Ladies' Repository," "Christian Leader," Santa Barbara "Press" and a number of church papers. Those articles were signed with her own name or the pen-name "Jennie Crayon." In 1889 she entered upon the career of an active journalist and accepted an appointment upon the staff of the "Sunday Herald," of Washington, DC. In addition to her work upon the local journal, she

contributes occasionally to the New York "Sun" and acts as special correspondent of the "World." As she is an all-round writer, she turns out with equal facility and grace of diction books, reviews, stories, character sketches, society notes and reports. She has recently published one novel, "Willis Peyton's Inheritance" (Boston). She is a member of the American Society of Authors, of New York City. She is a member of the National Society of the Daughters of the American Revolution, of the National Press League, and the Triennial Council of Women, besides several other women's organizations. She does a good deal of church work and is now corresponding secretary of the Woman's Centenary Association of the Universalist Church. She is social in her nature and is thoroughly a woman's woman.

SHERWOOD, Mrs. Kate Brownlee, poet and journalist, was born in Mahoning county, OH, 24th September, 1841. Her descent is Scottish, and her ancestors number many men and women of literary bent. Her maiden name was Brownlee. She was educated in Poland Union Seminary. Before graduating she became the wife of Isaac R. Sherwood, afterward General, Secretary of State and Congressman from Ohio. Her husband is the editor of the Canton "Daily News-Democrat," and Mrs. Sherwood, attracted to journalism, learned everything in the line of newspaper work from typesetting to leader-writing. While her husband was in Congress, she served as Washington correspondent for Ohio journals. She was for six years in editorial charge of the Toledo, OH, "Journal," and for ten years has edited the woman's department of the soldier organ, the Washington "National Tribune." Her career as a journalist and society woman has been varied and busy. She was one of the first members of the Washington Literary Club, and of the Sorosis of New York, to whose early annual receptions she contributed characteristic poems, and the vice-president for Ohio in the first call for a national congress of women. She was the organizer of the first auxiliary to the Grand Army of the Republic outside of New England, and is a founder of the national association known as the Woman's Relief

Corps, Auxiliary to the Grand Army of the Republic. She served that order as national president, organized the department of relief and instituted the National Home for Army Nurses, in Geneva, OH. Despite her versatile excellence, public instinct gives popular homage to her one gift, song. She has been the chosen singer of many national occasions, including army reunions, and is the only northern poet ever invited by the ex-Confederates to celebrate the heroism of a southern soldier. The broad, liberal and delicate manner in which she responded to that significant honor, in her poem at the unveiling of the equestrian statue of Albert Sidney Johnston, in New Orleans, LA, elicited praise from the gray and the blue. A student of French and German, her translations of Hein, Goethe and Frederich Bodenstedd have been widely copied. Her "Camp-fire and Memorial Poems" (Chicago, 1885) has passed through several editions. Her home is now in Canton, OH.

SHERWOOD, Mrs. Mary Elizabeth, author and social leader, born in Keene, NH, in 1830. Her father, General James Wilson, served as a member of Congress from New Hampshire. Her mother was Mary Richardson, a woman of great personal beauty and fine intellect. On her father's side she is of Irish extraction. Mary received a thorough education. When her father was in Congress, the family lived in Washington, DC, and soon after his election his wife died, and upon Mary fell the care of the large family. She was a young woman of strong intelligence and great beauty. She was acquainted with Bancroft, Motley, Bryant, Prescott and many other men of note. At the age of seventeen she published a criticism of "Jane Eyre," which attracted much attention. While living in Washington, she became the wife of John Sherwood, who is still living. Their union has been a happy one. Her literary work includes correspondence with eminent men and women abroad, and many contributions to the "Atlantic Monthly," "Scribner's Magazine," "Appleton's Journal," the "Galaxy," and the New York "Tribune," "Times" and "World." For years she corresponded for the Boston "Traveller." Her work in "Harper's Bazar," "Frank Leslie's Weekly" and other journals from Maine to Oregon would fill many volumes. Among her published books are "The Sarcasm of Destiny" (New York, 1877); "Home Amusements" (1881); "Amenities of Home" (1881); "A Transplanted Rose" (1882); "Manners and Social Usages" (1884); "Royal Girls and Royal Courts" (Boston, 1887), and "Sweet Brier" (Boston, 1889). She has written many poems, to which she signs the initials, "M. E. W. S." She has translated some poems from European languages. She has written hundreds of short stories, many of which appeared anonymously. During her seasons abroad she formed the acquaintance of Queen Victoria and other notable persons. She has had three interviews with the Queen of Italy. She has traveled extensively in Europe for years. In 1885 she gave readings in her New York City home in aid of the Mount Vernon Fund, and they became so popular that she continued them for several years, giving the proceeds to charity, realizing over $10,000 in that way. Her readings comprise essays on travel, literature and history. She is the president of the "Causeries," a literary club composed of women distinguished in New York society. Her family consisted of four sons, two of whom, James Wilson Sherwood and John Philip Sherwood, died in early manhood. Her living sons are Samuel Sherwood, the artist, and Arthur Murray Sherwood, the broker. In Mrs. Sherwood's parlors hang the original and imaginative drawings and paintings of her two artist sons. One is by Samuel Sherwood of his brother Philip, taken just before his death. Several done by Philip Sherwood show that in his early death a genius was lost to the world. In his name his mother has contributed to the funds of the Home for the Destitute Blind, the St. Joseph's Hospital, the Kindergarten for the Blind, the Woman's Exchange, the New York Diet Kitchen, the Manhattan Hospital and Dispensary, the Home of St. Elizabeth and many others, various schemes to care for children, and to many objects known to only her friends, who confide to her sufferings not made public, and especially for women in need and for young women who are striving to fit themselves for a profession by which they may earn an honorable livelihood. She has done much to advance literature and science in New York City. She is still active in benevolent and literary lines. Among her many testimonials of recognition abroad, she was decorated with the insignia of Officier d'Académie, an honor conferred by the French Minister of Public Instruction on persons who have distinguished themselves in literary pursuits. It is said to be the first time this decoration has been conferred upon an American woman.

SHERWOOD, Mrs. Rosina Emmet, artist, born in New York, NY, 13th December, 1854. Her maiden name was Rosina Emmet. She is a twin sister of Robert Temple Emmet, the soldier, and a direct descendant of Thomas Addis Emmet, the Irish patriot, who was born in Cork, Ire., 24th April, 1764, and died in New York City 14th November, 1827. He was an older brother of Robert Emmet, who was executed in Dublin in 1803. The family has produced many eminent persons, soldiers, lawyers, chemists, physicians, engineers and scholars. Rosina Emmet was educated in Pelham Priory, Westchester county, NY. She displayed remarkable artistic talents in youth, and she studied art with William M. Chase in 1879 and 1880. In 1885 and 1886 she studied in Paris, France. Her progress was rapid, and she was soon ranked with the most promising artists of the age. In 1879 she won the first prize in a Christmas-card competition. In London, England, in 1878, she won a first-prize medal for heads on china. She illustrated a juvenile book, "Pretty Peggy," collecting the poems and music for it, in 1880. In 1884 she made the illustrations for Mrs. Burton Harrison's "Old-fashioned Tales." Much of her illustrative work has appeared in prominent periodicals. She is a member of the Society of American Artists. Many of her oil and water-color pictures have been shown in exhibitions. In 1887 she became the wife of Mr. Sherwood, the son of Mrs. John Sherwood, of New York City, where they now live.

SHOAFF, Mrs. Carrie M., artist and inventor, born in Huntington, IN, 2nd April, 1849. She developed artistic talents at an early age, and after learning to draw and paint she turned her attention to plastic art. She invented a method of manufacturing imitation Limoges ware, which is utilized in the making of advertising signs, plaques and other forms. In that art she uses common clay and a glaze of her own invention, and the results are surprisingly fine. She established a school in Fort Wayne, IN, and trained a large number of students. Many business firms have given her orders for souvenirs and advertising plaques, made of her materials and from her designs, and her reputation has spread through the United States. She teaches women the art of using common clay and turning out imitations of the Limoges ware that almost defy detection, even by connoisseurs. She has received numerous invitations to open art-schools in New York and other large cities, but she remains in Fort Wayne, earning both fame and money. She teaches her classes the art of digging, preparing and modeling their own clay, the art of ornamenting the pieces properly, and the secret of glazing the finished wares into perfect copies of the fired wares. She has opened a new field, in which woman's ingenuity and artistic tastes may find profitable employment.

SHOEMAKER, Mrs. Rachel H., dramatic elocutionist and Shakesperean reciter, born near Doylestown, PA, 1st October, 1838. Her maiden name was Rachel Walter Hinkle. One of her ancestors on her father's side came to America with William Penn, with whom he was closely associated in the affairs of the colony of Pennsylvania. On her mother's side her ancestors were Hollanders. Her parents were farmers. Rachel lived on the homestead farm until she was twenty years old. She was the youngest of five children. In childhood she displayed a talent and liking for recitation. Her early education was such as the public schools gave in those days, and later she attended the State Normal School in Millersville, PA, where, after graduation, she remained as a teacher of English and French. On 27th June, 1867, she became the wife of Professor J. W. Shoemaker. They made their home in Philadelphia, where, in 1875, they opened the National School of Elocution and Oratory and later commenced the publication of elocutionary books. Professor Shoemaker died in 1880, leaving his wife with two young children, a son and a daughter. Mrs. Shoemaker has always maintained a connection with the school in some capacity, acting as president when no one else was chosen. She has compiled a number of books for elocutionists, and she has studied and written much upon the subject. She has taught thousands of students and has read in many cities, including Philadelphia, New York, Cincinnati and Minneapolis in the United States, and Toronto, Hamilton and Montreal in Canada. The school founded by herself and her husband has prospered from the beginning and has trained some of the most successful readers of the day.

SIBLEY, Mrs. Jennie E., temperance worker, is a daughter of the late Judge Thomas, of Columbus, GA, a leader in his State, and the wife of William C. Sibley, of Augusta, GA, president of the Sibley Cotton Mills. Her girlhood home was a beautiful estate near Columbus. With the exception of some reverses in her early married days, consequent upon the fortunes of war, her life has been one of comfort and luxury. Reared in wealth and married to a gentleman of means, her life has been one singularly free from care, but she has turned away from the allurements of social leadership to give her time, her money and her forces of mind and character to the alleviation of the woes and crimes of the vicious and unfortunate. For years she has taught a Sunday-school among the factory children of her husband's mills and has carried purity, strength and peace into many unenlightened homes. Her Sunday-school work has been in a Presbyterian Church, built and given to the factory people by Mr. Sibley, whose purse is ever open to the wise and sympathetic calls of his philanthropic wife. Mrs. Sibley has delivered many public addresses. One of the most important of these was her plea before the State Sunday-school convention on "Sunday-school Work Among the Factory Children." Her prominence and courage in temperance work have given her a reputation throughout the land. She labors with her hands, her purse, her pen, her eloquent tongue, with all the force and fervor of a crusader and the most purifying and regenerating results follow her efforts in every field. She has an immense correspondence in connection with her benevolent and reformatory enterprises, and has contributed a large number of strong and suggestive articles to various magazines and periodicals.

Her home life is exceptionally happy, luxurious and easeful. She has already met her reward for her unselfish devotion to all uplifting and and healing measures, in the blessed possession of five sons, all enthusiastic for temperance and all members of the church. She is at the head of many of the most successful reform organizations of the South, and honors and distinctions have been showered upon her.

SIDDONS, Mrs. Mary Frances Scott, actor, was born in India. Her father was Capt. William Young Siddons, of the 65th Bengal Light Infantry. Her mother was a daughter of Col. Earle, of the British army. Her paternal great-grandmother was the famous Sarah Siddons. Mary Frances Siddons was educated in Germany. At the age of eleven years she astonished her teachers and friends by her striking performance of a part in a French play, "Esther." She became fascinated with the stage and was constantly acting in French and German plays, playing the most difficult rôles in the dramas of Schiller, Racine, Molière and Corneille. Her rendition of Mortimer in Schiller's "Marie Stuart" led her teacher to introduce her to Charles Kean, who recognized her talents and advised her to wait till she was older before going on the stage. In 1862 she became the wife of Mr. Scott-Chanter, a British naval officer. In 1865 she took as her stage-name Mary Frances Scott-Siddons, and, against the wishes of her family, joined the company of the Theater Royal in Nottingham, England. She made her début as Portia in "The Merchant of Venice." In 1866 she appeared as Juliet in "Romeo and Juliet," in Edinburgh. On 1st April, 1867, she made her first appearance in London in the Hanover Square Rooms, where she read selections from Shakespeare and Tennyson. On 8th April she played Rosalind in the Haymarket Theater in London. In the fall of 1868 she came to the United States, and in New York City she gave readings from Shakespeare in Steinway Hall. Her theatrical début in that city was made in the Fifth Avenue Theater, where she played successfully in a long line of characters. In July, 1870, she played as Pauline in "The Lady of Lyons" in London, following with other impersonations. In 1872 she played as Coralie in "Ordeal by Touch" in the Queen's Theater in London. She then starred in the United States for several years, returning to London in 1879. In 1881 she assumed in London the management of the Haymarket Theater. Her death occurred in Paris, France, 19th November, 1896.

SIGOURNEY, Mrs. Lydia Huntley, author, born in Norwich, CT, 1st September, 1791, and died in Hartford, CT, 10th June, 1865. She was the daughter of Ezekiel Huntley, a soldier of the Revolution. She was a very precocious child. At the age of three years she read fluently, and at seven she wrote verses. She was educated in Norwich and Hartford, and she taught a private girls' school in Hartford for five years. In 1815 she published her first volume, "Moral Pieces in Prose and Verse." In 1819 she became the wife of Charles Sigourney, a literary and artistic man, of Hartford. She then devoted herself to literature. Her books became very popular. In her posthumous "Letters of Life," published in 1866, she names forty-six separate works from her pen, besides two-thousand articles contributed to three-hundred periodicals. Some of her books found a wide sale in England and France. Her poetry is refined, delicate and graceful. Her prose is elegant. All her work is of the purest moral stripe. Her literary labor was only a part of her work. She was active in charity and philanthropy, and she had many pensioners. In 1840 she visited Europe, and in 1842 she described her journey in "Pleasant Memories of Pleasant Lands." While in London, England, she published two volumes of poetry. Her best works are: "Traits of the Aborigines of America," a poem (1822); "Sketch of Connecticut Forty Years Since" (1824); "Letters to Young Ladies" (1833, twentieth American and fifth English edition in 1853); "Letters to Mothers" (1838, with several English editions); "Pocahontas, and Other Poems" (1841); "Scenes in My Native Land" (1844); "Voice of Flowers" (1845); "Weeping Willow" (1846); "Water Drops" (1847); "Whisper to a Bride" (1849); "Letters to My Pupils" (1850); "Olive Leaves" (1851); "The Faded Hope," a memorial of her only son, who died at the age of nineteen years

(1852); "Past Meridian" (1854); "Lucy Howard's Journal" (1857); "The Daily Counselor" (1858); "Gleanings," poetry (1860), and "The Man of Uz, and Other Poems" (1862). Her whole married life, with the exception of the time, he spent in Europe, was passed in Hartford.

SILLER, Miss Hilda, poet, born in Dubuque, IA, 7th August, 1861. Her father is Frank Siller, of Milwaukee, WI, who is known as "the German poet," but who emigrated to America from St. Petersburg, Russia, when a boy of fifteen. Her mother's maiden name was Sarah Baldwin. She was an English woman. Hilda Siller has inherited from her parents a love of literature and art. She excels the average amateur musician in the same degree that she excels the average local poet. Miss Siller wrote for "Our Continent" in its palmiest days, later for the Springfield "Republican," Boston "Transcript," New York "Post," Chicago "Inter-Ocean," "The South," St. Louis "Globe-Democrat," and for Wisconsin papers generally. She studied music with the best teachers abroad as well as in Milwaukee, and the works of Chopin and Beethoven found in her a skilled and sympathetic interpreter. She has written some very good stories. The fact that father and daughter are both poets and both possess conspicuous German traits gives them a sort of unified personality. Their poems have been widely translated from English into German and extensively copied in German periodicals.

SIMPSON, Mrs. Corelli C. W., poet, born in Taunton, MA, 20th February, 1837. She is one of a pair of twin daughters. Her father was Capt. Francis Dighton Williams. Corelli C. Williams was thoroughly educated in both public and private schools, chiefly in the Bristol academy, the Taunton high school and the Salisbury mission school, in Worcester, MA. She went to Bangor, ME, in March, 1863, to visit her sister, Mrs. S. C. Hatch. She opened the first kindergarten in that city, in 1864, becoming at once very popular. Mr. A. L. Simpson, a member of the Penobscot bar, at that time a widower, who led his daughter Gertrude daily to the kindergarten teacher, perceived her rare qualities and asked her to preside over his home-garden. They were married 20th September, 1865. In December, 1866, their daughter Maude was born, and in May, 1871, their son Howard Williams was born. She has written her poems mainly in moments of inspiration, and not as a serious task. Her productions have appeared in various popular periodicals and are warmly received. In 1883 a fair for the benefit of the Young Men's Christian Association was held in Bangor, and she was asked to give something salable. The result was a "Tete-a-tete Cook Book," of which one-thousand copies were sold. She published an enlarged edition in 1891. Her home in Bangor is a center of literature and refinement. She has painted many artistic works in oil. Her mother died in March, 1889, in the seventy-fifth year of her age.

SKELTON, Mrs. Henneriette, temperance worker, born in Giessen, Germany, 5th November, 1842, where her father was connected with the university. Parentless the children emigrated to Canada, where Henneriette became the wife of Mr. Skelton, traffic superintendent of the Northern Railroad. They had one son. In 1874 Mr. Skelton died in their home in Toronto, Canada, and soon after, the son, showing signs of pulmonary disease, accompanied his mother to southern California, hoping to find health. The hope was not realized. In 1882 he died. Mrs. Skelton then devoted herself to the cause of the Woman's Christian Temperance Union, with which for years, during her residence in Canada, she had been closely identified. Her name will be associated in the minds of thousands of the German citizens of the United States as one of the most fearless and indefatigable workers in the cause of temperance. For a time she conducted the temperance paper known as "Der Bahnbrecher," besides writing three books published in the English language, "The Man-Trap" (Toronto), a temperance story, "Clara Burton" (Cincinnati), a story for girls, and "The Christmas Tree" (Cincinnati), a picture of domestic life in Germany. Her energy and zeal in the reform to which she is devoting her life were early recognized by the national executive board of the Woman's Christian Temperance Union, and she was appointed one of its national organizers. In that capacity she has traveled over the United States, lecturing in both the English and her native tongue, and leaving behind her local unions of women well organized and permeated with earnestness. Her platform efforts are marked by breadth of thought, dignity of style and the very essence of profound convictions. Her home is in San Francisco, CA.

SLOCUM, Miss Jane Mariah, educator, born in Slocumville, NY, 1st May, 1842. Her paternal ancestor, Giles Slocum, came from Somersetshire, England, in 1642. Her father supported a little school for the children in Slocumville, and Jane began her education at the early age of two-and-one-half years. She learned to read without difficulty and developed an omnivorous taste for books. Fortunately, no trash came in her way. The district school, with a woman to teach in the summer and a man in the winter, had to suffice until she was fifteen, when she was permitted to go to a small boarding-school. The following year she went to the new Friend's boarding-school in Union Springs, NY. Graduating after a three-year course, just as the war broke out, she was turned from her purpose of entering Oberlin, or Antioch College, the only higher institutions of learning then open to women. She was yet too young to be allowed to go to the front, and she continued her studies in a collegiate institute. Before the close of the war her zeal to take some active part in the conflict led her to join the first volunteers for teaching the Freedmen. She received an appointment to teach in Yorktown, PA. A little school building was erected on Darlington Heights, on York River, and there she devoted eight months of labor to the new race problem. A severe attack of malarial fever made a return to that field impracticable. One school year was given to the teaching of a private school in Philadelphia, NY, and the summer was devoted to the study of book-keeping in the commercial college in Rochester, NY. An imperative call to Howland School, Union Springs, NY, resulted in further association with old teachers, and for ten years she continued to labor there, building up the first department for girls in civil government and political economy. In 1873, after being made principal, she took a leave of absence for two terms of the year, to pursue a law course in the University of Michigan, for the triple purpose of gaining more discipline by study, of acquiring a better foundation for political science, and to study the effects of co-education in college. In 1874 she took the degree of LL.B. In 1878, in company with three other women, she went to Canandaigua, NY, where they established Granger Place School. Miss Slocum was chosen vice-president, a position which she still occupies. Her departments of instruction include civil government, political economy, psychology, logic and ethics. Her success as an educator has been remarkable.

SMEDES, Mrs. Susan Dabney, author and missionary, born in Raymond, MS, 10th August, 1840, of Virginian parents. Her father, Thomas Smith Dabney, was of the old Huguenot family of D'Aubigné, a branch of which settled in Lower Virginia early in the eighteenth century. Susan was the second daughter in a family of nine sons and seven daughters. As a child she was gentle and devout, and her earliest ambition was to become a missionary. In 1860 she became the wife of Lyell Smedes, of Raleigh, NC. Their happy but brief union was terminated by his death at the end of eleven weeks. Having lost her mother about the same time, her life was henceforth devoted to the care of her father and her younger brothers and sisters. In 1882 the family removed from the plantation in Mississippi to Baltimore, MD, where she lived till the close of her father's life. In consequence of that event, at the age of forty-five, her early dream of missionary labors became a possibility, and she went out to the Sioux Indians, commissioned as a United States teacher. Her love and sympathy for those people brought her almost immediately into the closest sympathy with her charges, and the fourteen months spent by her in teaching and ministering to their spiritual needs

are reckoned as the happiest of her life. Living as she did in an isolated camp, in the rigorous climate of Dakota, her health failed, and she was taken by her friends to Helena, Mont., where she hoped to recruit her strength and return to the field. In this she was overruled, and having an offer of work in the Surveyor General's office, she labored for the next three years as clerk in that department of the government service. From there she removed, in October, 1891, to Washington, DC, where she now lives. She has been for several years a contributor to the leading magazines and newspapers of the country. The simple story of her father's life, as told in "A Southern Planter" (Baltimore, 1887), her greatest work, has not only attracted wide attention in the United States, but is well known in England through the London edition. That edition was issued at the request of Mr. Gladstone, who commended it to his countrymen, with a prefatory note from himself. Students and professors of history pronounce that work the most valuable contribution to the history of the ante-bellum South that has yet appeared.

SMITH, Mrs. Charlotte Louise, poet and author, born in Unity, ME, 20th September, 1853. She is the daughter of James Bowdoin Murch and Mary Lucretia Murch. On her mother's side she is descended from the Prescotts of Revolutionary fame, a family which has given the world a brave general and patriot, a great historian, and many valued workers in the field of literature. Her father was a lawyer and a man of scholarly tastes, who placed a volume of Shakespeare in his daughter's hands at an age when most children are reading nursery tales, and who encouraged her attempts at verse-making. Early in her youth her family removed from Unity to Belfast, the county seat of Waldo county, ME, where her girlhood was passed, and her first literary efforts were made. Before she was fifteen years of age two of her poems were published in the Boston "Traveller," and since that time she has been a contributor to the more important newspapers of Maine and to many journals in other parts of the United States. Her literary work has been chiefly in the line of journalistic correspondence, descriptions of natural scenery, translations from foreign literature, and the composition of poetry. To the stanzas of the great French poets she has given such careful study and patient effort as to make her successful in reproducing their subtle shades of meaning and the music of their intricate rhythm. In 1879 she became the wife of Bertram Lewis Smith, of Bangor, ME, a lawyer. After her marriage she lived in Bangor till 1889, when business interests took her husband to Patten, ME, which has since been her home.

SMITH, Mrs. Elizabeth J., editor, born in a suburb of St. John's, New Brunswick. For forty years she has been a resident of Providence, RI, to which city she removed when eight years of age. She is descended from a Scotch ancestry distinguished for scholarly attainments and spirituality; on her father's side from the Scotch covenanters, and from a maternal line marked in every generation, back to the crusaders, with brilliant intellects and religious fervor. In her earliest years she gave promise of great mental activity. On the removal of her parents to Providence, RI, she entered classes with pupils several years her senior. At fourteen she was a teacher in one of the public schools, and became its principal at sixteen. After a bright conversion, at the age of ten years, she united with the Chestnut Street Methodist Episcopal Church, of which she is now a member, and at thirteen became a Sunday-school teacher. She became the wife of Ransom L. Smith, of Winchester, NH, when eighteen, and two years later returned, a widow, to the home of her father and mother, where she now brightens their declining years. From her childhood her sympathetic nature was moved to help in every good cause. Her religious convictions were powerful and, manifestly called into public religious work in her own denomination, she resolutely turned from her profession of music and voice culture and entered into the work of an evangelist with devoted zeal. With a marked aptitude for pulpit work, she delivered sermons nightly for successive weeks to crowded audiences. Large numbers of converts were added to the churches where she labored. In 1886, when about to commence a series of winter engagements in New England churches, after her return from a National Woman's Christian Temperance Union, to which she was a delegate, an attack of pneumonia laid her up for some time. During her convalescence her thoughts were turned into a new channel for influencing the young, which has proved further reaching in its benefits than any work depending upon her personal presence. In addition to her other labors she filled the position of State superintendent of juvenile work in the Rhode Island Woman's Christian Temperance Union for over twelve years, and inaugurated the Loyal Temperance Legion, before it was made national. That organization flourished under her care. Her desire to interest young people in temperance work culminated in the publication of an eight-page illustrated paper, the "Home Guard," which has increased to twelve pages, and in its extensive circulation all over the country, in Sunday-schools of every denomination, demands her time and best efforts as its editor and publisher. When the effort was made to secure constitutional prohibition in Rhode Island, she, as a State lecturer, gave effective addresses in nearly every town and city of the State.

SMITH, Mrs. Elizabeth Oakes Prince, author, born in North Yarmouth, ME, 12th August, 1806. Her maiden name was Prince. She received a careful education in her native town. At an early age she became the wife of Seba Smith, the journalist and author, and for years she aided him in his editorial labors. For three years she edited "The Mayflower," an annual published in Boston, MA. In 1842 she and her husband removed to New York City, where they engaged in literary work. She was the first woman in the United States to become a public lecturer, and she has preached in different churches. At one time she acted as pastor of an independent congregation in Canastota, Madison county, NY. Her husband died 29th July, 1868, in Patchogue, NY, and she went to Hollywood, NC, where she thereafter made her home. She was for many years a regular contributor to magazines and periodicals. Among her published volumes are: "Riches Without Wings" (1838); "The Sinless Child" (1841); "Stories for Children" (1847); "Woman and Her Needs" (1851); "Hints on Dress and Beauty" (1852); "Bald Eagle, or the Last of the Ramapaughs" (1867); "The Roman Tribute," a tragedy (1850), and "Old New York, or Jacob Leisler," a tragedy (1853). She died in Hollywood, NC, 15th November, 1893.

SMITH, Mrs. Emily L. Goodrich, newspaper correspondent, born in the old Hancock house, Boston, MA, 1st June, 1830. She is the oldest daughter of the late Hon. S. G. Goodrich, widely known as "Peter Parley." Her mother was Miss Mary Boott, of an English family of position. Being obliged to go abroad, they placed their little daughter in the famous Inglis-McCleod school. Her education, begun thus auspiciously, was for years pursued in France and Italy, where every opportunity for study was given her, and she became an accomplished linguist. In 1846, in Paris, France, she was presented at the court of Louis Philippe and saw the throne of the "citizen king" broken and burned in the uprising of 1848. At that time she took her first lesson in caring for the wounded. The court of the hotel was filled with men shot down by the soldiery. A mob of ninety-thousand controlled the city three days. For twenty hours Lamartine held them by his eloquence, and Miss Goodrich stood on a balcony near when the rabble hurled down a statue and thrust him into its niche. While her father was Consul in Paris, she assisted her mother in entertaining numbers of their countrymen, as well as such dignitaries of other nations as were visiting the city. In the days so alarming for all Paris the American Consulate and Mr. Goodrich's house were filled with terror-stricken foreigners, who found their only place of safety under the protection of the American flag. Miss Goodrich was presented at the Court of St. James at the time of the first great exposition. In 1856 she returned to the United States and became the wife of Nathaniel Smith, of Connecticut, a grandson of the famous Nathaniel Smith who was Senator in the days when Congress sat in Philadelphia, and chief justice of Connecticut. In 1861 Mrs. Smith followed her husband to the Civil War, where she remained with him for two years. He was injured in an explosion, and, although his death did not occur till some years after the war had ended, he was a martyr to the cause of liberty. "Mrs. Colonel," as the soldiers called her, is mentioned in the State reports as being very efficient in tent and hospital. She has written many stories and some verse for various magazines. During the stormy years in Paris and the stirring times there-

after she was correspondent of a great New York daily. Her letters during the war and accounts of the Centennial were widely read and copied. In 1883, to help others, she took up the work of the Chautauqua Literary and Scientific Circle, and she is one of ten in Connecticut who, in 1891, were enrolled in the highest order of Chautauqua degrees. When Mount Vernon was to be purchased by the women of America, she was appointed first vice-regent of Connecticut, and her daughter was one of her most valued assistants. She has done much efficient work in the State as agent for the Humane Society. For many years she lived in Woodbury, but of late has lived in Waterbury, CT. For the last twenty years she has been more or less connected with the newspapers, and was for two years secretary of the large correspondence association of the "American."

SMITH, Mrs. Emma Pow, evangelist, born in Adams, MI, 11th March, 1848. She comes from a long line of American ancestry. Her father, J. Henry Smith, M.D., was born and bred in Royalton, NY, in which place he lived with his parents until he attained his majority. At the age of twenty-four he was married to Mariah Brooks, who was also a thoroughbred American. In 1843 they emigrated from New York State and settled on a farm in the heart of the dense woods of Michigan, where their daughter Emma was born, the seventh child of a family of twelve. As a child she was eccentric and given to seeking seclusion and solitude. Even in childhood she seemed to have a wonderful reverence for God in nature, and her thoughts then, as now, were of the spiritual rather than the temporal things of life. In April, 1867, she became the wife of a man who proved to have a fatal tendency to strong drink, and with whom she spent seven most unhappy years. Feeling that her life must pay the forfeit of her mistake, should she remain in that unholy state, she broke the bond, and, the court deciding in her favor, she regained her maiden name. Being converted, she was in the month of June, 1879, called and endowed by the spirit of God to preach the gospel. Closing her dressmaking business, she went directly from Grand Rapids, MI, to California, where she labored most earnestly for five years as a gospel missionary in the city of San Francisco. Her powers of oratory won for her a host of friends from all grades of society. Six years ago she was duly authorized and began her work in the field under the auspices of the Woman's Christian Temperance Union. When she is not in the field, where she is nearly constantly employed, she spends her time in her own "Sea Side Rest," Pacific Grove, CA. Among her literary and poetical productions none have received greater commendation than her new book, "Chrysolyte." She is a fine conversationalist upon ennobling subjects. One of her eccentricities is that she will not spend her time in talk to amuse people.

SMITH, Mrs. Estelle Turrell, reformer, born in Forest Lake, Susquehanna county, PA, 30th October, 1854. Her maiden name was Turrell. Her father's people were among the first settlers of Pennsylvania, emigrating at an early day from Connecticut. Her mother's family were Quakers. Her mother's maiden name was Gurney, and she was a descendant of John Joseph Gurney and Elizabeth Fry. In childhood Mrs. Smith was thought old for her years, was fond of poetry and music, and delighted in the studies of natural science. She became early acquainted with the fauna and flora about her country home. Her studies commenced at home and were pursued in the Montrose Academy, Montrose, PA. She commenced to teach when seventeen years of age, at the same time continuing her special studies, then among the masters of art and song. In 1875 she removed with her parents to Longmont, CO. She taught two years in the State Agricultural College in Fort Collins, CO. In 1878 she became the wife of P. M. Hinman, secretary of the State Board of Agriculture, who died a few years later. She then became more deeply interested in the problems of woman's progress. Having means and leisure at her command, she devoted much time to the study and support of social reforms. Her devotion to the work of reform and her frequent contributions to the press soon won for her a place as a leader. In 1884 she became the wife of Dr. A. B. Smith, of Des Moines, IA. She was shortly after elected president of the Polk County Woman Suffrage Society. She has been an efficient member of the State executive committee for four years, and is at present (1892) president of the State Woman Suffrage Asociation of Iowa. At her instigation a series of mothers' mass meetings was held in Des Moines. The large City Hall was filled again and again, hundreds of women taking active part. Mrs. Smith was chosen president of the meetings. Much good was accomplished, especially in banishing from the city disreputable posters, cigarette cards and other evils. Through those meetings a bill regulating the property rights of women was presented to the State legislature.

SMITH, Mrs. Eva Munson, poet and composer, born in Monkton, VT, 12th July, 1843. She is a daughter of William Chandler Munson and Hannah Bailey Munson. Her parents came of Puritan stock. Her father was descended from Capt. Thomas Munson, who was born in England in 1612 and came to the Colonies in 1639. He settled first in Hartford, CT, and afterward removed to New Haven, CT. Her mother is a direct descendant of Hannah Bailey, of Revolutionary fame, who tore up her flannel petticoat to make wadding for the guns in battle. Eva Munson received a good education in the Mary Sharp College, Winchester, TN. Her family removed to Rockford, IL, where her father died in 1867. She was graduated in 1864 in the female seminary in Rockford, and, being thrown upon her own resources after his death, she made good use of her attainments. She removed to Nebraska City, NE, where she had full charge of the musical department of Otoe University. She there became the wife of George Clinton Smith. Her musical and poetical gifts appeared in her childhood, and she was, while yet a girl, a proficient musician, a fine singer and a writer of meritorious verse. At the age of five years she composed little airs, and at fourteen she wrote her musical compositions in form for publication and preservation. She united early with the church, and her musical gifts were turned into the religious channel. She sang in church choirs, and she early observed that many of the choicest musical productions are the work of women. She decided to make a collection of the sacred compositions of women, and the result is her famous compilation, "Woman in Sacred Song" (Boston, 1885). The second edition, published in 1887, contains poetry written by eight-hundred-thirty women, and one-hundred-fifty musical compositions by fifty different women. The work is now known throughout the civilized world. Mrs. Smith has composed many popular pieces. Her "Joy" was published in 1868. Among her best known productions are "Woodland Warblings," "Home Sonata," "American Rifle Team March," and "I Will Not Leave You Comfortless." Her latest is a setting to music for voice and piano of Lincoln's favorite poem, "Oh, Why Should the Spirit of Mortal Be Proud?" She is now living in Springfield, IL, and her home is the resort of a large circle of temperance and religious workers, and musical, literary and patriotic persons. She is in sympathy with missionary and all moral and patriotic movements, and for two years, during 1890 and 1891, was the president of Stephenson Woman's Relief Corps, No. 17, which position she filled with untiring zeal and satisfaction to all.

SMITH, Miss Fannie Douglass, journalist, born in Middletown, OH, 3rd August, 1865. While she was yet a child, her parents removed to Hamilton, OH, where they have since resided. She was educated in the public schools of Hamilton. After leaving school she devoted her attention for some time to music, taking a course of vocal instruction in the College of Music in Cincinnati. She has a fine soprano voice and is a leading member of the Methodist Episcopal Church choir of Hamilton. She has a local reputation as a singer, and her vocal gifts give great promise for her future success in that line. She now holds the routine of society reporter on the Hamilton "Daily Democrat," where she has gained considerable reputation. She is a member of the Unity Club, the leading literary club of Hamilton, and she frequently contributes to the musical as well as the literary parts of its programmes.

SMITH, Miss Frances M. Owston, poet, was born in Peterborough, Ontario, Canada. She is of mixed English and Irish blood. Her father, Ralph Smith, was a native of King's county, Ireland, and her mother was a daughter of Captain William Owston, of the Royal Navy, Yorkshire, England. She was reared and educated in Peterborough, and her home has for some years past been in Lucan, in the western part of the Province of Ontario. She has written verses since her childhood, and her poems have been published in the "Irish Monthly," Ireland, in the "Canadian Monthly," and in several leading Canadian weeklies. Her poetry runs in the religious vein principally. Her work shows culture, earnestness and purity of thought and aspiration, and she is ranked with those other Canadian singers who are aiding powerfully to create and glorify a Canadian literature. She is known for her charitable deeds as well as her literary achievements.

SMITH, Mrs. Genie M., author, born on a farm in Vermont, 17th November, 1852. Her maiden name was Boyce. Her father was an invalid, and she was left to live an out-door life in childhood. She became the wife, at an early age, of Colonel Dwight T. Smith, and her home is in Dubuque, IA. Four children were born to them, two of whom died in infancy. Mrs. Smith is widely known by her pen-names, "Maude Meredith" and "Kit Clover." She has been a prolific author of serials, poetry, short stories and papers on home subjects for women. "Maude Meredith" began her literary career in the columns of the Chicago "Tribune" in 1880. The following year she issued "The Rivulet and Clover Blooms," a small volume of poems. In 1883 she wrote "St. Julian's Daughter" (Chicago), an interesting novel of Dubuque in pioneer days. In 1884 she edited and published the "Mid-Continent," a magazine which died young. In 1886–87–88 she edited the "Housekeeper" and created for that periodical the extensive reputation it has ever since enjoyed. Among other periodicals to which she has contributed are the "Independent," "Literary Life," "Peterson's Magazine," Chicago "Inter-Ocean," the "Current," "St. Louis Magazine," "Golden Days," "Journalist," "Godey's Lady's Book," the "Writer," St. Paul "Pioneer-Press," "Northwest Magazine," "Home-

Maker," "Ladies' World," and "Ladies' Home Companion." She has recently published two novels in book form, "Winsome but Wicked" (Chicago, 1892), and "The Parson's Sin" (Chicago, 1892), and has other novels in press, and also "The Columbian Cook-Book." In 1886 she published "Our Money-Makers," a practical poultry book. She is at present editing departments in five or six different publications. So far she has attempted to enter none of the higher fields of literature; she has addressed herself to the intelligent masses only, but she has written no worthless matter.

SMITH, Miss Helen Morton, journalist, born in Sullivan Harbor, ME, 12th December, 1859. She was a precocious child and a diligent student. She received a primary education in the school of her town. Her later education was obtained in a convent in Michigan. While quite young, she became a regular contributor to country papers, and many of her articles were copied by metropolitan journals. She enrolled herself in the ranks of overworked and underpaid school teachers and won the success sure to attend the efforts of a gifted woman. After three years of service in the cause of education, the craving for a broader life led her to abandon what she had once considered her chosen work and enter the profession which is always open to talents such as hers. Boston was her chosen field of labor, and the excellent training received in that city prepared her for the positions she has since held. In 1890, in addition to a large special correspondence and associated press reporting from Bar Harbor, she was local editor of the Bar Harbor "Record," and in the following year she was made managing editor. In connection with that work she furnished many of the leading newspapers with Bar Harbor matter, her letters reaching as far west as Cincinnati and Chicago. She has a beautiful home in Sullivan Harbor, but spends her winters in New York and Washington.

SMITH, Miss Isabel Elizabeth, artist, born in Clermont county, OH, in 1845. She is of Scotch descent. Her father, Alexander Smith, was born in Perthshire, Scotland. He came to this country in 1820 and located in Belmont county, OH. His wife was Miss Rachel McClain. They had a family of three children, a son and two daughters. The father was a man of great nobility of character, a lover of art and a philanthropist. The mother is a woman of excellent mind and given to the doing of kindly deeds. Miss Smith early developed a taste for art. She was educated in the Western Female College, Oxford, OH, and studied art during vacations in Cincinnati. After her education she went abroad and studied in Paris and Dresden. After an absence of nearly three years she returned to this country and opened a studio in Washington, DC, in 1871. She achieved marked success in portrait painting, having many prominent persons as sitters, among them Secretary Stanton, a full length portrait of whom was ordered from her by the representatives of the city government. She also painted the portrait of Mrs. Cramer, a sister of Gen. U. S. Grant. While in that city, she became a member of the Methodist Episcopal Church. During her years of labor in Washington her eyes failed her, but after a season of rest she again went to Paris to learn the Sévres method of painting on porcelain. She also studied in the Dresden Gallery, receiving criticisms from the celebrated Director Schnoor von Carroldsfeld. On her return she opened a studio in New York City, where she had the best possible recognition from the literary and art circles. While there she was elected a member of Sorosis, in which society she held the position of chairman of the art committee. She usually has several students, whom she teaches gratuitously. When fifteen years of age, she had a severe illness, during which she vowed to build a church for the poor in her native place, which through her aid and influence has been done, and to which she gives her interest and help. Her father owned a large tract of land in Florida, near the mouth of the St. John's river, where he had an orange grove and a winter home. There she spent several winters. Her father died several years ago. She has painted in Cincinnati, and her portraits there are highly praised. She has been the instructor in art in Chautauqua, NY, for four years, having her studio in the Kellogg Memorial Building. She gave up her studio in New York to devote her time and care to her invalid mother.

SMITH, Mrs. Jeanie Oliver, poet and romancist, was born in Troy, NY. Her maiden name was Davidson. Her father was of Scottish extraction and was long well known in Troy as a philanthropist, but is now a resident of New York City. Her mother was a member of the Oliver family, conspicuous in southern Scotland. From both strains she inherits poetic and artistic tendencies. When her mother died, the young girl went with an aunt to Scotland, and for five years she lived in Edinburgh, where she was educated thoroughly and liberally. After graduation she returned to the United States. At an early age she became the wife of Hon. Horace E. Smith, dean of the Albany Law School, and since her marriage she has lived in Johnstown, NY, and her home is known as a social and literary center. She has cared for her two young daughters and for the large family of her husband by a former marriage. Her time has been filled with literary, society and charitable work, and she is especially interested in religious and educational matters. Her literary productions have been numerous, including poems, tales and sketches of great merit. She has contributed to leading magazines, including the "Magazine of Poetry," "Christian at Work," and many others. She has published recently one volume of poems, "Day Lilies" (New York, 1890), which has passed into its second edition and won her substantial reputation as a poet. She is the author of "The Mayor of Kanameta" (New York, 1891), a story on sociological lines, showing marked powers in the author, also "Donald Moncrieff," a companion book to the former (Buffalo, 1892). Her finest work is done in verse. She has a number of tales in preparation.

SMITH, Mrs. Julia Holmes, physician, born in Savannah, GA, 23rd December, 1839. Her father was Willis Holmes, of South Carolina, a descendant of an old English family well known as planters in that State and Alabama. On her mother's side her grandfather was Capt. George Raynall Turner, of the United States navy. The early life of Miss Holmes was spent in New Orleans. Her education was entrusted to a maiden aunt, Miss Turner, who taught the child to read before she was four years old. Passing from the care of her aunt, the girl was sent to the famous seminary conducted by Gorham D. Abbott in Union Square, New York, under the name of the Spingler Institute. There she was graduated at the age of eighteen, and after one year in society became the wife of Waldo Abbott, oldest son of the historian, John S. C. Abbott. In 1864 her husband died, leaving her with one son, Willis John Abbott. The widowed mother labored for the next eight years to support herself and her child by literary and journalistic work and teaching. In 1872 she became the wife of Sabin Smith, of New London, CT, and removed to Boston, where she was first attracted toward the profession in which she has been so successful. Happening to summon a physician to treat a slight cold, she met for the first time a woman practicing medicine. The physician was Prof. Mary B. Jackson, who was at that time past seventy years old and an honored member of the faculty of the Boston University School of Medicine. So much impressed was Mrs. Smith by the character and profession of Dr. Jackson that she soon turned toward the same calling. Holding high ideals of womankind, it has always been the boast of Dr. Smith that, although receiving careful teaching during her life from many distinguished persons, her career was shaped by two women, the one in childhood inculcating a taste for study, and the other later in life directing that taste toward a profession, the practice of which has given her a national reputation. She began her professional education in Boston University School of Medicine in 1873. There she remained three years, but, her husband's business calling the family to Chicago, she was graduated in 1877 from the Chicago Homeopathic College, and has been in practice in that city ever since. She has been active in the intellectual work of the women of that city. She is a member of the Fortnightly and was for two years its secretary. Of the Woman's Club, one of the foremost institutions of its kind in the country, she was thrice elected president. She has long been a prominent member of the Association for the Advancement of Women. She was the organizer and first president of the Woman's Medical Association, the only society of the kind in America. Other organizations of a professional character with which Dr. Smith is allied are the American Institute of Homeopathy, of one of the bureaus of which she is the secretary, the Academy of Physicians and Surgeons, the Illinois Homeopathy Association, and the board of directors of the Illinois Training School for Nurses, in which she is a lecturer. In literary work Dr. Smith has always been active. Her articles upon literary and general topics have appeared in publications of the highest class and are quite numerous. Of her purely professional publications, two are worth special reference. In 1889 she contributed to the New York Ledger" a series of articles on "Common Sense in the Nursery," which met general approval. She is the only woman who contributed to "Arndt's System of Medicine," her share in that work, which is a generally accepted authority, being something more than one-hundred pages on medical topics. Dr. Smith is active in social life in Chicago, despite the heavy demands that her practice puts upon her.

SMITH, Mrs. Luella Dowd, poet and author, born in Sheffield, MA, 16th June, 1847. Her parents were Almeron and Emily Curtiss Dowd. In her second year the family removed to West Virginia, where they remained nine years. Her parents were teachers, and she was educated by them at home and in the schools which they conducted. They returned to Massachusetts, when Luella was eleven years old, and she continued her studies in the academy in South Egremont, in the high and normal schools in Westfield, and Charles F. Dowd's seminary in Saratoga Springs, NY. She was graduated in the last named institution and became a successful teacher for several years. With her school work she carried on Sunday-school and temperance work. In 1875 she became the wife of Henry Hadley Smith, MD. They lived in Sheffield, MA, until 1884, when they went to Europe. After a long trip abroad they returned to the United States and settled in Hudson, NY, where Dr. Smith practices medicine, and where they still live. Mrs. Smith's literary work dates from her youth. She has written much, in both prose and verse, and she has contributed to many magazines and periodicals. In 1879 she collected some of her productions and published them in a volume entitled "Wayside

Leaves" (New York). In 1887 she brought out a second volume, "Wind Flowers" (Chicago). Her work includes a series of temperance stories for children, and is impressive because of its artistic excellence and its high moral stamp.

SMITH, Mrs. Lura Eugenie Brown, journalist, born in Rochester, NY, 23rd June, 1864. Her father, Leverett Russell Brown, died in Little Rock, AR, in January, 1891. Her grandfather, Joseph Patterson Brown, was a citizen of Winsor, NY, where he married Lura M. Russell. Mrs. Smith's mother was Catherine Anne Ostrander, a member of the Knickerbocker community in the Empire State. Mrs. Smith is the second of a family of four children. She went to Little Rock, AR, in 1883, and has been engaged in journalistic work ever since 1884. She has become one of the most widely known journalists of the South, and she is well known also in the North. Her earlier work in that field included correspondence of the special sort for Arkansas, Tennessee, Texas and other journals. For a time she edited the "Arkansas Life," and has for several years been the poet of the Arkansas Press Association. She has been an earnest worker in the Chautauqua Circle in Little Rock. At one time she held a department editorship on the Milwaukee "Sunday Telegraph," which failing health compelled her to give up. She is joint author, with Octave Thanet, of "Victory's Divorcement" (New York, 1891). She contributed "The Autocrat of Arkansas" to the "Arkansas Press" in 1890, and in 1891 she wrote the serial "On the Track and Off the Train," which later was issued in book form. She became the wife of Sidney Smith, editor of the Cedar Rapids, IA, "Masonic Review," 20th April, 1892.

SMITH, Mrs. Martha Pearson, poet and musician, born in North Conway, NH, 29th September, 1836. Her parents were John M. and Laura Emery Pearson. Her paternal grandmother was related to Nathaniel Hawthorne. She is a descendant of a race of godly people. Her ancestry runs back to the Smithfield martyr. Her ancestors included the Gilmans, who came from England in the ship "Diligent," in 1638, and settled in Hingham, MA. Many of the most noted men and women of New England were members of her family in past generations. Her early life was passed amid the quiet and healthful scenes of the White Mountains. Her family removed to Meredith, and when she was seven years old, they made their home in Boston, MA, where she studied. Her mother, who had been a successful teacher, personally superintended the education of her family. The young Martha was able to read when she was only four years old, and before she was seven years old had read Milton's "Paradise Lost," Harvey's "Meditations" and other classical works. The Pearson family for generations had been a musical one. Her grandfather, John Pearson, was a singer and composer of both words and music that were sung in the Congregational Church in Newburyport, MA. He was a fine performer on several instruments, and from him Martha inherited her strong love and talent for music. She studied music and even ventured to compose airs, when she was six years old. Among her published songs are "Under the Lilies Sleeping" and "Go, Forget Me." She has many musical compositions in manuscript, and some of her temperance songs are published in the temperance department of "Woman in Sacred Song." Some of her verses have been set to music by Prof. T. M. Towne. When she was yet a child, her family moved to Cincinnati, O., and afterward to Covington, KY, where she attended school for a number of years. Her teacher trained her in composition, for which she early showed a strong talent. She attended a young ladies' seminary in Covington, and at the age of sixteen years published in the local papers several serial stories over the pen-name "Mattie May." Some of her poems appeared when she was eleven years old. At the age of ten she began to write a book founded on the Maine Liquor Law, in which a wonderful hero and an abundance of tragedy were conspicuous. The irrepressible author displayed itself in her on several occasions. During the cholera epidemic in Covington she was slightly indisposed, and her parents, imagining her a victim of the pest, hurried her to bed, bathed her aching head, and enjoined her to keep quiet. Shortly after her mother entered her room and was amazed to see the supposed cholera patient sitting up in bed, with flushed face, writing as fast as she could a poem entitled "The Song of the Pestilence." She was not allowed to finish the song. She lived in Kentucky until 1857, when she removed to Minnesota. In 1859 she became the wife of Edson R. Smith, a banker and mill-owner, of Le Sueur, who has served his State as Senator. Their family consists of three sons. Mrs. Smith does much charitable work. Her first years in Minnesota were troublesome ones, as the Dakota Indians were then murdering the pioneers. Mrs. Smith and her children were sent to Vermont for some months, until the Indian troubles were ended. She is a voluminous writer, but most of her best work has never been published. She is a lover of children and a most devoted home-maker and housekeeper.

SMITH, Miss Mary Belle, educator and temperance worker, born in that part of Middlefield, CT, now known as Rockfall, 18th December, 1862. On her father's side she traces her descent from the early settlers of the country, through a long line of men who were identified with the mercantile and manufacturing interests of the country. On her mother's side is strongly patriotic blood, and members of her line have fought for their country in every war that has taken place since the landing of the Pilgrims. She received a careful moral and mental home training and has been from childhood a thorough student. She was taught at home by her mother until ten years of age, when she was placed under the tuition of a teacher whose instruction prepared her to take the entrance examination of Mount Holyoke College, from which institution she was graduated in 1886. After graduating, she entered her father's office as a practical accountant and remained for two years, having entire charge of his books and correspondence and acquiring a thorough business education. She devoted much of her time to Sunday-school and missionary work and became an active member of the Woman's Christian Temperance Union, having joined the young woman's organization while in college. She has held various offices in the local union, has been county secretary and State superintendent of press-work, and is the State reporter of Connecticut for the "Union Signal." From having occasional pupils at home, she became interested in teaching and is now engaged successfully in that work. She has been a member of the Methodist Episcopal Church since childhood, and to it she is devotedly attached. Her home is in Rockfall.

SMITH, Mrs. Mary Louise Riley, poet, born in Brighton, Monroe county, NY, 27th May, 1852. Her maiden name was Mary Louise Riley. She was educated in the collegiate institute in Brockport, NY. She early showed her literary talent, and in youth wrote much in rhyme. In 1869 she became the wife of Albert Smith, of Springfield, IL. They soon removed to New York City, where they now live. She was for years corresponding secretary of Sorosis, and she belongs to other woman clubs, before which she has often spoken. Their family consists of one son. Her published books are "A Gift of Gentians and Other Verses" (New York, 1882), and "The Inn of Rest" (1888). She has contributed to many periodicals, and her poems are of the class that are widely copied. Among the best and most popular of her poems are "Tired Mothers," "If We Knew," "The Easter Moon," "Love is Sweeter than Rest" and "My Prayer." Among those that have been published separately as booklets are "His Name" and "Sometime," and they have found a wide sale.

SMITH, Mrs. Mary Stewart, author and translator, born in the University of Virginia, 10th February, 1834. She is the second daughter of Prof. Gessner Harrison and his wife, Eliza Lewis Carter Tucker. Dr. Harrison gave to his children the valuable idea that education is not finished with the school curriculum, but is a thing of eternal progressiveness. Private tutors were freely engaged or the children. They studied Latin, German, French and Italian. One daughter, Maria, began Hebrew, and Mary took up Greek. She began early to rhyme and show great fondness for poetry, natural scenery, and romances of the best description. When thirteen years old, being chosen Queen of the May by her companions, she composed a poem to recite upon her coronation. From that time until she arrived at maturity she wrote verse only occasionally. In spare hours from numerous duties she greedily devoured every work of fiction that came in her way. She became the wife of Prof. Francis H. Smith in 1853, and considers herself to be peculiarly blessed in being able to reside still in the University of Virginia, her beloved native place. After the Civil War was over, she took up her pen for the real and earnest literary work of her life. Besides original articles, her translations from the German for leading periodicals and publishing houses form in themselves a long list. From E. Werner she has translated "A Hero of the Pen," "Hermann," "Good Luck" "What the Spring Brought," "St. Michael," "A Judgment of God" and "Beacon Lights." Her translations from other German writers are "Lieschen," "The Fairy of the Alps," "The Bailiff's Maid," "Gold Elsie," "Old Ma'amselle's Secret," "The Owl House," "The Lady With the Rubies," "Seraps," "The Bride of the Nile," "Lace," by Paul Lindau, and others. She is thought by eminent critics to have an especial gift for translating German poetry, as for instance her "Chidhe" in the "Overland Monthly." She is one of those writers who have power to please children. Some of her books for children are translations from the German or adaptations from the French. Among the former are "The Canary Bird, and Other Stories," and "Jack the Breton Boy." From original work and French suggestion may be noted "How Lillie Spent Her Day," and "Little May and Her Lost A." Of her original books, "Heirs of the Kingdom" was published in Nashville, for which a prize of $300 was awarded by a select committee. "Lang Syne, or the Wards of Mt. Vernon" was published on the occasion of the Washington Centennial, held in New York in April, 1887. Mrs. Smith has made innumerable contributions of practical articles to "Harper's Bazar," some to the "American Agriculturist," "Good Housekeeping," and other periodicals of like trend. Of this sort of literature her "Virginia Cookery Book" (New York) is a valuable work; so also is her "Art of Housekeeping" (New York), which first appeared as a series of papers written for the New York "Fashion Bazar." Her series of "Letters from a Lady in New York" was published in the "Religious Herald."

Some of her good work has been in the form of review articles for the "Southern Review," the "Southern Methodist Quarterly" and the "Church Review." She translated from the French "The Salon of Mme. Necker." Some of her best review articles are: "Askaros Kassis Karis," "Robert Emmet," "Queen Louisa of Prussia," "John of Barneveldt," "What the Swallows Sang," "The Women of the Revolution," "The Women of the Southern Confederacy," "Madame de Stael and Her Parents," "The Necker Family," "Madam Récamier," "Mary and Martha Washington," and "The Virginia Gentlewoman of the Olden Time."

SMITH, Mrs. Olive White, author, born in Clarendon, VT, 25th December, 1846. She is generally known in literature as Mrs. Clinton Smith. Her ancestors were among the early settlers of Vermont. Her father, Charles White, was a pioneer geologist and the discoverer of several of the Vermont marble quarries. Her childhood was passed among the Green Mountains. She grew up with a mind imbued with a stern morality, tempered by a love of humanity, which led her in girlhood to be intelligently interested in the abolition of slavery. She was educated under Mrs. H. F. Leavitt, in the female seminary established by Mrs. Emma Willard, in Middlebury, VT. Home and foreign missions claimed her attention, and the Woman's Christian Temperance Union found in her an enthusiastic friend. Although her home has been in a retired corner of the great world, so deep has been her interest in public affairs that she has lived in the current of passing events. Possessing a reverence for law, she marveled at the ease with which the prohibitory liquor law of her State was evaded. After spending much time and energy in interviewing judges, justices, sheriffs and States' attorneys, she came to the conclusion that those officers, holding their positions through the votes of a political party, will go no further in good works than that party demands. Her parlors have been a gathering place for temperance people and prohibitionists. She has written some temperance articles and addresses, as well as short poems and stories, for New York papers and magazines. All of her life she has been connected with Sunday-school work in the Methodist Episcopal Church. Her husband sympathizes in all her hopes, and they have an interesting family of five children. She has been a contributor to the "Rural New Yorker," the New York "Weekly Witness," "Demorest's Magazine" and other periodicals. She has used the pen-names "Alicia" and "August Noon." Her home was in Middlebury, VT, until 1891, when her husband was called to a Government position in Washington, DC, and removed his family to that city, where Mrs. Smith is actively engaged in literary pursuits.

SOLARI, Miss Mary M., artist, born in Calvan, near Genoa, Italy, in 1849. She was brought by her parents, in 1849, to the United States. They made their home in Memphis, TN, with which city the family has ever since been identified. She was educated in the public schools and received her first lesson in drawing from Mrs. Morgan. The death of her mother during the epidemic of 1878, when all the members of her family were conspicuous for their courage and devotion as nurses and workers in the public interest, had a very depressing effect upon her, and on the advice of her surviving brother, Lorenzi Solari, she went to Italy, for the double purpose of recovering her health and studying art, toward which she had shown a decided inclination from her earliest childhood. On arriving in Florence, she was disappointed in finding the doors of the academy closed against her and all other women. In consequence she became a pupil of the renowned historical painter, Casioli, with whom she remained for two years, making rapid progress. She was determined to accomplish the greater work of causing the doors of the academy to be opened to her sex and to break down the opposition to women in the government schools of Italy. She plead her cause before Prof. Andrew De Vico, then (1880) director of the Academy of Florence. She was frequently told by those leading professors that she "had missed her vocation," that she "might better learn to cook a meal" or to "knit stockings," and similar belittling suggestions. She soon became noted as the eloquent advocate of the rights of her sex, reminding those whom she addressed that, when Italy was noted for her women students in the University of Bologna, and a few such noble and intelligent women as Vittoria Colonna, her men grew out and away from narrow grooves of thought and purpose and became the leaders of the world, and finally, in 1885, after a battle of six years, she was admitted to the academy. In that year she exhibited her first work there, in competition with the more favored students. It bore comparison well, was admired, proved that she was worthy, and it brought to her aid the press of Florence, hitherto silent or opposed to woman's advancement, which expressed the hope that succeeding years would see hung side by side studies of women with those of the male alumni. Through the door opened by her other women entered, and many now exhibit their work in competition with the members of the academy of the other sex. Beginning with only a dozen women, admitted in 1885, fully one-third the students in the academy now are of that sex. She, in 1887, won the first silver medal ever awarded a woman by the Florentine Academy. In 1888 she won the prize for composition from the antique and modeling. In 1889 she won the bronze medal for perspective and water-color, and also honorable mention for figure. In 1890 she received the highest awards in the Beatrice Exposition, open to women of all Italy, over one-thousand competitors, in ornamental drawing and water-colors. The Master of Arts degree was conferred upon her the same year, besides which she received letters of merit and the diploma which entitles her to teach in the government art-schools of Italy. She learned to speak Italian after going to Florence. She returned to Memphis after nine years of study in Florence.

SOUTHWORTH, Mrs. Emma Dorothy Eliza Nevitte, author, born in Washington, DC, 26th December, 1819. Her maiden name was Nevitte. Her mother was married twice, the second time to Joshua L. Henshaw, in whose school she was educated. Miss Nevitte was graduated in 1835, and in 1840 became the wife of Frederick H. Southworth, of Utica, NY. From 1844 to 1849 she taught in one of the public schools in Washington, and while there employed she began to write stories. Her first story, "The Irish Refugee," appeared in the Baltimore "Saturday Visitor." She then wrote for the "National Era," and in its columns her first novel, "Retribution," was published. That story was issued in book form in 1849. She became a prolific writer, averaging three novels a year, strong, dramatic and finely descriptive works, which attained a remarkable popularity. In 1853 she and her husband settled on Potomac Heights, near Washington, where they lived until their removal to Yonkers, NY, in 1876. Mrs. Southworth devised for her own use the manila box-envelope, which was afterward patented by others. Her published novels number over sixty. In 1872 she brought out a uniform edition of her works, consisting of forty-two stories, beginning with "Retribution" and ending with "The Fatal Secret." Her later stories are: "Unknown" (1874); "Gloria" (1877); "The Trail of the Serpent" (1879); "Nearest and Dearest" (1881); "The Mother's Secret" (1883), and "An Exile's Bride" (1887). Besides these she has published others as serials in the New York "Ledger." Many of her novels have been translated into French, German and Spanish, and republished in Montreal, London, Paris, Leipzig and Madrid. She is now living in Georgetown, DC.

SPALDING, Miss Harriet Mabel, poet, born in Gloversville, NY, 10th January, 1862. She is the daughter of Rev. N. G. Spalding, a prominent clergyman in the Troy conference of the Methodist Episcopal Church. Her parents possessed literary talents. Her father is a graduate of Union College and a brilliant orator. Her mother is a graduate of Mrs. Willard's Troy Seminary and an artist of merit. Miss Spalding inherits the talents of both parents. In 1868 the family removed to Schodack Landing, NY, which is now her home. Harriet was carefully and liberally educated. In 1877 she was graduated in the Albany Female Academy, where she won six gold medals offered by the alumnæ in various branches of composition. She began to write verses at the age of nine years. She has written much and her work has been widely copied.

SPALDING, Mrs. Susan Marr, poet, was born in Bath, ME. Her maiden name was Marr. Her youth was passed in Bath, and she studied in a seminary. Her parents died, while she was a girl, and she went to New York City to live in the family of an uncle, a clergyman. At an early age she became the wife of Mr. Spalding, a cultured and literary man. They settled in Philadelphia, PA, where Mr. Spalding died shortly after. She continues to make her home in that city, though her time is passed mostly among relatives and friends in answer to the demands made upon her as nurse and counselor. She is a woman of varied accomplishments. Her poetical career dates back to her girlhood. Her poems are artistic productions, and she excels in sonnet writing. Ranking among the most successful sonnet writers of the day, her work has a peculiar charm. She has contributed to many prominent periodicals.

SPARHAWK, Miss Frances Campbell, author and philanthropist, born in Amesbury, MA, 28th July, 1847. She will be remembered by posterity as one who was associated with efforts in behalf of the American Indians. She is of distinguished ancestry, descended on her mother's side from a Highland baronet, a Jacobite, who, through his adherence to the Stuarts, lost both his title and estate. On her father's side she is related to a branch of the Sir William Pepperell family. Her father was an eminent physician, a graduate of Dartmouth College and of the Harvard Medical School, and studied in the Massachusetts General Hospital under Dr. James Jackson. When a child, Frances was ill a great deal and was kept away from school. She drove about with her father, when he went to visit his patients, imbibing his thought and spirit, which was of the finest mold. Another strong formative influence in those early days was her friendship with their neighbor, the poet, John Greenleaf Whittier. She was graduated in the young ladies' seminary in Ipswich, MA, in 1867, the valedictorian of her class.

Soon after leaving the seminary she began to write for the press, contributing stones and sketches to various papers and magazines, and published her first book, "A Lazy Man's Work," in 1881. That was followed by "Elizabeth, A Romance of Colonial Days," a story of the siege of Louisburg. It was brought out as a serial in the "New England Magazine" in 1884. In 1886 "Gladys Langdon" came out in the "Christian Union" as a serial. The same paper published her other articles, and from time to time the greater number of the stories in "Little Folly Blatchley," afterward collected in book form (Boston, 1887). She then published "Miss West's Class" (1887); "The Query Club" in "Education," "A Chronicle of Conquest" (1890); "Onoqua," her last novel (1892). These last two stories deal with Indian life, with which Miss Sparhawk is thoroughly familiar, having spent some time in the Carlisle Indian School, where she edited the "Red Man," and having also visited other Indian schools and reservations. She is a member of the Woman's National Indian Association and puts much time, strength and enthusiasm into her great life-work. Her present home is in Newton Center, MA, where she lives with two sisters, all who are left of her immediate family.

SPEAR, Mrs. Catherine Swan Brown, reformer and educator, born in Worcester County, MA, in 1814. Her father, Samuel Swan, was of Scotch origin, an American by birth. Her mother, Clara Hale, was of English descent by both parents. Her mother was Joanna Carter, of Leominster. Their residence was in Hubbardston, MA. Her father was graduated from Cambridge University in 1799. Both parents were teachers. Her father was engaged as counselor-at-law forty years. Catherine was the oldest of seven children and was in immediate association with her parents and the society of maturer people. She began to attend school when three years of age, and continued until eighteen. She was engaged as a teacher three years. She was always opposed to slavery, and at nineteen years of age she became actively engaged in the anti-slavery organization. She became the wife of Abel Brown, of Albany, NY, in 1843. They had in charge many fugitive slaves. Her husband was corresponding secretary and general agent of the Eastern New York Anti-slavery Society. His office was in Albany. She lived with him only eighteen months, and during that time they traveled six-thousand miles. They were also engaged in the temperance movements. Her husband died at the age of thirty-five, a martyr to the cause of temperance and anti-slavery in Troy, 1845, in consequence of mob violence inflicted on his person. In 1855 Mrs. Brown became the wife of Rev. Charles Spear, of Boston, known as the "Prisoner's Friend." She visited with him many prisons and became interested in reformatories, by petitions and lectures in behalf of an industrial school for girls in South Lancaster, MA, and for boys in Washington, DC, through the influence of Charles Sumner. In the cause of temperance, she petitioned and labored for an asylum for inebriates in Boston, now under the management of Albert Day, M.D. In former days she was especially interested in the question of woman's rights as preliminary to that of suffrage. She now continues to work for the abolition of capital punishment. She has spoken in the senate of her native State on that subject, with others, and in all has addressed the legislature ten times, including one lecture in the House of Representatives. She was engaged in hospital work during the war of the Rebellion, her husband, Rev. Charles Spear, being chaplain, appointed by President Lincoln, in Washington, DC. He died in 1863, but Mrs. Spear remained until the close of the war. Although belonging to the Universal Peace Society, the war seemed to her the only way to conclude peace and to reëstablish the Union. In her work she was permitted to visit the rebel prison in the old capitol and give aid to the suffering. She is now living in Passaic, NJ.

SPENCER, Miss Josephine, poet, was born in Salt Lake City, UT. When a mere child, she was persistently writing in rhyme, and early constructed little dramas, in which there was the element of poetry. She attended the best schools in the Territory, but her education in literature has been acquired chiefly from reading the poets and the older English and American authors. While in school and a member of a class literary society, she attracted attention by her

contributions in poetry and prose to the manuscript paper issued periodically by the association. She was chosen editor of the paper. Thereafter occasional poems appeared in print over her name, and recently her contributions to magazines and the holiday editions of newspapers have been quite frequent. She has been the successful competitor in several poetic contests. In prose she is a pleasing and thoughtful writer. Her stories and essays in the literary periodicals are entertaining.

SPOFFORD, Mrs. Harriet Prescott, author, born in Calais, ME, 3rd April, 1835. She is a daughter of the late Joseph N. Prescott. Her father went to California in 1849, and there suffered a stroke of paralysis that made him an invalid for life. He was a lawyer and a lumber merchant. His wife was Sarah Bridges, and both families were of good New England stock. The family removed to Newburyport, MA, where Harriet was educated in the Putnam school. She went next to Derry, NH, where she entered Pinkerton Academy. There she was graduated in 1852. Her parents were both invalids at that time, and she began to use her literary talents to aid the family. She wrote stories for the Boston papers, for which she received small pay. Her stories of those day she has never collected or acknowledged. In 1859 she published her Parisian story, "In a Cellar," in the "Atlantic Monthly," which at once brought her into notice. Since then she has contributed both prose and poetry to the leading magazines. In 1865 she became the wife of Richard S. Spofford, of Boston, now disceased. Her home is now on Deer Island, a suburb of Newburyport, in the Merrimac river. Among her published books are "Sir Rohan's Ghost" (1859); "The Amber Gods, and Other Stories" (1863); "Azarian" (1864); "New England Legends" (1871); "The Thief in the Night" (1872); "Art Decoration Applied to Furniture" (1881); "Marquis of Carabas" (1882); "Poems" (i882); "Hester Stanley at St. Mark's" (1883); "The Servant Girl Question" (1884), and "Ballads About Authors" (1888).

SPRATT, Miss Louise Parker, journalist, was born in Aberdeen, MS. She received all the literary and musical advantages of her native and other towns and was graduated from the Tuscaloosa Female College. While continuing her musical studies in New Orleans, LA, the great expectations to which she had been born "vanished into thin air," and she was brought suddenly face to face with the problem of existence. With no moment given to idle regret, she turned to face that problem with all the hopeful fearlessness and proud confidence of youth. The efforts that she then made in the fields of literature and music soon brought her into prominence among those who appreciate the best and highest in those two arts. In 1888 she was engaged on the staff of the Birmingham, AL, "Age," as society editor and general writer. She made her departments on that paper exceptionally attractive by the brightness and piquancy of her articles, and by the fervor and honesty of her efforts in any work undertaken. Since that time she has been connected with the press of Birmingham, in nearly every department of editorial, reportorial and correspondence work on the different leading papers of that city. In every position, in every office, she has acquitted herself with a faithfulness always to be commended and with ability. In 1890 she established in Birmingham an independent journal, devoted to society and literature, and was making it a success, when an unfortunate fall, in which she broke her right wrist and injured her left, followed by protracted fever, incapacitated her temporarily for the work. Necessarily her pen was for a time idle. She has published a dialect story, entitled "A Dusky Romance," with pen-and-ink illustrations, showing her talent for that style of work. She possesses a talent for drawing and painting, though circumstances and work in other lines have so far prevented the development of that talent. She is an artist in her performances on the piano and organ, and has won as much success in her musical as in her literary work.

SPRINGER, Mrs. Rebecca Ruter, author, born in Indianapolis, IN, 8th November, 1832. She is the daughter of Rev. Calvin W. Ruter, a well-known clergyman of the Methodist Episcopal Church. She passed her youth in New Albany and Indianapolis. She was educated in the Wesleyan Female College, in Cincinnati, OH, and was graduated in 1850. She wrote much in youth, but allowed none of her productions to be published before she had grown to womanhood. The first of her poems to be known to the public was one which she read in college about the time of her graduation. She began to publish verses shortly after, and has since contributed to leading periodicals. In 1859 she became the wife of William M. Springer, the lawyer and congressman, and much of her time has been passed in Washington, DC. She is the mother of one son, Ruter W. Her health has at times been poor, and she has traveled abroad to gain strength. She has published two novels, "Beechwood" (Philadelphia, 1873), and "Self" (1881), and a volume of poems, "Songs by the Sea "(Chicago, 1890).

SPURLOCK, Mrs. Isabella Smiley Davis, philanthropist, born in Nodaway county, MO, 21st January, 1843. Her maiden name was Davis. Her father was of Jeff. Davis's lineage and born in Tennessee, but in the day of the nation's peril his love of country sent his first-born son, Maj. S. K. Davis, against the nation's foe, regardless of the kinsman commander in gray. Her mother's name was Windom, and she belonged to a good family. Miss Davis's child-life was one of care and responsibility, instead of play and pastime. Her life has been one of suffering or service. She became the wife, 1st November, 1860, of Burwell Spurlock, of Virginia, who belonged to one of the prominent families of the South, eminent in political and church work. They began home-keeping in Plattsmouth, NE. Her husband, connected with the church officially, aided in establishing the Methodist Episcopal Church in the new West. Her first public work was in the interest of foreign missions, organizing societies. During the temperance crusade she was one of the leaders who, with tongue and pen, waged warfare against the drink-evil. She twice represented the society in national conventions and was State superintendent of mothers' and social purity meetings. She was often a member of committees appointed to confer with influential bodies. In the spring of 1882 she was disabled physically, so that she was obliged to give up all public work, and a year of intense suffering followed. Through the prayers of herself and friends, as she believes, she was lifted out of darkness and received the command, "Go to Utah, and visit the sick and imprisoned." She heeded the call and spent two years among the women of Utah. That field of labor was one untried, and, though all doors were closed and all hearts sealed, she was gifted with the address and spirit of love that unlocked hearts and threw open doors from the "Lion House" of ex-President Brigham Young to the humblest hut of poverty and sorrow. While there, she assisted in opening a day nursery, where forsaken plural wives could leave their children and go out to earn their bread. That was the step that won the confidence of the Mormon women. She led in the movement to organize a Christian association, formed of the women of all denominations, for the assistance of the helpless women of Mormondom. In 1886 she was made trustee of an orphan's home on a farm in the West. Finally she persuaded the national executive committee of the Women's Home Missionary Society to adopt the movement, and in 1891 she and her husband were appointed to the superintendency of that work, the Mothers' Jewels' Home, near York, NE, which they now have in charge. She is the mother of two sons, of whom one died in infancy. The other was graduated with the law class of 1892 from De Pauw University, Greencastle, IN.

STAFFORD, Mrs. Maria Brewster Brooks, educator, born in Westmoreland, NH, in 1809. Her parents, of English origin, were enterprising and successful. Of their five daughters, all were married early, except Maria, who remained in school for thorough training. In 1833 she was invited by Rev. William Williams, whose wife was her friend, to go to Alabama as assistant teacher in the Alabama Female Institute. She became the central figure in that school and taught most successfully until she became the wife of Prof. Stafford, of Tuscaloosa. Prof. Stafford was a North Carolinian by birth and education, and his high scholastic attainments admirably fitted him for a chair in the Alabama State University, where they remained twenty years, until they were invited to take charge of the Alabama Female Institute, where Mrs. Stafford taught till 1872, and when widowed and alone in 1884 she went to live with her oldest daughter in Danville, KY.

STANFORD, Mrs. Jane Lathrop, philanthropist, born in Albany, NY, 25th August, 1825. Her early life was passed in her native place until her marriage to Leland Stanford, a young man of great industry, courage and ambition, but without competency, so far as mere material prosperity is concerned. During the earlier years of struggle and varying fortune she proved herself a true, devoted and faithful wife. Mrs. Standford's social life began in 1861, when Mr. Stanford was elected Governor of California. In 1874 Governor Stanford built a magnificent home in San Francisco, but during his closing years he and Mrs. Stanford preferred "Palo Alto," their country seat, situated some thirty miles from San Francisco. There they raised to the memory of their only child that seat of learning which bears the name "The Leland Stanford Junior University." In October, 1891, its doors were opened to over four-hundred students. In this memorial centered the interest of both Senator and Mrs. Stanford. In all the details incident to the completion of the university Mrs. Stanford had a hand. Not a building was erected without the plans being submitted first to her, and their interior arrangement, decoration and furnishing have been executed under her immediate supervision. She had erected, at her own individual expense, a museum which will contain works of art and a collection of curios gathered by her son during his tours in foreign lands. Senator Stanford gave his wife his closest confidence in all business matters, whether political or financial; she has consequently a wide range of experience in worldly affairs. Besides the gigantic endowment to the university she has given bountifully to many charitable institutions. In Albany the Children's Hospital was built from a gift of one-hundred-thousand dollars from her and is supported by an endowment of one-hundred-thousand dollars more. The kindergarten schools in San Francisco have also received a gift of one-hundred-sixty-thousand dollars from her. These are her public works of charity, done in remembrance of her son, but her silent deeds of mercy are almost as great as those about which the world knows. Mrs. Stanford's executive ability and capacity for business have been manifested since the Senator's death, in 1893. She has endeavored to carry out his every plan for the furtherance of the university. During the tedious lawsuit of 1895 and 1896, which threatened to involve the means her husband had left for the maintenance of the university, she sacrificingly used her personal means to help over until the suit was gained.

STANTON, Mrs. Elizabeth Cady, reformer and philanthropist, born in Johnstown, NY, 12th November, 1815. She is the daughter of the late Judge Daniel Cady and Margaret Livingston Cady. She took the course in the academy in Johnstown, and then went to Mrs. Emma Willard's seminary, in Troy, NY, where she was graduated in 1832. She had, in her youth, in her father's law office, heard much talk of the injustice of the laws, and she early learned to rebel against the inequity of law, which seemed to her made only for men.

In childhood she even went so far as to hunt up unjust laws, with the aid of the students in her father's office, and was preparing to cut the obnoxious clauses out of the books, supposing that that would put an end to them. She soon learned that the abolition of inequitable laws could not be thus simply achieved. She learned Latin and Greek, and she was active in sport as well as study. She was disappointed in her ambition to enter Union College, where her brother was graduated just before his death. Her life in Mrs. Willard's seminary for two years was made dreary through her disappointment and sorrow over not being a boy. She was full of mischief in school, and many of her pranks are told by the survivors of her class. While in Troy she heard a sermon preached by Rev. Charles G. Finney, ex-president of Oberlin College, which had an evil effect on her. She became nervous, convinced that she was doomed to eternal punishment, and finally grew so ill that she was forced to leave the seminary. After recovering from the prostration incident to that shock, she joined the Johnstown church, but was never contented or happy in its gloomy faith. She remained seven years in Johnstown, reading and riding, studying law, painting and drawing. Her studies in law have since served her well in her struggles for reform. In 1839 she met Henry Brewster Stanton, the anti-slavery orator, journalist and author, and in 1840 they were married. They went on a trip to London, England. Mrs. Stanton had been appointed a delegate to the World's Anti-Slavery Convention in that city. There she met Lucretia Mott, with whom she signed the first call for a woman's rights convention. On that occasion Lucretia Mott, Sarah Pugh, Emily Winslow, Abby Kimber, Mary Grew and Anne Greene Phillips, after spending their lives in anti-slavery work and traveling three-thousand miles to attend the convention, found themselves excluded from the meeting, because they were women. Returning to the United States, Mr. and Mrs. Stanton settled in Boston, MA, where Mr. Stanton practiced law. The Boston climate proved too harsh for him and they removed to Seneca Falls, NY. In that town, on 19th and 20th July, 1848, in the Wesleyan Chapel, the first assemblage known in history as a "woman's rights convention" was held. Mrs. Stanton was the chief agent in calling that convention. She received and cared for the visitors, she wrote the resolutions and declaration of aims, and she had the satisfaction of knowing that the convention, ridiculed throughout the Union, was the starting point of the woman's rights movement, which is now no longer a subject of ridicule. Judge Cady, hearing that his daughter was the author of the audacious resolution, "That it is the duty of the women of this country to secure to themselves their sacred right to the elective franchise," imagined that she had gone crazy, and he journeyed from Johnstown to Seneca Falls to learn whether or not her brilliant mind had lost its balance. He tried to reason her out of her position, but she remained unshaken in her faith that her position was right. Since that convention she has been one of the leaders of the women of the United States. In 1853, in Cleveland, OH, in the woman's rights convention, Lucretia Mott, who had tried to persuade Mrs. Stanton not to force the franchise clause in the Seneca Falls convention, proposed its adoption, as a fitting honor to Mrs. Stanton. In 1854 Mrs. Stanton addressed the New York legislature on the rights of married women, and, in 1860, in advocacy of divorce for drunkenness. In 1867 she spoke before the legislature and the constitutional convention of New York, maintaining that, during the revision of its constitution, the State was resolved into its original elements, and that citizens of both sexes, therefore, had a right to vote for members of the convention. In Kansas, in 1867, and Michigan, in 1874, when those States were submitting the woman-suffrage question to the people, she canvassed the States and did heroic work in the cause. From 1855 to 1865 she served as president of the national committee of the suffrage party. In 1863 she was president of the Woman's Loyal League. Until 1890 she was president of the National Woman Suffrage Association. In 1868 she was a candidate for Congress in the Eighth Congressional District of New York, and in her address to the electors of the district she announced her creed to be "Free speech, free press, free men and free trade." In 1868 "The Revolution" was started in New York City, and Mrs. Stanton became the editor, assisted by Parker Pillsbury. The publisher was Susan B. Anthony. She is joint author of "The History of Woman Suffrage," of which the first and second volumes were published in 1880 in New York City, and the third volume in 1886 in Rochester, NY. Her family consists of five sons and two daughters, all of whom are living and some are gifted and famous. Her latest work has been the "Woman's

Bible," a unique revision of the Scriptures from the standpoint of woman's recognition.

STARKEY, Miss Jennie O., 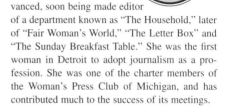 journalist, born in Detroit, MI, 29th July, 1863. She is the youngest daughter of the late Henry Starkey, of Detroit. Beginning work on the Detroit "Free Press," editing the puzzle column, she steadily advanced, soon being made editor of a department known as "The Household," later of "Fair Woman's World," "The Letter Box" and "The Sunday Breakfast Table." She was the first woman in Detroit to adopt journalism as a profession. She was one of the charter members of the Woman's Press Club of Michigan, and has contributed much to the success of its meetings.

STARKWEATHER, Miss Amelia Minerva, educator and author, was born in Starkville, town of Stark, Herkimer county, NY. Her first poem was published in the "Progressive Batavian," and many poems have followed in various periodicals. After some years spent in successful teaching in New York she removed to Pennsylvania and accepted a position in the primary department of the public schools of Titusville. A few years ago she published "Tom Tits and Other Bits," which has reached a second edition. Her hymns have been published in several Sunday-school and devotional books. She removed from Titusville several years ago to accept the superintendency of the Western New York Home for Friendless Children. Lately she has entered upon the work of a deaconess in the Methodist Episcopal Church.

STARR, Miss Eliza Ellen,  poet, author and art critic, born in Deerfield, MA, 29th August, 1824. While living in Philadelphia she published some of her earlier poems. In 1867 she published a volume of

Alice Thill.
From Photo Copyright, 1894, by B. J. Falk, New York.

Marie St. John.
From Photo Copyright, 1896, by Aime Dupont, New York.

Bessie Tyree.
From Photo by Schloss, New York.

Cora Tanner.
From Photo by Aime Dupont, New York.

Dorothy Sherrod.
From Photo by Morrison, Chicago.

Effie Shannon.
From Photo by Pach Bros., New York.

May Standish.
From Photo by Morrison, Chicago.

poetry, and soon after she brought out her two books, "Patron Saints." In 1875 she went to Europe, where she remained for some time, and on her return she published her art work, "Pilgrims and Shrines," which, with her "Patron Saints," has been widely read. In 1887 she published a collection of her poems, "Songs of a Lifetime," and in 1890, "A Long-Delayed Tribute to Isabella of Castile, as Co-Discoverer of America." That has been followed by "Christmastide," "Christian Art in Our Own Age," and "What We See." Gifted in art and poetry, her Chicago home is a center of art and education.

STEARNS, Mrs. Betsey Ann, inventor, born in Cornish, NH, 29th June, 1830. Her maiden name was Goward, and when fourteen she became a weaver in a mill in Nashua. Saving her money she attended the schools in Meriden, NH, and Springfield, VT. She taught for several years, then learned tailoring. She became the wife of Horatio H. Stearns, of Acton, MA, 5th June, 1851. In 1869 her dress-cutting invention received from the Massachusetts Mechanical Association a silver medal and diploma. It next received the highest award in the Centennial Exposition in Philadelphia, in 1876. The next year the American Institute, New York, awarded it a special medal for excellence, and in 1878 the Massachusetts Mechanical Association awarded its second medal for an improvement made. She then organized the Boston Dresscutting School and several other branch schools in other States, so that now the Stearn's tailor method for cutting ladies' and children's garments has become a household word.

STEARNS, Mrs. Nellie George, artist, born in Warner, NH, 10th July, 1855. She is the daughter of Gilman C. and Nancy B. George, and wife of George Frederick Stearns. She inherited from her mother a decided inclination toward art, even in her childhood. From her father she inherits poetic talents. Sketching was her constant amusement. Her parents early engaged art tutors for her in her own home. She was graduated with high honors in one of the best institutions of learning. After leaving school she taught for several years. She took a thorough course in the Boston Museum of Fine Arts, and later studied portrait painting with Monsieur Ernilie Lonigo. She has wide knowledge of technique. Her painting of "The Great Red Pipe Stone Quarry," a scene immortalized in Longfellow's "Hiawatha," was exhibited in the New Orleans World's Exposition in 1884. She most delights in painting the human face and form. Her home and studio are in Boston, and her time is spent in teaching art in its various branches. Her summers are devoted to classes throughout the New England States. During the season of 1891 she had charge of the art department in the East Epping, Chautauqua Assembly, NH.

STEARNS, Mrs. Sarah Burger, woman suffragist and reformer, born in New York City, 30th November, 1836. She went with her parents to Ann Arbor, MI, in 1845. Being a thoughtful child, she early felt the injustice of excluding girls from the State University. Of this she took note in a school paper, which she edited for a year, at the age of fourteen. At fifteen she served as president of an industrious literary society of girls. At sixteen she had the good fortune to attend a national woman's rights convention, held in Cleveland, OH. Inspired by the eloquence of Lucretia Mott, Lucy Stone and others to do her part toward securing a higher education for women, she left the Cleveland high school three years later, and returned to Ann Arbor to prepare, with others, for the classical course of the State University. Miss Burger succeeded in finding a dozen young women who could and would make with her the first formal application to the regents for admission. The only reply given them was that "It seems inexpedient, at present, for the University to admit ladies." The discussion thus aroused in 1858 never ceased until young women were admitted in 1869. In the meantime she had accepted, for a year, a position as preceptress and teacher of Greek and Latin in an academy for girls and boys, and made a second application. Receiving the same answer as before, she entered and soon was graduated in the State Normal School. After spending six months in her native city, she returned to Michigan and became the wife of Lieutenant Ozora P. Stearns, a young man who had won her heart, five years before, by advocating justice for women. As he was in the army, she after marriage, served one year as preceptress in a seminary for young women in Monroe, MI. Her husband, having obtained a position on staff duty in St. Paul, MN, wished her to be with him until he was sent south, after which she returned to her home in Detroit, MI, but not long to be idle. She sought to arouse the indifferent and employ the inactive by lectures upon the Soldiers' Aid Societies and the Sanitary Commission. While in Boston, MA, the Parker Fraternity invited her to give a lecture upon the "Wrongs of Women and Their Redress." That she repeated in some of the suburban towns. While waiting for her husband to be relieved from service, after the close of the war, she taught the Freedmen where Colonel Stearns was stationed. She was always busy. Even after going to housekeeping in Rochester, MN, she found time to lecture before the institutes upon primary teaching, moral instruction in the schools, and kindred subjects, and was fond of writing for the press upon educational topics. She helped to promote benevolent work, by her lectures upon "Woman and Home," "Woman and the Republic," and other subjects. Colonel and Mrs. Stearns moved to Duluth, MN, in the spring of 1872, since which time she has indulged less her fondness for study and literary work, and has become known as a woman of varied philanthropies. For three years she served as a member of the Duluth school board. She was for several years vice-president for Minnesota of the Association for the Advancement of Women. She served four years as president of a society for the maintenance of a temporary home for needy women and children. As a white-ribboner and a suffragist she was often a delegate to their State annual meetings. She was for many years vice-president for Minnesota of the National Woman Suffrage Association, and she helped to organize the state society and some local ones. She was for two years president of the State society, and is now president of the Duluth Suffrage Circle.

STEBBINS, Mrs. Catharine A. F., reformer, born in Farmington, near Canandaigua, NY, 17th

August, 1823. Her father, Benjamin Fish, and her mother, Sarah D. Bills, were of the Society of Friends, the former of Rhode Island and the latter of New Jersey. Both families removed to western New York about 1816. They were farmers. When Catharine was five years old, her family went to Rochester, NY. Her parents helped to form the earliest anti-slavery societies. Their moral and intellectual life was devoted to emancipation, total abstinence and moral reforms. Catharine was educated for the most part in the select schools of Rochester, but enjoyed the advantages of an excellent Friends' boarding-school in a near town for six months of her fifteenth year. She afterward taught her brothers and several neighbors' children in her home. She was requested to go before the board of examiners, that the people of the neighborhood might draw the school moneys to educate their children. Receiving a certificate, she took charge of the first public school in the ninth ward of Rochester. Her first reform work was in gathering names to anti-slavery petitions, between her twelfth and fifteenth years. For several years before and after marriage she was secretary of a woman's antislavery society. When she was fifteen years of age, Pollard and Wright, from Baltimore, total abstinence Washingtonians, held meetings and circulated the pledge in Rochester, and from that date her mother banished all wines from her house. A few years later Miss Fish and her sister kept on the parlor table an anti-tobacco pledge, to which they secured the names of young men. She became the wife of Giles B. Stebbins in August, 1846. She attended the first woman's rights convention in Seneca Falls, NY, in 1848. She spoke a few words in the convention and contributed a resolution in honor of Dr. Elizabeth Blackwell. The resolution was passed the next week in Rochester. She was one of the secretaries of the Rochester convention. While in Milwaukee, WI, in 1849 and 1850, she published her first letter, in the "Free Democrat," in protest against the subordinate position of women. The letter was much discussed. In the early part of the Rebellion she wrote for the Roch ester dailies a number of short letters on the conduct of war-meetings and of the war, criticising men and methods, and urging that more stress be put upon "Freedom" and less upon "Union." She visited the camps, when men were to be sent forward, and wrote letters to officers, suggesting what duties were likely to be overlooked. She occasionally organized both anti-slavery and woman-suffrage societies in southern New York and Michigan, and worked in aid societies in both States, and in 1862 and 1863 entered zealously into Gen. Fisk's work for clothing the refugees on the Mississippi and west of it. During winters spent in Washington, and since 1869 the years in Detroit, MI, one of her methods to further woman suffrage has been to write articles for the press and have slips struck off for distribution, and at other times to have able arguments of distinguished advocates put in that form for circulation in letters and meetings. She has always been an active member of the National Woman Suffrage Association from its beginning, and was most of the time on its executive board, proposing many measures, and taking part in hearings before judiciary committees of the House of Representatives and other bodies, and has repeatedly written letters to National nominating conventions in behalf of the equal representation of women in the State. She is also identified with the Association for the Advancement of Women, and signed the call for its first meeting.

STEELE, Mrs. Esther B., author, born in Lysander, NY, 4th August, 1835. She is the daughter of Rev. Gardner Baker, a distinguished minister of the Northern New York Methodist Episcopal Conference. From 1846 to 1852 Miss Baker studied in Mexico Academy and Falley Seminary, NY, where her talent as a writer attracted the attention of all her teachers, but no published literary efforts mark that period of her life. During those years her imagination and aspirations found expression in music. In 1857 she was installed as music teacher in Mexico Academy, whither the next year went J. Dorman Steele as professor of natural science. His keen intellect, stimulating conversation and strong character won her. In 1859 they were married. The first years of their married life were broken into by the Civil War, when, responding to the call of his country, Mr. Steele entered the service in command of a company he had raised. A wound received in the battle of Fair Oaks and long illness

of camp-fever incapacitated him for further military service, and he resumed his profession as educator, first in Newark, NY, and afterward in Elmira, NY. In 1857 there was among teachers an urgent call for brief scientific text-books, and Dr. Steele was invited to prepare a book on chemistry. From his study in Elmira then began to issue that series of school books which is known throughout the United States. How much their great success is due to Mrs. Steele it is impossible to estimate. In a personal reminiscence, written just before his death, Dr. Steele says: "My wife came at once into full accord with all my plans; she aided me by her service, cheered me by her hopefulness and merged her life in mine. Looking back upon the past, I hardly know where her work ended and mine began, so perfectly have they blended." Inspired by the success in the sciences, text-books on history, Mrs. Steele's favorite study, were next planned. During the years that followed four journeys were made to Europe, in order to collect the best and newest information on the subjects in hand. Libraries were ransacked in London, Paris and Berlin, distinguished educators interviewed, and methods tested. Fourteen months were spent in close study within the British Museum. Pervaded by the one idea of rendering a lasting service to education, husband and wife, aiding, encouraging and counseling each other, returned to their study in Elmira, laden with their rich spoils, to weave the threads so laboriously gathered into the web they had planned. Their conscientious literary work was successful. The books that issued from that workshop were original in plan and execution. They were called the Barnes Brief Histories, so named from the publishers, A. S. Barnes & Co., New York, as at that time Dr. Steele preferred that his name should be attached only to the sciences. The historical series includes "United States" (1871), "France" (1875), "Ancient Peoples" (1881), "Mediæval and Modern Peoples" (1883), "General History" (1883), "Greece" (1883), and "Rome" (1885). The last two books were prepared for the Chautauqua Course. In 1876 a large "Popular History of the United States" was issued. In the preparation of these histories Mrs. Steele had entire charge of the sections on civilization and of the biographical notes. In 1886 Professor Steele died. The entire management of the books then fell upon her, demanding her time, her heart, her brain. Since that time, many of the books have been revised under her supervision. In recognition of her intellectual attainments, the Syracuse University conferred upon her, in 1892, the honorary degree of Doctor of Literature. Mrs. Steele's generosity is continually drawn upon by her sympathy with every noble project. Among the public benevolences which have absorbed large sums of money may be mentioned the Steele Memorial Library of Elmira, and the physical cabinet connected with the J. Dorman Steele Chair of Theistic Science in Syracuse University.

STEELE, Mrs. Rowena Granice, journalist and author, born in Goshen, Orange county, NY, 20th June, 1824. She is the second daughter of Harry and Julie Granniss. At an early age she showed talent for composition, but, being of an extremely sensitive nature, her efforts were burned as soon as written. In 1856 she went to California. Through the force of circumstances she was compelled to offer her stories and sketches to the newspapers and magazines, and in less than two years the name of Rowena Granice had become a household word in every town in the new State of California. The newspapers were loud in their praise of the simple home stories of the new California writer. In 1862 she, with her husband, Robert J. Steele, started the "Pioneer" newspaper in Merced county, in the town of Snelling. They soon removed to Merced City, where the paper was enlarged. Mrs. Steele continued to act as associate editor until 1877, when the failing health of her husband compelled her to take entire charge, and for seven years she was editor and proprietor. In 1884, assisted by her son, she started a daily in connection with the weekly. In 1889 her husband died. After conducting successfully the newspaper business in the same county for twenty-eight years, she sold out. She has been married twice and has two sons, H. H. Granice and L. R. Steele, both journalists. She is still an active writer and worker in the temperance cause, and at present (1892) is editor and proprietor of the "Budget," in Lodi, CA.

STEIN, Miss Evaleen, poet, was born in Lafayette, IN, and has passed her whole life in that city. She received a liberal education and at an early age showed her poetic talents. Her father, the late John A. Stein, was a brilliant lawyer and a writer of meritorious verse and prose, and he directed her studies and reading so as to develop the talents which he discovered in her. Her training included art, and she has won a reputation as an artist of exceptional merit. She has done much decorative work for Chicago and New York societies, and recently she took an art-course in the Chicago Art Institute. She began to publish poems in local papers about six years ago, and her work at once attracted attention by its finish and mastery of form, as well as by its spirit and sentiment. She has contributed prose sketches to the local press, and has been a contributor to "St. Nicholas," the Boston "Transcript," the Indianapolis "Journal" and other periodicals. Poems from her pen have appeared in various collections, but she has never published a volume of her work. In her Lafayette home she is the center of a large circle of cultured persons.

STEINER, Miss Emma R., musical composer and orchestral conductor, was born in Baltimore, MD. Her father, Colonel Frederick Steiner, was well known in commercial and military circles. She was a precocious musician, but her family did not encourage her in the development of her talents. The only instruction she ever received in music was a three-month course under Professor Frank Mitler, while she was a student in the Southern Institute. She is a self-educated musician. She went to Chicago and entered the chorus of an operatic company, and there she attracted the attention of E. Rice, who engaged her as director in one of his companies in "Iolanthe." She conducted successfully in Boston, and later in Toronto, Canada, where she took the place of Harry Braham, who was taken ill. She succeeded in every attempt and was at once recognized as the possessor of all the qualities that make a successful orchestral conductor. Her ambition was next employed in the production of an opera of her own composition, and "Fleurette" was there sult. She then dramatized Tennyson's "Day Dream." She is engaged on several other operas, some of them of a higher grade. Four of her compositions were selected by Theodore Thomas, to be played in the Columbian Exposition in 1893. These are "I Envy the Rose," "Tecolotl," a Mexican love-song, a "Waltz Song" from "Fleurette," and an operatic "ensemble" for principals and choruses with full orchestral accompaniment. She is recognized as a composer of great merit, a conductor of much ability and a musician whose abilities are marked in every branch of the art. Her home is in New York City.

STEPHEN, Mrs. Elizabeth Willisson, author, born in Marengo county, near Mobile, AL, 21St March, 1856. Her maiden name was Willisson. Her paternal ancestry is English, and some of them were noted figures of the Revolutionary period. Her mother's family is of Huguenot descent, and the name of Marion is conspicuous on their family tree. Thomas Gaillard, her maternal grandfather, ranked high as an ecclesiastical historian. Her grandmother, Mrs. Willisson, was an intellectual woman, who fostered the little girl's love for books and cultivated her intellect. Elizabeth grew up in the world of books, writing stories and verses. Her mother, Mrs. M. Gaillard Spratley, is an author and joint worker with Mrs. Stephen in "The Confessions of Two." Her field of usefulness widened with her marriage, in 1888, to W. O. Stephen, an able Presbyterian clergyman. She takes an active interest in her husband's work and in all religious progress. Her home is in Rockport, IN. Her married life is a happy one, and one child, Walter Willisson, blesses their union. Beside the novel, "The Confessions of Two," she has written much, both in prose and verse, for various newspapers and periodicals.

STERLING, Mme. Antoinette, singer, was born in Sterlingville, Jefferson county, NY. She is the daughter of James Sterling, who is descended from old English stock. The first member of the family to come to the Colonies was William Bradford, who came in the Mayflower. At an early age she showed talent for singing, and in 1862 she went to New York City, where she studied with Abella. In 1864 she went to Europe and studied with Mme. Marchesi and Mme. Virdot-Garcia. Her voice is a contralto of exceptional strength, volume and purity of tone, and she has a range quite unusual with contraltos. In 1873 she made her début in Covent Garden, London, England, in a concert given under the direction of Sir Julius Benedict. In 1874 she sang before Queen Victoria in Osborne Palace. Her training has been on Italian methods, but she admires the German school of singing. She sang before the Emperor and Empress of Germany. In 1874 she became the wife of John Mackinlay. Her husband is a Scotch-American of musical tastes. Their family consists of three children. Her home is in London.

STEVENS, Mrs. Alzina Parsons, industrial reformer, born in Parsonsfield, ME, 27th May, 1849. She is one of the representative women in the order of the Knights of Labor, and her history is, in some of its phases, an epitome of woman's work in the labor movement in this country for the last twenty years. Her grandfather was Colonel Thomas Parsons, who commanded a Massachusetts regiment in the Continental Army during the Revolutionary War. Her father was Enoch Parsons, a soldier in the War of 1812, while her two brothers served in the late war in the Seventh New Hampshire Infantry. Mrs. Stevens has fought the battle of life most bravely. When but thirteen years of age, she began self-support as a weaver in a cotton factory. At eighteen years of age she had learned the printer's trade, at which she continued until she passed into other departments of newspaper work. She has been compositor, proof-reader, correspondent and editor, and in all of these positions has done well, but it is in the labor movement she has attracted public attention. In 1877 she organized the Working Woman's Union, No. 1 of Chicago, and was its first president. Removing from that city to Toledo, OH, she threw herself into the movement there and was soon one of the leading spirits of the Knights of Labor. She was again instrumental in organizing a woman's society, the Joan of Arc Assembly Knights of Labor, and was its first master workman and a delegate from that body to the district assembly. In the district she has been a zealous and energetic worker, a member of the executive board, organizer, judge, and for a number of years recording and financial secretary. In 1890 she was elected district master workman, becoming the chief officer of a district of twenty-two local assemblies of knights. She has represented the district in the general assemblies of the order in the conventions held in Atlanta, GA, Denver, CO, Indianapolis, IN, and Toledo, OH. She represented the labor organizations of northwestern Ohio in the National Industrial Conference in St. Louis, MO, in Feburary, 1892, and in the Omaha convention of the People's Party, July, 1892. She is an ardent advocate of equal suffrage, an untiring worker, a clear, incisive speaker and a capable organizer. She has been appointed upon the Women's Auxiliary Committee to the World's Fair Labor Congress. For several years she held a position on the editorial staff of the Toledo "Bee." She is now half owner and editor of the "Vanguard," a paper published in Chicago in the interests of economic and industrial reforms through political action.

STEVENS, Mrs. E. H., librarian, was born in Louisiana. Her maiden name was Hebert, and her family was of distinguished French Huguenot blood, She was educated by private tutors and in the seminaries in New Orleans. Her education is thorough and extensive, and she is master of both French and Spanish, to which fact she owes her success in her present arduous position as librarian of the agricultural department, Washington, DC, which she has held since 1877. She is the widow of a West Point officer who filled many prominent positions during his lifetime as a member of the Corps of Engineers. He traveled extensively and she always accompanied him, gaining wide knowledge of the world. He died abroad some years ago while building railroads. When he died, he left her in straitened circumstances, with two children dependent upon her for support. She applied for a government position in Washington. She says of her entrance in that field: "I came to Washington with only one letter of introduction in my pocket. That was to the Postmaster-General from the then district attorney of Baltimore, and a note from Mrs. Gen. Grant. The Postmaster-General turned my case over to the then Commissioner of Patents, Gen. Leggett, who gave me a place in the drafting office, but, upon its being made known that I was a fluent French and Spanish scholar, I was often called upon to translate, and finally they placed me at a separate desk and kept me at that during the whole Grant regime, giving me only translating to do. Indeed, I may be said to have inaugurated the desk of 'Scientific Translations' in the Patent Office. When Mr. Hayes came in, Mr. Schurz, Secretary of the Interior, put in a requisition for a 'new translator.' My salary had been $1,000, but the desk becoming a permanency, the salary was rated at $1,600, and Schurz, without ceremony, put in one of his political friends, transferring me to another place as correspondent, at $1,200. My friends were indignant, since I had done the work of organizing that desk, and, acting on their advice, I resigned, but was immediately reappointed in the agricultural department. I was the assistant of Mr. Russell, the librarian. His health soon failing, I was promoted, on his retirement, to the office of librarian." Mrs. Stevens in time past wielded a ready and facile pen. She is a member of the Woman's National Press Association of Washington, and is interested in whatever will help woman onward professionally. Her success in her conspicuous position is pronounced.

STEVENS, Mrs. Emily Pitt, educator and temperance worker, went to San Francisco, CA, in 1865, and her life has been devoted to educational and temperance work on the Pacific coast. In 1865 she started an evening school for working girls, by permission of the superintendent of the city schools. The night school was popular and successful. During the first year the number of students grew to one-hundred-fifty. Miss Pitt became the wife of A. R. Stevens in 1871, and her happiness in her domestic relations intensified her desire to aid the less fortunate. She organized the Woman's Coöperative Printing Association and edited the "Pioneer," a woman's paper produced entirely by women, on the basis of equal pay for equal work. She was aided by prominent men in placing the stock of the company, and through it she exercised great influence in advancing the cause of woman in California. Ill-health forced her to suspend the paper. She is a gifted orator, and she is known throughout California as an earnest temperance worker. She lead in the defeat of the infamous "Holland bill," which was drawn to fasten the degradation of licensed prostitution on California. She lectured for three years for the Good Templars and was for two years grand vice-templar, always maintaining a full treasury and increasing the membership. Since the organization of the Woman's Christian Temperance Union in California she has labored earnestly in that society. She has contributed to the columns of the "Bulletin," "Pharos" and "Pacific Ensign," and has served as State lecturer. She joined the prohibition party in 1882, and she led the movement, in 1888, to induce the Woman's Christian Temperance Union to endorse that party. She is a member of the Presbyterian Church, and is active in the benevolent work done in the Silver Star House, in sewing-schools and in various societies. In 1874 she instituted the Seamen's League in San Francisco, with her husband as president and herself an officer. In 1875 the old seamen's hospital was donated by Congress to carry on the work, and the institution is now firmly established. She attended the Atlanta convention of the Woman's Christian Temperance Union, as a delegate, and is now one of the national organizers.

STEVENS, Mrs. Lillian M. N., temperance lecturer and philanthropist, born in Dover, ME, 1st March, 1844. Her father, Nathaniel Ames, was born in Cornville, ME, and was a teacher of considerable reputation. Her mother, Nancy Fowler Parsons Ames, was of Scotch descent and a woman of strong character. Mrs. Stevens inherited her father's teaching ability and her mother's executive power. When a child, she loved the woods, quiet haunts, a free life and plenty of books. She was educated in Westbrook Seminary and Foxcroft Academy, and, after leaving school, was for several years engaged in teaching in the vicinity of Portland, ME. In 1857 she became the wife of M. Stevens, of Deering, ME, who is now a wholesale grain and salt merchant in Portland. They have one child, Gertrude Mary, the wife of William Leavitt, Jr., of Portland. Mrs. Stevens was among the first who heard the call from God to the women in the crusade days of 1873–74. She helped to organize the Maine Woman's Christian Temperance Union, in 1875, and was for the first three years its treasurer, and since 1878 has been its president. She has for ten years been one of the secretaries of the National Woman's Christian Temperance Union. She is corresponding secretary for Maine of the National Conference of Charities and Corrections, treasurer of the National Woman's Council of the United States and one of the commissioners of the World's Columbian Exposition. She is one of the founders of the Temporary Home for Women and Children, near Portland, one of the trustees of the Maine Industrial School for Girls, and a co-worker with Neal Dow for the prohibition of the liquor traffic. Her first attempt as a speaker was made in Old Orchard, ME, when the Woman's Christian Temperance Union for the State was organized. The movement fired her soul with zeal, and she threw her whole heart into reform work. She has become widely known as an earnest lecturer and temperance advocate. Her utterances are clear and forcible and have done much for the cause, not only in Maine, but also in many other States. As a philanthropist, she labors in a quiet way, doing a work known to comparatively few, yet none the less noble. She is known and loved by many hearts in the lower as well as in the higher walks of life. Her justice is always tempered with mercy, and no one who appeals to her for assistance is ever turned away empty-handed. Her pleasant home in Stroudwater, near Portland, has open doors for those in trouble.

STEWART, Mrs. Eliza Daniel, temperance reformer, known as "Mother Stewart," born in Piketon, OH, 25th April, 1816. Her grandfather, Col. Guthery, a Revolutionary hero, moved to what was, in 1798, the Northwest Territory, and settled on the banks of the Scioto, and on a part of his estate laid out the town where the future "Crusader" was born. Her mother was a gentle, refined little woman of superior mental ability. Her father, James Daniel, was a man of strong intellect and courtly manners. From her maternal ancestor she inherited her fearlessness and hatred of wrong, and a determination to vindicate what she believed to be right at any cost, and from her father, who was a southern gentleman in the sense used seventy-five years ago, she inherited her high sense of honor. These characteristics, toned and enriched by a religious temperament and a warm, genial nature, fitted her to be a leader in all movements whose purpose was the happiness and uplifting of humanity. Her child-life was shadowed at the age of three years by the loss of her mother. Before she had reached her twelfth year, her father died, and she was thrown upon her own resources, and prepared herself for teaching. At the age of fifteen she made a profession of religion, and at once became prominent as an active worker in the church. At eighteen she began to teach and was thus enabled to continue her studies, and she took her place among the leaders of her profession in the State. After years of efficient work in her chosen field of labor, she was married, but her husband died a few months afterward, and she resumed her work as a teacher. Some years later she again took upon herself the duties of wife and the care of home. In 1858 she became a charter member of a Good Templar Lodge organized in her town, and she has always been a warm advocate of the order. About that time she delivered her first public temperance address, before a Band of Hope in Pomeroy, OH, and continued thereafter to agitate the temperance question with voice and pen. When the booming of cannon upon Sumter was heard, she devoted her time to gathering and forwarding supplies to the field and hospital. At length she went south and visited the soldiers in the hospitals. From them she received the name "Mother" that she wears as a coronal, and by which she will be known in history. The war ended and the soldiers returned, many of them with the appetite for drink, and everywhere was the open saloon to entrap and lead them to destruction. Her heart was stirred as never before, because of the ruin wrought upon her "soldier boys" through the drink curse, and she tried to awaken the Christian people to the fact that they were fostering a foe even worse than the one the soldiers had con-

quered by force of arms. The subject of woman's enfranchisement early claimed her attention and received her full endorsement. Removing to Springfield, OH, her present home, she continued to agitate those subjects from the platform and with her ever vigorous pen. She organized and was made president of the first woman suffrage association formed in her city. On 22nd January, 1872, she delivered a lecture on temperance, in Springfield, which was her first step in the "Crusade" movement. Two days later a drunkard's wife prosecuted a saloon-keeper under the Adair Law, and Mother Stewart, going into the courtroom, was persuaded by the attorney to make the opening plea to the jury, and to the consternation of the liquor fraternity, for it was a test case, she won the suit. It created a sensation, and the press sent the news over the country. Thereafter she was known to the drunkards' wives, if not as an attorney, at least as a true friend and sympathizer in their sorrows, and they sought her aid and counsel. Her next case in court was on 16th October, 1873. A large number of prominent women accompanied her to the court-room. She made the opening charge to the jury, helped examine the witnesses, made the opening plea, and again won her case, amid great excitement and rejoicing. She had written an appeal to the women of Springfield and signed it "A Drunkard's Wife," which appeared in the daily papers during the prosecution of the case, and served to intensify the interest already awakened. She also, with a delegation of Christian women, carried a petition, signed by six-hundred women of the city, and presented it to the city council, appealing to them to pass, as they had the power to do, the McConneisville Ordinance, a local option law. Next, by the help of the Ladies' Benevolent Society and the cooperation of the ministers of the city, a series of weekly mass-meetings was inaugurated, which kept the interest at white heat. Neighboring cities and towns caught the enthusiasm, and calls began to reach Mother Stewart to "come and wake up the women." On 2nd December, 1873, she organized a Woman's League, as these organizations were at first called, in Osborne, OH. That was the first organization ever formed in what is known as Woman's Christian Temperance Union work. Soon after she went to a saloon in disguise on the Sabbath, bought a glass of wine, and had the proprietor prosecuted and fined for violating the Sunday ordinance. That was an important move, because of the attention it called to the open saloon on the Sabbath. Then the world was startled by the uprising of the women all over the State in a "crusade" against the saloons, and Mother Stewart was kept busy in addressing immense audiences and organizing and leading out bands, through her own and other States. She was made president of the first local union of Springfield, formed 7th January, 1874. The first county union ever formed was organized in Springfield, 3rd April, 1874, with Mother Stewart president. She then organized her congressional district, as the first in the work, and on 17th June, 1874, the first State union was organized in her city, her enthusiastic labors throughout the State contributing largely to that result, and because of her very efficient work, not only in her own, but other States, she was called the Leader of the Crusade. In the beginning of the work she declared for legal prohibition, and took her stand with the party which was working for that end. In 1876 she visited Great Britain by invitation of the Good Templars. There she spent five months of almost incessant work, lecturing and organizing associations and prayer unions, and great interest was awakened throughout the kingdom, her work resulting in the organization of the British Women's Temperance Association. In 1878 she was called to Virginia, and there introduced the Woman's Christian Temperance Union and the blue-ribbon work. Two years later she again visited the South and introduced the Woman's Christian Temperance Union work in several of the Southern States, organizing unions among both the white and the colored people. Age and overwork necessitated periods of rest, when she wrote "Memories of the Crusade," a valuable and interesting history, and in preparing for the press her "Crusader in Great Britain," an account of her work in that country. She was elected fraternal delegate from the National Woman's Christian Temperance Union to the World's Right Worthy Grand Lodge of Good Templars, which met in Edinburg, Scotland, in May, 1891. In 1895, by invitation of Lady Henry Somerset, she again visited England and the Continent, being the observed of all at the World's Woman's Christian Temperance Convention in London. Young in heart, she is passing her last years at Springfield.

STILLE, Miss Mary Ingram, temperance worker, born in West Chester, PA, 1st July, 1854,

and has always lived within a few squares of her present home. She is the oldest of the three daughters of Abram and Hannah Jefferis Stille. She represents on the father's side the fifth generation of the Philips family, who came to this country from Wales in 1755, and the members of which were noted for intellectual vigor. On her mother's side she is the seventh in descent from George and Jane Chandler, who came to America in 1687 from England. Her ancestors served with distinction in the Revolution, and her grandfather, Josiah Philips, was called out by President Washington to aid in the suppression of the Whisky Insurrection. Miss Stille's education was begun in Pine Hall Seminary, in the Borough, and was continued in Lewisburg Institute, now Bucknell University. From childhood she was associated with Sunday-school work, and for years was prominent in the primary department. She is a warm advocate of equal suffrage. She was the first woman appointed by the Pennsylvania Agricultural Society as superintendent of woman's work. In 1889 she had charge of the fine art display in their fair in Philadelphia. Without instructions from her predecessor, and under unfavorable circumstances, she worked the department up to such a condition as to win the commendation of the officers. Her systematic arrangements and business ability greatly contributed to the success of the exposition. By virtue of her ancestry Miss Stille is a member of the Washington Chapter of the Daughters of the American Revolution. The organization has been reconstructed recently, and she was made a charter member. In May, 1384, the first organization of the Woman's Christian Temperance Union was effected in West Chester, and, having ever had the cause of temperance at heart, she at once identified herself with the work and has always been a useful member. She has ably filled positions in the State and national divisions of the temperance work. In 1889 and 1890 she was actively engaged in the State headquarters, assisting in the great work of the State organization, and when the new State organ was published, she held the position of treasurer as long as that office existed. The early success of the venture was largely due to her efforts. She possesses a natural ability and special taste for journalism, but her home duties prevent her from devoting her time solely to that profession.

STIRLING, Miss Emma Maitland, philanthropist, born in Edinburgh, Scotland, 15th December, 1839, where her parents had gone to spend the winter. Their home was in St. Andrews, the scene of John Knox's labors and the place where so many of the Reformation martyrs suffered for their faith. Her father was John Stirling, the third son of Andrew Stirling, of Drumpellier in Lanarkshire, Scotland, a gentleman of an old family, the name of which is known in Scotch history. Her mother was Elizabeth Willing, daughter of Thomas Mayne Willing, of Philadelphia, PA, a granddaughter of the Thomas Willing who signed the American Declaration of Independence, and niece of Dorothy Willing, who previous to the war was married to Sir Walter Stirling, Bart., so that her father and mother were second-cousins. Emma was the youngest of twelve children. Although in her childhood the family usually spent the winters in England, St. Andrews was their home, and, when Emma was nine years old, they lived there steadily, in one of the pre-Reformation houses, situated directly opposite the ruins of the cathedral, in the midst of the quarter of the town inhabited by the fishing population. To this she attributes her early developed love and compassion for poor children, which was much aroused and sorely needed by those who lived on the other side of her garden walls. Truly the "fisher-folk" of those days on the east coast of Scotland were degraded, steeped in poverty, ignorance, dirt and whisky. At all events they drank, fought, swore and did everything that was shocking, and their poor children suffered accordingly. Miss Stirling says: "Ever since I can remember the suffering and cries of these children, 'my neighbors,' were a great distress to me. I don't remember trying to do much for them until I was twelve years old, except to speak kindly to the least rough of the tribe, and an occasional small gift of anything I had to the little ones. We were not rich ourselves. I was called by the Lord at twelve years of age, and, being brought by Him from darkness to light, felt that I must try to do something for those He loved so well as the children. From that time to help them in some way or other became the business of my life. It was, I can honestly say, my constant prayer to be shown what I could do; in short, it became a passion with me, part of my existence. This craving, for I can call it nothing else, to save and help poor suffering children has never ceased, never abated. It is the reason why I am living in Nova Scotia to-day. To show how it acted at that time of my life, when I was twelve years old I hated plain sewing, but the necessities of my small neighbors were so apparent and pressing that I practiced it for their sake, and ere long came to love it." Having thus grown up among those children, she was asked, when about seventeen years old, to become a lady visitor in the fisher's school, close by. She accepted willingly and enjoyed her work heartily. After some years a secretary was required for the school, and she was chosen and worked hard for several years more. There were six-hundred children in the various departments. She had clothing clubs for girls and boys, a penny-bank for all, and a work society for old women. Besides all this work, she had the care of keeping house for her mother, with whom she lived alone. In 1870 a great trial befell her. She slipped on the icy street, when on her rounds, and was so seriously hurt as to be an invalid for nearly six years, unable to walk. She became more anxious about saving children from accidents in consequence. About that time her mother died, and her old home was broken up. She went to live near Edinburg, and felt called on to open a day nursery in February, 1877, for the protection of the little ones whose mothers worked out. Soon the homes grew out of that, until in 1886 she had too many children to feed in Scotland, three-hundred every day. Being responsible for the debt of the institution, she found her own means melting away, and she had to find some country where food was cheaper and openings more plentiful for poor children than in Scotland, and she went to Nova Scotia, where she settled on Hillfoot Farm, Aylesford, Kings county. There she had a large house, and her heart has not grown smaller for poor children.

STOCKER, Miss Corinne, elocutionist and journalist, born in Orangeburg, SC, 21st August, 1871, but Atlanta, GA, claims her by adoption and education. Miss Stocker's great-great-grandfather fought under La Fayette to sustain the independence of the American colonies; her great-grandfather was prominent in the war of 1812, and her grandfather and father both lent their efforts to aid the Southern Confederacy. Her maternal descent is from the French Huguenot. At an early age Corinne showed a decided histrionic talent. In her ninth year she won the Peabody medal for elocution in the Atlanta schools, over competitors aged from eight to twenty-five years. In 1889 she was placed in the Cincinnati College of Music, where she made the most brilliant record in the history of the school, completing a four-year course in seven months. Prof. Pinkley, the master of elocution there, writes of her that among the thousands whom he has known and personally labored with he has found no one who gave surer promise of histrionic greatness. Her success as a parlor reader and as a teacher of elocution in the South has been pronounced. Her classes were large, and she numbered among her pupils some who were themselves ambitious teachers, and as old again in years. Her répertoire compasses a wide range of literature, from Marie Stuart and Rosalind to Stuart Phelps-Ward's "Madonna of the Tubs" and Whitcomb Riley's baby-dialect rhymes. After the first year of teaching Miss Stocker gave up her classes and accepted a position on the Atlanta "Journal," to do special work, in which line she has won great success. She continues her elocutionary studies and gives frequent parlor readings.

STOCKHAM, Mrs. Alice Bunker, physician and author, born in Ohio, 1833. Her maiden name was Bunker. Her parents were Quakers, and many of her relatives are ministers and philanthropists in that sect. When she was three years old her parents removed to Michigan, where they lived in a log cabin, among the Indians. She grew up out of doors and was a vigorous child. Advantages for education were limited, but she was educated in Olivet College, paying her way by manual labor and by teaching during vacations. Progressive theories in the art of healing interested and impressed Alice from her earliest years. Her parents had adopted the Thompsonian system, and in the new country treated their neighbors for miles around. The doctor early showed the instincts of a nurse and, when yet a child, was called upon for night and day nursing. When she was about fourteen, hydropathy became the watchword. Her parents espoused that new pathy, and the periodicals and books teaching it greatly interested the girl. With almost her first earnings she subscribed for "Fowler's Water Cure Journal." At the age of eighteen she met Emma R. Coe, a lawyer. Dissatisfied with school-teaching as a profession, she asked Mrs. Coe what she would advise for her lifework. "Why not study medicine? You have an education, and in the near future there certainly will be a demand for educated women physicians." Once being persuaded that this was lifework for her, she could not shake it off. Want of means and opposition of friends were slight obstacles. Her twentieth birthday found her in the Eclectic College of Cincinnati, the only college in the West at that time admitting women. Only three or four women are her seniors in the profession. For twenty-five years she engaged in an extensive general practice, but her sympathies were more enlisted in the welfare of women and children which led to the study of the vital needs of both, and out of this sprang the most beneficent work of her life, the writing of "Tokology," a book on maternity, which has been invaluable to thousands of women all over the civilized world. This book was published in Chicago in 1883, and has a constantly increasing circulation and has been translated into the Swedish, German and Russian tongues. The Russian translation was made by Count Leo Tolstoi. In 1881 Dr. Stockham visited Sweden, Finland, Russia and Germany, during which time she became much interested in the Swedish handicraft slojd which forms a part of the education of the Swedish and Finnish youth. She perceived its value and how worthily it might serve to the same purpose in the schools of her own country, and with the promptness and energy which so strongly mark her character, she set about at once upon her return home to introduce that method of teaching into the public schools of Chicago, which, after some opposition, she succeeded in doing. In November, 1891, she started on a trip around the world, visiting India, China, Japan and some of the islands of the Pacific, giving much attention to the schools, kindergartens and the condition of the women of those countries. There are few works of benevolence in Chicago in which she has not taken an active interest. Winning honor as a physician is but one of many in the life of this quiet, concentrated, purposeful woman. For many years she was an active member of the society for the rescue of unfortunate women, and of one to conduct an industrial school for girls. She has been publicly identified with the social purity and woman suffrage work for many years, giving both time and money for their help and advancement. Progressive thought along all lines has her ready sympathy, and her convictions are fearlessly acted upon. Her life is wrought of good deeds, her theories are known by their practical application, and her charity is full of manifestation. Her home is in Evanston, IL.

STODDARD, Mrs. Anna Elizabeth, journalist and anti-secret-society agitator, born in Greensboro, VT, 19th September, 1852. Her father was David Rollins, of English descent. Her mother was a Thompson, a direct descendant of the Scotch who settled in the vicinity of Plymouth, MA. The family removed to Sheffield, VT, when she was six years of age, and at eleven she was converted and joined the Free Baptist Church. Her parents then moved to Cambridge, MA, where she had an excellent opportunity to gratify her love of books and study. Foremost in Sabbath-school and other church work, she was recognized as a leader among her young associates. In 1880 she became the wife of John Tanner, Jr., of Boston, an earnest Christian reformer and strongly opposed to secret orders. He died in September, 1883, and she went south to engage in Christian work. In December, 1885, she became the wife of Rev. J. P. Stoddard, secretary and general agent of the National Christian Association, with headquarters in Chicago, IL. With her husband she has labored in several parts of the country along the lines of reforms. Always an advocate of temperance, she united at an early age with the Good Templars in Massachusetts, and occupied every chair given to women and became a member of the Grand Lodge. Finding that most of the time during the meetings was spent on trivial matters of a routine character, to the exclusion of practical, aggressive work against the liquor traffic, she came to the conclusion that it was a hindrance rather than a help to true gospel temperance work. She severed her connection with the order and gave her ener-

gies to the Woman's Christian Temperance Union, which had just come to the front. She has with pen and voice actively espoused that reform, organizing in different parts of the South Woman's Christian Temperance Unions and Bands of Hope. Having been located in Washington, DC, for a year or more, she was led to establish a mission-school for colored children, to whom she taught the English branches, with the addition of an industrial department and a young ladies' class. A Sabbath-school was organized in connection with that work, with a system of house-to-house visitations, and a home for the needy and neglected children of that class was established, largely through her efforts. Since January, 1890, her residence has been in Boston, MA. There her labors have been numerous, the most important of which is the publishing of a monthly paper for women, called "Home Light," designed to encourage those who are opposed to secretism and to enlighten others as to the evils of the same. The financial responsibilities have rested entirely on her from its inception. She espouses the cause of woman suffrage and takes an interest in all the reforms of the day, believing that to oppose one evil to the neglect of others is not wise nor Christian.

STODDARD, Mrs. Elizabeth Barstow, author, born in Mattapoisett, MA, 6th May, 1823. Her maiden name was Elizabeth Barstow. She received a thorough education in various boarding-schools and in her school-days showed her bent toward poetry and literature in general. In 1857 she became the wife of Richard Henry Stoddard, the author. Soon after her marriage she began to publish poems in all the leading magazines, and ever since she has been a frequent contributor. Her verses are of a high order. She has written for intellectual readers alone. She has never collected the numerous poems she has published in the periodicals, although there are enough of them to fill a large volume. In addition to her poetical productions, she has published three remarkable novels: "The Morgesons" (New York, 1862); "Two Men" (1865), and "Temple House" (1867). Those books did not find a large sale when first published, but a second edition, published in 1888, found a wider circle of readers. They are pictures of New England scenery and character, and they will hereafter become standard works. In 1874 she published "Lolly Dinks's Doings," a juvenile story.

STOKES, Miss Missouri H., temperance worker, born in Gordon county, GA, 24th July, 1838, in the old home of her maternal grandfather, Stevens, which had been occupied by the missionaries to the Cherokee Indians. Her paternal grandfather, Stokes, was a native of Ireland, who fought on the side of the Colonies in the Revolutionary War, and at its close settled in South Carolina. His family was a large one. The Stevenses were planters, and the Stokeses were professional men. Rev. William H. Stokes, a Baptist clergyman and an uncle of Miss Stokes, edited in 1834–1843 the first temperance paper ever published in the South. Her father was a lawyer and in those pioneer days was necessarily much away from home. He was killed in a railroad accident, while she was yet a child. She was tutored at home until she was thirteen years old, with the exception of several years spent in Marietta, GA. Her mother and her sister were her teachers. The family moved to Decatur, GA, where she attended the academy. She then became a pupil of Rev. John S. Wilson, principal of the Hannah More Female Seminary, from which institution she was graduated after a three-year course in the regular college studies. In 1853 she became a member of the Presbyterian Church. She had been religious from childhood, and was early a Bible-reader and Sabbath-school worker. She became interested in foreign missions, from reading the life of the first Mrs. Judson. She showed an early liking for teaching, and after graduating, in 1858, she taught for several years, including those of the Civil War. Her only brother, Thomas J. Stokes, was killed in the battle of Franklin, TN. Her mother died soon after the close of the war. Her widowed sister-in-law and little nephew were then added to the household, and she gladly devoted herself to home duties, abandoning all teaching for several years, excepting a music class and a few private pupils. In 1874 she took charge of the department of English literature and of mental and moral science in Dalton College, which she held till 1877. In 1880 and 1881 she taught a small private school in Atlanta, GA, and for the next four years she was in charge of the mission day school of the Marietta Street Methodist Church, working earnestly and successfully in that real missionary field. She was at the same time doing good service in the Woman's Christian Temperance Union, which she joined in Atlanta in 1880, a member of the first union organized in Georgia. She was made secretary in 1881, and in 1883 she was made corresponding secretary of the State union organized that year. She has held both those offices ever since. She worked enthusiastically in the good cause, writing much for temperance papers, and she was for years the special Georgia correspondent of the "Union Signal." She took an active part in the struggle for the passage of a local option law in Georgia, and in the attempts to secure from the State legislature scientific temperance instruction in the public schools, a State refuge for fallen women, and a law to close the bar-rooms throughout the State. She and her co-workers were everywhere met with the assertion that all these measures were unconstitutional. Miss Stokes was conspicuous in the temperance revolution in Atlanta. She has made several successful lecture tours in Georgia, and she never allowed a collection to be taken in one of her meetings. The last few years have been trying ones to her, as her health, always delicate, has been impaired. Since 1885 she has lived in Decatur with her half-sister, Miss Mary Gay.

STONE, Mrs. Lucinda H., educator and organizer women's clubs in Michigan, born in Hinesburg, VT, in 1814. Her maiden name was Lucinda Hinsdale. Her early years were passed in the quiet life of the sleepy little town, which was situated midway between Middlebury and Burlington, and the most stirring incidents of her youthful days were the arrivals of the postman on horseback, or the stage coaches, bringing news from the outside world. As a child she read eagerly every one of the local papers that came to her home, and the traditional "obituaries," the religious revivals called "great awakenings," the "warnings to Sabbath-breakers" and the "religious anecdotes" that abounded in the press of that country in those days were her especial delight. The reading of those articles left an impression upon her mind which time has never effaced. Her interest in educational and religious matters can be traced directly to the literature of her childhood days. Her early desire for knowledge was instinctive and strong. Study was life itself to her. Lucinda's father died, when she was three years old, leaving a family of twelve children, of whom she was the youngest. After passing through the district school, when twelve years old, she went to the Hinesburg Academy. She became interested in a young men's literary society, or lyceum as it was called, in Hinesburg, to which her two brothers belonged. That modest institution furnished her the model for the many women's libraries which she has founded in Michigan, and through which she has earned the significant and appropriate title of "Mother of the Women's Clubs of the State of Michigan." Lucinda spent one year in the female seminary in Middlebury. Acting upon the advice of a clergyman, she returned to the Hinesburg Academy, where she entered the classes of the young men who were preparing for college. She kept up with them in Greek, Latin and mathematics, until they were ready to enter college. That experience gave her a strong bias of opinion in favor of coëducation. From the Hinesburg Academy she went out a teacher, although she strongly wished to go to college and finish the course with the young men, in whose preparatory studies she had shared. She became a teacher in the Burlington Female Seminary, where the principal wished to secure a teacher who had been educated by a man. As she answered that requirement, she was selected. She taught also in the Middlebury Female Seminary, and finally a tempting offer drew her to Natchez, MS, where she remained three years. In 1840 she became the wife of Dr. J. A. B. Stone, who was also a teacher. In 1843 he went to Kalamazoo, MI, and took charge of a branch of the Kalamazoo University. He also filled the pulpit of a small Baptist Church in that town. Mrs. Stone could not resist her inclination to assist her husband in teaching, and she took an active part in the work of the branches, which were really preparatory schools for the university. The successor of the university is Kalamazoo College, of which Dr. Stone was president for twenty years. The college was a coeducational institution, and the female department was under Mrs. Stone's charge. Dr. Stone was always a warm advocate of the highest education for women and of coeducation in all American colleges. He believed also in equal suffrage and urged the abolition of slavery. The borne of Mrs. Stone was the resort of abolitionist and equal suf-

frage lecturers, and among the guests they entertained were some of the most advanced leaders of thought, Emerson, Alcott, Wendell Phillips, Fred Douglas, Mrs. Stanton, Mary Livermore, Lucy Stone and a host of others. In November, 1864, Mrs. Stone gave up her department in Kalamazoo College, after toiling a score of years. After leaving the college, she took up another line of educational work, that of organizing women's clubs, which are societies for the education of women. She spent some time in Boston, just after the formation of the New England Woman's Club. She returned to Michigan and transformed her old historical classes into a woman's club, the first in Michigan and the first in the West. The Kalamazoo Woman's Club, as it was named, was the beginning of the women's clubs in Michigan, and out of it have grown many of the leading clubs in the State. When the question of collegiate education for girls began to stir the public mind, Mrs. Stone was roused to the justice and importance of it, and exerted her energies and influence to forward the matter of admitting women to the University of Michigan. She fitted and sustained in her efforts the first young woman who asked admission to its halls. Now, when the annual attendance of women in Ann Arbor is recorded by hundreds, and many women graduates are filling high positions and becoming noted for their fine scholarship, Michigan University could do no more graceful and just thing than to call one of her own daughters to a professor's chair. To accomplish that Mrs. Stone is exerting her later and riper energies. The University of Michigan, in its commencement in 1891, conferred upon her the degree of Doctor of Philosophy, in recognition of her valued efforts in educational work.

STONE, Mrs. Lucy, reformer, born on a farm about three miles from West Brookfield, MA, 13th August, 1818. She was next to the youngest in a family of nine children. Her father, Francis Stone, was a prosperous farmer, a man of great energy, much respected by his neighbors, and not intentionally unkind or unjust, but full of that belief in the right of men to rule which was general in those days, and ruling his own family with a strong hand. Little Lucy grew up a fearless and hardy child, truthful, resolute, a good student in school, a hard worker in her home and on the farm, and filled with secret rebellion against the way in which she saw women treated all around her. Her great-grandfather had been killed in the French and Indian War, her grandfather had served in the War of the Revolution, and afterward was captain of four-hundred men in Shays's Rebellion. The family came honestly by good fighting blood. Reading the Bible when a very small girl, she came across the passage which says, "Thy desire shall be to thy husband, and he shall rule over thee." It had never occurred to her that the subjection of women could be divinely ordained, and she went to her mother, almost speechless with distress, and asked, "Is there no way to put an end to me?" She did not wish to live. Her mother tried to persuade her that it was woman's duty to submit, but of that Lucy could not be convinced. Later, she wished to learn Greek and Hebrew, to read the Bible in the original, and satisfy herself whether those texts were correctly translated. Her father helped his son through college, but, when his daughter wished to go, he said to his wife, "Is the child crazy?" She had to earn the means herself. She picked berries and chestnuts and sold them to buy books. For years she taught district schools, teaching and studying alternately. At the low wages then paid to women teachers, it took her till she was twenty-five years of age to earn the money to carry her to Oberlin, then the only college in the country that admitted women. Crossing Lake Erie from Buffalo to Cleveland, she could not afford a stateroom and slept on deck, on a pile of grain-sacks, among horses and freight, with a few other women who, like herself, could only pay for a "deck passage." In Oberlin she earned her way by teaching during vacations and in the preparatory department of the college, and by doing housework in the Ladies' Boarding Hall at three cents an hour. Most of the time she cooked her food in her own room, boarding herself at a cost of less than fifty cents a week. She had only one new dress during her college course, a cheap print, and she did not go home once during the four years. She was graduated in 1847 with honors, and was appointed to write a commencement essay. Finding that she would not be permitted to read it herself, but that one of the professors would have to read it for her, the young women in those days not being allowed to read their own essays, she declined to write it. She carried out her plan of studying Greek and Hebrew, and from that time forward believed and maintained that the Bible properly interpreted,

was on the side of equal rights for women. Her first woman's rights lecture was given from the pulpit of her brother's church in Gardner, MA, in 1847. Soon after, she was engaged to lecture for the Anti-Slavery Society. It was still a great novelty for a woman to speak in public, and curiosity attracted immense audiences. She always put a great deal of woman's rights into her anti-slavery lectures. Finally, when Power's Greek Slave was on exhibition in Boston, the sight of the statue moved her so strongly that, in her next lecture, she poured out her whole soul on the woman question. There was so much woman's rights and so little anti-slavery in her speech that night that Rev. Samuel May, the agent of the Anti-Slavery Society, who arranged her lectures, said to her, "Lucy, that was beautiful, but on the anti-slavery platform it will not do." She answered, "I know it; but I was a woman before I was an abolitionist, and I must speak for the women." She accordingly proposed to cease her work for the Anti-Slavery Society and speak wholly for women's rights. They were very unwilling to give her up, as she was one of their most popular speakers, and it was finally arranged that she should lecture for woman's rights on her own responsibility all the week, and should lecture for the Anti-Slavery Society on Saturday and Sunday nights, which were regarded as too sacred for a secular theme like the woman question. Her adventures during the next few years would fill a volume. She arranged her own meetings, put up her own handbills with a little package of tacks that she carried, and a stone picked up in the street, and took up her own collections. When she passed the night in Boston, she used to stay in a boarding-house on Hanover street, where she was lodged for six-and-a-quarter cents, sleeping three in a bed with the young daughters of the house. One minister in Malden, MA, being asked to give a notice of her meeting, did so as follows: "I am asked to give notice that a hen will attempt to crow like a cock in the Town Hall at five o'clock to-morrow night. Those who like such music will, of course, attend." At a meeting in Connecticut one cold night, a pane of glass was removed from the church window, and through a hose she was suddenly deluged from head to foot with cold water in the midst of her speech. She wrapped a shawl about her and went on with her lecture. At an open-air meeting in a grove on Cape Cod, where there were a number of speakers, the mob gathered with such threatening demonstrations that all the speakers slipped away one by one, till no one was left on the platform but herself and Stephen Foster. She said to him, "You had better go, Stephen; they are coming." He answered, "But who will take care of you?" At that moment the mob made a rush, and one of the ringleaders, a big man with a club, sprang up on the platform. She turned to him and said in her sweet voice, without a sign of fear, "This gentleman will take care of me." The man declared that he would. Tucking her under one arm and holding his club with the other, he marched her out through the crowd, who were roughly handling Mr. Foster and those of the other speakers whom they caught, and she finally so far won upon him that he mounted her upon a stump and stood by her with his club, while she addressed the mob upon the enormity of their conduct. They finally became so ashamed that, at her suggestion, they took up a collection of twenty dollars to pay Stephen Foster for his coat, which they had rent from top to bottom. Mobs that howled down every other speaker would often listen in silence to her. In one woman's rights meeting in New York the mob were so determined to let no one be heard that William Henry Channing proposed to Lucretia Mott, who was presiding, that they should adjourn the meeting. Mrs. Mott answered firmly, "When the hour set for adjournment comes, I will adjourn the meeting, not before." Speaker after speaker attempted to address the audience, only to have his or her voice drowned with uproar and cat-calls, but, when Lucy Stone rose to speak, the crowd listened in silence and good order. As soon as she ceased, and the next speaker arose, the uproar began again and continued till the end of the meeting. Afterward the crowd surged into the ante-room, where the speakers were putting on their wraps to go home, and Lucy Stone, who was brimming over with indignation, began to reproach some of the ringleaders for their behavior. They answered, "Oh, well, you need not complain of us; we kept still for you." In 1855 she became the wife of Henry B. Blackwell, a young merchant living in Cincinnati, an ardent abolitionist and an eloquent speaker. The marriage took place in her home in West Brookfield, MA. Rev. T. W. Higginson, then pastor of a church in Worcester, and who afterward went into the army and is now better known as Col. Hig-

ginson, performed the ceremony. She and her husband at the time of their marriage published a joint protest against the unequal features of the laws, which at that time gave the husband the entire control of his wife's property, person and earnings. She regarded the taking of the husband's name by the wife as a symbol of her subjection to him, and of the merging of her individuality in his; and, as Ellis Gray Loring, Samuel E. Sewall and other eminent lawyers told her that there was no law requiring a wife to take her husband's name, that it was merely a custom, she retained her own name, with her husband's full approval and support. Afterward, while they were living in New Jersey, she allowed her goods to be sold for taxes, and wrote a protest against taxation without representation, with her baby on her knee. In 1869, with William Lloyd Garrison, George William Curtis, Julia Ward Howe, Mrs. Livermore and others, she organized the American Woman Suffrage Association, and was chairman of its executive committee during the twenty years following, excepting during one year, when she was its president. She took part in the campaigns in behalf of the woman suffrage amendments submitted in Kansas in 1867, in Vermont in 1870, in Colorado in 1877, and in Nebraska in 1882. For over twenty years she was editor of the "Woman's Journal," and all her life gave her time, thought and means to the equal-rights movement. Lucy Stone died in Dorchester, MA, 18th October, 1893.

STONE, Miss Martha Elvira, postmaster, born in North Oxford, MA, 13th September, 1816, where she has always lived. She is the only daughter of the late Lieutenant Joseph Stone. Her early education was in the district school in her native village. She was graduated from the Oxford Classical School. Later she took a course of study in the academy in Leicester, MA. She was in August, 1835, bereft of her mother. To secure for herself an independence, she taught for several years near her home, in both public and private schools, until, on petitions of the citizens, she was appointed postmaster at North Oxford. The date of her commission was 27th April, 1857, under the administration of Hon. Horatio King, First Assistant Postmaster-General.

That office she has held thirty-six years. During all that time the office has been kept in her sitting-room. In February, 1862, her father died. In October, 1864, her brother died, leaving a family of young children, the oldest of whom, Byron Stone, MD, she educated. By vote of the town of Oxford she was elected a member of the examining school board in the spring of 1870, which office she held until 1873. Her time and talent outside of her public duties have been given to literary pursuits. She was for eight years a co-laborer with Senator George L. Davis, of North Andover, MA, in his compilation of the "Davis Genealogy." She was at the same time associated with Supreme Court Judge William L. Learned, of Albany, NY, in his compilation of the "Learned Genealogy." The Learned and Davis families were intimately connected by frequent intermarriages. From the former Miss Stone traces her descent. She is the great-granddaughter of Colonel Ebenezer Learned, one of the first permanent settlers of Oxford, in 1713. During the Civil War she entered into it with zeal and personal aid to the extent of her ability, in all that contributed to the comfort and welfare of the soldiers. Her room was the dépôt for army and hospital supplies.

STOTT, Mrs. Mary Perry, business woman, born in Wooster, Wayne county, OH, 18th August, 1842, of English parentage. In 1852 her father with his family commenced the perilous trip across the plains for Oregon, then a land of vague and magnificent promise. After much privation and danger from hostile Indians and cholera, they arrived in Oregon City, then the largest settlement, afterward locating in Yam Hill county, where Mrs. Stott has since lived. Her life at that time was full of the privation and dangers incident to frontier existence everywhere. The schools were poor, but, with limited opportunities, she succeeded in educating herself for a teacher. She taught until she became the wife of F. D. Stott, in 1866. Since that time she has been an earnest and enthusiastic worker for female suffrage, higher education and kindred reforms. For the last twelve years she has been railroad station-agent in North Yam Hill, a position that affords her pleasant mental occupation, and for which she is especially fitted by reason of her business capacity. In addition to that charge, she oversees the working of her farm. She has been a widow for some years and has four living children. Her life is a busy and well-regulated one.

STOWE, Mrs. Emily Howard Jennings, physician, born in Norwich, Ontario, Canada, 1st May, 1831. She was educated in her native place, and Toronto, Ontario, receiving a diploma of the grade A from the Toronto Normal School. She followed the profession of teacher prior and subsequent to her marriage. Her health becoming impaired, she determined that the infancy of her three children should not prevent the materialization of a long cherished desire to enter the field of medicine, at that time in Canada untrodden by women. That purpose received stimulus from the invalidism of her husband, whose feeble health demanded rest from business. She pursued her medical course in New York City, whither she was forced to go for the opportunity by that fear of intellectual competition with women which drives men to monopolize collegiate advantages. In 1866, obtaining the degree of Doctor of Medicine, she returned to Toronto to practice. A prevision of the difficulties which beset the path of a pioneer failed to daunt a courage born of the optimism of youth and a noble resolve forfreedom in the choice of life's rights and duties. The notable incidents in her professional life are focused in the fact of successful achievements, which may be summed up as, first, in the secured professional standing of women physicians in Ontario, and second, in her individual financial success over the many economic difficulties which beset a woman who, without money, seeks to cast up for herself and others a new highway through society's brushwood of ignorance and prejudice, by creating a favorable public sentiment through her own isolated and laborious efforts. A just tribute is cheerfully accorded by her to the sustaining and helpful encouragement she has received from husband and children. Two of her children have entered the professional arena. The oldest, Dr. Augusta Stowe Gullen, was the first woman to obtain the medical degree from an Ontario university. She is following in the professional footsteps of her mother and is now numbered among the faculty of the Toronto Woman's Medical College. Through the law of heredity to Dr. Stowe was bequeathed in more than ordinary degree the intuitive knowledge that natural individual rights have for their

STOWE, Mrs. Emily Howard Jennings

basis our common humanity, and all legislation to control the exercise of these individual rights is subversive of true social order, and therefore she was among the first women to seek equal opportunities for education by demanding admittance into the University of Toronto, which was refused to her. She has been in her native country a leader in the movement for the political enfranchisement of women, which is now in part accomplished.

STOWE, Mrs. Harriet Beecher, author, born in Litchfield, CT, 14th June, 1812. She was the sixth child and the third daughter of Rev. Lyman Beecher. When she was four years old, her mother died, and Harriet was sent to the home of her grandmother in Guilford, CT. She displayed remarkable precocity in childhood, learning easily, remembering well, and judging and weighing what she learned. She was fond of Scott's ballads and the "Arabian Nights," and her vivid imagination ran wild in those entertaining stories. After her father's second marriage she entered the academy in Litchfield, then in the charge of John Brace and Sarah Pierce. She was an earnest student in school, not fond of play, and known as rather quiet and absent-minded. She showed peculiar talent in her compositions, and at twelve years of age she wrote a remarkable essay on "Can the Immortality of the Soul be Proved by the Light of Nature?" That essay won the approbation of her father, although

she took the negative side of the question. After her school-days were finished, she became a teacher in the seminary founded in Hartford by her older sister, Catherine Beecher. When her father was called to the presidency of Lane Theological Seminary, in Cincinnati, OH, in 1832, Catherine and Harriet went with him and established another school. There, in 1836, Harriet became the wife of Prof. C. E. Stowe, one of the instructors in the seminary. Soon after arose the agitation of the slavery question, which culminated in the rebellion. The "underground railroad" was doing a large business, and many a trembling fugitive was passed along from one "station" to another. Prof. Stowe's house was one of those "stations," and Mrs. Stowe's pity and indignation were thoroughly awakened by the evils of slavery and the apathy of a public which made such conditions possible. The slavery question became at last a source of such bitter dissension among the students of the seminary that the trustees forbade its discussion, in hope of promoting more peaceful studies, but that course was quite as fatal. Students left by the score, and when Dr. Beecher returned from the East, where he had gone to raise funds for the conduct of the school, he found its class-rooms deserted. The family remained for a time, teaching all who would be taught, regardless of color, but shortly after the passage of the Fugitive Slave Law, in 1850, Prof. Stowe accepted an appointment in Bowdoin College, in Brunswick, ME, and there "Uncle Tom's Cabin" was written. The story is told that once, while Mrs. Stowe was walking in her garden in Hartford, a stranger approached and offered his hand, with a few words expressive of the pleasure it gave him to meet the woman who had written the book which had so strongly impressed him years before. "I did not write it," replied Mrs. Stowe, as she placed her hand in his. "You didn't!" exclaimed her caller. "'Who did, then?" "God did," was the quiet answer. "I merely wrote as He dictated." That celebrated book was first published as a serial in the "National Era," an anti-slavery paper of which Dr. Bailey, then of Washington, was editor. When it had nearly run its course, Mrs. Stowe set about to find a publisher to issue it in book form, and encountered the usual difficulties experienced by the unknown author treating an unpopular subject. At last she found a publisher, Mr. Jewett, of Boston, who was rewarded by the demand which arose at onces and with which the presses, though worked day and night, failed to keep pace. Mrs. Stowe sent the first copies issued to those most in sympathy with her purpose. Copies were sent to Prince Albert, the Earl of Shaftsbury, Macaulay, the historian, Dickens and Charles Kingsley, all of whom returned her letters full of the kindest sympathy, praise and appreciation. The following year she went to Europe, and enjoyed a flattering reception from all classes of people. A "penny-offering" was made her, which amounted to a thousand sovereigns, and the signatures of 562,448 women were appended to a memorial address to her. Returning to the United States, she began to produce the long series of books that have added to the fame she won by her "Uncle Tom's Cabin." In 1849 she had collected a number of articles, which she had contributed to periodicals, and published them under the title, "The Mayflower, or Short Sketches of the Descendants of the Pilgrims." A second edition was published in Boston in 1855. She had no conception of the coming popularity of "Uncle Tom's Cabin." Her preceding works had been fairly popular, but not until her serial was published in a book did her name go around the world. In the five years from 1852 to 1857, over 500,000 copies of "Uncle Tom's Cabin" were sold in the United States, and it has since been translated into Armenian, Bohemian, Danish, Dutch, Finnish, French, German, Hungarian, Illyrian, Polish, Portuguese, modern Greek, Russian, Servian, Spanish, Swedish, Wallachian, Welsh and other languages. All these versions are in the British Museum, in London, England, together with the very extensive collection of literature called out by the book. In 1853, in answer to the abuse showered on her she published" A Key to Uncle Tom's Cabin, Presenting the Original Facts and Documents Upon Which the Story is Founded, Together with Corroborative Statements Verifying the Truth of the Work." In the same year she published "A Peep Into Uncle Tom's Cabin for Children." The story has been dramatized and played in many countries, and the famous book is still in demand. After her trip to Europe, in 1853, with her husband and brother Charles, she published "Sunny Memories of Foreign Lands," a collection of letters in two volumes, which appeared in 1854. In 1856 she published "Dred, a Tale of the Dismal Swamp," which was republished in 1866 under the title "Nina Gordon," and has been recently published under the original title. In 1859 she published her famous book, "The Minister's Wooing," which

added to her reputation. In 1864 her husband resigned his Andover professorship, to which he had been called some years previous, and removed to Hartford, CT, where he died 22nd August, 1886. Mrs. Stowe has made her home in that city, and for some years passed her winters in Mandarin, FL, where they bought a plantation. She was treated rather coldly by the southern people, who could not forget the influence of "Uncle Tom's Cabin" in abolishing slavery. In 1869 she published "Old Town Folks," and in the same year she published "The True Story of Lady Byron's Life." A tempest of criticism followed, and in 1869 she published "Lady Byron Vindicated, a History of the Byron Controversy." Her other published books are: "Geography for My Children" (1855); "Our Charley, and What To Do with Him" (1858); "The Pearl of Orr's Island, a Story of the Coast of Maine" (1862); "Reply on Behalf of the Women of America to the Christian Address of Many Thousand Women of Great Britain" (1863); "The Ravages of a Carpet" (1864); "House and Home Papers, by Christopher Crowfield" (1864); "Religious Poems" (1865); "Stories About Our Dogs" (1865); "Little Foxes" (1865); "Queer Little People" (1867); "Daisy's First Winter, and Other Stories" (1867); "The Chimney Corner, by Christopher Crowfield (1868); "Men of Our Times" (1868); "The American Woman's Home," with her sister Catherine (1869); "Little Pussy Willow" (1870); "Pink and White Tyranny" (1871); "Sam Lawson's Fireside Stories" (1871); "My Wife and I" (1872); "Palmetto Leaves" (1873); "Betty's Bright Idea, and Other Tales" (1875); "We and Our Neighbors" (1875); "Footsteps of the Master" (1876); "Bible Heroines" (1878); "Poganuc People" (1878), and "A Dog's Mission" (1881). Nearly all of those books have been republished abroad, and many of them have been translated into foreign languages. In 1859 a London, England, publisher brought out selections from her earlier works under the title "Golden Fruit in Silver Baskets." In 1868 she served as associate editor, with Donald G. Mitchell, of "Hearth and Home," published in New York City. Four of her children are still living. During ner last few years she lived in retirement in Hartford with her daughters, being in delicate health, and her mental vigor impaired by age and sickness. She was a woman of slight figure, with gray eyes and white hair, originally black. In spite of the sale of about 2,000,000 copies of "Uncle Tom's Cabin," she did not average over four-hundred dollars a year in royalties from the sales. In her library she had fifty copies of that work, no two alike. Next to her brother, Henry Ward Beecher, she was the most remarkable member of her father's most remarkable family. Mrs. Stowe died in Hartford, CT, 1st July, 1896.

STOWELL, Mrs. Louise Reed, scientist and author, born in Grand Blanc, MI, 23rd December, 1850. She is a daughter of Rev. S. Reed, a Michigan clergyman. She was always an earnest student. At an early age she entered the University of Michigan, from which she was graduated in 1876 with the degree of D.S. Afterward she pursued postgraduate work for one year, and in 1877 received the degree of M.S. She was at once engaged as instructor in microscopical botany and placed in charge of a botanical laboratory, which position she held for twelve years. One of the leading features of that laboratory was the amount of original work accomplished in structural botany by both teacher and pupils. In 1878 she became the wife of Charles H. Stowell, M.D., professor of physiology and histology in the same university. Mrs. Stowell is a member of a large number of scientific associations, both at home and abroad. She is a member of the Royal Microscopical Society of London, England, ex-president of the Western Collegiate Alumnæ Association, and president of a similar organization in the East. She is now actively engaged in the university extension work. Her contributions to current scientific literature number over one-hundred. All of her writings are fully illustrated by original drawings made from her own microscopical preparations, of which she has nearly five-thousand. For seven years she edited the monthly journal called the "Microscope." She is the author of the work entitled "Microscopical Diagnosis" (Detroit, 1882). She has not confined herself to purely scientific literature, as she has written a large number of articles for popular magazines, illustrating each with charcoal, crayon or pen-and-ink sketches. While she has always felt and shown the deepest interest in the welfare and success of young women in pursuit of higher education, that interest has not prevented her from being engaged most actively in philanthropic work.

STRANAHAN, Mrs. Clara Harrison, author, was born in Westfield, MA. Her maiden name was Harrison. In her early childhood her father took his family to northern Ohio for a period of five years, from 1836 to 1841, and there his children had the benefit of the excellent schools of that country. Clara afterward received the advantages of the personal influence of both Mary Lyon and Emma Willard in her education, spending one year in Mount Holyoke Seminary, going thence to the Troy Female Seminary, where she completed the course of study instituted by Mrs. Willard. She had shown some power with her pen, and as early as her graduation from the Troy Seminary some of her productions were selected for publication. She has since published some fugitive articles, a poem or a monograph, as "The Influence of the Medici," in the "National Quarterly Review," December, 1863. Her crowning work is "A History of French Painting from its Earliest to its Latest practice" (New York, 1888). She became the wife of Hon. J. S. T. Stranahan, of Brooklyn, NY, in July, 1870. Mrs. Stranahan inherits the qualities, as she does the physiognomy, of the old New England stock from which she is descended. Energy in the pursuit of her aims, and elevation of aim, with a strong sense of justice and an earnest patriotism, are as marked in her as in the "builders" of New England. This is shown in her interest in and knowledge of the affairs of the Commonwealth. Whatever she may have done for the French in her history, or for the great army of the poor by her intelligent and practical benevolence of many years, or for education in her constant promotion of its interests, it is not among the least of her satisfactions that her husband is a sturdy supporter of all the patriotic movements of his city and country, as well as an efficient helper of all projects of progress. Passing from the State legislature to the United States Congress, he has served as member of both the conventions that nominated Lincoln for President, and as elector-at-large in the college that placed Benjamin Harrison in that office. in his municipal relations he has been honored by his compatriots under the title of "First Citizen of Brooklyn," with a bronze statue of heroic size, erected while he yet lived, 6th June, 1891.

STRAUB, Miss Maria, song-writer, born in De Kalb county, IN, 27th October 1838. She was the sixth of eight children. Her parents, who were of German origin, were Pennsylvanians. The family were greatly diversified in religious belief, representing the extremes as well as the more moderate views. The religious proclivity of Miss Straub is strongly indicated by the numerous hymns of hers sung in churches and Sabbath-schools throughout the land. Of a studious, quiet nature, a victim to bodily affliction, she early manifested fondness for reading and study. Unable, physically, to take a regular school course, and being ambitious to lose nothing, she planned her own curriculum and made up through home study, by the

assistance of her friends, what she failed to get otherwise. During those years she caught the spirit of verse-making. Especially was she aided in her endeavors in self-culture by a tender mother, who granted her all the opportunity possible to make the most of herself. After her father's death she was engaged for some time in teaching country schools in the vicinity of her home. She gradually became associated with her brother, S. W. Straub, the musician in music-book making. In 1873 she went to Chicago, IL, where she became a member of her brother's family. There she took a place on the editorial staff of her brother's musical monthly, the "Song Friend," a place she still holds, besides contributing occasionally in prose and poetry to other periodicals. She is interestedin current events and especially in reforms and philanthropies. Her love for the cause of temperance prompted the words of her and her brother's first published song, "Gird On, Gird On Your Sword of Trust," in 1868. Some of her happiest effusions were inspired by her love of country as shown in the titles of two of her highly popular pieces: "Blessed is the Nation whose God is the Lord," and "Wave, Columbia, Wave Thy Banner." These with many others of her secular poems have found musical expression in the various singing-books in use in homes and schools.

STRICKLAND, Mrs. Martha, lawyer, born in St. Johns, MI, 25th March, 1853. Her father was Hon. Randolph Strickland, well known in Michigan for his legal ability and broad and liberal mind. He represented the old Sixth Congressional District in Congress in 1869. Her mother was Mrs. Mary S. Strickland, one of the earliest friends of woman's advancement in that State. While her father was in Congress, Martha, then a bright, vivacious miss of sixteen, was his private secretary. When she was twenty, she began the study of law with her father, and after a few months she entered the law department of the Michigan University. Her eyesight failed soon after, and she was compelled to give up her studies. In the meantime she had become a forceful and eloquent platform orator, and for several years after she had quit the study of law she lectured on various phases of the movement to enlarge the field of activity for women. In 1875 she became the wife of Leo Miller. She has one son. She has always retained her maiden name, for she believes in the individuality of women. In 1882 she again entered the Michigan University, and in 1883 she was graduated from the law department. For three years thereafter she practiced in St. Johns, MI, the home of her parents, where she acted as assistant prosecuting attorney for the county, in which capacity she showed rare legal ability. Mrs. Strickland was the first woman to argue cases in the Supreme Court of Michigan, and it was due to her untiring efforts that there was won before that tribunal the greatest legal victory for women known up to that time. The case involved the right of women to hold the office of deputy county clerk. About ten days before the final hearing Mrs. Strickland was called into the case. She was satisfied that women were eligible to such offices, and she went to work to prove it to the highest court in the State. Some of the best lawyers doubted her position, but she prepared her brief, appeared before the court, made her argument and won. In 1886 she went to Detroit, MI, and entered a law office, and a few months later opened an office of her own. there she has formed a large circle of acquaintances. Her classes in parliamentary law and the active interest she took in every movement for the advancement of women brought her in contact with the more intellectual women of the city, and she occupies a leading place among the prominent women of Detroit.

STROHM, Miss Gertrude, author and composer, born in Greene county, OH, 14th July, 1843, and has always lived in a country home eight miles from Dayton. She is the oldest of four children. Her paternal grandparents were Henry Strohm, born in Hesse Darmstadt, and Mary Le Fevre, a descendant of the Huguenots. her mother, the late Margaret Guthrie, was the daughter of James Guthrie, who went from the East to Greene county in the early part of the century. Her mother was Elizabeth Ainsworth, whose first husband was Hugh Andrews. Miss Strohm's father, Isaac Strohm, has been engaged nearly all his life in Government service in Washington, DC, first in the Treasury, then for sixteen years the chief enrolling and engrossing clerk in Congress, and latterly in the War Department. He has written much for the press. When a young man, he was a contributor to Mr. Greeley's "New Yorker," and wrote poems and sketches for "Sartain's Magazine," the "Southern Literary Messenger," and other periodicals. Gertrude attended school principally in Washington, but her studies were interrupted by ill health. Her first publication was a social game she had made and arranged, entitled, "Popping the Question." It was published in Boston and afterward sold to a New York firm, who republished it, and it was again brought out in an attractive edition for the holiday trade of 1891. She made three games for a Springfield, MA, firm, the last called "Novel Fortune Telling," composed wholly of titles of novels. She has also published a book of choice selections, "Word Pictures" (Boston, 1875); "Universal Cookery Book" (1887); "Flower Idyls" (1871), and "The Young Scholar's Calendar" (1891). Another line of compilation in which she has engaged is from the Holy Scriptures. She has made many reward cards and Sabbath-school concert exercises.

SUNDERLAND, Mrs. Eliza Read, educator, born in Huntsville, IL, 19th April, 1839. Her father was Amasa Read, a native of Worcester county, MA, who removed to Illinois in 1838 as one of the earliest pioneer settlers in the central-western part of the State. Her mother, whose maiden name was Jane Henderson, was born in Ohio, of Scotch ancestry, and was a woman of remarkably vigorous mind and noble character. There were three children born into the home, who reached adult years, Eliza and two younger brothers. The father died when the children were very young, leaving the mother to face alone the hardships of pioneer life. Fully persuaded of the value of education, the mother made everything else yield to the attainment of that for her children. Until the age of ten Eliza attended the village school, a mile away. Then, for the purpose of obtaining greater educational advantages, the family removed first to St. Mary's and then to Abingdon, IL. The daughter's years from sixteen to twenty-four were spent partly in study in Abingdon Seminary and partly in teaching school. At the age of twenty-four she entered Mount Holyoke Seminary, in Massachusetts, at that time the most advanced school for young women in the country, and was graduated from that institution in 1865. Her highest ambition was realized when, on graduation day, she was invited to return as a teacher, but circumstances at home prevented. Later she became a teacher in the high school in Aurora, IL, where she was soon made principal, holding that important position for five years, until her marriage with Rev. J. T. Sunderland, a clergyman, in Milwaukee, WI, in 1871. From 1872 to 1875 her home was in Northfield, MA, for the next three years in Chicago, IL, and since 1878 it has been in Ann Arbor, MI. She is the mother of three children, a daughter of eighteen years, a son of seventeen, and a daughter of fifteen. Besides discharging with never-failing interest her duties as wife and mother, Mrs. Sunderland has always been very active in all that line of work which usually falls upon a minister's wife, and at the same time has carried steadily forward her literary studies, having taken nearly or quite every philosophical course offered in the University of Michigan, and many of the literary, historical and politico-economic courses. In 1889 she received from the university the degree of

Ph.B., and in 1892 the degree of Doctor of Philosophy. She has held many positions of honor in the Unitarian denomination, being one of the best known of its women speakers in its national and local gatherings. She has been for a number of years an active worker in the National Association for the Advancement of Women. Though not an ordained minister, she often preaches. She has more calls to preach and lecture than she can possibly fill. Few speakers are so perfectly at home before an audience, or have so great power to hold the attention of all classes of hearers. No woman in Ann Arbor, where her home has been for many years, is more esteemed by all than is she. She is especially honored and beloved by the young women students of the university, who find in her a constant and ever-helpful friend.

SWAFFORD, Mrs. Martina, poet, was born near Terre Haute, IN. She is widely known by her pen-name, "Belle Bremer." Her parents were Virginians, and each year she spends part of her time in the South, generally passing the winters in Huntsville, AL. She was reared in Terre Haute, and received a liberal education, which she supplemented by extensive reading and study. She is troubled by an optical weakness, which at times makes her unable to read or write, and her health is delicate. She was a precocious child and at an early age showed by her poetical productions that she was worthy to be ranked with the foremost of the rising authors of the Wabash Valley. Her first literary work was stories for the Philadelphia "Saturday Evening Post." She became a contributor to "Peterson's Magazine" and other periodicals, east, west and south, and her poems were extensively read and copied. The Atlanta "Constitution" introduced her to its extended southern constituency, and some of her best work appeared in that journal. Much of her work has been done during her winter residence in Huntsville. In poetry she belongs to the romantic rather than to the aesthetic school, though her verse is characterized by melody and a noticeable artistic treatment. Her muse is preeminently heroic and ideal, as her subjects generally indicate. She has published one volume of poems, entitled "Wych Elm" (Buffalo,

1891). Her husband, Dr. Swafford, is a prominent physician in Terre Haute. Her home is a social and literary center, and her time is devoted to good works and literature.

SWAIN, Mrs. Adeline Morrison, woman suffragist, born in Bath, NH, 25th May, 1820. Her father, Moses F. Morrison, was a graduate of the medical department of Dartmouth College and a distinguished practitioner. Her mother, Zilpha Smith Morrison, was a woman of ability and intelligence. Though burdened with the many cares arising from a family of three sons and five daughters, she managed to acquaint herself with the questions of the day. Both parents were freethinkers in the broadest and highest sense of that term, and both were in advance of the times. The home of the family was a continuous school, and what the children lacked in the preparation for the higher seminary and college course, they succeeded in gaining around their own hearthstone, assisted by parental instruction. At the age when most girls were learning mere nursery rhymes, Adeline Morrison spent a large portion of her time in pursuing the study of a Latin grammar. She received an education beyond the ordinary. She was accomplished in the fine arts, and her paintings have been recognized as works of superior merit. She taught several languages for many years in seminaries in Vermont, New York and Ohio. In 1846 she became the wife of James Swain, a prominent business man of Nunda, NY. In 1854 they removed to Buffalo, NY, where they resided several years. There her attention was called to the subject of spiritualism. She devoted much study to that subject, and finally accepted its claims as conclusive, and became an avowed advocate of its doctrines and philosophy. In 1858 they removed to the West and settled in Fort Dodge, IA. There she at once organized classes of young ladies in French, higher English, drawing and oil-painting. When the American Association for the Advancement of Science held its meeting in Dubuque, IA, Mr. and Mrs. Swain were elected members. In that assembly Mrs. Swain read an able paper, one of the first by a woman before the association. She was an active member of the

Iowa State Historical Society and a correspondent of the entomological commission appointed by the government to investigate and report upon the habits of the Colorado grasshoppers. She is a prominent and influential member of the National Woman's Congress and of the State and National Woman Suffrage Associations. In 1883 she was unanimously nominated by the Iowa State convention of the Greenback party for the office of superintendent of public instruction, being one of the first women so named on an Iowa State ticket, and received the full vote of the party. In 1884 she was appointed a delegate and attended the national convention of the same party, held in Indianapolis, IN, to nominate candidates for President and Vice-President. She was for several years political editor of "The Woman's Tribune." In 1877 her husband died suddenly. Her home is now in Odin, Marion county, IL.

SWARTHOUT, Mrs. M. French, educator, born in Sangerfield, Oneida county, NY, 15th September, 1844. She was educated in the Baptist Seminary in Waterville, NY, and afterward took the course in the State Normal School in Albany, NY. After finishing her school work, she removed with her parents to Lake county, IL. She soon after went to Chicago, where she has since

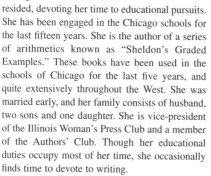

resided, devoting her time to educational pursuits. She has been engaged in the Chicago schools for the last fifteen years. She is the author of a series of arithmetics known as "Sheldon's Graded Examples." These books have been used in the schools of Chicago for the last five years, and quite extensively throughout the West. She was married early, and her family consists of husband, two sons and one daughter. She is vice-president of the Illinois Woman's Press Club and a member of the Authors' Club. Though her educational duties occupy most of her time, she occasionally finds time to devote to writing.

SWEET, Miss Ada Celeste, pension agent, born in Stockbridge, WI, 23d February, 1853. When the Civil War began, her father, Benjamin J. Sweet, a successful lawyer and State Senator, entered the Union army as Major of the Sixth Wisconsin Infantry. Afterward, as Colonel of the Twenty-first Infantry, he was wounded at Perryville. Left in broken health, he took command of Camp Douglas in Chicago, IL, as Colonel of the Eighth United States Veteran Reserve Corps. Ada spent her summers in Wisconsin and her winters in a convent school in Chicago. After the war, General Sweet settled on a farm twenty miles from Chicago and opened a law office in the city. Ada, the oldest of the four children, aided her father in his business. She was carefully educated and soon developed marked business talents. In 1868 General Sweet received from President Grant the appointment as pension agent in Chicago. Ada entered the office, learned the details of the business, and carried on the work for years. In 1872 General Sweet was made first deputy commissioner of internal revenue, and moved to Washington, DC. Ada accompanied him as his private secretary. He died on New Year's Day, 1874, and his estate was too small to provide for his family. President Grant then appointed Miss Sweet United States agent for paying pensions in Chicago, the first position as disbursing officer ever given to a woman by the government of the United States. The Chicago agency contained six-thousand names of northern Illinois pensioners on its roll, and the disbursements amounted to over one-million dollars yearly. She made the office independent of politics and appointed women as assistants. In 1877 President Hayes made all Illinois pensions payable in Chicago, and her office disbursed over six-million dollars yearly. She chose her own clerks and trained them for her work. She did so well that, in spite of pressure brought to secure the appointment of a man, she was reappointed in 1878 by President Hayes, and in 1882 by President Arthur. In 1885 the Democratic commissioner of pensions asked her to resign, but she appealed to President Cleveland, and he left her in the office until September, 1885, when she resigned, to take a business position in New York City. In 1886 she visited Europe. Returning to Chicago, she became the literary editor of the Chicago "Tribune." In 1888 she opened a United States claims office in Chicago, and she has done a large business in securing pensions for soldiers or their families. She is now living in Chicago with her brother, he and one sister, who lives in San Francisco, CA, being the only surviving members of her family. She is interested in all the work of women, a member of the Chicago Woman's Club, and president of the Municipal Order League of Chicago. In October, 1890, she gave the first police ambulance to the city, having raised money among her friends to build and equip it, and thus originated the present system in Chicago of caring for those who are injured or fall ill in public places.

SWENSON, Mrs. Amanda Carlson, soprano singer, was born in Nykiöping, near Stockholm, Sweden. When fourteen years old, her possession of a rare voice was discovered by her friends. Her mother was a widow in moderate circumstances, with seven children to support, and there was little hope of her receiving a musical education. The young girl built air-castles and dreamed of a fair future. When she was sixteen, Rev. Mr. Ahlberger, of her native town, determined that she should have a musical education. He secured the coöperation of some ladies and noblemen of the vicinity, and she was sent to the conservatory in Stockholm, where in three years she was graduated with honors, winning two silver medals. While there, she realized her childhood's dream of singing before the king and queen of Sweden. She remembers, with some pardonable pride, one occasion when she sang with the crown prince, now King Oscar, president of the conservatory. A few years after graduation, at the suggestion of her former teacher, Prof. Gunther, she accepted the position of first soprano in the Swedish Ladies' Quartette, then arranging for its tour. On the eve of departure a farewell concert and banquet, given in her honor, showed the esteem in which she was held by her native town. Giving their first concert with great success in Stockholm, the quartette started on their tour June 7th, 1875. Their route lay through Norway, Nortland and Finland, thence to St. Petersburg, where they remained three months, giving public and private concerts and meeting many European celebrities. They spent two months in Moscow, receiving cordial welcome

and entertainment. They visited Germany, Bohemia, Holland and Belgium, spending the summer on the Rhine. At Ems they met some Americans, who persuaded them to visit America. Soon after their arrival, Max Strakosch engaged them for a concert in New York. From that time their success in America was assured. They sang with Theodore Thomas in all the large eastern cities, and in several concerts with Ole Bull in the New England States. Afterward they made a tour of the United States, receiving welcomes in all the cities. Giving their last concert in San Francisco, CA, they returned to Chicago, IL, where they separated. Miss Carlson was persuaded to remain in the United States, and she spent the next two years in Reading, PA, where she held the position of first soprano in the Episcopal Church. Then she was married, and, her husband's health requiring change of climate, they removed to Kearney, NE, where, after five years, Mrs. Swenson was left a widow with two daughters. She is a genuine artist and has done much to raise the standard of musical culture in the city which has been her home for twelve years.

SWIFT, Mrs. Frances Laura, church and temperance worker, born Strongsville, OH, 6th February, 1837. She is descended from a long line of New England ancestors, the Damons, who settled in Massachusetts two-hundred years ago. Her mother removed to Ohio, after the death of her father. Miss Damon, was educated in the Springfield Female Seminary, and taught, subsequently, New-England-girl fashion, to round off her education. She became the wife of Dr. Eliot E. Swift, of Newcastle, PA, a young Presbyterian minister. He was called to the assistance of his father, pastor of the First Presbyterian Church of Allegheny, PA, whom he succeeded, and where he and his wife labored for twenty-six years. Dr. Swift died on 30th November, 1887. With her husband's encouragement, Mrs. Swift became an efficient worker in the Woman's Christian Temperance Union. With his sympathies and aid, she entered into the labors of the crusade. The calm strength of Dr. Swift's example won for the cause of temperance many friends, the cooperation of other ministers, and opened closed doors of opportunity and encouraged all workers. Mrs. Swift was the leader of the first crusade band in Pennsylvania. She was for eight consecutive years president of the State Woman's Christian Temperance Union of Pennsylvania. During all those years she was also president of the local union, where she first pledged herself. She is vice-president of the Woman's Board of Foreign Missions of her church, a member of the Board of State Charities, and actively identified with many benevolent institutions of the city. In 1887 she resigned the position of president of the State Woman's Christian Temperance Union, having had eleven-hundred unions under her care, and several thousands of officers and superintendents associated with her. She then went to Europe for eighteen months with her daughter and two other young ladies. Mrs. Swift has two sons, the younger a physician. As a presiding officer she is a woman of grace, gentleness and dignity.

SWITZER, Mrs. Lucy Robbins Messer, temperance worker, born in Lowell, MA, 28th March, 1844. Her maiden name was Lucy Ann Robbins. Both her parents are natives of Massachusetts and both of English and Scotch descent. The families of both Mr. and Mrs. Robbins were of the orthodox Congregational faith of New England. In 1855 the family moved to Wisconsin, and the next spring found them on a prairie farm in Minnesota, Greenwood Prairie, near Plainview. At thirteen years of age she took note of such remarks as "petticoat government of Great Britain" and "a woman's school," and, turning these matters over in her mind and believing that God gave women brains to use, she reasoned out the question of the entire equality of woman socially, politically and religiously, and has ever since held to those principles. She soon became a believer in and an advocate of total abstinence, after seeing something of the effects of the use of intoxicants by a young man who worked for her father on the farm, and on hearing the sneering and abusive language used in referring to him by a neighbor, who was a moderate drinker. In September, 1864, she became the wife of Frederick Messer, formerly of New Hampshire. His health had been injured by the exposure of army life, and after many changes of residence for his benefit he died in North Platte, NE, in 1880. Mrs. Messer united with the Methodist Episcopal Church with her husband in Plainview, MN, in 1869. In 1877 she took up the work of the Woman's Foreign Missionary Society and the Woman's Christian Temperance Union in Lynnville, IA. After the death of Mr. Messer she removed to Cheney, WA, stopping for a few weeks in Colfax, where she organized a union in October, 1880. She became the wife, 15th June, 1881, of W. D. Switzer, a druggist of Cheney. Immediately on the organization of the Cheney Methodist Church Mrs. Switzer was made its class-leader, and held the position three years. The work of the Woman's Christian Union was not forgotten. A union was formed in Cheney in 1881, and Bands of Hope were formed in Cheney and Spokane. In 1882 she was appointed vice-president of the Woman's Christian Temperance Union for Washington Territory, and before Miss Willard's visit in June and July, 1883, she had organized in Spokane Falls, Waitsburg, Dayton, Tumwater, Olympia, Port Townsend, Tacoma and Steilacoom. She arranged for eastern Washington a convention in Cheney, 20th to 23rd July, 1883. Many articles were written by her for the "Pacific Christian Advocate" and the "Christian Herald" on all phases of the Woman's Christian Temperance Union, thereby helping to institute the work over all the north Pacific coast. She has been president of the Eastern Washington State Union since 1884. The campaigns of 1885 and 1886 for scientific instruction and local option, and the constitutional campaigns for prohibition and woman suffrage are matters of record as representing arduous work and wise generalship, although in the constitutional campaign the right did not prevail. She has traveled thousands of miles in the work, having attended the national conventions in Detroit, Philadelphia, Minneapolis, Nashville, New York, Chicago and Boston, and also the Centennial Temperance Conference in Philadelphia in 1885, and the National Prohibition Convention in Indianapolis in 1888, as one of the two delegates from the Prohibition party of Washington. She served as juror on the petit jury in the district court in Cheney for twenty days in November, 1884, and February, 1885, and was made foreman and secretary of several cases. She was active during the years from 1883 to 1888, when women had the ballot in Washington, voting twice in Territorial elections and several times in municipal and special elections.

TAYLOR, Mrs. Esther W., physician, born in Sanbornton, NH, 16th April, 1826. Her parents were Ebenezer and Sally Colby. Eight children were born to those parents, of whom two survive, Dr. Esther and a sister, Dr. Sarah A. Colby, of Boston, MA. Dr. Taylor received her education in the public schools of her native place and in Sanbornton Academy. After devoting some time to teaching in the public schools, she paid a visit to her brother in Boston, and there made the acquaintance of N. F. Taylor, to whom she was married on 25th January, 1846. One child was born to them, a daughter, who is now Mrs. Charles F. Goodhue, of Boston. In 1855 Mr. Taylor and his family removed to Minnesota, where they spent a few years. After the Indian outbreak in the time of the Civil War, they went to Freeport, IL, where Mrs. Taylor decided to study medicine. She was aided by her husband and had the full sympathy and cooperation of her daughter in her efforts to obtain a thorough medical education. She attended the Hahnemann Medical College in Chicago, IL, from which she was graduated with honor on 22nd February, 1872. In 1875 she became a member of the Homeopathic State Medical Society of Illinois, and the same year a member of the American Institute of Homeopathy. In 1879 she received a diploma from the Homeopathic Medical College of Chicago. She located for practice in Freeport, remaining there till October, 1880, at which time she removed to Boston to join her sister. In 1881 she became a member of the Homeopathic State Medical Society of Massachusetts. Since her residence in Boston she has enjoyed the full confidence of a large circle of patrons.

TAYLOR, Mrs. Hannah E., poet, born in Fredricton, New Brunswick, 18th August, 1835. Her maiden name was Barker. She is of English descent and native American for five generations. Mrs. Taylor's father was born and bred in New Brunswick, where he was married to Miss Elizabeth Ann Sewell, He removed to Hartford, CT, and reared his family there. Hannah received her education in Fredricton and in Hartford. During her school life her compositions were spoken of highly. Music was her passion, and, possessing a fine voice, it was the wish of her parents that she should study music as a profession. She accepted a position as leading soprano in the First Baptist Church of Hartford, teaching music meanwhile. During all those years she was writing poems, but it is only of late years any of her compositions have been published. In 1874 she became the wife of George Taylor. Mr. and Mrs. Taylor reside in Pasadena, CA, where for several years Mr. Taylor has been general secretary of the Young Men's Christian Association. Mrs. Taylor has been an active member of the Woman's Christian Temperance Union for over ten years; she is corresponding secretary of the Pasadena branch of the Woman's National Indian Association, and is the recording secretary of the State Association.

TAYLOR, Mrs. Margaret, wife of Zachary Taylor, twelfth president of the United States, born in Calvert county, MD, about 1790, died near Pascagoula, LA, 18th August, 1852. She was a daughter of Walter Smith, a Maryland planter. She received her education at home, and early in life was married. She resided with her husband, before his election to the presidency, chiefly in garrisons on the frontier. She did good service in the Tampa Bay hospital during the Florida War. She was without social ambition, and considered Gen. Taylor's election as a "plot to deprive her of her husband's society and to shorten his life by unnecessary care." She surrendered to her youngest daughter the superintendence of the household, and took no part in social duties.

TAYLOR, Mrs. Martha Smith, author, born in Buxton, ME, in 1829. She is the daughter of David and Susan Warner Smith, formerly of Buxton, ME. Her father was educated in Derry, NH. Her mother was the daughter of Captain Nathaniel Warner. Her maternal great-grandfather was the son of Capt. James Gregg, one of the original settlers of the town, who emigrated from Ayrshire, Scotland, in 1720. He was a man of ability and means, and procured a grant for the land upon which the city of Manchester and other towns, including Derry, were built. Soon after her father had completed his studies, he married and removed to Buxton, ME, where he became a successful teacher. Martha is the sixth of eight children. She early manifested a fondness for books. When she was six years old, her mother died, and two years later her father died. She was adopted by her maternal grandfather in Derry, NH. At the age of seventeen she finished her education in the academy, in Derry, and soon after became the wife of George H. Taylor. He was active in business matters and filled many important official positions in his town and county. They have had three children, two daughters and one son. The son died in infancy. Mr. Taylor, with his family, removed to Pittsburgh, PA, in 1867, for the benefit of his health, which was impaired by asthma, from which disease he died in 1889. Mrs. Taylor and one daughter still reside in that city. Mrs. Taylor has written for many years for the leading newspapers of Pittsburgh and New England. She has been special correspondent for several years for the Pittsburgh "Dispatch" and "Commercial Gazette." She is a staunch advocate of temperance and all moral reforms. Her poems have been published in the different newspapers with which she has been associated. She has rendered important service in the temperance and charitable work of Pittsburgh, and has taken especial interest in its progress in literature. She was for several years president of the Pittsburgh Woman's Club, and is still an active member. She belongs to the Travelers' Club of Allegheny, PA.

TAYLOR, Mrs. Sarah Katherine Paine, evangelist and temperance worker, born in Danielsonville, CT, 19th November, 1847. Her father was Reuben Paine. Her mother's maiden name was Susan A. Parkhurst. Her father died when she was thirteen years of age, leaving a widow and three children. Sarah attended but two terms of school after the death of her father and then was obliged to leave home to do housework for two years, after which she entered a shoeshop. Not satisfied with that work, she studied evenings and fitted herself for a teacher. When eighteen years of age, she felt called to gospel work and began to hold children's meetings, to write for religious papers and to talk to assemblies in schoolhouses, kitchens, halls and churches. In 1868 she went to work in the office of the "Christian," in Boston, MA, where for the first time she met Austin W. Taylor, a young minister from Byron, ME, who afterward went south to teach the Freedmen. In January, 1869, Miss Paine went to Seabrook, NH, and gave herself wholly to gospel work, holding meetings evenings, and during each day visiting from house to house, reading the Bible and praying with the families. Many were converted. A church was organized and a church edifice was built. In April she went to Belmont, NH, and held a protracted meeting in the Christian Church. More than one-hundred-fifty professed conversion. That summer she held meetings in New Hampshire, Massachusetts and Rhode Island, seeing many converted. In August Mr. Taylor returned from the South, and on 3rd September, 1869, they were married. For several years they held meetings together in the New England States, often in summer using a large tent for a church. In 1875–76 Mrs. Taylor taught school in Atlantic City, NJ, preaching Sundays and having charge of a Sunday-school of about two-hundred members. From 1877 to 1887 her home was in Harrison, ME, from where she and her husband went out to labor. Mr. Taylor was pastor of a church in Kennebunk, ME, for two years, Mrs. Taylor assisting him by preaching half the time. She spent the years 1881–82 in Boston, editing the "Little Christian," a child's paper. While there, she became deeply interested in homeless children, and when she returned to Maine in the spring of 1883, she took six little ones with her, for whom she obtained good homes. That work was continued for many years, and more than forty children are indebted to her for homes in Christian families. Some of those little ones she kept with her for years, and one she adopted. That work was done almost entirely at her own expense. Although much of the time in delicate health and doing her own housework, she has always made it a rule to spend a short time each day in study, which included the sciences, Latin, Greek, Spanish, French and German. In 1889

Mr. Taylor accepted the pastorate of a church in Bridgeton, ME, and there they have since resided. Mrs. Taylor is engaged in preaching, lecturing, writing, holding children's meetings, organizing Sunday-schools and doing missionary work. As an example of a self-educated woman succeeding under adverse circumstances, Mrs. Taylor stands in the foremost rank.

TELFORD, Mrs. Mary Jewett, army nurse, church and temperance worker, born in Seneca, NY, March 18th, 1839. She was the fifth of ten children. Her father, Dr. Lester Jewett, was a physician and surgeon. Her mother, Hannah Southwick, was a Quaker of the Cassandra Southwick family. Her early life was spent on a farm. Her parents were uncompromising temperance people and shared fully in the abolition principles of the Quakers. Anti-slavery and temperance lecturers always found a refuge and a welcome at their fireside, and round that hearth there was much intelligent discussion of the live questions of the day. The "underground railroad" ran right through the farm, there being only one station between it and the Canadian line. Her earliest recollection is of a runaway slave; she stood clinging to her father's knees, watching the chattel as he examined a pistol, while the hired man was hitching up the team to convey him to the next station. "You would not shoot?" said her father. "I wouldn't be taken," was the reply. The conflicting passions on that slave's face indelibly impressed the mind of the child and doubtless had its influence in making her life work the relief of the oppressed and suffering. In 1846 the family moved to Lima, MI. Delicate health prevented regular attendance in school, but home instruction and the attrition and nutrition derived from an intelligent home life made her an acceptable district school teacher at the age of fourteen years. In 1859 she received the offer of a position as teacher of French and music in an academy in Morganfield, KY. The girl replied that she was an abolitionist. The offer was repeated and she accepted. When she returned home the next year she left many cherished friends and kept up a warm correspondence until it was hushed by the gun which was fired on Fort Sumter. On the organization of the Sanitary Commission in the early summer of 1861, Miss Jewett applied to Miss Dix for a position as army nurse.

She received only evasive answers and did not then know that the wise provision concerning age excluded her. She was at that time president of a girls' Soldier's Friends Society. A younger brother, who had enlisted, died in Nashville, TN, in December, 1862, in a hospital where there were one-thousand sick and wounded soldiers, and not one woman's care. She renewed her efforts to be accepted as a nurse in the western department. They were wisely shy of strangers, and she received the reply that they "had all the women they needed." She told no one of that letter, but throwing it into the grate made of it a "whole burnt offering to her righteous wrath." That day was Saturday. On Monday, with her parents' consent (this was the third child they had given for freedom), she started for Nashville, determined to find or make a way into the hospitals. On her arrival she called on Miss Chase at Hospital No. 8 as a visitor. Some one had given an organ to the hospital, but there was no one who could play. Discovering that her visitor was a musician, Miss Chase invited her to remain a few days and give the soldiers some music. She at once took up the work of the house, and soon the surgeon, Dr. Otterson, inquired for her papers. "How would you like," said he, "to have me send and get you a commission?" With a bounding heart, she handed him the letter from Governor Blair and other Michigan friends, and the coveted commission was hers. Soon Miss Chase's health compelled retirement, and for eight months Miss Jewett was the only active woman in a hospital with six-hundred patients. The following year she became the wife of Jacob Telford, a soldier, to whom she had long been betrothed. They removed to Grinnell, IA, in 1866, where they remained for seven years. Mrs. Telford took classes in French and music from Iowa College. They then removed to Denver, CO, and she began to contribute to papers in Boston, New York, Philadelphia and Chicago. She also wrote several juvenile stories. She edited the "Colorado Farmer" for two years. The establishment of Arbor Day in Colorado, during Governor Grant's administration, was largely her work. There being no temperance paper in the new West, in 1884 she established the "Challenge," which was immediately adopted by the Woman's Christian Temperance Union and the Prohibition party of Colorado. She was one of the organizers of the

Woman's Relief Corps in 1883, and was elected national corresponding secretary. From 1885 to 1887 she was president of the Department of Colorado and Wyoming, commanding the respect and love of all the veterans.

TERHUNE, Mrs. Mary Virginia, author, widely known by her pen-name, "Marion Harland," born in Amelia county, VA, 21st December, 1831. Her father was Samuel P. Hawes, a native of Massachusetts, who went to Virginia to engage in business. She received a good education, and in childhood displayed her literary powers in many ways. When she was fourteen years old, she began to contribute to a weekly paper in Richmond. In her sixteenth year she published in a magazine an essay entitled "Marrying Through Prudential Motives," which was widely read. It was quoted throughout the United States, republished in nearly every journal in England, translated into French and published widely in France, and finally retranslated into English for a London magazine. It at last appeared in the United States in its altered form. In 1856 she became the wife of Rev. Edward Payson Terhune, D.D., now pastor of the Puritan Congregational Church in Brooklyn, NY, where they have lived since 1884. Their family consists of one son and two daughters. Besides her church and charitable work, Mrs. Terhune has done a surprisingly large amount of literary work. She has contributed many tales, sketches and essays to magazines. She was for two years editor of the monthly "Babyhood," and conducted departments in "Wide Awake" and "St. Nicholas." In 1888 she established a magazine, "The Home-Maker," which she successfully edited. Her published books are: "Alone, a Tale of Southern Life and Manners" (1854); "The Hidden Path" (1856); "Moss Side" (1858); "Nemesis" (1860); "At Last" (1863); "Helen Gardner" (1864); "True As Steel" (1865); "Sunny Bank" (1867); "Husbands and Homes" (1868); "Phemie's Temptation" (1868); "The Empty Heart" (1869); "Ruby's Husband" (1870); "Jessamine" (1871); "Common Sense in the Household" (1872); "From My Youth Up" (1874); "Breakfast, Luncheon and Tea" (1874); "My Little Love" (1876); "The Dinner Year-Book" (1877); "Eve's Daughters, or Common Sense for Maid, Wife and Mother" (1880); "Loiterings in

Pleasant Paths" (1880); "Handicapped" (1882); "Judith" (1883); "A Gallant Fight" (1886), and "His Great Self" (1892). Besides these volumes she has published countless essays on topics connected with home management. To thousands of women throughout the civilized world she is known through her cookbooks and other household productions, and everywhere she is known to readers as one of the most polished and successful novelists of the century. She is a member of Sorosis and of several other literary and philanthropic organizations in New York City. She has done most of her book work on orders, and so many applications are made that she can accept only a small part of them. During the past few years she has been prominent in the Woman's Councils held under the auspices of a Western Chautauquan Association, lecturing on "The Kitchen as a Moral Agency," "Ourselves and Our Daughters," "Living by the Day," and "How to Grow Old Gracefully." She was the first woman to call attention to the ruinous condition of the unfinished monument over Mary Washington's grave, and the movement to complete that monument was started by her. In behalf of the movement she wrote "The Story of Mary Washington" (1892). She was selected to write "The Story of Virginia" in the series of stories of States brought out by a Boston house. Her children have inherited her literary talents. Mrs. Terhune has been a contributor to "Lippincott's Magazine," "Arena," "North American Review," "Harper's Bazar" and "Harper's Weekly," "Once a Week," "Youth's Companion" and other publications without number. Recently she has served editorially on the "Housekeeper's Weekly," of Philadelphia, PA. She works actively in church and Sunday-school. There are no idle moments in her life. She systematizes her work and is never hurried. The family home is in Brooklyn, and they have a summer home, "Sunnybank," in the New Jersey hills near Pompton. She is a thoroughly practical woman.

THAXTER, Mrs. Celia Laighton, poet, born in Portsmouth, NH, 29th June, 1835. When a child, her father, Thomas B. Laighton, removed his family to the Isles of Shoals, where he was keeping the lighthouse, which is described in her book, "Among the Isles of Shoals." All her summers were spent among those islands. In 1851 she became the wife of Levi Lincoln Thaxter, of Watertown, MA, who died in 1884. She never sought admittance to the field of literature, but the poet James Russell Lowell, editor of the "Atlantic Monthly," happened to see some verses which she had written for her own pleasure, and without saying anything to her about it, christened them "Landlocked" and published them in the "Atlantic." Persuaded by her friends, John G. Whittier, James T. Fields and others, she wrote and published her first volume of poems in 1871, and later the prose work, "Among the Isles of Shoals," which was printed first as a series of papers in the "Atlantic Monthly." Other books have followed, "Driftweed" (1878), "Poems for Children" (1884) and "Cruise of the Mystery, and Other Poems" (1886). Among her best poems are "Courage," "A Tryst," "The Spaniards' Graves at the Isles of Shoals," "The Watch of Boon Island," "The Sandpiper" and "The Song Sparrow." Her last and most popular collection of poems was "A Island Garden," published shortly before her death, which occurred 26th August, 1894.

THAYER, Mrs. Emma Homan, author and artist, born in New York, 13th February, 1842. She was educated in Rutgers. She was married to George A. Graves, a native of western New York, in her seventeenth year. Mrs. Graves was widowed after five years, and then turned her attention to art, entering the Academy of Design, afterward becoming one of the original members of the Art League. Many of her figure paintings have been exhibited in the National Academy of Fine Arts and in many of the large cities. One life-size piece, entitled "Only Five Cents!" won her two gold medals. In 1877 she became the wife of Elmer A. Thayer, of Worcester, MA. They lived in Chicago, IL, for the following six years, and she devoted her entire time to her art. In 1882 they moved to Salida, Colorado. Her first book, "Wild Flowers of Colorado," was published in 1883 (New York). Two years later "Wild Flowers of the Pacific Coast" was published, and proved even more beautiful than its predecessor. Her talent as a writer of fiction is shown in her novel, "An English-American," published in 1890.

THAYER, Miss Lizzie E. D., train-dispatcher, born in Ware, MA, 5th October, 1857. Her family removed to New London, CT, in 1871. She was educated thoroughly, and is a graduate of the young ladies' high school in New London. She has been a telegraph operator since 1878, and was employed in various New England offices. In 1889 she entered the service of the New London Northern Railroad, which extends a distance of one-hundred-twenty-one miles. Not a mile of the road is double-tracked. It does a large freight business and runs forty-eight regular trains besides many extra ones. Over all the immense business of the line she exercises supervision. She had been the train-dispatcher's assistant for nearly a year, when he resigned, and Miss Thayer was put in charge temporarily. The officials of the road looked in vain for a man to fill the bill, and finding that Miss Thayer's work had been satisfactory, she was made the official train-dispatcher. At first she held the place without assistance of any kind, and was on duty daily from 7 a.m. until 9 p.m. During the years of her service there has not been a single accident for which she was in any way to blame. She is the first and only woman in the world to hold the important position of train-dispatcher.

THOMAS, Miss Edith Matilda, poet, born in Chatham, OH, 12th August, 1854. While she was yet a student at Geneva, OH, several of her poems were published in Ohio newspapers, and they were widely quoted. Mrs. Helen Hunt Jackson introduced Miss Thomas to the editors of the "Atlantic Monthly" and the "Century," and she became a contributor to those and other magazines. In 1885 she published her first volume of verse, entitled a "New Year's Masque, and Other Poems." In 1886 she published in a volume a series of prose papers, entitled "The Round Year." In 1887 she published her second volume of verse, "Lyrics and Sonnets," and still later, "The

Sarah Truax.
From Photo by Baker, Columbus.

Lulu Tabor.
From Photo by B. J. Falk, New York.

Marie Shotwell.
From Photo by Aime Dupont, New York.

Marie Studholm.
From Photo by Morrison, Chicago.

Ellen Beach Yaw.
From Photo by B. J. Falk, New York.

Inverted Torch." In 1888 she went to New York, and her home is now in that city. She is one of the most popular of American poets.

THOMAS, Miss Fanny Edgar, author, was born in Chicago, IL. She became a bookkeeper in a publishing house, and worked hard and faithfully. As a diversion she wrote a small book during her leisure hours, which she published clandestinely by the aid of a printer. All the work was done outside of business hours. She signed the volume with the cabalistic pen-name "6-5-20," and the venture was successful, clearing her a comfortable sum of money. The small edition was soon exhausted. The book attracted the attention of Mrs. Ella Wheeler Wilcox, who invited the author to New York City and took her into her home. She soon became a contributor of taking sketches and essays, and the identity of "6-5-20" was established.

THOMAS, Mrs. Mary Ann, journalist, born near Lavergne, TN, 10th January, 1841. Her maiden name was Mary Ann Lane, and her father's family, the Lanes, were of English extraction. Her grandfather went from North Carolina to Tennessee in 1812 and settled in Davidson county. Her mother was descended from old Dutch and Irish stock, and was a native of New Jersey. Her father was nineteen and her mother sixteen years old when they were married in Nashville, TN, in August, 1839. Mary is the oldest of their family of seven children. During her youth the family lived in various places in Illinois, Kentucky and Tennessee. She was an intelligent child and was carefully educated. After leaving school, she became a teacher and taught until her marriage, 31st July, 1872, to Archie Thomas, part proprietor of' the Springfield, TN, "Record." In 1883 Mr. Thomas sold that journal and moved to Sumter, FL. They returned to Tennessee in 1884, and he repurchased the "Record," which he edited until his death, 10th October, 1888. After his death, Mrs. Thomas bought the "Record" and became both editor and publisher. She entered the journalistic field with diffidence, but she has made her journal very successful. She wrote for the press from youth, and was made an honorary member of the Tennessee Press Association in 1870. In 1873 she read a poem in the fall meeting of that body in Pulaski. She has written both poems and stories. Since her marriage she has done but little purely literary work, as her time was employed in the care of her daughter and several children of her husband by a former marriage. She has reared her family while working as proprietor, publisher, editor, clerk and proof-reader.

THOMPSON, Mrs. Adaline Emerson, educational worker and reformer, born in Rockford, IL, 13th August, 1859. Her father was Ralph Emerson, a son of Prof. Ralph Emerson, of Andover, MA, who was a cousin of Ralph Waldo Emerson. He was a man of singularly strong character. With discernment he read the signs of the times, and, before it was a usual thing for girls to go to college, when most men were still questioning their fitness for training, either mentally or physically, he decided that his daughters should have the most liberal education that could be obtained. Adaline entered Wellesley College in 1877 and was graduated with honor in 1880. The thesis which she presented on that occasion showed that she possessed literary ability. After graduating she returned to her home in Rockford, IL, and in 1883 became the wife of Norman Frederick Thompson. The first five years after her marriage were uneventful. Two children and the details of her home occupied her attention. Upon the removal of her household to New York, in 1888, her days of mental activity began. As president of the Woman's Club, of Orange, and also of the New York Associated Alumnæ, she has won recognition as a leader and presiding officer, but in the College Settlements' Association her organizing force has been most largely expended. Believing that the true way to reach and help the poor in the large cities is through the intimate personal contact which comes from living among them, and further, that the only way to solve the sociological problems pressing so heavily upon us is through knowledge gained at first-hand by thinking men and women, she has thrown her energy and enthusiasm into this home extension movement. As its president she has carried the association successfully through all the trials and difficulties which beset any new organization. She now lives in East Orange, NJ.

THOMPSON, Mrs. Eliza J., temperance reformer and original crusader, born in Hillsborough, OH, in 1813. She is the wife of Judge Thompson, of Hillsborough. She was early led into temperance work, both by her own inclinations and by the influence of her father, the late Governor Trimble, of Ohio. In her youth she accompanied her father to Saratoga Springs, NY, to attend a national temperance convention, and was the only woman in that meeting. On 23rd Decemher, 1873, in Hillsborough, she opened the temperance movement that in a few weeks culminated in the Woman's Temperance Crusade. She was, by common consent of all the churches in her town, chosen the leader of the first band of women who set out to visit the saloons. That movement was a success in many ways, and much of its success is to be credited to Mrs. Thompson. She is now living in Hillsborough. She has one son, a distinguished clergyman of the Methodist Episcopal Church.

THOMPSON, Mrs. Elizabeth Rowell, philanthropist and temperance reformer, born in Lyndon, VT, 21st February, 1821. Her maiden name was Rowell. Her childhood was full of the hardships of pioneer life, and she began, at the age of nine years, to earn money by serving as maid-of-all-work in a neighboring family, receiving a salary of twenty-five cents a week. Her early education was naturally neglected, but in later years she made up for the want of training that marked her childhood. She grew to womanhood, and in 1843 visited Boston, MA. There she met Thomas Thompson, a millionaire, a man of refinement and culture. He was captivated by her remarkable beauty. The attraction was mutual, and they were married. With great wealth at her command, she was able to carry out her wishes to do good. She engaged in charitable work on a large scale, and her methods include the removal of the causes of misery, quite as much as the relief of misery after it is caused. Her expenditures to aid worthy men and women in getting education amount to over one-hundred-thousand dollars, and her other benevolent enterprises represent an outlay of over six-hundred-thousand dollars. She has regularly expended her income in benevolence. She has aided actively in the temperance reform movement, and her aid has often taken the form of large sums of money when needed to carry on some particular work. One of her contributions to the literature of temperance is a statistical work entitled "The Figures of Hell." Her husband coöperated with her until his death on 28th March, 1869. He left her the entire income of his great estate. Being childless, she was free to give full play to her generous impulses. She purchased Carpenter's painting of the signing of the emancipation proclamation by Lincoln in the presence of his Cabinet, paying twenty-five thousand dollars for it, and presented it to Congress. She paid ten-thousand dollars for the expenses of the Congressional committee appointed to study the yellow-fever plague in the South. She gave liberally to support the Women's Free Medical College in New York City. She founded Longmont, in the Rocky Mountains. In Salina county, Kansas, she gave six-hundred-forty acres of land and three-hundred dollars to each colonist settled on it. She spent a large sum in bringing out a "Song Service" for the poor.

THOMPSON, Mrs. Eva Griffith, editor, born near Jennerville, Somerset county, IA, 30th June, 1842. Her father, Abner Griffith, a Quaker, died at the age of seventy-two. Her mother, Eliza Cooper Griffith, Scotch-Irish, an octogenarian, still survives. Miss Griffith was married at the beginning of the Civil War, and her husband joined the Union army. In six months she was a widow, at the age of twenty. School duties, never given up, were continued, and in 1868 she was graduated from the female seminary in Steubenville, OH. S. J. Craighead, county superintendent of common schools of Indiana county, PA, appointed her deputy superintendent. That is said to be the first time such an honor was conferred upon a woman. For years she has held the office of president of the Presbyterian Home Missionary Society. The Grand Army of the Republic men claim her as a comrade, and in many of their meetings she has been called upon to make addresses. At the inauguration of the Woman's Christian Temperance Union movement in Indiana county, she was appointed organizer, a position she still holds. As State superintendent of franchise in the Pennsylvania Woman's Christian Temperance Union she is doing an aggressive work. As editor and proprietor of the "News," Indiana, PA, she wields her pen in behalf of temperance and reform. The paper indorses the People's Party. Mrs. Thompson is active and earnest in her work.

THOMPSON, Miss Mary Sophia, Delsartean instructor and elocutionist, born in Princeton, IL, in 1859. Her father was a native of London, England. Her mother, a descendant of the Puritans, came from central Massachusetts. From her earliest childhood Mary possessed a wonderfully sweet voice and an equally wonderful aptitude in using it to the very best effect in childish exercises of recitation, dramatization and even weird improvisation. When she grew to womanhood, her talents attracted such attention that the usual inducements looking to a public use of her gifts were not wanting, but so long as the family circle, whose pride she was, continued intact, she preferred her life there. She varied the monotony of country-town existence by accepting an offer to teach in the high school in which she was graduated. Then her father died suddenly, and the daughter was left helpless by a bereavement so terrible as to plunge her into the profoundest dejection and to deprive her of all capacity for ordinary vocations. Feeling assured that then her only refuge lay in unceasing productive activity, she went to Chicago, IL, and, after some preliminary training under the mastership of Mrs. Abby Sage Richardson, went, by that lady's advice, to Boston, MA, where she was placed in the classes of the school of oratory of the Boston University, presided over by Louis B. Monroe. There she remained six or seven years as pupil, instructor, and eventually as chief instructor of that institution, where she had for professors and, in time, for colleagues, Alexander Graham Bell, Charles A. Guilmette, Robert Raymond and Prof. Hudson. At that time the doctrines and principles of Francois Delsarte were beginning to attract considerable notice, and Miss Thompson promptly threw herself into that art, in all its applications, with a zeal and an aptitude that insured success. Forming a partnership with Miss Genevieve Stebbins, who was at that time Mr. Mackaye's pupil, she went to New York, and they soon founded the first school of Delsarte in that city. From that time onward Miss Thompson's career has been successful. Hitherto the teachings of Delsarte had been regarded with suspicion, ridiculed by actors and doubted by the press, but in the famous Delsarte matinees, given by the women in the Madison Square Theater, the narrow provincialism which came to scoff found such genuine merit and sincere artistic enthusiasm and, above all, such exquisite performances, that its opposition was silenced, petty pique gave way to generous admiration, and now Delsarte is the fashion. Miss Thompson has taught in the schools of Mrs. Sylvanus Reed and of the Misses Graham. She is no specialist, in the narrower sense of the word, her achievements and performance ranging from the celebrated "bird notes," for which she has a national renown, to the delivery of a monologue, in which she is extremely successful. She has for some years contributed to various periodicals, mainly upon subjects to which she devotes her talents, and has recently published, in book form, "Rhythmical Gymnastics, Vocal and Physical."

THORP, Mrs. Mandana Coleman, patriot and public official, born in Karr Valley, Allegany county, NY, 25th January, 1843. She is the daughter of Colonel John Major. By her mother she is a descendant of Major Moses Van Campen, a Revolutionary patriot. She was brought up under the training of the most devoted mother and received a liberal education in Alfred University. The stirring events before and during the Civil War called out the sentiment of every patriotic person. The musical talents of Miss Major were actively enlisted from the echo of the first gun fired upon the national flag. The national airs and the stirring battle hymns were sung by her at nearly all of the meetings held in that part of the State. At the close of the first peninsula campaign, in the summer of 1862, President Lincoln requested the Governor of the State of New York to raise and equip two regiments at once for service in front of General Lee, whose forces were invading Pennsylvania. It was during the organization of those two regiments the patriotism of Allegany, Livingston and Wyoming counties was brought into activity. During the months of July and August, 1862, the loyal people of those communities filled the ranks of the 130th and 136th regiments, and after attending scores of war meetings, urging with song every stalwart yeoman to rally round the flag, Miss Major, on 6th September, 1862, at the military rendezvous on the banks of the Genesee in Portage, NY, was married in the hollow square of the 130th regiment by the Rev. Dr. Joel Wakeman, then a captain in the regiment in which her husband, Thomas J. Thorp, was lieutenant colonel, who had up to that time participated in every battle of the Potomac Army, and, although severely wounded at Fair Oaks and Malvern Hill, had refused to stay in the hospital. By permission of the Secretary of War, Col. Thorp was assigned to the new regiment, which became the famous First New York Dragoons, by an order of the War Department, after the battle of Gettysburg. During the years of the war Mrs. Thorp rendered devoted service in the ranks, with other noble women of that period, in their efforts, in gathering and distributing every needed comfort for the wounded and sick in camp and in hospital. She joined the regiment of her adoption and remained with it during the siege of Suffolk, VA. She rode with her full eagle at the head of the regiment in the grand review in Washington at the close of the war in 1865. She never once suggested to her husband that, as he had been several times wounded and made a prisoner of war, he could consistently leave the service, but she cheered him in the camp and field and, finally, with the star above the eagle, they rode side by side in the Second Brigade, First Division of the Cavalry Corps of the Army of the Potomac. Since the war she has raised a family and cheerfully aided her husband in all his various enterprises. In

Northern Michigan, where they were pioneers, she was made deputy clerk and register of deeds. In the later years, in Arizona Territory, she assisted her husband in the sheep and wool industry, often guarding the camp located in the valley of the Little Colorado river, adjacent to the reservation of the Navajo Indian Nation, while her husband was absent on business. During all her life she has been a quiet but earnest worker in all progressive temperance movements. Her home is now in Forest Grove, OR.

THORPE, Mrs. Rose Hartwick, poet, born in Mishawaka, IN, 18th July, 1850. Her family moved to Litchfield, MI, in 1861, and in that town Rose grew to womanhood and received her education. In 1871 she became the wife of Edmund C. Thorpe. She was introduced to the public by her famous poem, "Curfew Must Not Ring To-Night," which appeared in 1870 in the Detroit, MI, "Commercial Advertiser." That poem has made the circuit of the earth. It was written when the author was a school-girl, and she kept it in her desk for more than a year, never dreaming that it was destined to make her name known throughout the civilized world. In 1883, at the commencement exercises in Hillsdale College, MI, the president and faculty unanimously voted to confer upon her the honorary degree of Master of Arts. Among her earlier literary productions was a prose sketch, which she published in 1868. Her extreme diffidence and want of confidence in herself led her to keep her work in her desk. Her awakening came with "Curfew." Other well-known poems followed, among them being "The Station Agent's Story," "Red Cross," and "In a Mining Town." Although evidently a busy and prolific author, she has been in ill health for some years. In 1888 she and her family removed to San Diego, CA, where they are pleasantly domiciled in Rosemere, Pacific Beach. There, in the eternal summer, beneath the blue sky, surrounded by ever-blooming gardens of flowers, each member of the family has recovered health and strength, and there Mrs. Thorpe finds abundant inspiration and leisure. Her father's family were artists, but she has inherited none of their artistic talent. The fondness for the brush and pencil passed over her and reappears in her daughter, now coming into womanhood.

THURSBY, Miss Emma Cecilia, singer, born in Brooklyn, NY, 21st February, 1857. She was educated in the public schools of the city, and early showed her musical tastes. Her fine voice attracted the attention of musical people and they advised her to prepare for a professional career. She learned the rudiments of music with Julius Meyer, and, studied later with Achille Errani and Erminia Rudersdorff. In 1873 she went to Italy and took a short course with San Giovanni and Francesco Lamperti. Returning to New York, she sang in the Broadway Tabernacle for a time. In 1876 she made a concert tour with Gilmore's Orchestra. In 1877 she traveled with Theodore Thomas. In that year she signed an engagement for six years with Maurice Strakosch, under whose management she made a number of very successful tours in the United States and Europe. She has appeared only in concerts and oratorios, and has declined many tempting offers to go upon the operatic stage in Europe. Her specialty is sacred music, and she is the leading oratorio singer of her day. She is a woman of commanding presence. Her voice is a soprano of great volume and purity, and her singing is characterized by dramatic intensity and thorough refinement in method.

THURSTON, Mrs. Martha L. Poland, social leader and philanthropist, born in Morrisville, VT, 12th May, 1849. Her father, Col. Luther Poland, was one of three brothers distinguished for public service and ability. The family were among the original and uncompromising abolitionists. Her mother, whose maiden name was Clara M. Bennett, was of sturdy New England stock, her ancestors having been among the first settlers of Vermont. Her parents removed to Madison, WI, in 1854, and later to Viroqua, in the same State. In 1867 they returned to Madison,

where Martha completed her education in the University of Wisconsin. After leaving college, her parents removed to Omaha, NE, where she has since lived. Her school-life did not commence until she was twelve years of age, and was completed just after her twentieth birthday. During that time she taught several country and city schools, and showed a marked talent and brilliant and thorough scholarship. Her essays were characterized by literary ability. On Christmas, 1872, she became the wife of John M. Thurston, then a young attorney, of Omaha. He is at present the general solicitor of the Union Pacific Railway system. He is a leading Republican and a noted orator. After her marriage, Mrs. Thurston devoted herself almost exclusively to her home. She is noted as an exemplary wife and mother. Her two older sons, both of remarkable precocity, died in the late fall of 1880, and her family now consists of one son, twelve years of age, and two daughters, aged nine and seven. She has educated her children at home, personally arranging and supervising their studies, until the fall of 1892, when her son was admitted to the high school. She is known as a great traveler. She has visited all of the States and Territories in the Union but two, and is familiar with all American cities and points of interest. She has at times been a valued contributor to the press, her articles on Alaska and what she saw there having been copied throughout the United States. She has participated in several newspaper controversies on important public questions, always under a pen-name, and her authorship has been known only to a very few of her most intimate friends. For many years she has been identified with charity, having attended as a delegate all of the conventions of the National Board of Charities and Corrections since 1885. In the last one, in Denver, CO, July, 1892, she held prominent positions on committees and contributed by her efficient assistance to the success of the convention. She is the constant traveling companion of her husband, and has aided him in his public efforts and addresses. Her home is a model of modest elegance.

TILTON, Mrs. Lydia H., journalist and temperance worker, born in Tuftonborough, NH, 10th July, 1839. She is a daughter of Abel Heath, a minister of the Methodist Episcopal Church. She inherited a love of literature that has made her a life long student. She was educated in the public schools of Manchester, NH, and in the New Hampshire Conference Seminary. In the latter school she taught and in Henniker Academy. In 1866 she became the wife of R. N. Tilton, and has since resided in Washington, DC. As a newspaper correspondent and as a writer of occasional poems she has won a large circle of literary friends. Though the center of a united home circle she finds time for much outside work. She is the national legislative secretary of the Nonpartisan Woman's Christian Temperance Union, and is active in its work.

TODD, Miss Adah J., author and educator, was born in Redding, Fairfield county, CT. Descended on her father's side from Christopher Todd, one of the pioneer settlers of New Haven Colony, and on her mother's side from Jehue Burre, of Fairfield, she inherits sterling character from a double line of Puritan ancestry. As her father had a large family and little wealth, he could give his daughter only the advantages of the common schools and a preparatory school. Her thirst for knowledge was insatiable, and by teaching in summer and writing throughout the year she succeeded in paying her expense in college and received from Syracuse University the degree of A.B., in 1880. By her own efforts and in opposition to the wishes of her friends, she continued her studies in Greek and philosophy and won the degree of A.M., in Syracuse, in 1883. In 1886 Boston University conferred upon her the degree of Ph.D. for work in languages and literature. She was valedictorian of one of her classes and salutatorian of another. With the tastes of a student she combined practical and executive ability. In 1880–81 she was teacher of languages and lady principal in Xenia College, OH. She resigned to continue her studies. In 1883 she accepted the position of science teacher in the Bridgeport, CT, high school, and was the first to introduce the full laboratory method into the public schools of Connecticut. Her work in that department was very successful and she received for it about half the salary a man would have received. At a later period she took charge of Greek in the same school, fitting pupils for Yale, Harvard and women's colleges, and having many private pupils in both Greek and Latin. In the summer of 1887 she had care of the department of physiology in the summer school for teachers in Martha's Vineyard. She always had a strong inclination for literary work, and her first published articles appeared when she was sixteen. During the last ten years she has written for various papers and magazines, made translations, assisted in the revision of Shepard's "Elements of Chemistry," and furnished weekly papers on natural history for the "Living Church" of Chicago, in 1891. In the summer of 1892 her first hook was published under the title, "The Vacation Club." She is a member of several literary, philanthropic and social clubs. Her home is in Redding.

TODD, Mrs. Letitia Willey, poet, born in Tolland, CT, in February, 1835. Her father, Calvin Willey, was a lawyer of marked ability. In the early part of this century he took an active part in public life, filling with efficiency many prominent positions. In 1823 he was a member of the United States Senate. Among his colleagues were Henry Clay, Daniel Webster and John Randolph. At that time Mr. Willey formed many friendships, which extended through his long and honorable life. Letitia was his amanuensis for several years, and as her father continued his correspondence with the friends of earlier days, she derived no little benefit, as well as pleasure, from the opportunity thus afforded her. From childhood she spent much time with him in his library, and she never tired of hearing him relate incidents connected with his life in Washington. At an early age she showed literary tastes. In 1847 her first published poem was printed in the Hartford "Times." Subsequently, in periodicals then in circulation, poems and short stories from her pen appeared under the pen-name "Alice Afton," and still later "Enola." Under the latter a poem, "Lines Written on Reading the Life of Kossuth," appeared in print soon after his visit to this country. It excited considerable comment of an encouraging nature to the author, and for a few years her pen was busy. In 1857 she became the wife of Sereno B. Todd, of North Haven, CT. Mr. Todd is a descendant of the Yale family, of which Elihu Yale, the founder of Yale College, was a member. They have two children, a son and a daughter.

TODD, Mrs. Mabel Loomis, author, born in Cambridge, MA, 10th November, 1858. She is the daughter of the poet and astronomer, Prof. E. J. Loomis, and his wife Mary Alden Wilder Loomis, in the seventh generation of descent from John Alden and his wife Priscilla. Mabel was a precocious child. At the age of five she was laboriously printing her first blood-curdling novel, and singing airs. Her father taught her during the first ten years of her life. In 1868 the office of the "Nautical Almanac" was removed to Washington, DC, and Professor Loomis moved his family to that city. Mabel entered the Georgetown Seminary, and studied botany and ornithology with her father, until she was seventeen. In 1875 she went to Boston to study music and painting, and became proficient in both. In 1879 she became the wife of Professor Todd, professor of astronomy and director of the observatory of Amherst, MA, and after marriage she continued her studies in art and music. In 1882 her interest in astronomy was aroused, and she made an exhaustive study of the science. In 1887 she accompanied her husband, who had charge of the expedition to Japan to observe the total eclipse of the sun, and she gave him much valuable assistance. To her was intrusted the drawing of the filmy corona. She wrote accounts of the expedition for the New York "Nation," and contributed articles on Japan to "St. Nicholas," the "Century" and other magazines. In 1889 she rendered valuable aid in preparation for her husband's expedition to western Africa to observe a total solar eclipse. In 1890 she edited and arranged for publication the poems left by the late Emily Dickinson, the first volume of which passed through a dozen editions in less than a year. In 1891 she prepared a second volume of Miss Dickinson's poems, to which she contributed a preface. Recently she has given drawing-room

talks on the life and literary work of that remarkable woman, as well as upon Japan and other subjects. She does a good deal of book reviewing for periodicals, as well as occasional sketches and short stories. She is interested in all work for woman. Her home is in Amherst. She has one daughter, aged ten years.

TODD, Mrs. Marion, author, lawyer and political economist, born in Plymouth, NY, March, 1841. Her parents were educated New Englanders. Her father died when she was ten years old, and she was compelled to earn her living. At the age of seventeen she began to teach school, and she remained in the ranks until she became the wife of Benjamin Todd. Her husband was an able speaker, and he induced her to go on the lecture platform. In 1879 she began to study law in Hastings College, San Francisco, CA. Her husband died in 1880, leaving her with one child, a daughter. In 1881 she was admitted to the bar, and at once opened a law office. In 1882 she was nominated for attorney-general of California by the Greenback party of that State. Her nomination was the first of the kind, and she stumped the State, making speeches for the Greenback party. In 1883 she went as a delegate to the first national anti-monopoly convention, held in Chicago, IL, and in 1884 she again attended the convention in the same city. In that year she attended the Greenback convention in Indianapolis, IN, and served as a member of the committee on platform. She spoke in each campaign from 1883 to 1886. She then returned to California, to conduct a number of important law cases. She joined the Knights of Labor in Michigan, and was sent as a delegate to the convention in Richmond, VA. She was a delegate to the labor conference in Indianapolis in 1886, and in Cincinnati, OH, in 1887, where she made brilliant addresses. She has abandoned the practice of law and devotes her time to lecturing. In 1886 she wrote a small volume on "Protective Tariff Delusion." In 1890 she published a volume entitled "Professor Goldwin Smith and his Satellites in Congress," in answer to Professor Smith's article or a "Woman's Place in the State." She did much . . . work on the Chicago "Express" several years ago. She has recently completed another [work], titled "Pizarro and John Sherman." Residing for some time in Chicago, she removed to Eaton Rapids, MI, where she now makes her home.

TODD, Mrs. Minnie J. Terrell, woman suffragist, born in Lewiston, NY, 26th November, 1844. Her father, a member of the Stacy family, of Somersetshire, England, removed to New York in 1841, and was married to an American woman of good family. Both parents were interested in the fugitive slave question and gave protection to and fed day or night the fleeing slaves. Born under these influences, at a time of great agitation, she inherited a strong love and sympathy for the unfortunate. She began early in life to show marked interest in the distressed, a quality that has remained with her and influenced to a great extent her life and the lives of others. On 14th September, 1865, she became the wife of Davison Todd, of Toronto, Canada. For some years after marriage she was fascinated with housekeeping and devoted to the duties of wife and mother, but she found she could respond to the needs of others without neglecting home, and many a life was made happier by her help. She is one of Nebraska's stanchest woman suffragists, and was at one time president of the sixth district. She is a member of the State Board of Charities, and in her own town is an enthusiastic leader in literary and art clubs and in every reformative and progressive movement.

TOURTILLOTTE, Miss Lillian Adele, author, born in Maxfield, Penobscot county, ME, 28th April, 1870. She is the youngest of three daughters of Franklin and Mary Bryant Tourtillotte. The Tourtillottes are of French descent, and the family is first mentioned in this country in 1682, when 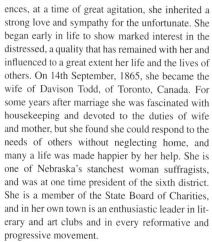 Gabriel Tourtillotte came from Bordeaux and settled in Rhode Island. Miss Tourtillotte's maternal ancestors were English. Her mother is a relative of the family to which William Cullen Bryant belonged. The daughter's schooling was obtained at home and in Foxcroft, ME. Her talent for poetical composition showed itself very early, in the singing of improvised songs to her dolls and the production of poems before she could write. Her first published attempt in verse appeared in 1885, since when she has written both poetry and prose. In 1887 she taught school, but recently, having learned the art preservative of all arts, she has been doing editorial and other work in a printing-office. Her home is now in Boston, MA.

TOUSSAINT, Miss Emma, author and translator, born in Boston, MA, 13th July, 1862. Her mother was German and her father Belgian, although the family are purely and anciently French, with Austrian intermarriages. The lineage entitled them to entertain royalty. When she was seven years old, her parents removed to Brookline, MA, which place is now her home. Through the panic of 1874 her father lost his fortune. Miss Toussaint is a fluent linguist, an able scholar and a ready thinker, as well as writer. Her short stories have been published over the pen-name "Portia." Her most important work has been the translation of the volume entitled "A Parisian in Brazil," by Madame Toussaint-Samson, which was published over her own name, and which received very favorable notices. She has also translated and adapted a number of plays. She possesses histrionic talent, and, had it not been for family reasons, she probably would have gone on the stage. She is a public-spirited woman, as is shown in her active membership in six clubs, the New England Woman's Club, The New England Woman's Press Association, the Castilian Club, the Ladies' Aid Association, the Woman's Charity Club and the Guild of the Church of our Savior, for she is an Episcopalian. Her life has been spent in attendance on an invalid mother, whose death occurred five years ago. It was mainly through her efforts the English actor, Henry Neville, was the first member of his profession who was invited to give a paper on the drama before the New England Woman's Club.

TOWNE, Mrs. Belle Kellogg, author and journalist, born in Sylvania, Racine county, WI, 1st

June, 1844. She is the daughter of the late Seth H. and Electa S. Kellogg. She began at an early age to display literary talent, but it was not until her marriage with Prof. T. Martin Towne, of Chicago, IL, the well-known musical composer, that she was induced to embrace penwork as a vocation. Ten years ago she was asked to take charge of the various young people's papers published by the David C. Cook Publishing Company, of Chicago. There she has found a wide field, not only for her literary gift, but executive ability. The "Young People's Weekly," the most noted of the periodicals published by that firm, is ranked among the foremost of religious papers for the young. Mrs. Towne reads the numerous manuscripts contributed for all the papers in her hands, and, although charitable to the young or obscure author, she has no sympathy with a writer who has no talent, or with one who has talent, but uses it unworthily or in a slipshod manner. All her business correspondence and original composition she dictates to a stenographer, and recently she has made large use of the phonograph in her literary work. She has written much and well. She is one of the rare examples of a successful author who is an equally successful editor.

TOWNSEND, Mrs. Mary Ashley Van Voorhis, poet, born in Lyons, NY, in 1836. She moved to New Orleans, LA, in early girlhood and has lived there ever since, save for a short time, when she lived in the West. Her husband, Gideon Townsend, is a wealthy banker, prominently identified with the business interests of New Orleans. Mrs. Townsend is the mother of three daughters. She has been writing since she was a young girl. Her first efforts were short stories, so popular that they went the "rounds of the press." Her first book was a novel, "The Brother Clerks: A Tale of New Orleans" (New York, 1859). In 1870 she published the well-known poem, "A Georgia Volunteer." Next came "Xariffa's Poems" (Philadelphia, 1870). This was followed by a fine dramatic poem of some length,

"The Captain's Story" (Philadelphia, 1874). In 1881 she brought out "Down the Bayou and Other Poems" (Boston). Her most important single poem, "Creed," appeared first in the New Orleans "Picayune," in 1869, and at once went ringing round the land, crossed the Atlantic, made itself famous in England and has never lost the hold upon the hearts of the people which it so speedily gained. She was selected as the writer of the poem for the New Orleans Cotton Exposition. She has made several visits to Mexico, and is a member of the Liceo Hidalgo, the foremost literary club in the city of Mexico, numbering among its members the most brilliant literary men of that country. At the time of her election she was the only American woman so honored. Her latest works are a book on Mexico and a volume of sonnets. Mrs. Townsend's life has been devoted to the highest and purest aims in literature, and her work has all been broad and uplifting. Her home-life is exceptionally happy and congenial. One of her daughters was married to a son of Edwin M. Stanton. Mrs. Townsend's intellect is stamped on her strong face.

TOWNSLEY, Miss Frances Eleanor, Baptist minister, born in Albany, NY, 13th September, 1850. Her parents were Gad Townsley, a commission merchant, large-hearted, free-handed and a strong abolitionist, and Charlotte Davis Townsley, of whom Frances says: "Of my mother there are no 'first memories.' She was always there. She always will be. A tiny, heroic, devoted woman, my saint. In her early widowhood she toiled for her children till midnight, and then eased her grief-smitten spirit by writing choice bits of prose and verse, which she modestly hid in her portfolio." Frances' "call to preach" was sudden, positive, undoubted. Once, when asked where she was educated, she said: "Partly in a village academy, partly in Wheaton College, partly in the studies of individual pastors, mainly in the University of Sorrow." Truly, from time to time one afflictive blow after another has fallen upon her heart, but she is known as "the happy woman." She spoke her first piece when five years old, the twenty-third psalm. To the faithful teaching of her mother she owes much of her training for a public speaker. Among the things committed to memory the first ten years of her life were Willis' "Sacred Poems," parts of "Paradise Lost," Pollock's "Course of Time," "The Miracles and Parables of Christ," His "Sermon on the Mount," the choicest portions of Hebrew poetry and prophecy, and many patriotic selections. She became a professing Christian before she was eighteen years old, after most turbulent struggles, mental and spiritual. She became a preacher against her previous ideas of woman's sphere, but has never held her work more holy than the ministry of home-life, considering that woman's first and best kingdom. She was licensed by the Shelburne Falls, MA, Baptist Church in 1874, after preaching a year, and after twelve years of work as an evangelist in Maine, New Hampshire, Vermont. Massachusetts, New York, Ohio, Illinois, Michigan, Minnesota, South Dakota and Nebraska, she was ordained by a council of Baptist Churches, after an examination spoken of as "most searching and satisfactory," which lasted three hours, on 2nd April, 1885, in Fairfield, NE. Her pastorate was greatly blessed in the upbuilding of the church in spirituality and members. She is a woman of rare consecration, of spotless character, especially remarkable for intensity, keen perceptions, tender sympathy, ready wit and broad love for all mankind, with strong common-sense, tact, eloquence and a great command of language. In addition to her special calling, she has been State evangelist for the Nebraska Woman's Christian Temperance Union, and a lecturer and a writer in prose and verse. Her present home is Ashland, NE, where she is now pastor of the Immanuel Baptist Church.

TRAIL, Miss Florence, author, born in Frederick, MD, 1st September, 1854. She is the second daughter of Charles E. Trail and Ariana McElfresh. Always of a buoyant disposition, a severe illness at ten years of age did not check her exuberant spirits, though it left her with impaired hearing. That would have been a great obstacle to her contact with the world, but her wonderful quickness of perception and heroic efforts to divine what others meant to say caused them to forget, or not to realize, that her hearing was not equal to their own. She graduated first in her class in the Frederick Female Seminary, in 1872, and the following year she graduated with highest honors in Mt. Vernon Institute, Baltimore, MD. Blessed in an unusual degree with the gift for imparting knowledge and inspiring others to study, she took classes in the Frederick Female Seminary in mental and moral philosophy, evidences of Christianity, modern history, mythology, rhetoric and composition, and achieved marked success. After teaching there four years, she announced her intention of leaving home for a position in Daughters College, Harrodsburgh, KY, where she afterward taught Latin, French, art and music. In Harrodsburg, as well as in Tarboro, NC, where she taught music in 1887 and 1888, and in Miss Hogarth's school, Goshen, NY, where she acted as substitute for some weeks in January, 1890, she made many devoted friends and did superior work as a teacher. In 1883 she visited Europe, and afterward published an account of her travels under the title "My Journal in Foreign Lands" (New York, 1885), a bright and instructive little volume, which passed through two editions and has been of great service as a guide-book. Miss Trail has been a member of the Society to Encourage Studies at Home for fourteen years, five as a student of modern history, French literature, Shakespeare and art, and nine as a teacher of ancient history. Her essay on "Prehistoric Greece as we find it in the Poems of Homer" was read before that society at the annual reunion at Miss Ticknor's, in Boston, MA, in June, 1883. Miss Trail is a brilliant musician, having studied music in the seminary in Frederick, in the Peabody Conservatory in Baltimore, and in Chickering Hall, New York. She has often appeared in concerts with success. Though gifted in many ways, she will be best known as a writer. Her crowning work, so far, is her last production, "Studies in Criticism" (New York, 1888). She has published over one-hundred articles in prose and verse, many without signature, in newspapers and magazines. Inheriting a taste for the languages, she is a fine translator and reads German, Italian, Latin and French.

TREAT, Mrs. Anna Elizabeth, author, born in the village of Brooklyn, OH, 28th February, 1843, where she was reared and still resides. She is the youngest child of Edward and Anna C. Fuller. Her father, a Harvard graduate and a minister of the Congregational Church, was a scholarly man and devoted to his books. He was a native of Connecticut. Her mother, Anna C. Greene, was also from the East. She was a woman of unusual refinement and intelligence and was highly educated. Miss Fuller was a constant reader and the well-selected volumes of her father's library proved the foundation of the liberal education which she afterward enjoyed. Besides her childhood love for books, she showed a strong taste for music and the study of language, acquiring especial proficiency in the German tongue. Her education was acquired in the schools of her native place, and she early became the wife of her teacher, William Treat. She began her literary work by contributing to various well-known periodicals, poems and articles which were favorably received. Her poems, published for the most part in eastern papers, were usually illustrated, especially those of a humorous nature. For a number of years she has been a contributor to the "Ohio Farmer," of Cleveland, many of her sketches and short stories appearing therein. She has also written much for various juvenile periodicals. Her name is upon the roll of the Ohio Woman's Press Association, and she takes an active interest in all local literary advancement. Two sons and two daughters, now grown, constitute her family.

TROTT, Mrs. Lois E., educator and philanthropist, was born near Oswego, NY. Her maiden name was Andrews. Her father was a pioneer farmer living remote from schools. At the age of three years Lois was sent to a school two miles distant. At fifteen years of age she became a teacher and earned a reputation for introducing new plans and methods of teaching. She was a pupil in the State Normal School of Albany in 1851, and left to engage again in teaching in Oswego. In 1857 Rev. L. M. Pease, of the Five Points House of Industry, visited Oswego and lectured on the condition of the poor in New York City. His recitals of the ignorance and sufferings of the poor children so affected Miss Andrews that she immediately volunteered to leave her work in Oswego and give her services to the instruction of the little children. Her offer was accepted, and she became principal of the school in the Five Points House of Industry. Again she became a student and was graduated with the New York City teachers. After some years of usefulness in her sphere of home missionary work, she became the wife of Eli Trott, who was employed in the same field. The darkness had become less dense, when Mr. and Mrs. Trott were called to labor in the interests of the Children's Aid Society. A lodging-house was to be opened for homeless girls, the first of the kind in America, and Mrs. Trott, without remuneration, took charge of the work. From one-thousand to one-thousand-two-hundred passed through the Home annually, and many of those girls are now filling places of trust and usefulness. Mrs. Trott left that work in 1872, that she might devote more time to her home and the education of her son and daughter. She retired to private life in Mt. Vernon, near New York City. Her husband still remains locating agent of the Children's Aid Society, finding homes for many thousands of poor children with the farmers of the West. In her early childhood the Washingtonian temperance movement originated, and her mother impressed its lessons on her heart. When the order of Daughters of Temperance was formed, she united with the organization and filled all of its honorary offices. As a child she was anxious to be a missionary in foreign lands. She became a church member when very young and has always been a Christian. When the Woman's Christian Temperance Union was organized, she at once entered the work. Having her summer home in Chautauqua, of which university she is now an alumnus, she became acquainted with many of the leaders in that movement. She has attended nearly all of its national conventions. She is deeply interested in all Chautauqua movements, and her last venture is a reading class for the domestics of her village. This is the largest and most important field which she has ever entered. It is exclusively for the kitchen-girl. In her home in Mt. Vernon she has been for many years president of the Woman's Christian Temperance Union, and has been largely instrumental in erecting a building as headquarters of the Union, named Willard Hall in honor of the national president.

TROTT, Miss Novella Jewell, author and editor, born in Woolwich, ME, 16th November, 1846. She traces her ancestry back to the Puritan emigrant, Thomas Trott, who came from England to Dorchester, MA, in 1635, and to Ralph Farnham, who, in the same year, settled in Andover, MA. Benjamin Trott and Joshua Farnham, descendants of the above, both removed to Woolwich about 1750, and there founded families whose children, from generation to generation, have been noted for their intelligence, integrity and public spirit. The parents of Novella Trott were worthy representatives of those two old families. Her mother was a woman of superior mental qualities and remarkable strength of character, and her father was a man of marked mental ability and moral worth. The daughter soon outgrew the educational advantages of her native town, and, at the age of thirteen, entered the public schools of Bath, afterward taking a special course of study in the State Normal School in Farmingron. Although she early showed decided literary tastes, she had intended to make teaching her profession. During a visit to Boston she was invited to take a position as proofreader in a prominent publishing house. There she had her introduction to the work which she was afterward to adopt as a profession. A sudden illness compelled her to give up her position and, upon her recovery, she resumed her original plans and taught successfully for several years. The five following years were devoted to the care of her invalid mother, after which circumstances opened the way for her return to literary life. In 1881 she entered the publishing establishment of E. C. Allen, in Augusta, ME, where she soon worked her way to a position upon the editorial staff. She became sole editor of the "Practical Housekeeper" and "Daughters of America." During the past ten years she has performed all branches of editorial work, selecting, compiling, condensing, revising, writing from month to month editorial, critical and literary articles, reading a large number of manuscripts and conducting the extensive correspondence of her office. In her private life she is much admired, and she is a bright and entertaining conversationalist. She was appointed one of seven women of national reputation to represent the press department of the Queen Isabella Association in the World's Fair, in Chicago, in 1893.

TRUITT, Mrs. Anna Augusta, philanthropist and temperance reformer, was born in Canaan, NH, in 1837. Her father was Daniel G. Patton. Her mother, Ruth Chase Whittier, was related to Governor Chase and the poet Whittier. At an early age her father emigrated to northern New York, where she was educated by private teachers. She subsequently spent two years in College Hills Seminary. After her first marriage she and her husband settled in the South, where they remained until the Rebellion, when they were forced to leave. Sacrificing valuable property and business interests, they returned to the North to begin again the battle of life. Her husband soon passed away. She afterward became the wife of Joshua Truitt, an energetic business man of Muncie, IN, where she has since lived, actively engaged in benevolent and philanthropic work. During the Civil War she labored constantly, preparing things useful and needful to the soldiers. She marched, sang and prayed with the crusaders. For the last sixteen years she has been a faithful worker in the Woman's Christian Temperance Union. She has been president of the Delaware county Woman's Christian Temperance Union for several years, and has often been selected by the Union to represent them in State and district meetings, as well as in the national convention in Tennessee. She was the temperance delegate to the international Sunday-school convention in Pittsburgh, PA. Her essays, addresses and reports show her to be a writer of no mean talent. She is well fitted for convention work. She has been an unfaltering worker in the temperance cause, earnestly seeking to bring all available forces against it. She is an advocate of woman suffrage, believing that woman's vote will go far toward removing the curse of intemperance. In the Woman's Christian Temperance Union she adheres to the principle of non-partisan, non-sectarian work. In a blue-ribbon club she has been an untiring worker and has spared neither time, effort nor means in advancing its interests. In the humbler fields of labor she has been equally active and successful. For years she has been identified with the industrial school of Muncie, not only as an officer and worker in its stated meetings, but her presence is familiar in the homes of the poor, carrying sympathy, counsel and needed food and raiment. She had no children of her own, but her mother love has been filled, for the four children of her deceased brother were received into her family, and she has discharged a mother's duty to them. Deeply sensitive, she has suffered keenly from various hostile attacks, but has not allowed criticism and persecution to turn her from the path of duty.

TRYON, Mrs. Kate, journalist, artist and lecturer, born in the village of Naples, ME, 18th March, 1865. She is the daughter of Charles A. Allen, of Portland, ME. In school in Portland she met James Libbey Tryon, and became his wife in Massena Springs, NY. Each was then but twenty years old. For three years Mr. Tryon was local editor of Portland and Bangor newspapers, and Mrs. Tryon, as his associate, gained a wide experience in journalism. In the fall of 1889 Mr. Tryon was able to fulfill his long-cherished plan of studying in Harvard University, and he is now working for his degree and enjoying the best literary courses the college affords. In the four-years of residence in Cambridge, MA, Mrs. Tryon has not neglected her opportunities. As member of the staff of the Boston "Advertiser" and its allied evening paper, the "Record," her name has become well-known to the newspaper-readers of New England. In 1891 she lectured upon the subject of New England's wild song-birds, her field being mostly in the scores of literary and educational clubs which abound in Massachusetts. She supplemented her lectures by illustrations in the shape of water-color drawings of each bird made by Lewell, showing its characteristic attitude and background. When actively engaged in newspaper work in Boston, she was especially happy as an interviewer.

TUCKER, Mrs. Mary Frances, poet, born in the town of York, Washtenaw county, MI, 16th May, 1837. Her maiden name was Mary Frances Tyler. In 1849 her family removed to Fulton, NY, where

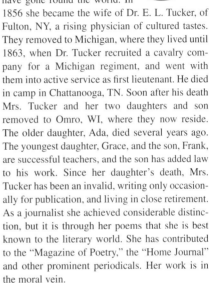

she was reared and carefully educated. In her early years she was inclined to poetical composition, and in her seventeenth year she published her two poems, "Going Up and Coming Down" and "Cometh a Blessing Down," which have gone round the world. In 1856 she became the wife of Dr. E. L. Tucker, of Fulton, NY, a rising physician of cultured tastes. They removed to Michigan, where they lived until 1863, when Dr. Tucker recruited a cavalry company for a Michigan regiment, and went with them into active service as first lieutenant. He died in camp in Chattanooga, TN. Soon after his death Mrs. Tucker and her two daughters and son removed to Omro, WI, where they now reside. The older daughter, Ada, died several years ago. The youngest daughter, Grace, and the son, Frank, are successful teachers, and the son has added law to his work. Since her daughter's death, Mrs. Tucker has been an invalid, writing only occasionally for publication, and living in close retirement. As a journalist she achieved considerable distinction, but it is through her poems that she is best known to the literary world. She has contributed to the "Magazine of Poetry," the "Home Journal" and other prominent periodicals. Her work is in the moral vein.

TUCKER, Miss Rosa Lee, State Librarian of Mississippi, born in Houston, MS, 1st September, 1868. She is a daughter of the late General W. F. Tucker, who served in the Confederate army during the Civil War. After the war, General Tucker, like most of the southern men, impoverished by the long struggle, resumed the practice of his profession, that of law, and became one of the most successful lawyers in Mississippi. Like the majority of the men of the South, he lived beyond his means. Consequently, when he died, in 1881, his family was left in straitened circumstances. Rosa Lee, who was then thirteen years old, remained in school until she was sixteen. After her graduation she taught school for one year. In 1886 she became the manager of the post-office in Okolona, MS, where her mother was postmaster. She managed the office acceptably for two years. In 1888 she was elected State Librarian of Mississippi, and has filled the position satisfactorily. As she was less than twenty years old when elected to that responsible position, she can doubtless claim to be the youngest woman ever chosen to fill an office of so high a grade. She is in every essential a southern woman, and in her career she has shown a wonderful degree of the energy and progressiveness which have enabled the women of the South to adjust themselves so readily to the new conditions following the overthrow of the social structure of the South.

TUPPER, Mrs. Ellen Smith, apiarist, born in Providence, RI, 9th April, 1822. Her father, Noah Smith, removed to Calais, ME, in 1828. Her mother died early and left a family of children, for whom Ellen cared. She studied diligently and followed the course of study of Brown University with her brother, Rev. James Wheaton Smith. She became the wife of Mr. Tupper, a man of great spirituality. Her ill-health made it necessary for them to move west soon after their marriage. They settled in Washington county, IA. In 1876 she again took up pioneer life in Lincoln county, Dakota. She died very suddenly in 1888, in El Paso, TX, of heart trouble, while visiting a daughter. Three of the women whose names appear elsewhere in this volume are her daughters. They are Mrs. Wilkes, Mrs. Galpin and Miss Tupper. Another daughter, Margaret Tupper True, is a leader in educational and philanthropic work in her home in El Paso, TX. One son, Homer Tupper, lives in Rock Valley, IA. Mrs. Tupper was for many years known as the "Queen Bee," because of her prominence as an authority in the culture of bees. For ten years prior to 1876 she was constantly writing on the subject, addressing conventions and caring for her fine apiary of Italian bees. During much of that time she was editor of the "Bee Keepers' Journal." For several years she was a non-resident lecturer on bee culture before the State Agricultural College of Iowa. A teacher she always was, although her actual employment in that capacity was for only a few months during the war, when she used to ride to school with one child on her lap and another behind her saddle. When, in the early Iowa days, she had to teach her own little ones, the children of the neighbors were invited to join. She was completely democratic in her spirit; indeed, it would be difficult to find one who had more absolutely escaped the consciousness of social lines. Born of a family running back into the New England stock on all lines, surrounded by refinement and luxury during her early life, she entered into the spirit of her pioneer life in both Iowa and Dakota, never recognizing hardships when they came, and entering into hearty comradeship with every neighbor. Mrs. Tupper was a scientist, a business woman, a lecturer, teacher, neighborhood nurse, citizen and mother, and above all a lover of her kind.

TUPPER, Miss Mila Frances, Unitarian minister, born on a farm near Brighton, IA, 26th January, 1864. Her mother was Mrs. Ellen Tupper, famous as the bee-culturist of Iowa. Miss Tupper's childhood was unusually free. She was very fond of outdoor sports, which have left their mark in her physical strength. She was particularly thoughtful as a child and studious, without much school discipline or incentive. During her years of residence in Des Moines, IA, she had the advantage of a public school, but when she was twelve years old, the family removed to the wild prairies of Dakota. There she found plenty of time and opportunity for continued physical culture, riding a great deal, chiefly to and from the post-office, which was three miles from her home. She had much time for reading, but, excepting two terms in a winter school taught by an older sister, there was no opportunity for mental culture outside of her home. In that home, where both parents were of intellectual tastes, there was less need of outside influences for culture. Evidence of that fact is shown in the mental life of all the daughters, who have become well known in their chosen professions. After three years spent in teaching in Sioux Falls, at the age of twenty-one, she entered the Whitewater Normal School, and had one year in preparation for college. She won a scholarship in mathematics on her entrance to Cornell University, where she was graduated in 1889. She at once entered the Unitarian ministry. Her first charge was in La Porte, IN, where she remained one-and-a-half years. She was called from that place to minister to a fast-growing society in Grand Rapids, MI, in which place she is now working successfully. The bent of her mind was always toward theological subjects. She united with the Baptist Church when she was nine years of age, but gradually drew away from that, until she took her place with the Unitarians. Her main characteristics are candor, generosity, conscientiousness, and notably the power of adapting herself to the minds of all ages and modes of thought. She has the happy faculty of meeting the young, the old and middle-aged on their own ground. Her discourses fulfill the promise of her early thoughtfulness, in their clear, logical and simple, yet forceful, presentation of the subject in hand, and her quiet dignity of manner gives added strength to the words that fall from her lips.

TURNER, Mrs. Alice Bellvadore Sams, physician, born near Greencastle, IA, 13th March, 1859. She was the second of a family of four children. She attended country schools and assisted in household duties until 1873, when she entered college in Indianola, IA. From that time until 1878 she was alternately engaged as teacher and pupil. On 21st October, 1878, she became the wife of Lewis C. Turner, who was making a like struggle for education. The first year after their marriage they were engaged in teaching, and the next year they entered school. Her husband gave instruction in penmanship and drawing, which paid for their books and tuition. Mrs. Turner, besides her school work, superintended and did a great portion of the work herself for boarders among their classmates, thus helping further to defray expenses. In 1880, in their last year's work, the school building where they were studying, Mitchellville, IA, was sold for a State industrial institution, and they had to relinquish the goal so nearly won. They at once entered the medical school in Keokuk, IA. There, in addition to their school work, they held the positions of steward and matron of the hospital for one year. In October, 1881,

a daughter was born to them. Dr. Turner entered her class when her babe was a month old, and was graduated in February, 1884, with high rating. They went to Colfax, IA, where they located for the practice of their profession, in their native county, and where they enjoy a large and lucrative practice. Besides their general practice, they have established an infirmary for the cure of inebriety. Dr. Turner is a student, a conscientious physician, a frequent contributor to the public press, and a prime mover in every cause for the betterment of humanity.

TUTTLE, Mrs. Emma Rood, author, born in Braceville, OH, 21st July, 1839. Her father was John Rood, Jr., a native of Connecticut. Her mother was Jane A. Miller. The ancestry is French and Welsh. The father was an advanced thinker, and the mother was a refined person of sensitive temperament. Emma was educated in the Western Reserve University, Farmington, OH, and in Hiram College, of which institution the late President James A. Garfield was then the head. In her school-days she wrote verse. At the age of eighteen years she became the wife of Hudson Tuttle, of Berlin Heights, OH, where she has passed her life. Her husband is also an author. Their family consists of three children. Their son, Dr. Carl Tuttle, is a well-known ornithologist. Their daughter, Miss Clair Tuttle, is a successful actor. After her marriage Mrs. Tuttle began the exercise of her dramatic power, which is second only to that of her gift of song. A part of her repertory was her own lyrical compositions. Her earliest publication was "Blossoms of Our Spring" (Boston, 1864), which was followed by "Gazelle," a tale of the rebellion, (Boston, 1866), "Stories for Our Children," and a joint work with others, "The Lyceum Guide" (1870). Her last volume is entitled "From Soul to Soul" (New York, 1890). She varies her domestic and literary work with the recreations of painting and elocution.

TUTWILER, Miss Julia Strudwick, educator, is a native of Alabama. She is the daughter of Dr. Henry and Julia Ashe Tutwiler. Henry Tutwiler, LL.D., was the first A.M. of the University of Virginia, having entered that institution in the first year of its existence, when Thomas Jefferson was chancellor. Through her mother Miss Tutwiler is descended from those well-known families of North Carolina, the Shepperds, Strudwicks and Ashes. In very nearly every Congress convened there has been a representative of the Ashe family. She was educated with great care. She was first instructed by her learned father and then spent some time in a French boarding-school of high repute in Philadelphia, PA. She spent some time in Vassar College. Afterward she passed three years of study in Germany. One year of that time she spent with the deaconesses of Kaiserwerth. In 1878 she was selected over many applicants to represent the "International Journal of Education" in the Paris Exposition. In 1890 she was appointed to read a paper before the National Educational Association in Minneapolis, MN, which brought forth much comment from the press of the United States. In August, 1891, she read by appointment a paper on "A German Normal School" before the International Educational Association in Toronto, Ontario, and in that meeting was chosen president for the next year of one of the departments of the association. Not only is she known as one of the leading teachers of the United States, but her poems, essays, stories and sketches have won her a reputation in the literary world. Her song, "Alabama," is sung in many of the schools of that State, and her sketches of people and scenes written during her stay in Europe for some of the leading magazines were widely copied. Alabama is the only State where the horrors of the lease-system of convict-government have been ameliorated by the establishment of prison-missions, in the form of night schools in the convict-camps. She has always taken a leading part in the establishment of these schools and in the accomplishment of other measures for improving the condition of the criminal administration of the State. Several measures conducive to this end have been passed through the legislature by her exertions. She has received from the State appointment as superintendent of prison schools and missions. She is State superintendent of two departments of work under the Woman's Christian Temperance Union organization, the department of prison and jail work and work among miners. She is preëminently a teacher, and is at present principal of the Alabama Normal School.

TWIGGS, Mrs. Sarah L., poet, born in Barnwell county, SC, 29th March, 1839. Her life from earliest infancy to womanhood was passed in one of the beautiful southern homesteads that lie along the Savannah river border, near Augusta, GA. Her great-grandfather, Gen. John Twiggs, figured as one of the Revolutionary heroes. Her ancestors were Swedish Norsemen. The first of the name came to this country in company with Gen. Oglethorpe, bearing a large grant of land from George III. Gen. David E. Twiggs, of Mexican War fame, was her great-uncle, and she is a sister of judge H. D. D. Twiggs, the distinguished Georgia barrister. Her father was a successful southern planter, who cared more for blooded horses and well-trained pointers than for literary pursuits. Her literary tastes were inherited from her mother, who was a woman of ability and culture. She is the only daughter in a family of five children. From a life of southern ease and affluence, on which were built the airy castles of a poetic temperament, she was awakened by the rude shock of war, in which her fortunes sank. Then followed the sorrow of an unhappy marriage and a succession of sad family bereavements. In 1885 she found herself, with two small children, in the national capital. There she succeeded in achieving a comfortable independence. The sterner phases of her altered life closed for her, in a measure, the literary avenues which were more in accordance with her taste, yet out of the shadow she occasionally sent flashes of a lamp not wholly extinguished. One of her poems, "Nostri Mortui," and several idyls, which appeared in southern journals, elicited flattering mention. She is now writing a book, which will be published in the near future.

TYLER, Mrs. Julia Gardiner, wife of John Tyler, tenth President of the United States, born on Gardiner's Island, near Easthampton, NY, in 1820. She was the oldest daughter of David Gardiner, a man of wealth. She was educated by private teachers at home until she was sixteen years old, when she was sent to Chegary Institute, in New York City, where she was graduated. After leaving school, she traveled with her father in Europe. Returning to the United States, she visited Washington, DC, in 1844. She and her father went with President Tyler on a steamboat excursion to Alexandria, and on the return trip the gun "Peacemaker" exploded while being fired, and Mr. Gardiner and several others were killed, and many others were injured. The body of Mr. Gardiner was taken to the White House, and President Tyler, then a widower, was thrown in the company of the grief-stricken daughter. They became engaged, and on 26th June, 1844, they were married in New York City. For the remaining eight months of President Tyler's term of office she presided in the White House with grace, dignity and success. Leaving Washington, they retired to Mr. Tyler's home, "Sherwood Forest," in Virginia. They remained there until Mr. Tyler died, 17th January, 1862, in Richmond. Since the Civil War she has lived in her mother's home on Castleton Hill, Staten Island, NY. She has several children. She is a convert to Roman Catholicism and is active in the charities of that church.

ULMAR, Mrs. Geraldine, singer, was born in Charlestown, a suburb of Boston, MA. In her eleventh year she made her début as "The Child Soprano" in three juvenile concerts in Worcester, MA. She was trained for the stage, and in November, 1879, she joined the Boston Ideals, singing first with that company in "Fatinitza." She then appeared in "The Sorcerer," "Boccacio," "Pinafore," "The Chimes of Normandy," The Bohemian Girl," and all the Sullivan operas except "Princess Ida." When the English "Mikado" company came to the United States, in 1885, Sir Arthur Sullivan, who heard her sing the part of Yum Yum, insisted that she should be engaged permanently to sing in that rôle. She went to England and there scored a brilliant success, both artistically and socially. She has since remained in London, where, on 30th March, 1891, she became the wife of an American musician, Felix Tilkin, known to

the musical world as Ivan Caryll. One of her greatest triumphs in London was won by her performance of "La Cigale." Her acquaintances in London include many persons prominent in society.

VALESH, Mrs. Eva McDonald, labor agitator, born in the village of Orono, ME, 9th September, 1866. The McDonald family is Scotch-Irish. Mrs. Valesh's father is a carpenter in Minneapolis. Her mother, from whom she inherits whatever of poetry there is in her nature, is at the age of fifty years a remarkably handsome woman. Mrs. Valesh is the oldest of a family of seven children. Her schooling developed no great promise. She was a bright child, but full of mischief, and she had an annoying habit of saying unpleasant truths in a blunt fashion without respect to the feelings of her teachers. In 1877 she moved with her family to Minneapolis, and so close was her application to her books that in four years, at the age of fifteen, she was graduated from the high school, to embark upon a career of many experiences. After leaving school she learned the printer's trade, and she began to take object-lessons to prepare her for the work before her. She was employed on the "Spectator." In due time she became a member of the Typographical Union and still holds a card from the Minneapolis Union. Her father had built a house in what was then a well out-of-town section, and Eva was put in charge of a little grocery store, which occupied the front of the building. The young girl harnessed up the delivery horse, delivered the goods to customers and brought to the store the supplies for the day. She grew fond of the horse and big black dog that always followed her. She also worked in stores and several factories until the age of twenty, when she attended the Minneapolis teachers' training-school for a year and was graduated. She had set her mind upon teaching, but by a chance recommendation of Timothy W. Brosnan, then district master-workman of the Knights of Labor of Minnesota, she began newspaper work, and printer's ink has clung to her fingers ever since. A shop-girls' strike had been in progress. Many of the girls, who were engaged in making overalls, coarse shirts and similar articles, belonged to the Ladies' Protective Assembly, Knights of Labor, into which Eva had been initiated but a short time before. She was not personally interested in the strike, but she attended all the meetings of the strikers and repeatedly addressed them, urging the girls to stand firm for wages which would enable them to live decently. The strike was only partially successful, but it opened an avenue for the talent of the young agitator. In March, 1887, she began a series of letters on "Working Women" for the St. Paul "Globe." These were continued for nearly a year and attracted wide attention. She began to make public speeches on the labor question about that time, making her maiden effort in Duluth in June, 1887, when not quite twenty-one years of age. After the articles on the workwomen of Minneapolis and St. Paul ceased, she conducted the labor department of the St. Paul "Globe," besides doing other special newspaper work. She continued her public addresses in Minneapolis and in St. Paul, and she was a member of the executive committee that conducted the street-car strike in Minneapolis and St. Paul in 1888, and subsequently wrote the history of the strike, publishing it under the title of "A Tale of Twin Cities." During the political campaign of 1890 she lectured to the farmers under the auspices of the Minnesota Farmers' Alliance. She was elected State lecturer of the Minnesota Farmers' Alliance on 1st January, 1891, and on the 28th of the same month, in Omaha, she was elected assistant national lecturer of the National Farmers' Alliance. Miss McDonald became Mrs. Frank Valesh on 2nd June, 1891. Mr. Valesh, like his wife, is a labor leader. He has been a prominent member of the St. Paul Trades and Labor Assembly for years and is president of the Minnesota State Federation of Labor. During the last year Mrs. Valesh has turned her attention more especially to the educational side of the industrial question, lecturing throughout the country for the principles of the Farmers' Alliance and in the cities for the trade-unions. By invitation of president Samuel Gompers she read a paper on "Woman's Work" in the national convention of the American Federation of Labor in Birmingham, AL, 12th December, 1891, and was strongly recommended for the position of general organizer among working women. Home duties prevented her from accepting the position, though she still manages an industrial department for the Minneapolis "Tri-

bune" and contributes an occasional magazine article on industrial or political matters.

VAN BENSCHOTEN, Mrs. Mary Crowell, author, was born in Brooklyn, NY. She was educated in Brooklyn and New York City. In youth she displayed dramatic and elocutionary talents, and gave many entertainments in aid of charities. Her maiden name was Crowell. At an early age she became the wife of Samuel Van Benschoten, of New York City, and they removed to Evanston, IL, where they now live. Their family consists of a son and a daughter. She began to publish poems and short stories in her early years, and she has contributed to the Chicago "Times" "Tribune," "Inter-Ocean" and other journals. She was one of the charter members of the Illinois Social Science Association, and one of the first secretaries of the Woman's Christian Temperance Union. She is a member of the Illinois Press Association and of the Chicago Woman's Club. She is one of the managers of the Chicago Woman's Exchange. She is interested in the Illinois Industrial School for Girls, and for eight years she edited the organ of that school, "The Record and Appeal." She is a busy woman at home, in society and in literature.

VAN BUREN, Mrs. Angelica Singleton, daughter-in-law of Martin Van Buren, the eighth President of the United States, and mistress of the White House during his term of office, was born in Sumter District, SC, in 1820, and died in New York, NY, 29th December, 1878. She was the daughter of Richard Singleton, a planter, and a cousin to President Madison's wife. Her grandfather Singleton and her great-grandfather, General Richardson, served in the Revolutionary War. Miss Singleton received a liberal education, and finished her school course with several years of training in Madame Greland's seminary in Philadelphia, PA. In 1837 she spent the winter season in Washington, DC. There she was presented to President Van Buren by her cousin, Mrs. Madison. In November, 1838, she became the wife of the President's son, Major Abraham Van Buren, and on New Year's Day, 1839, she made her appearance as mistress of the White House. President Van Buren was a widower, and his brilliant and beautiful daughter-in-law rendered him no small service in presiding over the White House during his eventful term of office. In the spring of 1839 Mrs. Van Buren and her husband visited Europe, where they were pleasantly received, especially in England. She showed great tact in her management of social affairs in the President's home. After leaving the White House, she and her husband made their home with the ex-President on his beautiful "Lindenwald" estate. In 1848 they settled in New York City, where she spent the remainder of her life. She was a devoted mother to her children, two of whom died in infancy. During her last years the family spent the winters in South Carolina, on a plantation inherited by Mrs. Van Buren. Her life was singularly pure and sweet, and in her last years she did much charitable work.

VAN DEUSEN, Mrs. Mary Westbrook, author and poet, born in Fishkill, NY, 13th February, 1829, where her father, Rev. Dr. Cornelius de Puy Westbrook, was pastor of the Dutch Church for a quarter of a century. Four years later Dr. Westbrook assumed charge of the Dutch Church in Peekskill, NY, where her girlhood days were passed. In 1865 she became the wife of James Lansing Van Deusen, of Rondout, NY, where she has ever since lived, sacrificing very largely the pleasures of "dream-life" that she might minister more constantly to husband and children. She has published much in prose and verse, pamphlet and book form, mostly through the Freeman Company, of Kingston, NY. Her "Rachel Do Mont" was published in 1883, and went through three editions in one year. Her "Christmas Rosary," "Dawn," "Eastertide," and "Merrie Christmas," all in verse, were published in 1884. Her "Mary Magdalene," in verse, and "Easter joy" were issued in 1886, and a third edition of "Dawn," a second one having been published in 1885. Her "Colonial Dames of America," "Voices of My Heart," a book of poems, and a novel called "Gertrude Willoughby" are her most recent works. The fourth edition of "Rachel Du Mont," with illustrations, was published in Albany, NY, in 1890.

VAN FLEET, Mrs. Ellen Oliver, poet, born in the town of Troy, Bradford county, PA, 2nd March, 1842. She is of English parentage. From her mother she inherited faithful domestic tendencies, together with an unswerving regard for duty. From her father she inherited a strong literary taste. Miss Oliver was educated by private teachers at home, in the public schools and private schools of her native town, in the Troy Academy, and in Mrs. Life's seminary for young women, then in Muncy, PA, now in Rye, NY. She never aspired to literary fame, and she has always written for a purpose. While her contributions to various periodicals and magazines are numerous, her choicest works are still in manuscript. Her lesson hymns are many and beautiful. She wrote a large number during a period of eight years, which were used by David C. Cook, publisher, of Chicago, IL. Among her hymns of note is the "Prayer of the Wanderer," which has been extensively sung in this country and in Europe. Her later writings bear the impress of mature thought toned by contact with the world. In September, 1887, Miss Oliver became the wife of Charles G. Van Fleet, a lawyer and a man of literary tastes. Her home is in Troy, PA.

VAN HOOK, Mrs. Loretta C., missionary and educator in Persia, born in Shopiere, WI, 4th July, 1852. Her maiden name was Turner. Her ancestors were New Englanders and Hollanders. Her father was a millwright, a native of New York, and her mother belonged to one of the old Dutch families of the same State. From her mother Loretta inherited a fine artistic taste and talent. She was a precocious child, and she generally led her classes. She acquired a varied education, and when fourteen years old she became a teacher. As a child she was deeply religious. She became the wife of Mr. Van Hook in 1870, and they moved to western Iowa. Her husband and her only child died in 1871, and Mrs. Van Hook consecrated her life to the service of others. She went to Rockford, IL, and took a course in the seminary there, graduating in 1875. She sailed for Persia in 1876. During that and the two succeeding years she spent her time in missionary work and in the acquisition of the language of the country, having in view the delivery of Persian women from the degradation in which they live. She went out under the auspices of the Presbyterian Board of Missions. She settled in Tabriz, a city of 200,000 people, where women were taught to believe that they have no souls, and where no woman had ever been taught to read. After learning the language of the people, in 1879 Mrs. Van Hook established a school for girls in a quarter of the city where no other foreigner resided. Prejudices and suspicions met her, but she conquered them, and now her school is a flourishing seminary, with large buildings in the heart of Tabriz. She has students from Erinam, Russia, Kars, Turkey, and Zenjan, Persia. Her graduates are holding influential positions from the Caspian Sea to the borders of Turkey and Kurdistan. She is assisted in her work by the bands of King's Daughters, and her Persian, Turkish and Armenian graduates scattered over the land are changing harems into homes and doing much to dispel the utter darkness in which the women of that country have for ages been kept. She is a quiet, sad-faced, delicate woman, but her work and accomplishments are those of a mental, moral and physical giant.

VAN ZANDT, Miss Marie, opera singer, born in Texas, 8th October, 1861. She is the daughter of the well-known singer, Mrs. Jennie Van Zandt, who was the daughter of Signor Antonio Blitz. Family reverses compelled Mrs. Van Zandt to use her musical talents in earning a livelihood. Marie early displayed strong musical tendencies, and her voice, even in childhood, was remarkable for range and quality. She was trained by her mother and other teachers, and in 1873 she went with her mother to London, England, where she studied in a convent school. There she sang before Adelina Patti, who advised her to train for an operatic career. She was associated with Patti for some time and learned much from that queen of the operatic stage. She went to Milan, Italy, and

studied with Lamperti, and in 1879 she made her operatic début in Turin as Zerlina, winning a triumph from the first. She sang there in "La Somnambula." In 1880 she appeared in London, in Her Majesty's Opera Company, repeating her success before the cold and unmusical English public. In 1881 she made her début in Paris, in the Opera Comique, in Mignon, and she sang there during four seasons. Her repertory is extensive. Her voice is a pure soprano, of remarkable volume and sweetness, and of great compass. She has sung in the principal music centers of Europe, and she is ranked among the foremost sopranos of the time.

VEEDER, Mrs. Emily Elizabeth, author, was born in the valley of Lake Champlain, NY. On one side she is the granddaughter of Judge McOmber. Her paternal grandmother was a poet of no mean order. The late Bishop Daniel Goodsell was her cousin. She was a student in Packer Institute, Brooklyn, NY. She wrote verses at the age of nine, but it was the direct influence of her brother-in-law, Professor Stearns, a professor of law, and of the notable people who gathered about him and her sister, which elevated her taste for literature and rendered it absorbing. Her culture has been increased by travel and by contact with many minds. Her first book, "Her Brother Donnard" (Philadelphia, 1891), was followed by "Entranced, and Other Verses" (1892). She has arranged several of her poems to music of her own composition. The world would hear more frequently from Mrs. Veeder, were she not much of the time prohibited from free expression by the exhaustion of invalidism. In her hours of pain she rises above physical suffering, and her habitual temper is buoyant and helpful. She possesses originality and piquancy. A keen observation of human nature and a nice discrimination of character give point to her conversation and her literary work. In anecdote is she especially fortunate. In private life she is eminently practical. Her home is in Pittsburgh, PA.

VERY, Miss Lydia Louisa Anna, author, educator and artist, born in Salem, MA, 2nd

November, 1823. At the age of eighteen she became a teacher, and continued in that profession for thirty-four years, for the greater part of the time in the public schools of her native city, and the last two years in the private school of her sister, Miss Frances E. Very. She has been noted for her independence of character, her contempt for fashionable foibles, her advocacy of all good causes, even when they were unpopular, and her love for and defense of dumb animals. She is also well known as a friend of horses. She is an artist, painting in oils and modeling in clay. Some of her statuettes are very artistic. Her artistic taste and fancy were displayed in her "Red Riding Hood," published some years ago. It was the first book ever made in the shape of a child or an animal, and wholly original in design and illustration. It had a large sale in this country and in Germany. The author was unable to get a patent for it, and she received but small compensation. Her next books were "Robinson Crusoe," "Goody Two Shoes," "Cinderella" and others. Poor imitations of these were soon in the market, and the original design was followed in late years by a multitude of booklets cut in various shapes. She has been a frequent contributor to the magazines and papers of the day. Two of her poems, "England's Demand for Slidell and Mason" and the "Grecian Bend," are widely known. The first volume of her poems was published in 1856, the last volume, "Poems and Prose Writings," in 1890. She has translated poems from the French and German. She is now living with her sister on the old homestead, in Salem, MA.

VICTOR, Mrs. Frances Fuller, author, born in Rome, NY, 23rd May, 1826. Her maiden name was Fuller. Her father was of an old Colonial family, some of whom were among the founders of Plymouth. She has on her mother's side a long line of titled and distinguished ancestry, descending through thirty-nine generations from Egbert, the first king of all England. The last titled representative of this line was Lady Susan Clinton, the wife of General John Humfrey, deputy-governor of the Massachusetts Bay Company, chartered in 1628 by Charles I. Lady Susan's granddaughter married Captain Samuel Avery, of New London, CT, and their daughter, Mary, married William Walworth, of Groton, who was a descendant of the William Walworth, Lord Mayor of London, who was knighted by Richard II for slaying Wat Tyler in defense of the king. This English ancestry became mixed with the sturdy Welsh blood of the Williamses, the founders of liberty on this continent. Mrs. Victor's mother was Lucy Williams, her grandmother a Mary Stark, of the race of General Stark, and her great-grandmother, Lucy Walworth, a granddaughter of William Walworth and a cousin of Chancellor Walworth, the last chancellor of New York. When Frances was nine years of age, she wrote verses on her slate in school, and arranged plays from her imagination, assigning the parts to her mates, to whom she explained the signification. At the age of fourteen she published verses which received favorable comment, and at the age of eighteen some of her poems were copied in English journals. At that time the family were living in Ohio, to which State her parents had removed, and it was a familiar boast of the Ohio press that the State had two pairs of poet sisters, the Carys and the Fullers. Frances and her sister Metta married brothers. The younger sister remained in the East, settling in the vicinity of New York City, and Frances followed her husband, then an officer in the naval service of the United States, to California. At the close of the Civil War he resigned and went to settle in Oregon. In that new world she began to study with enthusiasm the country and its history from every point of view. She wrote stories, poems and essays for California publications, which, if collected, would make several volumes. After the death of her husband, in 1875, she returned to California and assisted Mr. H. H. Bancroft on his series of Pacific histories, writing in all six volumes of that work, on which she was engaged for about eleven years Subsequently she resumed book-making on her own account. Besides the great amount of literary work done by Mrs. Victor which has never been collected, she has published "Poems of Sentiment and Imagination" (New York, 1851); "The River of the West" (Hartford, 1870); "The New Penelope, and other Stories and Poems" (San

Francisco, 1876); "All Over Oregon and Washington" (San Francisco, 1872), and "Atlantes Arisen" (Philadelphia, 1891), all of which, excepting the first volume of poems, deal with the history and the romance of the Northwest. Her home is in Portland, OR.

VICTOR, Mrs. Metta Victoria Fuller, author, born near Erie, PA, 2nd March, 1851. Her maiden name was Fuller. She was the third of a family of five children. From early childhood she showed literary tastes and inclinations. At the age of ten she was dreaming of poets and poetry and essaying rhymed composition. Her parents, fully appreciating the promise of their daughters, removed to Wooster, OH, in 1839, and there gave them the advantages of excellent schools for several years. Metta's literary career commenced at thirteen years of age, for she was then writing for the local press in prose and verse, winning a reputation which soon made her more than a local celebrity. Her "Silver Lute," written in 1840, was an extraordinary production for a girl of her age and was reprinted in most of the papers of the West and South. That success was followed by great activity in verse and story, and she and her sister, Frances A., became widely known as "The Sisters of the West." At fifteen years of age she produced the romance, "Last Days of Tul" (Boston, 1846), and it had a quick and extensive sale. In 1846, over the pen-name "Singing Sybil," she began to write for the New York "Home Journal," then edited by N. P. Willis and George P. Morris. The serial, "The Tempter," a sequel to "The Wandering Jew," published in the "Home Journal," created a decided literary sensation, and the identity of the writer was then first established. Numerous prize stories were produced by her for the "Saturday Evening Post" and "Saturday Evening Bulletin," of Philadelphia, all of which were afterward published in book-form. The first volume of poems by the Fuller sisters, under the editorship of Rufus Wilmot Griswold, was published in New York City, in 1850. The same year a Buffalo, NY, firm issued the volume, "Fresh Leaves from Western Woods." Her novel, "The Senator's Son: A Plea for the Maine Law," followed in 1851. It was issued by a Cleveland, OH, publishing house. It had an enormous circulation, and was reprinted in London, whence the

acknowledgment came of a sale of thirty-thousand copies. These successes made her work in great demand, and she produced in the succeeding five years a great deal of miscellany in the fields of criticism, essays, letters on popular or special themes, and numerous poems. In 1856 Miss Fuller became the wife of Orville J. Victor, then editing the Sandusky, OH, "Daily Register," and for two years thereafter she did a great deal of admirable pen-work for that paper. In 1858 Mr. Victor, having taken editorial charge of the "Cosmopolitan Art Journal," they removed to New York City, and from that date up to her death, in June, 1885, Mrs. Victor was a constant and successful writer, chiefly in the field of fiction. One engagement may be instanced, that with the "New York Weekly," which paid her twenty-five-thousand dollars for a five-year exclusive serial story service for its pages. Her published volumes, besides those already indicated, number over twenty, all in the fields of fiction and humor. The novel, "Too True," written for "Putnam's Magazine" (1860), was reissued in two forms in New York City. The romance, "The Dead Letter" (1863) was printed in four separate book-forms in New York City, and three times serially. It was also reproduced in "Cassell's Magazine," London. Her "Maum Guinea: A Romance of Plantation and Slave Life" (New York, 1862), had an enormous sale in this country and Great Britain. The humorous "Miss Slimmen's Window" (New York, 1858), and "Miss Slimmen's Boarding House" (New York, 1859), were from Mrs. Victor's pen, as also was the "Bad Boy's Diary" (New York, 1874). "The Blunders of a Bashful Man" (New York, 1875) was first contributed by her to the "New York Weekly" as a serial. Personally, Mrs. Victor was a beautiful and lovable woman. Her fine home, "The Terraces," in Bergen county, NJ, was the Mecca of a wide circle of friends and literary people.

VON TEUFFEL, Mrs. Blanche Willis Howard, author, born in Bangor, ME, in 1851. She is widely known by her maiden name Blanche Willis Howard, which has been signed to all of her work. She received a liberal education and is a graduate of the high school in Bangor. She showed her literary bent at an early age, and quietly, and without other attempts or disheartening failures, she published her novel, "One Summer" (Boston, 1875), and took her place among the foremost novelists of the day. Desiring to enlarge her world, she determined to go abroad for travel, study and observation. With a commission as correspondent of the Boston "Transcript" she went to Stuttgart, Germany, where she has since made her home. In that city she occupied a high social position and received and chaperoned young American women, who were studying art, music and languages. She there became the wife, in 1890, of Dr. Von Teuffel, a physician of the German court, a man of wealth and social standing. Her life since marriage has been a busy one. She is a model housekeeper, and she is at once employed in writing a novel, keeping house for a large family of nephews and nieces, and supervising the translation of one of her books into French, German and Italian, besides a number of other mental and physical activities. In 1877 she published her book of travel," One Year Abroad." Her other books are "Aunt Serena" (Boston, 1881), "Guenn" (1883), "Aulnay Tower" (1885), "The Open Door" (1889), and "A Fellow and His Wife" (1891). All her books have passed through large editions in the United States, and most of them have been published in the various European languages. Mrs. Von Teuffel is a woman of cheerful and charitable disposition, and her life is full of good deeds. Her generosity and self-sacrifice are immeasurable, and only her strong physical powers enable her to keep up her numerous occupations. She is fond of dress and society, and in the high social circles in which she moves in Stuttgart she is a woman of note. Her husband encourages her in her literary work and is proud of the position she holds in the literary world. Their union is one of the idyllic kind, and her happy life and pleasant surroundings since marriage have done much to stimulate her literary activity.

WAIT, Mrs. Anna C., woman suffragist, born in Medina county, OH, 26th March, 1837. Her parents were natives of Connecticut. Her maiden name was Anna A. Churchill. Her spirit of independence and self-helpfulness manifested itself very early. Her first ambition was "To be big enough to earn her own living," which was gratified when she was eleven years old through the need felt by a near neighbor of "a little girl to do chores." The only achievements in which she seems to take pride are that she has been entirely self-supporting since eleven years of age, and that she assisted in organizing the first permanent woman suffrage association in Kansas. Her second ambition was to go to Western Reserve College. When she learned that girls were debarred from that privilege, her indignation knew no bounds. At the age of sixteen she commenced to teach school, and continued to teach for thirty-two years. She became the wife of Walter S. Wait, of Summit county, OH, 13th December, 1857, and moved to Missouri in the spring of 1858, and resided there until the breaking out of the Civil War. Their son, Alfred Hovey Wait, was born there. The fact that he was less than a year old when his father enlisted was all that kept Mrs. Wait from going to the front. She returned to Ohio and filled those dreadful years by teaching to support herself and baby. Her husband rejoined her after three years of faithful service to his country, which had recognized his ability by promoting him to the captaincy of Company H, Fiftieth Illinois Volunteer Infantry. The hardships and severe exposure during the siege of Fort Donelson had undermined his health. The family removed to Indiana in 1869, and in 1871 they went to Salina, KS. In the spring of 1872 they located in Lincoln county. There Mrs. Wait helped to organize the school district in Lincoln, the county seat, and taught school there two years. Then came the "grasshopper year." She secured employment in the Salina public school that year, and then returned to her home in Lincoln, where she continued to teach until 1885, when the breaking down of her husband's health compelled her to abandon teaching and assume a part of his duties in the publication of the Lincoln "Beacon," a reform paper started by them in 1880, devoted to prohibition, woman suffrage and antimonopoly, in which her special department was woman's enfranchisement. To her more than to any other person does that cause owe its planting and growth in Kansas. The first work done in the suffrage line in Kansas since the campaign of 1867 was the organization of a local woman suffrage association in Lincoln, KS, 11th November, 1879, by Mrs. Anna C. Wait, Mrs. Emily J. Biggs and Mrs. Sarah E. Lutes. It began with three members, but increased in numbers and influence. The suffrage sentiment and work it brought out spread throughout the county, overflowed into other counties and eventually crystallized into the State Equal Suffrage Association, which was organized 26th June, 1884. Mrs. Wait was the first vice-president and second president, and since that time, except one year, has occupied an official position in it. During the first winter of its existence the State association held a convention in Topeka, during a sitting of the Kansas legislature, and caused the municipal suffrage bill to be brought before that body. After running the gantlet of three winters before that law-making body, it became a law, bestowing municipal suffrage upon the women of Kansas. Mrs. Wait is admirably endowed to be one of the leaders in the work.

WAIT, Mrs. Phœbe Jane Babcock, physician, born in Westerly, RI, 30th September, 1838. She is one of a large family of children of whom there were eight daughters and three sons. Her early education was acquired in the district school, and she afterward taught in district schools for two years, then graduated from Alfred University, Alfred Center, NY. In 1863 she became the wife of William B. Wait, the superintendent of the institute for the blind in New York City where she was teaching. In 1868 she entered the New York Medical College and Hospital for Women, in New York City, and in 1871 received the degree of M.D. In 1869 Alfred University conferred upon her the degree of A.M. In 1879 she received the diploma of the New York Ophthalmic Hospital and College. In 1880 she was elected to the chair of obstetrics in the New York Medical College and Hospital for Women, which position she now fills. In 1883 she was made chairman of the hospital staff, which position she has held uninterruptedly. Upon the death of Dr. Clemence Sophia Lozier, the founder and dean of the college, Dr. Wait was elected by the faculty to the vacant

office. She is secretary of the Society for Promoting the Welfare of the Insane, and is also a member of the consulting staff of the Brooklyn Woman's Homeopathic Hospital.

WAITE, Mrs. Catherine Van Valkenburg, lawyer and author, born in Dumfries, Canada West, in 1829. Her maiden name was Van Valkenburg. She was educated in Oberlin College and was graduated in 1853. In 1854 she became the wife of Judge C. B. Waite. In 1859 she established in Chicago, IL, the Hyde Park Seminary for young women. She became interested in law and took the course in the Union College of Law, graduating in 1886. She then started the Chicago "Law Times," which she has made a recognized authority in this country, Canada, England, Scotland and France. In 1888 she was elected president of the Woman's International Bar Association. While living in Utah with her husband, who held a commission in that Territory under President Lincoln, she wrote her famous book, "The Mormon Prophet and His Harem," an authority on the Mormon question from the social standpoint. She suggested the statue to Isabella for the Columbian Exposition. She was one of the original woman suffragists in Illinois, and for many years she served as State lecturer. She has, in addition to her legal, literary and reformatory work, been a successful financier, and has carried on extensive real-estate and building operations. Her home is in Hyde Park, a suburb of Chicago.

WAKEFIELD, Mrs. Emily Watkins, singer, educator and lecturer, was born in London, England. Her, father, Henry George Watkins, was an artist of great ability, being one of the old line engravers for Landseer, Herring and other celebrated painters. She was educated in Queen's College, London. Her first field of work was in St. Johns, New Brunswick, where her artistic ability was soon recognized, and she received for an original painting the highest award from the Dominion Exhibition. In 1873 she removed to Halifax, Nova Scotia, where her soirees, her musicales, her examination days, and her school exhibitions were of great renown. After two years of successful administration in Patapsco Seminary, Maryland, she was invited to Titusville, PA, in which place she has been since 1882. Mrs. Wakefield has been a teacher, a singer and a musical director, and a lecturer on the Chautauqua platform in 1892.

WAKEMAN, Mrs. Antoinette Van Hoesen, journalist, was born in a beautiful valley in Cortland county, NY. When Antoinette was little more than an infant her father went to Minnesota. At that time the Sioux Indians, while no longer legally in possession of the lands of the State, still lingered there, and as a child she was familiar with them and also very fond of them. When she was ten years of age she returned to her birthplace with her father. She was sent to a boarding-school, first to the female college in Evanston, IL, and later to Jennings' Institute in Aurora, IL, then called Clark Seminary, and graduated from the latter school with honors. In a few months she was married. She became bread-winner as well as bread-maker. About that time her brother, F. B. Van Hoesen, was in the Minnesota State Senate, and while in St. Paul with him she made the acquaintance of F. A. Carie, editor of the St. Paul "Pioneer-Press." He encouraged her to send letters of correspondence from Chicago to his paper. Later she corresponded for various papers throughout the country, in each case being paid for her work. During the time she was engaged in general newspaper correspondence she was also doing special writing for the Chicago "Times." For two years she edited and published the "Journal of Industrial Education," and also attended to its business conduct. Receiving what seemed to be a very flattering offer from a New York pattern company to go there and establish a fashion magazine, she went to New York and established the publication. The work and the situation proved most uncongenial, and she resigned and returned to Chicago. She then was employed on the regular staff of the "Evening Journal," and she also edited

"American Housekeeping." When the Chicago "Evening Post" was established, she became one of the staff. She has been a regular contributor of the American Press Association and the Bok Syndicate. She has written for the "Chautauquan" and other kindred publications, and also for the New York "Sun." The first story she ever wrote was widely copied both in this country and abroad, as also was a series of articles called "Dickens, the Teacher." A sonnet called "Nay," a poem entitled "The Angel's Prayer," and another "Decoration Day," which she wrote some years ago, still continue to be published. She is a member of the Chicago Woman's Club and is one of the founders of the Press League.

WALKER, Mrs. Harriet G., reformer and philanthropist, born in Brunswick, OH, 10th September, 1841. She is the youngest daughter of Hon. Fletcher and Fannie Hulet, who were natives of Berkshire county, MA. In her sixth year the family removed to Berea, OH, for educational advantages. Before her school days were ended she was a regular contributor to several publications, and the dream of her life was to write a book. On 19th December, 1863, she became the wife of Thomas B. Walker, her schoolmate and companion since their sixteenth year. They moved to Minneapolis, MN. Eight children were born to them. For many years Mrs. Walker has been secretary of the reformatory for women called the Bethany Home in Minneapolis. Mrs. Walker organized the Northwestern Hospital for Women and Children, at the head of which as president she stood. With a strong board of women directors, a training school for nurses, with women physicans, and women and children as patients, the history of that institution has been one of continued success and prosperity. The society owns one of the finest hospital buildings in the Northwest, which is valued, with the other property in their possession, at not less than $60,000. Mrs. Walker has always been strongly devoted to temperance principles, and she was one of the first to take up the work of the Woman's Christian Temperance Union. Minneapolis is indebted to her for the introduction of police matronship. She will never look upon this branch of work as complete until she sees a separate woman's prison under the care of a board of women, including reformatory features and indeterminate sentence for all women who come under the restraining or corrective hand of the law, and for that object she is now laboring. In 1892 she was elected to the presidency of a new organization, called the Woman's Council, which is a delegate association representing all the organized woman's work of Minneapolis. Fifty associations are included, each sending two delegates, who thus represent a constituency of over two-thousand women from all fields of organized woman's work. This council has been thus far a great success and furnishes a fine field for the exercises of the peculiar abilities which have made a success of Mrs. Walker's public efforts.

WALKER, Miss Mary E., physician, army surgeon, lecturer and dress-reformer, was born in Oswego, NY. She belongs to a family of marked mental traits, and was, as a child, distinguished for her strength of mind and her decision of character. She received a miscellaneous education and grew up an independent young woman. She attended medical colleges in Syracuse, NY, and New York City. She always had an inclination to be useful in the world. When the Civil War broke out, she left her practice, went to the front and served the Union army in a way that, in any other country, would have caused her to be recognized as a heroine of the nation. Of all the women who participated in the scenes of the war, Dr. Walker was certainly among the most conspicuous for bravery and for self-forgetfulness. She often spent her own money. She often went where shot and shell were flying to aid the wounded soldiers. While engaged on the battlefields of the South, she continued to wear the American reform costume, as she had done many years previous to the war, but eventually dressed in full male attire, discarding all the uncomfortable articles of female apparel. Her bravery and services in the field were rewarded by a medal of honor, and she draws a pension from the government of only $8.50 a month, a half pension of her rank, in spite of the fact that she really deserves the highest recognition of the govern-

ment and the public for her patriotic and self-sacrificing services in the army. Her career has been an eventful one, and she has been a pioneer woman in many fields. She is the only woman in the world who was an assistant army surgeon. She was the first woman officer ever exchanged as a prisoner of war for a man of her rank. She is the only woman who has received the Medal of Honor from Congress and a testimonial from the President of the United States. She has been prominent and active in the woman suffrage and other reform movements. She was among the first women who attempted to vote and did vote, who went to Congress in behalf of woman suffrage, and who made franchise speeches in Washington, DC. She is the author of a constitutional argument on the right of women to vote. In Washington, DC, when the patent office was converted into a hospital, she served as assistant surgeon and worked without pay. In 1864 she was in the service as a regular A.A. surgeon. Many stories are told by generals, other officers and soldiers of her bravery under fire. In 1866 and 1867 she was in Europe, and directed and influenced ten-thousand women to vote in the fall of 1869. Because of her determination to wear male attire, Dr. Walker has been made the subject of abuse and ridicule by persons of narrow minds. The fact that she persists in wearing the attire in which she did a man's service in the army blinds the thoughtless to her great achievements and to her right to justice from our government. No whisper against her character as a woman and a professional has ever been heard. During the past three years she has suffered severely from an injury caused by slipping and falling which has left her lame for the remainder of her life. She is now living on the old homestead, in Oswego county, NY.

WALKER, Mrs. Minerva, physician, born in Clintondale, NY, 12th May, 1853. Her maiden name was Palmer. Her parents and grandfather were born in the same State and were Quakers. Minerva lived in Clinton county, IA, from the age of two years to that of sixteen, on a farm. Her father was a farmer, nurseryman and fruit-grower. She was educated in a preparatory course for college in the Nurserymen's

Academy and in the union school of Geneva, NY. She took a three-year course in the department of letters in Cornell University. She left that school on account of a change in pecuniary circumstances, and taught a year in a private school. The next year she began the study of medicine in a doctor's office and in the Woman's Medical College of Pennsylvania. She was graduated there in 1880. She spent the next year in the New England Hospital for Women and and Children, in Boston Highlands, and in the dispensary connected with it. Her time since that has been occupied in general and sanitarium practice, with a few months of study in the hospitals of Paris, France. She was one of the resident physicians for over five years in the Elmira Water Cure, and during the four years after she had some patient living with her in her home, in Rochester, NY. She is a member of the Monroe County Medical Society, of the Western New York State Medical Society, of the Practitioner's Society of the City of Rochester, NY, and of the Provident Dispensary of the same place. She was one of two women physicians appointed on the board of city physicians, in the spring of 1890. On 12th May, 1892, she became the wife of C. S. Walker, of Charleston, WV, where she now lives.

WALKER, Mrs. Rose Kershaw, author and journalist, born on a plantation in Mississippi, in 1847. She, is descended from an old Charleston family and was reared in a cultured and refined home. The Civil War stripped her family of fortune, and she utilized her liberal education and her literary talent. She studied in youth at home, near Pass Christian, MS, and later attended a seminary in New York City. After leaving school, she traveled three years in Europe, where she learned several modern languages. Going to St. Louis, MO, she joined the staff of the "Globe-Democrat," after working for a time on the "Post-Dispatch." She still writes on society for the former journal, and she owns and edits "Fashion and Fancy," a magazine of fashion and society, which is very successful. She contributed a series of sketches to "Frank Leslie's Illustrated Newspaper." While she was in Europe, in 1876, she corresponded for a number of newspapers, and her European letters were widely copied. She is a leader in society and interested in various charities.

WALL, Mrs. Annie, author, born in Crawford county, WI, 19th September, 1859, Her father, J. B. Carpenter, died when Annie was three years old. After his death she lived for about three years with her maternal grandmother in Richmond county. Mrs. Carpenter was married again, and little Annie went home to live in Crawford county, until she was twelve years old. Then she went to live in Grant county. Her first poem was published when she was fourteen years old. She wrote regularly for a few years for "Farm and Fireside." She has written for many other papers, and most regularly for the Chicago "Sun" and Milwaukee "Sentinel." She wrote for the Pueblo, CO, "Press" for nearly a year, until failing health prevented regular literary work. She became the wife, 12th June, 1878, of B. T. Wall, of Marion, IN. Two of their children died in infancy, and one child is living. Mr. Wall removed to Pueblo, for the benefit of his wife's health. There they have a pleasant home.

WALLACE, Mrs. M. R. M., philanthropist, born in Lamoille, IL, 2nd September, 1841. Her maiden name was Emma R. Gilson. She received a careful education, and was at an early age interested in reform and charitable movements. She became the wife of Col. M. R. M. Wallace, 2nd September, 1863, and their wedding tour took them to the South, where Colonel Wallace was stationed. They remained in the South until the war ended, and then went to Chicago, IL, where they have since lived. They are members of St. Paul's Universalist Church, in that city, and Mrs. Wallace has been prominently identified with its interests. She has been for years president of the Women's Universalist Association of Illinois, and the work accomplished under her leadership has been of great importance to the denomination at large. She has suc-

Maud Ellyson Shaw.
From Photo by Morrison, Chicago.
Flora Wright.
From Photo by Morrison, Chicago.

Theresa Vaughn.
From Photo Copyrighted, 1895, by Morrison, Chicago.
Florence Lillian Wickes.
From Photo Copyrighted, 1895, by Morrison, Chicago.

cessfully managed church and charitable associations without number. She is a member of the Chicago Press Club, the Chicago Woman's Club, the Woman's Relief Corps, the Woman's Exchange, the Home of the Friendless and many other similar organizations. She was among the first to interest the public in a woman's department for the World's Columbian Exposition for 1893, and she is one of the lady managers of the exposition. She is now president of the Illinois Industrial School for Girls, in Evanston, and that institution owes much of its success to her.

WALLACE, Mrs. Susan Arnold Elston, author, born in Crawfordsville, IN, 25th December, 1830. Her maiden name was Susan Arnold Elston. She was an active, intelligent girl, and received a good education in the schools of her native town and New York. In 1852 she became the wife of Gen. Lewis Wallace, now famous as the author of "Ben Hur." During the Civil War she saw much of camp-life and war in general. They made their home in Crawfordsville, where General Wallace practiced law after the war. From 1878 to 1881 he was governor of New Mexico, and Mrs. Wallace passed those years in that Territory. From 1881 to 1885 she was with him in Turkey, where he was serving as United States minister. They were popular in that oriental land, and Mrs. Wallace was permitted to see more of the life of oriental women than any other woman before her had seen. General Wallace was the intimate friend of the Sultan. During their residence in the orient they gathered from travel and observation much of the material for their books. In 1885 they returned to their home in Crawfordsville, where General Wallace resumed the practice of law and wrote his famous books. Mrs. Wallace has been a frequent contributor to newspapers and magazines for many years, contributing stories and poems. Her most widely known poem is "The Patter of Little Feet." Her published books are "The Storied Sea" (Boston, 1884); "Ginévra, or the Old Oak Chest" (New York, 1887); "The Land of the Pueblos," with other papers, (1888), and "The Repose in Egypt" (1888). She gives a good deal of attention to charitable movements, and her home is a literary and social center.

WALLACE, Mrs. Zerelda Gray, reformer, born in Millersburg, Bourbon county, KY, 6th August, 1817. 17. She is the daughter of Dr. John H.

Sanders and Mrs. Polly C. Gray Sanders. Her father was of South Carolina descent, and her mother a member of the Singleton family. Zerelda was the oldest of five daughters. She received as good an education as could be had in the Blue Grass Region schools of those early days. When she was ten years old, she attended a grammar-school taught by Miss Childs, a Massachusetts woman. In 1828 she entered a boarding-school in Versailles, KY, where she remained two years, studying science and history, mythology and composition. In 1830 her father removed to New Castle, KY. At a sale of public lands in Indianapolis he purchased his homestead, and removed to Indiana and built up a large practice. After leaving Kentucky, Zerelda had only limited opportunities for education, only enjoying six months of study with a cultured Baptist clergyman. She assisted her father in his practice and became interested in medicine. She read works on hygiene, mental philosophy and other elevating subjects, and was acquainted with many prominent men. In 1836, in December, she became the wife of Hon. David Wallace, soldier and jurist, and then Lieutenant-Governor of Indiana. He was a widower of thirty-seven, with a family of three sons. In 1837 he was elected Governor of the State, and in 1840 he went to Congress as a Whig. During his term Mrs. Wallace spent some time in Washington, DC, with him. She urged him to vote against the Fugitive Slave Law, and she shared all his reading in law, politics and literature. Six children were born to them. They reared their family carefully, cultivating their particular talents, and developing all their powers in every way. Mr. Wallace died in 1857, and he left his family no estate beyond their homes. Not wishing to accept assistance from her relatives, who tendered it freely and in full measure for all her needs, Mrs. Wallace opened her home to boarders and supported the family until they were able to care for themselves. Two of her daughters died, one in youth, the other after marriage. All her living children have succeeded in life. Her husband's children by his first wife included General Lewis Wallace, the soldier, jurist, scholar, statesman and author of the immortal "Ben Hur." General Wallace never refers to her as "stepmother," but always as "mother." She is a member of the Christian Church and has often spoken in its mission meetings. She was one of the crusaders and joined the Woman's Christian Temperance Union, in which she has done a good deal of valuable service. She spoke before the Indiana legislature in advocacy of temperance, and was soon after a pronounced woman suffragist. As a delegate to temperance conventions she has addressed large audiences in Boston, MA, Saratoga Springs, NY, St. Louis, MO, Detroit, MI, Washington, DC, Philadelphia, PA, and other cities. Her physical and intellectual powers are yet full. Her mental characteristics are of the stripe usually labeled "masculine." She is living in Indianapolis, surrounded by her children an grandchildren.

WALLING, Mrs. Mary Cole, patriot, born in Pike county, PA, 19th June, 1838. She is a lineal descendant of the patrician families of Stephen Cole, of Scotland, and Hannah Chase, of England. She was known during the Civil War as "The Banished Heroine of the South." Her parents moved to Cass county, IL, in 1850, where, in the same year, she became the wife of Captain F. C. Brookman, of St. Louis, MO, who shortly after fell a victim to yellow-fever. The young widow went to Texas, where she became the wife of C. A. Walling. She was the mother of four children, in a happy and luxurious home, when the alarm of war was sounded, and her husband joined the Confederate army. The wife's patriotism and love for the Union was so pronounced that, in 1863, she was warned by the vigilance committee to "leave the country within a few hours." The heroic woman, with four little children, the oldest a mere baby, ordered the family carriage, and, with a brother eleven years of age for a driver, started through the wilds of Texas for the Union lines, with no chart or compass for her guide save the north star. The brave woman engineered her precious load for twenty-three days, and her joy at the first sight of the flag she loved so well repaid her for her trials. Upon learning that seven of her brothers were in the Union army, where they all fought and died, she determined to lecture in defense of the Stars and Stripes, and was so cordially received that, upon

being introduced to a large audience in Cooper Institute by Horace Greeley, he declared her "The greatest female speaker of the age." She delivered speeches in nearly all the large cities of the North. On 10th May, 1866, the United States Senate passed a resolution according to her the privilege of addressing that honorable body, which distinction was unprecedented in the history of our country. Before that distinguished body she delivered her famous argument on reconstruction. Surrounded by her children in her Texas home, as a last literary task, she is writing an autobiography of her ante-bellum days and of her subsequent trials and successes.

WALSWORTH, Mrs. Minnie Gow, poet, born in Dixon, IL, 25th July, 1859. Her family has given many persons to literary and professional pursuits. Her grandfather, John L. Gow, of Washington, PA, was a man of fine literary tastes and a writer both of poetry and prose. Her father, Alex M. Gow, was well known as a prominent educator and editor in Pennsylvania and Indiana. He was the author of "Good Morals and Gentle Manners," a book used in the public schools of the country. Before Minnie Gow was ten years of age, her poetic productions were numerous and showed a precocious imagination and unusual grace of expression. She is a graduate of Washington Female Seminary. On 4th December, 1891, she became the wife of Edgar Douglas Walsworth, of Fontanelle, IA, and their home is in that town. She has been a contributor to the New York "Independent," "Interior," "St. Nicholas," "Wide Awake," "Literary Life" and other periodicals.

WALTER, Mrs. Carrie Stevens, educator and poet, born in Savannah, MO, 27th April, 1846. She went to the Pacific coast with her parents ten years later, and has since lived in California. She inherited her poetic talent from her father, the late Josiah E. Stevens, a man of gentle, imaginative temperament, who was at one time a leading Mason and prominent politician of California. Carrie is the oldest of six children, and at an early age showed her leaning toward literary pursuits. She was carefully educated in the Oakland Seminary, and at eighteen years of age was the valedictorian of the first graduating class of that institution. Many of her verses had already found their way into leading periodicals of the coast. She soon achieved a popularity that was unique, even in that period of exaggerated personality in California's social circles. Some years ago she entered the communion of the Roman Catholic Church. Her maternal love has found expression in numerous poems of exquisite tenderness. It is this sympathetic appreciation of children that has made Mrs. Walter one of California's most successful teachers. Several years ago she laid aside her school-work, in which she had labored for twenty years, and has since devoted to literature all the time and strength she could spare from the care of her four children. In 1886 her "Santa Barbara Idyl" was published in book form. She has done and is now doing much newspaper and magazine work. In her prose productions her descriptions of California scenery are inimitable. Her present home is in Santa Clara county.

WALTON, Mrs. Electa Noble Lincoln, educator, lecturer and woman suffragist, born in Watertown, NY, 12th May, 1824. She was the youngest daughter of Martin and Susan Freeman Lincoln, with whom at the age of two she removed to Lancaster, MA. She resided afterward in Roxbury, and later in Boston. Under the pastoral care of Dr. Nathaniel Thayer, of Lancaster, and Dr. George Putnam, of Roxbury, she early assented to the doctrines of Unitarianism. During the ministration of Rev. J. T. Sargent and under the impulse occasioned by the preaching of Rev. Theodore Parker, she devoted herself to religious work. Her first and principal teacher was her father. In her seventeenth year she entered the State Normal School in Lexington, MA, and was graduated. She was immediately elected assistant in the Franklin school, Boston. After teaching there a few weeks, she was appointed assistant in her alma mater; to which she returned and taught successively under Mr. May, Mr. Peirce and Mr. Eben S. Stearns. In the interregnum between the resignation of Mr. Peirce and the accession of Mr. Stearns, she served as principal of the school. It was the expressed wish of Mr. Peirce that Miss Lincoln should be his successor, but such a radical innovation was not entertained with favor by the author-

ities, and she continued as assistant until she became the wife of George A. Walton, of Lawrence, MA, in August, 1850. She has had five children, of whom three are living, Harriet Peirce, wife of judge James R. Dunbar, of the Massachusetts superior court, Dr. George L. Walton, neurologist, Boston, and Alice Walton, Ph.D., at present, 1892, a student in Germany. After her marriage Mrs. Walton devoted her spare time to benevolent and philanthropic enterprises, and was always a leader in church and charitable work. She defended the Sanitary Commission when it was aspersed, turning the sympathies of the Lawrence people toward it and organizing the whole community into a body of co-laborers with the army in the field. She received thorough instruction in vocal culture from Professor James E. Murdock and William Russell. She was employed for years as a teacher of reading and vocal training in the teachers' institutes of Massachusetts. She has taught in the State Normal Institute of Virginia, and for five successive years, by invitation of Gen. Armstrong, conducted a teachers' institute of the graduating class in Hampton. She was co-author with her husband of a series of arithmetics. Her belief in the equal right of woman with man to be rated at her worth and to be credited with her work was intensified by the decision of the publishers, that her name should be withheld as co-author of the arithmetics. From being simply a believer in the right of woman suffrage, she became an earnest advocate for the complete enfranchisement of woman. She was always a zealous advocate of temperance and during a residence in Westfield held the office of president of the Woman's Christian Temperance Union of that town. Since her removal to West Newton, MA, where she now resides, she has been most actively interested in promoting woman suffrage, believing that through woman suffrage the cause of temperance and kindred reforms may be best advanced. She is an officer of the Massachusetts Woman Suffrage Association, an active member and director in the New England Women's Educational Club of Boston, and has been president of the West Newton Woman's Educational Club since its organization in 1880. Though not a prolific writer, she sometimes contributes to the press. She is an interesting speaker and an occasional lecturer upon literary and philanthropic subjects.

WALTON, Mrs. Sarah Stokes, poet and artist, born in Philadelphia, PA, 12th February, 1844. She is the third living child of Charles Crawford Dunn, sr., and Helen Struthers, his wife. Her ancestors on the male side originally were from the south of England. Her father's father, James Lorraine Dunn, a prominent lawyer of central Pennsylvania, was born in 1783, on the old homestead, located on the Chester river, Kent county, MD, where the family had lived for nearly one-hundred-fifty years prior to his birth. Mr. Dunn was the descendant in direct line from Sir Michael Dunn, an Englishman, who came to this country with the first Lord Calvert. On her mother's side Mrs. Walton is of Scotch descent. Her mother was the daughter of the late John Struthers, of Edinburgh, Scotland, more recently one of Philadelphia's successful business men. From her sixth to her tenth year Sarah attended a private school kept by Miss Sarah James. In, the spring of 1854 her father purchased a farm on the Delaware river, where he built their beautiful home, "Magnolia Hall." Her studies were continued in the Farnum preparatory school, Beverly, NJ. She was exceedingly fond of books, and remained in that school until 1858, when, at the age of fourteen years, her school days were brought to a close, as the duties of her home called on her with a strength that was irresistible. About the close of the Civil War some business affairs of importance required her father's presence in Washington, DC, for an indefinite time. From "Magnolia Hall" her family moved to Philadelphia, where she remained until October, 1866, when she became the wife of Louis N. Walton, a gentleman of good family, a Philadelphian by birth, but at that time doing business in Lexington, KY, to which place the newly wedded couple went. From that union there are two living children, a daughter and a son. Her husband's business affairs called him to Philadelphia in the course of three years, and there the family remained a short time. From that city she moved to Beverly, NJ, where they settled permanently. From her youth Mrs. Walton has been a member of the Protestant Episcopal Church, and she is prominent in everything that will advance the interests of the church and its people.

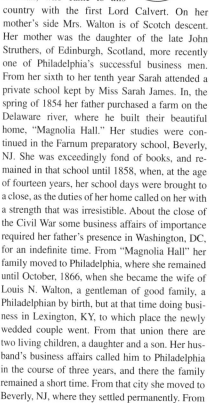

WALWORTH, Mrs. Ellen Hardin, author, educator and poet, born in Jacksonville, IL, 20th October, 1832. She is the daughter of John J. Hardin, a well-known lawyer, politician and soldier. He was the friend of Lincoln, Logan, Baker, Douglas and other renowned men of that time. He was in the Black Hawk War. He led the first Illinois regiment to the Mexican War, and was killed in the battle of Buena Vista. His strong character and intellectual qualities were transmitted to his oldest child, Mrs. Walworth. In 1851 her mother became the wife of Chancellor Reuben H. Walworth, of New York. When Chancellor Walworth went west to marry the mother, he took with him his gifted young son, Mansfield Tracy, afterward known as the author of many novels of the romantic school. The son captivated the fancy of Miss Hardin, a courtship followed, and they were married 29th July, 1852, in Saratoga Springs, NY, after he had finished his law studies in Cambridge. The young couple continued to reside in the family homestead, in Saratoga Springs, with the father and mother. Sons and daughters were born to them, and to the outside world no lives could seem more fair and smooth; but storms were gathering, which culminated with the disasters of the Civil War. Trouble and tragedy filled the life of Mrs. Walworth for many years, in which she held her children closely around her, carrying forward their education under the greatest difficulties. The older children were sent to college and the younger ones taught at home. In 1871 she established a boarding and day school in the homestead, and, with one interruption only, continued it until 1887. At that time the death of her oldest son and a temporary failure of her own health caused her to close the school. During those years she had been elected a member of the board of education in Saratoga, being one of the very first women for whom the school franchise was exercised. She served for three years, and by her energy and ability introduced many improvements in the public school system of the place. She was elected a trustee of the Saratoga Monument Association, and is chairman of important committees in that organization. By her personal exertions she has had erected many historical tablets on the battlefields of Saratoga. She has published numerous historical articles in the leading magazines, and has read papers before the Society for the Advancement of Natural Science, of which she is a member. In the interest of natural science she was largely instrumental in the founding of the Art and Science Field Club in Saratoga, which did much active service. She was vice-president of the Society of Decorative Art of New York City, and she succeeded in taking artists of the first order from Boston and other cities to Saratoga, and thus promoted the advancement of art in northern New York. She was for twelve years president of the Shakespeare Society of Saratoga, which is, with one exception, believed to be the oldest society devoted exclusively to Shakespeare in this country. In 1889 she went to Washington, DC, to make a winter home in a milder climate, and there she pursues her literary work. She has compiled a "History of the Saratoga Monument Association," which is published with other original material that shows historical Saratoga in an instructive and attractive form. She is engaged on a biography of Robert R. Livingston, first chancellor of the State of New York. She is the author of many fugitive poems, soon to be collected and published in a volume. She is a life member of the American Historical Association, and is actively concerned in its work. She is one of the founders and active officers of the National Society of the Daughters of the American Revolution, and she is editor of the "American Monthly Magazine," a successful publication of that society. Her time and labor are given to historical subjects, which may be pursued with unusual facility in the national capital. Her summer home is still in Saratoga Springs.

WALWORTH, Mrs. Jeannette Ritchie Hadermann, author, born in Philadelphia, PA, 22nd February, 1835. Her father was Charles Julius Hadermann, a German baron, who was a president of Jefferson College. He removed his family to Natchez, MS, where he died. The family then moved to Louisiana, and Jeannette, who had been carefully educated, became a governess at the age of sixteen years. At an early age she became the wife of Major Douglas Walworth, of Natchez. They lived for a time on his plantation in southern Kansas, and thence moved to Memphis, TN. They next removed to New York City, where she now lives. She has contributed many stories to newspapers and periodicals. Her published works are: "Forgiven at Last" (1870), "The Silent Witness" (1871), "Dead Men's Shoes" (1872), "Heavy Yokes" (1874), "Nobody's Business" (1878), "The Bar Sinister" (1885), "Without Blemish" (1885), "Scruples" (1886), "At Bay" (1887), "The New Man at Rossmere" (1887), "Southern Silhouettes" (1887)," True to Herself" (1888), "That Girl from Texas" (1888), "Splendid Egotist" (1889) and "The Little Radical" (1890).

WARD, Mrs. Elizabeth Stuart Phelps, author, born in Boston, MA, 31st August, 1844. Her father was Rev. Austin Phelps, professor of sacred rhetoric in Andover Theological Seminary. The family removed from Boston to Andover in 1848, and lived there until 1890. Professor Phelps was elected president of the seminary in 1869, and in 1879 he became professor emeritus. Elizabeth was a precocious, imaginative child, and her education was liberal and thorough. Her mother, Mrs. Elizabeth Stuart Phelps, was an author of note. After the death of her mother, in 1852, Miss Phelps, who had been christened with another name, took her mother's name in full. She began to publish sketches and stories in her thirteenth year, and her literary work in Andover was mingled with charitable, temperance and general reform work. In 1876 she delivered a course of lectures in the Boston University. Her published works are: "Ellen's Idol" (1864); "Up Hill" (1865); "The Tiny Series" (4 volumes, 1866 to 1869); "The Gypsy Series" (4 volumes, 1866 to 1869); "Mercy Gliddon's Work" (1866); "I Don't Know How" (1867); "The Gates Ajar," twenty editions in the first year (1868); "Men, Women and Ghosts" (1869); "Hedged In" (1870); "The Silent Partner" (1870); "The Trotty Book" (1870); "Trotty's Wedding Tour" (1873); "What to Wear" (1873); "Poetic Studies" (1875); "The Story of Avis" (1877); "My Cousin and I" (1879); "Old Maids' Paradise" (1879); "Sealed Orders" (1879);

"Friends, a Duet" (1881); "Beyond the Gates" (1883); "Dr. Zay" (1884); "The Gates Between" (1887); "Jack the Fisherman" (1887); "The Struggle for Immortality," essays; "Poetic Studies," and "Songs of the Silent World." Besides her books, she has written many sketches, stories and poems for "Harper's Magazine," "Atlantic Monthly," "Youth's Companion" and other periodicals. Her most famous work is "The Gates Ajar," which has passed through many large editions in the United States and Great Britain, and was translated into several European languages. In October, 1888, she became the wife of Rev. Herbert D. Ward. Since then she has published "Fourteen to One," a volume of stories, and, in collaboration with her husband, "The Master of the Magicians" and "Come Forth." In the summer she and her husband live in East Gloucester, MA, and in the winter their home is in Newton Highlands. Her productions throughout are marked by elevated spirit and thoughtfulness. She is interested in all philanthropic work, and she gives much time, labor and money for benevolent interests. Her circle of readers is a large one and is constantly growing.

WARD, Mrs. Genevieve, singer and actor, born in New York, NY, 27th March, 1833. She is a granddaughter of Gideon Lee. Her full maiden name was Lucia Genoveva Teresa, and the name by which she is known is only her stage-name. In childhood she lived in France and Italy. In 1848 her fine voice attracted the attention of Rossini, who trained her in music. She sang in "Lucrezia Borgia," in La Scala, Milan, and afterward in Bergamo and Paris. In London, England, she sang in English opera. In December, 1851, she sang in "Messiah," in London. She became the wife of Count Constantine Guerbel, a Russian officer, before she went upon the operatic stage, and for a time she used the name Madame Guerrabella on the bills. In 1862 she gave Italian operas in London, and in that year she came to the United States. She sang in New York, Philadelphia and Havana, Cuba. She was ill with diphtheria and lost her singing voice. She then gave vocal lessons in New York for several years and prepared for the dramatic stage. She was coldly received in New York City. In 1873 she went to England, and on 1st October made her début as Lady Macbeth in Manchester. She succeeded and added other standard tragedies to her list, and played successfully in all the larger English and Irish towns. In 1877 she went to Paris to study with François Joseph Regnier, and there she played a French version of Macbeth so successfully that she was invited to join the Comédie Française. She then repeated her success in London, and in 1878 she appeared in New York City. In 1879 she returned to London, and since then she has played in England and the United States with great success. In 1882 she started on a tour of the world, which was ended in November, 1885. She then became the manager of the Lyceum Theater in London. In 1888 she retired from the stage.

WARD, Miss Mary E., poet, born in North Danville, VT, 2nd May, 1843. The farm which has always been her home is the one to which her grandfather removed, when her father, now a man of eighty-one, was a boy less, than three years of age. Her mother was Amanda Willard, a granddaughter of Rev. Elijah Willard, of Dublin, NH, a "minute man" and chaplain in the Revolution. Her mother was Mary's first and best teacher. The love of poetry was a birthright. She could recite many hymns before she could read. She wrote her first poem in the summer following her thirteenth birthday, and since then she has written much. She has poems in "Poets and Poetry of Vermont," and has contributed to the "Vermont Chronicle" and other State papers, the "Golden Rule," "Union Signal" and others. She has a poem in "Woman in Sacred Song." She is now living in North Danville, VT.

WARD, Mrs. May Alden, author, born in Mechanicsburg, OH, 1st March, 1853. She is in the sixth generation from John and Priscilla Alden. As a school-girl her favorite studies were literature and the languages. At the age of nineteen she was graduated from the Ohio Wesleyan University, and one year later, in 1873, she became the wife of Rev. William G. Ward. Numerous translations and newspaper and magazine articles gave early evidence of Mrs. Ward's versatility. Her special liking for studies in Italian, French and German literature was strengthened by two years of travel in Europe, and in 1887 she published a comprehensive and attractive life of Dante, which at once won for her high rank as a thorough scholar and discriminating and graphic biographer. She issued in 1891 a life of Petrarch, no less fascinating than its predecessor. She has achieved popularity as a parlor lecturer. Her series of lectures on French and German literature was one of the most entertaining literary features of the season before her departure from her home in Cleveland, OH. A volume of essays on those subjects is to be issued, and a course of lectures on the early life and literature of New England is of yet more recent preparation. During her residence in Cleveland, she was a member of the Ohio Woman's Press Association, and was made president of the East End Conversational Club. Her home is now in Franklin, MA, where she is in touch with many of the literary circles of the East, while prosecuting her chosen work.

WARE, Mrs. Mary, poet, born in Monroe county, TN, 11th April, 1828. Her maiden name was Mary Harris, a name that has long been prominent in southern literature. Her early youth was spent amid the beautiful scenery of east Tennessee, and to the charm of her surroundings was added the intellectual companionship of a brother, Edmund K. Harris, whose poetic gifts were of an order that gave promise of a brilliant future, and the loving instruction of a father, who was not only eminent as a lawyer, but possessed discriminating literary taste. Just as she reached womanhood, her parents moved to Shelby county, AL, to which State her brother had preceded them, and he had already begun a successful literary career, when his sudden death in Mobile threw a shadow across the life of the sister. Her verses have more than sustained the merit they early

promised. They have been published by all the leading magazines and periodicals of the South, many of which belonged to ante-bellum days. "The South" published in New York City contained her contributions for twenty years. In 1863 she became the wife of Horace Ware, who was born in Lynn, MA, but reared in the South and widely known as a pioneer in the development of the iron industries of Alabama. Mr. Ware died in July, 1890, and Mrs. Ware has since resided in Birmingham, AL, where her home circle is brightened by the presence of four nieces, children of a surviving brother. Besides poetry she has written some interesting Indian legends, and a few romances further show her varied gift.

WARNER, Mrs. Marion E. Knowlton, poet and story writer, born in Geneva, OH, 15th June, 1839. She is a lifelong resident of the Western Reserve of Ohio, near Lake Erie. Her home is in Unionville, Lake county. A lineal descendant of the original Dutch of New York and of those who bore honorable part in the nation's struggle for liberty and independence, she inherits many strong traits of character. She in early life gave evidence of the literary instinct, and she was not long in developing a taste for standard literature that has been abundantly gratified. At the age of eighteen her first story was published in the Cleveland "Gleaner," followed by others at frequent intervals. Her stories appeared in the local papers, giving evidence of more than average ability and attracting attention. About the same time she began to write poetry. Though afflicted with oft-recurring and severe illness, and though since the demise of her husband some years ago she has been occupied with the care of a large portion of his estate and with the guardianship of her young daughter, still she has found time for literary pursuits, and has contributed a collection of poems, published from time to time, generally over the signature "M. E. W."

WARREN, Mrs. Mary Evalin, author and lecturer, born in Galway, NY, 14th March, 1829. On 26th April, 1847, she became the wife of George Warren, in the town of Balston. They moved to

Wisconsin and settled on a farm purchased directly from the government, where they now reside. The farm is situated near the village of Fox Lake. Mrs. Warren and her husband united with the Baptist Church in Fox Lake in 1859, and have had a continuous membership since that time. She has been for many years a faithful worker in the church, especially prominent in connection with the cause of home and foreign missions. She has taken great interest in Wayland University, the Baptist College in Beaver Dam, WI, and has furnished money to erect a dormitory for girls, which is called "Warren Cottage." Three sons were born to this couple, and one girl who died in infancy. Not satisfied with severe toil incident to "getting on in the world" in a new country, her kindly heart warmed to the needs of those less fortunate. She reared and cared for six motherless girls, at different periods, until most of them have found homes of their own. She has been for many years prominent intemperance reform. She joined the Good Templar Order in 1878. She has filled all subordinate lodge offices, is prominent to this day in district lodges, has filled all the offices in the grand lodge to which women usually aspire, and as grand vice-templar several terms has lectured to large audiences in nearly all parts of the State. She has attended several sessions of the right worthy grand lodge and filled several important offices of honor and trust therein. Wherever Good Templary is known in all the civilized world, she is honored because of her work for the good of mankind. She has been a member of the Woman's Christian Temperance Union ever since it was organized, and takes a deep interest in its success. She is a prominent member of the State Agricultural Society, and on invitation has furnished several papers at the annual meetings of the society. She has written and had published three books, two in pamphlet form, entitled "Our Laurels" and "Little Jakie, the Boot-Black," and a large volume in cloth entitled "Compensation," which has been widely read. Politically she was a radical Republican until long after the war, but for the past few years she has been identified with the Prohibition party. She is a woman suffragist. She is equally prominent as author, lecturer, church member, representative and officer in societies, home-keeper, neighbor and friend.

WASHINGTON, Mrs. Lucy H., poet and temperance reformer, born in Whiting, VT, 4th January, 1835. Her maiden name was Lucy Hall Walker. She is descended from New England ancestry running back to 1642. Her paternal lineage is traced to Deacon Philip Walker, of Rehoboth, MA, one of the founders of the commonwealth and also one of the principal characters in the bloody drama of King Philip's War. On her maternal side her descent is from Samuel Gile, one of the eleven first settlers of Haverhill, MA, in 1640. From her mother she inherited a love for the beautiful in nature and an ear and soul attuned to song. Her early educational advantages were such as the common school, select school and academy of her native State afforded. Her first printed verses appeared at the age of fourteen. With active intellect and strong ambitions, she resolved to enter upon a wider course of study, and became a pupil in Clover Street Seminary, Rochester, NY, where she was graduated with honors in 1856. In the seminary her talent met cordial recognition, and the aid of her muse was often invoked for special occasions. From that time her verses have frequently appeared, with occasional prose sketches. After graduation she devoted three years to teaching and was at the time of her marriage preceptress of the Collegiate Institute in Brockport, NY. Her husband, Rev. S. Washington, a graduate of Rochester University and of Rochester Theological Seminary, has during his professional life served prominent churches in both eastern and western States, and is now pastor of the Baptist Church in Port Jervis, NY. In Jacksonville, IL, in 1874, Mrs. Washington was made a leader in the crusade movement, and in response to the needs of the hour was brought into public speaking. Her persuasive methods, Christian spirit and eloquent language made her at once an effective speaker, acceptable to all classes. Her first address in temperance work, outside of her own city, was given in the Hall of Representatives in Springfield, IL. Commendatory press reports brought her to extended public notice, led to repeated and urgent calls and opened a door to service which has never been closed. During the succeeding years she has in various official capacities been largely engaged in Woman's Christian Temperance Union work, having given addresses in twenty-four States and extended her labors from the Atlantic to the Pacific. In the great campaigns for constitutional prohibition in Iowa, Kansas, Maine and other States, she has borne a helpful part. In difficult emergencies her electric utterance has been decisive of interests great and imperiled. With equally vigorous body and mind she has yet much history to make. She is the mother of four children, a son and three daughters, all finely educated and worthy of the parents who have so planned for their care as to enable their mother to devote much time to public work. In 1887 she published "Echoes of Song," a volume containing numerous selections from her poetical writings from early girlhood. She has subsequently added many contributions of merit, which, with selections from her first volume, were published under the title of "Memory's Casket" (Buffalo, 1891). She has contributed to the "Magazine of Poetry," and many other periodicals, and some of her hymns have been sung throughout the country.

WASHINGTON, Mrs. Martha, wife of George Washington, first President of the United States, born in New Kent county, VA, in May, 1732, and died in Mt. Vernon, VA, 22nd May, 1802. She was a daughter of Colonel John Dandridge, a wealthy planter. She was educated by private teachers. She was an accomplished performer on the spinet, and her education covered all the branches usually learned by the young women. of her day. In 1747 she was introduced to the vice-regal court, during the administration of Sir William Gooch. In June, 1749, she became the wife of Daniel Parke Custis, a wealthy planter. They settled in Mr. Custis' home, the "White House," on Pamunkey river, where they lived a life of refinement in the Virginia fashion. Four children were born to them, two of whom died in infancy. Mr. Custis died in 1757, leaving his widow one of the wealthiest women in Virginia. In the following year Mrs. Custis met George Washington, then a colonel, and in May, 1758, they became engaged. They were married in January, 1759, after Colonel Washington returned from his northern campaign. After their brilliant wedding, they settled in

Mount Vernon, and for seventeen years they lived in the style of aristocratic English people, entertaining much and taking the lead in all social affairs. Mrs. Washington sympathized with her husband in his patriotic resistance to British oppression and injustice. After he was made commander-in-chief, her life was full of care. In 1775 she joined him in Cambridge, MA, and afterward accompanied him to New York and Philadelphia, and joined him in camp wherever it was possible. During the severe winter in Valley Forge she shared the privations of the soldiers and worked daily from morning till night, providing comforts for the sick soldiers. During the war she discarded her rich dresses and wore only garments spun and woven by her servants in Mount Vernon. At a ball in New Jersey, given in her honor, she wore a homespun suit. She left the camp for the last time when General Washington was stationed in Newburg, NY, in 1782. When she became mistress of the executive mansion in New York City, she was fifty-seven years old, and was still a beautiful woman of dignity and sauvity of manner. Her social régime was brilliant in the extreme. During President Washington's second term they lived in Philadelphia. She disliked official life and was pleased when, in 1796, President Washington refused a third election to the presidency. They retired to Mount Vernon, where they lived the rest of their days. Before her death she destroyed her

entire correspondence with her husband, not wishing that their confidences should be seen by other eyes.

WASHINGTON, Mrs. Mary, mother of George Washington, the first President of the United States, born in Westmoreland county, VA, about 1713, and died in 1789. Her maiden name was Mary Ball, and her descent was English. On 6th March, 1730, she became the wife of Augustine Washington, the second son of Lawrence Washington and the grandson of John Washington, the first of the family to come from England to the Colonies. He purchased lands in Westmoreland county, became a wealthy planter, and was successively a county magistrate, a member of the house of burgesses, and colonel of the Virginia forces that drove away the invading Seneca Indians. In honor of his public services and private character, the parish in which he lived was named Washington. There his son, Lawrence, and his grandson, Augustine, were born. Augustine Washington was married twice. By his first wife he had four children, two of whom, Lawrence and Augustine, outlived their mother, who died in 1728. By his second wife, Mary Ball, he was the father of the immortal George Washington, who was the first child of his second marriage. Mrs. Mary Washington was a devoted mother, and her son George was a most faithful and affectionate son. He was born 22nd February, 1732, and his father died in 1743, leaving a family of five children for his widow to rear. She took the management of her estate into her own hands, and supervised the education of her children. To her George Washington owed as much as any other great man of history ever owed to a woman. While he was absent in the army, for nearly seven years, she managed the home and kept up the estate, and when the victory was won and Cornwallis had surrendered, he visited his aged mother. She consented to appear in a ball given in Fredericksburg in honor of her son, and she surprised the foreigners by her simple dress and quiet dignity. One of her most earnest commendations of her illustrious son was that "George had always been a good son." She lived to see him reach the proudest position in the newborn nation. He bade her farewell for the last time in the home of her childhood, in Stafford county, across the Rappahannock from Fredericksburg, where his father had purchased an estate several years before his death.

The parting was affectionate, and the venerable woman died shortly afterward, too suddenly to make it possible for her son to reach her. Mary Washington, more than any other one woman, is to be remembered for having given to the world one of the greatest men of history. Her simple virtues were reflected in her glorious son, and the name of George Washington will never be mentioned without calling up pleasant thoughts of the noble, simple mother who gave him birth—Mary Washington.

WATERS, Mrs. Clara Erskine Clement, author, born in St. Louis, MO, 28th August, 1834. She is the daughter of John Erskine. Her first attempt at writing was made in a description of travel in 1868, and was called "A Simple Story of the Orient." It was printed for private circulation only. Mrs. Clement Waters has traveled extensively, and mostly from her own note books compiled "Legendary and Mythological Art" (Boston, 1870). That was followed by "Painters, Sculptors, Architects, Engravers and Their Works" (1873). These books were written while she was an invalid, and but for the voluminous notes that she had made, could not have been done at that time. Subsequently, with Lawrence Hutton, she prepared "Artists of the Nineteenth Century" (1879). Her other works are: "A History of Egypt" (1880); "Eleanor Maitland," a novel, (1881); "Life of Charlotte Cushman" (1882); "Painting for Beginners and Students" (New York, 1883); "Sculpture for Beginners and Students" (1885), and "Architecture," belonging to same series, (1886); "Christian Symbols and Stories of the Saints," prepared for Roman Catholics, edited by Katherine E. Conway and dedicated by permission to the Very Reverend Archbishop Williams (Boston, 1886), and "Stories of Art and Artists" (1887). She has also written occasionally for magazines and newspapers; has translated "Dosia's Daughter," by Henry Greville, and the "English Conferences" by Renan. For the benefit of various charities, societies and clubs, she has given lectures upon "Women Artists," "The History and Symbolism of the Cross," "Travel in the Holy Land," "Parsifal," "The Passion Play at Ober Ammergau" and "Dravidian Architecture." In 1852 Miss Erskine became the wife of James Hazeri Clement, who died, leaving four sons and one daughter. Her second husband is Edwin Forbes Waters, for many years publisher of the Boston "Advertiser," with whom, in 1883–84, she visited Japan, China and India for the first time, and, after an interval of eighteen years, made for the second time the journey across the Holy Land and ascended the Great Pyramid. She has lived twice in Italy for lengthy periods, and has visited all the countries of Europe, except Russia, again and again. Her home for many years has been in Boston, and is well known for its generous hospitality to friends and acquaintances from near and far.

WATSON, Mrs. Annah Robinson, author, was born in the Taylor homestead, near Louisville, KY. She was the daughter of Mrs. Louise Taylor Robinson and the grand-daughter of Hancock Taylor, a brother of President Zachariah Taylor. The two brothers spent their boyhood in the old house which was built by their father, Col. Richard Taylor, who moved with his family from Virginia to Kentucky while the future president was a child. Annah was a romantic, poetic, imaginative child. After some years of quiet life in the old homestead, her family moved to Louisville, and in that city and Chicago she was educated. Her studies covered a wide range, and, after completing her course, she entered society in Louisville. Her poetic bent became very strong, and she did much literary work. In 1870 she became the wife of James H. Watson, a son of Judge J. W. C. Watson, of Mississippi. In spite of domestic cares that have taken most of her time, she has continued to write, and her productions in both verse and prose have been widely copied. Her poem, "Baby's Mission," has gone over the earth and was included in the London, England, "Chatterbox." Several years ago, when the New York "Churchman" opened a contest for the best lullaby, she sent one, which was one of the five selected from the many hundreds that were sent. Besides the poems and stories which she has published over her own name, she has done much important work unsigned, including reviews and editorials. Her earliest married life was spent in Mississippi, but several years ago the family removed to Tennessee and settled in Memphis, where Mr. Watson is practicing law. She has been recently elected president of the Nineteenth Century Club, the largest woman's club in the South. She is a member of the Episcopal Church and an earnest worker in the charitable institutions of the city.

WATSON, Mrs. Elizabeth Lowe, lecturer, born in Solon, OH, 6th October, 1842. Her maiden name was Low, which was changed to Lowe by the younger members of the family. Her father was of Teutonic descent, born in New York, and her grandfather, of the Knickerbocker type, had large landed possessions in "Old Manhattan Town." Her mother was of Scotch stock. Her grandmother, Mary Daniels, was a remarkably intelligent woman, with a poetic, religious temperament possessed of psychic gifts, the nature of which was then a profound mystery. Mrs. Watson was the ninth child in a family of thirteen, ten of whom are living. At the age of eight, remarkable psychic phenomena, of a physical nature, were manifested through her, and a few years later she became developed as an "inspirational" speaker, so-called. At fourteen her public ministry began, attracting great crowds of people to hear her discussion upon religion and social ethics. She then, as in later years, often answered all kinds of questions from the audiences, and usually the subject of her lecture was chosen by a committee. In 1861 she became the wife of Jonathan Watson, one of the oil kings of Titusville, PA. She was a devoted wife and the mother of four children, only one of whom is living. For some years after her marriage she discontinued her public work, except to officiate at funerals. Recently she has resumed her ministry of love, and, removing to California, for seven or eight years she lectured nearly every Sunday in San Francisco, for much of the time as the regular pastor of the Religious and Philosophical Society of that city. She lectured in 1882 through Australia, attracting large audiences. Her recent lectures in Chicago and other parts of the East were successful. Her work is principally devoted to the elevation of mankind morally and spiritually, to moral, social and religious reform, including the advancement of woman in all proper directions. After meeting many reverses and bereavements, she finds herself now possessed of a productive fruit farm, "Sunny Brae," in Santa

Clara county, CA, which brings an annual income of between four-thousand and five-thousand dollars. She superintends the entire business.

WATSON, Mrs. Ellen Maria, church worker, born near Fayetteville, Washington county, AR, 31st December, 1842. She is a daughter of W. T. and Maria Anderson. Her parents went to Arkansas from Virginia. Her father was a Methodist minister, and in the lap of Methodism she and her two sisters were reared. Early in life she showed fondness for the reading and study of the Bible. She became a member of the Methodist Church at twelve years of age. At fifteen she became a teacher in the Sunday-school. Her father's income being meager, she turned her attention to music as a means of self-maintenance and help to her family. At sixteen years of age she was able to draw a comfortable income from her class in vocal and instrumental music. In 1861 she became the wife of B. F. Perkins, a native of North Carolina, whose death eight months after, in the Confederate Army, and the exigencies of war, left her a widow and penniless. She put aside her own fate in administering to the sorrows of others. She nursed the sick and the dying in hospitals and visited the prisoners. Firm in her convictions of the justice of the southern cause, she rendered aid wherever she could. The war over, having lost both father and husband, she accepted a situation as governess in the family of the Rev. L. D Mullins, a Methodist minister, near Memphis, TN, where she remained two years. In 1867 she became the wife of Rev. Samuel Watson, D.D., a man of great prominence in the Methodist Episcopal Church South. By this marriage she had two daughters and three sons, one daughter and two sons are living. During those years the most important work of her life was done. Her first effort in charitable lines was sewing, making and supervising the making of garments for the poor. Her first contributions were devoted to the employing of a Bible-reader to the poor and ignorant of the city, and clothing and food to the destitute. She has been prominent in the Woman's Christian Association, visiting cities, attending conventions, acquainting herself with methods

and plans of work corresponding to that which engaged her mind, and in which she has occupied the highest official position for ten years successively. A home for self-supporting and unprotected young women is a monument to her as its inaugurator. The Woman's Christian Temperance Union has in her a most devoted adherent and strong advocate, so far as the Christian basis of organization and of total abstinence extends. The Woman's Foreign Missionary movement of the Methodist Episcopal Church South feels her power in her consecration to the work. She has been the conference president twelve years in succession.

WATTS, Mrs. Margaret Anderson, temperance worker, born in a country place near Danvile, KY, 3rd September, 1832. She is the daughter of Hon. S. H. Anderson, a lawyer and orator of distinction, who died while he was a member of the House of Representatives in Washington, DC. On the maternal side she is a granddaughter of Judge William Owsley, who was the fourteenth governor of Kentucky and a man of the highest order of legal ability. Her ancestors run back to the Rev. John Owsley, who in 1660 was made rector of the Established Church in Glouston, England, in which place he served sixty years. His son, Thomas Owsley, came to the Colony of Virginia, in America, in 1694, and settled in Fairfax county. From his line came Amelia G. Owsley, the mother of Mrs. Watts. Both the Owsleys and Andersons were talented, educated people, and from them Margaret Anderson inherited her talents. She is the sixth child of her family, and ample means gave her fine educational advantages, her studies including classical learning and all the "accomplishments" of the day. She became the wife of Robert Augustine Watts in 1851. She has three children grown to maturity. The oldest daughter is the wife of Commander H. W. Mead, of the United States Navy, the second daughter is the wife of a Florida orange-grower, and the son is a successful engineer. She has always been a deep thinker on the most advanced social and religious topics, and she has occasionally published her views on woman in her political and civil relations. She was the first Kentucky woman who wrote and advocated the equal rights of woman before the law, and who argued for the higher education of woman. During the recent revision of the constitution of Kentucky, she was chosen one of six women to visit the capital and secure a hearing before the committees on education and municipalities, and on the woman's property rights bill, which was under discussion. She is a successful adult bible-class teacher. She says that she regards the bible as "the Magna Charta of a true Republic." She felt a strong interest in the Chautauqua movement instituted by Rev. John H. Vincent. In the second year of that movement she became a student of the Chautauqua Literary and Scientific Circle. She caught the true Chautauqua idea and has formed several successful circles in her own State. When the Woman's Crusade movement was initiated, she was living in Colorado, where business affairs called her husband for several years, but her hearty sympathies were with the women of Ohio and with those who formed the Woman's Christian Temperance Union, which she joined as soon as she returned to Louisville. She has worked actively in various departments of that organization, but her special work has been given to scientific temperance instruction in the public schools. Her work has attracted much attention and resulted in much positive good. She has recently assumed the national superintendency of police matrons. In the autumn of 1875 she, in connection with some other efficient women of the Woman's Christian Association of Louisville, established a Home for Friendless Women. She was the first secretary of the board of managers and its president for eight years. The work was begun with a few thousand dollars and has been sustained and carried on by gratuitous contributions from the Christian people of the city. Hundreds of outcast women have slept beneath its roof since its doors were opened. A new and spacious building has recently been erected. Mrs. Watts, in the fall of 1887, gave a course of lectures, treating woman from a standpoint of culture, affection, industry and philanthropy, before the Woman's Ethical Symposium of Louisville. Of late years she has given much study to metaphysics and scientific subjects, and is a member of the Metaphysical Association of Boston, MA. She now has enjoyment in the consciousness of having made a happy home for her husband and children. Music is one of her accomplishments, and it has formed a part of her home life. Her home, her neighbors, her State and her country have been the recipients of her thought, her loving heart and generous hand.

WEATHERBY, Mrs. Delia L., temperance reformer and author, born in Copely, OH, 7th June, 1843. Her father, Col. John C. Stearns, was a stanch, old-time abolitionist and temperance worker. She received an academic education and afterward taught school in her native town. In 1868 she became the wife of Rev. S. S. Weatherby, then a member of the North Ohio Conference of the Methodist Episcopal Church. In 1870 they removed to Baldwin, KS, where for nine years he served as professor of languages in Baker University. She was at one time called to the chair of mathematics in that university, but declined. In 1880 Mr. Weatherby entered the ministry again, and for seven years she shared with her husband the toils and duties of an itinerant life, until failing health compelled him to retire from active work, and she now lives in their country home, near LeRoy, KS. Inheriting the same disposition which made her father an abolitionist, she early became an active worker in the order of Good Templars. She could endure no compromise with intemperance, and wherever she has lived she has been distinguished as an advanced thinker and a pronounced prohibitionist. She was a candidate on the prohibition ticket in 1886 for county superintendent of public instruction in Coffey county. She was elected a lay delegate to the quadrennial meeting of the South Kansas Lay Conference of the Methodist Episcopal Church in 1888. In 1890 she was placed in nomination for the office of State superintendent of public instruction on the prohibition ticket. She has always taken a great interest in the cause of education. In 1890 she was unanimously elected clerk of the school board in her home district. She was an alternate delegate from the fourth congressional district of Kansas to the National Prohibition Convention in 1892, and also secured, the same year, for the second time by the same party, the nomination for the office of superintendent of public instruction in her own county. She belongs to the white ribbon army and has been the president of the Coffey County Woman's Christian Temperance Union for several years. She is superintendent of the press department of the Kansas Woman's Christian Temperance Union and State reporter for the "Union Signal." She is the mother of three children. Notwithstanding her household duties pressing for attention, she has for four years edited a temperance department in one of the country papers, and she frequently contributes to the press articles of prose and poetry, chiefly on the subject of temperance reformation.

WEBB, Miss Bertha, violinist, was born in North Bridgeton, ME. She comes from a musical family on both sides. From her earliest infancy she gave evidence of extraordinary talent and ability for music. It is related of her that she could hum a tune before she could enunciate a single word. Through her earlier years her musical training was fraught with difficulty. She lived in Portland, ME, with no teacher of the violin nearer than Boston. Once or twice a week, when only a child, she made her trips to that city, where Prof. Julius Eichberg gave her her first instruction. She was often called upon to play before audiences in Maine, and on one of these occasions her uncle, Dr. Hawkes, of New York City, was so impressed with her talent that he proposed that she should go to the metropolis, where she could pursue her literary and musical studies without interruption. She went and was at once placed under the care of the late Dr. Damrosch. After his death she studied with Prof. Listemann, Prof. Dannreuter, Prof. Bouis and Camilla Urso. For ten years she studied earnestly, and she is to-day an example of what a woman may accomplish by determined effort. She is well known in musical circles as one of the most conscientious and painstaking musicians in the country. She has played in nearly every city in the United States. During the past season she played two-hundred-fifty nights in succession, and more than a quarter of a million people listened to her playing. She now makes her home in New York City.

WEBB, Mrs. Ella Sturtevant, author, born in Cleveland, OH, 15th December, 1856. Her early years were spent in the country home of her grandparents, her father, Ezra Sturtevant, having died shortly after the birth of his only child. Her first story was written under a pen-name for a Chicago child's magazine, but most of her work has been upon domestic topics, in the treatment of which she is particularly successful. Her bright handling of commonplace themes has made her a welcome contributor to the "Homemaker" and "Good Housekeeping," and other household journals. She has been for two years upon the regular staff of "Leisure Hours." She is a member of the Ohio Woman's Press Club. She is the wife of Chandler L. Webb, of Cleveland, OH, and the mother of one daughter.

WEBSTER, Miss Helen L., professor of comparative philology in Wellesley College, was born in Boston, MA. In her childhood her family removed to Salem, MA, where she was educated in the public schools; graduated in the normal school. After graduation she taught for several years in the high school in Lynn, MA. Afterward she went to Zurich, where she entered the university. She studied there over three years, when she passed with the highest credit the examinations for the degree of Ph.D. She handed in to the faculty a dissertation entitled "Zur Gutturalfrage im Gotischen," which attracted general comment by its wide research and scholarly handling. After receiving her degree, she traveled in Europe for a time. In 1889 she returned to the United States, and in the winter of that year she lectured in Barnard College, in New York City. During the last half of that college year she taught in Vassar College. In 1890 the chair of comparative philology was established in Wellesley College, which position she was called to fill.

WEISS, Mrs. Susan Archer, poet, author and artist, born in Hanover county, VA, 14th February, 1835, on a plantation. Her maiden name was

Gladys Wallis.
From Photo Copyright, 1897, by B. J. Falk, New York.

Bertha Westbrook.
From Photo by Chickering, Boston.

Berenice Wheeler.
From Photo by Morrison, Chicago.

Talley. The family moved to Richmond, VA, when she was eight years old. When she was ten years old, she developed a remarkable talent for drawing, which her father took pains to cultivate. She manifested equal skill in watercolors and oil paintings. She became interested in the work of her cousin, the young sculptor, Alexander Gait, and spent many hours in his studio. One day he gave her a small block of plaster, out of which, without assistance or model, she cut with a pen-knife a female head so plainly the work of genius that Mr. Gait took it with him to Italy, where it was seen by Crawford and Greenough, who were enthusiastic in their desire that she should devote herself to sculpture, but her father's death hindered her from doing so. She was but eleven years of age when, by accident, some of her little verses fell under the observation of her father. He showed them to Benjamin B. Minor, editor of the "Southern Literary Messenger," who published them in his magazine, where in a few years her contributions attracted much attention. During the war she became the wife of Colonel Weiss, of the Union army, with whom she for some years resided in New York City. The marriage proved an unhappy one, and Mrs. Weiss obtained divorce and bent her energies to support herself and child. She contributed to New York newspapers, to "Harper's," "Scribner's" and other magazines, until incessant application to writing brought on a painful affection of the eyes, which for some years incapacitated her for the use of her pen. Of late years she has published little. She now resides with her son, in Richmond.

WELBORN, Mrs. May Eddins, journalist, born near Demopolis, AL, 25th February, 1860. She is the youngest child of a family of eight children. She was educated in the Judson Female Institute, Marion, AL, where she was graduated in 1876. Her first literary work was done a year before graduation, when she began to write for the children's department of the Louisville "Courier-Journal." The first work of Miss Eddins that attracted much attention were papers in the "Home and Farm." Those papers attracted the attention of one of the most noted agricultural editors and writers of the South, Col. Jeff Welborn, who, learning after much effort the writer's name, for Miss Eddins had written over a pen-name, went from Texas to Alabama to see the writer whose work had so pleased him. The writer her-

self pleased him even more than her work, and they were married 23rd October, 1890. Her suburban home, an experimental farm in New Boston, TX, is an ideal one for an agricultural writer and scientific farmer and his wife.

WELBY, Mrs. Amelia B. Coppuck, author, born in St. Michaeis, MD, 3rd February, 1819, and died in Louisville, KY, 3rd May, 1852. She removed with her family to Louisville in 1835. She received a careful education, and in 1838 she became the wife of George B. Welby, a merchant of Louisville. In 1837, under the pen-name "Amelia," she contributed a number of striking poems to the Louisville "Journal," and she soon acquired a reputation as a poet of high powers. She published in 1844 a small volume of poems, which quickly passed through several editions. It was republished in 1850, in New York, in enlarged form, with illustrations by Robert W. Weir. Mrs. Welby was a petite, slender woman, dark-eyed and brown-haired. Her work was notable for its delicacy of diction, its elevation of sentiment and its fineness of finish, and was widely copied by many leading journals.

WELCH, Miss Jane Meade, journalist and historical lecturer, was born in Buffalo, NY. She comes of New England stock. She received a good education and had the ambition to pursue a college course. In her sophomore year she was taken seriously ill, and her college course was abandoned perforce. After recovering her health she entered journalism. She began with a year of service as a general writer on the Buffalo "Express." She next joined the staff of the Buffalo "Courier" as society editor and occasional writer of editorial articles. She added to her duties the preparation and conduct of a woman's work column. She served on the "Courier" for ten years, and was the first woman in Buffalo to make a profession of journalism. She kept up her studies in history, and finally prepared a series of lectures on historical subjects, which she first delivered to friends in her own home. She next presented her lectures in the Chautauqua Assembly, and her success was instant. She was at once engaged for the next year to deliver a series of lectures on American history in the university extension course. In February, 1891, she gave a series of six lectures in the Berkeley Lyceum Theater in New York City, and success crowned her venture.

WELLS, Mrs. Charlotte Fowler, phrenologist and publisher, born in Cohocton, Steuben county, NY, 14th August, 1814. She is the fourth in a family of eight children. Her father, Horace Fowler, was an able writer. Miss Fowler received most of her education in the district school, with only two winters, or six months, of instruction in the Franklin Academy. She is a self-taught woman, with her wide range of reading and thinking, her close observance of character, her mountain-born love of nature and her large-hearted tolerance. Her brothers, O. S. and L. N. Fowler, were among the first to examine and believe the doctrines of Gall and Spurzheim, and the present increasing interest in the science of phrenology is greatly the result of their lifelong labor. Their young sister, Charlotte, most carefully studied and became deeply interested in Spurzheim's works, teaching the first class in phrenology in this country, and thenceforth her life was devoted to the love and labor for humanity through unfolding its truths. Urged by her brothers, she closed her school and joined them in New York City in the work of establishing the present Fowler & Wells Publishing House. Possessing superior executive abilities, she was the oracle and moving spirit of the undertaking. In their early days of struggle and opposition, they would at times have abandoned the field and closed the office but for the young sister's inspiring presence. Timid, yet lion-hearted, she averted calamity and achieved success, until was established at length one of the most successful publishing houses in the city. When O. S. Fowler was in the lecture field and L. N. Fowler was establishing a branch in London, England, she had charge of all the large and complicated business in New York. In 1844 she became the wife of Samuel R. Wells, who was in the same year made a partner in the firm. They worked happily and harmoniously together for thirty-one years. She was left at different and long periods with entire control, while husband and brother were traveling for years through this and other countries, spreading the science and collecting the treasures for their valuable cabinet. When her husband died, in 1875, she was left entirely alone, the sole proprietor and manager for nine years, when a stock company was formed, now known as the Fowler and Wells Company, of which she is president. Her little enclosure in the office is a shrine, where unknown friends come from all parts of the world to take her hand. She goes to her office from her home on the Orange Mountain. She is vice-president and one of the instructors of the American Institute of Phrenology, which was incorporated in 1866. She has been active in every great enterprise for woman's advancement. She was one of the founders in 1863, and has ever since been one of the trustees, of the New York Medical College for Women. Never self-assertive, without a touch of vanity in her nature, she has declined nearly every conspicuous position, and yet has filled her life with kindly charities. Many a woman owes to her the timely aid, saving from despair, or relieving from financial disaster.

WELLS, Miss Mary Fletcher, philanthropist and educator, was born in Villenova, Chautauqua county, NY. Her father, Roderic McIntosh Wells, was of Scotch origin. She began to teach at fourteen years of age, still pursuing her studies. She taught successfully in high schools and seminaries in Indiana, and for several years was the associate editor of the "Indiana School Journal." Failing health obliged her to rest. When the Civil War broke out, she received the news with much seriousness. She saw, as by inspiration, that the war was to emancipate the slave, that the liberated slave must have teachers, and she must be one of those teachers. During the war she received a letter from President Lincoln, asking her to take charge of a contraband school near Washington. Her health was then insufficient, and she was obliged to decline. A few months later there came another call, to which she responded, and for nearly two years, in the hospital in Louisville, KY, she watched beside the sick and dying soldiers. With the close of the war came a renewal of the call to teach the freedmen, and she went to Athens, AL. She was cordially welcomed by Chaplain and Mrs. Anderson, and she had for her assistants Mrs. Anderson and Mr. Starkweather, a Wisconsin soldier. At the hour appointed for opening, there came in a multitude, three-hundred strong. Miss Wells remained at the head of Trinity School twenty-seven years. From the crude beginning in 1865 has been developed a flourishing institution, with boarding, industrial and normal departments, sending out every year many teachers, who do efficient work among their people. From that school, under the American Missionary Society, have grown a church and many auxiliary societies. Failing health has made rest and change imperative, and she is now living in her summer home in Chautauqua, where, in 1878, she was among the first to join the Chautauqua Literary and Scientific Circle. She was graduated in the class of 1882. She traveled with the Fisk Jubilee Singers the first four months of their introduction to the public.

WERTMAN, Mrs. Sarah Killgore, lawyer, born in Jefferson, Clinton county, IN, 1st March, 1843. She received from her parents, David and Elizabeth Killgore, a liberal education. She was graduated in Ladoga Seminary in 1862. She then engaged in teaching school for a number of years. She next began the study of law, and attended the law school in Chicago, IL, during 1869. Michigan University just then admitted women, and, on account of the greater convenience it afforded her, she went there during 1870. She was the first woman law student in Michigan University, and the first woman graduate in law of that school, in 1871. She was the first woman admitted to the supreme court of Michigan. Soon after she was taken sick and was an invalid for more than a year. Her naturally fragile body was long in recovering strength. She became the wife of J. S. Wertman, a practicing attorney, of Indianapolis, IN, 16th June, 1875. The statutes of Indiana required for admission to the bar "male citizens of good moral character," hence she was compelled to content herself with office work. In November, 1878, they changed their location to Ashland, OH. She has two living children, Shields K. and Helen M., and one baby, Clay, died in his infancy. For a number of years the higher duties of motherhood prevented her from actively engaging in her profession. As soon as practicable, she resumed her profession, and is now engaged with her husband in the practice of law and the business of abstracting in Ashland. She is a busy and successful woman, a consecrated Christian and a devoted wife and mother.

WEST, Mrs. Julia E. Houston, soprano singer, born in Ashburnham, MA, 22nd June, 1832. She is descended from the Treadwells, of Portsmouth, and other well-known families. Taste and talent for music were her inheritance from her father, who was a good general musician and 'cello player, and her mother, who was for several years the chief singer in Dr. Buckinersher's church, in  Portsmouth. At an early age her accurate ear and fine voice began to attract notice. She sang in public at fourteen, and at eighteen took the leading part when "The Song of the Bell" was given. in Fitchburg. Her singing attracted so much notice that she at once received an invitation from the organists, Bricker and Bancroft, to enter the quartet which they were directing in Boston. She sang for some years in Worcester, and in 1856 she accepted a place in Boston, in Dr. E. E. Hale's church. There she remained three years, when she accepted a call to the Old South Church. In 1867 she returned to Dr. Hale's church, where she remained until her withdrawal from church work, in 1881. The record of oratorio music in the principal cities of the country bears her name as that of one of its greatest exponents. During the war she was often heard in patriotic assemblies, and she sang in the "Ode to Saint Cecilia" at the dedication of the great organ in Music Hall, in the second jubilee in Boston, in the great celebration in that city of the Emancipation Proclamation, and lately in the festivities on the two-hundred-fiftieth anniversary of the foundation of Haverhill, MA. She has sung in oratorio in New York, Chicago, Philadelphia and Washington. She has appeared with Parepa, Formes, Adelaide Phillips, Nilsson, Guerrabella, Rudersdorf and many others. She visited Europe, where she studied with Randegger and Madame Dolby. She sang in a reception in Rev. Newman Hall's church, in London. Her voice is an extended mezzo-soprano of even quality. She was married in 1870 to James F. West, a well-known business man of Haverhill, MA, where she now resides.

WEST, Miss Mary Allen, journalist and temperance worker, born in Galesburg, IL, 13th July, 1837. Her parents were among the founders of Knox College, one of the earliest collegiate institutions in the Mississippi valley. Mary was a healthy, vigorous, studious girl, maturing early, both mentally and physically. She was prepared for college before she had reached the age for admission. She was graduated in her seventeenth year and at once began to teach school, which she then believed to be her life work. She was so successful in teaching and so influential in educational circles that she was twice elected to the office of superintendent of schools in Knox, her native county, being one of the first women to fill such a position in Illinois. She served in that capacity for nine years and resigned on accepting the presidency of the Illinois Woman's Christian Temperance Union. She attended many educational conventions and was a power in them, and continually wrote for school and other journals. She thus discovered to herself and others her marvelous capacity for almost unlimited hard work. Home duties were at that time pressing heavily, including as they did the care and nursing of an invalid mother and sister. She occupied a prominent social position, and her work included Sunday-school teaching. When the Civil War came, she worked earnestly in organizing women into aid societies to assist the Sanitary Commission. Her first editorial work was at long range, as she edited in Illinois the "Home Magazine," which was published nearly one-thousand miles away, in Philadelphia. Later she left the pen and the desk for active work in the temperance cause throughout the State. When the woman's crusade sounded the call of woman, the home and God against the saloon, her whole soul echoed the cry, and after the organization of the Woman's Christian Temperance Union she became an earnest worker in its ranks. She gave efficient aid in organizing the women of Illinois, and in a short time became their State president. In that office she traveled very extensively throughout Illinois and became familiar with the homes of the people. It was that knowledge of the inner life of thousands of homes, together with her intimate studies of children in the school-room, which efficiently supplemented her natural bias for the task of writing her helpful book for mothers, "Childhood, its Care and Culture." She

has written scores of leaflets and pamphlets, all strong, terse and full of meat, but that is her great work, and will long survive her. While she was State president of the Woman's Christian Temperance Union, she was often called upon to "help out" in the editorial labors of Mrs. Mary B. Willard, the editor of the "Signal," published in Chicago. Later it was merged with "Our Union," becoming the "Union Signal," under the editorship of Mrs. Willard. Before Mrs. Willard went to Germany to reside, Miss West removed to Chicago, and accepted the position of editor-in-chief, with Mrs. Elizabeth W. Andrew as her assistant. As editor of that paper, the organ of the national and the world's Woman's Christian Temperance Union, her responsibilities were immense, but they were always carried with a steady hand and an even head. She met the demands of her enormous constituency in a remarkable degree. A paper having a circulation of nearly one-hundred-thousand among earnest women, many of them in the front rank of intelligence and advancement of thought, and all of them on fire with an idea, needs judicious and strong, as well as thorough and comprehensive, editing. This the "Union Signal" has had, and the women of the Woman's Christian Temperance Union repeatedly, in the most emphatic manner, indorsed Miss West's policy and conduct of the paper. Soon after she went to Chicago to reside, some Chicago women, both writers and publishers, organized the Illinois Woman's Press Association, its avowed object being to provide a means of communication between woman writers, and to secure the benefits resulting from organized effort. Miss West was made president, and filled the position for several consecutive annual terms. Her work in that sphere was a unifying one. She brought into harmony many conflicting elements, and helped to carry the association through the perils which always beset the early years of an organization. She was a wise and practical leader, inaugurating effective branches of work, which have been of great value to the association. She was a member of the Chicago Woman's Club. She had no love for city life. Its rush and its roar tired her brain; its squalor, poverty, degradation and crime appalled her. She had an unusual capacity for vicarious suffering. The woes of others were her woes, the knowledge of injustice or cruelty wrung her heart. That made her an effective director of the Protective Agency for Women and Children, but the strain of that work proved too great, and she stepped outside its directorship, although remaining an ardent upholder of the agency. Her heart was in her Galesburg home, the home of her childhood and youth, and when she allowed herself a holiday, it was to spend a few days with the home folks, who were still the center of the universe to her. Miss West, in 1892, visited California, the Sandwich Islands and Japan in the interests of temperance work. She died in Kanazawa, Japan, 1st December, 1892.

WESTLAKE, Miss Kate Eva, editor, was born in Ingersoll, Canada. Her life was spent in the adjacent city of London. She is a Canadian by birth and in sentiment, though she comes of English parentage. Her first literary work, outside of occasional sketches for local newspapers, was a serial story entitled "Stranger Than Fiction," published in a western monthly magazine. She entered active journalistic work as sub-editor of the St. Thomas "Journal," which position she held until she assumed the editorship of the "Fireside Weekly," a family story paper published in Toronto, Ontario. Among the best known of her longer serial stories are "A Rolling Stone," "Eclipsed" and "A Previous Engagement." Two others of her stories have been published in book form in the United States and Canada, and it is, perhaps, in the field of fiction she does her best work, although her series of humorous sketches, written over the pen-name "Aunt Polly Wogg," is widely read and very popular. She is quiet and retiring, strongly sympathetic, with a keen sense of humor and a ready wit. In religion she is a Baptist, in politics a Liberal, and in all questions of progression and social reform she takes a warm interest.

WESTOVER, Miss Cynthia M., scientist, inventor and business woman, born in Afton, IA, 31st May, 1858. Her great-grandfather was Alexander Campbell, founder of the Campbellites. Her father is a descendant of the Westovers, of Virginia, who settled early in 1600 near the site where Richmond now stands, and her mother was from a well-known English family, named Lewis. Her father is a noted geologist and expert miner. From the age of four years, being a motherless girl, she accompanied him on all his prospecting tours from Mexico to British America. Naturally, from her early surroundings, she became an expert shot and horsewoman, and she also acquired an intimate knowledge of birds and flowers, the habits of wild animals and many other secrets of nature. After graduating from the State University of Colorado, she took a four-year course in a commercial college, where she was considered a skilled mathematician. In early womanhood she went to New York City to perfect her musical education, and after singing acceptably in several church choirs, she received an offer of a position in an opera. The practical side of her nature asserted itself, when she took the civil service examination for custom-house inspectors. She was promptly appointed and, with her usual force and energy, began to learn French, German and Italian, perfecting her Spanish and acquiring a general knowledge of languages, which placed her in an incredibly short space of time on speaking terms with most of the nationalities coming to our shore. Commissioner Beattie, of the street-cleaning department of New York City, appointed her his private secretary. She is the only woman who has held a position by appointment in any of the city departments. During the illness of the commissioner for several weeks, she managed successfully the affairs of the entire department. Many Italians were on the force, and for the first time in their experience they could air their grievances at headquarters. Lately she invented a cart for carrying and dumping dirt, for which the Parisian Academy of Inventors conferred upon her the title of Membre d' Honneur, with a diploma and a gold medal. She is joint author of a book entitled "Manhattan, Historic and Artistic," which was so favorably received that the first edition was exhausted in ten days. She is a newspaper writer, and secretary of the Woman's Press Club of New York City.

WETHERALD, Miss Agnes Ethelwyn, poet, novelist and journalist, was born in Rockwood, province of Ontario, Canada. Her parents were

Quakers. Her ancestry is English. She received a very careful and thorough education in a Friends' boarding-school in New York State. She showed literary talent in her youth. Although a Canadian by birth and citizenship, and a bright star among the rising authors of the Dominion of Canada, she is, by training, intellectual development and literary clientage, quite American. Some of her best work has appeared in American periodicals, such as the "Christian Union," the "Woman's Journal," the Chicago "Current," the "Magazine of Poetry" and various newspapers in the United States. Some of her stories were first published in the United States, and her novel, "An Algonquin Maiden," written conjointly with another Canadian author, was published in New York City. That novel was reprinted in England, and it has had a large sale in the United States, Canada and Great Britain. During the past few years she has devoted her time to the journals of Canada almost entirely. She has contributed largely to the "Week." Under the pen-name "Bel Thistlethwaite" she conducted for a long time a very successful woman's department in the Toronto "Globe." She contributed sketches, essays and poems to the "Canadian Monthly," while that magazine was in existence. The London, Canada, "Advertiser" and the Toronto "Saturday Night" have published a good deal of original matter from her pen. For several years she has been one of the conductors and editors of a woman's journal published in London, Ontario, called "Our Wives and Daughters." Her work shows, in prose, a vivid imagination, good sense, humor, clear judgment and acute powers of observation, and in poetry strong feeling, fine diction, marked creative powers, a musical ear and the true fire of the true poet. Miss Wetherald's home is in Fenwick, Ontario.

WETHERBEE, Miss Emily Greene, author, was born in Milford, NH, 6th January, 1845. She is a descendant of Gen. Nathanael Greene, of Revolutionary fame. Her earliest years were spent in Charlestown, MA, whence at the age of twelve she removed to Lawrence, MA, where she has since resided, with the exception of some years spent as a teacher in the public schools of Boston. She received her education in the schools of Lawrence, and since graduation, being of decided literary tastes, has improved all opportunities afforded for self-culture. She has been for many years one of the most successful teachers in the Lawrence high school. Poems from her pen have appeared from time to time in the "Journal," "Transcript" and "Globe," newspapers published in Boston, also in the New England "Journal of Education" and the publications of the American Institute of Instruction; but, though of a poetic temperament and having a keen perception of whatever is beautiful in nature and art, poetry has occupied by no means the larger share of her time and talent. Her contributions in the form of essays and lectures before many teachers' institutes, and before the Old Residents' Association, a very popular society of which Miss Wetherbee has been president for ten years, have been quite numerous and valuable. For many years she has been a constant contributor to the columns of the local press, her humorous papers attracting very general commendation. She has been one of the most important factors in the social and literary life of her city, and won fame and distinction not bounded by the limits of the commonwealth. She is an excellent reader, and has given public recitations to home audiences, and to many others in different parts of New England. Miss Wetherbee is president of the Lawrence Women's Club.

WETMORE, Mrs. Elizabeth Bisland, see BISLAND, MISS ELIZABETH.

WHEELER, Mrs. Cora Stuart, poet and author, born in Rockford, IL, 6th September, 1852. Her mother, Mrs. Harriet L. Norton, from whom her poetic talent was inherited, died when Cora was two years old. Both her parents were of New England birth, her mother of Scotch extraction. She was placed in school in the Emmittsburg, MD, convent, and later in the Convent of the Visitation Nuns in Georgetown, DC, where she passed the last years of the war, and was with her father in Ford's Theater, in Washington, when President Lincoln was shot. She witnessed the closing review of the Grand Army in Washington after the Civil War was ended. She was then sent to Howland College, Springport, NY, a school conducted under Quaker patronage. Eighteen months after leaving that college, she became the wife of a Moravian. Three children were born to them, one of whom, a daughter, survives. She lived among the Moravians two years, and then moved to the Southwest. Business reverses in 1882, while in Connecticut, threw her upon her own resources. She then began to give readings, and later wrote for the Hartford "Courant," in the office of Charles Dudley Warner. In 1884 she wrote her first story, "Twixt Cup and Lip," which took a prize in the Chicago "Tribune." Under the pen-name "Trebor Ohel" she contributed, the same year, regular articles to the Cleveland "Leader," the Kansas City "Journal," the Detroit "Post," "Tribune" and the "Free Press." She next took up biography, and wrote brief lives of prominent women. For one year she served as art critic on the Boston "Transcript." In November, 1885, with six other women, she formed the New England Women's Press Association. She was then, in addition to all other work, furnishing specials to the Boston "Advertiser" and "Record" and the Providence "Journal." In 1886 she wrote a series of social, dramatic and literary sketches for a Chicago syndicate, the A. N. Kellogg Company, and short stories, sketches and specials for the Hartford "Times," the Boston "Globe," New York "Herald" and other papers, which at once found favor. She edited the "Yankee Blade" at that time, and furnished largely the humor for the "Portfolio" of the "American Magazine." She won fame also as a household writer. Those of her biographical sketches which appear in the "Daughters of America" have been collected for publication in book form, as have also her short stories, "The Fardel's Christmas," "The Bings' Baby," "The White Arrow" and others. For over ten years she wrote under her own name. Since 1882 her permanent home was with her father and daughter in Boston, MA. Her best work, if not her most voluminous, was her poetry; but she showed a wide range of talent in all departments of prose. She was an industrious worker, and her home was the meeting place of literary persons of Boston. She published, from time to time, lyrics and verse in "Harper's Magazine," "Century," the "Ladies' Home Journal," "Youth's Companion," "Wide-Awake" and other literary publications. She lectured on "Authors Whom I Have Known," "Moravians as I Lived Among Them," "Cervantes," "Legends and Superstitions" and "Fallacies of

Family Life." In March, 1897, Mrs. Wheeler died while yet in the first prime of her literary work.

WHEELER, Miss Dora, artist, designer and decorator, born in Jamaica, Long Island, NY, 12th March, 1858. She is the daughter of Mrs. Candace Wheeler, well known for her work in developing the art of needlework in the United States. Miss Wheeler early showed her fine artistic talents. After receiving a liberal general education, she took up the study of art with William M. Chase, and next she went to Paris, France, where she studied with Guillaume Adolphe Bouguereau and other eminent artists. She painted a number of fine pictures, but she has devoted herself mainly to decorative designing. Her paintings include a series of portraits of American and English authors. Her decorative designs cover a wide range, including Christmas, Easter and countless fancy cards and many contributions to periodicals that publish illustrated articles. Her work is ranked with the best in its line. Her home is in New York City.

WHEELER, Mrs. Mary Sparkes, author, poet and preacher, born near Tintern Abbey, England, 21st June, 1835. At the age of six years she came with her parents to the United States and settled in Binghamton, NY, where her childhood and youth were spent. Her father was a man of rare intelligence and literary ability. Her mother was a woman of clear intellect and refined sensibilities, devoted to her family and her church. In childhood Mrs. Wheeler showed great fondness for books. In composition she excelled, and began to write for the press at a very early age. In former years she wrote more poetry than prose, and is the author of a volume entitled "Poems for the Fireside" (Cincinnati, 1888). Some of those have been republished and extensively used by elocutionists, especially her "Charge of the Rum Brigade." The lamented P. P. Bliss, Professors Sweeney, Kirkpatrick and others have set many of her poems to music. By request of Prof.

Sweeney, who composed the music, she wrote the two well-known soldiers' decoration hymns, "Peacefully Rest" and "Scatter Love's Beautiful Garlands Above Them." Before her marriage, 13th April, 1858, she was principal of the largest school in Binghamton, NY. She is the wife of Rev. Henry Wheeler, D.D., now of the Philadelphia Conference of the Methodist Episcopal Church. He is the author of "The Memory of the Just," "Methodism and the Temperance Reformation," "Rays of Light in the Valley of Sorrow," "Deaconesses: Ancient and Modern," and other works. They are united in heart, life and purpose. For many years after her marriage her life was mostly given to her children, who were in delicate health. Of the seven born to them, but three are now living. She has an innate love for the beautiful and is a lover of art, spending much time with her pencil and brush. In addition to "Poems for the Fireside," she is the author of two books, "Modern Cosmogony and the Bible" (New York, 1880); "The First Decade of the Woman's Foreign Missionary Society" (New York, 1884), and is a frequent contributor to periodical literature. She is president of the Woman's Foreign Missionary Society of Philadelphia, and national evangelist of the Woman's Christian Temperance Union. She is a member of the "National Lecture Bureau" of Chicago, IL. Her special delight is in preaching and conducting evangelistic services. She has spoken in many of the largest churches from Boston, MA, to Lincoln, NE. She has addressed large audiences in the open air in such summer resorts as Thousand Islands Park and Ocean Grove. She is an eloquent and forcible speaker. She was, in November, 1891, appointed superintendent of the World's Woman's Christian Temperance Union Mission. Her home is in Philadelphia, PA.

WHEELOCK, Mrs. Dora V., temperance worker, born in Calais, near Montpelier, VT, 1847. Her parents belonged to strong New England stock, with a mingling of French blood. Her great-grandfather was a captain in the Revolutionary War. Her father, a Christian minister, died when she was but three years old, leaving a family of small children, of whom she was the youngest. Her mother, a woman of ability

and force, proved equal to the charge. In 1865 Dora was graduated from the high school of Berlin, WI, and in July, three weeks after, became the wife of Oren N. Wheelock, a merchant of that city. They lived first in Iowa, and then in Wisconsin, till 1873, when they settled in Beatrice, NE, their present home. Mrs. Wheelock has always been interested in church, foreign missionary and school work. Since 1885 she has been an influential worker in the Woman's Christian Temperance Union, serving for several years as local president and three years as president of Gage county. In the spring of 1889 she was elected to a position on the board of education of Beatrice, which office she still holds. She is State superintendent of press work, and reporter for the "Union Signal" for Nebraska. She has written much and might have written more, but for the many paths in which duty called her. Her articles have appeared in the "Youth's Companion," "Union Signal" and various other publications. She is a variously gifted woman, a musician, both vocal and instrumental, and an artist who might have won recognition had she chosen to make painting a specialty. She is strong in the advocacy of woman's enfranchisement, though not known as a special worker in the field. She strives to be one of the advance guard in the cause of woman's progress.

WHEELOCK, Miss Lucy, educator, lecturer and author, born in Cambridge, VT, 1st February, 1857, in which town her father has been pastor for many years. She is of New England descent. Her education was begun under the care of her devoted mother, and was continued in Chauncy-Hall School, in Boston, where she became an excellent classical and German scholar and a writer of both prose and verse. Toward the close of her course in that school, she was drawn toward the education of very young children according to the kindergarten system, and took a thorough course of instruction to prepare herself for that work, receiving her diploma from the hand of Miss Elizabeth Peabody. She began to teach in the kindergarten that had been recently established in the Chauncy-Hall School, which position she has held for about ten years. Her work has made her a successful exponent and advocate of the system of Fröbel, which she is often called upon to expound before educational institutes and conventions. During the last four years she has taught a training class of candidates for the kindergarten service, coming from all parts of the Union and Canada, increasing in number from year to year. In addition to preparing numerous lectures, she has translated for "Barnard's Journal of Education" several important German works, and has contributed to other educational journals many practical articles. She has also translated and published several of Madame Johanna Spyri's popular stories for children, under the title of "Red Letter Tales." Her interest in young children early led her into Sunday-school work, and she soon became superintendent of a large primary class connected with the Berkeley Temple, in Boston. Her success in that work won her a reputation, and she is now a favorite speaker in Sunday-school institutes and gatherings, as well as those for general educational purposes in New England, Philadelphia, Pittsburgh, St. Louis, Chicago, Minneapolis, St. Paul and Montreal. She devotes a great part of her summer vacation to work of that sort. She also teaches a large class of adults in the Summer School of Methods in Martha's Vineyard, and gives a model lesson weekly, for eight months in the year, to a class of about two-hundred primary Sunday-school teachers. She publishes weekly in the "Congregationalist," "Hints to Primary Teachers," in the same line of work.

WHIPPLE, Miss M. Ella, physician, born in Batavia, IL, 20th January, 1851. Her parents were both of English descent, her father being a lineal descendant of the Whipple who was one of the signers of the Declaration of Independence. Her father was born and bred in Chautauqua county, NY, and her mother was born in New Jersey and bred in Orange county, NY. They both removed to Illinois, where they were married. In 1852 they started across the plains by ox team to Oregon, being six months on the way. Her mother was a teacher for many years and wrote for the papers of the day. Dr. Whipple's early childhood was spent on a farm. She was studious, industrious and persevering, and always at the head in school work. Her school-days were spent in Vancouver, Wash.,

where her parents went to educate their children. She was graduated in 1870 from Vancouver Seminary. Two years later she received the degree of B.S. from Willamette University, and had also completed the normal course in that institution. The nine years following were spent in teaching in the schools of Oregon and Washington, where she acquired the reputation of a very successful teacher. She was for two years preceptress of Baker City Academy, and later was principal of the Astoria public schools. Deciding to prepare herself for the medical profession, she gave up teaching and, after a three-year course of study, was graduated with honors from the medical department of the Willamette University in 1883. She received the advantage of special study and hospital practice in the sanitarium in Battle Creek, MI. She was an active practitioner in Vancouver, Wash., until her removal to Pasadena, CA, in 1888, where she is now located and in active practice. She has always been identified with the religious, temperance, philanthropic and educational interests of every place where she has resided. For ten years before the granting of equal suffrage Dr. Whipple was a stanch worker in the suffrage field and shared largely in the honors and benefits gained by suffrage in Washington. She was twice a delegate to the Clarke county Republican convention in 1884 and 1886, and twice a delegate to the Territorial Republican convention in the same year. In the first convention she was on the committee on resolutions, and in the second convention was chairman of the committee on platform. In the Clark county convention, in 1884, she was nominated for superintendent of public schools and was elected by a large majority, although there were three tickets in the field. She discharged the duties of her office in such a way as to win the respect and confidence of political opponents as well as friends. She has at different times occupied every official position to which a layman is eligible in the Methodist Episcopal Church, of which she is an earnest member, being thrice a delegate to the lay electoral conferences of 1874 and 1878. During her term as superintendent of public schools the Clarke County Normal Institute was organized, and still exists. She has been active in temperance reform, having been a Good Templar for many years and occupied nearly all the high and responsible positions in that order. She has been active in the Woman's Christian Temperance Union since the organization of Oregon and Washington, as she now is in California. She has been called to responsible offices in the two latter States. She is now filling a county and State superintendency. She is a thorough prohibitionist and is identified with that work in California. In 1890 she was the nominee on the Los Angeles county prohibition ticket for superintendent of public schools. For a number of years she has been a contributor to the press along the lines of suffrage, education and temperance. Dr. Whipple is the inventor of a bath cabinet. She stands high in her chosen profession and is conscientious and successful.

WHITE, Mrs. Laura Rosamond, author, was born in Otsego county, NY. Her parents removed when she was one year old, and part of her childhood was passed in Pennsylvania, and the remainder and her early girlhood in New York City. Her maiden name was Harvey. She is descended from an illustrious family of Huguenots, named Hervé, who fled from France to England during a time of great persecution. One branch settled in England, one in Scotland, and from a Franco-English alliance descended Dr. Harvey, who discovered the circulation of the blood. The family name became Anglicized from Hervé to Hervey, and then to Harvey. Her ancestors were among the Puritans and pioneers of America. She early showed her fondness for intellectual pursuits, and was educated mostly in private schools and under private tutors. It was through meeting with unsought appreciation and encouragement her work became a matter of business, and for several years she has been receiving substantial recognition. Her contributions have appeared in many journals and magazines, and some of them have been widely copied. She is a versatile writer, and excels in poems that express sentiment suggested by humanity, friendship and patriotism. She is not confined to the didactic and sentimental, and most of the time discards that style. Then she produces her finest poetic work. She possesses an element of the humorous, as frequently shown. As a jonrnalist, her prose articles cover a wide range of subjects. She has been

asked often to write for occasions the most recent being the dedication of the National Woman's Relief Corps Home in Madison, OH. She is a prominent writer in the Woman's Relief Corps and the Woman's Christian Temperance Union. Her home is in Geneva, OH.

WHITE, Miss Nettie L., stenographer, was born near Syracuse, NY. Her great-grandfather served in the War of the Revolution with the Massachusetts troops. On her mother's side she is connected with the Morses, from whom she inherited the persistent industry and independence which moved her in young womanhood to seek some means of earning her own maintenance. After much agitation in the choice of a profession by which to accomplish that, at the suggestion of a friend, she procured Pitman's "Manual of Phonography" and went to work without a teacher. She found the study of that cabalistic art by no means an easy one, but her ambition kept her working early and late. About 1876, when her first regular work began with Henry G. Hayes, of the corps of stenographers of the House of Representatives, in Washington, DC, women engaged in practical stenography in Washington could be counted on the fingers of one hand, and upon them fell the burden of introducing woman into a profession hitherto occupied entirely by men. In her extended congressional work of thirteen years she deeply appreciated the responsibilities of the situation, beyond merely doing the work well, in establishing a new field of labor for women, always insisting that, while she might not go upon the public platform and plead and argue for financial independence for womankind, she could help supply the statistics of what had been successfully done for the use of those who would speak. She is a young woman of pronounced individuality. Her sympathy for those struggling for place is warm, and her practical observations are always helpful to beginners. After several years of most difficult and rapid dictation work in the Capitol, she became ambitious to try her skill in the committees of Congress, but the conservative controlling power thought it would be most unbecoming for her to do what no woman had ever done before.

So she had to wait till one day when the committees in session outnumbered the official force, and a newly-arrived authority gave her the satisfaction of choosing which committee she would undertake. She decided upon the committee of military affairs. General Rosecrans, the chairman, being such a kind and genial man, she thought he would be less likely than the others to object to the radical change in having flounces and feathers reporting the grave and weighty proceedings under his charge. And so it turned out. After a few questions he seemed resigned, and she seated herself at a long table opposite the friend she had urged to accompany her to keep her as well as the "Members" in countenance. In her choice of chairman she had neglected the selection of matter to be reported, and she was obliged to plunge into the obscurity of "heavy ordnance," just as fast as General Benet saw fit to proceed. She presented her report, it was accepted, and the bill was approved just the same as though she had been a man, except that the manuscript was first thoroughly examined. Constant application to her business finally affected her health, so that she was obliged to seek rest and relief in change of climate. She spent one winter in Los Angeles, CA, and was greatly benefited. The year after her return, her friend, Miss Clara Barton, asked her services during the relief work of the Red Cross in Johnstown, PA. It was while there she received her appointment, through civil service examination, from the Pension Bureau, going in as an expert workman on a salary of one-thousand-six-hundred dollars per year.

WHITING, Miss Lilian, journalist, poet and story-writer, was born in Niagara Falls, NY, the daughter of Hon. L. D. and Mrs. Lucretia Clement Whiting. Her ancestry runs back to Rev. William Whiting, the first Unitarian minister of Concord, MA, in the early part of the seventeenth century. Her paternal grandmother was born Mather, and was a direct descendant of Cotton Mather. On her mother's side her ancestry is also of New England people, largely of the Episcopal clergy. While their daughter was an infant, Mr. and Mrs. Whiting removed to Illinois. For some time the young couple served as principals

of the public schools in Tiskilwa, IL, the village near which lay their farm. Subsequently Mr. Whiting became the editor of the "Bureau County Republican," published in Princeton. In that work he was assisted by his wife. Later Mr. Whiting was sent to the State legislature as representative from his district, and, after some years in the lower house, was elected State senator, in which capacity he served for eighteen consecutive years. He was one of the framers of the present constitution of Illinois. Books and periodicals abounded in their simple home. Senator Whiting was a man of ability and integrity. His death, in 1889, left to his three children little in worldly estate. Mrs. Whiting died in 1875. Their only daughter, Lilian, was educated largely under private tuition and by her parents. Both devotees of literature, they pursued a theory of their own with their daughter, and from her cradle she was fairly steeped in the best literature of the world. She inherited from her mother much of the temperament of the mystic and the visionary, and her bent was always toward books and the world of thought. This temperamental affinity led her to the choice of journalism, and, practically unaided, she essayed her work. In 1876 she went to St. Louis, MO, to enter upon her chosen pursuit. For three years she remained in that city. In the spring of 1879, through the acceptance of two papers on Margaret Fuller, Murat Halstead gave her a place on his paper, the Cincinnati "Commercial." After a year in Cincinnati she went, in the summer of 1880, to Boston, MA, where she soon began to work for the "Evening Traveller" as an art writer, and to her writing of the art exhibitions and studio work in Boston and New York she added various miscellaneous contributions. In 1885 she was made the literary editor of the "Traveller." In 1890 she resigned her place on the "Traveller," and, three days after, she took the editorship-in-chief of the Boston "Budget." In that paper she has done the editorial writing, the literary reviews and her "Beau Monde" column. For several years she has had her home in the Brunswick Hotel, in Boston. In person she is of medium hight, slight, with sunny hair and blue eyes. Her hand is ever open to those who need material aid.

WHITING, Mrs. Mary Collins, lawyer and business woman, born in the township of York, Washtenaw county, MI, 4th March, 1835. Her maiden name was Collins, and her parents,

George and Phebe Collins, were New Englanders, who settled in Michigan in 1832. Her ancestry runs back to the Pilgrim Fathers. She received a liberal education in the normal school and afterward taught for several years. In 1854 she became the wife of Ralph C. Whiting, of Hartford, CT, and they settled on a farm near Ann Arbor, MI. She kept up her literary work, writing for local papers, and in 1885 she began to study law, mainly for the purpose of handling her large estate, of which she took entire control. She entered the law department of Ann Arbor University and was graduated in 1887. She soon afterward began to practice, and she now has a large and lucrative business. She is one of the busiest women in Michigan. She possesses decision of character in a marked degree.

WHITMAN, Mrs. Sarah Helen, poet, born in Providence, RI, in 1803, and died there 27th June, 1878. She was the daughter of Nicholas Power. She became the wife of John W. Whitman, a lawyer, of Boston, MA, in 1828. She lived in Boston until her husband died, in 1833, when she returned to Providence. There she devoted herself to literature. In 1848 she became conditionally engaged to Edgar A. Poe, but she broke the engagement. They remained friends. She contributed essays, critical sketches and poems to magazines for many years. In 1853 she published a collection of her works, entitled "Hours of Life, and Other Poems." In 1860 she published a volume entitled "Edgar A. Poe and His Critics," in which she defended him from harsh aspersions. She was the joint author, with her sister, Miss Anna Marsh Power, of "Fairy Ballads," "The Golden Ball," "The Sleeping Beauty" and "Cinderella." After her death a complete collection of her poems was published.

WHITNEY, Mrs. Adeline Dutton Train, author, born in Boston, MA, 15th September, 1824. She is a daughter of Enoch Train, formerly a well-known shipping merchant and founder of a packet line between Boston and Liverpool. She was educated in Boston. She became the wife of Seth D. Whitney, of Milton, MA, in 1843. She contributed a good deal to various magazines in her early years. Her published works are "Footsteps on the Seas" (1859); "Mother Goose for Grown Folks" (1860), revised in 1870, and 1882; "Boys at Chequasset" (1862); "Faith Gartney's Girlhood" (1863); "The Gayworthys" (1865); "A Summer in Leslie Goldthwaite's Life" (1866); "Patience Strong's Outings" (1868); "Hitherto" (1869); "We Girls" (1870); "Real Folks" (1871); "Pansies," poems (1871); "The Other Girls" (1873); "Sights and Insights" (1876); "Just How: A Key to Cook-Books" (1878); "Odd or Even" (1880); "Bonnyborough" (1885); "Homespun Yarns," "Holy-Tides" (1886); "Daffodils" and "Bird-Talk" (1887). The last three volumes named are in verse. "Ascubney Street" and "A Golden Gossip," first issued as serials in the "Ladies' Home Journal," Philadelphia, were published in book form in 1888 and 1890.

WHITNEY, Miss Anne, sculptor, was born in Watertown, MA, the youngest child of a large family. She is descended from the earliest New England colonists, and can trace her ancestry to an eminent English family that flourished before the colonies were founded. Her parents were of the advanced liberal thinkers of their time, and were among the earliest converts to what is called Liberal Christianity. From them she inherits a large faith in humanity, a vital belief in the possibilities of human betterment, and an unflinching hostility to every form of oppression and injustice. Her childhood and youth were passed under most favorable conditions. Whatever would contribute to her development was furnished by her parents, and she was taught in the best schools, under the instruction of the noblest teachers. The center of a loving household, she was encompassed with affection and was wisely cared for in all respects. She very early expressed herself in poetry, for she possessed a high order of imaginative power, and it seemed certain, for some few years, that she would devote herself to literature. Her earlier poems have never been collected, and not until 1859 did she publish a volume of poems. Their quality was very remarkable, and they were as original as they were vigorous. Stately in rhythm and large in thought and feeling, they are earnest, strong and courageous. The ablest reviewers pronounced them "unexcelled in modern times." A mere accident gave a different bent to her genius, and she decided to make sculpture her profession, and began to work immediately. There were not a dozen persons in New England at that time working in sculpture, and there were no teachers. Her own genius and her native force were called into requisition, for she had no other resource. Her first work was portrait busts of her father and mother, which proved that she had not mistaken her vocation. Then she attempted her first ideal work, putting into marble her beautiful conception of "Lady Godiva," which was exhibited in Boston. That was followed by "Africa," a colossal statue of another type. It was a masterpiece of genius, and was received by the public in a most gratifying manner. "The Lotus-Eater," as fabled by the ancients and reproduced by Tennyson, was her next work, and then she went to Europe, where she spent five years, studying, drawing and modeling in the great art centers of the Old World. While abroad, she executed several very fine statues, "The Chaldean Astronomer," studying the stars; "Toussaint L'Ouverture," the St. Domingo chief, statesman and governor, and "Roma," which has been called a "thinking statue." She returned home with completer technical skill and larger conceptions of art, and has worked diligently since in her studio. The State of Massachusetts commissioned her to make a statue in marble of Samuel Adams, the Revolutionary patriot, for the national gallery in Washington, and one in bronze for Adams square, Boston. She went to Rome to execute the commission, and while abroad spent another year in Paris, where she made three heads, one of a beautiful girl, another of a roguish peasant child, and the third an old peasant woman, coiffed with the marmotte, who could not be kept awake, and so Miss Whitney modeled her asleep. The last, in bronze, is to be seen in the Art Museum, Boston. Her latest great works are a sitting statue of Harriet Martineau, the most eminent Englishwoman of the present century, which is of marble and of heroic size. It stands in Wellesley College, Massachusetts. The other is an ideal statue of "Lief Ericsson," the young Norseman, who, A.D. 1000, sailed from Norway, and, skirting Iceland and Greenland, sailed into Massachusetts Bay and discovered America. It is colossal in size and in bronze, and stands at the entrance of a park, near Commonwealth avenue, Boston. A replica of that statue stands in Milwaukee on the lake bluff. Of medallions, fountains and portrait busts Miss Whitney has made many. She has made portrait busts of President Stearns, of Amherst College; President Walker, of Harvard; Professor Pickering, of Harvard; William Lloyd Garrison, Hon. Samuel Sewall, of Boston; Mrs. Alice Freeman Palmer, ex-president of Wellesley College; Adeline Manning, Miss Whitney's inseparable friend and house-mate; Harriet Beecher Stowe, Frances E. Willard, Lucy Stone, Mary A. Livermore and others. She will exhibit several of her works in the World's Fair, in Chicago, in 1893. Her home is on the western slope of Beacon Hill, where she passes much of her diligent and devoted life, and where are clustered many of her most beautiful sketches, for her studio is peopled with "the beings of her mind."

WHITNEY, Mrs. Mary Traffarn, minister, born in Boonville, NY, 28th February, 1852. Her maiden name was Mary Louise Traffarn. Her father was a descendant of an old Huguenot family, and from that ancestry she inherited their love of truth and force of moral conviction. She received the rudiments of her education in the Whitestown Seminary, the Utica Academy, and the Clinton Industrial Institute, being graduated from St. Lawrence University in 1872. Her especial fondness was for the mathematical, scientific and logical branches of study. The next year she became the wife of Rev. Herbert Whitney and became an active assistant in his work, pursuing such lines of study as a busy life would permit, and teaching several terms with him in the old academy in Webster, NY. In 1881 she was graduated from the Chicago Kindergarten Training School, and taught that valuable system for two years. She had preached and lectured occasionally up to 1885, when she was asked to take charge of a church in Mt. Pleasant, IA, which she did, finding in the ministry the real work of her life. At present she has charge of the First Unitarian Church in West Somerville, MA. She is an ideal homemaker, finding the highest uses for her learning in its devotion to the problem how to make the happiest and most helpful home for her husband and her four boys. The trend of her ministry is in the direction of the practical and spiritual, rather than the theoretic. As a lecturer on reform subjects she has won popularity, and in all philanthropic work and the great social problems of the day she takes a deep interest. Earnestly desirous of the advancement of women, she has felt that she might do most to promote that advancement by practically demonstrating in her own work that woman has a place in the ministry. In accord with this thought, her aim has been to do her best and most faithful work in whatever place was open to her. The motive of her ministry has been to add something to the helpful forces of the world. The secret of her success is hard work, making no account of difficulties. The methods and means of her progress may be described as a habit of learning from experience and from passing events, taking great lessons for life from humble sources.

WHITTEN, Mrs. Martha Elizabeth Hotchkiss, author, born near Austin, TX, 3rd October, 1842. She is the daughter of Hon. William S. and Hannah B. Hotchkiss. She entered school when she was five years old and was educated principally in the Collegiate Female Institute in Austin. At the age of fourteen years she was sent to McKenzie College. She began to write verses at the age of eleven, and at twelve and thirteen she contributed to the press. The death of her mother, before she was ten years old, saddened her life and gave to all her early poems an undertone of sorrow. Soon after entering McKenzie College she wrote her poem "Do They Miss Me at Home?" She was married when quite young, widowed at twenty-four, and left without money or home and with but little knowledge of business. She resorted to teaching as a means of support for herself and fatherless boys, and made a grand success of it, and soon gained not only a competency, but secured a comfortable home and other property. She has written on a variety of subjects and displays great versatility in her poems, historical, descriptive, memorial and joyous. Her poems were collected in 1886 in book-form under the title of "Texas Garlands," and have won appreciation in the literary world and success financially. She has written many poems since the publication of her book. She read a poem before a Chautauqua audience on Poet's Day, 23rd July, 1888, and one written by request, and read in Tuscola, IL, 4th July, 1889, to a large audience. She is now engaged on her "Sketch-Book," which will contain both prose and poetry, letters of travel and fiction. She has been twice married and has reared a large family. Her home is in Austin.

WICKENS, Mrs. Margaret R., worker in the Woman's Relief Corps, born in Indianapolis, IN, 3rd August, 1843. Her father, Thomas Brown, was a native of Dublin county, Ireland. Her mother was Judith Bennett, of Cumberland county, New Jersey, a descendant of the Bennetts of Mayflower and Revolutionary fame. Margaret was the older of a family of two daughters. In 1854 the family moved to Henderson, KY. Their detestation of slavery was strong, and their house became a station on the underground railroad. For having aided needy colored fugitives, Mr. Brown was imprisoned in Frankfort, KY, for three years, and his family were compelled to remove to the North. In 1857 he was released and joined his family in Indianapolis. There he was honored by a public reception, in which Lloyd Garrison and other prominent men participated. In 1859 he removed to Loda, IL. In 1861 he enlisted in the Tenth Illinois Cavalry, but his strength was not sufficient to enable him to enter the service, and he was obliged to remain at home. Margaret taught in the Loda high school, where her sister, Harriet, was also employed. She did all she could do to aid the Union cause. In 1864 she became the wife of Thomas Wiley Wickens, and they removed to Kankakee, IL. Five children were born to them. Mrs. Wickens was a temperance advocate from childhood. She joined the Good Templars in Indianapolis, and was one of the first members of the Illinois Woman's Christian Temperance Union. In that order she worked for prohibition legislation in Kansas. She served as district president of her union for several years and went as delegate to the national convention in Minneapolis. After settling in Sabetha, KS, she was, in 1885, elected department president of the Kansas Woman's Relief Corps. She was reelected in 1886. Her department grew from fifty-nine to one-hundred-forty-nine organized corps in two years. She attended the national convention in California and was there appointed national inspector, which position she resigned in order to care for her State department. She has served her department two years as counselor, as a member of the department and national executive boards. In the St. Louis convention she was elected a member of the executive board. In 1891 she was made general agent for the United States of the National Grand Army of the Republic Memorial College. In Detroit, 5th August, 1891, she was elected national senior vice-president of the Woman's Relief Corps. In October of that year she was elected State president of the Rebekahs of Kansas. In the Washington, DC, convention, 24th September, 1892, she was elected national president of the Woman's Relief Corps. Her work is of the most valuable character. She lives in Sabetha.

WIGGIN, Mrs. Kate Douglas, philanthropist and author, was born in Philadelphia, PA. She is of Puritan descent, and her ancestors were prominent in the church, in politics and in the law. She was educated in New England, after which she removed to California, where she studied the kindergarten methods for a year. After that she taught for a year in a college in Santa Barbara, and was then called upon to organize the first free kindergarten in San Francisco. For a time she worked alone in the school, after which she interested Mrs. Sarah B. Cooper in the subject, and together they have made a notable success of kindergartens in that city, Miss Nora Smith, Mrs. Wiggin's sister, also laboring with them. From that opening have branched out over fifty other kindergartens for the poor in that city and in Oakland, CA, beside many others upon the Pacific coast. Upon becoming the wife of Samuel Bradley Wiggin, a brilliant young lawyer, she gave up her kindergarten teaching, but continued to talk to the training class twice a week, besides visiting all the kindergartens regularly, telling the children those stories which have

since been published to a wide circle of readers. Her first story was a short serial, entitled "Half-a-Dozen Housekeepers," which appeared in "St. Nicholas." For many years she wrote no more for publication, except in connection with kindergarten work. Her "Story of Patsy" was written and printed for the benefit of the school. Three-thousand copies were sold without its appearance in a book store. In 1888 Mr. and Mrs. Wiggin removed to New York. The separation from her kindergartens left so much leisure work on her hands that she again began her literary labors. Some of her works are: "The Birds' Christmas Carol," "A Summer in a Canon" and "Timothy's Quest." "The Story Hour" was written in conjunction with her sister Nora. Mrs. Wiggin has given many parlor readings for charity, which show that she is also an elocutionist of merit. She is an excellent musician, possessing a beautiful voice, and has composed some very fine instrumental settings for her favorite poems, notably her accompaniment to "Lend Me Thy Fillet, Love," and of Ibsen's "Butterfly Song." She has published a book of children's songs and games, entitled "Kindergarten Chimes." The death of her husband, in 1889, was a grievous blow, from which she bravely rallied, and returning to California, again took up her beloved work in a large normal school for the training of kindergarten teachers, of which she is the head.

WIGHT, Miss Emma Howard, was born in Baltimore, MD. She is the only daughter of J. Howard Wight, a well-known tobacco broker of that city. She is of English extraction, her father's ancestors having come over with Lord Baltimore. Her paternal grandmother was a Miss Howard, of the well-known Howard family, and a celebrated beauty in her youth. On the maternal side she is also descended from an old Maryland family. Miss Wight was educated in the Academy of Visitation, Baltimore, and early showed a decided talent for writing, her school compositions being always highly commended. For some years after leaving school her time was given to society, though she occasionally wrote a little for her own amusement. At length, acting upon the advice of friends, she submitted some of her writings with a view to their publication. They were promptly accepted, and her productions have since appeared in some of the best journals in the country. Some of her theological articles were especially commented upon by Cardinal Gibbons, and were copied in some of the leading English journals. Her novel, "Passion Flowers and the Cross," appeared in 1891 and made a great stir in the literary world. She is very fond of outdoor exercise as a panacea for nearly all physical ills and a great promoter of health and beauty.

WILCOX, Mrs. Ella Wheeler, author, was born in Johnstown Center, WI. Her parents were poor, but from them she inherited literary bent. Her education was received in the public schools of Windsor, WI, and in the University of Wisconsin. She began to write poetry and sketches very early, and at the age of fourteen years some of her articles were published in the New York "Mercury." Two years later she had secured the appreciation of local editors and publishers, and from that time on she contributed largely to newspapers and periodicals. Soon after, she published "Drops of Water" (New York, 1872), a small volume on the subject of total abstinence. Her miscellaneous collection of verse entitled "Shells (1883) was not successful, and it is now out of print. Her talents were used for the unselfish purpose of providing a comfortable home for her parents and caring for them during sickness. She has had the satisfaction of being a widely read author and of receiving a good price and ready sale for all she produces. In 1884 she became the wife of Robert M. Wilcox, of Meriden, CT, and since 1887 they have resided in New York City. Her other works are "Maurine" (Chicago, 1875); "Poems of Passion" (Chicago, 1883); "Mal Moulée," a novel (New York, 1885), and "Poems of Pleasure" (1888). She has published several novels and has written much for the syndicates.

WILCOX, Mrs. Hannah Tyler, physician, born in Boonville, NY, 31st August, 1838. Her father, Amos Tyler, was a cousin of President John Tyler. His liberal ideas on the subject of woman's education were far in advance of his generation. Her mother's father, Joseph Lawton, was a patron of education and one of the founders of the first medical college in New York, in Fairfield, Herkimer county. His home and purse were open to the students and professors, and thus Elizabeth Lawton learned to love the science of medicine, though not permitted to study it. Her daughter, Hannah, attended the academies in Holland Patent and Rome, NY, and, being desirous of a higher education than could there be obtained, she went to the Pennsylvania Female College, near Philadelphia, where she was graduated with honors in 1860. A call came to the president of the college for a teacher to take charge of an academy in southwest Missouri. This involved a journey three-hundred miles by stage coach south of St. Louis. Miss Tyler resolved to accept the position, and in one year she built up a successful school, when the war of 1861 made it unsafe for a teacher of northern views to remain, and she returned to her native town. In 1862 she became the wife of Dr. M. W. Wilcox, of Rochester, NY. They went to Warrensburg, MO, and there witnessed some of the stirring scenes of that period of national strife. Three times they witnessed the alternation of Federal and Confederate rule. She entered into the profession with her husband and studied in the various schools, the allopathic, eclectic, and later, desiring to know if there was any best in "pathies" of medicine, she took a degree in the homœopathic school in St. Louis, MO, where she resided many years. She is a believer in the curative powers of electricity, and many of her cures are on record, with the skillful use of various means of healing the sick. Her great aim is the advancement of her sex. She is prominent in all the great movements of and for women, the Woman's Christian Temperance Union, the Woman's Relief Corps and the educational and industrial unions. She is a member of the National American Institute of Homoenopathy, and was a delegate from St. Louis and Missouri to the convention in Saratoga, NY, in 1887. She has been medical examiner for ten years for the Order of Chosen Friends. In 1887 her health failed from overwork, and she sought the invigorating climate of southern California, in Los Angeles. When her health was restored, she returned to her home in St. Louis. Her lectures on health and dress for women have aided materially in reform. She has been a widow for many years and has one living son. In 1892 she removed to Chicago, IL, and is now permanantly located in that city.

WILDER, Mrs. S. Fannie Gerry, author, born in Standish, ME, 4th September, 1850. She is the daughter of Rev. Edwin J. and Sophia J. Gerry. Her father was settled over the Unitarian parish in that town seven years, then going to New York, where he was connected with the Children's Aid Society for five years, and finally accepted a call from the Benevolent Fraternity of Churches to settle in Boston, MA, as pastor of the Hanover Street Chapel, where he remained as minister for twenty-five years. Mrs. Wilder, although born in Maine, was essentially a Boston girl, as she was educated in the schools of that city and has lived in the vicinity nearly all her life. As she grew to womanhood, her interest became naturally identified with her father's work, in assisting the poorer class among whom he labored. She was looked upon by the people of his parish as a sister, friend and helper. Occupied by these various duties, the years went quietly by until 1881, when she became the wife of Millard F. Wilder, a young business man of Boston. Then every-day cares and interests, the death of her infant son and of her father filled her mind and heart for some years. She had always been very fond of history and literature in her school-days, taking a high rank in composition during that time. After the death of her father, her desire became so great to place his work and life before the public, that it might serve to inspire others, that she wrote, in 1887, his memoir, entitled "The Story of a Useful Life." The publication of that book was received with great favor, and the author was gratified to know that her work was fully appreciated. Afterward she wrote for different papers and magazines, making a specialty of stories for children. Her love for the work increased every year, and in 1890 she published a book for young people, entitled "Boston Girls at Home and Abroad." She will soon publish another book for young people, historical in character,

entitled "Looking Westward: A Romance of 1620." She is an active member of the New England Woman's Press Association, and is connected with various other societies. She was elected secretary of the Arlington, MA, branch of the Chautauqua Literary Social Circle for 1892.

WILHITE, Mrs. Mary Holloway, physician and philanthropist, born near Crawfordsville, IN, 3rd February, 1831, and died 8th February, 1892. Her maiden name was Mary Mitchell Holloway. Her father, judge Washington Holloway, a native of Kentucky, was one of the pioneers of Crawfordsville. Her mother was Elizabeth King, of Virginia. When Mary was but seventeen years of age, her mother died. At an early age Mary Holloway developed strong traits of character. At the age of fifteen she united with the Christian Church, and she continued through life an earnest and active member. Wishing to be self-supporting, she engaged in school-teaching and sewing. Her thirst for knowledge led her to enter the medical profession. She studied and fitted herself unaided, and entered the Pennsylvania Medical College, Philadelphia, in 1854. She was graduated in 1856. She was the first Indiana woman to be graduated from a medical college. She was also the first woman in Indiana, as a graduate, to engage in the practice of medicine. Returning to Crawfordsville, she opened an office. On account of her sex she was debarred from membership in medical associations, but she went forward in a determined way and gained a popularity of which any physician might be proud. She made several important discoveries regarding the effects of medicine in certain diseases. Her greatest success was in treatment of women and children. In 1861 she became the wife of A. E. Wilhite, of Crawfordsville, an estimable gentleman, who, with two sons and two daughters, survives her. Three of their children died in infancy. With all her work in public life, Dr. Wilhite was domestic in her tastes and was a devoted wife and mother. She lived to see marked changes in public opinion in regard to the principles she maintained. Her counsel was sought, and her knowledge received due recognition. She was, in the true sense of the term, a philanthropist. Her charity was broad and deep. She was especially interested in the welfare of young girls who were beset by temptations, and helped many such to obtain employment. She was unceasing in her warfare against the use of whiskey and tobacco. When employed as physician to the county almshouse, she was grieved at the condition of the children associated with the class of adult paupers, and she never rested until she had, with the help of others, established the county children's home. She was an advocate of woman's rights, even in childhood. In 1850 she canvassed for the first woman's rights paper published in America, the "Woman's Advocate," edited by Miss Anna McDowell, in Philadelphia. In 1869 she arranged for a convention, in which Mrs. Livermore, Mrs. Stanton and Miss Anthony were speakers. Subsequently she was a leading spirit in arranging meetings in the cause of the advancement of woman. She was a fluent and forcible writer, and contributed much to the press on the subjects which were near her heart. Her poetic nature found expression in verse, and she wrote many short poems.

WILKES, Mrs. Eliza Tupper, minister, born in Houlton, ME, 8th October, 1844. Her father was a native of Maine, her mother of Rhode Island, and all ancestors, except an honored Irish grandmother, were of New England since the earliest colonization. The Tuppers were established in 1630 upon a farm in Sandwich, MA, which is still occupied by a member of the family. On other lines the family is traced to the Mayhews, of Martha's Vineyard, and the Wheatons, of Rhode Island. Early in the childhood of Mrs. Wilkes, her parents moved to Brighton, Washington county, IA. Her early education was largely given her by her mother, Mrs. Ellen Smith Tupper, who became celebrated for her knowledge of bee culture. At sixteen she returned to New England with her grandfather, Noah Smith, then prominent in the public life of Maine, and for two years studied in the academy in Calais, ME. Returning to Iowa, she was graduated from the Iowa Central University after four years of study, during which time she had largely supported herself and economized

with heroic fortitude. Until toward the end of her college course, she was a devoted Baptist and planned to go as a foreign missionary. Her anxiety for the heathen, however, led her to question the truth of her belief in eternal punishment, and she became a Universalist. Association with a Quaker family made her realize that she might preach, although a woman, and, encouraged by the Reverend Miss Chapin, Mrs. Livermore and others, she became a Universalist minister, and was ordained 2nd May, 1871. Her first pastorate was in Neenah, WI, before her ordination, and in 1869 she accepted a call from the church in Rochester, MN. After the time of her entrance upon that pastorate she became the wife of William A. Wilkes, a young lawyer of great strength of character and of much professional promise, which has since been more than realized. Much of Mrs. Wilkes' success has been due to the inspiring sympathy and encouragement of her husband. He has always been active as a leader in reformatory measures and as a layman in church work. In 1872 she resigned her pastorate and went with her husband to Colorado Springs, where he found a fine professional field. In that year their first child was born, and from that time on for fifteen years she gave most of her time and strength to her home life, although her ministry really never ceased. She always kept a live and active interest in all the good work of the communities in which she lived, and preached occasionally, whenever her help was needed. Through her efforts a Unitarian church was started during that period in Colorado Springs, and later another in Sioux Falls, Dakota, to which place the family moved in 1878. In Dakota she gathered about her through post-office missions and occasional preaching tours a large parish of hungry truth-seekers, scattered all over the prairies of southeastern Dakota. Her influence was especially felt among the young women in the new communities in which she lived. Although young herself, her experience made her seem a natural adviser, and, whether by starting study classes, or kindergarten, or giving suggestions as to infant hygiene, her usefulness was unceasing. In 1887 she again entered actively into the ministry, accepting the pastorate of a church in Luverne, MN, a town a few miles from Sioux Falls, where her home remained. That work she still continues. She herself is mother, sister, friend or teacher to every man, woman or child in the congregation, and most of the life of the community centers in the activities she inspires. Together with that, she is virtual pastor of three mission churches, to which she preaches as there is opportunity. Five sons and one daughter were born to her.

WILKINS, Miss Mary E., author, born in Randolph, MA, in 1862. She is the daughter of Warren E. Wilkins, and is descended from an old New England family. In her infancy her family removed to Brattleboro, VT. She received her education in Mt. Holyoke Seminary. She early began to write, and her stories were published in various periodicals. In 1884 her father died, and she returned to Randolph, where she now lives. She is the last of her family. One of her earliest successes was the writing of a prize story for a Boston journal. She soon became well known as a regular contributor to the leading periodicals. Her first contribution to bring her a reward was a ballad, published in "Wide Awake." She wrote for the "Budget," Harper's "Bazar," "Weekly," "Magazine" and "Young People," and other periodicals for years. She has published several volumes of her stories. Among her best works are "The Humble Romance," "Two Old Lovers," "A Symphony in Lavender," and "A New England Nun." She is a prolific author, and all her work is carefully finished. Her work has been very popular, and her poems and stories are in large demand. A part of her time is spent in Boston and New York City.

WILLARD, Mrs. Allie C., journalist and business woman, born near Nauvoo, IL, 13th April, 1860, the oldest of ten children. Her parents were Cyrus E. Rosseter and Lydia A. Williams. In 1872 the family removed to Grand Island, NE, and from there to Loup City, NE, in 1873, where the greater part of her life has been spent. Being a frail and delicate child, she was deprived of educational advantages, but the love of knowledge could not be quenched, and all her education was obtained by her own hard effort. The extent of her

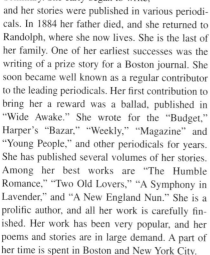

opportunities was five summers in school until twelve years of age, after which fifteen months in school enlarged her experience. Every spare moment was devoted to study. At the age of seventeen she had fitted herself to teach. Then she earned the means for a nine-months' course in an academy presided over by J. T. Mallalieu, of Kearney, NE. After a few months of application she began her business career under the guidance of L. B. Fifield, of Kearney, who had discerned her talents and ambition. She studied some months with Mr. Fifield, during which time she entered a printing office, where she worked at a case, read proof, attended to the mail list, reviewed books, did paragraphing and performed some of the outside business duties. Appointed postmaster in Loup City when only twenty-one years old, for five years she served the public in that capacity, performing faithfully the duties an increasing business demanded. In 1881 she became the wife of the man who had waited patiently for the little woman who had said, five years before: "No, we do not know enough to marry," realizing that marriage should be founded on a higher plane than the mere sentiment of inexperienced youth. Her husband was a successful politician and newspaper man, under whose training she developed as a writer. The husband died by an assassin's hand in May, 1887. Prostrated for a time by the terrible occurrence, Mrs. Willard rallied from the shock and, with undaunted courage, took up her husband's work. As editor of the Loup City "Times" she became a member of the Nebraska Editorial Association. During a part of the year 1889 she took a course in the business college of Lincoln, NE, and served three months as clerk in the Nebraska Senate, where she made a splendid record. Late in 1889 she entered the employ of the Western Newspaper Union in Omaha. She was later manager of that company's Chicago office, but resigned because physically unable to bear the strain. Since 1880 she has been a constant writer for the press in the line of news, sketches, temperance and politics. As a member of the Nebraska Press Association she received the homage of the editors of the State for her ability as a writer, editor and successful business woman. She is a member of the Woman's Christian Temperance Union and an earnest worker in the cause. She has always striven to advance the interests of her home town and surrounding country and has been instrumental in promoting moral and educational reforms. She is an uncompromising Republican, and, if she chose to enter the field, she is fitted to stand with the highest as a political or temperance orator. The amount of work which she has performed with indomitable perseverance and energy is marvelous. In a few years she paid debts of thousands of dollars which her husband's political career had entailed, besides performing unnumbered charities in a quiet, unpretentious way. She is a member of no church, but her creed embraces the good of all.

WILLARD, Mrs. Cordelia Young, missionary worker, born in Onondaga county, NY, 30th August, 1822. She grew to womanhood in DeWitt, her native village. Her father, Rev. Seth Young, was a lineal descendant of Rev. Christopher Young, vicar of Reyden, England, and chaplain of Windsor during the reign of Queen Elizabeth, and of Rev. John Young, his son, of Southwold, 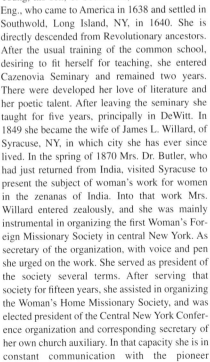 Eng., who came to America in 1638 and settled in Southwold, Long Island, NY, in 1640. She is directly descended from Revolutionary ancestors. After the usual training of the common school, desiring to fit herself for teaching, she entered Cazenovia Seminary and remained two years. There were developed her love of literature and her poetic talent. After leaving the seminary she taught for five years, principally in DeWitt. In 1849 she became the wife of James L. Willard, of Syracuse, NY, in which city she has ever since lived. In the spring of 1870 Mrs. Dr. Butler, who had just returned from India, visited Syracuse to present the subject of woman's work for women in the zenanas of India. Into that work Mrs. Willard entered zealously, and she was mainly instrumental in organizing the first Woman's Foreign Missionary Society in central New York. As secretary of the organization, with voice and pen she urged on the work. She served as president of the society several terms. After serving that society for fifteen years, she assisted in organizing the Woman's Home Missionary Society, and was elected president of the Central New York Conference organization and corresponding secretary of her own church auxiliary. In that capacity she is in constant communication with the pioneer

preachers on the frontiers of the nation, and with the struggling missions in destitute regions of the South and Southwest, and through her agency many comforts are carried into desolate homes and substantial aid is afforded to the heroic toilers in those remote fields. The Peck Memorial Home, of New Orleans, was suggested by her and carried to completion mainly through her efforts. Another phase of Christian work, to which she has given much thought and labor, is the Order of Deaconesses, recently established in the Methodist Episcopal Church, of which she is a member. Notwithstanding her active life on these lines, she still finds time to look well to the affairs of her household. Though unknown to the literary world as a writer and contributing little to the periodicals of the day, yet to the inner circle it is known that she has poetic genius of no mean order, and some of her poems, written on special occasions for friends, possess genuine merit.

WILLARD, Mrs. Emma, educator, born in Berlin, CT, 23rd February, 1787, and died in Troy, NY, 15th April, 1870. She was a daughter of Samuel Hart. She was educated in the academy in Hartford, CT, and, at the age of sixteen, began her career as a teacher. She taught in different institutions and finally took charge of a school in Middlebury, VT. In 1809 she became the wife of Dr. John Willard, then United States Marshal of Vermont. In 1814 she opened a girls' boarding-school in Middlebury, in which she adopted many new features. She decided to found a seminary for girls, and in 1819 she addressed a treatise on "The Education of Women" to the legislature. In that year she opened in Waterford, NY, a school, which was incorporated and partly supported by the State of New York. In 1821 she removed to Troy, NY, where an appropriate building for a seminary was given to her by the city, and her school became known as the Troy Female Seminary. In 1825 her husband died, and the business management of the school fell upon her hands. She conducted the institution until 1838, when she was succeeded by her son, John Hart Willard, and his wife. In 1830 she traveled in Europe, and in 1833 she published her "Journal and Letters from

France and Great Britain," devoting her share of the proceeds, over $1,200, to the support of a school that had been founded in Greece, through her influence, for the education of native women teachers. Her colleagues in that enterprise were her sister, Mrs. Almira Lincoln Phelps, and Sarah J. Hale, Lydia H. Sigourney and others. In 1838 she became the wife of Dr. Christopher C. Yates. In 1843 she was divorced from him and resumed her former name. She revised her numerous school-books and did much work in the cause of higher education. In 1846 she traveled eight-thousand miles in the western and southern States, addressing conventions of teachers. In 1854 she attended the world's educational convention in London, England. She was the pioneer in the higher education of women in the United States, and educated over five-thousand pupils. Her school-books had a large sale and were translated into the European and Asiatic languages. Her publications are: "The Woodbridge and Willard Geographies and Atlases" (1823); "History of the United States, or Republic of America" (1828); "Universal History in Perspective" (1837); "Treatise on the Circulation of the Blood" (1846); "Respiration and Its Effects, Particularly as Respects Asiatic Cholera" (1849); "Last Leaves of American History" (1849); "Astronomy" (1853); "Morals for the Young" (1857), and many charts, atlases, pamphlets and addresses. She wrote a number of poems, including the famous "Rocked in the Cradle of the Deep," which were published in a volume, in 1830, and afterward suppressed. She was a woman of great powers of mind, and she possessed marked executive capacity. All her work in the school-room was carried out on philosophical methods.

WILLARD, Miss Frances Elizabeth, educator, reformer and philanthropist, born in Churchville, near Rochester, NY, 28th September, 1839. Her father, Josiah F. Willard, was a descendant of Maj. Simon Willard, of Kent, England, who, with Rev. Peter Bulkeley, settled in Concord, MA, less than fifteen years after the landing of the Pilgrims at Plymouth. Major Willard was a man of great force of character and of distinguished public service, and his descendants included many men and women who inherited his talents with his good name. Miss Willard's great-grandfather, Rev. Elijah Willard, was forty years a pastor in Dublin, NH. His son, Oliver Atherton Willard, was a pio-

neer, first in Wheelock, VT, and later in Odgen, Monroe county, NY, where he died at the age of forty-two, leaving to his widow, Catharine Lewis Willard, a woman of strong character and remarkable gifts, the task of rearing a young family in a country then almost a wilderness. Josiah, the oldest child, grew to maturity. At the age of twenty-six he was married to Mary Thompson Hill, born in the same year as himself, in Danville, VT. Frances was the fourth of five children born to Josiah and Mary Willard, two of whom had passed away in infancy before her birth. Inheriting many of the notable gifts of both parents and of more remote ancestors, Frances grew up in an atmosphere most favorable to the development of her powers. In her second year her parents removed from Churchville to Oberlin, OH, that the father might carry out a long-cherished plan of further study, and that the family might have the advantages of intellectual help and stimulus. They remained in Oberlin five years, both parents improving their opportunities for study. Mr. Willard's health demanding change of climate and life in the open air, he removed with his family, in May, 1846, to Wisconsin, then a territory, and settled on a farm near the young village of Janesville. Their first advent was to the log house of a relative. Frances is remembered, as at that time a child of six-and-a-half years, small and delicate. The family were soon settled on an estate of their own, a beautiful farm, half prairie, half forest, on the banks of Rock river. Their abode was named "Forest Home." In the earlier years, without near neighbors, the family were almost entirely dependent upon their own resources for society. Mrs. Willard was poetical in her nature, but life was to her ethical and philosophical as well as poetical. With a memory stored with lofty sentiments in prose and verse, she was at once mentor and companion to her children. The father was "near to nature's heart" in a real and vivid fashion of his own. The children, reared in a home which was to their early years the world's horizon, lived an intellectual, yet a most healthful life. Frances enjoyed entire freedom from fashionable restraints until her seventeenth year. She was clad during most of the year in simple flannel suits and spent much of the time in the open air, sharing the occupations and sports of her brother and sister. Her first teachers were her educated parents. Later an accomplished young woman was engaged as family teacher and companion for the children.

Her first schoolmaster was a graduate of Yale College, and a former classical tutor in Oberlin. At the age of seventeen Frances, with her sister Mary, was sent from home to school, entering Milwaukee Female College in 1857. In the spring of 1858 they were transferred to the Northwestern Female College, in Evanston, IL, and thither the parents removed in the following autumn, that they might educate the children without breaking up the home circle. Miss Willard was graduated from that institution in 1859, with valedictory honor. A brief term of teaching in 1858 was the introduction to her successful life as a teacher, covering sixteen years in six locations and several prominent positions, her pupils in all numbering about two-thousand. Beginning in the district school, she taught a public school in Evanston and one in Harlem, IL. She then taught in Kankakee Academy, in the Northwestern Female College, in Pittsburgh Female College, in the Grove school, Evanston, was preceptress in Genesee Wesleyan Seminary, Lima, NY, and was president of the Ladies' College, Evanston, later the Woman's College of the Northwestern University, of which she was dean and professor of aesthetics in the University. Her success as a teacher was very marked. In coeducation she was ever an earnest believer, and she dealt with the unsolved problems of coeducation in its early stages with cheer, hopefulness and skill. As president of the Ladies' College, Evanston, she was free to work her will, as she says, "as an older sister of girls," and there was instituted her system of self-government, which bore excellent fruit and has been followed in other institutions with success. The Roll of Honor Club, open to all pupils, had for its general principles "to cooperate with the faculty in securing good order and lady like behavior among the boarding pupils, both in study and recreation hours, in inspiring a high sense of honor, personal responsibility and self-respect." Pupils were not regarded as on the roll of honor after they had transgressed a single regulation of the club, and their places were supplied by those whose lives were above reproach. From the roll of honor, girls were graduated after a specified length of time to the list of the self-governed and took this pledge: "I promise so to conduct myself that, if other pupils followed my example, our school would need no rules whatever, but each young lady would be trusted to be a law unto herself." At the close of the first year, twelve young ladies were on the self-governed

list, and all the rest were on the roll of honor. Thus with happy tact she smoothed the uneven path of diligence for young spirits and established them in a conscientious order of life that would prove a sure reliance in the stress and strife of future years. An extract from her journal tells of busy hours maintained by strictest routine: "Rose at six, made my toilet, arranged the room, went to breakfast, looked over the lessons of the day, although I had already done that yesterday; conducted devotions in the chapel; heard advanced class in arithmtic, one in geometry, one in elementary algebra, one in Wilson's 'Universal History'; talked with Miss Clark at noon; dined; rose from the table to take charge of an elocution class, next zoology, next geology, next physiology, next mineralogy; then came upstairs and sat down in my rocking-chair as one who would prefer to rise no more, which indeed is not much to be wondered at." In 1868 Miss Willard freed herself from the restraint of school, life and in company with a friend went abroad for an extended trip of over two years, and keeping in mind her school work, collected eight-hundred photographs relating to her travels. Using these to illustrate her instruction she tells how they prompted a cherished plan, never realized: "Many of these I had produced on glass so that they could be thrown on the screen of the stereopticon, and described to the entire class at once. It was my earnest hope that after I had taught the theory and history of the fine arts for a few years, I might be able to prepare a text-book that would be used generally in schools and would furnish the introduction—of which I so much felt the need—to a study of the European galleries and of art in our own land." Miss Willard's associates in the faculty of the Woman's College were a unit with her in aims, methods and personal affection. The Chicago fire swept away a large part of the financial aid which had been pledged to the college in Evanston as an independent enterprise, and in 1873 it became an organic part of the university with which, from the beginning, it had been connected as a sister institution with an independent faculty. The new arrangement led to complications in the government of the Woman's College, which rendered it impossible for Miss Willard to carry out her plans therefor, and she resigned her deanship and professorship in June, 1874. Her soul had been stirred by the reports of the temperance crusade in Ohio during the preceding winter, and she heard the divine call to her life-work. Of all her friends no one stood by her in her wish to join the crusade, except Mrs. Mary A. Livermore, who sent her a letter full of enthusiasm for the new line of work and predicted her success therein. In the summer of 1874, while in New York City, a letter reached her from Mrs. Louise S. Rounds, of Chicago, who was identified there with a young temperance association. "It has come to me," wrote Mrs. Rounds, "as I believe, from the Lord, that you ought to be our president. We are a little band without money or experience, but with strong faith. If you will come, there will be no doubt of your election." Turning from the most attractive offers to reenter the profession she had left, Miss Willard entered the open door of philan-throphy, left for the West, paused in Pittsburgh for a brief personal participation in crusade work, and, within a week, had been made president of the Chicago Woman's Christian Temperance Union. For months she prosecuted her work without regard to pecuniary compensation, many a time going without her noonday lunch down town, because she had no money, and walking miles because she had not five cents to pay for a street-car ride. She found that period the most blessed of her life thus far, and her work, baptized in suf-fering, grew first deep and vital, and then began to widen. With the aid of a few women, she estab-lished a daily gospel meeting in lower Farwell Hall for the help of the intemperate. Scores and hundreds of men were savingly reformed, and her "Gospel Talks" were in demand far and wide. She had made her first addresses in public three or four years before with marked success, but then, turning from the attractions of cultivated society and scholarly themes, even from church work and offered editorial positions, those little gospel meetings, where wicked men wept and prayed, thrilled her through and through. Thrown upon a sickbed the following year by overwork, she con-sented to accent a sum sufficient to provide for the necessities of her widowed mother and herself, but has ever steadfastly refused to receive, an amount which would enable her to lay up anything for the future. Every dollar earned by writing or lecturing, not needed for current expenses, has been devoted to the relief of the needy or to the enlargement of her chosen work. The Chicago Woman's Christian Temperance Union, from that "day of small things" in the eyes of the world, has gone on and prospered, until now it is represented by a wide range of established philanthropies. The Woman's

Temperance Temple, costing more than a million dollars, the headquarters of the National Woman's Christian Temperance Union and of the Woman's Temperance Publication Association, which scat-ters broadcast and around the world annually many million pages of temperance literature, are a few of its fruits. Soon after Miss Willard's election to the presidency of the Chicago union, she became secretary of the first Illinois State conven-tion of the Woman's Christian Temperance Union, and a few weeks later, in November, 1874, after having declined the nomination for president in the first national convention, was elected its corre-sponding secretary in Cleveland, OH. In that office, besides wielding a busy pen, she spoke in Chautauqua and addressed summer camps in New England and the Middle States. In 1876, while engaged in Bible study and prayer, she was led to the conviction that she ought to speak for woman's ballot as a protection to the home from the tyranny of drink, and in the ensuing autumn, in the national convention in Newark, NJ, disregarding the earnest pleadings of conservative friends, she declared her conviction in her first suffrage speech. She originated the motto, "For God and Home and Native Land," which was, first, that of the Chicago union, was then adopted by the Illi-nois State union, in 1876, became that of the national union, and was adapted to the use of the world's union in Faneuil Hall, Boston, MA, in 1891, then becoming "For God and Home and Every Land." Miss Willard was one of the founders of the National Woman's Temperance Union paper, "Our Union," in New York, and of the "Signal," the organ of the Illinois union, which, in 1882, were merged in the "Union Signal," and which is now one of the most widely circulated papers in the world. In January, 1877, she was invited by D. L. Moody to assist him by conducting the woman's meetings in connection with his evangelistic work in Boston. The Chris-tian womanhood of Boston rallied around her, and her work among the women was marked by suc-cess so great that soon she was put forward by Mr. Moody to address his great audience of seven-thousand, on Sunday afternoon in the Tabernacle. She had not lessened her temperance work, but accepted such invitations as her time and strength permitted to lecture on gospel-temperance lines. In the following autumn she sundered her engage-ment with Mr. Moody, in the best of mutual feeling, but with the decided conviction that she could not refuse to work with, any earnest, devout, reputable helper because of a difference in religious belief, and because she preferred to work with both men and women rather than confine herself to work among women. For a short time after the sudden death of her only brother, O. A. Willard, in the spring of 1878, Miss. Willard, with her brother's widow, Mrs. Mary B. Willard, assumed the vacant editorship of his paper, the Chicago "Post and Mail," rather for the sake of others than through her own preference. In the autumn of 1877 she declined the nomination for the presidency of the National Woman's Christian Temperance Union, but she accepted it in 1879, when she was elected in Indianapolis, IN, as the exponent of a liberal policy, including "State rights" for the State societies, representation on a basis of paid membership and the advocacy of the ballot for women. At that time no southern State, except Maryland, was represented in the national society, and the total yearly income was only about $1,200. During the following year the work of the national union was organized under five heads: Preventive, Educational, Evangelistic, Social and Legal, and a system of individual superintendence of each department established. In 1881 Miss Willard made a tour of the Southern States, which reconstructed her views of the situation and conquered conservative prejudice and sectional opposition. Thus was given the initial impetus to the formation of the home protection party, which it was desired should unite all good men and women in its ranks. In August, 1882, she became one of the central committee of the newly organized prohibition home protection party, with which she has since been connected. During the following year, accompanied by her private secretary, Miss Anna Gordon, she completed her plan of visiting and organizing every State and Territory in the United States, and of presenting her cause in every town and city that had reached a population of ten-thousand. She visited the Pacific coast, and California, Oregon, and even British Columbia, were thoroughly organized, and more than twenty-five-thousand miles of toilsome travel enabled her to meet the national convention in Detroit, MI, in October, 1883, to celebrate the completion of its first decade with rejoicing over complete organizations of the Woman's Christian Temperance Union in each one of the forty-eight subdivisions of the United States, Alaska not then included. In 1884, after the failure of endeavors to

have each of the three political parties, Democrats. Greenbackers and Republicans, endorse the prohibition movement, the prohibition party held its nominating convention in Pittsburgh, PA. There Miss Willard seconded the nomination of John P. St. John for president, in a brilliant speech. The general officers of the National Woman's Christian Temperance Union publicly endorsed the party, and in the annual State meetings nearly every convention did the same. While the position of the national society is not necessarily that of States and individuals, so great has been Miss Willard's influence and so earnest the convictions of her co-laborers, that the National Woman's Christian Temperance Union is practically a unit in political inifuence. In 1885 the national headquarters were removed from New York to Chicago, and the white-cross movement was adopted as a feature of the work of the national union. Because no other woman could be found to stand at the helm of this new movement, Miss Willard did so. No other department of the work ever developed so rapidly as this. A great petition for the better, legal protection of women and girls was presented to Congress, with thousands of signatures. Mr. Powderly, chief of the Knights of Labor, through her influence, sent out ninety-two-thousand petitions to local assemblies of the Knights to be signed, circulated and returned to her. Through the efforts of the temperance workers the same petition was circulated and presented for legislative action in nearly every State and Territory. In 1883, while traveling on the Pacific coast, she was deeply impressed by the misery consequent on the opium habit among the Chinese, and in her annual address in the national convention she proposed a commission to report plans for a World's Woman's Christian Temperance Union, which had been suggested by her in 1876. Mrs. Mary A. Leavitt was soon sent out as a missionary of the national union to the Sandwich Islands, whence she proceeded to Australia, Japan, China, India, Africa and Europe, returning to her native land after an absence of eight years, leaving Woman's Christian Temperance Unions organized in every country, while hosts of friends and intrepid workers had been won to the ranks. The British Woman's Temperance Union had been previously organized, and the most notable feature of the national convention in Minneapolis, MN, in 1886, was the presence of Mrs. Margaret Lucas, the sister of John Bright and first president of the World's Woman's Christian

Temperance Union, accompanied by Mrs. Hannah Whithall Smith. Her reception was magnificent, the convention rising in separate groups, first the crusaders in a body, then the women of New England, then of the Middle States, after these the western and the Pacific coast, and last the southern representatives, while the English and American flags waved from the platform, and all joined in singing "God Save the Queen." The Dominion Woman's Christian Temperance Union of Canada has had also a powerful influence as an ally of the national union. Mrs. Letitia Youmans, the earliest white-ribbon pioneer in Canada, went to the convention in Cincinnati, OH, in 1875, to learn its methods, and became, ten years later, the first president of the Dominion union. Thirty-five nations are now auxiliary to the World's Woman's Christian Temperance Union, and the wearers of its emblematic white ribbon number three-hundred-thousand. About half of these women are residents of the United States. Miss Willard has been reelected president of the national union, with practical unanimity, every year since 1879. She was elected president of the World's Woman's Christian Temperance Union, to succeed Mrs. Margaret Bright Lucas, in 1887, and has been since reelected for each biennial term. Besides sending out several round-the-world missionaries to nurture and enlarge the work initiated by Mrs. Leavitt, the world's union has circulated the monster polyglot petition against legalizing the alcohol and opium traffic, translated into hundreds of dialects, actively circulated in Great Britain, Switzerland, Scandinavia, India, China, Japan, Ceylon, Australia, Sandwich Islands, Chili, Canada and the United States, and signed by more than a million women. The president of the British Woman's Temperance Association, Lady Henry Somerset, is vice-president of the world's union, and Miss Willard finds in her a close friend and coadjutor. The sacrifices which Miss Willard has so freely made for this work have been repaid to her in abundant measure. She has been called by Joseph Cook "the most widely known and the best beloved woman in America." With a sisterly devotion to all of every creed who would "help a fallen brother rise," she has been ever loyal to the simple gospel faith in which she was reared. She is, first of all, a Christian philanthropist. Her church membership is with the Methodist Episcopal Church, which has honored itself in its recognition of her, though not to the extent of admitting her to its

highest ecclesiastical court, the general quadrennial conference, to which she has twice been elected by the local conference. She has been one of the greatest travelers of this traveling age. From 1868 to 1871, in company with Miss Jackson, she spent two-and-one-half years abroad, traveling in Great Britain and Ireland, Denmark, Germany, Belgium, Holland, France, Austria, Turkey in Europe and Asia, Greece, Palestine and Egypt, studying art, history and languages indefatigably, and returning to her native land rich in the benefits reaped only by the scholarly and industrious traveler. She has traversed her own land from ocean to ocean and from the lakes to the gulf, and made second and third trips to England in the autumn of 1892. She has contributed hundreds of articles to many prominent periodicals, is assistant editor of "Our Day," of Boston, and other magazines, and is editor-in-chief of the "Union Signal." Her published volumes are: "Nineteen Beautiful Years," "Hints and Helps in Temperance Work," "How to Win," "Woman in the Pulpit," "Woman and Temperance," "Glimpses of Fifty Years," "A Classic Town," and "A Young Journalist," the last in conjunction with Lady Henry Somerset. Her annual addresses to the Woman's Christian Temperance Union would form volumes unmatched in their way in the libraries of the world. In August, 1892, her devoted mother, the companion and inspirer of her life, without whose encouragement she believes her life-work never could have been done, one of the noblest women of this or any age, was transplanted to the life beyond, and Miss Willard, still in the prime of life, is now the last of her family. She is a member of societies in her own and other lands whose name is legion. She was president of the Woman's National Council, a federation of nearly all the woman's societies in America, in 1890, and is now vice-president of the same. She was at the head of the woman's committee of temperance meetings in the World's Fair, and of other World's Fair committees. She was interested in promoting plans to aid in sending help to the Armenian sufferers in 1896, and to provide homes and funds for refugees who fled to America for protection.

WILLARD, Miss Katherine, musician, born in Denver, CO, in April, 1866. Her parents, Oliver A. Willard and Mary Bannister Willard, were both of distinguished New England ancestry, and persons of remarkable intellectual gifts and acquirements.

Her maternal grandfather was Rev. Henry Bannister, D. D., for twenty-seven years professor of Hebrew in Garrett Biblical Institute, Evanston, IL, and her father was the only brother of Miss Frances E. Willard. In the infancy of Miss Katherine Willard her parents removed from Colorado to their former home in Evanston, IL. There, in a refined Christian home and with the best social and intellectual advantages, she spent her early youth. The death of her father occurred when she had reached the age of twelve, and in 1885 she accompanied her mother, Mrs. Mary Bannister Willard, to Germany, where, besides continuing her studies in languages, art and history, she devoted herself to the cultivation of her voice under the best musicians of Berlin. Under the faithful improvement of rare advantages her gifts of voice, person and manner united to win for her a marked success. In the autumn of 1885 she began years of industrious study with Fräulein Louise Ress, the most celebrated exponent o the old Italian method, and she also studied with other famous singers of the Italian school. She sang in Berlin two successive winters in the Sing-Akademie with Scharwenka, Heinrich Grünfeld, the celebrated 'cellist, and with M'me Madeline Schiller. During her residence of five years in Berlin, she made the acquaintance of many eminent Germans and Americans. She was invited by the Countess Waldersee to sing in a soirée given to Prince Bismarck and Count Von Moltke, and in Berlin and elsewhere she sang in many private and public entertainments. In London, England, she sang with great success. She was invited by her old school friend Mrs. Grover Cleveland, to Washington, and in 1889 she spent several weeks in the White House, where she passed a brilliant season in society and sang in many notable entertainments in the Executive Mansion, and elsewhere. She sang in New York, Baltimore, Chicago and other cities in concert and parlor musicales. In October, 1892, she returned to Europe, to study in Berlin and to sing in London during the season of 1893.

WILLARD, Mrs. Mary Bannister, editor, temperance worker and educator, born in Fairfield, NY, 18th September, 1841. She is the daughter of Rev. Henry Bannister, D.D., a. distinguished scholar, and Methodist divine, and his wife, Mrs. Lucy Kimball Bannister, a woman of rare gentleness and dignity of character. In the infancy of Mary, their oldest daughter, the father became principal of Cazenovia Seminary, and her childhood and early youth were spent as a pupil in that institution. When she was fifteen, the family removed to Evanston, IL. Possessing a love for study and rare talents, Mary made rapid progress in scholarship and was graduated with honor from the Northwestern Female College, in Evanston, at the age of eighteen. The following year she went to Tennessee as a teacher, but her career there was cut short by the approach of the Civil War. She became the wife of Oliver A. Willard, 3rd July, 1862, and went, with her husband to his first pastorate, in Edgerton, WI. In the following year they removed to Denver, CO, where her husband founded a Methodist church, and became presiding elder at the age of twenty-seven years. Two years later, the family, consisting of the parents, one son and one daughter, returned to Evanston, where they made their home for several years, and where another son and another daughter were added to their number. Mrs. Willard has always wielded a gifted pen. She wrote little during those years, giving such leisure as domestic care permitted to home study with her husband, who had become the editor of a Chicago daily paper. His sudden death, in the prime of his brilliant powers, was an overwhelming bereavement, and left to Mrs. Willard the responsibility of conducting his paper, the "Post and Mail," which she assumed with the assistance of her husband's sister, Miss Frances E. Willard. The financial burden proving too heavy, it was relinquished, and not long afterward Mrs. Willard was called to assume the editorship of a new paper, the "Signal," the organ of the Illinois Woman's Christian Temperance Union. Several years of most successful work as editor and temperance worker displayed her gifts, both in the editorial sanctum and as organizer and platform speaker. The "Signal" under her leadership came quckly to the front, and it was said that no other paper in America was better edited. In 1881 she made her first trip to Europe. Successfully editing the "Union Signal" for several years afterward, her health became impaired, and with her two daughters she spent a year in Berlin, Germany. In the autumn of 1886 she opened in that city her American Home School for girls, unique in its way, and which for six years has been carried out on the original plan with much success. It combines the best features of an American school with special advantages in German, French and music, and the influences and care of a refined Christian home. History, literature and art receive special attention. The number of pupils received never exceeds the limits of a pleasant family circle, and vacation trips are arranged under Mrs. Willard's personal supervision and escort. In the years of her residence in Europe, her gifts and wide acquaintance have ever been at the service of her countrywomen, and she has stood there, as here, as a representative of the best phases of total abstinence reform.

WILLARD, Madame Mary Thompson Hill, mother of Miss Frances E. Willard, born on a farm in North Danville, VT, 3rd January, 1805. Her father was John Hill, of Lee, NH, and her mother, Polly Thompson Hill, was a daughter of Nathaniel Thompson, of Durham and Holderness, in the same State. Both the Hills and the Thompsons were families of note, and their descendants include many well-known names in New Hampshire history. John Hill removed to Danville, VT, in the pioneer period of that region, and on his farm of three-hundred acres, a few miles west of the Connecticut river, he and his wife made a happy and well-ordered home. The father was a sort of Hercules, strong in body, mind and soul, and an active Christian. The mother's character was a rare combination of excellence, religious, cheerful, industrious, frugal, hopeful, buoyant, mirthful at times loving and lovable always, with a poet's insight, and fellowship with nature. Their oldest son, James Hill, was a youth of rare powers and high ambitions. Mary, strongly resembling her brother James, was the second daughter in the family, each one of whom possessed abilities of a high order. Her early education was obtained in the country district school and in the log school house of a new country, but the schools were taught usually by students or graduates of Dartmouth and Middlebury colleges, who often boarded in Mary's home, and whose attainments and character made deep impressions for good upon the susceptible child. In her twelfth year her father sold his Vermont farm and removed to the new region of the Genesee valley in western New

York. In the new settlement, fourteen miles west of Rochester, now known as the town of Ogden, Mary grew to young womanhood. She was a good student and a wide reader, and at the age of fifteen taught her first school. Teaching proved attractive, and she continued for eleven years with much success. She seemed not to have been made for the kitchen and she was never put there in her father's home. Fine needle work and fine spinning, the fashionable domestic accomplishments in those days, gave her pleasure. She possessed in an unusual degree an admiration for the beautiful, especially in language. She had the poetic faculty, was a sweet singer, had remarkable gifts in conversation, and rare tact, delicacy and appreciation of the best in others. Of fine personal appearance and dignified manners, she won the regard of a son of her father's near neighbors, the Willards, who had removed thither from Vermont. Josiah F. Willard was a young man of irreproachable character and brilliant talents, and when he became the husband of Mary Hill, 3rd November, 1831, and their new home was set up in Churchville, it was with the brightest prospects of happiness, comfort, and usefulness. Both were active members of the Union Church in Ogden. The family resided in their first home until four children had been born to them, the only son, Oliver, two daughters who died in infancy, and Frances Elizabeth, who was a delicate child in her second year, when her parents decided to remove to Oberlin, OH, in order to secure educational advantages for themselves and their children. Mr. Willard entered the regular college course, which he had nearly completed when hemorrhage of the lungs warned him to seek at once a new environment. The years they spent in Oberlin were happy years to Mrs. Willard. There her youngest child, Mary, was born, the year following their removal thither. Her domestic life was well-ordered, and her three children shared the most devoted love and the most careful training, while her intellectual and social gifts drew to their home a circle of choice friends from among the most cultivated women of Oberlin. They formed a circle for study, long before a "woman's club" had ever been heard of, and kept pace with husbands, brothers and sons among the college faculty or in the student ranks. When necessity was laid upon the family for removal to a drier climate for the husband's sake,

Mrs. Willard prepared for the long overland journey, and herself drove one of the three emigrant wagons which conveyed the family and their possessions to the Territory of Wisconsin. The summer of 1846 saw the Willards settled on a farm near Janesville, WI. The trials inseparable from pioneer life could not be avoided, but they were accepted by the parents with Christian fortitude, lofty philosophy and ceaseless industry. Soon the father was a leader in the church, a magistrate in the community and a legislator in the State, meantime having created a beautiful estate, which was named "Forest Home." There they passed twelve years, when Mrs. Willard bade adieu to "Forest Home" for Evanston, near Chicago, that the daughters might be educated without sending them from home. In June, 1862 the family met their first great grief in the death of their daughter Mary, just blooming into womanhood. In 1868 she was called to lay her husband beside the daughter, and in 1878 she buried her son, Oliver, in the meridian of his years. From the earliest years of her children the chief aspect of life to Mrs. Willard was that of motherhood, and so nobly did she reach her lofty ideal that in this respect her character was a model. Sympathizing with, guiding, stimulating and training each child according to its needs, the law of liberty in the development of every faculty and freedom for every right ambition were observed carefully. In early youth her daughter, Frances, wrote: "I thank God for my mother as for no other gift of his bestowing. My nature is so woven into hers that I think it would almost be death for me to have the bond severed, and one so much myself gone over the river. I verily believe I cling to her more than ever did any other of her children. Perhaps because I am to need her more." "Enter every open door" was her constant advice to her daughter, and much of the daughter's distinguished career has been rendered possible because of the courage and encouragement of her mother. The widened horizon and the fame which came to the mother in later years was in turn through her daughter, and thus the centripetal and centrifugal forces united in the shaping of an orbit ever trite to its foci, God and humanity. Preserving her mental powers undimmed to the last, Madame Willard died after a brief illness, 7th August, 1892, at the age of nearly eighty-eight years. At her funeral it was said, "She was a reformer by nature. She made the world's cause her own and identified herself with

all its fortunes. Nothing of its sorrow, sadness or pain was foreign to her. With a genius, a consecration, a beauty and a youth which had outlived her years, a soul eager still to know, to learn, to catch every word God had for her, she lived on, a center of joy and comfort in this most typical and almost best known home in America. She stood a veritable Matterhorn of strength to this daughter. Given a face like hers, brave, benignant, patient, yet resolute, a will inflexible for duty, a heart sensitive to righteousness and truth, yet tender as a child's, given New England puritanism and rigor, its habits of looking deep into every problem, its consciousness full of God, its lofty ideal of freedom and its final espousal of every noble cause, and you and I shall never blame the stalwart heart, well-nigh crushed because mother is gone." The birthday motto adopted in the famous celebration of Madam Willard's eightieth birthday was "It is better further on," and her household name was "Saint Courageous."

WILLIAMS, Miss Adéle, artist, born in Richmond, VA, 24th February, 1868. She comes of a family many members of which have been well known and conspicuous in the communities in which they lived. Her descent is thoroughly English. She is a descendant, on her mother's side, of Rev. Peter Bulkeley, who came from England to America in 1836; she is a great-great-granddaughter of Capt. Sylvanus Smith, of Revolutionary times, and a granddaughter of H. M. Smith, of Richmond, a man known throughout the country as an inventor and draughtsman. From him she inherited her talent. Her father, John H. Williams, was for many years a resident of San Francisco, CA, and there accumulated considerable wealth. In her eleventh year reverses came to the family, and her subsequent education was acquired in the public schools of Richmond. At the age of fifteen she was graduated from the high school at the head of her class. Her attention since then has been almost entirely devoted to art. She went to New York in 1886 and became a pupil in the Woman's Art School of Cooper Union. After three years of study she was graduated, having twice won medals in the different classes. During the period spent in New York she was at times a pupil of the Art Students' League, of the Gothani Art School and of many of the most prominent teachers. Her first picture on exhibition was accepted for the exhibition in the Academy of Design in 1888. Since that time she has been a regular contributor to the exhibitions of the American Water Color Society, and of the New York Club since its formation, in 1889, besides being represented in many minor exhibitions. As a pupil of Mrs. Rhoda Holmes Nicholls, her attention was chiefly directed to the study of watercolors. In June, 1892, she went to Europe, and, after spending three months in travel, settled down to study in Paris, France. Her home is in Richmond.

WILLIAMS, Mrs. Alice, temperance reformer, born in Gallatin, MO, 19th January, 1853. Her father, Franz Henry Von Buchholz, was the younger son of a titled German family. The older son inherited the family estate, and there was little left for the younger son, save the title, on which he found it difficult to live. At the age of twenty-eight he embarked for America. Here he found no difficulty in winning his way, and two years after settling in Lexington, KY, he was married to Miss Harriette Thwaits, the daughter of a wealthy slave-owner of Lexington. The mother had all the conservative ideas of the South concerning woman, her sphere and her work, and in Alice's girlhood was shocked the first time she heard a woman's voice in the social prayer meeting. At the immature age of sixteen, with the approval of her parents, Alice became the wife of R. N. Williams, a Christian gentleman, some years her senior. Into their home came a daughter and a son; then followed years of invalidism. During years of suffering Mrs. Williams read, studied and thought much. When the Woman's Christian Temperance Union was formed in Missouri, she became an active local worker. In 1884 she went with her husband to Lake Bluff, IL, to a prohibition conference. There, at the request of Missouri's State president, Alice Williams' voice was first heard from the platform in a two-minute speech. She was appointed superintendent of young woman's work in Missouri and was called to every part of the State to speak and organize. She is a national lecturer in the department of social purity, and is one of the few, whether of men or women, who can speak strongly, yet not offensively, before a mixed audience on this most difficult theme. She has four children, two daughters and two sons. Her home is in Cameron, MO.

WILLIAMS, Miss Florence B., editor and publisher, born in Bryan county, GA, 20th December, 1865. A part of her childhood was spent in Savannah, GA. At the age of sixteen she left home to battle with the world, not from necessity, but because she was ambitious. She began her life of independence by teaching. From the age of sixteen she continued to teach, to study and to read until 1889, when she took charge of the Statesboro "Eagle," the official organ of the county. She leads a busy life. Besides doing all of the work on her paper, her social duties are many. She is numbered with the few southern girls who have braved the prejudices of their neighbors to assume the duties of an editor. Besides her regular work on her own paper, she contributes articles to the "Sunny South," "Old Homestead" and other papers. In 1892 she established the Valdosta "Telescope," a news and literary paper, published in Valdosta, GA, which gives promise of a bright future in newspaperdom for its editor, who has already achieved a prominent place among the women writers of her State.

WILLIAMS, Mrs. Louisa Brewster, musician and composer, born in Philadelphia, PA, 25th June, 1832. She is in the direct line of descent from William Brewster, the Elder of Plymouth, the companion of Standish. One of his grandsons, Francis E. Brewster, settled in the southern part of New Jersey, where was born Dr. Horace Brewster, a prominent surgeon in his day, who gave his time and services to his countrymen through the war of the Revolution. He served in the army as one of its chief surgeons, and

endured with his copatriots all the ordeals and trials of that conflict. Dr. Brewster had several children, one of whom was Edmund Brewster, the father of Louisa. He was an artist of acknowledged ability, who gave his attention principally to portrait painting. He moved in early years to Philadelphia, where he died in 1850, leaving a widow and five children. The family were left with but little means, and it became necessary that each member should contribute in some way for their support. Louisa had developed a passionate fondness for music to such an extent that, before she was six years of age, she was in charge of a competent teacher. Her sister Angeline was also possessed of the same devotion to music, and together they pursued their studies with such success that, when it became necessary for them to do their share, they immediately turned their knowledge of music to advantage and started a school of music. Success crowned their efforts, and soon their students came in such numbers as to enable them to support the entire family with their earnings. Louisa has taught music from that time to the present. During all those years they took care of their mother and an invalid sister until her death. Her sister Angeline died some years ago, and of the family three survive, a brother, Dr. Thomas Brewster of Missouri, a widowed sister who now lives with her, and herself. Besides teaching the piano and organ, she has also found time to compose several pieces of music, which have won success in all quarters. Among these compositions are "The Union Bell March," "President's Dream Waltz," and "The Dying Nun." She has written a new and improved piano instructor, which is one of the standard works for beginners. She now lives in the old home of her father in Philadelphia, where she has always, resided. She is still active and energetic and possesses all the traits of her ancestry to a very marked degree.

WILLING, Mrs. Jennie Fowler, author, preacher, lecturer and educator, born in Burford, Canada West, in 1834. She has a mixture of heroic English, Scotch and Irish blood in her veins. Her maternal grandmother was disinherited because she chose to share the wilderness perils with an itinerant minister. Her father was a Canadian "patriot," who lost all in an attempt to secure national independence. He was glad to escape to the

States with his life and his family, and to begin life again in the new West. He could give his children little more than a hatred of tyranny, constant industry, careful economy and good morals. With this simple outfit and an irrepressible love of study, his daughter began to teach school when she was fifteen years old. The next year, though a timid little body, she finished teaching the winter term of a village school, from which the "big boys" had "turned out" their young man teacher. At the age of nineteen she became the wife of a Methodist minister, and went with him to western New York. The multitudinous duties of a pastor's wife left small time for study, but she has always had a language or a science on the tapis. She began to write for the press at the age of sixteen years, and, besides constant contributions to papers and magazines, she has produced two serials for New York papers and ten books of no mean quality. In 1873 she was elected professor of English language and literature in the Illinois Wesleyan University. Since then she has been connected as trustee or teacher with several first-grade literary institutions. In 1874 she was nominated, with a fair prospect of election, to the superintendency of public instruction in the State of Illinois. On account of other duties she was obliged to decline the nomination. Her inherited love of reform brought her to the fore when the great crusade swept over the land. For several years she was president of the Illinois Woman's State Temperance Union. With Emily Huntington Miller she issued the call for the Cleveland convention, and she presided over that body, in which the National Woman's Christian Temperance Union was organized. For a few years she edited its organ, now the "Union Signal." Mrs. Willing was drawn into public speaking by her temperance zeal, and soon she found herself addressing immense audiences in all the great cities of the land. As one of the corresponding secretaries of the Woman's Foreign Missionary Society, she presented its claims at conferences of ministers, and in scores of large towns in different parts of the United States, interesting thousands of people in its work. For seven or eight years past she has rendered similar service to the Woman's Home Missionary Society. As an evangelist she has held many large and important revival services, and with marked success. Since her removal to New York

City, in 1889, she has had her hands full with her home mission work, her evangelistic services, her Italian mission and the bureau for immigrants, with its immigrant girls' home, in New York, Boston and Philadelphia. Clear of head, warm of heart, steady of faith, her English sturdiness, Scotch persistence and Irish vivacity make her ready for every good work for Christ and his poor. She bears the university degree of A.M.

WILLIS, Miss Louise Hammond, artist, born in Charleston, SC, in 1870. From her mother, Elizabeth Louise Hammond, she inherited a love of nature and a scientific mind. From her father, Major Edward Willis, she inherits ambition, an indomitable will and perseverance. The Willis home is the resort of men and women of talent and distinction. She was graduated with first-honor medal and diploma from the Charleston Female Seminary, where she had charge of the painting and drawing classes. She was the assistant teacher in the Carolina Art School. In her chosen profession she works with steady purpose. Her studies have been carried on in Charleston, SC, under E. Whittock McDowell, and in New York under J. Carroll Beckwith and H. Siddons Mowbray. She purposes to study in Paris and the German schools. Her specialty is portraiture, in which art she is already successful. Believing that everything helps everything else, she applied herself to the study of architecture, originating clever plans. She is familiar with a half-dozen languages and plays on a number of musical instruments. She writes both prose and poetry for the best magazines. She has studied the theory of music and she composes easily, showing originality. Her illustrations, pen-and-ink drawings, are meritorious. She excels in the womanly art of fine and artistic needle work, point-laces and art embroideries. Her writings appear over the pen-name "Louis Hammond Willis." All her surroundings are literary and artistic. Her paintings have always received favorable comment and attracted attention. She is a Daughter of the American Revolution. She now lives in New York City.

WILLSON, Mrs. Mary Elizabeth, gospel singer and song-writer, born in Clearfield county, PA, 1st May, 1842. Her father, Mr. Bliss, was a man of godly principles, of simple and childlike faith. Her mother, Lydia Bliss, was a noblehearted Christian woman. Her only brother was the singing evangelist and hymn-writer, P. P. Bliss. Of the two daughters, Mary Elizabeth is the younger. While she was still a child, the family removed to Tioga county, PA, where Mr. Bliss bought a tract of wild land and built a modest home in a great forest of hemlocks and maples. She recalls the happy time when she roamed those grand old woods with her beloved brother, both shouting and singing in the gladness of their youthful hearts, and to their free life in the balsamic air of the forest may be attributed, in a measure, the strength of body, the clearness of voice, the naturalness of tone and manner that have distinguished her brother and herself in their rendering of Zion's songs. When she was fifteen years old, she accompanied her brother into the adjoining county of Bradford, where the latter taught a select school. They made their home with a family named Young, who were very musical. Miss Young gave P. P. Bliss his first lessons in singing and eventually became his wife. Mrs. Willson does not remember learning to read notes by sight; it seems to her that she always knew them. In 1858 she commenced to teach, and she taught until 1860, when she became the wife of Clark Willson, of Towanda, PA, where they still have a pleasant home, to which they resort for occasional rests from their evangelistic labors. For the first sixteen years of their married life Mr. and Mrs. Willson spent considerable time in teaching music and holding musical conventions. When her brother, the author of "Hold the Fort," with his beloved wife, was killed in the disaster of Ashtabula Bridge, on 29th December, 1876, the first great sorrow of her life fell on the devoted sister. Mrs. Willson then said: "I can never again sing merely to entertain people, but if the Lord will use my voice for the salvation of men, I will go on singing." Very soon a friend and co-worker of the lamented P. P. Bliss, Major Whittle, called husband and wife to aid him in evangelistic work in Chicago. They accepted the call, and their work as gospel singers was so successful in Chicago and many other places that they at once and without reserve laid themselves on the altar of God's service. In 1878 Francis Murphy, the apostle of temperance, invited Mr. and Mrs. Willson to "sing the gospel" for him in what was known as the 'Red Ribbon Crusade." They visited the principal cities of the Northern and Southern States, and everywhere Mrs. Willson won the admiration and respect of all who heard her. Thurlow Weed, in an article in the New York "Tribune," named her the "Jenny Lind of sacred melody," a term that has clung to her ever since. In 1882 she and her husband spent several months in Great Britain, in the gospel temperance work, under the leadership of Francis Murphy. She sang to great audiences in Liverpool, Birmingham, Manchester, Edinburgh, Aberdeen, Glasgow, Dublin and other cities. The British press was enthusiastic in her praise. She has written several hymns and sacred songs that, like her brother's, are being sung around the world. Among the most popular ones are "Glad Tidings," "My Mother's Hands" and "Papa, Come this Way." She is the author of two volumes of gospel hymns and songs, one entitled "Great Joy" and the other "Sacred Gems." She has contributed words and music to most of the gospel song-books published within the, past twelve years. She is in the prime of her powers as a singer, composer and evangelist.

WILSON, Mrs. Augusta C. Evans, author, born near Columbus, GA, in 1836. Her maiden name was Augusta C. Evans. In her childhood her family removed to Texas, and afterward to Mobile, AL, where, in 1868, she became the wife of L. M. Wilson, a prominent citizen of Alabama. She has since lived near Mobile, in a fine old country home. Her first novel, "Inez, a Tale of the Alamo," was brought out in New York. It was only moderately successful. In 1859 her second book, "Beulah," was published, and its success was instantaneous. It is still a popular book and has passed through many editions. When the Civil War broke out, she was living near Columbus, GA, and her devotion to the Confederacy kept her from doing any literary work for several years. Her next book was "Macaria," a copy of which she sent with a letter to her New York publisher, by a blockade runner, which carried it to Havana,

Cuba, whence it was mailed to New York. It was printed on coarse brown paper, copyrighted by the "Confederate States of America," and dedicated "To the Brave Soldiers of the Southern Army." It was printed in Charleston, SC, and published by a bookseller in Richmond, VA. The book was seized and detroyed by a Federal officer in Kentucky. It was brought out in the North and found a large sale. After the war she went to New York City and published her famous "St. Elmo," which had a very large sale. Her later works include "Vashti," "Infelice," and "At the Mercy of Tiberius." She has large wealth through her marriage and her literary earnings. During the past few years she has lived in retirement.

WILSON, Mrs. Augustus, reformer, was born in Ensor Manor, MD. She is the daughter of Gen. John S. Ensor and his wife, Mrs. Elizabeth B. Ensor. She comes of English stock, and her ancestors were distinguished in history. Her great-grandfather was a descendant of King James, and came to the colonies with Lord Baltimore. The land he received by grant is still in the possession of the family. Her male ancestors were soldiers, patriots and statesmen. Her mother was of Scotch descent. Miss Enson served as her father's private secretary during the Civil War. She became the wife, on 1st December, 1863, of Augustus Wilson, of Ohio, in which State they settled, after traveling extensively in the United States and British America. In 1874 Mr. and Mrs. Wilson removed to Parsons, KS, where Mr. Wilson engaged in business. He died in July, 1885, in that town Mrs. Wilson's only child, a son, died in 1869, while they were living in New Madison, OH. She has long been identified with the woman suffrage movement, and in 1870 she was elected president of an association. In Ohio she was active in temperance work, and while living in Kansas she wrote much for temperance journals. In 1879 she was made a life member of the Kansas temperance union. In July, 1881, she was a delegate to the national prohibition convention, held in Chicago, and she has attended many State and national conventions of the woman suffragists. From childhood she has been a church and missionary worker, having worked on the woman's board of foreign missions of the Methodist Episcopal Church. In 1875 she assisted in raising money to found the mission home in Constantinople, Turkey. In the West she became a member of the Congregational Church. In 1880 she was elected president of the congressional work of the Woman's Christian Temperance Union in Kansas. She aided in founding the Parsons Memorial and Historical Library. In 1881 she memorialized both houses of Congress to secure homes in Oklahoma for the "Exodusters." She has served in many public enterprises, such as the Bartholdi monument fund, the relief association for drouth-smitten farmers in Kansas and the New Orleans expositions. She is a trustee of the State Art Association of Kansas, a member of the State Historical Society and of a score of other important organizations. She is a member of the press committee and the Kansas representative in the Columbian Exposition of 1893. After her husband's death she managed her estate. She started the Wilsonton "Journal" in 1888, and still edits it. She lives in the town of her founding, Wilsonton, KS.

WILSON, Mrs. Jane Delaplaine, author, born in Hamilton, OH, in 1830. She was educated in the academy for young women in her native town. At an early age she became the wife of E. V. Wilson, then a lawyer. They removed to northeastern Missouri, where they settled in Edina. Her husband is now Judge Wilson. As a child she was inclined to literature, and during youth she wrote much, which was never allowed to see the light. In 1880 she began to publish short stories and poems under the pen-name "Mrs. Lawrence" After using that name for a short time, she laid it aside and signed her work with her husband's initials. Both her poems and stories have been widely copied. She has contributed to a number of periodicals.

WILSON, Mrs. Martha Eleanor Loftin, missionary worker, born in Clarke county, AL, 18th January, 1834. She was educated in the Dayton Masonic Institute, in that State. She became the wife, 14th November, 1850, of John Stainback Wilson, MD. During the Civil War she had a varied experience in the hospitals of Richmond, VA, with her husband, who was a surgeon. At that time she wrote a little book, "Hospital Scenes and Incidents of the War," which was in the hands of the publishers, with the provision that the proceeds should go to the sick and wounded. The manuscript was burned in the fall of Columbia, SC. A part of the original manuscript was deposited in the cornerstone of the Confederate Home, in Atlanta, GA. She is the mother of five sons and one daughter. She has been a member of the Baptist denomination from early childhood, having been baptized in 1845. She has always been connected with the benevolent institutions of the vicinity in which she lived. She accepted as her life work the duties of corresponding secretary of the central committee of the Woman's Baptist Missionary Union of Georgia. The central committee was organized by the home and foreign boards of the Southern Baptist Convention, 19th November, 1878, in Atlanta, with Mrs. Stainback Wilson as president. Besides filling the position of corresponding secretary, she is the Georgia editor of the "Baptist Basket," a missionary journal published in Louisville, KY. She was for some time president of the Southside Woman's Christian Temperance Union and of the Woman's Christian Association of Atlanta, both of which she aided in organizing. At the same time she taught an infant class of sixty to seventy-five in her church Sabbath-school. Her entire time is given to works of benevolence. Her husband died on 2nd August, 1892. Her two-fold work goes on without interruption.

WILSON, Mrs. Zara A., reformer and lawyer, born in Burnettsville, IN, 8th October, 1840. She was the fourth in a family of eight children. Her maiden name was Mahurin, to which form it had been Americanized from the Scotch Mac Huron. Her father was of southern birth and education, a native of the Carolinas. He was twice married, his second wife being Matilda C. Freeman, the mother of Mrs. Wilson, to

whom he was married near Troy, OH, in 1832. Mrs. Wilson's early life was spent on a farm, but she had the advantages of a seminary education in an institution founded and presided over by a half-brother, Isaac Mahurin. She had always shown a fondness for books, and during her student days mathematics was to her a fascinating study. At the age of seventeen she began to teach. After one year in Fort Wayne College, then in thriving condition, she became assistant in that school. The sudden death of her father called her home to the support of a sorrowing mother, whom she assisted, during the next year, in the settlement of a large estate. Then she resumed teaching and served with success in Lafayette and other towns of Indiana. In the former city she took her first public stand in favor of the equality of sex, refusing to accept a position as principal because the salary offered was ten dollars per month less than was paid to a man for the same work. She had already suffered from the disability custom had laid upon her sex. She had, in her earnest longing to do good, a strong desire to enter the ministry, but found that, because of sex, she would not be admitted to the Biblical Institute in Evansville, IN. In 1867 she became the wife of Port Wilson, a merchant of Goodland, IN. Owing to broken health, her energies were for ten years confined mostly to home duties and the care of her only child, a son. During that time she organized the Woman's Foreign Missionary Society of the Methodist Episcopal Church in Goodland, and was corresponding secretary of that district until, her health demanding change of climate, the family home was removed to Lincoln, NE, in 1879. She gradually improved in the climate of Nebraska. She has been an efficient member of the Nebraska Woman's Christian Temperance Union, delivering addresses and publishing State reports. She was three times elected corresponding secretary of the Nebraska body, resigning because of overwork. For four years she was a member of the national convention. She has always been active in the cause of woman's advancement and has been a warm advocate of woman's political enfranchisement, wielding a ready pen in its favor. Since her admission to the bar, in 1891, she is making the legal status of women a specialty, and she has in that line written much for the press. At present she is the State superintendent of franchise for the Woman's Christian Temperance Union and district corre-

sponding secretary of the Woman's Foreign Missionary Society of the Methodist Episcopal Church. In the fall of 1892 she was a candidate on the prohibition ticket for county attorney.

WING, Mrs. Amelia Kempshall, author and philanthropist, born in Rochester, NY, 31st May, 1837. She is the oldest of a family of eight children. Her father, the son of an English gentleman and a representative man, gave his children the best educational advantages of the time. Mrs. Wing was a student in the Wyoming Academy and in Ingham University. Although reared with a prospect of continued affluence, her earnestness of purpose was early shown, for, at the age of sixteen, during financial trouble, she, eager to feel herself in touch with the world, went to teach in a public school in Brooklyn, NY. At twenty years of age she became the wife of Frederick H. Wing, and in Newark, OH, began her wedded life. The stirring needs of the war were arousing the women into action, her capabilities were quickly recognized, and she was made secretary and treasurer of a local branch of the Sanitary Commission, in which position she did active service. On her return to Brooklyn she continued her connection with philanthropic work, and was chairman of the executive committee of the Maternity Hospital and recording secretary for the Home for Consumptives. In January, 1886, she was elected president of the Brooklyn Woman's Club, and by unanimous reelection remained in office five years. Her executive ability is shown by the enlarged scope of the work of the club committees, which is due to her personal interest. Her literary work, begun after her two sons were grown, shows much merit, and the mother-love is effectively portrayed in her stories written for children. She has written on many subjects. A deep religious spirituality pervades her hymns and poetry, and when she speaks of the "Coming Woman," a favorite subject, she exalts her topic by the high standard of her ideal.

WINKLER, Mrs. Angelina Virginia, journalist, born in Richmond, VA, 2nd June, 1842. Her father, John Walton, and her mother, Elizabeth

Tate Smith, were both of English descent, her father, a direct heir of Lady Mary Hamilton, of Manchester, England. Her mother was the owner of a valuable slave property, inherited from the Tates, of Virginia. At the time of Angelina's birth, her father was a merchant of Richmond, where he spent fifty years of his life, and reared and educated a family. She was educated in the Richmond Female Institute. Her early home life was of the domestic order. When the war-cloud broke upon the South, she devoted herself to the care of the sick, the wounded and the dying soldiers in the hospitals. During those terrible years she lost her father, mother, a brother and other near relatives. The war swept away her estate, and the parental home was left a ruin, carrying with it valuable papers proving her right to a large estate in England. In June, 1864, she became the wife of Lieutenant Colonel Winkler, of the 4th Texas regiment, who shared the fortunes and misfortunes of Hood's famous Texas brigade. Mr. Winkler, at the opening of the war, was a prominent lawyer of Corsicana, TX. After the surrender of Appomattox, Mrs. Winkler, with her husband, went to Corsicana, where they established a new home, and a family grew up around them. Mr. Winkler was absent most of the time, being a member of the State Legislature and a factor in the politics of the State, until called to serve as judge in the Court of Appeals, where, after six years of valuable service to his State, he died. Mrs. Winkler, before her husband's death, had contributed some popular articles to the "Southern Illustrated News" and "Magnolia," published in Richmond, VA, and newspapers and magazines in Texas and other Southern States. She then undertook the publication of a literary magazine, "Texas Prairie Flower," which she managed for three years. She was a member of the Texas Press Association. She was appointed honorary commissioner for her State to the World's Exhibition in New Orleans, and organized associations for work in the woman's department of Texas. Her chief work has been the preparation of a historical work, entitled "The Confederate Capital, and Hood's Texas Brigade." She is now associate editor and business manager of the "Round Table," a monthly magazine published in Texas.

WINSLOW, Mrs. Caroline B., physician, born in Kent, England, 19th October, 1822. She came to the United States with her family in 1826. She received a good education. Becoming interested in medicine, she entered the Eclectic College, in Cincinnati, OH, and was graduated in June, 1856. She was the first woman graduated in that college and the fifth woman in the United States to graduate in medicine. She practiced successfully in Cincinnati until 1859, and then took a postgraduate course in, and received a diploma from, the Homeopathic College in Cleveland, OH. She then went to Utica, NY, the home of her parents, where she remained over seven years. After the death of her parents she went to Washington, DC, in April, 1864. There she served as a regular visitor in military hospitals, under the auspices of the New York agency. After the Civil War she went to Baltimore, MD, for eight months. She then returned to Washington, where she has since lived. In that city she has practiced homeopathy very successfully. In 1877 she opened the first homeopathic pharmacy in Washington, which flourished for some years. She became the wife of Austin C. Winslow on 15th July, 1865. Their life has been a happy one. Dr. Winslow has succeeded in her profession in spite of several accidents and much sickness. Besides her work in medicine, she has done much in other fields, especially in the Moral Education Society of Washington, of which she was president for fourteen years. She edited the "Alpha," the organ of that society, for thirteen years. She has always been a woman-suffragist and an advocate of higher education for all. Notwithstanding her advanced age, she is still active.

WINSLOW, Mrs. Celeste M. A., author, born in Charlemont, MA, 22nd November, 1837. Her mother, Mary Richards Hall, was known as the author of much poetry and prose, especially of popular temperance tales. Her great-grandfather, Richardson Miner, a soldier of the Revolution, who lived to the age of ninety-four, was descended from Thomas Miner, who moved to Connecticut, in 1642, from Somerset county, England. The family name originated with Sir Henry Miner, who was knighted by an early king for bravery. The family poetic taste was largely derived from the Lyons ancestors. In her eighth year, Celeste's home in the valley of the Deerfield was changed for one in Keosauqua, IA, and later for a pioneer home on a prairie. There she studied and wrote stories and rhymes. Her first printed story appeared in a southern journal, when she was twelve years old. Shortly afterward the Hall family removed to Keokuk, where her education was completed in the Keokuk Female Seminary. There she became the wife of Charles H. Winslow, MD, and, her two sons were born. Removing to Chicago, IL, in 1884, Mrs. Winslow assisted her son in the editorial work of his periodical "Happy Hours," afterward "Winslow's Monthly." She has published both poetry and prose enough for volumes, but devotion to her family has interfered with systematic work in literary fields. Her writings have appeared in the "Atlantic Monthly," "Scribner's Magazine," "Lippincott's Magazine," "Independent," "Advance," "Manhattan Magazine," "Brooklyn Magazine" and "Good Company," and she has contributed to numerous newspapers in various parts of the United States. She now lives in New York City, where her son, Herbert Hall Winslow, is known as a successful dramatic author.

WINSLOW, Miss Helen M., author, born in Westfield, VT, 13th April, 1851. She is in the ninth generation of descent from Kenelm Winslow, a brother of Governor Winslow, of the Plymouth Colony. Her great-grandmother Winslow was Abigail Adams. In her infancy her family removed to Greenfield, MA, and afterward to St. Albans, VT, where her father was a leader in musical circles. He was a musical composer of note and a member of the first English opera company organized in the United States. Mrs. Winslow was a scholar, a linguist and a poet. Helen was educated in the Vermont schools and finished with the normal course. She began early to write. She published her "Aunt Philury Papers" first, and

next her story, "Jack," both of which were well received. After her mother's death and her father's re-marriage, she went to Boston, MA, where she has since lived in the Roxbury District with her three sisters. Her first, serial story, "The Shawsheen Mills," was published in the "Yankee Blade." In 1886 she published "A Bohemian Chapter" as a serial in the Boston "Beacon," a story telling of the struggles of a woman artist in Boston. In poetry she has written equally well. Many of her poems are devoted to nature, and they all show finished work in form. She has done much journalistic work. She served first on the Boston "Transcript," and later she became one of the regular staff of the Boston "Advertiser," doing work at the same time for the Boston "Saturday Evening Gazette." Besides doing work on almost every Boston daily, "The Christian Union," "Christian at Work," "Interior," "Drake's Magazine," "Demorest's Magazine," the "Arena," "Journal of Education," "Wide Awake," "Youth's Companion," "Cottage Hearth," and other periodicals were mediums through which she addressed the public. Her work covers a wide range, and all of it is well done. She has been treasurer of the New England Woman's Press Association since its foundation, and was one of its six founders. She is vice-president of the Press League.

WINTERMUTE, Mrs. Martha, poet, born in Berkshire, OH, in 1842. Her maiden name was Martha Vandermark. She is descended from a patriotic soldier ancestry. Her grandfather, Benjamin Hitchcock, of Connecticut, entered the Revolutionary army at the age of seventeen years and served to the close of the war. He was the father of Samuel Hitchcock, the philanthropist, and of the late Benjamin Hitchcock, for many years an author and the editor of the New Haven "Palladium." His oldest daughter became the wife of a son of Elbridge Gerry, one of the signers of the Declaration of Independence, and also a vice-president of the United States. Another daughter was the mother of Orvil Hitchcock Platt, one of the present United States Senators from Connecticut. Roswell Dwight Hitchcock, the theologian, and Allen Hitchcock, the soldier and author, and Edward Hitchcock, the geologist, were of the same ancestors. Mrs. Wintermute's father was a descendant of the Symmeses, of Holland, who at an early period settled upon the Island of Barbadoes, and acquired title to a large portion of it. She wrote verses at the age of ten. At the age of sixteen she wrote a poem entitled "The Song of Delaware," which she brought before the public by reading it on her graduation from the Ohio Wesleyan University, Delaware, OH. That poem was soon followed by others, which were received with favor by the public. She became the wife, at the age of nineteen, of Dr. Alfred Wintermute, of Newark, OH, and for a number of years thereafter she did not offer any poetry to the public. In 1888 she began the revision and publication of her writings. In 1890 she brought out in a volume a prose story in the interest of temperance, closing the volume with about one-hundred pages of her poetry, revised and corrected. Since the publication of that volume, she has published in the newspapers much miscellaneous verse. She resides in Newark, OH.

WINTON, Mrs. Jenevehah Maria, poet and author, born in Orrville, NY, 11th May, 1837. Her maiden name was Pray, and she belongs to a family with many branches throughout the Union. Three brothers of her father's ancestry came over from France with Lafayette and joined the American forces. One of these gave his means and ships, another became an officer in the Continental army, and the third gave his life for the American cause. Her father, a native of Rhode Island, was educated in Oxford University, England, and became art eloquent preacher. Her mother, the daughter of an English earl and otherwise related to some of England's most exemplary and noted nobility, was very highly educated and wrote considerable prose and poetry, some of which was published in book form, under a pen-name. Mrs. Winton early began to write, and while attending Lima Seminary, Lima, NY, wrote much poetry. Many of her poems were printed and copied extensively, under some pen-name or unsigned, in magazines and other periodicals. In her younger years she wrote much and earned considerable means. Being then

in affluent circumstances, it was her custom to give what she earned to the poor and unfortunate. In after years, when the wife of William H. Winton, and living in Indianapolis, IN, and other cities of the West, her productions were identified and copied far and near. Many of her original poems were set to music by Thomas P. Westendorf and others. For several years her residence has been in Rochester and Kingston, NY, where, up to the time of the death of her daughter, her manuscripts were given to the press. Since that event, which nearly took the mother's life, but few productions have been sent out. For nearly two years, to escape the rigors of a northern climate, she resided in southern New Jersey, among the rustic surroundings of her farm on Landis avenue, East Vineland. More recently she has resided in New Haven, CT. She is a devoted member of the Methodist Episcopal Church.

WITTENMYER, Mrs. Annie, reformer, Woman's Relief Corps and temperance worker, born in Sandy Springs, Adams county, OH, 26th August, 1827. She is the daughter of John G. Turner, descended from an old English family. Her paternal grandfather, James Turner, fought in the War of 1812. Her maternal grandfathers fought in the Colonial War between France and England and in the Revolutionary War. Her mother's ancestors belonged to an Irish family. She received a good education. In 1847 she became the wife of William Wittenmyer, a merchant, of Jacksonville, OH. In 1850 they removed to Keokuk, IA. Five children were born to them, all but one of whom died in infancy. She now lives in Sanatogo, PA, with her only surviving child. In Keokuk she engaged in church and charity work, and opened a free school at her own expense before public schools were started. When the war broke out, she became Iowa's volunteer agent to distribute supplies to the army, and was the first sanitary agent for the State, being elected by the legislature. She received a pass from Secretary of War Stanton, which was endorsed by President Lincoln. Throughout the Civil War she was constantly in the field, ministering to the sick and wounded in the hospital and battle-field. She was under fire at Pittsburgh Landing, and was under the guns in Vicksburg every day during the siege, when shot and shell were flying and balls filled the air with the music of death. When warned of her danger, her reply was: "I am safe; He covers me with His feathers and hides me under His wings." She was personally acquainted with the leading generals of the army, was a special friend of General Grant, and accompanied him and Mrs. Grant on the boat of observation that went down the Mississippi to see six gunboats and eight wooden steamers run the blockade at Vicksburg. While in the service, she introduced a reform in hospital cookery, known as the Special Diet Kitchens, which was made a part of the United States army system, and which saved the lives of thousands of soldiers, who were too ill to recover on coarse army fare. In 1863 she started the Soldier's Orphans' Home in Iowa, the first in the Union. She was the first president of the Woman's Christian Temperance Union, serving five years without a salary. Beginning without a dollar in the treasury, she won the influence of the churches, and her efforts were crowned with success. She established the "Christian Woman" in Philadelphia, and was its editor for eleven years. She now is associate editor of "Home and Country," a magazine published in New York, edits a Relief Corps column in the New York "Weekly Tribune," and is a frequent contributor to the "National Tribune" and other periodicals. As an author she has taken high rank. Her "Women of. the "Reformation" is a standard work, and her hymns are found in numerous collections. In Relief Corps work she has been a leader, first serving as national chaplain, then as national president, and later as national counselor. She compiled the Red Book, made up of official decisions, now the recognized code of laws of the order. She is chairman of the board of directors of the National Relief Corps Home, Madison, OH. After five months of earnest work she secured the passage of a law by the Fifty-second Congress to pension army nurses. The establishment of the Kentucky Soldiers' Home is largely due to her efforts. As an orator she is intense and persuasive. She has lectured to multitudes at hundreds of camp-fires on her personal experience in the war, which she tells with pathos and fire. She is still active, untiring and full of vigor, and is very popular among the veterans wherever she goes.

WIXON, Miss Susan Helen, author and educator, was born in Dennisport, Cape Cod, MA. She is of Welsh descent. Her father was Captain James Wixon, a man of sturdy independence and honesty. Her mother, Bethia Smith Wixon, was a woman of firmness, integrity and uprightness. Miss Wixon was from infancy a thoughtful child, of a dreamy, studious and poetic nature. She was an apt scholar and, before she was thirteen years old, she was teaching a district school. The committee hesitated about appointing her, on account of her extreme youth and diminutive size. "Indeed, I can teach," she said. "Give me a chance, and see!" They did so, and her words proved true. She followed teaching with success for several years, and desired to make that profession her life-work. Early in life, after the loss of four brothers at sea, all at one time, the family removed from their country home to Fall River, MA, where Miss Wixon now lives with her sister. In 1873 she was elected a member of the school board of that city, serving three years. In 1890 she was again elected to that position, where she is now serving. For several years she has had the editorial charge of the children's department of the New York "Truth Seeker." She is a contributor to several magazines and newspapers, and at one time was a regular reporter on the staff of the Boston "Sunday Record." She is an easy, graceful writer, both in prose and poetry. Her poem, "When Womanhood Awakes," is considered one of the most inspiring among the poems written in the behalf of women. She is the well-known author of several books, "Apples of Gold" (Boston, 1876); "Sunday Observance" (1883); "All In a Lifetime" (Boston, 1884); "The Story Hour" (New York, 1885); "Summer Days at Onset" (Boston, 1887), besides tracts and pamphlets. She is a lecturer of ability on moral reform and educational topics. She is interested in scientific matters and is president of the Humboldt Scientific Society, and president of the Woman's Educational and Industrial Society, of Fall River. She is a member of the Woman's Relief Corps, and takes an active interest in several other organizations. She was elected a member of the committee on woman's industrial advancement,

World's Columbian Exposition, in the inventors' department. She is an ardent supporter of all reformatory measures, and it was her suggestion to Gov. Russell, and her able representation of the need of women as factory inspectors in Massachusetts, that caused the appointment of two women to that position in 1891. She is a member of the executive council of the Woman's National Liberal Union, whose first convention was held in Washington in February, 1890. She especially espouses the cause of women and children. In both politics and religion she holds radical views, boldly denouncing all shams and hypocrisies, wherever they appear. In 1892 she made a tour of Europe, studying principally the tariff question. Upon her return her opinions, published in Fall River, aroused much interest and discussion.

WOLFE, Miss Catherine Lorillard, philanthropist, born in New York City, 28th March, 1828, and died there 4th April, 1887. She was the daughter of John David Wolfe, the New York merchant, and the granddaughter of David Wolfe, who served in the Revolutionary War under Washington. Her mother was Dorothea Ann Lorillard, a daughter of Peter Lorillard. Miss Wolfe inherited from her father and grandfather an invested fortune of $10,000,000, and from her father she inherited her philanthropic tendencies. She was carefully educated, and from early childhood she was interested in benevolent work. After coming into control of her fortune, she at first spent $100,000 a year in charity, and, as her income increased, she increased her expenditures to $250,000 a year. She supported the charities which her father had established, and carried out his design in giving a site for the Home for Incurables in Fordham, NY. She gave $100,000 to Union College, $30,000 to St. Luke's Hospital in New York City and $65,000 to St. Johnland, Long Island. She aided in building the American Chapel in Rome, Italy, and gave a large sum of money to the American Chapel in Pans, France. She founded an Italian mission costing $50,000, a newsboy's lodging-house, and a diocesan house costing $170,000. She built schools and churches in many southern and western towns, added to the funds of the Alexandria Seminary, the American school in Athens, Greece, Griswold College, and gave large sums for indigent clergymen and deserving poor through the Protestant Episcopal Church. In 1884 she sent an expedition to Asia Minor, headed by Dr. William H. Ward, which resulted in important discoveries in archaeology. To Grace Church, in New York City she gave a chantry, reredos and other buildings that cost $250,000, and she left that church an endowment of $350,000. Her home was filled with costly paintings, which she willed to the Metropolitan Museum of Art, together with $200,000 for its preservation and enlargement. Her benefactions during her life amounted to millions.

WOOD, Mrs. Frances Fisher, educator, lecturer and scientist, was born in Massachusetts while her mother was on a visit to that State. Her home was in Ohio. During her collegiate course in Vassar she was distinguished in mathematical and astronomical studies. She was a pupil and friend of Maria Mitchell. Some of her telescopic discoveries were considered of sufficient importance for publication in scientific journals. Finding the demands of conventional dress detrimental to health and success, the young girl applied to the authorities for permission to wear in college her mountain dress, consisting of a short kilted skirt and a comfortable jacket. Dress reform at that time had not been incorporated in fashionable ethics, but the departure in costume, though requiring considerable courage in the introduction, soon became popular, and has been influential in establishing in the college a more hygienic dress régime. Since that time, though she has not sought recognition among the agitators of dress-reform, she has been a strong advocate of a rational dress for women. During her college life she held several important offices, and was graduated with high honors. Renouncing voluntarily the enjoyment of a brilliant social career, she began her educational work by preparing the boys of Dr. White's Cleveland school for college entrance examinations in higher mathematics. Later she purchased a school for girls in Cleveland, and conducted it with financial and educational success until her marriage with Dr. William B. Wood, of New York. Since then her educational activity has broadened and embraced a wide area of interest. She is one of the founders of the Public Education Society in New York which is devoted to investigating and reforming the public school system. She is also on the executive board of the University Extension Society, and one of the organizers and incorporators and a trustee of Barnard College. Simultaneously with her educational work, Mrs. Wood began to write for the press and to speak on scientific subjects and on current topics, including evolution, at that time an unfamiliar and unpopular theory. Political economy, scientific chanty, the higher education of women and other kindred themes were her favorite topics until recently, when the scientific care of young children employed her attention. At present she is engaged in writing a book for mothers upon the prevention of disease in children. She is a close student of current literature, and reads for her husband the medical periodicals and books as soon as issued. She has a gift of rapid scanning, swift memorizing and instantaneous classification, which enables her to catch and retain the salient points of a book in an afternoon's reading, and to dispose of a scientific periodical in the time occupied by the ordinary woman in looking over her fashion journal. In 1888 Mrs. Wood's accustomed interests were interrupted by the birth of a son. Finding artifical nourishment a necessity, within three months she had mastered all the literature of infant's food and its digestion obtainable in the English and German languages. From that research she deduced the theory that the only proper artificial food for infants was sterilized milk in its most perfect form. Sterilized mik is a modern discovery, and in 1888 its preparation was comparatively unknown in this country. Mrs. Wood devoted her energies to the work of preparing and perfecting artificial food, conducting the experiments in her home; for nearly a year. Having found that the only possible way to sterilize milk was to have an establishment in the country, she organized it on such a scale that its benefits extend to other mothers. Thus out of her own need was gradually developed the industry of the Kingwood Farms, Kingston, NH, the only establishment of its kind in this country, where, from a herd of blooded jersey cows, milk is so sterilized that it will keep for years. The series of exhaustive experiments has been directly under Mrs. Wood's supervision, the financial affairs of the successful business are still entirely controlled by her, and one of the principal inventions for the accomplishment of the seemingly impossible, which had baffled savants as well as dairy men, was made and patented by this scientific woman. She is a member of the Association for the Advancement of Women, of the Wednesday Afternoon and Women's University Clubs and of the Association of Collegiate Alumnæ.

WOOD, Mrs. Julia A. A., author, born in New London, NH, 13th April, 1826. She is widely known by her pen-name, "Minnie Mary Lee." She is a daughter of Ezekiel Sargent and his wife, Emily Everett Adams. She was educated in the New London Literary and Scientific Institution, Colby Academy, and later was for some time pupil in a seminary in Boston. In 1849 she became the wife of William Henry Wood, a lawyer, of Greensburg, KY, and soon after with him removed to Sauk Rapids, MN, which place is the permanent home of the family. Mr. Wood, a person of literary tastes and ability as a writer and orator, filled many public positions of trust, and was widely known until his death, in 1870. Mrs. Wood became a convert to the Roman Catholic faith, to  which she is ardently attached, and has written several novels more or less advocating the claims of that faith. Among them are "Heart of Myrhaa Lake" (New York, 1872), "Hubert's Wife" (Baltimore, 1873), "Brown House at Duffield" (1874), "Strayed from the Fold" (1878), "Story of Annette" (1878), "Three Times Three" (1879) and "From Error to Truth" (New York, 1890). She served as postmaster of Sauk Rapids for four years under the Cleveland administration. She has been engaged at different times in editorial work and is at present, with her son, conducting the Sauk Rapids "Free Press." She is a writer of serial tales and shorter stories for the "Catholic Times and Opinion" and for the "Catholic Fireside," both published in Liverpool, England. She has two sons, both of them journalists, and a married daughter, living in Minneapolis, MN. She believes in woman doing with her might whatever she is able to do well, but has had little or no fellowship with the movement for woman's rights and woman suffrage. She believes that woman should lend every effort to the suppression of the present divorce laws.

WOOD, Mrs. Mary C. F., poet, editor and author, was born in New York City. Her maiden name was Mary Camilla Foster. At an early age she became the wife of Bradley Hall, a promising young lawyer. Migrating with him to California, they settled in San Rafael. He became district attorney of Marin county, and was rapidly rising in his profession when he died, leaving her in easy circumstances, with an only son. Removing to Santa Barbara, CA, which has since been her home, she subsequently was married to Dr. Edward Nelson Wood, a young man of rare intellect and a brilliant writer, who appreciated her poetic gifts and encouraged her to write for the press. Her first poem was published in a Santa Barbara journal in 1872. They established the Santa Barbara "Index" in the fall of 1872, but, her husband's health was failing and he died in 1874. His long illness and unfortunate investments had dissipated her little fortune, and Mrs. Wood found herself face to fact with the necessity of making a living for herself and son. Turning naturally to literature as the only congenial or possible means, she entered a newspaper office and made herself familiar with the practical details of the business. In 1883 she helped to establish the "Daily Independent" of Santa Barbara, which she has since edited with ability and success, writing poetry for her own amusement and the pleasure of her readers as the inspiration came. Her first volume, "Sea Leaves," was published from her office in 1887. The book received much attention from the press, and some of the poems were translated into French. Although never regularly placed upon the market, it has been a financial as well as a literary success. She has used the pen-name "Camilla K. Von K.," but lately she has been known by her full name, Mary C. F. Hall-Wood.

WOODBERRY, Miss Rosa Louise, journalist and educator, born in Barnwell county, SC, 11th March, 1869. She is next to the oldest in a family of nine, and comes from a long line of ardent Carolinians. She spent the first thirteen years of her life in a small town, Williston, SC, and there received her early education. Her parents then removed to Augusta, GA, where she was graduated with first honor as valedictorian of her class. It was during her school-life in that city she began her literary work and became a contributor to various journals. At the same time she learned shorthand, and soon took a position on the staff of the Augusta "Chronicle." She resigned that position to take a collegiate course in Lucy Cobb Institute. Athens, GA, in which institute she has been teaching since her post-graduate year. She now has charge of the current literature class in that school. During vacations her home is in Savannah, GA. She finds time to do a great deal of literary work, and gets through a large amount of reading, both in books and newspapers. Her stories, sketches, poems and critical reviews have appeared in various papers and magazines. She has given much of her time to the study of science, and is a close observer of all scientific phenomena. From her earliest years she has discussed State and political themes with her father. Reared in such an atmosphere, one can readily account for one of her chief characteristics, fervent patriotism and devotion to her native State and sunny southland. She eloquently upholds all its customs, peculiarities and beliefs. Her eager interest and patriotic devotion have made her keenly alive to all political, social and humanitarian movements, and have led her to give close attention to the study of political economy, especially in its bearing upon the industrial present and future of the South. She won a prize of fifty dollars for the best essay on the method of improving small industries in the South, offered by the Augusta "Chronicle." She has an intense sympathy with girls who earn their own living, and she is warmly interested in all that concerns their progress and encouragement. Having been a stenographer herself, she knows from experience the realities of a vocation. She is an officer in the Woman's Press Club of Georgia, and the chairman of all confederated woman's clubs in the State.

WOODBRIDGE, Mrs. Mary A. Brayton, temperance reformer, was born in Nantucket, MA. She was a daughter of Captain Isaac Brayton and his wife, Love Mitchell Brayton. Her mother belonged to the family of Maria Mitchell, the astronomer. Mary A. Brayton received a fair educational training, and in youth she excelled in mathematics. At the age of seventeen years, she became the wife of Frederick Wells Woodbridge, a merchant, whom she met while living in Ravenna, OH. They settled in Cleveland, OH. Several children were born to them, one of whom died early. She was too busy to do much literary work, but she was interested in everything that tended to elevate society. She was the secretary of a literary club in Cleveland, over which General James A. Garfield presided upon his frequent visits to that city. She was particularly interested in temperance work and, when the crusade opened, she took a leading part in that movement. She joined the Woman's Christian Temperance Union, and filled many important offices in that organization. She was the first president of the local union of her own home, Ravenna, then for years president of her State, and in 1878 she was chosen recording secretary of the National Woman's Christian Temperance Union, a position which she filled with ability. Upon the resignation of Mrs. J. Ellen Foster, in the St. Louis National Woman's Christian Temperance Union convention, in October, 1884, Mrs. Woodbridge was unanimously chosen national superintendent of the department, of legislation and petitions. Her crowning work was done in her conduct of the constitutional amendment campaign. She edited the "Amendment Herald," which gained a weekly circulation of one-hundred-thousand copies. From 1878 she was annually reelected recording secretary of the national union. She was Secretary of the World's Woman's Christian Temperance Union, and in 1889 attended the world's convention in England. She died in Chicago IL, 25th October, 1894.

WOODRUFF, Mrs. Libbie L., journalist, born in Madison county, IL, 20th October, 1860. Her maiden name was Piper. As a child she was ambitious, truthful and determined. She attended college in Valparaiso, IN, and fitted herself for teaching, which occupation she successfully followed for several years. She became the wife, 28th January, 1890, of S. C. Woodruff, editor of the Stromsburgh, NE, "News." At that time her husband was in need of assistance, and, though she was entirely unacquainted with newspaper work, she entered into the work immediately. She soon showed her powers. She is a facile, forcible writer, with broad views and firm principles of right and justice, which her pen never fails to make plain to the people. She is an uncompromising advocate of Republican principles and a warm adherent of that party, which owes much to her editorials in the districts where the Stromsburgh "News" and the Gresham "Review," of which she is associate editor, find circulation. Her home is in Stromsburgh, NE.

WOODS, Mrs. Kate Tannatt, author, editor and poet, born in Peekskill-on-the-Hudson, NY, 29th December, 1838. Her father, James S. Tannatt, was a descendant of an old Welsh nobleman, who came to the United States for the pleasures of hunting. The father of Kate was born in Boston, MA, but left that city when very young and went abroad. He afterward became an editor in New York, and there was married to the brilliant woman who was the mother of Mrs. Woods. Both parents were intelligent and fond of literary life and books. The mother, Mary Gilmore, came of literary stock, being a descendant of Sir John Gilmore, the owner of Craigmiller Castle, near Edinburgh, Scotland. In her childhood Kate was very delicate, but an excellent scholar. A rheumatic affection of the hip kept her for some years from joining girls of her age in active sports, and her books were her delight. Her taste was fostered by her parents, although novels, save Sir Walter Scott's, were strictly forbidden to her. Owing to poor health and an affection of the eyes, which was the result of incessant reading and study, the young and ambitious girl was compelled, after leaving her New York home, to continue her studies with private tutors. She had been a pupil in the Peekskill Seminary, where she made rapid progress. Upon the death of her father, his widow decided to move with her family to New England, where her sons could enjoy the advantage of public schools. For a time she made her home in New Hampshire with her eldest daughter, a half-sister of Kate, then the wife of a young physician. When the doctor removed to Manchester-by-the-Sea, the family went also. They remained but a short time, as Salem offered unusual advantages. Miss Tannatt was for a short time a teacher in the public schools, where nearly every pupil was as old as, or older than, herself. Her work was so well performed that a higher position was offered to her as a teacher. She declined the position to spend a year in New York, devoting herself to study and music. At the end of the year she became the wife of George H. Woods, a graduate of Brown University and the Harvard Law School. Mr. Woods was already settled in Minneapolis, MN, where he took his young bride. Her first child was born in Minneapolis, and there she wrote some of her best poems and stories. After a time the physicians ordered her to the seaboard, as the climate of Minessota was too bracing for her. While visiting in New England, in the home of her husband's parents, the war broke out, and Mr. Woods raised a company for the First Minnesota Regiment and was sworn into service as first lieutenant. When the regiment was ordered to the front, Mrs. Woods joined him, taking her two babies with her, and ever after was the devoted nurse and friend of the soldiers. Her husband, who rose to high official position, was seriously injured while on duty, but he lived on for nineteen years, suffering constantly from his injuries. His death was sudden at last, and, worn out with the care of the family and a succession of deaths in her own and her husband's family, Mrs. Woods took the advice of her physcian and friends and sailed for Europe. For six months she quietly enjoyed study and travel, and then returned to America. During her husband's semi-invalid years she followed him wherever he chose to locate, until necessity compelled her to care for his parents and to educate her children, when she settled in the homestead in Salem, MA, where she now lives. Her first production was published when she was but ten years old, and she has since kept her pen in active service. She is one of the editors of the "Ladies' Home journal," of Philadelphia, a regular contributor to the leading magazines, and usually publishes one book each year. Her paintings in oil and water-color have received commendation. She is fond of music, is an excellent horsewoman, and is considered high authority in

culinary matters, besides excelling in embroidery. Her short stories and poems have never been collected, although the former are numbered by hundreds, and the latter are copied far and wide. Among her books are the following juveniles: "Six Little Rebels," "Dr. Dick," "Out and About," "All Around a Rocking-Chair," "Duncans on Land and Sea," "Toots and his Friends," "Twice Two" and several others now out of print. Among her so-called novels, which are in reality true pictures of life, are "That Dreadful Boy," "The Minister's Secret," "Hidden for Years," "Hester Hepworth," "A Fair Maid of Marblehead," "Barbara's Ward," and "A Little New England Maid." Two beautifully illustrated poems from her pen are called "The Wooing of Grandmother Grey" and "Grandfather Grey." She is one of the officers of the Federation of Clubs, a member of the New England Woman's Club, vice-president of the Woman's National Press Association, an active member of many charitable organizations and literary societies, including the Unity Art Club of Boston and the Wintergreen Club. She is a member of the Author's Society of London, England, and is president of the Thought and Work Club of Salem. Much of her early work was done under the penname "Kate True." Until her sons were old enough not to miss her care, she declined to leave her home for public work. Now she is in demand as a speaker and lecturer. She frequently gives readings from her own works for charitable purposes, while her lectures on historical subjects are very popular.

WOODWARD, Mrs. Caroline Marshall, author and artist, born in New Market, NH, 12th October, 1828. Her father, Capt. John Marshall, was a native of Concord, MA. Mrs. Woodward early showed a strong individuality. At the age of eight years she commenced a diary, which she never neglected, often writing in rhyme. On 25th December, 1848, she became the wife of William W. Woodward, in Concord, NH. In 1852 they removed to Wooster, OH. There they buried their son, aged four years. They then removed to Ft. Wayne, IN, where she commenced the study of French and German. Having mastered those languages, she turned her attention to oil-painting, and commenced to take lessons. Finding that she was being instructed falsely, she gave up her tuition and proceeded to find the true art for herself. She had also kept up her writing. Her poems, "The Old, Old Stairs" and "Dumb Voices," rank her among the best writers of our day. She became a contributor to some of the leading magazines of the country. She died in Ft. Wayne, IN, 28th November, 1890, of heart-failure, following an attack of influenza.

WOODWARD, Mrs. Caroline M. Clark, temperance worker, born in Mignon, near Milwaukee, WI, November 17th, 1840. Her father, Jonathan M. Clark, was a Vermonter of English descent, who, born in 1812, of Revolutionary parentage, inherited an intense American patriotism. Her mother, Mary Turch Clark, of German and French ancestry, was born and bred on the banks of he Hudson river. Both were persons of more than ordinary education and, though burdened with the cares of a family of one son and seven daughters, were life-long students. Caroline was the oldest daughter. She attended the district school in a log house till seventeen years of age. To that was added one year of study in German in a private school. At the age of eight years she was considered quite a prodigy in her studies. At the age of seventeen she began to teach. After two years of study in the Milwaukee high school under John G. McKidley, famed as a teacher and organizer of educational work, she taught in the public schools of that city. She became the wife of William W. Woodward in 1861. For eighteen years they made their home on a farm near Milwaukee, a favorite resort for a large number of cultivated friends and acquaintances. In 1879 they removed to Seward, NE, where they still reside. Since 1875 she has been engaged in public affairs, serving as secretary of the Woman's Foreign Missionary Society and as president of the Milwaukee district association. She has been identified with the same work in Nebraska. In 1882 she entered the field of temperance as a newspaper writer, and she has shown herself a consistent and useful worker in that cause and in all the reformations of the times. In 1884 she was elected treasurer of the Nebraska Woman's Christian Temperance Union, and in 1887 vice-president-at-large of the State, which office she still holds. In 1887 she was appointed organizer for the National Woman's Christian Temperance Union, and was twice reappointed. In the Atlanta convention she was elected associate superintendent of the department of work among railroad employes. She has been a member of each national convention of the Woman's Christian Temperance Union since and including the memorable St. Louis convention of 1884. She was a delegate to the National Prohibiton Party Convention of 1888, held in Indianapolis. She was nominated by that party for regent of the State University in 1891, and led the State ticket by a handsome vote. Mrs. Woodward is one of the clearest, most logical and forcible speakers in the West.

WOODY, Mrs. Mary Williams Chawner, philanthropist and educator, born in Azalia, IN, 22nd December, 1846. She is of English blood. Her grandfather, John S. Chawner, was an English lawyer, who came to America early in this century, and married and settled in eastern North Carolina. The other ancestors, for several generations, lived in that section. Among them were the Albertsons, Parkers and Coxes. Both families were Friends for generations. Mary's parents were very religious, and gave to their children the guarded moral and religious training characteristic of the Friends a half-century-ago. She was educated in the preparatory schools, supplemented by training in the Friends' Academy and in Earlham College, to which was added a year of study in Michigan University. In all those institutions coeducation was the rule, and the principles of equality therein inbibed gave shape to the sentiments of the earnest pupils. She entered, as teacher, the Bloomingdale Academy, where her brother, John Chawner, A.M., was principal. In the spring of 1868 she became the wife of John W. Woody, A.M., LL.B., of Alamance county, NC. Together they entered Whittier College, Salem, IA, as teachers. Mrs. Woody threw the utmost vigor into her teaching. At the end of five years Prof. Woody was elected president of Penn College, an institution of the Friends, in Oskaloosa, IA, and Mrs. Woody entered that institution as teacher. In 1881 they returned to North Carolina to labor in Guilford College. There her poor health and the care of her little family prevented her from teaching, but with her home duties she found time for religious work, for which perfect liberty was afforded in the Friends Church, while her husband still filled his favorite position as professor of history and political science in Guilford College. When the Woman's Christian Temperance Union was organized in North Carolina, she entered its ranks, and in the second State convention, held in Asheville, in October, 1884, she was chosen president, a position to which she has been elected every year since that date. At the time of her election to the presidency, the church at home was completing its proceedings in setting her apart for the ministry of the Word. The requirements in that double position were not easily met. In the Woman's Christian Temperance Union work she cheerfully seeks and presents to her followers what can be most readily undertaken. Her annual addresses before her State conventions are models.

WOOLLEY, Mrs. Celia Parker, novelist, born in Toledo, OH, 14th June, 1848. Her maiden name was Celia Parker. Shortly after her birth her parents left Toledo and made their home in Coldwater, MI. With the exception of a few months in the Lake Erie Seminary in Painesville, OH, Miss Parker's education was received in her own town. She was graduated from the Coldwater Seminary in 1866. In 1868 she became the wife of Dr. J. H. Woolley. In 1876 Dr. and Mrs. Woolley removed to Chicago, IL, where they now reside. Until 1885 Mrs. Woolley's literary work was limited to occasional contributions to Unitarian papers, both eastern and western. These contributions were mainly devoted to social and literary subjects, and she earned the reputation of a thoughtful and philosophic writer. For eight years she was the Chicago correspondent of the "Christian Register" of Boston, MA. Occasionally she published poems of marked merit. Her first story was published in 1884 in "Lippincott's Magazine," and a few others have followed in the same periodical. When she planned a more ambitious volume, it was only natural that she should touch upon theology and other questions of current interest, as she had seen much of the theological unrest of the day. Her father, while still young, broke away from "orthodox" associations, going first with the Swedenborgians and later with

more radical thinkers. Her mother, bred in the Episcopal Church, withdrew from that organization and aided her husband in forming a "liberal" society. Naturally, the daughter was interested in all those changes, and her book, "Love and Theology" (Boston, 1887), took on a decidedly religious or theological character. That work in one year passed into its fifth edition, when the title was changed to "Rachel Armstrong." Since then it has been still more widely circulated. Her second book, "A Girl Graduate" (Boston, 1889), achieved another remarkable success. Her third volume, "Roger Hunt" (Boston, 1892), is pronounced her best book. Mrs. Woolley's literary connections are numerous. For two years she served as president of the Chicago Woman's Club, an organization of nearly five-hundred members, devoted to literary culture and philanthropic work. She is a member of the Fortnightly, a smaller, but older, social and literary organization of women. For a year she was president of the Woman's Western Unitarian Conference, and she is especially interested in that line of work, having served as assistant editor of "Unity," the, western Unitarian paper, whose editor is Rev. Jenkin Lloyd Jones. Much of her work has been done on the platform, lecturing before women's clubs and similar organizations.

WOOLSEY, Miss Sarah Chauncey, poet, known to the world by her pen-name "Susan Coolidge," born in Cleveland, OH, in 1845. She is descended from noted New England families, the Woolseys and Dwights, of Connecticut. Her father was the brother of President Theodore Dwight Woolsey, of Yale. She received a careful education, but her literary work did not begin till 1871. She has contributed many excellent poems and prose sketches to the newspapers and magazines, and her productions are widely quoted. She has published two volumes of verse: "Verses," in 1880, and "A Few More Verses," in 1889. She has contributed to various periodicals. Some of her best known poems are "Influence," "When?" "Commissioned," "Benedicam Domino," "The Cradle Tomb," "Before the Sun," and "Laborare Est Orare." Her "Katy-Did" series is best known of her juvenile books. She has also published" A Short History of Philadelphia," a translation of Théophile Gautier's "My Household of Pets," and edited the life and letters of Mrs. Delany and Madame D'Arblay in an abridged form. Her home is in Newport, RI.

WOOLSON, Mrs. Abba Louise Goold, author, born in Windham, ME, 30th April, 1838. She is the daughter of William Goold, the well-known author of "Portland in the Past" (1886), and of several papers in the "Collections" of the Maine Historical Society, of which he was for many years corresponding secretary. Miss Goold was reared and educated in Portland, ME, where she was graduated in the high school for girls in 1856. In that year she became the wife of Prof. Moses Woolson, the principal of that school. They lived in Portland until 1862, and there Mrs. Woolson began to publish poems. Her first sonnet was published in 1856 in the New York "Home Journal," and she contributed to that journal occasionally. In 1859 she began the publication of an anonymous series of poems in the Portland "Transcript," which attracted much attention. She contributed for four years to that journal and to the Boston "Transcript." She served for a short time as professor of belles-lettres in the Mt. Auburn girls' school, and afterward went with her husband to Concord. In 1868 they removed to Boston, where her husband was professor in a high school, and where she now lives. She contributed a notable essay, entitled "The Present Aspect of the Byron Case," to the Boston "Journal," which drew general attention to her. She soon afterward began to publish her work in volumes. She has given courses of lectures on "English Literature in Connection with English History," "The Influence of Foreign Nations Upon English Literature" and "The Historic Cities of Spain." She is a member of several literary and benevolent societies, and has served as president of the Castilian Club, of Boston. In 1871 she went to Utah, and there interviewed Brigham Young for the Boston "Journal." Her other published works include "Women in American Society" (1872), "Browsing Among Books" (1881) and "George Eliot and Her Heroines" (1886). She edited "Dress Reform," a series of lectures by women physicians of Boston on "Dress as It Affects the Health of Women" (1874). She aids liberally the charities of her city.

WOOLSON, Miss Constance Fenimore, author, born in Claremont, NH, in 1848. She was the daughter of Charles Jarvis Woolson and Hannah Cooper Pomeroy Woolson. Her mother was a niece of James Fenimore Cooper, and a woman of literary talents of a high order. While Constance was a child, the family removed to Cleveland, OH. She was educated in a young ladies' seminary in Cleveland, and afterward studied in Madame Chegary's French school in New York City. Her father died in 1869. She soon afterward began to use her literary talents. In 1873 she removed with her mother to Florida, where they remained until 1879. In that year her mother died, and Miss Woolson went to Europe. During her later years she lived in Italy, but also visited Egypt and Greece. Her first books were two collections of short stories, called, respectively, "Castle Nowhere" and "Rodman the Keeper." Her first novel, "Anne," appeared as a serial in "Harper's Magazine" in 1881. Other novels were "For the Major" (1883); "East Angels" (1886); "Jupiter Lights" (1889). For some years she spent a part of her time in England. Some of her widely known single poems are "Me Too!" "Tom," and "Kentucky Belle," which have been much used by elocutionists. This gifted woman committed suicide in Venice, Italy, 24th January, 1894.

WORDEN, Miss Sarah A., artist, born in Xenia, OH, 10th October, 1853. Her father was a New Englander, of Puritan stock, and her mother was born in Kentucky, of Scotch parents. Miss Worden in childhood showed her artistic bent. Her parents gave her good educational advantages, but her father's death threw her upon her, own resources at an early age. She entered Cooper Institute in New York City and was soon admitted to its most advanced classes, and to those of the Art Students' League. Her struggles as an art student and as a stranger in the city, dependent upon her own exertions, were successful means of vigorous development of character. She continued her studies for several years, until overwork and intense study impaired her health. She was subsequently invited to become a member of the faculty of Mt. Holyoke Seminary and College. She accepted the position as one of the instructors in art, and has filled it for several years. She participated in the transformation of the seminary into a college, and was instrumental in raising the standard of the art department and establishing a systematic course of study. She has made a specialty of landscape painting. Her pictures have been displayed in the exhibitions in New York and other large cities. Her literary inclinations have found expression in stray poems and prose, articles in newspapers and magazines. She is deeply interested in all the questions of the day, artistic, social, political and religious. Her home is now in South Hadley, MA.

WORLEY, Mrs. Laura Davis, dairy farmer, was born in Nashville, TN. She is a descendant of Frederick Davis, one of the original settlers of Nashville. She was graduated at the age of sixteen from St. Cecilia's Convent, in Nashville, where she laid the foundation of a liberal education and devoted much time to the study of music, painting and the French language. After leaving school she continued her studies with private teachers. She traveled much in the United States and Canada. She became the wife of Frank E. Worley, a banker, of Ellettsville, IN, where she now lives. Mr. Worley is a large land-owner. Finding the need of occupation and amusement in a little country village, Mrs. Worley turned her attention to dairy farming. She owns a large herd of Holstein and Jersey cattle and makes a high grade of butter. She has been secretary of the Indiana State Dairy Association since its organization, and is a writer on subjects connected with dairying in all its branches. She is a member of the World's Fair Congress Auxiliary in the labor department, vice-president of the Indiana Farmers' Reading Circle, and a member of the advisory board of the National Farmers' Reading Circle. She is interested in all that pertains to bettering the condition of the farmer's life socially and financially. She is a woman of energy and finds time to entertain in her home many of the gifted and cultured people of the day. She is a member of the executive committee of the World's Fair Managers for Indiana.

WORMELEY, Miss Katherine Prescott, translator, born in Ipswich, England, 14th January, 1830. She is the second daughter of Admiral Wormeley, active during the war in connection with the Sanitary Commission. She served under McOlmsted on the James river and the Pamunky, and was afterward made lady superintendent of the hospital for convalescent soldiers in Portsmouth Grove, RI. She published many of her letters in a book called "Hospital Transports," and in another volume on the work of the Sanitary Commission. These works have been recently republished under another name. Miss Wormeley resides principally in Newport, RI, where she engages actively in all matters touching sanitary improvement, charity organization, the employment of women, instruction for girls in household duties and in cooking schools. She is the translator of Balzac for a Boston publishing firm, and her work is praised as an almost unrivaled translation. She has also translated works by George Sand.

WORTHEN, Mrs. Augusta Harvey, educator and author, born in Sutton, NH, 27th September, 1823. She is the daughter of Col. John and Sally Greeley Harvey. Col. John Harvey was a younger brother of Jonathan and Matthew Harvey, who both became members of Congress. Matthew was, in 1831, governor of New Hampshire. When Augusta was eight years of age, she went to live with the last-named uncle, in Hopkinton, NH, and remained six years, during which time she enjoyed the advantage of tuition in Hopkinton Academy. At the age of sixteen she commenced to teach in district schools, which occupation she followed for two years. Weary of idleness during the long vacations, she found employment in a Lowell cotton factory. There she remained three years, doing each day's work of fourteen hours in the factory and pursuing her studies in the evenings in a select school. The first article she offered for print was written during that time, and was printed in the Lowell "Offering," a magazine devoted exclusively to the productions of the mill operatives. After three years she resumed teaching, and was at one time pupil-assistant in the Andover, NH, academy, paying for her own tuition by instructing some of the younger classes. On 15th September, 1855, she became the wife of Charles F. Worthen, of Candia, NH, who died on

15th January, 1882. After marriage to Mr. Worthen, she set herself to work to carry her share of their mutual burdens, but, after a time, comfort and competence being attained, she engaged in study and composition, and wrote prose sketches and poems. The great work of her life has been the preparation of a history of her native town, extending to over eleven-hundred pages. It was published in 1891. It is the first New Hampshire town history prepared by a woman. This heavy work being accomplished, she is again employing her ready pen in writing articles of a lighter and more imaginative character. Her home is in Lynn, MA, to which city she removed from Danvers, MA, with her husband, in 1858.

WRAY, Mrs. Mary A., actor, born in 1805 and died in Newtown, NY, 5th October, 1892. Her maiden name was Retan. She became the wife of Mr. Wray in 1826, and soon afterward she went on the stage, making her début as a dancer in the Chatham Street Theater, in New York City. She made rapid progress in the dramatic art, and appeared as Lady Macbeth with Edwin Forrest in the Walnut Street Theater, Philadelphia, PA. She then played for six years in the Old Bowery Theater, in New York City, where she supported Junius Bruitus Booth, the father of Edwin Booth. She traveled through the South with a company in which Joseph Jefferson and John Ellsler appeared in Charleston, SC. In 1848 she was a member of the Seguin Opera Company. In 1864 she retired from the stage. Her family consisted of four children. One of her sons was known on the minstrel stage as "Billy Wray." He lost his life in the burning of the "Evening Star," on the way from New York to New Orleans, in 1866. Her other son, Edward, died in the same year in Illinois. Two daughters and a number of grandchildren survive her. Mrs. Wray was for over thirty-five years a member of the American Dramatic Fund. She was a woman of conspicuous talents and high character, and was, at the time of her death, the oldest representative of the American stage.

WRIGHT, Miss Hannah Amelia, physician, born in New York City, 8th August, 1836. She is a daughter of Charles Cushing and Lavinia D. Wright. Her father was a native of Maine. Her mother was born in Charleston, SC, and was in direct lineal descent from the second settlers of that city, the Huguenots. Dr. Wright's father was

an artist of merit. The daughter received her education at home. Until her thirteenth year she lived in Louisiana, but returned to New York in 1849, where she has since resided. While still a young girl, Miss Wright decided upon an independent career. Her first effort was in writing fiction. Her stories were published, but, dissatisfied with her work in that line, she turned her attention to the study of music. In 1860 she obtained a position as teacher of music in the Institution for the Blind in New York. After spending eleven years in teaching in that school, she was preparing to go abroad to pursue the study of music, when she became interested in the care of the insane. She determined to study medicine, with the hope that she might render service to that unfortunate class. In 1871 she entered the New York Medical College for Women, and in 1874 she received the diploma of that institution. Shortly after her graduation, and again some years later, backed by influential friends, Dr. Wright sought admission to one of the State asylums for the insane as assistant physician, but great was her disappointment to find, after preparing herself especially for that branch of work, that women were not considered eligible for the position of physician in those institutions, sex being the only ground upon which she was rejected. The better to care for her own patients, Dr. Wright was in 1878 made an examiner in lunacy, being the first woman so appointed. As a physician she has been successful, having established a large and remunerative practice. Realizing the necessity for women physicians in the field of gynæcology, she has for the past five or six years devoted herself to that branch of the practice of medicine as a specialist. In 1878 she was made a trustee of the medical college from which she was graduated. While serving as secretary of the board of trustees, she used her influence to establish women in the chairs of that college, and it was mainly through her determination and perseverance that women succeeded men as professors in that institution. Dr. Wright was one of the organizers of the Society for Promoting the Welfare of the Insane, chartered in 1882. She served for many years as president of that society. She was also instrumental in organizing the alumni association of her alma mater, serving for several years as its secretary and afterward as its presiding officer. She is a member of the Medico-Legal Society, the Woman's Legal Education Society, the State and County Homeopathic Medical Societies, and the American Obstetrical Society.

WRIGHT, Mrs. Julia McNair, author, born in Oswego, NY, 1st May, 1840. She is the daughter of John McNair, a well-known civil engineer of Scotch descent. She was carefully educated in private schools and seminaries. In 1859 she became the wife of Dr. William James Wright, the mathematician. She began her literary career at sixteen by the publication of short stories. Her published works include "Almost a Nun" (1867); "Priest and Nun" (1869); "Jug-or-Not" (1870); "Saints and Sinners" (1873); "The Early Church in Britain" (1874); "Bricks from Babel," a manual of ethnography (1876); "The Complete Home" (1879); "A Wife Hard Won," a novel (1882), and "The Nature Readers," four volumes (1887–91). Her works have been very popular. Most of her stories have been republished in Europe, in various languages, and several of them have appeared in Arabia. Mrs. Wright has never had a book that was a financial failure; all have done well. "The Complete Home" sold over one-hundred-thousand copies, and others have reached ten, twenty, thirty and fifty thousand. Since the organization of the National Temperance Society, she has been one of its most earnest workers and most popular authors. She has two children, both married. Her son is a distinguished young business man; her daughter, Mrs. J. Wright Whitcomb, a member of the Kansas bar, is a promising young author.

WRIGHT, Mrs. Laura M., physician, born in Royal Oak, Oakland county, MI, 25th April, 1840. She is a descendant of Pilgrim stock, through both the parents of her mother. Her father, Joseph R. Wells, is of Welsh origin. She inher-ited pluck and thrift and early developed an insatiable thirst for knowledge, while an unselfish labor for others became apparent in her childhood, and in active work in the Baptist Church, of which she early became a member. Later in life, still indefatigable in the pursuit of knowledge, she was graduated from two medical colleges, and has taken her place in the active field of professional life. Dr. Wright possesses a gentle but firm character, supported by perseverance and a strong conscience. Born of parents poor in this world's goods, but abounding in energy, frugality, good sense and superior management, of which she possesses a full share, she is ready now to give and extend the helping hand with even more than early helpfulness. She believes that genius consists in the sum of doing the little things about you well. As a local worker in the Woman's Christian Temperance Union ranks, she has been active and earnest. Her home is in New York City.

WRIGHT, Mrs. Marie Robinson, journalist, born in Newnan, GA, 4th May, 1853. Her father, John Evans Robinson, was a cultured and wealthy planter. He was descended from an honorable English family, of 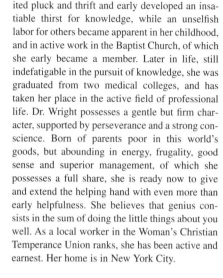 which the knightly Sir George Evans was the head. Marie was a precocious girl, well matured in body and mind at the age of sixteen, when she made a romantic marriage by running away with Hinton Wright. Mr. Wright was the son of a prominent lawyer, Judge W. F. Wright, a gentleman distinguished for his scholarly attainments. Being a bright, ambitious girl, she studied law with her husband, and sat by his side when he passed his final examination for the bar. She was blessed with two children, a daughter and a promising son. Loss of fortune followed soon after her marriage. Reared in the greatest affluence and trained to the old-fashioned southern idea that a woman should never venture outside the shelter of home in quest of a career, it was a cruel struggle to her when she realized that she would be compelled to go out into the hard and untried world to earn a living for herself and little ones. She was too proud, as well as too delicately reared, to go into any of the few situations, mostly menial, open to women at that time.

Without preparation she launched into journalism. Her first work was done for the "Sunny South," a literary weekly published in Atlanta, GA. She was immediately engaged upon that paper, and served it with marked ability for several years. She has been in newspaper work for eight years, and has been regularly connected with the New York "World" for three years. She has used her pen so that she has earned a handsome support for herself and children. She has been a hard-working woman. Her special line, descriptive writing and articles on new sections of the country, has called for a peculiar order of mind and character. As special correspondent of the New York "World" in that department, she has traveled from the British Provinces to Mexico. One of her noteworthy achievements during 1892 was her superb descriptive article of eight pages in the "World" on Mexico, supplemented by a handsomely illustrated souvenir on that romantic and interesting country. She is a member of several press clubs and literary societies. She was sent to Paris as commissioner from the State of Georgia to the exposition. While she has been absorbed in her regular work, she has occasionally contributed to other papers and magazines. Her home is now in New York City.

WYLIE, Mrs. Lollie Belle, journalist and poet, was born at Bayou Coden, near Mobile, AL. Her maiden name was Moore. From Alabama her parents moved to Arkansas. As the father died when she was five months old, she was reared by her maternal grandfather, William D. Ellis, residing always in Georgia, chiefly in Atlanta. Between that fine old gentleman and herself there existed a congeniality rare and delightful. It was he who fostered in the girl those distinguishing traits for which today her friends admire the woman, the tastes and culture which places upon her lifework the crown of success. At seventeen, she became the wife of Hart Wylie. During the next nine years of domestic quiet it never occurred to her that she had talents lying dormant, except for occasional verse written for her own amusement. Those beautiful years of dreaming closed sadly in the lingering illness of the young husband. Want soon thrust its shadow across the threshold of the home. What to do to protect from need those three dearest to her, husband and two baby girls, was

the problem presented for solution. She could think of no talent, no gift of hers that might be turned to account, save her little verses. The sudden thought brought help. The waifs were quickly collected, and a friendly publisher agreed to bring out the small book. Several hundred volumes were immediately sold, paying the expenses of publication and relieving the pressing necessities of the household, but the first copy was placed on the young wife's desk while the husband lay sleeping through death's earliest hour. Two days later Mr. Hoke Smith, president of the Atlanta "journal," offered her the place of society editor on his paper She took up the work at once, and at once succeeded. Her first "write-up" was of the reception given to President and Mrs. Cleveland in Atlanta, and filled seven columns of the paper. Having filled that place most satisfactorily for three years, and having refused several offers from papers north and south, the dauntless woman now well known in her profession and vice-president of the Woman's Press Club of Georgia, decided, in December, 1890, to have her own organ of her opinion. In ten days after the decision there appeared the first issue of "Society," a weekly publication under her editorship. It was immediately successful. On account of ill health Mrs. Wylie was not able to prosecute this venture for any length of time. Her pen has not been idle, however; she has written for as many as fifty periodicals at one time. When the Woman's Board of the Atlanta Exposition was seeking to honor their most- gifted southern writer, they selected Mrs. Lollie Belle Wylie, and set apart a day for the celebration of her compositions, the program being made up entirely of her musical and literary productions. During the leisure intervals of her busy life Mrs. Wylie has found time for the composition of several songs, all of which she has set to music. These songs have become favorites in many households. The rich melody of the southland is theirs, and they strongly appeal to the true musician's heart. A still more recent recognition of Mrs. Wylie's ability in the realm of letters came through the will of Judge Richard H. Clark, who designated her the literary executor of his manuscripts, which contain valuable data on Georgia history. It is Mrs. Wylie's intention to edit these papers into a comprehensive and attractive history of the State, which, under such a facile pen, should produce from the bones of dry facts a work at once readable and of permanent historic value. Aside from her success in the literary world Mrs. Wylie would win recognition for her attractive personality. She is a woman of unusual force of character, with an earnestness of purpose and power of conviction that capacitate her to discuss with ability the important questions of the day, whether in politics, social or literary life. Her present success is considered by her critics but the dawning of a more brilliant future.

WYMAN, Mrs. Lillie B. Chace, author and philanthropist, born in Valley Falls, RI, 10th December, 1847. She is the daughter of Samuel B. and Elizabeth B. Chace. Growing up in an anti-slavery but very retired village home, where the visits of anti-slavery speakers and the harboring of fugitive slaves were the chief occurrences of interest, her thoughts were early turned upon the moral duties of the members of society. She read old anti-slavery papers, listened to discussions and formed her social philosophy upon a fundamental belief that men are worth saving from misery and sin. She was taught to be liberal and unorthodox in theology, and was left largely to find her own religious belief. She attended the school which Dr. Dio Lewis conducted in Lexington, MA. She went to Europe in 1872, and spent more than a year there. She got some notion of the significance of history when she was in Rome, and became interested in liberal Italian politics. She soon began to feel very strongly that the labor question and kindred social questions were the most pressing and important ones of her time, and that they should engage the attention of all conscientious persons. She remained in Valley Falls for five or six years after her return from Europe. Her family were cotton manufacturers, and she made some study, as her strength permitted, of the conditions of factory operatives. In 1877 she published in the "Atlantic Monthly" a short story, called "The Child of the State," which narrated the experiences of a child who was born in a factory operative family and early became an inmate of a reform school. It was studied very closely from life, both as regards existence in the factory village and in the reform school. Its subject caused it to receive much attention. The school described was recognized, and the superintendent thereof, whom she had drawn from life, was also recognized. She continued to publish short stories

at intervals, and a number were afterward collected and published in a book called "Poverty Grass" (Boston, 1886). Since its appearance she has published no other book, but she has written a number of other stories and sketches. Her most serious work since then, has been a series of studies of factory life, four of which appeared in the "Atlantic Monthly," two in the "Christian Union" and one in the "Chautauquan." Besides these she has written out her own anti-slavery reminiscences in a paper entitled "From Generation to Generation," which was published in the "Atlantic Monthly." She has spent two years in southern Georgia, where she and her husband have been instrumental in establishing a free library for the colored people in that State. They have also helped to start some work in industrial education among the negroes. She embodied the results of her studies of the condition of the Georgia negroes in two papers, which appeared in the "New England Magazine." She is a believer in woman suffrage, prohibition and total abstinence, and in Henry George's theories as to land tenure. She is interested in socialism, and looks to a conciliation of the seemingly opposing ideas socialism and individualism into a harmony which may bring about a better state and a happier social condition. She has no definite philosophy, but she is wholly opposed to materialistic ways of regarding things. In 1878 she became the wife of John C. Wyman, a Massachusetts man, born in 1822. He was a Garrisonian abolitionist before the war, entered the Union army as captain in a Massachusetts regiment, was made United States provost-marshal at Alexandria, and afterward served for some time on General McCallum's staff. He is now executive agent for the Rhode Island commissioners of the World's Fair. They have one son, Arthur, born in 1879. Mrs. Wyman is very much interested in Russian affairs, and helped to organize the society of American Friends of Russian Freedom.

YATES, Miss Elizabeth U., lecturer, born in Bristol, ME, 3rd July, 1857. Her ancestors on both sides were characterized by intellectual strength and religious character. During her school days she gave evidence of oratorical gifts that have been developed by special training. She studied in the Boston School of Expression and has had private instruction from the leading professors of elocution in this country. She is one of the few women to whom the Methodist Episcopal Church ever granted a license to preach. Her pulpit efforts are remarkable for simplicity and power. In 1880 she went as a missionary to China. She has given an interesting and graphic account of oriental life in her book, "Glimpses into Chinese Homes." In 1886 she returned to the United States, where she has devoted herself to moral and religious reforms. She is a national lecturer of the Woman's Christian Temperance Union, and one of the leading speakers of the National American Suffrage Association. She is especially interested in the subject of woman's advancement in all countries, of which she is an able exponent and persuasive advocate. She is also winning success as a lecturer. Her home is in Round Pond, ME.

YOUMANS, Mrs. Letitia Creighton, temperance reformer, born in Coburg, Ontario, Canada, in January, 1827. Her maiden name was Letitia Creighton. She was educated in the Coburg Female Academy and in Burlington Academy, in Hamilton, Ontario. After graduation, she taught for a short time in a female academy in Picton. In 1850 she became the wife of Arthur Youmans. She became interested in the temperance movement and was soon a successful lecturer. She was superintendent of the juvenile work of the Good Templars of Canada, and served on the editorial staff of the "Temperance Union." She organized the Woman's Christian Temperance Union in Toronto, and was president of the Ontario Temperance Union from 1878 till 1883, when she was elected president of the Dominion Woman's Christian Temperance Union. She was reelected in 1885. She was one of the Canadian delegates to the World's Temperance Congress in Philadelphia, PA, in 1876. In May, 1882, she visited the British Woman's Temperance Association, in London, and afterward lectured throughout England, Ireland and Scotland. She has delivered many lectures in the cities of the United States. She has traveled and lectured through California,

from San Diego and National City to Nevada City. She went by steamer from San Francisco to Victoria, British Columbia, and spent several months in that province, lecturing in every available point. On leaving British Columbia she took the new Canadian Pacific Railroad, then just opened, and went through the Northwest Territories, holding meetings in many towns. She was thus the means of introducing the temperance question in the Northwest Territory She then lectured in Manitoba, which she had visited before. She at that time formed a Provincial Woman's Christian Temperance Union for Manitoba. Since July, 1888, Mrs. Youmans has been a helpless invalid, confined to her room.

YOUMANS, Mrs. Theodora Winton, journalist, born in Dodge county, WI, 1st February, 1863. Her predilection for newspaper work began to be evident before she had reached womanhood, and showed itself in the form of original essays, poems and translations from German authors, which appeared over her maiden name, Theodora Winton, during her course of study in Carrol College, Waukesha, WI. She was graduated as valedictorian of her class at the age of seventeen. Her family resided near Waukesha and Milwaukee, so that it was not difficult for her to keep in touch with the serial publications of both towns, though it was not until 1887 that she was regularly enrolled as a local reporter on the staff of the Waukesha "Freeman," a daily edition of which was issued during the resort season in Waukesha. The small chronicling of local news from day to day was not very attractive to a young lady educated as Miss Winton has been, but she devoted herself to the duties of her position with intelligent fidelity and industry and achieved a marked success in the business from the beginning. A few months later she was permitted by the editor, now her husband, Mr. H. M. Youmans, to establish a department in the newspaper particularly for women, of which she took the sole management, and which proved to be successful. After remaining associated in editorial work for nearly two years, Miss Winton and Mr. Youmans were married in January, 1889, and immediately went on a tour of the Pacific States, the story of which was related in a series of highly interesting newspaper letters from Mrs. Youmans' pen. After that pleasant vacation she returned to her favorite work on the "Freeman," to which she has given continuous attention. Her productions have received warm commendation from all her readers. Her views of the relations between a country newspaper and its constituency were set forth in a paper read before the Wisconsin Press Association, in the meetings of February, 1890, which was pronounced by the "National Journalist" of the following month to be the clearest, most practical and entertaining of any paper presented at the session. She has found time for the accomplishment of much special work for city newspapers and for the preparation of several papers of interest, read in meetings of various literary, social and agricultural organizations. She is a typical New Englander by ancestry and in the characteristics of enterprise, self-possession and persistency.

YOUNG, Miss Jennie, ceramic artist, lecturer and writer, is a native of New York. When a child she was taken to Minnesota and grew up in an unfettered atmosphere of social freedom. She taught in a pioneer school-house built of logs, but the gift of song which she possessed made her long for the advantages of a large city. Friendless, she went to New York, and made her living while she studied. Gaining an entrance to the columns of the New York "Tribune" she gradually established herself as a writer. When the china craze became prevalent Miss Young attained her fame as an authority on ceramic art. She made a study of ceramics and enamels from an historical point of view and contributed articles on this subject to magazines. A leading publisher asked her to write a volume upon pottery and porcelain, in the compilation of which she traveled far and wide, viewing all the great collections and visiting the leading manufactories of the country. This book, "The Ceramic Art," is a thorough treatise on the subject and met with great success. Soon after its publication Miss Young went abroad to live, for a time in Paris, but settled finally in London, still studying the more practical forms of art in the

metropolitan collections. Her cherished love of music was not forgotten, and upon a visit to Scotland she conceived the happy idea of combining literature and music in a series of public entertainments on poetical, musical themes, which were enthusiastically received. To rest from her lecture work Miss Young visited the highlands of Mexico, and there became interested in a financial and industrial scheme for colonizing and developing the country. She returned to England to lecture for this cause, and to procure funds to push the enterprise of Mexican improvement, which she perseveringly champions.

YOUNG, Miss Jennie B., artist, born, in Grundy county, Missouri, 23rd May, 1869. In 1882 she removed with her parents to El Dorado, KS, where she now resides. She is an only child. Her grandfather was one of the pioneers of the Christian Church, and with her parents she has always been enthusiastic in her efforts to promote the cause of Christianity. There is scarcely any line of Christian work that has not received a new impetus from her thought and labor. She is a born artist. When a very small child, she was continually, drawing, and when she was fourteen, she painted in oil. She is very fond of still-life pictures and has done many excellent pieces. She paints flowers, figures, landscapes and marine scenes in oil, and excels in painting animals. There is hardly any line of art work that is not familiar to her, designs of fabric painting and decorative work as well as many others. She was graduated with honor from the El Dorado high school when she was fifteen years old. She began to teach at sixteen and taught several terms, after which she took a classical and art course in Garfield University, Wichita, KS. She is a ready writer and a pleasant speaker in public.

YOUNG, Mrs. Julia Evelyn Ditto, poet and novelist, born in Buffalo, NY, 4th December, 1857. Her father, the late John A. Ditto, was a noted civil engineer, who twice served as city engineer of Buffalo. Her mother, Mrs. Margaret McKenna Ditto, was a woman of both literary and artistic talents, who finally chose art and became a successful painter in oils. The family on both sides is a talented one. Julia early showed that she had inherited literary talent of a high order. She was educated in the grammar and normal schools of Buffalo. After completing a thorough educational course, she became the wife of Robert D. Young, 30th December, 1876. Mr. Young is now cashier of the Erie County Savings Bank. Two sons were born to them. The older, born in 1877, died in 1882. The younger is living. Mrs. Young, when a mere child, began to write stories and verses. As soon as she had learned to write, she utilized her accomplishment to commit to paper a gloomy poem, "The Earl's Bride." In 1871 she published a story in the Buffalo "Evening Post," which opened in this alarming style: "Shriek upon shriek rent the air, mingled with yells." She next published in the Buffalo "Express," an essay on Fort Erie, which aroused protest on account of its inaccuracies. She then became a contributor to "Peterson's Magazine" and to the Frank Leslie periodicals. Recently she has written many short stories for a newspaper syndicate. These stories show many remarkable and artistic qualities in the author. She has written much poetry also, and her poems, like her stories, show her to be the possessor of vivid imagination and a master of diction. She has translated standard poems from the French and German into English. In November, 1889, she published a novel, "Adrift: A Story of Niagara," a finished work, the plot of which is laid in the neighborhood of Niagara Falls. The book was successful. She is now engaged on more important works. Her home is on Bouck Avenue, Buffalo, NY, and is a center of simple and cordial hospitality and of refinement and culture. In her literary work she has the encouragement of her husband, who is a man of intelligence. Her married life is an ideally happy one.

YOUNG, Miss Martha, author and poet, was born in Hale county, AL. She is the daughter of Dr. E. Young, of Greensborough, AL. Her grandfather, Col. E. Young, was a Virginian by birth, an honor graduate of Princeton and in his day a leader of law and politics in Alabama. His wife was Miss Martha Lucia Margaret Strudwick, of North Carolina, a family of note in that State since the days of the Revolution. Her maternal ancestor was Dr. Henry Tutwiler, owner and principal of Green Springs high school. He was the first full graduate of the University of Virginia, and a Virginian by birth. His wife was Miss Julia Ashe, of North Carolina, a member of a prominent family that has represented the State in many high offices. One of her ancestors was governor of North Carolina in 1795, and members of that family have in every generation since that year held many positions of honor and trust in North Carolina. Miss Young was graduated from the college in Livingston, AL. The most valued part of her education was gained from the reading of innumerable volumes in the old family library. Her reading was always supervised by her mother, who was a woman of wonderfully clear mind and many accomplishments. Miss Young's introduction to the reading public was a story published in a Christmas number of the New Orleans "Times-Democrat," entitled "A Nurse's Tale." Many other stories and ballads appeared during the following year in the "Southern Bivouac," Detroit "Free Press," "Home and Farm" and other journals, all signed "Eli Sheppard." These writings attracted attention because of their versification and faithful reproduction of the old-time negro character and language. Only a few friends knew the name of the author. Her identity was unveiled in the "Age-Herald" of Birmingham, which published an article signed Martha Young ("Eli Sheppard"). Joel Chandler Harris was among the first to recognize Miss Young's gift, and, showing his faith by his works, asked her to co-operate with him in the preparation of a work entitled "Songs and Ballads of Old-Time Plantations." "The First Waltz," a serial story by her, published in the New York "Home Journal," was a finished production. Her contributions have been published in the "Atlantic Monthly," "Cosmopolitan Magazine," "Belford's Magazine," "Century," "Youth's Companion," "Home-Maker," "Wide-Awake" and many papers, among the latter the Boston "Transcript."

YOUNG, Mrs. Sarah Graham, army nurse, born in Tompkins county, NY, five miles north of

Ithaca, in 1831. She was the only daughter in a family of ten children. Her maiden name was Sarah Graham. When the Civil War broke out, she went to the South with the 109th Regiment of New York Volunteers. She was in the field hospital from 1862 to 1865, being absent from active service only eight days in three years. Miss Dix appointed her matron of the Ninth Corps Hospital. She served faithfully among the sick and wounded, never breaking down nor faltering under the terrible work of those terrible days. She was known among the soldiers by a pet name, "Aunt Becky." She is now living in Des Moines, IA.

ZAKRZEWSKA, Miss Maria Elizabeth, physician and medical college professor, born in Berlin, Germany, 6th September, 1829. She is descended from a Polish family of wealth, intelligence and distinction. She was liberally educated, and is master of several, modern languages. She became interested in the study and practice of medicine, and took a medical course in the Charite Hospital in Berlin, and after finishing the prescribed course, taught in the college and served as assistant in the hospital. Desiring to find a wider field of action she came to this country in 1853. She studied in the Cleveland Medical College, and was graduated in that school. In 1859 she was called to the chair of obstetrics in the New England Female Medical College. At her suggestion the trustees of the college added a hospital, or clinical department, to the school, to give the students practical instruction. She had, after graduation, taken an active part in establishing and managing the New York Infirmary for Indigent Women. In that work she cooperated with Elizabeth and Emily Blackwell, the eminent pioneer women physicians. In 1863 she went to Boston,

MA, and there she founded the New England Hospital for women and children. She served three years and resigned, being one of the incorporators of that institution.

ZEISLER, Mrs. Fannie Bloomfield, piano virtuoso, born in Bielitz, Austria, 16th July, 1866. Her maiden name was Fannie Bloomfield. In 1869 her parents left Austria and came to the United States, making their home in Chicago, IL. She studied at first with Carl Wolfsohn and came out at an early age as a juvenile musical prodigy. Miss Bloomfield went to Vienna, where she studied a year in the Conservatory, and then began to study with Leschetizky, remaining in his charge for four years. In 1882 she made her debut in Vienna, where she carried the musical public by storm. Although one of the youngest pianists before, the public, she was at

once ranked with the foremost in all the essentials that make a great piano virtuoso. After further study she returned to the United States, and made her debut in this country in a concert of the Chicago Beethoven Society, 11th January, 1884. She afterward played in Chicago, in the Milwaukee orchestral concerts, in the Peabody Conservatory concerts, in Baltimore, in the Thomas concerts, in the Boston Symphony Society concerts, in the St. Louis symphony concerts, in Van der Stucken's novelty concert in New York City, making her debut in Steinway Hall, in the Mendelssohn Glee Club concert in Chickering Hall, in the New York Philharmonic concerts, in the Damrosch symphony concert, and in the Music Teachers' National Association concerts in Cleveland, OH, in 1884, in New York City in 1885, in Indianapolis in 1887, and in Detroit in 1892. In 1885 she became the wife of Sigmund Zeisler, a lawyer of Chicago.

LADIES OF THE
McKINLEY ADMINISTRATION

ALGER, Mrs. Russell A., the wife of the Secretary of War, has long been prominent in the best circles of Detroit, where they have made their home for over thirty years. As Annette Henry, the daughter of a leading citizen of Grand Rapids, she became the wife of Russell Alger in April, 1861. Through all those trying years of the war and the subsequent exigencies of her husband's business and political career, she has ever been the truest of help-meets. Mrs. Alger is the mother of a family of five grown-up children, and graciously does she wear the responsibilities of her station in life. Her first introduction to official society promises to be a repetition of the tactful hospitality for which she is famed in Detroit. General Alger has a penchant for fine pictures, which his wife shares, and her discriminating taste will be appreciated in art circles at the capital.

GAGE, Mrs. Lyman J., the wife of the Secretary of the Treasury, is a native of Albany, NY. Her maiden name was Cornelia Lansing, of a family long known and honored in that part of the State. Mrs. Gage is every way a typical American woman, first of all home-loving and home-keeping, and will count the four years as the wife of a Cabinet officer her first experience in administrative social circles. She will be greatly missed from Chicago, where she has lived since childhood, and where she has figured as a leader among the brightest women of that city.

GARY, Mrs. James A., the wife of the Postmaster-General, meets the demands of her position with the prestige of an aristocratic Baltimore family and a thoroughly womanly personality. Though the mother of a family of eight children, who have all gone from the home nest, yet she carries her years with the fresh-heartedness of youth. As in her Baltimore home she will exemplify the bountiful hostess of Southern hospitality.

LONG, Mrs. John D., the wife of the Secretary of the Navy, is familiar with Washington society, to which she came as a bride in 1883 during Governor Long's term in Congress. Her home is at Hingham, MA, and her New England birthright has been a self-poised intellectuality.

McKENNA, Mrs. Joseph E., the wife of the Attorney-General, came from the Golden Gate to Washington once before when Senator McKenna represented California from 1885 to 1892. Mrs. McKenna's tastes are quite suited to social life, and she entertains extensively with the aid of her eldest daughter.

Mrs. Russell A. Alger.
From Photo by
Hayes, Detroit.

Mrs. James A. Gary.
From Photo by Cummins, Baltimore.
Mrs. Joseph E. McKenna.
From Photo by Thors, San Francisco.

Mrs. Lyman J. Gage.
From Photo by Ciz, Chicago.
Mrs. John D. Long.
From Photo Copyrighted, 1897,
by Taylor, Higham, Mass.

Ladies of the McKinley Administration.

CLASSIFIED INDEX

ACTORS

Anderson, Mary
Bateman, Isabel
Bateman, Kate
Bert, Mabel
Booth, Agnes
Bowers, Mrs. D. P.
Campbell, Miss Evelyn
Cayvan, Miss Georgia
Cheatham, Miss Kitty Smiley
Claxton, Kate
Coghlan, Rose
Collins, Mrs. Miriam O'Leary
Crabtree, Miss Lotta
Cushman, Miss Charlotte Saunders
Duavray, Helen
Davenport, Fanny Lily Gipsy
Drew, Mrs. John
Ellsler, Miss Effie
Fiske, Mrs. Minnie Maddern
Fry, Mrs. Emma V. Sheridan
Haswin, Mrs. Frances R.
Hearne, Miss Mercedes Leigh
Kimball, Miss Corinne
Kimball, Miss Grace
Kimball, Mrs. Jennie
Marlowe, Miss Julia
Mather, Margaret
Modjeska, Mme. Helena
Morris, Miss Clara

Potter, Mrs. Cora Urquhart
Rehan, Miss Ada C.
Ritchie, Mrs. Anna Cora Mowatt
Siddons, Mrs. Mary Frances Scott
Ward, Mrs. Genevieve
Wray, Mrs. Mary A.

ARCHAEOLOGISTS

Le Plongeon, Mrs. Alice D.
Peck, Miss Annie Smith

ARCHITECTS

Bethune, Mrs. Louise
Nichols, Mrs. Minerva Parker

ARMY NURSES

See also PHILANTHROPISTS

Barry, Mrs. Susan E
Bickerdyke, Mrs. Mary A
Brinton, Mrs. Emma Southwick
Gillespie, Miss Eliza Maria
Stewart, Mrs. Eliza Daniel

Telford, Mrs. Mary Jewett
Wittenmyer, Mrs. Annie
Young, Mrs. Sarah Graham

ART EDUCATORS

See also ARTISTS AND DESIGNERS

Carter, Mrs. Hannah Johnson
Carter, Miss Mary Adaline Edwarda
Cobb, Mrs. Sara M. Maxson
Hicks, Mrs. Mary Dana

ARTISTS

See also CERAMIC ARTISTS

Abbatt, Miss Agnes Dean
Blackwell, Miss Sarah Ellen
Boyd, Mrs. Kate Parker
Braumiller, Mrs. Luetta Elmina
Brownscombe, Miss Jennie
Campbell, Miss Georgine
Carpenter, Miss Ellen M
Dillaye, Miss Blanche
Donlevy, Miss Alice
Durgin, Miss Harriet Thayer
Durgin, Miss Lyle
Dyer, Mrs. Clara L. Brown
Eggleston, Miss Allegra
Ficklen, Mrs. Bessie Alexander
Foote, Mrs. Mary Hallock
Granberry, Miss Virginia
Greatorex, Mrs. Eliza
Gregory, Mrs. Mary Rogers
Gutelius, Mrs. Jean Harrower
Hawes, Miss Franc P.
Hirschberg, Mrs. Alice
Humphrey, Miss Maud
Hurlbut, Miss Harietta Perris
Jackson, Miss Lily Irene
Loop, Mrs. Jennette Shephard Harrison
Lutz, Mrs. Adelia Armstrong
Moore, Miss Sarah Wool
Morse, Miss Alice Cordelia
Mumaugh, Mrs. Frances Miller
Nicholls, Mrs. Rhoda Holmes
Nieriker, Mrs. May Alcott
Owen, Mrs. Ella Seaver

Sartain, Miss Emily
Scott, Mrs. Emily Maria
Selinger, Mrs. Emily Harris McGary
Shaw, Miss Annie C.
Sherwood, Mrs. Rosina Emmet
Smith, Miss Isabel Elizabeth
Solari, Miss Mary M.
Stearns, Mrs. Nellie George
Thayer, Mrs. Emma Homan
Very, Miss Lydia Louisa Anna
Wheeler, Mrs. Dora
Williams, Miss Adele
Willis, Miss Louise Hammond
Worden, Miss Sarah A.
Young, Miss Jennie B.

ASTRONOMER

Mitchell, Miss Maria

AUTHORS

See also POETS, LITERARY CONTRIBUTORS, DRAMATISTS, HISTORIANS, HUMORISTS, HYMN-WRITERS, JOURNALISTS, NOVELISTS

Adams, Miss Hannah
Alcott, Miss Louisa May
Alden, Mrs. Isabella Macdonald
Alden, Mrs. Lucy Morris Chaffee
Allen, Mrs. Esther Lavilla
Ames, Mrs. Eleanor M.
Ames, Miss Lucia True
Andrews, Miss Eliza Frances
Austin, Mrs. Jane Goodwin
Banks, Miss Mary Ross
Barnes, Miss Annie Maria
Bates, Mrs. Clara Doty
Bates, Miss Katharine Lee
Bates, Mrs. Margaret Holmes
Baylor, Miss Frances Courtenay
Beat, Mrs. Eva
Beauchamp, Miss Mary Elizabeth
Bedford, Mrs. Lou Singletary
Beecher, Miss Catharine Esther
Benedict, Miss Emma Lee
Bingham, Miss Jennie M.
Blackwell, Mrs. Antionette Brown
Blake, Mrs. Euphenia Vale

DELSARTEAN INSTRUCTORS

Bishop, Mrs. Emily Mulkin
Thompson, Miss Mary Sophia

DENTIST

Cuinet, Miss Louise Adele

DESIGNERS

See also ARTISTS AND ART EDUCATORS

Carter, Miss Mary Adaline Edwarda
Cory, Mrs. Florence Elizabeth

DRAMATIC READERS

See also ELOCUTIONISTS

Adams, Mrs. Florence Adelaide Fowle
Babcock, Mrs. Helen Louise B.
Biggert, Miss Mabelle
Collins, Miss Laura Sedgwick
Conner, Mrs. Elizabeth Marney
Howard, Mrs. Belle
Parker, Miss Helen Almena
Pond, Mrs. Nella Brown
Potter, Miss Jennie O'Neill

DRAMATISTS

See AUTHORS, POETS, LITERARY CONTRIBUTORS

Logan, Mrs. Celia
Morton, Miss Martha

DRESS REFORMERS

Bloomer, Mrs. Amelia
Miller, Mrs. Annie Jenness

EDITORS

See also JOURNALISTS, PUBLISHERS, LITERARY CONTRIBUTORS

Aikens, Mrs. Amanda L.
Ames, Miss Julia A.
Amies, Mrs. Olive Pond
Barnes, Miss Catharine Weed
Bradwell, Mrs. Myra
Burlingame, Mrs. Emeline S.
Cameron, Mrs. Elizabeth
Churchill, Mrs. Caroline M.
Dortch, Miss Ellen J.
Duniway, Mrs. Abigail Scott
Housh, Mrs. Esther T.
Logan, Mrs. Mary Cunningham
Loud, Miss Hulda Barker
Mallory, Mrs. Lucy A.
Michel, Mrs. Nettie Leila
Miller, Mrs. Annie Jenness
Miller, Mrs. Mary A.
Pritchard, Mrs. Esther Tuttle
Robinson, Mrs. Abbie C. B.
Smith, Mrs. Elizabeth J.
Thompson, Mrs. Eva Griffith
Towne, Mrs. Belle Kellogg
Trott, Miss Novella Jewell
West, Miss Mary Allen
Westlake, Miss Kate Eva
Williams, Miss Florence B.

EDUCATORS

See also ART EDUCATORS, DELSARTEAN INSTRUCTORS, ELOCUTIONISTS, KINDERGARTNERS, MUSICAL EDUCATORS

Abbott, Mrs. Elizabeth Robinson
Adams, Mrs. Jane Kelley
Alden, Miss Emily Gillmore
Amies, Mrs. Olive Pond
Avann, Mrs. Ella H. Brockway
Baggett, Mrs. Alice
Barber, Mrs. Mary Augustine
Bartlett, Mrs. Maud Whitehead
Beck, Miss Leonora
Beecher, Miss Catherine Esther
Bond, Mrs. Elizabeth Powell
Boughton, Mrs. Caroline Greenbank

Bradley, Miss Amy Morris
Brownell, Mrs. Helen M. Davis
Buck, Mme. Henriette
Cabell, Mrs. Mary Virginia Ellet
Carhart, Mrs. Clara H. Sully
Carson, Mrs. Delia E.
Chandler, Mrs. Mary Alderson (Stenography)
Clerc, Mme. Henrietta Fannie Virginie
Cleveland, Miss Rose Elizabeth
Cobb, Mrs. Mary Emelie
Coe, Mrs. Emily M.
Collins, Mrs. Delia
Cone, Miss Helen Gray
Conway, Miss Clara
Cooper, Mrs. Sarah Brown Ingersoll
Cummins, Mrs. Mary Stuart
Cunningham, Miss Susan J.
Dicklow, Miss Adelaide Lynn
Dodge, Miss Hannah P.
Dowd, Miss Mary Alice
Durrell, Mrs. Irene Clark
Edgar, Mrs. Elizabeth
Edwards, Miss Anna Cheney
Edwards, Mrs. Emma Atwood
Fisher, Mrs. Anna A.
Foxworthy, Miss Alice S.
Gale, Mrs. Ada Iddings
Galpin, Mrs. Kate Tupper
Garner, Miss Eliza A.
Gibbs, Miss Eleanor Churchill
Granger, Miss Lottie E.
Graves, Mrs. Adelia C.
Hall, Mrs. Sarah Elizabeth
Haskell, Miss Harriet Newell
Haven, Mrs. Mary Emerson
Hogue, Mrs. Lydia Evans
Howland, Miss Emily
Keysor, Mrs. Jennie Ellis
Kidd, Mrs. Lucy Ann
Lamson, Miss Lucy Stedman
Leland, Mrs. Caroline Weaver
Lippincott, Mrs. Esther J. Trimble
Little, Mrs. Sarah F. Cowles
Lord, Mrs. Elizabeth W. Russell
Lyon, Miss Mary
Meech, Mrs. Jeannette Du Bois
Merrick, Mrs. Sarah Newcomb
Miller, Mrs. Addie Dickman
Morgan, Miss Anne Eugenia Felicia
Mortimer, Miss Mary
Nash, Mrs. Mary Louise
Nixon, Mrs. Jennie Caldwell

O'Donnell, Miss Nellie
Orum, Miss Julia Anna
Palmer, Mrs. Alice Freeman
Peabody, Miss Elizabeth Palmer
Peck, Miss Annie Smith
Picken, Mrs. Lillian Hoxie
Pollock, Mrs. Louise
Rambaut, Mrs. Mary L. Bonney
Ripley, Miss Mary A.
Roach, Miss Aurelia
Robinson, Mrs. Jane Bancroft
Rogers, Mrs. Effie Louise Hoffman
Rutherford, Miss Mildred
Sabin, Miss Ellen Clara
Sewall, Mrs. May Wright
Shafer, Miss Helen Almira
Shattuck, Miss Lydia White
Shoemaker, Mrs. Rachel H.
Slocum, Miss Jane Mariah
Stafford, Mrs. Maria Brewster Brooks
Stone, Mrs. Lucinda H.
Sunderland, Mrs. Elisa Read
Swarthout, Mrs. M. French
Todd, Miss Adah J.
Tutwiler, Miss Julia Strudwick
Walton, Mrs. Electa Noble Lincoln
Webster, Miss Helen L.
Wells, Miss Mary Fletcher
Wheelock, Miss Lucy
Willard, Mrs. Emma
Willard, Mrs. Mary Bannister
Willing, Mrs. Jennie Fowler
Woody, Mrs. Mary Williams Chawner

ELOCUTIONISTS

See also DRAMATIC READERS

Bailey, Mrs. Sara Lord
Beasley, Mrs. Marie Wilson
Brace, Miss Maria Porter
Furman, Miss Myrtie E.
Immen, Mrs. Loraine
Noble, Mrs. Edna Chaffee
Peirce, Miss Frances Elizabeth
Shoemaker, Mrs. Rachel H.
Stocker, Miss Corinne
Thompson, Mrs. Eva Griffith

ETHNOLOGIST

Fletcher, Miss Alice Cunningham

EVANGELISTS

See also CHURCH WORKERS AND TEMPERANCE WORKERS

Barney, Mrs. Susan Hammond
Butler, Miss Clementina
Henry, Mrs. Sarepta M. I.
Isaac, Mrs. Hannah M. Underhill
Jenkins, Mrs. Francis C.
Lathrap, Mrs. Mary Torrans
Meech, Mrs. Jeannette Du Bois
Pratt, Miss Hannah T.
Prosser, Miss Anne Weed
Smith, Mrs. Emma Pow
Taylor, Mrs. Sarah Katherine Paine
Wheeler, Mrs. Mary Sparkes
Willing, Mrs. Jennie Fowler

FINANCIERS

See also BANKERS AND BUSINESS WOMEN

Carse, Mrs. Matilda B.
Dow, Mrs. Mary E. H. G.
Plumb, Mrs. L. H.

HARPIST

Morgan, Miss Maud

HISTORIANS

Barnes, Mrs. Mary Sheldon
Lamb, Mrs. Martha Joanna

HORTICULTURISTS

Austin, Mrs. Helen Vickroy
Jack, Mrs. Annie L.

HUMORISTS

Goza, Miss Anne
Holley, Miss Marietta
Huntley, Mrs. Florence

HYMN-WRITERS

See also POETS AND AUTHORS

Crosby, Fanny J.
Hawks, Mrs. Annie Sherwood
Miller, Mrs. Emily Huntington
Morton, Miss Eliza Happy
Starkweather, Miss Amelia Minerva
Van Fleet, Mrs. Ellen Oliver
Willson, Mrs. Mary Elizabeth
Wittenmyer, Mrs. Annie

INSURANCE AGENTS

Adsit, Mrs. Nancy H.
Richmond, Miss Lizzie R.
Schaffer, Miss Margaret Eliza

INVENTORS

Bailey, Miss Ellen Alice
Blanchard, Miss Helen Augusta
Brown, Mrs. Harriet A.
Frackleton, Mrs. Susan Stuart
Gilbert, Miss Linda
Hughes, Mrs. Kate Duval
Stearns, Mrs. Betsey Ann
Westover, Miss Cynthia M.

JOURNALISTS

See also EDITORS, PUBLISHERS, LITERARY CONTRIBUTORS

Abrich, Mrs. Emma B.
Ames, Mary Clemmer
Andrews, Mrs. Mary Louise
Austin, Mrs. Helen Vickroy

KINDERGARTNERS

LABOR CHAMPIONS

See also POLITICAL ORATORS

Blackall, Mrs. Emily Lucas
Bohan, Mrs. Elizabeth Baker
Boyd, Mrs. Louise Esther Vickroy
Braden, Mrs. Anna Madge
Bradford, Mrs. Mary Carroll Craig
Briggs, Mrs. Mary Blatchley
Brooks, Mrs. M. Sears
Brown, Mrs. Charlotte Emerson
Buck, Mrs. Mary K.
Bucknor, Mrs. Helen Lewis
Burnham, Miss Bertha H.
Bush, Mrs. Jennie Burchfield
Cardwill, Miss Mary E.
Case, Mrs. Marietta Stanley
Chandler, Mrs. Lucinda Banister
Clarke, Mrs. Mary Bassett
Clarke, Mrs. Mary H. Gray
Cleary, Mrs. Kate McPhelim
Coit, Miss Irene Williams
Colby, Mrs. H. Maria George
Cole, Miss Elizabeth
Conklin, Mrs. Jane Elizabeth Dexter
Cook, Miss Amelia Josephine
Cornell, Mrs. Ellen Frances
Cotes, Mrs. Sara Jeannette Duncan
Crawford, Mrs. Alice Arnold
Crawford, Mrs. John
Dana, Miss Olive Eliza
Davis, Mrs. Ida May
Davis, Miss Minnie S.
Dayton, Mrs. Elizabeth
De Jarnette, Mrs. Evelyn Magruder
Dieudonne, Mrs. Florence Carpenter
Dole, Mrs. Phoebe Cobb Larry
Dufour, Mrs. Amande Louise Ruter
Dunham, Mrs. Emma Bedelia
Engle, Mrs. Addie C. Strong
Fenner, Mrs. Mary Galentine
Fletcher, Mrs. Lisa Anne
Forney, Miss Tillie May
Frank, Miss Rachel
Fryatt, Miss Frances Elizabeth
Furber, Miss Aurilla
Gage, Mrs. Frances Dana
Gannett, Mrs. Abbie M.
Giles, Miss Ella A,
Goldthwaite, Mrs. Lucy Virginia
Gordon, Mrs. S. Anna
Goza, Miss Anne
Gray, Mrs. Mary Tenney
Green, Mrs. Julia Boynton
Greene, Miss Frances Nimmo
Gregory, Mrs. Elizabeth Goadby

Groenevelt, Mrs. Sara
Hager, Mrs. Lucie Caroline
Hall, Mrs. Margaret Thompson
Hamilton, Miss Anna J.
Harby, Mrs. Lee C.
Harrell, Mrs. Sarah Carmichael
Harris, Mrs. Ethel Hillyer
Hatch, Mrs. Mary R. P.
Hawley, Mrs. Frances Mallette
Hazelrigg, Mrs. Clara H.
Helm, Miss Lucinda Barbour
Henderson, Mrs. Frances Cox
Herrick, Mrs. Christine Terhune
Hewitt, Mrs. Emma Churchman
Hibbard, Mrs. Grace
Higginson, Mrs. Ella Rhoads
Hiles, Mrs. Osia Joslyn
Hill, Mrs. Agnes Leonard
Hinman, Miss Ida
Hobart, Mrs. Sarah Dyer
Hodgkins, Miss Louise Manning
Hooper, Mrs. Lucy Hamilton
Howe, Mrs. Emeline Harriet
Humphreys, Mrs. Sarah Gibson
Huntley, Mrs. Florence
Ingham, Mrs. Mary Bigelow
Ives, Miss Alice Emma
Jeffrey, Mrs. Isadore Gilbert
Johnson, Mrs. Carrie Ashton
Johnson, Miss E. Pauline
Johnston, Mrs. Maria I.
Jones, Mrs. Jennie E.
Judson, Miss Jennie S.
Kahn, Mrs. Ruth Ward
Keating, Mrs. Josephine E.
Keezer, Mrs. Martha Moulton Whittemore
Kipp, Mrs. Josephine
Lauder, Mrs. Maria Elisa Turner
Lawson, Mrs. Mary J.
Leonard, Mrs. Cynthia H. Van Name
Lincoln, Mrs. Martha D.
Linn, Mrs. Edith Willis
Longbead, Mrs. Flora Haines
Lyon, Miss Anne Bozeman
McCabe, Miss Lida Rose
McClain, Mrs. Louise Bowman
McComas, Mrs. Alice Moore
McCracken, Mrs. Annie Virginia
McKinney, Mrs. Kate Slaughter
McManus, Miss Emily Julian
Manning, Mrs. Jessie Wilson
Manville, Mrs. Helen Adelia
Marble, Mrs. Callie Bonney

Tyler, Mrs. Julia Gardiner
Van Buren, Mrs. Angelica Singleton
Washington, Mrs. Martha

MUSICAL EDUCATORS

See also MUSICIANS AND SINGERS

Cheney, Mrs. Abbey Perkins
Dussuchal, Miss Eugenie
Eddy, Mrs. Sarah Hershey
Hahr, Miss Emma
Hanna, Miss Sarah Jackson
Hibler, Mrs. Nellie
Howard, Miss Mary M.
Millar, Mme. Clara Smart
Sherman, Miss Marietta R.

MUSICIANS

See also COMPOSERS, HARPIST, PIANISTS, MUSICAL
EDUCATORS, ORCHESTRAL CONDUCTORS, SINGERS,
VIOLINISTS

Atwood, Miss Ethel
Berg, Miss Lillie
Bigelow, Mrs. Ella Augusta
Bloudner, Mrs. Alme Reese
Brainard, Mrs. Kate J.
Bullock, Mrs. Helen Louise
Collins, Miss Laura Sedgwick
De Fere, Mrs. A. Litsner
Fay, Miss Amy
Fonda, Mrs. Mary Alice
Keating, Mrs. Josephine E.
Lawton, Mrs. Henrietta Beebe
Raymond, Mrs. Carrie Isabel Rice
Searing, Miss Florence E.
Willard, Miss Katherine
Williams, Mrs. Louisa Brewster

NATURALISTS

Agassiz, Mrs. Elizabeth Cabot
Lewis, Mrs. Graceanna
Miller, Mrs. Olive Thorne

NOVELISTS

See also AUTHORS AND LITERARY CONTRIBUTORS

Barr, Mrs. Amelia E.
Bellamy, Mrs. Emily Whitfield Croom
Burnett, Mrs. Frances Hodgson
Burnham, Mrs. Clara Louise
Cruger, Miss Mary
Darling, Mrs. Flora Adams
Deland, Mrs. Margaret
Elliott, Mrs. Maud Howe
Evans, Mrs. Lizzie P. E.
French, Miss Alice ("Octave Thanet")
Goodwin, Mrs. H. B.
Holmes, Mrs. Mary Jane
Kirk, Mrs. Ellen Olney
Leprohon, Mrs. Rosanna Eleanor
Litchfield, Miss Grace Denio
Murfree, Miss Mary Noailles ("Charles Egbert
    Craddock")
Reno, Mrs. Itti Kinney
Southworth, Mrs. Emma Dorothy Eliza Nevitte
Woolley, Mrs. Celia Parker

OFFICIALS (CIVIC)

Baxter, Mrs. Annie White (County Clerk)
Chenoweth, Mrs. Caroline Van Deusen (Vice
    Consul)
Couzins, Miss Phoebe (United States Marshal)
Diehl, Miss Cora Victoria (Register of Deeds)
Dodge, Miss Grace Hoadley (School Com-
    missioner)
Grisham, Mrs. Sadie Park (President City
    Council)
Hawes, Mrs. Flora Harrod (Postmaster)
Leonard, Mrs. Anna Byford (Sanitary Inspector)
Lewis, Miss Ida (Lighthouse Keeper)
Lowman, Mrs. Mary D. (Mayor)
Morris, Mrs. Esther (Justice of the Peace)
Rogers, Mrs. Effie Louise Hoffman (County
    Superintendent of Public Schools)
Stone, Miss Martha Elvira (Postmaster)
Sweet, Miss Ada Celeste (Pension Agent)
Thorp, Mrs. Mandana Coleman (Register of
    Deeds)

Mather, Mrs. Sarah Ann
Meyer, Mrs. Annie Nathan
Mitchell, Mrs. Martha Reed
Moore, Mrs. Clara Jessup
Mott, Mrs. Lucretia
Quinton, Mrs. Amelia Stone
Rose, Mrs. Martha Parmelee
Russell, Mrs. Elizabeth Augusta S.
Schaffner, Mrs. Ernestine
Spear, Mrs. Catherine Swan Brown
Spurlock, Mrs. Isabella Smiley Davis
Stanford, Mrs. Jane Lathrop
Stearns, Mrs. Sarah Burger
Stewart, Mrs. Eliza Daniel
Stirling, Miss Emma Maitland
Stone, Lucy
Thompson, Mrs. Elizabeth Rowell
Trott, Mrs. Lois E.
Walker, Mrs. Harriet G.
Wallace, Mrs. M. R. M.
Wells, Miss Mary Fletcher
Wolfe, Miss Catherine Lorillard
Wyman, Mrs. Lillie B. Chace

PHOTOGRAPHER

Barnes, Miss Catherine Weed

PHYSICIANS

Aldrich, Mrs. Flora L.
Allen, Mrs. Mary Wood
Armstrong, Miss Sarah B.
Baker, Mrs. Charlotte Johnson
Bennett, Mrs. Alice
Blackwell, Miss Elizabeth
Blackwell, Miss Emily
Brewster, Miss Cora Belle
Brewster, Miss Flora A.
Brinkman, Mrs. Mary A.
Brooks, Miss Ida Joe
Brown, Miss M. Belle
Bushnell, Miss Kate
Butin, Mrs. Mary Ryerson
Cady, Mrs. Helena Maxwell
Canfield, Mrs. Corresta T.
Chapman, Miss Millie Jane
Cleaves, Miss Margaret Abagail
Colby, Miss Sarah A.

Comfort, Mrs. Anna Manning
Conant, Miss Harriet Beecher
Dabbs, Mrs. Ellen Lawson
Davis, Miss Minta S. A.
Davis, Mrs. Virginia Meriwether
Dight, Mrs. Mary A. G.
Dixon, Mrs. Mary J. Scarlett
Dodds, Mrs. Susanna May
Dodson, Miss Caroline Matilda
Dunlap, Miss Mary J.
Fairchild, Miss Maria Augusta
Frisby, Miss Almah J.
Frissell, Miss Seraph
Gavitt, Mrs. Elmina M. Roye
Gilchrist, Mrs. Rosetta Luce
Gleason, Mrs. Rachel Brooks
Gordon, Mrs. S. Anna
Green, Mrs. Mary E.
Haensler, Mrs. Arminta Victoria Scott
Hall, Miss Lucy M.
Hall, Mrs. Sarah C.
Hammond, Mrs. Loretta Mann
Hersom, Mrs. Jane Lord
Holcombe, Mrs. Elizabeth J.
Howard, Mrs. Elmira Y.
Hughes, Mrs. Marietta E.
Jackson, Mrs. Katharine Johnson
Jacobi, Mrs. Mary Putnam
Jones, Miss Harriet B.
Keller, Mrs. Elizabeth Catharine
Kemp, Mrs. Agnes Nininger
Kurt, Miss Katherine
Lankton, Mrs. Freeda M.
Longshore, Mrs. Hannah E.
Lozier, Mrs. Jennie de la Montagnie
Lukens, Miss Anna
Lummis, Mrs. Dorothea
Mark, Miss Nellie V.
Miller, Mrs. Elizabeth
Moody, Mrs. Mary Blair
Mowry, Miss Martha H.
Peckham, Mrs. Lucy Creemer
Pettet, Mrs. Isabella M.
Post, Miss Sarah E.
Potts, Mrs. Anna M. Longshore
Preston, Miss Ann
Ripley, Mrs. Martha George
Safford, Miss Mary Jane
Severance, Mrs. Juliet H.
Smith, Mrs. Julia Holmes
Stockham, Mrs. Alice Bunker
Stowe, Mrs. Emily Howard Jennings

PIANISTS

POETS

See also AUTHORS, SONG-WRITERS, LITERARY CONTRIBUTORS

POLITICAL ORATORS

See also LECTURERS, TEMPERANCE WORKERS, WOMAN SUFFRAGISTS

SOCIAL ECONOMIST

See also Reformers and labor Champions

Cohen, Miss Mary M.

SOCIAL LEADERS

Beban, Miss Bessie
Breed, Mrs. Alice Ives
Carlisle, Mrs. Mary Jane
Churchill, Lady Randolph
Clarke, Mrs. Lena Thompson
Cross, Mrs. Kate Sneed
Cruger, Mrs. S. Van Rensselaer
Davis, Mrs. Varina Howell
Downs, Mrs. Sallie Ward
Eagle, Mrs. May Kavanaugh
Fremont, Mrs. Jessie Benton
Guzman, Mme. Marie Esther
Henderson, Mrs. Augusta A. Fox
Hendricks, Mrs. Eliza C. Morgan
La Follette, Mrs. Belle Case
Larrabee, Mrs. Anna Matilda
McMurdo, Mrs. Katharine Albert
Mims, Mrs. Sue Harper
Morton, Mrs. Anna Livingston Street
Overstolz, Mrs. Philippine E. Von
Palmer, Mrs. Bertha Honore
Reno, Mrs. Itti Kinney
Routt, Mrs. Eliza Franklin
Scranton, Miss Lida
Sherman, Mrs. Eleanor Boyle Ewing
Sherwood, Mrs. Mary Elizabeth
Thurston, Mrs. Martha L. Poland

SONG-WRITERS

Crosby, Fanny J.
Gordon, Miss Anna A.
Marble, Mrs. Callie Bonney
Miller, Mrs. Emily Huntington
Newell, Mrs. Laura Emeline
Straub, Miss Maria

SPELLING REFORMER

Burnz, Mrs. Eliza B.

STENOGRAPHERS

Ballou, Miss Ella Maria
Burnz, Mrs. Eliza B.
Churchill, Miss Lide A.
Latrop, Miss Clarissa Caldwell
Saunders, Mrs. Mary A.
Seymour, Miss Mary F.
White, Miss Nettie L.

TELEGRAPH OPERATORS

Kelley, Miss Ella Maynard
Thayer, Miss Lizzie E. D.

TEMPERANCE WORKERS

See also Church Workers, Evangelists, Philanthropists, Reformers

Acheson, Mrs. Sarah C.
Ackermann, Miss Jessie A.
Adkinson, Mrs. Mary Osburn
Aldrich, Mrs. Mary Jane
Allen, Mrs. Mary Wood
Ames, Miss Julia A.
Archibald, Mrs. Edith Jessie
Armstrong, Mrs. Ruth Allen
Bailey, Mrs. Lepha Eliza
Barnes, Mrs. Frances Julia
Bateham, Mrs. Josephine Penfield Cushman
Benjamin, Mrs. Anna Smeed
Bigelow, Mrs. Belle G.
Black, Mrs. Sarah Hearst
Blair, Mrs. Eilen A. Dayton
Bradley, Mrs. Ann Weaver
Brown, Mrs. Martha McClellan
Browne, Mrs. Mary Frank
Buell, Mrs. Caroline Brown
Bull, Mrs. Sarah C. Thorpe
Bullock, Mrs. Helen Louise
Burlingame, Mrs. Emeline S.
Burnett, Miss Cynthia S.

Burt, Mrs. Mary Towne
Bushnell, Miss Kate
Campbell, Mrs. Eugenia Steele
Carse, Mrs. Matilda B.
Chapin, Mrs. Clara Christiana
Chapin, Mrs. Sallie F.
Chase, Mrs. Louise L.
Coit, Mrs. Elizabeth
Cole, Mrs. Cordelia Throop
Collins, Mrs. Delia
Colman, Miss Julia
Cooley, Mrs. Emily M. J.
Cornelius, Mrs. Mary A.
Crane, Mrs. Mary Helen Peck
Cranmer, Mrs. Emma A.
Doe, Mrs. Mary L.
Douglas, Mrs. Lavantia Densmore
Dow, Miss Cornelia M.
Dunham, Mrs. Marion Howard
East, Mrs. Edward H.
Elmore, Mrs. Lucie Ann Morrison
Esmond, Mrs. Rhoda Anna
Fawcett, Mrs. Mary S.
Foster, Mrs. J. Ellen Horton
Foster, Mrs. Susie E.
Frazier, Mrs. Martha M.
Goff, Mrs. Harriet Newell Kneeland
Gordon, Miss Anna A.
Gordon, Miss Elizabeth P.
Gray, Mrs. Jennie T.
Greenwood, Miss Elizabeth W.
Griffith, Mrs. Eva Kinney
Grub, Mrs. Sophronia Farrington Naylor
Hammer, Mrs. Anna Maria Nichols
Harrell, Mrs. Sarah Carmichael
Hitchcock, Mrs. Mary Antoinette
Hodgin, Mrs. Emily Caroline Chandler
Hoffman, Mrs. Clara Cleghorn
Holmes, Mrs. Jennie Florella
Housh, Mrs. Esther T.
Hunt, Mrs. Mary H.
Ingalls, Mrs. Eliza B.
Kendrick, Mrs. Ella Bagnell
Kepley, Mrs. Ada Miser
Kinney, Mrs. Narcissa Edith White
Knox, Mrs. Janette Hill
La Fetra, Mrs. Sarah Doan
Lathrap, Mrs. Mary Torrans
Leader, Mrs. Oliver Moorman
Leavitt, Mrs. Mary Clement
McCabe, Mrs. Harriet Calista Clark
Meriwether, Mrs. Lide

Merrick, Mrs. Caroline Elizabeth
Miller, Mrs. Addie Dickman
Moots, Mrs. Cornelia Moore Chillson
Morris, Miss Ellen Douglas
Neblett, Mrs. Ann Viola
Nichols, Mrs. Josephine Ralston
O'Donnell, Mrs. Martha B.
Palmer, Mrs. Hannah Borden
Perkins, Mrs. Sarah Maria Clinton
Porter, Mrs. Florence Collins
Pugh, Miss Esther
Ramsey, Mrs. Lulu A.
Reese, Mrs. Mary Bynon
Riggs, Mrs. Anna Rankin
Rittenhouse, Mrs. Laura Jacinta
Rude, Mrs. Ellen Sergeant
Scott, Miss Mary
Sibley, Mrs. Jennie E.
Skelton, Mrs. Henriette
Smith, Miss Mary Belle
Stevens, Mrs. Emily Pitt
Stevens, Mrs. Lillian M. N.
Stewart, Mrs. Eliza Daniel
Stille, Miss Mary Ingram
Stoddard, Mrs. Anna Elizabeth
Stokes, Miss Missouri H.
Swetzer, Mrs. Lucy Robbins Messer
Thompson, Mrs. Eliza J.
Tilton, Mrs. Lydia H.
Truitt, Mrs. Anna Augusta
Walker, Mrs. Harriet
Warren, Mrs. Mary Evalin
Washington, Mrs. Lucy H.
Watts, Mrs. Margaret Anderson
Weatherby, Mrs. Delia L.
West, Miss Mary Allen
Wheelock, Mrs. Dora V.
Willard, Miss Frances Elizabeth
Willard, Mrs. Mary Bannister
Williams, Mrs. Alice
Willing, Mrs. Jennie Fowler
Wittenmyer, Mrs. Annie
Woodbridge, Mrs. Mary A. Brayton
Woodward, Mrs. Caroline M. Clark
Woody, Mrs. Mary Williams Chawner
Yomans, Mrs. Letitia Creighton

TRAIN DISPATCHER

Thayer, Miss Lizzie E. D.

TRANSLATORS

Booth, Miss Mary Louise
Bull, Mrs. Sarah C. Thorpe
Hapgood, Mrs. Isabel F.
Ireland, Mrs. Mary E.
Moore, Mrs. Aubertine Woodward
Sheldon, Mrs. Mary French
Smith, Mrs. Mary Stewart
Toussaint, Miss Emma
Wormeley, Miss Katherine Prescott

TRAVELERS

Brinton, Mrs. Emma Southwick
Carpenter, Mrs. Alice Dimmick
Shaw, Miss Emma

VIOLINISTS

Powell, Miss Maud
Webb, Miss Bertha

WOMAN SUFFRAGISTS

See also PHILANTHROPISTS, REFORMERS, TEMPER-
ANCE WORKERS

Anthony, Miss Susan B.
Avery, Mrs. Rachel Foster
Babcock, Mrs. Elnora Monroe
Bascom, Mrs. Emma Curtiss
Beckwith, Mrs. Emma
Blake, Mrs. Lillie Devereux
Bloomer, Mrs. Amelia
Bones, Mrs. Marietta M.
Catt, Mrs. Carrie Lane Chapman
Claflin, Mrs. Adelaide Avery
Clay, Mrs. Mary Barr
Collins, Mrs. Emily Parmely
Cones, Mrs. Mary Emily Bennett
Curtis, Mrs. Martha E. Sewall
Devoe, Mrs. Emma Smith
Drake, Mrs. Priscilla Holmes
Du Bose, Mrs. Miriam Howard
Everhard, Mrs. Caroline McCullough
Fray, Mrs. Ellen Surrey

Gage, Mrs. Frances Dana
Gage, Mrs. Matilda Joslyn
Greenleaf, Mrs. Jean Brooks
Harbert, Mrs. Elizabeth Boynton
Henry, Mrs. Josephine Kirby Williamson
Hill, Mrs. Eliza Trask
Holmes, Mrs. Mary Emma
Hooker, Mrs. Isabella Beecher
Howell, Mrs. Mary Seymour
Humphreys, Mrs. Sarah Gibson
Iliohan, Mrs. Henrica
Jenkins, Mrs. Theresa A.
Johns, Mrs. Laura M.
McKinney, Mrs. Jane Amy
Marble, Mrs. Ella M. S.
Pope, Mrs. Cora Scott Pond
Post, Mrs. Amalia Barney Simons
Read, Mrs. Elizabeth C. Bunnell
Ricker, Mrs. Marilla M.
Rose, Mrs. Ellen Alida
Saxon, Mrs. Elizabeth Lyle
Segur, Mrs. Rosa L.
Sewall, Mrs. May Wright
Shaw, Miss Anna H.
Shaw, Mrs. Cornelia Dean
Smith, Mrs. Estelle Turrell
Stanton, Mrs. Elizabeth Cady
Stone, Lucy
Swain, Mrs. Adeline Morrison
Todd, Mrs. Minnie J. Terrell
Wait, Mrs. Anna C.
Walker, Dr. Mary
Walton, Mrs. Electa Noble Lincoln

WOOD-CARVER

Fry, Miss Laura Ann

MISCELLANEOUS

Alger, Mrs. Russell A.
Bailey, Mrs. Ann (Scout)
Bailey, Mrs. Anna Warner (Patriot)
Blavatsky, Mme. Helene P. (Theosophist)
Bonaparte, Mme. Elizabeth Patterson
Bridgman, Miss Laura D. (Blind Deaf-mute)
Brown, Mrs. Corinne Stubbs (Socialist)
Cheney, Mrs. Armilla A. (W.R.C. Worker)
Converse, Mrs. Harriet Maxwell (Chief Six
    Nations Indians)